THE
CRISIS YEARS

Books by Michael R. Beschloss

KENNEDY AND ROOSEVELT: THE UNEASY ALLIANCE (1980)

MAYDAY: EISENHOWER, KHRUSHCHEV AND THE U-2 AFFAIR (1986)

THE CRISIS YEARS: KENNEDY AND KHRUSHCHEV, 1960–1963 (1991)

THE
CRISIS YEARS

KENNEDY and KHRUSHCHEV

1960 – 1963

Michael R. Beschloss

Edward Burlingame Books
An Imprint of HarperCollins*Publishers*

FIRST EDITION

Library of Congress Cataloging-in-Publication Data

Beschloss, Michael R. (1955–)
    The crisis years: Kennedy and Khrushchev, 1960–1963 / by Michael R. Beschloss.—1st ed.
        p. cm.
    Includes bibliographical references and index.
    ISBN 0-06-016454-9 (cloth)
    1. United States—Foreign relations—Soviet Union. 2. Soviet Union—Foreign relations—United States. 3. World politics—1955–1965. 4. Cold War. 5. Kennedy, John F. (John Fitzgerald), 1917–1963. 6. Khrushchev, Nikita Sergeevich, 1894–1971. I. Title.
    E183.8.S65B469 1991
    909.82'6—dc20   90-55946

91 92 93 94 95 CC/RRD 10 9 8 7 6 5 4 3 2 1

For Afsaneh Mashayekhi

PREFACE

This volume examines the relationship of John Kennedy and Nikita Khrushchev and its impact on the Cold War. Why did these two leaders, who both came to power with genuine hopes of reducing the harshness of Soviet-American relations, take humankind instead to the edge of nuclear disaster and into the most ferocious arms race in world history?

The book benefits from new scholarship and new information on the Kennedy-Khrushchev period. Like every scholar, I stand on the shoulders of many others and am happy to here express my debt to all of those who have gone before me. Recent years have seen the opening of the majority of John Kennedy's papers bearing on the Soviet Union and of other archives shedding light on his relations with Nikita Khrushchev. American political, military, and intelligence officials of the period have become more willing to be interviewed at length about sensitive aspects of their service. Thanks to a Harvard group, Soviet and American officials and historians have gathered to reexamine the crises over Berlin and Cuba.

In my last book, *Mayday: Eisenhower, Khrushchev and the U-2 Affair,* * I complained about the "paucity of Soviet sources open to Western scholars". The increased openness of the Soviet government has ex-

---

*Harper & Row, 1986, p. xvi.

cited expectations that at last historians can write with equal access to Soviet and American sources. This book does benefit from hundreds of oral and written reminiscences by Soviet figures that were not until recently available. These expand our knowledge and understanding of Soviet decision-making.

Still I have used them with considerable self-restraint, for they are subject to the same partisan motives, faulty memories, and other limitations that distort Western oral history and memoir. Unlike in the West, we do not yet have access to a substantial number of contemporaneous official Soviet documents that might help us to better judge their accuracy. Until the Soviet government opens its classified archives to Western scholars, volumes such as this one must be more tentative in their treatment of the Soviet than the Western side. Until that time, no scholar can aspire to write a fully comprehensive or reliable history of any portion of the Cold War.

Information is not the only ingredient vital to historiography. So is the passage of time. It is difficult to think of two leaders whose reputations have oscillated more wildly in three decades than those of Khrushchev and Kennedy. The distance of thirty years allows us to look at both men with greater dispassion.

The end of the Cold War enables us to study that dangerous half century not as an earlier phase of current politics but as a discrete epoch. By exploiting the assets of retrospect and increasing information, historians in both East and West can begin to work toward consensus on the overarching questions of why that epoch started, why it ended, and how to prevent another such tragic and costly struggle.

MICHAEL R. BESCHLOSS

Washington, D.C.
March 1991

CONTENTS

ILLUSTRATIONS

(following page 274)

John Kennedy campaigning in Buffalo (John F. Kennedy Library)

Kennedy and Adlai Stevenson arriving at Carlyle Hotel
    (UPI/Bettmann Newsphotos)

Kennedy greeting RB-47 pilots (John F. Kennedy Library)

"Skull session" in the Cabinet Room (John F. Kennedy Library)

Fidel Castro and Nikita Khrushchev (Wide World)

Kennedy, William Thompson, and George Smathers (Wide World)

Kennedy and his father (Joe Scherschel/*Life* Magazine)

Cuban exiles preparing to retake Cuba (Wide World)

The invasion begins

Prisoners of war displayed (Wide World)

The Kennedys and Prime Minister and Mrs. Constantine Caramanlis
    (Noel Clark/*Life* Magazine)

Robert Kennedy (Wide World)

Georgi Bolshakov (UPI/Bettmann Newsphotos)

The President and First Lady monitor the Alan Shepard flight (John
    F. Kennedy Library)

With Charles de Gaulle, Élysée Palace (UPI/Bettmann Newsphotos)

At Versailles (UPI/Bettmann Newsphotos)

THE
CRISIS YEARS

CHAPTER

1

Almost Midnight

O N SUNDAY MORNING, OCTOBER 14, 1962, JOHN FITZGERALD Kennedy awoke at the Penn Sheraton Hotel in Pittsburgh, there to campaign for Democrats running in the 1962 elections. He did not know it yet, but this was the eve of a military confrontation between the United States and the Soviet Union that was potentially the most dangerous ever.

The President attended Sunday Mass and flew to Niagara Falls, New York, where he climbed into an open car for a motorcade into Buffalo. A girl jumped up and down, shouting, "I can see his hair! I can see his hair!" After speaking on the steps of the Buffalo City Hall, he was scheduled to fly back to Washington in midafternoon.

Then his press secretary, Pierre Salinger, told reporters that there had been a "sudden shift of plans": now the President would stop in New York City on Sunday evening to consult with Adlai Stevenson, his Ambassador to the United Nations.

1

Stevenson had been spending a weekend with friends at Rhinebeck on the Hudson when asked to rush to the President's side. Flown by helicopter to New York City's Idlewild Airport at 6:35 P.M., he was still wearing a country tweed jacket and sweater when he shook Kennedy's hand and followed him into the presidential limousine.

The two men were driven to the Carlyle Hotel, where the President kept a thirty-fourth-floor duplex with antique French furniture and glittering night views of Manhattan. He chatted with Stevenson for an hour about Cuba and the Congo. Then Stevenson left the hotel, telling reporters, "Just a routine briefing."

The newsmen did not discover that Stevenson was quietly followed into Kennedy's suite by the President's gregarious old Harvard roommate, Torbert Macdonald, a Congressman from Malden, Massachusetts. Dinner was brought in. After three hours, Kennedy and Macdonald emerged from the Carlyle and were driven to La Guardia Airport, where they boarded *Air Force One,* bound for Washington.

Far below the presidential plane as it swept over Washington was an outpost of the Central Intelligence Agency, hidden on an upper floor of a car dealership five blocks from the floodlit U.S. Capitol. Inside the darkened suite, photo experts leaned over light boxes, staring at images taken that morning of Fidel Castro's Cuba. A U-2 spy plane had provided the first close look in five weeks at the western reaches of the island.

Secret agents and Cuban exiles had reported to the CIA that the Soviet Union was moving missiles into western Cuba capable of launching nuclear warheads against the United States. Kennedy had sent the U-2 to assure himself that these reports were wrong.

His Sovietologists had reminded him that Nikita Khrushchev had never allowed Soviet nuclear missiles to go outside the Soviet Union. They had insisted that the Chairman would never be so reckless as to send them in secret to an area so close to the United States and an island ruled by a leader so erratic and unpredictable as Castro.

On Monday, weary from campaigning and his late night at the Carlyle, the President did not arrive at the Oval Office until 11:27 A.M., almost three hours later than usual. As he sat down at the famous desk carved from the timbers of the H.M.S. *Resolute,* his back hurt. On the South Grounds of the White House, the Army Band was tuning up and crowds were gathering for the landing by Marine helicopter of Ahmed Ben Bella, Prime Minister of newly independent Algeria.

Every morning, in bed or in his office, Kennedy donned the horn-rimmed reading glasses he never wore in public and looked through a top-secret document called *The President's Intelligence Checklist.* The CIA tailored this paper to the reading habits of each President it served. Under Kennedy, the *Checklist* used the almost wise-guy language that the President and his intimates used in private.

This morning's edition said, "The Saudis, fed up with the unending overflights of their territory by Egyptian aircraft, have obliquely warned Cairo to knock it off. . . . A well-placed source in Vientiane tells us that the cabinet on Friday was treated to a blistering harangue by Phoumi Vongvichit of the Pathet Lao."

The men at the Agency knew that this President's attention could be caught by salacious secrets about foreign leaders. Kennedy was intrigued to hear that the President of Brazil, João Goulart, had had his wife's lover shot to death. He was given a transcript showing what the belligerent West German Defense Minister, Franz-Josef Strauss, "talks like when drunk."

Ben Bella's chopper landed on the South Grounds at Monday noon. As the President and his dark young state guest marched past an honor guard, the nearly five-year-old Caroline Kennedy and her kindergarten class watched from an upstairs window of the White House. Each time the cannon boomed in its twenty-one-gun salute, the children cried out, "Bang!" The President looked up at the window and barely managed not to smile.

Charles de Gaulle, with his exquisite conception of statesmanlike behavior, would have been outraged. The Algerian was charmed. Kennedy led him into the Rose Garden, where his wife, Jacqueline, was crouching with her arms around little John, Jr., who was frightened by the sound of the cannon. Grinning, Ben Bella pinched the cheek of the President's son.

In the aerie above the car dealership, a CIA man cried, "Take a look at this!" Bleary-eyed colleagues looked over his shoulder at a blowup of San Cristóbal, one hundred miles west of Havana. He showed them a rude series of tents, propellant vehicles, missile transporters, erectors, and a launching pad. His superior, Arthur Lundahl, said, "Don't leave this room. We might be sitting on the biggest story of our time."

Lundahl dialed Ray Cline, the CIA's Deputy Director for Intelligence, who said, "You know all the shit is going to hit the fan when you tell him that." Feeling that he lacked the seniority to give

Kennedy the grim news, Cline called the President's national security adviser, McGeorge Bundy, whom he had known since they were both Junior Fellows at Harvard in 1941.

Bundy and his wife, Mary, were giving a small dinner for Charles and Avis Bohlen, who were about to sail for Paris, where the lifelong diplomat and Soviet expert was to accept the difficult mission of serving as Kennedy's envoy to de Gaulle. When the telephone rang, Bundy left the room to take the call. Cline spoke guardedly: "Those things we've been worrying about—it looks as though we've really got something."

Bundy asked, "You sure?" Cline was sure. Bundy said, "I'll handle it at my end. Will you guys be ready in the morning?"

Bundy knew that within hours the United States and Soviet Union would probably be "closer to nuclear war than at any time during the age of the atom." His telephone call to the President could prove more fateful than the call to Franklin Roosevelt after Pearl Harbor or to Harry Truman after North Koreans swarmed across the Thirty-eighth Parallel.

Then he thought again: why call the President now? Among the dinner guests talking and laughing in the next room were French diplomats and at least one reporter. The group "would clearly be startled if the dinner party broke up, or if I spent the evening on the phone, because it could only be the President and nobody else." The highest officials of the U.S. government were "scattered around town." If the President convened them all tonight, everyone in the city could learn the secret.

Bundy knew that his boss was tired after his late flight from New York. As he told Kennedy much later, "I decided that a quiet evening and a night of sleep were the best preparation you could have in the light of what would face you in the next days."

At eight-thirty on Tuesday morning, October 16, Bundy took the tiny elevator up to the family quarters on the second floor of the White House. He walked down the wide hall past paintings by Catlin, Homer, Prendergast, and Sargent and paused before the oaken door to the President's bedchamber. Once inside the room, he saw Kennedy sitting in a wing chair, wearing a nightshirt and slippers and eating breakfast from a tray.

Bundy told him that the worst had come to pass. The angry President's first reaction was a sense that Khrushchev "can't do this to me."

He was certain that "one way or another, the missiles have to go." Both he and Bundy knew without saying it that bombing the missile sites could sentence millions of Americans, Europeans, and Soviets to their deaths.

Kennedy lowered himself into a steaming bath with his children's toy yellow dogs and pink pigs along the rim of the tub. Then, as he quickly dressed, he told Bundy to call an urgent secret meeting in the Cabinet Room and rattled off names to be invited. He telephoned his brother Robert, Attorney General of the United States, and told him they were facing "great trouble."

At the Justice Department, Robert Kennedy kept a morning appointment with Richard Helms, the CIA's poker-faced Deputy Director for Plans. Helms had asked to see the Attorney General about a recent Soviet defector, knowing that Kennedy rarely minced words. Once when Helms told him of a plan to use a Latin American Jesuit order in a CIA operation, the Attorney General shook his head: "You can't trust the Jesuits."

As Helms walked into the vaulted office, his piercing eyes took in the crayon drawings by Kennedy's children tacked onto the mahogany-paneled walls. The shirtsleeved Kennedy looked up from behind his big desk. "Dick, is it true they've found Russian missiles in Cuba?"

"Yes, Bob, they have."

"*Shit!*"

Helms and Kennedy discussed the defector, but their attention remained on Cuba. Later in the morning, the two men went to the old Executive Office Building, across from the White House, for a scheduled engagement with the Special Group (Augmented), a group invented by the President to oversee covert action against the island. Few of its members were cleared to know about the missiles in Cuba. Helms and Kennedy knew that canceling the meeting might arouse suspicions.

Since the failed effort to retake the island by landing at the Bay of Pigs in April 1961, Helms had felt what he called "white heat" from the President about Cuba. In the absence of intolerable provocation by Castro or the Soviets, Kennedy lacked the stomach to approve a full-scale American military invasion that could cost more than a hundred thousand lives. The American war against Castro would thus have to be a secret campaign.

As Helms recalled, "The whip was on the Agency all the time from the President through Bobby: 'Get on with this thing! God, you've got to do something about it!' He wanted Castro *out* of there." In January 1962, Robert Kennedy had called Helms to his office and told him that getting rid of Castro was "the top priority in the U.S. government. All else is secondary. No time, money, effort, or manpower is to be spared."

The result was Operation Mongoose, which soon became the largest of the CIA's covert operations. The program consisted of at least thirty-three different schemes intended to culminate in Castro's removal—paramilitary raids, espionage, counterfeiting of money and ration books, and attacks on oil refineries and farms that would make the Cuban economy scream. The CIA contaminated Cuban sugar fields, detonated bombs in department stores, set factories aflame.

For two years, Helms and his men had also collaborated with Mafia leaders like Sam Giancana of Chicago to murder Fidel Castro. By October 1962, Helms had concluded that the plots were going nowhere. He suspected that at least one of the Mob's hit squads in Cuba had been captured and tortured by Castro's forces. But as he recalled years later, he saw little harm in letting the gangsters keep on trying to kill the dictator in order to see whether the Mafia actually had any valuable intelligence assets on the island.

During this morning's Special Group session, to avoid betraying the secret of the missiles on Cuba, Robert Kennedy behaved as if there were no special news from the island. With more heat than usual, he complained that the job of Castro's removal had been "botched." Mongoose had been going for a year without success. Why couldn't they *do* something? The President was *not happy.*

After the meeting, he went to Bundy's office in the White House basement to look at the U-2 pictures for himself. Bending over the pictures with a magnifying glass, he hissed, "*Shit! Shit! Shit!*"

In the Oval Office, the President asked his close aide and speech writer Theodore Sorensen to look up what kind of public warning he had issued against Soviet offensive missiles in Cuba. The answer: before July 1962, Kennedy had never formally cautioned the Soviet Union against such an installation on the island. By then, the missiles had to have been already on their way.

White House aides not cleared to know the Cuba secret wondered why Kennedy was so edgy this morning. He kept pulling at the wattle under his chin, tracing his lips with his index finger, jamming his foot against the drawers of his desk, and bouncing his knee up and down. David Powers, the man-of-all-work who had served the President since his first campaign for Congress in 1946, thought, *God, he looks like someone has just told him the house is on fire.*

Salinger assumed that Kennedy was angry about Ben Bella. After the imposing White House welcome and what the President had thought was an amiable conversation in the Oval Office, the Algerian had confirmed Kennedy's private prejudices about the opportunism of nonaligned leaders by flying straight to Havana and joining Castro to demand that the United States abandon the ninety-nine-year lease to its Guantanamo naval base on the island.

At 11:50 A.M., Kennedy walked into the Cabinet Room and sat down with Secretary of State Dean Rusk, Secretary of Defense Robert McNamara, and other liege men around the coffin-shaped table. The President was the only one present who knew that he had ordered this session secretly recorded by a tape machine connected to microphones hidden in the draperies.

As the reels began to turn, Kennedy asked Arthur Lundahl and a CIA missile expert, Sidney Graybeal, to explain the U-2 pictures to the laymen present. The tape of the dialogue has been preserved:

LUNDAHL: This is a result of the photography taken Sunday, sir.

KENNEDY: Yeah.

LUNDAHL: There's a medium-range ballistic missile launch site and two new military encampments on the southern edge of Sierra del Rosario in west central Cuba. . . .

KENNEDY: How do you know this is a medium-range ballistic missile?

LUNDAHL: The length, sir.

KENNEDY: The what? The length?

LUNDAHL: The length of it. . . . Mr. Graybeal, our missile, uh, man, has some pictures of the equivalent Soviet equipment that has been dragged through the streets of Moscow. . . .

KENNEDY: Is this ready to be fired?

GRAYBEAL: No, sir.

KENNEDY: How long have we got? We can't tell, I take it.

GRAYBEAL: No, sir. . . .

* * *

This same morning in Moscow, Kennedy's new Ambassador to the Soviet Union, Foy Kohler, had gone to the Kremlin for his first official audience with the man who was both Chairman of the Council of Ministers and First Secretary of the Soviet Communist Party's Central Committee.

Nikita Sergeyevich Khrushchev's face was still pink and glowing from two months of swimming, sunbathing, and badminton-playing with his wife, son, daughters, and grandchildren at his estate at Pitsunda on the Black Sea. The two months were not merely frivolous. Since the days of Stalin, who rarely left Moscow, Soviet leaders had been almost honor-bound to spend long periods away from the capital as earnest of their intention not to reimpose a Stalin-style rule.

While relaxing at Pitsunda, Khrushchev liked to stroll the beaches and woods and ponder what he insisted was the "radiant future" of the Soviet Union. With his eyes half closed, he stayed up late into the night with friends and family, singing folk songs from his Ukrainian childhood like "The Wide Dnieper Roars and Moans," "Black Lashes, Brown Eyes," and "I Wonder at the Sky." Semiliterate into his thirties, he now professed to read *War and Peace* at least once a year.

At the Kremlin, standing behind Khrushchev as he greeted Kohler and his political counselor, Richard Davies, were Vasily Kuznetsov and Mikhail Smirnovsky of the Soviet Foreign Ministry and the Chairman's crack young translator, Viktor Sukhodrev. As always, the Americans were seated across from Khrushchev at the green-baize-draped table, the sun streaming into their eyes.

Khrushchev complained that American spy planes were "harassing" Soviet merchant ships heading for Cuba. Why was the United States so worried about Cuba? The Soviet government had "no intention of putting any offensive weapons in there." Kohler explained that one reason Americans were so worried about Cuba was Castro's recent announcement that the Soviet Union was building a new port on the island.

The Chairman said, "Just because I am building a fishing port in Cuba, you want to go to war. After all, I'm not doing anything you haven't done to me in Turkey and Iran." He inveighed against the Jupiter missiles placed by the United States in 1959 along the Soviet border in Turkey. While insisting that the Cuban port would have no military value, he conceded that Castro's announcement had caused Kennedy political trouble: "If I had been in Moscow, the announcement would never have been made. . . . After the elections, there will be plenty of time to talk about these things."

After returning to the American Embassy, Kohler cabled Washington that Khrushchev had been "charming" and "extremely amiable." In his ignorance about the missiles in Cuba, Kohler reported that the conversation had been "very reassuring."

In the afternoon, the President went to the State Department auditorium for an off-the-record session with five hundred editorial writers and broadcasters. Several in the audience wondered why Kennedy seemed so distracted and intense.

He declared that the overriding problem for the United States was to ensure "the survival of our country" without igniting "the third and perhaps the last war." He recited a Spanish bullfighter's verse that Robert Kennedy carried in his wallet:

> *Bullfight critics ranked in rows*
> *Crowd the enormous Plaza full;*
> *But only one is there who* knows.
> *And he's the man who fights the bull.*

That evening, after another Cabinet Room council on the missiles, he and Jacqueline were driven to Georgetown for a dinner given by the columnist Joseph Alsop and his wife, Susan Mary. As Alsop recalled, the President "sat at the head of the table and damn near threw a ruin on the evening because he was in such a deep brown study." Twice Kennedy asked two other guests, Chip Bohlen and the Oxford historian Isaiah Berlin, what the Soviets had done in the past when backed into a corner.

Mrs. Alsop was surprised that the President "wanted to go back for more on a subject that didn't even seem interesting." That night in bed, she told her husband, "I may be crazy, but I think something is going on." Berlin left the dinner wondering whether "deep in the President's mind he may not have a presentiment that he may not live a long time . . . and that he must make his mark on history quickly."

Buoyancy and optimism were hallmarks of Kennedy's political persona. "Like a lot of flags on a ship," observed his Harvard friend Charles Spalding. But as his admirer the historian William Manchester observed, "Under the facade there is, though scarcely suspected, a dark vein of sadness." The President's foreign policy aide Walt

Rostow noticed that Kennedy's "voracious enjoyment of life" was always balanced against "a sense of the possibility of failure and tragedy."

Fatalism was a rational response to Kennedy's life experience. Son of a deeply pessimistic Irish father, he never lost sight of how his own career had been shaped by accident. Had his father not amassed a fortune, had his older brother, Joe, survived World War II to enter politics, had one voter per precinct in 1960 changed his vote to Nixon, he probably would never have become President of the United States. He privately joked that he owed his job to "Cook County, Illinois."

He was fascinated by the subject of death by violence and accident. His friend Senator George Smathers of Florida recalled that "twenty times or more" Kennedy asked him what would be the best way to die: "What would it be like to drown? Would you rather be in an airplane and crash? Would you rather be shot? Is it the best way to get hit in the head or in your chest somewhere and have time?" He wondered whether you would "think about all the good things that had happened to you, or regret all the things you hadn't done."

Sitting on the *Honey Fitz,* the presidential yacht he had renamed for his maternal grandfather, Mayor John Fitzgerald of Boston, Kennedy would watch a passing jet and wonder whether if the pilot died, he could fly it, wrestling with the controls. As a macabre joke while relaxing with Jacqueline and friends at Newport, he once pantomimed his own death, clutching his chest and falling to the ground with make-believe blood gushing from his mouth as a friend's motion picture camera rolled.

Kennedy's Choate School friend LeMoyne Billings felt that in the late 1940s, after Kennedy's beloved sister Kathleen was killed in an air crash and he was told that he too might soon die of Addison's disease, "he just figured there was no sense in planning ahead anymore. The only thing that made sense . . . was to live for the moment, treating each day as if it were his last, demanding of life constant intensity, adventure, and pleasure."

Even as President, Kennedy's tomorrow-we-die streak remained, evinced by his promiscuity with women and his indifference to physical risk. Secret Service men complained that he was "a notoriously poor driver who drove through red lights and took many unnecessary chances." Sometimes he dismissed the agents, saying, "Whoever wants to get me will get me."

In November 1963, the weekend before he left for Texas, he told Lyndon Johnson, "Get in my plane." The agents pleaded with him to follow custom and let the Vice President fly in a separate aircraft.

Kennedy laughed. "Don't you fellows want McCormack as President?"*

Once at a Washington horse show, the novelist and playwright Gore Vidal, whose mother and Jacqueline's had successively married the same man, remarked to Kennedy on how easy it would be for someone to shoot the President—"only they'd probably miss and hit me." Kennedy chuckled: "No great loss."

The President went on to relate the surprise ending of the thriller *Twenty-four Hours* by Edgar Wallace. A British prime minister was told he would be assassinated at midnight. Guards from Scotland Yard surrounded Number Ten Downing Street. Midnight came and went. The telephone rang. Relieved, the prime minister picked up the receiver—and was electrocuted.

Near midnight, driven away from the Alsop house in his black Lincoln with Jacqueline sitting on his left, Kennedy stared out at the almost-deserted streets of Washington.

He often said that being President would be "the best job in the world if it weren't for the Russians. . . . You never know what those bastards are up to." That afternoon Rusk had brought him Kohler's cables from Moscow about his conversation with Khrushchev. Kennedy had flushed with anger. No offensive weapons in Cuba? No desire to embarrass him before the elections? When had a Soviet leader told an American President more brazen lies?

The President told his brother that Khrushchev's behavior was "how an immoral gangster would act, and not as a statesman, not as a person with a sense of responsibility." As Robert later said, "It had all been lies. One gigantic fabric of lies. We had been deceived by Khrushchev, but we had also fooled ourselves."

Kennedy knew what thermonuclear war would mean: the flight to the underground presidential Doomsday headquarters in Virginia, the rioting and panic, the death clouds over American and Soviet cities. Within days, he and Khrushchev would embody the image that Dwight Eisenhower had used in 1953 to describe the Cold War: two colossi eying each other across a trembling world.

The President could not later ignore the irony that this global confrontation had been ushered in by accident and miscalculation,

---

*John McCormack of Massachusetts, the parochial Speaker of the House and sometime Kennedy foe, was in his seventy-second year and uncertain health.

exactly the dangers he had preached against in public and private for two years. In the fall of 1962, he was reading the best-selling thriller *Fail Safe* by Eugene Burdick and Harvey Wheeler, about the accidental release of an American nuclear bomber, leading to the incineration of Moscow and New York.

This October evening was three years and one month to the day after Kennedy's first encounter with the leader of the Soviet Union, during Khrushchev's American tour. Kennedy was a junior member of the Senate Foreign Relations Committee, and, as the Chairman never forgot, he was late.

CHAPTER

2

"He's Younger Than My Own Son"

O N WEDNESDAY AFTERNOON, SEPTEMBER 16, 1959, THE JUNIOR
Senator from Massachusetts stepped out of his family's new
eighteen-seat Convair, the *Caroline,* at National Airport in Washington, D.C. He found his driver, a *Last Hurrah* Bostonian named Muggsy
O'Leary, and slipped behind the wheel of his battered blue Pontiac
convertible. O'Leary sat in what he called the "death seat" for one of
his boss's breakneck rides to the Old Senate Office Building.

Kennedy had interrupted what his office called a "pulse-feeling"
tour of Ohio in order to take tea at the Capitol with Nikita Khrushchev, leaders of the Senate, and fellow members of the Foreign
Relations Committee, led by its chairman, J. William Fulbright of
Arkansas. Several Senators had announced their refusal to sit in the
same room as the best-known Communist on the planet.

Khrushchev was in Washington for the first American visit by a
supreme Soviet leader. His week-long rail and air journey to New

13

York, Los Angeles, San Francisco, Des Moines, and Pittsburgh was scheduled to end with a private weekend with President Eisenhower and their chief aides at Camp David.

Usually Kennedy was irritated by having to rush back to Washington for an important Senate vote or another mandatory occasion. Not this time. He was curious to see Khrushchev in person, and he could ill afford to be seen skipping the chance to do so in order to barnstorm in Ohio.

A Gallup poll released this week showed that in a presidential trial heat, Richard Nixon had surged ahead of Kennedy for the first time this year. The Vice President's new lead was attributed to his "kitchen debate" with the Soviet leader in Moscow in July, allowing him to advertise himself as the man who had stood up to Khrushchev. Kennedy knew that attending a Senate tea with the Chairman was a meager substitute, but it would at least enable him to tell voters that he too had dealt with the leader of the Soviet Union.

Kennedy envied the prestige that Hubert Humphrey had gained from seeing Khrushchev in Moscow for twelve well-publicized hours in 1958. Only four years after the plague time of Joseph McCarthy, the Minnesota Senator had managed to win the approval even of Henry Luce's *Life* in a glowing cover story. Kennedy thought briefly of trying to arrange his own audience with Khrushchev but abandoned the idea so as not to seem to be imitating Humphrey.

Early in 1959, the unctuous American-baiting Soviet Ambassador Mikhail Menshikov, sardonically known in Washington as "Smiling Mike," began calling on Senators cited as presidential possibilities in 1960. When Menshikov came by the Kennedy office, the Senator "gave him very short shrift," as his foreign affairs adviser Frederick Holborn recalled. "Kennedy was very resistant to dealing directly with Soviets. . . . It didn't last very long and Kennedy wasn't very interested in having any significant conversation. I think he was just very wary. He didn't know what Menshikov would say or try to—he didn't like the politics of it."

Some weeks later, Menshikov invited Kennedy by letter to come for a weekend at the Soviet estate on the Eastern Shore of Maryland. Holborn noted that Kennedy's response was "wry but contemptuous": he disliked the Ambassador, feared that the Soviets or the Right might use the visit to "embarrass" him, and was certain he would be "bored to death."

Arriving at his Senate office, Room 362, Kennedy looked through his telephone messages. Some concerned Ohio. Last night in Columbus, Kennedy and his twenty-seven-year-old brother, Edward, had dined with the state's rotund Democratic Governor, Michael DiSalle (the *Washington Evening Star:* LOOK-ALIKE KENNEDYS MEET GOVERNOR). Two and a half hours of haggling had failed to capture DiSalle's early endorsement for 1960.

Now it was almost five o'clock. The Khrushchev meeting was about to begin. Kennedy brushed aside a warning that he would be late. He returned some political telephone calls, then walked with Holborn to the Capitol, where they had never seen so many security men. Americans and Soviets with screeching walkie-talkies were guarding the soundproof door of F-53, the ceremonial chamber of the Foreign Relations Committee.

As Kennedy was let into the room, Khrushchev looked up. Although the Senator was only a few minutes late, five years as the most powerful man in the Kremlin had made the Chairman unaccustomed to tardiness. Always alert to the remotest hint of American affront, he may have wondered whether this was a deliberate insult. Was the young man showing his contempt for the great socialist state and its leader?

By laws of seniority, Kennedy was compelled to remain silent while Senate elders like Fulbright, Lyndon Johnson, Everett Dirksen, Richard Russell, Theodore Green, and Carl Hayden badgered Khrushchev about American overseas bases, outer space, Soviet subversion, censorship, and radio jamming. As Kennedy sat and listened, he took notes: "Tea—vodka—if we drank vodka all the time, we could not launch rockets to the moon. . . . Tan suit—French cuffs—short, stocky, two red ribbons, two stars."

At the end of the ninety minutes, Fulbright introduced the guest of honor to each Senator. Kennedy was impressed by the way Khrushchev seemed to know exactly who in the room had enough influence in the Senate or presidential potential to merit special attention. Khrushchev told him that he looked too young to be a Senator: "I've heard a lot about you. People say you have a great future ahead of you." Walking back to his office, Kennedy told Mike Mansfield, "It was very important to see Khrushchev in the flesh."

Dictating his memoirs years later, Khrushchev said he was "impressed with Kennedy. I remember liking his face, which was sometimes stern but which often broke into a good-natured smile." The Soviet diplomat Georgi Kornienko recalled that when Khrushchev asked Menshikov and his embassy staff about Kennedy, "I gave the most positive picture. I said that, while Kennedy was not yet another Roosevelt, he was independent and intelligent and could be counted on for new departures. Khrushchev listened."

Several weeks later, Kennedy received a note from Fulbright along with his place card from the Khrushchev tea, which the Chairman had autographed for each Senator: "Dear Jack. . . . Maybe this will enable you to get out of jail when the revolution comes, but it may have some other value that I do not now recognize."

Too junior to be invited to Khrushchev's dinner for Eisenhower at the Soviet Embassy that evening, Kennedy flew back to Columbus and arrived late for an address to the Ohio Bankers Association. Reporting on his meeting, Kennedy said that Khrushchev had an "inferiority complex," which surfaced in his answers to "harmless questions": "He has a sense of humor that runs through everything. He looks tireless. . . . He is built close to the ground, and it looks as if he will survive for a long time."

In speech after speech during the year to come, Kennedy noted Khrushchev's prediction to the Senators on the Foreign Relations Committee that their children and grandchildren would live under communism: "I don't believe it. . . . I believe *his* children can be free. But it depends on us."

As an adolescent in the 1930s, John Kennedy was considerably more aware of foreign affairs than the average Choate or Harvard student. During these years, his father was increasingly drawn to the international arena, doing film and liquor business in Europe, negotiating with bankers, businessmen, and foreign officials as chairman of Franklin Roosevelt's Securities and Exchange Commission and Maritime Commission, and dealing with Neville Chamberlain and Winston Churchill in London during his fateful term as Roosevelt's Ambassador to the Court of St. James's.

Believing that commanding knowledge of world affairs would help them to have the social and political eminence he wished for them, Joseph Kennedy led his sons in the famous family dinner table arguments, sent them on foreign trips, and, while serving in London, hired Joe, Jr., and Jack for various tasks in the Embassy.

In the spring of 1934, carrying a tennis racket, Joe, Jr., boarded a train to Moscow and Leningrad with Harold Laski, the British Socialist with whom he was studying at the London School of Economics. When he returned home with enthusiastic tales of Soviet life and challenged his father on capitalism versus communism, his brother Jack gibed that "Joe seems to understand the situation a little better than Dad."

In 1936, Rose Kennedy and her eldest daughter, Kathleen, went to see the mysterious land for themselves. In Moscow, they stayed at Spaso House with Ambassador William Bullitt, whom Roosevelt had appointed after recognizing Stalin's regime in November 1933. Mrs.

Kennedy was dismayed by the compulsory atheism and the secret police but enthralled by Moscow's new Metro, finding every station "a work of art in marble and mosaic."* By tour's end, she conceded that the masses were "better off in a good many ways than they had been under the czarist system."

In the summer of 1937, Jack toured France, Italy, and Spain and read John Gunther's bestseller *Inside Europe,* which described Stalin's purges and show trials as well as the rising Soviet standard of living. Gunther concluded that however much world revolution still lurked in Stalin's mind, Soviet foreign policy could be "expressed in one word—peace."

Kennedy wrote in his journal, "Finished Gunther and have come to the decision that Facism [sic] is the thing for Germany and Italy, Communism for Russia, and Democracy for America and England." As a Harvard junior in 1938, he took a popular Russian history course taught by Professor Michael Karpovich, a White Russian émigré, who gave him a B-minus.

He left Harvard in the spring of 1939 to take a job arranged by his father in the American Embassy in Paris, where Bullitt was now Ambassador. In May, Jack wrote his Choate friend Lem Billings, now at Princeton, "Am living it up at the Embassy and living like a King. . . . Big Bull Bullitt is his usual genial self and has been as a matter of fact very nice to me."†

Carrying a letter of introduction from Secretary of State Cordell Hull, Kennedy traveled to Poland, Latvia, Moscow, Leningrad, and the Crimea, Turkey, Palestine, and the Balkans. There is little record of his journey through the Soviet Union. Kennedy found it "a crude, backward, hopelessly bureaucratic country." Later he suggested that his mother read Alice-Leone Moats's *Blind Date with Mars,* which limned a grim, regimented Soviet people resigned to eternal imprisonment.

Assigned to entertain Joseph Kennedy's son at the American Embassy in Moscow, Chip and Avis Bohlen were both struck by what

---

*Construction of the subway had been overseen by Nikita Khrushchev of the city's Communist Party.

†Bullitt assigned him to his aide Carmel Offie, a homosexual whom Jack called "La Belle Offlet." He wrote Billings, "Offie has just rung for me so I guess have to get the old paper ready and go in and wipe his arse." He complained that Bullitt's aide "is always trying, *unsuccessfully,* to pour Champagne down my gullet." He added, "Met a girl who used to live with the Duke of Kent and who is as she says 'a member of the British Royal family by injections.' She has terrific diamond bracelets that he gave her and a big ruby that the Marajah [sic] of Nepal gave her. I don't know what she thinks she is going to get out of me but we'll see."

Bohlen later called the young man's "charm and quick mind"—especially his "openmindedness about the Soviet Union," which Bohlen called "a rare quality in those prewar days."

"Had a great trip," Jack wrote Billings from London in mid-July. "The only way you can really know what is going to go on is to go to all the countries—I still don't think there will be a war this year. . . . Germany will try to break Danzig off gradually making it difficult for Poland to say that at *this* point her independence is being threatened.* However, I don't think she will succeed." After the outbreak of war in September, he returned to Harvard to write his senior honors thesis on "Appeasement at Munich," which was published in July 1940 as the bestseller *Why England Slept.*

After Pearl Harbor, by then a lieutenant in Naval Intelligence, Kennedy wrote Billings, who was on his way to North Africa, "It seems a rather strange commentary that it will take death in large quantities to wake us up, but I really don't think anything else ever will. I don't think anyone realizes that nothing stands between us and the defeat of our Christian crusade against paganism except a lot of chinks who never heard of God, and a lot of Russians who have heard about Him but don't want Him.

"I suppose we can't afford to be very choosy at a time like this. When you get to Africa make friends with any brown, black, or yellow man you happen to meet. In *The Decline of the West,* Mr. Spengler, after carefully studying the waves of civilization, prophesied that the next few centuries belonged to the yellow man. After the Japs get through uniting Asia it looks as though Mrs. Lindbergh's 'wave of the future' will certainly have a yellow look."

In May 1945, returned from his PT-109 adventure in the South Pacific, he covered the United Nations' founding conference at San Francisco for the Hearst papers. From the turbulent meetings and "talk of fighting the Russians in the next ten or fifteen years" he concluded that much time would have to pass before the Soviets entrusted their safety to anyone but the Red Army: "There is a heritage of twenty-five years of distrust between Russia and the rest of the world that cannot be overcome completely for a good many years."

After Kennedy was elected to Congress in 1946 from an ethnic working-class district in Massachusetts, his pronouncements on the Cold War reflected his constituents' fury about Soviet domination of Eastern Europe. Kennedy told a Polish-American group that Franklin Roosevelt had given Poland to the Communists "because he did not

---

*This is almost word for word the way President Kennedy described his anxiety about what Khrushchev might do to West Berlin in 1961.

understand the Russian mind." In 1949, he lambasted "a sick Roosevelt" for giving up the Kurile Islands and strategic Chinese ports at Yalta.

Travel and ambitions for higher office helped to pull Kennedy's views toward the mainstream of the national Democratic Party. A 1951 trip to Western Europe reassured him that a Red Army invasion was unlikely. In Paris, he asked General Eisenhower if there was not a great danger that Western military preparations in Europe might provoke Russia to attack. In his notes he recorded Eisenhower's view "that these were only two chances for a deliberate war: 1st, If the Russians believed they could win a quick victory; 2nd, If they could win a long war of exhaustion. They can't do either of these now.

"He doesn't eliminate the possibility of an accidental war. I asked him what he would do if he were advisor to the Russians. He replied that he would advise them to continue doing exactly what they are now doing—but more so, would keep up the pressure in the hopes of an economic collapse in the U.S. 'or these countries here' falling into Russian hands. . . . Said $64 question was whether Kremlin leaders were fanatical doctrinaires or just ruthless men determined to hold on to power. If first, chances of peace much less than 2nd."

By the time Kennedy reached the Senate in 1953, he had discarded much of his brash critique of the Roosevelt-Truman approach to the world. But only in 1957, as a new member of the Foreign Relations Committee preparing to run for President, did he move strongly into foreign affairs. In July, speaking on the Senate floor, he antagonized much of the American foreign policy establishment by endorsing Algerian independence from the French. The next month, in another floor speech, he called for the United States to promote diversity in Poland and other Soviet bloc countries through trade and economic assistance.

By the late 1950s, the Democratic Party was divided about how to deal with the Soviets. Dean Acheson and kindred spirits argued that the world had changed little since his term as Truman's Secretary of State and that Khrushchev's nuclear threats were intended to achieve Stalin's old goal of world domination. Adlai Stevenson, Chester Bowles, Averell Harriman, and other Democrats believed that Khrushchev genuinely wished to reduce his military budget in order to improve the Soviet standard of living.

Kennedy was too allergic to ideology and too eager for broad Democratic support in 1960 to side with either camp. He used Cold War language that a Stevenson would never have used. After the Geneva summit of 1955: "The barbarian may have taken the knife out of his teeth to smile, but the knife itself is still in his fist." When George

Kennan in 1957 made his controversial proposal for East-West talks on disengagement from Central and Eastern Europe, Kennedy wrote him to praise its "brilliance and stimulation."

In 1958 and 1959, he jabbed at the Eisenhower diplomacy from both left and right: the President was laggard on arms control, over-reliant on nuclear weapons, indifferent to the Third World and to the Soviet missile buildup. Along with other Democrats and Republicans he warned of a "missile gap" that would give the Soviets "a new shortcut to world domination" through "Sputnik diplomacy, limited brushfire wars, indirect non-overt aggression, intimidation and subversion, internal revolution . . . and the vicious blackmail of our allies. The periphery of the free world will slowly be nibbled away."

The text of a tape-recorded conversation in July 1959 with his first biographer, James MacGregor Burns, reveals Kennedy's private pessimism about improving relations with Moscow:

> You have to first decide what is the motive force of the Soviet Union. Is it merely to provide security for them, and in order to provide security for the Russian mainland, do they have to have friendly countries on the borders? . . . Or is it evangelical, that communists can, by continuing to press on us, weaken us so that eventually they can—the world revolution?
>
> I guess probably, obviously, a combination of the two. So therefore, I don't think that there is any button that you press that reaches an accommodation with the Soviet Union which is hard and fast. . . . What it is is a constant day-to-day struggle with an enemy who is constantly attempting to expand his power. . . . You have two people, neither of whom—who are both of goodwill, but neither of whom can communicate because of a language difference. . . .
>
> I don't think there's any magic solution to solve or really ease East-West at the present time. Now maybe a successor to Khrushchev—or even Khrushchev himself. . . . It's like those ads you see in the Sunday [New York] Times in the back about some fellow with a beard about "he releases the magic powers within you." The magic power really is the desire of everyone to be independent and every nation to be independent. That's the basic force which is really, I think, the strong force on our side. That's the magic power, and that's what's going to screw the Russians ultimately.

Khrushchev's Camp David weekend with Eisenhower brought unexpected results. He suspended his demand that the West get out of Berlin. The two leaders agreed to a full-fledged summit with the leaders of Britain and France, after which Eisenhower would tour the

Soviet Union with Khrushchev at his side. Despite the President's caution, newsmen heralded a "Spirit of Camp David" that would begin to rid the world of Cold War.

Republican campaigners were delirious: Eisenhower would sign ground-breaking accords with the Soviets, travel the Soviet Union one month before the party conventions, and sweep Richard Nixon into the White House as the man to continue the President's work for peace.

At the University of Rochester, Kennedy scoffed: the Khrushchev he had met had not "in the slightest" changed his belief in the inevitable triumph of communism. "The real roots of the Soviet-American conflict cannot be easily settled by negotiations. Our basic national interests and their basic national interest clash—in Europe, in the Middle East, and around the world." The *Washington Star* felt that Kennedy's speech showed that he "at this stage of the game does not know which way to jump. If we were in his shoes, we wouldn't know either."

In the early spring of 1960, neither Kennedy nor his rivals wished to undercut the President as he prepared for the mid-May Paris summit at which he would bargain with Khrushchev over Berlin and a nuclear test ban treaty. As Kennedy won primaries in New Hampshire, Wisconsin, and Indiana, he stuck mainly to domestic issues.

Then, on May Day, an American U-2 crashed thirteen hundred miles inside the Soviet Union. Eisenhower pledged to stop further such flights but refused Khrushchev's demand for an apology. The Chairman stalked out of the summit meeting in Paris, revoked his invitation to the Soviet Union, and declared that he would deal only with the next American President.

Campaigning in Oregon, Kennedy said that Khrushchev had made "a clumsy attempt to divide us along partisan lines." He promised, if elected, to maintain Eisenhower's ban on future espionage flights, but said that the President should never have let "the risk of war hang on the possibility of an engine failure." As a result of the U-2 affair Americans were now "living through the most dangerous time since the Korean War."

Two mornings after the summit collapse, a high school student in St. Helens, Oregon, asked Kennedy what he would have done in Eisenhower's place. He replied that Khrushchev had set two conditions to continue the summit: "First, that we apologize. I think that that might have been possible to do. And that, second, we try those responsible for the flight. We could not do that. . . . It was a condition Mr. Khrushchev knew we couldn't meet, and therefore it indicated that he wanted to break it up."

Kennedy instantly knew that he should have been more careful. He had someone call the Portland *Oregonian*'s political reporter, Mervin Shoemaker, who was present, to say he had meant to say "express regrets." But Shoemaker wrote a story accusing Kennedy's "henchmen" of "semantic sidestepping" to "explain away a statement by Kennedy that they fear might have important aftereffects."

Wire services sent Kennedy's gaffe all over America. On the Senate floor, Hugh Scott of Pennsylvania demanded that he relieve himself of the suspicion of "appeasement"—a word that had a special sting for the son of Joseph Kennedy. Before replying, Kennedy wanted to make sure that he had undeniably said "apologize." He called the St. Helens principal, who located a tape of his appearance and played it for him over the long-distance telephone.

On the Senate floor, he argued that he could not have proposed apologizing to Khrushchev to save the summit because the summit was by then already beyond saving. But bundles of angry telegrams descended on Room 362: "When one apologizes to Khrushchev, it's the same as apologizing to the Devil. . . . Saying or implying Eisenhower goofed at the summit will breed disgust for you and your party. . . . YOU'RE UNFIT TO BE PRESIDENT. They need your kind of double-dealers in Russia. Go to Russia."

Lyndon Johnson, campaigning in the Northwest, asked audiences, *"I'm* not prepared to apologize to Mr. Khrushchev—*are you?"* ("No-o-o-o-o-o!" they cried.) David Kendall of the White House staff told colleagues that Kennedy had made himself "the candidate of the Kremlin."

Richard Nixon called Kennedy's "naive" comments new evidence of his inexperience: no President must ever apologize "for trying to defend the United States." *Time* reported that the "new cold air mass" from Moscow had brought "an entirely new atmosphere in U.S. political life." Senator Henry Jackson of Washington said, "The public is going to expect a tough, tough line."

With Kennedy on the threshold of the Democratic nomination, surveys now showed that Americans were having second thoughts about entrusting their security to a forty-three-year-old back-bench Senator. The new atmosphere did not cause Kennedy to lose the remaining primaries, but had the U-2 wrecked the Paris summit in March rather than May, he might have been defeated by someone such as Adlai Stevenson who was more experienced in world affairs.

In June 1960, on the Senate floor, Kennedy proposed a twelve-point plan including increased defense spending to resist the "Soviet program for world domination": "As a substitute for policy, President Eisenhower has tried smiling at the Russians, our State Department has tried frowning at them, and Mr. Nixon has tried both. . . . So long as Mr. Khrushchev is convinced that the balance of power is shifting his way, no amount of either smiles or toughness—neither Camp David talks nor Kitchen Debates—can compel him to enter fruitful negotiations."

That summer, in Havana, Castro expropriated American property and asked for Soviet aid. Anti-American rioters in Tokyo forced the President to cancel a visit to Japan. Soviet forces were invited to the Congo. The Soviets walked out of Geneva disarmament talks. In July, they downed an American RB-47 over the Barents Sea and jailed the two survivors. In August, they subjected the U-2 pilot, Francis Gary Powers, to a humiliating show trial ending in a prison sentence.

Nikita Khrushchev had already twice remolded the 1960 campaign, first by meeting Eisenhower at Camp David and then by destroying the Paris summit. In September, emboldened by his summer's gains, he sailed to New York to attend the UN General Assembly. For twenty-five days, he competed with the two presidential nominees for the attention of nervous Americans, giving press conferences from the balcony of the Soviet mission, embracing Castro in Harlem, gasconading at the UN, and, in the most famous gesture of his career, removing his shoe and beating his fists on the desktop.

The 1952 election had not been particularly fought in the vernacular of which candidate could stand up to Stalin. But Khrushchev's three meetings with Eisenhower, his rocket-rattling, and his flamboyant visits to the United States had so personalized Soviet behavior that Americans in 1960 thought in terms of which man could best confront Khrushchev. Nixon boasted of his encounters with the Chairman and warned that Kennedy was "rash and immature," the kind of man "Mr. Khrushchev would make mincemeat of."

The truth was that neither candidate enjoyed the towering experience in foreign affairs that Nixon claimed for himself. Indeed, the Vice President had traveled on numerous vice presidential goodwill trips, including the Soviet tour in 1959 that included the "kitchen debate" with Khrushchev. He boasted about his talks with thirty-five presidents, nine prime ministers, two emperors, and one shah. His campaign used the slogan "It's Experience That Counts."

But for the past seven years, the small circle on whom Eisenhower called for foreign affairs and defense advice had seldom included Nixon; when it did, the President tended to consult him about the domestic context. The Vice President privately complained that Eisenhower "regards me as a political expert only. If I try to speak up on defense matters, say, from a strictly military point of view, he says, 'What does this guy know about it?' "

Despite Kennedy's international-minded upbringing and foreign travel, his writing and speaking, he had no serious history in diplomatic bargaining or managing an organization. Critics noted that the largest enterprise he had ever run was the PT-109, which had been sunk. During his three years on the Senate Foreign Relations Committee, he was largely away from Washington campaigning.

In his campaign broadside *Kennedy or Nixon: Does It Make Any Difference?* the Harvard historian and Kennedy supporter Arthur Schlesinger, Jr., sensibly did not try to argue that his man had a deep foreign policy background: "Experience is helpful. Especially experience in doing good things. But experience in doing stupid things is no advantage." Years later Schlesinger wrote that "anyone with political judgment, intellectual curiosity, a retentive memory, a disciplined temperament, and sense of the way history runs can grasp the dynamics of foreign policy quickly enough."*

Kennedy defended himself with a strong offense: "Mr. Nixon is experienced—experienced in policies of retreat, defeat, and weakness. . . . Waving your finger under Khrushchev's face does not increase the strength of the United States."†

Still, Kennedy's polls showed that Khrushchev's rantings at the UN were scaring voters into the Nixon camp. He privately expected Nixon to try to "put us on the defensive as the soft-on-communism party." Walt Rostow warned him that this was the only way Nixon "knows how to operate. . . . Don't leave any fishhooks lying around. Be prepared for the issue and the thrust."

Rostow was correct. Nixon quietly asked his friend William Rogers, the Attorney General, to "try your hand" at speech material, noting

---

*In 1965, Jacqueline Kennedy bridled when she read in a draft of Schlesinger's *A Thousand Days* that her husband had entered the White House "knowing more about domestic than foreign matters." With more loyalty than historical judgment, she insisted to the historian that her husband "knew as much about foreign as domestic affairs & certainly more than any other American President coming into office." Schlesinger chivalrously revised his text to say that Kennedy "had had a considerably more varied and extensive international experience than most men elected President."

†Stevenson had written Kennedy after his nomination that "the 'youth and inexperience' argument is an essentially false argument. . . . You either have leadership qualities or you don't. . . . Since it is apparent that the Republican emphasis will be on Nixon's 'experience' in dealing with the Communists . . . it is essential to make it clear that . . . the question is not who can face a mob or shake his finger in a dictator's face, but who can build a program and supply a leadership which will prevent such incidents from occurring."

that Kennedy "would be a very dangerous President, dangerous to the cause of peace and dangerous from the standpoint of surrender. Here we can put a fear into them."

Kennedy thus began the fall campaign with anti-Communist rhetoric that would have pleased John Foster Dulles. In September, at the Mormon Tabernacle in Salt Lake City, he said, "The enemy is the Communist system itself—implacable, insatiable, unceasing in its drive for world domination. . . . This is not a struggle for supremacy of arms alone. It is also a struggle for supremacy between two conflicting ideologies: freedom under God versus ruthless, godless tyranny."

The Harvard economist John Kenneth Galbraith soon wrote the Kennedy pollster Louis Harris, "JFK has made the point that he isn't soft. Henceforth he can only frighten." The Senator's chief foreign policy adviser, Chester Bowles, wrote him that he had "brilliantly" brought the campaign "to a point where no one can call us soft on communism."

But Kennedy's problems in the fall of 1960 ran far beyond the need to assert his anticommunism. He had the unhappy task of running against the heir to a President who had brought the United States to the zenith of its power and influence in the Cold War. The nation enjoyed a preponderance in nuclear strength and economic productivity it would never know again.

Aware of the fact that he could not easily win unless he gave voters a bleaker portrait of the American position in the world, Kennedy fashioned an argument that the United States was behind or falling behind the Soviet Union in long-range missiles, economic growth, and political influence.

Central to Kennedy's charge that Eisenhower and Nixon had weakened the nation was his use of the missile gap issue. In its purest form, the argument ran that Eisenhower's obsessive concern with a balanced budget had forced him to shortchange the intercontinental ballistic missile program: while the United States built ICBMs at a leisurely pace, Soviet factories were, as Khrushchev bragged, turning out ICBMs "like sausages."

This issue allowed Kennedy to assert his toughness and show that Democratic doctrine on the value of deficit spending was compatible with the building of American strength. The problem was that there was no missile gap. Eisenhower had access to closely held U-2 and other intelligence that was enough to convince him that, whatever Khrushchev's boasts, there had been no crash Soviet buildup: the United States was firmly in the lead.

Nixon wanted the President to kill the issue by sharing the facts of

American nuclear superiority with the American people. But Eisenhower did not wish to compromise secret intelligence sources. Nor did he wish to disrupt the tacit agreement he had developed with Khrushchev.

When confronted in public with the Chairman's boasts that the Soviet Union was outproducing America in ICBMs, Eisenhower simply summoned his credibility as the hero of World War II and replied that American strength was awesome and sufficient. As long as Eisenhower did not disturb the illusion that the Soviets exceeded the United States in long-range missile strength, Khrushchev was willing to forego the huge expenditure that a crash Soviet ICBM buildup would actually require.

The President indirectly tried to signal Kennedy not to disturb this delicate arrangement and scare the nation about a missile gap that did not exist. One of Eisenhower's science advisers, Jerome Wiesner of MIT, who had seen the intelligence showing American superiority, was "astounded" when the President approved his request to advise Kennedy during the campaign. Wiesner thought that Eisenhower's intention was to let the Democrat know the truth about the missile gap.

In August, before CIA Director Allen Dulles went to Hyannis Port for the intelligence briefing offered to both presidential candidates, Eisenhower asked him to stress America's commanding military strength. But when Kennedy asked Dulles how the nation stood in the missile race, the CIA man coyly replied that only the Pentagon could properly answer the question.*

Later in August, when the Strategic Air Command briefed Kennedy in Omaha, the candidate was annoyed not to be given a full top-secret accounting of American-Soviet bomber and missile power. He complained that he had been given more information as a member of the Foreign Relations Committee: if SAC and the Air Force were this complacent, he would remember next year at budget time. Assured that there was no missile gap during a Joint Chiefs of Staff briefing in September, Kennedy said, "Don't you have any doubting Thomases in the Pentagon?"

Kennedy could argue that he had not been shown the raw intelligence that had persuaded the President there was no missile gap. But

---

*Dulles later explained his caution by saying that, until the United States enjoyed full satellite coverage of the Soviet Union, a missile gap could not be absolutely ruled out. Richard Nixon later suspected that Dulles had framed his answer in order to allow Kennedy to keep exploiting the issue—a favor that a victorious Kennedy might remember after the election when pondering whether or not to replace him.

Eisenhower, the Joint Chiefs, and SAC had all affirmed that if there was a missile gap it was strongly in America's favor. Despite this considerable body of evidence, Kennedy persisted in exploiting the issue.

He knew this would frighten Americans and limit the next President's freedom to act by generating public pressure on him to escalate the arms race. He knew it might goad the Soviets to respond, if he was elected, in kind. He did exercise some caution by referring to the Soviet missile "advantage," avoiding numbers and dates, citing nonpartisan experts. But he continued to issue the accusation, telling crowds that Republicans were "the party which gave us the missile gap."

More fairly, Kennedy charged the administration with overreliance on nuclear weapons, "tying our hands in a limited war." He promised a conventional defense buildup and efforts to keep the United States from being second in science, education, and outer space.

He issued the specious complaint that the Soviet Union enjoyed "an economic growth of two or three times as much as the great productive country of the United States" and that in 1959 "the United States had the lowest percentage of economic growth increase of any major industrial society in the world." Sophisticated as he was about the severe limitations of the command economy and Kremlin manipulation of Soviet growth figures, Kennedy knew full well that the United States was not in danger that the Soviet economy would soon exceed America's.

The disturbing statistics he cited were a manipulation. The American figure was artificially low because 1959 was a recession year, the Soviet figure artificially high because it reflected the Soviet Union's recovery from the devastation of World War II. In 1960, the Soviet economy was still a fraction of the size of America's. The United States was producing nearly one third of the world's goods.

Kennedy charged that the incumbents had let down American world prestige. He noted secret United States Information Agency surveys that found sagging American prestige and demanded their release.* By November, a Gallup poll found that nearly half of Americans felt that world respect for the United States had declined in the past year.

In one of his standard lines, Kennedy said, "I ask you to join with

---

*When these polls were leaked to the press, a furious Eisenhower had the same suspicions about USIA Director George Allen that Nixon did about Allen Dulles. He privately carped that the USIA man was "playing politics" to keep his job in the event of a Kennedy victory.

me in a journey into the 1960s, whereby we will mold our strength and become first again. Not first *if.* Not first *but.* Not first *when.* But first *period.* I want the people of the world to wonder not what Mr. Khrushchev is doing. I want them to wonder what the United States is doing."*

American presidential campaigns are inclined to treat foreign issues with cartoonish simplicity. Nineteen-sixty was no exception. Kennedy's utterances offered little insight into how he would act on the two Cold War trouble spots that would prove to dominate his term as President—Cuba and Berlin.

He found that voters asked him more often about Cuba and Castro than any other foreign issue. As his speech writer Richard Goodwin recalled, the emergence of a pro-Soviet dictator ninety miles off the American coast had done "more than Khrushchev could to anger and alarm the American people." Cuba gave Kennedy another chance to attack Nixon from the right. He asked his staff, "How would we have saved Cuba if we had the power?" Then: "What the hell, they never told us how they would have saved China."

He scored the Republicans for permitting "a Communist menace" to arise "only eight jet minutes from Florida": "We must make clear our intention not to let the Soviet Union turn Cuba into its base in the Caribbean—and our intention to enforce the Monroe Doctrine." He demanded more propaganda and sanctions to "quarantine" the Cuban revolution, more support for Cubans who opposed the Castro regime. His campaign manager, Robert Kennedy, worried that the Eisenhower administration might invade Cuba before the election, thereby improving Nixon's election chances.

In late October, flying to New York, the candidate told Goodwin to "get ready a real blast for Nixon." That evening Goodwin drafted a new assault for the morning papers on the Republicans and Cuba: the United States must strengthen democratic anti-Castro Cubans "who offer eventual hope of overthrowing Castro. Thus far these fighters for freedom have had virtually no support from our government."

---

*With such statements he rejected Nixon's public suggestion that neither candidate discuss the subject of national weakness while Khrushchev was in the country. "I want to make it clear that nothing I am saying will give Mr. Khrushchev the slightest encouragement," Kennedy told crowds. "He is encouraged enough." He proposed to "discourage him" by "rebuilding national strength and vitality. The most ominous sound that Mr. Khrushchev can hear . . . is not of a debate in the United States but the sound of America on the move, ready to move again."

According to Goodwin, Kennedy was asleep when the draft was finished and it became the only such statement in the campaign to be released without the candidate's clearance.

When Nixon saw the morning headlines (KENNEDY ADVOCATES U.S. INTERVENTION IN CUBA), he was furious. He assumed that Dulles had briefed his opponent on the CIA's plans to invade Cuba; was Kennedy so craven that he would jeopardize the operation for votes? On a secure line, his adviser Fred Seaton, Secretary of the Interior, called General Andrew Goodpaster, the President's staff secretary, who informed him that Kennedy had been "fully briefed."*

---

*In March 1962, Nixon's memoir *Six Crises,* charging that Kennedy had subordinated national security to political ambition, caused a public sensation. Nixon wrote that Dulles had told the Democratic nominee that for months the CIA had "not only been supporting and assisting, but actually training Cuban exiles for the eventual purpose of supporting an invasion of Cuba itself."

McGeorge Bundy wrote the President, "This subject turns out to be more complicated than I had hoped." He had talked to the retired Dulles and his colleagues, who "agree that you did not receive any briefing on an actual plan for an invasion of Cuba, but unfortunately this is not what Nixon asserts. . . . Allen Dulles reports that his notes for a July briefing do indicate that he was prepared to tell you that CIA was training Cuban exiles as guerrilla leaders. . . . He says he could not have briefed you on anything beyond that because nothing beyond this then existed. . . . But it can be argued that what Nixon says is not wrong.

"On the other hand . . . it appears that you had only sketchy and fragmentary information about covert relations to Cuban exiles and no briefing at all on any specific plan for an invasion. The difficulty is that the notes that Dulles has would give some support to Nixon's stated position. Dulles is obviously in the middle and I am sure his preference will be to keep out of it if he can."

Bundy recommended issuing a statement that the President was given a "general briefing" by Dulles in July, but that not until after the election did the CIA Director "give the President-elect a full briefing on covert plans relating to Cuba." Kennedy did not heed this graceful effort to repair his political problems without resorting to a presidential lie. On March 20, the White House flatly announced that Kennedy "was not told before the election of 1960 of the training of troops outside of Cuba or of any plans for 'supporting an invasion of Cuba.' "

The President also asked Dulles to issue a statement saying "that the President never knew about it." But Dulles told reporters only that Nixon must be victim of "an honest misunderstanding." Soon thereafter, he was stripped of certain of his CIA retirement privileges. On the day of Dulles's statement, John McCone called Nixon in California and told him "categorically" that Dulles had actually informed him privately that he had "told Kennedy about the covert operation" in 1960. He added that Senator Smathers had confirmed for him that Kennedy knew about the Cuban plans "before the election."

Goodpaster informed this author that Allen Dulles told him in October 1960 that he had indeed briefed Kennedy "about the planning, which was to form the unit and to train the unit, that this was what had been approved." Richard Goodwin said in 1981 that Kennedy "may very well have known" in October 1960 about the CIA's

Nixon called the White House and said he felt he had been "put into a corner by this." After consulting the President, he tried to preserve the operation's secrecy by saying the opposite of what he actually believed. In their fourth television debate, he attacked Kennedy's idea as "the most dangerously irresponsible recommendation that he's made during the course of this campaign. . . . It would be an open invitation for Mr. Khrushchev to come in, to come into Latin America and engage us in a civil war, and possibly even worse than that."

In response to this and to liberal criticism, Kennedy said he did not favor intervention that would violate American treaty obligations, only letting the freedom fighters know that America "sympathized with them." The *New York Times* called the reversal a "major blunder." Adlai Stevenson privately wrote a friend that Kennedy's mistake on Cuba had been "appalling."

The bizarre result was that many Americans who did not wish to intervene in Cuba voted for Nixon, who was privately prodding the CIA to get the job done before Election Day. Many Americans who wanted more militance against Castro voted for Kennedy, who was privately ambivalent at best about ousting Castro by force.

Kennedy said even less about what he intended to do about Berlin. The reason for this was statesmanlike. In August 1960, Stevenson had privately advised him to avoid "extended discussion" of the issue because it would be "difficult to say anything very constructive about a settlement in Berlin without embarrassing future negotiations. Beyond a declaration of our intention to preserve our rights and do our duty lies the temptation to assert greater rigidity and inflexibility than the other fellow."

Stevenson recalled that, as Democratic nominee, "I 'unilaterally' took a similar position in September 1956—that I would not discuss Suez because the situation was 'too delicate,' although I was aching to have at 'em. A month later came the disaster and Eisenhower was the beneficiary of my restraint. So I write you with misgivings and diffidence."

Throughout the fall of 1960, Kennedy raised the Berlin issue in only a half dozen speeches, and then in nothing more than a single applause line: "Can you possibly say that our power is increasing when you know that next winter and next spring the United States will

---

invasion planning. In his 1988 memoir *Remembering America,* Goodwin wrote more directly that Kennedy's CIA briefings during the campaign "revealed that we were training a force of Cuban exiles for a possible invasion of the Cuban mainland." One may safely presume that this whole episode did nothing to relieve Nixon's already-great bitterness toward the Kennedys, Dulles, and the CIA.

face a most serious crisis over Berlin at a time when our strength is not rising in relation to that of the Communists?"

He devoted greater attention to Quemoy and Matsu, challenging the administration's implied pledge to defend the long-disputed Chinese offshore islands, perhaps at risk of nuclear war. He accused Nixon of eagerness to "involve American boys in an unnecessary and futile war." Republicans called Kennedy's comments "an open invitation" for the Chinese Communists to "take these islands the day Kennedy takes office, if he does." He announced that "in the interests of bipartisanship" he would drop the issue.

During his twenty-five days in New York, sitting upstairs in the old beaux arts Eben Pyne mansion on Park Avenue that served as the Soviet mission, Khrushchev was no doubt delighted by how frequently his name popped up during the first two Kennedy-Nixon debates.

During his opening statement in the first debate, Kennedy said, "Mr. Khrushchev is in New York, and he maintains the Communist offensive throughout the world because of the productive power of the Soviet Union itself." In the second debate, Nixon on the U-2: "I don't intend ever to express regrets to Mr. Khrushchev or anybody else if I'm doing something . . . for the purpose of protecting the security of the United States."

Khrushchev had never had much respect for the American electoral process. "The American people have practically no influence on the policies of the U.S.A.," he had once said. "They are cleverly tricked during election campaigns and virtually do not even know for what they are voting." His experience in New York did not change his mind: "The battle between the Democrats and Republicans is like a circus wrestling match. The wrestlers arrange in advance who will be the loser before they even enter the arena."

He later said that "political advertising in America is quite noisy and, I would say, theatrical. Imagine it! Into the head of the poor voter, around the clock from morning to night, pour torrents of television speeches by representatives of a donkey or an elephant."

Despite his fealty to Marxist notions that personalities were far less important than grand historical forces, he knew that America's choice in 1960 could do much to determine his country's fate and his own. The year before, after Camp David, he had assured members of the Presidium that Eisenhower was a "sincere" man with whom he could do business. By sending the U-2 a fortnight before the Paris summit, Eisenhower had made him look like a fool and caused Kremlin colleagues to question his judgment. Now Khrushchev wished to ensure that the President in 1961 would be someone with whom he could deal.

His official preference was Gus Hall, the old warhorse of the American Communist Party. But, as Khrushchev conceded, America's inevitable march toward communism was not yet advanced enough to let Comrade Hall enter the White House. So he began 1960 as a partisan of Adlai Stevenson, whom he considered to have "a tolerant—I'd even say friendly and trustworthy—attitude toward the Soviet Union." They had met in 1958 when the Governor toured the Soviet Union with two sons. Khrushchev advised the boys to marry Soviet girls and told their father, "In 1956, I voted for you in my heart."*

During the 1956 campaign, Khrushchev had clumsily arranged for his then–Prime Minister, Nikolai Bulganin, to issue a public letter lauding "certain public figures" for endorsing a nuclear test ban. Eisenhower fired off an angry complaint about Soviet meddling "in our internal affairs." Richard Nixon used the Soviet letter to show how Stevenson's "dangerous scheme" would play "disastrously into the Communists' hands."

This time Khrushchev was determined not to meddle in a way that would boomerang against him. In late 1959, when Ambassador Menshikov took home leave in Moscow, Khrushchev asked him to pay a secret call on Stevenson and ask "which way we can be of assistance."

Stevenson thought Menshikov a mildly comic figure; he told friends how, at a Georgetown garden party, the envoy insisted on using his not-quite-working English to toast the ladies present, saying, "Up your bottoms!" In January 1960, he accepted the envoy's invitation to the old George Pullman mansion on Sixteenth Street in Washington that housed the Soviet Embassy.

Over caviar, fruit, and drinks, Menshikov told him that Khrushchev thought Stevenson more likely to "understand Soviet anxieties and purposes" than other presidential candidates. Should the Soviet press praise him, and for what? Should it criticize him, and for what?

Afterward Stevenson wrote a friend, "As I think about it, I get more and more indignant about being 'propositioned' that way, and at the same time, more and more perplexed, if that's the word, by the *confidence* they have in me. I shall do one thing only *now*: politely and

---

*Khrushchev did not mind telling a whopper if unlikely to be caught. When Anastas Mikoyan saw Eisenhower in the Oval Office in January 1959, he said that Khrushchev had confided to him that had he been permitted to vote in the 1956 American elections, he would have voted for the President!

decisively reject the proposal—and pray that it will never leak, lest I lose that potentially valuable confidence."

After Nixon and Kennedy were nominated, Khrushchev told colleagues in Moscow that they had to "make a choice in our own minds": "We can influence the American election." Richard Nixon was his nemesis, a "puppet" of the American Cold War establishment, an "unprincipled careerist," an ally of "that devil of darkness McCarthy." Khrushchev's anxieties may have been somewhat eased by the fact that the Vice President was no longer quite the anti-Communist of old, but, he feared, "We'll never be able to find a common language with him."

Still, the choice was not so easy. "We had little knowledge of John Kennedy," Khrushchev later said. "He was a young man, very promising and very rich, a millionaire. We knew from the press that he was distinguished by his intelligence, his education, and his political skill."

He and his advisers realized that Kennedy's world view had grown more rounded since the anti-Soviet oratory of his House and early Senate years. The Senator favored a nuclear test ban and wider Soviet-American contacts. Khrushchev liked his regret over the U-2 and his vow to observe Eisenhower's pledge of no more such spy flights. But he worried about Kennedy's rhetoric about the missile gap and the need to rebuild American defense.

Izvestia echoed Khrushchev's misgivings about the Democrat—not by accident, for its editor was Khrushchev's son-in-law and close adviser Alexei Adzhubei: "He is furiously attacking the Eisenhower-Nixon policies but has not yet proposed anything to replace them." Another Soviet journal found Kennedy a straddler, a "young millionaire who promises everything to everyone." He had taken the "flexible if not to say unprincipled position" of siding sometimes with Big Labor, sometimes with Big Business; all sorts of "bourgeois political leaders—conservatives and liberals alike" saw Kennedy as "their man."

However, Kennedy's anti-Sovietism had lacked Nixon's consistency. He was surrounded by such moderate figures as Stevenson, Bowles, Fulbright, Mansfield, and Harriman. As the junior Foreign Ministry official and later defector Arkady Shevchenko recalled, Khrushchev "saw what he wanted to see" in Kennedy's calls for negotiation. Khrushchev himself later said, "We thought we would have some hope of improving Soviet-American relations if Kennedy were in the White House."

He may have thought that Kennedy would be easier than Nixon to hornswoggle. He knew that much of the Washington establishment considered Kennedy a light and insubstantial figure, a playboy. (In 1959, James Reston of the *New York Times* asked Rostow, "Do you *really* believe that man can be President of the United States?") When Kennedy retreated under campaign fire on Quemoy and Matsu and Cuba, the Soviets noticed.

No one exulted more in his own rise from obscurity than Khrushchev. "You all went to great schools, to famous universities—to Harvard, Oxford, the Sorbonne," he once told Western diplomats. "I never had any proper schooling. I went about barefoot and in rags. When you were in the nursery, I was herding cows for two kopeks. . . . And yet here we are, and I can run rings around you all. . . . Tell me, gentlemen, why?"

Since 1917, the very year Kennedy was born, Khrushchev had been clawing his way up the treacherous Soviet hierarchy, enticing and betraying patrons, sending thousands to death during the purges and the war, resisting Stalin's paranoia to keep his job and his life and then, at the pinnacle of power, resisting two coups d'état by his own colleagues. This induced self-confidence in his powers against a man who rode on the back of a millionaire father.

Khrushchev could not fathom how a man who had been so junior in the American government could suddenly become President. KGB psychological profiles suggested that a Kennedy presidency would be more unpredictable than Eisenhower's. Khrushchev privately noted, "He's younger than my own son."*

In public, Khrushchev put on a show of dazzling nonpartisanship. "Mr. Nixon has dressed himself in the garb of an anti-Communist," he declared in Moscow in August. "Well, he will not be the first to demonstrate that this raincoat does not cover the nakedness of the capitalist world or hide its sores. . . . Of Mr. Kennedy I know less. I met him when I was in Washington and we exchanged a few sentences. But I do know that both Nixon and Kennedy are both servants of monopoly capital. . . . As we Russians say, they are two boots of the same pair: which is better, the left or the right boot?" While in New York, asked which candidate he favored, Khrushchev invoked the patron saint of Soviet-American cooperation: "Roosevelt!"

Both Nixon and Kennedy knew that if Khrushchev so desired, he could influence the election by causing some kind of international incident designed either to stampede voters to the more experienced candidate or to show Eisenhower's and Nixon's inability to handle the

---

*Leonid Khrushchev, evidently born in 1917, was killed in June 1943 on the Voronezh front. His widow, Lyubov, was imprisoned on charges of being some sort of "Swedish spy" and was not released until after Stalin's death in 1953.

Soviets. Neither candidate was willing to leave this wild card wholly up to chance. Unbeknownst to the American people, key supporters of both Nixon and Kennedy made confidential contact with Khrushchev and asked him to do things to help their man.

In February 1960, Henry Cabot Lodge, who had served Eisenhower for seven years as Ambassador to the UN, went to the Soviet Union. Meeting with the Chairman in Moscow, Lodge said that as "a man who deeply hopes for good relations between the U.S.S.R. and the United States," he felt he should point out that "there is always a minimum of flexibility in foreign relations in the United States in an election year. What is hard or impossible to do in 1952 or 1956 or 1960 is often quite susceptible of accomplishment in 1953 or 1957 or 1961."

He assured Khrushchev that he could work with Nixon: "Don't pay any attention to the campaign speeches. Remember, they're just political statements. Once Mr. Nixon is in the White House, I'm sure—I'm absolutely *certain*—he'll take a position of preserving and perhaps even improving our relations." On his return, he told the Vice President that he had "had a talk with Khrushchev" that he had "not reported to the State Department."

Ambassador Llewellyn Thompson wrote Nixon from Moscow, "Several top Soviets have indicated to me their opposition to you. I have always taken the line with them that you are a staunch and effective anti-Communist just as they are staunch anticapitalists, but that they made a mistake in assuming that you were opposed to negotiations or agreements with the Soviet Union whenever these were possible with benefit to both sides."

Khrushchev's chief link to the Democrats was Averell Harriman, the Union Pacific heir and two-time presidential candidate who had served as Franklin Roosevelt's wartime envoy to Stalin. Defeated in 1958 by Nelson Rockefeller for reelection as Governor of New York, Harriman may have been considered out of power by Americans, but Khrushchev had no doubt who ruled Washington. In September 1959, Harriman entertained the Chairman at his Upper East Side brownstone, inviting a small pantheon of the American financial establishment. In October 1960, through Menshikov, Harriman reminded Khrushchev to be tough on both candidates: the surest way to elect Nixon was to praise Kennedy in public.

That fall, the Eisenhower government was quietly pressing the Soviets to release Francis Gary Powers and the RB-47 fliers. As Khrushchev recalled, a high-ranking Republican "with whom I had established not bad relations at the time of my trip to the U.S.A." met with Ambassador Menshikov and appealed for the airmen's freedom: if Nixon became President, the old Eisenhower policies would be reviewed. "We, of course, understood that Nixon wished to make political capital out of this for himself in advance of the elections. . . . Nixon wanted to make it appear as if he had already arranged certain contacts with the Soviet government."

In Moscow, Khrushchev told his colleagues, "We would never give Nixon such a present." The two candidates were in stalemate. "If we give the slightest boost to Nixon, it will be interpreted as an expression of our willingness to see him in the White House." Khrushchev kept the fliers in prison and thereby cast his early ballot against "that son of a bitch Richard Nixon."

At Spaso House, on Wednesday, November 9, Llewellyn and Jane Thompson held an Election Day luncheon. A large Zenith radio was set up so that guests could listen through static to the Voice of America's election coverage.

An American correspondent among the guests asked the Ambassador whom he would have voted for. Thompson replied that he was a Foreign Service officer: Washington, D.C., was his official address, so he couldn't have voted anyway.* His daughter Jenny evoked laughter when she piped up, "Don't be silly, Daddy. You'd have voted for Kennedy!" The group responded to the news of Kennedy's victory with applause and cheers. Thompson's sea-blue eyes gleamed. As his wife recalled, he was "delighted and thrilled."

Thompson had known the new President since 1951, when as counselor in Rome he had given a luncheon for Kennedy and other visiting Congressmen. That same year, Jane Thompson entertained Jacqueline and Lee Bouvier, daughters of her friend Janet Auchincloss, who were touring Europe that summer. In 1953, the Thompsons were invited to the Kennedy-Bouvier wedding in Newport but had to remain at their post.

During the middle 1950s, as U.S. High Commissioner in Austria, Thompson would drop in on Kennedy when in Washington to defend his budget before Congress. During a closed Foreign Relations Committee session, Thompson referred to a recent book and was "much impressed" by the fact that Kennedy was "the only member of the Committee to get the name of the book and its author from me."

Thompson was a Democrat, but he adeptly hid his sympathies. Even Khrushchev, who knew him well and who saw messages intercepted between the American Embassy and Washington, had him pegged as

---

*Nineteen-sixty was the last year in which the Constitution forebade citizens of Washington, D.C., from casting ballots for President.

a Nixon supporter. On November 7, at a Kremlin celebration of the forty-third anniversary of the Russian Revolution, he said, "I know who *you're* going to vote for."

"No, you don't," replied Thompson with his crinkle-eyed smile.

"Yes, I do. *I* wish *Nixon* would win because I'd know how to cope with him. Kennedy is an unknown quantity." Khrushchev voiced his apprehension about Kennedy's youth and ambiguous record. Republicans, he said, made no secret of their subservience to Wall Street and Cold War weapons makers. Democrats tried to hide it and were therefore less predictable. Khrushchev said his advisers were telling him Kennedy would win.

Thompson now allowed himself to dream of having the President's ear. Since his arrival in Moscow three years earlier, he had been frustrated that Eisenhower had paid his cables and other advice so little heed. The President and Foster Dulles had sought little advice on Soviet policy: for seven years, it had been the Dark Age for Soviet experts like George Kennan and Harriman, whom Eisenhower classed with Truman and the Democrats.

Thompson thought Kennedy "more intelligent and well read" than Eisenhower. Now, as the newsmen left Spaso House to file their stories, Thompson went to his embassy office and began planning the education of the next President.

In Hyannis Port, after accepting victory on national television at the local armory, John Kennedy lunched at his father's house with his wife, brothers, and sisters, his painter friend William Walton, and Ted Sorensen. Freed from last night's tension, they laughed and argued over who had performed best in the campaign and needled those responsible for states lost to Nixon.

After rising from the table, the President-elect was handed a telegram from Nikita Khrushchev expressing the hope that Soviet-American relations would return to the warmth of Franklin Roosevelt's time. All mankind, it said, was "longing for deliverance from the threat of a new war. . . . There are no insurmountable obstacles to the preservation and consolidation of peace." Worried that an ill-chosen word might start things off with Khrushchev on a bad note, Kennedy telephoned Chip Bohlen at the State Department.

3

"Our Clue to the Soviet Union"

BY CALLING BOHLEN, KENNEDY HAD RETURNED TO THE START OF his own history with the Soviets. He remembered how the renowned Soviet hand had entertained him in Moscow in 1939. With his debonair sangfroid of the kind that Kennedy admired and tried to emulate, Bohlen was one of the Sovietologists who had suffered under Eisenhower.

Bohlen's career in Soviet affairs had begun in the twenties at Harvard, where he read Russian literature, sang Russian songs, and found a Russian girl, which he thought to be the "correct way" to learn the language. In late-night bull sessions over bathtub gin, he defended aspects of the Bolshevik experiment in the exclusive precincts of the Porcellian Club. As a foreign service officer, he joined William Bullitt's embassy in 1934 and kept returning to Moscow with higher and higher rank. He served as Roosevelt's translator at Yalta.

To win confirmation in 1953 as Eisenhower's Ambassador to Moscow, Bohlen had to withstand Joseph McCarthy's insinuations about his sexual inclinations and his "ugly record of great betrayal" at Yalta. Foster Dulles refused to risk being photographed with Bohlen. Eisenhower stood more firm: he and Bohlen had been golfing partners while serving together in Paris. After the nomination was pushed through, Eisenhower's Senate leader, Robert Taft, told him, "No more Bohlens."

Bohlen later lamented his failure to move heaven and earth to convince the President to exploit the hopeful atmosphere after Stalin's death. But Dulles was not eager for rivals. When Bohlen returned to Washington in 1956, the Secretary of State barred him from addressing the Cabinet: "It would build him up too much. . . . He is not working with us."

In 1957, Dulles removed him with an opaque letter saying that he knew Bohlen wished to "take up writing as a profession." Bohlen had no such wish or ability. Told that Thompson would be his successor, he almost broke off their friendship before he learned that Thompson had not known he was being used to wrench Bohlen out of Moscow.

Bohlen refused the Karachi Embassy and bitterly accepted Manila. To a Dulles query about Soviet matters he acidly replied that he could not comment on the Soviet Union "from this great distance." After Dulles's death in 1959, the new Secretary of State, Christian Herter, a fellow St. Paul's School man, brought Bohlen back from exile and hired him as his counselor on Soviet affairs, which did not require Senate confirmation.

Now, when Kennedy called him for aid on a reply to Khrushchev, Bohlen told him he would have to clear it "through channels." Called in Augusta, Georgia, where he was golfing, Eisenhower asked Herter to make sure he saw Bohlen's draft before it was sent out.

On the telephone with Kennedy, Bohlen fumbled: even after the long campaign, he still lacked the "foggiest notion" of Kennedy's views toward the Soviet Union. He asked whether Kennedy wanted to start off with a "great gesture" or "play it cool." Told to play it cool, Bohlen recommended being courteous and avoiding substance. He drafted a one-sentence reply. Kennedy thought this too brusque and added two more sentences.

At a press conference at the Hyannis Armory the next morning, he read from his finished wire thanking Khrushchev for his courtesy and good wishes: "The achievement of a just and lasting peace will remain a fundamental goal of this nation and a major task of its President."

* * *

Throughout the campaign, Ambassador Menshikov had invited Bohlen, dozens of Senators, and other officials such as Supreme Court Justice William O. Douglas to the opulent dining room of the Soviet Embassy for chicken Kiev and interviews on what the Soviet Union could expect from the next President.

Menshikov had always been inclined to cable Khrushchev what he wanted to hear: millions of Americans were out of work; the United States was on the verge of a workers' revolution. After the Chairman saw America for himself in 1959, he began heavily discounting what he heard from Menshikov.* A member of Menshikov's own staff referred to him as *"Nash Durak"*—"Our Fool."

The week after the 1960 election, Menshikov told Adlai Stevenson in his New York law office that Khrushchev had "high hopes" for new understandings with the United States, including a test ban treaty. But such agreements could be reached only if the two leaders used private channels. If Kennedy and Khrushchev communicated in public, they would have to repeat "old accusations."

A Khrushchev emissary named Alexander Korneichuk saw Averell Harriman. Korneichuk was a Ukrainian writer and Central Committee member who had known Khrushchev when he was Stalin's viceroy in the Ukraine and had known Harriman when he served as wartime Ambassador to Moscow. Harriman later reported to Kennedy that Korneichuk "asked me whether you would follow FDR's policies. . . . He asked me how I thought you and Mr. Khrushchev would get along if you met. I said Mr. Khrushchev would find you were not interested in scoring points in debate."

At the Soviet Embassy in Washington, Menshikov read Harriman a message from Khrushchev. The Chairman said he understood that during the campaign Kennedy had had to make anti-Soviet statements; he was willing to overlook them. Now the two nations must return to the warm relations of Harriman's years in Moscow. Harriman replied that if Khrushchev was serious, he might try to show Americans that his angry mood of the summer and fall was over. Perhaps he could stop complaining about the U-2 affair and release the RB-47 fliers.

* * *

---

*While flying from New York to Los Angeles with the Chairman and his escort, Henry Cabot Lodge, Deputy Foreign Minister Kuznetsov told Lodge that the trip was proving "an education for Khrushchev, and I am glad that he is traveling with someone who vigorously expounds the United States point of view."

In late November, Kennedy's campaign advisers Walt Rostow and Jerome Wiesner flew to Moscow for a meeting of disarmament experts. At Dartmouth, just before the election, Rostow had seen Korneichuk, who urged him to "take disarmament seriously" because soon certain forces in Moscow would "move in and make a movement toward peace impossible."

Deputy Foreign Minister Kuznetsov called on the two Americans and said, "What can we do to help the new administration?" Wiesner and Rostow presented a list of items drafted with Ambassador Thompson's help. The RB-47 pilots should be freed "without Kennedy's having to ask for them or bargain for them." Pressure on Berlin should be relaxed. During test ban talks, the Soviets must be "very generous" about on-site inspections.

Rostow warned, "We are a country that can't work on a two-track policy very well. If we have a Berlin crisis, we are not going to be able to talk very seriously about arms control." When the Americans asked Kuznetsov what they could do in return, the Soviet said, "Take disarmament negotiations seriously."

During another talk, Rostow reminded Kuznetsov and his colleagues that Kennedy was a man of tangible action. There could be no summit unless it was "well prepared and concerned with very concrete business." He suggested that if the RB-47 fliers were freed and a test ban accord was ready, a Kennedy-Khrushchev summit and signing ceremony could be held in New York. But the visit must be "melodramatically different" from Khrushchev's appearance in New York that fall. He should "arrive with his top hat, wearing his shoes."

The Soviets asked, "How does Kennedy's intent to raise the military budget square with his interest in arms control?" Rostow explained that the changes Kennedy had called for would reduce American fears about surprise attack and confirm "once and for all" that in "our military dispositions as well as our political structure and values," the United States had no intention of waging a first-strike nuclear attack against the Soviet bloc.

Kuznetsov warned that if Kennedy went through with his defense plans, he could not expect the Soviet Union to "sit still." Rostow later reported to the President-elect that while the Soviets might be ready to move on arms control, they were rigid about Berlin and were "going to give us hell in the underdeveloped areas."

On Monday, December 12, Menshikov landed Robert Kennedy for luncheon at the Soviet Embassy. He praised the new President's "intelligence and vigor" and blamed old troubles on mid-level American officials who had "distorted" Soviet positions. Now the two nations could achieve a "clear and friendly understanding."

Two days later Menshikov told Harriman that Khrushchev wanted him or some other American to act as a secret, informal emissary between the two leaders before Inauguration Day. Harriman replied that the new administration could not hold talks of substance until Kennedy could meet with his new Cabinet and advisers and decide what his policies would be.

The next day, Menshikov spoke off the record to Harrison Salisbury of the *New York Times,* another old Soviet hand and advocate of better relations. He said, "Time is of the essence." The two leaders must meet "before those who would not like to see agreement have had a chance to act and prevent it. . . . There is more to be gained by one solid day spent in private and informal talk between Khrushchev and Kennedy than all the meetings of underlings taken together."

Salisbury noted that the President-elect was staying at his father's house in Florida: "Maybe Khrushchev would like to spend a vacation in Palm Beach." Menshikov replied, "But it takes two to make that possible."

Never before had a Soviet leader badgered an American President for a summit meeting before his inauguration. Much of the reason for Khrushchev's impatience lay in a closed session of eighty-one Communist delegations in Moscow that had begun the morning after Kennedy's election.

In November 1960, although the West did not know it, the most dramatic change in the world balance of power in a decade was taking place. The Soviet Union's "unshakable" alliance with China was breaking apart. Mao Tse-tung was racing to build nuclear weapons and challenge Khrushchev for leadership of the world Communist movement.

As early as 1955, Khrushchev had complained to the West German Chancellor, Konrad Adenauer, "Think of it. Already six hundred millions of them and every year twelve million more. . . . We have to do something for our people's standard of living, we have to arm like the Americans, we have to give all the time to the Chinese, who suck our blood like leeches."

He recalled how, in 1957, Mao had told him not to shrink from war with the West: " 'If the imperialists unleash war on us, we may lose more than three hundred million people. So what? War is war. The years will pass and we'll get to work producing more babies than ever before.' " Two years later Mao told the Soviet Foreign Minister, Andrei Gromyko, that in the event of war, Russia should allow the United States to penetrate deep into Chinese territory: "Only when the Americans are right in the central provinces should you give them everything you've got."

Khrushchev concluded that Mao was a "lunatic on a throne." In June 1959, he secretly reneged on his pledge to give the Chinese a sample atomic bomb. After Khrushchev's weekend with Eisenhower at Camp David, Mao privately accused him of selling out China and world communism to make a deal with the United States.

This had its truth. By negotiating with the United States, Khrushchev was rejecting the Chinese notion that global war with the imperialists was inevitable. When the U-2 affair killed his accommodation with Eisenhower, the Chinese exploited the episode to demonstrate that Khrushchev had been taken in by the West. In June 1960, at a secret conference in Bucharest, they denounced him to his face. In August, Khrushchev replied by withdrawing twelve thousand Soviet technical advisers from China.

Still, he hoped to conceal the Chinese-Soviet rift from the West. The illusion that he commanded a billion people gave him vital bargaining power against the United States. He had called the eighty-one Communist delegations to Moscow mainly to hammer out a proclamation that Sino-Soviet solidarity was still undiminished.

Behind closed doors, Khrushchev violently rebutted Chinese charges that he had strayed too far from Lenin and Stalin and gone soft on capitalism. He called Mao a "megalomaniac warmonger," oblivious to anyone's interests but his own. China evidently wanted a demigod to "blame when things go wrong . . . someone you can piss on. . . . If you need Stalin that badly, you can have him—cadaver, coffin, and all!"

Nevertheless he reached a fragile compromise with the Chinese, who conceded that war might not be inevitable after all in exchange for Khrushchev's pledge of more energetic political warfare in the newly independent states of the Third World. The meeting ended with a public proclamation of the unshakable unity of the socialist camp.*

---

*Western leaders were already more aware of the Sino-Soviet split than Khrushchev might have hoped. In January 1960, Stevenson had privately told Menshikov he was aware of Soviet difficulties with China. The Ambassador smiled. "Yes, we may be allies again." That same month, Thompson reported to Washington that Sino-Soviet friction was "profound" and would "probably worsen," although he expected no "complete break in the foreseeable future."

* * *

The Western press liked to call Khrushchev the "dictator" and "absolute leader" of the Soviet Union, an appearance he was happy to maintain. But no one knew better than he how far from absolute his authority really was. In 1957, he had barely survived an overthrow attempt by Georgi Malenkov, Vyacheslav Molotov, and other old-line Stalinists that he branded the "Anti-Party Coup."

In May 1960, after the U-2 embarrassment, new authority had accrued to domestic rivals like Frol Kozlov and Mikhail Suslov, who had criticized Khrushchev for proposing that the Soviet armed forces be cut by 1.2 million men, for bargaining with the imperialists, and for alienating the Chinese. As the historian Adam Ulam has written, Khrushchev might have been thrown out in the summer of 1960 but for the fact that his firing might have been taken "as a sign of capitulation to the Chinese."

Khrushchev's fewer-guns-more-butter policy and his break with the Chinese were contingent on a period of rapprochement with the United States. He knew that if he was going to regain respectability for negotiation with the West, he had better meet with Kennedy fast and produce results: a Berlin settlement, a test ban that might keep Peking and Bonn from getting nuclear weapons, relaxation of Kennedy's campaign pledges to escalate the conventional arms race.

Khrushchev feared that the longer a summit with Kennedy was delayed, the weaker his bargaining position against the United States might be. Each month that passed would give the Americans more certainty that the missile gap was in their own favor and that Peking had split with Moscow. He knew if the two superpowers continued for long in confrontation, he would have to drop his troop reductions and

---

In October 1960, Thompson wrote that Khrushchev's truculence at the UN showed the "depth of the Chinese-Soviet split and Khrushchev's apparent need to undercut Chinese influence with other satellites on grounds that he was too soft toward the West." On November 28, the Ambassador cabled that one effect of the eighty-one-party meeting would be the "weakening of Khrushchev personally. . . . Presumably the Soviets will find it more difficult to impose decisions on other bloc members. Khrushchev's need for success will have increased and his ability to make compromises on such questions as Berlin will have diminished."

By April 1961, the CIA's Sino-Soviet Task Force had gathered enough information to send the President a 99-page report on "The Sino-Soviet Dispute and Its Significance." Citing an "intelligence breakthrough" based on "covert sources," the document quoted from the secret eighty-one-party sessions and concluded that the struggle was "genuine, serious, and bitter." Still the Soviet Union and China would "find it very difficult to contemplate an open and final rupture. . . . We believe that they will not permit it to occur."

his plans to help the Soviet consumer. He might lose his job to hard-line Kremlin rivals allied with the Soviet armed forces and the Chinese, who had argued that the Soviet Union could never do business with the United States.

An early summit with Kennedy would allow the Chairman to assess who and what he was up against. As Thompson once put it, Khrushchev's "whole way of doing business" was that "only the tops could decide." With inordinate faith in his ability to judge motives and personality, Khrushchev was determined to gain a fix on the new President, whose record and statements were so ambiguous.

Kennedy's youth and seemingly effortless rise suggested to Khrushchev that he might be easier to manipulate than other leaders he had known (like Stalin and Mao Tse-tung). He wanted to influence the President-elect before his policies were set in stone.

For much of November and December, the President-elect stayed at his father's house in Palm Beach, planning his government. He filled jobs, read task force reports, met the press, and relaxed, stripping off his clothes to sun himself in the "bullpen" behind the white-stucco Mizener house, playing golf, watching films (*The Sundowners, Fanny, Where the Boys Are*), and swimming in the Atlantic under watch by a Coast Guard cutter, which displeased him: "Are they expecting Castro to invade Palm Beach?"

One day he was sitting on his father's cabin cruiser, the *Marlin,* when another yacht knifed across the bow. Kennedy jumped up. "Who the hell was that?" It was Armand Hammer, the wily old capitalist who had traded with Lenin, made fortunes in liquor and oil, and given money to the Kennedy campaign. The next day, Kennedy boarded Hammer's boat for Bloody Marys and talk about Hammer's adventures with the Soviets.

Khrushchev was much on Kennedy's mind. Stevenson, Harriman, Bohlen, Salisbury, and others had all kept him informed of the messages being flashed from Moscow. Weary of Khrushchev's indirection, Kennedy asked his friend the veteran diplomat David Bruce to ask Menshikov exactly what the Soviets had in mind. The Soviet Ambassador responded by handing Bruce a letter with no letterhead or signature, setting forth what he claimed were his "own personal thoughts." The message pleaded for urgent bargaining and a Kennedy-Khrushchev summit.

*   *   *

If Khrushchev thought that working through Harriman, Stevenson, Bowles, and others who wanted better Soviet relations might move the new President to give them top positions, he was severely disappointed. "The most graphic example of Kennedy's approach to forming his administration was the fate of the Democrats' past idol, the truly unfortunate Adlai Stevenson," wrote a Soviet observer who reflected Khrushchev's views. "He was not only rejected as Secretary of State but offered a second-rate post, Ambassador to the United Nations." Harriman was given the largely decorative post of Ambassador-at-Large.

Kennedy's Secretary of State would be none other than Dean Rusk, president of the Rockefeller Foundation. At Defense: Robert McNamara, president of the Ford Motor Company, whom the Soviets considered to be pressed on Kennedy by the Michigan family whose fortune depended on automobiles and armaments. At Treasury would be Douglas Dillon, the financier who had been Eisenhower's Under Secretary of State. Khrushchev recalled him from Camp David: "It was obvious Dillon couldn't stand us."

Nor was the Chairman charmed by the reappointments of J. Edgar Hoover and Allen Dulles, whom the Soviet press habitually called "the most dangerous man in the world." Whatever frustration he felt about Kennedy's personnel selections, it could not have been much more acute than that of liberal Democrats, who might have reconsidered their enthusiasm for Kennedy had they known that, once elected, he would deflect the claims of Stevenson and other liberals and install Republicans at Defense, Treasury, and the National Security Council.

In Moscow on New Year's Eve, under a moonlit filigree of frost, two thousand guests flowed into St. George's Hall. Llewellyn Thompson was suffering from ulcers, so his wife, Jane, went alone. All eyes were on Khrushchev, laughing and grinning, exposing several iron teeth as he bobbed back and forth, moving from ballet stars to Bulgarian diplomats.

For Khrushchev, 1960 had been a disaster. Privately he was glad to see it go. In public he may have boasted about Communist advances in Cuba, the Congo, and Southeast Asia, the propaganda victories of the U-2 downing and his UN trip. But in his mind these events were dwarfed by the deterioration of American relations, the perils of Mao Tse-tung, the challenges to his domestic political position.

The Kremlin clock struck midnight. With no candor, Khrushchev raised his glass and cried, "No matter how good the old year has been, the new year will be better still!" There were shouts and applause.

"Dear Comrades! Friends! Gentlemen! The Soviet Union makes every effort to be friends with all peoples. But I think no one will reproach me if I say that we attach great importance to improving our relations with the U.S.A. . . . We would like to believe that the U.S.A. wants the same thing—that with the coming of a new President, a fresh wind will blow."

It was "well known" that relations had deteriorated after the U-2 episode. "During the election campaign, Mr. Kennedy said that if he had been President, he would have expressed regret to the Soviet Union. . . . We would like our bad relations with the U.S.A. to become a thing of the past with the departure of the old year and the old President." He hoped that the two nations could turn over a new leaf. "For peaceful coexistence among nations! For peaceful coexistence among all peoples!"

On Tuesday, January 10, 1961, lunching as they flew on the *Caroline* from New York to Washington, Kennedy asked George Kennan what to do about the feelers from Khrushchev. Over the plane's droning engines, he described the Soviet approaches and showed Kennan a copy of Menshikov's unsigned letter calling for a summit. Kennan thought the letter "considerably stiffer and more offensive" than what Menshikov had been saying in person. It seemed to have been "drafted in Khrushchev's office but cleared with a wider circle."

Kennan told the President-elect, "I would make no reply to Menshikov or to Khrushchev before taking office." The Soviets had "no right whatsoever" to rush him this way. After the Inaugural, Kennedy might want to send Khrushchev a private message that if the Soviets seriously wanted to talk about outstanding differences, the United States would respond. But the "burden of proof" was on anyone suggesting a summit "to show why these questions could not be better treated at lower and more normal levels."

Kennan told Kennedy that he should "insist on the right of privacy in the handling of the Soviet problem": Eisenhower had gone "much too far in accepting the thesis that nothing should be done with the Soviets which should not immediately be made known to the press."

In Palm Beach, after rising in his father's house, Kennedy put on sport clothes and sat down on the patio overlooking the gray-blue Atlantic. Puffing on a small cigar, he pressed a yellow legal pad against his knees and scribbled out language for his Inaugural Address.

Adlai Stevenson called to say that the "most important first thing" to do after the Inauguration was to learn what was on Khrushchev's mind. Perhaps a presidential emissary should fly to Moscow, find out what Khrushchev's troubles were, and "explore ours with him": "I think we will not find anyone easier to deal with than Khrushchev is. I think it is important to find out whether he wants to expand the Cold War."

Kennedy asked Stevenson whom he had in mind. The reply: "I think the unhappy thing is the best one is me. . . . The alternative would be Harriman. He has disadvantages in view of the fact he always insists on talking, and his difficulty in hearing. I think it would be best to send someone Khrushchev knows and with whom he has had dealings before, someone he would be quite sure would represent you, someone influential—not just a diplomat."

For Kennedy, the idea had no appeal. He was still irritated by Stevenson's reluctance to endorse him before the Democratic Convention, insisting that he must remain uncommitted in order to unify the party after a nominee was chosen. Kennedy thought Stevenson had acted like "an old woman."

Even had Kennedy looked kindly on Stevenson, he was haunted by his own fragile victory margin. He told the columnist Walter Lippmann that Stevenson had "too many enemies" and that if he went to State, "they'll chew him alive. They'll call him an appeaser, a Communist." Kennedy knew that critics who would be angered by Stevenson as Secretary of State would be incited to riot if he sent him to Moscow as his agent for secret dealings with Khrushchev.

Thus he closed their conversation with a polite brush-off: "Good. We will have a chance to talk before we come to a final judgment on this. . . . I'll see you at the Inauguration."

After his hairbreadth victory, Kennedy knew the surest way to unite the Congress and people behind his leadership was through foreign policy. This coincided with his natural instincts: compared to foreign affairs, he once privately asked, "Who gives a shit about the minimum wage?" He told Sorensen that their inaugural language on domestic goals sounded too much like the campaign: "Let's drop the domestic stuff altogether. It's too long anyway."

The final version of his address combined tough warnings with overtures for peace. The United States would not permit "the slow undoing" of human rights. It would "oppose aggression or subversion anywhere in the Americas." The nation would "pay any price, bear any burden, meet any hardship, support any friend, oppose any foe" to assure liberty's survival.

Still, both sides must begin anew "the quest for peace." They could not "take comfort from our present course—both sides overburdened by the cost of modern weapons, both rightly alarmed by the steady spread of the deadly atom, yet both racing to alter that uncertain balance of terror that stays the hand of mankind's final war. So let us begin anew, remembering on both sides that civility is not a sign of weakness, and sincerity is always subject to proof. Let us never negotiate out of fear, but let us never fear to negotiate."

On Friday, January 20, Radio Moscow said, "Several hours from now, the new President will be inaugurated, marking the end of the infamous eight years of the Eisenhower regime." In Washington, Senator Barry Goldwater sat on the inaugural platform and clapped wildly after the most bellicose passages of Kennedy's speech: "God, I hope he follows it up, but I don't think he will." The ever-cautious Menshikov sat stock-still, his gloved hands firmly in his lap.

As parade floats passed the White House, Kennedy was handed a telegram from Khrushchev and the figurehead Soviet President Leonid Brezhnev endorsing a "fundamental improvement" in the "whole international situation." That evening, while attending the inaugural balls, Jacqueline Kennedy "just crumpled," as she later said, and let her husband continue his rounds alone, returning to the White House long after midnight.

In Moscow, where it was Saturday morning, the American Ambassador to the Soviet Union climbed into his Cadillac to be driven to his first private audience with Khrushchev in months. The Chairman rarely held formal meetings on a weekend, and he had never telephoned Thompson at the Embassy. But so eager was he to start his relationship with the new President that he had broken both rules. After putting down the receiver, Thompson had told an aide, "You'll never guess who just called me."

On Saturday morning, a few minutes before ten, the black car with snapping American flags passed through the Kremlin gates. Followed by his second secretary, Culver Gleysteen, Thompson emerged, wearing a black karakul hat and long black coat, his breath a white cloud. He started up the familiar steps to Khrushchev's second-floor headquarters.

Llewellyn Thompson was closer to Khrushchev than any American had ever been to a Soviet leader. The miner from Kalinovka was excruciatingly sensitive to his treatment by Western diplomats. After swimming with the West German Ambassador at the Black Sea, Khrushchev was furious when the envoy spread the news all over Moscow that the Chairman used a black rubber inner tube.

He regarded Bohlen as a class enemy. When Bohlen chuckled with friends about "our little fat friend" and "Nikita's customary suavity" and called Mrs. Khrushchev "Anastasia," such remarks got back to Khrushchev, who was furious. In 1959, he insisted to Harriman he had "documentary proof" that Bohlen had spread the rumor that Khrushchev was a drunkard.*

Such behavior would have been unthinkable from Thompson. In fact, his staff complained that he held his relationship with Khrushchev so tightly to his vest. Later, flooded with offers to write his memoirs, Thompson refused, noting that no Soviet leader would confide so freely in an American if he had to fear his comments would wind up in print. Khrushchev often used Thompson to check up on Menshikov's reports from Washington, saying, "I wonder if what I'm hearing is true."

With his self-effacing manner and his ruddy, kindly face, Thompson was something of a diplomatic Gary Cooper. He had ulcers and usually kept a glass of milk and graham crackers within easy reach. Born in 1904 in Las Animas, Colorado, to a poor Baptist ranching family, he joked with Khrushchev that they had both herded sheep in their youth. He had worked his way through the University of Colorado by washing dishes. Diplomacy beckoned "because I had so many interests and could follow them all."

The Foreign Service sent him to Moscow in 1940 as second secretary. When German panzers ripped across the Soviet border, much of Stalin's government and the diplomatic corps were evacuated to Kishinev on the Volga. But Thompson stayed on under firebombs in the blacked-out capital to report home on Soviet chances of survival. Soviet officials later expressed their gratitude that he hadn't "abandoned" them. After VE-Day, Thompson participated in almost every major international conference called to bring the West and the Soviet Union to better terms.

His shyness and addiction to work had been the enemies of romance. In 1948, engaged to be married, he was sailing to Europe when he met a vivacious Boston divorcée, Jane Goelet, who was also engaged. By the end of the voyage, they had forgotten their fiancés. Jane's warmth and aversion to pomposity strengthened his self-con-

---

*Thompson tried to correct the damage by not too credibly telling Khrushchev that Bohlen had actually called Khrushchev a "normal drinker" and had said that "the heavy drinker among the Presidium was Mr. Bulganin."

fidence and his humanity. He always reminded her, "Remember that neither the honors nor the insults in this trade are meant personally for you."

In 1952, they went to Vienna. Through almost four hundred sessions and a brutal last fortnight of horse-trading with the Soviets, Thompson negotiated the treaty that made Austria neutral and independent. Years of dealing with Moscow gave him confidence in his judgment. During the Hungarian uprising in 1956, someone woke him to warn that Soviet tanks were heading for the Austrian border. Certain that the Soviets would not enlarge the conflict, he said, "Forget it," and went back to bed.

Thompson was about to retire from the Foreign Service when Foster Dulles told him he was slated to succeed Bohlen in Moscow. Thompson said he hoped he would not have to stay long: Moscow was not the best place to raise two American girls. Although Bohlen and Thompson were old friends, fellow golfers, skiers, and poker players, their conflict over the Moscow Embassy almost destroyed their friendship.

Thompson wrote a conciliatory letter. Bohlen replied, "While I can very well understand your desire to avoid any 'impression' that you were pushing me out here, nevertheless, according to Dulles, this is actually the case." Finally Thompson told his wife, "I'm just going to withdraw my candidacy" and, as Jane recalled, "Chip woke up and stopped acting like a prima donna."

The Thompsons flew in 1957 to a Moscow electrified by stories of Khrushchev's defeat of the cabal known as the "Anti-Party Group." The new Ambassador wrote Bohlen in Manila that the "most striking thing" he observed was "the skepticism and uneasiness of the people."

"I have built up a relationship with Khrushchev which is, I think, something we can exploit, to some extent at least," Thompson once told Senators in private. "Because I have always been straight with him, he will take what I say with at least a certain amount of acceptance if this is a straight story. And I am also anxious not to in any way spoil that."

Thompson's relationship with Khrushchev had begun to flower soon after Khrushchev won supreme power in 1958 by ousting Bulganin to make himself Chairman of the Council of Ministers as well as leader of the Soviet Communist Party. At a reception in Moscow that summer, the Canadian Ambassador noted that Khrushchev left the head table to sit with Thompson for more than an hour, showing "about a thousand guests" that he wanted better relations with the West.

At another reception, with colleagues present, Khrushchev dressed down Thompson so fiercely that the Ambassador bit his lip to the point of bleeding. This may have been to show colleagues that he could stand up to the Americans. Later he told Thompson, "You know me. I was just letting off steam." Thompson observed that "any diplomat who softsoaps him earns contempt. He scolds me and I scold him."

Over private dinners in a Kremlin orangery, Jane Thompson was one of the few who could tease Khrushchev to his face. When the Chairman hinted in 1959 that he would like to tour the United States but might be considered too dangerous a visitor, she said, "Perhaps you should go in a beard." When she gave him a pair of English toasting cups designed to reduce the amount of liquor drunk, Khrushchev's wife, Nina Petrovna, gave her a great hug. The Thompsons were not spared Khrushchev's depressions or tantrums. "There he goes again," Mrs. Khrushchev said. "He's either way up here or way down there."

Thompson's cables on his conversations with the Chairman had the texture of a seventeenth-century French diplomatic diary. November 1959: "As I was taking my leave, Khrushchev remarked he had hoped our families could get together socially soon but he could tell me a secret—namely, that he . . . expected soon to go to the Caucasus. He said he had personally shot three bears in Romania and his party had shot six in all. . . . On such occasions he could not escape heavy dinners and accompanying toasts and this was not really a rest."

At the 1960 Kremlin New Year's Eve ball, Khrushchev took the Thompsons before dawn into an anteroom and "pushed the booze at us," as Thompson recalled. The Chairman used the opportunity to declare that peace was essential if they did not wish to "commit suicide." He merrily noted that fifty Soviet nuclear bombs were earmarked for France—"more than enough to destroy that country"—thirty each for West Germany and Britain. Jane asked, "How many do you have for us?" Khrushchev replied, "That is a secret."

Later that month, he invited Thompson, his number-three man Boris Klosson, and their families for a weekend at his dacha. No Americans had ever been invited there for a weekend with the Chairman. On a Friday night, the Thompsons were driven to the stone mansion where Stalin had egged on Khrushchev and his other minions in infamous all-night drinking bouts.

The next morning, the lord of the manor appeared, his beaming face encircled by a fur hat with earpieces. With six-year-old Sherry

Thompson on his lap, Khrushchev drove the fathers and their children to stables the size of a small hippodrome. A groom placed the boys and girls atop horses presented by Arab leaders and the Shah of Iran.

The previous September, on his American trip, Khrushchev had watched Frank Sinatra and Shirley MacLaine film *Can-Can* and denounced the dancing as "pornography." Asked the name of one horse, Khrushchev repeated the question to his stable man, who cried, "Khan-Khan!" When his little grandson Nikita refused to ride, the Chairman said, "Never mind, he's the intellectual. He's going to be the philosopher in the family."

Jane Thompson was shocked to see that the embassy-grown hyacinths she had brought for Mrs. Khrushchev had been crudely replanted. Nina Petrovna closed her eyes and flicked her hands; the secret police guard had been at work.

When the party sat down in Stalin's dining room to a feast of black bread, soup, fish, and quail, two Thompson girls, three Klosson boys, and numerous Khrushchev grandchildren raced in and out, chased by nurses in starched white headdresses. Deputy Premier Anastas Mikoyan said, "If Stalin could only see us now, with the American Ambassador here, he'd turn in his grave."

Khrushchev's son-in-law, Alexei Adzhubei, put some popular music records on a gramophone. The Chairman said, "Can't we get that thing turned down?" He announced that on doctor's orders he would drink not vodka but white wine: "All Russians who can speak English, give your toasts in English! All Americans who can speak Russian, give your toasts in Russian!" When Klosson took only a sip, the drunken Frol Kozlov held his glass over his head and turned it upside down: "In Russia, we drink *this* way."

Klosson toasted the next generation. Kozlov heckled again: "We should toast the *present* generation and not just the future!" Khrushchev motioned him to be quiet.

Klosson went on: "Mr. Chairman, there's something about the Russian language. When I speak in Russian, I find it difficult to do in just a few words." Khrushchev slammed the table and guffawed: "That is what I've been telling my people. They say I talk too much. Listen to what the American says!"

Khrushchev demanded song. "The only songs *he* knows are the old revolutionary songs from 1905," murmured Lidiya Gromyko. The Khrushchev grandchildren sang ballads about the coming of spring. Jenny and Sherry Thompson responded by singing, to the tune of "Frère Jacques," "I like vodka, I like vodka / Drink it up, drink it up! / Mix it with martini, mix it with martini! / Drink, drank, drunk—

drink, drank, drunk!" There was silence until Khrushchev laughed and everyone followed. The girls' mortified mother wondered why they couldn't have chosen "Home on the Range."

That night, hulking secret policemen dragged the children on sleighs through the freshly fallen snow. Inside the guesthouse, Thompson hushed his wife as he scribbled notes about the day's events and stuffed them into his pajama pockets.

On this and later visits, Khrushchev showed the Thompsons his beloved home-grown corn, defended the Soviet system ("The United States is so rich that, for the time being, it can postpone revolution by buying off or bribing the workers"), and reminisced: "I will tell you how Stalin died. We all went out to his dacha on Saturday and had a good dinner. . . . Usually he called us on Sundays, but he did not that day. On Monday night, his guards called and said that he was ill."

Khrushchev lay down, shut his eyes, and assumed the role of the comatose tyrant, arching an eyebrow in a flicker of consciousness. After telling the story, he said, "We wanted him dead." But when Stalin died, "I wept. I was his pupil. We were all indebted to him. Like Peter the Great, he combated barbarism with barbarism. But he was a great man."

Four months after the dacha weekend came the U-2 affair. At a reception after the downing, Khrushchev told reporters, "I respect the U.S. Ambassador and am sure that he had nothing to do with this incursion. . . . I am convinced of the moral qualities of this man. . . . I suppose he is feeling very bad about this incident both for himself and for his country." He took Thompson into a side room and said, "This U-2 thing has put me in a terrible spot. You have to get me off it."

But Thompson could not save the American-Soviet rapprochement. In September 1960, before hundreds of diplomats, Khrushchev berated him for the U-2 and RB-47 flights and stamped on his foot: "If you do that, you should say, 'Excuse me!' " Thompson asked him to return the captured airmen. Khrushchev replied, "This is your first position. But your second position is not to put them on trial before the elections."

Now it was January 1961. Sitting across from Khrushchev at the green-baize-draped table, Thompson thought he looked tired and sounded hoarse. From confidential information he knew the Chairman had just spent a week fighting new battles with internal rivals. He asked, "Have you read the Inaugural Address?"

"I read it this morning," said Khrushchev. "Kennedy obviously has a different point of view from mine, but I see constructive things in the speech. I will ask our newspapers to print the full text"—he laughed—*"if* they will agree to do so!"

Kuznetsov read out an aide-mémoire: although the RB-47 had violated Soviet airspace, the Soviet government was now willing to release the plane's two surviving crewmen. There was "every reason to clear away the rubbish and residue of the Cold War." Khrushchev said he would let the airmen go as soon as the United States endorsed the Soviet statement. It must promise no more aerial violations and no use of the freed airmen for propaganda. "If not, the only logical outcome will be to put them on trial."

Thompson said he had no instructions yet from President Kennedy and must speak for himself. He appreciated the spirit of the offer. But at the risk of sounding ungrateful, he must note that, unlike the U-2, the RB-47 had not violated Soviet airspace. As he understood the Chairman's offer, the fliers would only be released if Washington confessed that the RB-47 had made a deliberate incursion.

"No, each side is welcome to maintain its own view." Changing subjects, he said he felt sorry for Thompson, who had had to defend the "uneven" Eisenhower-Dulles policies for eight years.

"I'm convinced I have been a poor Ambassador, because there is clearly wide misunderstanding on both sides—particularly the Soviet." Thompson said what troubled the West was Moscow's wish to dominate the world. Once a nation joined the Communist bloc, the bloc used full force to keep it there, whatever the people's own wishes: look at Hungary.

Khrushchev shook his head; the United States was the one trying to police the world. In Laos, guerrillas were fighting against the reactionary "drunkard" the Americans had put in power. What importance did "tiny Laos" have to Moscow or Washington? "Let us put out the flames." And what about the Congo? Now that the Belgians had gone, there was no more "white king," but obviously the Belgians now intended to oppress the Congolese people by other means. Why not disband both power blocs? The Soviet Union would agree to pull its troops from Eastern Europe.

"But the Soviet Union would still have a monolithic system," said Thompson. "I cannot believe the contrary until some country which has become Communist is allowed to change its system." Perhaps the Soviet people, "in general," supported the Communist system. "But this is not true of most other Communist countries."

"Hitler counted on the people turning against the regime when he invaded the Soviet Union," Khrushchev replied. "Hitler was a fool. If he had been wise, he would have been not Hitler but Stalin." He said there was no point in "belaboring" the issue. Perhaps they could talk more leisurely one weekend at the dacha. Khrushchev asked, "Will you remain as Ambassador?"

"I don't know."

"We will gladly give you our vote. But I am not sure this would be helpful." He asked Thompson to send his regards to President Kennedy, Stevenson, and the other American officials he had met.

At the White House on Saturday morning, Kennedy awoke in the Lincoln Bedroom. Jacqueline joined him, and they sat for a time on the bed while sunlight poured in through the tall windows. Before ten o'clock, Kennedy walked jauntily to the West Wing to receive his first official visitor, Harry Truman, the first President of the Cold War, whom the Soviets reviled as much as they loved Roosevelt.

Truman's assault on Kennedy before his nomination ("Senator, are you certain that you are quite ready for the country, or that the country is ready for you?") was forgotten this morning as the new President took him to see Jacqueline. When they opened her bedroom door, she was in bed on her back, leg in the air, while Kennedy's doctor, Janet Travell, worked a kink out of one of her calf muscles. Truman blushed.

That evening, after attending the annual Alfalfa Club dinner at the Statler Hilton, the President read Thompson's cables on his meeting with Khrushchev, which advised him to accept Khrushchev's bargain on the RB-47 fliers. On Monday afternoon, Kennedy, Rusk, and his new deputy, Chester Bowles, discussed the matter with McNamara, Bundy, and Sorensen. As Bundy recalled, the President regarded Khrushchev's offer with "a certain wariness. You know, 'Is there a trick here?' "

Kennedy decided to say yes. He hoped to announce the airmen's release at his first news conference as President on Wednesday. Rusk cabled Thompson that the United States would not exploit the crew's release and that "flights of American aircraft penetrating the airspace of the Soviet Union have been suspended since May 1960. . . . President Kennedy has ordered that they not be resumed." Rusk relayed the President's hope that the men could be freed before his press conference.

That evening, the Kennedys dined at the White House with Charles and Martha Bartlett. The men took off their jackets and lit cigars. The President said, "I slept in Lincoln's bed last night." Bartlett: "Any strange dreams?" Kennedy: "No, I just jumped in and hung on." Tailed by a pair of Secret Service men, they went off into the snow to explore the Executive Office Building and encountered Walt Rostow of the National Security Council. Why was he working so late? "I have a tough boss."

Bartlett took the President off to see the Indian Treaty Room, where Eisenhower had met the press. "It was probably the happiest moment of Jack Kennedy's life, and Jackie's too," he recalled. "There was this wonderful and exhilarating sense that all things were possible. He was just bursting with all the things he could do. There was an enormous amount of goodness in his spirit then." Ted Sorensen agreed: "Everyone had told him he didn't have a chance, and now he had reached the Number One power center."

True to Khrushchev's word, *Pravda* and *Izvestia* ran the full text of the Inaugural Address—without comment. The Soviets reduced their jamming of the Voice of America, stepped up after the U-2 affair. Moscow newspapers, radio, and television reported the Soviet people's "great hopes" for improved relations with the United States.

Kuznetsov told Thompson it might be difficult to release the two fliers in time to put them on a flight leaving Moscow at Wednesday noon. But shortly after Tuesday midnight, he called to say that Khrushchev had been reached in Kiev. The airmen would be brought to the Embassy at ten o'clock Wednesday morning.

In Washington, David Wise of the *New York Herald Tribune* learned that something important would happen at 2 A.M. Washington time. He called Pierre Salinger at his home in Falls Church, Virginia. "Don't tell anyone about this," said the press secretary. "It's a matter of the highest secrecy, and I have no comment."

Armed with more facts about the release, Wise called Salinger again and warned that his paper had stopped the presses to run large numbers of its Late City Edition. Salinger replied that he could speak for the President: the story would be "inimical to the national interest" and might jeopardize the fliers' release. Wise and his editors decided not to "jeopardize the first diplomatic breakthrough between Washington and Moscow, four days after the inauguration of a new President."

On Wednesday morning, dressed in Russian overcoats and hats, captains Freeman Olmstead and John McKone were delivered to the American Embassy in Moscow. Thompson briefed them on arrangements to get them out of the country incognito. The Soviets had also produced the body of the dead pilot. Thompson's staff had his coffin lined with zinc to conform with American law. (The three other crewmen were never found.)

As the KLM jet taxied for takeoff, two of its tires blew out. The President was not informed that the plane was airborne until less than an hour before his first press conference. Rising from his desk, he borrowed a hairbrush from his secretary, Evelyn Lincoln, raked it over his hair, and was driven to the vast new State Department Auditorium, where 418 newsmen sat waiting on orange theater seats.

For the first time, sixty million people were watching on live television. Eisenhower's press conferences had been filmed and cleared by the White House for the networks. Kennedy wished to do it live, but Rusk, Sorensen, and Bundy advised him not to: a slip of the tongue could cause an international incident. But as Salinger recalled, the President was "absolutely confident of his ability to handle himself."

Gripping the sides of his podium beneath a huge presidential seal, Kennedy said that he was "happy to be able to announce" the airmen's release, which "removes a serious obstacle to improvement of Soviet-American relations."

Three days later the President flew by helicopter to Andrews Air Force Base, where he greeted the airmen. While McKone kissed his wife for twenty-seven seconds, Kennedy scuffed his shoes and stared at the tarmac. Over coffee with the airmen and their families in the White House Red Room, the President teased McKone: "You had lipstick all over you." Salinger refused requests to interview the fliers, citing "our relations with the Soviet Union."

Walt Rostow considered the release "just a small, cheap dowry to Kennedy." Dean Rusk told his staff, "The one thing I fear is that Americans will think the Russians have really changed, that they're softening, that the worst is over." A KGB man in Washington later told an American that whatever had been said in public about no quid pro quo, the Soviet Union expected "a number of American concessions" in return for the RB-47 release.

The following week, Kennedy's relations with Khrushchev came close to being fractured at the start. An American reconnaissance plane passed near Vise Island in the Karsk Sea. In Moscow, Kuznetsov privately complained to Thompson that the United States had once again violated Soviet airspace: was Kennedy's pledge of no more such flights worth the paper it was written on?

Furious, the President ordered the Pentagon to find out what was going on. The incident had the potential to be another U-2 or RB-47 affair. The President cabled Thompson to tell Kuznetsov that "a thorough investigation" was being made: he hoped the two governments could handle the problem "quietly and without publicity."

In July 1960, it had been in Khrushchev's interest to fan the flames of the RB-47 incident as evidence of American "perfidy." This time, it was not. In order "not to aggravate the international situation," Khrushchev accepted Kennedy's assurance that there would be no more such incursions, said nothing in public, and closed his books on the matter. It has remained secret until this writing.

Kennedy set about trying to improve the climate with Moscow by ordering the U.S. Post Office to stop censoring Soviet publications. The Soviets were invited to resume civil aviation talks that had broken down in 1960.

The Chief of Naval Operations, Admiral Arleigh Burke, and other officials were asked to take harsh anti-Soviet language out of speeches. Burke complied—and then leaked word of the admonition to the *New York Times.* Senators Strom Thurmond and Barry Goldwater denounced the "silencing" of Admiral Burke, along with the RB-47 airmen, as "gag-rule diplomacy."*

For a decade, Soviet crabmeat had been barred from American stores because of its reputation for being the product of slave labor. Through the intercession of Senator Albert Gore of Tennessee, Ar-

---

*Burke's transgression was not an isolated instance. In May 1959, Eisenhower's doctor, Howard Snyder, noted that the President was "exercised" and "in a bad humor" because the Admiral had made a public statement "to the effect that neither the Nike-Hercules nor the Bomarc defense missiles were worth a damn."

In April 1961, Rear Admiral Samuel Frankel, Deputy Director of Naval Intelligence, wrote a speech for delivery in Austin, Texas, suggesting that Presidents Eisenhower and Kennedy were deluded in their willingness to negotiate with the Russians in certain circumstances. When Assistant Secretary of Defense for Public Affairs Arthur Sylvester asked for revisions, Navy officials took the matter up with the President, who backed Sylvester. When this became known, the privately published *Navy Times* complained of the "air of secrecy, of censorship, of arbitrary rulings" in Kennedy's Pentagon.

That same month, the *Overseas Weekly* documented the radical-right activities of Major General Edwin Walker. This led to an official "admonishment" for his efforts to influence the voting of his troops. Walker later resigned from the Army, became a spokesman for the John Birch Society, and moved to Dallas. There he flew the American flag upside down, questioned the patriotism of Dean Rusk and Walt Rostow, and decried Kennedy's "no-win" foreign policy. In September 1962, he went to Oxford, Mississippi, and was arrested while egging on a mob opposing James Meredith's entrance into the University of Mississippi. One evening in April 1963, Lee Harvey Oswald, who thought Walker a potential Hitler, took a shot at the General through the window of his home and missed. The sniper was not caught.

mand Hammer was asked to examine the problem during a Soviet trip. Khrushchev called the old concessionaire to the Kremlin, insisting, "There is no slave labor any more in Russia! Not since Stalin died!" The President approved lifting the ban.

But the glowing promise of better relations with the Soviet Union was fast eclipsed in Kennedy's mind by a secret speech Khrushchev had given in Moscow.

On Friday, January 6, in a closed-door session with Soviet ideologists and propagandists, Khrushchev had declared that capitalism was retreating all over the world. Socialism was on the march. The Soviets had surpassed the United States in long-range missiles. Revolutionary ferment from Vietnam to Cuba showed that the Third World would pass into the Communist camp.

The Chairman insisted that a world war was unacceptable because it would destroy civilization. There was now "only one way of bringing imperialism to heel"—the "sacred" struggles of colonial peoples. The Soviet Union would fully support these wars of national liberation: "Communists are revolutionaries, and it would be a bad thing if they did not exploit new opportunities."

Khrushchev's speech was kept secret until the Kremlin released a condensed version two days before Kennedy's inauguration. When Eisenhower read it, he was unruffled. Long accustomed to Khrushchev's bluster about Berlin, Soviet missiles, and world revolution, he privately observed that the Chairman rarely fulfilled his threats; the tough talk usually substituted for action.

Most of what Khrushchev said had already been said in the eighty-one-party declaration of December 1960. By renouncing the option of world war, he was once again defying hard-liners in Moscow and Peking and, he presumably thought, reassuring the West. Blinded by his internal problems, he did not realize the extent to which Kennedy might take the timing and content of his address as a provocation and test of a new young President.

Lacking Eisenhower's experience with Khrushchev, Kennedy did not have the background to set what he soon called the "January Speech" against Khrushchev's years of false boasting and false threats. He still knew too little about Soviet politics to view the speech in terms of Khrushchev's problems with Chinese and Kremlin rivals.

Since Election Day, Kennedy had been trying to read the conflicting signals from Moscow. Did Khrushchev intend to cooperate or drive for world domination? With this speech, the new President thought he had the answer. Since 1957, he had warned that the Soviets would use their missile strength and other advantages to attack the periphery of the free world. Now Khrushchev seemed to have proved him right.

Just after taking office, Kennedy read a cable from Thompson saying that the speech "brings together in one place Khrushchev's point of view as Communist and propagandist. (There are other sides to him.)" Thompson noted that, if taken literally, the statement was a "declaration of Cold War." He presumed Kennedy would be asked about the speech at his first press conference:*

"Solely from a tactical point of view toward the Soviet Union, it might be advantageous for the President to take the line that he cannot understand why a man who professes to wish to negotiate with us publishes a few days before his inauguration what amounts to a declaration of Cold War and determination to bring about the downfall of the American system. . . . Such a statement would be balanced by some reference for its part to find the way to peace."

As Thompson advised, the President gave copies of Khrushchev's speech to his top people and told them to "read, mark, learn, and inwardly digest" it. As Robert McNamara recalled, "It was a significant event in our lives."

But Kennedy ignored Thompson's warning that the statement showed only one side of a complex world leader. Badly overreacting, he took it as a comprehensive account of Khrushchev's intentions. He told his highest officials, "You've got to understand it, and so does everybody else around here. This is our clue to the Soviet Union." Ten days after the Inauguration, he used his first State of the Union address to respond in kind to what he thought to be Khrushchev's challenge.

---

*Thompson was wrong. More curious about the RB-47 release and a possible Kennedy-Khrushchev summit, reporters ignored Khrushchev's speech.

4

Novosibirsk

O N MONDAY EVENING, JANUARY 30, WHEN KENNEDY WALKED down the center aisle of the House of Representatives through cheering members of Congress, Hugh Sidey of *Time* thought the new President was trying to look "as solemn as a forty-three-year-old man can look" but that the effort was "not quite successful."

Kennedy declared that it was "an hour of national peril and national opportunity. Before my term has ended, we shall have to test anew whether a nation organized and governed such as ours can endure." American domestic problems paled "beside those which confront us around the world." The United States must never be "lulled" into believing that the Soviet Union or China had "yielded its ambitions for world domination—ambitions which they forcefully restated only a short time ago."

Asia was menaced by Communist China's "relentless pressures." The Congo was "brutally torn by civil strife." In Latin America,

"Communist agents seeking to exploit that region's peaceful revolution of hope have established a base on Cuba, only ninety miles from our shores." He had asked the Secretary of Defense "to reappraise our entire defense strategy." He would accelerate the Polaris submarine and missile programs and order fifty-three new transport planes designed for airlifts in time of crisis.

Jabbing his right hand into the air, he read phrases he had scrawled onto Sorensen's text: "Each day, the crises multiply. Each day, their solution grows more difficult. Each day, we draw nearer the hour of maximum danger, as weapons spread and hostile forces grow stronger.* I feel I must inform the Congress that our analyses over the last ten days make it clear that, in each of the principal areas of crisis, the tide of events has been running out—and time has not been our friend."

Americans who had read Eisenhower's reassuring final message to Congress eighteen days before must have thought they were now living in another country and world. For a decade, no President had spoken in such apocalyptic terms.

The speech was far more alarmist than Kennedy was in private. For ten days, he had been closeted with his foreign policy circle, reviewing fresh intelligence information. From this he knew that the Soviets and Chinese were no longer working in harmony, that the Soviet military buildup was not frenzied. He knew that while Khrushchev was exploiting opportunities in Laos, the Congo, and Cuba, he had refused Chinese demands to mobilize Soviet resources in an absolute drive for world communism.

He knew that, with the exception of the Wars of Liberation speech, the signals Khrushchev had sent since the election were more conciliatory than at any time since May 1960. But in Kennedy's mind, Khrushchev's speech had dwarfed all the Chairman's other post-election words and actions.

The President's alarming rhetoric also had domestic political uses.

---

*Kennedy's use of the term "hour of maximum danger" was not random rhetoric. The 1950 Cold War tocsin NSC-68 referred to 1954 as the "year of maximum danger," by which time the Russians would have enough atomic bombs to "seriously damage this country" and thus might "be tempted to strike swiftly and with stealth." During the missile gap controversy, the term came to refer to the moment that the Soviets would feel so secure in their missile superiority that they might blackmail the West into negotiation on Soviet terms or actually wage a surprise nuclear attack. Kennedy's use of this code phrase in his State of the Union showed his continuing willingness to use the missile gap issue against his predecessor.

Kennedy wished to vindicate his campaign charges that Eisenhower had been too complacent about the Soviet danger. With his slender victory margin, he needed to build national support that would help him to push his defense, foreign policy, and other programs through Congress. He knew Americans were more likely to rally to him in an atmosphere of mounting world crisis.

The man whose campaign slogan was "A Time for Greatness" knew that great Presidents are not easily made in tranquil times. With his Churchillian penchant for stirring rhetoric and theater, Kennedy as President moved naturally into the role of rousing a complacent people against the external danger he had celebrated in *Why England Slept*. He had warned Democrats at Los Angeles that the New Frontier would be the opposite of Eisenhower, that he promised "more sacrifice instead of more security."

Kennedy knew it was politically safer to err on the side of seeming too tough on the Soviets than too soft. During his early Senate years, anxiety about Joseph McCarthy's large Massachusetts following had kept him from making a public stand against the demagogue, even though it would have been unlikely to make a serious dent in his reelection majority.

Kennedy's worry about the Right had not ended when he entered the White House. He did not enjoy Eisenhower's immense popularity and the public's confidence that, even if Eisenhower's words and deeds seemed diffident about the Soviets, the Supreme Commander of World War II would never put the nation in danger. Kennedy knew that Cold War rhetoric would help to immunize him against accusations that he was too intellectual or too surrounded by people like Stevenson and Bowles to oppose the Russians with adequate fervor.

There is little evidence that Kennedy devoted much thought to the effect of this speech on the Soviets, aside from responding in kind to Khrushchev's Wars of Liberation speech. He had yet to have a serious extended discussion with his Soviet experts on what his policy toward Khrushchev should be. He knew that portraying a nation besieged by "hostile forces," nearing an "hour of maximum danger," would make it more difficult for himself to negotiate with Khrushchev and hold down the arms race.

Khrushchev almost surely thought Kennedy's State of the Union address a deliberate slap in the face. By his own lights, he had praised the new President in public as another Roosevelt, signaled through Menshikov and Thompson that he wanted better relations, released the RB-47 fliers.

With his eternal assumption that American leaders were telepathic enough to read his mind, he probably thought that Kennedy knew his

Wars of Liberation speech had been delivered mainly for Chinese consumption. In return, the President had seemed intentionally to undermine Khrushchev's effort to show his rivals that negotiation with the imperialists would be more fruitful than confrontation. After Kennedy's State of the Union speech, *Izvestia* dropped its politeness toward Kennedy. It complained that the address evoked "irksome echoes of the Cold War."

On Wednesday, February 1, the United States conducted the first test launching of its Minuteman ICBM. The American press predicted deployment in large numbers by the middle of 1962. The Kremlin knew that these missiles, placed in hardened silos, could be used for a first-strike nuclear attack against the Soviet Union.

At the same time, the United States was rumored to be planning to shift ownership of its Jupiter missiles in Turkey, perhaps even some kind of access to atomic weapons to the Turkish government newly arousing the ancient Russian and Soviet anxieties about encirclement and threats along the border. In Ankara on February 3, Soviet Ambassador Nikita Ryzhov demanded that the Turkish foreign minister tell him what was going on.

On Monday evening, February 6, at Robert McNamara's first background session with reporters at the Pentagon, someone asked about the missile gap that Kennedy had so dramatized in the campaign. The Secretary of Defense candidly replied that he had been going through the classified evidence: "There is no missile gap."

He reported that the United States and the Soviet Union had about the same small number of missiles in the field. (He did not go on to reveal the far more secret information that the United States had roughly six thousand nuclear warheads against roughly three hundred for the Soviets—a twenty-to-one advantage.)

As McNamara recalled, he knew almost instantly that he had made a "terrible mistake": "They broke the damn door down. They went out and the headline on the late afternoon edition of the [Washington] *Evening Star* says, 'McNamara declares no missile gap.' And the next day, perhaps with tongue in cheek, the Republicans asked that the election be rerun."*

With rising anger, Kennedy read the columns and news articles

---

*One result of the fracas was the Defense Intelligence Agency, which McNamara established in August 1961 to integrate estimates of such services as the Air Force, whose wildly excessive assessments of Soviet missile capabilities had originally inspired public fears about a missile gap.

suggesting that he had won the Presidency by exploiting a fraudulent issue. At his February 8 press conference, he tried to obscure the matter: "It would be premature to reach a judgment as to whether there is a gap or not a gap." Later, during military discussions in the Cabinet Room, he sardonically asked, "Who ever believed in the missile gap?"

The President was chiefly worried about the political embarrassment of having exploited a campaign issue that now had been proven false. Far more serious was the Soviet reaction to McNamara's declaration. The Secretary of Defense had unwittingly overturned the tacit understanding by which Eisenhower had never specifically refuted Khrushchev's bombast about a crash missile buildup in order not to compel the Chairman to escalate his missile program and other military spending and avoid being branded a liar.*

Khrushchev was inclined to view American actions in Soviet terms, as the deliberate result of decisions made by a highly centralized bureaucracy. The rebuffs of his pleading for an early summit, the unpublicized air incident over the Karsk Sea, Kennedy's harsh State of the Union speech and his broad review of American defense, the Minuteman launching, the Jupiters in Turkey, and now McNamara's declaration that there was no missile gap had all occurred within seventeen days of Kennedy's Inauguration.

Khrushchev found Kennedy's previous views on the Soviet Union so difficult to decipher that he inevitably read too much into what he now saw. He may have assumed that the seeming provocations of Kennedy's first seventeen days were not isolated events but a deliberate campaign to herald a harsh new American strategy for dealing with Moscow.

In early February, the President convened his Soviet experts. He had wired Thompson to come home "both to get your advice and demonstrate highest level confidence in you." His reappointment thus assured, Thompson wrote a friend from Moscow, "It was not easy to forego the possibility of a post with a normal life but I do think this will be a critical year and not the best time to change nags here, even though I feel most incompetent in the face of the enormous problems we have with these people."

The Ambassador took off from Moscow in an Air Force plane and

---

*In private, Khrushchev was more reserved about Soviet power. In Moscow in February 1960, Henry Cabot Lodge dropped a comment about the Soviet Union's having superior missiles and Khrushchev replied, "No, not really."

landed at Idlewild Airport. He took the train to Washington, arriving in a blinding night storm of sleet and snow. Noting that the Soviet winter had been probably the warmest in fifty years, he said, "It looks like we're on the wrong end of a cultural exchange!" From Union Station he went to his quarters in the fine old Georgetown house of his CIA friend Frank Wisner.

Before leaving Moscow, he had sent Kennedy a series of long tutorial telegrams of the kind Eisenhower had disliked. He told Jane, "It's wonderful to work for someone you know will read what you write." He wrote the President that events were already forcing him to decide "our basic policy toward the Soviet Union." He assumed that Kennedy was willing to take risks to reach accommodation: "We should be under no illusions as to what can be accomplished within a reasonable period of time." But to do anything else would probably divide the West, estrange the Third World, and lead to war.

In the Kremlin, "Khrushchev is the dominant personality, but it is quite possible that he could disappear from the scene within the next few years from natural or other causes." The President must always remember that Soviet leaders "have an almost religious faith in their beliefs, and this motivates them to a larger extent than generally believed." Even Khrushchev, the least doctrinaire of them all, justified his position by working for world communism: "The degree of effort and the methods used are factors which our own policies can influence."

The great problem? "We both look at the same set of facts and see different things." But there was reason for optimism. The Soviet people ardently wished for peace as the best way to gain a better life. Thus they exerted "constant pressure toward accommodation with us."

Thompson wrote that Khrushchev believed that if he reduced tension and diverted resources from weapons to the Soviet consumer, perhaps with Western aid, he could make an example of the Soviet Union and thus lead the world to communism: "I believe the Soviet leadership long ago correctly appraised the meaning of atomic military power. They recognized that a major war was no longer an acceptable means of achieving their objective." But "we shall, of course, have to keep our powder dry and plenty of it."

The Ambassador noted that Communists felt that if their movement lost its dynamism, it would risk disintegration: "Unfortunately, the Chinese Communists have considerably rejuvenated the revolutionary posture of the Soviet party." Still, the Soviets had a "strong strain of nationalism." If Khrushchev could "offer hope of a period

of tranquillity, I would not exclude an eventual complete break between the Soviet and Chinese Communists."

At the start of his Presidency, Eisenhower had characteristically
sought to shape his general approach to the Soviet Union by devising
formal machinery. He assigned three teams of advisers to make the
case for three levels of aggressiveness: rolling back the Iron Curtain,
containment, and Fortress America. After weeks of debate and study,
the President called the teams to the third-floor White House solarium, where he listened to their presentations and asked questions.

Kennedy's method, honed through years in the Senate, was the
opposite of Eisenhower's. As Bundy later put it, "All Senators are
disorderly." On Saturday morning, February 11, the new President
gathered Lyndon Johnson, Rusk, Bundy, Thompson, and three previous envoys to Moscow—Harriman, Kennan, and Bohlen—for a free-
form skull session to "chart our future relations with the Soviet
Union." Kennan was about to leave for Belgrade as Ambassador.
Bohlen was staying on at the State Department.

Kennedy opened the meeting by saying, "Now tell me about
Russia." As the four diplomats spoke, the President interrupted only
to stimulate and clarify. Dean Rusk was surprised at how he "wanted
to look at everything from the beginning, the ground up." Through
the entire two and a half hours, Vice President Johnson said virtually
nothing.

Kennan argued that Khrushchev was faced with "considerable opposition" from Stalinists, who opposed negotiation with the West:
"Control over the Party apparatus is today being exercised collec-
tively . . . and not personally by Khrushchev."

Thompson agreed but thought that Khrushchev would be "seriously threatened" only if he faced "unusually grave difficulties" in
farming and foreign affairs: the Soviet Union had had "two really
disastrous years in agriculture, and right now the prospect is pretty
good for another one."

He said that the Soviet government would keep showing off its
economic growth in flamboyant ways, such as building the world's
largest heated swimming pool. Everyone in Moscow seemed to have
a friend with a new house, and "the appetite grows with eating."
Recently Thompson had sent a member of his staff to a community
meeting: "The people got so out of hand that they were just pounding
the table and screaming and yelling and demanding. Once you abolish
terror as the way to operate this system, you run into this."

Thompson suggested that the Pentagon was probably overestimating Soviet conventional strength but agreed with Bohlen that Moscow's growing faith in its military position had made it bolder in recent years. Kennan replied that Soviet leaders did not indulge in pure military calculus: "They expect to win by the play of other forces, while their military strength protects the 'forces of history' from the imperialists."

Thompson said, "Khrushchev's own deepest desire is to gain time for the forthcoming triumphs of Soviet economic progress. For this he really wants a generally unexplosive period in foreign affairs. . . . While the Soviet attitude toward the world is fundamentally optimistic, Khrushchev would very much like some specific diplomatic successes in 1961." The Soviet Union's "great long-run worries" were West Germany and Red China. Khrushchev was deeply anxious that both nations would acquire the Bomb.

Meanwhile, the Chairman and his colleagues were "cheerfully taking advantage of targets of opportunity." Recent successes in Laos, the Congo, and Cuba had made them "perhaps overconfident about their prospects in such adventures."

Thompson felt that the United States was better off with Khrushchev in power than an alternative: "He is the most pragmatic of the lot of them and he is tending to make his country more normal. . . . This is evident in their quarrel with the Chinese, and I think that is our one hope of the future. This evolution inside there is going very fast. These people are becoming bourgeois very rapidly."

Thompson noted that Khrushchev had been talking about flying to the UN in March as a means of staging a get-acquainted meeting with the President. All four ambassadors endorsed such an informal meeting, but not a full-fledged summit with serious bargaining. Bohlen dreaded the thought of an encore of the fall of 1960 at the UN: Khrushchev would be "incapable of resisting a rostrum" and it would be "unlikely to add to the sum of goodwill."

Bohlen warned Kennedy to move quickly if he wished to prevent Khrushchev from flying to New York. Perhaps he should tell the Chairman that while he looked forward to seeing him "before too much time has passed," a meeting connected with the General Assembly session would be "unproductive." Harriman suggested that Kennedy tell Khrushchev it would be hard to see him before he had seen the leaders of Britain, France, and West Germany.

Kennedy closed the meeting by asking what the United States should do. Thompson shrewdly framed his reply in the language of Kennedy's own campaign speeches: "Make our own system work. . . . Maintain the unity of the West. . . . Find ways of placing ourselves in new and effective relations to the great forces of nationalism and anticolonialism. . . . Change our image before the world so it becomes plain that we and not the Soviet Union stand for the future."

Later, Bohlen told Thompson that when he was in Moscow he would have given "a good deal" to have had anything "remotely approaching" their talk with the President: "I never heard of a President who wanted to know so much." Like Rusk, he was amazed at how few fixed ideas Kennedy had about relations with Moscow: "He had a mentality extraordinarily free from preconceived prejudices, inherited or otherwise . . . almost as though he had thrown aside the normal prejudices that beset human mentality."

Bohlen was startled that the President's private talk bore so little resemblance to the fierce language of his State of the Union message. "He saw Russia as a great and powerful country and we were a great and powerful country, and it seemed to him there must be some basis upon which the two countries could live without blowing each other up." Bohlen worried that, if anything, Kennedy privately underestimated the seriousness of Khrushchev's commitment to dynamic world communism.

On a Saturday morning one week later, as rain spattered the Cabinet Room windows, Kennedy reconvened his council to consider whether he should ask for a meeting with the Chairman. Sitting on the President's right, the back of his rounded head and shoulders lit by the tall windows behind him, Dean Rusk was appalled by the notion that the President should go to the summit with Khrushchev so early in his administration.

Rusk once said, "I am more comfortable on the inside than on the outside." In this most personality-conscious of administrations, he insisted that processes were more important than people: "I don't think the United States should be represented by someone hamming it up." He wired American envoys that they should stop using the word "feel" in their cables.

Years later, after leaving office, Rusk wrote Bohlen that his old superior George Marshall ("the greatest man I've ever known") had "a very strong feeling both as a soldier and as a Secretary of State that the public business should not be influenced by personal considerations and friendships. . . . In my own case, this trait has always been part of a dour man from Cherokee County, Georgia—such people just don't talk very much about the things they feel most deeply. . . . Let me surprise you by sending my love to you and Avis!"

Using Marshall as his role model, Rusk sought to be Kennedy's chief adviser on questions men "should approach on their knees." No one must overhear or interfere with the advice the Secretary of State gave the President. In large meetings, he would deliberately "act the position of a dumb dodo" while others spoke. When they were done, he would summarize what had been said, let the meeting end, and then follow Kennedy into the Oval Office to offer his own views in private.

One of the few subjects that conspicuously aroused him was leaks. He allowed few written records to be kept of his Oval Office conversations and ended the practice of allowing someone to listen in on presidential telephone talks in order to write an action memo. Suspicious of wiretapping by the FBI or the Soviet bloc, he preferred not to speak with Kennedy over the telephone about grave subjects altogether. This handicapped him in gaining the good opinion of a President who liked to do business by telephone. In early 1961, Rusk told J. Edgar Hoover in Kennedy's presence that if he ever found a tap on his telephone or a bug in his office, he would resign immediately and go public with the evidence.

Rusk's demand for secrecy extended to history. Later, when he retired, he destroyed those records of his presidential meetings that he could find. Like Marshall, he resolved not to write memoirs; future Presidents might not be candid with their Secretaries of State if they had to worry about publication of what they said.* "There are some things that history does not deserve to know," he told this author in 1987. "Ninety-nine percent of the information historians will get. As for the other one percent, I say, 'What the historians don't know won't hurt 'em.' "

After World War II, Rusk had enjoyed the swiftest ascent of anyone in the Truman State Department, rising to the number-three post by the age of forty-two. A principal source of success had been his ability to win the admiration of patrons—generals Joseph Stilwell and George Marshall, Truman, Dean Acheson, and John Foster Dulles. But in each of these relationships, he had had time for the careful building of confidence.

Appointed Secretary of State, he had entered the most important partnership in the American government with a man he had never known before December 1960. He lacked the strength of the indepen-

---

*Late in life, Rusk reluctantly acceded to his son Richard's request to collaborate on an autobiography. In that volume, *As I Saw It* (Norton, 1990), the son lamented that his father "would say nothing at all about areas crucial to the story"—"personal disappointments; moments of failure; differences with his presidents; critical observations of the men he served with."

dent political base that Stevenson had or the personal relationship with the President that Robert Kennedy had. Rusk knew enough about his new boss to know that, unlike Truman with Acheson, Kennedy would not be reluctant to fire a Secretary of State who became heavy political baggage.

During the Truman years, Rusk had made friends in Congress and the press but not many steadfast allies. By 1960, probably no more than one in a thousand Americans had ever heard of him. As for his new department, Rusk was in the opposite position of most new Secretaries of State: those loyalists he had were more in the Foreign Service than at the top of the hierarchy.

Before agreeing to serve at Defense, McNamara had exacted the President's written promise that he could choose his own people. Rusk was unable to be so demanding. He was saddled with Kennedy political creditors like Bowles, Stevenson, Harriman, and G. Mennen Williams, Assistant Secretary for Africa, all of whom the President had appointed before he had decided on his Secretary of State.

Chester Bowles later recalled that at the start of the Kennedy administration, Rusk felt "very insecure. . . . He had no political experience, he knew no one on Capitol Hill, he was afraid of Capitol Hill, and he had no press connections at all—almost none. . . . And he worried about these things."

Dean Rusk's father was considered the most accomplished man in Cherokee County, Georgia: a violinist, the first college graduate in his family, an ordained Presbyterian minister rendered inactive by a bad throat. Robert Hugh Rusk married a schoolteacher, rented forty acres of red-clay farmland, built a three-room house, and grew cows, chickens, hogs, corn, and cotton, the only cash crop. But as one of his sons said, "The land didn't want us."

Born in 1909, David Dean Rusk was named for a great-grandfather and for the horse that had carried an aged doctor through a stormy night for his delivery. (For much of his life, Rusk was under the mistaken impression that the doctor had been a veterinarian.) When floods ravaged the Rusk acres in 1912, the desperate father moved the family to Atlanta, where he found a job as a letter carrier.

The young Dean walked to school in flour-sack drawers sewn by his mother, carrying hot bricks in a woolen sack on cold days, spelling girl "G-A-L," and admiring General Robert E. Lee for his "patient courage, patriotism, and his love for his men." In 1918, when Woodrow Wilson rode through Atlanta, Rusk turned out with a placard touting the League of Nations.

When Rusk played basketball at Davidson College in North Carolina, his manner and already-receding hairline led teammates to call him "Elijah" or "Old Folks." Captivated by politics and international relations, he shifted his ambitions from the ministry to college teaching. As a Rhodes Scholar he went to Oxford, which gave him "digs" and "a man" and changed his orthodox Southern views on race. On his return, he taught political science at Mills College in California and married a student named Virginia Foisie.

When war came, Rusk served in military intelligence, enrolled in the elite Fort Leavenworth command school for General Staff, and left for New Delhi and the China-Burma-India Theater as the legendary General Stilwell's chief of war plans. He wrote Virginia, "I feel deeply this loss of time from a life that should be concerned with other things than war."

After VE-Day, Rusk was appointed to the staff of the State-War-Navy Coordinating Committee in Washington. With his insistence on orderly procedure, he was appalled that Truman did not seek a systematic range of advice for his decisions on Hiroshima and Nagasaki or about the bomb's political impact on Stalin. He had not outgrown his Wilsonian ardor for international law and was pained by George Kennan's championship of a balance-of-power approach to the Soviet Union.

At the Truman State Department, Rusk worked on the Soviet threat to Iran, the founding of the United Nations, the first Soviet-American arms talks, the birth of Israel, the Berlin Blockade, the drafting of NSC-68, and Korea. By March 1950, when the department was buffeted by the Alger Hiss affair and "Who Lost China?" inquisitions, he manfully asked for demotion to the hot seat of Assistant Secretary of State for Far Eastern Affairs.

Dean Acheson told Rusk that he deserved "a Purple Heart and a Congressional Medal of Honor, all in one." Enemies later gibed that no one remembered what Rusk did in the job, but this was exactly the point: a more attention-grabbing official would have deepened the Truman government's misery. As fondly as Rusk looked on the Truman years, he was angry at the "meddling" of White House aides in what he saw as the department's business.

Like every President-elect, Kennedy had no shortage of eager candidates to head the State Department. The New Dealer Adolf Berle had noted after a summer cocktail party at Averell Harriman's house in New York that "half the men in the room were running for Secretary of State."

Three weeks after the election, Kennedy went to the Georgetown house of the last Democratic Secretary of State and told Dean Acheson that the person he knew best in foreign affairs was Bill Fulbright. He did not know that in 1952 and 1956 Stevenson had planned, if elected, to make Fulbright Secretary of State. Acheson complained to the President-elect that Fulbright was a dilettante: "He likes to call for brave, bold new ideas and he doesn't have many brave, bold new ideas. . . . You either think of them or you don't, and if you don't, you better shut up."

Acheson suggested the sixty-two-year-old diplomat David Bruce or John McCloy, Republican alumnus of the Roosevelt and Truman diplomacy, the epitome of the postwar bipartisan foreign policy establishment, chairman of the Chase Manhattan Bank. Kennedy replied that it would seem too bad for a Democratic President to seem unable to find a Democrat able to be Secretary of State.

Next Acheson brought up Rusk. Kennedy said he only knew the name. Acheson told of Rusk's voluntary demotion in 1950: he was "strong and loyal and good in every way. I would recommend him without reservation." He added that someone so good as a number two or three might, of course, prove not so good in full command, but that the only way to find out was to try him.

Three days later, Kennedy summoned the sixty-five-year-old Robert Lovett for lunch at his house on N Street. Son of the president of the Union Pacific Railroad, Lovett had risen like Acheson and McCloy through State and Defense under Truman and returned to private life under Eisenhower. Lovett lacked Acheson's sarcasm, Cold War adamance, and enemies as well as McCloy's conspicuous identification with Big Business and the Republican party. He must have passed the muster of the President-elect's father, who had served alongside him on Eisenhower's intelligence advisory board.

For a new President worried about his slender victory and a skeptical foreign affairs establishment, Lovett would provide reassurance. "Henry Stimson was one of those New York Republicans, and Roosevelt was glad to get him," Kennedy told aides. "I'm going to talk with Lovett and see what he can do for me." Pleading ill health, Lovett refused Kennedy's offer of State, Defense, or Treasury. He said that choosing a Secretary of State was easy: Dean Acheson. Kennedy shook his head. He said that Eisenhower had given Foster Dulles too much license. He intended to make foreign policy himself.

"Do you want a Secretary of State," asked Lovett, "or do you really want an *Under* Secretary?" Kennedy laughed. "Well, I guess I want an Under Secretary." Lovett said that Dean Rusk would be "perfect." Kennedy asked his staff to get "all the information you can" on Rusk.

* * *

The gentleman himself, from his place at the Rockefeller Foundation, was not above discreet campaigning for the job. Eliminating any doubts the President-elect might have about his stand on race, he wrote Kennedy "as a Georgia-born citizen" advising him to make no deals with Democratic members of the Electoral College who were threatening to vote against him unless he pledged to go slow on civil rights. He also arranged a breakfast between the President-elect and the UN Secretary-General, Dag Hammarskjöld, at the Carlyle.

On Wednesday, December 7, Rusk was at a Rockefeller Foundation board meeting in Williamsburg, Virginia, along with Bowles and Lovett, when he was called from the room for a message from Sargent Shriver, the President-elect's brother-in-law and talent scout. Rusk later said, "I knew so little about the Kennedys that I thought this was probably a military aide that had been assigned to Kennedy." He asked Bowles, "What in hell does he want to see me about?" Bowles said, "He wants to make you Secretary of State."

Tipped off by the President-elect, Lovett told Rusk that his breakfast with Kennedy, scheduled for the next morning, was indeed an audition: "I spoiled his sleep for that night and probably digestion as well." That night, Rusk dined at Bowles's Georgetown house, talking long into the evening about Kennedy and his views on foreign policy.

When he arrived at Kennedy's house the next morning, Kennedy asked him what kind of man would make a good Secretary of State. Rusk said that the most important quality was loyalty to the President. He found Kennedy vaguely unsure of himself. He was not charmed by the mess of papers on the floor or Kennedy's informal manner. Bowles recalled that after the meal Rusk called him to say that the breakfast had been "a complete dud. . . . I'm not going to become Secretary of State because Kennedy and I simply found it impossible to communicate. He didn't understand me and I didn't understand him."*

After Kennedy's breakfast with Rusk, he still preferred Fulbright, with whom he felt "humanly comfortable," while admitting, "He's lazy." Robert Kennedy was determined to block the Arkansas Senator, who had signed the Southern Manifesto opposing public school desegregation: every time the United States had to take a position against an African nation, the Soviets would say it was because America had a white supremacist as Secretary of State. Friends of Israel

---

*Reminded of this in 1987, Rusk could not remember saying that he and Kennedy could not communicate: "That was never a problem."

were outraged by Fulbright's frankly pro-Arab approach to the Middle East.*

The brothers argued strenuously about the matter. Kennedy changed his preference to David Bruce, although he worried that Bruce had "no fire in his belly." Marguerite Higgins of the *New York Herald Tribune* assured Robert that Bruce would be "tough with the Russians," but the President's brother concluded that Rusk would be the least of three evils.

Rusk recalled that when Kennedy called him to take the job, "it came as a complete surprise." He replied, "Now, wait a minute. There're a lot of things we ought to talk about before you come to that conclusion." Kennedy: "Come on down to Palm Beach and we can talk about it further."

Sitting behind his father's house and walking down the beach, Kennedy asked Rusk if there was anything about him he should know before making the appointment. So that Kennedy would not hear it from others, Rusk mentioned that he had wired Harriman during the Los Angeles convention, DON'T BE A DAMN FOOL. SUPPORT ADLAI STEVENSON. Kennedy laughed.

Rusk told Kennedy that serving at State would place him "on a thin financial margin." He could only serve for one term. Kennedy said he understood. At noon, the President-elect told reporters perhaps a bit too candidly that Rusk was "the best man available" for the job.

The incoming Secretary of State flew north to New York, still uncertain about his compatibility with the incoming President. After selecting Rusk, Kennedy told Galbraith, "I must make the appointments now. A year hence, I will know who I *really* want to appoint."

Part of Rusk's opposition to an early summit meeting with Khrushchev may have come from his fears about Kennedy's newness to foreign policy. Much of it was the professional diplomat's aversion to American-Soviet summitry. In a 1960 *Foreign Affairs* article he wrote that negotiation required patience and precision, qualities not usually abundant at the highest levels of government:

"Picture two men sitting down together to talk about matters affecting the very survival of the systems they represent, each in a position to unleash unbelievably destructive power. . . . Is it wise to

---

*In August 1960, an FBI wiretap on the telephone of the United Arab Republic's Ambassador to Washington revealed, for example, that after Kennedy spoke to a Zionist group in support of Israel, Fulbright called the Egyptian, "apologized for Kennedy's speech, and explained it was dictated by political expediency."

gamble so heavily? Are not these two men who should be kept apart until others have found a sure meeting ground of accommodation between them?"

When Rusk made these arguments to the President in private, Kennedy was not unmoved. During the campaign, he had criticized the kind of informal meeting Eisenhower and Khrushchev had held at Camp David as a "soft sentimentalism" and "diffuse desire to do good" that had become "a substitute for tough-minded plans and operations."

But as Rusk said years later, "Kennedy had the impression that if he could just sit down with Khrushchev, maybe something worthwhile would come out of it—at least some closer meeting of the minds on various questions. Secretaries of State are very skeptical of summits, but there's something about the chemistry of being President that causes them not to agree with Secretaries of State on that."

Thompson understood the degree to which Khrushchev was affected by personal relationships. He wanted Kennedy to understand at first hand Khrushchev's aspirations and anxieties: "The President has *got* to know this man." He had cabled from Moscow, "I believe that Soviet policy was for a time influenced by the conviction Khrushchev gained from his meeting with Eisenhower that the latter was a man of peace."

The President was burning with curiosity about the second most powerful man in the world. Bohlen observed that Kennedy "really felt he had to find out for himself. The issues and consequences of mistakes of a serious nature in dealing with the Soviet Union are so great that no man of any character or intelligence will really wholeheartedly accept the views of anybody else."

Kennedy said, "I think we'll go and see Khrushchev." Later he told his aide Kenneth O'Donnell, "I have to show him we can be just as tough as he is. I can't do that sending messages to him through other people. I'll have to sit down with him and let him see who he's dealing with."

On Tuesday afternoon, February 21, the President brought his council to the Cabinet Room for the last time to work on his first substantial letter to Khrushchev. Thompson produced a one-page draft, which Kennedy thought too brief. At the bottom of the sheet he wrote, "Am interested in harmonious relations—recognize the different systems." Sorensen finished the letter, which Bundy later thought "as gentle an opening ploy as you can find."

In the Oval Office the next morning, Kennedy asked Thompson to explore Khrushchev's attitudes on disarmament, nuclear testing, defense spending, the Congo, Laos, Berlin. He produced the final two-page letter to Khrushchev with his illegible signature at bottom:

> Dear Mr. Chairman:
>
> I have had an opportunity, due to the return of Ambassador Thompson, to have an extensive review of all aspects of our relations with the Secretary of State and with him. . . .
>
> I have not been able, in so brief a time, to reach definite conclusions as to our position on all of these matters. . . . I think we should recognize, in honesty to each other, that there are problems on which we may not be able to agree. However, I believe that while recognizing that we do not, and in all probability will not, share a common view on all of these problems, I do believe that the manner in which we approach them, and, in particular, the manner in which our disagreements are handled, can be of great importance. . . .
>
> I hope it will be possible, before too long, for us to meet personally for an informal exchange of views in regard to some of these matters. Of course, a meeting of this nature will depend upon the general international situation at this time, as well as on our mutual schedules of engagements.
>
> I have asked Ambassador Thompson to discuss the question of our meeting. Ambassador Thompson, who enjoys my full confidence, is also in a position to inform you of my thinking on a number of the international issues which we have discussed. . . . I hope such exchange might assist us in working out a responsible approach to our differences with the view to their ultimate resolution for the benefit of peace and security throughout the world. You may be sure, Mr. Chairman, that I intend to do everything I can toward developing a more harmonious relationship between our two countries.

After his post-Inaugural meeting with Thompson, Khrushchev had left Moscow for a long tour of the Soviet farming regions that were giving him such trouble. In Kiev, Rostov-on-the-Don, Tbilisi, and Voronezh, he spoke of the American-Soviet competition in the most peaceful economic terms. Ukrainian meat production could overtake the United States "in two to three years—four at the most." Soviet industry would surpass its American counterpart by 1970. "In saying this, we do not threaten anyone. . . . Our success and our growth do not harm other peoples."

During Khrushchev's cavalcade came the harsh signals of Kennedy's first seventeen days, culminating with McNamara on the missile gap. Then on Saturday, February 11, the same day Kennedy was meeting with his advisers on the Soviet Union, Khrushchev was suddenly called back to Moscow. There, in the opinion of the diplomatic historian Robert Slusser, his rivals apparently convened a surprise Presidium meeting and demanded a more tough-minded response to what they considered the new American militance.

On Friday, February 17, Khrushchev reinflamed the Berlin problem. In Bonn, his envoy gave Chancellor Konrad Adenauer a demarche charging the West German government with "extensive military preparations" and proclaiming Moscow's "unshakable determination" to achieve a German peace treaty.

A week later, at a hastily called farming conference in Moscow, Khrushchev discarded the moderate language he had used since Kennedy's inauguration and sang a hymn to Soviet nuclear weapons and ICBMs: "All the advantages the Americans won by establishing bases around our country they lost at the moment our rocket soared and, flying thousands of kilometers, landed precisely at the spot planned by our scientists and engineers."

The same day, Khrushchev's marshals implicitly acknowledged that McNamara had called their bluff about the missile gap. For years, they had boasted that Soviet missile power was "superior" to the United States. Now for the first time in public, they declared only that Soviet ICBMs were "sufficient" to defend the nation.

Khrushchev's early relations with Kennedy were further aggravated by the Congo. After being granted independence by the Belgians, the Congo's richest province, Katanga, had seceded in June 1960 with the aid of Belgian mining interests. Members of the new Congolese army, resentful of Belgian troops who remained, robbed, raped, and murdered white settlers. Paratroopers arrived from Belgium to protect them. The Congo's erratic new premier, Patrice Lumumba, complained that colonial rule was being reimposed. Twenty thousand UN troops arrived to keep the peace.

At his Kremlin reception the night before Kennedy's election, Khrushchev declared, "They say that in the Congo, the Soviet Union was beaten. We say that those who laugh last laugh best." Lumumba accepted the Chairman's offer of military help and accused the West of plotting against him. President Joseph Kasavubu fired Lumumba and expelled Soviet-bloc personnel. The Soviets demanded Lumumba's restoration. He was arrested and jailed. On February 13, the Katangans announced that Lumumba had been murdered.

When Khrushchev threatened to intervene, Kennedy told reporters, "I find it difficult to believe that any government is really planning to take so dangerous and irresponsible a step." He implied that Soviet intervention would be resisted by American force.

Khrushchev restrained himself from charging the United States in public with Lumumba's killing. But he blamed "Western colonialists" led by the UN and Hammarskjöld: "The murder of Patrice Lumumba and his comrades in the dungeons of Katanga climaxes Hammarskjöld's criminal actions." Khrushchev demanded that the UN get out of Africa and that Hammarskjöld be replaced by an East-West-neutral troika.

Before Thompson left Washington, Kennedy asked him to tell Khrushchev that he hoped their differences over the Congo would not pose a "serious obstacle" in improving relations.

By the Ambassador's return to Moscow on Monday, February 27, Khrushchev had been informed that Thompson was carrying back an important message from Kennedy. But the next morning, in a calculated insult, the Chairman boarded his plane and resumed his agricultural tour without making any effort to receive the letter from Thompson.

During his tour, maintaining the new Soviet hard line, Khrushchev worked to overcome the damage of McNamara's missile gap revelation. At his first stop, Sverdlovsk: "The Soviet Union has the most powerful rocket weapons in the world and as many atomic and hydrogen bombs as are needed to wipe aggressors from the face of the earth!"

Back in Moscow, Thompson told Gromyko that he would "go anywhere and at any time" to see Khrushchev, but the Foreign Minister made no promises. A week after the Ambassador's return, Khrushchev went to Novosibirsk for a meeting of Siberian farm workers. Two thousand miles east, the city was normally closed to Americans, but Gromyko asked Thompson to fly there.

Carrying the letter in his brown satchel, Thompson and Boris Klosson went to Vnukovo Airport outside Moscow in a driving snowstorm. With Anatoly Dobrynin of the Foreign Ministry, they boarded a silver Tupolev-104 passenger jet. Arriving in Novosibirsk after nightfall, they were driven to the city's only hotel. Dobrynin told Thompson, "It would speed things up if we could write a translation of the President's letter." He promised not to give it to Khrushchev until their morning meeting. Thompson agreed and later smoothed out the Soviet translation.

Khrushchev was staying on the edge of Academy City, the three-year-old Siberian headquarters of the Academy of Sciences. In the mid-1950s, the Chairman himself had been the one to command that a "town of science" be built in the heart of Siberia. Now members of the faculty found him in a foul mood, perhaps the result of his recent political frustrations.

Like other autocrats, when Khrushchev encountered problems that were not in his control, he turned his wrath to problems that were. When he learned that the Academy City faculty included a geneticist who did not believe in the theories of his beloved Lysenko, he held a tantrum and ordered him fired. An architectural model of a new academy building was brought for the Chairman's perusal. Unlike the usual such Soviet edifice of five stories, this one had nine. Violently Khrushchev shook his head and swung his right hand in a chopping gesture. The design was changed to five stories.

Past the sunlit steel mills and nineteenth-century log cabins of Novosibirsk, Thompson and Klosson were taken to the dacha where the Chairman was holding court. They were met by one of his bodyguards. "He was five by five," Klosson recalled, "and could break a man in half with one fist." He took the Americans upstairs, where Khrushchev sat at an oblong table in a small room with Dobrynin and other aides. The Chairman showed the strains of his past few weeks. Thompson thought he looked "extremely tired, and his appearance shocked even the Soviets who accompanied me."

Khrushchev read the Russian translation of Kennedy's fifteen-day-old letter and said, "It could serve as a good beginning." He would have to ponder Kennedy's proposal but was "inclined" to say yes: it would be "useful to become acquainted with the President." He had had the pleasure of meeting him in 1959, when he was on the Senate Foreign Relations Committee, but they had only exchanged "a few words."

Thompson mentioned that the President planned to see Harold Macmillan and Konrad Adenauer in April in Washington. After that he would fly to Paris to see de Gaulle. Perhaps he could see the Chairman on the same trip and avoid crossing the ocean twice. Khrushchev said, "I know well these transatlantic flights." Thompson proposed a meeting at the beginning of May in Vienna or Stockholm. Khrushchev said, "That might be suitable." He preferred Vienna.

Moving on, Khrushchev said that he held Dag Hammarskjöld "personally responsible" for Lumumba's murder. With Hammarskjöld's connivance, Kasavubu had sent him to Katanga, where the Katangan leader, Moise Tshombe, "the stooge of the Belgian mining monopoly," had killed him. The UN had been used by "colonialists" to retain their colonies and oppress Third World peoples.

Thompson replied that the United States was not always pleased with the UN's decisions. The Cold War must be kept out of Africa. Nothing in the Congo was basic to American or Soviet interests.

Khrushchev said, "You have your Belgian allies!" The UN's policy was "colonialist." The Soviet Union would oppose it "with all its means." The United States had once raised the "banner of democratic bourgeois freedom": "Now, unfortunately, it has shown that it does not support popular movements." He demanded Hammarskjöld's replacement by a troika of three leaders—"yours, ours, and neutral"—with a veto for each.

Thompson assured him that in late March, when American-Soviet-British test ban talks resumed in Geneva, the President would make a "vigorous effort" to achieve a fair treaty; Kennedy saw the talks as a partial bellwether of détente. Khrushchev replied, "We have had no tests for two years and are not living badly." But testing was not the main question. "Even if tests stopped, weapons production would not. The main question is disarmament." Thompson said that a test ban must be the first step.

Khrushchev: "The U.S.S.R. is willing to conclude such an agreement, but would France sign?"

Thompson: "What about China?"

Khrushchev said, "France is conducting tests. China is not. China does not produce atomic weapons today but may achieve progress in this field." A test ban accord must be signed by both France and China. "Agreement must be universal." (Thompson later reported home, "I believe the foregoing indicates that the Soviets have less interest than formerly in a test agreement and will probably use the French as the excuse for failure to conclude it.")

Downstairs, lunch was served: *zakuski,* soup, fish, beefsteak, chicken cutlets. Khrushchev took some pills, drank only a small amount of red wine, and eschewed the steak. He noted, "My father promised me a gold watch if I didn't smoke."

Raising a glass of *pertsovka,* the pepper-flavored vodka he favored, he said he would not offer the usual toast to the President's health; "Being so young, he does not need such wishes." He added that he hoped it would soon be "possible" to invite President Kennedy to the Soviet Union. The Soviet people would like to welcome him and his family and show him their country. But the time was not yet ripe.

Khrushchev told Thompson that he was leaving for Akmolinsk and Alma-Ata and would be back in Moscow by the last week in March. Perhaps he would have an answer to the President's confidential offer by then.

That evening, at the Moscow airport, reporters asked Thompson whether he was optimistic after the Khrushchev meeting. He said, "I shall always be an optimist." The next day, in his series of cables to Washington, he reported that Khrushchev was "obviously pleased" with the President's proposal of a summit: "I believe it moderated the position he took on various problems discussed."

But Thompson noted that the hopeful spirit of Menshikov's private messages and his post-Inaugural meeting with Khrushchev was almost gone. It was "noteworthy" that Khrushchev had "refrained from any mention of possible patterns of settlement" in the Congo and that his enthusiasm for a test ban seemed to be ebbing. He had not been able to speak with Khrushchev about the President's proposed military increases. "I hope there may be an occasion in the future to do so, as I gather from the Soviet press that this is causing them serious preoccupation."

On Monday, March 20, Alexander Fomin of the Soviet Embassy lunched with Robert Estabrook, editorial page editor of the *Washington Post,* who was known to be close to high officials of the Kennedy government. Fomin's actual surname was Feklisov. His official title was Counselor, but the FBI knew him as the KGB's *rezident* in Washington. In 1959, he was a member of Khrushchev's party during his tour of the United States.

Fomin was not the first Soviet diplomat to cultivate an American close to the New Frontier. During the campaign, Mikhail Smirnovsky had interrogated Charles Bartlett about his friend the Democratic nominee. As Bartlett recalled, "I had the feeling that they were hungering for a better relationship with the United States. He would always say the idea was to try not to give arguments to those in the Soviet Union who favored the Cold War."

After the Inauguration, J. Edgar Hoover told the President, "You've got to be careful of Bartlett because he has lots of Russian friends."* Kennedy asked Bartlett why he knew so many Russians. "When you're in the newspaper business, you talk to people," Bartlett replied. "I've always been interested in the Soviet Union and what you might be able to do in the way of making peace. There are some people I like very much over there."

At an early National Security Council meeting, someone noted that the President's British friend Henry Brandon of the *Sunday Times* "has

---

*At about the same time, Hoover warned the Attorney General that a prominent journalist and friend of the President's had been "compromised" by homosexuals during a visit to Moscow. Kennedy ignored the warning and continued to see the journalist socially.

had a conversation with some Russian." Someone else followed with: "Bartlett has been talking to Smirnovsky and Smirnovsky says—" Kennedy gave out an acid laugh: "Our sources are getting better all the time!"

Over luncheon, Fomin told Estabrook that the Soviets were "disappointed" that the Americans had not reciprocated for the release of the RB-47 fliers. The Soviet Union was "pleased" by suggestions that the crabmeat ban would be lifted. "Nothing very significant" would happen at the spring UN session.

Raising the subject of Laos, he said that the only way to solve the problem was an international control commission. "What is needed is a neutral government on the Austrian model." The "Austrian solution" could be a model for "settlement of many situations around the world." The Soviets were hampered by the fact that the Chinese were creating "difficulties on any solution in Laos." If the United States intervened with force, it would "fight alone."

Tomorrow the Geneva test ban talks were to reconvene for the first time since Kennedy took office. The West had been holding out for twenty annual inspections of nuclear test sites, the Soviets for three. Fomin believed that a compromise between the two figures was "possible."

Since 1956, John Kennedy had endorsed a nuclear test ban accord with the Soviet Union. His Senate colleague Clinton Anderson of New Mexico had convinced him that, if tests were stopped, America would remain comfortably ahead of the Soviets. Kennedy thought a test ban the best way to stop the Bomb from spreading to other nations.

His prewar London friend David Ormsby-Gore, chief British delegate to the Geneva talks, tutored the Senator on the subject. As he recalled, "Jack was not passionate about nuclear disarmament at first. He was logical and unemotional, just as he was about every other issue, national or international."

Like his other campaign rhetoric, Kennedy's treatment of the test ban issue in the fall of 1960 reflected the post-Paris-summit chill and his new courtship of Republicans and independents. Unlike Nixon, he wished to continue the voluntary moratorium on nuclear testing that the Americans, British, and Soviets had observed since 1958. He had raised the matter of a test ban only twice, in almost identical speeches during a swing through Wisconsin one day in late October:

"If we are to ever hope to negotiate for an effective arms control agreement, we must act immediately. For as each year passes, the control of increasingly complex, mobile, and hidden modern armaments becomes more difficult, and the chances for country after country to possess an atomic capacity. By 1964 or 1965, we may see a world in which twenty countries have a nuclear capacity. . . . No problem is more vital."

One of Kennedy's first acts as President was to ask the Soviets to postpone reopening the Geneva talks until late March to allow the United States to review its position. He asked his new Special Adviser on Disarmament, John McCloy, to see what concessions might be made. After reviewing transcripts of the more than 250 Geneva sessions since 1957 and calling on an ad hoc panel of scientists, McCloy concluded that current methods ensured detection from outside the Soviet Union of Soviet nuclear tests in the atmosphere and under water, but not in space or underground. The key sticking point was on-site inspections.

The number twenty, sacrosanct to some members of Congress, was a considerable distance from the Soviet offer of three. McCloy recommended that the President agree to an annual minimum of ten, with one additional inspection for each of five unidentified seismic events beyond fifty, up to an annual total of twenty. Despite opposition from the Joint Chiefs of Staff, Kennedy agreed to this and other serious concessions. Reading the classified record of the 1960 test ban talks, he had learned how close the Americans and Soviets had come to agreement before the Paris summit fiasco.

He told Congressmen over a White House lunch, "If we could gain agreement on a test ban, it might enable us to move on toward agreement on other East-West issues, such as Berlin and Laos." With Rusk and Bundy he mused about the path they might have to tread if there were no agreement—an endless arms race, the spread of nuclear weapons to other nations like Israel and China. They had to "make a serious effort at Geneva."

But when the talks resumed on March 21, the Soviets did not even wait to hear the new American offer before unveiling a new hard-line stand. The Soviet position had obviously toughened since December and January, when Menshikov had quietly assured Kennedy's people that the Chairman was serious about a test ban treaty.

The chief Soviet delegate, Semyon Tsarapkin, now made a new demand. The control board to police an accord should be chaired not by a neutral, as agreed, but by a troika: "It is impossible to find a completely neutral person." Told of this development, Rusk said, "Utterly unacceptable."

The new Soviet hard line may have been imposed by the Presidium against Khrushchev's preference in February. Why had Fomin flashed word to the White House the day before the Geneva talks opened that a test ban compromise was possible? If the source of the KGB man's message was Khrushchev or his close aides, it is possible that the Chairman was trying to signal Kennedy not to let the formal opening Soviet position dissuade him from genuine bargaining.

At noon on Monday, March 27, a Soviet Embassy Cadillac stopped in front of the West Wing. Andrei Gromyko and Menshikov stepped out. Kennedy's military aide General Chester Clifton escorted the two Soviets to the Oval Office, where they shook hands with the President, Rusk, Stevenson, Bohlen, and Kohler.

The main subject was Laos, which Kennedy privately called "the worst mess the Eisenhower administration left me." In December, the Soviets had begun airlifting arms to Pathet Lao rebels. Now battalion-sized units were sweeping up the northwestern part of the country and moving toward the cities against the hapless American-backed Premier, Prince Boun Oum, and his deputy, General Phoumi Nosavan.

During the Cabinet Room sessions in February, the President's Soviet experts told him that "disunity and the failure of the West to find and support an esteemed non-Communist leader have played into the hands of the Communists."

The Pentagon advised Kennedy that if American troops were committed to battle, the United States might again face the Chinese. To keep the Chinese out of Southeast Asia could require three hundred thousand troops and Western help. At some stage, it might involve nuclear weapons. The Soviets would probably reply by sending their own volunteers with nuclear support.

Thompson and Bohlen told the President that Khrushchev was probably just as eager to keep the Chinese out and did not want to flirt with American power. But the President must demonstrate his readiness to use force to protect the Phoumist government.

Kennedy had five hundred Marines flown to the Thai side of the Mekong River. The U.S.S. *Midway* moved toward the Gulf of Siam, the Seventh Fleet into the China Sea. American bases near Laos were provisioned and fortified.

Especially after Khrushchev's Wars of Liberation speech, the President was gripped by "something approaching an obsession about guerrilla war," as one journalist friend wrote. He read from Mao Tse-tung, Che Guevara, and the Irish Republican Army on guerrilla tactics. In a special defense message sent to Congress in March, he said, "We need a greater ability to deal with guerrilla forces, insurrections, and subversion."

Kennedy's public calls for a neutral Laos did not stop the Communist offensive. He asked Rusk to make one last plea to Gromyko at the UN. When that failed, Kennedy read out a sharply worded threat at a news conference: "If these attacks do not stop, those who support a truly neutral Laos will have to consider their response." The next day, Gromyko asked Stevenson for an appointment to see the President; he had just received a message from Khrushchev, who shared Kennedy's desire for a "neutral, independent Laos."

In the Oval Office, both Gromyko and the President declared themselves for peace and neutrality in Laos. Gromyko said that both their countries must work for a peaceful settlement and "take steps to prevent the conflict from spreading."

Gromyko said that he hoped someday their two countries would establish "genuine friendship." The President noted that there were differences in their systems and national interests in certain areas like Laos, Africa, and Cuba. The problem was to "create an atmosphere where these problems can be settled without bringing the military situation to the brink."

Kennedy suggested that they go outside into the Rose Garden, where they sat on a white wrought-iron bench. Caroline came running out of the White House, Jacqueline behind her. The President briefly introduced them to his Soviet visitor.

When the formal talk resumed, Kennedy raised one of his most abiding anxieties, the danger of miscalculation. At Harvard, he had studied the origins of World War I and been shocked by how easily one nation's misunderstanding of another's intentions could bring global conflict.

He repeated the necessity of "avoiding the brink." The Soviets should not try to "push" the United States where its prestige was involved. Gromyko and the Chairman should know that the United States would not idly watch the Communists move across Southeast Asia. He also mentioned Cuba and its "belligerent attitude."

Before the end of their fifty-two minutes together, Kennedy repeated that he was still willing to meet with Khrushchev. Gromyko said that the Chairman "liked" the idea but refused to offer a formal reply.

Exhausted from his provincial tour, Khrushchev returned to Moscow on Friday, March 24. He planned a vacation on the Black Sea, where he would sleep, swim, and work on the program for the autumn Twenty-second Party Congress. He had left Kennedy's letter unanswered for two weeks.

Why not accept the very summit he had once bid for so eagerly?

Now that Kennedy had already set certain of his foreign and defense policies in train, Khrushchev could not argue in the Presidium that a meeting would help him to push in directions agreeable to Soviet interests. A meeting now, after Kennedy had revealed his intentions in military spending, Laos, and other areas, might seem to reward the President for what the Soviets considered Kennedy's unwarranted hard line. Khrushchev knew that if he met with Kennedy and achieved nothing, it would help to discredit negotiation with the West and strengthen his enemies in Moscow and Peking.

But the main reason Khrushchev refused to commit himself to a summit probably lay in the Caribbean. Khrushchev had suspected that Kennedy would someday try to invade Cuba and destroy the Castro regime with American forces, but he apparently never thought this would happen soon after the Inauguration.

At least one Soviet diplomat reasoned that the new President had people around him like Rusk, Bowles, and Stevenson, all known for their reluctance to use military force. So new in office, would Kennedy overrule such advisers? Would he jeopardize his relationships with the Soviet Union and Latin America, still in their infancy?

Khrushchev thought Kennedy more deliberate than that. Through the winter, Soviet and Cuban intelligence had sent him growing evidence that the President would soon unleash Cuban exiles and other troops being organized for such an invasion. But as one later Soviet defector said, the more such information Khrushchev received, "the less he believed."

The Chairman probably suspected, not without reason, that the Cubans were inflating the danger to scare the Kremlin into sending more aid. His KGB chief, Alexander Shelepin, evidently defended the soundness of his evidence but deferred to Khrushchev's political wisdom, resorting to the classic intelligence caveat that it was possible to judge the enemy's capabilities but not its intentions.

Still Khrushchev could not be certain that Kennedy would not soon invade Cuba. He did not want to commit himself to a summit with a President whose forces might have just dislodged the first government in the world to move toward Soviet communism of its own free will.

Khrushchev's nervousness showed in his public silence about Cuba. As Soviet intelligence sent him more and more information that Kennedy might soon give the fateful order, the Chairman's public utterances notably avoided the subject of the island. He knew that if Kennedy committed American force, there was little he could do to save Castro, short of threatening to rain nuclear weapons on the United States.

*   *   *

On Wednesday, March 29, before the President flew to Palm Beach for the Easter weekend, Richard Bissell of the CIA came to the Cabinet Room and presented a progress report on Operation Zapata, the top-secret plan to invade Cuba from the Bay of Pigs. In Cuba, CIA-equipped confederates of Sam Giancana were stalking Fidel Castro with botulinum-toxin pills.

CHAPTER

5

"I'm Not Going to Risk an American Hungary"

AT THE SESSIONS WITH HIS SOVIET EXPERTS IN FEBRUARY, Kennedy had raised the idea of invading Cuba and replacing Castro with a more traditional, pro–U.S. regime. The record of the meetings shows that his advisers agreed that Khrushchev would not respond violently: "A quick fait accompli would probably lead to only verbal reactions. On the other hand, a long civil war might well generate strong pressures upon the Soviet government to prove its greatness on behalf of an embattled ally in the great contest against imperialism."

George Kennan told the President, "Whatever you feel you have to do here, be sure that it is successful, because the worst thing is to undertake something of this sort and to undertake it unsuccessfully."

Later in February, Chip Bohlen assured Kennedy that "Khrushchev would not go to war over as strategically unimportant an area as Cuba. If the invasion led to a long, protracted struggle, the Soviets would deliver arms to Cuba, but not military forces." Bohlen nonetheless opposed an early move against Castro; he could not recall a single case in history when refugees returned and successfully overthrew a revolutionary regime, "particularly before that revolution had had any chance to use up its initial capital."

Leaving the White House in a car with Allen Dulles and two other CIA men, he asked, "Wouldn't it be better to infiltrate people into the mountains of Cuba and set up a local government?" The United States could recognize the shadow regime and use it as a base for guerrilla operations. Dulles and his colleagues dismissed the notion. As Bohlen recalled, he knew he "had not thought the idea through sufficiently to put up a good argument and did not press my point."

Before 1959, the island of tobacco, sugar, melancholy legends, tarpon fishing, cockfights, and the mambo would not have seemed a likely candidate to become the first Soviet client state in the Western Hemisphere. Cuba had been an American vassal since 1898: at the end of the Spanish-American War, the United States occupied the island for four years and departed only after saddling the Cuban constitution with the notorious Platt Amendment, which authorized the U.S. to intervene at any time necessary to preserve Cuban independence.

For most of its more recent history, one Cuban leader after another had taken power pledging reform and then ruled by graft and violence. None did so more vigorously than the vainglorious and corrupt President Fulgencio Batista. As an army sergeant in 1933, he masterminded a coup that allowed him to pull the strings controlling five successive presidents of Cuba while he amassed a private fortune.

In 1940, Batista deigned to accept the presidency in name. During World War II, he enlisted Cuba behind the Allies, protecting the American naval base at Guantanamo and selling Cuba's 1941 sugar crop to the United States at bargain prices. After the war, he retired to his Florida estate but in 1952 retook power in another bloodless coup.

By the 1950s, Americans owned 40 percent of the Cuban sugar industry, 80 percent of Cuban utilities, 90 percent of Cuban mining. The island ranked near the top among Latin American nations in per capita income, education, social services. But the wealth on such garish and provocative display in Havana casinos and nightclubs was mainly denied to the nonurban and nonwhite. Cuba's main industry, "His Majesty King Sugar," was in decline, throwing vast numbers out of work and fueling opposition to Batista.

The dictator reacted with violence. Dangling from the royal palms along the island's country roads were the bloody corpses of Cubans who had made the mistake of supporting the mountain rebel Fidel Castro.

Like Lenin, Mao, and other great revolutionaries, Castro was not a son of the working class. His orphaned father, Angel Castro y Argiz, had left Spain at thirteen to live with an uncle in the Mayarí region of Cuba. The American presence was more intense in this district than almost anywhere else on the island, thanks largely to the United Fruit Company, which in 1954 helped the CIA to evict the leftist Guatemalan government of President Jacobo Arbenz Guzmán after he threatened expropriation of the firm's Guatemalan holdings.

Angel laid track for a United Fruit railway, rented some of the company's land, and peddled merchandise from *finca* to *finca.* He used the profits to become a landowner in Oriente province, but what Fidel Castro later professed to remember was the "shame" of growing up a citizen of an American-dominated "pseudo-republic."

Castro's mother, Lina, was evidently a servant in Angel's house whom Angel married in 1926 after Fidel's birth. The boy matured under the spell of José Martí, champion of Cuban independence, who had been ambushed and killed nearby in 1895. Excitable, devious, defiant, the young Castro accused his father of "abusing" his sugarcane workers with "false promises" and vainly tried to organize them against him. Later, after he began his political career, he set the family fields afire.

Castro was sent to Belén, the leading school of the Cuban establishment. At graduation, he won a long ovation for his basketball prowess, but a friend later felt that classmates from the Havana Establishment had "inflamed him" with "hatred against society people." At the University of Havana, noted for its volatile student politics, he joined a self-proclaimed anti-imperialist league and orated against the status quo. When the Cuban secret police chief warned him to lower his voice, he began carrying a gun.

In 1947, he joined twelve hundred Cubans, exiles from the Dominican Republic, and others in an effort against Rafael Trujillo, archetype of the bloody Latin American tyrant who opened his country to foreign interests which gave him the weapons to murder potential foes. The invasion was aborted by Cuban and American forces.

Castro went to Bogotá to help other students harass Latin American foreign ministers gathered to sign the charter of the Organization of American States. He married a schoolmate's sister, Mirta Díaz-Balart, and, perhaps in emulation of Martí, took her on a wedding trip to America. (He divorced her in 1954, claiming that her family was too close to Batista.) In New York, he bought some books by Marx and Engels, including *Das Kapital.* After law school in Havana, he opened a poor people's practice and planned to run for the Cuban parliament.

By March 1952, Batista had returned from Florida to his estate outside Havana. Before dawn, he strutted into Cuban army headquarters and was restored the next day to the Presidential Palace. Elections were canceled.

On July 26, 1953, Castro led a failed charge against the Moncada army barracks in Santiago. Seventy anti-Batista rebels were killed. In court, holding a volume of Martí quotations, Castro defended himself in a two-hour tour de force that later gave the Cuban revolution its credo: "Dante divided his hell into nine circles. What a hard dilemma the Devil will face when he must choose the circle adequate for the soul of Batista!"

Demanding free elections, land reform, profit-sharing, and public housing, Castro proclaimed that he was struggling for hundreds of thousands of unemployed Cubans: farmers "who work four months and go hungry the rest of the year," factory workers "whose pensions have been stolen," teachers "badly treated and poorly paid." He cited Aquinas, Luther, Calvin, Rousseau, Balzac, and the revolutions of Britain, America, and France: "Condemn me! It does not matter. History will absolve me!"

Freed from prison after nineteen months, Castro went to Mexico, where he worked with other Cubans on a plan to land on the island and vanish into the Sierra Maestra mountains as guerrillas. In November 1956, drenched by a midnight rain, he and eighty-one other armed men boarded a white yacht and set off for Cuba. Landing at Alegría de Pio, they crawled on elbows and knees through cane fields toward the mountains. Batista's forces attacked. All but sixteen surrendered, fled, or were killed. The following month, the United States sold Batista sixteen new B-26 bombers for use against the rebellion. These bombers were refueled and equipped with napalm at the Guantanamo naval base.

In the Sierra Maestra, Castro's guerrilla army grew. He may not have known it, but the CIA, which liked to hedge its bets, was said to be the source of at least fifty thousand dollars slipped to his movement.* But after one of Batista's raids using American bombers and bombs, Castro wrote his mistress, "I have sworn that the Americans

---

*In 1958, the United States also used the Agency to aid both the Sukarno regime and its rebel opposition.

will pay very dearly for what they are doing. When this war has ended, a much greater war will start for me, a war I shall launch against them. I realize that this will be my true destiny."

By 1958, the tide was moving toward Castro. Landowners and businessmen fed up with Batista were showering the 26th-of-July Movement with so much money that Castro had the luxury of ordering his men to pay a dollar for a single bullet, if necessary. The British Ambassador reported home from Havana, "He undoubtedly has a considerable number of sympathisers throughout the island and has come to be regarded as a romantic hero of the Robin Hood type." He added that Castro was "suspected of Communist sympathies."

On December 5, 1958, Arthur Gardner, a Republican financier who was Eisenhower's Ambassador to Batista from 1953 to 1957, sent a cryptic message "of the gravest importance" to Richard Nixon's Northwest Washington home: "The Miami matter . . . should be started at once. Also, outside of ordinary Embassy channels, in an extremely confidential and personal manner, a check should be made of the situation, and probably the Head Man should be seen and given a little moral support that might save the situation for the time being, offering time for our own judgment as to what is best to do."

Gardner knew that the Vice President had long had a special interest in Cuba. As a young man, Nixon had half seriously looked into prospects for a legal career in Havana. His great friend Charles "Bebe" Rebozo was a Cuban expatriate in Miami. As soon as the Vice President read the message, he scheduled an immediate appointment with Gardner to discuss how to keep the Havana government from collapsing in a way that would damage the United States.

William Pawley was a wealthy former Ambassador to Brazil and Peru who spoke fluent Spanish, had large Cuban interests, and was close to the CIA. As Eisenhower discreetly wrote a friend, he used Pawley "frequently, as a private citizen, for chores of different kinds during my two Administrations." In December 1958, Pawley went to Havana "to ask Batista to resign," as Nixon was later informed, "in order that a new and responsible president might be named to forestall an irresponsible president taking over."

It was too late. After midnight on New Year's Day 1959, Batista and his family fled to the Dominican Republic.* From the Moncada bar-

---

*According to a British diplomat's report to London, the Dominican dictator, Rafael Trujillo, "extracted about $3 million from Batista. . . . Just what . . . for I could not elucidate—perhaps Dominican expenses for military operations, present or future, against Fidel Castro. Anyway when Batista jibbed at paying up after the first couple of million, the Saviour of the Fatherland threw him into a dungeon and tipped in a

racks, where his movement began, Fidel Castro gave his first speech
as the leader of the new Cuba: "The Revolution begins now. . . . It
will not be like 1898, when the North Americans came and made
themselves masters of our country. . . . For the first time, the Republic
will really be entirely free and the people will have what they deserve. . . . This war was won by the people!"

Cubans in Chevrolets with 26th-of-July flags honked their horns
and ran stoplights. Some ransacked casinos and knocked down the
parking meters that were an infamous source of graft. As Castro rode
into Havana with his semiautomatic slung over the shoulder of his
green fatigues and his trademark cigar jammed between his teeth,
people wept, sang, embraced, and cried, *"Gracias,* Fidel!"

Issuing orders from his new Havana Hilton penthouse, El Líder
Maximo refrained from twisting Uncle Sam's tail so badly that American forces would quickly be once again be sent to stamp out independence. Still when the North Americans were outraged by his trials and
executions of Cuban "war criminals," he asked why they had been so
silent during Batista's torture and killing: "If the Americans don't like
what's happening in Cuba, they can land the Marines and then there
will be two hundred thousand gringos dead!"

In April 1959, he flew to Washington to speak to the American
Society of Newspaper Editors and promised his audience a free Cuban
press. He told the Senate Foreign Relations Committee (John
Kennedy was off campaigning) that he would not seize American
property. Eisenhower refused to receive him. As a British diplomat in
Washington recorded, "The wishes of the President's doctor that he
should take a rest coincided with the strong desire of the State Department to get the President out of Washington during the Castro visit,
and he is now in Georgia."

Instead, Castro saw Nixon and Secretary of State Christian Herter,
assuring them that he could "handle" the Communists. Later Herter
told the President that Castro was "very much like a child": "quite
immature" and "puzzled and confused by some of the practical difficulties now facing him." He had "made a plea for patience while his
government tries to deal with the situation in Cuba." In English, he
spoke "with restraint and considerable personal appeal." But in Spanish, he became "voluble, excited, and somewhat wild."

Castro addressed thirty thousand people at night in New York's

---

box of hungry rats for company, and after 24 hours, Batista's purse strings soon
loosened again."

Central Park and ten thousand more in Harvard's Dillon Field House. Nathan Pusey, Harvard's president, was unavailable (perhaps after consulting one or more Harvard Corporation members who had large Cuban holdings subject to expropriation). Thus the job of escorting Castro fell to the Dean of the Faculty, McGeorge Bundy.

Bundy recalled, "I couldn't get anywhere with him. He wouldn't talk Spanish. My Spanish is a lot better than his English, which isn't saying a whole hell of a lot. . . . He struck me as interested in public gain and not interested in private conversation." Later, as Kennedy's national security adviser, Bundy did not mention the experience to his boss: "It wasn't relevant. I didn't learn much about Castro. . . . It certainly didn't leave me with the feeling that he was the first thing to be removed in 1961."

Castro knew that nothing would galvanize Americans more quickly against him than suspicion that he would turn the island over to communism. His brother Raul and his colleague Che Guevara were known Marxist-Leninists, but Castro himself had always held back from such open commitment. Since at least 1958, he had quietly collaborated with old-line Cuban Communists, but this was hardly the same thing as aspiring to transform Cuba into a Soviet satellite.

The Soviet Union had done little to exploit the ancient resentment against the United States in Latin America. Stalin and his successors had not considered courtship of the banana republics to be worth challenging America's commitment to its Monroe Doctrine. In 1959, Moscow had diplomatic relations with only three countries in the region. That fall, as he sought better relations after Camp David, Khrushchev was loath to inflame Eisenhower by forming an open alliance with an erratic young rebel whose days in power might well be numbered.

Castro needed the Soviets more than they needed him. Cuba's bitter history taught that America would never accept a hostile regime so close by. Eisenhower's government was already trying to keep him from buying arms usable for defending himself against mountain guerrillas or for subverting other regimes in Latin America. He concluded that if he planned to defy the United States, he could not do it forever without the help of the other superpower.

The Soviets put out a secret feeler to the new Cuban leader. In October 1959, Alexander Alexeyev installed himself in Havana. He was ostensibly a correspondent for the Soviet news agency TASS but actually a Soviet intelligence agent whose surname was Shitov. As he later recalled, he was "the first Soviet citizen on the island" after Castro: "We knew next to nothing about the Cuban revolution. . . . I found that at least ninety percent of the people were for Fidel. . . . They idolized him. . . . Every Cuban house had graffiti saying, 'Fidel, this is your home!' "

Alexeyev called on Castro and told him that the Soviets had "great admiration" for his work for social progress. Castro replied that he would be happy to trade with Moscow. Perhaps Mikoyan could open the Havana trade fair planned for February 1960. Adzhubei warned Mikoyan, "Fidel is an ordinary American dictator. He already went to bow down to Washington and met with Nixon."

Still the Soviet Deputy Premier went to Havana and signed a Soviet-Cuban trade pact. According to Alexeyev, Castro "never" asked Mikoyan to sell him weapons. Then in March, the French freighter *La Coubre* was blown up in Havana Harbor. Alexeyev: "It was clear to everyone that the time bomb was planted by CIA agents. . . . Only after the *La Coubre* explosion did Fidel and his government request Soviet military aid." Esso, Texaco, and Shell refused Castro's demand to process crude Soviet petroleum. As Alexeyev said, "Castro asked us for oil and bought our oil—and paid much less." Castro seized the three companies' refineries.

As early as June 1959, Eisenhower had privately told Cabinet members that if the Soviet Union were to "take over Cuba," he "would have to go to Congress to start war against Cuba." Now he retaliated by banning Cuban sugar imports to the United States. "This meant death to the Cuban revolution," recalled Alexeyev. "So Fidel spoke to me. . . . He asked if we could buy some of his sugar—at least a symbolic quantity. He was preparing a rally and wanted to tell the Cubans that there *was* an alternative."

The response came in the form of a cable from Khrushchev to Alexeyev, who recalled, "When I handed this to Fidel, it said that we, the Soviet Union, were ready to buy *all* the sugar, those 700,000 tons rejected by the Americans. And not only *that* year's consignment but also all the *next* year's. That was really an event! I was at the rally. There were one million people there. I could see for myself the joy of the Cuban people. They were throwing their berets in the air. They were dancing."

Castro declared that Eisenhower's sugar embargo would "cost Americans in Cuba down to the nails in their shoes." Despite his earlier promises, he nationalized $850 million worth of U.S. sugar mills, ranches, refineries, and utilities. Disillusioned followers and much of the Cuban middle class departed for the United States. The President privately vowed that if American citizens were endangered, he would "blockade Cuba with the Navy and Air Force and intervene as a last resort."

By the summer of 1960, Khrushchev's rapprochement with the United States had vanished and there was little need to soft-pedal the opportunity in Cuba. The island offered a priceless strategic asset in America's backyard, a chance to demonstrate to the Chinese and other skeptical allies that he was committed to world communism and that Soviet communism was indeed the wave of the future. Llewellyn Thompson informed Washington that Khrushchev and the Soviets "see in this Cuban thing their own revolutionary movement all over again."

In exchange for Cuban sugar, Khrushchev offered credits for Cuban purchase of Soviet materials, machinery, equipment, and weapons. In July 1960, he declared the Monroe Doctrine dead: "The only thing you can do with anything dead is to bury it so that it will not poison the air." It was "obvious" that Washington was plotting "perfidious and criminal acts" against Cuba. "Should the aggressive Pentagon forces wish to attack Cuba, then Soviet artillerymen can support the Cuban people with rocket fire."

Khrushchev's aides quickly explained that this pledge to defend Cuba with missiles was merely "symbolic." But Che Guevara boasted that the Castro regime would henceforth be defended by "the greatest military power in history." Eisenhower replied by warning that the United States would not "permit the establishment of a regime dominated by international communism in the Western Hemisphere." That fall, during his turbulent trip to the UN, Khrushchev went to the Hotel Theresa in Harlem and gave Castro the famous bear hug.

John Kennedy's history with Cuba began with an unpublicized trip there in December 1957. It was evidently during an unhappy period in his marriage.* Kennedy quietly flew to Havana for a bachelors' holiday with his chum Senator George Smathers, Democrat of Florida.

Their friendship dated to Smathers's acquaintance with Joseph Kennedy as a young district attorney in southern Florida. Smathers accompanied the older man to the Hialeah racetrack, pretending to

---

*In July 1956, after Kennedy lost his bid to run for Vice President with Adlai Stevenson, he and Smathers flew off to the Riviera, where they and female guests relaxed aboard a yacht. During the cruise, Kennedy's wife lost their first child, a girl, in Newport. Hampered by bad communications, he did not fly home for several days. The columnist Drew Pearson, a Georgetown neighbor, wrote that "for a long time, she wouldn't listen to his overtures for a reconciliation. He blamed himself for the estrangement."

be the escort of a young lady who was actually there with the old Ambassador. As friends in the House and Senate, Smathers and John Kennedy reputedly acquired a hideaway used for assignations with air hostesses and secretaries. The conservative Floridian conceded that their politics differed: "Sometimes we argue and he gives me hell. But we understand each other."

Arriving in Havana in December 1957, Kennedy called on Ambassador Earl Smith, an old Palm Beach friend, and Smith's wife, Florence, with whom he had once had a great romance. He addressed the American Embassy staff and admired the Embassy's commanding view of Havana Harbor.

He looked up a wartime friend named Mal McArdle, played golf, sailed off Varadero Beach, visited the Tropicana and Casino Parisien, and, as Smathers years later said, "went our various ways." The widow of Meyer Lansky, a leader of the Miami and Havana underworld, insisted that her husband gave Kennedy advice on where to find women.

"Kennedy wasn't a great casino man," recalled Smathers, "but the Tropicana nightclub had a floor show you wouldn't believe. There was a girl named Denise Darcel, a French singer, whom we got to meet. . . . Kennedy liked Cuba. He liked the style. He liked the people. The people were warm everywhere you went, they were friendly as they could be. . . . Cuba had everything, a lot of wealthy people. Once they started looking after you, which naturally they would a senator, why it was just elegant."

Later, during the 1960 campaign, Kennedy condemned the Batista regime as "one of the most bloody and repressive dictatorships in the long history of Latin American repression" and complained that Batista had "murdered twenty thousand Cubans in seven years." These facts did not faze him during his 1957 visit. "I don't think I ever heard Kennedy express any feeling about Batista or Castro either way," Smathers recalled. "We were just going frankly for a vacation." The two Senators returned for another Cuban respite in early 1958.

Batista's security police were routinely ordered to perform surveillance on eminent American visitors to Havana. Their targets were unlikely to have excluded the Massachusetts Senator described in a December 1957 *Time* cover story as a possible future President. When Castro took power in 1959, he presumably inherited whatever information the files contained on Kennedy's two Havana visits, contents of which may have helped to inform his public verdict on Kennedy's election: "Four years of a rich illiterate."

During the winter before his inauguration, Kennedy asked his friend the *Look* writer Laura Bergquist about Castro's messianic appeal. Could it be compared to Hitler's in the thirties? Why the long harangues? Did he have any kind of personal life, a love life? "Kennedy was the complete contrast to Castro: cool, self-possessed, a disciplined rationalist," she later wrote. "The emotional appeal of a Castro seemed to elude him, and along with some people, I then wondered whether Kennedy for all his brightness had a visceral understanding of the angry revolutionists loose in the world."

In the same way that he leaned on his friend David Ormsby-Gore for advice on nuclear testing, Kennedy had sought informal counsel on Cuba during the 1960 campaign from Smathers and Earl Smith, a Republican and investment banker who lacked Kennedy's sense of detachment and humor. Kennedy's Senate aide Fred Holborn recalled how his boss lampooned Smith after the older man departed Room 362, having delivered himself of a blistering lecture against Castro.

Smith had married one of the most important women in Kennedy's life. Florence Pritchett was a model with whom Kennedy spent much time at the Stork Club in New York at the close of World War II. His friend Charles Spalding's wife, Betty, recalled that after the romance died, their bond remained Kennedy's "closest relationship with a woman I know of. She was very bright, very amusing, and by far the most intelligent, competent girl I ever saw him with. But it could never have resulted in marriage because she didn't have what he would need politically."

When visiting New York as President, Kennedy would slip over to her Fifth Avenue apartment, where she gathered glossy women and other friends for what one guest called a "nightclub-style evening" of the kind he could no longer have in public. Later, when Mrs. Smith entered Lenox Hill Hospital for the leukemia that finally killed her, Kennedy and his Secret Service agents rushed up the back stairs to her sickroom.

The President had tried to appoint Earl Smith as Ambassador to Switzerland, but the Swiss refused to accept a diplomat who had been so close to Batista out of fear that Swiss interests in Cuba might be jeopardized. Chip Bohlen had never found Kennedy so angry as the moment when he demanded American retaliation by showing "no intimacy" with the Swiss as long as he was President. When the order was violated, Kennedy told Bohlen in what the latter recalled as a "very sharp, unpleasant, and unmistakable" voice, *I want this stopped.*

As a Senator whose state included a growing number of Cuban

exiles, Smathers lobbied Kennedy hard against Castro. At the start of the 1960 campaign, Smathers thought his friend too oriented toward Europe, too diffident about the danger from Havana: "Kennedy always identified me with pushing, pushing, pushing."

In *The Strategy of Peace*, the anthology of his foreign policy statements published in early 1960, Kennedy described Castro as "part of the legacy of Bolívar" and wondered whether Castro would have behaved more rationally had the U.S. government not backed Batista "so long and so uncritically" and "had it given the fiery young rebel a warmer welcome in his hour of triumph."

The Senator privately told a friend, "I don't know why we didn't embrace Castro when he was in this country in 1959, pleading for help. . . . Instead of that, we made an enemy of him, and then we get upset because the Russians are giving them money, doing for them what *we* wouldn't do." But by the fall of 1960, as Castro's anti-Americanism was more obvious than ever, Kennedy moved sharply to the right on Cuba. "There are two people I'd like to get out," he told aides. "Jimmy Hoffa and Castro. . . . Why doesn't he take off those fatigues? Doesn't he know the war is over?"

In Cincinnati in early October, Kennedy criticized the Eisenhower government for ignoring warnings about Communists in Castro's circle: "Castro and his gang have betrayed the ideals of the Cuban revolution and the hopes of the Cuban people. . . . He has transformed the island of Cuba into a hostile and militant Communist satellite—a base from which to carry Communist infiltration and subversion throughout the Americas." Later that month came the Senator's call for American assistance to Cuban exile freedom fighters who might overturn the Castro regime.

Watching the campaign from the Rockefeller Foundation in New York, Dean Rusk thought that Kennedy "had it in for Castro." Later, when he became Secretary of State, he was startled by the "intensity" of the antagonism: "It was a natural animosity in Kennedy's mind that was not just political posturing. It was emotional."

One reason for Kennedy's campaign intensity against Castro was fear that Eisenhower would stage an October invasion of Cuba that would oust Castro and elect Nixon. It was good for his peace of mind that he did not know how relentlessly Nixon was pressing behind the scenes for action. In early October, Nixon asked the Republican chairman, Leonard Hall, to badger the President about Cuba. He asked his foreign policy aide why the CIA was taking so long to make its move:

"Are they falling dead over there? What in the world are they doing that takes months?"

Secret American efforts to depose Castro had begun as early as March 1959, when Eisenhower's National Security Council pondered how to bring "another government to power in Cuba." Castro had yet to seize American property or establish diplomatic relations with Moscow. The announced American policy was still friendliness toward the new Havana government.

In January 1960, a dozen veterans of the 1954 Guatemala coup gathered in the office of J. C. King, the CIA's Western Hemisphere chief. Why not use the Cuban underground to stage "a typical Latin political upheaval?" Thirty Cuban exiles could be trained in the Panama Canal Zone to serve as a guerrilla cadre. Allen Dulles showed Eisenhower how a Cuban sugar refinery might be sabotaged. The President replied, "If you're going to make any move against Castro, don't just fool around with sugar refineries."

Dulles returned in March with "A Program of Covert Action Against the Castro Regime," including a government-in-exile, a propaganda offensive, covert action and intelligence-gathering, and a paramilitary force. Dulles suggested that the coup might be ready to roll before the November election. When it was not, the defeated Nixon suspected that, just as he felt the CIA had "given" Kennedy the potent issue of the missile gap, Agency "liberals" had postponed action on Cuba to ensure Kennedy's victory.*

On Saturday morning, November 18, 1960, Dulles and his deputy for operations, Richard Bissell, went to Palm Beach for the President-elect's first full intelligence briefing. The CIA Director had golfed with Kennedy in the 1950s while vacationing in Palm Beach with the oilman and Kennedy neighbor Charles Wrightsman. Nevertheless, his intelligence deputy Robert Amory felt that the old man "didn't really feel comfortable" with the new President, who was "young enough to be his son."

Before the meeting, Dulles evidently studied an assessment of Kennedy's personality by CIA psychologists using files dating to the 1930s, including material from British surveillance of Joseph Kennedy's London Embassy as well as his son's wartime service in the Navy. Such assessments predicted how the subject would respond

---

*Privately Nixon included Eisenhower in his criticism. He wrote a friend in 1963 that both Eisenhower and Kennedy deserved blame for what had happened in Cuba— Eisenhower "for not acting sooner" and Kennedy "for not acting decisively."

when informed of the full range of CIA operations, showing Dulles the most effective method of appeal.

Included in the new President's FBI files, and presumably in his CIA files, was evidence of his 1942 affair with Inga Arvad Fejos, a suspected Nazi spy, while he served in Naval Intelligence. There were transcripts of telephone and hotel room conversations, on which the FBI had eavesdropped by order of J. Edgar Hoover.

Kennedy and his father knew this material had the capacity to destroy his political career. If Americans learned of the wartime romance, it would seem to demonstrate the truth of suspicions, raised especially by Jewish groups during the 1960 campaign, that Kennedy had inherited what was thought to be his father's diffidence about Nazism while Ambassador to London. Americans would have demanded to know how the young Naval Intelligence officer could have put himself literally in bed with a woman whom he knew to have been close to Hitler and Göring at a time when his country was at war with Nazi Germany.

Joseph Kennedy's anxiety about this information had more than a little to do with his efforts to cultivate J. Edgar Hoover and Allen Dulles through the 1950s. He wrote Hoover numerous flattering letters and volunteered for service as an FBI special contact. After exerting himself to win appointment to Eisenhower's intelligence oversight board, he improved his acquaintance with Dulles. His insistence that Hoover and Dulles be kept friendly was a vital factor in his son's immediate announcement after the 1960 election that both men would stay at their posts.

Fear that Hoover or Dulles would destroy him was hardly the chief influence on the new President's relations with the two men. Kennedy knew that now he was in power, the two men could be tempered by the considerable ability of a President to make life miserable for a disloyal appointee who tried to blackmail or kill the king. Nevertheless the potentially explosive material in the FBI and CIA files made Kennedy less free to overrule Hoover or Dulles on an important matter than a President who did not have embarrassing secrets to hide.

In the gloomy Moorish revival living room of Joseph Kennedy's house, musty from decades of exposure to salt air, Bissell used large maps and charts to show the President-elect what the CIA was doing about Castro. As Bissell recalled, Kennedy seemed to be surprised only by the scale of the plans.

He and Dulles reminded their new boss that Soviet military aid was now flowing into Cuba: the longer an invasion was postponed, the more difficult it would be. Kennedy said he needed to consider the matter. Dulles replied, "That's understandable, Mr. President, but there isn't much time."

By January 1961, there were even more urgent reasons to do something about the Maximum Leader. As Dulles privately told Senators, Cuba was "being rapidly absorbed into the Sino-Soviet bloc." The island could soon be "a significant military power that could pose great security problems to the United States."

Not only were the Soviets sending arms in large numbers, but Czech-trained Cuban pilots would arrive "almost any day" to fly MiG jets provided by the Soviets. Inside Cuba, the "totalitarian apparatus" used by Communist powers to control "an entire population" would soon be firmly in place. Castro was supporting revolutionaries in Panama, Nicaragua, the Dominican Republic, and Haiti. The CIA feared that one or more of these states might "go like Castro in the next few months."

Most alarming of all, "Cuba might become a Sino-Soviet bloc missile base in this hemisphere, right close to our own coastline, a threat which would be formidable not only because it would greatly threaten the United States directly if short-range and intermediate-range missiles should be established in Cuba. . . . If efforts were made politically or diplomatically to try to prevent or stop such a development or have them withdrawn, we would be involved in a difficult bargaining position . . . with . . . the Soviet Union."

The day before the Inauguration, Eisenhower told Kennedy that the CIA's Cuban project was going well; it was the new President's "responsibility" to do "whatever is necessary" to make it succeed.

On Saturday, January 28, Dulles told Kennedy and his National Security Council that "Cuba is now for practical purposes a Communist-controlled state." Castro's military power and "popular opposition to his regime" were both growing rapidly. "The United States has undertaken a number of covert measures against Castro, including propaganda, sabotage, political action, and direct assistance to anti-Castro Cubans in military training." Now they must decide whether to use "a group of such Cubans now in training in Guatemala, who cannot remain indefinitely where they are."

In its race against time, the CIA had abandoned the idea of a guerrilla-infiltration-airdrop campaign in favor of a military operation. This meant securing a beachhead while B-26s took control of the air and destroyed Cuban transport and communications. At the same time, just as with Arbenz in Guatemala in 1954, Castro would be overwhelmed with rumors of numerous landings; dissidents would be encouraged to take up arms. By February, the plan had evolved into a dawn amphibious-airborne assault at Trinidad, on the southern coast, which was reputed to be a hotbed of anti-Castro sentiment.

On Wednesday, February 8, Bundy told the President, "Defense and CIA now feel quite enthusiastic about the invasion. . . . At the worst, they think the invaders would get into the mountains, and at the best, they think they might get a full-fledged civil war in which we could then back the anti-Castro forces openly. State Department takes a much cooler view, primarily because of its belief that the political consequences would be very grave both in the United Nations and in Latin America."*

Kennedy wanted to get rid of Castro without suffering such political consequences. He believed what he had said in 1960 about aligning a new, young, freedom-loving United States with the emerging nations of the world—especially in Latin America, where he had high hopes for the "Alliance for Progress" proclaimed in his inaugural speech. To start his Presidency by openly ordering the demolition of the Cuban government could cast him and his country as the old imperialistic bogeyman with a younger face. He felt that if he committed full American military force to a Cuban invasion, the result could be another Hungary, with horrifying pictures of tanks crushing bodies in the streets of Havana.

More profound was Kennedy's worry that if he moved openly against Castro, in an area in which American conventional forces were superior, then Khrushchev would feel compelled to retaliate by moving against Berlin, where the Soviets had the conventional advantage. Unlike the Soviets with Cuba, the West had guaranteed the survival of Berlin. If Khrushchev acted, Kennedy would then have to make hard choices he preferred not to have to make, especially after only three months in office. He would be forced to renege on the Western commitment, be called an appeaser, and watch NATO collapse—or else call Khrushchev's bluff and possibly pull the two great powers into nuclear war.

As Kennedy weighed the CIA's plans for Cuba, he confided his worries about Berlin to almost no one. If someone leaked a single such offhand presidential comment to a reporter, the result could be

*That same month, Bundy unsuccessfully suggested to Kennedy that he move Bissell to State, where he could "keep a sharp eye" on covert operations: "If Dick has a fault, it is that he does not look at all sides of the question, and of course, the State Department's trouble is that it is usually doing exactly that and nothing else."

disastrous: headlines shouting that Kennedy was hesitant about ful-
filling the Western commitment to defend its position in the city with
nuclear weapons, that he was paralyzed by Khrushchev's threats.

The President therefore asked Bissell to consider a quieter landing
in Cuba, with fighting from the mountains, instead of showing the
world "an invasion force sent by the Yankees." On March 11,
Kennedy said he could not endorse a plan that would "put us in so
openly, in view of the world situation." Trinidad was "too spectacular": "This is too much like a World War Two invasion."

Dulles said, "Don't forget that we have a disposal problem." The
Cuban exiles in Guatemala might resist being disarmed. Even if they
did not, they would spread the word that the United States had turned
tail, which might inspire Communist coups all over Latin America.
Dulles did not need to add that when the noisy exiles let it be known
they had been abandoned, the President would be vilified by the
American Right.

On Wednesday, March 15, the CIA presented a new plan, code-
named Zapata, for a landing at the Bay of Pigs, west of Trinidad.
Bundy wrote Kennedy that the Agency had done "a remarkable job
of reframing the landing plan so as to make it unspectacular and quiet,
and plausibly Cuban in its essentials." The President asked Bissell to
"reduce the noise level" of the landings still further and ensure that
all ships would be unloaded at night. Somehow neither Kennedy,
Bundy, nor McNamara were made to realize that, unlike Trinidad, if
the new plan failed the exiles could not "melt into the mountains"
from Pig Bay.

The President left Washington on Thursday, March 30, to spend
the long Easter weekend at Palm Beach, using *Air Force One* for the first
time. He still had not made up his mind about Cuba. Before hitching
a ride with Kennedy to Florida, William Fulbright had asked an aide,
Pat Holt, to draft a paper showing why an invasion of Cuba would be
a terrible idea. Soon after the plane took off, he gave it to the President.

The paper said that American planning against Castro was an
"open secret": "To give this activity even covert support is of a piece
with the hypocrisy and cynicism for which the United States is constantly denouncing the Soviet Union in the United Nations and elsewhere." If the United States then had to intervene with military force,
Cuba would become another Hungary: "We would have undone the
work of thirty years in trying to live down earlier interventions."
Better to tolerate and isolate the island. Castro was a "thorn in the
flesh" but not a "dagger in the heart."

*   *   *

On Good Friday, the President and First Lady went to Earl and
Florence Smith's house for lunch. That afternoon Kennedy golfed
with his father and Bing Crosby at the Palm Beach Country Club,
predominantly Jewish, which Joseph Kennedy had joined after the war
partly for its proximity and partly to dispel his reputation for anti-
Semitism.

The President's troublesome back was bothering him, so he only
played eleven holes. During the game, Secret Service agents told him
that pro-Castro Cubans were rumored to be plotting to kidnap Caroline or otherwise harm his family. A Cuban couple and two accom-
plices were soon located near Palm Beach and interrogated. As the
First Family attended Easter services at St. Edward's Church, they
were tightly surrounded by the Secret Service and Palm Beach police.

Throughout the weekend, in the family custom, Kennedy watched
films every night at his father's house: *One-eyed Jack, Posse from Hell, All
in a Night's Work.* He swam in the ocean with Jacqueline and Caroline,
played more golf with Earl Smith, his father, and his brother-in-law,
the British actor Peter Lawford, and pondered the invasion of Cuba.

After the President's return to Washington on Tuesday, April 4,
Bundy was startled by the change in Kennedy's thinking about Cuba.
Before the Easter weekend, Arthur Schlesinger had written in his
journal that the President seemed to be "growing steadily more skeptical" and the tide was "flowing against the project." Now Bundy
discovered that Kennedy "really wanted to do this," as he recalled
years later. "Not necessarily all the way through, but when he came
to the moment of truth—the decision to go or not go—he had made
up his mind and *told* us. He didn't *ask* us."

Bundy suspected that someone had gotten to Kennedy in Palm
Beach: "There are candidates—Smathers would certainly be one, his
father would be another, Earl Smith would be a third. In any event,
he went down there and something happened that made him come
back and say, 'We're going ahead.' If I'd known him and had the kind
of relationship with him that we both developed, I would have said,
'What the hell has happened to you on the weekend?' But I didn't say
that. I said, '*Yes, sir.*' "

Bundy's speculation about who might have influenced his boss was
probably correct. The two men with whom the President had spent
the most time that weekend were Joseph Kennedy and Earl Smith.
The senior Kennedy was gung-ho for the Cuban operation; the Presi-

dent saw him almost constantly. He saw Earl Smith on five separate occasions that weekend, for a total of more than seven hours. He talked with George Smathers over lunch before his Easter Sunday golf game. All three men spoke their mind on Cuba, pushing, pushing, pushing.

The views of Smith and Smathers were unlikely to carry the same weight as Joseph Kennedy's. Schlesinger recalled that after the President's Florida weekend "some of us darkly suspected that he had been talking to his father."

Despite his efforts to conceal the patriarch's role as a sounding board, the President called him as many as a half dozen times a day. Had this been publicly known at the time, it would not have helped the administration. Joseph Kennedy's views were scarcely in the Democratic mainstream. He opposed foreign aid, considered the Western commitment to Berlin "a bloody mistake," and, after the onset of the Congo crisis, referred to American blacks as "Lumumbas." Years later, reminded of Joseph Kennedy's efforts to influence the President on foreign affairs, Bundy rolled his eyes.

At six o'clock on the evening of his return from Florida, the President went to the State Department to meet in secret with a dozen men, including his secretaries of State and Defense, Bissell, two of the Joint Chiefs of Staff, and Fulbright. The press was told that the meeting was on Laos. The actual subject was Zapata.

McNamara was enthusiastically in favor of going ahead. Not Rusk. He thought irregular warfare "self-legitimizing" if it succeeded; had the American Founders failed, "they'd have been hanged as traitors." But he was worried about the effect of an invasion on international law and world opinion. He was willing to endorse the plan so long as Kennedy foreswore U.S. military intervention.

Rusk said little at this meeting. Striving to win the confidence of a President he had known for only four months, believing always that Secretaries of State should advise Presidents in private, he was, as he later said, "very noncommittal."

Kennedy was worried that the operation might still be "too noisy" but said, "If we decided now to call the whole thing off, I don't know if we could go down there and take the guns away from them." Schlesinger, who opposed the invasion, was surprised at how much "more militant" the President had become since his weekend in Florida.

* * *

As early as October 1960, the *Hispanic American Report* had revealed that anti-Castro guerrillas were being trained in Guatemala. Through the fall and winter, the *Nation, St. Louis Post-Dispatch, Los Angeles Times, Miami Herald, Washington Post,* and *U.S. News & World Report* had all added further fragments to the puzzle.

At the start of April, Gilbert Harrison, owner and editor of the *New Republic,* showed galleys of a pseudonymous piece on anti-Castro training camps called "Our Men in Miami" to Schlesinger, who took them immediately to the President. As Harrison recalled, Schlesinger called him back with a "stutter" and "shaky voice": "I must ask you on the highest authority not to publish this piece." Harrison was willing to pull the article, but the author saved him the trouble by doing so himself.

Scheduled to run as the lead story under a four-column headline in the April 7 *New York Times* was a report by the diplomatic correspondent Tad Szulc that the CIA had trained anti-Castro insurgents for an imminent invasion. The President persuaded the *Times* publisher, Orvil Dryfoos, to considerably muffle the story.* "I can't believe what I'm reading!" he told Salinger. "Castro doesn't need agents over here. All he has to do is read our papers!"

Resting at his Black Sea estate, Khrushchev was suspicious about intelligence reports predicting an imminent American invasion. His son Sergei recalled that the Chairman was always skeptical of such information, assuming that much of it was "planted." Nonetheless Khrushchev expected the United States to reclaim the island sooner or later: "The Cuban coast is only a few miles from the American shore and it is stretched out like a sausage, a shape that makes it easy for attackers and incredibly difficult for the island's defenders."

In July and October 1960, the Chairman issued and then relaxed his threats to use Soviet missiles in retaliation against an American invasion, if it came. On January 2, 1961, he told a Kremlin audience, "Aggressive American monopolists are preparing a direct attack on Cuba. What is more, they are trying to press the case as though the rocket bases of the Soviet Union are being set up or are already established in Cuba. It is well known that this is a foul slander."

Without mentioning Kennedy by name, he added, "I hope that there are people in the United States with enough common sense not to allow the execution of such aggressive plans, but will prevent the

---

*Managing editor Clifton Daniel said later that Dryfoos "could envision failure for the invasion, and he could see the *New York Times* being blamed for a bloody fiasco."

forces of reaction from placing the world on the brink of war." Mikoyan shouted, *"Cuba da! Yankee nyet!"* and the room went wild. Careful about his relations with the incoming President, Khrushchev smiled but did not join in the shouting.

Four days later, on the same day Eisenhower broke diplomatic relations with Castro, Khrushchev declared in his Wars of Liberation speech that "solidarity with revolutionary Cuba" was the "duty" of all socialist countries but went no further. More evidence of the Chairman's unwillingness to engage his prestige came when he saw Llewellyn Thompson in January and March. During these discussions, he barely mentioned Cuba. He left the job of sounding the Americans out on the subject to much lower-ranking officials.

In early April, Georgi Kornienko, the round-faced, sharp-eyed Counselor of the Soviet Embassy, asked Arthur Schlesinger for an immediate appointment: why did the United States care so much about the rise of a regime with ties to the Communist world? Schlesinger asked him to imagine that recent events in Cuba had occurred instead in Poland: would the Soviet Union remain so composed?

The Soviet diplomat asked whether Washington had ruled out negotiation with Castro. Under Schlesinger's questioning, he conceded that Castro would probably refuse to discuss internal Cuban questions such as the Communist party's monopoly on power. As Kornienko recalled many years later, the purpose of his call was to gain insight into how quickly and forcefully Kennedy was ready to back an invasion. He did not mind trying to take some wind out of the Americans' sails by tantalizing them with the prospect of bargaining over their differences with Castro.

On Tuesday, April 11, Walter Lippmann and his wife, Helen, arrived at Khrushchev's Black Sea retreat. Before leaving Washington, the columnist was briefed by Bohlen and the CIA and had lunch with the President. Kennedy once complained, "I know Khrushchev reads him and he thinks that Walter Lippmann represents American policy. Now how do I get over that problem?"

While boarding his plane for Europe, Lippmann was handed a note from Menshikov saying that Khrushchev was on vacation and wished to postpone the meeting for a week. "Impossible," said Lippmann. Khrushchev had never underestimated Lippmann's influence. When the couple arrived in Rome, they were told that the Chairman would see them as scheduled, but on the Black Sea rather than Moscow. As their car swung through the iron portals, their host came out to greet them and took them on a tour of his estate.

On the Pitsunda peninsula, eighteen miles south of Gagra, Khrushchev's preserve was surrounded on three sides by a huge state farm, on the fourth by a broad, rocky beach with boardwalks, piers, and cabanas. Once when a chilling wind blew in from the Black Sea, Khrushchev told an American visitor, "It's coming from your ally Turkey. I presume we could expect nothing else but a cold wind from a NATO country."

The Chairman often came here when he had to ponder an important problem or write an important speech. Ordering the telephones shut off, he would stroll down the beach or through his ancient grove of silvery pines. "A chicken has to sit quietly for a certain time if she expects to lay an egg," he said. "If I have something to hatch, I have to take the time to do it right." Here at Pitsunda he had decided to deliver his immortal Secret Speech against Stalin in 1956.

Khrushchev jovially told the Lippmanns that since his doctor was in Moscow for the day, he would break his diet. Arriving from an adjoining villa for luncheon, Mikoyan complained that the Lippmanns were "ascetics" who only sipped wine: his Armenian native custom demanded glasses of vodka drunk to the bottom after every toast. Khrushchev finally provided a bowl into which the Americans discreetly poured their wine as soon as the Deputy Premier filled their glasses.

He showed off his indoor swimming pool, which had a roof made from old Soviet bomber wings and great retractable steel-and-glass doors that opened to the outdoors. Then they went to the badminton court, a parquet floor with Oriental rug and no net. Khrushchev announced, "Now we play." The Lippmanns obediently picked up their racquets. The Chairman teamed up with a portly female press aide from his Foreign Ministry and surprised the Americans by besting them easily.

During their formal interview, Khrushchev told Lippmann that in recent years the two main powers in the world had concluded it was useless to "test" each other by military means. What had compelled the West to reduce the threat of war was growing Communist strength. The Chairman said that Kennedy's policies would be determined by the forces behind him—in a word, "Rockefeller."

He flatly declared that the United States was preparing a landing in Cuba, using not American troops but Cubans armed and supported by Washington. When and if that happened, the Soviet Union would "oppose" the United States. Lippmann later wrote, "I hope I was not misled in understanding him to mean that he would oppose us by propaganda and diplomacy, and that he did not have in mind military intervention."

Lippmann's impression was that Khrushchev considered it "normal" for a great power to undermine an unfriendly government within its own sphere of interest: "He has been doing this himself in Laos and Iran, and his feeling about the American support of subversion in Cuba is altogether different in quality from his feeling about the encouragement of resistance in the satellite states of Europe. Mr. Khrushchev thinks more like Richelieu and Metternich than Woodrow Wilson."

The Chairman gave the Lippmanns no inkling that the Soviet Union was hours away from launching the first man into outer space. This was one reason he was staying in Pitsunda. If the launching failed and the world discovered the failure, he did not wish to be caught in the public eye. Only the next morning, after Major Yuri Gagarin completed his mission in triumph, did Khrushchev rush back to Moscow to bask in the cosmonaut's reflected glory.

Khrushchev masterfully used space spectaculars to conceal Soviet military inferiority and entrance the world, especially the Third World, into believing that communism was the future. He later said, "We tried to exert pressure on the American militarists and also influence the minds of more reasonable politicians so that the United States would start treating us better."

In October 1957, the launching of Sputnik panicked much of the world into accepting the false notion that the Soviets had overnight become the greatest power on earth. This was despite the fact that Moscow was not even close to perfecting a guidance system that could pinpoint military targets. In 1959, to bolster his prestige, he timed the first Soviet moon landing for three days before his arrival in Washington.

Khrushchev evidently wished to engineer another such triumph during his visit to the UN in 1960. In his luggage were miniature spaceships for unveiling at the magic moment. But two Soviet rockets said to be bound for Mars fizzled on the launching pad.

McNamara's well-publicized insistence that the United States was ahead of the Soviet Union in missiles may have moved Khrushchev to order his scientists to hasten the first Soviet manned space flight. On March 23, 1961, during top-secret final training, the chosen cosmonaut, Lieutenant Valentin Bondarenko, was locked into a pressure chamber. After medical tests he removed the sensors from his body, used alcohol-soaked cotton wool to clean himself, and then tossed the wad onto the ring of an electric hot plate. Flame raced through the oxygen-charged atmosphere, burning off Bondarenko's skin, hair, and eyes. He died within hours.

On Khrushchev's orders, his government concealed the accident from the Soviet people and the world. Before Moscow released photographs of the first group of cosmonauts, Bondarenko's image was removed by airbrush. We do not know whether the Chairman ever reflected on the fact that Bondarenko might not have died had Khrushchev not pressured his space scientists to get him into the skies so quickly. If Khrushchev had any regrets, they did not deter him from demanding that his men try again immediately.*

On Wednesday, April 12, Yuri Gagarin, who had stood over the cosmonaut's deathbed, was strapped onto a rocket and launched into a single orbit. Only after the mission was clearly successful was it revealed to the public. With Khrushchev's enthusiastic approval, the mission was called Vostok ("the East"), signifying the rising of communism. *Pravda* claimed that during his 108-minute trip, Gagarin sent greetings to the African peoples struggling below to break the chains of imperialism.

Now that he knew he had a hero, Khrushchev greeted the cosmonaut in Moscow with an enormous bear hug and repeated kisses on both cheeks. A national holiday was declared. People sang and danced in the streets. Hundreds of thousands of happy Soviets paraded in Red Square under huge Gagarin portraits. Three decades later, there were statues of Gagarin in every corner of the Soviet Union; there were none of Bondarenko.

Khrushchev boasted that Gagarin's success demonstrated Soviet military might and the sweep of advanced technology through the Soviet economy; soon per capita production would surpass the United States. Actually it represented only the inordinate resources that Khrushchev had lavished on his space program. Nevertheless, as with Sputnik, many people around the world mistook the flight to demonstrate the predominance of the Soviet military, social, and economic system.

At the White House, told that Gagarin had returned safely, Kennedy approved a prewritten statement praising the Soviet "technical accomplishment." At a news conference, he tried to minimize the event: "A dictatorship enjoys advantages in this kind of competi-

---

*Soviet secrecy about the Bondarenko accident may have cost the lives of the three Apollo One astronauts who died in an oxygen-rich fire in their cabin during training in January 1967. Knowledge of the Soviet mishap would have warned NASA about the highly flammable materials in the Apollo One cabin and the absence of a quick-release hatch and effective fire-fighting equipment.

tion over a short period by its ability to mobilize its resources for a specific purpose."

Still, Edwin Newman said on NBC that evening, "This is the end of an uncomfortable day for the great mass of American people, as well as for President Kennedy and his associates. Today belonged to the Russians." *Time* reported that Americans were feeling "frustration, shame, sometimes fury."

Privately the President said, "Russian housing is lousy, their food and agricultural system is a disaster, but those facts aren't publicized. Suddenly we're competing in a race for space we didn't even realize we were in. No matter what progress you make, the critics bomb away that we're second in space."

Kennedy himself had made no effort to publicize such facts about the Soviet system in 1960. Such private talk showed how far he had come from his campaign complaints that the United States was second in space and elsewhere falling behind. With the new pressure for a dramatic American success somewhere in the world, he continued to supervise planning for the landing at the Bay of Pigs.

Sorensen noted that by now his boss was committed enough to the Cuban project to be irritated by doubters. The President told his aides, "I know everybody is grabbing their nuts on this." On Wednesday, April 12, someone suggested that if the invasion succeeded but a new Cuban exile government needed military help to establish itself, the United States might have to send in some supporting forces.

"Under no circumstances!" Kennedy exploded. "The minute I land one Marine, we're in this thing up to our necks. I can't get the United States into a war and then lose it, no matter what it takes. I'm not going to risk an American Hungary. And that's what it could be, a fucking slaughter. *Is that understood, gentlemen?*"

That afternoon, at the same press conference at which he commented about Gagarin, someone asked how far the United States would be willing to go "in helping an anti-Castro uprising or invasion of Cuba." Kennedy declared, "There will not be, under any conditions, an intervention in Cuba by the United States armed forces."

After numerous delays, the President had to make the final "go" decision by Friday, April 14. He read a telegram from a Marine colonel who had just inspected the exile group, Brigade 2506, in Guatemala. It reported that the officers had "a fanatical urge to begin battle" and that they "do not expect help from the U.S. armed forces."

Kennedy called Bissell and approved the air strikes against the three main Cuban airfields that were scheduled for Saturday; how many B-26s would be sent? Bissell said, "Sixteen." The President said, "I don't want it on that scale. I want it minimal." Bissell reduced the number.

On Saturday morning, the world learned that six B-26s with Cuban markings had bombed Cuban air bases, destroying less than half of Castro's small air force. Following the CIA's instructions, another exile pilot landed his bomber at Miami International Airport and claimed that he and two other "defectors from Castro's air force" had done the bombing. At the UN, Castro's ambassador scoffed at the pilot's story and blamed the attack on the United States as the "prelude to a large-scale invasion attempt."

Adlai Stevenson had not been informed that the Miami "defector" and his story were counterfeit. That afternoon, as requested by Washington, he defended the story before the UN General Assembly. Then he was told that he had disseminated a lie.

Stevenson sputtered that he had been "deliberately tricked" by his own government. Back at his Waldorf Towers suite, looking ill, he told a friend, "I've got to resign. There's nothing I can do but resign. My usefulness and credibility have been totally compromised." Then: "I can't resign—*can't*—the country is in enough trouble."* He later complained about Kennedy's "boy commandos" and wrote a friend that the "Cuban absurdity" made him "sick for a week."

Stevenson feared that open U.S. action against Castro would taint the American image around the world. He cabled Rusk that "if Cuba now proves any of the planes and pilots came from outside, we will face an increasingly hostile atmosphere. No one will believe that bombing attacks on Cuba from outside could have been organized without our complicity."

Worried that Stevenson might resign and denounce Kennedy, worried that the U.S. government was about to be humiliated, as during the U-2 affair, by revelation of its public deceptions, Rusk and Bundy telephoned the President on Sunday at Glen Ora, his newly rented 600-acre estate in the Virginia hunt country.

Kennedy would have preferred a place on the Eastern Shore of Maryland, near the water, but consented to Glen Ora in deference to Jacqueline, who often spent four days a week here riding. The Presi-

---

*Breakfasting with Stevenson in New York on Monday morning, Bundy found him "very decent" about the matter: "He did *not* fuss about the box he was in. All he wanted was more information so he would not dig deeper holes."

dent found it "pretty deadly." He asked friends, "Can you imagine me ending up in a place like this?"

This Sunday afternoon, he had played nine holes of golf and was in the master bedroom with Jacqueline when the telephone rang. The Secretary of State gave his report. Kennedy said, "I'm not signed on to this." He forbade further air strikes that could have decimated the remainder of Castro's air force: the strikes were not to be flown until after the exiles had secured a Cuban beachhead. Then the new attacks could be plausibly portrayed as launched from Cuban soil.

Kennedy put down the receiver and paced the bedroom in obvious distress. Jacqueline thought he seemed less upset by what he had told Rusk than by the confusion in planning. What would go wrong next? Knowing how easily he made decisions, she had never seen him so low.

Bundy called Bissell and crisply told him that the President had ordered no further air strikes. Bissell and Dulles's number-two man, General C. Pearre Cabell, pleaded into the night with Rusk to reconsider: without another strike, Castro's planes would easily vanquish the invaders. Rusk replied that "political requirements" were now "overriding": Stevenson had "insisted" that further air strikes would make it "absolutely impossible for the U.S. position to be sustained." Rusk suggested to Cabell and Bissell that they talk to the President themselves. Perhaps worried that Kennedy might cancel the entire Cuban project, they declined.

Later, after rerunning that fateful Sunday night endlessly in his mind, the President reproached himself about barring the second air strike. He thought this decision an error, although not a decisive one. Still, he told Lem Billings that if he "hadn't stayed all weekend in Glen Ora and had gone back Sunday night," he "might have learned more about the situation" in Cuba that might have changed the course of events.

At four-thirty on Monday morning, April 17, Cabell woke up Rusk at his Sheraton Park Hotel quarters with a new proposal: Why not let the invasion ships return to international waters and then gain air cover from the nearby U.S. carrier *Essex*? The Secretary of State replied that this would violate the President's ban on U.S. military involvement. He arranged to have Cabell make his pitch directly to Kennedy at Glen Ora by telephone. Cabell awakened the President, made his appeal, and was turned down.

Through the blue darkness of Pig Bay, the lumbering old invasion ships, now protected only by machine guns, crashed into coral reefs under blinding floodlights. With infinite irony, the invasion fleet in-cluded boats from the United Fruit Company, whose domination of Oriente province had been the earliest inspiration for Castro's anti-Americanism. Soon the vessels were bombarded by Castro's planes.

This morning was Khrushchev's sixty-seventh birthday. Back at Pitsunda after celebrating the Gagarin success, the Chairman was listening to Radio Moscow, which announced, "An armed interven-tion against Cuba has begun."

Sergei Khrushchev said years later, "That was his present from the United States. He was very upset and honestly didn't think that Cuba could put up serious resistance against the landing troops."

CHAPTER

6

"A Big Kick"

ON SUNDAY, APRIL 16, AT THE GRAVE OF SEVEN AIRMEN KILLED by the American air strike, ten thousand Cubans cried *"Guerra! Guerra!"* Raising his eyes toward the heavens, swinging his cupped hands up and down, Castro told them, "The whole world knows that attack was made with Yankee planes flown by mercenaries paid by the United States Central Intelligence Agency." He quoted from wire service reports about the Miami "defector": "Even Hollywood would not try to film such a story!"*

Reading the speech in Pitsunda, Khrushchev was astonished by its peroration. Castro had said, "The United States sponsored the attack because it cannot forgive us for achieving a socialist revolution under

---

*Castro may have filched some of his lines from Khrushchev. After the U-2 crashed eleven months before, the Chairman had in almost identical fashion publicly and elaborately ridiculed the deceptions in the American cover story.

their noses." This was the first time in public that the Cuban had called his movement "socialist." The Chairman felt that tactically it "didn't make much sense" because it "narrowed the circle of those he could count on for support against the invasion."

Pravda told its readers that Allen Dulles, "the notorious American master spy," had gone to direct the invasion from a "secret command post" in Puerto Rico. (Actually Dulles had kept a weekend speaking engagement to a business group on the island in order to keep the Cubans and Soviets from knowing that something unusual was about to happen.) *Izvestia* said, "Cuba is not alone. All of progressive mankind is with her."

In London, Anthony Eden, the Prime Minister who had led Britain to disaster at Suez, wrote a friend that since the Americans had "only eighty miles of sea to cover and not a thousand, as we had at Suez from Malta, they ought not to have underestimated the job they have to do, and Kennedy ought to know that exiles are always optimistic. Maybe the Americans have calculated better than it appears on the surface. I pray so."

On Monday morning at ten, the President called the Attorney General away from a speech in Williamsburg, Virginia, and asked him to return to Washington "right away": "I don't think it's going as well as it should."

Since the Inauguration, Kennedy had rarely used his brother on foreign policy matters. Robert's first serious exposure to the invasion planning had been only the previous week, when the President asked Bissell to brief him. With the operation in trouble, the President needed someone of incontestable loyalty.

Now that the landed exile forces were under pounding attack, the President agreed to allow the U.S. Navy to move closer to the Cuban shore; he would "rather be called an aggressor than a bum." But he had few illusions that this would save the operation. Robert told his press aide Edwin Guthman, "I think we've made a hell of a mistake." Guthman asked if there was anything he could do. Kennedy said, "You can start praying for those fellows on the beach."

Despite the events in Cuba, Llewellyn Thompson left Moscow on a U.S. Air Force plane for Frankfurt and a scheduled holiday in central Europe. At noon on Tuesday, April 18, Thompson's chargé d'affaires, Edward Freers, was called to the Soviet Foreign Ministry and handed a message from Khrushchev to President Kennedy. The statement had already been broadcast by Radio Moscow forty-five minutes before. Giving the message to the world before it was given to Freers was a deliberate insult.

Khrushchev's message, polished in the tranquillity of Pitsunda, warned that the invasion was "fraught with danger to world peace." It was no secret that America had trained and armed the exiles. Only recently he and Kennedy had each spoken "about the common desire of both sides to make joint efforts to improve relations between our countries and avert the danger of war." And what about the President's pledge last week against military involvement in Cuba?

The United States must now keep the "flames of war" in Cuba from "spreading into a conflagration which will be impossible to cope with." Kennedy must halt the aggression. "Any so-called 'small war' can produce a chain reaction in all parts of the world. As for the Soviet Union, there should be no misunderstanding of our position: We shall render the Cuban people and their government all necessary assistance in beating back the armed attack on Cuba."

That afternoon in Moscow, the fun began. Hoisting Cuban flags and banners (WE ARE WITH YOU FRIENDS . . . VIVA CUBA . . . DO NOT PLAY WITH FIRE), thousands of students and workers hurled ball bearings and bottles of blue-black ink at the U.S. Embassy, shouting "Hands off Cuba!" and "Interventionists into the sea!"

A Red Army general, militiamen, and police on white horses arrived to wind things down. Some of the African students refused to stop protesting. "They didn't realize this was a pageant," recalled Boris Klosson. "The Soviet police pulled them off the fence, and if they didn't come off they'd knock the living daylights out of them. These kids were not brought up in the Russian way of protest, which was to do the ballet and then go home." Later a Soviet official told Klosson, "How terrible it is, invading a small country!" Klosson replied, "We won't trade invasion stories."

American embassies were stoned in Warsaw, Cairo, Tokyo, and New Delhi. The official Chinese news agency announced that "angry condemnation" of the United States was "sweeping through Chinese cities." Kennedy was particularly pained by the bloody Latin American demonstrations against "Yankee imperialism." In Recife, workers holding torches and Castro portraits demanded that Brazilian troops be sent to aid Cuba. In Mexico City, students shouted, *"Castro si, Kennedy no!"*

The President read Khrushchev's message before he sat down in the family dining room for his regular Tuesday breakfast with leaders of Congress. He told the congressional leaders that he doubted Khrushchev would send "volunteers" to Cuba, as he had threatened to do during the Suez War of 1956, or resupply the island with military equipment: Khrushchev knew that the United States "wouldn't stand" for a large number of Soviets in Cuba.

With the same exquisite caution he had shown throughout the weeks of secret meetings on the Bay of Pigs, Kennedy did not mention Berlin. The last thing he needed now was to have Congressmen walking out onto the White House steps and complaining before television cameras that the President was so paralyzed by fear of what Khrushchev might do in Berlin that he was about to abandon the courageous exiles on the Cuban beaches.

Nevertheless, Kennedy took the Chairman's message as a blanket threat to march against West Berlin if the United States persisted against Cuba. He later privately told Cuban exile leaders that Khrushchev's message had forced on him a choice between risking a Berlin confrontation, which could touch off a large-scale war, or maintaining world peace and suffering the loss of fourteen hundred men in Cuba. It was a difficult and painful decision, but the priority clearly had to be world peace.

Late on Tuesday morning, Kennedy read a note from Bundy: "I think you will find at noon that the situation in Cuba is not a bit good. The Cuban armed forces are stronger, the popular response is weaker, and our tactical position is feebler than we had hoped. Tanks have done in one beachhead, and the position is precarious at the others." Bundy predicted that the CIA would "press hard for further air help—this time by Navy cover to B-26s attacking the tanks."

He recommended saying yes "because it cannot be easily proven against us and because men are in need." But the real question was "whether to reopen the possibility of further intervention and support, or to accept the high probability that our people, at best, will go into the mountains in defeat." (Even at this late moment, the President's people had not discovered that from these beachheads there was no such escape.) Bundy thought "the right course now is to eliminate the Castro air force, by neutrally painted U.S. planes if necessary, and then let the battle go its way."

Over luncheon with James Reston of the *New York Times,* Kennedy said that defeat in Cuba would be an incident, not a disaster; if the Cuban people were not ready to back a revolt, the United States could not impose a new regime on them by invasion. Reston asked whether American prestige would not suffer. The President said, "What is prestige? Is it the shadow of power or the substance of power? . . . No doubt we will be kicked in the ass for the next couple of weeks, but that won't affect the main business."

Robert Kennedy, Lyndon Johnson, McNamara, Bohlen, and others generally agreed that Khrushchev would not risk war over a country like Cuba that was so far from the Soviet Union. His message had pledged "all necessary assistance" but did not mention the rockets he had in 1960 twice specifically threatened to use for Castro's defense.

At seven on Tuesday evening, Rusk called Menshikov to the State Department and gave him Kennedy's response. It said that the Chairman was "under a serious misapprehension" about Cuba: "It cannot be surprising that, as resistance within Cuba grows, refugees have been using whatever means are available to return and support their countrymen in the continuing struggle for freedom." The United States would not intervene militarily in Cuba but, if "any outside force" became involved, it would "honor our obligations to protect this hemisphere against external aggression."

The President's message noted Khrushchev's comment that the events in Cuba might affect peace elsewhere: "I trust this does not mean that the Soviet government, using the situation in Cuba as a pretext, is planning to inflame other areas of the world."

At 11:58 P.M., after the annual White House reception for members of Congress, Kennedy returned to the Cabinet Room, where the long table was littered with notes and newspapers. On a metal easel was a map of Cuba and the Caribbean adorned by tiny magnetic ships. Still in white tie and dress uniforms, the President and Vice President, Robert Kennedy, Rusk, McNamara, and General Lyman Lemnitzer and Admiral Arleigh Burke of the Joint Chiefs of Staff listened as Bissell laid out the options that now remained.

The CIA man argued that the operation could still be saved if the President allowed the use of jets from the *Essex*. Admiral Burke said, "Let me take two jets and shoot down the enemy aircraft." Kennedy said he had told the Pentagon "over and over again" that he would not commit U.S. forces. Burke suggested an American show of strength by letting unmarked jets roar over the beach—or they could bring in a destroyer. The President said, "Burke, I don't want the United States involved with this."

The Navy chief cast off his deference: "Hell, Mr. President, we *are* involved!"

Finally Kennedy approved a compromise. For one hour, six jets from the *Essex* could fly over the beachhead to protect the Brigade's ammunition supply flights and their B-26 escorts. The jets must not fire at Castro's planes or ground targets unless the Brigade's aircraft should be attacked. Rusk reminded him of his pledge not to use American forces: "The President shouldn't appear in the light of being a liar." Kennedy raised his right hand to the base of his nose: "We're already into it up to here."

Ken O'Donnell thought that his boss was as close to weeping as he had ever seen. Off to the side of the room, a miserable Robert Kennedy kept murmuring, "We've got to do something." After the meeting ended, with tears in his eyes, Robert put both hands on his brother's shoulders: "They can't *do* this to you!"

Without a jacket, the President opened one of the French doors and walked out into a gentle breeze on the South Grounds. Secret Service men kept their distance as he strolled until almost three in the morning by himself through the damp grass, his head bent, his hands thrust in his pockets.

On Wednesday, April 19, after dawn, the U.S. Navy jets approved by the President took off from the *Essex*. A timing mistake brought them too early over the beaches of the Bay of Pigs. Without proper defense, the Brigade's supply flights were driven away and two of its B-26s were downed. That afternoon, the demoralized exiles began surrendering. One hundred and fourteen were dead. The other 1,189 were captured by Castro's troops.

Told what was happening, Kennedy returned to the family quarters for a nap and lunch with Jacqueline. He was haunted by the image of the brave men on the beaches who would now be shot like dogs or taken off to Castro's jails. The only times his wife had seen him weep before were in the hospital at moments of sheer frustration over his back. He did not cry, but tears would fill his eyes and roll down his cheeks. That day in Jacqueline's bedroom, he put his head into his hands and almost sobbed. Then he took her into his arms.

Rose Kennedy, who was visiting the White House, later wrote in her diary that she had "phoned Joe, who said Jack had been on the phone with him much of the day, also Bobby. I asked him how he was feeling and he said 'dying'—result of trying to bring up Jack's morale. . . . Jackie walked upstairs with me and said he'd been so upset all day. Had practically been in tears, felt he had been misinformed by CIA and others. I felt so sorry for him."

In the Cabinet Room, Robert Kennedy barked at colleagues that they must now "act or be judged paper tigers in Moscow."* They could not just "sit and take it." With all that talent around the table, somebody ought to find something to do.

Walt Rostow later recalled that he "had what I can only describe as a tender feeling" toward the President's brother. He took him outside and said, "If you're in a fight and get knocked off your feet, the most dangerous thing is to come up swinging." That was the way to get badly hurt. Now they should "pause and think." There would be plenty of times and places to show the Russians that they were not paper tigers: "Berlin, Southeast Asia, and elsewhere."

Robert said, "That's constructive." He wrote his brother a prophetic memo: "If we don't want Russia to set up missile bases in Cuba, we had better decide now what we are willing to do to stop it." They could send American troops into Cuba, which "might have to be reconsidered," or they could blockade the island, an act of war that would bring "worldwide bitterness."

A third option was to ask the Organization of American States to ban all arms shipments to Cuba and guarantee the island's territorial integrity "so that the Cuban government could not say they would be at the mercy of the United States." The OAS might agree to such a course "if it was reported that one or two of Castro's MiGs attacked Guantanamo and the United States made noises. . . . Maybe this is not the way to carry it out, but something forceful and determined must be done. . . . The time has come for a showdown, for in a year or two the situation will be vastly worse."

The President and First Lady attended a dinner at the Greek Embassy given by visiting Prime Minister Constantine Caramanlis. Jacqueline later told Lem Billings that she and Jack had given Caramanlis "a very boring state gift," but at the last moment she had picked up one of her "favorite snuff boxes" and given it to the Prime Minister's wife.

After returning from the dinner, Kennedy returned to the Cabinet Room. As Robert recalled, "Everybody really seemed to fall apart." The Attorney General told the assembly, "We should pick ourselves up and figure out what we are going to do that would be best for the country and the President over the next six to twelve months. . . . What worries me most is now nobody in the government will be

---

*In 1957, Mao Tse-tung had gained much attention with his gibe that the West was a "paper tiger." Khrushchev not only did not share Mao's view, but it was one of the Chinese articles of faith he decried at the eighty-one-delegation Communist Party meeting in Moscow in November 1960.

willing to stick his neck out, to take a chance, to plan bold and aggressive action against the Communists."

Chester Bowles observed that by now the consensus was to "get tough with Castro." He felt that had the President now wished to send in troops or bomb Cuba, 90 percent of the room would have approved. Bohlen strongly argued for sending U.S. troops. Rusk objected. Others spoke of blockading the island. Robert Kennedy later recalled having "a slight flare-up" with Lyndon Johnson: during a discussion of who had been in favor of the Cuban project, "we had the impression he was just trying to get off it himself."

The President's immediate task was to write a speech for delivery on Thursday to the American Society of Newspaper Editors, the same group that had invited Castro to the United States in 1959. He loped down the checkered linoleum hallway lined with filing cabinets to Ted Sorensen's office.

This intense young man was perhaps the most serious liberal in Kennedy's inner circle. Sorensen had the instinctive distrust of easy charm and emotionalism that was characteristic of both New England and the American Midwest. Central to his admiration for Kennedy was his conviction that "the liberal who is rationally committed is more reliable than the liberal who is emotionally committed."

This view was tested in October 1959, when Sorensen read a draft of *John Kennedy: A Political Profile,* by James MacGregor Burns. Based on access to the Senator, his family, and his papers, Burns's admiring volume concluded with a reservation: although Kennedy would bring "bravery and wisdom" to the Presidency, "whether he would bring passion and power would depend on his making a commitment, not only of mind but of heart, that until now he has never been required to make."

Sorensen wrote Burns, "The impression should never be given that he does not believe deeply in what he says or will not fight fiercely for the causes in which he believes. . . . I really think he is a unique figure in American politics—where he combines extraordinary qualities of strong leadership and intellectual brilliance with an uncanny sense of public relations and the public mood. Not only do I think he will be President—more than any other living man he ought to be."*

*Burns's conclusion was not all that rankled Kennedy and Sorensen. After Burns's editor mailed Sorensen a sampling of praise from prominent liberals who had read the manuscript, Sorensen replied by sending Burns a list of revisions he and the

Sorensen's father was a progressive Nebraska lawyer who managed campaigns for the maverick Senator George Norris and was himself twice elected the state's attorney general. Known as a crimebuster and foe of corporate wealth, C. A. Sorensen met his Russian Jewish wife, Annis Chaikin, while defending her along with other pacifists during World War I.

Born in 1928, the son registered with draft authorities after World War II as a noncombatant and helped to form local chapters of the Congress of Racial Equality and Americans for Democratic Action. Arriving in Washington after the University of Nebraska Law School, he worked for two years as a government lawyer before presenting himself for an interview with the newly elected Senator from Massachusetts in January 1953.

He much later said, "I felt I could have had the job right then. . . . But I also felt that if I was going to throw in with him, then there were things I wanted to know. . . . We had another interview, and this time I asked the questions—about his father, Joe McCarthy, the Catholic Church. He must have thought I was an odd duck . . . but I know we satisfied each other." For the next decade, Kennedy "was the only human being who mattered to me."

A friend thought Sorensen saw Kennedy as "his work of art." From the start, he worked to help the Senator become a figure of presidential quality, steering him toward the liberalism of the national Democratic Party. Sorensen also gave the Senator his voice. The hackneyed speeches of Kennedy's congressional years gave way to the staccato phrases, contrapuntal sentences, soaring rhetoric, and quotations from the great for which Kennedy would always be remembered.* Sorensen once said, "A Kennedy speech has to have class."

His hand was not absent from *Profiles in Courage,* the book that allowed Kennedy's supporters to call him "the Pulitzer Prize-winning

---

Senator wanted. These, he said, were "the basis for our judgment that publication of this book in the form in which we read it would be a disaster—a major setback to the campaign and a real weapon in the hands of our opponents. We are not impressed by the fact that the liberal bigots feel the book is slanted the other way—we know that is inevitably their attitude and we know it is useless to pander to their prejudices."

Burns made some changes in cases where he felt Kennedy and Sorensen were "justified in your point of view" but insisted to them that "there has to be ultimately only one author of the book." This greatly irritated the candidate, and especially his brother Robert. Although Burns campaigned for Kennedy in the Wisconsin primary, their relations were never the same again. Unlike scores of academics less close to the candidate than Burns, he was never offered a place in the new administration.

*In a high school valedictory address, Sorensen said, "To prove ourselves, we must improve the world."

Senator." Sorensen told the historian Herbert Parmet in 1977, "I do not want current history books—and maybe not even future history books—to say that Sorensen . . . took credit for all things that appeared with Kennedy's name.

"That was a very sensitive subject while he was alive—*very*. . . . Nothing upset him more than the charge that he was not the author of *Profiles in Courage,* and I still feel some inhibitions in talking about this matter frankly even today. . . . I'll tell you that I did have a substantial role in all of the output, and his role was that of being the final responsible person who signed it."*

In 1957 and 1958, Sorensen traveled with Kennedy to all forty-eight states, filing the names of thirty thousand Democrats on index cards. Sorensen occasionally saved the Senator time by impersonating him on the telephone. When someone told him that he was "getting more like Jack than Jack himself," Kennedy took the man aside and said, "Don't—he gets that from all sides." Sorensen took full part in the Senator's political life and almost no part in his social life. The political scientist Richard Neustadt, who later helped Kennedy organize his White House staff, observed that "never have two people been more intimate and more separate."

When the Senator hired new people in 1959 in order to run for President, Sorensen was not immune to a natural possessiveness about his boss. That fall, when Kennedy recruited the Stevenson Democrat Hy Raskin of Chicago, Kennedy said, "Don't worry about Sorensen. Bobby's coming onto the campaign next week, and he hates him even more than you do." Still, the morning after the 1960 election, it was Sorensen who awakened Kennedy with the news that he was President-elect.

Kennedy worried that formal titles might tend to ossify his staff but relented when Sorensen insisted on being called Special Counsel to the President. Neustadt noticed that once Sorensen got his title, he "accepted intellectually the fact that the new situation was too much for him to dominate. Now he was established in control of speeches and programs."

Roaming Sorensen's large, bare office after midnight, Kennedy told his aide that he wanted his speech to the editors to forestall demands

---

*After examining the Senate papers of Kennedy and Sorensen, Parmet concluded that Kennedy "served principally as an overseer or, more charitably, as a sponsor and editor" of the book: "The burdens of time and literary craftsmanship were clearly Sorensen's, and he gave the book both the drama and flow that made for readability."

for violent retaliation against Castro, reassure the free world of America's prudence, and dissuade the Communists from presuming that restraint meant weakness. Here, in private with the trusted Sorensen, the President said what he would not say in the larger meetings: the main reason he had been so allergic to American force against Cuba was fear that Khrushchev might use it as a pretext to move against Berlin.

As Kennedy bade Sorensen good night, he snatched a magazine from the desk. At 1:30 A.M., Sorensen telephoned the family quarters to ask him a question, but the operator said the President was still presumed to be with him. Sorensen put down the telephone, walked down the corridor, and almost fell over someone slumped in a chair, reading. With a start, he realized it was Kennedy.

On Thursday, April 20, over breakfast and throughout the morning, the President worked on his ASNE address. "Never did he look back," recalled Bohlen. "He was always looking forward." But during a walk together on the South Grounds, Sorensen found his boss "depressed and lonely." Kennedy complained that he had "unnecessarily worsened" relations with the Soviet Union just as test ban talks were starting again. He had handed his critics a stick with which they would forever beat him.

At the Statler Hilton, he told the editors, "Our restraint is not inexhaustible. . . . I want it clearly understood that this government will not hesitate in meeting its primary obligations, which are to the security of our nation." The next line went to the heart of Khrushchev's Tuesday message: "Should that time ever come, we do not intend to be lectured on 'intervention' by those whose character was stamped *for all time* on the bloody streets of Budapest!" The ballroom rocked with applause.

"We face a relentless struggle in every corner of the globe that goes far beyond the clash of armies or even nuclear armaments. . . . They serve primarily as the shield behind which subversion, infiltration, and a host of other tactics steadily advance, picking off vulnerable areas—one by one—in situations that do not permit our own armed intervention. . . . We dare not fail to grasp the new concepts, the new tools, the new sense of urgency we will need to meet it, whether in Cuba or South Vietnam."

He closed: "History will record the fact that this bitter struggle reached its climax in the late 1950s and the early 1960s. Let me then make clear as the President of the United States that I am determined upon our system's survival and success, regardless of the cost and regardless of the peril!"

Cuban exile leaders in Miami who heard the speech on radio slapped one another on the back. Ambassador Menshikov had been scheduled to breakfast with Stevenson on Friday; after hearing Kennedy's address, he canceled his appointment.

Robert Kennedy thought his brother's speech "very effective." Richard Goodwin, now a White House aide, told the President that his hint about a future invasion of Cuba sounded like a vague threat, especially if the United States had no such intention. As Goodwin recalled, his boss replied in a "mild, barely distinct" voice. "I didn't want us to look like a paper tiger. We should scare people a little, and I did it to make us appear tough and powerful." Kennedy shrugged. "Anyway, it's done. You may be right, but it's done."

Scaring people a little was calculated to protect the President against the criticism that was already being unleashed upon him. Barry Goldwater declared that Kennedy's Cuban fiasco should fill every American with "apprehension and shame." General Lauris Norstad, Supreme Commander of Allied Forces in Europe, told a friend that Cuba was the worst American defeat "since the War of 1812."

The Cold War braggadocio of Kennedy's ASNE address helped to vent his frustration at his inability to make the invasion succeed. It put Khrushchev on notice to think twice before moving massive armaments and Soviet troops onto the island. But the President's pledge to fight the "new concepts" and "new tools" of Communist insurgency suggested that he was still so mesmerized by Khrushchev's Wars of Liberation speech that he missed the meaning of the Bay of Pigs.

Khrushchev had gained an ally not by subversion of Cuba but mainly by sheer luck. Castro had come to power not because the KGB or Red Army installed him, as they had the dictators of Eastern Europe, but through a genuine popular revolution. After reading the ASNE speech, Llewellyn Thompson cabled, "At the risk of being considered an apologist, I suggest we should keep in mind that in recent trouble spots—Iraq, the Congo, Cuba, and, so far as I am informed, Laos—the Soviets did not initiate the crisis but followed their usual policy of taking advantage of opportunities."

One of the debacle's chief lessons was that, until Castro's popularity crumbled, his regime would be resistant to American tactics like counterinsurgency. Nevertheless, anyone who scrutinized Kennedy's speech, including Khrushchev's analysts in Moscow, would have divined that the President would make another effort to topple Castro, either by covert action or full-scale invasion by United States armed forces.

The Soviet poet Yevgeny Yevtushenko wrote a poem about a Cuban mother camping on the beach near the grave of her son, killed at the Bay of Pigs:

> The sea . . .
> That is where the murderers came from!
> I know—
> They can come back again!

Kennedy faced the press on Friday morning, April 21. With a lordly stroke that later Presidents would envy, he foreclosed questions on Cuba by saying that no "useful national purpose" would be served by further public discussion: "I prefer to let my statement of yesterday suffice for the present." Sander Vanocur of NBC asked why they could not explore the "real facts" behind the Bay of Pigs.

Kennedy replied, "There's an old saying that victory has a hundred fathers and defeat is an orphan. . . . Further statements, detailed discussions, are not to conceal responsibility, because I'm the responsible officer of the government—and that is quite obvious—but merely because I do not believe that such a discussion would benefit us during the present difficult, uh, situation." For the remainder of the session, no one challenged Kennedy on his silence about this most important event of his administration thus far.

The President took responsibility, but there were efforts to spread the blame. A White House aide told reporters on background how the Joint Chiefs had selected the landing beaches and the CIA had promised uprisings: "Allen and Dick didn't just *brief* us on it. They *sold* us on it." Hedley Donovan complained to *Time-Life* colleagues that Kennedy was getting "preposterous praises" for stating the constitutional fact that he was responsible while "telling scores of friends, senators, journalists, only slightly privately, that his mistake was to pay any attention to the CIA and military brass."

The President told Jacqueline, "My God, the bunch of advisers we inherited. . . . Can you imagine being President and leaving behind someone like all those people there?" He told one reporter that Allen Dulles had assured him the operation's chances for success were "as great as in Guatemala." Telling the tale to someone else, he attributed the quote to the Joint Chiefs. On another occasion he carped, "I'll bet Dean Rusk wishes he had spoken up in a louder voice."

* * *

Back in his office after his Friday press conference, Kennedy was already speaking of the Bay of Pigs in the past tense. "We can't win them all," he told Johnson and Schlesinger, "and I have been close enough to disaster to realize that these things which seem world-shaking at one moment you can barely remember the next. We got a big kick in the ass—and we deserved it. But maybe we'll learn something from it."

On Saturday morning, April 22, he received Khrushchev's response to his Tuesday message and his ASNE speech: "Mr. President, you are taking a highly dangerous road. Think about it. . . . No one can have any commitment to defend rebels against the lawful government of a sovereign state like Cuba."

The Chairman noted that some Americans were suggesting that Moscow was turning Cuba into a Soviet base: "We do not have any bases in Cuba, and we do not intend to establish any." If the President felt aggrieved by Cuba, the Soviet Union had "no lesser grounds" against states along its border whose territory was being used to threaten Soviet security.

Khrushchev noted that Kennedy "did not like my words in my previous message that there can be no stable peace in the world if there are flames of war anywhere. But . . . the world is a single whole, whether one likes it or not. I will only repeat what I said: it would not do to put out the flames in one area and thereby kindle a new conflagration in another."

The President regarded this message as one last volley in the propaganda battle over the Bay of Pigs. His Soviet experts recalled Khrushchev's threats to send Soviet volunteers to the Middle East only after the Suez War had cooled: "He's got this very good habit of jumping all over things when the danger is over, and not before."

Now that the tumult over Cuba was over, Kennedy did not bother to reply to the Chairman's message. The State Department highhandedly announced that he would not be "drawn into an extended debate with the Chairman" over "this latest . . . Communist distortion of the basic concepts of the rights of man."

In retrospect, Khrushchev's message was of cardinal importance. For perhaps the first time, the Chairman made the clear public argument that he considered Soviet interests in Cuba now to be parallel with American interests in countries along the Soviet perimeter like Turkey, where the United States maintained a substantial military establishment.

What logically followed from this was that if the United States continued to commit hostile acts against Cuba, it gave the Soviet Union the right to harass American allies along its border. For the United States to place missiles in Turkey that the Soviets considered offensive, for instance, granted the Soviet Union similar license in Cuba. As with so many other subtleties in the long history of the Cold War, this signal to Washington was overlooked.

When the failure of the Bay of Pigs was certain, Kennedy had asked Sorensen, "How could I have been so stupid as to let them go ahead?" With his narrow election margin, Kennedy had not been eager to rile the national hero who preceded him. "It was Eisenhower's plan," Robert Kennedy wrote in a note to himself. "Eisenhower's people all said it would succeed." If the President had not gone forward, "everybody would have said it showed he had no courage."

By the time Dulles and Bissell briefed the President-elect, they had done much to tie his hands. As Dulles kept reminding him, they had a "disposal problem." If Kennedy shut down the project, thousands of exiles trained for the invasion would fan out through the Americas, calling him a coward and his country a helpless behemoth.

The President's anger at Castro ran deep. This was not primarily because of the Cuban's ideology or his bloody methods; Kennedy could easily think of two dozen foreign leaders who behaved more abominably. What he resented more were the costly political choices forced upon him by Castro's rise to power and his alliance with Moscow. He told friends that sooner or later, every politician acquired an albatross: "I've got Cuba."

He knew that early 1961 could be his last chance to shake off the albatross. If Khrushchev continued to strengthen Castro's armed forces, even a full-scale American invasion could only mire the island in civil war and threaten nuclear confrontation with the Soviet Union. Bundy later felt that Kennedy was looking for ways to make the CIA plan work: "He wanted it to work and allowed himself to be persuaded that the risks were acceptable."

So new in office, so unaccustomed to failure, so prone to what Schlesinger called the "autointoxication" of the early New Frontier, Kennedy was poorly equipped to make the operation work. The Bay of Pigs turned out to be a textbook case of the problems inherent in the covert method of shaping foreign affairs. Planned by a small, closed group, lacking exposure to the press, Congress, bureaucracy, and other institutions that monitor, criticize, and thus improve other government initiatives, the Cuban operation had defects that remained largely undetected.

Eager to sell the project to the President, its planners were naturally inclined to minimize its risks. Kennedy might have avoided disaster had he given a group of experienced experts the same security clearances as Dulles and Bissell in order to police the operation for flaws and false assumptions and coldly assess the degree of probability that, in the event of failure, the President and the country would be damaged.

But Kennedy had abolished much of the apparatus devised by Eisenhower to scrutinize covert projects. This forced him to accept at face value the judgments of novice secretaries of State and Defense and other officials with their own axes to grind. With his superficial experience in management and in national security matters, he was overimpressed by its mandarins: "You always assume that the military and intelligence people have some secret skill not available to ordinary mortals."

As he weighed the Cuban project, he was hamstrung by the same ambivalence that showed in his campaign statements on Cuba and the Soviet Union. He did not want to be indicted for softness on communism. Nor did he wish to inflame Latin America, the Third World, and the Stevenson liberals by approving an all-out invasion. He was anxious that American action against Cuba not trigger a Soviet action against Berlin. Wishing to intervene without paying the price of intervention, he therefore ordained an operation too small to succeed and too big to hide American involvement.

Kennedy's concern about Berlin may have been exacerbated by the fact that three days before the start of the Bay of Pigs operation, Konrad Adenauer came to the White House for his first meetings with Kennedy. This may have caused the President to focus more than he might otherwise have done on the dangers of a Soviet move against Berlin.

Through all his deliberations on the Cuban venture, he did not once gather his Soviet experts for exhaustive consideration of his highly questionable assumption that open American involvement would provoke Khrushchev to retaliate in Berlin. Bundy said, "He would have thought more about the Russian aspect of a Cuban adventure two years later."

Robert Kennedy later wrote in his notes that his brother "never would have tried this operation if he knew that Cuba forces were as good as they were and would fight." The President suffered from other large misconceptions—that the exiles' landing would be greeted by massive Cuban uprisings, that the invaders if defeated could head for the mountains and fight on as guerrillas, that the American role could be kept secret or at least plausibly deniable.

The CIA was hardly blameless. Dulles later conceded in his notes that he had not alerted Kennedy to certain issues that might "harden" him against the project, such as the falsity of the notion that the exiles could melt into the mountains. He blamed himself for failing to make the President see that "air cover for the landing was an absolute prerequisite." Bissell insisted years later that "if we had been able to drop five times the tonnage of bombs on Castro's airfields, we would have had a damned good chance."

Dulles admitted in his notes that he accepted Kennedy's constraints on the invasion plan because he presumed that, if it should falter, "we would gain what we might lose if we provoked an argument" before it was launched. During his decade in the CIA, he had seen "a good many operations which started out like the Bay of Pigs." When the Guatemalan coup of 1954 seemed near collapse, Eisenhower had saved it by openly rushing airplanes to the rebels. The CIA Director expected the same reaction from Kennedy on Cuba: "We felt that when the chips were down, when the crisis arose in reality, any action required for success would be authorized rather than permit the enterprise to fail."

Dulles bitterly concluded that Kennedy had been only "half sold on the vital necessity of what he was doing." Proceeding "uncertainly toward defeat," he was surrounded by "doubting Thomases and admirers of Castro": "I should have realized that if he had no enthusiasm about the idea in the first place, he would drop it at the first opportunity to do the things necessary to make it succeed."

Throughout the invasion planning, the CIA had been quietly working on another track to increase the chance that the operation would succeed. Track Two was the assassination of Fidel Castro.

Bissell said years later that Track Two was "intended to parallel" the invasion preparations: "Assassination was intended to reinforce the plan. There was the thought that Castro would be dead before the landing." If Castro were killed, Bissell said, it could have made Track One "either unnecessary or much easier."

One Sunday evening in March 1960, during a lull in the presidential primaries, John and Jacqueline Kennedy had held a dinner at their house on N Street in Georgetown. One of the guests brought along the British novelist Ian Fleming, then at work on *Thunderball.* Over coffee, Fleming said that the Americans were making "too much fuss" about Castro: it would be perfectly simple to take the steam out of him. Kennedy asked how.

"Ridicule, chiefly." Fleming opined that the Cubans only cared about three things: money, religion, and sex. Cuban money should be scattered over Havana, crosses painted in the skies. Pamphlets should be dropped on the island warning that atomic testing had made the Cuban atmosphere radioactive: radioactivity made men impotent and lingered longest in beards. Cubans would shave off their beards. Without bearded Cubans, revolution would cease.

Kennedy might have guessed but did not know how close Fleming's fantasy mimicked reality. Around this time, CIA experts were debating how Castro's shoes could be dusted with a depilatory that would make his beard fall out and damage his virile image.

Such shenanigans were merely a sideshow. In December 1959, J. C. King of the CIA wrote a memo suggesting that "thorough consideration" be given to the "elimination" of the Cuban dictator, which would "greatly accelerate the fall of the present government." Bissell approved, assuming that King meant "incapacitating" Castro, resorting to his murder only "if we can't do anything else." He asked Dr. Sidney Gottlieb of the Agency's Technical Services Division to investigate techniques of assassination.

In September 1960, Bissell's subordinate Sheffield Edwards met in Los Angeles with a former FBI man named Robert Maheu, who undertook free-lance assignments for the CIA and Howard Hughes. The following month, Maheu met in Miami Beach with the Chicago mobster Sam Giancana, his West Coast associate John Roselli, and Santos Trafficante, a Havana underworld chief who had been jailed by Castro in 1959.* Giancana asked for poison that could be slipped into Castro's food or drink: something "nice and clean, without getting into any kind of out-and-out ambushing."

Bissell thought that hiring gangsters to kill Castro was the "ultimate cover," because there was "very little chance that anything the Syndicate tried to do would be traced back" to the U.S. government.

During congressional hearings in the 1970s, CIA officials insisted under oath that the plotting against Castro was approved by someone at a high political level of the Eisenhower administration. No name was ever established. One key to the mystery may be that at the time of the conspiracy, Maheu was in business partnership with

---

*During his time in prison, Trafficante had American visitors, evidently including the Dallas nightclub owner Jack Ruby.

one of the closest friends of the Vice President of the United States.

Robert King was a former FBI man who had met Richard Nixon during the war when he was investigating possible Soviet spies in San Francisco and Nixon was a lieutenant in the Navy. In 1955, the Vice President hired him away from the management of the Southern Comfort distillery to serve as his chief foreign policy aide. Nixon told reporters that King was "a sort of alter ego." After two years, King left the Nixon office and later went into partnership with Maheu in Los Angeles.

On January 4, 1960, the CIA's confederate William Pawley called Nixon's secretary, Rose Mary Woods, to pursue a dinner conversation he had had with Nixon a few evenings before "about a problem we are having just south of Miami." The Vice President told Woods to "call Pawley" and say that "RN has been in the middle of some very intense discussions on the Cuban situation with people in government outside of State and with people outside of government. Within the next week to ten days, he will know more about what he thinks our position should be than he does now and he will contact you then."

On January 9, Nixon invited Pawley to his home for lunch. On January 12, he met at home with King. Afterward he cryptically wrote Pawley, "On the matter we were discussing, we had a very satisfactory conversation with the President on Monday morning. Your name was well and favorably mentioned. . . . I have not yet heard from our West Coast inquiries, but will be in touch with you just as soon as I get some news."

Did the "West Coast inquiries" refer to King and/or Maheu? King said in 1991 that if Cuba came up during his 1960 talks with Nixon, there was a "large blank in my memory." He insisted that he was not aware at the time of Maheu's collaboration with the Mafia against Castro: "Bob was interested in me because of my connection with Nixon. . . . When Nixon lost, the gleam faded very quickly." He said that he did not know whether the Vice President was in direct contact with Maheu. In July 1960, Pawley wrote Nixon, "I'm in touch with Allen Dulles's people almost daily and things are shaping up reasonably well. The matter is a very delicate problem and every care should be taken to handle it so as not to affect our Nation adversely, nor our political campaign."

As President in 1971, Nixon showed an extraordinary interest in making sure that the CIA's files on Cuba were not released. He told his aide John Ehrlichman to order the Agency to turn over "the *full* file" on the Cuban project "*or else.*" The President "must have the file," said Ehrlichman's notes. He had been "deeply involved."

We will probably never know for certain whether Vice President Nixon flashed the green light for a CIA-Mafia attempt against Castro. But it is hard to believe that as President he would have made such a heavy-handed demand of Ehrlichman merely to retrieve evidence of his support for invading Cuba in 1960. If anything, such evidence would have helped him politically by demonstrating his foresight into Castro's danger to the hemisphere. The demand makes more sense if Nixon was worried about public embarrassment by information showing his involvement in a murder plot against a foreign leader.

This concern may have led to Watergate. As many have noted, the risk of breaking into the office of Lawrence O'Brien, Democratic chairman in 1972, would not, on the face of things, have seemed worth the potential reward. But Nixon knew O'Brien had recently worked alongside Maheu as a consultant to Howard Hughes. He may have feared that Maheu had told O'Brien about the Nixon-King-Maheu-Roselli connection and that O'Brien might use this information to taint the President during his reelection campaign.

There is no evidence that Nixon sent the burglars into Democratic headquarters in the Watergate Office Building. But if it was generally known at the Nixon White House that the President wished to know what was in O'Brien's files, Nixon's anxieties might have inspired the operation.

This leads to the question of what Kennedy knew about the effort to murder Castro. It was in February 1961, the month after the inauguration, that Sheffield Edwards gave Roselli a batch of CIA-produced botulinum-toxin pills. By early March, Roselli reported that his contact in Castro's entourage had lost his access to the Cuban leader or, as Roselli thought more likely, his nerve. That same month, Trafficante arranged another effort to poison Castro.

In early April, as the Cuban exiles prepared their landing at the Bay of Pigs, the plotters were waiting to hear word of Castro's illness and death. During these weeks, Kennedy kept postponing final approval for the invasion of Cuba. Did he do so because he was waiting to hear the same news?

As with Nixon, whether Kennedy gave a clear go-ahead for the CIA's assassination plots against Castro will probably never be conclusively resolved. The Agency's accountability to White House and Congress in the early 1960s was less codified than in a later age.

Presidents did not normally sign written orders to assassinate foreign leaders.*

During the investigations of the 1970s, Rusk, McNamara, and Bundy all testified that they had never heard of a CIA plot against Castro. Sorensen insisted that assassination was "totally foreign" to Kennedy's "reverence for human life and his respect for his adversaries," his "insistence upon a moral dimension in U.S. foreign policy." In November 1961, the President told Tad Szulc of the *New York Times* that "morally" the United States must not be a party to assassinations. A day or two later, he told Dick Goodwin, "If we get into that kind of thing, we'll all be targets."

But Kennedy was in the habit of making comments intended to throw writers, aides, and friends off the scent of a potentially injurious subject. To his campaign aide John Bartlow Martin he scoffed at rumors that he was a "skirt chaser": "You've heard them; they always do that." He told Ben Bradlee, "You're all looking to tag me with some girl, and none of you can do it because it just isn't there."

The fact that no authorization appears on paper or in the memories of Kennedy's lieutenants does not prove that the President never signaled the CIA that he would not object to Castro's murder. Richard Helms told this author in 1988 that "a lot of people probably lied about what had happened in the effort to get rid of Castro." Bissell gave his "pure personal opinion" in 1975 to the Senate that during the Palm Beach meeting at which he and Dulles briefed the President-elect on Cuban invasion planning, the CIA Director told Kennedy "obliquely of this auxiliary operation, the assassination attempt."

It is only remotely possible that the President was told of the murder plot so obliquely that he did not know what he was hearing. Dulles and Bissell would have been unlikely to take the chance that an irate Kennedy would discover what he thought to be an unauthorized Castro murder plan that could upend his foreign policy and, should Castro retaliate, endanger his life. McNamara conceded years later that the CIA was "a highly disciplined organization, fully under the control of senior officials of the government."†

---

*Although when President Gerald Ford read a secret report in 1975 on the CIA's "family jewels," Ford said it would ruin the reputation of "every President since Truman."

†When the Castro plots were revealed during the Senate investigations of the mid-1970s, Helms, Bissell, and other former CIA officials "walked a fine line," as Thomas Powers, the student of the CIA, has written. "They refused to take the rap, but declined to incriminate the President. They were good soldiers—up to a point. Kennedy Administration officials wisely decided not to press them. Head-scratching

Helms said, "There are two things you have to understand. Kennedy wanted to get rid of Castro, and the Agency was not about to undertake anything like that on its own."

George Smathers recalled in a 1964 oral history that while walking on the White House grounds in March 1961, Kennedy had asked him whether "people would be gratified" if Castro were assassinated. In a 1988 interview with this author, he expanded upon his memory: the President told him that he had been "given to believe" by the CIA that when the invaders hit the beaches of the Bay of Pigs, Castro would no longer be alive. As Smathers recalled, "Someone was supposed to have knocked him off and there was supposed to be absolute pandemonium."

If Kennedy knew that the CIA's murderers were loose in Cuba and ready to strike, this would help explain his approval of an invasion plan that seems otherwise so implausible. It is not inconceivable that the President forbade vital air support for the invaders after learning that the assassination attempts against Castro had failed.

We do know that Robert Kennedy later received a memo from J. Edgar Hoover reporting that "in connection with CIA's operation against Castro," Sheffield Edwards had contacted Maheu about "using Maheu as a 'cut-out' in contacts with Sam Giancana." Since this was "dirty business," Edwards "could not afford to have knowledge of the actions of Maheu and Giancana in pursuit of any mission for CIA." Hoover referred to the fact that Bissell had already told the Attorney General that "some of the associated planning included the use of Giancana and the underworld against Castro."

Had Kennedy and the President found Hoover's information a disturbing surprise, one would have expected them to order a thorough investigation to find out what "dirty business" really meant and exactly what kind of "contacts" the CIA had with one of the most notorious criminals in the United States. There is no record of such an investigation.

After becoming Attorney General, Robert Kennedy announced that fighting organized crime would be his "number one concern": "I'd like to be remembered as the guy who broke up the Mafia." He compiled a target list of forty criminals, including Giancana, Roselli, Trafficante, and his old nemesis James Hoffa, president of the Teamsters Union. In the spring of 1961, the Justice Department deported

bafflement was the only answer these officials chose to give when asked how it could have happened."

the New Orleans mob leader Carlos Marcello to Central America. (He soon returned.)

Therefore, at the same time the CIA was collaborating with Giancana and other mobsters on the murder of Fidel Castro, the Attorney General was working to put them in jail. Roselli complained on a telephone line tapped by the FBI, "Here I am, helping the government, helping the country, and that little son of a bitch is breaking my balls."

Decades later, investigation of the Kennedy-Mafia-Castro connection has become a cottage industry. Kennedy's severest critics argue that in 1960 he made some kind of secret unholy alliance with Giancana and other organized crime leaders. The result: once Kennedy was President, he had to navigate between his brother's insistence on prosecuting the Mob and whatever pledge he or his representatives might have made to Giancana and his men. Such a pledge might have included a promise to move slowly on prosecuting the Mob and fast on removing Castro.*

For Giancana, the dictator's ouster was of no small importance. Castro's crackdown on gambling, drug, and other interests was said to have cost the Chicago boss and his allies as much as a billion dollars per year. "That syphilitic bastard," Giancana said in his daughter's hearing. "Do you have any idea what he's done to me, to our friends?"

John Kennedy's FBI files contain considerable evidence hinting at links with underworld figures during the 1960 campaign. A March 1960 document, for instance, reports an informant's claim that Joseph Fischetti, Meyer Lansky, and "other unidentified hoodlums" were "financially supporting and actively endeavoring to secure" Kennedy's election at the behest of the Senator's friend Frank Sinatra.† Another report has Giancana sending his ally Paul "Skinny"

---

*Giancana and partners may have hedged their bets by asking a similar pledge of Kennedy's opponent. Trafficante and Marcello were rumored to have given Jimmy Hoffa $500,000 in a satchel for the Nixon campaign. In December 1959, former California Congressman Oakley Hunter called on Hoffa in Miami Beach. Afterward Hunter wrote Nixon that he had told Hoffa he was interested in the Vice President's "political future and the effect the activities of the Teamsters Union might have upon it."

The columnist Drew Pearson later charged that in August 1960 a Florida grand jury was ready to indict Hoffa for misusing union funds but that the Eisenhower administration had "sat on it while Hoffa was helping the Republicans in the presidential campaign." Pearson wrote that Teamster influence had been vital in "switching Ohio, considered safe for Kennedy, into the Nixon column."

†The singer's files included so much material on alleged Mafia connections that Eisenhower spurned Sinatra's frequent requests through their mutual friend Freeman Gosden for a presidential audience. In January 1961, Eisenhower said he could not

D'Amato into West Virginia during the state's crucial primary to use his influence on Kennedy's behalf with local politicians who gambled in D'Amato's parlors.

In the summer of 1960, before the Democratic convention, Joseph Kennedy sequestered himself at the Cal-Neva Lodge in Lake Tahoe—an eccentric choice for a man straining that year not to embarrass his son. Partly owned by Sinatra and Giancana, the resort had a reputation as a favorite Mob gambling place and watering hole. D'Amato was its sometime manager. A report in John Kennedy's FBI files claims that, during his stay, Joseph Kennedy was "visited by many gangsters with gambling interests."*

In November 1960, after Giancana's West Side Chicago bailiwick helped to win Illinois for Kennedy by 8,858 votes, the gangster boasted that he had stolen the margin responsible for Kennedy's election. This assertion ignored the fact that Illinois's twenty-seven electoral votes alone were insufficient to swing the election to Kennedy; if any ballots were stolen, they were more likely stolen by Mayor Richard Daley's Democratic machine.

A more verifiable tie between Kennedy and organized crime is his relationship with the young starlet and painter Judith Campbell of Beverly Hills. The affair began in February 1960 with an introduction from Sinatra. Within a year it had enmeshed the President of the United States with a woman he knew to be the paramour of Giancana.

White House telephone logs record seventy calls in 1961 and 1962 between Campbell and the West Wing. George Smathers remembered watching Campbell being taken into the President's private quarters by William Thompson, a railroad lobbyist and roguish mutual friend who had accompanied Kennedy and Smathers on their 1958 trip to Cuba. Smathers recalled, "When Kennedy and Thompson and I were together, they would talk about her."†

---

fathom how Kennedy could let a man like Sinatra become "so prominent in his preelection activities."

Kennedy had met Sinatra through Peter Lawford. In 1959 and 1960, he stayed at the singer's Palm Springs house and accompanied him to Las Vegas nightclubs. A Justice Department report from Las Vegas said that "show girls from all over the town were running in and out of the Senator's suite."

*Rumors of association with organized crime had floated about the father since the 1920s and 1930s, when he earned a fortune in liquor and conducted a romance with the widow of a Mafia don who had been gunned down in New York. The radio commentator Walter Winchell recalled that in the mid-thirties, after he broadcast the blind item "A top New Dealer's mistress is a mobster's widow," Kennedy became "a fruitful source of news."

†The President was more discreet with others not of his innermost circle. When Thompson began talking in Hy Raskin's presence about women he and Kennedy had

Like his father's odd choice of the Cal-Neva, it is doubtful that this supremely self-protective President would have risked pursuing his relationship with Campbell except for a purpose. He certainly had access to other women who lacked underworld connections that made him vulnerable to blackmail by the Mafia. Campbell herself claimed in 1988 that, at Kennedy's request, she arranged secret meetings during the 1960 campaign during which Kennedy asked and received various forms of help from Giancana—and that during 1961 she took numerous sealed envelopes back and forth between the President and the mobster.*

Thanks to FBI eavesdropping on Giancana's telephone, we know that as 1961 wore on, the mobster was growing more and more angry at Kennedy's failure to call off the Justice Department. One such transcript shows Roselli egging on his boss: "You fuck them, you pay them, and then they're through. . . . Now let them see the other side of you." Giancana told an FBI agent who was trailing him that he knew "all about the Kennedys" and would one day "tell all."

We will never be able to finally verify Campbell's assertions about the meetings and the envelopes. Scholarship on the Mafia and on Presidents' private lives is not subject to the same precision as the study of diplomatic history, for which there are official documents drafted and preserved according to professional standards in public archives.

In 1988, Campbell said the reason she did not tell this part of the Kennedy-Giancana tale in her 1977 memoir *My Story* was fear for her life. If her claim is true, the President may have continued their relationship in order to use her as courier and intermediary in an effort to move between the shoals of Robert's insistence on pursuing the Mafia and Giancana's threats to tell all about the President's liaison with Campbell and about whatever alliance he felt he had formed with the Kennedys in 1960.

Campbell wondered in 1988 whether by delivering the envelopes

---

seen several nights earlier, the President jerked his head in Raskin's direction and cut off Thompson in mid-sentence.

*She also claimed that on April 28, 1961, Kennedy and Giancana briefly met in secret at the Ambassador East Hotel in Chicago: "Sam arrived first and then Jack, who put his arms around me. . . . Sam said hello; he called him 'Jack,' not 'Mr. President.' . . . To give them privacy, I then went into the bathroom, sat on the edge of the tub, and waited until they were finished." The President's official log (which Sorensen has described as "far from complete") asserts that on April 28 he arrived at his Conrad Hilton Hotel suite at 4:55 P.M. and remained there before departing at 7:11 P.M. for a Democratic dinner. Of course, the log mentions no meeting with Giancana, but this does not exclude the possibility that the two men did meet.

to Giancana, she may have been "helping Jack orchestrate the attempted assassination of Fidel Castro." This is doubtful. Logistics were the CIA's province. Giancana in 1961 was more concerned about staying out of jail. The Chicago boss may nonetheless have used what opportunities he had to pressure the President to fulfill the CIA's plans against Cuba and the removal of the Mob's nemesis, Fidel Castro.

The Bay of Pigs dampened the "exhilarating sense that all things were possible" that Bartlett noticed during Kennedy's first week. The President threw a copy of *Time* into the fireplace to avoid reading about his failure. Robert Kennedy recalled, "We'd been through a lot of things together, and he was more upset this time than he was any other."

In a memo on the Bay of Pigs, Robert recorded, "He felt very strongly that the Cuba operation had materially affected . . . his standing as President and the standing of the United States in public opinion throughout the world. We were going to have a much harder role in providing leadership. The United States couldn't be trusted. The United States had blundered." The President told his attorney and confidential adviser Clark Clifford that a "second Bay of Pigs" would "destroy this administration."

During the campaign, Kennedy had promised one hundred days of "exacting presidential leadership" in the style of Woodrow Wilson and Franklin Roosevelt. Columnists and reporters now noted that he was spending his own hundredth day digging out of the rubble of the Bay of Pigs.

Being President was the "most unpleasant job in the world," he told his friend LeMoyne Billings. "Lyndon can have it in 1964." Billings replied that he couldn't believe that Kennedy wanted to "turn the country over to Lyndon." The President quickly agreed; he hadn't been "too impressed with Lyndon in the different crises that have come up to date." Nevertheless Billings was astonished by Kennedy's self-deprecating gloom. When he tried to cheer him up by mentioning his post-presidential library, Kennedy retorted, "Who would want to erect a monument to a tragic administration?"

A New York advertising man, Billings had known Kennedy since they led a Choate School group of rebels that called itself "the Muckers."* He was assigned his own room on the third floor of the White

---

*In 1939, Kennedy wrote him, "I got an especially sickening letter from Choate wanting me to recommend a boy 'who will carry on the traditions of the present Sixth.'

House, where he kept a set of clothing. Years later, Billings said that Kennedy "may have been the reason I never got married. I mean, I could have had a wife and a family, but what the hell. Do you think I would have had a better life having been Jack Kennedy's best friend . . . having had the best friend anybody ever had—or having been married, and settled down, and living somewhere?"

After a late April luncheon at Glen Ora, Billings recorded in his diary that Kennedy "constantly blamed himself for the Cuban fiasco. . . . However he is still extremely upset about the advice given him by the Joint [Chiefs of] Staff. . . . Looking back he wonders how he could have made any other decision with all his top advisers recommending he go ahead with the plan."

The President complained that "things can't get better," that "the Communists will constantly be making inroads by creating crises in all parts of the world," getting "tougher and tougher." The "Cuban mistake" was "so far-reaching" that even the British and other allies were now "taking cracks" at him, which "they never would have done if it hadn't been for Cuba."

"It was the only thing on his mind, and we just had to let him talk himself out," recalled his friend Charles Spalding. "Before the Bay of Pigs, everything was a glorious adventure, onward and upward. Afterward, it was a series of ups and downs, with terrible pitfalls, suspicious everywhere, cautious of everything, questioning always."

Kennedy quickly protected his political flanks by conferring with Eisenhower, Nixon, Goldwater, Rockefeller, and other eminent Republicans. He told aides that he would maintain Dulles in office for the time being to keep the Republicans off his back. "Dulles is a man," said Robert Kennedy. "He never complained, he took all the blame on himself."

During a private meeting with Eisenhower at Camp David, the President had to bite his tongue while his predecessor dressed him down like an errant schoolboy: "Why on earth" hadn't he provided the exiles with air cover? Kennedy said he had feared the Soviets "would be very apt to cause trouble in Berlin."

The veteran of Iran, Guatemala, Berlin, and the early Cuban plan-

---

So far I have not been able to think of a big enough prick but I'm giving it a lot of thought." After a 1945 visit to Choate, he wrote Billings, "I'm enclosing a card from the head [master] which will give you the spirit of the occasion. . . . I wish you would send it back as I want to save it for my children to show them what their old man's preparatory school thought of him."

ning gave Kennedy one of the chilling stares that the public never saw: "That is exactly the *opposite* of what would really happen. The Soviets follow their own plans, and if they see us show any weakness, then is when they press us the hardest. . . . The failure of the Bay of Pigs will embolden the Soviets to do something that they would not otherwise do."

Kennedy said, "Well, my advice was that we must try to keep our hands from showing in the affair." Eisenhower was aghast: "How could you expect the world to believe we had nothing to do with it? Where did these people get the ships to go from Central America to Cuba? Where did they get the weapons? . . . I believe there is only one thing to do when you go into this kind of thing: it must be a success."

The President agreed. Eisenhower pledged to support "anything" that would prevent Communist penetration of the Western Hemisphere, but he noted that Americans would "never approve direct military intervention by their own forces, except under provocations against us so clear and so serious that everybody will understand the need for the move."

Kennedy remained polite during Eisenhower's stiff lecture but later blew off steam with Billings: he had been "exceedingly unimpressed" with the General, who was "completely misinformed" and "rather pleased that all the troubles inherited from him had come to roost with the new administration because it makes Eisenhower look better." He hoped this would be "clearly pointed out by the press."

When Goldwater came to the Oval Office, Kennedy said, "So you want this fucking job, eh?" Later the Arizonan recalled asking Kennedy why he had ruled out the follow-up air strikes. By Goldwater's account, the President replied that if he had not, Stevenson would have told the UN that the United States was behind the Bay of Pigs invasion. Goldwater said he told the President that he should have "let that two-time loser tell them. Then I'd fire him so fast he'd barely have time to get his coat and leave the UN."

Kennedy asked Nixon what he would do now in Cuba. The old rival said, "I would find a proper legal cover and I would go in." Nixon felt that the President could justify a full-fledged invasion by protecting American citizens in Cuba or the Guantanamo naval base.*

The President shook his head: "Both Walter Lippmann and Chip Bohlen have reported that Khrushchev is in a very cocky mood. . . . This means that there is a good chance that if we move on Cuba, Khrushchev will move on Berlin." Nixon's reply was almost identical

---

*Later American Presidents, of course, used similar justifications to invade Grenada and Panama in 1983 and 1989.

to Eisenhower's: "Khrushchev will prod and probe in several places at once. When we show weakness, he'll create crisis to take advantage of us. We should act in Cuba and Laos, including, if necessary, a commitment of U.S. air power."

While working to disarm Republican leaders, Kennedy also considered trying to insulate himself from their criticism on Cuba by instigating a congressional study of how the problem had been handled before 1961. Bundy dissuaded him: "There would be the heaviest Republican pressure to extend the time frame up through our own period."

Kennedy's feeling of betrayal by the CIA, the Joint Chiefs, and to a lesser extent the State Department moved him to increase his grip on his foreign policy government. Although Sorensen had never traveled outside the United States, the President asked him to plunge into foreign affairs: "That's what's really important these days." He made the same request of Robert and considered appointing him CIA Director. But the Attorney General felt the job should not go to a Democrat or a presidential brother.

Shortly after the Cuban operation had begun to collapse, Henry Brandon had encountered Bundy, who looked "absolutely white in his face" and told him, "I'm guilty." With his lofty sense of public service, Bundy scrawled out his resignation.* Kennedy refused the letter and moved him from the Executive Office Building across the street to the West Wing basement, where Bundy would be more accessible to him and more able to dominate the flow of foreign policy information in and out of the White House.

The President established a board of inquiry on the Cuban project, chaired by the D-Day hero General Maxwell Taylor, with Robert Kennedy, Dulles, and Arleigh Burke as the other members. In *The Uncertain Trumpet* (1959), which Kennedy had much admired, Taylor had criticized Eisenhower for overdependence on nuclear weapons

---

*"You know that I wish I had served you better in the Cuban episode. . . . If my departure can assist you in any way, I hope you will send me off. . . . Your assistants are yours to use—and one use is in changing the air when that is needed." Henry Kissinger, who was commuting from Harvard to serve the NSC as a consultant on Germany, wrote Bundy by hand, "Our society is not good at encouraging people to say the things which really matter. . . . If you permit me to say something which may sound corny: It is important not to be discouraged or defensive, but things must still be done, and your friends and admirers would rest easier if they knew that you will continue to play a unique, indeed a leading, part in them."

and diffidence about equipping American forces for brushfire wars and counterinsurgency.

A week after the Bay of Pigs, Kennedy convened his National Security Council. Chester Bowles found the NSC meeting the "grimmest" in his government experience. Bowles thought the atmosphere "emotional, almost savage. . . . The President and the U.S. government had been humiliated and something must be done."

After Bowles read aloud a long argument that Castro's authority was untouchable by anything short of an American invasion, the Attorney General exploded: "That's the most meaningless, worthless thing I've ever heard. You people are so anxious to protect your own asses that you're afraid to do anything. All you want to do is dump the whole thing on the President. We'd be better off if you just quit and left foreign policy to someone else."

As Robert ranted on, his brother tapped a metallic pencil cap against his gleaming white teeth. Richard Goodwin later wrote, "I became suddenly aware—am now certain—that Bobby's harsh polemic reflected the President's own concealed emotions, privately communicated in some earlier, intimate conversation. I knew, even then, there was an inner hardness, often volatile anger beneath the outwardly amiable, thoughtful, carefully controlled demeanor of John Kennedy."

Dean Rusk was more worried than ever that Khrushchev might next move offensive missiles into Cuba. In early May he privately reminded the Senate Foreign Relations Committee that in the absence of a large long-range bomber force, Russia's ability to threaten the United States rested on a small number of submarines and ICBMs. Jet bombers and missiles based in Cuba "could reach parts of this country which may be more difficult to reach otherwise." This would "impose a degree of blackmail upon the United States in dealing with our problems in all parts of the world."

Someone asked why the United States did not simply blockade Cuba to keep out Soviet matériel. The Secretary of State replied that a blockade would "certainly be looked upon as an act of war. Now if we get to the point if we see missile bases and things of that sort going in there—and we can watch that very closely—we may . . . have to force that sort of decision."

Kennedy's NSC resolved in May that the United States should "retain the right to intervene" in Cuba if it became a "direct military threat to the United States" or "if Castro commits aggression against any American republic." The Taylor Board concluded in June,

"There can be no long-term living with Castro as a neighbor. . . . While inclining personally to a positive course of action against Castro without delay, we recognize the danger of dealing with the Cuban problem outside the context of the world situation." Still the United States was locked in a "life-and-death struggle" with the Soviet Union "which we may be losing."*

Robert Kennedy wrote to himself that month, "The Cuban matter is being allowed to slide. Mostly because nobody really has the answer to Castro. Not many are really prepared to send American troops in there at the present time, but maybe that is the answer. Only time will tell."

From Moscow, the Canadian Ambassador, Arnold Smith, advised his government that the Bay of Pigs, so soon after the Gagarin feat, had endowed Khrushchev with new "if perhaps exaggerated self-confidence. . . . I think they really believe that most broad historical forces are going their way." He thought the mood "comparable to that of the English at the end of the Victorian Era."

Like many Americans that spring, Smith made the mistake of falling for Khrushchev's rhetoric. The Chairman in private was anything but self-confident. He knew that in nuclear strength his country was falling farther than ever behind the United States. Soviet advances in the Congo, Laos, Cuba, and elsewhere warmed his heart ideologically but drained rubles that he might have preferred to spend on his domestic economy. Privy to economic facts he was too embarrassed to reveal to the world, Khrushchev knew how difficult it would be to "overtake and surpass" the United States by 1970 or 1980 or 1990.

The American defeat in Cuba gave Khrushchev a propaganda opportunity. But the greater effect of Kennedy's roll of the dice in the Caribbean was probably to upset the Chairman's plans. Arkady Shevchenko of the Foreign Ministry, who later defected to the United States, recalled that the Bay of Pigs "intensified the anti-American temper" in the Soviet military and Presidium: by forcing Khrushchev to speak in defense of Cuba, it had the effect of "exacerbating his

---

*Dulles may have had some influence over this language. In 1954, Eisenhower had appointed a similar board, chaired by General James Doolittle, to examine the CIA. The board concluded that "we are facing an implacable enemy whose avowed objective is world domination. . . . We must . . . learn to subvert, sabotage, and destroy our enemies by more clever, more sophisticated, and more effective methods than those used against us."

relations with Kennedy instead of improving them, as he had wanted."

After Kennedy's election, the Soviet leadership had worried that the new President's inexperience and narrow victory margin might provoke him into international adventures that a more secure and popular President like Eisenhower would have rejected. They were baffled as the rhetoric of Kennedy's first three months oscillated between conciliation and militance (supposing that this was a privilege only Khrushchev should enjoy).

Then came Kennedy's decision to launch the invasion of Cuba and let it fail. From their own intelligence and postmortem articles in American magazines, the Soviets learned of Stevenson's role in the President's ban against a second air strike.* Some wondered whether Kennedy was so inexperienced, so intimidated by his liberal intellectual advisers, and so hypnotized by his own rhetoric about self-determination and nonintervention that when it came to using force to reclaim a nation clearly embedded in the American sphere he was immobilized. Shevchenko said the Bay of Pigs "gave Khrushchev and the other leaders the impression that Kennedy was indecisive."

An Eastern European diplomat reminded Chester Bowles that "once Khrushchev had started to face up to the problem of Hungary, he had plowed ahead, even at the cost of thirty-two thousand dead on the streets of Budapest. . . . Khrushchev assumed that Kennedy would do the same thing."

Burned into Khrushchev's memory was the unhappy outcome of his experience with the first American President he had ever dealt with. After Camp David, he had assured colleagues that Eisenhower was a sincere "lover of peace." Then came the U-2 affair, which caused them to wonder whether the President had not played Khrushchev for a fool.

The Chairman was not about to make the same mistake again. After Kennedy's election, he had allowed himself to hope in public that the young man might be a "new Roosevelt." If Kennedy could have been relied upon not to embarrass him as Eisenhower had with the U-2, it might have been in Khrushchev's political interest to try to form a

---

*After a rash of such articles, one of McNamara's rebellious generals, James Van Fleet, a Pentagon consultant after retiring from the Army, publicly declared that Stevenson "should have been fired" when he "would not support the armed action" at the Bay of Pigs and caused the United States to "withhold air support" for the rebels. Stevenson demanded an apology. Van Fleet announced that his comments had been taken "out of context."

relationship with Kennedy. Even during a time of tension, if the Chairman could present himself to the rest of the Soviet leadership as someone who understood and could deal with Kennedy, this would lend him an indispensability that might make his rivals more loath to throw him out.

But after watching what he considered the inconsistency of Kennedy's early policies toward Moscow and now the Bay of Pigs, Khrushchev was doubly nervous about harnessing his political future to what he saw as an unpredictable, immature new President too doubtful about his own priorities and domestic standing to act decisively. Several weeks after the Bay of Pigs, Khrushchev seemed to reveal his current private feelings about Kennedy during a speech on other matters when he interjected that he had not become head of the Soviet government because his father was a rich man.

Khrushchev now sought to protect himself with his colleagues and Chinese critics by taking a harder line toward the United States. The three months of American militance culminating in Cuba seemed too great a challenge to ignore. The slapstick incompetence and weakness displayed at the Bay of Pigs seemed too great an opportunity not to exploit.

In Washington, a Soviet official informed an American that Kennedy had "not stood his test" in the eyes of the Soviet government. The President had "uselessly wasted the political credit granted him by Khrushchev."

Despite Kennedy's extreme care to confide to almost no one his fear that Khrushchev would move against Berlin, it took the Chairman and his analysts little effort to notice the diamond in the chandelier. They almost certainly concluded that Kennedy was so uncertain about the American commitment to the divided city that he was willing to brook the humiliation of the Bay of Pigs rather than face a new Berlin crisis now. At a time when Khrushchev felt he had few levers of power against Kennedy and the West, he could now conclude that Berlin might serve nicely.

Nine weeks had passed since Novosibirsk, when Thompson handed Khrushchev the President's secret letter proposing a summit meeting. For nine weeks there had been no response.

Kennedy's proposal of a summit had been based on the hopeful atmosphere of February. Now, after his embarrassment over Cuba and the souring of relations with Moscow, he was glad to be spared the ordeal of seeing Khrushchev. In a private letter to Konrad Adenauer, he wrote that the "deterioration in the general situation" had caused him to "suspend active consideration of a meeting with Khrushchev." As Bohlen recalled, the President "thought the matter was dead."

The Chairman had postponed his reply for nine weeks because he was waiting to see what happened in Cuba. He had no desire to embarrass himself by meeting Kennedy in the wake of a successful American invasion that had retaken the island despite Soviet promises to defend Castro. But if there was a summit now, it would be Kennedy on the defensive. After the months of confusing signals from Washington, Khrushchev also thought it important to take Kennedy's measure.

Another reason to ask for a summit was that Khrushchev expected the President to stage another action against Cuba in the near future, before Castro liquidated his internal enemies and the Soviets had the chance to send great numbers of weapons and advisers onto the island. He knew that Kennedy would be unlikely to invade Cuba during the period immediately before or after a summit. Thus the scheduling of a meeting would give Castro several crucial months in which to eliminate his opposition and begin building a serious defense.

At the end of April, the Chairman flashed word to a Soviet intelligence agent in Washington to contact the Americans and ask the President to make good on his offer of a Kennedy-Khrushchev summit.

CHAPTER

7

The Secret Agent

A SOVIET OFFICIAL NAMED GEORGI NIKITOVICH BOLSHAKOV AC-costed his friend Frank Holeman of the *New York Daily News:* "I'd like to meet the Attorney General. Could you help arrange it?" He added, "I'm the only person in the Embassy who can communicate directly with Khrushchev." A meeting with the President's brother, he said, could bear important fruit.

Jovial, hard-drinking, clownish, with unruly dark hair, blue eyes, and a barrel chest, Bolshakov had first met Holeman while serving in the early 1950s under shallow cover in Washington as a TASS correspondent. In late 1959, he had returned to the capital as an information secretary at the Soviet Embassy and editor of the Soviet English-language magazine *USSR*.

Bolshakov's formal rank among the sixty-seven members of the Embassy was fortieth. But the gaggle of FBI and Soviet intelligence agents who followed him around Washington attested to his actual importance. As Holeman recalled, "Georgi was being tailed by everybody on earth."

According to Alexei Adzhubei many years later, Bolshakov was a Soviet military intelligence agent who had served in the mid-1950s as an aide to the Soviet Defense Minister, the World War II hero Marshal Georgi Zhukov. After Khrushchev fired Zhukov, Adzhubei rescued Bolshakov by commending him to his father-in-law, who was pleased to have him edit *USSR* and serve as his personal representative in Washington.

As Soviet intelligence surely divined from psychological profiles of the Kennedy brothers, working through a secret agent conformed to their predilection for secrecy and circumvention of the bureaucracy for speed and flexibility. If custom was followed, Bolshakov was briefed on almost everything Soviet intelligence knew about the President and his brother: their ideology, methods, likes, dislikes, and eating, drinking, and sexual habits.

Holeman told the Attorney General's aide Edwin Guthman that Bolshakov wanted to meet him. Robert consulted the President, who was advised that Bolshakov was "an important agent of the Soviet secret police." The President told him to find out what the man wanted.

This was not the first time a Soviet agent had been sent to communicate with a high American official. In the late 1950s, distressed by polls showing that Richard Nixon might well be elected to succeed Eisenhower, Khrushchev and his colleagues thought it essential to build bridges to the Vice President so fabled for his anticommunism.

Chosen as the American go-between was Holeman, who was known to be friendly with Nixon and not unduly anti-Soviet. As a practical joke at the end of the 1952 campaign, Nixon had put the *Daily News* man alongside his wife, Pat, in a Seattle motorcade, allowing him to play candidate and wave at baffled crowds. Against bitter opposition, Holeman had persuaded fellow National Press Club governors to grant membership to Soviet diplomats in Washington, including one Yuri Gvozdev.

In February 1958, Gvozdev sought out Holeman and asked him, "on behalf of the Soviet Union," what would happen if Moscow's Syrian allies moved into Lebanon. Holeman went to the Nixon staff and obtained a reply, which he relayed to Gvozdev: "You've got to stop at the Lebanese border or you'll be in real trouble."*

The Soviets may have thought that Holeman was a spook himself. He told Nixon's secretary, Rose Mary Woods, "I keep telling them I have no influence, I have no connections, and the more I protest the more they think I am not telling the truth." He called himself "Frank Holeman, Boy Spy."

After Eisenhower sent the Marines into Lebanon that July, Gvozdev gave Holeman another urgent message for Nixon: "The Russians feel war is close. There are many places Russian volunteers can go, including Egypt. . . . Any United States or British move toward Iraq will mean war. If war, the Russians will ignore European bases and attack the United States directly."

When Khrushchev laid down his Berlin ultimatum, Gvozdev asked Holeman to assure his highly placed friends, "Don't worry about Berlin. There is not going to be any war over Berlin." This message may have fortified the President's inclination not to escalate the crisis.

In December 1958, Gvozdev told Holeman that Khrushchev was "very interested" in a Nixon visit to the Soviet Union. He would "bid very high for it in terms of constructive proposals on Berlin." What was the Vice President's "attitude toward visiting?"

Nixon conferred with the President and Secretary of State. Holeman was asked to tell Gvozdev that Nixon would come to Moscow "under certain conditions." The main one was "a period of relative quiet" between the United States and Soviet Union, especially over Berlin. The Soviets complied with Nixon's terms.

The Vice President's relationship with the Soviet agent has remained secret until this writing. His contacts with Gvozdev were at such arm's length that he may not have even known the man's name. By the time Nixon departed for his trip to the Soviet Union in July 1959, Gvozdev had vanished from Washington. Six years later, he was posted to Brasilia and expelled as a spy.

Now Holeman brought Georgi Bolshakov to the Justice Department, where the man took the private elevator to Kennedy's office. In almost perfect English, he told the Attorney General that he had once been a farmer and a laborer. Since Khrushchev's American tour in 1959, he had enjoyed a special relationship with the Chairman.

---

*Told the story years later, Eisenhower's foreign policy aide, Andrew Goodpaster, presumed that Nixon would have conferred with the Secretary of State and the President before allowing such a message to be sent in his name.

The President and the Chairman, he said, would surely have things to say to each other that could not be conveyed through official channels. He could offer a more true-to-life portrait of what was happening in the Kremlin than the Kennedys might get from the press or other sources.

Then Bolshakov got down to business. In his February letter, the President had proposed a summit meeting with the Chairman. Did the offer still stand?

Robert took the query to the President, who was startled and annoyed: now, in the wake of the Bay of Pigs embarrassment, Khrushchev had decided he wanted a summit after all. Kennedy wrote Adenauer that he was "faced with the problem" of consenting to a summit or else "withdrawing from my previous indication of my willingness to do so."

Bohlen reminded the President that Eisenhower had laid down conditions before agreeing to meet with Khrushchev. Kennedy decided to employ the same tactic. He asked Robert to tell Bolshakov that he was "leaning" toward a summit and would give the Chairman a final answer by May 20. That judgment would depend on whether America's allies approved and whether there was "genuine progress" in talks on Laos and nuclear testing.

Bolshakov assured Robert that there would be progress in both negotiations. According to Kennedy, Bolshakov suggested that Khrushchev would make substantial concessions in order to clinch an agreement on nuclear testing. As Robert recalled, "He indicated to me here quite clearly that they would reach an agreement on the test ban." If Bolshakov could be believed, this was a tantalizing reason for the President to accept a summit.

By the Attorney General's account, he and Bolshakov also debated what the two leaders might discuss: Laos, the "importance of their understanding that we were committed on Berlin," as well as "trying to reach some understanding" about the "control of nuclear weapons."

For the next year and a half, Robert Kennedy met with Georgi Bolshakov roughly two or three times a month. The Attorney General explained to his brother that "they didn't want to go through their Ambassador, evidently." Bolshakov had told him that Menshikov "wasn't giving accurate reports to Khrushchev." Thus the Chairman "didn't really understand the United States."

Holeman helped to cement the relationship: "Bobby was my client, but I liked Georgi." When Bolshakov did not wish to risk telephoning Robert's office directly, Holeman would call Guthman: "My guy wants to see your guy."

The *Daily News* man picked Bolshakov up by taxi away from the Soviet Embassy in an effort to give the slip to American or Soviet agents: "My interest was in making sure my friend and the Attorney General were not embarrassed by these bastards." Kennedy usually saw Bolshakov in his office. Sometimes they met in a doughnut shop next to the Mayflower Hotel or strolled up Constitution Avenue toward the Capitol.

Bolshakov's clandestine business with Robert Kennedy was camouflaged by his large acquaintanceship in New Frontier Washington. On first-name terms with presidential aides like O'Donnell and Sorensen and presidential friends like Bartlett, Bradlee, and William Walton, he was appreciated for his refusal to spout the Soviet party line. Bolshakov told anyone who would listen that his heroes were Nikita Khrushchev and John Kennedy.

Of the highest officials in the American government, only the President and his brother knew everything that Robert was saying to Bolshakov and hearing back. The Attorney General later recalled, "I unfortunately—stupidly, never—I didn't write many of the things down. I just delivered the messages verbally to my brother and he'd act on them. And I think sometimes he'd tell the State Department and sometimes perhaps he didn't."

Thompson's misgivings about the Bolshakov channel went beyond the professional's aversion to informal diplomacy. He thought it an "error of judgment. . . . They tried to sell the idea 'Well, the State Department is so biased against us that we can't get anywhere. If we could just get direct contact, why we could do this.' This way, they hoped to avoid any staff work and to avoid having all the facts known—and to persuade the President to make a judgment simply on the basis of their presentation on the assumption that they could do business that way. I think this was a great mistake."

Thompson warned the President that the Soviets "might attach great importance to careless remarks": American officials who spoke with anyone from the Soviet Embassy must be told to keep records of their conversations. Kennedy nodded but ignored Thompson's advice.

Rusk and Bundy were also unenthusiastic about the channel. Neither knew that the President's brother was seeing Bolshakov so frequently. The Attorney General's assistant James Symington resented Bolshakov's "insinuating jocularity" and "almost unlimited access to the inner sanctum." He thought his boss was playing a "dangerous game."

The President was never seen with Bolshakov except in meetings with Soviet delegations. But for his brother to meet so often with a known Soviet agent had its risks. The FBI had both Bolshakov and the Attorney General under surveillance: when Bolshakov dined at Holeman's Virginia home, Holeman saw FBI photographers "hanging out of the trees." But as Bartlett observed, Robert was protected by his background of conspicuous anticommunism: "I don't think Bobby thought he'd be in danger of being attacked as a Communist sympathizer."

The greater problem with the channel was that it gave the advantage to the Soviets. The Soviets could count on Robert Kennedy not to give their man false information: if the President's brother lied, it would directly taint the President. But Bolshakov was a deniable agent. If he should be deliberately used to deceive the Kennedys and was found out, all the Kremlin had to do was say its man had been "misinformed" and yank him back to Moscow.

The Chairman used a similar method to communicate with Castro. Their most sensitive dialogues were conducted not through Khrushchev's Ambassador in Havana, whom the Cuban leader reviled, but through Alexander Alexeyev, the agent who operated, as Bolshakov had, under shallow cover as a TASS correspondent.

An important reason for Khrushchev's use of such channels with Kennedy and Castro was that he did not fully trust his own Foreign Ministry. The Chairman once said that if he asked Gromyko to "drop his trousers and sit on a block of ice for a month," Gromyko would do it. But he never forgot that Gromyko's patron had been Molotov, Foreign Minister under Stalin and a chief conspirator in the 1957 Anti-Party Coup.

Had Khrushchev gained absolute power after 1957, he might have removed Molotov from government altogether and chosen a new foreign minister with few ties to the Stalin group. Instead he had sent Molotov to the Soviet Embassy in Ulan Bator, a not inconsequential assignment, and installed Gromyko as Foreign Minister.*

By 1961, Khrushchev had moved Molotov to the UN Atomic Energy

---

*Gromyko's immediate predecessor was Dimitri Shepilov, a young man in a hurry whom Khrushchev had appointed Foreign Minister to replace Molotov in 1956. Shepilov made the mistake of choosing the losing side and betraying his patron during the Anti-Party Coup.

Agency in Vienna.* The Chairman remained worried about Molotov loyalists in the Foreign Ministry and elsewhere in Moscow. Most were suspicious of Khrushchev's openings to the West. The Chairman may have suspected that they might sabotage any overtures he made to Kennedy or use them to show that Khrushchev was "soft on capitalism."

Nevertheless, using agents as a diplomatic conduit was subject to most of the same risks as using the Foreign Ministry. His efforts to reduce tensions with the West and the harshness of the Soviet police state undermined the raison d'être of the KGB, threatening its chieftains' power and privileges. The KGB chairman was thought to be a critic of the Chairman's tough line with China and his efforts to improve American relations.

After Khrushchev's message, Kennedy had little choice but to accede to a summit. If he tried to escape it, the Soviets might release the contents of his February letter and crow that after his Bay of Pigs humiliation the President seemed to be afraid to go into the same room as Khrushchev.

Necessity forced Kennedy to see the benefits of going ahead with a summit. He noted that "each crisis that I've faced so far in this job has really stemmed from Russia": already the Congo, Laos, and Cuba had all threatened to drag the two powers into confrontation. Berlin and South Vietnam had the same potential.

The President had conceded to Nixon in April that his Cuba failure may have suggested to Khrushchev that he could "keep pushing us all over the world." A summit would allow Kennedy to demonstrate the contrary. He told O'Donnell, "Getting involved in a fight between Communists and anti-Communists in Cuba and Laos was one thing. But this is the time to let him know that a showdown between the United States and Russia would be entirely something else again."

Since the Inauguration, Kennedy had been attracted to the idea of sitting down with Khrushchev to arrange a standstill in the Cold War. Such a cooling-off period would keep both powers from finding themselves committed to actions that risked their essential security and

---

*Khrushchev may have removed Molotov from Mongolia because Chinese leaders across the border took every opportunity to lavish praise on Molotov as Stalin's pupil and rightful heir and hence show contempt for their antagonist Khrushchev. The Chairman heard rumors of Chinese conspiracies with Molotov and other enemies against him. He may have felt that Molotov would be less dangerous in Vienna, where there were fewer chances to rub shoulders with high-level Chinese.

threatened the equilibrium of peace. It would give the two leaders the opportunity to build some kind of rational framework for Soviet-American relations that would take account of both leaders' aims and domestic needs.

It did not escape the President that a summit would fortify his domestic and international position. Eisenhower's Geneva and Camp David meetings, even the disaster at Paris, had unified the American people and the West. As in the television debates with Nixon, for Kennedy to hold his own against Khrushchev would help to quash the talk now recurring after the Bay of Pigs that he was too young and inexperienced.

Kennedy marveled at how Americans rallied to a President at moments of foreign challenge—even when the danger was his own fault, as with Eisenhower and the U-2 affair. Reading a post–Bay of Pigs poll showing his approval by an unprecedented 82 percent of Americans, he said that it was just like Eisenhower: "The worse I do, the more popular I get." (Later he added, "If I had gone further, they would have liked me more.")

The President wrote Adenauer, "I would assume you would share my view that since I have not previously met Khrushchev, such an encounter would be useful in the present international situation. If the meeting in fact takes place, I would expect to inform you of the content of these discussions with Khrushchev, which I anticipate will be quite general in character."

Lyndon Johnson feared that in the aftermath of the Cuban fiasco, Khrushchev might take Kennedy's willingness to meet as a sign of weakness. There is no evidence that the President ever took this notion seriously. Neither did Bohlen, who felt that "Soviet rulers usually pay more attention to United States power than tactical errors." Other American officials worried nevertheless that Khrushchev would come to the summit, make some outrageous demand that Kennedy would have to reject, and then, as in Paris in 1960, blast the meeting apart in order to escalate the Cold War to his own advantage.

As Bolshakov and Robert Kennedy conferred secretly in Washington, Gromyko approached Thompson in Moscow on Thursday, May 4, with a formal proposal for a summit, saying, "Recent events make a meeting even more necessary."

Thompson cabled Washington that he hoped the President would "maintain" his plan to meet with Khrushchev. Knowing Kennedy's critics might charge that the Bay of Pigs had stampeded him into a summit, he suggested that the President reveal to the public that he had proposed the meeting two months before the Cuban fiasco: "Moreover, on the questions of the Congo, Laos, and Cuba, the President has made clear his firm stance in the face of Soviet actions."

The Ambassador thought scheduling a summit would make Khrushchev "more reasonable" during the months ahead. The Chairman was now making important decisions about his October Twenty-second Party Congress, "and it is in our interest to influence these decisions." The "mere fact of a meeting" would "exacerbate Soviet-Chinese relations." Despite "recent sharp exchanges and Soviet actions," Thompson felt there had been no major change in Khrushchev's intentions: "While it has always been clear that the Soviets seek the communization of the world, Khrushchev continues to advocate peaceful means."

On Friday morning, May 5, the United States launched its first man into space. The nervous Kennedy said that after Gagarin's success and the Bay of Pigs, a failure in space would usher in "a very difficult time for NASA and for us all."

After the fifteen-minute, three-hundred-mile suborbital flight, Kennedy was relieved to learn that the astronaut, Commander Alan Shepard, was safely in the helicopter. Billings wrote in his diary that the President "wasn't too happy to note that . . . everyone wanted to get into Shepard's act, including the Vice President.* He remarked that if the flight had been a failure, he would have been placed in the act fast enough."

The President had been especially anxious about the Shepard mission because he was fighting off a new challenge in Laos. Khrushchev once asked Thompson why the Soviet Union should bother taking risks over the little country: "It will fall into our laps like a ripe apple." Now the Chairman's prophecy seemed to be coming true. The White House was informed that American-backed Royalist forces in Laos were "on the ropes."

From Vientiane, Ambassador Winthrop Brown asked Rusk for permission to authorize air strikes that would deprive the enemy of key objectives. Brown realized that such an attack "would blow the whole cease-fire negotiations wide open" and "most likely" bring American intervention. The Joint Chiefs of Staff prepared contingency plans for a move against North Vietnam and perhaps southern China.

---

*Johnson served as chairman of the President's new council on space.

So soon after the Bay of Pigs, the President did not wish to give Khrushchev or the Republicans the impression that he was pulling punches in Laos as well as Cuba. But he knew if the United States acted "we might find ourselves fighting millions of Chinese troops in the jungles." He told Billings he could not "afford to make another mistake." He would "rather not" send troops into Laos "if there were any other way. I feel so much more strongly about Cuba." But if the Communists were not stopped in Laos, "Vietnam would be next. Then Thailand, et cetera."

Rusk thought the Royalist regime unworthy of "the life of a single farm boy." The leaders of Congress agreed. From New Delhi, Ambassador John Kenneth Galbraith wrote the President that, as a military ally, "the entire Laos nation is clearly inferior to a battalion of conscientious objectors from World War I."

The Joint Chiefs were divided. Robert Kennedy recalled, "The head of the Army said that we would have forty-percent casualties within a short period of time—I think thirty days—this based on disease and dysentery. So that we would send these troops in and have them wiped out for a country that really wasn't interested in defending itself." After one such briefing, Robert said, "If the Marines aren't willing to go in, even *I'm* against it."

As the Attorney General recalled, someone estimated that "the Communists could send five men into Laos for every one that we sent in, that they could destroy the airports and therefore cut off our people after getting only a thousand or several thousand into Laos," and that to preserve the Royalist regime "we had to be prepared to engage in a major atomic war both with China and with Russia."

Unwilling to risk such a nuclear confrontation, the President barred the use of American forces in Laos. He was grateful to the Bay of Pigs for making him more skeptical of military advice, saying that if it hadn't been for Cuba "we would be into Laos up to our necks."

Quiet British-Soviet bargaining produced a cease-fire. On Friday, May 12, a fourteen-nation conference on Laos met in Geneva. As his envoy Kennedy sent Averell Harriman, who had argued for the more limited commitment to Laos. The President told him not to come back to Washington without a settlement.

After an official trip to Southeast Asia, Lyndon Johnson privately told Senators that he was "very depressed about Laos. . . . I don't think anything is going to come out of the conference. I think the Russians are going to bust it up, and I think that the Communists will practically have it."

Robert Kennedy consulted Bolshakov about an American-Soviet effort to wind down the conflict. Nevertheless he feared that a Laos settlement could exacerbate the President's problems in Southeast Asia by offering "the Russians and the Communists a tunnel right into the heart of South Vietnam."

In support of his effort to lure the President to the summit, Khrushchev said at Tbilisi on Friday, May 12, "Although President Kennedy and I are men of different poles, we live on the same earth. . . . We have to coexist on our planet, and consequently we have to find a common language on certain questions." The State Department told Kennedy that Khrushchev's remarks were "probably the most moderate he has made in a public address since before the U-2 incident of last year."

By mid-May, as Western allies were consulted about a Kennedy-Khrushchev encounter, the news was leaking all over. Golfing during a long presidential weekend in Palm Beach, the President's military aide General Chester Clifton told Sander Vanocur of NBC that when he flew with Kennedy to Paris at the end of May he had better take extra clothes. Vanocur had noted Khrushchev's new moderation; he needed no further hint. He told Salinger he would go with the story "unless there is some overriding reason of national security." The press secretary said, "I can't stop you."

On Tuesday morning, May 16, Mikhail Menshikov went to the White House and gave the President an English translation of a Khrushchev letter dated May 12. In it, the Chairman complained once more about the Bay of Pigs and accepted Kennedy's summit proposal.

Having waited sixty-eight days for Khrushchev's reply, the President did not hasten to answer. He coolly noted that when Gromyko had broached the subject with Thompson, it had not been clear whether Laos and other aspects of the international climate would be "conducive" to a summit. Now he would consider the matter with Rusk and reply within forty-eight hours. If he decided to meet with the Chairman, the summit should be held in Vienna.

Kennedy mentioned the speculation in the American press during the previous week about a summit. With his surly manner Menshikov retorted that no leaks had appeared in the Soviet press. The President explained that he had consulted de Gaulle about the meeting; "inevitably" this had spread the news. One reason he wished to talk with Khrushchev was the "crucial" nuclear test ban talks. He did not want official statements to suggest that he and the Chairman expected to reach an agreement on Laos or a test ban. Public expectations must not be raised.

Bohlen called the Secretary of State, who was in Geneva at the conference on Laos: Kennedy wanted to go ahead, unless the Secretary objected. Even less happy about a summit than he was before the Bay of Pigs, Rusk replied that the Laos situation was "not very good from the Russian point of view, which might be a consideration."

Bohlen told him that word about a summit was already leaking; the President wanted a decision today. Rusk replied that "in the circumstances" the President should "go ahead." With this exuberant endorsement from his Secretary of State, Kennedy notified Khrushchev that he would meet him in Vienna.

The next day, John and Jacqueline Kennedy flew to Ottawa for their first official foreign trip. The President detested the Canadian Prime Minister, John Diefenbaker, whom he thought ponderous and insincere. He resented Diefenbaker's public suggestion that Canada mediate between the United States and Cuba. The Prime Minister thought Kennedy a "young pup" and a "boastful young son of a bitch."

Diefenbaker was newly provoked when Kennedy publicly asked the Canadian Parliament to overrule Diefenbaker's opposition to Canadian membership in the OAS. When the President left the Prime Minister's offices, someone left behind a memo from Rostow urging Kennedy to "push" the Canadians on the OAS and Laos. (The President thought the culprit was Bundy.)

Diefenbaker later claimed that the memo bore the letters "S.O.B." in Kennedy's handwriting. The President later said, "I didn't think Diefenbaker was a son of a bitch"—he paused—"I thought he was a prick." He wondered why the Prime Minister "didn't do what any normal, friendly government would do: make a photostatic copy and return the original."

An Ottawa ceremony had been staged in which Kennedy was to plant two red oaks. Perhaps from the tension of dealing with Diefenbaker, he neglected to crouch, as his back doctors had trained him. Instead, he bent over the pile of black earth. Pain seized the lower lumbar region of his back, site of football and war injuries that had almost killed him when infection set in after a 1954 spinal fusion operation. He thrust one hand into a side pocket of his jacket and gripped his forehead with the other.

The next day in the Oval Office, his secretary, Evelyn Lincoln, found him "cranky" and "almost exhausted." In the privacy of the

White House family quarters, he resorted to crutches for the first time in years.

On Saturday, May 20, while the President and Jacqueline were at Glen Ora, the Khrushchev summit was announced simultaneously in Moscow and Washington. White House aides told reporters of their certainty that Khrushchev would "quickly" recognize the President as "a man of decision."

The announcement of earlier summits such as Geneva, Camp David, and Paris had been greeted by vast hope. But this time the reaction in Western countries ran from mild expectation to outright worry. As William Fulbright conceded, there was now "great nervousness" about the young President going to see Khrushchev. A Jacksonville businessman said, "You don't negotiate with somebody who has just given you a beating." According to a Carson City laborer, "Khrushchev will kick him around the block."

Columnists quoted past Kennedy statements that Presidents should not go to summits unless results were negotiated in advance. In the *New Yorker,* Richard Rovere warned that "Mr. Khrushchev may not see in our young President quite all that Theodore Sorensen and Charles Bohlen see in him."

From Madrid, Ambassador Anthony Biddle cabled, "There is worry here which, reduced to simple terms, is that somehow the wily and corrupt old Soviet leader may get some advantage at Vienna from meeting with the youthful President of 'idealistic young' America." A *Newsweek* correspondent reported that diplomats of Western Europe thought the meeting would "merely serve to enhance Khrushchev's prestige" and that "Khrushchev is unlikely to worry very much about American warnings."

Senator Albert Gore called the summit "ill-advised and untimely." Senator Bourke Hickenlooper, Republican of Iowa, said, "No justification . . . no hope of success." George Ball, the number-three man at State, told a friend it was "unfortunate" that Kennedy should see Khrushchev just after the "series of defeats we have suffered" in space, Cuba, and Laos. Secretary of Labor Arthur Goldberg bluntly told Kennedy he was not ready to talk to Khrushchev because he hadn't been President long enough.

Kennedy's friend and Senate leader Mike Mansfield of Montana wrote him a letter noting that since January his foreign policy had left "much to be desired. . . . If the meeting degenerates into a slugfest of words, with each trying to prove he is stronger and more adamant than the other, then it would have been better had the meeting not taken place."

By May 1961, in Kennedy's campaign formulation, the people of the world seemed to be growing less interested in what the United States was doing than in what Mr. Khrushchev was doing. In a column reprinted by *Pravda,* James Reston noted that the Chairman was "having a ball. He has us over a barrel in Laos. He has made us look foolish in Cuba."

The American setbacks in foreign affairs and space caused the President to feel overtaken by events. He said, "I'm going to start doing like Eisenhower and have my staff cut up the paper." With his approval, the U.S. Information Agency quietly stopped taking the polls on American prestige that he had used so effectively to needle Eisenhower and Nixon during the 1960 campaign.

During his mid-May trip to Palm Beach, Kennedy had pondered how to regain the initiative before the summit with Khrushchev. Fred Holborn of the White House staff said, "There's a feeling that the next ten days are crucial."

The President decided to break with tradition by delivering a second State of the Union address on Thursday, May 25, twelve weeks after his first. (Wags called it a *"Re-*state of the Union.") With this noon speech on "urgent national needs," he hoped to make a powerful new start before he went to Vienna. Cautioned by aides against a new military request on the eve of Vienna, he said that if Khrushchev was offended, that was the way it would have to be.

Augmenting his earlier defense appeal to Congress in March, Kennedy now asked for fifteen thousand more Marines, new emphasis on guerrilla warfare, howitzers, helicopters, personnel carriers, more battle-ready Army reserve combat divisions—and tripled funds for fallout shelters across the nation.* He also asked for the most open-ended financial commitment ever made in peacetime in order to land an American on the moon by 1970.

During his first months in office, the President had been cautioned to distance himself from Project Mercury, lest his stature be damaged

---

*The shelters would strengthen his leverage not only against Khrushchev but also against Nelson Rockefeller, the nation's most vocal champion of a major shelter program, who, as Sorensen recalled, the President felt was "likely to be his opponent in 1964."

by exploding rockets or dead astronauts. In March, he had rejected a NASA request for funds that would go to man-in-space projects. But after the Gagarin coup, when Congressmen accused the President of tolerating a "Soviet space monopoly," Kennedy asked his experts, "Is there anyplace where we can catch them? . . . Can we put a man on the moon before them?"

Cuba and Southeast Asia had further sapped the President's political ability to defend a measured effort in space. Using Kennedy's own campaign rhetoric, Lyndon Johnson wrote him, "In the eyes of the world, first in space means first, period." Scientists warned that there was only a fifty-fifty chance of beating the Soviets to the moon and that the huge expense of a hurry-up moon landing program could not be justified on scientific or technical grounds. The deciding reason would have to be political.

Political advisers reminded the President that a moon project would stimulate the national economy. It would help to mollify Congressmen, generals, and aerospace tycoons angry about McNamara's Pentagon reforms. It would also bolster Kennedy's popularity; they imagined the President greeting the courageous young spacemen at Cape Canaveral and in the Rose Garden.

Kennedy knew that if the United States held the lead in an all-out moon program, it would help to protect him and his government through Cold War setbacks. As Khrushchev had done with Sputnik, the President could use successes in outer space to divert public attention from domestic and foreign frustrations on earth.

With his unassailable reputation on defense and foreign matters, Eisenhower had resisted post-Sputnik demands for an expensive American rush to the moon, just as he had resisted demands for a massive defense buildup. Kennedy did not. Twenty billion dollars, the ultimate cost of an American moon landing, was a large price to pay for the primary purpose of recapturing Cold War prestige.

Eisenhower wrote a friend that Kennedy's decision was "almost hysterical" and "a bit immature." He complained to the astronaut Frank Borman in 1965 that the moon effort "was drastically revised and expanded just after the Bay of Pigs fiasco. . . . It immediately took one single project or experiment out of a thoroughly planned and continuing program involving communication, meteorology, reconnaissance, and future military and scientific benefits and gave the highest priority—unfortunate in my opinion—to a race, in other words, a stunt."

Senator Prescott Bush of Connecticut complained that Kennedy would "unleash the forces of inflation" by refusing to recommend the taxes to pay for his new defense and space programs. Joseph Kennedy agreed. He told White House aides, "Damn it, I taught Jack better than that! Oh, we're going to go broke with this nonsense. *I* told him that I thought it was ridiculous."

During the last week of May, the President lay in his four-poster bed with a moist heating pad under his back. He pored over galleys of *The Grand Tactician,* a new Khrushchev biography by a Soviet émigré named Lazar Pistrak, and read black leather-bound State Department and CIA briefing books. Bundy wrote, "Here are the beginnings of some of the interesting dope on Vienna."

Kennedy was advised by State that Vienna offered him an opportunity to show Khrushchev his "grasp of the world situation" and his intention to shape it. Worried about China, the Chairman "would prefer that the talks end on a note of accord." Khrushchev believed "that a détente atmosphere would establish a political deterrent of sorts to forceful U.S. action against Cuba and against Laos. . . . He might also hope that this atmosphere would take some of the steam out of an expanding U.S. arms program."

A CIA profile noted that Khrushchev's "speech is larded with peasant proverbs and even biblical phrases. . . . He is at his folksiest best in the fields of a collective farm, dispensing advice to the assembled peasants on the best means of planting potatoes or corn."

The Chairman was "the poor man's universal genius with solutions to all problems . . . an expert on everything from silage to outer space. An uninhibited ham actor, who often illustrates his points with the crudest sort of barnyard humor, he is endowed on occasion with considerable personal dignity. Proud of his proletarian origin, he is nonetheless determined to receive full recognition and honor as the authentic leader of a great world power."

Although "capable of extraordinary frankness, and in his own eyes no doubt unusually honest," Khrushchev was also "a gambler and dissembler, expert in calculated bluffing. . . . While priding himself on his realism and particularly his mastery of the realities of the balance of power, he is imbued with the idea that he can utilize Soviet power to move the world toward communism during his lifetime."

The CIA warned the President that Khrushchev might deliberately try to knock him off balance at Vienna. As the briefing paper noted, this was an old Khrushchev tactic: in Moscow, he had once arrived late for an American television interview, ordered the cameras turned off, and "launched into a tirade against the methods of the American press. Just when the production seemed doomed, Khrushchev told the crew to proceed and became completely charming for the interview. Throughout the program, the reporters, not Khrushchev, were on the defensive."

The Agency also submitted the findings of more than a dozen internists, psychiatrists, and psychologists whom it had secretly convened in 1960 to assess Khrushchev's personality. The experts had watched films of the Soviet leader greeting Indians, dozing off during ceremonies, removing his shoe and pounding his fists at the United Nations. After scrutinizing telephone intercepts, letters, speeches, and Agency debriefings of Westerners who had watched and bargained with Khrushchev, they concluded that the Soviet leader was a "chronic optimistic opportunist."

One member of the project, a social psychiatrist named Bryant Wedge, warned Kennedy by letter that efforts to change Khrushchev's mind about important issues were useless: "There can be only one mode of argument—to state the realities of Western positions in unmistakable terms so that miscalculation will be avoided and practical accommodation achieved. Explanation as to *why* U.S. positions are taken on any other than pragmatic grounds will fall on deaf ears."

The President read transcripts of Khrushchev's conversations with Eisenhower, Nixon, Stevenson, Humphrey, the Iowa corn grower Roswell Garst, and the United Auto Workers leader Walter Reuther, whom the Chairman had told, "You are like a nightingale. It closes its eyes when it sings, and sees nothing and hears nobody but itself." (Khrushchev would have known.)

Stevenson gave Kennedy a memo on "the way Soviet leaders see things." The President asked Humphrey and James Reston whether logic worked with Khrushchev. Bohlen told him that the Chairman's personality was best described by the French word *"méchanceté"**: "I can't really translate this for you. You had better ask your wife to elaborate." Khrushchev's chief characteristic, he said, was "an extraordinary amount of animal energy."

Walter Lippmann told the President over lunch that he could get along with Khrushchev by being self-confident and, above all, patient: "This man moves very slowly. He cannot be hurried, and you've just got to make up your mind that it's going to be a terribly long affair or it won't work. . . . Three hours for Khrushchev? He hasn't started." He warned that Khrushchev was a "committed revolutionist."

"He's not a *real* revolutionist," said Kennedy. "He's never going to carry a revolution to the point where he thinks it is going to produce a war with us."

---

*Best translated as a sort of wicked mischievousness.

* * *

The third great leader of the Soviet Union was born in 1894 in the village of Kalinovka, near the border between Russia and the Ukraine. The young *muzhik* worked as a shepherd before being sent at sixteen to the coal pits, which he later called "a working man's Cambridge, the university of the dispossessed of Russia." During the Civil War, he reputedly led a battalion of metalworkers to victory over a Cossack army. After the cannons died, his first wife died of scarlet fever, leaving their children, Leonid and Julia.

Khrushchev entered a miners' school where, backed by Cheka, the infamous secret police, he was student, commissar, police informer, and interpreter of the news. He married a schoolteacher named Nina Petrovna Kukharchuk, attached himself to the Ukrainian boss Lazar Kaganovich, and followed him to the Soviet capital. Chief of the Moscow Communist Party by 1935, Khrushchev became a minor member of Stalin's circle, mutely watching as hundreds of thousands of Soviets were murdered in the Great Purge.

He returned to Kiev in 1938 as Stalin's viceroy to wipe out those Ukrainian enemies of the people who still survived. In the early months of World War II, he followed Red Army tanks into eastern Poland to oversee the region's incorporation into the Soviet Union. He helped plan the disastrous assault on Kharkov and served as political adviser when the Soviets defeated the Nazis at Stalingrad and Kursk.

In 1946, during a Ukrainian famine, Khrushchev greeted a UN mission in Kiev headed by Marshall MacDuffie, one of the first Americans he had ever met, who recalled, "He stared at me quizzically and with great curiosity, like a man studying a bug on a rock." Before the mission members left, Khrushchev surprised them by entertaining them and their wives and "sat on the porch with them until long past midnight, discussing their personal lives and plans."

Stalin in 1949 gave Khrushchev back his old post as Moscow Party chief and made him a secretary of the Central Committee, one of the half dozen most powerful men in the Soviet Union. These were the years of Stalin's wildest paranoia, leading to the arrest of members of the so-called Doctors' Plot and rumors of a new purge at the highest level.

Then, in March 1953, Stalin died. As the new Party chief, Khrushchev quickly began undermining the new Premier, Georgi Malenkov, from the right. Opportunistically he grabbed for support from the military and the secret police by criticizing Malenkov's overtures to the West, the resources being shifted from arms to consumer goods, and Malenkov's un-Stalinist laments that nuclear war would end civilization. (All these were policies that Khrushchev later championed as soon as he took full power.)

By 1956, Malenkov was out. Khrushchev served alongside Premier Nikolai Bulganin. At a secret session of the Twentieth Party Congress, he gave the speech that gave him immortality. Delegates wept as he exposed Stalin's transgressions, the "intolerance, brutality, and abuse of power," policy mistakes, the "grave perversions" of Party principles, the personality cult. The CIA obtained a copy of the address, soon called the Secret Speech, and passed it to the *New York Times*. Stalin's political prisoners staggered out of labor camps.

Khrushchev's indictment of the Great Father encouraged satellite governments in Eastern Europe to liberalize. Nationalist rebellion spread through East Germany and Poland. By fall, the revolutionary danger was so great that Khrushchev flew to Warsaw, where he demanded a crackdown and crushed the Hungarian revolution, earning his reputation in the West as the "Butcher of Budapest." By January 1957, the domestic backlash against de-Stalinization was so great that Khrushchev was compelled to declare that when it came to fighting imperialism, "we are all Stalinists."

With Khrushchev's blood on the water, more genuine Stalinists like Molotov, Malenkov, Kaganovich, and Bulganin saw their opportunity. In June 1957, while Khrushchev was in Finland, they convened the Presidium and demanded his resignation.

Khrushchev refused to quit unless the verdict was ratified by the Central Committee: "You are afraid to face its members." He knew the larger group was weighted toward officials outside Moscow who appreciated his efforts to increase their authority. His Defense Minister, Marshal Zhukov, flew in Central Committee members from the most distant corners of the Soviet Union on Army planes. His gamble succeeded.

With his talent for the political use of language, Khrushchev called the episode the Anti-Party Coup, portraying it as a crime against the Communist Party. Once reconfirmed in power, he ousted his Anti-Party foes. Marshal Zhukov's critical role in his survival convinced him that the Defense Minister was too powerful. With rank ingratitude, he forced out Zhukov on a trumped-up charge of "Bonapartism."

As for Bulganin, "the fool didn't realize that they would have got rid of him the next day if they had succeeded," Khrushchev said. "The post of Prime Minister of the Soviet Union is not intended for an idiot." Adding Bulganin's portfolio to his own chieftainship of the Party, Khrushchev in 1958 became supreme leader of the Soviet Union as only Lenin and Stalin had been before.

* * *

During the negotiations in early May, the Americans had proposed that the first order of business at Vienna be a nuclear test ban: then Kennedy and Khrushchev could turn to other issues like Berlin and Laos. But the Soviets insisted that the Chairman's first concern would be Berlin.

Meeting at Potsdam in 1945, the leaders of the United States, the Soviet Union and Britain divided Germany into four zones and established four-power control of Berlin. They intended this accord to prevail until the four victors agreed on a final German peace treaty and an all-German regime. This hope was dashed by the Cold War. The occupied nation was converted into opposing East and West German states: the German Democratic Republic (GDR) and the Federal Republic of Germany (FRG).

One hundred and ten miles inside the GDR, Berlin was, as Khrushchev said, a bone in the throat of East Germany and all Eastern Europe. The Western sector of the city was a staging point for anti-Soviet propaganda and espionage, a rebuff to the notion that communism produced prosperity, a holdout against Stalin's attempt to incorporate every hectare of Eastern Europe into the Soviet sphere.

In 1948, Stalin tried to eliminate these problems with a blockade to starve the two million people of West Berlin into submission. But when the West responded with the Berlin Airlift, he was unwilling to escalate the conflict. In 1949, he declared the GDR a sovereign nation, with a Soviet-controlled government operating East Berlin, which the West refused to recognize.

Khrushchev renewed Stalin's offensive in November 1958. Thirteen years after the war, he said, there was still no German peace treaty. If the West did not come to terms on a treaty within six months, he would sign a separate peace with the GDR, which would put the East Germans in control of access routes to West Berlin. If the East Germans blocked the routes and the West tried to crash through with tanks, the conflict could spiral into nuclear war.

The Chairman brandished his new force of missiles that could attack all of Western Europe: "We don't even have to fire them from East Germany. We can send them from the U.S.S.R. . . . Our troops are not there to play cards. We mean business."

Khrushchev's peace treaty was designed to compel the Western powers to recognize two German states, sanctioning the division of Germany and Europe. Berlin would become a "free city." Stripped of its twenty-five thousand Western troops, it would naturally fall into the Soviet sphere.

Such an accord would cauterize the growing exodus of refugees to the West and buttress Soviet power in Eastern Europe. A peace treaty on Soviet terms would undermine faith in other Western guarantees and demonstrate to the uncommitted nations that the Soviet bloc was indeed the rising force in the world. It would make reunification of Germany less likely, which would suit Khrushchev just fine.

Like most Soviet leaders, one of his darkest nightmares was a reunified "revanchist" Germany, a NATO member whose "Hitlerite generals" had access to nuclear weapons. The CIA profile warned that Khrushchev's anxiety was "deadly and dangerous. . . . The Soviet Union lost twenty million people to Hitler—ten percent of her population. Khrushchev himself acted as political commissar at Stalingrad during the German siege. Thus a prime concern of Khrushchev is to keep Germany weak, and this desire should not be underrated."

The United States, Britain, and France wanted a plebiscite enabling both East and West Germans to vote for an all-German government. They had little doubt that if such a vote were fairly held, the result would be a Western-oriented member of NATO.

Foster Dulles once told Mikoyan that the East German government was "a form of masked occupation" that was "wholly imposed upon" and "hated" by the Germans. Mikoyan retorted that the GDR leaders "did not spring to power by accident. They were people who are well known there." Many had been in the Bundestag at the time of the Kaiser. The GDR had to fear "neither the Soviet government nor Soviet forces." The two countries were "allies," just as the United States and West Germany were allies.

Khrushchev told Humphrey in 1958, "If you try to talk about German reunification, the answer is no. There are two German states and they will have to settle reunification by themselves." Any other kind of settlement would "come only through force. An attack on the GDR is war, and we will support our partner in that war." The best hope for reunification was a "kind of confederation" between the GDR and the FRG.

Humphrey asked whether such a confederation would require West Germany to leave NATO. Khrushchev said "NATO would disappear anyhow." Humphrey countered, "What about the Warsaw Pact? Will it disappear?"

"Yes, any time now. . . . You must remember that many of your friends, the English and French, do not really want a reunited Germany. They are afraid of German reunification. The U.S.S.R. is not afraid.* The situation isn't like it was before the war. The U.S. and the Soviets need have no fear of a reunited Germany. Let's test our mutual strength by economic competition. If the U.S.S.R. and the U.S.A. are on the same side on this Berlin issue or any other, there will be no war. Only a madman or a fool would think of such a thing."

Despite their public rhetoric about the sacred need for German "self-determination," most American leaders of the time, including John Kennedy, expected never to see a reunited Germany. Like Khrushchev and the Soviets they were queasy about a resurgent German nation that might draw the world into a third great global war. During the 1956 campaign, Stevenson confided to an aide that one truth an American politician could never tell the American people was that Germany would never be reunified.

Eisenhower was an exception. Having overseen Germany's conquest and occupation, he continued to hope that it would someday be reunited through free elections and tied to NATO, ensuring that the new nation served as counterweight to Soviet power and that the German military would never again menace the world. In a prophetic letter to a friend in 1953, he predicted that West Germany's "steady social, political, military, and economic advance" would one day make it a magnet to East Germany: "It might even become impossible for the Communists to hold the place by force."

Through Eisenhower's efforts, the FRG gained its sovereignty in 1955 as a NATO member. Its army was limited to twelve divisions, under the ultimate command and control of the Supreme Allied Commander in Europe. The Bonn government pledged never to make or acquire atomic weapons.

This pledge did not convince Khrushchev. As Mikoyan's son Sergo recalled, the Chairman believed that the West Germans were about to get the Bomb: "We knew that officially they would not get it, but we knew that Germany felt like a second-class power and wanted nuclear weapons so as to feel like a nation." When NATO announced that nuclear missiles would be placed at the disposal of the Supreme Allied Commander, Khrushchev wondered whether some subordinate FRG commander might not be able to launch a nuclear attack against the Soviet Union and Eastern Europe, reversing the verdict of World War II.

So deep was the Chairman's anxiety that in March 1958 he en-

---

*With his determination never to concede any form of Soviet weakness, Khrushchev was as unwilling to confess anxiety about a reunified, rearmed Germany in NATO as he was Soviet weaknesses in nuclear weapons, space, farming, and economic productivity.

dorsed the Rapacki Plan, put forward by the Polish Foreign Minister, Adam Rapacki, but almost certainly drafted in Moscow. It proposed a ban against atomic, hydrogen, and rocket weapons in Poland, Czechoslovakia, and both Germanys.

Eisenhower made the mistake of rejecting the offer. Since the West was not planning to arm the West Germans with nuclear weapons, it had little to lose. A nuclear-free zone in Central Europe would have meant some form of international control in East Germany, Czechoslovakia, and Poland that could have shaken the Soviet dominion.

By leaving open the possibility of nuclear weapons in West German hands, Eisenhower's rebuff helped to provoke Khrushchev into his Berlin ultimatum of 1958. The President replied by reinforcing American troops in Central Europe enough to prevent an easy seizure of Berlin by East German guards. Despite congressional demands, he refused to mobilize U.S. armed forces and increase the defense budget. One purpose of "Khrushchev's manufactured crisis," he said, was to "frighten free populations and governments into unnecessary and debilitating spending sprees."

The Chairman's deadline came and went. At Camp David, Eisenhower conceded to Khrushchev that Berlin's status was "abnormal." He agreed to discuss Western concessions to ease the problem, such as thinning out Western forces in Berlin and scaling down espionage and propaganda. This negotiation was halted by the collapse of the Paris summit.

During the 1960 campaign, Khrushchev's foreign policy advisers advised him to go easy on Berlin because otherwise it would force Nixon and Kennedy to outbid each other with his toughness. But at the Kremlin celebration of New Year's 1961, Khrushchev told the West German Ambassador, Hans Kroll, that the question must be "solved" within the year.

Kennedy's own statesmanlike silence on Berlin during the 1960 campaign meant that, unlike Cuba, he came to office unencumbered by campaign promises on the subject. But it also meant he had to concoct a policy almost from scratch. Khrushchev, Adenauer, and other leaders would scrutinize each of his utterances on Berlin and Germany far more intensely than if he had come to office with a well-articulated position on the issue.

The President knew that, of all his foreign problems, Berlin had the greatest immediate danger of forcing a choice between "holocaust and humiliation." He did not ever wish to have to make such a choice—certainly not during his first months in office, before he had closely studied the issue and before he had earned the respect of the Soviet Union, the American people, and the remainder of the West as a world leader.

Kennedy thus tried to sweep the issue under the rug. In January, he instructed Thompson to ask Khrushchev for time to prepare his position. In his first State of the Union message, despite his extended treatment of other world problems like the Congo, Cuba, and Laos, the President did not once mention Berlin. Asked by a reporter about the omission, he lamely explained that it was "very difficult to name every area" of trouble. For the next four months he did not once speak the word Berlin in public, as if his continued silence might encourage Khrushchev to wave the problem away.*

In February, Thompson reminded him that West Germany would hold parliamentary elections in September. If Kennedy informed Khrushchev that "real progress" on the Berlin problem "could be made after the German elections," the Chairman might be "disposed not to bring matters to a head before that event." Kennedy could resume the Eisenhower policy by scheduling a September meeting of Soviet and Western foreign ministers, which would lead if successful to a summit meeting on Berlin.

Thompson warned that unless the President took the bull by the horns, Khrushchev would "almost certainly proceed with his separate peace treaty" and attempt the "gradual strangulation of Berlin." This would be "a highly dangerous situation, and one which could get out of control."

Kennedy ignored Thompson's excellent advice. Before the Ambassador called on Khrushchev in Novosibirsk in March, the President told him not to mention Germany and Berlin. When Khrushchev inevitably raised the matter, Thompson replied, as instructed, that Kennedy found it "difficult to understand" why the Soviets found it necessary to question a situation with which, "despite obvious disadvantages to both sides, we have managed to live for many years."

As further instructed, Thompson warned that if Khrushchev created a new Berlin crisis, he would be "surprised at the unanimity with which the American people will support a firm governmental policy. . . . If there is anything which will bring about a massive increase in U.S. arms expenditures of the type which took place at the time of the Korean War, it would be the conviction that the Soviets indeed are attempting to force us out of Berlin by utilizing geographic

---

*Even in two communiqués issued jointly by the President and the West German foreign minister and Chancellor after White House meetings in February and April, Berlin was buried amid lists of other foreign policy problems that Kennedy was said to have discussed with the Germans.

advantages which the Soviets and East Germans admittedly enjoy."

After the Novosibirsk meeting, Thompson cabled a warning to Kennedy: "All my diplomatic colleagues . . . consider that in the absence of negotiations, Khrushchev will sign a separate treaty with East Germany and precipitate a Berlin crisis this year." The Chairman, he said, was disturbed by the fact that Kennedy had shown "greater militancy" than Eisenhower, which gave support to "Chinese arguments that accommodation between East and West is impossible."

Thompson suggested that the President "hold out the prospect of negotiations, which would at minimum enable Khrushchev to save face somewhat and maintain his position. . . . If we expect the Soviets to leave the Berlin problem as it is, then we must at least expect the East Germans to seal off the sector boundary in order to stop what they must consider the intolerable continuation of the refugee flow through Berlin."

Instead, Kennedy persisted in his fantasy that Khrushchev might be willing to live with the problem. As Lippmann recalled, before he himself went to see the Chairman in April, an "American authority" told him, "See if you can find out whether he wouldn't at least be willing to . . . leave everything where it is for, say, five years. In five years, we'll all be older and wiser . . . and maybe then we can negotiate." When Lippmann made the suggestion, Khrushchev looked at him as if he were insane.

If Khrushchev did not gain some sort of satisfaction on Berlin soon, he risked becoming a laughingstock. As his enemies bitterly noted, he had dropped his 1958 Berlin ultimatum after gaining Eisenhower's promise to negotiate, which proved hollow. He had politely granted Kennedy's request for time to form his Berlin position. In return, Kennedy had merely hinted that Khrushchev should be a gentleman and forget the whole matter.

The Chairman rightly felt that had it not been for his 1958 Berlin demands, Eisenhower would never have agreed to negotiate about the city. Khrushchev knew that the vulnerable position of the West in Berlin gave him a rare chance to win the Western powers' attention and force them to bargain about other issues. Experience had shown him that the Americans were inclined to rest on their sense of nuclear and economic superiority unless pressured: "If I go to a cathedral and pray for peace, nobody listens. But if I go with two bombs, they will."

For Khrushchev, removing the Berlin "cancer" from Eastern Europe and codifying the permanent division of Germany would stabilize the western frontier of the Soviet empire. A new Berlin crisis that ended in triumph would give him a new instance with which to claim that the tide was turning in favor of communism. It would serve his old aim of fracturing NATO and faith in American guarantees. It would show Soviet generals that Khrushchev had not gone soft on the West.

By May 1961, he had evidently concluded that Kennedy could be pushed on Berlin. He knew that world leaders did not duck issues in public and ask for stand-still agreements in private out of strength. The Bay of Pigs and Laos had given credence to those Khrushchev advisers who argued that Kennedy was enraptured by his liberal campaign rhetoric and immobilized by intellectual advisers when it came time to use force.

The Chairman knew that a primary reason for the President's failure to save the Bay of Pigs invasion had been fear of retaliation against Berlin. This suggested that Kennedy had little stomach to fulfill American guarantees on Berlin requiring use of nuclear weapons.

In the wake of his Cuba failure, the President was on the defensive. If Khrushchev treated him with kid gloves at Vienna, his rivals would chide him for forsaking a splendid opportunity to exploit Kennedy's misery. After the Eisenhower experience, the Chairman was eager to show that he was not subject to some kind of lovesickness that made him weak at the knees when in the presence of an American President.

More urgent crises in the Congo, Cuba, and Laos and domestic problems had kept Kennedy from convening a full-dress review of Germany and Berlin. In March, he had consulted Dean Acheson, the hawkish veteran of the Berlin Blockade, who told him that no agreement was possible that would not "open the way to early Western elimination from Berlin."

That same month, the administration publicly renounced the concessions that Eisenhower had made and evidently planned to make on Berlin at the Paris summit. Averell Harriman told the press, "All discussion on Berlin must begin from the start."

Allan Lightner, U.S. Minister in West Berlin, endorsed a further hard line. He proposed by cable that Kennedy "tell Khrushchev in blunt language" at Vienna that the "Soviets should keep their hands off Berlin": "Any indication that the President is willing to discuss interim solutions, compromises, or a modus vivendi if the Soviets sign a separate peace treaty would reduce the impact of warning Khrushchev of dire consequences of his miscalculating our resolve."

Thompson urged Kennedy to offer something to Khrushchev: "We owe it to ourselves and to the world to make every possible effort to see if some way around the present impasse can be achieved. . . . If we hope to arrive at a peaceful solution, some formula must be found which would enable both sides to save face. This is difficult but not impossible. This is an area it seems to me that the President might most usefully explore with Khrushchev in private, stating frankly what his purpose is." Otherwise Berlin would lead to "a really major crisis." War would "hang in the balance."

Bundy wrote the President, "At one extreme are those who feel that the central Soviet purpose is to drive us out of Berlin and destroy the European Alliance as a consequence. On the other extreme are those who feel that if we think in terms of accommodation, we should be able to avoid a real crisis. . . . The one thing which must be avoided . . . is any conclusion that the United States is feeble on Berlin itself. . . . We ourselves might indeed have new proposals at a later time."

Rusk suggested that Kennedy ask Khrushchev "what the Soviets really find so unsatisfactory" in the present situation. Bundy agreed: "There is a chance that you might draw him into some clearer statement of their purposes here. It's not a very good chance, though, because he will probably be cautious in tipping his hand, just as you must be." Robert Kennedy insisted to Georgi Bolshakov that the United States was "committed on Berlin."

On Saturday night, May 27, through a rainstorm, the President and Lem Billings flew on *Air Force One* for Kennedy's first stay in Hyannis Port as President. Waiting for his son, Joseph Kennedy said, "He's the President of the United States! You'd think he could at least order somebody to make a telephone call and tell his family what goddamn time he'll be home!" As a practical joke, he had spread pictures of voluptuous women all over the President's bedroom.

The next morning, a cold wind and fog knifed across Nantucket Sound. The President hobbled out of his father's house on crutches, wrapped himself in a gray Navy blanket, and sat on a lawn chair to read more Vienna briefing papers. The pain in his back was growing worse.

Cruising with Billings on his father's yacht *Marlin,* he complained, "I don't have any gift for Khrushchev." As Billings later recalled, when choosing presents for foreign leaders, the President "always wanted to give Americana. I mean everything had to be historical and with some reason. He didn't just give out stupid Steuben glass like Eisenhower did."

Billings thought of Kennedy's own new replica of the U.S.S. *Consti-*

tution. When Kennedy had first seen it, he was deterred by the price, about five hundred dollars: "Maybe Dad will buy it for my birthday." Billings had passed the word to the patriarch. Now the President realized that Old Ironsides was the ideal gift for Khrushchev at Vienna, representing the United States in 1812: "a young republic— strong, youthful, in love with freedom—exactly the kind of message I want to send Russia." As Billings recalled, "He hated to give it up, it was something he adored," but "there was no time to find anything as appropriate."

Before leaving Hyannis on Monday afternoon, Kennedy thrust his hands into his pockets and sheepishly told his father that he did not have "a cent of money." Joseph Kennedy sent his secretary upstairs for a packet of large bills. The President said, "I'll get this back to you, Dad." Watching him walk down the front steps of the house, the father muttered, "That'll be the day."

It was Kennedy's forty-fourth birthday. That evening he attended a hundred-dollar-a-plate celebration by five thousand Massachusetts Democrats in the Boston Armory, festooned in green, red, white, and blue. Kennedy's aides had asked to let him speak early so that he could get a good night's rest. After frantic negotiations, he was moved up to thirteenth place on the schedule—after party hacks, the Kennedy family priest Richard Cardinal Cushing, and Robert Frost, who famously urged the guest of honor to be "more Irish than Harvard" in Vienna.

When the President rose to speak, his ovation was hardly greater than that for the sheriff of Middlesex County, who was under indictment and whose firm had catered the dismal meal. Kennedy declared that when he went to Vienna, he would go "as the leader of the greatest revolutionary country on earth."

In 1960, he had often told of how Samuel Adams had threatened the British colonial governor with revolution, later writing, "It was then I fancied that I saw his knees tremble." This time Kennedy flubbed the tale by referring to "John Quincy Adams." None of the pols seemed to notice. He went on, "Our knees do not tremble at the word revolution. We believe in it. We believe in the progress of mankind."

Driving to the armory, he had spotted the statue of the Boston abolitionist William Lloyd Garrison and sent a state trooper back to copy the words on its base, which he now read aloud: " 'I am in earnest, I will not equivocate, I will not excuse, I will not retreat a single inch, and I will be heard.' "

* * *

Khrushchev was gliding toward Vienna on a five-car train with his wife, Anatoly Dobrynin, Gromyko, Menshikov, and the Adzhubeis. Thousands in Kiev cheered their old viceroy. In Bratislava, the Chairman told a huge crowd that while the Soviet Union was "always in favor of relaxing international tensions," he did not want to "anticipate the results of this meeting."

Before Khrushchev left Moscow, he had invited Thompson to join him at that evening's performance of the American ice-skating troupe, the Ice Capades, at the Lenin Sports Palace. The Ambassador had not seen Khrushchev in private since Novosibirsk. When he and Jane arrived at the stadium, the Chairman was sitting in his box with his son Sergei and daughter Yelena. At intermission, he took them into an adjoining salon for dinner.

Khrushchev said he had "seen enough ice shows" in his life. He had only come here tonight as an "excuse" to discuss the Vienna meeting. He bluntly warned Thompson that if he and Kennedy reached no agreement on Berlin, he would sign a separate peace treaty after the September German elections and his October Party Congress. He knew this act would "bring a period of great tension."

Thompson replied with "utmost seriousness" that Khrushchev must understand the American position: If force were used to block access to Berlin, it would be met with force. Khrushchev replied that "only a madman" would want war, but if the Americans wanted war they would get it.

Kennedy flew to New York, where he met with the Israeli Prime Minister, David Ben-Gurion, who had thought him cool toward Israel and wondered whether the President had inherited his father's anti-Semitism. On Tuesday night, May 30, Kennedy joined Jacqueline aboard *Air Force One* at Idlewild Airport. Before the plane reached the North Atlantic, the couple slipped into the two bunk beds in the stateroom behind the pilot's cabin.

Worried that the summit would create unrealistic expectations, the President had asked Salinger to deprecate the chances for success. Privately Georgi Bolshakov's assurances had led him to assume that Khrushchev was ready to deal on a test ban. Whatever went badly in Vienna would be overlooked if the summit produced what would be the first major nuclear agreement between the United States and Soviet Union. A test ban would help Kennedy to overcome the setbacks of his first spring in office and grant him considerable new world stature.

Robert Kennedy later recalled that he and his brother were "reasonably hopeful about what would happen" at Vienna on nuclear testing. They did not know that Bolshakov's insistence that Khrushchev was ready to compromise was, at best, premature or, at worst, a deliberate deception to entice the President to a summit that might not otherwise be in Kennedy's interest.

8

"Not as a Cripple"

O N WEDNESDAY MORNING, MAY 31, *AIR FORCE ONE* TAXIED TO A
stop at Orly Field in Paris. Inside the plane, Kennedy pulled
up his tie knot and brushed his hair. As drums rolled, he stepped out
the forward hatch, followed by Jacqueline, and gave his customary
choppy wave. Towering at the foot of the stairs, Charles de Gaulle
paid him the compliment of employing his rarely used English: "Have
you made a good aerial voyage?"

Kennedy toyed with the button on his jacket and mistakenly walked
past the waiting color guard. De Gaulle grasped his arm, motioning
him to stand still and accept a salute. An American diplomat translated Kennedy's arrival statement into arcane, stilted French. A
French official muttered, *"Mon Dieu,* the translator is playing Mo-
lière!" Later, Kennedy was philosophical: "You can't crucify somebody for not being as witty as I might be, but we won't use him again."

Waiting in the Orly reception room was Rose Kennedy, in Paris for her annual survey of the fashion houses. She thought her son "looked a little surprised when he spotted me." Lem Billings recalled that Kennedy was "terribly sensitive about his friends and particularly his family going on those trips. He was a new young President who had won a very close election. . . . But there wasn't anything he could do about it because Mrs. Kennedy was determined to be in on everything."

From the airport, fifty black Citroëns escorted by the mounted, saber-armed Garde Républicaine swept past a million cheering Parisians chanting "Kenn-a-dee!" and "Zhack-ee!" Dave Powers opened his car window and called out, "Commen-tally vous, pal?"

At the Quai d'Orsay, the President was shown into the blue-gray, silk-paneled bedroom of Louis XVI, his back in excruciating pain. He stripped off his clothes and with a grateful moan lowered himself into a huge golden tub of steaming water: "God, we ought to have a tub like this in the White House." Powers told him that if he played his cards right with de Gaulle, he might take it home as a "souvenir."

Before lunch, the President was driven to the Élysée Palace. He had long been fascinated by de Gaulle, one of the last great figures of World War II, who had been summoned to rescue France from the chaos of the Fourth Republic. Jacqueline had once read him passages from the General's memoirs evoking de Gaulle's image of France, which Kennedy used in speeches. Before leaving for Paris, Kennedy had memorized phrases from de Gaulle to quote during their meetings and read briefing papers on the General's efforts to assert French independence from NATO.

The President also read a memo that Bundy had requested from the Harvard political scientist Nicholas Wahl, who had met with de Gaulle half a dozen times: "Even when there is a dialogue, one usually emerges with the impression that it has all been carefully 'managed' by de Gaulle from the beginning. . . . He often uses the third person to refer to himself, which is more his own historian speaking than the megalomaniac, the latter not being completely absent."

De Gaulle had been fighting as a captain on the Western front for three years when Kennedy was born in 1917. He was almost as determined as the Soviets not to tolerate a rearmed Germany. Especially after the Bay of Pigs, he thought Kennedy "somewhat fumbling and overeager" and worried that the "young man" might not be resolute on Berlin.

In an effort to dampen the French President's anxieties and ensure Western unity before the Khrushchev summit, Kennedy began by citing Khrushchev's recent harangues to Thompson about a German peace treaty. The Allies, he said, had two options: refuse to bargain, because Western rights in Berlin were nonnegotiable, or give the "appearance of negotiation" as Eisenhower had done, by offering minor concessions.

In this palace a year before, de Gaulle had told Eisenhower that the "entire Berlin problem" came down to whether or not the Soviets wanted détente. Now he wearily reminded Kennedy that Khrushchev had been setting deadlines for two and a half years. If the Chairman planned to go to war over Berlin, he would have done so already. Kennedy said the problem was whether Khrushchev really believed in the Western commitment: even President de Gaulle had questioned whether the United States would defend Paris if it meant annihilating New York.

De Gaulle advised him to remind Khrushchev that it was the Soviets, not the West, who wanted a change. The Chairman must be made to understand that the first moment he used force against the West in Berlin, he would have general war: "That is the last thing he wants."

Jacqueline had still not recovered from John, Jr.,'s difficult birth six months before, but a week at Glen Ora had allowed her to sleep and build strength. Speaking with her during luncheon in French about Louis XVI, the Duc d'Angoulême, and the later Bourbons, de Gaulle leaned across the table and told Kennedy that his wife knew more history than most Frenchwomen.

Gesturing at Bundy, he asked, *"Qui est ce jeune homme?"* She said that he was a brilliant Harvard professor who now ran the President's national security staff. De Gaulle slowly said something about Harvard to Bundy as if he were speaking to someone who did not know the language. Bundy responded in fluent French. Jacqueline thought, *Score one for our side.*

After lunch, Kennedy returned to the Berlin problem. Existing Allied military plans assumed that any Soviet probe of Western intentions would be very limited. But what if a brigade or division was sent in? De Gaulle recommended that if access was blocked, it be restored with a new Berlin airlift. If a Western plane was downed, there would be no ambiguity. Russia was also vulnerable to economic retaliation. The Western position in Berlin was not so weak as people thought.

Kennedy asked de Gaulle to increase the French military presence in Laos. The General replied that Laos and its neighbors were "fictitious" countries, their terrain good for neither Western troops nor Western politics. Neutralization was the best solution: "The more you become involved out there against communism, the more the Communists will appear as the champions of national independence, and the more support they will receive, if only from despair. . . . You will sink step by step into a bottomless military and political quagmire, however much you spend in men and money."

That night, while dressing for de Gaulle's white-tie dinner at the Élysée, Salinger was telephoned by O'Donnell: Rusk would not be arriving in Paris tomorrow as scheduled "because of the situation in the Dominican Republic." Trujillo had been murdered. As Salinger recalled, O'Donnell said this "so matter-of-factly" that he presumed that the news had already been broken. At the Hotel Crillon, therefore, Salinger announced that Rusk would be delayed by "the assassination of General Trujillo."

After calling in the story, newsmen wondered how the United States had known so quickly of Trujillo's death, which was still being denied in the Caribbean; was the CIA involved? Salinger confessed his mistake to the President, whom he found "never angrier with me than at that moment." Rusk called Salinger from Washington: *Are you out of your mind?"*

Kennedy almost surely knew that the CIA had smuggled guns into the Dominican Republic for Trujillo's murder before backing off after the Bay of Pigs. Might Salinger's mistake now cause reporters to link Kennedy to American plotting against Trujillo? The President may have worried that on the eve of the summit, the story might lead to revelations of American assassination efforts against Castro.

That evening Salinger learned that Trujillo's death had been confirmed. Overjoyed, he went out drinking and did not return to bed until six the next morning.

Despite Kennedy's gracious references to French influence "which stretches around the globe" and its place as "America's oldest friend," de Gaulle remained bent on making his country more independent and influential in world politics. On Thursday, he told Kennedy that while France would not disrupt NATO during a Berlin crisis, he must expect it to chart its own course thereafter.

The President replied with the standard American position that if the Russians attacked Western Europe, he would retaliate with nuclear weapons. If European nations built separate defense establishments, those without the Bomb might be forced into resentment and neutralism.

When Kennedy said that he regarded European and American defense as the same, de Gaulle replied, "Since you say so, Mr. President, I believe you," but asked how anyone could be certain. The Soviet

Union had perhaps "ten times the killing power of France," but she might not attack if she knew that France could "tear off an arm" of Russia.

The General that night gave his grand dinner for the Americans in the Hall of Mirrors at Versailles, followed by a ballet and fireworks. Earlier that day Jacqueline had toured Josephine Bonaparte's home with the French Minister of Culture, André Malraux. She did not object when Malraux said that her husband spoke French "with a bad Cuban accent." Kennedy was proud of his wife's exuberant reception everywhere in Paris. He told aides, "De Gaulle and I are hitting it off all right, probably because I have such a charming wife." Watching the General and Jacqueline at Versailles, he murmured, "God, she's really laying it on, isn't she?"

Before the two leaders finished their talks on Friday, Kennedy said, "You've studied being head of a country for fifty years. Have you found out anything I should know?" De Gaulle told him not to pay too much attention to advisers or inherited policies; what counted for every man was his own judgment.

At the end of Kennedy's visit, the General uttered a compliment that he expected the Americans to publicize: "I have more confidence in your country now." Kennedy later told friends that de Gaulle cared only for his country's "selfish" interests but that he was grateful for the General's concealment of their differences over Berlin, Laos, and NATO.

He took a quiet Friday dinner at the Quai d'Orsay with Rusk, Bundy, Sorensen, Thompson, Bohlen, and Kohler. Harriman had arrived from Geneva with a late report on the deadlocked talks on Laos. He advised the President to speak gently with Khrushchev about how they both saw the world: "Go in and relax and take it easy and be humorous and funny and open."

On Saturday morning, June 3, *Air Force One* moved away from the Orly terminal. A Secret Service man cried out, "Stop that plane!" Onto the field careened a station wagon carrying Mrs. Kennedy's maid, social secretary, and luggage, which were put aboard the aircraft. During the flight to Vienna, the President gave his briefing papers one more look. Over rolls and orange juice, he consulted with Thompson, who gave him a final warning: "Avoid ideology, because Khrushchev will talk circles around you."

Kennedy's back was still contorted with pain. His doctors had told him that if he must go to Europe, he should use crutches. He had shaken his head: he was "simply not" going to meet Khrushchev "as a cripple." As a Congressman in 1949, Kennedy himself had charged that the Kurile Islands and other strategic points had been "given" to Stalin by a "sick" Roosevelt at Yalta. He wanted no such talk about his performance at Vienna.

On the day of Kennedy's inauguration, Admiral Arthur Radford, former Chairman of the Joint Chiefs, had arrived early for an F Street Club luncheon being given for Eisenhower after the ceremonies. Watching the new President deliver his speech on television, Radford was startled to note that although Kennedy was standing without coat or hat in frigid weather, heavy beads of perspiration were rolling down his forehead.

"He's all hopped up!" called out General Howard Snyder, the retiring White House physician. Privy to FBI and Secret Service information that Eisenhower had also seen, Snyder told Radford that Kennedy was "prescribed a shot of cortisone every morning to keep him in good operating condition. Obviously this morning he was given two because of the unusual rigors he must endure, and the brow sweating is the result of the extra dose."

Snyder added that people dependent on cortisone moved from a high to a low when the medicine's effect wore off: "I hate to think of what might happen to the country if Kennedy is required at three A.M. to make a decision affecting the national security."

In June 1960, the co-chairman of Lyndon Johnson's presidential campaign, India Edwards, had told reporters that Kennedy had Addison's disease: "If it weren't for cortisone," he "wouldn't be alive." Sorensen deflected the charge by saying, "I don't know that he is on anything any more than you and I are on."

That fall burglars tried to break into the offices of both of Kennedy's New York doctors. They were almost surely looking for his medical records, which had been wisely filed under a different name. The burglars were not the only ones interested in Kennedy's health; William Casey, the New York Republican who twenty years later ran the CIA for Ronald Reagan, investigated the subject for the Nixon campaign.*

Serious people who raised the issue of Kennedy's health worried that it might affect his decision-making on national security. Raymond Moley of *Newsweek* warned Nixon after the 1960 election that the new

---

*Despite Casey's later appetite for covert action, there is no evidence that he or anyone else in the Nixon campaign was behind the burglary. Nevertheless, one must note the resemblance to the 1971 break-in at the office of Daniel Ellsberg's psychiatrist in quest of information that could be used by the Nixon White House to discredit the man who had disseminated the "Pentagon Papers" on Vietnam.

President might suffer "palpable mental lapses" that could usher in "a serious crisis. Perhaps you know all or more than I do, but with Bill Casey I went into it thoroughly. And it is frightening. There are several contingencies which may well mean a one-term Presidency—even the succession of Johnson."

Long before such cases as Woodrow Wilson's stroke and Roosevelt's terminal weariness at Yalta, historians have tried to assess the impact of physical disability on political decision-making. The chief problem with such retrospective diagnosis is the lack of reliable and comprehensive information. In the absence of a Lord Moran, the private physician to Churchill who recorded his patient's daily condition and treatment, we shall probably never know the exact state of Kennedy's health as he flew to Vienna.

Aside from his bad back, the President's most enduring problem was Addison's disease, which impairs the adrenal glands and weakens the body. Once almost always fatal, by the time Kennedy's case was diagnosed in 1947, the illness was treated by pellets of corticosteroid hormones implanted in the patient's thigh, which extended life expectancy to five or ten years. By 1953, Kennedy began using a new orally administered cortisone, which promised a normal life span.

Nonetheless he knew that the treatment was not foolproof and that Addison's rendered one more prone to infection, especially during surgery. After his 1954 spinal fusion operation, he was given the last rites of the Catholic church. Awareness of his vulnerability had much to do with his private fascination with men dying young, the incessant inquisition about what was the best way to die, the insistence on treating each day as if it were his last.

He hated the bloating effect of the cortisone treatment. Looking in a mirror, he said, "This is not my face." Cortisone could also inflate the user's stamina, libido, and sense of well-being, causing the patient's mood to oscillate.

Replying to rumors, Kennedy's managers declared that he did not have Addison's disease, reasoning that the "classic" form of the illness came from tuberculosis. Dr. Travell issued a statement which said that Kennedy's adrenal glands "do function" but did not mention that the reason was cortisone. The cover-up succeeded, but it denied Americans the knowledge that they were electing a President whose treatment for a chronic illness might affect his decision-making and negotiation skills and, conceivably, his survival.*

---

*The cover-up continued in November 1963. At the possible behest of Robert Kennedy, the version of the autopsy report released to the public omitted the finding that "the President suffered from bilateral adrenal atrophy."

Superimposed upon Kennedy's history of Addison's disease was his ancient back problem. He once told Billings that he would trade all his political successes and all his money "just to be out of pain." One of his doctors thought that he was "born with an unstable back," perhaps aggravated by football. He badly injured his back when the PT-109 was split in half by a Japanese destroyer. He submitted to a life-threatening spinal fusion operation because he "couldn't take any more pain."

Still suffering, he began seeing Dr. Travell, one of the first physicians to treat muscular disorders with injections of the anesthetic procaine. Jacqueline later recalled that the treatments "changed Jack's life." In 1960, he asked Travell not to leave the United States for the duration of the campaign.

During his visit to Paris, the President spent almost every spare moment soaking in his golden bathtub at the Quai d'Orsay. Travell injected him with procaine two or three times a day. This distressed the White House physician Admiral George Burkley, an Eisenhower holdover. Burkley wished that Kennedy would use the more conventional approach of strengthening his back through exercise and physical therapy. Once numbness from procaine wore off, the pain returned, requiring larger doses. Burkley feared that the President might next require narcotics.

There were more grounds for this worry than Burkley may have known. Kennedy was also being treated by an eccentric known in Manhattan café society as "Doctor Feelgood" for boosting his patients' mood and stamina with what he called "vitamin and enzyme shots." The doctor's syringes may have contained vitamins and enzymes but they also contained amphetamines, steroids, hormones, and animal organ cells, which he used to keep celebrity clients such as Eddie Fisher, Truman Capote, Alan Jay Lerner, and Tennessee Williams coming back. At least one patient later died of what the New York medical examiner called "acute amphetamine poisoning."

Max Jacobson was a German-Jewish refugee who emigrated to the United States in 1936. With his thick dark hair, horn-rimmed glasses, and fingernails stained black with chemicals, he looked like a mad scientist. He experimented in his East Side office and a Long Island shack with magnets, precious stones, boiling vials, and cauldrons, professing to search for a cure for multiple sclerosis. Drawn to famous names, he claimed to have invented the world's first laser microscope and that a "completely insane" partner had absconded with the device.

Eddie Fisher recalled that Jacobson "prided himself on being able to diagnose his patients at a glance, and his injections were designed to treat them for fatigue, nervous tension, vitamin deficiencies, or anything else he thought was wrong with them." After injecting the singer backstage, the doctor would boom, "Anybody else? You, *ja*? You want it in the arm or the ass?" Sometimes he injected patients in the solar plexus, the back of the neck, and the spinal column. Using oranges, he also showed them how to inject themselves.

Kennedy was evidently referred to Jacobson in September 1960 by his friend Charles Spalding, who was concerned about his exhaustion from campaigning. By his own account, Jacobson saw Kennedy at the White House, Palm Beach, New York, and Hyannis Port, where Joseph Kennedy's chauffeur recalled being told, "Dr. Jacobson's here. . . . Do you want a vitamin shot?"

Another of the President's doctors later said he warned him to stop seeing Jacobson: "I said that if I ever heard he took another shot, I'd make sure it was known. No President with his finger on the red button has any business taking stuff like that." But as late as 1963, Jacobson was still close enough to Kennedy to be photographed with him in sport clothes in Palm Beach.

William Manchester recorded in his 1983 volume *One Brief Shining Moment* that after the President arrived in Paris, while his golden bathtub was being filled, he "gave himself a novocaine injection." But if the injection was one of Travell's prescriptions, Kennedy would almost certainly have summoned her from her nearby room to administer it. This suggests that he may have actually been injecting himself with one of Jacobsen's amphetamine formulas.

This explanation is not incompatible with Jacobson's own account. In an unpublished autobiography, he recorded that he did not arrive in Paris until later that day. He recalled being brought that evening to Kennedy's suite, where he injected him once to give him "a restful night" and again the next morning, before the talks with de Gaulle resumed. By Jacobson's account, he flew on with the President to Vienna on *Air Force One* to provide more treatments during the summit with Khrushchev. As Mrs. Jacobson said years later, "The last thing Kennedy wanted the Russians to know was that he was in anything but the best of health."

The President's resort to the New York doctor was not quite as bizarre as it may at first seem. In late May 1961, he found himself locked into a summit with Khrushchev, doubled over with pain, and surrounded by advisers admonishing him to extinguish any suspicion Khrushchev had that he might be soft or indecisive on Berlin or other matters. He was facing the possibility that when he confronted the

Chairman he would be on crutches and exhausted from pain—especially after three densely packed days with de Gaulle in Paris.

Kennedy's long medical history had instilled in him roughly the same lack of awe for medical experts as he held for the political experts who had told him he had no chance to win the Senate in 1952 or the Presidency in 1960. He knew that more orthodox doctors looked askance at Travell's procaine injections, but as far as he was concerned she had succeeded where the so-called experts had failed.

He had not found Jacobson in some back alley. His brother-in-law Stanislas Radziwill, Charles Spalding, and other respectable friends were among the doctor's clientele. The President evidently felt that if Jacobson was able to put him in fighting condition for Paris and Vienna, he would have done what his other doctors could not. Better to take whatever was in Jacobson's shots and ask questions later. Kennedy reputedly said, "I don't care if it's horse piss. It works."

The President's use of mutually resentful doctors was perfectly matched to the way he sought political advice. He preferred to assign a problem to several advisers and let them compete. Thus he avoided being on what he called the "leading strings" of a single aide.

The problem with this was that medicine was not the same thing as politics. Now that Kennedy was President, he should have been vastly more careful in pursuing his medical experimentation than he had been as a Senator. The stakes now were not one political career but literally the fate of the world.

At no time during the European trip was a single doctor supervising Kennedy's entire medical treatment. No one was in overall charge to anticipate or deal with the danger that an interaction of cortisone, procaine, amphetamines, or whatever else Jacobson had in his syringe could cause the President to behave at Vienna in a way that could have had dire consequences.

Even in small doses, amphetamines cause side effects such as nervousness, garrulousness, impaired judgment, overconfidence, and, when the drug wears off, depression. What if Kennedy should display these qualities in Vienna, when Khrushchev would be scrutinizing every aspect of his behavior, assessing his capacity, mettle, and judgment?

On Friday afternoon, Khrushchev's train had reached the Austrian border, where it was coupled to an Austrian locomotive for its last forty miles to Vienna, arriving at five o'clock. Among the welcoming committee at the Vienna station was the Chairman's enemy Molotov, smiling sardonically. With no conviction, Khrushchev told him, "We must get together." The old rival replied, "Nice weather we're having."

Unbeknownst to both men, the CIA in 1961 thought Molotov might be discouraged enough about his prospects in the Soviet Union to accept a million dollars, funneled through an American magazine, to defect to the West or at least submit to a debriefing. An offer was being prepared.

Scattered crowds lined the streets as Khrushchev rode by in an open car to the presidential palace, where he called on the Austrian chief of state, Adolf Schärf. Then he rode on to the Soviet Embassy residence, equipped with swimming pool and tennis courts. His aides were disturbed by the inflexibility about Berlin that had emerged from Kennedy's talks with de Gaulle in Paris: "A militaristic exercise and poor preparation for the meeting here."

It was raining on Saturday morning when *Air Force One* landed at ten-fifty. Placards cried, GIVE 'EM HELL, JACK! . . . HELP BERLIN . . . LIFT THE IRON CURTAIN . . . INNOCENTS ABROAD SAY HOWDY. Austrians handed out leaflets saying, "Mr. Kennedy, Europe does not forget Yalta."

Nervous that the President would attract more enthusiastic throngs, the Soviets had tried to suggest no parades for either Kennedy or Khrushchev. The Americans had responded by adding more limousines and flags. As in other cities, the local CIA station worked overtime to make sure that the President's welcome was warm.

As the Kennedys rode through the rains to the presidential palace and on to the American residence, Lem Billings saw "more people than I had ever seen before, all of them roaring with enthusiasm." He later recalled that Kennedy's "attitude toward great crowds was always the same. The bigger the crowd, the greater was his pleasure. . . . Obviously the Austrians wanted to show their preference for the President of the United States over the Premier of Russia."

A chill wind shook the pines and rattled windows as the President and First Lady walked into the grim stone American residence. Surrounded by a barbed-wire fence and police dogs wearing wire-mesh muzzles, the mansion had once belonged to a Jewish merchant driven out by the Nazis. During the war, it served as a local headquarters for Hitler's SS.

Kennedy paced the upstairs hallways. He wondered whether Khrushchev would remember meeting him at the Foreign Relations Committee tea in 1959. According to Jacobson, the President summoned him and said, "Khrushchev is supposedly on his way. You'd better give me something for my back."

At 12:45 P.M., Kennedy and his aides heard the ZIL limousine crunching up the circular gravel driveway. He stepped out onto the red-carpeted front steps. When the black car halted, Khrushchev swung out his short legs and stood below the President. Two medals were pinned to his breast and lapel.

Constrained by a tight corset to keep his back straight, Kennedy leaned stiffly forward, wearing a fixed smile. Thrusting out his hand, he looked Khrushchev in the eye and said in his best Boston street manner, "How are you? Glad to see you." Looking up with a slightly patronizing upturn of the lips, Khrushchev shook Kennedy's hand and then started up the stairs.

Photographers shouted, "Another handshake!" Kennedy told his interpreter, "Say to the Chairman that it is all right to shake hands if it is all right with him." After a second handshake, the President stepped backward. Menshikov followed and stamped on Dean Rusk's foot, apologizing profusely.

His mouth a straight line, Kennedy thrust his hands into his coat pockets and looked Khrushchev up and down. Reporters scribbled fiercely in their notebooks. Later he told O'Donnell, "After all the studying and talking I've done on him in the last few weeks, you can't blame me for being interested in getting a look at him."

Frank Holeman, who was in Vienna to cover the summit for the *New York Daily News,* received a telephone call from his old Soviet contact Yuri Gvozdev, who asked him to meet him at a coffeehouse. The two men had not seen each other since Nixon's trip to Moscow in 1959. Now, as Holeman recalled, "Yuri was trying to find out if I knew the American position at the summit. I was trying to find out if he knew the Soviet position. We met at a different place each time. When we came to one place, he said, 'Let's get out of here.' "

During the Geneva summit in 1955, the local CIA station had a clandestine source with contacts in the Soviet delegation. Every evening the source came to a nightclub for debriefing on Soviet reactions to the day's proceedings, information which was slipped to Eisenhower when he awoke the next morning. In Vienna, neither Holeman nor Gvozdev could shed much light on what their leaders were about to say to each other. As Holeman recalled, "Neither of us struck oil."

* * *

Khrushchev walked into the American residence, his heavy footsteps shaking the rafters. The President introduced him to members of his staff, including O'Donnell, who glared. Later Kennedy told his aide, "He must have thought you were a spy from the IRA." The two leaders sat down side by side on a rose-colored sofa in the red, gray, and gold music room. Seated on a half-circle of chairs were advisers: Gromyko, Dobrynin, Menshikov, Rusk, Kohler, Bohlen, Thompson. Underneath the room was the entrance to an SS escape tunnel.

The President started off by saying that, of course, Khrushchev knew "our Ambassador to Moscow." Khrushchev retorted, "You mean *our* Ambassador." All laughed.

Kennedy said how pleased he was to see the Chairman again: as he had mentioned to Gromyko and Menshikov, he was "extremely interested" in discussing "at least to a certain extent" matters affecting their relations. He hoped that during the next two days "a better understanding of the problems confronting us could be reached."

Khrushchev replied that he too wanted the conversations to be useful. Recalling their first meeting in 1959, he needled Kennedy by noting that he had been late. There had been "no opportunity to say much except hello and goodbye." He recalled mentioning that he had heard he was "a young and promising man" in politics. Now he was pleased to meet him as President.*

"I remember you said that I looked young to be a Senator, but I've aged a lot since then."

"Did I *really* say that to you?" Khrushchev said that young people always wanted to look older and the old to look younger. As a boy, he had been offended when people misjudged his youthful appearance. Then his hair had begun to turn gray at twenty-two, which solved the problem. He would be happy to exchange ages or even split his years with the President.

Turning to business, Kennedy declared that their common objective should be to conduct their competition without endangering peace: "The problem is to find means of avoiding situations in which our two countries become committed to actions involving their security." How could two great nations with different social systems, con-

---

*The account of the private Kennedy-Khrushchev conversations in Vienna in this book benefits from interviews by the author and other primary sources but is based on the official memoranda of conversations drafted by the President's interpreter, Alexander Akalovsky, available at long last. The U.S. government sealed these documents for twenty-nine years after the Vienna summit, until September 5, 1990, when they were released by the Archivist of the United States in response to this author's four years of appeal.

fronting each other around the world, avoid head-on collision in an era of great change?

Khrushchev replied that the Soviet Union had long worked for friendly relations with the United States but would not do so at the expense of other peoples: "The United States is a rich country and has all the necessary resources. So far, the Soviet Union has been poorer than the United States and it recognizes that fact. However the Soviet Union will develop—not at U.S. expense, because it has no predatory intentions, but rather by developing its own human and natural resources." He did not wish to conceal that the Soviet Union wanted "to become richer than the United States." But it did not wish to "stand in the way of U.S. economic development."

Kennedy replied that he was impressed with the Soviet economic growth rate: surely this was a "source of satisfaction" to the Chairman, as American growth was to the United States.

Khrushchev said he could not expect to convert the President to communism, but "the West must recognize that communism exists and has won the right to develop. Such recognition should be *de facto* and not *de jure.*" American policy under John Foster Dulles had been based "on the premise of liquidation of the Communist system." But communism would finally triumph "through the spread of ideas."

Kennedy said that Khrushchev's remarks raised a very important problem: "You wish to destroy the influence of my country where it has traditionally been present. You wish to liquidate the free system in other countries." At the same time, the Soviet Union objected to any efforts to liquidate Communist systems.

Khrushchev called this "an incorrect interpretation of Soviet policy. The Soviet Union is against implanting its policy in other states. As a matter of fact, this would be an impossible task. What the Soviet Union says is that communism will triumph. This is a different proposition. . . . The Soviet Union proceeds from one assumption alone—namely, that any change in the social system should depend on the will of the peoples themselves."

He said that the Soviet Union was challenging the capitalist system just as the French Revolution was a response to the Holy Alliance created by feudalist Russia. His country had "proposed general and complete disarmament" to demonstrate "its intention not to use arms." The U.S.S.R. believed in its system, just as the President believed in his, but this was "not a matter for argument, much less for war."

Kennedy replied that the American position was that "people should have free choice." When Communist minorities seized control, the Chairman considered this historical inevitability. The United

States did not. Obviously they could not avoid disagreement, but he hoped that they could at least avoid direct military confrontation.

Khrushchev said he hoped he had misunderstood: had the President said that if communism moved into new areas, the United States would be in conflict with the Soviet Union? Dams could not be placed in the way of the development of the human mind. "The Spanish Inquisition burned people who disagreed with it, but ideas did not burn and eventually conquered."

History should be the judge: "People will judge capitalism and communism by the results of their respective efforts. If capitalism ensures better living for people, it will win. . . . If communism achieves this goal, it will be the winner." He wanted to "emphasize" that what he had in mind was "a victory of ideas, not a military victory. In any event, the military aspect has become unimportant today. . . . Ideas should not be borne on bayonets or missile warheads."

Kennedy wryly noted that Mao Tse-tung had said political power came out of the barrel of a rifle. Khrushchev doubted that Mao had really said such a thing: "Marxists have always been against war."

The President said that he and the Chairman owed it to their people to "have this struggle for ideas, which is part of our times, conducted without affecting the vital security interests of the two countries." Both the Americans and the Soviets had certain essential interests. "The struggle in other areas should be conducted in a way which would not involve the two countries directly and would not affect their national interest or prestige."

As the Chairman knew from history, it was very easy to get involved in a struggle that would affect the peace of the world. "My ambition is to secure peace. If we fail in that effort, both our countries will lose. . . . Our two countries possess modern weapons. . . . If our two countries should miscalculate, they would lose for a long time to come."

Khrushchev cried, "Miscalculation! All I ever hear from your people and your news correspondents and your friends in Europe and everyplace else is that damned word miscalculation." Did America want the Soviet Union to sit like a schoolboy with hands on top of the desk? "We don't make mistakes. We will not make war by mistake." Moscow would defend its vital interests whether the United States called it miscalculation or not. "You ought to take that word and bury it in cold storage and never use it again." The U.S.S.R. did not want war but would not be "intimidated."

Kennedy retorted that, as Khrushchev knew, history had shown that it was "impossible to predict the next move of any country. . . . Western Europe has suffered a great deal because of its failure to foresee with precision what other countries would do." Just recently, he had himself conceded "certain misjudgments" by the United States. In the Korean War, the United States had "failed to foresee what the Chinese would do. . . . The purpose of this meeting is to introduce precision in judgments of the two sides and to obtain a clearer understanding of where we are going."

Khrushchev agreed: if their meeting succeeded, the "expenses in- curred" would be "well justified." If they failed, "the hopes of the peoples would be frustrated." At 2 P.M., they adjourned for lunch.

In the dining room, Khrushchev downed a dry martini: "Like vodka." Accompanied by nine aides each, the two leaders sat down to a luncheon of beef Wellington. Kennedy asked the Chairman about his medals. Khrushchev touched his chest with his chin: "This one is the Lenin Peace Price." Kennedy told the interpreter, "Tell him I hope they never take it away from him." Khrushchev laughed.

Trading stories about outer space, Khrushchev revealed that Soviet scientists had feared the psychological effects of orbital flight. They had encoded Gagarin's instructions so that only a sane person could use them. The precaution had happily proved unnecessary; Gagarin had even sung songs while in orbit. The President asked why their countries could not fly together to the moon. Khrushchev said he must be cautious: space flight could be used for military advantage. Then he said, "All right, why not?"

Briefed on Khrushchev's favorite subject, Rusk told the Chairman about a new fast-growing American corn that would produce two or more annual crops in the same field. "Remarkable," said Khrushchev, "but do you know that we have found a way to make vodka from natural gas?" The President said, "It sounds like another of Dean Rusk's corn stories."

Khrushchev told Kennedy that he had "voted" for him in 1960 by waiting until after the election to release the RB-47 fliers: "We kept Nixon from being able to claim that he could deal with the Russians." The President laughed. "You're right. I admit you played a role in the election and cast your vote for me."

Khrushchev asked Kennedy how he got along with Gromyko. "All right," replied the President. "My wife thinks he has a nice smile. Why do you ask?" Khrushchev: "Well, a lot of people think Gromyko looks like Nixon." Laughter up and down the table.

Raising his glass, Kennedy stood up and said that having welcomed Khrushchev to the United States in 1959, he was now glad to welcome him to this small piece of the United States in Vienna. Khrushchev rose and reminisced about Eisenhower. He was "almost certain" that the old General had not known about the U-2 plane sent on May Day 1960 but had chivalrously taken the blame. He had respected Eisenhower and was sorry that his Soviet tour had had to be canceled. He hoped to welcome Kennedy to the U.S.S.R. "when the time is ripe. . . . The road is open."

Playing to his audience, Khrushchev recalled that Nixon had tried to convert the Soviet people to capitalism by showing them a "dream kitchen" which did not exist and never would. "I apologize for referring to a citizen of the United States, but only Nixon could think of such nonsense."*

He complained of the commercial language so often used in dealings with the Soviet Union: "You give this and we'll give that." What was he supposed to concede? "We are blamed for Communist parties in other countries, but I don't even know who their leaders are. I am too busy at home." He decried the idea of mutual concessions in negotiation.

He said that Russians admired Americans—especially their technological success. He and the President should work together to improve their peoples' futures. Hadn't the Soviet Union decorated American engineers who helped build the country after the Revolution? He recalled that one engineer came back to the Soviet Union for a visit and mentioned that he was building houses in Turkey. Of course, the Soviets knew "that in fact he was building military bases there. But this is a matter for his own conscience."

Khrushchev toasted Kennedy's health. He envied the President's youth: "If I were your age, I would devote even more energy to our cause. Still, even at sixty-seven, I am not renouncing the competition."

After lunch, Kennedy took Khrushchev for a stroll in the residence gardens, accompanied only by interpreters. Reading the minutes of Eisenhower's Camp David conversations with Khrushchev in 1959, he had noted that the Chairman became more temperate during a walk in the woods, away from the others in his entourage.

As Kennedy and Khrushchev walked in the newly emerged sun, O'Donnell watched from a second-floor window, drinking a glass of

---

*This referred to the American exhibition in Moscow in 1959 where Khrushchev and Nixon had held their "kitchen debate." Although every appliance in the model kitchen was available to American consumers, Khrushchev still refused to believe it.

Austrian beer. He noticed that Khrushchev was shaking his finger and "snapping" at the President "like a terrier."

By Kennedy's account, he started the conversation by saying that they both had a special responsibility for peace: "I propose to tell you what I can do and what I can't do, what my problems and possibilities are, and then you can do the same." According to Khrushchev, the President described the narrowness of his 1960 victory and his weakness in Congress and asked him not to demand too many concessions because he could be turned out of the Presidency.

Khrushchev replied with a harangue on Berlin. He complained about the American insistence on German reunification: his own son had been killed by the German army. Kennedy replied that his brother had also been killed by the Germans. He had not come to Vienna "to talk about a war of twenty years ago." The United States could not turn its back on the West Germans and pull out of Berlin.

To ease the tension, Kennedy asked how Khrushchev managed to have such long conversations as those with Humphrey and Lippmann without interruption. His own White House schedule was "very crowded." He was "constantly wanted on the telephone." The Chairman replied that the Soviet system had been decentralized under his leadership.

Kennedy explained that the American system of consultation between the President and Congress was a "time-consuming process." Khrushchev seized the opening: "Well, why don't you switch to our system?" The President invited him inside for further talk without their advisers. At 3:20 P.M., they returned to the music room, this time sitting on pink damask chairs.

The President restated his morning thesis in terms more likely to appeal to Khrushchev. Noting the Chairman's reference to the death of feudalism, he said he understood this to mean that capitalism would be succeeded by communism. This was "disturbing." As the Chairman well knew, the French Revolution had brought "great disturbances and upheavals throughout Europe.

"Even earlier, the struggle between Catholics and Protestants . . . caused the Hundred Years War. . . . When systems are in transition, we should be careful, particularly today, when modern weapons are at hand. Whatever the result of the present competition—and no one can be sure what it will be—both sides should act in such a way as to prevent them from coming into direct contact and thus prejudicing the establishment of lasting peace." Even the Russian Revolution had produced convulsions and "intervention by other countries."

He wanted to restate what he had meant by miscalculation. In Washington, he had to try to make judgments about events—"judgments which may be accurate or not." Hoping to win Khrushchev over with a self-deprecating remark, he said that he himself had miscalculated at the Bay of Pigs. "It was more than a mistake. It was a failure."

This admission did not have its desired effect. Frustrated, he blurted out to Khrushchev, "We admit our mistakes. Do you ever admit you are wrong?" The Chairman said, "Oh, yes, in the speech before the Twentieth Party Congress I admitted Stalin's mistakes." Kennedy replied, "Those weren't *your* mistakes."

The Chairman went on to say that he had liked the President's May statement to Congress that it was difficult to defend ideas that would not improve people's living standards. But the President had drawn the "wrong conclusion" if he thought that "when people rise against tyrants, that is a result of Moscow's activities. That is not so. Failure by the U.S. to understand this generates danger. The U.S.S.R. does not foment revolution, but the United States always looks for outside forces whenever certain upheavals occur."

Khrushchev asked how he and the President could work anything out if the United States was inclined to regard revolution everywhere simply as the result of Communist machinations. The Soviet Union "supports the aspirations of the people." The instigator of revolution was the United States, with its support of "tyrannical regimes."

Look at Cuba! During Castro's battles in the late 1950s, American capitalists had supported Batista: "This is why the anger of the Cuban people turned against the United States." The President's decision to launch a landing against Cuba had "only strengthened the revolutionary forces and Castro's own position, because the people of Cuba were afraid that they would get another Batista and lose the achievements of the revolution."

Khrushchev warned that while Castro was no Communist, "you are well on the way to making him a good one." The President had claimed that the United States attacked Cuba because the island threatened American security: "Can six million people really be a threat to the mighty U.S.?" If the United States felt threatened by tiny Cuba, what was the Soviet Union to do about Turkey and Iran? "These two countries are followers of the United States. They march in its wake, and they have U.S. bases and rockets."

Khrushchev mocked the Shah's claim that his power was granted by God; in fact, "everyone" knew the Shah's power had actually been seized for him by his father, who was no God but only an army sergeant. "If the U.S. believes that it is free to act, then what should the U.S.S.R. do? The U.S. has set a precedent for intervention in internal affairs of other countries. The U.S.S.R. is stronger than Turkey and Iran, just as the U.S. is stronger than Cuba." He warned that, "to use the President's term," this situation might generate some miscalculation too.

Kennedy said he held "no brief for Batista." And if the Shah did not improve his people's condition, Iran would have to change too.* He objected to the Castro regime not because it had ousted commercial monopolies but because of "Castro's destruction of the right of free choice and his stated intent to use Cuba as a base for expansion in the neighboring area." This "could eventually create a peril to the United States." As for American bases in Turkey and Iran, "these two countries are so weak that they could be no threat to the U.S.S.R.—no more than Cuba to the U.S."

The President reminded Khrushchev that the Soviet Union had said it would not tolerate hostile governments in areas it regarded as of vital interest. What would the Chairman do if a pro-American government were established in Warsaw? "The United States stands for the right of free choice for all peoples." If Castro had acted in that spirit, he might have won American support.

Kennedy reiterated that it was "critical to have the changes occurring in the world and affecting the balance of power take place in a way that would not involve the prestige or the treaty commitments of our two countries." If certain governments should fail to give their people a better standard of living and worked "in the interest of only a small group," their days would be numbered.

Khrushchev replied, "If Castro has not held any elections, this is an internal affair and it grants no one the right to intervene. If Castro fails to give freedom to his people, he will detach himself from them and be just as removed as Batista was. It would be a different situation if our two countries took it upon themselves to decide this question."

He hoped that American-Cuban relations would improve. "Such a statement might sound strange to the United States, but the U.S.S.R. believes that this would improve relations not only in the Western Hemisphere but also throughout the world." Once again he compared Cuba to Turkey: when the Ankara government was toppled in May 1960, the Soviet Union had remained neutral "because it regarded the change as an internal affair of that country."

---

*This comment was soon leaked to the Shah, who began worrying whether Kennedy was pondering an effort to remove him from power. After the Vienna summit, Dean Rusk told NATO officials that there now seemed a chance that Khrushchev would move against Iran later in 1961.

* * *

Turning to Laos, Khrushchev said that the President "knew very well" that the United States was behind the coup against Souvanna Phouma in December 1960. They should "be frank and recognize" that both of their countries were sending arms to Laos. But just as with Mao Tse-tung's defeat of Chiang Kai-shek, "the side supported by the U.S.S.R. will be more successful because the arms supplied by the United States are directed against the people."

He and the President must be patient about Laos: "If the United States supports old, moribund, reactionary regimes, then a precedent of intervention in internal affairs will be set, which might cause a clash between our two countries."

Kennedy replied, "We regard . . . Sino-Soviet forces and the forces of the United States and Western Europe as being more or less in balance." He said that he did not wish to discuss the details of each of their military postures, but this was how he saw the situation.*

The President's declaration sent Khrushchev into near ecstasy. For the rest of his life he boasted that at this summit the leader of the United States had finally acknowledged that there was rough parity between the two great powers. Dictating his memoirs in the late 1960s, he praised Kennedy for understanding that the Soviet bloc had amassed such economic and military might "that the United States and its allies could no longer seriously consider going to war against us."

In Washington, when the Joint Chiefs learned of Kennedy's comment, they were furious.

The President went on to say that the United States had three basic objectives. First, "free choice through elections for all people." Second, "defense of our strategic interests." Third, ensuring that events in the 1960s would not be "greatly disturbing to the balance of power" in the world. One such disturbing event, he said, would be the growing military potential of the Chinese. Kennedy may have raised the subject of China to see whether Khrushchev might suggest some joint effort to keep Peking from acquiring nuclear weapons.

The Chairman said only that the United States should recognize China, allow it into the UN, and end the "occupation" of Taiwan. If

---

*After their Camp David talk in April, Eisenhower recorded Kennedy's belief "that the two great powers have now neutralized each other in atomic weapons and inventories, but that in numbers of troops, and our exterior communications as opposed to the interior communications of the Communists, we are relatively weak. He did not seem to think that our great sea power counteracted this situation completely."

the Soviet Union were in China's place, it would have attacked Taiwan long ago. (This was balderdash; the Soviets had in fact restrained Mao in his efforts against the island.) The President replied by citing the "constant hostility" of Peking toward the United States and noting that the Taiwan question involved American strategic interests.

Knowing that Laos was one of the areas on which Bolshakov had suggested that Khrushchev was ready to make concessions, Kennedy said that while Laos was "relatively unimportant from the strategic standpoint," the United States had commitments in the area under the Southeast Asia Treaty Organization. He added that, "speaking frankly," American policy in Southeast Asia had not always been "wise."

He had not yet been able to ascertain "what the people's desires in that area are." There were nine or ten thousand Pathet Lao, who had two distinct advantages. "One is that they are for change." Second, the Pathet Lao were getting "support not only in the form of supplies, but also in the form of Viet Minh manpower, which has made them a stronger force." Last March he and the Chairman had agreed on a "neutral and independent Laos." Now they must find "a solution not involving the prestige or the interests of our two countries," including a cease-fire and a mechanism to verify it.

Khrushchev changed the subject; he wanted to say "a few words about the so-called guerrilla warfare against regimes that are not to the liking of the United States. There has been a lot of talk about this kind of warfare in the United States, and this is a dangerous policy."

The President should believe him when he warned that if the United States sent in guerrillas unsupported by the people, that would be a "hopeless" cause. "If guerrilla troops are local troops, belonging to the country, then every bush is their ally." He recalled his own service in the Red Army: "In spite of its being very poor, the Red Army won because the people were on its side."

Khrushchev argued that "modern times are not like the past. Modern weapons are terrible." He did not know whether the balance of power was exact, but that did not matter. "Both sides know very well that they have enough power to destroy each other. This is why there should be no interference."

America was supporting colonial powers: "This is why the people are against it. There was a time when the United States was a leader in the fight for freedom. As a matter of fact, the Russian czar refused to recognize the United States for twenty-six years because he regarded it as an illegitimate creature. Now the United States refuses to recognize the new China. Things have changed, haven't they?"

Kennedy said that Americans were concerned about the Chairman's

January speech endorsing wars of national liberation: "The fact is that certain groups seize power, frequently by military means." Some were supported by the Soviet Union, some by the United States. "If one takes the situation in Vietnam, there are some seven to fifteen thousand guerrillas there. We do not believe that they reflect the will of the people. . . . The U.S.S.R. may believe so. The problem is to avoid getting involved in direct contact as we support the respective groups."

Khrushchev replied that he and the President had different conceptions of liberation struggles. When the "people's only recourse is to rise in arms," the Soviet Union called it a sacred war. "The United States itself rose against the British. The Soviet Union has been proud of the United States in this respect. But now the U.S. has changed its position and is against other people's following suit."

If some country in Africa were to adopt the socialist system, "that might mean that a few drops would be added to the bucket of Communist power. . . . But this would be an expression of popular will. If there were to be interference, there would be a chain reaction and ultimately war between our two countries."

The Chairman aired his standard complaint about American bases surrounding the Soviet Union: "This is very unwise and aggravates the relations between the two countries. The countries where the bases are located spend money on their military establishments while their people live like paupers. Thus these people have the choice of developing along militarist lines or rising. We must be reasonable and keep our forces within our national boundaries."

Kennedy wished to make it clear that he did not oppose all countries with different social systems: "Yugoslavia, India, and Burma are extremely satisfactory situations, as far as the United States is concerned. . . . If the Communist cause were to win in certain areas and if those areas were to associate themselves closely with the Soviet Union, that would create strategic problems for the United States."

In case Khrushchev did not realize that he was referring to Cuba, the President once again noted that Chairman would be disturbed if Poles were given the opportunity to turn toward the West: "Certainly one could think that they might not necessarily support the present government."

The Chairman angrily replied that what happened in Poland was none of the President's business: "Poland has a fine government, more democratic than the United States. Its election laws are more honest than those in the United States." In America, parties existed only to deceive the people. If the premise of American policy was to preserve the existing balance of power, the United States must not really want peaceful coexistence. Maybe it was seeking a pretext for war.

Khrushchev said that the President was mistaken in thinking that Viet Minh forces were involved in Laos: "What is an actual fact is that military action was started from Thailand by the United States."

Despite Bolshakov's assurances, Kennedy found the Chairman little interested in Laos. He and Khrushchev agreed to prod their Laotian clients to cooperate with the commission policing the cease-fire. With a smile, the President said they might unite on this even if they could not unite on the merits of the American electoral system. Unamused, Khrushchev said that elections were "an American internal affair."

At a quarter to seven, Kennedy saw the Chairman to his car. The President's friend Henry Brandon of the *Sunday Times* thought he looked "dazed." After Khrushchev's departure, Kennedy asked Thompson, "Is it always like this?" The Ambassador said, "Par for the course."

By Dr. Jacobson's account, during an intermission in the afternoon conversations, he had asked Kennedy how he was feeling. The President had replied, "May I be permitted to take a leak before I respond?" When he returned, he said that he was "fine" and that Jacobson could retire to his hotel. When Kennedy returned to his quarters, Jacqueline was having her hair styled. He asked Evelyn Lincoln for a cigar. He said he wanted to rest but instead paced the floor, deep in thought. She asked him how the first day's meetings had gone. He said, "Not too well."

As the President soaked in a hot bath, Dave Powers told him that he had watched him walking with Khrushchev in the garden: "You seemed pretty calm while he was giving you a hard time out there." Recalling the Chairman's tirade, Kennedy said, "I'm trying to remind myself: the next time I'm talking to Khrushchev, don't mention miscalculation."

Knowing that Khrushchev had disdained Eisenhower's reliance on advisers, the President had guided the conversations in a way calculated to impress the Chairman with his self-assurance, boldness, energy, and command of facts, his willingness to say what he thought without prompting by notes or aides.

His error was in allowing Khrushchev to draw him into debate over ideology. After debating Humphrey and Nixon in 1960 and gaining excellent reviews for his presidential news conferences, Kennedy was more confident than he should have been about his ability to best Khrushchev in an argument over communism versus capitalism.

The Chairman had the advantage not only of his half century as an agitator but of his overflowing idealism about communism. Against this, Kennedy the skeptical pragmatist, armed mainly with speech material from the 1960 campaign, could not stand up. The President was in the position of arguing that the United States, patron of Boun Oum, the Somozas, and the Shah, was a revolutionary and anticolonial nation. When he said that a government's days would be numbered if it worked "in the interest of only a small group," only politeness stopped Khrushchev from replying that the President had just described his own system.

Kennedy's streak of cynicism about politicians and his impatience with ideologues served him badly with Khrushchev. He ignored Thompson's warning that Khrushchev's rhapsodies about communism were not just words: "He really believes it." Khrushchev no doubt took Kennedy's comment that he could not defend all of his predecessors' policies and commitments as a sign of irresolution.

Asking Khrushchev to agree to a standstill in the Cold War implied that Kennedy considered the Chairman's public views about dynamic world communism a political stance that could be discarded in private. It asked Khrushchev to discard his life's beliefs and guarantee American predominance in the world. In the Chairman's mind, this embodied the arrogance of American power. For himself and for those in the Kremlin who would later read his remarks, Khrushchev was compelled to reject Kennedy's appeal and defend his own doctrines in fighting language.

There is no evidence that Kennedy's performance was hampered by a drug interaction or by amphetamine injections. By his freewheeling approach to his own medical treatment, the President had tempted fate and won.

Charles Bartlett said years later, on the basis of a talk with Kennedy, "I think his problem at Vienna was his damned back. . . . When that back went off, Jack was off. . . . Jack got sort of borne down by going to Paris first. . . . He was trying to impress de Gaulle and live up to the French love of formality. . . . My impression was that he wasn't in top shape when he hit Vienna."

A thousand journalists waited in the vast marble ballroom of the Hofburg Palace, an appropriate place for briefings in light of the President's interest in miscalculation: it was once the home of Archduke Franz Ferdinand, whose murder ignited the escalating misjudgments that led to World War I.

"Achtung! Achtung!" cried an Austrian official. Salinger and Mikhail

Kharmalov read out an American-Soviet statement saying that the first day's talks had been "frank, courteous, and wide-ranging." Kharmalov said he hoped the Sunday meeting would be "as fruitful as today." Chalmers Roberts of the *Washington Post* asked Salinger if he agreed that the talks had been fruitful. Salinger referred him to the official statement, which Roberts thought "an obvious tipoff that all was not as rosy as Kharmalov would have them believe."

As other journalists vainly tried to pry information out of the two spokesmen, Randolph Churchill of the London *Evening Standard* declared himself "bored": "I will not listen to any more of this rot!" Walking out, he was stopped by a security guard. Churchill asked where the man thought he was—in Russia? When he was finally released, the son of the wartime leader staged his own news conference and, so a colleague wrote, "spoke more freely than anyone else had all day."

During the day's meetings, someone in the Austrian Foreign Ministry had shown a wicked sense of humor by arranging for Mrs. Khrushchev to attend a Cézanne exhibition and sending Mrs. Kennedy to a factory. As in Paris, Jacqueline stopped traffic when she moved about the city. As she lunched at a candlelit restaurant, the maître d'hôtel went outside to announce that Mrs. Kennedy had "come to the dessert." The crowds cheered. That afternoon, she begged off a monastery tour to rest.

On Saturday evening was a black-tie state dinner at the 1400-room Schönbrunn Palace. Built in 1694, the old Habsburg country estate was filled tonight with spring flowers. When the car bearing the Kennedys reached the floodlit gates, there was a cry from the dark: "The American princess!"

Greeting Khrushchev, the President had to apologize for being five minutes late. The Chairman wore no black tie. Averse to bourgeois dress, he had decreed business attire for his entire delegation. He would have preferred not to bring Nina Petrovna to Vienna but bowed, as he had on his 1959 American trip, to Western custom. When photographers asked him to shake hands with the President, he leered at the First Lady in her glittering, sleeveless floor-length Cassini and long white gloves: "I'd like to shake *her* hand first."

"Kennedy's wife was a young woman whom the journalists were always describing as a great beauty," Khrushchev later recalled. "She didn't impress me as having that special, brilliant beauty which can haunt men, but she was youthful, energetic, and pleasant. . . . As the head of the Soviet delegation, I couldn't care less what sort of wife he had. If he liked her, that was his business—and good luck to them both.''

As vermouth and pineapple juice was served, the President introduced Khrushchev to his mother, who had followed the presidential party to Vienna. ''We knew she was a millionaire, and consequently we had to keep in mind whom we were dealing with at all times,'' Khrushchev recalled. ''We could smile courteously and shake hands with her, but that didn't change the fact that we were at opposite poles.''

After meeting Nina Petrovna, Rose Kennedy wrote in her diary that Khrushchev's wife was ''strong, sturdy, capable of hard physical exertion. Wears her hair drawn straight back. No makeup.'' Without a scintilla of irony, she wrote that Khrushchev's wife was ''the kind of woman you'd ask in perfect confidence to baby-sit for you if you wanted to go out some evening.'' Kennedy's mother was delighted when Nina Petrovna recalled having read about her in *McCall's,* saying, ''I must learn your beauty secrets.''

De Gaulle had warned Jacqueline about Khrushchev's wife: *''Plus maline que lui.''* [''More malicious than he.''] Perhaps overinfluenced by the warning, she thought Nina Petrovna ''hard and tough.'' But this judgment was dead wrong. Khrushchev's wife was indeed a strong woman; she was probably shrewder about people than her husband, and as idealistic or more so about communism. But she was also a woman of uncommon sweetness and had much to do with keeping Khrushchev's more humane instincts and aspirations alive through the Stalin years in which they were so brutally tested.

Jacqueline liked the Khrushchevs' daughter Rada Adzhubei but could not stand her boastful husband. She had been told of Adzhubei's influence on Khrushchev but after seeing the two men together concluded that ''Khrushchev doesn't really like him'' and was not ''particularly close to him.''

The President's favorite sister, Eunice Shriver, had also come to Vienna. As Billings recalled, Kennedy ''always loved having her around, got a big kick out of her humor. For this reason, Eunice was able to make the atmosphere at this meeting more pleasant. . . . Khrushchev roared with laughter over something Eunice said. I can't remember what it was, but I'm sure it was something at her brother's expense.'' Gromyko asked her whether her brother was hard to live with. She replied, ''Very.'' Gromyko said, ''I hadn't noticed.''

Guests dined on Habsburg china as they listened to ''The Blue Danube'' and other waltzes. Dr. Travell wrote in her journal, ''I never in my wildest dreams thought that I would sit at dinner with Khrushchev!'' During the meal, the Chairman regaled Jacqueline with anecdotes. He found her "quick with her tongue. In other words, she had no trouble finding the right word to cut you short if you weren't careful with her."

Moving his chair closer to hers, Khrushchev spun off one gag after another, reminding her of Abbott and Costello. Feigning amazement at one story, she put a gloved hand over her mouth. Enchanted by the horses and dances in Lesley Blanch's *Sabres of Paradise,* she asked him about the nineteenth-century Ukraine. When Khrushchev told her that the region now had many more teachers than the Ukraine of the czars, she said, "Oh, Mr. Chairman, don't bore me with statistics."

Khrushchev laughed, and for a moment she found him "almost cozy." Running out of things to say, she recalled hearing that one of the Soviet canine space travelers had had puppies: "Why don't you send me one?"

Following dinner, an opera, and ballet, the Kennedys returned to the American residence. Bohlen found the President "a little depressed" at his failure to persuade Khrushchev to preserve the existing balance of power in the world. He tried to console him: "The Soviets always talk tough."

Privately Bohlen believed that during the day's talks, Kennedy may have been "quiet" with Khrushchev but he had been "perfectly firm." The problem was that Kennedy had let Khrushchev draw him into ideology: "He got a little bit out of his depth."

Thompson was "very upset" that Kennedy had ignored his advice to stay off ideology; the President still did not seem to realize "that a Communist like Mr. Khrushchev could never yield" in this area of argument "even if he wanted to." Kohler wondered whether Kennedy should have met with Khrushchev so soon after the Cuban debacle: "After the Bay of Pigs, if you knew Khrushchev, this would just whet his appetite."

Bohlen, Thompson, and Kohler urged the President to stick to concrete issues on Sunday. Kennedy resolved to make sure that before Khrushchev left Vienna, he was "going to understand the United States point of view." Rusk suggested that he take the approach, "You aren't going to make a Communist out of me and I don't expect to make a capitalist out of you, so let's get down to business."

On Sunday morning, the Kennedys attended early Mass at St. Stephen's Cathedral and heard the Vienna Boys' Choir. Khrushchev laid a wreath at a Soviet war memorial locally known as "The Unknown

Plunderer." An American reporter asked him how he liked his counterpart. "That is for the American public to say," said Khrushchev. "Some people like short men, some tall men, some fat men. Everyone likes different types." Khrushchev invited the American to visit Moscow: "And bring your President with you."

Kennedy and Rusk were driven to the chestnut-shaded Soviet Embassy, which stood next to a Russian Orthodox Church. Thousands of Viennese who had turned out to see the First Lady were dismayed to find only the Secretary of State. Kennedy said, "Rusk, you make a hell of a substitute for Jackie!" Rusk feared that when Khrushchev compared such public enthusiasm to his own mild reception when he moved about Vienna, it would make him even more truculent.

The President emerged from the car. A beaming Khrushchev shook his hand: "I greet you on a small piece of Soviet territory. Sometimes we drink out of a small glass, but we speak with great feelings." Kennedy nodded: "I'm glad to hear this." Then they went inside.

CHAPTER

9

"He Just Beat Hell Out of Me"

At the Soviet Embassy, Khrushchev led the President up the grand staircase and into a parlor upholstered in melancholy red damask. Rusk, Bohlen, Thompson, Kohler, Gromyko, Dobrynin, and Menshikov clustered around an oblong table. Khrushchev called out to the two foreign ministers, "You look so aloof. Move closer and join us!"

Using the crisp new approach suggested by his Secretary of State, Kennedy began by saying that if they couldn't agree on anything else, at least they might agree on Laos. The United States had treaty commitments to the little nation but wished to reduce its involvement. He hoped the Soviet Union would do the same. "Laos is not so important as to get us as involved as we are."

Khrushchev replied that the Soviet Union had no desire to assume responsibilities in remote geographical areas. It was in Laos at the request of Souvanna Phouma, the "only legitimate government." He was not impressed when the President spoke of American commitments: "The U.S. has no right to distribute indulgences, as it were, and to interfere in the various areas of the world." What business did the United States have claiming special rights in Laos?

If the President would pardon his bluntness, he said, the American policy stemmed from delusions of grandeur, from megalomania. "The United States is so rich and powerful that it believes it has special rights and can afford not to recognize the rights of others."

The Soviet Union would not stop helping other peoples win independence. "As the President has stated, the forces of the two sides are now in balance. . . . A great deal of restraint is required because the factors of prestige and national interests are involved here. We should not step on each other's toes and should not infringe upon the rights of other nations, small or big."

Responding with excessive candor, Kennedy said that "frankly speaking," the American obligations in Laos were made before he took office on January twentieth. Why they were made was not at issue here. He wanted to decrease U.S. commitments: "What is at issue here is how to secure a cease-fire and to have the fighting stop."

Khrushchev rejoined that he could see the President's "own hand" in Laos. "I've read all your speeches." Hadn't the President ordered U.S. military advisers in Laos to wear American uniforms? Hadn't he ordered and then canceled a Marine landing in Laos?

The President insisted that he had never ordered in the Marines. Khrushchev said that was not what he had read in the American press. He pointed out that when Molotov opposed the Austrian State Treaty in 1955, he had "overruled" him. On taking supreme power, he had canceled all "unreasonable decisions" made by Malenkov and Bulganin.

Westerners were "much better than the Easterners at making threats in a refined way. Every once in a while it is intimated that Marines might be used. But as engineers know, the law of physics says that every action causes a counteraction. So if the United States were to send Marines, other countries might respond with their Marines or some other forces. Another Korea or an even worse situation might result."

Khrushchev pledged every effort to influence the Laotian forces to establish a truly neutral government. The American and Soviet foreign ministers "should be locked into a room and told to find a solution." Chuckling, Gromyko noted that the Palais des Nations in Geneva was "a big place with a lot of rooms."

The President said he was "anxious to get the U.S. military out of Laos." He had been reluctant even to consider a Marine landing because he recognized that such an action would bring a "counteraction, and thus peace in that area might be endangered."

Khrushchev agreed: "The situation at the front lines is always unstable. Even a shot fired accidentally by a soldier could be regarded by the other side as a violation of the cease-fire. Therefore other questions should not be made contingent upon a cease-fire. . . . The basic question is to bring about agreement among the three forces in Laos so that the formation of a truly neutral government can be secured."

Now the Chairman raised the subject of nuclear testing. In May, Georgi Bolshakov had given Robert Kennedy the impression that Khrushchev was ready to tolerate up to twenty inspections per year in order to reach a test ban agreement.

If this was the President's expectation, he was badly disappointed. Khrushchev declared that three inspections per year should be sufficient. "A larger number would be tantamount to espionage, which the Soviet Union cannot accept." The West should simply agree to complete and general disarmament. Then espionage would be impossible "because there would be no armaments." If both sides showed goodwill, they should be able to reach such an agreement within two years.

The Chairman added that any commission devised to monitor a nuclear test ban agreement would have to be run by troika: the behavior of Hammarskjöld's UN forces in the Congo had shown that there were neutral nations but no neutral men. Disheartened, Kennedy asked whether Khrushchev really thought it "impossible to find any person that would be neutral both to the U.S. and the U.S.S.R." The Chairman nodded.

Kennedy dismissed the idea of a treaty allowing the Soviets to veto control measures. It would be as if he and Khrushchev lived in adjoining rooms and "could not go to each other's rooms without the consent of the occupant" to inspect suspicious events. Such a treaty "could not be confirmed by the U.S. Senate." Without proper verification, how could the Chairman assure those of his own people who charged the United States with secret testing? He conceded that the problem was less acute for the Russians because the United States was an open society.

Khrushchev grinned: "But what about Allen Dulles? Isn't that secret?" Kennedy said he wished it were.

The Chairman said a test ban was not so important. "The danger of war would remain because the production of nuclear energy, rockets, and bombs would continue full blast. What people want is peace.

Therefore, agreement should be reached on general and complete disarmament." In that case, the Soviet Union would agree to any controls, "even without looking at the document."

Kennedy acknowledged that a test ban would not of itself lessen the number of American and Soviet nuclear weapons. "Nor would it reduce the production of such weapons. However, a test ban would make development of nuclear weapons by other countries less likely— although, of course, no one can guess what will happen in the future. . . . Great Britain possesses certain quantities of such weapons and France is also getting some capability.

"If we fail to reach agreement on a nuclear test ban, then other countries will undoubtedly launch a nuclear weapons program." He was too diplomatic to speak the name of China. "If no agreement is reached, then in a few years there might be ten or even fifteen nuclear powers." The Chairman must balance his fear of espionage "against the risks involved in the proliferation of nuclear weapons."

Khrushchev confessed that Kennedy's position had "some logic." This was why the Soviet Union was negotiating at Geneva. "But practice has shown that this logic is not quite correct, because while the three powers are negotiating . . . France simply spits at them and goes on testing. . . . Without a link between a nuclear test ban and disarmament, other countries may say that they are in an unequal position and might act like France."

Under general and complete disarmament, "nuclear weapons would be eliminated and other countries would be in an equal position" and would not have to spend money on the development of nuclear weapons. This was "the most radical means of preventing war. . . . Let us now begin with the main issue and include the test ban in it."

The President replied that under the current draft of a test ban treaty, a signatory could abrogate it "if any country associated with any party to the treaty should conduct tests. The United States does not support French testing. We hope that once a treaty has been concluded, most other countries will join in it. The question of a nuclear test ban is a relatively easy problem to resolve because the controls are based on scientific instrumentation. . . . So why not start with this relatively easy question?"

Khrushchev did not respond. Kennedy went on to ask whether a Soviet plan for general and complete disarmament would include "inspection anywhere in the U.S.S.R." The Chairman said, "Absolutely."

Kennedy said in that case why not declare that both nations were committed to such a plan in stages, including a nuclear test ban as the first stage? Khrushchev asked him "not to start with this measure because it is not the most important one." Better to start with a ban on the manufacture of nuclear weapons "or elimination of military and missile bases."

The President said, "A nuclear test ban would be if not the most important step, at least a very significant step and would facilitate a disarmament agreement. There is a Chinese proverb saying that a journey of a thousand miles begins with a single step. So let us take that step."

Khrushchev looked at him quizzically: the President seemed to know the Chinese very well, but he too knew them quite well. Kennedy retorted that the Chairman "might get to know them even better." Khrushchev evidently took this as a taunting signal that the President knew of Mao's designs against him. He primly retorted, "I already know them very well."

Kennedy complained that on a test ban, they were now back to where they had started. For three years, their countries had observed an unpoliced moratorium on testing. If the test ban were now to be tossed into discussions on general disarmament, the unverified moratorium would have to be extended for several more years. This would be "of great concern" to Americans. He insisted that they try for a test ban now.

Khrushchev said he was happy to negotiate, but the Soviet Union would not accept controls amounting to espionage. This was "what the Pentagon has wanted all along. Eisenhower's Open Skies proposal in 1955* was a part of that scheme." The West wanted inspection stations inside the Soviet Union: "This is also espionage."

The President warned, "This is bound to affect the national security of our two countries and increase the danger of major conflicts."

Now they turned to Berlin. Khrushchev became more intense than he had been all weekend. "Sixteen years have passed since World War Two. The U.S.S.R. lost twenty million people in that war, and many of its areas were devastated. Now Germany, the country which unleashed World War II, has again acquired military power and has assumed a dominant position in NATO." This threatened a third world war.

The Soviet Union wanted to "draw a line" through World War II: "There is no reason why, sixteen years after the war, there is still no

---

*Eisenhower proposed that the two countries exchange blueprints of and allow surveillance flights over each other's military-industrial establishment.

peace treaty." He was simply observing the reality "that two German states exist. Our own wishes or efforts notwithstanding, a united Germany is not practical because the Germans themselves do not want it."

Emphatically he told the President that he wanted to reach agreement "with *you*" on the German question. Otherwise he would sign a peace treaty with the GDR. Then "all commitments stemming from Germany's surrender will become invalid. This would include all institutions, occupation rights, and access to Berlin, including the corridors."

If a "free city" were established in West Berlin, he was willing to offer guarantees "to ensure noninterference and the city's ties with the outside world. If the U.S. wants to leave its troops in West Berlin, this would be acceptable under certain conditions. However the Soviet Union believes that in that case, Soviet troops should be there too." If the United States rejected his proposal, he would regard the rejection as the result of the "pressure of Adenauer." Then the Soviet Union would "sign a peace treaty unilaterally. . . . All rights of access to Berlin will expire because the state of war will cease to exist."

Kennedy thanked the Chairman for being so frank. "At the same time, the discussion here is not only about the legal situation but also about the practical facts, which affect very much our national security. Here we are not talking about Laos. This matter is of the greatest concern to the U.S. We are in Berlin not because of someone's sufferance. We fought our way there, although our casualties may not have been as high as the U.S.S.R.'s. We are in Berlin not by agreement of East Germans but by contractual rights.

"This is an area where every President of the United States since World War II . . . has reaffirmed his faithfulness to his obligations. If we were expelled from that area and if we accepted the loss of our rights, no one would have any confidence in U.S. commitments and pledges. . . . If we were to accept the Soviet proposal, U.S. commitments would be regarded as a mere scrap of paper. Western Europe is vital to our national security, and we have supported it in two wars. If we were to leave West Berlin, Europe would be abandoned as well. So when we are talking about West Berlin, we are also talking about Western Europe."

He noted that Khrushchev seemed to agree "that the ratios of power today are equal. Therefore it is difficult to understand why a country with high achievements in such areas as outer space and economic progress should now suggest that we leave an area where we have vital interests."

Khrushchev said that under the President's definition of national security, the Americans could justify forging on to Moscow. Kennedy replied, "We are not talking about the U.S. going to Moscow, or of the U.S.S.R. going to New York. What we are talking about is that we are in Berlin and have been there for fifteen years. We suggest that we stay there."

He conceded that the Berlin situation was not satisfactory; Eisenhower had told Khrushchev at Camp David that it was "abnormal." Nevertheless "because conditions in *many* areas of the world are not satisfactory today, it is not the right time now to change the situation in Berlin and the balance in general." The Soviet Union "should not seek to change our position and thus disturb the balance of power. If this balance should change, the situation in Western Europe as a whole would change, and this would be a most serious blow to the U.S." Khrushchev would not accept a comparable shift in the world balance away from his country: "We cannot accept it either."

These were almost the most ill-chosen words that Kennedy could have used with Khrushchev. He had not stopped trying to persuade the Chairman to accept that since the world balance of power was in equilibrium, he should consent to a standstill in the Cold War. This would have required Khrushchev to renounce the ideal of dynamic world communism that he privately cherished and publicly championed, especially under the new pressures of the Chinese.

Kennedy's insistence that Khrushchev not change the power balance came just six weeks after he himself had tried to change it at the Bay of Pigs. As he had done for five months through Thompson, Lippmann, and other emissaries, he was asking the Chairman simply to drop the Berlin demands that he had been making since 1958, whatever the political humiliation.

Twenty months before, at Camp David, Eisenhower had suggested compromise to ease the Berlin situation. Kennedy had renounced Eisenhower's concessions. Now, in Khrushchev's view, he was arrogantly brandishing the superior might of the United States. Despite his earlier rhetoric about parity, Kennedy seemed to be saying that since America was more powerful, it could afford to ignore Soviet concerns about Berlin.

The Chairman's anger grew slowly. He began by saying that Berlin was "the most dangerous spot in the world. The U.S.S.R. wants to perform an operation on this sore spot, to eliminate this thorn, this ulcer." A peace treaty would "impede the revanchists in West Germany who want a new war. . . .

"Today they say that boundaries should be changed. . . . Hitler spoke of German's need for *Lebensraum* to the Urals. Now Hitler's generals . . . are high commanders in NATO." He was "very sorry," but "no force in the world will prevent the U.S.S.R. from signing a peace treaty." How long should it be delayed? "Another sixteen years? Another thirty years?"

In World War II, "the U.S. lost thousands and the U.S.S.R. lost millions. But American mothers mourn their sons just as deeply as Soviet mothers shed tears over the loss of their beloved ones." He had lost a son, Gromyko two brothers, Mikoyan a son. "There is not a single family in the U.S.S.R. or its leadership that did not lose at least one of its members in the war."

His proposal of a German peace treaty was not designed "for the purpose of kindling passions or increasing tensions" but "just the opposite—to remove the obstacles that stand in the way of develop-ment of our relations." After the treaty was signed, the Soviet Union would regard violations of the GDR's sovereignty as "open aggres-sion against a peace-loving country" and would act accordingly.

Kennedy opposed "a buildup in West Germany that would consti-tute a threat to the Soviet Union. The decision to sign a peace treaty is a serious one. . . . The U.S.S.R. should consider it in the light of its national interests." He repeated that his own brother had been killed in the last war. Khrushchev's proposal would "bring about a basic change in the situation overnight and deny us our rights. . . . No one can foresee how serious the consequences might be. . . . What is discussed here is not only West Berlin. We are talking here about Western Europe and the United States as well."

Khrushchev said, "The Polish and Czech border should be formal-ized. The position of the GDR should be normalized and her sover-eignty ensured. To do all this, it is necessary to eliminate the occupa-tion rights in West Berlin. . . . It would be impossible to imagine a situation where the U.S.S.R. would sign a peace treaty with the U.S. retaining occupation rights based on the state of war."

The President replied that the Soviet Union had no right to break the Potsdam agreement. Khrushchev insisted that the war had been over for sixteen years. "In fact, President Roosevelt indicated that troops could be withdrawn after two or two and a half years." Kennedy replied that Roosevelt "was not able to foresee this situation or the fact that our two countries would be on different sides."

Khrushchev said that they both knew "very well that Berlin has no military significance. The President speaks of rights, but what are those rights? They stem from war. If the state of war ends, the rights end too."

He recalled that at Camp David he and Eisenhower had discussed an "interim arrangement" that "would not involve the prestige of our two countries. Perhaps this could serve as a basis for agreement. The U.S.S.R. is prepared to accept such an arrangement even now. Adenauer says that he wants unification, but this is not so. As far as unification is concerned, we should say that the two German governments should meet and decide the question of unification.

"A time limit of, say, six months should be set, and if there is no agreement we can disavow our responsibilities. And then anyone would be free to conclude a peace treaty." This would be "a way out" that resolved "this question of prestige."

He said that in May 1960 he had hoped to reach such an agreement with Eisenhower at the Paris summit, "but the forces which are against improvement of relations between the U.S. and U.S.S.R. sent the U-2 plane. . . . The U.S.S.R. decided that in view of the tensions prevailing as a result of that flight, this question should not be raised." Now the "time for such action is ripe."

They must not act "like crusaders in the Middle Ages" and "start cutting each other's throats for ideological reasons." The Soviet Union could no longer delay on Berlin. "It will probably sign a peace treaty at the end of the year. . . . If the U.S. refuses to sign a peace treaty, the U.S.S.R. will have no other way out than to sign such a treaty alone."

History would be the judge of their actions. "The West has been saying that Khrushchev might miscalculate. . . . If the U.S. wants to start a war over Germany, let it be so. Perhaps the U.S.S.R. should sign a peace treaty right away and get it over with. This is what the Pentagon has been wanting. But Adenauer and Macmillan know very well what war means. If there is any madman who wants war, he should be put in a straitjacket."

Kennedy said, "It is an important strategic matter that the world believe the U.S. is a serious country."

In cold anger, Khrushchev declared that American intentions led to "nothing good." After the peace treaty, the Soviet Union would "never, under any conditions," accept U.S. rights in West Berlin. He was "absolutely convinced" that the world would understand. The United States had stripped the Soviet Union of its rights and interests in West Germany and unilaterally signed a peace treaty with Japan.

"If the U.S. refuses to sign a peace treaty, the U.S.S.R. will do it alone. East Germany will obtain complete sovereignty, and all obligations resulting from the German surrender will be nullified." The United States could not longer follow its policy of "I do what I want."

Kennedy replied, "There is every evidence that our position in Berlin is strongly supported by the people there, and we are committed to that area. Mr. Khrushchev says that we are for a state of war. This is incorrect. It would be well if the development of U.S.-U.S.S.R. relations were such as to permit solution of the whole German problem."

He said that during the Chairman's stay in power, he had seen many changes. Now Khrushchev wanted "a peace treaty in six months, an action which would drive us out of Berlin." He may be a young man, as the Chairman had noted, but he had not "assumed office to accept arrangements totally inimical to U.S. interests."

Again Khrushchev suggested an interim agreement on Berlin that "would give the semblance of the responsibility for the problem having been turned over to the Germans themselves. If the U.S. does not wish such an arrangement, there is no other way but to sign a peace treaty unilaterally. No one can force the U.S. to sign a peace treaty, but neither can the U.S. make the Soviet Union accept its claims."

Kennedy refused to discuss an interim agreement that might allow the Chairman to postpone a Berlin crisis without public embarrassment. Unlike Eisenhower at Camp David, he felt that to show any flexibility on Berlin during this meeting would suggest to Khrushchev that he would not fulfill the American commitment to the city.

After the two leaders adjourned for lunch, the President told aides that he wanted to see Khrushchev once more alone for about twenty minutes to pin down the Soviet position on Berlin and leave the Chairman with no doubt of his firmness: "I can't leave here without giving it one more try." Someone cautioned that another meeting would keep the President from leaving Vienna on time. Kennedy barked, "No, we're *not* going on time! I'm not going to leave until I know more."

The banalities of diplomacy proceeded. Mrs. Khrushchev and Mrs. Kennedy lunched at the Pallavicini Palace with the daughter of the Austrian President. Outdoor mobs shouted, "Jah-kee! Jah-kee!" The two ladies walked to an upstairs window. Nina Petrovna later said that she felt "motherly" toward Jacqueline, who looked "like a work of art." She appreciated her intelligent conversation, so unusual in public life. Smiling, she took Mrs. Kennedy's gloved hand in hers and held it aloft.

At the Soviet Embassy, the Chairman and the President and their delegations were served caviar, fish cartilage pie, and crabmeat. Khrushchev said he had studied the President's May defense message to Congress: obviously America was controlled by monopolists and could not afford to disarm.

Lighting his cigar, Kennedy replied that not one of the financiers and industrialists Khrushchev had met at Harriman's house in New York in 1959 had voted for him. Khrushchev was certain it was all a trick: "They are clever fellows." Kennedy mentioned that the auto union leader Walter Reuther had endorsed him; hadn't the Chairman met him on his trip to San Francisco? Khrushchev said, "We *hanged* the likes of Reuther in Russia in 1917."

He warned that the American military buildup would force him to increase the size of the Soviet armed forces. Kennedy replied that he had no plans to increase his own force, "except for ten thousand Marines to bring three Marine Corps divisions up to full strength."

Khrushchev said that "missiles are the gods of war today." He noted that both he and the President were being pushed by their scientists to resume nuclear testing: "We will wait for you to resume testing—and if you do, we will. . . . We will never be the first to break the moratorium. You will break it, and that will force us to resume testing."

As for the joint moon project they had discussed yesterday over lunch, he said that on further reflection the United States should go itself. Without disarmament, a joint flight would be impossible because rockets could also be used for military purposes. The project would be so expensive it would divert resources that should go to Soviet defense. He said he was resisting pressure from Soviet scientists to send a man to the moon. The United States was rich. It should go first. The Soviets would follow.

Kennedy suggested that their two countries save money by coordinating their space efforts: "This would not involve Soviet rockets." Khrushchev did not rule out the idea but confessed that so far there had been "few practical uses of outer space launchings." The space race was not only expensive but "primarily for purposes of prestige."

The President presented him with the replica of the U.S.S. *Constitution,* chosen so late that Billings had had to bring it to Europe. Kennedy's good manners kept him from revealing to Khrushchev that the model had been his own birthday gift from his father. The Chairman would never have been so self-restrained under similar circumstances. He reciprocated with a silver Czechoslovak coffee service, a gold humidor, caviar, and phonograph records.

Billings later recalled that Kennedy regarded the coffee set "as plunder from a captive people and felt that while he had taken it on the chin in other respects, he had at least gotten the best of the exchange of gifts. . . . But afterward he wished that he had kept the *Constitution* for himself. . . . We could never find as good a model again."

The Chairman rose and lifted his glass of champagne. Personal contacts were "always better than acting through even the best ambassadors." If the leaders of states could not resolve "the most complex problems between themselves," how could lower officials accomplish that task? He and the President had heard each other out and reached "no understanding."

But "if people could resolve all difficult questions in their first meeting, no difficult questions would exist." The German peace treaty would be "a painful process, and it is similar to a surgical operation. However, the U.S.S.R. wants to cross that bridge and it will cross it." It would cause "great tensions" with the United States, but he was sure that "the clouds will dissipate, the sun will come out again and shine brightly.

"The U.S. does not want Berlin. Neither does the Soviet Union. It is true that U.S. prestige is involved in this matter, but the only party really interested in Berlin as such is Adenauer. He is an intelligent man, but old." Nodding to Kennedy, he said, "The Soviet Union cannot agree to having the old and moribund hold back the young and vigorous."

He called Franz-Josef Strauss, the GDR Defense Minister, "the most aggressive-minded man in West Germany. But even a man like himself, whose mind is in eclipse, can apparently see the light. On one occasion, Strauss wisely admitted that he fully understood how greatly Germany would suffer in a new war and how complete its destruction would be."

The Chairman drank to the President and to solution of their problems. "You are a religious man and would say that God should help us in this endeavor. For my part, I want common sense to help us."

Kennedy replied that both their countries were strong. Their peoples wanted peace and a better life. As he had told Mr. Gromyko, his ambition was "to prevent a direct confrontation between the U.S. and U.S.S.R. in this era of evolution, the outcome of which we cannot foresee." He had never underestimated the power of the Soviet Union. Both countries had "vast supplies of destructive weapons."

Swinging an open hand at the *Constitution* model, he noted that the vessel's guns had reached only a half mile. In the *Constitution*'s day, nations had been able to recover from war. No longer. He hoped not to leave Vienna "with a possibility of either country being confronted with a challenge to its vital national interests." Germany was "extremely important because of its geographic location." He and Khrushchev could keep the peace only "if each is wise and stays in his own area."

He recalled that at Schönbrunn Palace last night, he had asked the

Chairman what job he had held at the age of forty-four. Mr. Khrushchev had replied that he was head of the Moscow Planning Commission. Kennedy said that when he was sixty-seven, he hoped to be head of the Boston Planning Commission and possibly national chairman of the Democratic Party. Khrushchev said, "Perhaps the planning commission of the whole world?" Kennedy grinned: "No, Boston would be fine."

At 3:15 P.M., the two leaders sat down one last time, accompanied only by interpreters. Kennedy said he hoped that Khrushchev understood the importance of Berlin. He hoped the Chairman would not present him "with a situation so deeply involving our national interest." Evolution was under way all over the world. "No one can predict what course it will take."

Khrushchev thanked Kennedy for being frank but complained that "the U.S. wants to humiliate the U.S.S.R. We cannot accept this." He would be glad to have an interim agreement on Germany and Berlin "with a time limit." But force would be met by force. The President asked whether an interim agreement would allow the West to stay in Berlin and maintain its access. Khrushchev said yes—"for six months." Then it would have to go.

The President said that if Khrushchev was going to take this "drastic action," he must not believe the American commitment to Berlin was "serious." He was about to see Prime Minister Macmillan in London. He would have to tell him that the U.S.S.R. had presented him with a choice of "accepting the Soviet action on Berlin or having a face-to-face confrontation."

Khrushchev replied that in order to save Western prestige "we could agree that token contingents of troops, including Soviet troops, could be maintained in West Berlin. However, this would be not on the basis of some occupation rights, but on the basis of an agreement registered with the UN. Of course, access would be subject to the GDR's control because this is its prerogative." With steel in his eyes, he slammed his open hand on the table. *"I want peace. But if you want war, that is your problem."*

The chamber was deathly silent but for a loudly ticking mantel clock. As de Gaulle had recommended, Kennedy replied, *"It is you, and not I, who wants to force a change."*

Khrushchev said that the Soviet Union had "no choice other than to accept the challenge. It must respond and it will respond. The calamities of war will be shared equally. War will take place only if the U.S. imposes it on the U.S.S.R. It is up to the U.S. to decide whether there will be war or peace." His decision to sign a peace treaty was "firm and irrevocable. . . . The Soviet Union will sign it in December if the U.S. refuses an interim agreement."

Tight-lipped, Kennedy said, "If that is true, it's going to be a cold winter."

Years later, Khrushchev recalled that the President "looked not only anxious, but deeply upset. . . . I would have liked very much for us to part in a different mood. But there was nothing I could do to help him." Politics was "a merciless business." The two leaders walked onto the front step of the Embassy to shake hands one final time. Photographers wondered why Kennedy's smile had vanished.

Riding back to the American residence with Rusk and Salinger, the President thumped the shelf beneath the car's rear window. The Secretary of State was in shock over Kennedy's final exchange with Khrushchev. "In diplomacy, you almost never use the word war," he noted long afterward. "Kennedy was very upset. . . . He wasn't prepared for the brutality of Khrushchev's presentation. . . . Khrushchev was trying to act like a bully to this young President of the United States."

The Soviet delegation quietly gave the Americans an aide-mémoire demanding a German settlement in "no more than six months." Kennedy decided not to publicize it unless the Russians did. He knew that when his critics learned that Khrushchev had exploited the summit to start a new Berlin crisis, they would question his wisdom in meeting the Chairman so soon after the Bay of Pigs. Publicizing the deadline would only increase the pressure on Khrushchev to fulfill it.

The President wanted no false "Spirit of Vienna" that would boomerang against him when the world finally discovered Khrushchev's new demand on Berlin. The unfortunate Bohlen was briefing reporters on the "amiable nature" of the talks when Kennedy decided to let reporters know that in truth the atmosphere had been "somber." He asked Salinger to stay behind in Vienna for a few hours and see as many influential correspondents as he could.

The President had already agreed to see James Reston of the *New York Times,* who was waiting in a dark room at the American residence with the blinds drawn so that no other journalists could see him. Kennedy dropped onto a sofa next to Reston, pushed a hat over his eyes, and sighed loudly. The columnist said, "Pretty rough?"

"Roughest thing in my life." Kennedy said he had tried to tell Khrushchev what he could and couldn't do, proposing that the Chairman do the same. The result: a violent attack on American imperialism, especially in Berlin. "I've got two problems. First, to figure out why he did it, and in such a hostile way. And second, to figure out what we can do about it.

"I think the first part is pretty easy to explain. I think he did it because of the Bay of Pigs. I think he thought that anyone who was so young and inexperienced as to get into that mess could be taken. And anyone who got into it and didn't see it through had no guts. So he just beat hell out of me. . . . I've got a terrible problem. If he thinks I'm inexperienced and have no guts, until we remove those ideas we won't get anywhere with him. So we have to act."

Air Force One took off for London. Kennedy's Air Force aide, Godfrey McHugh, noted how silent and depressed the President and his party seemed: "It was like riding with the losing baseball team after the World Series."

Jacqueline Kennedy was also on edge. When she asked McHugh to proofread a handwritten letter in French to de Gaulle, he suggested that she not use the male form of address, *"mon général"*; the French leader was so exacting about etiquette. She replied, "In that case, the State Department can write its own goddamn letter."

Summoning O'Donnell to his stateroom, the President denounced Khrushchev as a "bastard" and "son of a bitch." So controlled for two days as he had tried to convince the Chairman of his firmness on Berlin, he now unburdened himself of his actual feelings. "We're stuck in a ridiculous situation. It seems silly for us to be facing an atomic war over a treaty preserving Berlin as the future capital of a reunited Germany when all of us know that Germany will probably never be reunited."

He kept thinking "of the children, not my kids or yours, but the children all over the world. . . . God knows I'm not an isolationist, but it seems particularly stupid to risk killing a million Americans over an argument about access rights on an *Autobahn* . . . or because the Germans want Germany reunified. If I'm going to threaten Russia with a nuclear war, it will have to be for much bigger and more important reasons than that. Before I back Khrushchev against the wall and put him to a final test, the freedom of all Western Europe will have to be at stake."

He thought that the main reason Khrushchev wanted to shut down West Berlin was the drain of manpower from East Germany: "You can't blame Khrushchev for being sore about that." He complained about Adenauer's obstruction of American and British efforts for a peaceful settlement. The four-power occupation of Berlin was "a mistake that neither we nor the Russians should have agreed to in the first place."

Now the West Germans wanted the United States "to drive the Russians out of East Germany. It's not enough for us to be spending a tremendous amount of money on the military defense of Western Europe . . . while West Germany becomes the fastest-growing industrial power in the world. Well, if they think we are rushing into a war over Berlin, except as a last desperate move to save the NATO alliance, they've got another thing coming."

From Heathrow Airport, the Kennedys rode into London in an open beige Bentley with Harold Macmillan and his wife, Lady Dorothy. They passed demonstrators in Trafalgar Square: NO POLARIS . . . BAN THE BOMB . . . FREE US FROM FEAR! The Prime Minister recorded in his diary that Kennedy "talked all the way up on his experiences." He had "laid great hopes" on the summit but for the first time in his life "met a man wholly impervious to his charm."

The presidential couple was to spend the night at the Radziwills' Georgian town house in Belgravia. Dr. Jacobson recorded that a Secret Service agent summoned him from Claridge's: "The driver escorted me through the garden to the back door. . . . I walked into Lee Radziwill's bedroom where Lee, the President, and Jackie were . . . chatting. The President and I retired to an anteroom, where I attended to him."

On Monday morning, June 5, Kennedy went to Admiralty House for formal talks with Macmillan.* Observing that his guest was very tired, the Prime Minister flung out his hand. "Let's not have a meeting—the Foreign Office and all that. Why not have a peaceful drink and chat by ourselves?" He found the President "grateful and relieved."

The previous November, Macmillan had worried about getting along with the "cocky Irishman" twenty-three years his junior: "I was an aging politician . . . and of an altogether different experience and background." The Prime Minister shared the British establishment's loathing for Joseph Kennedy, who as Roosevelt's Ambassador in London had opposed American aid to Britain's fight against Hitler. It helped that Kennedy's late sister Kathleen had been married during the war to Lady Dorothy's nephew, Lord Hartington, before Hartington's death in the invasion of France.

Ambassador David Bruce once cabled the President from London

---

*Number Ten Downing Street was closed for repairs.

that Macmillan gave the "impression of being shot through with Victorian languor" but in fact he was "a political animal, shrewd, subtle in maneuver." Embodiment of "Edwardian and eighteenth-century England in the grand tradition of the Establishment," the Prime Minister had "charm, politeness, dry humor, self-assurance, a vivid sense of history, dignity, and character."

Meetings in Washington and Key West had helped to cement Kennedy's closest relationship with a foreign leader. Before Vienna, Macmillan wrote the President a birthday letter: "I value our friendship. I rejoice that relations between the United States and my country are so close and happy."

Years later he carped that Kennedy spent "half his time thinking about adultery, the other half about secondhand ideas passed on by his advisers." But he said, "You know how it is when you meet someone and feel immediately as if you had known him always? That is the way I felt with Jack. We could talk in shorthand."

Now the President told him that Khrushchev had been "much more of a barbarian" than he had expected. Macmillan wrote in his diary that Kennedy "seemed rather stunned . . . like somebody meeting Napoleon (at the height of his power) for the first time."

Khrushchev returned to Moscow determined to look like the victor. At an Indonesian Embassy celebration of the visiting President Sukarno's sixtieth birthday, a Western reporter thought that Khrushchev looked "more exuberant and relaxed" than in years. *Time* observed that he was "apparently without a care in the world."

As the band struck up "Indonesia / Is free / Cha cha cha," the Chairman shouted at Mikoyan and Brezhnev, "Dance, you two!" Brezhnev whipped out a white handkerchief, fluttered it over his head, and sashayed with the Deputy Premier. Beating on a bongo drum, Khrushchev said that Mikoyan was "a good dancer. That's why we keep him on the job."

Sukarno ordered decorative Indonesian women to kiss the Soviet leaders and demanded to be kissed by a Russian girl. Mrs. Khrushchev asked a Russian girl to do her duty: "Oh, please come. You only have to kiss him once." The Chairman thanked the girl for "upholding Russian honor."

At the Kremlin, he gave colleagues a mixed report on Vienna: Kennedy did not need to consult his Secretary of State "the way

Eisenhower always depended on Dulles." Still, the President seemed "too intelligent and too weak."

Khrushchev told of his astonishment when Kennedy undercut his own arguments by saying he had inherited many of his policies and had no choice but to defend them. To a leader of Khrushchev's belief, this absence of emotional conviction hinted at weakness; if Kennedy was motivated only by abstract geopolitical gamesmanship, he might fold under pressure. He also worried about the "very small majority in the presidential election" that Kennedy had mentioned at Vienna. During a world crisis, the President might be excessively warlike in order to shore up his domestic standing.

Khrushchev's aide Fyodor Burlatsky felt that, to Khrushchev, Kennedy had "more the look of an adviser, not a political decision-maker or President. Maybe in a crisis he would be an adviser, but not even the most influential." He felt that Khrushchev looked on Kennedy with the condescension of the self-made man: "This guy was here as a result of his own activities. And he understood the feelings of simple people. John Kennedy had no such feeling. Maybe his relations with workers or peasants were like a political game."

Sergei Khrushchev recalled that his father saw Kennedy "as a worthy partner and a strong statesman, and as a simply charming man to whom he took a real liking. . . . He trusted Kennedy and felt real human sympathy toward him, and such likes and dislikes played a big part in Father's life." He thought the President a "serious political figure" with whom it "would be possible to do business."* Georgi Kornienko recalled that Khrushchev cited his 1959 report that Kennedy was "independent and intelligent and could be counted on for new departures": "You were right and the others were wrong."

In London, the President and First Lady attended the christening of Antony Radziwill and a party afterward, attended by the Macmillans, the Duke and Duchess of Devonshire, Randolph Churchill, Douglas Fairbanks, and David and Cissie Ormsby-Gore. David Bruce's wife, Evangeline, thought Kennedy looked "very depressed." Joseph Alsop was unnerved when the President told him, "I won't give in to the Russians no matter what happens." Alsop thought the

---

*Sergei Khrushchev's memory of Vienna may be colored by Kennedy's later rise in Khrushchev's estimation, especially after November 1963. The son also recalled that, in Vienna, Khrushchev and Kennedy "discussed an idea that was daring for its time, the idea of joint Soviet-American flight to Mars." The joint flight discussed, of course, was to the moon.

comment "a little chilling among the duchesses and the champagne."

Before going to Buckingham Palace for dinner, the President sat in a bathrobe on his bed autographing a picture of himself for Elizabeth II. The two heads of state had first met in 1938, when Kennedy was visiting his parents at the London Embassy. He wrote Billings, "Met Queen Mary and was at tea with the Princess Elizabeth, with whom I made a great deal of time. Thursday night I'm going to Court in my new silk knee breeches which are cut to my crotch tightly and in which I look mighty attractive."

The Queen disliked Radziwill, but to accommodate the President she included the couple and addressed them by their royal Polish titles, which the Palace ordinarily did not recognize. While flying to London, Jacqueline had asked the American Chief of Protocol, Angier Biddle Duke, whether she should bend her knee to the Queen. He told her that the wife of a head of state never curtsied to anyone.

After the dinner, she and her sister flew off for eight days in Greece, where the Greek government had provided a villa and a yacht for a tour of the Greek islands. Still wearing his tuxedo, the President boarded *Air Force One* for Washington. After takeoff, he ordered some hot soup, looked through the London newspapers, and called in Hugh Sidey of *Time,* who found him sitting in boxer shorts, his eyes "red and watery, dark pockets beneath them."

Kennedy told him that the meeting with Khrushchev had been "invaluable." Before going to sleep, he scribbled out a Lincoln quotation that he had used at the end of the campaign: "I know there is a God, and I see a storm coming. If he has a place for me, I believe that I am ready."

The next morning, Charles Bartlett was working in his office at the National Press Building when he heard the President's helicopter roaring overhead from Andrews Air Force Base to the White House. Earlier in the spring, when Kennedy asked why Bartlett had so many Russian friends, the columnist had defended himself by saying, "Every man has his Russian."

Now, a few minutes after hearing the presidential chopper, Bartlett received a call from the Oval Office: "Well, I want you to know that I've now got a Russian of my own!"

Salinger had asked the three networks for television time on Tuesday evening. Bundy advised Sorensen that the President's speech should portray Vienna as a "direct, frank, and civil exchange" in which Kennedy had shown American "vigor and confidence. . . . No one ever expected that a weekend of talk would bridge the gap" between the two countries. He suggested the "Churchill custom" of describing "the moments of color and beauty" and "the overwhelming crowds that lined the streets."

Kennedy called congressional leaders to the upstairs Oval Room for an off-the-record briefing. Under Jacqueline's supervision, the room was being transformed into an elegant salon. He reported that Khrushchev was "confident and cocky." Berlin was the only subject on which the Chairman had raised his voice. Fulbright asked whether Khrushchev had set a deadline for signing a peace treaty.

"He said December." The President added that in his speech he intended to concede that Berlin was serious but would not "press it home too sharply. We shall soon send back an aide-mémoire on our own rights, and we must consider what else we can do." He would "give no sense of a time limit." He asked the leaders to "say nothing that would seem to put Khrushchev in a corner where he must fight back."

Shortly before seven that evening, Kennedy sat a technician behind his Oval Office desk, peered through the camera, and asked for changes in lighting: "These TV lights sometimes give me a double chin." The naval desk had been swept clear except for leather-bound copies of *Why England Slept* and *Profiles in Courage,* his olive-green telephone, and a calendar. Jammed with people and equipment, the room was sweltering.

He sat down on three cushions stacked upon the seat of his upholstered swivel chair. As the camera's red light blinked on, a fly buzzed around the room, too late to be swatted.

"Good evening, my fellow citizens. I returned this morning from a week-long trip to Europe, and I want to report to you on that trip in full. . . . To lay a wreath at the Arc de Triomphe, to dine at Versailles and Schönbrunn Palace, and with the Queen of England—these are the colorful memories that will remain with us for many years to come."

But "this was not a ceremonial trip." After describing his talks with de Gaulle, he turned to Vienna. "I will tell you now that it was a very sober two days." Still, the talks had been "immensely useful." He and Khrushchev needed as "much direct, firsthand knowledge" of each other as possible. He had spoken to the Chairman "directly, precisely, realistically." The talks had reduced chances of a "dangerous misjudgment on either side."

Nevertheless "the Soviets and ourselves [*sic*] give wholly different meanings to the same words—war, peace, democracy, and popular will. We have wholly different views of right and wrong, of what is an internal affair and what is aggression. And above all, we have wholly different concepts of where the world is and where it is going."* Khrushchev "believes the world will move his way without resort to force." The one "prospect of accord" was in Laos. But hopes for a test ban had been "struck a serious blow."

The "most somber" exchange, he said, had been over Germany and Berlin: "We and our allies cannot abandon our obligations to the people of West Berlin." Kennedy was so determined to conceal Khrushchev's December ultimatum that he told the American people a falsehood, claiming that there had been "no threats or ultimatums by either side."

The evasion succeeded. Wednesday's *New York Times* headline did not even mention Berlin: KENNEDY SAYS KHRUSHCHEV TALKS EASED DANGER OF A "MISJUDGMENT."

The next day, the President learned that Pathet Lao forces in Laos had seized the mile-high hamlet of Padong. The news made him angry: hours after his speech insisting that he and Khrushchev had agreed on Laos, the new attack would cause Americans to wonder whether he had been tricked.

Rusk cautioned him that Padong was "something of a special case," only fifteen miles from the Pathet Lao headquarters, "a thorn in its side, an embarrassment for them from the very beginning." Thompson reminded him that Khrushchev's main reason for getting into Laos had been to keep the Chinese out; Padong was no reason to presume that he was not serious about a "temporary deal."

Kennedy's critics ridiculed his failure to act after warning Khrushchev that he would protect American interests in Laos. He ordered Harriman to boycott the Geneva conference but, when the cease-fire resumed, told him to return to the table: "I want to have a negotiated settlement. I do not want to become militarily involved."

Kennedy had hoped to return from Vienna with a test ban accord, a working relationship with Khrushchev, and other achievements that would help to overcome his narrow victory margin and the international setbacks of the spring of 1961. Instead, Khrushchev's Berlin ultimatum had thrown the two great powers into the most potentially dangerous confrontation since the early 1950s. As Kennedy had told

---

*The President had obviously been impressed by the post-Inaugural cable from Thompson, which said, "We both look at the same set of facts and see different things."

Reston, he could not understand why the Chairman "did it, and in such a hostile way."

In fact, Khrushchev would have been hard pressed to ignore Berlin in 1961, even if he had wished. For two and a half years, he had insisted on the fundamental importance of resolving the problem of Berlin and Germany. During that time, he had allowed his demand to be postponed and postponed. In May 1959, he had surrendered his peace treaty deadline in favor of Geneva talks.

When these failed, he agreed with Eisenhower on four-power negotiation at the Paris summit of May 1960. When that collapsed, he had tabled the problem until a new American President took office. After the inauguration, he had granted Kennedy's request for a few months in which to shape the new American policy on Berlin. He could not keep deferring the problem forever without looking fatally soft.

For Khrushchev in June 1961, the cost of tolerating the German status quo was higher than ever: the growing number of East Germans escaping to the West, the growing danger of a rearmed "revanchist" West Germany with access to nuclear weapons. Taking a hard line on Berlin would help him avoid charges that he was soft on Washington and impress his Soviet critics, the Chinese, and the Third World with his assertion of Soviet power. His acceptance of a cease-fire in Laos had put extra pressure on him to prove that his rhetoric about the rising tide of communism was not merely words.

These facts would have compelled Khrushchev to gain some kind of satisfaction on Berlin no matter who was President in 1961. The ferocity with which he now sought that satisfaction was largely Kennedy's doing. During his first five months, the President had given Khrushchev the dangerous impression that he was at once more passive and more militant than Eisenhower.

Some of Khrushchev's advisers suggested that if Kennedy was so ambivalent about retaking Cuba, an island embedded in the American sphere, why expect him to be bolder elsewhere? Khrushchev knew of the President's private qualms about the American commitment to Berlin and his fear during the Bay of Pigs of Soviet retaliation against the city. If he did not push Kennedy hard, his critics would charge him with forsaking a golden opportunity to bully a President who was vulnerable to intimidation.

During these same months, Khrushchev felt that Kennedy had behaved with unnerving belligerence. The new President had abandoned Eisenhower's caution about brandishing American nuclear superiority. Despite Moscow's warnings, he had three times asked Congress to increase the defense budget, the last in his "second State of the Union" of late May. Khrushchev may have thought the timing an effort to send him a threatening message one week before Vienna.

Most galling was Kennedy's insistence that Khrushchev drop his demands on Berlin, despite the Chairman's frequent warnings that the problem must be solved in 1961. To Khrushchev, this was a provocative insult. Not only did it presume that he did not mean what he said about Berlin, it suggested that Kennedy was trying to rub his nose in the fact of Soviet nuclear inferiority.

Hypersensitive to signs of American condescension, he felt that if the President genuinely respected the Soviet Union as an equal power, he would negotiate on Berlin as Eisenhower had. Not irrationally, he believed that if he did not manufacture a new Berlin crisis, Kennedy might go on ignoring the issue.

Had the President announced in early 1961 that he would revive the four-power negotiating mechanism used by Eisenhower to deal with Berlin, Khrushchev might have felt less compelled to seize Kennedy's attention by issuing a new Berlin ultimatum. At Vienna, he suggested that he might be satisfied with some kind of interim solution. Kennedy's insistence that Khrushchev simply like or lump the existing Berlin situation left the Chairman with few choices other than to ignite a major confrontation.

This accounts for Khrushchev's almost theatrical bellicosity at Vienna—a performance so studied that he said years later he could not help "feeling sorry for Kennedy" as he spoke his brutal lines. He had to convince the President that he was ready to go to nuclear war over Berlin. Otherwise Kennedy might assume that once again he was crying wolf.

Why did Khrushchev renege on Georgi Bolshakov's assurances about a test ban agreement at Vienna? Bolshakov later told Robert Kennedy that somehow the Chairman had "changed his mind" before the summit. It is possible that Khrushchev had never had any intention of making concessions on the issue and deliberately sent Bolshakov to lie to the Kennedys in order to lure the President to the summit. But it is difficult to imagine that Khrushchev would have so casually risked poisoning his relations with a President whom he expected to remain in power for eight years.

More likely it was in May that Khrushchev decided to launch a new Berlin crisis. Agreement on nuclear testing would have been incompatible with his aim of scaring the President with his pugnaciousness about Berlin. Soviet scientists and generals were pressing him for permission to detonate the largest hydrogen bombs ever produced. Khrushchev realized that in the context of a Berlin crisis, this would demonstrate Soviet nuclear might and his willingness to use it.

He probably believed it when he told Kennedy that the Soviets would not be the first to resume testing. Knowing that a majority of Americans favored resumption, he presumed that once they knew a test ban would be impossible to achieve in 1961, they would pressure the President into ending the three-year moratorium.

If the United States was the first to test, the brunt of world outrage would come down on Kennedy. Then, with a conspicuous show of regret, Khrushchev could respond by exploding his much larger "superbombs," evoking, as with Sputnik and Vostok, the world's awe at Soviet might.

Lem Billings found that Khrushchev's belligerence "absolutely shook" Kennedy; the President had "never come face to face with such evil before." Harriman found Kennedy "shattered." Robert Kennedy felt it was the first time his brother "had ever really come across somebody with whom he couldn't exchange ideas in a meaningful way." The President complained that dealing with Khrushchev was "like dealing with Dad. All give and no take."

Ben Bradlee noted that for weeks after the summit, the President "talked about little else." The *Newsweek* man was among the friends to whom Kennedy read aloud from the official transcript. When excerpts appeared in the press, the President exploded. Acheson wrote a friend that "while JFK was giving us his lecture on security, he told us that newspaper men had even seen copies of his report of his talks with Mr. K. This did not come as a surprise to me since one of them, a neighbor of mine, told me that over the weekend JFK had read the best parts to him and a colleague."

Mike Mansfield concluded that Khrushchev had looked on the President "as a youngster who had a great deal to learn and not much to offer." Lyndon Johnson told cronies, "Khrushchev scared the poor little fellow dead." Later, as President, he dropped to his knees in dramatic replication of what he thought to be Kennedy's begging of Khrushchev at Vienna, saying that he would never behave the same way on Vietnam.

Angry at the criticism that got back to him, Kennedy told Dave Powers, "What was I supposed to do to show how tough I was? Take my shoe off and pound it on the table?"

Georgi Bolshakov told Frank Holeman that the Russians were "amazed" that the President appeared to be so "affected and scared" by Khrushchev: "When you have your hand up a girl's dress, you expect her to scream, but you don't expect her to be scared."

* * *

Kennedy's back problem was worse than ever. On Thursday, June 8, he flew to Palm Beach to recuperate at the vacant home of his Palm Beach neighbor Charles Wrightsman, where there were dust covers on the furniture. He slept late and lounged in his pajamas, hobbling on crutches to the heated saltwater pool. In the evening, he entertained friends and several of the White House secretaries with daiquiris and Frank Sinatra records on the phonograph.

Salinger announced the President's malady to the press. Reporters asked why, if Kennedy was in such pain, the First Lady had proceeded with her trip to Greece. After consulting the President, he improbably explained that Mrs. Kennedy had not known of the back problem until their departure from London, when "he said in passing that his back was bothering him." Told in Greece that the problem was serious, she had wanted to fly home "immediately" but her husband had "discouraged" her. Asked if the President was taking drugs for his pain, Salinger said, "I don't know if he is or not."

Kennedy had speculated in private that Khrushchev might call a peace conference on Berlin before the end of 1961 but noted that the Chairman's threats were rarely carried out: "As de Gaulle says, Khrushchev is bluffing and he'll never sign that treaty.... It would be crazy, and I'm sure he's not crazy."

Rusk advised the President that if the Soviets kept Khrushchev's six-month ultimatum secret, it would show their willingness to avoid a new crisis over Berlin. But on Saturday, June 10, *Pravda* published the full text of Khrushchev's aide-mémoire, revealing the deadline to the world.

Kennedy left for Washington. Photographers at the West Palm Beach airport gasped when they saw him using crutches and being lifted aboard *Air Force One* by a hydraulic cherry picker. At the White House, his doctors restricted him to his four-poster bed with a heating pad. He told advisers ranged gravely around the room that the United States could soon be "very close to war" with the Soviet Union.

Later he mused with David Ormsby-Gore about what had gone wrong to disappoint his early, modest hopes for improving Soviet relations. He wondered whether his March and May defense messages to Congress had been too menacing—not in substance, but in presentation.

Robert Kennedy considered Berlin "the first effort by Khrushchev to test the President, figuring that after the Bay of Pigs he was going to back out on everything." In London, Macmillan wrote in his diary, "We may drift to disaster over Berlin—a terrible diplomatic defeat or (out of sheer incompetence) a nuclear war."

The President told aides that he didn't know exactly how Khrushchev would move against West Berlin; perhaps he would repeat Stalin's effort to take the sector over by blockade. He asked McNamara what supplies would be available for American troops in Berlin and 2.4 million West Berliners, should Khrushchev and the East Germans halt access.

10

The Ticking Clock

ON WEDNESDAY, JUNE 21, KHRUSHCHEV WENT TO THE GREAT Hall of the Kremlin for a televised military observance of the twentieth anniversary of Hitler's invasion. He wore his green lieutenant general's uniform: during World War II he had served as political adviser on the Stalingrad front.

Bidding for support at the outset of his Berlin crisis, he told the assembled marshals, generals, and admirals that the Red Army would get whatever it needed to defend the motherland. As he later recalled, "the hands of the clock were ticking."

In Alma-Ata three days later, Khrushchev rambled almost incoherently on the tastiness of horsemeat. Suspecting that their leader was drunk, censors worked hard to produce an acceptable official text. The next day, Khrushchev called Berlin "the most important problem" but spent the greater part of his speech unreeling his vision of

a peaceful economic competition with the United States. He pledged
that the Soviet Union would overtake the "aged runner" by 1970.

Ambassador Menshikov arrived at the White House with a terrified
small white fluffy dog named Pushinka. A letter from Khrushchev said
that she was "a direct offspring of the well-known cosmos traveler
Strelka." The President asked his wife, "How did this dog get here?"
She put her hand to her mouth. "I'm afraid I asked Khrushchev for
it in Vienna. I was just running out of things to say."

The Chairman's gift was heartfelt, but Khrushchev also enjoyed the
idea of placing an emblem of Soviet dominance of space in the President's own household. During the campaign, Kennedy had complained that the first creatures to orbit the earth had been named
"Strelka and Belka, not Rover or Fido."* Pushinka was checked for
eavesdropping devices and, as O'Donnell recalled, became a "pam-
pered member of the family."

Khrushchev also sent a hand-carved model of an American whaler:
"Such sail-steam vessels were in use at the end of the nineteenth
century in the Chukchi Sea for whale-fishing, and they would visit
Russian harbors." The President replied that the whaler "now rests
in my office here at the White House." While Pushinka's long flight
from the Soviet Union had not been "as dramatic as the flight of her
mother," she had "stood it well. We both appreciate your remembering these matters in your busy life."

At Vienna, Kharmalov and Salinger had agreed, along with Adzhubei and Harrison Salisbury, to debate the merits of their systems on
American and Soviet television. On Saturday, June 24, the sixty-min-
ute program was taped in New York and aired by NBC.† Kennedy
called Salinger from Glen Ora: "I thought you won hands down."

On Monday morning, the President received Kharmalov, Adzhubei,
and Georgi Bolshakov in the Oval Office. Briefed on the Chairman's
barbs about the "aged runner," he told Adzhubei, "Your father-in-
law has his view, but I want to tell you ours. . . . You're like the
high-jumper. He can raise the bar a foot at a time until he reaches a
certain height—say, six feet. But for the next foot, he must raise it by
inches, and after that, by fractions of inches."

---

*"Or even Checkers," as he sometimes added in Richard Nixon's honor.
†The Russians later reneged on their pledge to air the debate, claiming that the
videotape was incompatible with Soviet television equipment.

Adzhubei said, "You use one set of figures to measure our growth, and we use another." Kennedy replied, "I'm not minimizing your effort. You've made remarkable economic advances. This is the kind of peaceful competition I would like to see us have. But you must do more than you are doing to see that the peace is kept. Do that, and we'll all be around in 1970 to find out whether Mr. Khrushchev's estimates are correct."

Adzhubei asked why the United States kept troops in West Berlin if its intentions were peaceful. The President replied that the ten thousand men were a "token" force. Adzhubei said, "I think you ought to let *us* have a token force in West Berlin." Perhaps drawing from dossiers on Kennedy's private life, he said, "We would start with seventeen pretty nurses."

The President laughed. "We might just be able to work *that* out!" Resuming his gravity, he called the American troops "a symbol of our commitment to West Berlin, a commitment we intend fully to maintain. . . . I just want to make sure that you and your father-in-law have no doubts about our position in Berlin."

Kennedy had made no public comment on Berlin since the day *Pravda* publicized Khrushchev's six-month deadline. During the weeks of the President's silence, Mike Mansfield had publicly declared that "sooner or later, Berlin is likely to become the pivot of a new disaster for mankind." He proposed that NATO and the Warsaw Pact guarantee Berlin as a "free city" in a first step toward German reunification.

At a press conference on Wednesday, June 28, the President said that Mansfield did not speak for him: Khrushchev's proposed "free city" would be one in which "the rights of the citizens of West Berlin are gradually but relentlessly extinguished—in other words, a city which is not free. . . . The Soviets would make a grave mistake if they suppose that Allied unity and determination can be undermined by threats or fresh aggressive acts."

He noted Khrushchev's boast that the Soviet Union would outproduce the United States by 1970: "Without wishing to trade hyperbole with the Chairman, I do suggest that he reminds me of the tiger hunter who has picked a place on the wall to hang the tiger's skin long before he has caught the tiger. This tiger has other ideas."* He insisted that the Russians were being far outpaced by the United

---

*Staff members chuckled at this. In the West Wing, Kennedy was colloquially known as "the tiger."

States and would not catch up even by the year 2000.

In the *New York Herald Tribune,* Roscoe Drummond recalled Kennedy's campaign charge that American economic growth was falling dangerously behind that of the Soviet Union: "I thought I was at the wrong press conference, or that . . . the man who was talking was President Richard Milhous Nixon."

As with Kennedy's effort to reveal Soviet nuclear inferiority, Khrushchev may have wondered why the President wished to humiliate him by puncturing his economic bragging. It would not have occurred to him that by igniting a Berlin crisis he had compelled the President to ensure that the Western allies and the rest of the world knew the full extent of American strength.

Few world leaders had been more unsettled by Kennedy's election than the eighty-five-year-old Chancellor of West Germany. Konrad Adenauer wished that Eisenhower and Dulles were still in power.

Grandson of a baker, deeply Catholic, Adenauer was a Rhinelander who felt more affinity with the southern Germans, the Dutch, and the French than with the "heathen steppes" of Protestant northeastern Germany, which he considered "almost in Asia." Berlin was to him an "un-Christian" Babylon. As Lord Mayor of Cologne from 1917 to 1933, he had scrutinized a plan to detach the Rhineland and unite it with France.

Adenauer hated Hitler most of all for the pagan mystique that separated children's souls from their parents. Dismissed by the Nazis, twice arrested by the Gestapo, he sat out most of the Third Reich cultivating roses and tinkering with clocks at his home in Rhöndorf, across the Rhine from Bonn. In 1949, when the Federal Republic was founded, Truman and Acheson promoted the Christian Democratic Adenauer for Chancellor over the objections of the Labour Prime Minister Clement Attlee, who would have preferred the Socialist Kurt Schumacher.

As leader of the Christian Democratic majority in the West German parliament, "Der Alte" helped West Germany to achieve its new place as the most prosperous nation on the continent, its politics, defense, and economy firmly anchored in the Western alliance. His regional prejudices and his anxiety about what he considered to be the German propensity for folly prevented him from being passionate about reunification.

Adenauer was incensed about a *Foreign Affairs* piece Kennedy had published in 1957 suggesting that the Chancellor's time was past and that Eisenhower was leaning too heavily on the Christian Democrats.

He feared that Kennedy's Secretary of State might be Stevenson, whom he considered dangerously relaxed about the idea of American recognition of the GDR. He told friends that Kennedy had "much to learn" and as President could be "fatal." Kennedy considered him almost openly pro-Nixon.

Hours after hearing of Kennedy's victory, Adenauer tried to recover by announcing that he would meet with the new President in February 1961. With a hint of retaliation for Adenauer's partisanship, Kennedy's circle replied that February would be too early: the Chancellor would have to wait his turn.

When his White House visit was scheduled for early April, Adenauer was determined to win Kennedy's reassurance that he would be as stalwart as Eisenhower about Berlin and West Germany. Facing new elections in September, he wished to show his domestic constituency that he could work with Kennedy. Polls showed the Christian Democrats were slipping against the coalition led by Willy Brandt, the young West Berlin Mayor often described as "Kennedyesque."

Before Adenauer's arrival, Henry Kissinger wrote the President that the intense American interest that spring in William Shirer's *The Rise and Fall of the Third Reich* and in the Israeli trial of the Nazi executioner Adolf Eichmann had aroused the West Germans' old "vague fears of being abandoned." Urging Adenauer to be flexible would be "like telling a member of Alcoholics Anonymous that one martini before dinner will not hurt him."

Heavily coached, the Chancellor gamely tried to give Kennedy the impression of spontaneity and informality, but the President sensed that he was "talking not only to a different generation but to a different era, a different world." He told Jacqueline that Adenauer had hung on too long and was turning mean and bitter. He was impatient with Adenauer's unquenchable thirst for what Sorensen called "repetitious reassurances of our love and honor."

After his return to Bonn, Adenauer privately praised Kennedy's ability to focus on basics but complained that the President was "a cross between a junior naval person and a Roman Catholic Boy Scout," presiding over an entourage of "cooks," "whiz kids," and "prima donnas."

The Chancellor was further unsettled by the Bay of Pigs. His military intelligence chief, General Gerhard Wessel, recalled, "It was a catastrophe that the world's number-one power could do a thing like this. Unbelievable! It was a shock to us. . . . Our feeling of trust in the American leadership diminished to a very low level." This mistrust was deepened by Vienna: "Our feeling was that Kennedy was not tough enough in his conversation with Khrushchev."

On Thursday, June 29, the President called the NSC to the Cabinet Room and asked Dean Acheson what he should do about Berlin. The elegant, sardonic diplomat had never been a Kennedy acolyte. Before 1960, he had viewed the President's father as a social-climbing boot-legger and prewar appeaser who had bought his spoiled son a seat in Congress. After the nominations of Kennedy and Nixon, he wrote a friend that the best campaign cheer he knew was "They can't elect *both* of them."

Acheson turned down the President-elect's offer to be ambassador to NATO. The only full-time job he would have accepted was his old one. But when Kennedy in March 1961 publicly called on him to advise on Germany and Berlin, Acheson's secretary noted that "DA is buoyed up by it all and looks better and younger than I have seen him in years."

His modest return to government did not restrict his sharp tongue. In a speech to the Foreign Service after the Bay of Pigs, he reported the feeling among Europeans that they were "watching a gifted young amateur practice with a boomerang when they saw, to their horror, that he had knocked himself out." Kennedy heard about the speech and, as Acheson recalled, "didn't like this at all."

Now, in the Cabinet Room, he argued that Khrushchev had started his newest Berlin crisis to weaken NATO, buttress the East German regime, and legalize the Oder-Neisse Line with Poland that the Sovi-ets recognized as the GDR's Eastern frontier.* Most of all, the Chair-

---

*At the Potsdam conference in July 1945, the Allies had provisionally established the Oder and Neisse rivers as the boundary between the old western and eastern German provinces, the latter of which were allocated to postwar Poland. The extrusion of the eastern provinces from what had been Germany before the war remained a live political issue in the FRG. Adenauer's aide Felix von Eckhardt brought a secret request from the Chancellor to both Kennedy and Nixon in July 1960 not to mention the Oder-Neisse Line during the campaign: "He realizes there may be some pressure from Poles in this country. . . . All sensible Germans recognize that there cannot be a change in the Line. But with the German elections coming up in September 1961, any state-ments in the U.S. would be used in . . . local campaigns to the disadvantage of the Chancellor and his party."

Von Eckhardt transmitted his message to Kennedy through Harriman, who told him that "the sooner all hands agreed to the Oder-Neisse Line, the better it would be for everybody." Since Kennedy was eager to avoid the issues of Berlin and Germany anyway, he was happy to comply with Adenauer's request. The closest he came to discussing the Oder-Neisse Line in the fall campaign was to tell the Polish-American

man was testing America's will. America could not back down from such a sacred commitment as the defense of Berlin. Khrushchev would take willingness to negotiate as a sign of weakness. He had only dared start this crisis because rising Soviet strength had reduced his fear of a nuclear confrontation.

The Eisenhower State Department had quietly drafted "three essentials" to protect in Berlin even at the risk of nuclear war: access by air and ground, continued Western garrisons and other forms of presence in West Berlin, and the freedom and survival of the Western sector.*

Acheson said that Khrushchev must be made to know that the United States was "irretrievably committed" to these three interests. The President must order a rapid buildup of conventional and nuclear forces, put two or three additional divisions in West Germany, hold three to six more in reserve for transport overseas on short notice, declare a national emergency.

If Khrushchev signed a peace treaty, Kennedy should not quibble. But if the Soviets and East Germans blocked access to Berlin, the President should launch a new airlift. If they interfered with the Western planes, he should order a ground probe of two divisions—too large for East Germany to stop without Soviet help. The President must show Khrushchev that he had the resolution to go on, if necessary, to nuclear war. That done, he might offer face-saving concessions, such as barring espionage and subversion from West Berlin or even recognition of the Oder-Neisse Line.

Some in the room were upset by Acheson's seeming nonchalance about risking nuclear war. They thought that starting off with negotiation would show Khrushchev that the West was ready to reduce West Berlin's irritation value while protecting Western rights.

Llewellyn Thompson, back in Washington to advise on Berlin, said that Khrushchev's chief motive in starting a new Berlin crisis was not to humiliate the United States but to improve the Communist position in Eastern Europe and disrupt NATO. Thompson favored a quiet Western military buildup, followed by a diplomatic offensive after the West German elections in September. Then the Soviet Union would have to suffer the world's hostility for opposing the Western plan to avert a nuclear war over Berlin.

Congress of Chicago, "We must eliminate Poland's fear of the West, fears that are very real, and this includes in particular fear of Germany."

*When the West Germans were told of the three essentials at a NATO meeting in May 1961, Mayor Brandt's aide Egon Bahr had complained, "This is almost an invitation for the Soviets to do what they want with the Western sector."

Thompson argued that a national emergency declaration would make the United States look "hysterical." It might force a rash countermove from Khrushchev that he did not really want to make.

Kennedy asked whether it was "really to our advantage" to press the old Western demand for reunification of Berlin. Rusk said that "self-determination is a better ground than unification." The President asked him to draft a proposal for a plebiscite allowing Berliners to choose their own destiny: no one could doubt who would win. He worried aloud that a new military buildup might be matched by the Soviet Union. Acheson agreed that "such back-and-forth challenges" should be avoided "as far as possible."

Kennedy asked what to do "if Khrushchev proposes a summit this summer." Acheson said, "It would not be hard to find answers as we go along." The President should propose lower-level talks first. There were "plenty of elderly, unemployed people" like himself who could "converse indefinitely without negotiating at all." He could easily do so "for three months on end." Listening to Acheson, Robert Kennedy thought that he would never wish "to be on the other side of an argument with him."

That week *Newsweek* published secret information on contingency planning for Berlin by the Pentagon, including a mobilization of American armed forces. Professing concern about how Khrushchev would view the information, Kennedy ordered the FBI to investigate. In fact, like the transcripts of the Vienna talks, the President or his aides may have themselves authorized the leak—in this case, to send a stiff alarm to Khrushchev.*

Khrushchev got the message. In a Moscow speech, he scoffed at "reports" of Western mobilization plans. While attending a performance by Dame Margot Fonteyn at the Bolshoi Theater, he called Sir Frank Roberts, the British Ambassador, to his box and warned that any effort to resist his German peace treaty would be futile; if the Western powers sent a new division to Germany, the Soviet Union could respond a hundredfold.

Six of his hydrogen bombs would be "quite enough" to destroy the British Isles. Nine would take care of France. Exploiting his awareness that the British were more willing than the Americans to bargain over Berlin, Khrushchev asked, "Why should two hundred million people die for two million Berliners?"

---

*David Klein of the NSC, whose mandate included Berlin, supposed that the culprit was in the White House or Defense Department.

* * *

On Tuesday evening, July 4, for the first time in three years, Khrushchev and his wife turned up at Jane and Llewellyn Thompson's Independence Day reception at Spaso House. They were followed by Mikoyan and Kozlov, Defense Minister Rodion Malinovsky, and five other Soviet marshals. The Chairman's visit was in character; he tended to make such calls when he was anxious that a crisis with the West might be about to grow overheated.

Boris Klosson entertained him until the Ambassador could gracefully leave his own receiving line: "I have a complaint. You're going to exploit me. You're going to print your new Twenty-year Plan on Sunday, so I am going to have to work on Sunday."

Khrushchev said, "You mean you're going to *read* that?" Jane Thompson gave him a Scotch highball, which he nursed and then gave to Nina Petrovna, saying, "I want to live. Mikoyan does all the drinking."

Seven-year-old Sherry Thompson took the Chairman by the hand and showed him her vegetable garden. Khrushchev inevitably demanded to see her corn patch, but she told him that the stalks were not yet high enough to display.

Someone cried, "The assault of correspondents has begun!" Khrushchev said, "We will repel it, but not with rockets." A reporter: "Our only weapon is a typewriter. Have you a secret weapon?" Khrushchev: "We need no weapons and no uniforms. All we need is brains." Mikoyan: "His tongue is his weapon." Another reporter: "That is a good weapon, and it gives us plenty of ammunition, but it is not a secret weapon."

On Saturday, July 8, Khrushchev scrapped his program to reduce the Red Army by 1.2 million men. Under military pressure, he abandoned his argument that missile forces could substitute for troops. The Soviet defense budget would be increased by one third. "These are forced measures, comrades. We take them because we cannot neglect the Soviet people's security."

He noted that Adenauer was "shouting himself hoarse for nuclear weapons." Kennedy had increased military spending. "This is how the Western powers have replied to the Soviet Union's unilateral reduction of armed forces and military expenditures over the past several years."

To remove the edge from his announcement, Khrushchev cited the President's call for a peaceful competition. "This, of course, is much better than competing in the development of ever more destructive types of weapons." Arkady Shevchenko recalled that "a crisis atmosphere prevailed as we waited to see what kind of countermeasures Kennedy would take."

The President was at Hyannis Port. Told of the announcement, he said that Khrushchev had just hardened his Berlin challenge. The previous week, he had sent John McCloy to Moscow in an effort to jump-start the Geneva disarmament talks.* Now he asked Bundy, "Should we break them off, using the recent Soviet increases as our argument, and ask that the matter be taken to the UN?"

Earlier that day, wearing a beige tweed jacket and chinos, Kennedy had joined his wife, Rusk, McNamara, Maxwell Taylor, and the Charles Spaldings for fish chowder and hot dogs aboard the *Marlin.* Jacqueline hopped over the side to water-ski. Taylor and McNamara swam. Still wearing his business suit, the Secretary of State sat on the fantail with Kennedy, who complained that a month had passed since Vienna, and still State had produced no reply to Khrushchev's Berlin aide-mémoire.

Rusk reminded him that the text had to be cleared with the Western allies: the Soviets would seize on the slightest nuance to wrench the alliance apart. The President bloviated that he did not intend to make himself dependent on the Allies. Didn't Rusk understand? The *United States* bore the main responsibility for Berlin. In the end, it alone would decide the policy.

Kennedy had read a memo from Schlesinger and two other staff members criticizing Acheson's fixation on the military aspects of the Berlin problem and what they thought to be the "least likely eventuality"—an immediate blockade of West Berlin. He agreed. He gave Rusk ten days to give him a plan for negotiations on Berlin.

Taylor and McNamara climbed back onto the boat. Still irritated, the President complained about the military planning on Berlin. If the Soviets severed access, NATO would be hard pressed to respond by conventional means. He wanted a wider choice than "holocaust or humiliation."

He gave McNamara ten days to draw up a plan for non-nuclear resistance on a scale large enough to demonstrate that the West would resist a "cheap and easy" seizure of Berlin by East German

---

*McCloy wrote Eisenhower that he was leaving "for another session with the Russians which I really do not relish, as my hands are pretty well tied, due to our relations with the Allies as well as to the other government agencies."

guards. It must be large enough to allow a true pause—a month instead of an hour—for himself and Khrushchev to choose retreat or nuclear war.

In the Cabinet Room on Thursday, July 13, Rusk told Kennedy that "Khrushchev's timetable is not under our control." If the President offered negotiations now, he could "take the fever" out of the crisis. The problem was that, as Acheson had said, the United States was "not currently in a good position to negotiate." If Khrushchev was "willing to protect our basic rights," he would not have started this confrontation.

McNamara recommended a national emergency declaration to arouse Americans to the dangers over Berlin and prepare them for sacrifice. The President should call up the reserves and the National Guard, extend the service of those on active duty, retrieve American dependents from Europe, and ask Congress for an additional $4.3 billion for defense.

Rusk worried that an emergency declaration "would have a dangerous sound of mobilization. . . . We should try to avoid actions which are not needed for sound military purposes and which would be considered provocative." Khrushchev would be more impressed if the "more drastic of our preparations" were "taken later on, as the crisis deepens." As an alternative, the President could ask Congress for a resolution to let him call up armed forces as needed.

Acheson complained that if the President did not call up reserves until late in the crisis, it would not affect Khrushchev's judgment any more than "dropping bombs after he had forced the issue to the limit." Lyndon Johnson argued that the President "should take the lead" because otherwise Congress would assume that Kennedy was shifting the burden to them.

After the meeting, the President took McNamara into the Oval Office: he should proceed on the assumption that America would act with force only if West Berlin were directly threatened. Only two things mattered in this crisis: "our presence in Berlin" and "our access." The United States would not challenge the Soviet Union in its own sphere of influence.

The U.S. government had still not responded to Khrushchev's Berlin aide-mémoire. Members of the Kennedy circle later transformed the long delay into a famous parable demonstrating the torpor of the State Department. In an interview, the President later complained that it took "many weeks to get our answer out through the State Department. . . . It seems to me that one of the functions of the President is to try to have it move with more speed. Otherwise you can wait while the world collapses."

The actual story was not so clear-cut. Martin Hillenbrand of State later recalled that a draft reply was sent shortly after Vienna, but that "White House administrative procedures were so sloppy it ended up in the safe of a presidential aide named Ralph Dungan, who then went off on a two-week holiday. . . . Finally we provided another draft when it was admitted that the first version couldn't be found in the White House. Obviously none of this was told to the President by his staff, and the State Department took the blame."

When the text finally reached the Oval Office, Kennedy and Bundy found it a paste-up of stale proposals and statements from the Berlin Crisis of 1958. They felt it had not been taken seriously: just another Cold War document to be ground out and soon forgotten.

The President asked Sorensen to write a "shorter, simpler version." Foy Kohler complained that any new version would have to be cleared with the Allies, which would take more time. As Kohler recalled, Kennedy had yet to decide his Berlin policy, "and I was goddamned if we were going to let a note go out without a basis for something to say." Kohler found that such arguments had "little effect" on Robert Kennedy, "who thought we were ineffective." The reply to Khrushchev's aide-mémoire was finally sent six weeks after Vienna.

That same month, the President complained to Bundy that a draft letter from Lyndon Johnson to Chiang Kai-shek was "hopeless": "I am shocked that it could be approved by them." After the Inauguration, unhappy with suggested replies to heads of state, he had finally sat down and dictated his own. Robert Kennedy recalled that major documents "all had to be done or redone by the President or somebody over at the White House, and that disgusted him. . . . Not only did they not have any ideas, but they were badly written."

John Kenneth Galbraith later distilled the Kennedy view of the State Department in his pseudonymous novel *The McLandress Dimension*. In Galbraith's rendering, the department acquires a large computer that enables it to realize its dream of a "fully automated foreign policy": in reply to a Soviet harangue, the machine spits out enough boilerplate and clichés to avoid the cardinal sin of innovation.

Kennedy felt that much of the State Department "really objects to my being President." He said, "They're not queer, but, well, they're sort of like Adlai." Galbraith wrote him from New Delhi, "If the State Department drives you crazy, you might calm yourself by contemplating its effect on me. The other night I woke with a blissful feeling and discovered I had been dreaming that the whole goddamn place had burned down. I dozed off again hoping for a headline saying no survivors."

Increasingly the President relied on McGeorge Bundy. He told Jacqueline that with the exception of David Ormsby-Gore, his national security adviser was the brightest man he had ever known: "Damn it, Bundy and I get more done in one day in the White House than they do in six months at the State Department."

Bundy made it his business to supply the loyalty, speed, and imagination that Kennedy felt he could not get from the State Department. He hired audacious young men for his NSC staff to act as presidential eyes and ears, keep the bureaucracy from sabotaging Kennedy's purposes, and bring the President options that might otherwise be filtered out in the struggle for bureaucratic consensus. Asked what he would have done if he were Secretary of State with Bundy at the NSC, Dean Acheson said, "Resign."

Kennedy's acquaintance with his foreign policy aide had been so slight at first that he frequently called him "McBundy." By the summer of 1961, Bundy spent more time in the Oval Office than any other senior aides except O'Donnell and Sorensen.

Encouraged by the President, he departed from precedent by giving speeches that set policy and by refusing to act, as Andrew Goodpaster had, mainly as a neutral conveyor of information between the White House and the agencies.* Kennedy joked, "I only hope he leaves a few residual functions to me." He told Ben Bradlee, "You can't beat brains, and with brains, judgment. . . . He does a tremendous amount of work. And he doesn't fold or get rattled when they're sniping at him."

To documents and cables Bundy often appended a note in the jocular we-own-the-world shorthand that amused his boss: "A shocker from the Italian mail. . . . Intercept conversation of the UAR [Egypt] Ambassador in Bonn with [Franz-Josef] Strauss which I send

---

*Under Eisenhower, Goodpaster's official title had been Staff Secretary, but he performed most of the functions later fulfilled by men like Bundy, Rostow, Kissinger, and Zbigniew Brzezinski, all of whom held the title of Assistant to the President for National Security Affairs. Gordon Gray, who held this title under Eisenhower, concentrated on long-range foreign policy planning.

along because it tells a good deal about Strauss and a little about us.* . . . Background explanation of Saud's bad temper. . . . An Afghan thriller. . . . The Shah gives the Secretary the business. . . . If you disapprove, we can turn around next week. . . . Memorandum showing that the Africans neither like nor dislike us as much as we think."

With his well-developed sense of public service, Bundy was admirably willing to take the fall if a decision was likely to cause Kennedy political damage, writing, "I think the White House should gang up again on that convenient scapegoat McBungle."

In September 1962, after a Chester Bowles speech on Cuba, Bundy reported to the President, "A semi-comedy of low-level errors. . . . All concerned were sloppy (and clearance within State was even sloppier). I have spread enough terror so that I doubt if this particular mistake will occur again. . . . I have also explained to the bright young Yale man who works for Bowles that his boss, when he speaks in this vein, is not heard by the Great American Public and is only a target for the cabbages of the Republicans."

Another service Bundy performed was to enhance the ethnic diversity of the West Wing. He was the only full-fledged Anglo-Saxon Protestant on the first string of the Kennedy staff. Like McNamara, Dillon, McCloy, and others, he satisfied the President's self-protective instinct to use Republicans in foreign policy. In 1962, Bundy asked Kennedy whether it would be "useful" if he reregistered as a Democrat since, after working for him, he now "felt like a Democrat." The President replied that it was "marginally more useful to me to be able to say that you're a Republican." Bundy dropped the idea.

Kennedy consulted him on all manner of things. Worried that he and Jacqueline would seem like "a couple of swells," he asked Bundy in May 1962 whether he thought it politically wise to let the First Lady go to a Virginia horse show in formal riding clothes. Bundy replied with a poem:

> "Shall I let her in the Horse Show?"
> The President was gloomy.
> "Will our critics strike a worse blow
> Than on Steel or Trib or Phoumi?"† . . .

---

*This refers to a report of a conversation intercepted by American intelligence in Bonn, perhaps by an eavesdropping device placed in the West German Defense Ministry or the Egyptian Embassy.
†"Steel" and "Trib" referred to the President's 1962 confrontation with U.S. Steel president Roger Blough over a steel price increase, and his cancellation of White

It is a sign of pride—a horse,
But not a thing to hide—a horse,
Assuming you provide—of course,
A brave and lovely lady who can ride.

For voters dare to admire the fair,
And voters crave to honor the brave;
Only the rich are likely to bitch,
But which rich itch for us anyway?

So smothering doubts the President shouts,
"I who decide say, 'Let her ride!'
I can't say No—on with the Show;
All systems GO—*and* A-OK.*"**

Third of three sons, Bundy was born in 1919 to what he called a "cold roast Boston" family. His mother was a Lowell. His father, born in Grand Rapids, Michigan, had finished first in his Harvard Law School class. The family saint was Henry L. Stimson, the legendary public servant under whom Harvey Bundy served when he was Herbert Hoover's Secretary of State and Franklin Roosevelt's Secretary of War.

The young Bundy grew up knowing Stimson, Acheson, and other members of the northeastern foreign policy patriciate, maturing in a household that demanded brilliance, excellence, competition, and logical, persuasive argument. From an early age, he seemed governed by his own gyroscope. At Groton he resisted the hero worship for the famous rector Endicott Peabody, whom he found anti-intellectual and anti-meritocratic. Despite his considerable Harvard ancestry, he enrolled at Yale, where he was the first freshman matriculant to win three perfect scores on his entrance exams.

After graduation in 1940, Bundy gravitated to Harvard as a member of the Society of Fellows, which had been endowed by his great-uncle, the Harvard President A. Lawrence Lowell, to free promising young scholars from what he feared to be the deadening influence of gradu-

---

House subscriptions to the *New York Herald Tribune* out of pique at what he took to be its anti-Kennedy line.
*As with most of Kennedy's presidential life, this episode had its subtext. Attending the horse show caused Mrs. Kennedy to miss her husband's vast forty-fifth birthday celebration at Madison Square Garden, at which Marilyn Monroe sang her famous sultry chorus of "Happy Birthday," joining the President afterward at a private party.

ate school. Invited to run for the Boston City Council in a heavily Republican district, Bundy was defeated by a Democratic unknown in what he later called "the worst-conducted campaign in history."

After Pearl Harbor, Bundy memorized the eye chart to enter Army Intelligence. A family friend, Vice Admiral Alan Kirk, commander of amphibious forces in the Atlantic, took him on as his aide-de-camp in the invasion of Sicily.* In 1943, Bundy wrote his friend John Mason Brown, the drama critic, "Wars are full of glory and greatness, but they are not of themselves, as a whole, either one or the other—they are ugly." Later he wrote, "Why did we all so much together—in spite of our astonishing and general loneliness? None of the novels help on this—for me at least."

In June 1944, when the U.S.S. *Augusta* reached Normandy, Bundy stood on the flag bridge with Kirk. He used his excellent French to help the Admiral set up headquarters in Paris. After VE-Day, he won a transfer to the infantry in the Pacific for the invasion of Japan that never came. In 1946, he moved into the guesthouse at Stimson's Long Island estate to collaborate on the Colonel's memoirs, the story of America's rise from isolationism to great power. He worked in 1948 under his old Yale economics teacher Richard Bissell on the Marshall Plan and wrote foreign policy speeches for Thomas Dewey.

Bundy joined Harvard as a lecturer on "The United States and World Politics" and became Dean of the Faculty at thirty-four, serving as a counterweight to what Galbraith called the "far from compelling rule" of President Nathan Pusey. He kept a hand in Republican politics. "I go to Temple Israel to preach the gospel according to Eisenhower," he wrote Brown in 1952. "Come and be converted, if you're a backslider to Adlai."

In September 1953, Eisenhower's national security adviser, Robert Cutler, asked Bundy to leave Harvard to serve as his deputy. Bundy had to say no; he had just been appointed Dean and could not leave after one month. He also "felt no great love" for Foster Dulles. Had Bundy taken the job and then succeeded Cutler, he would have been one of the chief defenders of the Eisenhower foreign policy against John Kennedy's fusillades in the fall of 1960.

Bundy had attended Dexter School in Brookline with the future President and his older brother: "I doubt if I knew which Kennedy was

*In 1961, Bundy persuaded Kennedy to appoint Kirk Ambassador to Taipei, arguing that the Admiral's experience with amphibious landings would allow him to show Chiang Kai-shek how difficult it would be to retake the mainland.

which. . . . We wound up in the same college class at two different colleges, and I used to see him around Boston socially then. I saw more of his sister Kathleen, but that is the way those things work."

In the spring of 1952, Arthur Schlesinger, Jr., invited Bundy to lunch in Cambridge to "talk about whether Jack should run for the Senate." Bundy told Kennedy that Henry Cabot Lodge was a shoo-in: "You could obviously become the Speaker of the House if you would just stay where you are." After watching Kennedy recoil from the notion of a lifetime in the House, Bundy noted that he never asked him for this kind of political advice again.

Bundy saw Kennedy more often after the Senator was elected a Harvard overseer. In 1958, Republican advertisements quoted Bundy as saying that the Democratic Governor, Foster Furcolo, was not a bad man, just a bad governor. Kennedy laughingly asked Bundy, "What makes you think he's not a bad man?"

By 1960, Bundy feared that the Eisenhower regime was losing the initiative in the Cold War. Finding Kennedy "much better than Nixon," he told the Senator at the Harvard commencement that he would support him. He knew from the Dewey campaign that "you can't help much from the outside," but he fed ideas to the Kennedy caravan from a distance.

After the election, over drinks at the Boston Ritz-Carlton, he told Sargent Shriver he would be interested in joining the government "but it would depend on the job." When Robert Lovett and Walter Lippmann suggested him for Secretary of State, Kennedy said, "He's rather young, isn't he?"

The President-elect was momentarily captured by the idea of Bundy at State. Bright, unconventional, Bundy was nationally unknown and hence had few enemies in Washington and no independent political following. He was an iconoclastic Republican and had the Establishment credentials to quell doubts about Kennedy's age, his father, his seriousness, and his narrow plurality. Finally the President-elect observed that "two baby faces like mine and his are just too much."

After choosing Dean Rusk, he suggested Bundy as number two, but Rusk preferred Chester Bowles. Kennedy called Bundy to the Carlyle and said that he did not want to create new jobs: he didn't want "New Deal bureaucrats lousing up the government." Did Bundy know Rusk and would he consider being Under Secretary for Political Affairs? This would make him number three in the Department. Bundy agreed; he knew and liked Rusk from the Rockefeller Foundation.

Embarrassed, the President-elect soon had to tell Bundy that Bowles had decided to specialize in political affairs. By statute, that meant the number three man had to specialize in economics: "I don't

think *either* of us could keep a straight face if we put you into *that* job."
As Bundy recalled, the next weeks passed in "awful silence." Then
Kennedy offered him Under Secretary for Administration. Bundy replied that he had been an administrator for years: he didn't have it in
him to straighten out "that crazy department."

As Bundy and his family were trimming their Christmas tree,
Kennedy called once more to offer him Special Assistant to the President for National Security Affairs. Bundy accepted. In 1960, this position lacked the prominence that Bundy and later incumbents of the
job gave it. But Bundy shrewdly judged that the post would at least
allow him to work closely with Kennedy: "That seemed to be worth
whatever I didn't know about it."

By May 1961, he had moved across West Executive Avenue into the
West Wing basement. Soon he informed O'Donnell that his quarters
were too small: "The President called it a pigpen and my pride is
hurt. . . . In the olden days of Eisenhower, the NSC people all stayed
on the other side—but I can't do my job from over there. . . . It all
comes from having a President who has taken charge of foreign affairs."

Bundy genuinely admired Kennedy and made certain allowances
for the Kennedy style. He would probably not have been seen dancing
at a party with the actress Angie Dickinson had Eisenhower brought
him to the White House. On occasion he set himself apart from the
Kennedy subculture. When the public learned of the President's taste
for spy novels, Bundy firmly told a reporter, "I am not an Ian Fleming
fan."

He never let off steam or tried to improve his own reputation in the
manner of later presidential aides by making disloyal private cutting
comments about the boss to reporters. His ample skepticism and
self-esteem prevented him from becoming a yes-man. When he challenged the President, he heeded his finely tuned instinct about what
would cross the line into insolence; with Kennedy, the threshold was
higher than with most Presidents.

Bundy much later recalled that when he and his colleague Myer
Feldman once dropped in on Kennedy, "he was having one of his
pretty girls rubbing some goo on his hair, some perfect prescription
that somebody had recommended for healthy hair. I said I didn't think
this kind of thing was sufficiently dignified for the Oval Office. He
looked around at Mike and me—both of us without much hair—and
said, 'Well, I'm not sure you two *plan* your hair very well.' "

Years later Bundy could not recall Kennedy saying thank-you five
times: "It wasn't that he was ungenerous, but you don't get to be
President without being concerned about Number One." Still, for

Bundy these were glorious years when the world seemed to be young and bright with hope, a period that may have seemed especially appealing in retrospect after Bundy had the experience of working under President Lyndon Johnson on Vietnam.

In July 1961, Ambassador Menshikov was telling everyone in Washington who would listen that "when the chips are down, the American people won't fight for Berlin." Khrushchev's aide Fyodor Burlatsky recalled that virtually no one in the Soviet government believed Americans would use nuclear weapons to protect Berlin: "Maybe we were wrong, maybe we were stupid."

Robert Kennedy arranged a meeting with Bolshakov. He was evidently willing to excuse the bald misinformation that the Russian had transmitted about Khrushchev's willingness to compromise on nuclear testing at Vienna; the Kennedys had concluded that the Chairman had had an honest change of heart. Bolshakov warned that, as usual, Menshikov was telling Khrushchev "what he'd like to hear," that if he used pressure, the President would collapse and the Soviet Union would "take over Berlin." Bolshakov said he was trying to correct the misimpression.

Over lunch at the Soviet Embassy, the Attorney General insisted to Menshikov that he and the President would prefer death to surrender. The envoy replied with polite incredulity. Kennedy became so angry that he almost left the room. Glaring at Menshikov, he declared that the United States would never abandon Berlin: the Ambassador had better tell that to Mr. Khrushchev—without editing.

Other Americans supplemented Kennedy's message. Paul Nitze had Menshikov to lunch at the Metropolitan Club and warned him that the Soviet Union would be devastated by the multimegaton nuclear attacks prescribed in American war plans. Walt Rostow reminded Menshikov that when backed against the wall, people were inclined to bravery.

McNamara's aide Henry Rowen and Carl Kaysen of the NSC staff were alarmed, as Kaysen recalled, that if the confrontation in central Europe "reached a military level and it started to go against us," the existing plans were to "just let go with all our strategic forces against the Soviet Union, the Eastern bloc countries, and China as well."

Kaysen and Rowen decided to ask themselves, "How small a strike can you make that will . . . be a warning and only do such carnage as is absolutely inevitable if you're going to use nuclear weapons at all?"

They drew up a "back-of-the-envelope" first-strike plan that would disable Soviet nuclear forces before they could attack. Tactical nuclear weapons in Europe, nuclear aircraft carriers, and alert bombers would be used to "take out Soviet missile and bomber bases" with the least possible destruction of people and property not directly involved with Soviet military sites.

Paul Nitze opposed the idea, noting that it could not be certain of preventing the Kremlin from launching its many short- and medium-range nuclear weapons against Western Europe, killing tens of millions of people. The maverick Marcus Raskin of the NSC staff asked Kaysen, "How does this make us any better than those who measured the gas ovens or the engineers who built the tracks for the death trains in Nazi Germany?"

Kaysen took the plan to Sorensen, who said, "You're crazy! We shouldn't let guys like you around here." He said it was "an outrageous thought" and the President "would never consider it." Years later Sorensen was not certain that the plan ever made it to the Oval Office.

On Wednesday afternoon, July 19, the President convened what Bundy called "the most important NSC meeting that we have had." Kennedy had to rule on the rapid conventional buildup proposed by Acheson to show that the United States had "irretrievably committed ourselves to the defense of Berlin."

During his Berlin crisis, Eisenhower had rebuffed such a notion. Certain that there was nothing that the Soviets wanted so badly they would risk the annihilation of the Kremlin, he felt that the United States must simply stand "right and ready"; as long as Khrushchev was convinced that the President would use the Bomb to defend Western rights in Berlin, there was no need for additional troops.*

Kennedy could not be so sure that Khrushchev respected his will. A conventional buildup would help to show the Chairman that he was not a pushover. It could also relieve a stark presidential choice between "holocaust and humiliation"—or "suicide and surrender," the other catch phrase of the time. Kennedy was worried that Khrushchev would reduce access to Berlin so gradually that the United States

---

*Eisenhower wrote John McCloy in June 1961, "I think the evidence is clear that Russia respects and fears our destructive power. . . . She is so determined to avoid an out-and-out military challenge with us that ever since World War II she has used only satellite or puppet forces, except in the single case of Hungary, an area already behind the Iron Curtain."

would lose the city before it was provoked into waging a nuclear attack: "If Mr. Khrushchev believes that all we have is the atomic bomb, he is going to feel that we are . . . somewhat unlikely to use it."

The Berlin Crisis provided both reason and a pretext for the President to promote his doctrine of "flexible response." Even aside from the Berlin problem, McNamara's people had found important defects and shortages in the American conventional force structure: large numbers of torpedoes without batteries, rifles without bullets, antiaircraft guns in disrepair.

Kennedy approved a substantial buildup. The United States would prepare a new Berlin airlift and the capability to move six more divisions to Europe by the time of Khrushchev's December peace-treaty deadline. It would increase naval strength and the number of bombers on ground-alert status and tactical and transport aircraft. The additional $3.5 billion incurred by this buildup would bring the total Kennedy increase in military spending since the Inauguration to $6 billion. The President would ask Congress for standby authority to triple draft calls, call up reserves, and impose economic sanctions against the Warsaw Pact nations.

Kennedy had trimmed Acheson's original request by $800 million and refused his demand for immediate mobilization of American forces. He was influenced in part by a Thompson cable from Moscow arguing that a measured, long-term buildup would impress Khrushchev more than sudden escalation.

Reflecting the views of Bohlen, Thompson, and most of his White House colleagues, Sorensen cautioned Kennedy not to "engage Khrushchev's prestige to a point where he felt he could not back down from a showdown, and provoke further or faster action on his part in stepping up the arms race." Opposing Acheson's view that Khrushchev would interpret any bargaining offer as weakness, the President resolved to "lean forward" on negotiations as soon as he had established American resolve. He did not intend to let Khrushchev choose the "framework of discussion."

Kennedy also vetoed Acheson's suggestion of a national emergency declaration. Kissinger had warned that this would seem "unnecessarily bellicose, perhaps even hysterical." Not for the first or last time, the President complained that he did not know where Rusk stood on the matter. Kennedy now felt that a national emergency "was an alarm bell which could only be rung once." It would only convince the Soviets "of our panic."

Some presidential advisers suggested financing the new military spending with an income tax increase of one percent or more. Robert

Kennedy thought that the tax would help Americans "understand the seriousness of the situation and everybody therefore would feel involved in it." Rusk, McNamara, and Lyndon Johnson agreed. The President overruled them when Douglas Dillon warned that the increase might kill the nation's recovery from recession.* Kennedy later told O'Donnell that he "couldn't believe" that his brother, a "supposedly experienced" politician, could "even think of raising income taxes at a time like this."

The President raised the matter of fallout shelters, which he saw as a means to reduce the Soviet Union's estimate of its ability to harm the American land mass. Kennedy had been told that without shelters, seventy-nine million people would be killed in a nuclear attack. The number could be reduced to fifty million. The President decided to ask Congress for $207 million for civil defense.

Indignant that his recommendations were not being fully adopted, Acheson now rose to the attack. He insisted on declaring a national emergency and on calling up reserves no later than September 1961. McNamara replied that it would be "wrong to accept a rigid timetable in advance." He did not want "large reserve forces on hand with no mission." The six newly created Army divisions and the two new Marine divisions could be sent to Europe at the moment trouble broke out. Reserves would be summoned to replace them.

Acheson later told colleagues, "Gentlemen, you might as well face it. This nation is without leadership."

One of the two main purposes of Kennedy's new Berlin policy was to reduce the chance that Khrushchev could quickly and easily take over the city. The other was to convince him that if the Western position were seriously challenged, Kennedy might well choose holocaust over humiliation.

That summer, with only Bundy present, Kennedy asked Acheson at what stage in the crisis he thought nuclear weapons might have to be used. More measured and quiet than usual, Acheson replied, "If I were you, I'd think about it very hard and tell no one what I'd decided."†

---

*After consulting Wilbur Mills, Chairman of the House Ways and Means Committee, O'Donnell told Robert that his tax proposal "would have been stuck in the House of Representatives for the next twenty-five years."
†In a 1959 *Saturday Evening Post* article, Acheson had written that the correct final choice might be to accept defeat if the only alternative was nuclear war. Bundy years later wrote that Acheson "may have consoled himself with the thought that nothing

McNamara later insisted that during the Berlin Crisis "there was absolutely no thought given by the President or me or Secretary Rusk to the use of nuclear weapons."* Bundy wrote more prudently that "nobody ever knew" what Kennedy would do if forced "to choose between defeat and the release of nuclear weapons."

The President was scheduled to speak to the American people on Tuesday evening, July 25, at ten o'clock. Bundy told Sorensen, "The President will do well in a quite literal sense to speak softly while he describes his new big stick."

Late on Tuesday afternoon, Sorensen sent pieces of the final text to Kennedy in the upstairs West Hall of the White House. Kennedy read each passage aloud so that Dave Powers could time it for length. Sorensen considered the text more somber than any presidential speech since the Soviet acquisition of nuclear weapons. Kennedy scribbled a personal note to go at the end of the speech and asked Evelyn Lincoln to type it up.

The Oval Office was jammed with seven television and newsreel cameras and burning lights, White House aides, Secret Service men, technicians, still photographers, and print reporters, including Tom Wicker of the *New York Times,* Mary McGrory of the *Washington Star,* and a TASS correspondent. When Kennedy walked in, one reporter thought he looked "tense and nervous." The President complained about the heat, mopping his upper lip, and strode out into the night air before taking his place at his desk.

Watching from Hyannis Port, Jacqueline felt "a little shooting pain of fright." She worried that "even Jack" might not be able to make this crisis "turn out for the best."

Kennedy looked into the camera: "Seven weeks ago tonight, I returned from Europe to report on my meeting with Premier Khrushchev and the others. . . . In Berlin, as you recall, he intends to bring to an end, through a stroke of the pen, *first* our legal rights to be in West Berlin—and *secondly* our ability to make good on our commit-

---

is more secret than a sentence buried in a two-year-old weekly." In fact, in 1961, some enterprising reporters unearthed and published his view. The fact that even this most militant of Kennedy's advisers on Berlin questioned the wisdom of nuclear war over the city was almost certainly noted by Khrushchev's circle and would have further convinced him that the President would not use the Bomb if pushed to the brink.

*He recalled that at one point he privately advised Kennedy never to initiate the use of nuclear weapons and Kennedy agreed. If this exchange conveyed Kennedy's genuine views, it very likely took place later and was the partial result of the President's experience in the Berlin Crisis.

ment to the two million free people in that city. That we cannot permit."

He restated the American commitment: "We have given our word that an attack upon that city will be regarded as an attack upon us all. . . . We cannot and will not permit the Communists to drive us out of Berlin." In a passage suggested by General Taylor, he went on, "I hear it said that West Berlin is militarily untenable. So was Bastogne. And so, in fact, was Stalingrad. Any dangerous spot is tenable if men—brave men—will make it so. We do not want to fight, but we have fought before."

Announcing his Berlin defense buildup and the call-up of reserves, he said, "I am well aware of the fact that many American families will bear the burden. . . . Studies or careers will be interrupted. Husbands and sons will be called away. Incomes in some cases will be reduced. But these are burdens which must be borne if freedom is to be defended. Americans have willingly borne them before, and they will not flinch now."

He was asking for new funds to "identify and mark space" for "fallout shelters in case of attack" and to stock them with "food, water, first-aid kits, and other minimum essentials for survival." No President had ever spoken so directly about the possibility of nuclear attack. "The lives of those families which are not hit in a nuclear blast and fire can still be saved—*if* they can be warned to take shelter, and *if* that shelter is *available.*"

To convey willingness to negotiate, Sorensen had included something Kennedy had said during his Berlin deliberations: "We do not want military considerations to dominate the thinking of either East or West." At Bundy's suggestion the President acknowledged the Soviet Union's "historical concern" about its European security after "ravaging invasions." The United States was ready to "remove any irritants in West Berlin" but not the city's freedom. He used a line provided by Edward R. Murrow, the fabled broadcast newsman whom he had appointed Director of the U.S. Information Agency: "We cannot negotiate with those who say, 'What's mine is mine, and what's yours is negotiable.'"

He spoke to his international audience: "The source of world trouble and tension is Moscow, not Berlin. And if war begins, it will have begun in Moscow and not Berlin. . . . It is the Soviets who have stirred up this crisis. It is they who are trying to force a change.* . . . To sum it all up, we seek peace, but we shall not surrender."

---

*Here the President was quoting himself to Khrushchev at Vienna in a line provided by de Gaulle.

Now he read from the peroration he had scrawled out in his bedroom. "I would like to close with a personal word. When I ran for the Presidency of the United States, I knew that this country faced serious challenges. But I could not realize—nor could any man realize who does not bear the burdens of this office—how heavy and constant would be those burdens. . . . I know that sometimes we get impatient. . . . But I must tell you that there is no quick and easy solution. The Communists control over a billion people, and they recognize that if we should falter, their success would be imminent. . . .

"I ask for your help and your advice. I ask for your suggestions, when you think we could do better. All of us, I know, love our country. And we shall do our best to serve it. In meeting my responsibilities in these coming months as President, I need your goodwill and your support—and above all, your prayers. Thank you, and good night."

After the hot lights were dimmed, Kennedy did not smile or say a word to the dozens of people in the Oval Office. He walked back to the family quarters alone.

"That boy is cool," said Lyndon Johnson. "If he has to press that button, he will. . . . He's tough. I know. He beat *me!*" Richard Nixon backed Kennedy's toughness on Berlin but asked why he did not also resume nuclear testing and move against Castro. Nixon and other Republicans said that the President should have increased taxes or cut social programs to support his new military proposals. So did the largest number of the twenty thousand letters and telegrams sent to the White House. A few proposed assassinating Khrushchev.

Robert Hartmann wrote in the *Los Angeles Times* that Kennedy was "trying very hard to be a great leader of a troubled nation, yet he conveyed the impression that he was the most troubled citizen of all." The *Indianapolis News* said that "America has been waiting for that kind of talk from the White House." TASS claimed that the President's defense buildup was intended to rescue his industrialist masters from their economic slump.

The *Times* of London said, MR. KENNEDY "READY TO SEARCH FOR PEACE."* Most American newspapers ignored the President's refer-

---

*The previous week Ambassador David Bruce had cabled from London, "The prospect of the Berlin Crisis provoking or leading, through inadvertence or accident, to nuclear war is regarded here with horror." Bruce noted that stout as the British were in a showdown, "their national political temperament inclines them to compromise, even at the expense of principle. . . . Nor do German prosperity, rates of

ences to negotiation, stressing instead the defense buildup and fallout shelters. To send a message to the Russians that Kennedy was serious about bargaining once American resolve had been demonstrated, anonymous government officials leaked specific items on which they said the President might be flexible.

In the *New York Times,* James Reston reported that "the eastern boundary of Germany is negotiable. So is the level of forces in Berlin, all of Germany, and Eastern Europe." Marguerite Higgins of the *New York Herald Tribune,* whose daughter's godfather was the Attorney General, reported that Kennedy was thinking of "some kind of 20- to 50-year nonaggression pact" with the Soviet Union, providing "reciprocal guarantee against a revival of German nationalism."

After learning that Kennedy would announce his Berlin decisions on July 25, Khrushchev had invited John McCloy to fly from Moscow to Pitsunda. He almost certainly wanted to use the diplomat as a means of direct communication with the President after his Berlin speech, if it proved necessary.

McCloy arrived with his wife, his twenty-year-old daughter, and a niece. The next morning, Khrushchev buzzed over to the McCloys' villa by motorboat. Wearing a pair of the Chairman's oversized bathing trunks, McCloy leaped into the Black Sea with Khrushchev. A photographer was called to photograph the smiling Communist in the water with his fleshy arm around the bare shoulder of the smiling capitalist.

Khrushchev was in a jolly mood as they strolled in the lush gardens and played badminton. Exchanging diplomatic notes, he said, was like kicking a football back and forth: this would continue until a treaty was signed and the Soviet Union kicked a different kind of ball. Then the Chairman was sent a Russian translation of Kennedy's Berlin speech. His merriment ended.

The next morning, he told McCloy that the United States had just declared "preliminary war" on the Soviet Union. What he had said in his speech on wars of liberation had been right: the capitalist world had clearly lost faith in its ability to prevail by peaceful means. President Kennedy seemed a "reasonable young man," filled with energy

---

taxation . . . and tranquil subordination to leadership endear their citizens and institutions to the British. Joy through work is not a British ideal, as it is in West Germany. Envy of nascent German power is galling to those who for more than a century considered the exercise of power in Europe their peculiar prerogative. The same reflection applies, in diminished force, to their suspicion and envy of ourselves."

and doubtless eager to display it. But if war broke out, Kennedy would be "the last President of the United States." The next war would be decided by the biggest rockets. These were under the Soviet Union's command.

He warned McCloy that the Russians now had a hundred-megaton hydrogen bomb, the largest in the world. His scientists were eager to test it. He had assured them that the United States would soon give them the opportunity by breaking the moratorium, saying, "Don't piss in your pants. You'll have your chance soon enough."

Khrushchev told McCloy that he would sign a German treaty "no matter what." Access would be cut off, and the United States would have to "make a deal" with East Germany. "If you attempt to force your way through, we will oppose you by force. War is bound to be thermonuclear, and though you and we may survive, all your European allies will be completely destroyed."

As he did when he habitually promised to drop hydrogen bombs on London, Paris, and other cities, Khrushchev softened his threat by saying that he still believed in the President's good sense. After thunderstorms, people cooled off and thought problems over. The Soviets and the Americans were both great peoples and should be friends. There was nothing to go to war about if both sides were reasonable. They should negotiate to guarantee access to Berlin and settle the German problem—"the only serious one between us."

After returning to Moscow, McCloy wired Kennedy at Hyannis Port that Khrushchev was "really mad on Thursday after digesting the President's speech. He used rough, warlike language, returning to cordiality after the storm had passed. . . . My estimate is that the situation is probably not yet ripe for any negotiation proffers by us but too dangerous to permit it to drift into a condition where cramped time could well lead to unfortunate action."

McCloy reported that both Ambassador Thompson and he felt the Soviets would soon be pressing the Western allies "with threats of destruction to weaken their determination to go along with us." He was flying to Europe and wished to "personally emphasize to NATO heads the importance of standing firm." He wrote that "de Gaulle may wish to see me in Paris." He assumed he could "talk freely with him re Khrushchev's comments."*

The President liked McCloy but was wary that this self-made, willful, loquacious Republican might try to tie his hands by conducting

---

*The French Ambassador, Herve Alphand, had already complained to Bundy on de Gaulle's behalf about sending McCloy to the Soviet Union at a time when the United States was supposed to demonstrate fortitude on Berlin.

his own diplomacy in Europe. He had Rusk wire McCloy, "Believe you should report personally to President prior to any report to NATO representatives. . . . President and I therefore request that you return directly to Washington."

East Germans were more fearful than ever that their access to the West through Berlin would soon be closed. The refugee flow had been quickened in recent years by East Germany's brutal efforts to collectivize agriculture and reform heavy industry. Khrushchev had urged the East Germans not to be "so quick" with the changes. But as his aide Burlatsky recalled, "We were not in control. Khrushchev knew he was not like Stalin, who felt he could but move his little finger in order to be in control of the Eastern bloc."

Since Khrushchev's July 8 speech increasing the Soviet defense budget by one third, twenty-six thousand East Germans had fled to the West. Harold Macmillan noted in his diary that this was "a record number of refugees leaving the Marxist Heaven of East Germany for the Capitalist Hell (or at least Purgatory) of West Berlin."

In Washington on Sunday morning, July 30, Senator Fulbright was asked on national television whether he thought the Berlin Crisis should be eased by closing the West Berlin escape hatch. He said, "The truth of the matter is, I think, the Russians have the power to close it in any case. I mean, you are not giving up very much because . . . next week, if they chose to close their borders, they could, without violating any treaty. I don't understand why the East Germans don't close their border because I think they have a right to close it."

Outraged, *Der Tagesspiegel* of West Berlin noted that Dean Acheson had helped to provoke the Korean War by declaring South Korea outside the American defense perimeter. East German papers exulted that Fulbright had offered a "realistic" formula for compromise. Bundy gave Kennedy what he called "a variety of comment from Bonn and Berlin, including reference to the helpful impact of Senator Fulbright's remarks."

Years afterward Bundy insisted that his use of the word "helpful" was meant to be sarcastic. But many wondered whether Fulbright's suggestion, along with Mansfield's about a "free city" in June, spoken by the two Senate Democrats with the greatest foreign policy influence, were inspired by the President in order to telegraph Khrushchev about a possible Berlin compromise that he dare not mention in public himself.

On Monday evening, July 31, Kennedy saw McCloy in the White House family quarters and interviewed him about his sessions with

Khrushchev. A few days later, striding with Rostow down the colonnade outside the Oval Office, he pondered what would happen next. Thompson had cabled from Moscow in March, "If we expect the Soviets to leave the Berlin problem as is, then we must at least expect the East Germans to seal off the sector boundary in order to stop what they must consider intolerable continuation of the refugee flow through Berlin."

Now the President told Rostow, "Khrushchev is losing East Germany. He cannot let that happen. If East Germany goes, so will Poland and all of Eastern Europe. He will have to do something to stop the flow of refugees. Perhaps a wall. And we won't be able to prevent it. I can hold the Alliance together to defend West Berlin, but I cannot act to keep East Berlin open."

CHAPTER

11

"A Wall Is a Hell of a Lot Better Than a War"

Aт THE KREMLIN ON SATURDAY, AUGUST 5, WALTER ULBRICHT, THE goateed, bespectacled party chief of East Germany, pleaded with Khrushchev for permission to seal the East Berlin border. Since January, Ulbricht had badgered the Chairman about the subject by letter or telephone at least two or three times a month.

At the end of March, Khrushchev had told Ulbricht that a border closing would be "premature." The Americans were planning the Bay of Pigs: the Chairman may have been loath to give Kennedy a pretext for sending U.S. armed forces into Cuba. Khrushchev and his circle merely told Ulbricht to "prepare everything" for a possible sealing at a later moment.

Ulbricht came to Moscow on Monday, July 31, and suggested blocking the air lanes between Berlin and the West, which were being used to fly out hundreds of refugees a day. Khrushchev refused, saying that it might provoke war. Once again Ulbricht asked about closing the

266

border. Khrushchev told him to wait until the Warsaw Pact leadership conference, scheduled, at Ulbricht's request, for the following Thursday.

At the Thursday meeting, Ulbricht warned that if nothing were done to stop the drain of valuable East German workers and professionals—two and a half million since 1949—as well as the forty thousand daily *Grenzgänger* [border-crossers] employed in West Berlin, the GDR could not meet its production commitments to the Soviet bloc. He warned that signs of unrest were everywhere. An uprising like the one that nearly toppled his government in 1953 could succeed this time. The refugee problem must be solved "here and now."

Khrushchev said he would approve a border closing if Ulbricht could promise that his security forces could preserve order and that his economy could survive, should the West Germans break off trade. Claiming in public that he had to deal with a West German "polio epidemic," Ulbricht rushed back to East Berlin and summoned his security chief, Erich Honecker, and other top ministers to his plush villa in suburban Wandlitz.

Through the night, he sought their reassurance about the East German economy and maintenance of order. They all agreed that construction of the barrier should begin on a weekend, when East and West Berliners would not be traveling to jobs across the boundary and when political leaders around the world would be relaxing.

By early Saturday morning, Ulbricht was back in Moscow. Perhaps to discipline the arrogant party boss whom he ultimately trusted no more than he did any other German, Khrushchev compelled him to wait for hours while he attended to other matters. Then, surrounded by other Warsaw Pact leaders, Ulbricht renewed his appeal. He evidently insisted that the Americans would do nothing to stop a border closing and quoted Fulbright's statement that the GDR had the "right."

Khrushchev gave his consent. In support of Ulbricht's argument that Kennedy would not interfere, he said that in Vienna he had been impressed by the President's wish to be an independent leader, unbossed by military or industrial interests, a man of peace. According to one of those present, he refused Ulbricht's plea to erect a steel-and-concrete wall around West Berlin: instead, seal the border with barbed wire. If the West did not respond with force, replace it with a wall. Under no circumstances were Ulbricht's forces to venture into Western territory.

"Thanks, Comrade Khrushchev," said the jubilant Ulbricht. "Without your help we could not solve this terrible problem." The Chairman repeated, "But not one millimeter further."

Ulbricht flew back to East Berlin and ordered implementation of blueprints for a border sealing updated since the 1950s. Since Khrushchev's amber light in March, Honecker had been secretly assembling concrete and barbed wire.

Ulbricht and Honecker decreed that until shortly before H-Hour, midnight on Saturday, August 12, only about twenty GDR officials should know about the plan. Other key members of their military and political staffs were told only of impending "exercises." Until just before construction began, orders would be transmitted not on paper but orally. Honecker's staff was working around the clock. To avoid attracting attention, he crowded his men into four rooms.

On Monday, August 7, in a television speech to the Soviet people, Khrushchev said he would not match Kennedy's new military buildup with another escalation of his own. The imperialists were "using West Berlin for subversive activities against the GDR and the other socialist countries." But they were being told, "Stop, gentlemen! . . . We are going to sign a peace treaty and close your loophole into the GDR."

East Germans thought they knew what Khrushchev meant. During the twenty-four hours after the speech, almost two thousand refugees swarmed into West Berlin, the highest number that year.

The next day, at the Soviet Defense Ministry, Khrushchev privately told his generals about his decision to close the border: "We'll just put up serpentine barbed wire, and the West will stand there like dumb sheep. And while they're standing there, we'll finish a wall."

Among the applauding guests was Colonel Oleg Penkovsky, a military intelligence officer who was the most valuable Western mole in the Soviet Union. If he wished to warn the West about the border sealing, he could have left a dead drop for a Western agent in Moscow, but this would be highly dangerous. He later told his handlers, "I knew you'd want to know. But I could tell you only at great risk to me, and I knew it would be impossible for you to do anything about it."

At the White House, Kennedy read a secret report from the Italian Prime Minister, Amintore Fanfani, who had seen Khrushchev for three days at the Kremlin. The Chairman had told him "about twelve times" that if war came over Berlin, it would be nuclear from the start. The Chairman wished that John Foster Dulles were still alive.

Kennedy's "complex foreign policy" posed a "great problem" for him. Khrushchev said that he believed "there will be no war" but that the President had better not "wait too long" to negotiate. He referred several times to the statements by Mansfield and Fulbright: although Kennedy could not say so in public, he probably agreed with the two Senators "about eighty percent."

By sending this message, which he knew would reach Kennedy, Khrushchev may have been testing his supposition that the President would not interfere with a border sealing. If the supposition was incorrect, Kennedy could be expected to send a warning back through public or private channels. During the Bay of Pigs, for example, he had not been shy about warning the Chairman against exploiting the episode for a move against Berlin. This time there was no such warning. Khrushchev felt emboldened to proceed.

On Thursday morning, August 10, at Kennedy's news conference, someone asked about Fulbright's comment about a border closing: "Could you give us your assessment of the danger and could you tell us whether this government has any policy regarding the encouragement or discouragement of East German refugees moving West?"

Kennedy did not repudiate Fulbright's statement. He did not use the opportunity to warn Khrushchev against a border closing. He said only that the U.S. government did not "attempt to encourage or discourage the movement of refugees, and I know of no plans to do so."

That same day Dean Rusk lunched with Adenauer at the Chancellor's villa in Cadenabbia, Italy. Kennedy had asked him to make sure that Adenauer would remain on the reservation if and when the United States negotiated with the Soviets over Berlin.

The Secretary of State gently told his host that if the President had to use military force in the Berlin Crisis, it had to be "clear to all" that "every effort was made to find peaceful solutions and that war was forced on us by the other side." Bargaining must take place "under conditions wherein we have some control over the subjects to be discussed and not occur at a late stage of the crisis where we would talk only about subjects Khrushchev wants."

He confided that Kennedy was "considering whether the West should take the initiative to bring about negotiations this fall." Reporting on a visit to Paris, he said that "General de Gaulle believes we are in Berlin and that if the Soviets disturb us we will shoot. This is not an adequate position in the sixties when we are considering a nuclear war."

Adenauer reminded Rusk that Khrushchev was a dictator: "A dictator gets reports from his ambassadors which do not reflect the full truth." What counted therefore was not reality but what Khrushchev believed. The Chancellor said that he would not object to negotiations but that "since 1949, the margins of compromise have been exhausted. There is little meat on the bone. Khrushchev has his prestige involved, and it will be difficult for him to save face."

Rusk said, "We might say to Khrushchev that the mess he has made in Eastern Germany is bad. He has had a gangster in charge who has created this. He puts pressure on the Soviets and poses danger for us. Perhaps this can be reduced by having a decent regime in East Germany. Then he could forget about it and the Berlin problem and concentrate on building up Russia." He told Adenauer that his own greatest ambition was to pass the Berlin question on to his successor.

At a Soviet-Romanian friendship meeting in the Kremlin on Friday, August 11, Khrushchev warned that if the imperialists unleashed a war over Berlin, the Soviet Union would crush Western allies—not only "the orange groves of Italy but also the people who created them." He would not quail before ordering his generals "to crush the NATO military bases in Greece. And of course, they will not have mercy on the olive orchards or on the Acropolis. . . . In cutting off the head, nobody worries about the hair."

Afterward he went out of his way to chatter amiably with diplomats from Canada, Britain, and France.* He said there would be negotiations over Berlin and no war if the West did not turn the issue into a "trial of strength."

The next day, the Chairman left for Kiev to deliver a speech on farming. Then he would relax at Pitsunda until early September. August was Khrushchev's annual recreation time, but his absence from the capital also allowed him to give the West a false sense of confidence that nothing vital would happen on Berlin. As with the Gagarin flight, he may have also wished to be away from Moscow to avoid a close connection with the border closing in case it turned into a donnybrook.

* * *

*Thompson was in the United States on home leave.

Kennedy spent the weekend at Hyannis Port, where Bundy gave him "a checklist of the actions that you are obligated to take if and when you contemplate a decision on the use of nuclear weapons." If nuclear war erupted while he was at his summer home, he was to be rushed to the new secret presidential fallout shelter on Nantucket Island. Built under a forty-five-acre submarine surveillance base, the Navy disguised it as a "jet assist takeoff fuel bottle storage area."

Outside the twelve-mile territorial limit, Soviet trawlers customarily tried to eavesdrop on communications between the presidential yachts and the "Hyannis White House" command post onshore.

At Saturday noon, the President and Billings sailed the *Caroline K* to Oyster Harbor, where they met Jacqueline and Caroline, who were on the *Marlin.* Before lunch was served on the larger boat, Kennedy went for a swim as the First Lady waterskied. He dropped by a neighbor's cocktail party and then took Jacqueline, Billings, and assorted Kennedy children to the Hyannis News Store.

That evening, all gathered at Joseph Kennedy's house for dinner and a film. Among the titles ordered by the senior Kennedy that summer were *Tiger Bay* and *Expresso Bongo.*

At midnight, heavy trucks and troop carriers rolled up to the perimeter of West Berlin. East German guards with machine guns were posted at crossing points. As officers shouted through bullhorns, crews jackhammered pavement and swung axes at trees. They jammed cement posts into the ground and connected them with mad circles of barbed wire.

The guards had been told to get the job done before anyone had time to react. By Khrushchev's order, Soviet infantry and armored divisions stood in tactical positions around the city, ready to move in case East Germans rebelled or the West counterattacked.

Upon news of the barricade, thousands of East Berliners ran to subway and train stations, only to be told that it was too late. Some shouted, some wept, some were arrested. West Berliners shook their fists at East German guards, who ignored them.

Ulbricht and Honecker issued a statement portraying the border sealing as a minor event: controls "appropriate for all sovereign states" were being imposed to block the hostile activities of "revenge-seeking and militaristic forces," including "spies and saboteurs." The West was offered one reassurance that Khrushchev had insisted upon: "It goes without saying that these measures must not affect existing provisions for traffic and control on routes between West Berlin and West Germany."

* * *

Communications in 1961 were so primitive that the State Department's new Operations Center heard almost nothing about the events in Berlin until midnight Washington time—six hours after the border sealing began. Someone called John Ausland, duty officer for Foy Kohler's Berlin Task Force, at home: a news agency was reporting "that something is going on in Berlin," but it was "not clear what." Ausland went back to sleep.

Just before four, Ausland was awakened again. An urgent cable had arrived from the CIA station in Berlin: East German forces were "cutting off movement into West Berlin." So far there was "no interference with movement between West Berlin and West Germany." The message included a code word suggesting that the President be notified immediately.

Ausland rushed to the State Department and searched for a contingency plan. Finally a vault was opened and a folder taken out. It was empty. The Department had for years been obsessed by the worry that West Berlin would be cut off from West Germany, not from the GDR and East Berlin.

Wearing a seersucker suit, Dean Rusk arrived at his office shortly before ten. Foy Kohler reminded him that the Western powers had "never considered" East Berlin in itself an issue over which they were willing to go to war. However much they should "deplore" the partitioning, they should not think of "changing the lines of demarcation by force."

Rusk agreed. He later said, "We might very well have looked around and said, 'Where is everybody?'" He saw the border sealing as a defensive move, not a "play against West Berlin." He decided not to call the President until harder information came in; Kennedy would demand details and he wanted to put his "ducks in a row."

The Kennedys attended ten o'clock Sunday Mass at St. Francis Xavier Church and at 12:17 P.M. boarded the *Marlin* for Great Island and lunch with John Walker, the National Gallery director who was assisting Jacqueline's White House restoration. Wearing a polo shirt and white ducks, the President still knew little or nothing of the drama that had started in Berlin eighteen hours before.

The boat was called back for a "triple-priority" message from Washington. Waiting near the dock in a golf cart, General Clifton gave the yellow teletype copy to Kennedy, who read it and glared: "How come we didn't know anything about this?" He called Rusk in

Washington: "What the hell is this? How long have you known? Was there any warning in the last two or three days?"

Rusk said they could not be sure that the Russians were trying to end, not just control, the refugee flow. Access routes to West Berlin had not been impeded. He saw no need for the President to rush back to Washington.

He read Kennedy a proposed U.S. statement saying that the "violations of existing agreements will be the subject of vigorous protest through appropriate channels." This bland response was designed to avoid triggering an East German uprising like the one the United States had encouraged in Hungary in 1956 with such tragic results. It was intended to assure the Soviets that the United States would not overreact.

The President told Rusk to issue the statement and ensure that no one did anything to aggravate the situation. Rusk had intended to go to a Yankees-Senators baseball game that afternoon. "Go to the ball game as you had planned," said Kennedy. "I am going sailing."

At the State Department, Kohler gave the statement to Ausland, who warned that "people are going to be asking what we are going to do about this besides protest." Kohler said, "Let's wait and see how things develop. After all, the East Germans have done us a favor. That refugee flow was becoming embarrassing."

Khrushchev was on his way to Pitsunda. "We kidded among ourselves that in the West the thirteenth is supposed to be an unlucky day," he later recalled. "I joked that for us and for the whole socialist camp it would be a very lucky day indeed."

Campaigning as Social Democratic nominee for Chancellor, Willy Brandt had been sleeping in a special car of the Nuremberg-to-Kiel express when brought the telegram from Berlin. Hung over from what he called a "frolicsome" Saturday night, the Mayor fled the train at Hannover, flew to Berlin, and rushed to the Brandenburg Gate, now blocked by East German militiamen with submachine guns.

Brandt demanded to see the Allied governing commission. He told the Western generals, "You let Ulbricht kick you in the rear last night! . . . At least send some patrols to the sector border immediately to combat the sense of insecurity and show West Berliners that they are not in jeopardy." Advised that such a show of force was out of the question, Brandt told reporters, "The entire East is going to laugh from Pankow to Vladivostok."

Son of an unmarried Lübeck saleswoman, Brandt was born in 1913 as Herbert Frahm. After Hitler's rise, he departed for twelve years in

Norway, where he worked as a journalist and in the resistance to the Nazis. Returning after the war, he joined the circle of the postwar West Berlin Mayor Ernst Reuter and led the city's house of representatives before he ran for mayor, succeeding on his second try in 1957.

Relations between Brandt and Adenauer had been icy from the start. As fellow Bundestag members, the old man had once slipped a note to Brandt saying that Premier Bulganin had asked him if Kempinski's, the most fashionable West Berlin hotel, was still standing. Lampooning the Chancellor's remoteness toward his city, Brandt replied by asking whether Adenauer had known the answer.

The Chancellor warily eyed the obvious communion between Brandt and the new American President, much noted by the American and West German press. Though not inclined to hero-worship, the Mayor was intrigued by Kennedy, whom he considered "an ultramodern conservative" but "remarkably free from prejudice and endowed with a felicitious combination of political acumen and intellect, personal authority, and mental drive." They were men of the same generation who laughed "at the same remarks and jokes."

His first White House meeting with Kennedy was in March 1961.* The President thanked him for a comment to the press that repeated protestations of American loyalty were superfluous: that was not the kind of thing he heard from Adenauer, and he was grateful. When Brandt spoke of his campaign for Chancellor, he referred to "neglected social responsibilities." Kennedy grinned: "That sounds familiar."

But now Brandt wondered whether his esteem for the President was misplaced. On the day the border was sealed, he exclaimed to his aide Egon Bahr, "*Kennedy* is making mincemeat out of us." Friends thought that the President's seeming diffidence about the West Berlin border closing was one of the central influences on Brandt's later political thinking, a reason for his search for accommodation with the Soviet Union when he finally became West German Chancellor in the 1970s.

"On August thirteenth, we became adults," Bahr later said. "Too bad it had to happen that way." Brandt believed that with the border closing "the Soviet Union had defied the major power in the world and effectively humiliated it." He later said, "The curtain went up, and the stage was empty."

* * *

---

*It did not go unnoticed that Kennedy did not receive Adenauer for the first time until a month later.

Sunday, October 14, 1962: On the eve of the Missile Crisis, John Kennedy campaigns in Buffalo and arrives with his Ambassador to the United Nations, Adlai Stevenson, at the Carlyle Hotel, New York City.

January 1961: The new President greets RB-47 spy pilots released by the Soviets, Andrews Air Force Base, Maryland. The following month, he holds his first private "skull session" on the Soviet Union in the Cabinet Room. *From left:* Llewellyn Thompson, Lyndon Johnson, W. Averell Harriman, Charles Bohlen, George Kennan, Kennedy, and Dean Rusk.

The Cuban "albatross." *Right:* Fidel Castro greeted by Nikita Khrushchev in Harlem, October 1960. *Below:* John Kennedy (*right*) and his friends William Thompson, a railroad lobbyist, and Florida Senator George Smathers, with whom he took little-known trips to Batista's Cuba in the late 1950s.

Above: Tuesday, April 4, 1961: After a Palm Beach weekend during which he has decided to forge ahead with the CIA's plans to invade Cuba, Kennedy (*left, wearing hat*) bids farewell to his father (*in short sleeves on right*). *Below:* Cuban exiles prepare to retake their homeland.

Opposite above: The flawed effort begins. *Middle:* Prisoners of war displayed. *Below:* Grimly proceeding with their duties, the President and Mrs. Kennedy greet the Greek Prime Minister, Constantine Caramanlis, and his wife at the White House.

Attorney General Robert Kennedy (*left*) and Georgi Bolshakov, the Soviet intelligence agent with whom he began meeting in secret in the spring of 1961.

Beleaguered after setbacks in Cuba and Laos, the President watches the progress of Commander Alan Shepard, first American in space. Jacqueline Kennedy is at right.

June 1961: The Kennedys with French President Charles de Gaulle outside the Élysée Palace, Paris (*above*), and arriving at Versailles.

Saturday, June 3, 1961: At the U.S. Embassy residence, Vienna, Kennedy greets Khrushchev for their first summit encounter. On left and right of the Chairman are Ambassador Mikhail Menshikov and Foreign Minister Andrei Gromyko. *Left:* At 6:45 P.M., the President sees Khrushchev off.

That evening, the two leaders are guided to their places at Schönbrunn Palace (*right*). Khrushchev exchanges quips with his wife, Nina Petrovna, and Jacqueline. Rose Kennedy is at rear.

At the Soviet Embassy, the Sunday confrontation over Berlin, of which Kennedy later said, "That was the real nutcutter." *Opposite above:* Khrushchev escorts the President out the front door after the meetings break up. *Below:* In the aftermath of Vienna, knowing that a Berlin crisis is about to erupt, the President returns to Washington from Palm Beach on crutches.

July 1961. *Right*: At the annual Independence Day garden party at Spaso House, Moscow, Khrushchev greets Jane and Llewellyn Thompson and a Thompson daughter. *Below:* At Hyannis Port, during meetings on Berlin, Kennedy points out landmarks to General Maxwell Taylor, Dean Rusk, and Robert McNamara.

August 1961: East Germany and the Soviet Union build a wall around West Berlin.

Above: Sent by President Kennedy to reaffirm the American commitment to West Berlin, Vice President Johnson is welcomed by West German Chancellor Konrad Adenauer. *Below:* Kennedy debriefs Johnson, General Lucius Clay, and Charles Bohlen.

American children in a duck-and-cover drill, rehearsing for the possibility that the Berlin Crisis might explode into nuclear war with the Soviet Union.

October 1961, Checkpoint Charlie, Berlin: American and Soviet tanks face one another, the only such confrontation of the Cold War.

With braggadocio Khrushchev conceals his grave political problems at the Twenty-second Party Congress, Moscow, October 1961. He is cheered by (*left to right*) Anastas Mikoyan, Leonid Brezhnev, Frol Kozlov, Mikhail Suslov, and Alexei Kosygin.

December 1961: Kennedy ends what his brother Robert calls "a very mean year."

On Monday at the White House, Kennedy met with Thompson and Bundy, who told him that "from Hour One" this was something the Soviets "have always had the power to do. It is something they were bound to do sooner or later."

Earlier that morning, Bundy had asked Robert Amory of the CIA, "What the hell should we do now?" Amory advised him to "vividly enhance your commitment to Berlin." Send a "combat team in this afternoon over the Autobahn" to ensure continued Western access to the city.

Bundy liked the suggestion, but Maxwell Taylor did not. "We're in a dangerous situation here. . . . Any troops that we have in Berlin will be casualties in the first six hours of fighting." The President sided with Taylor.

Bundy advised Kennedy that his senior staff all thought the United States should take a "clear initiative" during the next ten days for negotiations on Berlin. The President felt that the aftermath of the border closing was not the right time. As Americans grew outraged by the border closing, there would be "more and more pressure for us to adopt a harder military posture."

He dictated a memo for Rusk: "What steps will we take this week to exploit politically propaganda-wise the Soviet-German cutoff of the border? This seems to me to show how hollow is the phrase 'free city' and how despised is the East German government, which the Soviet Union seeks to make respectable. . . . It offers us a very good propaganda stick which, if the situation were reversed, would be well used in beating us."

On Tuesday, the President received a visitor from Belgrade, George Kennan, who advised him to stay cool; Khrushchev had closed the border to head off a confrontation, not cause one. Kennan was the man who in 1957 had proposed talks on disengagement from Central and Eastern Europe. Kennedy saw him in the family quarters, which allowed the meeting to be concealed from the press.

On Wednesday, August 16, three hundred thousand West Berliners poured into the square in front of their city hall, the Schöneberg Rathaus, shouting slogans and hoisting signs: BETRAYED BY THE WEST . . . WHERE ARE THE PROTECTIVE POWERS? . . . THE WEST IS DOING A SECOND MUNICH.

Sweating, Brandt rose to speak from the Rathaus steps. He knew that if his people were not reassured that the freedom of West Berlin would survive, they could desert. He reminded the crowd that the Western powers had preserved their basic rights: "Without them, the tanks would have rolled on." Still, "Berlin expects more than words!" He said that he had written a private letter to President Kennedy stating "our views in all frankness."

Brandt's letter arrived at the White House by teletype. It said, "The illegal sovereignty of the East German government has been acknowledged through acceptance." Warning that West Berliners might begin to leave the city in droves, it suggested that the Western garrison be strengthened: "I assess the situation to be serious enough to write you this frankly, as is possible only among friends who trust each other fully."

Kennedy angrily read the letter, his political sensitivities tight as a drum: "Trust? I don't trust this man at all! He's in the middle of a campaign against old Adenauer and wants to drag me in." Showing the letter to his friend Marguerite Higgins, he said that instead of grandstanding, the Mayor should have telephoned him or flown to Washington. Higgins was unsympathetic: "I must tell you frankly. The suspicion is growing in Berlin that you're going to sell out the West Berliners."

Konrad Adenauer had taken the border closing more calmly than Brandt. After he was awoken by the news on Sunday morning and told that West German intelligence expected no Soviet-bloc assault on West Berlin, he went back to sleep. The next day, he rejected advice to fly to the city, telling aides that he did not want to induce an East Berlin uprising that, as in 1953, would ultimately be crushed by Soviet tanks.

The new emergency did not dim his partisanship. Before twenty-five thousand supporters that evening in Regensburg, the Chancellor referred to his opponent as "Herr Brandt, alias Frahm." Informed of the slur during a West Berlin senate meeting, the disconsolate Brandt left the chamber and issued a statement: "Three days after the event that has brought the German people to its most severe test, I can only state my absolute incomprehension at the unworthiness of the attacks by the Chancellor."

Khrushchev's Ambassador in Bonn, Andrei Smirnov, told Adenauer that the Soviet Union did not intend to exacerbate the Berlin Crisis, but the West must show equal composure. The Chairman was evidently worried that American outrage or demands by Brandt and his West Berliners might goad Kennedy into escalating the crisis—especially because the East Germans were about to replace the barbed wire with a permanent concrete wall, stanching any hope that the border closing might be temporary.

*   *   *

In West Berlin, Allan Lightner of the U.S. Mission sent home alarming reports about flagging morale in West Berlin. Edward R. Murrow, who happened to be in the city, cabled that West Berliners might flee: "What is in danger of being destroyed here is that perishable commodity called hope." CIA agents reported "sudden fear among the West Berliners that there would be a military coup against them."

Walt Rostow wrote the President, "Remember that what is at stake here—and has always been at stake from Khrushchev's point of view—is the long-run expectations of the West Berliners. Their will to go on living and working in that setting depends primarily, of course, on whether or not they feel secure about Western access."

To reaffirm the American commitment, Kennedy decided to send a battle group of fifteen hundred Americans across East Germany to West Berlin. As his special envoy he would send the Vice President, along with Bohlen and General Lucius Clay, hero of the Berlin Blockade period. Johnson would be the highest-ranking American official to visit Berlin since the end of World War II. When the President called him, Johnson was visiting his mentor, Speaker Sam Rayburn, who was dying of cancer.

The Vice President protested that he had planned to go fishing with Rayburn, but the Speaker said they could go fishing another weekend. O'Donnell, no Johnson admirer, claimed later that the Vice President was nervous about the troop movements and said, "There'll be a lot of shooting and I'll be in the middle of it. Why me?"

Harold Macmillan wrote in his diary, "The President sent me a message about sending more troops into Berlin. Militarily, this is nonsense. But I have agreed to send in a few more armoured cars, etc., as a gesture. I still feel that from Khrushchev's point of view, the East German internal situation was beginning to crumble and something had to be done. But I also believe that he does not want to produce a situation which may lead to war. The danger is, of course, that with both sides bluffing, disaster may come of mistake."

For eight days after the border was closed, and as the barbed-wire fence was replaced by a concrete wall, Kennedy did not say a word in public about what was happening in Berlin. Nor did he allow any statement on the subject to be issued in his name. As in the winter and spring of 1961, the President's public silence was no doubt inspired by his desire to keep Berlin from becoming a bruising domestic political controversy that might force him to take a harder line than he wished to take.

Amazingly enough, it succeeded. In a later age, the American press and public would have been unlikely to tolerate a President's refusal to comment for more than a week on such a momentous event as the building of the Berlin Wall. But in August 1961 not a single major publication objected to Kennedy's silence.

Members of the White House staff used this period to disseminate the notion that the President was "shocked and depressed" by the border closing and the Wall.* This may have been true, but it was hardly the whole story. As O'Donnell later wrote, "Actually he saw the Wall as the turning point that would lead to the end of the Berlin crisis."

Privately Kennedy told his aides, "Why would Khrushchev put up a wall if he really intended to seize West Berlin? There wouldn't be any need of a wall if he occupied the whole city. This is his way out of his predicament. It's not a very nice solution, but a wall is a hell of a lot better than a war." On another private occasion, he suggested more crudely that his sympathy for the East Germans was limited: they had had fifteen years "to get out of their jail."

The President would not have dared to say such things in public. Were Americans and Western Europeans to learn what some may have suspected—that Kennedy privately saw the Wall less as a problem than as a solution—he would have been subject to charges of appeasing Khrushchev. In the overheated language of the time, critics

---

*During the weeks and months after the Wall went up, there were published reports of Kennedy's anger at American intelligence for failure to give him earlier warning of the border closing. The President's pique was genuine, although he accepted the CIA's contention that the secret Moscow and East Berlin meetings and the secret movement of building materials would have defeated almost any intelligence agency.

The magnification of Kennedy's anger in the press may have been a deliberate White House effort to suggest that the Wall had caught him by surprise and, by implication, that, had he known it was coming, he would have acted to prevent it. It was certainly never reported at the time that in late July the President was already anticipating some effort by Khrushchev to stop the refugee flow—"perhaps a wall," as he told Rostow.

Kennedy was hardly unfamiliar with the political charges of the 1940s that Franklin Roosevelt had known the Pearl Harbor attack was coming and ignored the signals in order to achieve his own larger international purposes. The lesson of this would have been that it was more prudent for a President to incur blame for intelligence services that had failed to give fair warning, as Roosevelt did, than for what would have appeared to be the cynical acceptance of Pearl Harbor or a Berlin Wall in order to achieve other aims in foreign policy. After the Missile Crisis, Kennedy similarly tried to divert blame from himself (for failing to warn the Russians not to send missiles to Cuba) to the CIA, for failing to predict Khrushchev's gambit.

might have demanded to know what other peoples he was willing to sell out, what other Soviet violations of postwar agreements he was willing to ignore in order to avoid the use of American force.

Khrushchev needed no explicit message from the President to be reasonably certain that the Americans would not fight over a border closing and a wall. Although NATO's consensus on the "three essentials" in Berlin for which the West would fight was supposed to be informal, the Chairman had enough spies with access to NATO secrets to know that a border closing was not among them.*

Insistence on the free access between East and West Berlin guaranteed in the Potsdam agreement of 1945 was conspicuously absent from Kennedy's July 25 speech. He said, "Today, the endangered frontier of freedom runs through divided Berlin. . . . The Soviet government alone can convert Berlin's frontier of peace into a pretext of war." Referring to the boundary as a "frontier of peace" hardly suggested disapproval. The President repeatedly referred in his address to the defense of "West Berlin" instead of "Berlin."†

Bundy years later conceded that Kennedy's speech "may have given advance encouragement to Khrushchev" to close the border: "It can be argued that it might have been wise at least to be less clear about it—to leave Khrushchev with greater uncertainty—to leave room in his mind for the possibility that a wall might mean a war. Certainly Kennedy could have spoken more vaguely, more of Berlin and less of West Berlin." Bundy believed that "the speech thus revised" might have been "more broadly deterrent to Khrushchev" but "distinctly less persuasive to Americans," who were being asked to make painful sacrifices.

Unlike Eisenhower, Kennedy was not comfortable with ambiguity when the stakes were as high as they were over Berlin. He was always

---

*One such agent was Georges Paques, a Frenchman on the NATO staff who passed information to Moscow on the "three essentials" and nuclear contingency plans before his arrest in late 1961. Another was Lieutenant Colonel W. H. Whalen, a U.S. Army intelligence officer working at the Pentagon for the Joint Chiefs of Staff, who obtained other classified information, including U.S. intelligence estimates suggesting that the Allies would stand firm on defending Berlin. Whalen was arrested in 1966. Dean Rusk recalled years later that he presumed there to be Soviet spies in NATO and thus used his communications with the alliance to convince Moscow that the United States would stand firm on Berlin. He expected such information to receive more urgent attention from the Russians if they stole it from NATO channels than if Thompson transmitted it to Khrushchev and Gromyko in Moscow.

†Absent also was the call for German reunification that had long been a staple of American statements on Germany and Berlin. This may have strengthened the message that Kennedy might be willing to tolerate a border closing that would make the division of city and nation more permanent.

afraid of nuclear war by miscalculation. As Bundy recalled, the President's efforts that July and early August were devoted to "definition and clarification" of what he would and would not fight for. These efforts included Kennedy's press conference three days before the border closing, when he failed to disavow Fulbright's contention that the East had the "right" to stop the refugee flow and said the United States would not "encourage or discourage the movement of refugees."

Such comments, however, would not have been as effective as sending a direct secret message to Khrushchev. This raises the question of whether Kennedy might have used some private channel to make absolutely certain the Chairman knew that, if erecting a wall should be the price of defusing the Berlin Crisis, he would not try to stop him.

The most obvious conduit would have been the secret talks between Georgi Bolshakov and Robert Kennedy, the only New Frontiersman the President really trusted except himself. During oral history interviews in 1964 and 1965, when Robert provided the only account he ever gave of his relations with the Soviet agent—a highly incomplete account—he never mentioned sending such a message. In fact, he claimed that he refused to meet with Bolshakov "after they put the Wall up because I was disgusted with the fact that they had done so. Finally I saw him three or four months later."

With this recollection, Robert may have been straining to protect his brother against later charges of encouraging the hated Berlin Wall. If he was "disgusted" by the Wall, he felt much more strongly against it than the President did.*

It would have been one thing for the United States to make a play for world opinion by protesting the Wall in public. But it seems doubtful that the younger Kennedy would have surrendered a channel that he and the President deemed important for three or four crucial months simply to make an emotional gesture that, because it was secret, would have no public impact. The President did not protest to Khrushchev about the Wall in any other serious way, so why should Robert have done so by turning his back for a while on Bolshakov?

In his oral history, Robert said that during the early summer of 1961 he kept insisting to Bolshakov that the United States would fight if access to Berlin were blocked. Bolshakov's general assignment was to find out how the United States would respond to other provoca-

---

*Also casting doubt on Robert's claim that he stopped meeting with Bolshakov out of disgust at the Wall is that in the same set of interviews, he says that he saw Bolshakov in mid-October—two months after the building of the Wall, not three or four.

tions, such as the sealing of the border between West Berlin and Eastern Europe. If he asked this question, Robert would not have undercut his brother's efforts to define what the United States would fight for by claiming that the President would use force to reverse a border closing. It almost defies belief that the intense talks between Robert and Bolshakov on Berlin did not touch on this part of the subject.*

By indirect or direct communication with Khrushchev, Kennedy managed to achieve an interim solution to the Berlin Crisis. By encouraging the Chairman to close the border and stop the refugee flow, he removed much of Khrushchev's incentive for pressing the confrontation. As a side benefit, the Wall gave Western propaganda organs a magnificent example with which to decry the brutal failure of the Soviet system.

In those years in which Americans were less inclined than later to scrutinize or question their President's actions in foreign affairs, Kennedy's complicity in the building of the Wall virtually escaped public attention. Critics focused instead on his failure to use force against it once it was built. Eisenhower did not criticize the President in public but in private told friends of his revulsion at Kennedy's failure to enforce the Potsdam agreements.† Dean Acheson agreed that "if we had acted vigorously . . . we might have been able to accomplish something."

There is some evidence that Ulbricht and East German leaders feared an effort to tear down the barrier. Lucius Clay thought "we might have been able to have stopped the Wall from having been built that night." If the American commandant in Berlin had "run trucks up and down the street" with "unarmed soldiers in the trucks," he felt that "we never would have had a war." Had the commandant acted, "even if he had been in violation of his instructions, he would have succeeded and he would have been forgiven and he would have become a very great man." Clay felt that by the time the matter reached Kennedy, "it was already too late."

---

*Fourteen months later, the President ended the most acute phase of the Missile Crisis in exactly this manner—by proposing a solution in talks of the highest secrecy with a private Khrushchev emissary, taking extraordinary pains to assure that the concession remained secret out of fear of deep political harm should Americans discover what he had done. See Chapters 18 and 19.

†Ironically, Kennedy and Eisenhower had first met in Potsdam in July 1945 while Truman, Stalin, Churchill, and his successor, Clement Attlee, were writing those agreements. Eisenhower was there as the victorious commander of Allied forces in Europe, Kennedy as a junior aide to his father's friend James Forrestal, then Secretary of the Navy.

The French Foreign Minister, Maurice Couve de Murville, recalled years later that he and de Gaulle thought "that it might have been better to have an immediate reaction against the Wall . . . and maybe the Russians would have withdrawn." The West German commentator Wolfgang Leonard said later, "We know now—we learned later from refugees—that the leadership in East Berlin would have backed down if the West had stood up to them. But the West, as usual, was too late."

In the United States, the President was much less politically vulnerable for failing to knock down the Wall than he would have been had the public learned the full extent to which he had encouraged Khrushchev to build it. Most Americans knew, as Sorensen later noted, that "had we torn it down, and the Germans had then built another one a hundred yards back or five hundred yards back, or a mile back, we sooner or later would have been involved militarily in East Germany."

Even without military conflict, as Burlatsky said, the East Germans could have kept on rebuilding the Wall "until the other side is just too tired to destroy it." At the time, Franz-Josef Strauss was certain that immediate action against the barrier "would risk World War III." Not until October did a reporter ask the President why he did not "use force to stop the building of the Wall." Kennedy replied, "As you know, Eastern Berlin and East Germany have been under the control of the Soviet Union really since 1947 and '48."

Whether because he disliked demagoguery or because he did not want to stir up embers that might burn him politically, Kennedy ostentatiously avoided mentioning the Berlin Wall in public. For a President who often spoke of the tragic differences between capitalism and communism, such an omission required a Herculean effort: there was no more vivid and moving symbol of America's superior moral position in the Cold War than the gruesome partition around West Berlin.

Between August 1961 and the day of his death—except for his visit to West Germany in June 1963—Kennedy mentioned the Wall in only three speeches. Each reference was merely in passing and consisted of no more than a sentence.*

---

*In December 1961, during a speech in Bogotá, the President noted that the Communist "failure is etched in the dramatic contrast between a free and powerful and prosperous Western Europe and the grim, drab poverty of Communist Eastern Europe, or the hunger of China, or the wall which separates West Berlin from East Berlin." In March 1962, at a Miami Beach fund-raising dinner for George Smathers: "The wall in Berlin, to lock people in, I believe, is the obvious manifestation, which can be demonstrated all over the world, of the superiority of our system." In May 1963, speaking at the Tennessee Valley Authority's thirtieth anniversary celebration,

* * *

Kennedy was prudent in deciding that preserving free movement between West Berlin and the East was not an issue for which he could ask Americans to fight. He knew that if a border sealing was inevitable and might relieve the crisis, he would personally pay a lower political price if the Russians and East Germans were to do it on their own hook, furtively and without warning, than if the West had to consent to a border closing during a public negotiation.

The President's effort to evade criticism for encouraging or allowing the Wall by making no statement after it rose and scarcely mentioning the subject in public for the rest of his life was hardly in the tradition of great leadership. The American people never had the benefit of their President's explaining to them why the Wall had been built, why it was not in their interest to oppose it with military force, and how it would never be allowed to still the abiding American insistence on the ultimate reunification of Germany.

Kennedy's public silence on the Wall was not only bad leadership but also risky politics. By failing to set the matter in context for Americans, he left himself highly vulnerable to a major investigation by reporters or congressional Republicans into why he had not prevented the Wall or how he might have encouraged it for his own political purposes, just as Roosevelt was charged with provoking Pearl Harbor. It was only Kennedy's luck that no such investigation occurred.

On Friday morning, August 18, the Vice President, General Clay, Bohlen, and the rest of their party landed in Bonn. During the flight, Bohlen had reminded Johnson that his main objective must be to "restore the morale of the West Berliners." Bohlen later recalled that Johnson "asked my advice so often I felt flattered, and he was careful to make no mistakes."

In a statement written for him, the Vice President told reporters, "I want to see at first hand the effects of this tragic situation . . . the separated families, the refugees who have had to abandon home and friends, tearing up their roots in order to start life anew in freedom."

Kennedy mentioned those critics who compared the TVA with the Berlin Wall "as threats to our freedom."

Bundy wrote years later that "it would also have been better if Kennedy himself had publicly denounced the wall more quickly than he did." It is difficult to disagree, especially when one notes that the President never denounced the Wall in public in any serious fashion until June 1963!

Even this string of clichés was more daring than what had passed Kennedy's lips.

At the Bonn airport, Adenauer pointed out a sign demanding AC-TION NOT WORDS, carried by an old woman with whom, he told Johnson, he would personally want neither. The Chancellor still had not seen the Wall. He offered to join the Americans on their flight, but Bohlen quietly convinced the Vice President that this might seem to favor Adenauer over Brandt in the September elections.

The Air Force Constellation landed in the late afternoon at Tempelhof Field, site of the Berlin Airlift that Clay had so well commanded. Jack Bell of the Associated Press sensed that Johnson had been "scared" about the flight over East Germany: "He thought that maybe the Russians would make this the real thing and shoot his plane down." The Vice President and Brandt rode through streets clogged by a half million people cheering and throwing flowers. Johnson kissed babies, shook hands, and gave out ballpoint pens. Egon Bahr concluded that he was already running for President in 1968.

At the City Hall, before another 350,000 cheering Berliners, Johnson delivered a speech drafted by Walt Rostow under Kennedy's line-by-line supervision to keep the Vice President from "talking nonsense," as Robert Kennedy put it. He said, "To the survival and to the creative future of this city we Americans have pledged, in effect, what our ancestors pledged in forming the United States—'our lives, our fortunes, and our sacred honor.' The President wants you to know and I want you to know that the pledge he has given to the freedom of West Berlin and to the rights of Western access to Berlin is firm. . . . This island does not stand alone!"

On Saturday evening, Johnson asked to see the famous blue china at the Staatliche Porzellanwerke. Brandt told him that the factory was closed. The Vice President exploded: "Well, goddamn it, you're the Mayor, aren't you? It shouldn't be too difficult for you to make arrangements so I can get to see that porcelain. I've crossed an entire ocean to come here."

Protocol officers dragged the factory manager out of bed, and Johnson ordered several sets of china. From his Berlin Hilton suite, he also ordered large numbers of shoes, electric shavers, and ashtrays from local vendors. Of the ashtrays he gloated, "They look like a dollar and cost me only twenty-five cents!"

The President had ordered the fifteen hundred men of the First Battle Group of the U.S. Army's Eighth Infantry Division to Berlin early on Sunday. Kennedy stayed at the White House; if the worst happened, "we shouldn't declare war from Hyannis Port."

After sending the battle group, the President had second thoughts. Though well within Western rights, the expedition might provoke the Russians. Robert Kennedy recalled, "It was a dangerous time. . . . He didn't know whether they would try to stop them." Restless, the President decided to screen a film. A mediocre Western was all that could be found. He walked out of the White House theater after an hour and ordered General Clifton to wake him if there was an emergency.

At midnight Washington time, the fifteen hundred men crossed the East German border and rolled down the Autobahn toward Berlin.* Kennedy had put American air and ground forces in Europe on alert in case of fighting. On Election Night 1960, although several states hung in the balance, he had managed to get several hours of sleep. Now, knowing once again that he could do little to affect the outcome, he retired.

Eight hours later, the President was up, demanding news. Clifton told him that the first contingent had passed into Berlin without trouble. Delighted, Kennedy went to nine o'clock Sunday Mass at St. Matthew's Cathedral and then boarded his helicopter for the flight to Cape Cod.

In West Berlin, the trucks moved down the Kurfürstendamm past shouting, weeping Berliners throwing flowers, which the soldiers tucked into helmet straps. Their commander thought it like the liberation of Paris. An Army band played as Johnson and the other Americans greeted troops until late afternoon. He told them, "All the resources of the mightiest nation in the world stand behind you."

At Hyannis Port, the President and First Lady spent Sunday afternoon on the *Marlin* with Jacqueline's couturier, Oleg Cassini, and one of her old suitors, John P. Marquand, Jr. The exhilarated Vice President sent word that he wanted to fly to Hyannis Port for a dramatic televised welcome. The President sent word back that a Washington meeting would be sufficient. Salinger told the press that "weather conditions" would make it difficult for the Vice President to land on the Cape.

On Monday afternoon, Kennedy received Johnson's report in the

---

*To expedite the battle group's passage onto the Autobahn, the commander deferred to a Soviet request to dismount his troops for a head count, a request previous commanders had refused. This unpublicized American concession remained as official practice.

White House Fish Room and made his first public utterance on Berlin since the border closing. This consisted of one sentence: "We are going to pass through difficult weeks and months in the time ahead in maintaining the freedom of West Berlin, but maintain it we will."

The Vice President told reporters off the record that Kennedy had sent him to Berlin not only because of the Berlin Crisis but also because of Laos and the Bay of Pigs: Khrushchev "has tasted blood in Cuba and Laos and now Berlin, and he's out for more. He thinks he can push a young President and a new administration and is probing to see how far he can go."

Worried that Eisenhower might upend his delicate effort to keep the Wall out of domestic politics, Kennedy dispatched Allen Dulles to brief the General in Gettysburg. Eisenhower predicted that Khrushchev would "merely chuckle" at the President's reinforcement of the Berlin garrison. Kennedy's conventional buildup would provoke Khrushchev into "a larger buildup of ground forces in order to stay ahead of us." He ridiculed the idea that "we can fight a conventional war in Europe without using nuclear weapons."

Harking back to one of his deepest concerns, the General told Dulles that the Kennedy administration must ask itself "how long we can continue to spend ever greater sums of money. . . . Any squeeze on the civilian economy with ever-growing government control could finally lead to a managed economy with everything centralized and controlled by the government."

Once Khrushchev had provoked him into action, Kennedy had proved better at managing the Berlin Crisis than he had been in avoiding it. Learning from his Bay of Pigs mistakes, he deployed his NSC and Berlin task force to attack the problem systematically from various angles and political points of view. These deliberations were all the more important because, just as Rusk and Bohlen had noted during the February Cabinet Room sessions on the Soviet Union, the President himself was so extraordinarily free of preconceived ideas about action on Berlin.

In devising his approach to Berlin, Kennedy had to overcome the damage he had done himself during his first half year in office. The Berlin policy announced in the July 25 Oval Office speech was largely designed to convince Khrushchev, the U.S. Congress, and the American people of his resolution and commitment to defend Western rights in the city.

In this effort, the President was brilliantly successful, demonstrating to Khrushchev that full pursuit of his maximum aim of driving the West from Berlin could indeed risk nuclear war. But had Kennedy succeeded in demonstrating his firmness and mastery on the Berlin issue during the spring and at the Vienna summit, there would have been less of an urgent need for him to alarm Americans and the world with a $3.5-billion military increase and hurry-up bomb shelter program.

The President did not need to contrive a sense of alarm that he did not feel. He took Khrushchev's challenge with utmost gravity. But he undeniably knew that an alarming speech and the sense of national unity that followed would make it easier for him to push through Congress the conventional buildup that he would have wanted even had there been no Berlin crisis—and to command widespread national support for whatever course he should take on Berlin, including negotiation with the Soviets.

Before the Berlin Wall went up, the President had asked Rusk to suggest a graceful means to start negotiations with Khrushchev on Berlin. Rusk had recommended having Thompson quietly speak with Khrushchev about means of assuring Western access to Berlin. The United States might ask for a summit meeting with the British, French, and West Germans, perhaps in Bermuda, at which they could agree on a Western position before Khrushchev's December treaty deadline.

In early August, the President had not been ready to move. Now Khrushchev had solved his refugee problem. Western access to Berlin had been reasserted. As Sorensen recalled, Kennedy "felt that a turning point in the crisis had been reached." On the day after the fifteen hundred troops reached Berlin, the President dictated a memo to Rusk that was a striking departure from his previous temporizing:*

"I want to take a stronger lead on Berlin negotiations. . . . I no longer believe that satisfactory progress can be made by Four-Power discussion alone. . . . We should, of course, be as persuasive and

---

*He may have been influenced by a memo he read that day from Bundy on a talk two days before with Stevenson: "His own immediate concern is the imbalance between our own military buildup and our negotiating posture. . . . He thinks we should proceed promptly to show that we are in fact calling for negotiations. He knows of Dean Rusk's plan for a call toward the end of the month, and he would like to move even sooner if possible. . . . Beyond this, he seemed more cheerful and less worried about his own problems than usual."

diplomatic as possible, but it is time to act. . . . We should this week make it plain to our three Allies that this is what we mean to do and that they must come along or stay behind." He wanted to issue an invitation to Khrushchev to negotiate before the end of August. Bohlen could discuss ways and means with the Soviets in September. Talks could begin in November.

Kennedy wrote to Rusk that Acheson's proposals had been a "good start" but *"not* a finishing point. What you and I need is a *small* group of hard workers who can produce alternatives for our comment and criticism on an urgent basis. This, in my judgment, should be a labor separated from the day-to-day operational work and planning under Kohler."

He suggested as members Bohlen, Bundy, and Sorensen—men who did not share Acheson's and Kohler's orthodoxies on Berlin. He wanted the strings in his own hands and did not want the public to learn that he had chosen three men whom critics might deem insufficiently tough on Berlin. Unlike with Acheson's much-heralded March appointment to advise on Berlin, he told Rusk that the group "should be as nearly invisible as possible, and it should report directly to you and me."

He issued staccato instructions: "Make the framework of our proposals as fresh as possible—they should *not* look like warmed-over stuff from 1959. . . . Examine all of Khrushchev's statements for pegs on which to hang our position. He has thrown out quite a few assurances and hints here and there, and I believe they should be exploited."

Two days later, a Soviet proclamation charged that since the West was moving "extremists, saboteurs, and spies" to Berlin, access must be stopped. Kennedy thought the statement might signal a new effort, now that Khrushchev had built the Wall without challenge, to go one step farther and halt Western access to Berlin.

The Chairman was in Pitsunda. The statement may have been issued in his absence by colleagues in Moscow who expected the President to give in to further challenges over Berlin. Less probably, Khrushchev may have written the document himself as another test of Kennedy's will; if the President reacted badly, he could always withdraw the statement or claim he had been misunderstood.

Whatever the reason, Khrushchev quickly acted to muffle the effect of the statement. He expressed his eagerness to negotiate on Berlin in a letter to Italy's Prime Minister Fanfani and in a hastily scheduled interview with the American columnist Drew Pearson.

* * *

After a cruise of Norwegian fjords with Chief Justice Earl Warren and other guests on a boat chartered by Agnes Meyer, widow of the *Washington Post* publisher Eugene Meyer, Pearson and his wife, Luvie, had flown to Moscow in hopes of an interview with Khrushchev.

They were flown in an old Viscount airplane to Sochi for the first interview Khrushchev had granted an American journalist since Lippmann in April. Arriving at Pitsunda, they found the Chairman wearing a Panama hat, a Ukrainian peasant shirt, and tan trousers pulled up almost to his chest.

He led them to the indoor-outdoor swimming pool—the best place for meetings, he said, because when talks became too heated, everyone could jump in the water and cool off. Over and over he insisted that there would be no war; if their nations stood together, "no other country in the world can ever make war." He was ready for a summit with President Kennedy and other Western leaders on Berlin.

Mrs. Pearson asked why he thought so many East Germans had fled to the West. Khrushchev explained that there were few consumer goods in the GDR; the East Germans had had to pay reparations to other countries in Eastern Europe. Unlike West Germany, there had been few factories in the East before World War II.

Pearson assured him that Kennedy was "a man with a good heart, a man who suffered greatly during the last war . . . and who doesn't want another war." Still, the President had to deal with "the opposition of the extreme Right. . . . The more you in the Soviet Union pressure him, the more difficult it becomes for him to settle the Berlin question, because it then looks as if he was surrendering under fire." He warned the Chairman not to "undermine moderates such as Kennedy"; most Americans "would not want to go to war over Berlin, but they would go to war to defend their President if they felt he was being kicked around."

Khrushchev invited his guests to swim in the Black Sea and stay the night. Then Pearson could type up his interview notes and gain his immediate clearance. He noted that, as a boy, he had worked in a mine and never properly learned to swim. "I noticed that Mr. McCloy does not swim very well either, so now I am not so embarrassed. And I have rubber lifesaving tubes for all. So if you do not swim very well, please do not feel embarrassed."

As the Chairman floated in his red rubber ring, a plane roared overhead. He joked, "I don't think it's a U-2!" Then: "I'm going to show you that I can swim without this tube." Climbing onto a pier, he shook the tube off, dove back into the water, and dog-paddled.

During lunch the next day, they heard a loud, distant explosion from across the Black Sea. Khrushchev said that the noise was probably from an American base in Turkey. "Maybe they are going to blow us up. I understand they are having maneuvers over there now." Mrs. Pearson said, "You don't seem very worried." The Chairman replied, "I'm not. There isn't going to be a war."

Pearson wrote an article affirming Khrushchev's peaceful intentions, which was published on Monday, August 28. This timing served the Chairman's purposes, for he was about to escalate the confrontation with the United States.

CHAPTER

12

"I Want to Get Off"

O N MONDAY AFTERNOON, AUGUST 28, THE PRESIDENT WAS RIS-
ing from a nap when told the bad news. An American listening post had picked up a signal that the Soviet government was about
to announce a new series of nuclear tests.

Kennedy scowled: "Fucked again." At the Vienna summit, Khrushchev had assured him that the Soviet Union would "never be the
first" to break the voluntary moratorium on testing that both sides
had observed since 1958. He had repeated this pledge during his visit
with McCloy at Pitsunda in late July.

The President was furious at Khrushchev for deceiving him and
furious at himself for believing him. His scientists told him that the
Russians had to have been secretly preparing this new series of tests
at the very time of Khrushchev's assurance at Vienna. Bundy and
Sorensen years later felt that Kennedy was more disappointed by this
betrayal than by any other Soviet action during his Presidency.

* * *

Since January, the President had courageously resisted domestic pressures to resume nuclear testing. A July Gallup poll showed that Americans by two to one thought that he should give the order, whatever the Soviets did.

Eisenhower wrote friends that he had planned to resume testing in December 1960, "assuming as I did then that Dick Nixon would be elected President," but that in light of the election's "unfortunate outcome" he had decided that Kennedy "should have a free hand." The Joint Chiefs were also pressuring the President for resumption.

In early August 1961, most of Kennedy's advisers felt that renewed American testing was inevitable if the Soviets remained so steadfast against a test ban treaty. The President wrote Macmillan that he was "not very hopeful" about delaying resumption much beyond the start of 1962: "We simply cannot be sure, without a control system, that the Soviets are not testing, and if they are testing, they can be learning important things. . . . What we don't know can hurt us."

At Thompson's instance, Kennedy toyed with the notion of asking the Soviets to agree to a limited test ban. Banning tests in the atmosphere and underwater would prevent the wind-carried nuclear fallout that horrified the world, and it would outlaw areas of testing presumed to help the Russians more than the United States. But the President worried that a limited approach might weaken the American position: better to fight for a comprehensive ban and then accept a limited treaty, if necessary.

By mid-August, the Geneva negotiations had reached an impasse. Kennedy authorized preparations for underground testing, but he did not wish to give the order until the whole world was convinced that he had done all he could for a test ban and that Western security required resumption. On August 28, he sent Ambassador Arthur Dean back to Geneva with a new concession. The Russians showed no interest.

After the President heard about Khrushchev's decision to resume, Drew Pearson came by the Oval Office to report on his talks with the Chairman. Distracted by Khrushchev's announcement, the President said he wondered whether history might record "Khrushchev and Kennedy as having brought the world to nuclear war."

Pearson wrote Khrushchev that the President was "upset" by his decision to test: "This, I'm afraid, is going to arouse American public opinion to a state of resentment which will not be easy to overcome." If the Chairman was renewing the tests for the purpose of "pressuring Kennedy on Berlin, then please remember our conversation regarding some of the political forces in the United States."

Kennedy recalled Ambassador Dean from Geneva and issued a statement: the Soviet Union's resumption of testing had increased "the dangers of a thermonuclear holocaust" and shown "the complete hypocrisy of its professions about general and complete disarmament."

After the Bay of Pigs, Robert had told the President that Khrushchev "must have thought there was something sinister and complicated behind it all or otherwise we would not have done anything quite as stupid." The brothers now felt the same way about Khrushchev's resumption of testing. The President said that Khrushchev was "obviously" trying to "intimidate the West and the neutrals" but he was still "at a loss" to explain the decision.

Khrushchev had announced his decision to Andrei Sakharov and other Soviet nuclear scientists at a secret Kremlin meeting on Monday, July 10, two days after announcing his Berlin defense buildup. The Chairman told them that the world situation had deteriorated; the Soviet Union must add to its nuclear might and show the imperialists what it could do.

Sakharov was certain that Khrushchev's decision was motivated by politics. He slipped the Chairman a note saying that in technical terms a resumption of testing "would only favor the U.S.A. . . . Don't you think that new tests will seriously jeopardize the test ban negotiations, the cause of disarmament, and world peace?"

At lunch, Khrushchev rose and raised a goblet of wine, as if to propose a toast. Then he put down the glass and spoke with rising fury. As Sakharov recounted the harangue, the Chairman said, "Sakharov writes that we don't need tests. But I've got a briefing paper which shows how many tests we've conducted and how many more the Americans have conducted. Can Sakharov really prove that with fewer tests we've gained more valuable information than the Americans? Are they dumber than we are?

"There's no way I can know all the technical fine points. But the *number* of tests, that's what matters most. How can you develop new technology without testing? But Sakharov goes further. He's moved beyond science into politics. Here he's poking his nose where it doesn't belong. . . . Politics is like the old joke about the two Jews traveling on a train. One asks the other, 'So, where are you going?' 'I'm going to Zhitomir.' What a sly fox, thinks the first Jew. I know he's really going to Zhitomir, but he told me Zhitomir so I'll think he's going to Zhmerinka.*

"Leave politics to us—we're the specialists. You make your bombs and test them. . . . But remember, we have to conduct our policies from a position of strength. We don't advertise it, but that's how it is! . . . Our opponents don't understand any other language.

"Look, we helped elect Kennedy last year. Then we met with him in Vienna, a meeting that could have been a turning point. But what does he say? 'Don't ask for too much. Don't put me in a bind. If I make too many concessions, I'll be turned out of office.' Quite a guy! He comes to a meeting but can't perform. What the hell do we need a guy like that for? Why waste time talking to him? Sakharov, don't try to tell us what to do or how to behave. . . . I'd be a jellyfish and not Chairman of the Council of Ministers if I listened to people like Sakharov!"

Khrushchev's resumption of testing satisfied his growing need to impress the world once again with Soviet power. As early as his meeting with the nuclear scientists, he knew he was unlikely to achieve his maximum aim in starting this new Berlin crisis—using nuclear threat to scare the West into recognizing the GDR and allowing Berlin to fall under the dominion of the Soviet bloc.

The Berlin Wall had achieved his minimum aim: halting the East German refugee flow and scoring a minor propaganda victory by showing that the Soviet bloc could violate an agreement such as Potsdam without serious Western retaliation. Arguably Khrushchev had known all along that since he was unwilling to press his Berlin demands to the point of nuclear war, his chances of getting his maximum goal had always been slim. His aide Burlatsky recalled that, in the Berlin Crisis, the Chairman had "demanded much" but was "satisfied with what he received."

If Khrushchev failed to win his maximum ambition, he would have new political problems. His generals would complain as in 1959 that he had embarrassed the Soviet Union by abandoning his Berlin ultimatum. They already wanted to know why he had not matched

---

*Like most of Khrushchev's stories, it was not the first time he told this one, which appeared in slightly altered version (Cherkasky substituted for Zhitomir) in the biographical material sent to Kennedy by the CIA before Vienna.

Kennedy's new defense increases with a further buildup of his own and pressed the crisis to the brink. As Sergei Khrushchev recalled, Soviet military leaders "in their mind understood that force would not resolve the question, but in their hearts they hoped it would."

The Chairman was worried that leaders of the Third World and other countries might interpret his willingness to negotiate as a tacit admission that, whatever his claims, American nuclear strength was far superior to that of the Soviet Union. If there were to be talks with the West on Berlin, he did not wish to deal from a position of weakness.

Khrushchev knew that resumption of nuclear testing might infuriate Kennedy, Macmillan, and some of the neutrals, but he knew it would strengthen the Soviet nuclear and political arsenal. He hoped any world leaders who doubted his claims of Soviet strategic strength might assume that the nation enjoying the capacity to detonate the biggest and ugliest hydrogen bombs had the capacity to control the earth.

In the wake of Khrushchev's announcement of resumed testing, Kennedy convened his NSC on Thursday morning, August 31. Robert Kennedy thought it the "most gloomy" White House meeting "since early in the Berlin Crisis." The President asked whether he should order immediate resumption of American testing.

Lyndon Johnson said, "I personally think it would be a good thing if you let Khrushchev take the heat for a little while. Also, you ought not to give the impression of reacting every time he does something." He thought that Khrushchev's move "might be a reaction to their failure to intimidate the West in the Berlin situation."

Rusk proposed issuing a statement that the President had ordered preparations but not a final decision to resume. This would keep the President from looking indecisive without having to renew testing now. Edward Murrow complained that issuing such a statement would forfeit "the greatest propaganda gift we have had for a long time."

Kennedy agreed with Murrow but doubted that he could long resist congressional pressure for resumption: "The Russians are not fools. They thought they would lose less than they would gain by this decision. They must believe they will gain most by appearing tough and mean." Worried that the Chairman might now further test him with an effort to down Western planes flying to West Berlin, thus escalating the crisis, the President approved McNamara's proposal to require such aircraft to obtain permission before firing at ground targets.

After the meeting, the Attorney General told his brother, "I want to get off." The President said, "Get off what?" Robert said, "Get off the planet." Robert added that he would not take a friend's jocular advice to run against his brother for President in 1964: "I don't want the job."

Dictating a memo to himself, Robert mused that the Russians felt "that if they can break our will in Berlin we will never be able to be good for anything else and they will have won the battle in 1961. . . . Their plan is obviously not to be the most popular but to be the most fearsome and to terrorize the world into submission. My feeling is that they do not want war, but they will carry us to the brink." He agreed with Bohlen's late-winter observation that 1961 would be the year the Russians brought the world closest to nuclear war.

The travails over Berlin and the resumption of nuclear testing illuminated Robert Kennedy's new place near the center of his brother's foreign policy government. When the President gathered advisers in February and March to discuss a summit with Khrushchev and an invasion of Cuba, the Attorney General had been virtually absent. After the Bay of Pigs, the elder brother had said, "I should have had him involved from the beginning."

When Joseph Kennedy first demanded that Robert be brought into the Cabinet, the President-elect had considered it an irritating example of his father's tribal Irish thinking. "But now he realized how right the old man had been," recalled Lem Billings. "When the crunch came, family members *were* the only ones you could count on. Bobby *was* the only person he could rely on to be absolutely dedicated. Jack would never have admitted it, but from that moment on, the Kennedy Presidency became a sort of collaboration between them."

"Every time they have a conference, don't kid anybody about who is the top adviser," Lyndon Johnson told a friend. "It's not McNamara, the Chiefs of Staff, or anyone else like that. Bobby is first in, first out. And Bobby is the boy he listens to." Johnson later said, "That upstart's come too far and too fast. He skipped the grades where you learn the rules of life."

Born in 1925, Robert Francis Kennedy was eight years younger than the President, and his childhood was different. The older brother could remember growing up in a modest house in Brookline, summer holidays in Irish Catholic ghetto resorts, a mother scrimping for an expanding family, a father still anxious about making his first million.

John Kennedy's early adolescence demanded adjustment to the family's rapidly improving financial and social circumstances. During these years, the Kennedys moved from the Hibernian Boston of his grandparents and the upper-middle-class strivers' world of Brookline to the mansions in Palm Beach, Bronxville, and Hyannis Port; New Deal Washington, in which his father was lionized as a Roosevelt crony; London and the Court of St. James's.

John could remember a time when it was not clear that he would never have to worry about earning a living, when the family socialized mainly with other Irish Catholics and did not rub shoulders with the great and famous. This experience revealed itself in certain aspects of his adult personality—the unfeigned respect for men who had worked their way up like his father (as long as they did not cross him politically)*, his anxiety about his social position even after he became President. Jacqueline privately called this her husband's "immigrant side."

Lem Billings believed that "in many ways Jack still felt something of an upstart, an Irish Catholic who looked to the Brahmins for a model of how to act." His social friends tended to be upper-class Protestants. His rhetoric and other aspects of his public style were self-consciously reserved and patrician.†

Although he frequently quoted the biblical maxim about much being expected of those to whom much is given, John Kennedy showed no sense of guilt about his privileges. As Sorensen and others have written, he always felt torn between the contending pulls of political struggle and a life of well-financed luxury, sitting on a

---

*One example was Henry Luce: "I like Luce. . . . After all, he made a lot of money through his own individual enterprise, so he naturally thinks that individual enterprise can do everything. I don't mind people like that. They have earned the right to talk that way. After all, that's the atmosphere in which I grew up. My father is the same way."

†In his private life, as if throwing off these constraints, he almost exulted in behaving in ways that would have outraged the Establishment. This mirrored Joseph Kennedy, who guffawed with his New Deal chum Thomas Corcoran about the time in the 1930s when a Washington dowager arrived at his rented Maryland mansion for tea. Walking down the stairs to greet her, he had made no effort to conceal that he had been upstairs in bed with a young woman and enjoyed watching the old woman's discomfort.

After the *Boston Globe* revealed in 1962 that Edward Kennedy had cheated on a Harvard Spanish test, the President told Ben Bradlee, "It won't go over with the WASPs. They take a very dim view of looking over your shoulder at someone else's exam paper. They go in more for stealing from stockholders and banks."

beach.* His unabashed attitude toward his wealth was in harmony with that of his parents, which his mother once expressed too frankly during a Kennedy campaign: "It's our money, and we're free to spend it as we please."

In contrast to his brother's early experience, Robert Kennedy had been a millionaire almost since birth. When he started a stamp collection, Franklin Roosevelt sent him contributions. Less compelled to prove himself than John, he did not make grand friends in London or employ a valet at Harvard. He was certainly far more relaxed about his Irishness and Catholicism. The Brahmin poet Robert Lowell once observed, "My, he's unassimilated."

This sense of social and financial security perhaps gave Robert the psychological freedom to brook being perceived as an upstart. He did not share John's outwardly conformist nature, his lack of unease with big businessmen or wealthy playboys. It is impossible to imagine Robert Kennedy saying, as John did of one of his chums, that the best thing about him was that "he really doesn't give a damn."†

Physically slight, as the seventh child Robert was so surrounded by sisters that his mother worried he would grow up a "sissy." This may have made him feel more obliged than his older brothers to prove his fortitude—especially to his tenacious father.

The toughness and nonconformism were combined in Robert's political approach. One of John Kennedy's heroes was Melbourne; were it not for ideology, Robert's might have been Castro. Told once that he should be in the hills with the Cuban leader and Che Guevara, he replied, "I know it." The Attorney General was the champion of counterinsurgency, displaying a Green Beret on his desk and flying Special Forces units to Hyannis Port, where his children, nieces, and nephews watched the soldiers swing from trees and fences.

Graduating from Harvard in 1948 after a war's-end tour on the *Joseph P. Kennedy, Jr.,* Robert espoused his father's isolationism, opposing the Truman Doctrine and aid to Greece and Turkey. He apparently did not disagree with his father's public demand two years later that the United States get out of Korea and Berlin and let communism collapse of its own weight instead of wasting American blood and treasure.

On a six-month tour of Europe and the Middle East in 1948, Robert wrote his parents from Vienna that "everybody in [the] Embassy wants to go to war with their comprehension of results built not on

---

*He once greeted an Oklahoma playboy as the man who "lives the life we'd all like to lead" and seemed to mean it.
†This referred to Smathers.

history but on [their] own rather idealistic beliefs. I'm afraid they might sweep us right into war." In a piece for the *Boston Advertiser* he wrote, "We can look back over the last four or five years and see the colossal mistakes that we have made."

As a University of Virginia law student, he wrote a paper embracing much of the right-wing critique of Yalta: "President Roosevelt felt that the way to beat the Common Enemy as well as to have future peace was to stay friendly with Russia. . . . This was the philosophy that he and his lieutenants, Hopkins, Harriman, Winant*, etc., kept as their guiding star . . . and a philosophy that spelled death and destruction for the world."

Traveling in a broad arc from Israel to Japan with Congressman John Kennedy in 1951 drew him closer to his brother than ever before. The trip exacerbated the Kennedys' impatience with the Foreign Service subculture, risk-averse diplomats who did not speak the local language and who insisted that the only problems that mattered were those between Moscow and Washington. In India, the brothers dined with Nehru, who, looking bored, warned them that communism thrived on discontent. In his journal Robert noted Nehru's observation that communism was "something to die for. . . . Must give the same aura to democracy. . . . We only have status quo to offer these people."

After the trip, Robert began his legal career by investigating Soviet agents for the Truman Justice Department, then switched to the Criminal Division, where he helped to press a corruption case against two former Truman officials. Reluctantly he left the job to manage John's 1952 Senate campaign against Henry Cabot Lodge. After the victory, Joseph Kennedy arranged with his friend and financial benefactee Joseph McCarthy of Wisconsin for Robert to be assistant counsel for McCarthy's Permanent Subcommittee on Investigations.

"At that time, I thought there was a serious internal security threat to the United States," Robert later said. "I felt at that time that Joe McCarthy seemed to be the only one who was doing anything about it." John Kennedy may have thought his brother's new job might send an agreeable signal to Massachusetts voters who thought their new Senator insufficiently McCarthyite. While McCarthy and his chief counsel, Roy Cohn, hunted Communists in government, Robert analyzed commercial statistics, finding that at the same time Chinese troops had killed Americans in Korea, seventy-five percent of ships carrying goods to China had sailed under Western flags.

He quit in August 1953 to serve as his father's aide on the second

---

*John Gilbert Winant, who was Joseph Kennedy's successor in London.

Hoover Commission on executive reorganization. Billings found him during this period a "really very cross, unhappy, angry young man," always telling people off and getting into fights. The next year, Robert returned to the Investigations Subcommittee as Democratic counsel and, after the infamous Army-McCarthy hearings, wrote a minority report lacerating the methods of McCarthy and Cohn.

In July 1955, Robert joined his father's friend Justice William O. Douglas on a five-week tour of Soviet Central Asia. In their hotel rooms at Baku, Douglas loudly complained before concealed microphones that the Soviets had broken their promise to provide an interpreter; he would call Khrushchev and tell him of their wretched treatment. Soon an interpreter arrived.

Douglas found that "everywhere we went," Robert "carried ostentatiously a copy of the Bible in his left hand." Behaving like an investigator, the twenty-nine-year-old man irritated the Justice by incessantly asking the Russians hostile questions. Refusing Intourist caviar and other Russian food because it was "dirty," he subsisted mainly on watermelon.

Flying to Omsk, Kennedy developed a fierce chill. Douglas felt his forehead and was sure his temperature must be at least 105 degrees. Robert said, "No Communist is going to doctor me." The Justice said, "I promised your daddy I would take care of you." Kennedy was showing signs of delirium when a large female doctor gave him a penicillin shot and put him to bed. When Kennedy and Douglas arrived in Moscow, they were met by Ethel, Jean, and Patricia Kennedy and dined at Spaso House with Ambassador Charles Bohlen.

Douglas later felt that the Soviet journey had brought a "transformation in Bobby. . . . In spite of his violent religious drive against communism, he began to see, I think, the basic, important forces in Russia—the people, their daily aspirations, their humanistic traits, and their desire to live at peace with the world." Douglas thought the Russian trip showed Kennedy that the Russian people were not soulless fanatics but human beings and achievers, "people with problems," and that for Kennedy it was "the final undoing of McCarthyism."

In a lecture to the Virginia State Bar Association, Robert said that the Soviet record "qualifies as colonialism of a peculiarly harsh and intractable kind." Unlike more severe Cold Warriors, he did not propose an American empire as a bulwark against it or suggest that African and Asian anticolonial movements were commanded from Moscow. Still, in a Georgetown University lecture, he warned that history had proven it "suicidal" to make major concessions to Moscow without a quid pro quo: "All I ask before we take any more drastic steps is that we receive something from the Soviet Union other than a smile and a promise—a smile that could be as crooked and a promise that could be as empty as they have been in the past."

When Chester Bowles's aide Harris Wofford began planning a Soviet trip for his boss in early 1957, he called on Kennedy, who gave him a "short, glum account of his Russian trip, warned that they spied on you night and day. . . . Then he went into a diatribe against the Soviet regime, which he explained was a great evil and an ever-present threat, and bid me goodbye." Wofford later recalled that the meeting with Robert "did nothing to make me want his brother to become President."

In August 1956, attending his first Democratic convention in Chicago, Robert helped to manage his brother's effort to win the Vice Presidential nomination. After the defeat Robert "was bitter," said a delegate who flew back with him to Boston. "He said they should have won and somebody had pulled something fishy and he wanted to know who did it." Robert assured his brother that he had "made a great fight, and they're not going to win, and you're going to be the candidate the next time."

That fall, he joined the Stevenson entourage, largely to school himself in presidential campaign management. By Election Day, he concluded that Stevenson had "no rapport with his audience—no feeling for them—no comprehension of what campaigning required—no ability to make decisions. It was a terrible shock to me." He was so disillusioned that he quietly cast his ballot for Eisenhower. The antipathy was mutual: Stevenson referred to the abrupt young man as the "the Black Prince."

Robert became chief counsel for the Senate's new Select Committee on Improper Activities in Labor and Management, whose members included the junior Senator from Massachusetts. This was where he pursued Jimmy Hoffa for flouting democratic procedure in the Teamsters, arranging the beating and perhaps murder of union opponents, misusing at least $9.5 million in union funds, using gangsters to buttress his control. For the first time, he gained some understanding of the hidden power of organized crime over American life.

One committee witness was Sam Giancana, who had employed an electrical workers' local to seize the Chicago jukebox and vending machine business. While Pierre Salinger of the committee staff read out charge after charge, the gangster thirty-three times took the Fifth Amendment. Robert hectored, "Will you tell us when you have opposition from anybody that you dispose of them by having them stuffed in a trunk? . . . Will you just giggle every time I ask you a quest-ion? . . . I thought only little girls giggled, Mr. Giancana."

In a best-selling book, *The Enemy Within*, Robert wrote that "the gangsters of today work in a highly organized fashion and are far more powerful now than at any time in the history of the country. They control political figures and threaten whole communities." He and his brother called for a National Crime Commission as a central clearing-house for intelligence on criminals. Speaking for both, Ken O'Don-nell complained in 1959 that "the FBI has never been aggressive on big crime. It went after Communists and stayed there." This criticism did not please J. Edgar Hoover.

In July 1959, the younger Kennedy wrote Richard Nixon that the Labor Rackets Committee was disbanding; would the Vice President like to hire one of his excellent investigators? Nixon did not even consider the request, which his aides suspected to be an effort to slip an agent into the enemy camp.* A member of the Nixon staff scrib-bled on Kennedy's letter, "Part of their spy system!!"

John McCormack of Massachusetts once said that Joseph Kennedy advised his son, "When you get to the White House there are two jobs you must lock up—Attorney General and director of the Internal Revenue Service."† Unhappy at the prospect of starting his term amid charges of nepotism, the President-elect enlisted his lawyer and friend Clark Clifford as well as George Smathers to talk his father out of the appointment.

The day before the announcement, Sam Rayburn sent a warning in his spidery handwriting, the letters one inch high: "Dear Jack—Be careful about your Attorney General—Too much talk." Lyndon John-

---

*The Nixon staff did this themselves in 1960, when John Ehrlichman served as a chauffeur in Nelson Rockefeller's entourage, sending regular reports on the New York Governor's doings and whereabouts.

†As early as 1957, the Ambassador had predicted to a reporter that John would one day be President and Robert Attorney General. A chief reason for the elder Kennedy's ambition may have been to place Robert in direct supervision of J. Edgar Hoover and, he would have hoped, of Hoover's files.

As Ambassador to London, Kennedy had seen how involved Franklin Roosevelt's attorneys general Frank Murphy and Robert Jackson had been with diplomacy. This experience may have shown him that, more than other Cabinet posts, being Attorney General would enable Robert to straddle both domestic and foreign policy and thus be of maximum help to the President. The elder Kennedy told Mortimer Caplin, whom his son had appointed as Director of the IRS, that he had "the third toughest job in the United States."

son told a friend that Senator Richard Russell of Georgia was "absolutely shittin' a squealin' worm. He thinks it's a disgrace for a kid who's never practiced law to be appointed."* Bundles of mail to the Democratic National Committee ran one hundred to one against Robert's appointment.

Ken O'Donnell felt that "Bobby did not want to be Attorney General" because he "loved his brother so much that he didn't want to hurt him. . . . The President wanted Bobby with him because they loved each other as brothers, and Bobby's another that's never going to screw him."

For their first three months in office, a distance was created between the brothers by Robert's absorption in learning how to run the Justice Department. It was accentuated by the President's sensitivity about the nepotism charge and his awareness that he had passed into a new league. At the start, especially in foreign policy, Kennedy turned for daily advice not to his brother but to those with statutory responsibility. Robert's exposure to Soviet affairs during the early months of 1961 was limited mainly to the Justice Department's work on counterintelligence.

After the Bay of Pigs, frustrated by unsound advice received from men he had barely known, the President discarded any qualms he had had about openly using his brother on matters outside Justice. Eisenhower provided something of a precedent: he had leaned on his devoted youngest brother, Milton, for confidential counsel, ordering installation of a special White House telephone line and flying him in by chopper from Baltimore, where he was president of Johns Hopkins University. But Milton had remained a shadowy figure to the American public; under his brother he never held a full-time government post and had almost nothing to do with implementation.

On the contrary, Robert Kennedy became his bother's troubleshooter, lightning rod, spokesman, adviser, no-man, eyes and ears ("Little Brother Is Watching"), whiphand overseer of the FBI and CIA, and tribune of presidential wishes and thoughts that the President would not let himself be heard to speak. Lampooning the cliché of the time, the President would cover his telephone receiver and say it was "the Second Most Important Man in the Capital calling." He told Robert that "there's only one way for you to go, and it ain't up!"

The Attorney General served as a conscience on matters like civil rights and poverty for a brother who had little use for mixing emotion with political action in the manner of their Boston Irish grand-

---

*Russell came to feel that Robert was "by far the smartest of all the Kennedys, but definitely lacked the personality that Jack had."

fathers. Billings recalled that when Robert gave a civil rights speech at the University of Georgia in May 1961, the President "wasn't too happy. . . . He said it wouldn't do him any good to bring that kind of civil rights talk directly into the heart of the South."

Robert did not feel compelled to behave like more orthodox Cabinet secretaries, who were in greater danger of exhausting the President's goodwill. Concerned above all with results, he once said, "Let Jack be charming with them." Over dinner at Hickory Hill, his estate in McLean, Virginia,* he once asked Averell Harriman, one of the villains of his law school dissertation on Yalta, about a directive he had asked for. Harriman said he was planning to get to it soon. Kennedy slammed his hand on the table: "You get on that first thing in the morning!"

In 1962, when the Gallup poll recorded the "bad things" Americans most frequently heard about the President, one was "too many Kennedys in public life." (Another was "too many parties, swimming pool dunkings,† running around too much.") Eisenhower's friend William Robinson, formerly of the *New York Herald Tribune*, complained to the General about "the little bully who is now Attorney General" and his "thinly veiled and arrogant intention" to have the Kennedys "take over complete control of the lives, activities, and destinies of the American people."

Admirably, the Attorney General refused to exempt men like the unscrupulous foreign agent Igor Cassini and Joseph Kennedy's old crony and former Harvard Law School Dean James Landis from prosecution because they were family friends. If the mastiffs of organized crime felt they had extracted some sort of tacit campaign pledge from the Kennedys to soft-pedal prosecution, this was strenuously contradicted by Robert's pursuit of the Mafia, which he fought more aggressively than any previous Attorney General.

After the Bay of Pigs, Robert Kennedy was not his brother's chief adviser on the Soviet Union; that portfolio remained with Bohlen and Thompson, to whose experience he could not pretend. But he was the man assigned to scrutinize and regroup his brother's counselors so that a Bay of Pigs could never happen again. The President now

---

*The house had belonged to Robert Kennedy's predecessor, Robert Jackson, and was the Civil War headquarters of General McClellan, whom Robert did not admire because "McClellan didn't press!"

†A reference to the many garbled stories of an overpublicized Hickory Hill dinner at which Ethel Kennedy's chair slid off a catwalk into the pool and Arthur Schlesinger dove in to rescue her. To show his distance from the New Frontier in-crowd, Dean Rusk later proudly noted that he had never been "pushed into Ethel's swimming pool."

realized that Robert was his only adviser who operated almost purely from the presidential point of view and with only the President's welfare at heart, undiluted by the aspirations of State, Defense, or the NSC staff.

As the President's back channel to the CIA, Robert was probably the only man other than his brother who knew virtually the full range of covert actions the President had approved and how Kennedy considered them to serve his foreign policy. The Kennedy brothers were the only two men in the Administration who knew everything that was said between Robert and Georgi Bolshakov.

For a man who had been so emotional about Soviet communism in the 1950s, the Attorney General was surprisingly nonideological about the subject once in power. He secretly met with a known Soviet agent without apparent discomfort. During Berlin and later foreign crises, he often proved to be the least militant man in the room. But on other matters, such as Castro's removal from power, no presidential adviser was more fierce.

He shared the President's strong preference for crisis management over the kind of planning and forethought that must be grounded on some pattern of ideology. With their deeply held convictions about Soviet motivation and behavior, Acheson and Stevenson required little self-searching before counseling Kennedy whether or not, for instance, to negotiate with Khrushchev over Berlin. Robert instead took the role of helping the President to seek and exhaust all available advice, questioning assumptions, demanding action-oriented conclusions.

As a politician who wanted his brother reelected in 1964, Robert never forgot that the President had to sustain support from a party that included an Acheson wing opposing serious negotiation with the Soviet Union as well a Stevenson wing that demanded it. Like the President, he always kept one eye on the American Right, which since the mid-1940s had policed the anticommunism of Democratic Presidents.

Always looking for ways to demonstrate American moral superiority over the Soviet Union to the world, the Attorney General saw the Soviet resumption of nuclear testing as a superb opportunity. "You see, I was nothing but a troublemaker," he recalled. "I thought it was outrageous that . . . there weren't parades and demonstrations and people throwing bricks through public relations offices at the Russians—as they would have if we had started testing.

"I thought if we could . . . use the elements within American society and have them get in touch with their counterparts in other countries—businessmen with businessmen, lawyers with lawyers, labor un-

ions with labor unions, students with students . . . plus what we could
do with our own government, although we didn't have such a thing
as an internal political party, as the Communists did . . . we still could
do a great deal more."

On Friday, September 1, the Russians fired off their first nuclear
blast in three years, a huge fireball over the central plains of Soviet
Asia. Gathered in Bundy's basement office, Arthur Dean and John
McCloy wanted the President to announce American resumption immediately. Kennedy's science adviser, Jerome Wiesner, preferred a
statement asking for world condemnation of the Russians, as did
Murrow, Bundy, and Schlesinger.

Kennedy was in his bedroom, resting after a noontime swim. Since
his Senate days, the President had used this hour for a full nap. When
Bundy and his colleagues knocked on Kennedy's bedroom door, he
emerged after a moment's delay, wearing a bathrobe. Obviously tense
and annoyed at being disturbed, he listened impatiently as Bundy
asked what they should do about the Soviet resumption. McCloy told
the President that they must not keep standing still while the Communists kicked them in the teeth.

Kennedy said he was not inclined to announce resumption now but
did not know how long he could hold back. Bundy showed him two
possible statements. After reading and tearing them apart, the President dismissed his aides.

In the Oval Office that afternoon, Schlesinger found him "much
more relaxed." Of their earlier discussion, Kennedy said, "McCloy
was certainly reverting to Republicanism—and to think that only a few
days ago, he was all over Khrushchev!"

In Paris, Charles de Gaulle told the American Ambassador, General
James Gavin, that the Soviet resumption of testing was just another
sign of the continuing Soviet military buildup: "It would be a grave
mistake for the West to run to the U.S.S.R. asking for negotiations."
At the end of their talk, the French President asked Gavin to give
Kennedy a "personal" message:

"I understand full well, better than anyone else, the weight and
scope of President Kennedy's responsibilities. He is the head of the
state in the West which is the most powerful. Therefore everything
depends, more or less, on him. . . . If the state of affairs turns from
bad to worse, we will enter a catastrophe. If such a catastrophe occurs,
France will enter it together with the United States. . . . If there is to

be no catastrophe, it will have been important for the West to have shown firmness."

On Saturday, September 2, in a last effort to avoid American resumption, Kennedy called Rusk from Hyannis Port to suggest that he and Macmillan propose an immediate atmospheric test ban with no inspection. This would be a serious concession; until now, the West had always insisted on controls. An Anglo-American note was sent to Moscow.

The next afternoon, General Clifton called the President back to shore from a *Marlin* cruise; the Soviets had fired off a second nuclear test. Arriving at his house by golf cart, Kennedy said, "Get Dean Rusk on the phone! Get my brother!" Carl Kaysen of the NSC staff suggested that the President exploit the situation by piously refusing to play the Russians' dirty game. Kennedy replied, "They'd kick me in the nuts. I couldn't get away with it."

Neutral and nonaligned nations meeting in Belgrade refused to censure the Soviets at the same time as they passed their usual resolution against Western colonialism. Kennedy responded with profanity.

In the Oval Office on Tuesday, Bundy reported that the Soviets had conducted a third nuclear test. The President's patience was exhausted. He gave the order for resumption of American nuclear testing, but only in the laboratory and underground, which would yield no fallout. "I had no choice," he later said. "I had waited two days for an answer to the message that Macmillan and I sent to Khrushchev. That was plenty of time. All they did was shoot off two more bombs."

He told Rusk the reason the Russians were showing so little interest in negotiations on Berlin was that "it isn't time yet. It's too early. They are bent on scaring the world to death before they begin negotiating, and they haven't quite brought the pot to boil. Not enough people are frightened."

When Stevenson complained about the decision to resume, Kennedy said, "What choice did we have? They had spit in our eye three times. We couldn't possibly sit back and do nothing at all." Stevenson replied that America had been ahead in the propaganda battle.

"What does that mean?" asked the President. "I don't hear of any windows broken because of the Soviet decision. The neutrals have been terrible. The Russians made two tests *after* our note calling for a ban on atmospheric testing. . . . All this makes Khrushchev look pretty tough. He has had a succession of apparent victories—space, Cuba, the Wall. He wants to give out the feeling that he has us on the run. . . . Anyway, the decision has been made. I'm not saying that it was the right decision. Who the hell knows?"

In a private memo to *Newsweek* colleagues, Ben Bradlee reported the President's belief that "the foul winds of war are blowing" and that "Khrushchev is really moving inevitably toward the brink."

Bundy recalled the late summer and fall of 1961 as "a time of sustained and draining anxiety. . . . There was hardly a week . . . in which there were not nagging questions about what would happen if . . . or what one or another of our allies would or would not support, or whether morale in West Berlin itself was holding up." When he later read Robert Lowell's poem "Fall 1961," he felt it captured his own emotions:

> *All autumn, the chafe and jar*
> *of nuclear war;*
> *we have talked our extinction to death.*

In early September, after a conversation with the President, James Reston wrote in his *New York Times* column that Kennedy was frustrated by his failure to "get down to rational discussion" with Khrushchev about Berlin. If the Soviets wished to negotiate an "honorable accommodation," the President was "ready to go along. . . . He will negotiate in good faith but he will not be bullied. He has been trying now ever since Vienna to make this clear to Khrushchev without success."

Khrushchev used his own *Times* columnist to send a message to Kennedy. At the Kremlin on Tuesday, September 5, he told C. L. Sulzberger that he was ready for another summit. At Vienna, they had "felt each other out." Now they must both be "prepared to relieve tension and reach agreement on the conclusion of a German peace treaty, on giving West Berlin the status of a free city, and especially on the more important problem of disarmament."

The Chairman complained that Kennedy was "too young. He lacks the authority and the prestige to settle this issue. . . . If Kennedy appealed to the people, if he voiced his real inner thoughts and stated that there is no use fighting over Berlin . . . the situation would be settled quickly." Had Eisenhower said this, "no one could have accused him of being young, inexperienced, or afraid." But if Kennedy did, "the opposition will raise its voice and accuse him of youth, cowardice, and a lack of statesmanship. He is afraid of that."

Under the atmospheric test ban proposed by Kennedy and Macmillan, France would still have been free to keep testing on NATO's behalf. The West had carried out many more nuclear tests than the Soviet Union. The Soviet Union had a "moral right" to catch up.

"What the hell do we want with tests? You cannot put a bomb in soup or make an overcoat out of it." He would test the new Soviet hundred-megaton bomb and "make would-be aggressors think twice."

When Sulzberger's transcript was cleared, the Russians asked for two important changes that softened its effect. Instead of linking a Kennedy-Khrushchev summit to progress on disarmament and Berlin, Khrushchev wished to say that he would "always be glad to meet" with the President. Instead of threatening to test his hundred-megaton bomb, Khrushchev wished to say that the Soviets would simply test the bomb's detonator.

At a Kremlin reception, the Chairman thanked Sulzberger for the way he had handled the interview. Sulzberger daringly replied, "You know, we must have had to cut down twenty thousand spruce trees in Canada to print all that crap." Khrushchev roared.

Before the end of their interview, the Chairman had asked Sulzberger to take a secret message to Kennedy: "I would not be loath to establishing some sort of contacts with him to find a means, without damaging the prestige of the U.S., to reach a settlement—but on the basis of a peace treaty and a free Berlin. And through such informal contacts, the President might say what is on his mind in ways of solving the problem."

Sulzberger had told Khrushchev that the fastest way to send such a message was through Thompson. Khrushchev said, "Thompson is very able, but he is an ambassador. He would have to send such a message to Secretary Rusk. Rusk would tell Kennedy what was wrong with it . . . and Kennedy would end up wearing Rusk's corset. Kennedy could not get a fair initial reaction, and Rusk is just a tool of the Rockefellers."

Walking in the Spaso House garden, away from Soviet eavesdropping devices, Sulzberger told Thompson that Khrushchev had put him "in the embarrassed position" of sending a message to Kennedy that the Chairman had asked him not to divulge: as soon as he sent it, he would ask the President to inform Thompson of its contents immediately.

Sulzberger flew to Paris, sealed Khrushchev's message in an envelope, and sent it by special courier to the White House. Kennedy read it and said it was "hard to figure" out just what it meant.

In the Cabinet Room on Wednesday, September 13, the Chairman of the Joint Chiefs, General Lemnitzer, briefed the President on secret plans for general nuclear war against the "Sino-Soviet bloc."

Using new satellite information, he reported that while the Soviet

Union could pulverize Western Europe with short- and medium-range nuclear missiles, it had only ten to twenty-five missiles on launchers capable of striking the United States. The Soviet Union had roughly twenty-eight nuclear-equipped submarines and roughly two hundred bombers that could be put over North America in a first-strike attack. It posed "a great threat to U.S. urban areas" but a more limited danger in the months ahead to American nuclear striking forces.

Little of the Soviet force was on alert. The ICBMs and bombers could take an hour or more to launch. Few of the submarines were thought to be able to launch warheads immediately against the United States. Lemnitzer warned Kennedy that even if the United States were to launch a first strike against the Soviet land mass, he had to expect that "some portion of the Soviet long-range nuclear force would strike the United States."

The bottom line: the United States enjoyed vast nuclear superiority, but it was not invulnerable. If the President learned of an impending Soviet surprise attack, he could almost instantly launch 1,004 delivery systems carrying 1,685 nuclear warheads in a preemptive first strike against the Soviet bloc. The United States would have to tolerate perhaps two to fifteen million American casualties, not to mention European deaths in the "low tens of millions." Nevertheless Soviet society would be much destroyed.

Lemnitzer said that if the President ever launched a "bolt-out-of-the-blue" first strike, without the provocation of impending attack, as some strategists and Pentagon officials had openly demanded in the 1940s and 1950s and as Khrushchev always feared, the imbalance of terror would be even greater.

Kennedy was scheduled to deliver his maiden speech to the United Nations in late September. Still fuming about the neutralist failure to condemn Soviet resumption of testing, he wondered whether Nehru, Nkrumah, and other nonaligned leaders would be in New York: "Khrushchev certainly drew the pick of the litter."*

He asked Stevenson, "What do you think of the idea of moving the UN to West Berlin?" Such an idea, which had originated under Eisenhower, would help to prevent a Russian attack on the city and keep world attention focused on the embarrassing Wall. Stevenson replied

---

*Later that month, Rostow wrote the President about "Nkrumah's plans to send 400 cadets to the U.S.S.R. for training. . . . The British have already helped knock the number way down, but he's a great little fellow."

that, as the host country, the United States should not call for such a move: it would lend the Soviet bloc prestige and make the UN almost a hostage behind Eastern lines.

While drafting his UN speech, the President considered presenting a four-point plan to reframe the Berlin problem in favor of the West: submit the legal aspects of the dispute to the World Court, put the Autobahn to Berlin under UN control, let Berliners decide how they should be governed by UN plebiscite, consider moving the UN to Berlin. Kennedy said in private, "There are two possibilities about Berlin: war, or losing West Berlin gradually to the Communists. I don't think enough of the UN not to be prepared to trade it for a nuclear war."

Using the press once again to send a new message to Khrushchev, the President told his friend James Wechsler of the *New York Post* for publication that he might one day have to run the supreme risk to convince Khrushchev that conciliation did not mean humiliation: "If Khrushchev wants to rub my nose in the dirt, it's all over." Wechsler told his readers that for Kennedy nothing was nonnegotiable "except the dignity of free men": "There can be full negotiations about the future of Germany and of China and almost any explosive area if Mr. Khrushchev is ready to negotiate rather than to dictate."

At Hyannis Port on Monday, September 18, the President awoke to learn that Dag Hammarskjöld's plane was presumed to have crashed in the Congo. He said, "It couldn't have happened at a worse time." Then word came that Hammarskjöld was dead. Kennedy knew that Khrushchev would now find it easier to replace the Secretary-General with a troika.

Kennedy had already asked Rusk to feel out Gromyko at the UN about the possibility of talks over Berlin. The next day, the Secretary of State tried to buttonhole the Russian after a General Assembly session, but Gromyko escaped down an escalator into a crowd of reporters. Unwilling to seem as if he was chasing after the Foreign Minister, Rusk turned away.

Bohlen arranged for the two men to meet over luncheon on Thursday, September 21, in the Waldorf Towers' seedily elegant Windsor Suite, so named for its frequent tenants, the Duke and Duchess of Windsor. Rusk told Gromyko that serious negotiation on Berlin was "difficult, if not impossible, while the air is full of threats. On the other hand, if the atmosphere can be improved, we are quite ready for businesslike and constructive discussion."

Rusk said that "our basic objection is to the Soviet threat to end our rights in West Berlin." America would "surely fight" for the three essential rights outlined by the President in his July address. "Our presence in West Berlin rests fundamentally not only on occupation rights but on the will of the people of that city. We are for what they are for." Gromyko replied that war over Berlin would be folly: "Unthinkable and unnecessary." Afterward Bohlen said, "There may well be some real give in the Soviet position."

At a return luncheon, Gromyko gave Rusk a package of Russian cigarettes before noticing that the brand was called Troika. He apologized: "Pure coincidence."

At Hyannis Port, the President spent the weekend sailing with Jacqueline and working with Sorensen on his UN address. Weekend guests at what the press now called the "Kennedy Compound" included the Dominican playboy Porfirio Rubirosa, Rubirosa's latest wife, and Frank Sinatra.

The White House press office specified that Sinatra and Rubirosa were visiting Peter Lawford and Edward Kennedy—not the President. Joseph Kennedy's chauffeur saw Sinatra arrive "with a crowd of jet-setters and Beautiful People" for a "big party. . . . The women they had trucked in that afternoon had looked like whores to me."

On Sunday evening, the President and Lawford boarded a noisy Air Force propeller plane for New York. The noise forced Kennedy and Sorensen to crouch in the aisle as they collated pages of his speech. At the Carlyle, the President took the unusual precaution of reading the address aloud for criticism by Rusk and other advisers.

Salinger had arrived at the Carlyle the previous evening. Georgi Bolshakov had called him and said it was "most important" that he dine with Kharmalov, who was in town with Gromyko. Salinger agreed to dine with the Russian in his hotel room on Sunday evening.

Half French, half Jewish, the President's press secretary was bluff, jovial, grandiloquent, and plump, fond of wine and brandy, food, women, music, and politics. Theodore White thought that with ten or fifteen more years of age, Salinger could have been "mayor of any Burgundian village." Robert Pierpoint of CBS recalled that Salinger "could drink and carouse with the best—or worst—of correspondents, and frequently did."

Watching Nixon's spokesman, Herbert Klein, conceding the 1960 election on television, Kennedy said, "He looks more like a New Frontiersman than you do." Later he told Oleg Cassini that Salinger seemed to have the "best life," spending "every other week in Paris, eating at the best restaurants, and smoking Cuban cigars."

Peter Lisagor of the *Chicago Daily News* recalled that in terms of "sitting down and talking to Pierre about presidential attitudes toward NATO or toward the New Frontier domestic programs, except where they spilled over into politics," Salinger was "not very useful" because the President was careful about what he told his spokesman: "Kennedy often felt . . . that he's his own best press secretary—he'll decide what goes out and how it goes out and when it goes out."

Salinger was born in San Francisco in 1925. His father took the family to Toronto, where he worked as a mining engineer, and Salt Lake City, where he worked as an impresario. The son studied piano, composition, conducting, and violin, but since he "had no friends of my own age, and had rarely swung a baseball bat or thrown a football," he gave up hopes for a concert career at eleven. After serving as skipper of a Navy minesweeper in the Pacific and graduating from the University of San Francisco, he served as night city editor of the *San Francisco Chronicle* and was working on a Teamsters exposé for *Collier's* when the magazine folded on Christmas 1956.

Out of work, he received two calls—one from the Teamsters, which tried to hire him as its publicist, and one from Robert Kennedy, who was setting up his Senate labor rackets investigation. On Salinger's first day on the labor rackets staff, Robert took him to Hickory Hill for dinner. Salinger was startled that, when he asked for a glass of wine, Robert said he did not have any in the house. By Salinger's account, Kennedy was "more than a little surprised" when he returned from his car with a bottle he "had in reserve for just such emergencies."

At Robert's behest, John Kennedy hired Salinger as campaign press secretary, although the two men barely knew each other. Salinger so gained the confidence of candidate and press corps that Theodore White wrote that "no one who followed the Kennedy campaign through 1960 remembers Salinger with anything but respect and affection."

After the Bay of Pigs, Salinger was the victim of the President's sudden interest in government censorship: "The publishers have to understand that we're never more than a miscalculation away from war and that there are things we're doing that we just can't talk about." Salinger replied with a suggestion he later regretted and would never have made, had he had more national experience: a presidential speech on the subject of press self-restraint on matters of national security.

Speaking to publishers in New York, Kennedy declared that "if the press is awaiting a declaration of war before it imposes the self-discipline of combat conditions, then I can only say no war ever posed a greater threat to our security. . . . For we are opposed around the world by a monolithic and ruthless conspiracy that relies primarily on covert means for expanding its sphere of influence." Editorial writers and columnists howled at what they saw as a presidential effort to divert blame for the Bay of Pigs onto the press.*

Following Salinger's careful instructions, Bolshakov brought Kharmalov to a side entrance of the Carlyle. A Secret Service agent took the two Soviets upstairs in a back elevator. Salinger opened his door. Kharmalov beamed: "The storm in Berlin is over." Salinger was dumbstruck: *"Over?"*

Kharmalov asked him to tell Kennedy that Khrushchev was willing to have an early summit and consider American proposals on Berlin. He would leave the timing up to Kennedy because of the President's "obvious political difficulties." But the summit must be soon. Socialist nations were pressing the Chairman. The danger of a major military incident in Berlin was great. Kharmalov said that Khrushchev "hopes your President's speech to the UN won't be another warlike ultimatum like the one on July 25. He didn't like that at all."

Salinger left a message for the President, who was said to be dining in his apartment upstairs with friends. Kennedy sent for him at one o'clock Monday morning. When Salinger arrived, the President was sitting up in white pajamas in bed, reading and chewing on an unlit cigar.

Salinger gave him the message from Khrushchev. The President rose from his bed and stared out at the glittering Manhattan skyline: "There's only one way you can read it. If Khrushchev is ready to listen to our views on Germany, he's not going to recognize the Ulbricht regime—not this year, at least—and that's good news."

Kennedy called Rusk, who agreed that since Khrushchev had not put his message on paper, he should reply the same way. The President dictated some sentences, which Salinger wrote down on Carlyle

---

*Despite or because of this reaction, Kennedy tried again. He suggested to news executives in the Oval Office that they appoint someone to come to Washington as their "adviser on information affecting the national security." If news organs were uncertain about whether a story would betray secrets to the enemy, they could submit it to the adviser, who, after being given a full briefing by the White House, CIA, State, or Defense, could suggest whether or not the story should run. The newsmen were unmoved. As Salinger later said, Kennedy saw "the futility of further overtures."

stationery. Then Kennedy took another look at his UN text in light of Khrushchev's warning against a "warlike" speech. He did not change a word.

Early the next morning, by his own account, Dr. Jacobson was summoned to the President's suite where, he noticed, there were "half-empty glasses and full ashtrays strewn about the room." Still in his nightclothes, Kennedy "greeted me with a whisper so hoarse that I could barely understand him." By Jacobson's account, he gave the President "a subcutaneous injection slightly below the larynx. . . . I can still see the surprised expression on Kennedy's face when he could speak again in a normal voice."

Jacqueline Kennedy had not planned to attend her husband's UN speech but changed her mind at the last minute. She could not have been disappointed. Its literary quality surpassed the high standard of most of Kennedy's presidential addresses.

Scrawled on his reading copy were the words "Deep . . . Slow." He began by noting that while Hammarskjöld was dead, the United Nations lived. "Mankind must put an end to war, or war will put an end to mankind. So let us here resolve that Dag Hammarskjöld did not live, or die, in vain."* Kennedy argued that the dead man's place could be better filled by one man than three: "Even the three horses of the troika did not have three drivers, all going in different directions."

Today "every man, woman, and child lives under a nuclear sword of Damocles, hanging by the slenderest of threads, capable of being cut at any moment by accident or miscalculation or by madness. The weapons of war must be abolished before they abolish us." He would "challenge the Soviet Union not to an *arms* race, but to a *peace* race."

On Berlin, "we believe a peaceful agreement is possible which protects the freedom of West Berlin and Allied presence and access, while recognizing the historic and legitimate interests of others in assuring European security."

Kennedy and Sorensen had each written a peroration and then woven together the best parts of both. Speaking in distinct phrases for emphasis, the President closed by saying, "We in this hall / will be remembered / either as part of the generation / that turned this planet / into a flaming funeral pyre / or as the generation that met its vow / 'to save succeeding generations / from the scourge of war.' / The decision is ours. / For together we shall save our planet—or together we shall perish in its flames."

---

*Perhaps unwittingly, Sorensen paraphrased this line when he drafted President Lyndon Johnson's first address to Congress on November 27, 1963.

To ensure that no one mistook this rhetoric for weakness, Robert Kennedy had gone on *Meet the Press* the previous day and warned that if Khrushchev miscalculated, "the world could be destroyed. I would hope that in the last few weeks he would have come to the realization that the President will use nuclear weapons."

While the President finished his speech to the General Assembly, Kharmalov and Bolshakov went to Salinger's room at the Carlyle, where the press secretary orally gave them Kennedy's reply to Khrushchev. He said that if the Soviet Union was ready to honor its commitments on Laos, a summit on the much more difficult question of Germany would be more likely to produce agreement. The President was "most encouraged" by the Chairman's willingness to reexamine his position on Germany.

The presidential entourage flew to Newport, where the Kennedys were to spend a week at Hammersmith Farm, the seaside summer home of Jacqueline's mother and stepfather. By courier Bundy sent the President some "special intelligence material" from Richard Helms at the CIA suggesting that "we are in a calm before a further squeeze" on Berlin.

On Friday afternoon, September 29, Salinger returned from golf to answer a call from Bolshakov in New York. The Russian told him they must meet "immediately." He would charter a plane and fly to Newport that evening. Salinger asked Bolshakov to do nothing until he heard back from him.

He called the President and Rusk, who both guessed that Bolshakov had Khrushchev's response to the President's secret message. With two dozen White House correspondents in Newport, Salinger feared that Bolshakov's sudden appearance might cause a "minor sensation." He suggested a meeting at three-thirty the next day at the Carlyle. Bolshakov said, "If you knew the importance of what I have, you wouldn't keep me waiting that long."

The next morning, Salinger flew to New York. Rusk told him that he wondered why Gromyko couldn't have given him Khrushchev's response when they had met earlier that day. At precisely three-thirty, Bolshakov appeared at Salinger's Carlyle room with newspapers under his arm. Concealed inside them was a thick manila envelope. He opened it and pulled out a sheaf of pages: "You may read this. Then it is for the eyes of the President only."

CHAPTER

13

"Dear Mr. President" and "Dear Mr. Chairman"

BOLSHAKOV HAD BROUGHT RUSSIAN AND ENGLISH VERSIONS OF A twenty-six-page private letter that Khrushchev had sent to Kennedy from Pitsunda. He said he had spent the whole night on the English translation. The only Russians in the United States who knew ·about Khrushchev's letter were himself and Gromyko. Ambassador Menshikov had not been informed.

After the Russian departed, Salinger called Newport. Kennedy told him, "Get that letter over to Dean Rusk as quickly as possible. Then bring it up here to me."

Salinger took the letter to the Secretary at the Waldorf. Rusk read it twice but was unwilling to offer a snap judgment. He took the letter along with him to Washington that evening and then sent it by courier to Salinger in New York the next morning. Salinger flew to Providence and delivered the precious envelope to the Auchincloss house in Newport, where the President had just returned from Sunday Mass.

Opening with "Dear Mr. President," Khrushchev's missive began with a homey note about resting at Pitsunda with his children and grandchildren. He said he had planned to write earlier in the summer after Kennedy's meeting with his son-in-law. But the President's statements on Berlin had been so belligerent they led to an exchange of militant actions by both countries that must now be restrained.

Replying to Kennedy's private message on Laos and Berlin, Khrushchev said he saw no reason why negotiation in good faith could not produce settlements in both places. He was willing, if the President was, to take another look at positions frozen hard through fifteen years of Cold War. He favored his Catholic counterpart with a biblical metaphor. The postwar world was like Noah's Ark. Both the "clean" and the "unclean," whatever their disagreements, wished it to stay afloat.

As leaders of the two mightiest states, he wrote, he and the President had a special obligation to prevent another war. It might be useful to start a purely informal correspondence that would bypass the American and Soviet bureaucracies, omit propaganda statements written for public consumption, and convey their positions without the necessity of a backward glance at the press.

If the President disapproved, he could consider that this letter did not exist. In any event, Khrushchev would not refer to the correspondence in public. He closed, "Accept my respects, N. Khrushchev, Chairman of the Council of Ministers of the U.S.S.R."

Khrushchev had corresponded with Eisenhower, but these were mainly formal documents.* Why did the Chairman now send such a personal letter? At this perilous moment, he may have feared leaving the Soviet-American relationship to the tender mercies of Rusk and Gromyko, two bureaucrats he distrusted. He had tried to send public and private messages to the President through Pearson and Sulzberger, but these had not brought a serious response.

He presumably felt that if he built a fruitful personal relationship with the President by letter, this could be cited to Kremlin critics as

---

*Although it never became as personal as his Kennedy correspondence, Khrushchev and his predecessor as Prime Minister, Bulganin, corresponded with Eisenhower more frequently and substantively than legend has come to suggest. There were twenty-two letters between Eisenhower and Bulganin, for instance, between the Geneva summit of 1955 and Bulganin's ouster in 1958. In March 1960, before the Paris summit, Khrushchev privately wrote Eisenhower of his anxieties about the possibility of nuclear weapons controlled by Bonn. The President replied by calling for a verifiable test ban and other disarmament measures: "You and I must recognize . . . that the secrets of the production of nuclear weapons . . . cannot long remain hidden from many of the states in the modern world which have advanced scientific and industrial resources."

evidence of Khrushchev's indispensability in foreign affairs. It would also lend Kennedy stature and might give him a stake in helping to keep Khrushchev in power as a man he knew and with whom he could deal. The Chairman felt that the stronger Kennedy felt his domestic standing to be, the more likely he was to follow what Khrushchev assumed were private views on the Cold War that were close to those of Mansfield, Stevenson, and Fulbright.

The Chairman was worried about his Twenty-second Party Congress, scheduled for Moscow in October. He knew that the meeting could be rocky and unpredictable, with people saying many harsh things against the United States. A private correspondence would allow him to maintain quiet contact with the President and keep hostilities from escalating.

Why the cloak-and-dagger? Under Eisenhower, Khrushchev had allowed such letters to be delivered to the President by Menshikov and Smirnovsky. But as Foy Kohler recalled, each time one of the Russians appeared at the West Wing, "the entire press corps laid siege to the U.S. government until they managed to find some inkling of what the message was about."

In March 1960, Eisenhower had been forced to wire the Chairman, "I deeply regret that the substance discussed in our recent correspondence has leaked to the press. I assure you that I believed that I had taken every precaution to safeguard against the exposure of these matters." He arranged to have the Embassy transmit Khrushchev's future letters more discreetly through the State Department.

Secrecy was restored, but Khrushchev did not like to imagine his letters appearing on the President's desk under some kind of disclaiming cover note attached by the Cold Warriors of the State Department. Sending the letters through Bolshakov and other secret emissaries would avoid this problem. It would appeal to what he knew to be Kennedy's penchant for secrecy and convey the implied compliment that he was willing to use a channel with Kennedy that he had never used with his predecessor.

After reading Khrushchev's letter, Kennedy called Rusk in Washington. They agreed to have Salinger inform Bolshakov that the President would respond, probably within the week.

Kennedy felt that a correspondence would be in keeping with his often-expressed desire for open communication, and it might postpone or muffle a showdown over Berlin. But he also saw dangers. A strongly negative reply to Khrushchev on Berlin might hasten Soviet action. If he sent a strongly positive reply, Khrushchev might trick him by quietly sending it to the French and West Germans as proof that Kennedy was conspiring behind their backs. If he took the precaution of showing his letter to the notoriously leaky Western allies, Khrushchev might find out and, outraged, halt their private correspondence forever.

The President dictated a memo to himself to "have Bundy and Sorensen analyze K's letter." Bohlen observed that Kennedy's reply "may be the most important letter the President will ever write."

The following Wednesday, October 4, Kennedy saw C. L. Sulzberger in the upstairs Oval Room. He thanked him for sending on the message from Khrushchev in September about using "informal contacts" to settle Berlin.

He said that he had recently studied the 1959 Western "peace plan," proposing free elections in both Germanys. It "was obviously not serious and we knew it could never be accepted." Now, at least, the United States was serious. Without disclosing Khrushchev's private letter, he reported that the Chairman had lately been "much softer" on Berlin. At Vienna, he had showed no recognition that American prestige was involved: "Now he does, and his attitude is less rigid."

Sulzberger asked if the Vienna summit had been useful. Kennedy said, "Yes, it was useful for me in judging this man. One always has a tendency to think that reason will prevail in personal conversation, but now I have been able to judge him. Now I know that there is *no* further need for talking. The only reason to meet again would be to make the final arrangements in any previously prepared agreement." In personal contacts, Khrushchev had one great advantage: known as a "rough, tough man," he was therefore more impressive to people when he was polite, just like Joe McCarthy and Jimmy Hoffa.*

Kennedy said he had no doubt that the American people were "ready to go to the brink of war" on Berlin: "The chances of settling this without war are not yet too good." More than once, he used the words, "If we push the button." Rocking jerkily in his chair, he said he had been concerned by Senator Margaret Chase Smith of Maine

---

*This was not the first or last time Kennedy compared Khrushchev to Hoffa. He once told reporters in a background session that "there is nothing like organization and discipline in international affairs, as in politics. . . . The Communists' ability to hold power once they have gained it makes them formidable, and the same thing is true here at home in the Teamsters Union." Just as telling is the President's comparison of Khrushchev to McCarthy, another erratic figure who had caused him terrible political problems.

and others who said he lacked the will to use nuclear weapons, but "I think we have convinced Khrushchev on that."

Sulzberger reminded Kennedy that Khrushchev had told him the Laos situation would soon improve. The President replied that this was the line Khrushchev was "putting out" but he figured the Chairman expected Laos to "soon fall into his lap." It was perfectly plain how the United States would fight over Berlin, he said, but how to defend Southeast Asia was not so clear-cut.

On Friday evening, October 6, Andrei Gromyko came to the White House. Kennedy told O'Donnell it was "really the first time since Vienna that they've wanted to talk." A week before, Gromyko had confided to Rusk that his government would not insist on signing a German peace treaty before the end of 1961. Kennedy told Rusk, "It looks like a thaw."

The President had first met Gromyko while reporting for the Hearst papers on the founding UN conference in San Francisco in 1945. He had found Gromyko polite, agreeable, and human; when he smiled, it was with a real smile—"not like our Russian Ambassador here."

Others observed that Gromyko combined the durability of Talleyrand, who consistently retained power through the French Revolution, Napoleon, and the Bourbon restoration, with the self-effacement of Tolstoy's Alexy in *Anna Karenina,* the minister "who reveals so little of himself that his every remark and gesture was a source of mystery." Asked once whether he had enjoyed his breakfast, he said, "Perhaps."

He once told a reporter, "My personality does not interest me." Harriman thought that Gromyko had "schooled himself out of any human foible." A British diplomat noted his "impatience, coldness, and heavy, somewhat macabre sense of humor." His daughter observed that since the 1930s, he had scarcely set foot on the streets of Moscow: "All he sees is the view of his car window."

Gromyko was born in 1909, son of a father whom he described as "semi-peasant, semi-worker," a Russo-Japanese War veteran. In 1931, the son left for Minsk, where he joined the Communist Party, married a fellow student, and studied Marxist theory and agricultural economics. By the end of the decade, he was on the Moscow fast track as a senior researcher at the Academy of Sciences.

At thirty, he was recruited to help fill the enormous new vacuum in the Soviet diplomatic service. In the spring of 1939, Stalin was mowing through the first postrevolutionary generation of Soviet diplomats; many were executed or sent to labor camps. His Jewish, anti-Fascist Foreign Minister Maxim Litvinov had negotiated the first

Soviet-American diplomatic ties with Franklin Roosevelt in 1933. Stalin replaced him with Molotov, who on taking power said, "Enough of Litvinov liberalism! I am going to tear out that kike's hornet nest by the roots!"*

As Stalin and Molotov renounced their pact with Hitler and then spun around into alliance with the United States and Britain, Gromyko's sea legs kept him on the winning side of the diplomatic bureaucracy. He was appointed as Counselor in Washington, where Litvinov had been sent as Ambassador to help weld together the Allied war machine. In 1943, more confident of victory and eager to fight for Soviet power in the postwar world, Stalin fired Litvinov and called Gromyko to Moscow. Stalin's aides reputedly joked that Gromyko would either be sent west, back to Washington, or east, to Siberia.

At thirty-four, Gromyko became Ambassador to Washington, where he fought for Stalin's interests in the postwar firmament.† During talks on a United Nations, he insisted that every major power have a veto, thus ensuring that the Soviet Union would not be thwarted as it did its business in Eastern Europe.

Stalin made him a Deputy Foreign Minister and his first permanent representative to the UN Security Council. Western reporters called him "Mr. Nyet" and "Grim Grom." So many times did he stalk out of the chamber that when American baseball players walked off the field, radio commentators began to say that they were "pulling a Gromyko."

By 1949, Gromyko was back at the Foreign Ministry. Molotov was replaced by the rabidly anti-American Andrei Vishinsky, who charged that Gromyko was too mild and had used official workmen and materials to build a weekend dacha. This practice was hardly unusual, but Vishinsky managed to have Gromyko censured and shunted off to the Court of St. James's in 1952. The next year, after Stalin's death, Molotov and Gromyko were restored to their old jobs.

Convinced that Khrushchev was conceding too much to the West,

---

*This was said despite the fact that Molotov's own wife, Paulina, was Jewish. She was sent in 1949 to a labor camp as an "international Zionist" without evident protest from Molotov, who was unwilling to jeopardize his standing with Stalin. The day of Stalin's funeral in 1953 was Molotov's sixty-third birthday. Leaving the mausoleum, Khrushchev and Malenkov asked him what he would like as a present. He replied, "Paulina." One wonders what she said to him after her release.

†Stalin advised him to improve his English by attending American churches and listening to sermons; the dictator had himself been educated by the Russian Orthodox Church while a seminarian. Flustered by the prospect of explaining why an atheist Soviet envoy was attending church, Gromyko committed the rare sin of disobeying Stalin's order.

Molotov tried to block the Austrian State Treaty and improved Soviet relations with Japan and Yugoslavia. In 1956, Khrushchev fired him as Foreign Minister in favor of a young man in a hurry, Dimitri Shepilov. Then Shepilov betrayed his benefactor by joining Molotov and others in the Anti-Party Coup. Gromyko was not unsettled by the newest shake-up. In a rare effort at wit, he once said, "It's a bit like the Bermuda Triangle. Every now and then one of us disappears."

Appointed Foreign Minister, he remolded himself to serve Khrushchev as he had Stalin. The Chairman teased him as an "arid bureaucrat." He once told a young Soviet diplomat in Gromyko's presence, "Andrei Andreyevich is an excellent diplomat and tactician. . . . But as an ideologist and theoretician, he's rather poor. . . . We'll make something of him yet."

Gromyko hated being ridiculed in front of an underling but bore it in silence. When Khrushchev pounded his fists on his UN desk in 1960, Gromyko manfully did the same. As he pounded, the sides of his thin mouth were curled downward in distaste.

Arriving at the Stalinist tower that housed the Foreign Ministry, Gromyko rose in a private elevator to a seventh-floor office whose desk and walls were bare but for the portrait of Lenin facing his chair. A visitor to the family's Moscow flat found it "so impersonal as to be modest." He relaxed by playing chess with his congenial wife, Lidiya, or reading Tolstoy, Shakespeare, Twain, and the confidential archives of the czarist diplomatic service. He had Western films screened at home and, like Stalin, offered running commentaries on the actors and their performances.

Gromyko's passion was not to reshape the world but political survival. This was not easy in the subculture of the Bermuda Triangle. He recoiled from Soviet domestic issues, concluding no doubt that more Soviet political careers had been broken by the economy and intra-Party feuds than by shifts in foreign policy. One aide noted that whenever a conversation threatened to grow personal or ideological, Gromyko changed the subject.

He lacked the sentimental idealism of Khrushchev and Mikoyan about the 1917 Revolution or their emotional commitment to communism. Still, Gromyko was a champion of his system and its spread throughout the world. Living in New York after the war had confirmed his view of capitalist America. "Profit is the pitiless filter through which everything to do with culture and art and the country's spiritual life has to pass," he wrote in memoirs late in life. "Only that which promises a return on capital can survive."

His relations with Khrushchev were probably the unhappiest of those with any of the five Soviet leaders he ultimately served.* The Chairman very likely suspected that Gromyko had not entirely surrendered his loyalty to Stalin and Molotov. He knew that Gromyko was quietly cultivating Brezhnev, a not unlikely future leader of the Soviet Union. As human beings, Khrushchev and Gromyko were oil and water.

The Chairman felt he must take audacious gambles if he was to advance the Soviet cause without bankrupting the economy with vast military spending. Gromyko looked on many of Khrushchev's bright ideas as those of an amateur who had to be watched to avoid serious damage to Soviet interests. If Khrushchev ever thought of firing Gromyko, he presumably concluded that it was not worth losing his expertise or the patina of continuity that Gromyko brought to his tumultuous foreign policy.

His impatience with Gromyko resembled nothing so much as Kennedy's impatience with Rusk. Kennedy and Khrushchev both solved their problem in the same way. The President increasingly relied on his brother, White House aides, and other loyalists for advice on foreign policy, using Robert Kennedy and others as emissaries for private communication with the Russians. Khrushchev increasingly relied on his son-in-law, political aides, and Mikoyan for advice, using Adzhubei and others to communicate with the Americans.

Born within five months of each other, Gromyko and Rusk each felt in the early 1960s that part of his task was to keep a theatrical, inexperienced, sometimes erratic boss on track. Each was privately irritated by the meddling of "amateurs" like Robert Kennedy and Adzhubei in foreign policy. More than one diplomat noted that Gromyko seemed to feel a unique professional empathy with his American counterpart. When a Soviet diplomat once needled Rusk on some minor technical point, Gromyko cried, "Leave the Secretary alone!"

The President took Gromyko to the upstairs Oval Room and showed him the dazzling view of the Washington Monument and

---

*This excludes Mikhail Gorbachev, who fired him as Foreign Minister and gave him the honorific post of President of the Soviet Union soon after taking power. A year before his death in July 1989, Gromyko resigned after a public meeting in which he was heckled as "too old." The timing of Gromyko's death was merciful. It came just before the collapse of the communist regimes in Eastern Europe which were such a part of his raison d'être.

Potomac beyond the Truman Balcony. He said, "I'm sorry Mrs. Kennedy isn't here. She's up in Rhode Island with the babies."

The Foreign Minister consumed an hour reading from a position paper on Berlin. Smoking a cigar, Kennedy felt there was nothing new but that Khrushchev seemed more resigned to accept the status quo. He told Gromyko that while he sensed a "softening" in the Soviet position, the Soviet Union had still made no acceptable proposal for negotiations on Berlin.

Gromyko mentioned the Chairman's stale offer to internationalize West Berlin in exchange for ill-defined access guarantees. Kennedy shook his head: "You're offering to trade us an apple for an orchard. We don't do that in this country." He suggested that Gromyko confer with Thompson in Moscow about a Berlin settlement that would lead to a "clear and stable relationship" between their countries.

Gromyko declaimed on the virtues of a troika. The President was prepared. At the suggestion of a Polish-born congressional aide, he picked up a Russian-language book and turned to a fable by the Russian Aesop, Ivan Krylov:

> *A swan, a pike, and crab once took their station*
> *In harness, and would drag a loaded cart;*
> *But when the moment came for them to start,*
> *They sweat, they strain, and yet the cart stands still.*

Gromyko replied, "But those are animals. We are talking about people." Kennedy said, "It's a delightful little book. I want you and Mr. Khrushchev to share it as a gift." He gave his visitor two leather-bound copies.

That evening, at a dinner for the Sudanese president, Kennedy told Lippmann that he had gotten "nowhere" with Gromyko. Lippmann said, "Gromyko is the most wooden man you'll ever have to deal with." Kennedy agreed: "I don't like him." Later, exact quotations from the meeting were leaked to the press to show that the President had not been soft with Gromyko.

After the Foreign Minister stopped to see Macmillan in London, the Prime Minister wrote, "I think the Russians are looking for a way out (as we are) if they can do so without too much loss of 'face.'"

At Hyannis Port, on the weekend of Saturday, October 14, Kennedy polished his reply to Khrushchev's private letter, working from drafts supplied by Sorensen and Bundy. Starting "Dear Mr. Chairman," he wrote of his retreat, his children, and their cousins: getting away from Washington gave him a clearer, quieter perspective. He tried to make the tone cordial and hopeful, using first-person references that he eschewed in speeches.

He welcomed the idea of a personal, informal, but meaningful exchange of views in frank, realistic, and fundamental terms. It could supplement official channels, but he would want to show the correspondence to his Secretary of State. Their letters could never convert each other, but at least they would be free from the polemics of Cold War debate. That debate would, of course, proceed, but they would direct their messages only to each other.

He liked the Chairman's reference to Noah's Ark: of course they must collaborate if they were to avoid destroying everything. He agreed with Khrushchev's emphasis on their special obligation. They two were not personally responsible for the events at the end of World War II that led to the current Berlin situation, but they would be held responsible if they could not deal with it peacefully.

He chose points from Khrushchev's letter with which he could agree, sometimes restating them to his own liking, but pulled no punches: the Chairman's suggestion to station Soviet troops in West Berlin was "not acceptable to the United States, nor to the other two Powers whose troops are in that City." He closed with best wishes from his family to Khrushchev's; through these letters and otherwise, he hoped for concrete progress toward a just and enduring peace. This, he wrote, was their greatest responsibility and their greatest opportunity.

The Chairman liked Kennedy's reply enough to pursue the secret correspondence, which Bundy dubbed the "pen pal letters." To avoid Foreign Ministry channels and underscore the notion that he was offering the President access to his private thoughts, Khrushchev sent later letters with the same aura of mystery as the first. Someone from the Soviet Embassy would meet Robert Kennedy, Sorensen, or Salinger on a street corner or in a saloon and slip a manila envelope out of his trench coat or folded newspaper.

Bundy gave the President a mid-October "report from Charlie Bartlett on his meeting with Smirnovsky. This is worth reading because it implies that the Soviets are hoping you will be 'reasonable.' Be wary!"

In the Kremlin's vast new red-and-gold Palace of Congresses, Khrushchev opened the Twenty-second Congress of the Soviet Communist Party with a six-hour speech. Of Gromyko's meeting with

Kennedy he said, "We hear the reproach that someone is trying to give an apple for an orchard in settling the German question. This figure of speech may please its authors, but it does not reflect the true picture."

The new Soviet nuclear tests were "coming along very well. . . . We shall probably wind them up by detonating a hydrogen bomb with a yield of fifty million tons of TNT." The Soviet Union also had a hundred-megaton bomb. "But we are not going to explode it, because even if we did so at the most remote site, we might knock out all our windows!" Resounding applause.

"May God grant—as they used to say—that we are never called upon to explode these bombs over anybody's territory. This is the greatest wish of our lives!" More resounding applause.

A White House statement called on the Russians not to test the fifty-megaton bomb because it would add more radioactive fallout to that "unleashed in recent weeks." It noted that the United States had the "technical know-how and materials to produce bombs in the fifty- to one-hundred-megaton range and higher."

Another passage in Khrushchev's speech disturbed the President: "We believe that the forces of socialism . . . are today more powerful than the aggressive imperialist forces." A German peace treaty "must and will be signed," making West Berlin a "free, demilitarized city." This passage suggested that the West would now accept Khrushchev's demands on Berlin out of fear that the world power balance had shifted toward the Soviet Union.

At a press conference just the week before, Kennedy had been asked about recent charges that he had not maintained the "strength and credibility of our nuclear deterrent" or convinced Khrushchev "that we are determined to meet force with force in Berlin or elsewhere." The President had replied by describing the military buildup since January. He skirted the issue of which superpower was stronger.

If he allowed Khrushchev to go unchallenged now, as he intimidated the world with the most powerful nuclear tests in history, any negotiation over Berlin might be viewed as a sign of American weakness. The Allies might reassess their dependence on the United States. Kennedy's Republican opposition would tear him to shreds.

At a White House luncheon that autumn, the venomous publisher of the *Dallas Morning News,* E. M. "Ted" Dealey, shocked those present by reading out a challenge to the President: "We can annihilate Russia and should make that clear to the Soviet government." Unfortunately "you and your Administration are weak sisters." What was needed was "a man on horseback. . . . Many people in Texas and the Southwest think that you are riding Caroline's tricycle."

Flushed with anger, Kennedy replied, "Wars are easier to talk about than they are to fight. I'm just as tough as you are—and I didn't get elected President by arriving at soft judgments."*

Since February, McNamara and others around the President had periodically assured the public that American strength was second to none. These assurances had always been deliberately imprecise. Like Eisenhower, Kennedy did not want to provoke the Soviets into a massive buildup. Nor could he be absolutely certain what the Russians did and did not have.

When McNamara told reporters in February that the missile gap was in the American favor, he was relying largely on primitive spy satellite photographs of Soviet territory, which were often dark and ill-defined. That spring, Western intelligence asked its agent Penkovsky for new information on the Soviet missile program. Using three rolls of microfilm passed by Penkovsky as well as other intelligence sources, the CIA concluded in June that the Russians had fifty to a hundred operational ICBMs.

In August, as the President grappled with Berlin, he asked the CIA for a new emergency assessment. On September 6, the Agency reported that its June estimate had been too high: the Soviet Union in fact had fewer than thirty-five operational ICBMs. Briefing Kennedy one week later, General Lemnitzer put the figure at ten to twenty-five. Unlike America's, none were in hardened silos; all were cumbersome to launch.

As long as their locations were secret, the Soviet missiles had been usable for a Pearl Harbor–style attack and a retaliatory second strike against the United States. But now that satellites had shown the Pentagon the location of virtually every Soviet ICBM, the system had only limited value for a first strike and almost none for a second. As the State Department intelligence chief Roger Hilsman recalled, "The whole Soviet ICBM system was suddenly obsolescent."

Kennedy knew that if the United States revealed Soviet inferiority, Khrushchev might speed up his ICBM program. Nevertheless, letting the Chairman know that the United States had absolute faith in its own superiority might make him less cavalier about pressing his Berlin demands to the point of war. For the President, Khrushchev's opening speech to his Party Congress demonstrated the danger of allowing

---

*The News reported that in response to its account of Dealey's exchange with the President, it received over two thousand telephone calls, telegrams, and letters, including a tribute from the eccentric right-wing tycoon H. L. Hunt, and that over 84 percent approved.

him to keep spinning public fantasies about Soviet dominance in nuclear weapons.

Kennedy decided to let the world know who was the dominant power but would not say so himself: "When I get up and say those things, it sounds too belligerent."

McNamara's deputy, Roswell Gilpatric, was scheduled to speak on Saturday, October 21, to the Business Council.in Hot Springs, Virginia. The fifty-five-year-old Gilpatric was a Wall Street lawyer, by way of Hotchkiss and Yale, who had served as Truman's Undersecretary of the Air Force.

Time said, "In many ways Gilpatric is McNamara's personality opposite—he is socially gregarious and skilled in the ways of handling admirals, generals, and politicians." Joseph Alsop told the President that Gilpatric provided a "badly needed human lubricant" at the Pentagon. Kennedy joked that Jacqueline thought him the "second most attractive man" at the Pentagon—after McNamara. She invited Gilpatric to small White House dinners and Camp David without his wife and visited his Maryland farm. Kennedy told her, "I think it's that father image of yours."

The President, Bundy, Rusk, and McNamara collaborated with Gilpatric on a text for his Business Council speech. The address would reveal more explicitly than ever before the immense nuclear superiority of the United States.

As Gilpatric said years later, it was designed "to convince the Soviet Union that we were ready to take on any threat in the Berlin area" and to persuade the West Germans and other allies "to beef up the conventional forces of the alliance." In the wake of the new Soviet nuclear tests and before the expected Berlin talks, Kennedy wished to remind the American people of the military might that had been preserved and enhanced under his administration.

Hilsman recalled that the President decided to authorize the address "only after much agonizing, since everyone involved recognized that telling the Soviets what we knew entailed considerable risk. Forewarned, the Soviets would undoubtedly speed up their ICBM program." Nevertheless, if Khrushchev "were allowed to continue to assume that we still believed in the missile gap, he would very probably bring the world dangerously close to war."

Drafting of the speech was assigned to Daniel Ellsberg, the young Pentagon strategist who a decade later disseminated the "Pentagon Papers" on Vietnam. Ellsberg asked Kaysen why Kennedy instead did not privately inform Khrushchev that he knew the full facts of Soviet nuclear inferiority. He could send the Chairman the precise coordinates of the Soviet ICBMs of Plesetsk or copies of satellite photos. Kaysen told him, "John Kennedy isn't going to talk that way to Khrushchev."

Gilpatric told his Business Council audience that the President was "determined that our strategic power must be sufficient to deter any deliberate nuclear attack on this country or its allies by being able to survive a first strike by the enemy with sufficient arms to penetrate his defenses and inflict unacceptable losses upon him."

He listed the conventional measures taken to deal with Berlin but argued that the "fundamental question" was the nuclear balance of power: "This nation has a nuclear retaliatory force of such lethal power that an enemy move which brought it into play would be an act of self-destruction on his part.

"The U.S. has today hundreds of manned intercontinental bombers . . . six Polaris submarines at sea, carrying a total of ninety-six missiles, and dozens of intercontinental ballistic missiles. Our carrier strike forces and land-based theater forces could deliver additional hundreds of megatons.

"The total number of our nuclear delivery vehicles . . . is in the tens of thousands, and, of course, we have more than one warhead for each vehicle." Even if the Russians tried to wage a Pearl Harbor–style assault, they could not hope for victory: "Our forces are so deployed and protected that a sneak attack could not effectively disarm us.

"The destructive power which the United States could bring to bear even after a Soviet surprise attack upon our forces would be as great as, perhaps greater than, the total undamaged force which the enemy can threaten to launch against the United States in a first strike. In short, we have a second-strike capability which is at least as extensive as what the Soviets can deliver by striking first. Therefore, we are confident that the Soviets will not provoke a major nuclear conflict."

Gilpatric taunted Khrushchev further by showing that the United States knew about the growing Sino-Soviet split: threatening to set off a fifty-megaton bomb was "the Soviet Union's answer to the discordant voice from its populous neighbor to the south."*

To show that Gilpatric was not speaking merely for himself, Rusk gave a television interview the next morning: "Mr. Khrushchev must

---

*At Khrushchev's opening Party Congress speech, Chou En-lai had been ostentatiously unenthusiastic. When other officials congratulated the Chairman, Chou brushed past him. On October 21, after laying a wreath at Stalin's tomb, the Chinese leader left Moscow before Khrushchev's Congress was over. TASS explained this away by saying that Chou had to prepare for a new session of his own National People's Congress. But this session was not held until March 1962.

know that we are strong. . . . When we talk about exploratory talks or about contacts with the Soviet government on one or another point, there is no problem that turns on whether we feel that we are weak or not. We are not weak."

Asked if the President had not recently conceded that American and Soviet power were equal, Rusk said, "Well, I think when we use the word equal, what is meant there is that in this confrontation of two great power blocs, each side has a capacity to inflict very great damage upon the other. . . . But that does not necessarily mean that, in the total situation, the two situations are equal."

That week McNamara said, "I believe we have nuclear power several times that of the Soviet Union." Classified briefings were given to allies that the United States knew to be penetrated by Soviet moles in order to strengthen the effect of Gilpatric's message.

At a news conference, in reply to a question, the President declared that the United States would "not trade places with anyone in the world. . . . I've stated that I thought that the United States was in a position that was powerful—Mr. Gilpatric said 'second to none.' I said it was our obligation to remain so. And that is what we intend to do."

Christian Herter wrote Eisenhower that "if what is now being said by the Administration had been said by the Democrats during the last two years, as it should have been, then . . . Khrushchev's present attitude might well be quite different from what it is." The General replied, "Amen. I marvel at how the opposition manages to get away with its switch in position without once being called on it or being reminded of previous statements."

By asking Gilpatric to make this speech, Kennedy may have strengthened his own domestic political standing and reassured American allies, but he also provocatively undermined Khrushchev's position in the Kremlin and in the world.

The Chairman's entire domestic and foreign strategy was based on creating the illusion of Soviet nuclear might. Now, as the world learned that the emperor had no clothes, Khrushchev must have imagined that the Third World and perhaps even Soviet allies, previously mesmerized by Soviet power, might begin turning away from Moscow. The Chinese would crow that his fakery and softness on capitalism had been revealed once and for all. His Kremlin rivals would ask why he had spent on consumer goods and agriculture at the cost of leaving the Soviet Union in such a humiliating position.

Khrushchev had fashioned an illusion of Soviet strength most of all so that the United States would treat his country as an equal. Now

Kennedy seemed to have deliberately chosen to humiliate him—and in the middle of a Party Congress at which he was already under fire by the Chinese and more hard-line Soviet leaders.

He may have wondered whether the "madmen of the Pentagon" might now press a President worried about his own domestic political weakness to order a nuclear first strike against the Soviet Union. The Kremlin had worried for years about Pentagon demands for a nuclear "bolt out of the blue." Soviet intelligence almost certainly picked up some hint of the daydreaming in Washington about an American first strike. Even if Kennedy stood up to his generals, who could say that he would not now exploit his nuclear advantage to demand that Cold War disputes be resolved on American terms?

To remedy the immediate damage of Gilpatric's speech, Khrushchev approved the detonation of a thirty-megaton nuclear blast. Two days after the speech, the world heard the shattering roar of the most mammoth explosion yet unleashed by man against the earth.

Defense Minister Malinovsky told the Party Congress that Gilpatric had "addressed a meeting of the Business Council in Virginia, presumably not without President Kennedy's knowledge, and, brandishing the might of the United States, threatened us with force. What is there to say to this latest threat, to this petty speech? Only one thing: *the threat does not frighten us!*

"They are threatening to reply with force to our just proposals for a German peace treaty and the ending of the abnormal situation in West Berlin. . . . A realistic assessment of the picture would lead one to believe that what the imperialists are planning is a surprise nuclear attack on the U.S.S.R. and the socialist countries."

Malinovsky insisted that America's claim of nuclear superiority was erroneous: Gilpatric's assessment was based on five-megaton warheads. The Soviet Union, he said, had many warheads from twenty to fifty megatons that could be delivered "to any spot on the globe." The Americans "must obviously make fundamental corrections" in their estimates. As for Western Europe, "You must understand, madmen, that it would take really very few multimegaton nuclear bombs to wipe out your small and densely populated countries and kill you instantly in your lairs!"

The thirty-megaton blast and Malinovsky's tough language may have temporarily consoled the Party Congress delegates, but the deeply serious problems created for Khrushchev by Gilpatric's speech remained. It pressured him to do something spectacular to change the world's perception of the nuclear balance between the Soviet Union and the United States.

* * *

On the day after the Gilpatric speech, Allan Lightner, the senior American civilian in West Berlin, and his wife were headed into the Eastern sector along Friedrichstrasse to see a Czechoslovak theater company perform. At Checkpoint Charlie, the East German police, the "Vopos" (*Volkspolizisten*—"People's Police"), refused to let the Lightners' Volkswagen into East Berlin without scrutinizing their passports. Lightner retorted that official American license plates had always been considered sufficient identification.

Since the United States did not recognize the GDR or its authority over East Berlin, Lightner demanded to see a Soviet official. The Vopos refused. Lightner referred the matter to Lucius Clay, now in Berlin as Kennedy's resident personal representative.

On leaving his post as chief of the Continental Can Company, Clay had won Kennedy's consent to have him report directly to the President. "I'm the President's man," he told a friend, "but I cannot abide that little brother of his." Bundy feared that the General might at some point resign in protest over Kennedy's moderation on Berlin. He found Clay "difficult. At least once a week, he would send a cable saying if A, B, or C didn't happen or if the current instruction or intent to do D and E should persist, he couldn't answer for the consequences."

By Clay's order, American troops armed with rifles escorted Lightner's car into East Berlin. As Lightner recalled, if the Vopos had tried to stop it "by shooting one of us, we would have had to kill all of them. . . . All hell would have broken loose."

In Moscow, Khrushchev may have wondered whether, in the wake of the Gilpatric speech, Lightner's display was the harbinger of new American belligerence around the world. He could not have known that authority for Lightner's stand came from the strong-minded General Clay, not the White House. When Kennedy was told about the incident, he reputedly carped, "We didn't send him over there to go to the opera in East Berlin."

The next day, with Soviet approval, the East Germans announced that only Allied personnel in uniform would be allowed into East Berlin without identity papers. Clay called the President and said that something had to be done or else the Communists would keep nibbling away at Western rights. Reluctant to provoke the General, Kennedy consented.

On Wednesday morning, October 25, two young members of the American military police drove through Checkpoint Charlie in an Opel sedan with official American plates. They refused to show their passports. When Vopos stopped them, three U.S. Army jeeps with battle-ready soldiers escorted them into East Berlin, defying the East German decree.

Taking up positions at the boundary line were three armored personnel carriers and ten American tanks equipped with bulldozer blades serviceable for an attack on the Berlin Wall. American jeeps escorted more civilian vehicles in and out of East Berlin in the most important Communist setback since the border closing.

On Friday, ten Soviet tanks rolled up to the boundary, facing the American tanks one hundred yards away. This was the first time in history that American and Soviet tanks had ever confronted each other. The U.S. tank commander, Lieutenant Colonel Thomas Tyree, feared an unexpected event that would touch off open military conflict with the Russians, "such as a nervous soldier discharging his weapon" or "some tanker stepping accidentally on his accelerator leading to a runaway tank."

The President called Clay in Berlin. By Clay's account, as he and Kennedy talked, he was handed a slip saying that twenty more Russian tanks had rolled up to the boundary. He told the President, "This proves they are good mathematicians. . . . We have thirty tanks in Berlin, so they brought up twenty more tanks so that they will have a tank for every tank that we have." He called it further evidence that "they don't intend to do anything."

"Well, I'm glad of that," said Kennedy. "I know you people over there haven't lost your nerve." Clay boldly replied, "Mr. President, we're not worried about our nerves. We're worrying about those of you people in Washington."

Without telling Clay, Kennedy had the Attorney General inform Bolshakov that he would like the Russians to remove their tanks within twenty-four hours. Valentin Falin, later Soviet Ambassador to Bonn, insisted years afterward that the American message included a suggestion that if the American and Soviet tanks "parted without damage to each other's prestige," the President would evince "certain flexibility" on the Berlin issue in a "productive, purely political exchange of opinions."*

---

*One pattern in Robert Kennedy's discussion of the meetings with Bolshakov and other Russians in his 1964 and 1965 oral histories is his inclination to suggest that the Soviets caved in at crucial moments to unilateral demands by himself and the President without mentioning American concessions that were actually the key to solutions. The most prominent example of this is his treatment of the bargaining that ended the Cuban Missile Crisis, distorted to suggest that he and his brother were tougher bargainers than they actually were.

In this, Kennedy demonstrates an extreme version of Dean Acheson's thesis that no diplomat comes out in his own recollection second-best. In his defense, one must

Bolshakov relayed Robert's message to Khrushchev. Adzhubei later recalled that while the American tanks made Soviet generals nervous, the Chairman himself was calm. By Khrushchev's own account, he told his commander in Berlin that the Americans "can't turn their tanks around and pull them back as long as our guns are pointing at them. . . . They're looking for a way out, I'm sure, so let's give them one."

The next morning, the Soviet tanks left the border. The United States followed suit. Robert may have offered Bolshakov another face-saving concession: American civilians were asked, for the time being, to keep out of East Berlin.

Falin later said that Moscow had information that American tank officers had been given orders "to destroy the Berlin Wall." The Soviets suspected that Clay favored an assault upon the Wall. Unbeknownst to Washington, the General had overseen Army plans to set up walls in a West Berlin forest and practice knocking them down.

As Falin recalled, had there been a move against the Wall, Soviet tanks would have opened fire, bringing the United States and Soviet Union "closer to the third world war than ever. . . . Had the tank duel started then in Berlin—and everything was running toward it—the events most probably would have gone beyond any possibility of control."

Khrushchev had hoped that the Twenty-second Party Congress would enshrine him as the full successor to Marx, Engels, and Lenin and architect of full-scale communism by 1980, at which time Soviet sporting events, national defense, and other public functions would be conducted by the spontaneous initiative of the masses. Instead, he had to cope not only with the Gilpatric speech but also with Soviet, Chinese, and Albanian critics.

Before the Congress ended, the Chairman tried to strengthen himself by resuming the anti-Stalin campaign begun with his Secret Speech in 1956. On Monday evening, October 30, the old dictator's mummy was evicted from the monument now no longer called the Lenin-Stalin Tomb. New place names were ordered for the Soviet Union's sixty-two Stalinskis, seven Stalinos, two Stalinsks, and one Stalingrad.

Almost none of the Party Congress speakers, save Khrushchev in

recall that Kennedy conducted these interviews not long after his brother's assassination, at a time when powerful emotions compelled him to try to burnish the Kennedy administration's historical reputation.

his opening address, mentioned the Berlin Crisis. Demands for a UN troika were dropped; the Soviets accepted the election as Secretary-General of U Thant of Burma, who was confirmed unanimously.*

On Tuesday, November 7, at a Kremlin celebration of the forty-fourth anniversary of the Russian Revolution, Khrushchev told reporters that he would not "wait indefinitely" to solve the Berlin problem, but that "for the time being, it is not good for Russia and the United States to push each other."

Two days later, he told the West German Ambassador, Hans Kroll, that relations between their countries must be improved: "Final reconciliation of the German and Soviet peoples would mean the crowning of my life's work in the field of foreign policy." He was playing for time.

In Washington, Bolshakov reported to Robert Kennedy on the Party Congress. The Chairman was "Kennedyizing" the Soviet government, "bringing in young people with new vitality, new ideas." Robert told this to the President, who laughed: "We should be Khrushchevizing the American government."

On November 9 and 10, Khrushchev sent the President two more private letters, a tough message on Berlin and a softer one on Southeast Asia. Bundy thought the Berlin letter a natural "raising of the price before negotiations begin." Bohlen advised Kennedy to let it "cool off a while."

The President agreed, responding instead to the letter on Southeast Asia: "I am conscious of the difficulties you and I face in establishing full communication between our two minds. This is not a question of translation but a question of the context in which we hear and respond to what each other has to say. You and I have already recognized that neither of us will convince the other about our respective social systems and general philosophies of life.

"These differences create a great gulf in communications because language cannot mean the same thing on both sides unless it is related to some underlying common purpose. I cannot believe that there are not such common interests between the Soviet and the American people. Therefore, I am trying to penetrate our ideological differ-

---

*Rusk privately told Senators that Thant was "an entirely reliable person. . . . He is strongly anti-Communist domestically, although a neutral internationally, and is a man of very considerable integrity and experience and ability."

ences in order to find some bridge across the gulf on which we could bring our minds together and find some way in which to protect the peace of the world."

A Laos agreement "ought to be possible" if he and Khrushchev took the "necessary steps" for the country's neutrality and independence. "I have explained to you quite simply and sincerely that the United States has no national ambitions in Laos, no need for military bases or any military position, or an ally."

Kennedy said that he had agreed to the formation of a coalition government headed by Prince Souvanna Phouma and was "pressing the leadership of the Royal Laotian Government to negotiate these questions in good faith." In contrast, the Communist Prince Souphanouvong had "remained consistently at a distance from these discussions": "I can only venture to hope that you, for your part, will likewise exert your influence in the same direction."

Khrushchev's letter had also criticized America's dealings with its ally, the President of South Vietnam, Ngo Dinh Diem, and dismissed Kennedy's complaints about North Vietnamese action against the South.

In April 1961, after the Bay of Pigs, while Laos was referred to the conference table, Kennedy's preoccupations about Vietnam had shifted from aiding the counterinsurgency to finding ways of showing that American willingness to compromise on Laos did not portend a similar retreat from Vietnam.

Robert Kennedy was advised that the best place to stand and fight in Southeast Asia was not Laos but Vietnam. It was a more unified nation, its forces were larger and better trained, it had direct access to the sea, its geography made it more subject to American air and naval power. When Lyndon Johnson visited the area in May, he took a letter from Kennedy to Diem pledging American readiness to "join with you in an intensified endeavor to win the struggle against communism."

At Vienna, just after the final bruising talk with Khrushchev about Berlin, the President told James Reston, "Now we have a problem in trying to make our power credible, and Vietnam looks like the place."

Walt Rostow wrote him several weeks later that Khrushchev's strategy was to exert pressure "on our side of the line" to "create a situation in which we can only reply at the risk of starting a nuclear war or escalating in that direction. Faced with this prospect, we look for compromise. He backs down a little, and a compromise is struck which, on balance, moves his line forward and shifts us back."

This was "the essential point of the exercise on Berlin, from Khrushchev's perspective, and before very long we shall be offered a 'compromise' on Vietnam in which a relaxation of guerrilla warfare will be offered for Vietnam's 'neutrality.' " Rostow suggested that they consider putting Moscow, Peking, Hanoi, and the world on notice that "expansion of the attack on Diem may lead to direct retaliation" against North Vietnam.

By September, the Viet Cong were inflicting military defeats that devastated the morale of the Diem regime, which asked for a defense treaty with the United States. Kennedy sent General Taylor and Rostow on a fact-finding mission to Vietnam. They reported that Saigon was suffering a crisis of confidence. The Laos experience had made the South Vietnamese worry that the United States would not stand by them. Viet Cong successes suggested that Diem's corrupt, unpopular, and inefficient government could not repel the enemy in any case.

Taylor and Rostow recommended that the President approve a U.S. military commitment to Vietnam and a generous infusion of Americans at all levels of the Saigon government to reform it "from the bottom up." Taylor proposed sending a task force, mainly of Army engineers, to the Mekong Delta, where there had been a major flood and where the Viet Cong guerrillas were strongest. He warned that the force would have to run some combat operations and expect to take casualties.

McNamara and the Joint Chiefs doubted that eight thousand men would show the Communists "we mean business." They would consent to Taylor's proposal only if the United States pledged to defend South Vietnam "by the necessary military action," requiring as many as 205,000 ground troops if North Vietnam and China should openly intervene.

Kennedy worried that sending combat troops might upset the Laos cease-fire and risk escalation in Vietnam. He told Schlesinger, "It will be just like Berlin. The troops will march in, the bands will play, the crowds will cheer, and in four days everyone will have forgotten. Then we will be told we have to send in more troops. It's like taking a drink. The effect wears off, and you have to take another."

Rusk and McNamara warned the President in a joint memo that a Communist victory in Vietnam would probably move the rest of Southeast Asia "to complete accommodation with communism, if not formal incorporation in the Communist bloc." Losing South Vietnam "would not only destroy SEATO but would undermine the credibility of American commitments everywhere." Coming at the same time as the Berlin Crisis, such a defeat would "stimulate bitter domestic controversies in the United States and would be seized upon by extreme elements to divide the country and harass the Administration."

Kennedy approved their recommendation to send U.S. military advisers to the South. Lemnitzer reminded McNamara that the Joint Chiefs saw the war as "a planned phase in the Communist timetable for world domination"; if the new program failed, he and his colleagues saw "no alternative" to sending in American combat troops.

Lunching with his father's old friend, the *New York Times* columnist Arthur Krock, in mid-October, Kennedy said he believed American troops should not be involved on the Asian mainland, especially in a country whose people cared neither about the Cold War nor about issues like freedom and self-determination. The United States couldn't interfere in civil disturbances created by guerrillas, and it was "hard to prove" that this wasn't largely the situation in Vietnam.

He doubted the continuing validity of the "domino theory," which held that one country's fall to communism would condemn the others in the region. "The Chinese Communists are bound to get nuclear weapons in time. And from that moment on, they will dominate Southeast Asia." It was "a hell of a note" to handle Berlin at the same time the Communists were "encouraging foreign aggressors all over the place." He said he was thinking of urging Khrushchev by letter to call off these aggressors in Vietnam, Laos, and elsewhere.

Now he wrote the Chairman that South Vietnam was suffering "a determined attempt from without to overthrow the existing government, using for this purpose infiltration, supply of arms, propaganda, terrorization, and all the customary instrumentalities of Communist activities in such circumstances, all mounted and developed from North Vietnam."* This was "completely at variance" with the 1954 Geneva accords.

Kennedy asked Khrushchev to persuade North Vietnam to observe the accords. "This would be a great act in the cause of peace which you refer to as the essence of the policies of the Twenty-second Party Congress." He asked him "to insure that those closely associated with you leave South Vietnam alone." In return, the United States would

---

*On December 15, Kennedy replied to a letter from President Diem: "Our indignation has mounted as the deliberate savagery of the Communist program of assassination, kidnapping, and wanton violence became clear. Your letter underlines what our own information has convincingly shown—that the campaign of force and terror now being waged against your people and your Government is supported and directed from the outside by the authorities at Hanoi."

"insure that North Vietnam will not be the object of any direct or indirect aggression. . . . I am leaving for a few days for a visit to the western part of our country and will be in touch with you on other matters when I return."

One reason for Kennedy's western speaking tour was to prepare American opinion for the negotiations on Berlin that he expected to begin soon. Polls showed voters in the region to be more resistant to talks with Moscow than any other Americans outside the South.

In a speech at the University of Washington in Seattle, Kennedy reminded his audience, "We must work with certain countries lacking in freedom in order to strengthen the cause of freedom. . . . We must face problems which do not lend themselves to easy or quick or permanent solutions. . . . As long as we know what comprises our vital interests and our long-range goals, we have nothing to fear from negotiations. . . .

"With respect to any future talks on Germany and Berlin, for example, we cannot, on the one hand, confine our proposals to a list of concessions we are willing to make. Nor can we, on the other hand, advance any proposals which compromise the security of free Germans and West Berliners, or endanger their ties with the West. . . . It is a test of our national maturity to accept the fact that negotiations are not a contest spelling victory or defeat."

As another precaution before talks with the Russians on Berlin, Kennedy invited Konrad Adenauer to Washington. Restored to power by a Christian Democratic victory in September, the Chancellor and his Ambassador in Washington, Wilhelm Grewe, had been much alarmed by the prospect of Gromyko and Thompson discussing Berlin.

Robert Amory of the CIA refined an oral briefing, which the Agency rehearsed before the President, to calm Adenauer's fears about the Soviet Union and encourage a larger West German contribution to NATO. Using McNamara's new systems analysis techniques, the presentation argued that Soviet divisions were only about one third the size of NATO's and were hence probably only one third as effective. As Amory recalled, it showed "that the Russian armies on the ground in Germany and their potential reinforcements were not invincible in a conventional war."

Lemnitzer privately complained to General Lauris Norstad at SHAPE that the briefing was "overoptimistic and in many cases overdrawn." He had had a "considerable argument" with the President about the fact that it included classified information going "far beyond" anything Adenauer had ever been shown. The briefing did not persuade Franz-Josef Strauss. He thought it was "influenced more by wishful thinking than reality."

In an October letter to fifty-nine British Labour Members of Parliament, Khrushchev had suggested a Berlin settlement including guarantees of Western access to West Berlin, recognition of the Oder-Neisse Line, and UN admission for both Germanys. He had also demanded a ban on nuclear weapons for both the FRG and GDR and military disengagement from Central Europe.

During his White House talks, Adenauer acceded to Kennedy's insistence on discussing the status of Berlin with the Soviets, as long as Western rights were preserved. He obliged the President's request to increase Bonn's investment in NATO from eight to twelve divisions. In return, Kennedy pledged not to bargain with Khrushchev over recognition of the GDR, the Oder-Neisse Line, or neutralization of Central Europe. But he rejected Adenauer's demand to have a share in NATO decision-making at the moment a European war reached the point of possible nuclear exchange.

During their meeting the night before the President's September UN speech, Salinger had complained to Kharmalov that all Khrushchev had to do to command a huge American audience was to invite Lippmann or Pearson or Sulzberger to see him. Why couldn't the Soviets reciprocate?

Kharmalov said it was "a very bad time to ask"; the State Department had just denied visas to fifteen Soviet correspondents. When Salinger corrected the problem, Adzhubei was scheduled to interview Kennedy for *Izvestia* on Thanksgiving weekend at Hyannis Port. As Adzhubei later recalled, his father-in-law asked him to try to improve relations with the President.

Before Adzhubei went to Hyannis Port, Salinger invited him and Bolshakov for dinner at his Virginia home. Imbibing Armenian brandy, which he had brought from Khrushchev, Adzhubei complained that his father-in-law had not given him and his wife a present in fifteen years of marriage. When Adzhubei was rushed from a hunting trip with the Chairman into the hospital with appendicitis, Khrushchev had merely said he hoped he would be all right: "That was the only personal interest he has ever shown in me."

Salinger refused Adzhubei's offer of an advance look at his questions. The Russian told him, "Well, don't blame me if it doesn't go your way." Dining in a Hyannis restaurant the night before his interview with Kennedy, he looked out of the corner of his eye at someone sitting at another table. Finally he spun in his chair and cried, "You agent!"

Before Kennedy's Oval Office meeting with Adzhubei in June, the CIA had told him that Adzhubei combined "native ability and marriage to Khrushchev's daughter to climb to the top of the Soviet journalistic profession and to gain . . . an unofficial position of influence in governmental affairs. Adzhubei doubles as a speech writer for his father-in-law, and during the past two or three years he has become one of the Premier's closest advisers, particularly in matters relating to the United States."

He was "ruthless" and "supremely confident of his own position and of the superiority of the Soviet Union." During his father-in-law's American trip in 1959, several Americans had insisted he was "the most completely arrogant man they had ever met." His attitude toward the United States was a "mixture of contempt, admiration tinged with envy, and the devout Communist's conviction that the capitalist world is doomed." While drinking heavily, Adzhubei had once argued with an American, saying, "We are so strong that we can crush you like this." He broke the neck of a wine bottle.

Thompson reported that according to a Soviet Jew who had been a diplomat under Litvinov, Foreign Ministry officials were complaining that they had had "no voice in foreign policy" since Adzhubei's appointment as a foreign affairs adviser to his father-in-law: "Khrushchev hesitates to grant Adzhubei party or government status commensurate with his advisory responsibilities, if only because he would open himself to charges of nepotism."

Born in 1924 in Samarkand, Adzhubei grew up in Moscow before joining the wartime Soviet Army and studying journalism and literature at Moscow State University. There he was handed what the Chairman would have called a "lucky lottery ticket"*—acquaintance with Khrushchev's daughter Rada, whom he married.

He joined *Komsomolskaya Pravda,* the voice of the Young Communist League, and with no small aid from Khrushchev became editor-in-chief in 1957. After Stalin's death, Khrushchev had demanded that Soviet papers become more lively and original. After his first visit to

---

*This was how Khrushchev described his immensely helpful acquaintance with Stalin's second wife while in school during the 1930s.

the United States in 1955, Adzhubei made his paper more American-looking, with a more eye-catching format, human-interest stories, and letters to the editor.

Smarting from conservative opposition in 1957, Khrushchev made an about-face and declared that originality for its own sake had no place in Soviet journalism. An ordinance was issued against "sensationalism" in *Komsomolskaya Pravda*. The experience may have shown Adzhubei the danger of depending on merely one political patron. As he continued to cultivate his father-in-law, he made important and lasting connections with Alexander Shelepin, a Komsomol organizer who headed the KGB from 1958 to 1961 and went on to other powerful positions, as well as Shelepin's KGB successor, Vladimir Semichastny.

In May 1959, Adzhubei became editor-in-chief of *Izvestia*, long one of the dullest Soviet papers, a digest of bureaucratic decrees under Stalin. He gave it punchier headlines, colloquial language, more pictures and foreign news, a Sunday magazine with cartoons, and letters soliciting Miss Lonelyhearts advice and reporting local malfeasance. Circulation doubled.

Adzhubei had shown Khrushchev color slides of his 1955 trip to the United States. He had found the Americans "exuberant people, easily carried away by novelties. They behave like children who fall for various epidemics, now the hula hoop, now a new movie star." Their leaders were "weak, stupid men who betray the people."

He accompanied Khrushchev to Washington in 1959, the UN in 1960, Vienna in 1961. It was said that when the Chairman learned that Adzhubei was involved with a woman not his wife, he merely told him to be more discreet.* Khrushchev basked in the young man's public devotion. At the Twenty-second Party Congress, Adzhubei boasted of his UN trip with the Chairman: "It may have shocked the ladylike diplomats of the Western world, but it was just great to see Comrade N. S. Khrushchev, when a Western diplomat was delivering one of those provocative speeches, take off his shoe and start pounding on the table with it."

---

*The CIA reported to Kennedy, perhaps using material transmitted by French Intelligence, that "the only close look at the Adzhubeis together was provided by their visit to Paris in November 1959." The couple had toured Les Invalides, the Louvre, and the Eiffel Tower, attended a midnight Mass at Notre Dame, sat in nightclubs in the Latin Quarter and Montmartre and the Lido, which Mrs. Adzhubei found "boring, not shocking," and saw a Brigitte Bardot film, which she also disliked. "She arrived in Paris in a mink coat and hat; she and her husband stayed at the Crillon in a suite which reportedly cost an unproletarian $40 a day."

Adzhubei was the incarnation of the Soviet New Class. The British journalist Edward Crankshaw called him "a most dubious mixture of the 'jet set' at its most lurid and the ambitious, intriguing politician: a protector of the very young and talented when it suited him, but also fathomlessly cynical. There must have been times when the young writers, the young painters, economists, and thinkers, would have been happier if Khrushchev had not had in his house a son-in-law who liked abstract painting and understood the problems of contemporary youth; they would have known better where they stood."

On Friday, November 24, the day before the President was to see Adzhubei, he called McNamara and White House aides to his father's Hyannis Port living room. Wearing a red jumpsuit, Robert Kennedy was outside playing touch football with his sisters and assorted children. The President called him in. Robert vaulted the porch rail, joined the group and gave what Carl Kaysen recalled as a "passionate speech" about "every citizen's duty" to build a fallout shelter: "The President metaphorically poured a bucket of cold water on him."

Then they all heard final arguments about the size of America's new ICBM force. McNamara considered the ability to destroy 20 to 50 percent of Soviet society sufficient to deter a Soviet attack on the United States. This would require roughly four hundred one-mega-ton bombs.* Kaysen and Wiesner agreed, but to help protect Kennedy against Congressmen who wished a mammoth buildup, they proposed a force of six hundred ICBMs. Everyone agreed that a thousand was a round number, and thus more salable to Congress.

Sorensen noted that a thousand missiles would spur the arms race. McNamara warned that the Administration would be "politically murdered" on the Hill if Kennedy proposed a smaller missile force. The President agreed that one thousand was "the best that we can live with."†

---

*McNamara's aide Alain Enthoven noted that an increase to 2,400, as SAC proposed, would add little to American destructive power and "only make the rubble bounce." The main reason for this was that almost half of the Soviet population was clustered in a small number of major cities. Before leaving office, Eisenhower had recommended nine hundred Minutemen but left the matter of funding for the new President. Told in April 1960 that some at the Pentagon wanted a production capacity of four hundred ICBMs per year, Eisenhower had replied, "Why don't we go completely crazy and plan on a force of ten thousand?"

†In January 1962, Bundy set down Kennedy's thoughts for a talk to the NSC staff: "To be honest with you, we would probably be safe with less." Congressional demand "for

* * *

On Saturday morning, Salinger brought Adzhubei and Bolshakov to the same cluster of houses where the President and his men had discussed the annihilation of the Soviet Union by ICBMs the day before. In the living room of Kennedy's cottage, Jacqueline introduced the two Russians to Caroline and John, for whom Adzhubei had brought a doll with a weighted bottom: "Like the Russian people—you can keep pushing it down, but it will always come up."

With sun shimmering into the room from over Nantucket Sound, Kennedy rocked in his chair and drank coffee. Adzhubei and Bolshakov sat on a facing sofa.

Adzhubei began by recalling Kennedy's "good intentions" at the beginning of the year to improve relations. The President agreed that relations now were "not as satisfactory as I had hoped when I first took office. . . . We want the people of the Soviet Union to live in peace." The "great threat to peace" was "this effort to push outward the Communist system, onto country after country."

Adzhubei complained that the United States was interfering in many areas of the world: "We would be happy if you, Mr. President, were to state that the interference in Cuba was a mistake." Kennedy said that the American dispute with Cuba was Castro's failure to hold free elections.

Adzhubei retorted that when the Bolsheviks came to power, "all the capitalist world was shouting that . . . there was no freedom in Russia, but in forty-four years our country became a great power." The President interjected, "You are a newspaperman and a politician." Adzhubei: "In our country, every citizen is a politician because we like our country very much."

Kennedy said, "The Soviet Union suffered more from World War Two than any other country. . . . The United States also suffered, though not so heavily as the Soviet Union, quite obviously. My brother was killed in Europe. My sister's husband was killed in Europe. The point is that that war is over now. We want to prevent another war arising out of Germany."

He said that neither he nor Khrushchev was responsible for the postwar arrangements on Berlin: "We have had peace, really, in Europe for fifteen years. . . . Nobody knows what is going to happen

---

more missiles and more nuclear weapons is pretty strong. I don't think such sentiment can be rationally defended, but there it is."

in the world over the long run, but at least we ought to be able to settle this matter of Berlin and Germany." Nothing would make Americans more satisfied than to see their two countries at peace, "enjoying a steadily increasing standard of living."

Adzhubei later recalled that after the interview, Kennedy took him down to the sea: "It was very cold. He'd given me a jacket, but we weren't very well dressed and shivered. I asked him, 'You're not cold here?' And he said something I'll always remember."

By Adzhubei's recollection, the President said, "When Stalin and Churchill and Roosevelt gained their victory, they were already very old men. . . . The world was very mixed up when they found it, and they didn't want to straighten it out. They couldn't. . . . But if there's a chance for us to do it now, we should do it. Otherwise in twenty years it'll be a world that we can't undo."

Kennedy had ordered the Secret Service's Protective Research unit to equip his living room with a secret taping system to protect himself in case Adzhubei misquoted him. Usually such an assignment would have been given to the Army Signal Corps, but he thought the Secret Service could do the job with fewer people knowing about it.

In time, Protective Research rigged the Cabinet Room, the White House library, the Oval Office, and his bedroom telephone for sound, the wires running to a Tandberg tape recorder in the basement. After each reel ran out it was slipped into a plain brown envelope, sealed, and brought upstairs to Evelyn Lincoln, who locked it in a special safe.

She and O'Donnell were evidently the only staff members who knew the full truth about the system.* One day, the President told Dave Powers, "I want you to be careful about your profanity because I don't want to hear your bad words coming back to me." Powers asked O'Donnell, "Kenny, what the hell is he talking about?"

When Kennedy asked for the system, he gave Secret Service men the impression that he wanted to "record understandings that may have been had" in American-Soviet relations. But he used the device on hundreds of conversations on all subjects.

Like his predecessor, who had installed a more rudimentary secret taping system and used it less, Kennedy may have wanted to use this confidential record to keep political antagonists from embarrassing him. After the Bay of Pigs, Pentagon and CIA officials had quietly told

---

*Years later, when it was revealed that President Richard Nixon had taped people without their knowledge, alumni of the Kennedy government said it was "inconceivable" that their boss would have done such a thing.

reporters that they had advised the President against the fiasco. Tape-recorded evidence could be used to make such people think twice before taking Kennedy's name in vain. It would allow him to correct the final record in his own favor when he and Sorensen wrote his presidential memoirs.*

Kennedy's use of electronic means to protect himself against potential foes extended to wiretapping. Taps were placed on the telephone of Robert Amory of the CIA, who was suspected of being too close to an undercover Eastern European agent before he quit in 1962. The military correspondents Hanson Baldwin of the *New York Times* and Lloyd Norman of *Newsweek* were evidently also surveilled.

One reason Kennedy may have spoken so freely to reporter friends was that he may have known what they were learning before their editors did. Bradlee years later was evidently convinced that his telephones were tapped: "My God, they wiretapped practically everybody else in this town."† According to Vernon Walters, later Deputy Director of the CIA under Nixon, those upon whom Kennedy eavesdropped included the Attorney General and Jacqueline.

After Adzhubei left the house, the President told Salinger, "Your arrogant Russian friend got in as many shots as I did." Bolshakov and Adzhubei lunched with Robert Kennedy, who found Khrushchev's son-in-law "a tough Communist" and disliked him. When American reporters asked what the President had said, Adzhubei called out, "Subscribe to *Izvestia!*"

Three days later, *Izvestia* ran the interview, the first time in history that five million Soviet readers had been exposed to an American President's extended views on the Cold War, including his complaints that the Soviets lacked "inclination toward serious talks."‡

---

*Robert Kennedy used the tapes in exactly this fashion to write his heroic memoir of the Missile Crisis, *Thirteen Days.*

†A technician Robert Kennedy had met during the Senate labor rackets hearings later claimed that the Attorney General asked him to bug the twenty or thirty telephones in the large room used by the White House press corps during a presidential visit to Newport. According to the man, Robert said he could not entrust the job to the FBI and gave him a "substantial" down payment. The technician said that when he told the Attorney General he was out on bail in a criminal case, Kennedy said, "Try to be as inconspicuous as possible, and if you get into trouble call me at this number and I'll take care of it."

‡One alteration was imposed on the text. At Hyannis Port, Adzhubei had mentioned that Khrushchev's 1959 American visit had not been "completely satisfactory." In *Izvestia*'s version, Adzhubei revised his own quote to spare the Chairman any hint of criticism: "The positive results of that trip were wrecked and brought to nothing by

In Washington, the President told his staff that the interview had been worthwhile, "if only to try to convince them that we're not all that bloodthirsty. But it was a propaganda stroke for Khrushchev too. Just by letting the interview run, he took the steam out of the argument that the Kremlin is afraid to let the Russian people hear the truth. . . . Maybe the biggest plus is that Khrushchev held still for it. Do you think he might be softening up a little?"

The next week, Kennedy drafted another private letter to Khrushchev: "As you know, I had an interview with your son-in-law . . . at my place in Hyannis Port, where I was spending the Thanksgiving weekend." He was "particularly glad to hear that you had successfully gone through the arduous proceedings of your Party Congress in Moscow and were in good health."

The Chairman had complained in his November 9 letter that an "aggressive" West Germany wished to upset postwar territorial arrangements by force. In fact, Kennedy wrote, West Germany was "the only nation of any size in the world whose armed forces are entirely under international control." It "only began rearming in 1955 at a time when it was fully apparent to the entire world that the regime in East Germany had been arming for some time."

It was the Soviets who had walked out of the four-power Berlin control commission in 1948. "Having incorporated East Berlin into the East German regime, the Soviet Union, in honesty, cannot object to any . . . status which the Western Powers desire to put in effect in West Berlin. . . . What is, however, a proper subject for negotiation would be the arrangements for the exercise of our access rights."

He warned, "I should tell you that we would not be prepared to agree to any renunciation of existing rights and their transference to the East German regime with authority to control, limit, or otherwise inhibit the existing rights of access between West Berlin and the rest of the world. . . . I fear informal correspondence of the type we are having is not . . . the proper basis to try and negotiate so complex and serious a problem. . . . I send you my best regards and hope that the next time we communicate, we shall have somewhat better news to discuss."

* * *

the well-known actions of the then American administration." Salinger later joked that he would have done the same thing had the combustible Khrushchev been his father-in-law.

On Saturday, December 9, in a speech to trade unionists, Khrushchev alluded to the private letter he had just received from Kennedy. He wanted "genuine" talks on Germany, but "some statesmen in the West would like to reduce the negotiations to the enhancement of the occupation regime in West Berlin."

For the first time in public, he showed his own determination to refute Gilpatric's assertions of American superiority. He warned the West, "Here is the might that will oppose your might—here it is: you do not have fifty- and one-hundred-megaton bombs, and we have them already and even more." These superbombs would hang over the heads of "imperialist aggressors" like the sword of Damocles.* The same Soviet missiles that put cosmonauts in orbit could strike any point on the globe.

He complained that the West had responded to Soviet proposals on Berlin with "war hysteria and an increase in the arms race. They began to increase their military potential . . . and to openly threaten us with war if the Soviet Union signed a German peace treaty. *But it is impossible to intimidate us!*"

At the end of the long year, Thompson told Khrushchev that his family was planning a Christmas skiing vacation: could he please keep things quiet for a while? The Chairman laughed. "You are the ones who are stirring things up."†

Kennedy flew to Bogotá, Caracas, and a Bermuda conference with Macmillan. He ended the long year in Palm Beach, where his father had been struck mute and crippled by a stroke six days before Christmas. Robert Kennedy later said that the President often spoke of "how he wished my father was well" when there were "matters that he would ordinarily talk to my father about."

Robert recalled that his brother had found 1961 "a very mean year" because of Berlin "and the fact that the Russians thought they could kick him around." When he asked his brother how he enjoyed being President, Kennedy replied that it would be the most "fantastic" job in the world "if it weren't for the Russians." When a reporter told him that he wished to write a book on his first year, the President shot back, "Who would want to read a book about disasters?"

* * *

---

*He may have lifted the reference to Damocles from Kennedy's UN speech.
†Thompson did not get his wish. The President asked him to stay in Moscow in case the Russians decided to start talks on Berlin.

Bundy argued many years later that during the four months after the Wall, the President displayed no "nuclear pushiness" toward Khrushchev that exploited the new American confidence in its nuclear superiority. In the October tank confrontation at Checkpoint Charlie, Kennedy's calm supervision and private diplomacy indeed relieved a conflict that could have quickly escalated. Throughout the autumn, he showed an impressive and growing willingness to persuade the allies and the American people that negotiations on Berlin were in their interest.

But his aversion to nuclear pushiness did not extend to his decision to authorize the Gilpatric speech. This was the final expression of Kennedy's determination to overturn his predecessor's method of dealing with the Soviet Union. Presented by Khrushchev with a similar Berlin ultimatum in 1958, Eisenhower had muffled his Berlin crisis by refusing to alarm the American people.

He had refused to increase conventional forces out of belief that no war in Europe would be limited to ground forces, because he did not wish to undercut the nuclear deterrent, and in order to hold down the trajectory of the arms race. He had refused to puncture Khrushchev's public claims of nuclear superiority and hence provoke the Chairman into a mammoth strategic buildup.

Kennedy lacked the Eisenhoverian instinct to muffle foreign policy crises. He did not enjoy Eisenhower's reputation for firmness and supreme competence on national security. Like Truman in the late 1940s, he knew that generating a sense of alarm would help him to push his defense requests through Congress and, when it came time to negotiate, insulate him against charges that he had not taken the Soviet threat with due seriousness.* And at some level of Kennedy's thinking there was always the conviction, as he wrote in *Profiles in Courage,* that "great crises make great men."

His commitment to flexible response had caused him to dismiss the Soviets' private pre-Inauguration warnings that if he pursued the conventional buildup he had promised in the campaign, the Soviet Union would not "sit still." He was far more unsettled than Eisenhower by the prospect of a rapid escalation of a European conflict to nuclear weapons and, unlike Eisenhower, did not feel that Khrushchev would assume that he was willing to use them.

He wished to strip Khrushchev of the benefits employed in courting the Third World of suggesting that the Soviet Union was the mightiest

---

*This view may have been influenced by the goodly representation of Truman administration alumni in the President's immediate circle, including Rusk, Gilpatric, Nitze, and Acheson.

nation in the world and was growing more so. He wished to convince the allies and the American people that if he negotiated with the Soviet Union, it would be out of strength. He wanted to ensure that Khrushchev was not emboldened into truculence over Berlin and elsewhere by the mistaken notion that Kennedy was still fooled into thinking that the Soviets enjoyed a missile gap over the United States.

These were good reasons for Kennedy to authorize Gilpatric to present the most detailed and provocative revelation of American strategic power ever made by a high American official. But, as later events demonstrated, they were not good enough.

The speech violated the President's own rule against backing an enemy into a dangerous corner.* Kennedy never gave sufficient thought to how Khrushchev might receive the speech. Khrushchev almost certainly wondered why the President had decided to publicly humiliate him by rubbing his nose in the fact of Soviet inferiority, and amid a crucial Party Congress. Did the address foreshadow an American first strike against the Soviet Union?

Khrushchev knew that his Kremlin and military critics would now demand that he relax his opposition to a huge Soviet military buildup. The forces set in motion by the Gilpatric speech and Kennedy's other efforts to demonstrate superiority compelled Khrushchev to look for a quick, cheap way to remake the nuclear balance of power so that he could genuinely claim that the Soviet Union was the superior force in the world. As Khrushchev might have put it, by authorizing the Gilpatric speech, the President of the United States was playing with fire.

Khrushchev's Berlin Crisis achieved few of the aims he had hoped for at the beginning of 1961. His threats and demands did not produce Western submission to the Soviet position on Berlin or provide the world with a melodrama of Western deference to Soviet power.

Instead, they provoked what the Chairman did not want: greater Western unity and resolution, the $6-billion American military buildup that shattered his own plans to hold down military spending, West German promises to endow NATO with more divisions, American revelation that his claims about Soviet nuclear power were a fraud. When Khrushchev suspended his six-month peace treaty deadline, just as in 1959, his critics in West and East crowed that once again he had been caught crying wolf.

---

*In a review of Liddell Hart's *Deterrent or Defense* in 1960, Kennedy praised the author's credo: "Never corner an opponent, and always assist him to save his face. Put yourself in his shoes—so as to see things through his eyes."

Bundy marveled at Khrushchev's rigidity as a negotiator. He recalled that in the White House at the height of the Berlin Crisis, there was greater interest in compromise "than Kennedy ever chose to show publicly." In late August 1961, Bundy privately suggested a shift substantially toward acceptance of the GDR, the Oder-Neisse Line, and a nonaggression pact. Years later he observed that if Kennedy had "heard proposals of this sort from Moscow, coupled with a prospect of reassurances on West Berlin, we would have had powerful reasons to press Bonn for concessions that did not come for another decade."

At no time did Khrushchev risk nuclear war over Berlin by seriously challenging the three American essentials. Before allowing the Wall to be built, he took the precaution of moving his two Soviet divisions into positions around Berlin to ensure that Ulbricht did not escalate the crisis beyond his control.

Two days before the border sealing, he used his normal combination of threats against Western Europe and reassurance to put the West off balance and also insist that there would be no war. In October, he withdrew his tanks from Checkpoint Charlie. Khrushchev knew that whatever the nuclear balance, a nuclear war would bring millions of deaths on both sides for which a German peace treaty was insufficient inducement.

Sergei Khrushchev recalled his father as "relaxed" throughout the crisis: "All military forces were possessed by you and by us. And since he didn't intend to take measures from our side which would call forth from you military measures, he therefore believed that the possibility of a military clash was minimal." Burlatsky years later described the Berlin Crisis as "one more step in the Cold War. . . . We pressed you, you pressed us, but it was not that dangerous. Only games—political games. That is all."

On Friday, December 29, Kennedy wired Khrushchev from Palm Beach that 1961 had been a "troubled" year: "It is my earnest hope that the coming year will strengthen the foundations of world peace and will bring an improvement in the relations between our countries, upon which so much depends."

The Chairman replied, "At the Vienna meeting, we agreed that history imposed a great responsibility on our peoples for the destiny of the world. The Soviet people regard the future optimistically. They hope that in the coming New Year, our countries will be able to find ways toward closer cooperation for the good of all humanity. As always, the Soviet Union will do everything in its power to ensure a durable and lasting peace on our planet."

For Khrushchev, ensuring a durable peace required doing something dramatic to improve the humiliating picture of Soviet inferiority painted for the world by Gilpatric two months before—especially if he wanted to keep his job and bargain with Kennedy on Berlin and other theaters of the Cold War as an equal power. As 1962 began, Fidel Castro was pleading with Khrushchev to do something to help him resist another American invasion of Cuba.

CHAPTER

14

"Your President Has Made a Very Bad Mistake"

A T THE KREMLIN NEW YEAR'S CELEBRATION, CHIMES SOUNDED AS Khrushchev stood and raised his glass at midnight: "The main achievement of the past year was that on most of the planet there was no war. . . . We shall do everything to prevent a new war in 1962."

Western diplomats felt that the Chairman looked "far from well" and that his entourage seemed "preoccupied, under serious tension." His text was uncommonly trite and devoid of his usual improvisations and jokes. He left at the earliest opportunity without speaking to a single foreigner.

The Kremlin announced that he was suffering from influenza, but rumors swept Moscow that Khrushchev was gravely ill or about to resign. These were not dispelled by his first major speech of the year at Minsk on Friday, January 12: "I am at the retirement age, and it is highly disagreeable when one finds oneself without an occupation. . . . This is the state of mind that is most painful to a man."

While the Chairman was in Minsk for a hunting trip, he was said to have been punched in the jaw at a party or stabbed in the shoulder by his chauffeur. The Italian Communist newspaper *L'Unità* reported a rumor that one of Khrushchev's bodyguards, while raising rifles in a triumphal arch, had lowered his gun and taken a shot as he walked through.* Another story had it that his hunting lodge had been set aflame. The Soviet Foreign Ministry took the rare step of denouncing the "lying rumors and nonsense."

At the White House, Chip Bohlen advised Kennedy that Khrushchev was not in serious trouble; otherwise he would never have taken the risk of leaving Moscow. The new CIA Director, John McCone, counseled the President that Khrushchev did not need to "fear for his position. But he does have to maneuver among colleagues who are less than equal to him but more than the terrorized lackeys who surrounded Stalin."

McCone and his analysts felt that odds were now "about even" that China and the Soviet Union would file for a complete and public divorce. Llewellyn Thompson warned from Moscow that "any indication that we were moving to exploit the quarrel" might force Khrushchev to heal it: "The less we discuss the situation in official statements, the better."

Georgi Bolshakov conceded to Ben Bradlee that the Soviet Union was having "serious difficulties" with China, Albania, and other radical Communist states. The problem for the West was simple: "You know you can live with Khrushchev, and you will never have it so good with Albanians." The way to help Khrushchev was to solve the problem in Berlin: "Give us the tools to strengthen our hand against the firebrands who charge our coexistence policy is a dismal failure, and we can live in peace forever."

Khrushchev had hoped that the October Party Congress would help to foil his enemies and enshrine his plans to shift resources to agriculture and consumer goods, achieving the blissful state of full communism by 1980. Instead Frol Kozlov, the Deputy Prime Minister whom he had once called his successor but who now attacked him from the Right, was given the number-two post in the Secretariat.

Despite his assaults on Stalin's personality cult, Khrushchev more than ever encouraged his own as a source of influence. A documentary called *Our Nikita Sergeyevich* was playing in Soviet movie houses. A

---

*The *L'Unità* story was thought to be inspired by Palmiro Togliatti, the Italian Communist leader known to be furious at Khrushchev's newest attacks on his hero Stalin.

highly fictionalized book was published on the Chairman's early years called *The Tale of an Honorary Miner*. The *New York Times* lampooned a new Soviet novel on Siberian farm problems whose protagonist was Khrushchev: "Sure Success for Novel—Khrushchev Is the Hero."

By January 1962, the harvest in Khrushchev's cherished Virgin Lands was confirmed to be the leanest in five years. Soviet citizens were demanding food, cars, and apartments, not fifty-megaton bombs. Critics cited the contrast between Khrushchev's rodomontade and reality. His three years of Berlin threats had not been followed by action.

Now that he was prosecuting his quarrel with China, the Soviet Union could no longer challenge the West with the combined force of more than a billion Communists. Tiny Albania had defied him. For all his rhetoric about expanding world communism, the only country to enter the Communist camp since Khrushchev took supreme power was Cuba—and not by Soviet premeditation.

During a brief Washington visit, Thompson privately told Senators that U.S. policy must not be "geared to whether Khrushchev is good or not good for us." Even if they wished to strengthen the Chairman against his rivals, "we don't know what action we could take. . . . Certainly as far as internal affairs go, Khrushchev is the best in sight because he is doing more to make the country more normal. . . . If we ever are going to work out a way of living with them, they have to become more normal than they were."

Thompson conceded that, in foreign affairs, Khrushchev had championed "some pretty dangerous policies, particularly over Berlin." But anyone who deposed him would take years to gather the authority to reach agreements with the United States. That leader "wouldn't be able to do the things which he could do and get away with."

Early in 1962, while researching a profile of Dean Rusk for *Life*, Theodore White interviewed the President and his staff. Kennedy warned his aides that White had better not hear "a discouraging word" about the Secretary.

Nevertheless, when he spoke to White off the record, he could not keep himself from complaining about Rusk: "He never gives me anything to chew on, never puts it on the line. You never know what he is thinking. . . . Take Acheson—a brilliant advocate, sarcastic but too bitter. I couldn't have worked with so bitter a man." Rusk was "calm, wise, thoughtful," an "excellent Secretary if you're not interested in foreign affairs—but I am." The problem with State was execution: "That's why Dick Goodwin is over there. They hate him, but he's needling them every minute."*

Worried that he had been too critical, he called White back for another conversation but still could not summon much praise: Rusk "knows more than anyone else in the White House or State about all these problems—the alliance of free peoples. But he's too busy to run the Department. It is understandable. McNamara can do things— moves divisions around the map—and Rusk can't do things on his job. His job is harder."

As early as the Bay of Pigs, Kennedy had privately complained, "How do you fire a Secretary of State who does nothing—good or bad?" He told Oleg Cassini a few months later that while Rusk was brilliant, "he always gives me twenty options and argues convincingly for *and* against each of them." In January 1962, while trying to dissuade Roger Hilsman from leaving State, he told Hilsman that Rusk was "certainly no Dean Acheson" and that he was "unhappy" with Rusk, but there wasn't much he could do about it except to keep on acting as his own Secretary of State.

Such presidential criticism got back to Rusk. This proud and sensitive man could not have helped but feel wounded that his ostentatious loyalty to the President was not reciprocated. Stoical as always, he said nary a word of complaint to anyone, but it surely must have crossed his mind that neither Truman nor Eisenhower would ever have dreamed of complaining about his Secretary of State to a reporter or, worse yet, one of the Secretary's own subordinates.

Kennedy benefited from Rusk's discretion and self-effacement, his excellent relations with Congress, and his willingness to announce bad news from Foggy Bottom.† But Rusk lacked the eagerness to use the telephone, the verbal shorthand, the informality, originality, impatience, flexibility, aggressiveness, acerbic humor, social ease, physi-

---

*In November 1961, the President had moved Goodwin from the White House to State as Deputy Assistant Secretary for Inter-American Affairs.

†Although it was later widely believed that Rusk was the only Cabinet member whom Kennedy did not call by his first name, this was true only for the first eight months of the Administration. That the President came to call Rusk "Dean" is confirmed by a transcript of a 1963 telephone conversation between them. Years later, in a letter to Bohlen, Rusk noted that early in the Administration, Mrs. Kennedy had told him over dinner, "You know, it is very significant that you are the only member of the Cabinet whom my husband calls Mr. Secretary." He wrote that it was "clear from the context that she considered it a compliment. . . . The last thing in the world I can imagine is that I would have said to him, 'Jack, why don't you call me Dean?'"

cal grace, and near-absolute loyalty that attracted the President to other key figures he had scarcely known, such as Bundy and McNamara.*

Robert Kennedy complained in a 1965 oral history interview that Rusk "would never follow anything up. He'd never initiate ideas. . . . I would think sixty percent of new concepts or plans about matters came from the President—maybe eighty percent came from the President and the White House, of which probably sixty of the eighty percent came from the President himself. . . . When we had letters from Khrushchev, he would either have to rewrite them himself or have someone in the White House rewrite them."

Unlike the Attorney General and McNamara, who brought in battalions of New Frontiersmen to bend their departments to the President's purposes, Rusk took seriously his role not only as Kennedy's action officer at State but as champion of the permanent State Department, especially the Foreign Service, assuring that its needs won a fair hearing at the White House.

During the early Eisenhower years, Rusk saw what could happen when a Secretary refused to defend the Foreign Service from political tampering: Foster Dulles had thrown one diplomat after another to the wolves rather than stand up to Joseph McCarthy. As Secretary, Rusk tried to rehabilitate one such victim, the China hand John Paton Davies, but Robert Kennedy refused to intervene in the case. He was evidently worried about political embarrassment to the President.

Such behavior opened Rusk to charges of disloyalty and obstructionism, especially from the Attorney General. Years later he recalled, "Robert Kennedy wanted people in the government who were Kennedy men. . . . In some cases I had a little tussle with Bobby Kennedy about getting some names approved. . . . Sometimes he would go for blood. . . . McNamara and Bobby got to be good personal friends, but that never developed between Bobby and me."

Rusk once complained to the President about the Attorney General's demand to have the State Department ask American corporations abroad to stage demonstrations in support of American foreign policy. Kennedy told him, "Let Bobby have his say in some of these matters because he is very interested in them. But if he ever gets in your way, I want you to speak to me about it."

For Robert Kennedy and, much more tacitly, his brother, Rusk

---

*When he spoke late in life to historians and journalists about his career, Rusk often used language that varied little from interview to interview. One such refrain: "My relationship with President Kennedy was very close, but . . . I didn't play touch football in Hyannis Port. I didn't go yachting at Palm Beach."

became a conspicuous symbol of State Department resistance to presidential aims. Notes taken by Arthur Schlesinger for his memoir *A Thousand Days* provide the essential view of Rusk taken by the Attorney General and his allies:

> He lived under a constant fear of inadequacy and threat of humiliation. . . . His colorlessness of mind seemed almost convulsive, the evenness of tone and temper purchased at inner cost. . . . One wondered whether the reality of the world, harsh revolutionary aspirations, underdeveloped countries, could ever penetrate the screen of clichés through which foreign affairs found their form for him.
>
> As he talked on in his even Georgia/Rockefeller Foundation voice, the world seemed to lose reality, everything became some bureaucratic fantasy, a film of the thirties seen on the Late Show. . . . Public stance stopping just short of self-righteousness; he knew that he spoke for the Establishment but, unlike John Foster Dulles, was not sure that he spoke for God too. He had a Foundation mind—his eyes sparkled when he thought of hospitals and universities and laboratories spreading benignly around the world.
>
> On Soviet Union had a matter-of-fact rigidity of a professional sort rather than missionary conviction of evil. PATIENT—endured with fortitude White House relationship—knew he did not fit into swift, irreverent, gay mood, considered it all frivolous and flippant. Yet State did not own foreign policy.*

The President covertly egged on Rusk's critics but stopped short of firing him. When he asked O'Donnell if they shouldn't find someone "with a little more pep," the aide replied, "Do you want somebody like Dean Acheson over there? Somebody who would be fighting everything you want to do and antagonizing the Congressmen . . . and talking to the newspapers?" Kennedy said, "Thanks for reminding me."

Kennedy told a friend that Rusk was "a tremendous operations man. He fits in exactly where I want him." To Justice Douglas he described him more bluntly as "a good errand boy." He kept the pressure on State by sending over operatives like Goodwin, encouraging Kennedy men to make alliances with like-minded diplomats

---

*Reading his son's treatment of Rusk in the manuscript, Arthur Schlesinger, Sr., scrawled, "Pretty rough on a nice guy!" The junior Schlesinger's enmity was fully reciprocated by Rusk, who privately grumbled that Schlesinger was too academic, inexperienced, and "talky," too eager to deal with the Chinese and Russians, "over in the East Wing with the social secretary." Rusk unfairly told an aide he had refused to discuss Berlin with the President while Schlesinger was present because "Schlesinger is the biggest gossip in town."

throughout the Department, and turning more and more to his brother, McNamara, special task forces, Bundy, and his staff for advice on major foreign issues.

Rusk worried about what he thought of as the casual attitude toward note-taking in the West Wing* and the President's wont to meet with foreign leaders without the presence of someone from State. He could not bear it when the President called mid-level officials in his department, "scaring the hell out of the desk officer and disrupting my system of organization."

Over highballs on an airplane, he inveighed against the intolerable "interference" by "people with no responsibility" on the White House staff. His relations with Bundy were civilized and cordial, but not all members of the NSC staff were as oblique and polished as their boss. Rusk once said, "It isn't worth being Secretary of State if you have a Carl Kaysen at the White House."† He told an assistant, "For God's sake, try to get the White House under control. They're all over this building, at every level."

Khrushchev knew that Thompson was planning to leave the Moscow Embassy in mid-1962. In January, Bolshakov and Smirnovsky told Ben Bradlee and his *Newsweek* colleague Edward Weintal over a private dinner at the Soviet Embassy that they were anxious for Thompson to be succeeded by "a prominent political New Frontier type, and a known friend of JFK, rather than a career ambassador." Leaving no doubt whom he meant, Bolshakov repeatedly expressed his "admiration and respect" for the Attorney General.

Bradlee later told the Attorney General that "bad food and good vodka" had been served "by pretty waitresses against the dreary background of the Ambassador's private dining room. It was a joshing, kidding affair with both hosts and guests in excellent humor." There was "an endless number of vodka toasts to *mir y druzhba* [peace and friendship], the New Frontier, Caroline, etc."

Bradlee reported that the Russians attached "great importance" to the appointment of Thompson's successor: "They seem to look to it as evidence of American intentions not so much toward the Soviet

*This problem was discovered by James Reston, who in 1962 complained in the *New York Times* that records were being "poorly kept": "The big decisions of this Administration are often taken in small private meetings, usually without the benefit of any chronological account of what happened."

†In November 1961, Kaysen had become Bundy's deputy, succeeding Walt Rostow, who went to State as Director of Policy Planning.

Union as toward Chairman Khrushchev personally. It was apparent our hosts thought a prominent U.S. Ambassador would be a boost to Mr. K's prestige."

That same month, in the Hay-Adams Hotel bar, Bolshakov told Salinger that the Chairman had agreed to Salinger's proposal for a series of American-Soviet television exchanges with President Kennedy. The Soviets would be "most receptive" if Robert Kennedy would stop in Moscow as part of the world tour he was about to begin. The Adzhubeis were in Havana and would soon be "passing through Washington."

Salinger saw the President in the Oval Office at midnight, after a dinner for Igor Stravinsky. Kennedy decided to invite the Adzhubeis for lunch but vetoed a Moscow trip by his brother: "The press would blow it up into something it wasn't, and it would certainly ruffle a lot of feathers over in State."

Someone leaked the invitation to the *New York Times*. Salinger thought that Bolshakov might have done it himself as a means of pressuring Robert into accepting. When he told Bolshakov that the Attorney General's "tight scheduling" precluded a visit, the Russian told reporters that it was "a direct affront to the Soviet Union." This extreme language suggested to the Kennedys that Khrushchev had been placing great stock in a visit by the President's brother. Robert wrote the Chairman a mollifying letter and received a twelve-page reply.

On Tuesday, January 30, Bolshakov arrived at the White House with Adzhubei and his blond wife, Rada, who wore a sable coat. Over luncheon the *Izvestia* editor discounted the rumors about his father-in-law's political problems: Khrushchev had told him that if there had been a plebiscite in 1957, the result would have been 95 percent for Molotov and 5 percent for him. Now it would be just the reverse. Jacqueline brought out Pushinka, the dog sent her by Khrushchev, and had coffee served in the cups that Khrushchev had given her in Vienna.

Kennedy took Bolshakov and Adzhubei into the Oval Room and warned them once again about misjudging American resolution over Berlin. During an exchange on Cuba, Adzhubei asked whether the United States would invade, and the President said, "No." At a press conference, Kennedy introduced Adzhubei to reporters as a man who combined the "two hazardous professions of politics and journalism."

Adzhubei recalled years later that during his White House visit, "little Caroline ran toward us. She'd woken up . . . and she was crying.

Jacqueline took her in her arms, took her to her bedroom, and put her to bed." In the child's room was a Russian doll and a crucifix. By Adzhubei's account, the President told him, "Your father-in-law said that our children should live under communism. But I prefer to put these two objects in front of her bed for her to choose—a present from Khrushchev and a present from the Pope. Let her decide."

Fidel Castro later recalled that the Soviets gave him a copy of Adzhubei's report on his talk with Kennedy. By Castro's recollection, the President had insisted that increased Soviet influence in Cuba would be "intolerable" and that Adzhubei should remember that when the Russians invaded Hungary, the United States had not intervened.

Castro assumed that Kennedy was asking the Russians not to intervene in the event of a full-scale action against Cuba. By his account, he used Adzhubei's report to persuade Soviet leaders that, despite Kennedy's insistence to the contrary, the United States was planning another invasion and that resisting the attack would require some dramatic kind of Soviet support. Many years later, reviewing the origins of the Missile Crisis, Castro said, "It was the copy of the report that started everything."*

At Bermuda in December, Macmillan had asked Kennedy if they and Khrushchev could not get together and make a "great new effort" to break the cycle of the nuclear arms race. The President replied that Soviet behavior suggested that they did not want a test ban. Hadn't they been preparing their latest series of tests since February 1961?

---

*Perhaps at the time and certainly later, Castro confused the Adzhubei conversation with the Kennedy-Khrushchev exchange on Cuba at the Vienna summit. In the early 1980s, he told the journalist Tad Szulc, who was researching a Castro biography, that "from the terms in which Kennedy expressed himself" in Vienna, "it could be deduced that he considered he had the right to use the armed forces of the United States to destroy the Cuban revolution. He referred to different historical events . . . on that occasion made a reference to Hungary. Having received information about that conversation, we reached the conclusion, as did the Soviets, that the United States persisted in the idea of an invasion."

By Bundy's contemporaneous recollection of the talk with Adzhubei, the President did not say that the Cuban situation was "intolerable," only that it was most difficult for the United States. Kennedy had gone on to say that if Adzhubei wanted to know how important Cuba was to the United States, he should remember Hungary. Bundy said that this remark was intended only to show how vital the United States considered Cuba to be.

He said that the problem was what would happen in 1964 if the Russians kept on testing and the West didn't. He could not "afford to be taken twice." He was a "great anti-tester" but felt they should prepare for a test series and carry it out unless there was a serious breakthrough on Berlin or disarmament.

He was also worried about Western intelligence reports that the new Soviet tests had made progress toward an anti-missile missile. Following on earlier experiments in 1958, plans for a new American series included tests to find whether high-altitude nuclear blast, heat, and radioactivity were able to destroy incoming Soviet missiles, neutralize their warheads, or foil their guidance systems.

Kennedy agreed to make one last stab at disarmament. For his part, the Prime Minister agreed that if it failed he would approve Kennedy's request to carry out atmospheric nuclear tests on Christmas Island, a British possession one thousand miles south of Hawaii.*

In early January, he wrote Kennedy that if the capacity for human destruction ended up in the hands of "dictators, reactionaries, revolutionaries, madmen," then "certainly, I think by the end of this century, either by error or folly or insanity, the great crime will be committed. . . . On the whole it is not the things one did in one's life that one regrets but rather the opportunities missed."

As Bundy worked on a presidential reply, Foy Kohler asked, "Why are we taking so much trouble over this hysterical document? . . . We can't let Macmillan practice this emotional blackmail on us."

Kennedy and Macmillan jointly wrote Khrushchev: "The three of us must accept a common measure of personal obligation to seek every avenue to restrain and reverse the mounting arms race." At the eighteen-nation Geneva disarmament talks scheduled to open in March, their foreign ministers should "ascertain the widest measure of disarmament" possible at the "earliest possible time."

The Chairman replied by asking why they should limit themselves to foreign ministers. Heads of government had the final authority. The leaders of all eighteen countries should go to Geneva: "Perhaps this idea will appear somewhat unusual but, you will agree, it is fully justified by the greatness of the goal." Kennedy responded that it would be more effective to start with foreign ministers; if and when there was progress, he would be "quite ready" to see the Chairman in Geneva.

---

*Kennedy did not wish to use the Nevada test site, adamant that the "political cost of another mushroom cloud visible in the United States" would be too high.

In a twenty-page reply, Khrushchev wrote that he was "chagrined" by the President's attitude: "The guiding precept of my life is to be where the main work is being done. . . . How long can one continue to engage in eliciting, studying, and clarifying each other's positions with negotiations, meetings, and contacts at various levels, endless arguments, and disputes?"

He charged that America and Britain were only trying to "sweeten the bitter pill" of resuming nuclear testing by making a "gesture" toward disarmament: "The life of the great American writer Hemingway was ended by an accidental shot while a shotgun was being cleaned. . . . An accident in handling rocket and nuclear weapons would cause the death of millions upon millions of people. Many more would be condemned to slow death by radioactive contamination."

Kennedy wrote Khrushchev that Rusk could present his views with complete authority; he hoped that progress at Geneva would lead to a summit before June. He asked the Attorney General to tell Bolshakov that since they were deadlocked on Berlin, he thought it necessary to try to find the area in which the earliest American-Soviet agreement was possible—disarmament and a nuclear test ban.

In a television address on Friday, March 2, the President announced that unless the Soviets agreed to a test ban treaty, the United States would resume nuclear testing in April. He told Bradlee, "There was always a chance that if we could make a deal on Berlin, or if the Soviet tests had been unimpressive, we could have called it off." Asked whether everyone in the administration was happy with the decision, he said, "I suppose if you grabbed Adlai by the nuts, he might object."

Three days later, a nervous Bolshakov summoned Salinger to the Hay-Adams bar and told him that Moscow was calling off the Kennedy-Khrushchev television exchange. Salinger was furious. He knew that the President was already hard at work on his first script.* Bolshakov said, "The fault is your own President's for deciding to resume the nuclear tests. The Soviet people would not understand if their Premier would consent to a joint appearance with him at a time like this."

Salinger had been planning to visit Adzhubei in Moscow in late spring. Bolshakov told him, "None of this affects your visit to the Soviet Union." Salinger slammed his fist on the table. "It sure as hell does affect my visit. What's the use of trying to open up lines of

---

*The President had told Sorensen to use a few Russian words, invoke Franklin Roosevelt's magic name, and ask the Soviets to reverse the course Stalin had started.

communication if your people are going to behave this stupidly?"

Kennedy first ordered Salinger to call Bolshakov and cancel his trip: "You might add that this is just another example of why it's so difficult for us to come to any agreement at all with the Russians." Then Bohlen advised a milder reaction: suggest to Bolshakov that they announce the suspension of the television exchange as a joint decision.

The President consented: "But tell him also that we are greatly displeased. Point out the criticism we've had from our own press and the great lengths we went to in good faith to bring this agreement to fruition. And you might stress *good faith*."

Kennedy's announcement that he would resume nuclear testing reached Khrushchev on the eve of an important Central Committee meeting. The Chairman wrote him, "Your military are openly boasting that they can allegedly wipe the Soviet Union and all the countries of the Socialist camp from the face of the earth. On the other hand, you now say that the United States has to conduct nuclear weapon tests for the alleged purpose of not lagging behind the Soviet Union in armaments."

Several days later Bolshakov told Sorensen that his government had been obliged to say a few harsh words about the American resumption, but that they had been comparatively low-key: Chairman Khrushchev still liked the President. The television exchange would be held later.*

From the Central Committee, Khrushchev now suffered one of his most painful rebuffs since taking power. It barred him from shifting money from defense production to agriculture, forcing him to raise butter and meat prices by 25 and 30 percent. Soviet citizens nostalgically remembered the last years of Stalin, when many retail prices had been annually reduced. Western intelligence heard that, across the Soviet Union, Khrushchev was being reviled in demonstrations and riots.

Since January, during repeated meetings on the seventh floor of the Foreign Ministry, Gromyko had told Thompson that the Soviet Union would not yield an inch on Berlin. Once again he vetoed internationalization of the Autobahn and demanded the placement of Soviet troops in the Western sector.

---

*It never was.

Privately Rusk hoped that both sides would talk on and on, tacitly agreeing to leave the city as it was. Berlin itself had been relatively calm, except for harassments of planes flying to and from the Western sector. The Soviets buzzed Western commercial traffic and dropped large masses of metal foil to defeat Western radar, but after the United States quietly complained, the interference stopped.

Frustrated by the failure of Thompson and Gromyko to make progress on Berlin, the President took up the matter in an early March letter to Khrushchev. He complained of the aerial harassments and reminded the Chairman that their "essential interests" did not collide over Berlin.

The Chairman replied, "Neither you, Mr. President, nor I know for how long the two German states that emerged on the ruins of the Reich will exist, if they ever unite. . . . Once upon a time, so the story goes, two goats met head to head on a narrow bridge across an abyss. They would not give way to each other and down they fell. They were stupid and stubborn animals."

He was prepared to discuss Kennedy's proposal for an international commission on access to West Berlin, but only "under the condition that the troops now stationed there by virtue of occupation are withdrawn from West Berlin. . . . All of this, of course, is connected with the transformation of West Berlin into a free, demilitarized city, and with the simultaneous achievement of an agreement on a final legalization and consolidation of the existing German borders and also on other questions which are well known to you."

The President was not willing to surrender the Western position in Berlin and recognize Soviet domination of Eastern Europe in exchange for Khrushchev's vague promise of an international commission on access to West Berlin. The talkathons in Moscow and Geneva ground on. Thompson privately told Senators that Soviet-American relations were "not so dangerous now as they were a year or two ago" but warned that Khrushchev and the Russians were "given to surprises, and they can make a sudden change at any time."

Two weeks after the first American orbital space flight by Colonel John Glenn in February, Kennedy wrote to Khrushchev suggesting a program of radio tracking stations on each other's territory, joint communications, weather and mapping satellites: Americans and Soviets might go on to explore the moon, Mars, and Venus together. The costs and risks were "so grave that we must in all good conscience try every possibility of sharing these tasks and costs and minimizing these risks."

The Chairman consented to medium-level talks on the subject, but the only result was an exchange of meterological data and a communications test using America's Echo 2 satellite. Cooperation would be easier, he said, when they agreed on disarmament.

During these weeks, Kennedy compartmentalized his myriad lives as much as ever. While touring Pakistan and India, Jacqueline was worried about the welfare of Sardar, the horse given her by Ayub Khan, President of Pakistan, during his 1961 Washington visit. Her husband cabled, DAVE, KENNY, TED, TAZ, MCHUGH, EVELYN, BOB, DEAN, AND MAC ARE DOING NOTHING BUT TAKING CARE OF SARDAR—DON'T WORRY. ALL LOVE, JACK.*

On Thursday, March 22, over lunch, J. Edgar Hoover told the President that the FBI knew of his relationship with Judith Campbell and hers with Sam Giancana. Within a few months, Hoover found that the relationship had ceased.

The day after his luncheon with Hoover, Kennedy flew to California, where he and McNamara toured the Lawrence Radiation Laboratory for nuclear research at Berkeley before flying to Vandenberg Air Force Base to watch a missile firing. They were greeted by the commander of the Strategic Air Command, General Thomas Power, who climbed into the back seat of the open car between President and Secretary.

Chatting as they drove, Power referred to the buildup of Minuteman ICBMs: "Mr. President, after we get the ten thousand Minutemen—" Kennedy interrupted: "Bob, we're not getting *ten thousand* Minutemen, are we?"

At the Lawfords' beach house in Santa Monica, Kennedy rode a Lawford child's toy car around the pool despite his sister's complaint that he would "wreck it": "Pat, how can you deny your President a little relaxation?" Over the Lawford mantel was a Senate campaign poster for Edward Kennedy, with the President's old slogan, "He Can Do More for Massachusetts." Kennedy crossed out the words and jovially scrawled, BULLSHIT. That same weekend the President went to Palm Springs, where he called on Eisenhower and, according to several witnesses, Marilyn Monroe.

---

*This referred to Powers, O'Donnell, Sorensen, the President's naval aide Tazewell Shepard, his air aide Godfrey McHugh, Evelyn Lincoln, McNamara, Rusk, and Bundy. During Mrs. Kennedy's trip, Nehru made a point of installing the First Lady and her sister in the apartment once inhabited by Lady Mountbatten, wife of the last British viceroy, who had apparently been his mistress.

* * *

Back in Washington, he accepted the credentials of Anatoly Dobrynin, the forty-two-year-old new Soviet Ambassador to the United States. Khrushchev wrote the President, "I recommend him to you, and I am confident that he will represent the Soviet Union in your country well."

The Chairman had finally recalled Menshikov in January and demoted him to what was then the non-job of Foreign Minister of the Russian Soviet Republic.* Thompson explained that this was a way to "give him some pay without too much to do." Menshikov spent the rest of his life writing elaborate accounts of how the United States was run by Wall Street conspiracies.

Dobrynin found New Frontier Washington different from the city of his first stint as Embassy Counselor from 1952 to 1955: "Suddenly all the diplomats talk like newspapermen and all the newspapermen talk like diplomats."

Son of a Moscow architect, he had been trained as a historian. He and his wife, Irina, had both spent World War II as aircraft engineers before he was reluctantly drafted into the Soviet diplomatic service. In the late 1950s, he was a UN Undersecretary-General before returning to the Foreign Ministry as chief of the U.S.A. section, in which post he accompanied Khrushchev to Vienna.

Thompson advised the President that Khrushchev had sent Dobrynin to Washington because he embodied the "new generation" in Russia and could thus relate to Kennedy. He told Senators, "Our relations with him have been about as good as with anybody we have over there. . . . He has lived here long enough that he does understand how we operate. You can at least get on the same wavelength with him."

Bolshakov soon raved that Dobrynin was "the best ambassador we ever had. He goes out and listens—not like some of our diplomats who sit behind closed embassy doors and interview each other." This enthusiasm was not reciprocated. Dobrynin regarded Bolshakov as a symptom of what was wrong with the Menshikov regime and did not

---

*Before leaving, Menshikov wrote characteristically leaden farewell letters. To Adlai Stevenson: "I am carrying with me my most genuine feeling of high consideration for your impressive personality and I will remember with pleasure our meetings and conversations, which I always found very interesting." Perhaps feeling that Khrushchev might have let him remain had he not been so contentious in Washington, when Menshikov departed on the *Queen Elizabeth,* he said that Kennedy was "a very good President. As far as internal affairs are concerned, it is up to you to judge. He is very thoughtful and trying to do things to preserve peace."

wish to be circumvented as his predecessor was. Frank Holeman found that the new Ambassador "hated Bolshakov's guts."

Dobrynin told Salinger over lunch that he knew all about Bolshakov's service as middleman between Kennedy and Khrushchev: "All that will stop now. All further communications from the Chairman to the President will go directly through me."*

In Washington, Rusk and the new Soviet Ambassador resumed talks on Berlin. The President felt sanguine enough about the problem to allow General Clay to resign from his post and return home.

After discussing a test ban with Gromyko in Geneva, Rusk had reported to Kennedy that the Foreign Minister had left "no room for maneuver . . . by declaring that there should be zero inspections." He advised the President to "continue to prepare for a test series to start late in April, barring any diplomatic miracle."

On the night of Wednesday, April 25, the United States fired off its first atmospheric nuclear blast since 1958 over Christmas Island. Kennedy's restrictions kept the total yield of the six-month-long series, labeled Operation Dominic—forty tests in all—down to roughly twenty megatons, one tenth the yield of the Soviet detonations.†

Life reported that tourists lined up on Hawaiian beaches to watch: "The blue-black tropical night suddenly turned into a hot lime green. It was brighter than noon. The green changed into a lemon pink . . . and finally, terribly, blood red. It was as if someone had poured a bucket of blood on the sky."

Andrei Sakharov found that Soviet intelligence "spared no effort" trying to find out the purposes of the new Western tests: "Once we were shown photographs of some documents. . . . Mixed in with the photocopies was a single, terribly crumpled original. I innocently asked why, and was told that it had been concealed in panties."

---

*Khrushchev had written Kennedy of Dobrynin that "whenever you need to convey something to me in a confidential way, he will be able to transmit this to me personally."

†British scientists were worried that the antimissile tests especially would harm the Van Allen radiation belt by significantly adding to its electrons. Despite American reassurances, one test in the series proved them correct. Seaborg thought this "should have a sobering effect on any who believe that the earth's outer environment could emerge from a full nuclear exchange without severe damage." Rusk's memory of how the American scientists had erred in 1962 helped to inform his opposition in the 1980s to Ronald Reagan's efforts for a space-based anti-ICBM system: "Spreading the arms race into outer space is politically inflammatory, militarily futile, economically absurd, and aesthetically repulsive. Otherwise it is a great idea."

* * *

In February 1962, Robert McNamara had told the Senate Foreign Relations Committee in private that American nuclear forces "have a great and growing capacity to survive surprise attack." Half the 1,550 bombers of the Strategic Air Command were on fifteen-minute ground alert. The United States had already hardened some of its ICBM sites and was hardening many more. Its Polaris submarines required no warning "and can launch their missiles from a submerged position at a range of at least 1,200 miles."

The United States enjoyed "a clear military superiority for major nuclear conflict . . . even if the Soviet Union strikes first. Moreover, this superiority is growing and we are determined that it shall be maintained." After a full nuclear exchange, the nuclear power and social and economic fabric of the Soviet Union would be virtually destroyed. The United States and Western Europe would suffer "very serious damage to their human and material resources," but they would survive.

With Kennedy's blessing, McNamara gave this recital of American strategic power not only to impress the allies but also to gain support for the President's conventional buildup, foreclose charges that he was soft on defense, and show that if Kennedy negotiated with the Russians in 1962 over Berlin, a test ban, or other issues, he would do so from a position of massive nuclear strength. As with the Gilpatric speech in October, another principal audience was Khrushchev and the Russians. McNamara knew that much of what he had said would leak to Soviet intelligence.

By now, Kennedy and McNamara felt Khrushchev had been reasonably convinced that the President was willing to use nuclear weapons to defend West Berlin. Giving the Chairman hard, precise facts about what nuclear war would mean would prevent him from believing his own rhetoric about hundred-megaton bombs and Soviet strength. In this, they were not wrong; almost from the moment of Gilpatric's speech, Khrushchev had eased serious pressure on Berlin.

To keep from needlessly antagonizing Khrushchev and scaring the world, Kennedy had left most of the job of heralding American superiority to McNamara, Gilpatric, Nitze, and other subordinates. But during an interview one late afternoon in March with his friend Stewart Alsop, he threw aside this caution.

"As late as 1954, the balance in air power, in nuclear weapons, was all on our side. The change began about 1958 or 1959, with the

missiles. Now we have got to realize that *both* sides have these annihilating weapons. . . . Of course in some circumstances, we must be
prepared to use the nuclear weapon at the start, come what may—a
clear attack on Western Europe, for example. But what is important
is that if you use these weapons, you have to control their use."

In his *Saturday Evening Post* article, "Kennedy's Grand Strategy,"
published in late March, Alsop reported that the President had "quietly discarded" the doctrine "that the United States would never
strike first with the nuclear weapon. . . . Khrushchev must *not* be
certain that, where its vital interests are threatened, the United States
will never strike first. As Kennedy says, 'in some circumstances we
might have to take the initiative.' "

Chalmers Roberts of the *Washington Post* asked Bundy if the President had actually uttered the words "might have to take the initiative." Bundy did not deny it; they had somehow been overlooked
when the White House cleared the article before publication.

Kennedy, Bundy, and Salinger had all read the article before its
release. None of them expected that the quote might be taken to mean
that Kennedy was considering a bolt out of the blue against the Soviet
bloc. At an off-the-record session with newsmen at the State Department, the President tried to backpedal by saying, "I was not talking
about a preemptive act or aggression by us." But the damage had
been done.

The President's chief purpose in giving the interview had been to
gain support in Western Europe for flexible response. But the leader
most affected by Alsop's article was Khrushchev. He had never heard
an American President so baldly raise the specter of a first strike
against the Soviet Union.

Immediately after the article's publication, the Kremlin ordered a
special military alert. *Pravda* declared itself "astonished": Kennedy's
comment meant that the United States "believes it has the right to be
the first to inflict a nuclear blow, to be the instigator of an aggressive
war. . . . It is incomprehensible what upside-down logic prompted him
to make this rash and provocative statement about a possible preventive nuclear attack against the Soviet Union."

Combined with the Gilpatric speech and the other assertions of
American superiority, Kennedy's comment almost certainly made
Khrushchev wonder whether the Pentagon and the American Right
were pressuring the President for a first-strike attack against the Soviet Union. He knew that the President knew that the United States
would probably never enjoy such unchallenged nuclear predomi-

nance again: if it was ever to wage a preemptive strike against the Soviet Union, now was the time.

The Chairman almost surely thought that however unpredictable and vulnerable to political pressures Kennedy was, he was not so mad as to attempt a first strike. Nevertheless, by brandishing American strength so provocatively, the President had badly aggravated Khrushchev's political problems.

The Chairman had tried to offset and conceal Soviet nuclear inferiority through such devices as space spectaculars, scaring the world over Berlin, and testing fifty-megaton bombs.* Now that Kennedy and his men had stripped him of his political cover, whatever their reasons, Khrushchev had been shown once and for all that stopgap measures were not enough.

On Friday, May 11, Salinger arrived in Moscow. At the airport, Thompson told him, "Adzhubei insists on taking you from here to the government dacha outside the city. You will spend most of tomorrow there with Khrushchev." Unaware until now that he would see the Chairman, he insisted on first cabling the President, who told him to avoid substance and assure Khrushchev that he would transmit his views to Washington.†

The next day, perhaps to avoid the indignity of giving such attention to a lesser official, Khrushchev made it clear that Salinger's visit was in exchange for Kennedy's hospitality to the Adzhubeis: "I thank your President for having my daughter to the White House. No other American President has had the courage to do that." He took the guest for a chilly cruise up the Moscow River, skeet-shooting ("Don't feel badly—I've got generals who can't hit anything either"), and a five-mile expedition through the woods ("You have to walk for your lunch").

Pulling his Panama hat down over his cold ears, he named the bushes and trees along the way: "I don't know why I waste my time explaining all this to you. You don't know anything about agriculture. . . . That's all right. Stalin didn't either." When no carp surfaced in his pond, Khrushchev grumbled, "I guess they don't know the Chairman of the

---

*Georgi Arbatov of the U.S.A.-Canada Institute in Moscow even heard that the Soviet Union had "phony missile launch sites" and inflatable mockups of submarines to deceive American spy planes and satellites.

†Every day of Salinger's Soviet visit, a cable also had to be sent to Bonn to reassure Adenauer that the President's press secretary was not secretly negotiating Germany's future with Khrushchev.

Party is here." Then a fish appeared. "They got the word."

Khrushchev himself avoided substance, except for a reference to Adenauer as a "dangerous and senile old man" and to a recent Kennedy comment on the importance of Berlin talks as "very good." He told Salinger that he was staying at the dacha of "Gospodin Averell Harriman": "I like that man very much and I tried to hire him. I said that if he would come to the Kremlin and be my adviser, I would give him this dacha, but he refused."

After dessert, Dr. Jekyll abruptly turned to Mr. Hyde. Khrushchev glared at Salinger: "Your President has made a very bad mistake for which he will have to pay. . . . He has said that you will be the first to use the Bomb. . . . This warmonger Alsop—is he now your Secretary of State? Not even Eisenhower or Dulles would have made the statement your President made. He now forces us to reappraise our own position."

Salinger explained that American policy was to avoid using nuclear weapons first unless the West was the target of mass Communist aggression. Khrushchev said, "I have seen that statement, but I take the President's words literally in the article. This is clearly a new doctrine." Shaking his finger, he said that he would apply exactly the same policy to the defense of East Germany after a peace treaty. If Western troops crossed its borders, he would respond with an immediate nuclear attack. "And I am talking facts, my friend, not theory."

Then Khrushchev clapped his hands and smiled: "I am now going to tell you an official state secret." During the tank confrontation at the Berlin Wall the previous October, he had consulted Marshal Malinovsky. "West Berlin means nothing to us, so I told Malinovsky to back up our tanks a little bit and hide them behind buildings where the Americans couldn't see them. If we do this, I said to Malinovsky, the American tanks will also move back. . . . We pulled back. You pulled back. Now that's generalship! . . . I personally ordered the construction of the Wall. A state is a state and must control its own borders."

The sun was sinking fast. Khrushchev rose: "Come, Gospodin Salinger. It is time that we speak to each other privately." Sitting in an arbor overlooking the river with only Khrushchev's interpreter along, he repeated how disturbed he had been about Kennedy's statements on nuclear policy. Still, "your President has accomplished much and shown himself to be a big statesman.

"Please convey to the President that I want to be his friend. . . . Of course, Kennedy is no kith or kin of mine. He is a big capitalist and I, as a Communist, have a very definite attitude toward capitalists. . . . It is unwise to threaten us with war. . . . Adenauer himself says that not a single fool wants to fight over West Berlin." The United States needed West Berlin "like a dog needs five legs."

He did not know how their relations would develop. "The key is in the hands of President Kennedy, because he will have to fire the first shot. You see, it was he who said that a situation could arise in which the U.S.A. would be the first to deliver an atomic strike. . . . So what? We are ready to meet this strike. But I want to warn you: we will not be slow to deliver a retaliatory strike."

During his talks with Salinger, Khrushchev said almost nothing about Cuba. During the year since the Bay of Pigs, Castro had strengthened his dominion over the island. In December 1961, he had openly ordained "a Marxist-Leninist program" for Cuba, "adjusted to the precise objective conditions of our country."*

In April 1962, Bundy gave Kennedy the CIA's "latest estimate," which was "not encouraging." Castro's lavish use of political murder, his anti-Americanism, and Soviet arms shipments had helped him to win the support or acquiescence of a "substantial portion" of the Cuban people. Cubans who might have fought him from within were said to be "resigned" not only because of the terror but because they saw "no feasible alternative." Castro was quietly sending weapons and supplies to Communist revolutionary movements elsewhere in Latin America.

That same month, the dictator ordered a three-day first-anniversary celebration of the defeat of the United States at the Bay of Pigs. In Havana, after a performance of Copland's "A Lincoln Portrait," Castro warned in a two-and-a-half-hour speech that if any more American "mercenaries" planned to attack Cuba, "let them write their wills first. . . . The new aggressors will have to fight against a force better organized and trained . . . and the revolution is more invincible!"

As with Khrushchev, Castro's boasts were often in proportion to his anxieties. The Cuban farm economy was collapsing. Despite his cleanup operations in 1960 and 1961, roughly three thousand anti-Castro guerrillas had reappeared in the Escambray Mountains—ten times the number of Castro's men in the Sierra Maestra before the revolution. The new rebels had no unified leadership or communica-

---

*After this speech, Eisenhower wrote a friend that Castro had given the United States "a definite opportunity to intervene. . . . That statement of Castro's definitely linked him with the Kremlin; to my mind it was his acknowledgment that Khrushchev was his overlord. . . . It seemed to me rather strange that it caused no reaction from us."

tion, but Castro's brother and Defense Minister, Raul, thought they threatened a "second civil war."

Castro heard that conspiracies against him were being woven by Cuban Communists with ancient ties to Moscow whom he had kept out of his government and denounced as "an army of domesticated and coached revolutionaries." Encouraged by the Soviet Ambassador in Havana, Sergei Kudryatsev, reputed to be a Soviet intelligence agent who had once stolen British and American nuclear information, the old-line Communists had managed to oust Castro as chief of the agrarian reform movement and were daring to ridicule him in public.

All these problems were flea bites compared to the danger from North America. By the spring of 1962, Cuban intelligence had concluded that the Kennedy administration would use "all means possible" to remove Castro. Another invasion seemed imminent, this time with the full military force of the United States.

In the late spring of 1961, as the Taylor Board secretly resolved that there could be "no long-term living with Castro as a neighbor," Allen Dulles had privately told Senators that the "menace" must be removed "as soon as possible, because if it stays there year after year, I have grave questions as to what will happen in the Caribbean and more broadly in Latin America."

The President required no persuasion. Castro was a symbol of Khrushchev's claim that communism was on the march, a beachhead for Soviet influence in Latin America, a lingering sign of his own failure at the Bay of Pigs. Dean Rusk was surprised that "this man with ice water in his veins" was so "emotional" about Castro. McNamara recalled that they were all "hysterical."

Behind closed doors, Robert Kennedy demanded that the "terrors of the earth" be invoked against the Cuban dictator. One method was diplomacy. The United States persuaded other members of the Organization of American States, except Mexico, to expel Cuba, portraying Castro as the enemy of the Western Hemisphere. An economic embargo was imposed against Cuba.

The other method was covert action. At the White House in November 1961, the Attorney General said, "My idea is to stir things up on the island with espionage, sabotage, general disorder, in an operation run essentially by the Cubans themselves." The President ordered use of "our available assets to overthrow Castro."

Operation Mongoose was born under the statutory command of General Edward Lansdale, a counterinsurgency specialist with experience in Manila and Saigon, where he had helped Diem to consolidate control. Its overseers included Bundy, Taylor, McCone, Lemnitzer, Gilpatric, and U. Alexis Johnson of the State Department, but their de facto leader and back channel to the Oval Office was Robert Kennedy. The target date for Castro's overthrow was October 1962.

The contamination of Cuban sugar exports, counterfeiting of Cuban money and ration books, other sabotage, paramilitary raids, propaganda, espionage, and guerrilla warfare enjoyed a budget of fifty to one hundred million dollars and a massive nerve center on the campus of the University of Miami called JM/WAVE, said to be the largest CIA installation in the world outside Langley.

American case officers ran some three thousand Cuban agents out of false business fronts with fleets of airplanes, ships, and speedboats. Former owners of Cuban factories, sugar mills, refineries, and mines gave the CIA blueprints on how to wreck their confiscated installations.*

"Bobby was his brother's wire-brush man," recalled Helms. "And he was tough as nails on Cuba." When agents tried to sabotage the Matahambre copper mines, the Attorney General called junior CIA officers again and again. Had they landed? Had they reached the mines? Were they destroyed?

Helms felt that boom-and-bang and "nutty schemes born of the intensity of the pressure" were unlikely to trigger a Cuban counter-revolution. The CIA credited Castro with having built, after the Bay of Pigs, a farreaching internal police apparatus for surveillance and repression.

A March 1962 intelligence estimate said that "increasing antagonism toward the regime is likely to produce only a manageable increase in isolated acts of sabotage or open defiance on the part of a few desperate men." About the only good news, from Washington's point of view, was the decline of the Cuban economy, which might inspire Cubans to rise up against their leader.

This implied skepticism about causing a change of government in Havana by covert action may have spurred the CIA's continued efforts to murder Castro. In April 1962, the Mongoose chieftain William Harvey handed four poison pills to John Roselli in Miami. During the same month, American soldiers were known in Havana and Moscow to be training in the Caribbean for an island invasion.

Castro saw the OAS expulsion, the economic blockade, Mongoose,

---

*The pace and number of these operations allowed a writer with close links to the CIA to observe in 1986 that John Kennedy had initiated more covert activities by the Agency than any other President.

and the American military maneuvers not as the substitute for the assault by hundreds of thousands of American troops that Kennedy was unwilling to authorize, but as its prelude: "We informed the Soviet Union that we were concerned about a direct invasion of Cuba by the United States and that we were thinking about how to step up our country's ability to resist an attack."

As one of Khrushchev's diplomats recalled, the Chairman was still a "romantic" about Cuba: "He completely believed . . . that socialism should triumph in Cuba and the entire world." In November 1961, Castro's son Felix, a Cuban Young Pioneer, had visited Moscow. Khrushchev had gaily posed with him for pictures.

By the spring of 1962, Castro was not making himself easy to love. Especially at a time when Khrushchev was hard pressed to finance his own military while improving the lot of the Soviet consumer, his advisers found it difficult to square Castro's increasing appetite for Soviet military and economic aid with his erratic behavior and rhetoric, his rudeness to Ambassador Kudryatsev, his persecution of the old Cuban Communists, and other demonstrations of independence such as his flirtation with Peking, evidenced by the Chinese-Cuban trade treaty he signed in March.

Wary of making a quixotic commitment to defend Cuba with conventional forces, Khrushchev had rebuffed Castro's efforts to join the Warsaw Pact and even reduced Soviet military shipments for the first half of 1962.* In spite or because of the Chinese accord, the Chairman approved an April increase from $540 to $750 million in Soviet trade with Cuba, which was the euphemism for economic aid. He acceded to Castro's demand that he fire Kudryatsev and install a Soviet envoy with whom he could get along.

That spring it was in both Castro's and Khrushchev's interest to persuade each other that an American invasion of Cuba was imminent. Castro hoped this would overwhelm any Soviet reservations about helping his regime: how would it look if Khrushchev made no conspicuous effort to hold on to the one country that had peacefully opted for communism, the single Soviet ally in the Americas? The

---

*Thompson privately told Senators in April 1962 that the Russians "don't like the fact that Cuba has declared itself a Marxist country and wants to be considered a member of the club, because this involves them in implied responsibilities which they don't want to assume. It is too far away, and they know they couldn't fulfill them."

Soviets hoped that alarming Castro about the danger from North America might erode his reservations about Soviet encroachment on Cuban sovereignty and exploitation of the island for Soviet aims.

The distortion of intelligence by both Moscow and Havana for political purposes helped to lead both Khrushchev and Castro to a fatefully incorrect conclusion—that Kennedy was about to authorize a massive invasion of Cuba, possibly costing hundreds of thousands of lives.

In fact, the President had no more inclination than in April 1961 to initiate "another Hungary" that would besmirch the American image around the world, especially in Latin America. He remained worried that Khrushchev would retaliate for a full-scale invasion of Cuba with a similar move on Berlin. McNamara said years later, "I can state unequivocally that we had *absolutely no intention* of invading Cuba. . . . Obviously there were contingency plans . . . for a host of circumstances which the government had no intention then to carry out."*

There is no evidence that Kennedy or his advisers paid sufficient heed to the danger that Khrushchev and Castro might interpret the American military preparations and diplomatic, economic, and covert actions against Cuba as the forerunner of a full-scale invasion. In retrospect, McNamara conceded, "If I had been a Cuban leader at that time, I might well have concluded that there was a great risk of U.S. invasion. . . . If I had been a Soviet leader at the time, I might have come to the same conclusion."

Khrushchev's and Castro's hazardous misperception was fortified by what Bundy called the President's "public balancing act" on Cuba. The Russians and Cubans certainly noted that between the Bay of Pigs and the end of April 1962, Kennedy never uttered another flat public assurance that American armed forces would not intervene in Cuba like the one he had offered the week before the failed invasion.

On the contrary, in his first speech after the Bay of Pigs, the President had warned that if there should be "outside Communist penetration" of the Western Hemisphere, he would meet America's "primary obligations" to its own security. That same week, James Reston had written in the *New York Times* after a talk with Kennedy that there was a "limit" to the President's promise not to use American armed forces against Cuba: "Massive military aid from the Communist world to

---

*In response to McNamara's statement, made at an American-Soviet-Cuban conference on the Missile Crisis in January 1989, Gromyko replied, "Mr. McNamara, you state that there was no intention. OK, we accept it as information that there was no intention." Gromyko made it clear that even after twenty-seven years he did not believe that Kennedy intended no invasion.

Cuba in the coming weeks and months will not be tolerated."

Answering a question in March 1962 about what he might do if Castro threatened Guantanamo, the President said, "We're always concerned about the defense of American territory wherever it is and would take whatever proper steps were necessary." To an anxious Cuban or Soviet listener, this might have suggested that the United States might use defense of Guantanamo (which despite Kennedy's reference was not legally American territory, only leased) as a pretext for invasion.*

The President warned congressional leaders in private, "Let the United States make a move against Castro in Cuba and Khrushchev will heat up the Berlin Crisis, move into Laos, strike at Iran or into the Middle East." But why did he in public leave open the tantalizing and provocative possibility of a full-scale invasion?

He hoped that fear of such an action would deter Khrushchev and Castro from dangerous behavior toward the United States in the Western Hemisphere. And in the political year of 1962, he was nervous about the Cuban issue, which was growing hotter by the week.

His pollster Louis Harris warned him that "the vast bulk of public opinion favors doing everything possible short of armed intervention." A *San Francisco Chronicle* poll sent to Sorensen found that, on Cuba, the Kennedy administration received a 62 percent negative rating. The President did not wish to harm himself and other Democrats by publicly closing the door now on an invasion of Cuba.†

Thus Khrushchev and his colleagues considered it almost certain that the United States would launch a full-fledged invasion of Cuba, probably before the year was out. They presumed that this time Kennedy would brook no defeat—especially with his potential for conventional superiority in the Caribbean enhanced by the 1961 buildup over Berlin.

An American invasion that toppled Castro would be the first time John Foster Dulles's old pledge to roll back the Communist tide was fulfilled. This could damage the Soviet Union in its relations with

---

*Weighing against this was the President's private negative response when Adzhubei asked him in January 1962 whether the United States would invade Cuba. Adzhubei and his colleagues put greater stock in what they thought to be Kennedy's statement that increased Soviet influence in Cuba would be "intolerable" and his admonition that Adzhubei remember Hungary.

†This approach to Cuba as a political issue was similar to what friends claimed to be the President's attitude toward Vietnam and 1964: defer withdrawal of American forces until after he was safely reelected.

Eastern Europe, its struggle with China, and its efforts to attract the uncommitted nations. The "Who Lost Cuba?" faction in Washington would be replaced by one in Moscow. Khrushchev knew that he would be the chief defendant.

With the Gilpatric speech and other American statements, Kennedy had revealed Soviet nuclear inferiority to the world. Khrushchev himself had publicly rejected the notion that a few nuclear weapons were all a nation needed to deter aggression, that no rational leader would risk even a few retaliatory hydrogen blasts on his territory. His own philosophy was that the more nuclear missiles and bombs a nation had, the more military and political power it had.

Therefore by the Chairman's own standard, the Soviet Union was in great danger, especially in light of the hints that the United States might be planning a first-strike attack. Khrushchev had often said that the uncommitted nations would be attracted to the Soviet camp by Soviet power. But what would the Third World do once it fully discovered Soviet weakness?

Khrushchev's failure to drive the West from Berlin after four years of ostentatious trying threatened to turn him into a joke among the Soviet leadership and people. Now that Kennedy had demonstrated the power and perhaps the will to destroy the Soviet Union in the event of a Berlin attack, the Chairman foresaw only more frustration and embarrassment.

Khrushchev's frustrations on Cuba, nuclear strength, and Berlin were exploited and exacerbated by Kremlin rivals, who complained that he was betraying Leninist ideology and shortchanging Soviet defense, and the Chinese and Chinese allies, who charged that he had abandoned the dream of world communism and who were on the verge of developing nuclear weapons themselves.

Throughout his career, Khrushchev had taken calculated gambles against monumental odds. In 1956, he had given the Secret Speech against Stalin although he knew that 95 percent of the Twentieth Party Congress opposed such views, or so his aide Burlatsky said years later. The gamble succeeded: by unleashing the forces of anti-Stalinism and placing himself at their head, he tapped a vast wellspring of political power.

During the Anti-Party Coup, with the highest echelon of the Kremlin demanding his resignation, Khrushchev had forced the Central Committee to deal with the question and flown in enough supporters to prevail. Understanding world reaction to a first success in space far better than Eisenhower, he used Sputnik to create the illusion that the

Soviets had the power to dominate the world. In 1958, although he privately knew that his nuclear strength was vastly inferior, he issued his ultimatum on Berlin and succeeded in getting the West to bargain with the Soviet Union on the full range of world issues as an equal.

Each time, he had used his inventive brain to remake the circumstances of a seemingly hopeless situation. Khrushchev had almost unlimited faith in his own superior wiliness and nerve. These qualities had been honed in the mines, during his rise to power, while preserving his sanity and his life under Stalin, and as supreme Soviet leader.

Since 1956, he had kept one step ahead of the sheriff as he defeated bloodthirsty Kremlin rivals, repealed major tenets of Stalinism, held off consumer and military rebellions, devised farming remedies, and stripped Moscow bureaucrats of much of their power. During these years, although a foreign policy novice, he had convinced most of the world of Soviet military superiority without actually having to pay for it, brought the West into serious negotiation, and exploited Soviet space successes and local opportunities like Laos, the Congo, and Cuba to bolster his claims that Soviet power and prestige was eclipsing that of the imperialists and that the Soviet economy would surpass the United States by 1970.

Khrushchev had done all this despite the fact that more "educated" advisers might have warned him that he could not keep power as an anti-Stalinist, or that the West would never bargain seriously with a nation so weak as the Soviet Union. It was hardly irrational that he should have such faith in his power to break his political shackles by devising brilliant schemes.

In April 1962, with new dangers on his horizon, Khrushchev's natural reflex was to devise an even more brilliant scheme that would protect Castro, cheaply and quickly repair the Soviet missile gap, force serious new Western concessions on Berlin, dazzle the Chinese and domestic opponents, and perhaps reap other rewards, such as forcing the West to give up the military bases along the Soviet border that the Chairman had railed against for years.

That month Khrushchev walked with Malinovsky along the Black Sea. The Defense Minister noted that the Turkish bases on the other side "could in a short time destroy all our southern cities. . . . Why do the Americans have such a possibility? They have surrounded us with bases on all sides, and we have no possibility and right to do the same!"

Khrushchev had long badgered American visitors about the missile sites along the Soviet periphery. In 1958, he complained to Stevenson, "We see ourselves surrounded by military bases. . . . How can we take a different attitude toward you if we are encircled by your bases?"

Stevenson had replied that the bases were "defensive—not aggressive." But Khrushchev had insisted, "The Americans have bases in England, Turkey, Greece, and I don't know where they don't have them, and yet you want us to respect you. But how can we applaud this? What would the Americans think if the Russians set up bases in Mexico or some other place? How would you feel?"

When Harriman called at the Kremlin in June 1959, he was struck by Khrushchev's apparent feeling of "humiliation" by the "nuclear bases close to their borders." It was in August 1961, when Drew Pearson visited Pitsuada, that the Chairman waved his finger at the bases across the Black Sea and wondered whether they would "blow us up."

Late in April, Khrushchev and Mikoyan strolled in the garden near their dachas outside Moscow. "They had a curious relationship," recalled the Deputy Premier's son Sergo, who served as his confidential aide. "They were friends, but Khrushchev was envious of my father's background and education. Khrushchev did not think of himself as my father's superior."

By Sergo's account, Khrushchev told Mikoyan that the United States was about to repeat the Bay of Pigs, but that this time Kennedy would not make the same mistakes. Even if Kennedy did not wish to invade Cuba, he was "not in a strong position and would submit to CIA preference." Khrushchev "thought an invasion was inevitable, that it would be massive, and that it would use all American force."

Khrushchev's solution: send nuclear missiles to Cuba! Sergo recalled, "The idea was that their very existence would deter an American invasion. It would not be necessary to launch them. . . . The intention was to do it very speedily, in September and October, but not to reveal it before the American elections in November."

After the elections, Khrushchev would notify Kennedy by letter. He expected the President to tolerate the news, just as he himself had had to accept it when the Americans installed missiles in Turkey.

These assumptions revealed the depth of the Chairman's misunderstanding of Kennedy and the United States. He guessed that such a monumental operation could be concealed from American intelligence for eight weeks. He seriously expected that, if Kennedy discovered the missiles, he might conceal the distressing news from the American people until the November elections, after which he could afford to take a more benign attitude toward them.

These assumptions were not without grounds. The Chairman felt that Kennedy was more affected by domestic politics than Eisenhower. He knew that the President considered the 1962 elections an important chance to improve his position in Congress.

He knew the President was in the habit of concealing information from the public that might be politically embarrassing. Throughout the Bay of Pigs, he had obscured his fear about Soviet retaliation in Berlin. After Vienna, he had tried to conceal Khrushchev's Berlin ultimatum until the Kremlin would no longer stand for it. After the Berlin Wall, he had done a surprisingly effective job of diverting attention from the fact that the United States had given Khrushchev and Ulbricht something tantamount to a green light.

The Chairman knew that, in the past, Moscow and Washington had tacitly joined to conceal certain secrets for mutual benefit. Until May 1960, they had both obscured the fact that the United States was able to send U-2s over Soviet territory for almost four years. Until 1961, the Americans had not revealed the degree to which his boasts about nuclear strength were false.

Going on past history, Khrushchev might have suspected that if Kennedy discovered the missiles before November and wanted them out, he might use Bolshakov or some other secret channel to ask Moscow for their removal. He almost certainly did not guess that the President would risk nuclear war to get the missiles out of Cuba.*

Perhaps he thought that Kennedy would be paralyzed by the same fear of Soviet retaliation in Berlin that had impelled him to accept humiliation at the Bay of Pigs. If the President had not used his nuclear superiority to dictate terms on Berlin, where the United States had treaty commitments, why should he use it over Cuba? Perhaps he would once again be immobilized by his liberal advisers, as during the Bay of Pigs.

Despite Khrushchev's hints as early as July 1960 that Soviet nuclear missiles might one day defend Cuba, as of the spring of 1962,

---

*Khrushchev's expectation that Kennedy would not go to the brink over missiles in Cuba is suggested by the massive Soviet investment in the missile operation. As the political scientist Richard Ned Lebow has noted, the MRBMs and IRBMs sent to Cuba were costly fixed installations: had Khrushchev had any intention of trading them for Cold War concessions by the United States, he could have probably won the same results with a more limited MRBM force. Such a force, capable of striking the southeastern United States, would have been less vulnerable and easier to disguise.

Kennedy had yet to issue a single serious warning against them. Khru-shchev must have assumed that this omission was not by accident. In contrast, during the Berlin Crisis, Kennedy had carefully defined for the Soviet Union which vital interests the United States would and would not risk war to defend in the German city.

The Chairman might have allowed himself to think that the President might explain the missiles away as defensive, or even that Kennedy might be secretly pleased if Soviet missiles were placed in Cuba: perhaps by failing to warn against such missiles, Kennedy was encouraging him to install them as a way of cooling off the Cuban situation, just as he had signaled that he would not oppose the sealing off of West Berlin as a means of cooling the Berlin Crisis. This is doubtful but, in light of Khrushchev's ample misinformation about American politics, not impossible.

The Chairman's expectation that Kennedy would not seriously object to the missiles might have been buttressed by the President's comment at a news conference in March 1962 that it did not matter whether a missile was fired from close range or from five thousand miles away. In his frame of mind at the time, Khrushchev could have interpreted this to mean that Kennedy would no more complain about Soviet mid-range missiles stationed near the United States than he would about ICBMs stationed in the Soviet Union.

Khrushchev expected that by presenting the missiles in Cuba to the world as a justified effort to defend Cuba from American aggression, comparing them to American missiles in Turkey and Italy which the United States defined as defensive, he could win world approval for his move. He never anticipated how the secrecy and deception he used to install the missiles would affect their reception by world opinion.

From Khrushchev's point of view, as Burlatsky recalled, secrecy was a fact of life in Soviet politics. The Chairman did not realize how furious Kennedy would be at having been deceived by Soviet assurances against offensive weapons in Cuba.

This was partly the President's own fault. When Bolshakov's assurance that Khrushchev would be willing to discuss a test ban treaty at the Vienna summit proved to be false, Kennedy had not called him on it. After Khrushchev's insistence at Vienna that he would not be the first to resume nuclear testing proved a lie, the President had not complained. The Chairman may have presumed that Kennedy accepted such trickery as a staple of international politics.

Even had Khrushchev known how his secrecy and deception would infuriate Kennedy and undermine his case for the missiles in world opinion, he knew there was probably no other way. Not irrationally, he felt, as with the Berlin Wall, that the President would be politically more able to tolerate a fait accompli than a Soviet announcement that nuclear missiles were going to Cuba.

By Sergo's account, Mikoyan opposed Khrushchev's idea. He predicted that the Americans would never accept the missiles. Not only would the United States discover them before Kennedy received the Chairman's letter, but Castro would also object because he knew that the presence of missiles in Cuba might trigger an immediate American invasion.*

Sergo believed that "Khrushchev did not think through the U.S. reaction. He thought that after they were informed of the missiles, U.S.-Soviet relations would improve." Presumably this belief was based on the Chairman's thought that once the United States knew that nuclear missiles were in Cuba, the Americans would cease to act with what he found to be such arrogant superiority.

The Deputy Premier had the impression that in his missile gambit, Khrushchev was interested first in defending Cuba and only secondarily in correcting the balance of power. His son Sergo years later said that the Chairman was "worried about the possibility that somebody in the United States might think that a seventeen-to-one superiority would mean that a first strike was possible. . . . Our inferior position was impossible for us."

Sergei Khrushchev recalled that the nuclear imbalance "naturally tormented our leadership a great deal." His father also "felt the pinch of a great state around which were placed military bases where the aircraft of a possible adversary could reach any vital center of the Soviet Union."

Sergo Mikoyan believed that Khrushchev had "only two thoughts" in sending the missiles: "Defend Cuba and repair the imbalance. But defending Cuba was the first thought."

By emphasizing Cuban defense in his talks with the senior Mikoyan, Khrushchev may have been concealing his real thinking. He knew that Mikoyan loved Castro and his revolution and that the best way to win him over to a risky plan was to harp on protecting Cuba.

Khrushchev may have been so sensitive about Soviet nuclear inferiority and his culpability for it that he even avoided mentioning it in private. His hypocrisy and duplicity were not so great that he could easily go from a public speech boasting of Soviet strength (hundred-megaton bombs, rockets being turned out like sausages) into private

---

*Sergo years later said, "He was mistaken on this, as specialists always are."

talks in which he spoke the raw facts of Soviet nuclear weakness.

Soviet inferiority may have been one subject Khrushchev's men tacitly knew not to mention in his presence. Trained in the conspiratorial school of Stalin, Khrushchev was accustomed to pursuing certain political aims, such as changing the nuclear balance, which he might not have been willing to mention even to close colleagues like Mikoyan.

Khrushchev's determination to champion his system sometimes led him to use Orwellian reasoning even with intimates. He might have considered admitting Soviet military inferiority in private or public as unpatriotic and defeatist as conceding that his economy might not actually surpass America's by 1970 or that, in 1980, national defense and other activities might not actually be performed by spontaneous initiative of the masses.

Thus the Chairman probably commended missiles in Cuba to Mikoyan and other colleagues not as an embarrassing ploy to repair a Soviet missile gap, for which he was largely to blame, but mainly as a noble and characteristic act of Soviet generosity to defend little revolutionary Cuba from the CIA and the Pentagon's aggressive designs and generally to advance the socialist camp. He certainly planned to use this line of argument when the missiles were revealed to the world.

Bolstering such a claim was Khrushchev's intention to send Cuba a substantial contingent of operational Soviet combat military forces, numbering more than 42,000 men, which would protect the missile sites and serve as a tripwire against an American invasion.

Dictating his memoirs years later, without documents to prompt his memory, Khrushchev said that he conceived of his missiles-in-Cuba plan not in late April but during a trip to Bulgaria from May 14 to 20, just after he received Salinger in Moscow: "All these thoughts kept churning in my head the whole time I was in Bulgaria. I paced back and forth, brooding over what to do. I didn't tell anyone what I was thinking. I kept my mental agony to myself."

As the Chairman recalled, "My thinking went like this: if we installed the missiles secretly and then if the United States discovered the missiles were there after they were already poised and ready to strike, the Americans would think twice before trying to liquidate our installations by military means. . . . If a quarter or even a tenth of our missiles survived—even if only one or two big ones were left—we could still hit New York, and there wouldn't be much of New York left. . . . The installation of missiles in Cuba would, I thought, restrain the United States from precipitous military action against Castro's government."

Khrushchev conceded that "in addition to protecting Cuba, our missiles would have equalized what the West likes to call 'the balance of power.' " He claimed that the imbalance had been created because "the Americans had surrounded our country with military bases and threatened us with nuclear weapons."

His speeches in Bulgaria showed the churning in his head. At Varna, May 16: "Would it not be better if the shores on which are located NATO's military bases and the launching sites for their armed rockets were converted into areas of peaceful labor and property?" At Sofia, May 19, about Kennedy's *Saturday Evening Post* statement about an American first strike: "Anyone who dared unleash a military conflict of that kind would receive a shattering retaliatory blow using all the very latest weapons of war."

Flying the next day from Sofia to Moscow, by Gromyko's account, Khrushchev told him, "I would like to speak with you alone about an important matter." As the Foreign Minister recalled, "No one else was about, so I knew that the conversation would be about something very important. Khrushchev did not like 'narrow' conversations on political subjects. . . . What was he going to speak with me about? I decided that he had developed or was developing some new idea that he needed to share with a person who was involved in foreign affairs professionally."

The Chairman noted that the situation in Cuba was dangerous: "In order to save it as an independent state, it is essential to deploy a certain number of our nuclear missiles there. This alone can save the country. Last year's failed assault at the Bay of Pigs isn't going to stop Washington. What is your view on this?"

Gromyko paused and replied, "I must say frankly that putting our missiles in Cuba would cause a political explosion in the United States. I am absolutely certain of that, and this should be taken into account." He feared that these words might make Khrushchev "fly into a rage." The Chairman did not, but Gromyko knew "that he had no intention of changing his position."

Khrushchev declared, "We don't need a nuclear war and we have no intention of fighting." When Gromyko heard this he "felt a sense of relief. Even Khrushchev's voice . . . had become a bit milder." The Chairman resolved to raise the question before the Presidium.

* * *

Khrushchev used to joke with his advisers that Presidium members were so inclined to talk about secret meetings that the Voice of America could broadcast their contents within a half hour of adjournment. Thus as Sergo Mikoyan recalled, the Chairman resolved to confide his missile scheme to only five officials: Mikoyan, Kozlov, Malinovsky, Gromyko, and Marshal Sergei Biryuzov, a Deputy Defense Minister and commander of Strategic Rocket Forces. To reduce the danger of revelation, Khrushchev excluded even note-takers.

By his own account, he convened a secret meeting on his return from Bulgaria where he "warned that Fidel would be crushed if another invasion were launched against Cuba and said that we were the only ones who could prevent such a disaster from occurring."

According to Sergo Mikoyan, Khrushchev asked Malinovsky how long it would have taken the Soviet Union to invade an island ninety miles away and win. The Marshal replied, "Three or four days, a week maybe." The Chairman reasoned that action against Cuba would take the Americans the same amount of time—not long enough for Moscow to defend the island even by retaliation elsewhere. Thus an invasion must be deterred beforehand by sending missiles to Cuba.

Malinovsky would not have been delighted to have to pay the mind-boggling cost of the operation out of his existing defense budget.* Nor would he have been enchanted by sending the most dangerous and secret Soviet weapons to such a strange, distant, highly exposed place as Cuba, where Americans or Cubans might conceivably capture them. The Soviet Union had never before moved missiles capable of bearing nuclear warheads outside its borders. Still Gromyko felt that Malinovsky's demeanor suggested "that he supported Khrushchev's proposal unconditionally."

The Foreign Minister recalled that Khrushchev "repeatedly elaborated his position on the basic questions. How to preserve Cuba as a sovereign socialist state? . . . When time was required to think carefully through the questions, they were postponed to the next discussion."

Sergei Khrushchev recalled that such talks were his father's "usual way to check himself." Khrushchev said in his memoirs, "It wasn't until after two or three lengthy discussions of the matter" that he and his colleagues "decided it was worth the risk."

Gromyko was relieved by the Chairman's insistence "that the Soviet Union should not and would not go so far as to risk a nuclear con-

---

*The CIA later estimated that the cost was one billion dollars.

flict," stated in private talks with several Presidium members.* As Gromyko recalled, "Of course, none of this eliminated the risk of nuclear war, as we did not know the American side's precise intentions."

According to Sergo Mikoyan, his father restated his objections. Khrushchev told the group, "Let's send Marshal Biryuzov to Cuba to find out the possibility of installing missiles without American discovery and take with him my letter to Fidel, in which I shall ask Fidel's opinion."

Alexander Alexeyev was the TASS correspondent and Soviet intelligence agent who called himself the first Soviet citizen in postrevolutionary Cuba and who had served as an informal emissary to Castro. In early May, he was mysteriously summoned from Havana to Moscow. Mikoyan showed him in to Gromyko: "Andrei Andreyevich, this is our new Ambassador to Cuba, Alexeyev." This was how Alexeyev learned of his appointment, a choice which delighted Castro.

In late May, Alexeyev was called to Khrushchev's office, along with Gromkyo, Malinovsky, Mikoyan, Biryuzov, and Sharaf Rashidov, an alternate member of the Presidium. As Alexeyev recalled, the Chairman was "very interested in the defense capability of Cuba." After some talk, he asked, "How would Fidel Castro respond if we placed our missiles in Cuba?"

Alexeyev recalled that Khrushchev's question "put me in a state of complete shock because I could never suppose that Fidel Castro would agree to such a thing." He advised the Chairman that Castro "will not accept such a proposal from us because he is building his security on first strengthening their defense capability and public opinion in Latin America and world public opinion."

Malinovsky disagreed: how could a socialist country refuse Soviet aid when Spain had accepted? Khrushchev told Alexeyev, "You are going to Cuba—Comrade Rashidov, Biryuzov, and you—and explain to Fidel Castro our concerns." By Sergo Mikoyan's account, the Chairman asked them to find out whether Castro would be willing to accept the missiles and whether they could be installed and deployed in secret.

---

*According to General Dimitri Volkogonov, deputy chief of the political directorate of the Soviet armed forces in 1989, one of the written orders given to Malinovsky stated, "The rocket forces are to be used only in the case of a U.S. attack, unleashing a war, and under the strict condition of receiving a command from Moscow."

As Alexeyev recalled, just before his trio's departure ten days later, Khrushchev summoned them to his dacha along with Gromyko and the Presidium: "For the salvation of the Cuban revolution, there is no other path than one which could equalize, so to say, the security of Cuba with the security of the United States. And this logically could be done only by our nuclear missiles, our long-range missiles. So try and explain it to Fidel."

As delegation leader, Rashidov was the highest-ranking Soviet to visit Cuba since Mikoyan in 1960, yet sufficiently junior to keep from arousing American suspicions. Not yet accredited as Ambassador, Alexeyev traveled as an adviser to the Soviet Embassy in Havana.

Arriving in early June "to study irrigation problems," as it was officially announced, they met privately with Fidel and Raul Castro and explained Khrushchev's plan for "saving the Cuban revolution." According to Alexeyev, the Cuban leader fell into thought and then said, "If this will serve the socialist camp, and if it will hinder the actions of American imperialism on the continent, I believe that we will agree. But I will give you an answer only after I consult with my close comrades."

Castro confided Khrushchev's request to Che Guevara, President Osvaldo Dorticos, the old Cuban Communist leader Blas Roca, and Castro's close aide Major Emilio Aragones. They endorsed it unanimously. "But we six and especially Fidel Castro were sure that we were doing this . . . not so much as to defend Cuba as to change the correlation of forces between capitalism and socialism," recalled Aragones. "Why? Because we believed that to defend Cuba, other measures could be taken without resorting to installing missiles."

Castro called the Soviets back, along with Raul, Guevara, Dorticos, and Blas Roca, and told them, "Yes, place missiles in Cuba and they will serve both the salvation of the Cuban revolution and assistance to the socialist camp."

Alexeyev was surprised by Castro's assent: "But Fidel knew the circumstances with regard to the Americans better than we did. . . . He added that as a sign of solidarity, that if it would really help world socialism, actually prevent the American threat not only to Cuba but to other regions, other countries, then he was willing to accept the proposal." Sergo Mikoyan recalled, "Fidel believed he could take the risk. He was always ready to fight to the last soldier, but he knew if the United States used all of its force, he would fail."

Back in Moscow, the delegation reported to Khrushchev that Castro would accept the missiles. Biryuzov assured him that they could be deployed in secret: there might even be places in the Cuban mountains where the United States would not even find the missiles. (The senior Mikoyan thought him "a fool.") Malinovsky said the missiles could be installed quickly; if the operation were properly camouflaged, they would not be found.

As Alexeyev recalled, the Chairman "thought that if we would act very carefully and not send immediately a stream of ships, we would take it to the point that on the sixth of November, we would announce openly our measures." The sixth of November was the date of the American midterm elections.

Castro later said that Khrushchev's proposal "surprised us at first and gave us great pause. . . . We finally went along because, on the one hand, the Russians convinced us that the United States would not let itself be intimidated by conventional weapons and secondarily because it was impossible for us not to share the risks which the Soviet Union was taking to save us." He felt he "had no right to refuse." Better to risk "a great crisis" than wait "impotently" for an American invasion.

Castro later complained that Khrushchev had not told him the truth about Soviet nuclear inferiority: "It did not occur to me to ask the Soviets about it. It did not seem to me that I had the right to ask, 'Listen, how many missiles do you have, how many do the North Americans have, what is the correlation of forces?' We really trusted that they, for their part, were acting with knowledge of the entire situation."

After the Russians left Havana, Castro donned his battle fatigues and rifle and departed with great fanfare for a week in the Sierra Maestra, birthplace of his revolution. Emboldened by his secret knowledge of Khrushchev's plan to thwart the American invasion that he presumed was imminent, El Líder Maximo declared, "Once more, I have raised the banner of rebellion!"

Khrushchev was undisturbed by Mikoyan's warnings that Kennedy would not tolerate missiles in Cuba. "He did not necessarily think through all possible permutations," recalled Burlatsky. Like Kennedy when he planned the Bay of Pigs, the secrecy Khrushchev had imposed on the operation prevented him from gaining the broad range of advice that might have shown him that the President might respond strongly.*

---

*After speaking with some of the principals, Georgi Arbatov of the U.S.A.-Canada Institute in Moscow complained that the missile decisions "were taken in a closed

Khrushchev may have expected the President to pretend he did not know about the missiles if he discovered them before the congressional elections, just as he may have believed that Kennedy pretended he did not know about planning for the Berlin Wall in order to avoid political embarrassment. Even if the President revealed the missiles to the public, it would probably take him many weeks to orchestrate a NATO response. Khrushchev recalled how it took almost two months during the summer of 1961 for Kennedy to draft an Allied response to his Vienna ultimatum on Berlin.

He may have assumed that the President would be deterred from strong action by fear that the Soviets would retaliate over Berlin. This had been so important during the Bay of Pigs that Kennedy had been willing to suffer an American defeat.

Khrushchev felt that sending missiles to Cuba was within his rights, just as the Americans had installed them in Turkey, Britain, and Italy. The missiles in those three nations were not in hardened sites and thus suited only for a first-strike attack, but the Americans called them "defensive." The Chairman intended to use the same adjective for the missiles in Cuba.

Gromyko bitterly remembered that when he once complained to Foster Dulles that the United States was secretly setting up missile bases along the Soviet border, Dulles had told him, "Matters involving the establishment of American military bases are decided by the United States, and only the United States, at its own discretion, and by agreement with the country on whose territory these bases are established." Gromyko recalled that South Korea had been covertly "jammed with nuclear weapons."

Khrushchev might have expected the President to respond to the sudden and secret installation of missiles in Cuba just as he had responded to the sudden and secret installation of the Berlin Wall: he would claim surprise, send Moscow a formal protest, and then tell the American people that this was not an issue on which the West was prepared to go to war. Gromyko years later said, "If this measure were not carried out in secrecy, it just would not have worked."

The Chairman recalled how Senator Fulbright had seemed to signal beforehand that the Soviets and East Germans had the right to close the Berlin border. In June 1961, Fulbright had told the Senate, "I suppose we would all be less comfortable if the Soviets did install missile bases in Cuba, but I am not sure that our national existence would be in substantially greater danger than is the case today." If

---

coterie. They were not analyzed from all sides. I think that a more or less serious analysis would have prevented such a step."

Khrushchev assumed that Fulbright tacitly spoke for Kennedy on Berlin, he may have also assumed that Fulbright spoke for Kennedy on Cuba.

If the Chairman needed further reassurance that the President would not react strongly against missiles in Cuba, he could note the Kennedy administration's failure as late as May 1962 to issue a formal warning against Soviet missiles on the island. After the Bay of Pigs, Khrushchev had pointedly written the President that while he did not "intend to establish" a missile base on Cuba, the United States did use other nations' territories for "preparations . . . that really do pose a threat to the security of the Soviet Union."

Even to this blatant hint Kennedy had not responded. In the summer of 1961, the President had carefully defined for Khrushchev those interests surrounding Berlin and Germany that the United States would and would not defined. The Chairman could be excused for presuming that Kennedy's failure to warn against nuclear missiles in Cuba was not accidental.

Now that Khrushchev felt he had found a way out of his quandary, his sense of frustration lifted. What did not lift was his private bewilderment and anger at the United States and its President.

At this solemn moment of decision, the leader of the Soviet Union was still a "very emotional man," as Burlatsky recalled. Khrushchev could not understand why Kennedy and his people had chosen to embarrass him by revealing Soviet weakness and seeming to threaten a first-strike attack. Among the deep swirl of Khrushchev's emotions in the late spring of 1962 was an almost childlike feeling of spite and revenge.

"It was high time America learned what it feels like to have her own land and her own people threatened," he thundered in his memoirs. "We Russians have suffered three wars over the last half century. . . . America has never had to fight a war on her own soil, at least not in the past fifty years. She's sent troops abroad to fight in the two World Wars and made a fortune as a result. America has shed a few drops of her own blood while making billions by bleeding the rest of the world dry."

Khrushchev savored giving the Americans "a little of their own medicine": "Now they would learn just what it feels like to have enemy missiles pointing at you."

CHAPTER

15

"No One Will Be Able Even to Run"

A T THE END OF MAY, KHRUSHCHEV ATTENDED A BENNY GOODMAN concert at the Red Army sports palace. He found jazz "decadent" but, under prodding by Jane Thompson, had agreed to a tour of the Soviet Union by the King of Swing. Sitting in his box with the Thompsons and the Adzhubeis, he said, "I just came to drink beer. I don't understand this music." But when Goodman's beautiful female vocalist, Joya Sherrill, appeared in a low-cut white gown, Khrushchev led the cheering.

He left at intermission, telling Jane Thompson, "It's a little too much." She said, "Well, it's your first time hearing it." Khrushchev said, "No matter. Let them enjoy it." Adzhubei later recalled that his father-in-law considered jazz "an invention of uncultured people. . . . Although he was a Marxist, and although he understood that blacks and whites are equal, he could still say that."

After the concert, the Thompsons threw a large reception at Spaso

House, one of their last before their planned departure in July. "Tommy and I went to bed before it was over," recalled Jane. "The Adzhubeis were still having a good time when we left. There was improvisation, with the windows wide open. The next two weeks, jazz mushroomed all over the city. It was a wonderful finale to our time in Moscow."

On Tuesday, June 5, Kennedy wrote Khrushchev, "I noticed with appreciation your friendly gesture in attending the concert offered by Benny Goodman in Moscow last week. I myself look forward to attending a performance of the Bolshoi Ballet when it comes to us in the fall."

He also thanked the Chairman "for the generous hospitality which you and your associates offered to Pierre Salinger while he was in the Soviet Union. He has given me a full account of his visit, with particular emphasis on your own generosity in giving him so much of your time." He recognized "that your kindness to him was in part a friendly gesture to me."

Berlin was being discussed by Rusk and Dobrynin: "I think it may be best to leave the discussion in their capable hands at this time. I am glad to learn again from Mr. Salinger that Ambassador Dobrynin has your confidence in unusual measure. He has already made a place for himself here in Washington as an intelligent and friendly representative of your Government."

In the spring of 1962, as Kennedy's and Khrushchev's men bargained in Geneva over a "neutral and independent" Laos under Prince Souvanna Phouma, the Communist Pathet Lao had resumed their military offensive. "I fear there is little Washington or Moscow can do on this," Dean Rusk said privately in March. "I have the impression the Russians would like to see a settlement of the situation, but the Chinese are messing things up."

In January, the President had warned Adzhubei that the United States would move more strongly in Southeast Asia if the Laotian Communists continued to harbor forces attacking South Vietnam. But that same month he told his NSC that after "careful weighing of the risks" and "examination of the supply problem" (there was no seaport), he had "decided to disengage" from Laos. At a February press conference, to keep a strong hand at Geneva, he denied that this was so. Sorensen years later observed that on Laos, Kennedy "combined bluff with real determination . . . in proportions he made known to *no one.*"

In March, the President used his *Saturday Evening Post* interview to issue a new threat to Khrushchev about Laos. With deceptive off-handedness, he said that the Chairman was as aware as he that if the United States was pushed to intervene in Laos, it might lead to use of nuclear weapons.

In early May, with North Vietnamese support, Prince Souphanouvong and the Pathet Lao broke the cease-fire. The Royal Laotian Army fled. The Communists seemed to be driving toward the Thai border. Kennedy considered how to convince the Pathet Lao to renew the cease-fire without encouraging the rightist General Phoumi Nosavan into thinking that he could block a coalition government and sink the Geneva talks.

Working through Thompson in Moscow, Rusk asked Gromyko to "use his influence" on the Pathet Lao. George Ball asked Dobrynin whether the Soviets had scrapped Khrushchev's Vienna pledge to seek an independent, neutral Laos: "The United States has been putting pressure on Phoumi. It is now to be expected that the Soviet Union will exercise control over the reckless actions of Souphanouvong." Dobrynin reaffirmed the Chairman's pledge and demanded that the Americans force the "Boun Oum–Nosavan clique" to stop sabotaging a coalition government.

On Thursday, May 10, the President considered a limited show of force, including the dispatch of portions of the Seventh Fleet to the Gulf of Siam. Verging on insolence, General Bernard Decker, the Army Chief of Staff, said, "Last spring you made some startling noises and then you had to back down, and I'm just afraid, if you are not prepared to follow through on this, we will look silly again."

That day in Washington, General Eisenhower told reporters that Kennedy's efforts for a coalition government in Laos were "the way we lost China." Kennedy asked McCone to "try to get him back onto the track." When McCone called on his old boss, Eisenhower agreed to support a limited response. He added that unless Phoumi's forces were disintegrating, it would be a "very splendid move" to reinforce them "so as to hold a firm position abreast of the northern border of South Vietnam—roughly the Seventeenth Parallel."*

---

* Honoring McCone's promise to keep his conversation with Eisenhower secret, Kennedy referred to the General as "X" when he called Roger Hilsman later that evening: "McCone talked to X. He wants to put troops in there." He acidly noted that "X" had once told him that the Royal Laotian forces were "a bunch of homosexuals,"

On Saturday, May 12, the Seventh Fleet was sent. Thompson cabled that it was "highly significant" that Khrushchev and Gromyko did not publicly complain: "The Soviets are almost encouraging us to demonstrate that the Pathet Lao are following a dangerous policy. . . . I find it difficult to believe that in a matter as important as this Khrushchev would have remained silent if the Soviets intended to seriously oppose us in this area." He suggested "taking the line that the Pathet Lao are out of control or being egged on by the Chinese." Washington should also tell the Soviets that "we are now really going to put the bite on Phoumi."

Four days later, after the United States quietly persuaded Bangkok to request aid, two American air squadrons, five thousand American Marines and infantrymen, and contingents from Britain, Australia, and New Zealand moved through Thailand to the Laotian border. Khrushchev complained to a Western diplomat that the President was playing "a reckless game."

Suggesting that Kennedy write to the Chairman, Rusk sent a draft to the White House.* Instead, Robert Kennedy asked Georgi Bolshakov to tell Khrushchev that the President had relied on Soviet assurances that there would be no more fighting, and that the new Pathet Lao action had made him feel "double-crossed."

Bolshakov returned several days later with a "personal" message from Khrushchev: there would be no more armed action in Laos. The Soviet Union was "anxious that the whole matter be resolved peacefully." After consulting his brother, the Attorney General reported that he was "pleased with the message." The United States would do all it could with Souvanna Phouma, but the Chairman must "also work with his people on the other side."

---

adding that "politically" help from "X" would make a limited display of force "a little less tricky."

*It said, "If your policy remains the same as you expressed to me at Vienna, then you will agree with me that immediate reestablishment of an effective cease-fire is the first and essential step. This must be accompanied by satisfactory assurances from the side you support that you will in the future honor this cease-fire and will restore to the Royal Laotian Government the territory that its aggressors of the past week have seized."

Otherwise the United States would have to act to honor its commitments to the Royal Laotians: "With this in mind I have ordered elements of the Seventh U.S. Fleet to the Gulf of Thailand and I am prepared to take such additional measures as the circumstances may call for. The United States government and the United States people will simply not permit Laos to be overrun by the Souphanouvong forces. This is particularly true since it is well known that the Soviet Union is in a position to restrain these forces and thereby permit a peaceful settlement."

The Pathet Lao reentered talks. A coalition government was formed on June 12 with Souvanna as Prime Minister and Phoumi and Prince Souphanouvong as deputies.

Khrushchev cabled Kennedy. "Good news has come from Laos. . . . There is no doubt that this may be the turning point not only in the life of the Laotian people but in the consolidation of peace in Southeast Asia. . . . Our mutual understanding at our Vienna meeting in June of last year on support for a neutral and independent Laos has begun to become a reality." The President replied, "I share your view that the reports from Laos are very encouraging."

A "Declaration on the Neutrality of Laos" was signed six weeks later in Geneva. Bolshakov reported to Robert Kennedy that Khrushchev was "very pleased with the settlement in Laos" but unhappy about the continuing presence of Western troops in Thailand. The Chairman understood that they had been sent because of a possible outbreak in Laos. He hoped that it was now possible to withdraw them.

Robert checked with his brother and asked Bolshakov to inform Khrushchev that the President would start the pullout within ten days. Khrushchev sent back a message that this meant "a great deal" to him.

The Laotian settlement did not hold. The Pathet Lao withdrew from the new government. The North Vietnamese continued using the Laos corridor to supply Viet Cong rebels in South Vietnam. Kennedy stepped up CIA covert action against the two enemy forces.

In early July, Castro sent his brother, Raul, and his aide, Major Aragones, to Moscow. In secret the Cubans persuaded Khrushchev, Mikoyan, and Malinovsky that the nuclear missiles should be brought to Cuba in the context of a formal Soviet-Cuban military accord.

Raul and Malinovsky drafted a document pledging the Soviet air force to respect Cuban sovereignty and law. The pact was to be in effect for five years, thereafter renewable, but could be terminated with one year's notice by either party. In that case, Soviet installations on Cuba would become Cuban government property; Soviet troops would have to leave with their equipment and war matériel.

According to Jorge Risquet, later of the Cuban Politburo, the Cubans suggested to Khrushchev that he make a public announcement that the Soviet Union was shipping missiles to Cuba: this was in both countries' rights. Otherwise, "led into a blind alley," the United States would "find itself faced with a fait accompli and it would have to react with a certain degree of violence . . . when faced with something that could be seen as some sort of deception, as something done dishonestly."

Khrushchev refused. As Aragones recalled, he "wanted to buy time. He said there would be no problems, he believed that was not going to happen, that it would not be discovered."

The Cubans insisted that if Washington discovered the missiles before they were combat-ready, "we could expect a preemptive attack by the United States with very grave consequences for ourselves and no ability to respond." Khrushchev replied that, in that case, he would still defend them and would send a letter to Kennedy telling him what he had done.

The Soviets and Cubans agreed that the pact would take effect as soon as it was initialed. Khrushchev and Castro could sign it publicly during a triumphant visit by the Chairman to Cuba in November, after the missiles were installed. When Castro was given the document in late July, he drafted his own preface. This would be published at the grand moment in November when he welcomed Khrushchev to Havana.

On Wednesday, July 4, Khrushchev went to the annual Independence Day lawn party at Spaso House, where he toasted President Kennedy and said, "I want to congratulate the American people. I wish for peace and success." Benny Goodman greeted him: "Ah, a new jazz fan." The Chairman replied, "I don't like Goodman music. I just like *good* music!"

The next day, he wrote the President to demand a solution to Berlin. Bolshakov had warned Robert Kennedy in June that the unsolved Berlin problem "makes our relations more difficult and . . . is full of possibilities of dangerous collision between states. The Soviet Union sincerely wants to reach an agreement with the United States which would *not* hurt vital interests or prestige for both sides."

Bolshakov told the Attorney General that he had informed Khrushchev of Robert's insistence that "the President and his government are realists and trying to reach an agreement and would not like to have a military conflict with the U.S.S.R." But if the West did not act soon, the Berlin Crisis would be reignited.

On Tuesday, July 17, Bundy gave the President "an AP report of a plane-buzzing incident in the Berlin corridor." At six o'clock in the Oval Office, Kennedy complained to Dobrynin about the harassment. He rejected Khrushchev's latest offer of a settlement requiring removal of Allied troops from West Berlin: this "would get us out" of Berlin "without so much as a fig leaf of concealment. This would mean a major retreat. Europe would lose confidence in U.S. leadership. It would be a major victory for the Soviet Union and a major defeat for the West."

Dobrynin said that the Chairman would be "greatly disappointed." He rudely asked Kennedy whether his position was "related to German interests or American interests." The President kept his cool: "There might well be other issues on which we would be willing to press the Germans quite hard, such as, for example, on the structure of an access authority." But "our presence in Berlin" was "of vital interest to all." He thought he had made that point clear to Gromyko when they met the previous autumn.

Kennedy reminded the envoy that "Soviet-created tensions in Berlin" had already caused increased Western rearmament: "Any new crisis would have a similar effect." Noting his disagreements with his allies on the spread of nuclear weapons (read France), he warned that a new Berlin crisis "could only increase the danger of results which the Soviet government would not like."

Dobrynin insisted it was the Western troops in West Berlin that created these dangers. The President replied that the best way to reduce tension over Berlin would be for the Soviet Union to understand that the troops were a Western vital interest.

In Geneva three days earlier, Arthur Dean had told reporters that improved nuclear detection methods might foreclose the need for inspection stations within the Soviet Union. After angrily reading Dean's remarks in a newspaper, Rusk had issued a statement saying that there had been no change in the American position. Kennedy was furious that in public the administration seemed to be so confused.

Now Dobrynin asked him what Dean had had in mind. Evading the question, the President simply said that if the Soviets renewed their nuclear tests, "American scientists would urge the need for additional American testing. . . . It would help if any new series of Soviet tests could be short." Dobrynin insisted that since the Americans had conducted "many more tests" than his government, the Soviet Union intended to resume nuclear testing.*

During the summer of 1962, the influence of the nation's Secretary of Defense was nearing its peak. On taking office, Robert Strange McNamara had surrounded himself with young men "who are smarter

---

*TASS publicly announced this decision four days later.

than I am": Alain Enthoven, Charles Hitch, Adam Yarmolinsky, and others who had tutored him about the new innovations in defense doctrine that had percolated in universities and think tanks during the late Eisenhower years.

With his white presidential telephone behind him, hunched in shirt-sleeves over his nine-foot General Pershing desk, his eyes racing down one document after another, McNamara had swiftly begun to fulfill the assignment implicit and explicit in Kennedy's 1960 campaign speeches—to build American nuclear forces, expand conventional forces to respond more flexibly to provocations short of war, and reduce costly intraservice rivalries by bringing the military under clear civilian control.

Arguing for his policies, McNamara always spoke in italics. "He really runs rather than walks," observed the Secretary of Agriculture, Orville Freeman, who noted that McNamara even ran "up and down the escalator steps." Generals, admirals, and Congressmen complained of his abruptness. McNamara authorized for direct attribution his wife's comment that "Bob suffers fools badly."

He was fastidious in his relations with the Secretary of State, avoiding the public impression of encroachment upon Rusk's terrain ("I have never taken actions bearing upon foreign policy without the complete concurrence of the Department of State"). But it was in his nature to fill a power vacuum. Whether in a debate behind closed doors or in public with his ferociously articulate Pentagon counterpart, Rusk could not compete.

McNamara began the custom of issuing an annual one- or two-hundred-page posture statement defining political purposes, military threats, and how the United States proposed to meet them. Foy Kohler said years later, "I tried to persuade Dean that we ought to issue our own foreign affairs summary every year before McNamara got his out. . . . I thought he let Bob run over him. . . . I thought he should have stood up more."

With his disdain for conventional procedure, the President more and more sought McNamara's advice on matters beyond defense. He had never met a self-made big businessman so literate and so able to hold his own against academics, Congressmen, and the press. He was dazzled by McNamara's toughness, quickness, fluency, competence, incorruptibility, freedom from political cant, and force of personality.

Except for Douglas Dillon and Robert Kennedy, McNamara was the only Cabinet member who made his way across the great divide into the President's social life. Jacqueline said, "Men can't understand his sex appeal." He became especially close to the Attorney General, who said, "Why is it they all call him 'the computer' and yet he's the one all my sisters want to sit next to at dinner?"

Naturally McNamara knew that intimacy with the Kennedys would increase his public influence. Still, he was genuinely attracted by the family's toughness, rationality, intellectual curiosity, and athleticism, their increasingly liberal instincts, and their hard work and play. He was grateful for deliverance from the anti-intellectual, illiberal realm of automobile men and their wives he had endured for fifteen years.

No one took more seriously the "Hickory Hill seminars" organized by Robert Kennedy and Arthur Schlesinger at which the inner circle of the New Frontier government and social worlds was quietly invited to question visiting academics on subjects ranging from presidential greatness to psychoanalysis.* Not impervious to the Kennedy style, McNamara once danced the twist with Jacqueline at a private White House dinner. Asked by a reporter to name those he called when he wished to chew the fat or have a beer, he said, "The Kennedys—I like the Kennedys."

Frank with himself about his own managerial deficiencies, the President admired the speed with which McNamara rationalized the Pentagon. He appreciated the Secretary's one-two-three method of doing business: unlike Rusk, he'd "come in with his twenty options and then say, 'Mr. President, I think we should do this.' I like that. Makes the job easier." Kennedy said McNamara was "one of the few guys around this town who, when you ask him if he has anything to say and he hasn't, says, 'No.' That's rare these days, I'm telling you."

McNamara was the embodiment of Kennedy's increasing conviction that the problems of the 1960s were more subject to "administrative" than ideological solutions. As the President put it in a major speech at Yale in June 1962, these were problems "so complicated and so technical that only a handful of people really understand them," forcing the average man to fall back on "a bunch of outdated if not meaningless slogans."

As time went on, the President became more aware of McNamara's shortcomings. O'Donnell, who disliked him, warned Kennedy that McNamara's political inexperience would one day get the President into bad trouble. When in 1963 the Secretary suggested to Congress

---

*Schlesinger called himself the Assistant Dean and Robert Kennedy the Dean. In December 1961, for instance, he wrote Jacqueline Kennedy's social secretary about "the next meeting of the Robert F. Kennedy Academy of Higher Learning" to be held at his Georgetown house: "The speaker will be Professor A. J. Ayer, the Oxford philosopher. . . . If Mrs. K. would like by any chance to come for dinner, I need hardly say that nothing would delight us more."

that some missiles sold to Canada had been mainly intended to attract a few Soviet missiles away from U.S. territory, Kennedy privately said, "Everyone ought to run for office. That's all there is to it."

Although he admired the Secretary of Defense, Joseph Alsop was exasperated when he heard Kennedy saying that "on a mathematical basis, the chances of a nuclear war within ten years were at least even." As Alsop recalled, "Bob had this complicated business about if China gets the bomb . . . it goes up to quadruple sizes. A lot of garbage: it doesn't go up like that at all. But the President had been given this information by McNamara, and hadn't really thought about it, and was just repeating it."

The columnist was also concerned about McNamara's uneven domestic political instincts. He wrote Kennedy, "Bob is your great discovery, but he resembles my old General, [Claire] Chennault,* in the last war, in the sense that his astonishing qualities are potentially counterbalanced by large gaps in his experience. . . . Give a short lecture to Bob on the need to be open and frank about his problems with the public, and therefore with people in Congress and in my business. He thinks if you do right, support will be automatic. It's a beautiful belief but alas not justified by the record.

"Tell him every great officer of state needs to command public support and confidence, and the only way to get it is to explain what he is up to. . . . I only write you all this because I foresee bad trouble for Bob unless preventive action is taken. . . . The enemies Bob is forced to make will get him yet, unless he is protected in the way I've outlined or in some other way."

Born in 1916, McNamara grew up in what was described as a "somewhat crowded, rigidly lower-middle-class area" in the northern hills of San Francisco. His father was the Boston Irish Catholic son of immigrants from County Cork, his mother a Scottish-English Protestant. Sales manager of a wholesale shoe firm, the father moved the family in 1924 to Oakland, which allowed the son to attend the excellent high school in the wealthy town of Piedmont.

---

*Simultaneously wartime chief of the U.S. Air Force in China and chief of staff of the Chinese air force, Chennault was a crony of Chiang Kai-shek ("one of the world's great men") who had founded the "Flying Tiger" flying force which bagged an impressive number of Japanese aircraft. He resigned in July 1945 after concluding that his command was being encroached upon, blamed his demotion on pressure from Chinese Communists, and became a pillar of the pro-Chiang "China Lobby" in the United States.

After Berkeley, he attended and taught accounting at the Harvard Business School. During World War II, as an Army Air Corps logistics expert, he used new statistical techniques. At war's end, he intended to return to Harvard, but when his new wife, Margaret, contracted polio, the medical bills compelled him to make money in business. He joined a management and control team of veterans dubbed the "Whiz Kids," hired by young Henry Ford II to revise the archaic, chaotic methods of the Ford Motor Company.

McNamara rose at Ford not through the usual combination of corporate politics and love of cars but through sheer managerial ability. He said, "I agree that I don't have the rapport that some of the backslappers do. I can't help it. . . . I just analyze every situation with all the tools at my command."

McNamara settled his family not in the suburbs but in the university town of Ann Arbor. Nominally a Republican, he joined the Citizens for Michigan committee formed by George Romney of American Motors to advise on public policy. In 1960, he was named president of Ford, the first time the company had been headed by someone outside the family. He let it be known that year that he was voting for Kennedy, but somehow the Kennedy campaign failed to note and exploit the fact.

After the election, Robert Lovett suggested McNamara among three or four others for the Pentagon. As civilian chief of air, Lovett had known his logistics work during the war. Eager to hire palatable Republican businessmen, the President-elect was relieved when Lovett told him that McNamara was not a Catholic. O'Donnell telephoned the United Automobile Workers and was assured that McNamara had a "liberal outlook."

Sargent Shriver flew to Detroit and suggested Treasury or Defense. McNamara replied that entering the Cabinet would mean a sacrifice of several million dollars, although he conceded that he already had "more money than I'm ever going to need or use," and that he had been president of Ford for only a month. By the end of their talk, Shriver left enchanted: "How many other automobile executives or cabinet ministers read Teilhard de Chardin?"

Meeting with the President-elect the next day in Georgetown, McNamara said that he was not qualified for Treasury (he was not candid enough to say that the idea bored him) but was fascinated by the challenge of the Pentagon. Perhaps because he knew that assertive leaders are impressed by assertiveness, he asked Kennedy if he had actually written *Profiles in Courage*. Kennedy replied that he had, although others had "of course" done much of the research. Afterward the President-elect said, "I think he is just the right man."

When McNamara saw him again, he brought a letter insisting that he be allowed to choose his own people, that he make up his own mind about the controversial findings of a Kennedy task force report on defense, and have direct operational and administrative authority in a chain from the President through the military commands. It concluded by saying that if Kennedy agreed to these understandings, he was prepared to accept the offer.

Other Presidents might have found it impudent for an incoming Cabinet minister to put such demands in writing. But, as was Robert Kennedy, his brother was "impressed with the fact that he was so tough about it."

The tug-of-war between the parents' Irish and Scottish ancestries seemed almost to play itself out in the son. McNamara was an emotional, partisan, driven man who worked hard to contain and conceal these instincts behind a facade of rational, self-confident, apolitical Olympian efficiency.

He told one reporter, "You can never substitute emotion for reason. I still would allow a place for intuition in this process, but not emotion." To another: "I've got to think precisely. The cost of being wrong is very high." The record of McNamara's utterances while at the Pentagon is suffused with such comments. If Kennedy was a realist brilliantly disguised as a romantic, McNamara was—if not a romantic—a man of intense emotion who aspired to coldly logical realism.* He knew that men of conspicuous self-doubt do not survive as president of Ford or Secretary of Defense.

At the White House, he argued for his policies with such consistent force and absolute certainty that Robert Kennedy, who greatly liked and admired him, made certain that his brother heard opposing arguments for balance. Robert thought McNamara "the most dangerous man in the Cabinet, because he is so persuasive and articulate." Someone else said that he hoped the Secretary was "never seriously wrong. Just think what happens when Bob comes up against someone else in

---

*This effort evidently failed by the third year of massive American involvement and casualties in Vietnam, when under great stress he finally resigned from Lyndon Johnson's Pentagon. Some of his friends told one of his biographers, Henry Trewhitt, off the record, of their worry that McNamara might take his own life. Johnson, by then angry at McNamara's change of heart on Vietnam, meanly told intimates that he was worried about "another Forrestal" (referring to the first Secretary of Defense, who leaped from a Bethesda Naval Hospital window to his death). Twenty years later, McNamara demanded of interviewers that they refrain from asking him about Vietnam.

a gray area of discussion. The other guy hasn't a chance."

James Reston once complained in the *New York Times,* "The issue about the Secretary of Defense is not over his inefficiency but his decisive efficiency in putting over dubious policies. . . . He is tidy, he is confident, and he has the sincerity of an Old Testament prophet, but something is missing: some element of personal doubt, some respect for human weakness, some knowledge of history."

From the Harvard Business School to the Pentagon, McNamara's passion had always been to impose rational procedures that would reduce the system's vulnerability to human error, chance, and accident.* The virtue in his approach was the greater exactitude it brought to American defense policy and statecraft. The weakness was that it lacked an equally sophisticated understanding of the emotional and seemingly irrational impulses that governed a people like the Vietnamese† or a leader like Nikita Khrushchev.

That winter, McNamara pondered an important shift in American nuclear strategy: in the event of impending Soviet nuclear attack, the United States would try to assault not Soviet cities but Soviet bomber and missile sites.

He hoped that such a counterforce strategy would reduce de Gaulle's doubts that the President would sacrifice New York for Paris, and thus his demands for a French nuclear *force de frappe.* In February, he declared in a Chicago speech, "We may be able to use our retaliatory forces to limit damage done to ourselves and our allies by knocking out the enemy's bases before he has had time to launch his second salvos."

One of his aides later said, "He was listening to his Whiz Kids and accepting too much of what they said at face value. In any case, he should have known there could be no such thing as primary retaliation against military targets after an enemy attack. If you're going to shoot at missiles, you're talking about first strike."‡

---

*As Secretary of Defense, he was appalled by how little had been done to prevent accidental nuclear war. One of his early acts was to order installation of Permissive-Action Links—PALs—to thwart unauthorized missile firings. (He also ordered that the technology be quietly provided to the Russians.)
†As McNamara later conceded.
‡McNamara said in the 1980s, "I don't know anybody who thinks that a nuclear war, once started today, can be limited. But that was our hope then." During the 1980s, Dean Rusk imagined a presidential call to a Soviet leader after a counterforce attack: "We launched our missiles a few minutes ago, but I want to assure you that we are

* * *

Combined with Kennedy's comments about taking "the initiative," McNamara's talk about counterforce deepened Khrushchev's anxieties that the United States was considering a preemptive nuclear attack against the Soviet Union. Like a child outshouting a rival, he was now all the more desperate to refute American claims of superiority.

On Wednesday, July 11, he told a Moscow "peace congress" that Eisenhower and Kennedy had once been "realistic," declaring that American and Soviet strength were equal: "That position was stated by President Kennedy during our meeting at Vienna. But now U.S. leaders have started trying to implant in the minds of their people and their allies that the balance of forces has shifted in favor of the United States. . . .

"This dangerous concept is designed to aggravate . . . the threat of war. But it is quite without foundation." He said that the Soviet Union was more dominant than ever, not only because of its hundred-megaton bombs but also a new anti-missile missile.* McNamara's "monstrous proposal" was "permeated with hatred for human beings, for mankind. . . . Are there no armed forces in and near big cities? Wouldn't atom bombs exploded according to McNamara's rules in, say, the suburbs of New York bring fiery death to that great city?"

Alluding to Kennedy, he said, "Some statesmen in positions of responsibility even declare openly their willingness to 'take the initiative' in a nuclear conflict with the Soviet Union. . . . Their reasoning is: hurry up and start the war now, or the situation may change."

A few days later Khrushchev boasted to visiting American editors that his anti-missile missile was so precise it could "hit a fly in outer space." The Soviet Union, he blustered, was "not Laos, not Thailand or some other small state." No doubt animated by visions of missiles in Cuba, he said, "Those who threaten us will get back everything they are planning for us!"

* * *

---

aiming them only at military targets, and so we hope that you will leave our cities alone. . . . And by the way . . . we ought to keep this conversation short, because since Moscow is your central command and control center, I want to give you time to get down into your shelter."

*McNamara's aides quickly told reporters that they doubted Khrushchev's assertion, although the Secretary privately said that the Soviets might be able to develop some kind of anti-missile missile by 1965 or 1966. In fact, we now know that Khrushchev's claim was correct, but that his anti-missile missile was primitive and inaccurate.

Faced with choosing a successor to Thompson at the Moscow Embassy, the President asked his brother whether he was interested. Robert reminded him that he had "spent ten years learning second-year French." Kennedy said, "You certainly don't need Russian in going," but concluded that his brother was "too greatly needed in Washington."

Jacqueline suggested John Glenn, whom she thought "the most controlled person on earth": "Even Jack, who is highly self-controlled and has the ability to relax easily and to sleep when he wishes, to shrug off the problems of the world, seems fidgety and loose compared to Glenn." The press sent up trial balloons for John Kenneth Galbraith. Then Republicans cried out against sending a "Socialist" to Moscow. Kennedy told Bradlee that it would not be Galbraith: "We've got to get a man who speaks Russian. A little give and take is so important."

The Foreign Service was fighting hard to keep the prize post. Its consensus choice was Foy Kohler. The Attorney General told his brother that Kohler gave him "the creeps." He wasn't "the kind of a person who could really get anything done with the Russians."

Kohler was the kind of stubborn bureaucrat whose influence the brothers had been fighting to reduce. He lacked the social grace that made them feel simpatico with other Soviet specialists such as Harriman, Kennan, Bohlen, and Thompson. Before joining the diplomatic service in 1931, he had been a Toledo bank teller. Kohler privately considered Kennedy a bright but inexperienced creature of public relations and wondered whether the Republicans might use information on the President's women to defeat him in 1964.

As Charles Bartlett recalled, Kennedy finally concluded that "if you send people outside the Foreign Service to countries where there is serious business, that person is going to be screwed by the Foreign Service." Kohler won the appointment.

Over lunch that July, Frank Holeman asked Bolshakov what the Russians thought of Kohler's selection. It had been six months since Bolshakov told the Americans that Khrushchev was anxious to have a "known friend" of the President, not a career ambassador. Now Bolshakov complained that Foy Kohler was "no New Frontiersman."

He said he was returning home for summer leave at the start of August. Concealing his rivalry with Dobrynin, he added that he had wanted to go home earlier but his "good friend" the Ambassador had asked him to stay. He reported that he and Dobrynin talked often "about many things": they both agreed "that the President wants an accommodation with the Soviet Union."

Bolshakov asked whether Kennedy might be persuaded to send a message to a forthcoming disarmament meeting in Moscow. Holeman replied that the conference was "just a Communist operation." Bolshakov said all he wanted was greetings. He warned that if the President signed a congressional proclamation for Captive Nations Week, it "might affect talks on Berlin."*

At a Kremlin reception that month, Nina Khrushchev asked Jane Thompson why she and her husband were leaving Moscow. The Ambassador's wife reminded her that they had been there for five years: "The kids have to get back to American schools. They've never lived in their own country."

Mrs. Khrushchev almost certainly knew of the missiles planned for Cuba. She threw out an ominous hint: *"I would say that it is very important that you do not change ambassadors at this time."*

Puzzled, Mrs. Thompson replied, "Maybe my husband can do more things in Washington than he can in Moscow."

On Wednesday morning, July 25, Khrushchev received Thompson in the Kremlin for a valedictory talk and that evening gave the envoy and his wife an eight-course dinner on the lawn of his dacha.

He insisted that he wanted to get Berlin settled and resume the road to coexistence: the Soviet Union could win a peaceful competition, and he wanted to get on with it. He also wanted good relations because of the Chinese. He had a "genuine fear" that the United States military might one day seize control of the U.S. government and then "really let go" on Berlin. At they parted, he told his American friend, "Go home and tell President Kennedy what I said."

Poised to replace Bohlen as the Secretary of State's adviser on Soviet affairs, Thompson reported home that "seldom has there been such a lack of a general pattern in Kremlin politics as there has been in the last six months." On domestic issues, Khrushchev was in re-

---

*This was not the first time Khrushchev's objections to the resolution, signed annually by Presidents since 1950, had been made known. In 1959, when Nixon called on Khrushchev in Moscow a week after Eisenhower had signed the document, the Chairman launched a harangue, saying that he could not "understand why your Congress would adopt such a resolution on the eve of such an important state visit. . . . This resolution stinks. It stinks like fresh horseshit, and nothing smells worse than that."

treat. Spending cuts were announced for housing, education, and culture. Prices of meat and dairy products were raised by almost a third, provoking a riot near Rostov.

Walt Rostow explained the Chairman's international problems in an August memo called "Khrushchev at Bay." He noted that Khrushchev was stalled on Berlin and in the Congo. His Southeast Asian prospects had been eroded in Laos and by Kennedy's commitment to South Vietnam. Cuba had been isolated. The East Germans and Chinese were pressing for action. By shattering the myth of Soviet nuclear superiority, the West had compelled him to increase defense spending, retarding the Soviet economy.

Rostow argued that Khrushchev must be looking for a "quick success" that would enhance his power and prestige in Moscow and in the international Communist movement. It must cheaply redress the military balance of power, give him leverage on Berlin, and allow the diversion of Soviet resources to consumer goods. Rostow said the United States might be about to see "the greatest act of risk-taking since the war."*

Dean Acheson shared Rostow's sense of foreboding. He wrote Harry Truman, "I have a curious and apprehensive feeling as I watch JFK that he is a sort of Indian snake charmer. He toots away on his pipe and our problems sway back and forth around him in a trancelike manner, never approaching but never withdrawing; all are in a state of suspended life, including the pipe player, who lives only in his dream. Someday one of these snakes will wake up, and no one will be able even to run."

Khrushchev spent August sunning himself and swimming with his grandchildren on the Black sea, except for a brief return to Moscow to welcome a pair of cosmonauts back from space.†As he relaxed, the

---

*He was correct about almost everything but the site of Khrushchev's gamble, although Ray Cline of the CIA told him, "Maybe we're seeing it in Cuba." After a private talk two months later, C. L. Sulzberger recorded Rostow's insistence that "we are *not* concerned about Cuba and that it is not an ultimate danger." Rostow told Sulzberger that "despite Russia, Castro was being squeezed out and there was no denying that."
†The timing of the mission, three weeks before the first ships bearing nuclear missiles reached Cuba, suggested that once again Khrushchev had staged a space spectacular to give his country an added boost in prestige on the eve of a pivotal world event. If this was the Chairman's aim, he succeeded. At Kennedy's next press conference, the President was forced to concede, "We're trying to overtake them, and I think by the end of the decade we will, but we're in for some further periods when we are going

Kremlin announced that he was considering a fall trip to New York to attend the UN General Assembly and see Kennedy. What the Chairman may have had in mind was to announce the missiles in Cuba from the UN rostrum and then, with his hand strengthened, bargain with the President about the most pressing Cold War issues. He may have been planning to fly on to Havana, where he could bless the new missile sites and sign the new military pact with Castro.

Khrushchev's bargaining with Kennedy might have included some kind of arrangement to ensure that China and West Germany were barred from acquiring nuclear weapons. In late August, Dobrynin told Rusk that the Soviets "might be willing to sit down and work out an arrangement that would try to interfere with the transfer of nuclear weapons to presently non-nuclear powers."

That same month, according to Chinese documents, the Soviets secretly informed Peking that Rusk had proposed an agreement banning the nuclear powers from transferring weapons and know-how to other nations and that the Soviet Union had agreed. Peking replied by warning Moscow against infringement on Chinese rights.

Operation Mongoose had not flagged. In August, the Special Group pondered what it could do to foment an anti-Castro uprising by October. Robert Kennedy said, "I am in favor of pushing ahead rather than taking any step backward."

McCone cautioned that they must be prepared to support the forces in Cuba encouraged to rise up against Castro by all necessary measures, including military force. General Taylor agreed. Rusk argued in favor of trying to create friction between Castro and the old-line Cuban Communists. McNamara worried about the damage to the United States in the world if its hand were exposed.

According to Senate testimony in 1975, the group also discussed the "liquidation of Castro." By Richard Goodwin's account, McNamara said, "The only way to get rid of Castro is to kill him . . . and I really mean it." Goodwin recalled that Robert Kennedy did not object.

---

to be behind." In a Houston speech the following month, he tried to put a more positive face on the American position, saying that some forty of forty-five orbital satellites had been made by the United States, "and they were far more sophisticated and supplied far more knowledge to the people of the world than those of the Soviet Union."

McNamara testified that he had no recollection of the exchange.

Taylor told the President that month that they should aim at causing the failure of the Castro regime rather than its overthrow.
Kennedy approved a top-secret decree on Thursday, August 23, demanding immediate implementation of Mongoose "Phase B"—massive propaganda and other provocations to damage the Cuban economy and create friction between the Soviets and the Cubans. The CIA
contaminated Cuban sugar destined for the Soviet Union while a
freighter was docked in San Juan. Sabotage teams were sent into
Cuba.*

On Thursday, August 30, an American U-2 soared for nine minutes
across the southern tip of Soviet-held Sakhalin Island, a key American
intelligence target. The Pentagon told Rusk that the plane had blown
off course. Remembering the U-2 fiasco in 1960, he and the President
decided to "just tell the truth and thereby prevent the Soviets from
making a great issue out of it." They issued a statement.

As his nuclear missiles were moving toward Cuba, Khrushchev was
jittery. Moscow issued a protest of the U-2 incursion in language
which sounded like his own: "What is this, a rebirth of the former
government's bandit practice, which President Kennedy himself condemned? Or is it the provocational act of the U.S. military circles, who
want to create a new international conflict like the 1960 conflict and
to heat up the situation once again to the limit?"

Soviet ships were heading toward Cuba bearing thousands of combat troops, along with the concealed first elements of the missile force

---

*Arthur Schlesinger wrote the President on September 5 of his concern about "intelli-
gence reports describing plans for an uprising inside Cuba in the next few weeks.
. . . If . . . we went to its support, we would find ourselves in a difficult war in which,
so far as we can presently tell, the majority of Cubans (and very likely the majority of
the nations of the world) would be against us. . . . If we did not go to its support, we
would be charged with betraying our friends and letting them be slaughtered by a
brutal dictatorship. . . . Our failure to act in Cuba would be far worse than our failure
to act in Hungary in 1956. . . . It is indispensable to be sure that no one down the line
is encouraging the Cubans into rash action."

Kennedy wrote Schlesinger an icy reply, using language that seemed designed to
betray no presidential awareness of Mongoose. It said in total, "I read your memorandum of September 5th on Cuba. I know of no planned 'uprisings inside Cuba within
the next few weeks.' Would you send me the intelligence reports to which you refer.
In any case, I will discuss the matter with the CIA."

intended for the island—apparently twenty-four MRBM and sixteen IRBM launchers, each to be equipped with one nuclear warhead and two missiles.*

Most of the troops aboard the vessels had not been told where or why they were going. To preserve the mystery, their high commanders had equipped them with winter clothes and skis. Some were told the truth only when their ships passed the Rock of Gibraltar.

As Alexander Alexeyev recalled, Marshal Biryuzov believed that the missiles could be sent to Cuba without detection, "but unfortunately our military wanted quickly to fulfill the directive. Instead of ten vessels, they sent so many. Of course, any fool could see that something was not right." Sergo Mikoyan said that the mistake was "absolutely Russian. We had to do it speedily, so too many ships were used and the Americans noticed."

The CIA's aerial pictures of the Soviet ships showed that they had unusual crates on deck and oversized hatches. The vessels were riding high on the water, suggesting that their cargo was large and lightweight.

Reports from Cuban agents and refugees flowing into the CIA's JM/WAVE station suggested that the Soviets were building surface-to-air missile (SAM) sites and radar and communications facilities as part of a major air defense system. The CIA warned the White House that "clearly something new and different is taking place."

There had never been such an influx of Soviet personnel and equipment into a non-bloc country: "Together with the extraordinary Soviet bloc economic commitments made to Cuba in recent months, these developments amount to the most extensive campaign to bolster a non-bloc country ever undertaken by the U.S.S.R."

With his background in business, engineering, and defense, John McCone could not believe that the Soviets would build anything so expensive as an air defense system unless they had some excellent reason to stop American spy planes from flying over Cuba. He concluded that Khrushchev might be on the verge of installing nuclear missiles in Cuba.

McCone wrote out his suspicions in a memo to the President. Kennedy viewed McCone's warning in terms of the CIA Director's

---

*The range of the MRBMs has been variously estimated at from 200 to 1,200 miles, the IRBMs at 1,300 to 2,200 miles. The above rendering of the size of the force is based on General Dimitri Volkogonov's reading of Defense Ministry archives. Cuban sources in 1991 claimed that the force was to be upward of a hundred missiles:

fierce anticommunism. At the White House on Wednesday, August 22, Kennedy, Rusk, and McNamara all doubted that Khrushchev would take such a risk. Seven days later, a U-2 found two SAM sites in Cuba and six other locations where SAMs might be installed, as well as a "substantial" number of Soviet personnel and missile-equipped torpedo boats.

After more such flights, McCone's deputy, General Marshall Carter, privately told the Senate Foreign Relations Committee that there was a Soviet "crash program" to build as many as twenty-four SAM sites on Cuba. Since mid-July, about sixty-five Soviet bloc ships had been discovered sailing to the island: roughly ten were known to have carried military equipment and technicians.

Dean Rusk told the Senators that the Soviet buildup resembled the military aid Moscow gave to other non-Warsaw Pact nations such as Indonesia, Iraq, and Egypt. The situation would change "if the Soviets were to establish their own military base there—submarine base— or if there were to be established in Cuba ground-to-ground missiles that would directly threaten the continental United States or Cuba's neighbors in the Caribbean."

Marines in the Caribbean were rehearsing amphibious landings to topple an island dictator code-named Ortsac. To the island dictator in Havana whose name was Ortsac spelled backwards, these maneuvers made him all the more certain that the United States was about to invade.

In September, Senator Kenneth Keating and others charged that Khrushchev was installing MRBMs and IRBMs in Cuba and that the Kennedy administration was covering up secret evidence of the buildup.* The New York Republican gave interviews in the corridor outside his office, saying that he had "good reason to believe" that the Kennedy brothers had bugged his office and telephone system.

Richard Helms suspected that Keating was just spreading rumors: "In those days, leaking by the intelligence community just wasn't done. . . . Keating probably just took a flier. If it's wrong, you just say, 'I was misinformed. Outrageous!'" Asked later by a friend where he thought Keating got his information, the President replied that there were "fifty thousand-odd Cuban refugees in this country, all living for the day when we will go to war with Cuba and all putting out this kind of stuff."

---

*In the latter charge, these critics may have shared Khrushchev's judgment of the President's political timidity.

Other Republicans did not need to believe Keating's charges to be angry about the Soviet buildup in Cuba. Richard Nixon and Senators Barry Goldwater, Strom Thurmond of North Carolina, John Tower of Texas, and Hugh Scott all demanded that Kennedy order a naval blockade of Cuba to prevent further Soviet military shipments. Nixon warned that the five thousand Soviet troops known to be in Cuba were a "clear and present danger" to the United States.*

The President asked for and won congressional authority to call up 150,000 reservists if necessary to defend American interests in response to the Soviet buildup in Cuba. But when he spoke in September at Rice University in Houston, Cuban refugees displayed signs: "The Cubans remind you Cuba is still alone and we remind you of your promises." A light plane circled overhead trailing a banner: ENFORCE THE MONROE DOCTRINE.†

Kennedy had deferred action on issues ranging from civil rights and poverty to China and Vietnam, complaining that he had been thwarted by his slim 1960 mandate and the power balance in Congress.‡ Democrats controlled the Senate by 65–35 and the House by 263–174, but he was obstructed in the House by conservative Southern committee chairmen, in the Senate by a coalition of Republicans and Southern Democrats. Now he hoped to reverse the usual pattern for off-year elections by which the party in the White House usually lost an average of forty seats in the House and Senate.

Coming at the outset of the 1962 congressional campaign, the outcry over Cuba hit the President where it hurt. The *New Republic* gibed that the Kennedy administration was taking its cue from the Rodgers and Hammerstein hit *The King and I:* "I hold my head erect / And whistle a happy tune / So no one will suspect / I'm afraid."

---

*Nixon's Cuban-born, Castro-hating friend Bebe Rebozo sent him an article reporting that the President considered the Cuban issue above politics: "I just can't read the paper more than once a week anymore—this'll hold me for another week at least."

†The Houston FBI office heard in advance of the Cuban picketing from a confidential source and cabled J. Edgar Hoover that the demonstrators were said to be "good people but are fanatical against Castro." Immigration records were searched to ensure that they were no danger to the President. As Kennedy entered the stadium, a seventeen-year-old boy decided to "test" the Secret Service by pulling from his shirt a convincing replica of a .45-caliber Colt automatic pistol. Secret Service agents and Houston police detectives grabbed him. An FBI man recorded, "This boy was questioned for two hours and then sent home after a lengthy lecture."

‡In 1960, for the first time in the century, the party that regained the White House failed to increase its strength in Congress. Kennedy ran further behind the candidates for Congress on his ticket than any President elected since the start of the two-party system. Many Democrats were certain that they had helped Kennedy more than he helped them. This did not increase his popularity on the Hill.

* * *

Robert and Ethel Kennedy had become close to John McCone since his appointment to the CIA in September 1961 and the death of his beloved wife, Rosemary, three months later. As the Attorney General recalled, "He liked Ethel very much because when his wife died, Ethel went over and stayed with him. So he had a good deal of feeling for us. . . . But he liked one person more, and that was John McCone."

With his rimless eyeglasses, white hair, roseate complexion, and three-piece suits, McCone looked like the Republican tycoon he was. An aide called him "something of a snob and a puritan," the kind of man who "demanded the best room in the best hotel." He was an Irish Catholic who in 1958 had attended Pope Pius XII's funeral as Eisenhower's representative, the kind of Catholic of whom Kennedy said that, in the crunch, money counted more than religion.

Born in 1902 to an affluent San Francisco Republican family, McCone had an engineering degree from the University of California. After working as a riveter, surveyor, and construction manager, he became executive vice president of the Consolidated Steel Corporation at age thirty-one. He was a founder of the Bechtel-McCone-Parsons Corporation, which designed and built oil refineries, factories, and power plants in the Americas and the Middle East.

During the war, he helped to form the Seattle-Tacoma Corporation, which built merchant ships for the United States and Britain.* Truman appointed him to a postwar commission on air warfare and as Under Secretary of the Air Force. In 1956, when ten Cal Tech scientists endorsed Adlai Stevenson's test ban proposal, McCone, a trustee, complained that they had been "taken in" by Soviet propaganda. He denied the allegation that he tried to have the professors fired.

In 1958, Eisenhower appointed McCone chairman of his Atomic Energy Commission, a striking example of his tendency to put men who did not share his ambitions to relax the Cold War into positions from which they could sabotage his purposes. When McCone fought

---

*In 1946, Ralph Casey of the Congress's General Accounting Office castigated McCone and his colleagues in public testimony as war profiteers who had made $44 million on an investment of $100,000: "At no time in the history of American business, whether in wartime or peacetime, have so few men made so much money with so little risk—and all at the expense of the taxpayers, not only of his generation but of future generations." McCone disputed the figure, claiming that the initial investment had been over $7 million and that the government had retrieved 95 percent of the profits in taxes.

the President's efforts for a test ban treaty, Eisenhower told Christian Herter to remind him that he was "an operator, not a foreign policy maker."

Squeamish about firing his own appointees, Eisenhower allowed McCone to lead the opposition to a test ban from within his own administration. He publicly denounced the idea as a "national peril" and threatened to resign if it came to pass. Before the U-2 affair killed Eisenhower's test ban efforts, his science adviser, George Kistiakowsky, complained in his diary that McCone was "maneuvering public opinion, including the Senate, so that the President will have a very difficult time getting a treaty ratified."

In November 1960, McCone voted for Nixon, an old California friend, and cabled the loser, "Let's look forward to 1964." During the summer of 1961, he lampooned the "Phi Beta Kappas" surrounding Kennedy and wrote Nixon that he was "deeply concerned" that Khrushchev believed the President would not use nuclear weapons to defend Berlin.

McCone was not Kennedy's first choice to succeed Allen Dulles. He had half seriously pondered sending his brother to Langley but knew it would scarcely be credible to place him in charge of operations of which presidential knowledge was supposed to be plausibly deniable.

The President's telephone call interrupted McCone as he was playing golf with Nixon in Los Angeles. Eager to acquire conservative Republican cover for controversial policies, Kennedy felt that McCone would deflect opposition to his intention to reduce the CIA's size and autonomy in the wake of the Cuban failure.*

As a Senator, he had watched McCone operate on the Hill and was impressed by his knowledge of Soviet missile strength. He considered him a quiet, keen, and steady manager who would ensure that covert operations were subordinated to his foreign policy and "preceded by more planning and less advertising than preceded the Bay of Pigs."

Before announcing McCone's appointment, Kennedy consulted almost none of his aides out of fear that they would undermine it. O'Donnell was already indignant that prizes like Defense and Treasury and the embassies in London and Paris had gone to people who

---

*As with Dillon, Eisenhower disliked the idea of his former official being used to provide Republican respectability for Kennedy's aims. He wrote McCone, "This morning's news says that you have accepted the post of Director of the CIA. As you know, I was not in favor of it, but certainly I want you to know that I shall be wishing you every possible success in the post."

had nothing to do with the President's domestic political constituency. A Washington columnist warned Roger Hilsman that "McCone is an alley fighter who will stop at nothing."

When McCone moved into Dulles's gleaming new white CIA headquarters at the end of November 1961, he banned the intercom that allowed senior officers to interrupt the Director at his desk and ordered that the doorway to the office of his newly appointed deputy, General Marshall Carter, be sealed overnight. (Carter mounted a replica of a hand on his side of the newly paneled wall as if it had been sliced off by the closure.)

Anyone who expected the new Director to preside over the CIA's dissolution was soon corrected. McCone swiftly replaced his inherited deputies, as well as most of his division chiefs. He quashed the recommendation of the President's newly revived board of outside intelligence advisers that his job be absorbed into the White House. He battled McNamara for influence over espionage by planes and satellites, better logistical support, and top-secret Pentagon data on American strategic capabilities and force dispositions.

When the CIA Inspector General, Lyman Kirkpatrick, drafted a highly critical Bay of Pigs postmortem, McCone reputedly destroyed most or all of the copies and kept the original in his own locked files, where it could do no damage. The launching of Operation Mongoose the month of McCone's arrival was a vote of presidential confidence in the CIA and its new Director.

McCone's success in winning Kennedy's confidence had no little to do with the close relationship he quickly formed with the Attorney General. The new Director did not interfere with Robert's direct communication with CIA officials and covert operators on the second and third echelons of the Agency. Robert may have known better than to inform McCone if he knew of the CIA's efforts to assassinate Castro. Deputy Director Ray Cline recalled that McCone "at all times expressed total disapproval of consideration of assassination as a CIA covert action, opposing it on both personal moral and political grounds."*

McCone never developed the faith in Kennedy's leadership that

---

*When the possibility of murdering Castro was raised at the Special Group (Augmented) meeting in August 1962, McCone evidently opposed it. He told McNamara later of his worry that he might be excommunicated were it ever known that he had entertained the idea of assassination.

Douglas Dillon, another Eisenhower Republican, did. His Air Force and AEC background made him skeptical of the President's commitment to flexible response and a test ban treaty.

Unlike most of those around Kennedy, McCone continued to believe that tiny changes in the nuclear balance with the Russians were crucial: a nation did not simply need a minimum number of warheads and missiles or bombers for deterrence. The more it had, the stronger its military and political position. Convinced that Khrushchev felt the same way, he was more receptive than Kennedy's other advisers to the possibility that the Chairman might try to correct his deficiency by sending nuclear missiles into Cuba.

In late August 1962, McCone married a Seattle widow, Theiline Pigott, who commanded an even larger shipping fortune than his. Despite his worries about missiles in Cuba, he sailed for a honeymoon in the south of France. Stopping in Paris, he conveyed his suspicions over lunch with the visiting Roswell Gilpatric.

From his honeymoon cottage on Cap Ferrat, McCone every few days cabled Langley, evidently demanding more probing assessment of the possibility that the new SAM buildup on Cuba foretold nuclear missiles from Khrushchev: "Why would they be putting all these SAM sites around the island unless they were putting something in there to worry us?"*

* * *

---

*Stung by the notion that his brother had ignored McCone's prescient advice on the most pivotal issue of the Kennedy Presidency, Robert Kennedy inaccurately told an oral history interviewer in 1965, "As far as ever putting anything in writing, as far as ever communicating his thought to President Kennedy or to anybody else, he didn't. And to indicate the fact that he wasn't really concerned about it himself, he went to Europe for a honeymoon for a month during that period of time. So if he was so concerned and thought that something should be done, number one, he should have written and told the President, number two, he should not have gone off to Europe for a month during that critical period of time. . . . He should have come home and worked at it, not be sending a letter from Cannes, France [sic]."

In *Thirteen Days*, written in 1967 for publication in *McCall's* the following year and published as a book in 1969 after his death, Robert went so far as to claim that "no official within the government had ever suggested to President Kennedy that the Russian buildup in Cuba would include missiles."

Later historians who took *Thirteen Days* as gospel neglected the fact that one reason for its writing was to bolster Robert Kennedy's credentials as a potential President. In 1968 Kenneth O'Donnell evidently chided Robert for taking credit for himself in the memoir that more properly belonged to the President. Robert replied, "Well, *he's* not running for President this year, and *I am.*"

Fearing that McCone might be right, Robert Kennedy conceded that "Cuba obtaining missiles from the Soviet Union would create a major political problem here." On Tuesday, September 4, at the Justice Department, he told Dobrynin that the President was "deeply concerned" about the amount of military equipment going to Cuba.

The Ambassador told him that Khrushchev had asked him to assure the President that there would be "no ground-to-ground missiles or offensive missiles placed in Cuba." The Chairman would do "nothing to disrupt the relationship of our two countries during this period prior to the election." He liked the President and did not want to embarrass him.

Kennedy replied that Khrushchev had "a very strange way of showing his admiration." Skeptical about Dobrynin's assurances, he persuaded the President to issue a public warning to the Soviets that if the United States ever found "offensive ground-to-ground missiles" in Cuba, "the gravest issues would arise."

Bundy explained years later, "We did it because of the requirements of domestic politics, not because we seriously believed that the Soviets would do anything as crazy from our standpoint as placement of Soviet nuclear weapons in Cuba." Bundy said it had "never occurred to us" to issue such a warning earlier.

Sorensen much later reasoned that by saying he would accept large-scale Soviet military aid to Cuba but not offensive missiles, "the President drew the line precisely where he thought the Soviets were not and would not be. . . . If we had known that the Soviets were putting forty missiles in Cuba, we might under this hypothesis have drawn the line at one hundred, and said with great fanfare that we would absolutely not tolerate the presence of more than one hundred missiles in Cuba."

Kennedy therefore issued a warning that was too late to stop Khrushchev's Cuba operation and so precise that it caused him to forfeit the option of responding to the discovery of missiles in Cuba with anything less than a full-fledged confrontation with the Soviet Union. Had the President issued such a warning five months earlier or not painted himself into a corner now, history might have been different.

Dobrynin asked Sorensen for an urgent meeting. After checking with Kennedy, the aide went to the Soviet Embassy on Thursday, September 6. Lunching with Dobrynin a fortnight earlier, Sorensen had tried to dispel any Soviet assumption that the congressional campaign would inhibit the President from responding to "any new pressures on Berlin."

The Ambassador now said that his report of their luncheon had brought a personal message from Chairman Khrushchev, which he read aloud: "Nothing will be undertaken before the American congressional elections that could complicate the international situation or aggravate the tension in the relations between our two countries . . . provided there are no actions taken on the other side which would change the situation."

If Khrushchev should come to the United States that fall, "this would be possible only in the second half of November. The Chairman does not wish to become involved in your internal political affairs." Sorensen replied that Khrushchev's message seemed "both hollow and tardy." The buildup in Cuba had "already aggravated world tensions and caused turmoil in our internal political affairs."

After the meeting, Sorensen told Kennedy that Dobrynin had "neither contradicted nor confirmed my reference to large numbers of Soviet military personnel, electronic equipment, and missile preparations. He repeated several times, however, that they had done nothing new or extraordinary in Cuba . . . and that he stood by his assurances that all the steps were defensive in nature and did not represent any threat to the security of the United States."*

By signaling the President that the Soviet Union would not do anything to harm him until after his elections, Khrushchev was not only trying to throw Kennedy off guard but he may have been encouraging the President, if the missiles were found before November, to explain them away to his own generals as purely defensive and conceal them from the public until the balloting was done.

In Pitsunda, Khrushchev received Secretary of the Interior Stewart Udall, who was touring with an American delegation on electric power. Wearing a collarless embroidered white shirt, the Chairman said he hoped to see President Kennedy soon, perhaps in the United States in November.

As usual, he combined geniality with threat: the President must agree to a Berlin settlement and treat the Soviet Union as an equal. Before long he should come to visit and be sure to bring Mrs. Kennedy. The Soviet people would give him a warm welcome. They could go bear-hunting together. He gave Udall a traditional drinking horn and a case of wine for the President.†

---

*Dobrynin said essentially the same thing to Stevenson.
†The Secret Service barred the President from drinking the wine. FBI laboratories tested it for "anti-personnel drugs which cause a personality change" and for "volatile

The next day, Khrushchev saw Robert Frost, who had been traveling with Udall. At Kennedy's inauguration, the blinding sunlight had
memorably kept the old poet from reading a preface hailing a new
"golden age of poetry and power," but he had managed to recite
"The Gift Outright," amended for the occasion.*

In July 1962, the President had asked Frost to represent the United
States in a Soviet cultural exchange. The eighty-eight-year-old poet
had replied, "How like you to take the chance of sending anyone like
me over there affinitizing with the Russians. . . . Great times to be
alive, aren't they?"

Frost had felt insulted when he was not asked to accompany Udall
to Pitsunda, but when Khrushchev's invitation came, he felt wobbly
and unwell. Flying to Sochi, he was put to bed in a state guesthouse.
After sending over his own doctor, Khrushchev arrived and pulled a
chair up next to the poet's bed: he had better follow doctor's orders
if he was going to live to be a hundred!

Frost implored him to avoid petty squabbles in favor of a "noble
rivalry" between Russia and the United States. When Frost suggested
reuniting Berlin, Khrushchev warned that in less than thirty minutes,
Soviet missiles could blast all of Europe to smithereens. The United
States should sign a German peace treaty: the President himself had
said that he wished to do so but couldn't "because of conditions at
home."

Khrushchev said that the United States and Western Europe resembled Tolstoy's adage—too old and infirm to make love but still with
the desire. Frost chuckled: this might be true for him and the Chairman, but the United States was too young to worry about that. All
Khrushchev had to do was offer a simple solution on Berlin and the
United States would accept it. The Chairman said, "You have the soul
of a poet."

At a press conference in Moscow, affected by illness, travel, and his
own prejudices, Frost recalled Khrushchev's comment about the West
being too infirm to make love and announced instead that the Chairman had called the Americans "too liberal to fight." Republicans
quickly adopted this crack to embarrass Kennedy, who privately

---

poisons, methyl alcohol, cyanides, acetone and formaldehyde, unusual residues of
metals and metalloids, the barbiturates and other acid drugs, basic drugs such as
strychnine, the amphetamines, alkaloids of opium, and others." None were found.
*During the Eisenhower years, when Frost was not invited to dinner at the White
House, he said, "Do you know why they don't invite me? They are too honest. They
are too decent honest to pretend they are interested in what I am interested in."

snapped, "You can't believe what Frost tells you. He is not very reliable as a reporter."

On Tuesday, September 11, TASS responded to the President's warning against ground-to-ground missiles in Cuba: Soviet missiles were so powerful that there was "no need" to locate them in any other country. The armaments being sent to Cuba "are designed exclusively for defensive purposes."

At his Wednesday news conference, Kennedy read out a more specific warning. If the Communist buildup in Cuba interfered with U.S. security, if Cuba tried to export aggression by force or threat of force "against any nation in this hemisphere" or became "an offensive military base of significant capacity" for the Soviet Union, then the United States would do "whatever must be done" to protect its own security and that of its allies.

In Moscow, Khrushchev told an official Austrian visitor that the Soviet Union would fight any U.S. blockade of Cuba. As the Chairman certainly expected, the message was relayed to Washington. Kaysen gave it to the President under the heading, "More rude noises from Khrushchev." Bundy advised Kennedy that he "may need to put some fairly tough talk back on both the public and private wires."

The Soviet freighter *Omsk* reached Cuba on September 8 with its secret shipment of MRBMs. In the dark, under the baleful stare of KGB guards, Soviet drivers hauled the first of the dismantled launchers out of Havana.

A U-2 had soared over Cuba on September 5 but found no new evidence of MRBMs or IRBMs.* For more than two years, the spy planes had raced over Cuba about twice a month. American satellites were of little help because they were not targeted on Cuba. The intelligence community's Committee on Overhead Reconnaissance (COMOR) now asked for much more frequent spy flights.

On September 9, Mainland Chinese SAMs downed a Nationalist Chinese-owned U-2. With similar SAMs going up on Cuba, this incident suggested that the Americans had better be more cautious about overflights of the island. As with Eisenhower and the U-2 missions

---

*It did return with pictures of a MiG-21 supersonic fighter parked in front of four shipping crates apparently containing additional MiGs, as well as more SAMs.

over Russia from 1956 to early 1960, each proposed run over Cuba was remanded to Kennedy.

On September 15, the Soviet freighter *Poltava* evidently brought the second shipment of MRBMs. Construction of launching sites began, but Washington did not find out. During a U-2 flight two days later, already delayed for nine days by bad weather, American cameras were shrouded by cloud cover.

Reports kept pouring into JM/WAVE in Miami. A subagent in Cuba had seen a missile segment dragged past his house corresponding to CIA profiles of Soviet MRBMs, but the report did not reach Washington until late September. Hundreds of other reports were mostly rumors and error.*

On September 19, a special CIA estimate advised the President that Khrushchev might wish to send offensive missiles to Cuba in order to bolster Soviet subversion of Latin America or a new move against Berlin, but the odds were low. The Chairman knew how violently the United States would react to such a discovery. MRBMs and IRBMs had often been reported in Poland, Albania, and other bloc nations: all had been false alarms. Drawing on advice from Bohlen and Thompson, the estimate stated that keeping nuclear weapon systems within Soviet borders was a firm Soviet policy.

McCone had demanded that the estimate be revoked because it did not consider how much Khrushchev's bargaining power would be increased by strategic missiles in Cuba. He failed. Writing to Nixon, who was running for governor of California, he said, "We are back in Washington after a very pleasant trip to southern France, and Theiline is attempting to accustom herself to living in the capital. . . . I wish you every success, Dick, and I'm confident of your victory in November."

On Tuesday, September 25, Castro announced that the Soviets would build a Cuban fishing port at Mariel. Republicans charged that the port could turn out to be a base for Soviet nuclear submarines.

Through these weeks, partly to throw Kennedy off guard, Khrushchev continued their secret correspondence, holding out the possibility of a test ban. Later, after he knew about the missiles in Cuba,

---

*A CIA postmortem later found that of more than two hundred reports by Cuban agents about Soviet offensive missiles on the island, only six were accurate. Rusk recalled that many were missightings of SAMs: "When you look at a surface-to-air missile as a layman not accustomed to missiles, you think you're looking at a hell of a missile."

the President compared this duplicity to that of Japanese negotiators in Washington in December 1941 as Tokyo prepared to bomb Pearl Harbor.

At Geneva in late August, the United States and Britain had proposed two draft treaties—a comprehensive ban, requiring monitoring stations and on-site inspections on the soil of each signatory, and a partial treaty banning all but underground tests, which would require less intrusive verification.

On Tuesday, September 4, Khrushchev wrote Kennedy that he was willing to accept a limited test ban in the "immediate future," as long as the agreement included France.

The President replied on September 15 with a private message delivered by the Attorney General: "I think we should make a serious effort to work out such an agreement in time to meet the target date of January 1, 1963. . . . We can then look at the problem of continued testing underground. . . . In your message you mention the role that France should play. . . . For its part, the United States would work in close consultation with France and would hope that France would adhere to the treaty."

Replying on Friday, September 28, Khrushchev agreed to the New Year's 1963 target date for reaching a test ban. He may have expected to discuss the matter with Kennedy in the United States in November, after he revealed his successful installation of missiles in Cuba.

In late September, avoiding known SAM sites, U-2s twice flew over eastern Cuba, the Isle of Pines, and a portion of western Cuba. These were supplemented by other missions along the island's periphery.

Photointerpreters studying the pictures of the SAM installations noticed the same trapezoidal pattern that U-2 cameras had found around missile bases in the Soviet Union. The center of the trapezoid was San Cristóbal in western Cuba. Two U-2 flights over eastern Cuba during the first week of October found no strategic missiles. The President ordered a dangerous run over western Cuba, but for days bad weather kept the spy planes grounded.

Bolshakov was on home leave in the Soviet Union. By his account, Khrushchev and Mikoyan called him in. The Chairman asked him to tell President Kennedy that he was a "man of his word" and that his "word could be relied upon." He was "not pleased" by the President's request for congressional authority to call up 150,000 reservists. The Soviet Union was doing only what it was "absolutely obliged" to do in Cuba. Castro was being sent only "defensive weapons."

Interjecting, Mikoyan told Bolshakov to tell the President that the Soviet Union was sending Castro only "short-range missiles to be used against airplanes."

Khrushchev went on to say that Kennedy should be told that he was "in a calm and moderate mood." There was no reason for the United States to be concerned about Cuba. This was "the time to lower the temperature and calm the atmosphere and not to raise tensions." He and his colleagues did not like the American talk about invading Cuba. Bolshakov should remind the President "that he said at Vienna that we are equal nations. If we are equal, we must respect each other's rights."

Bolshakov penciled the message into his small blue notebook and flew back to Washington.*

The Chairman and Mikoyan may have chosen their words carefully to try to stick to the literal truth. By Khrushchev's lights, only defensive weapons *were* going to Cuba. When Mikoyan said that Castro was getting only short-range anti-aircraft weapons, he might have argued that he was not lying: the MRBMs and IRBMs were being sent to Cuba, but since they remained in Soviet possession they were not being given to Castro.

Nevertheless Khrushchev certainly knew that he was sending Kennedy a message that the President would in time consider a deliberate lie. He may have convinced himself that the President might tolerate the deception as a tool of diplomacy. Perhaps he comforted himself with the notion that he had gotten away with deceiving Kennedy before, with the assurance that he would be serious about a test ban treaty at Vienna, and by insisting at the summit that the Soviet Union would not be the first to resume testing.

---

*Charles Bartlett recalled that during this period he was contacted by Dobrynin's subordinate Alexander Zinchuk, whom he thought of as "a very close friend." Over lunch, Zinchuk said he'd just come back from vacation in Moscow. He said that before he left, the Chairman called him in and asked if he could convey a message to President Kennedy: "The message was that he understood the problems of the congressional elections. He understood that the President would be preoccupied . . . and wanted him to know that he would do nothing during this period that would in any way divert him or create problems for him." Bartlett gave Khrushchev's message to the President. Asked years later if he might have been confusing Zinchuk with Bolshakov, he insisted that it was Zinchuk whom he had seen. If Bartlett's account is correct, Khrushchev was taking extraordinary care to ensure that his message reached Kennedy.

More likely he felt that the risk of a bold-faced lie to the President was worth the chance that it might throw the Americans off the trail of his Cuban venture or encourage Kennedy to defer a missile crisis until after the November elections.

The State Department sent the White House a pedestrian draft of a presidential thank-you note for the wines and drinking horn Khrushchev had sent back with Udall. Bundy called the text "preposterous." Kennedy decided to send no letter at all.

He continued to pursue Khrushchev's apparent interest in a limited test ban. On Monday, October 8, he wrote the Chairman, "I am glad that we can continue to use this channel as a means of communicating privately and frankly." He and Khrushchev were "within striking distance" of a limited ban: "I believe that we should keep at it to see if we cannot promptly reach the understanding which the world wants and needs."

The New York lawyer James Donovan was on his way to Havana to bargain with Castro for release of the more than a thousand Cuban exile invaders jailed after the Bay of Pigs.

In May 1961, the dictator had offered to exchange the prisoners for an "indemnity" of five hundred D-8 Super Caterpillar bulldozers. Around this time, the President told O'Donnell that he had not slept the night before: "I was thinking about those guys in prison down in Cuba. I'm willing to make any kind of a deal with Castro to get them out of there." He asked Eleanor Roosevelt, Walter Reuther, Milton Eisenhower, and George Romney to lead a fund-raising committee.

Since the bulldozers specified by Castro seemed more suited for building airfields and missile bases, the panel offered farm tractors instead. The "Tractors for Freedom" Committee was denounced for trading in human lives, surrendering to Communist ransom demands, and violating the Logan Act forbidding private intervention in American diplomacy. The publicist William Safire wrote Nixon, for whom he had drafted campaign speeches, "Millions for defense but not one damn penny for tribute." The committee disbanded.

When Castro's demand for $28 million was refused, he held a four-day show trial in March 1962. At Robert Kennedy's behest, Richard Goodwin persuaded the Brazilian president, João Goulart, to tell Castro that if the prisoners were executed, Americans would force their President to take strong action against Cuba. The Cubans sentenced the exiles to thirty years at hard labor and increased their ransom demand to $62 million.*

The Attorney General wondered how the United States could "send $60 million worth of equipment to Cuba with part of our population and a number of political leaders calling for an invasion of Cuba." At his suggestion, Donovan was hired to bargain with the Castro regime on behalf of a newly established "Cuban Families Committee," whose sponsors included Richard Cardinal Cushing, Lucius Clay, Lee Radziwill, and the television host Ed Sullivan. By mid-September, Donovan had persuaded Castro to accept medicine and drugs instead of cash.

In October, nominated as Democratic candidate against Senator Jacob Javits of New York, Donovan arranged to see Castro once again. On Monday evening, the eighth, Bundy asked Richard Helms to send word to Donovan via Robert Kennedy or General Carter that "before Donovan signs on, another hard effort should be made to include the twenty-two Americans in the deal." This referred to U.S. citizens in Castro's prisons. Helms replied, "I got the message."

Dean Rusk advised the President that Khrushchev may have intended his buildup in Cuba as a diversion from a new Soviet move against Berlin. The President sent for the Pentagon's large package of contingency plans for a new Berlin crisis. As Sorensen recalled, he felt that Berlin had "every chance of becoming very alive."

On Wednesday, October 10, a reporter asked Rusk why the administration had not discussed the military buildup in Cuba with the Russians. Rusk replied that the Soviets would then raise the issue of American nuclear weapons in Turkey and support for Iran, two countries on their border, just as Cuba was on the periphery of the United States.

Three days later, CIA photointerpreters concluded that ten huge crates photographed on the decks of the Soviet ship *Kasimov* near Cuba exactly resembled crates containing Il-28 nuclear light bombers that had been spotted in Egypt and Indonesia. The Il-28's radius was perhaps six hundred miles—too short to strike Atlanta or New Orleans, but enough to reach Tampa and thus considered deployable as an offensive weapon against the United States. McCone tried and failed to reach Robert Kennedy.

Chester Bowles, now an Ambassador-at-Large, was leaving for

---

*In April, Castro released sixty of the sick and wounded, announcing that he would collect his payment of $2.9 million for them later.

lunch with Dobrynin when his aide Thomas Hughes told him about the Il-28s: "We just got the most shocking news here that the Russians are really moving stuff into Cuba." Bowles told Dobrynin, "We have reports that you are introducing offensive weapons into Cuba." Hadn't Dobrynin read the President's September warnings? "Don't play around. If this is true, and I think it is true, it's absolute folly. . . . Our relations will be in grave trouble."

Looking surprised, Dobrynin insisted that the report was untrue. He was "fully aware" of how risky such a move would be. Bowles replied that if Dobrynin was wrong, he wouldn't be the first or last ambassador in history to be deceived by his own government.

Dobrynin no doubt sent a report on the conversation to Khrushchev, who by now was back in Moscow. The Chairman probably assumed that what Bowles told Dobrynin had been carefully worked out beforehand with Kennedy.

The President's September warnings had referred to offensive weapons of "significant capacity." Since the Il-28s were unlikely to be so considered, Khrushchev may have taken Bowles's words to mean that the United States had discovered the nuclear missiles moving into Cuba. If so, Khrushchev may have wondered why Kennedy's initial response to this discovery was merely a mild, private protest by a second-level diplomat known to have lost his confidence.

Whether or not in reaction to Dobrynin's cable, Khrushchev evidently ordered his forces to speed up their work on the missile sites in Cuba—even before the SAM defenses were completed. At a New York hotel, Gromyko saw the Cuban President, Osvaldo Dorticos, who had flown in for the UN General Assembly. Worried about American eavesdropping devices that might pick up discussion of the missiles in Cuba, they scribbled messages to each other on slips of paper.

On Sunday afternoon, October 14, Bundy was questioned on ABC's *Issues and Answers* about the buildup in Cuba. He said there was "no present evidence," nor was there any likelihood that the Soviets and Cubans would try to install a "major offensive capability."

He said that whether a gun was offensive or defensive depended "a little bit on which end you are on." MiG fighters and other planes had a "certain marginal capability for moving against the United States. But I think we have to bear in mind the relative magnitudes here. . . . So far, everything that has been delivered in Cuba falls within the categories of aid which the Soviet Union has provided, for example, to neutral states like Egypt and Indonesia, and I should not be surprised to see additional military assistance of that sort."

* * *

At the Kremlin that evening, Khrushchev and most of the Presidium held a farewell dinner for the Chinese Ambassador, Liu Hsiao, departing after eight years in Moscow. The envoy had recently confided to Peking that Khrushchev had found an ingenious "new way" to solve the Berlin Crisis. In the blackness outside the windows, the first snowflakes of the season were falling. The Chairman raised a glass to "unbreakable and eternal Soviet-Chinese friendship."

That evening in New York, on the thirty-fourth floor of the Carlyle, Kennedy held his hastily called meeting with Adlai Stevenson and his private dinner with his Harvard roommate Congressman Torbert Macdonald before *Air Force One* soared at midnight to Washington, where the government's best photointerpreters were spinning through the U-2 film shot that morning over western Cuba.

The next day, the photoanalysts alerted McCone's executive assistant, Walter Elder, who telephoned his boss: "That which you alone said would happen, did."

CHAPTER

16

"He's the One Playing God"

AROUND THE CABINET TABLE, TUESDAY, OCTOBER 16, AT NOON, with the reels of the President's secret tape recorder turning and microphones hidden in the curtains, Kennedy and his advisers stared at the two-day-old aerial pictures of MRBM sites in Cuba.

The enlargements were propped up on an easel in front of the fireplace, above which loomed a Stuart portrait of George Washington. The President summoned his photographer, Captain Cecil Stoughton, to capture the meeting for history. Roswell Gilpatric noted that Kennedy was "very clipped, very tense. I don't recall a time when I saw him more preoccupied and less given to any light touch at all."

Just before this meeting, Kennedy had called Bohlen to his office and told him the secret that Bundy had confided to him in his bedroom after breakfast. Bohlen thought it "almost purely a Khrushchev

431

venture." He found the President "absolutely determined" that the missiles would leave Cuba.

Dean Rusk had learned of the missiles on Monday night. Now he told the men in the Cabinet Room, "We, all of us, had not really believed the Soviets could carry this far. . . . Now I do think we have to set in motion a chain of events that will eliminate this base. I don't think we can sit still. The questioning becomes whether we do it by sudden, unannounced strike of some sort—or we build up the crisis to the point where the other side has to consider very seriously about giving in, or even the Cubans themselves take some . . . action on this."*

Throughout the secret meetings on Mongoose, Rusk had asked for covert action to promote a split between the Russians and Cubans. Now he suggested using some channel to tell Castro privately "that Cuba is being victimized here, and that the Soviets are preparing Cuba for destruction or betrayal."

The Secretary noted that on Monday the *New York Times* had reported that the Russians might wish to trade Cuba for Berlin: "This ought to be brought to Castro's attention. It ought to be said to Castro that . . . the time has now come when he must take the interests of the Cuban people—must now break clearly with the Soviet Union, prevent this missile base from becoming operational."†

Rusk said he was "very conscious" that "there is no such thing . . . as unilateral action by the United States. It's so heavily involved with forty-two allies and confrontation in many places that any action that

---

*This quotation and those that follow from the Cabinet Room meetings of this date are taken from transcripts made from the President's secret tapes and from those audio copies of the actual recordings that are available. In the case of the latter, what appears in the transcript has been very occasionally revised in slight degree to conform more exactly with the audiotapes. Most of the "uhs" and "ums" have been omitted.
†Someone wrote a draft of a twenty-four-hour ultimatum to "Mr. F. C.," saying that "to serve their interests," the Soviets had "justified the Western Hemisphere countries in making an attack on Cuba which would lead to the overthrow of your regime." Unless the United States "can receive assurances from you . . . by public or private channels that you will not tolerate this misuse of Cuban territory . . . then we and our friends shall, of course, have to act."
An accompanying note conceded that Castro was "unlikely on short notice to be able to accustom himself to the idea of help from the U.S. for any internal struggles a favorable response might cause. We must, of course, be prepared for a 4-hour TV appearance, revealing and denouncing our approach. But it seems likely that he is aware that Soviet offers of support have not been made in categorical terms and that his internal position is not one of great strength. . . . Presumably the old-line Communist elements would plump for a flat rejection of the U.S. approach. This might lead to a major flare-up between the two groups, of considerable potential advantage to us."

we take will greatly increase the risks of direct action involving our other alliances and our other forces in other parts of the world."

Aside from notifying Castro, they had two broad alternatives: "One, the quick strike. The other, to alert our allies *and* Mr. Khrushchev that there is an utterly serious crisis in the making here. . . . Mr. Khrushchev may not himself really understand that or believe that at this point." The situation "could well lead to general war." They must "do what has to be done" in light of the President's September warning against offensive weapons in Cuba. But they must try to settle the problem "before it gets too hard."

McNamara said that any air strike against the missiles had to be scheduled before they became operational. If the missiles were launched, "there is almost certain to be chaos in part of the East Coast or the area in a radius of six hundred to a thousand miles from Cuba."

Such an air strike would have to include not only the missile sites but airfields, hidden aircraft, and possible nuclear storage sites. They must assume that the planes had nuclear warheads or at least "high explosive potential." This kind of broad air strike would mean perhaps two or three thousand Cuban casualties.

McNamara reported that the Joint Chiefs would prefer to have several days to prepare such an assault. But if "absolutely essential, it could be done almost literally within a matter of hours. . . . The air strike could continue for a matter of days following the initial day, if necessary. Presumably there would be some political discussions taking place either just before the air strike or both before and during. In any event, we would be prepared, following the air strike, for an . . . invasion both by air and by sea."

The air strike option must involve mobilization of American forces "either concurrently with or somewhat following, say, possibly five days afterwards, depending upon the possible invasion requirements." The first phase could be carried out under the congressional resolution on Cuba signed by the President just a week ago. The second would require declaration of a national emergency, as Kennedy had considered doing in 1961 over Berlin.

Newly sworn as Chairman of the Joint Chiefs, Maxwell Taylor said, "Once we have destroyed as many of these offensive weapons as possible, we should . . . prevent any more coming in, which means a naval blockade. . . . At the same time, reinforce Guantanamo and evacuate the dependents." Then, "continuous reconnaissance." The results of the air strike would help them decide "whether we invade or not. I think that's the hardest question militarily in the whole business—one which we should look at very closely before we get our feet in that deep mud in Cuba."

Rusk: "I don't believe myself that the critical question is whether you get a particular missile before *it* goes off because if they shoot *those* missiles, we are in general nuclear war." If Khrushchev wanted nuclear war, he did not need to launch MRBMs from Cuba.

With his abiding worry about nuclear war by accident, McNamara noted that someone might somehow get his thumb on the nuclear trigger against the wish of the Kremlin: "We don't know what kinds of communications the Soviets have with those sites. We don't know what kinds of control they have over the warheads."

The President broke his silence: "What is the advant—must be some major reason for the Russians to set this up as a—must be that they're not satisfied with their ICBMs. What'd be the reason that they would—"

Taylor argued that missiles in Cuba would supplement the Soviet Union's "rather defective ICBM system."

Kennedy: "Of course, I don't see how we could prevent further ones from coming in by submarine. I mean, if we let 'em blockade the thing, they come in by submarine."

McNamara: "I think the only way to prevent them coming in, quite frankly, is to say you'll take them out the moment they come in. You'll take them out and you'll carry on open surveillance and you'll have a policy to take them out if they come in."

Rusk: "About why the Soviets are doing this. Mr. McCone* suggested some weeks ago that one thing Mr. Khrushchev may have in mind is that he knows that we have a substantial nuclear superiority, but he also knows that we don't really live under fear of his nuclear weapons to the extent that he has to live under fear of ours. Also, we have nuclear weapons nearby—in Turkey and places like that."†

The President asked how many missiles the United States had in Turkey. The reply: about fifteen Jupiter IRBMs.

Rusk said McCone believed "that Khrushchev may feel that it's important for us to learn about living under medium-range missiles, and he's doing that to sort of balance that . . . political, psychological fact. I think also that Berlin is very much involved in this. For the first time, I'm beginning really to wonder whether maybe Mr. Khrushchev is entirely rational about Berlin."

Perhaps the Russians thought they could "bargain Berlin and Cuba against each other or . . . provoke us into a kind of action in Cuba which would give an umbrella for them to take action with respect to Berlin"—just as Khrushchev had exploited Suez in 1956 to deflect

---

*McCone was arranging the funeral of his stepson in Seattle after the boy's death in a sports-car accident.
†The Chairman himself could not have said it better.

world attention and scorn from his invasion of Hungary. "But I must say I don't really see the rationality of the Soviets pushing it this far unless they grossly misunderstand the importance of Cuba to this country."

With the benefit of his eight years of diplomacy under Eisenhower, Douglas Dillon warned that "OAS action and telling people in NATO" in advance of an air strike on Cuba had the danger of forcing the Russians "to take a position that if anything was done, they would have to retaliate. Whereas a quick action, with a statement at the same time saying this is all there is to it, might give them a chance to back off and not do anything."

Bundy worried about the "noise we would get from our allies saying that they can live with Soviet MRBMs, why can't we?" and the "certainty that the Germans would feel that we were jeopardizing Berlin because of our concern over Cuba."

Rusk: "And if we go with the quick strike, then . . . you've exposed all of your allies . . . to all these great dangers . . . without the slightest consultation or warning or preparation."

Kennedy: "But, of course, warning them, it seems to me, is warning everybody. And I, I—obviously you can't sort of announce that in four days from now you're going to take them out. They may announce within three days they're going to have warheads on 'em: if we come and attack, they're going to fire them. Then what'll—what'll we do? Then we don't take 'em out. Of course, we then announce, well, if they do that, then we're going to attack with nuclear weapons."

Adamant about telling only "the minimum number of people that we really have to tell," the President asked how long they could expect to keep the secret before it became known beyond the highest levels of the government.

McNamara said, "I think, to be realistic, we should assume that this will become fairly widely known, if not in the newspapers, at least by political representatives of both parties within . . . I'd say a week. . . . I doubt very much that we can keep this out of the hands of members of Congress, for example, for more than a week." Rusk said, "Not later than Thursday or Friday of this week."

Kennedy warned the group that whatever course of action they ultimately chose must be the "tightest" secret of all: "Because otherwise we bitch it up."

Listening to the discussion of an air strike, Robert Kennedy had passed a note to Sorensen: "I now know how Tojo felt when he was planning Pearl Harbor." This comment was an abuse of history: there was only the most surperficial comparison between Japan's un-provoked surprise attack and a surprise assault against an offensive base in Cuba against whose construction the United States had warned the Soviet Union, however belatedly.

The Attorney General warned the group that with a full-fledged air strike, "you're going to kill an awful lot of people and we're going to take an awful lot of heat on it. . . . You're going to announce the reason that you're doing it is because they're sending in this kind of missiles. Well, I would think it's almost incumbent upon the Russians then to say, 'Well, we're going to send them in again, and if you do it again . . . we're going to do the same thing to Turkey, or . . . Iran.' "

The President asked how the Cuban people would react to an air strike. Taylor said, "Great confusion and panic." McNamara said, "There's a real possibility you'd *have* to invade. If you carried out an air strike, this might lead to an uprising such that in order to prevent the slaughter of—of—of the free Cubans, we would have to invade to—to reintroduce order into the country. . . . It's not probable, but it's conceivable that the air strike would trigger a nationwide uprising."

Bundy argued that there should be an "enormous premium" on making the air strike as "small and clear-cut" as possible.

Kennedy said, "The advantage of taking out these airplanes would be to protect us against a reprisal by them. I would think you'd have to . . . assume they'd be using iron bombs and not nuclear weapons, because obviously why would the Soviets permit nuclear war to begin under that sort of half-assed way?"

He returned to the heart of the matter: "I don't think we've got much time on these missiles. . . . It may be that we just have to—we can't wait two weeks while we're getting ready to—to roll. Maybe just have to take *them out,* and continue our other preparations if we decide to do that. That may be where we end up. . . . Because that's what we're going to do *anyway.*

"We're certainly going to do Number One—we're going to take out these missiles. The questions will be . . . what I describe as Number Two, which would be a general air strike. . . . The third is the—is the general invasion. At least we're going to do Number One, so it seems to me that we don't have to wait very long. We—we ought to be making *those* preparations."

Bundy worried that the President had seemed to leap so hastily to a decision in favor of an air strike. Gently he said, "You want to be clear, Mr. President, whether we have *definitely* decided *against* a political track."

* * *

Why had the revelation of the missiles caught Kennedy by such surprise? Khrushchev had publicly warned in the summer of 1960 and during the Bay of Pigs that missiles might be used to defend Cuba. In early 1961, Dean Rusk and Allen Dulles had privately raised the matter with the Senate Foreign Relations Committee. In August 1962, Walt Rostow had issued an alarm with his "Khrushchev at Bay" memo. John McCone repeatedly raised the possibility in August and September, saying that if he were Khrushchev he would send offensive missiles to Cuba.

Nevertheless until mid-October 1962, Kennedy accepted—oddly, with almost none of his usual skepticism—the consensus view of his Soviet experts that the Chairman would not violate his self-imposed ban against stationing nuclear missiles outside Soviet territory.* As Bundy recalled, the President and his circle assumed that Khrushchev "was much too sensible to challenge us in the way that nuclear weapons in Cuba so obviously would."

Kennedy's partisans later lauded his detached ability to see things from his opponents' point of view and his care not to push them to the wall. This quality was not in consistent evidence in his relations with Khrushchev through 1961 and early 1962. The President had almost no understanding of the extent to which his allusions to American nuclear superiority and a possible first strike had made Khrushchev feel trapped and deeply insecure.

Bundy recalled how in 1962 Kennedy and his aides "believed that in the overall contest with the Soviet Union we were still on the defensive. It was not we who threatened destabilizing changes in Berlin or in Southeast Asia. . . . We did not suppose that nuclear superiority conferred on us the opportunity for political coercion that Khrushchev took for granted."

By the summer of 1962, the President had been persuaded by McNamara's insistence that nuclear superiority mattered little as long as a nation had sufficient warheads and delivery systems to inflict unacceptable damage on another. So captured was Kennedy by this reasoning that he did not pause to think that Khrushchev might not share it. He gave short shrift to McCone's arguments that Khrushchev had both the motive and the ability to quickly repair his missile gap by sending MRBMs and IRBMs to Cuba.

Kennedy's inclusion of ground-to-ground missiles in his September public warning reflected not that he had realized his mistake but instead that he still had no notion Khrushchev might need or want to

---

*One analyst later quipped that it wasn't the Kremlinologists who had erred, but Khrushchev.

send such weapons to Cuba. He issued the warning on the basis of Robert Kennedy's reminder that offensive missiles would "create a major political problem here." Its main purpose was to provide a showy demonstration to Republican critics that the President was capable of drawing the line on Cuba. He did not know that he was closing the barn door after the cows were out.

Kennedy gave only secondary thought to how the warning might influence the course of world history. He did not canvass a full range of advisers before making it. Despite the warnings of Allen Dulles, Rusk, McCone, and the Chairman himself, the President was still so certain Khrushchev would not dream of sending offensive missiles to Cuba that he assumed he was issuing a challenge he would never have to back up with force.

Had the President issued his warning in March 1962, it is not so likely that Khrushchev would have defied it, especially in his then-current gloom about American first-strike capability. By September, the Chairman could not have reversed course without becoming a laughingstock in the Kremlin and throughout the Communist bloc, when his ignominy became known. Castro might have cried out to the world about how the Soviets had failed to fulfill their treaty commitment to send him missiles.

Had Kennedy taken the time to convene a cross-section of his advisers and examine the dangers of issuing such a warning, they might have impressed on him that mid-range missiles might go to Cuba and counseled him to word the statement more ambiguously.

It can be argued that in the fall of 1962 and the hot political climate over Cuba, Americans would never have tolerated nuclear missiles in Cuba and that anyone who was President would have felt compelled to demand their removal. The problem with Kennedy's warning was that it locked him into a specific course of action. In his haste to remedy his domestic political worries and his excessive certainty about his judgment of Khrushchev and Soviet motives, Kennedy had issued a blanket warning that had the effect of foreclosing any presidential action if missiles were found in Cuba short of risking nuclear war.

On Tuesday afternoon in the Oval Office, Kennedy pored over Kohler's cables on his three-hour morning meeting with Khrushchev. The Chairman had assured him, "I am most anxious not to do anything that will embarrass the President during the campaign."

Khrushchev had told Kohler he would do nothing new about Germany and Berlin until after the American elections in November. But then a German solution must finally be found. He was still considering a visit to the UN and to President Kennedy in November.

Khrushchev's complaint about the Jupiter missiles in Turkey and Italy took Kohler by surprise. The State Department had not briefed him on how to respond to such a complaint because it considered the matter so extraneous. Not so Khrushchev. He almost certainly knew that in six days the Jupiters were scheduled to be turned over to Turkish command.

To help relieve post-Sputnik fears about a missile gap, NATO had decided in late 1957 to install IRBMs on European soil. Sixty Thors were earmarked for Britain, thirty Jupiter launchers for Italy, fifteen for Turkey.

In June 1959, after Khrushchev complained to Washington about the IRBMs, Eisenhower privately told his Defense Secretary, Neil McElroy, that he could see good reason for them to go into West Germany, France, and Britain, but that provoking the Russians by going so close to their border as Greece seemed "very questionable."

McElroy reminded the President that Khrushchev had threatened "to obliterate Western Europe" and the allies were "showing signs of being shaken by the threat." One day the IRBMs could be used as bargaining chips. Eisenhower rejoined that the missiles would hardly "reduce tensions between ourselves and the Soviets." He worried that the Soviets might equate the deployment of missiles on NATO's southern flank with the installation of Soviet missiles in "Cuba or Mexico."

The Jupiters went into Turkey at about the time of Khrushchev's first visit to the United States in 1959. Eisenhower's aide Karl Harr reminded the President that "in terms of public relations" the installation must be handled carefully in light of Khrushchev's "particular political sensitivity" about IRBMs along his border.

American ICBMs and missiles launchable from Polaris submarines soon made the Jupiters obsolete. Dean Rusk was told that Turkish motorists could strike the above-ground missiles with a BB-gun and that the Jupiters were so out of date that, if launched, the United States could not be certain which way they would fly.

Like the Russians, the Congressional Joint Committee on Atomic Energy worried that American control over the missiles in Turkey might be too lax. Kennedy had asked for a review of the matter in March 1961 but was advised in June that in light of Khrushchev's "hard posture" at Vienna, withdrawing the Jupiters "might seem a sign of weakness." General Norstad warned him that the Turks would feel insulted. The President gibed, "What the Turks want and need is the American payrolls these represent."

The British announced in August 1962 that the Thors were being phased out. (The job was completed by December.) Kennedy again pondered pulling out the Jupiters but knew this would require negotiation within NATO. As Rostow recalled, "Neither the Pentagon nor the State Department had gotten on with the diplomacy of getting them out of Turkey and Italy."

Were the President aware that the missiles in Turkey were being turned over on October 22 with ceremony to the command of Turkish armed forces, he would have seen the gesture as a sop to good alliance relations. He would have presumed that the question of ownership meant little as long as the United States controlled their nuclear warheads.

Khrushchev may not have known that their nuclear warheads were to remain under strict American control. He was always worried that some local commander in West Germany or elsewhere might be able to put his finger on the nuclear trigger. Misapprehension that the Turks might be about to gain the ability to launch nuclear warheads against the Soviet Union would have caused him to place high value on getting the Jupiters out of Turkey.

At six-thirty, Kennedy and his men returned to the Cabinet Room. McCone's deputy, General Carter, reported that the latest reconnaissance of Cuba showed "a capability of from sixteen or possibly twenty-four missiles." There was "no evidence whatsoever" of nuclear warheads, although this did not prove the absence of such weapons. The Soviet launchers in Cuba "could be operational within two weeks" or, in the case of one, "much sooner." Once operational, "they could fire on very little notice."

Rusk pursued his idea of persuading Castro to evict the Soviet missiles from Cuba. He thought that Castro might "break with Moscow if he knew that he were in deadly jeopardy. Now this is one chance in a hundred, possibly. But in any event, we're very much interested in the possibility of a direct message to Castro as well as Khrushchev."

If the United States took the air-strike route, "we would expect, I think, maximum Communist reaction in Latin America." About six Latin American governments "could easily be overthrown."* After an air strike, "the Soviets would almost certainly take some kind of action somewhere." Could Washington take such an action "without letting

---

*He did not specify which ones or how.

our closer allies know of a matter which could subject them to very great danger?" The United States could find itself "isolated and the alliance crumbling."

McNamara opposed any discussion with Castro, Khrushchev, or NATO leaders before an air strike occurred: "It almost *stops* subsequent military action." He raised a new, middle option: "a blockade against offensive weapons entering Cuba in the future" and constant reconnaissance of the island.

He warned that any form of direct military action "will lead to a Soviet military response of some type someplace in the world." American military action could generate an anti-Castro uprising in Cuba: the United States might be forced to accept an "unsatisfactory uprising," like the Bay of Pigs, or else have to invade.

Now the President spoke: "I completely agree that there isn't any doubt that if we announced that there were MRBM sites going up . . . we would secure a good deal of political support after my statement. And the fact that we indicated our desire to restrain, this really would put the burden on the Soviet."

He agreed that if the United States revealed the missiles to the world before it used force against Cuba, "we lose all the advantages of our strike. Because if we announce that it's there, then it's quite obvious to them [the Soviet Union] that we're gonna probably do something about it—I would *assume.*" He doubted that a message to Castro about the missiles would turn the dictator against Moscow: "I don't think he plays it that way."

Nor did he think a message to Khrushchev would work. He noted that the Chairman had obviously ignored his September warnings against missiles in Cuba: "It seems to me my press statement was so *clear* about how we *wouldn't* do anything under these conditions,* and under the conditions that we *would.* He must know that we're going to find out [about the missiles], so it seems to me he just—"

Bundy: "That's, of course, why he's been very, very explicit with us in communications to us about how dangerous this is, and the [September 11] TASS statement and his other messages."

Kennedy: "That's right. But he's—he's initiated the danger really, hasn't he?"

As the President's tape machine churned on, he made a muffled comment on Khrushchev that could be interpreted as "He's the one playing his card"—"cahd" in the Boston accent—"not us." He may also have said, "He's the one playing God, not us."

---

*Meaning a defensive military buildup in Cuba.

Rusk: "And his statement to Kohler on the subject of his visit and so forth. *Completely hypocritical.*"

McNamara warned again that the Soviet missiles on Cuba could be placed "in operational condition quickly." Whether six hours or two weeks, "we don't know how much time has started."

Rusk: "We could be just utterly wrong, but we've never *really* believed that Khrushchev would take on a general nuclear war over Cuba."

Kennedy: "We certainly have been wrong about what he's trying to do in Cuba. There isn't any doubt about that. . . . [Not] many of us thought that he was going to put MRBMs on Cuba."

Bundy: "Yeah. Except John McCone."

Carter: "Mr. McCone."

Kennedy: "Yeah."

Now, for the first time in the Cabinet Room all day, Bundy finally raised the most fundamental issue: "Quite aside from what we've said—and we're very hard-locked onto it, I know—what is the strategic impact on the position of the United States of MRBMs in *Cuba?* How gravely does this change the strategic balance?"

McNamara: "Mac, I asked the Chiefs that this afternoon, in effect. And they said, 'Substantially.' My own personal view is, *not at all.*"

Defending the Joint Chiefs, Taylor said, "They *can* become a very"—he corrected himself—"a *rather* important adjunct and reinforcement to the strike capability of the Soviet Union. We have no idea how far they will go. But more than that . . . to our nation, it means, it means a good deal more—you all are aware of that—in Cuba and not over in the Soviet Union." By this he meant that Americans would feel more insecure when they learned that Soviet missiles had been placed in the Western Hemisphere, only ninety miles away.

Dillon did not speak, but he and Paul Nitze considered the missiles in Cuba "a major step toward nuclear parity" by the Soviet Union, as Nitze said years later: "Not in numbers but in military effectiveness, because their capability in an initial strike from those sites would be tremendous. . . . Between the MRBMs and the IRBMs there was hardly any part of the United States that wasn't vulnerable to these missiles."

Kennedy returned to the possibility that the missiles were already operational: "Then you don't want to knock 'em out. . . . There's too much of a gamble. Then they just begin to build up those air bases there and then put more and more. . . . Then they start getting ready to squeeze us in Berlin." He embraced McNamara's view that the Soviet nuclear danger was not now necessarily greater than it had been before the missiles were sent to Cuba: "You may say it doesn't make any difference if you get blown up by an ICBM flying from the Soviet Union or one that was ninety miles away. Geography doesn't mean that much."

Taylor: "We'd have to target them with our missiles and have the same kind of—of pistol-pointed-at-the-head situation as we have in the Soviet Union at the present time."

Kennedy noted that if he had pressed the April 1961 invasion of Cuba to the point of success, he would not be facing this monumental crisis: "That's why it shows that the Bay of Pigs was really right."

Robert Kennedy said, "The other problem is in South America a year from now. And the fact that you got *these* things in the hands of Cubans here and then you—say, your—some problem arises in Venezuela. You've got Castro saying, 'You move troops down into that part of Venezuela, we're going to fire these missiles.' "

Edwin Martin, Assistant Secretary of State for Latin America: "It's a psychological factor. It won't reach as far as Venezuela is concerned."

McNamara: "It'll reach the U.S. though. This is the *point.*"

Martin: "Well, it's a psychological factor that we have sat back and let 'em do it to us. That is more important than the direct threat."

The President agreed: "Last month I said we weren't going to." By this he meant allowing offensive weapons in Cuba. He laughed caustically: "Last month I *should* have said we're—that we don't care. But when we said we're *not* going to and then they go ahead and do it, and we do nothing, then our risks increase. . . . I think it's just a question of, after all, this is a political struggle as much as military."

He assessed the options: "Don't think the message to Castro's got much in it." He proposed that "twenty-four hours ahead of our doing something" with military force, the U.S. government should announce the presence of missiles in Cuba: "That would be notification in a sense that, of their existence, and everybody could draw whatever conclusion they wanted to."

McNamara disagreed: the missiles could be readied "between the time we in effect *say* we're going to come in and the time we *do* come in. This—this is a very, very great danger to this, this coast. . . . If you are going to strike, you shouldn't make an announcement."

Kennedy renewed discussion of how widespread the military attack against Cuba should be: "I don't think we ought to abandon just knocking out these missile bases. . . . That's much more defensible, explicable, politically or satisfactory-in-every-way action than the general strike which takes us—us into the city of Havana."

Bundy agreed: "It corresponds to the—the punishment fits the crime in political terms." They would be "doing only what we *warned* repeatedly and publicly we would *have* to do."

Kennedy: "Once you get into beginning to shoot up those airports, then you get in, you get a lot of antiaircraft. . . . I mean, you're running a much more major operation. Therefore the dangers of the world-wide effects* are substantial to the United States, are increased. I quite agree that if we're just thinking about Cuba, the best thing to do is to be bold if you're thinking about trying to get this thing under some degree of control."

He asked why the Russians put in the missiles if they "did not increase very much their strategic strength." Hadn't Khrushchev been cautious throughout his dealings on Berlin?

George Ball called attention to the Chairman's trial balloon about a New York visit in November: perhaps he had intended to reveal that "here is Cuba armed against the United States, or possibly use it to try to trade something in Berlin, saying he'll disarm Cuba if we'll yield some of our interests in Berlin and some arrangement for it."

Bundy: "I would think one thing that I would still cling to is that he's not likely to give Fidel Castro nuclear warheads."

Kennedy: "That's right, but what is the advantage of that? It's just as if we suddenly began to put a major number of MRBMs in Turkey. Now that'd be goddamn dangerous, I would think."

Someone said, "Well, we *did,* Mr. President."

Kennedy: "Yeah, but that was five years ago. . . . That was during a different period then." The President betrayed no knowledge that the Jupiters were to be transferred to the Turks next week. No one else raised the subject.

Someone speculated that Khrushchev's generals "have been telling him for a year and a half that he had—was missing a golden opportunity to add to his strategic capability."

Robert Kennedy said, "One other thing is whether we should also think of whether there is some *other* way we can get involved in this through Guantanamo Bay or something, or whether there's some ship that—you know, sink the *Maine* again or something." This was a dangerous suggestion: using a transparent pretext to justify a military action against Cuba for which the United States had substantial reason would have undermined the American case in the court of world opinion.†

The President remembered that he was scheduled to see Gromyko

---

*Almost certainly meaning a Soviet attack on Berlin.
†In retrospect, Robert may have thought so too. He omitted his suggestion about Guantanamo and the *Maine* from *Thirteen Days.*

in the Oval Office two days hence. He asked for advice on "whether we ought to say anything to *him,* whether we ought to indirectly give him sort of a—give him an ultimatum on this matter, or whether we just ought to go ahead without him." Dobrynin had told the Attorney General and others "that they were not going to put these weapons there. Now either he's lying or doesn't know."

Bundy said he "wouldn't bet a *cookie*" that Dobrynin knew.

Kennedy suggested that Robert tell Dobrynin that if offensive missiles were found in Cuba, the United States "would have to take action." Perhaps this would make the Soviets "reconsider their decision. . . . I can't understand their viewpoint, if they're aware of what we said at the press conferences. . . . I don't think there's any record of the Soviets ever making this direct a challenge ever, really, since the Berlin Blockade."

Courageously Bundy told his boss what he could not have wanted to hear: "We have to be clear, Mr. President, that they made this decision, in all probability, *before* you made your statements."

McNamara: "Uh-huh."

Bundy read aloud from the September TASS statement that the Soviet Union had such powerful missiles that it had "no need" to place them outside of its own territory.

Kennedy: "Well, what date was that?"

Bundy: "September eleventh."

The President remained baffled by the Soviet boldness in Cuba: "We never really ever had a case where it's been quite this—after all, they backed down in—Chinese Communists in '58.* They didn't go into Laos, agreed to a cease-fire there. . . . I don't know enough about the Soviet Union, but if anybody can tell me any other time since the

---

*This referred to the Formosa Straits crisis of 1958, when Mainland China tried using shelling and a naval blockade to reduce Nationalist China's ability to resupply Quemoy and Matsu. Eisenhower had warned that if Quemoy seemed about to be overwhelmed, he would do whatever was necessary. To the area he ordered what was called the "most powerful air-naval striking force" in American history, which was known to include nuclear weapons. Khrushchev complained to the President by letter about American "threats and atomic blackmail" but withheld Soviet support from the Chinese adventure.

In a September 1959 speech, Kennedy said that one lesson from the Formosa episode was that a minor power like Chiang Kai-shek must not be allowed to make unilateral decisions that "dragged" the world into world war—a lesson he did not forget in both the Berlin and Cuban crises.

The first day of the Missile Crisis was not the first time the parallel between Formosa 1958 and Cuba 1962 had occurred to Kennedy. In September, Republicans had modeled their demands for a congressional resolution about Cuba on a similar document enacted at the time of the Formosa crisis.

Berlin Blockade where the Russians have given us so clear provocation, I don't know when it's been. Because they've been awfully cautious really. . . . Now maybe our mistake was in not saying sometime *before* this summer that if they do this, we're [bound] to act."

McNamara said, "I'll be quite frank. I don't think there *is* a military problem here. . . . This is a domestic political problem. The announcement—we didn't say we'd go in . . . and kill them. We said we'd *act*. Well, how will we act? . . . First place, we carry out open surveillance, so we know what they're doing. . . . Twenty-four hours a day from now and forever. . . . We prevent any further offensive weapons coming in. In other words, we blockade offensive weapons."

The United States should also make "a statement to the world, particularly to Khrushchev, that . . . if there is ever any indication that they're to be launched against this country, we will respond not only against Cuba, but we will respond directly against the Soviet Union with—with a full nuclear strike. Now this alternative doesn't seem to be a very acceptable one, but wait until you work on the others. . . . As I suggested, I don't believe it's primarily a military problem. It's primarily a domestic political problem."

Ball: "Yeah? Well, as far as the American people are concerned, action means military action. Period."

In his emphatic way, McNamara threw out more questions: "What do we expect *Castro* will be doing after you attack these missiles? Does he survive as a—as a political leader? Is he overthrown? . . . How could Khrushchev *afford* to accept this action without *some* kind of rebuttal? I don't think—he *can't* accept it without some rebuttal. . . . Where? How do *we* react in relation to it? What happens when we *do* mobilize? How does this affect our *allies'* support of us in relation to Berlin?"

Gilpatric suggested that they all study American "points of vulnerability around the world," especially Berlin, Iran, Turkey, Korea. McNamara warned the group that if Khrushchev struck back at Berlin, "the risk of disaster would go way up."

The record of Kennedy's Tuesday Cabinet Room meetings does not quite bear out the later claims made on his behalf that this was a President superbly in command of the crisis from the start.* Even allowing for the fact that he may not have wished to inhibit the conversations by dominating them, he made little effort to provide disci-

---

*The complete record of these meetings only became known to historians when transcripts and copies of the President's secret tapes, with excisions for national security reasons, were released by the Kennedy Library in 1983.

pline, other than by injecting questions and comments. Not until halfway through the evening session did the conversation, thanks to Bundy, meander to the central question of whether MRBMs in Cuba actually changed the American-Soviet balance of power.

The Tuesday meetings rested on Kennedy's immediate assumption that the United States was "certainly going to . . . take out these missiles"—by diplomacy or force, perhaps at risk of nuclear war. This was despite the fact that at a March 1962 press conference, he had said that there was not "a significant difference" between a nuclear warhead "stationed in this area" and one five thousand miles away.

McNamara was confident that while nuclear missiles in Cuba might increase the speed, power, and accuracy of a Soviet first strike, they could not remotely upset the vast American advantage. As he said years later, if Khrushchev in 1962 "thought he was numerically behind by seventeen to one or thereabouts, do you think an extra forty-two missiles in Cuba, each carrying one warhead, would have led him to think he could use his nuclear weapons? No way!"

The reason the President felt he had to take out the missiles was not because he felt they violated the Monroe Doctrine. He privately thought that the doctrine lacked meaning in international law. But he was unwilling to take the heat of being the first President to say in public that the doctrine had little value.

Asked in August 1962 what the doctrine meant to him, Kennedy replied that it "means what it has meant since President Monroe and John Quincy Adams enunciated it, and that is that we would oppose a foreign power extending its power to the Western Hemisphere. And that's why we oppose . . . what's happening in Cuba today."* Two weeks later in private, told by a Justice Department official that the doctrine gave the United States special hemispheric rights, Kennedy snapped, "The Monroe Doctrine—what the hell is that?"

He was angry at the secrecy and deception by which Khrushchev had conducted his Cuba operation, in defiance of the assurances the Chairman had given him publicly and privately since early September.† Otherwise it was not easy to argue that the Soviet missiles in

---

*Arthur Krock felt this endorsement of the Monroe Doctrine was insufficient. He accused the President of substituting for it a "Kennedy Doctrine" under which the United States would act only if a foreign power was "endangering our peace and safety." Krock was correct. It was another instance of the President's extraordinary good fortune that his critics never succeeded in forcing him to articulate and defend such a "Kennedy Doctrine," which could have caused him serious domestic political damage.

†Bundy recalled the "intense feeling that we had been deliberately deceived." Sorensen later felt that had the Soviets announced the missiles in Cuba, as the United

Cuba could be any less acceptable to the United States than NATO's IRBMs along the Soviet border were to the Soviet Union.

Bundy had had to remind the President that he had issued his warning against missiles in Cuba considerably after the moment at which Khrushchev must have decided to send them. Kennedy now knew he had erred badly by brushing aside McCone's numerous warnings that Khrushchev might be taking such a gamble. Instead, in September he had issued the American people an unambiguous pledge to "do whatever must be done" if Khrushchev moved ground-to-ground missiles into Cuba.

How different these Cabinet Room conversations might have been had Kennedy phrased his September pledge more vaguely or not at all. Instead of discussing how to take the missiles out, he and his advisers would now be able to consider the option of explaining to Americans that they had little to fear from the missiles in Cuba.

As when Eisenhower reassured Americans during the Sputnik and missile gap hysteria, this approach might have forced Kennedy to brave charges that he was too sanguine about the Soviet threat, especially because Kennedy lacked Eisenhower's military prestige. It might have caused the Democrats to lose the 1962 elections.

Still, this would have been preferable to the Kafkaesque nightmare that now faced the President—risking nuclear war to eliminate missiles that, in his own opinion and that of his Secretary of Defense, did little to harm American security.

The clock could not be turned back now. Kennedy had issued his warning. Like Khrushchev's decision to install the missiles, he had made exactly the kind of fateful miscalculation he had cautioned the Chairman against at Vienna. He could not discard his September warning now without shattering his political career and the world's faith in American threats and promises. He later told his brother Robert that if he hadn't acted against the missiles, "I would have been impeached."

Wednesday, October 17. After seeing the German Foreign Minister, Gerhard Schröder, the President went swimming and asked Dave Powers to ride with him to St. Matthew's Cathedral: "Have you forgotten that I proclaimed today as a National Day of Prayer?"

The previous day, after a luncheon for the Libyan Crown Prince, he had taken Adlai Stevenson up to the family quarters and told him of

States had its missiles in Turkey, Kennedy "would have found it much more difficult to mobilize world opinion on his side."

the missile secret. Stevenson's mind may have drifted back to his first meeting with Khrushchev in 1958, when the Chairman had complained of American missile bases in Turkey and Greece and said, "What would the Americans think if the Russians set up bases in Mexico or some other place? How would you feel?"

Today Stevenson gave Kennedy a handwritten note: "We must be prepared for the widespread reaction that if we have a missile base in Turkey and other places around the Soviet Union surely they have a right to one in Cuba. If we attack Cuba, an ally of the U.S.S.R., isn't an attack on NATO bases equally justified?" The President must make it "clear that the existence of nuclear missile bases anywhere is *negotiable* before we start anything."

Kennedy showed the memo to Sorensen and meanly said, "Tell me which side he is on."

To balance Stevenson's advice, he summoned Acheson, McCloy, and Robert Lovett, requesting highest secrecy, to join his crisis council. Acheson's presence ensured that the hard-line wing of the Democratic Party would be represented and that the President could draw on Acheson's institutional memory on Berlin.

The President asked Bohlen to cancel his voyage to France, where he was about to start his tour as Ambassador. Bohlen replied that unless he broke "a leg on the station platform," this would arouse suspicions, not to mention de Gaulle's sensitivities. Instead he left the President a written suggestion that an air strike "will inevitably lead to war." A private message to Khrushchev would allow the Chairman to back down gracefully.*

That afternoon Kennedy flew to Connecticut for a four-hour campaign tour with his longtime supporter Abraham Ribicoff, now running for the Senate to succeed the retiring Prescott Bush. The President presumed that when the missiles were revealed, the Republicans would crow that they had been right all along about Cuba. Privately he told aides, "The campaign is over. This blows it—we've lost anyway."

He gave no hint of his pessimism in public. On the village green in Waterbury, Connecticut, where he had ended the last campaign, he said, "Our meeting here two years ago at three o'clock in the morning was the high point of the 1960 campaign, and we will meet at three o'clock in the morning the last week of the 1964 campaign. . . . I don't

---

*Robert Kennedy, indulging his unfortunate tendency to decide who was a patriot and who was not, later said he was "shocked" that Bohlen "ran out on us" and left "this country in a crisis." This was especially unfair because, to fulfill his responsibilities, Bohlen knew he was missing the greatest challenge of his career.

want to see the next two years spent with a Congress in the control of the Republicans . . . and nothing being done which must be done if this country's going to move ahead."

In Washington, to avoid attention, the President's crisis team met in George Ball's windowless conference room at the State Department. When told of the missiles on Tuesday, Kennedy had simply rattled off the names that came to mind.

The crisis group was soon styled the Executive Committee of the National Security Council—"Ex Comm." It included the President, Rusk, Ball, U. Alexis Johnson, Thompson, Edwin Martin, McNamara, Gilpatric, Nitze, Robert Kennedy, General Taylor, Chief of Naval Operations George Anderson, Sorensen, and Bundy. The official members were joined, when duties allowed, by the Vice President, Stevenson, Dillon, and either McCone or General Carter.

As with Berlin, Kennedy proved himself better able to manage the Missile Crisis than to avoid it. And like the group he selected to provide systematic advice during Berlin, Ex Comm showed an impressive diversity of experience and ideology, more varied than a comparable group would have been under Eisenhower. As the students of the Missile Crisis James Blight and David Welch have argued, the council was roughly divided into two schools of thought on Soviet behavior.

Members like Acheson, Nitze, McCone, and Dillon, who had gained power during the age of the American nuclear monopoly, believed that as in the Berlin crises of 1948, 1958, and 1961, America's nuclear advantage would force Khrushchev to accept the President's demands. Others, like McNamara, Robert Kennedy, and Sorensen, who had come to power during the years of mutual American-Soviet vulnerability, thought there to be a higher danger that an air strike on the missile sites, killing Russian troops, might risk everything.

Each faction could cite the Berlin Crisis of 1961 as evidence for its point of view. The Achesonians could argue that even in Berlin, where he enjoyed clear conventional superiority, Khrushchev had been compelled to swallow his ultimatum out of fear of the huge American nuclear advantage. The McNamara faction could cite the success of Kennedy's Berlin policy as evidence of the value of responding to provocation by Khrushchev with a carefully calibrated, gradual application of force.

When Kennedy issued his September warning, he had never confronted the question of whether MRBMs and IRBMs in Cuba would gravely change the nuclear balance of power between the United

States and the Soviet Union. Dillon, McCone, Nitze, and the Joint
Chiefs felt the missiles had greatly increased the Soviet threat. They
noted that the United States had no early warning system on its
southern flank and that the new Soviet missiles might increase the
temptation for a Soviet first strike. A majority of Ex Comm accepted
McNamara's view that the missiles did "not at all" change the nuclear
balance.

On Tuesday, with little soul-searching, Kennedy had agreed with
McNamara, saying it made no difference if "you get blown up" by an
IRBM or a missile five thousand miles away. Later he reflected that
the importance of missiles in Cuba was that they "would have appeared to" change the balance of power, "and appearances contribute
to reality."

In fact, according to Volkogonov, the Soviet Union had deployed
only twenty ICBMs in 1962, not the thirty-five or fifty estimated by
McNamara that February. Thus the IRBMs and MRBMs earmarked
for Cuba could have quadrupled the number of nuclear warheads that
Soviet missiles could drop on the United States.

Since the President felt compelled to fulfill his September warning
in any case, the matter was academic. But his ready acceptance of the
notion that the missiles on Cuba had little military meaning suggested
that, even at this late date, he continued to presume that Khrushchev
and his generals affected the same indifference to the military significance of nuclear imbalance that he and McNamara did.

Rusk tried to keep his regular public schedule in order to preserve
secrecy. When he met with Ex Comm, he saw his function as preventing the group from moving too far or too fast.* Deferring to Rusk's
Constitutional role, McNamara tried with mixed success to rein in his
natural take-charge instincts.

In the President's absence, Robert Kennedy became the group's de
facto leader. His performance did much to suggest that every group
considering a paramount matter of state should include at least one
participant who need not fear for his job.

With no necessity to convey his ideas in genteel language or respect
the political dynamics of the room, he issued a constant, almost
prosecutorial challenge to his colleagues' assumptions. His talent for
criticizing propositions from all angles, without the filter of ideology,
helped to foreclose the perils of the Bay of Pigs deliberations, in which

---

*Noting Rusk's comment that he had been "playing the role of the 'dumb dodo,'"
Robert Kennedy later said, "I thought it was a strange way of putting it."

no one had seemed to have the courage to bell the cat.

At the same time, his presence imposed a certain degree of inhibition. All present knew from experience that anything said in Robert's hearing might well be reported to the President, and that the rendition was not always flattering. As one Ex Comm member recalled, "We all knew Little Brother was watching and keeping a little list of where everyone stood."*

Amazingly some Ex Comm members suggested on Wednesday that the problem should be handled "as the 1960 U-2 episode should have been—in effect, to pretend it hadn't happened." The United States could pretend that the missiles were "a mistake by the Kremlin in contradiction of Khrushchev's repeated promises. . . . Wiping them out with a few non-nuclear bombs would correct the mistake. That would be the end of the affair, on the assumption that the Soviets would not choose to make an issue of being caught red handed in an embarrassing situation."

The official record says that "most of the group favored this course of action in the first hours of discussion." This was before it became clear that "an air strike to destroy all the offensive missiles would be a major effort, not an affair of a few bombs and a few minutes."

Hospitalized the previous month for ulcers, Sorensen recorded the options: "Political action, pressure, and warning, followed by a military strike if satisfaction is not received. . . . A military strike without prior warning, pressure, or action, accompanied by messages making clear the limited nature of this action. . . . Political action, pressure, and warning, followed by a total naval blockade. . . . Full-scale invasion, to 'take Cuba away from Castro.' "

---

*For example, in an oral history interview years later, Robert charged that Rusk, his chief major antagonist in the administration, "had a virtually complete breakdown mentally and physically." It is virtually impossible to find evidence that this accusation had any basis in fact. Rusk himself later denied it. Historians who rely on Robert Kennedy's oral histories must remember the degree to which his recollections were distorted by a prism of intense loyalties and antipathies. By 1965, when Kennedy, by then Senator from New York, gave this particular interview, he and Rusk were no longer uneasy colleagues in his brother's administration but open political enemies.

During retirement, in his quiet way, Rusk was not averse to settling scores. In an interview with this author, he said that Robert "didn't have all that much influence at the time of the Cuban Missile Crisis. His role has been somewhat exaggerated. . . . There was a heavy emotional content through that book *Thirteen Days*. But that emotion was personal to Bobby Kennedy. This was a first experience for him. But fortunately, President Kennedy and other principal advisers were very calm and cool during this period."

He listed random points of disagreement: Would Moscow be willing or able to prevent Soviet or Cuban commanders from firing the missiles against the United States? Might the Soviets threaten an "equivalent attack" on U.S. missiles in Turkey or Italy, "or attack Berlin or somewhere else?" How would an air strike affect the fate of the Bay of Pigs prisoners?

That evening, Sorensen and the Attorney General met the President at National Airport. While riding to the White House, Robert convinced his brother to let Ex Comm meet on its own for a while: if the President were present, he might show his own leanings and "cause the others just to fall into line."

The President was amazed that the missile secret was being kept. Remembering that Kennedy had dined in Georgetown the previous evening, Sorensen joked, "We don't know of any leak at all other than your conversation with Joe Alsop." With a flash of anger that betrayed his inner tension, Kennedy said he had never mentioned the missiles to Alsop.

Thursday morning, October 18. At 11:10 A.M., the President called Ex Comm to the Cabinet Room. Sorensen reported that the Secretary of State favored a "surgical" air strike without warning. This was opposed "by the diplomats (Bohlen, Thompson, probably Martin), who insist that prior political action is essential . . . by the military (McNamara, Taylor, McCone) who insist that the air strike could not be limited . . . by advocates of the blockade route."

He reported that Bohlen had left a message favoring "a prompt letter to Khrushchev, deciding after the response whether we use air strike or blockade." This was supported by all blockade advocates and opposed by General Taylor, "unless the decision had already been made to go the blockade route."

Thompson warned that if an air strike killed thousands of Russians, Khrushchev might "give an order for a Soviet counteraction" against the Turkish missile sites or Berlin, which could result "eventually if not immediately in nuclear war." If there must be an air strike, the Chairman must be given "time to reflect on his actions" so that "his advisers would have an opportunity to counsel him." Knowing how well Thompson knew Khrushchev's mind, the President was much affected.

Someone asked what the United States should do if Khrushchev struck the missiles in Turkey. Attack the home bases of the attacking Soviet missiles, said someone else. In a later meeting, someone asked,

"Where will we be if Khrushchev knocks off Berlin?" Kennedy replied, "In World War Three."

Sorensen worked on a possible television address to be given by the President after an air strike. His draft began, "This morning, I reluctantly ordered the armed forces to attack and destroy the nuclear buildup in Cuba." The assault was to show that the United States would "defend liberty with all the means at its disposal. This applies elsewhere in the world as well as in Cuba. I refer particularly to Berlin." Americans should "remain calm, go about your daily business, secure in the knowledge that our freedom-loving country will not allow its security to be undermined."

Sorensen was attracted by Bohlen's suggestion to send a private message to Khrushchev.* He worked on an "airtight letter" that could be carried by a high-level American envoy from Kennedy to Khrushchev.

It began by saying that for the first time since Korea, the United States had been confronted with an event to which it had an "inescapable commitment" to respond with force: "Consequently, the purpose of this note is to inform you that . . . I have no choice but to initiate appropriate military action against the island of Cuba."

If Khrushchev could assure the bearer of the letter that he would remove his offensive weapons from Cuba, the President could withhold the use of force. Should the Chairman come to New York, Kennedy would be "glad to meet with you" and "discuss other problems on our agenda, including, if you wish, the NATO bases in Turkey and Italy to which you referred in your conversation with Ambassador Kohler but which are in no way comparable in the eyes of history, international law, or world opinion."

Sorensen read his draft, dissatisfied. He found that "no matter how many references I put in to a summit, to peaceful intentions, and to previous warnings and pledges," the letter "still constituted the kind of ultimatum which no great power could accept." He told Ex Comm

---

*Adlai Stevenson felt the same way. In his Wednesday note he had written the President that *"talking* with K" through an emissary "would afford a chance of uncovering his motives and objectives far better than correspondence through the 'usual channels.' " He went on to recommend that Kennedy's first public announcement of missiles in Cuba not mention that an attack was imminent: "Because an attack would very likely result in Soviet reprisals somewhere—Turkey, Berlin, etc.—it is most important that we have as much of the world with us as possible. To start or risk starting a nuclear war is bound to be divisive at best, and the judgments of history seldom coincide with the tempers of the moment."

that to send Khrushchev a letter saying that "this messenger is going to stay in this room until you give us an answer" was "ridiculous."

On Thursday afternoon, Thompson said that if there was a blockade, the probability that Soviet ships would turn back or allow inspection was "high but not certain." The United States might be forced to fire at them first.

Rusk suggested that if the Russians were still working on the missiles by Tuesday, the United States should inform Britain, France, West Germany, Italy, and Turkey that it would use force to remove them. As the Air Force struck Cuba, the Russians would be warned against retaliation: "If we don't do this, we go down with a whimper. Maybe it's better to go down with a bang."

After a swim and two private hours in the family quarters, Kennedy saw Acheson in the Oval Office. The older man was impatient with Ex Comm, which he found "repetitive, leaderless, and a waste of time." Consensus decision-making was not the way Truman had done things. When the President used the Pearl Harbor analogy to describe the problems of an air strike, Acheson told him that he was repeating his brother's clichés.

Gromyko was scheduled to come to the Oval Office at five o'clock. Rusk and Thompson advised the President not to show Gromyko the U-2 pictures of the missiles and demand their removal. This would give Khrushchev the initiative. American policy was still undecided. Thompson later said, "It is rather like finding your wife unfaithful. She may know, but when you tell her, things are different. Then you had better be prepared, for things will begin to happen."

Bundy advised Kennedy that if Gromyko raised the subject of the missiles himself, "you will probably want to hear him before you reply. But you will want to be ready to cut him off if he tries to express any direct threats."

When Dobrynin and Gromyko and their interpreter, Viktor Sukhodrev, arrived, the President showed them to the cream-colored sofa to the right of his rocker. Rusk and Thompson sat on the sofa across from the Russians. Also present were Vladimir Semyonov, Soviet Deputy Foreign Minister for German affairs, Martin Hillenbrand of the Berlin task force, and Alexander Akalovsky, the interpreter who had accompanied the President to Vienna.

Gromyko recited the Soviet mantra on Berlin: after the November elections, if they could not agree on making Berlin a "free city," the

Soviet Union would be compelled—*compelled,* he said again—to sign a German peace treaty. Kennedy replied with the American mantra: the United States was always ready to talk about Berlin, but Western troops were vital to the city's survival and freedom.

Gromyko said that Khrushchev planned to come to the General Assembly in late November, after the elections. He felt that a meeting with the President would be useful. Kennedy said he would be glad to talk with Khrushchev, but not to bargain about Berlin. Other friendly nations had an interest in the city's future. Such a meeting must have no fixed agenda.

When the Foreign Minister said he wished to raise the subject of Cuba, the Americans wondered whether he was about to reveal the missiles. He did not. Instead he complained of America's "anti-Cuba campaign." By sending Cuban exiles to attack the island's shipping, the United States was committing "piracy on the high seas." Apparently it intended to blockade all of Cuba.

All of this, he said, could lead only to great misfortunes for mankind. The Soviet Union could not observe the situation idly when aggression was planned and threat of war loomed. Cuba belonged to Cubans, not the United States. It was a "baby facing a giant"—no threat to anyone. Hadn't Castro repeatedly stressed his desire for peace?

Gromyko said he knew the President appreciated frankness. This was not the nineteenth century, "when the world was divided up into colonies and . . . the victims of aggression could only be heard weeks after any attack." The congressional resolution enabling the President to call up 150,000 reservists had "no military significance." Modern weapons had changed all that.

Taking out notes carefully written after consultation with Khrushchev, Gromyko said he had been "instructed to make it clear" that Soviet aid to Cuba was "by no means offensive." It was solely for "the purpose of contributing to the defense capabilities of Cuba. . . . If it were otherwise, the Soviet government would never become involved in rendering such assistance."

Impassive, Kennedy sent for one of his September warnings against offensive weapons in Cuba and read a key passage aloud. Rusk noticed that while Gromyko kept a straight face, Sukhodrev blanched. The President later told O'Donnell, "I was dying to confront him with our evidence. In effect I told him that there had better not be any ballistic missiles in Cuba. And he told me that such a thing had never entered Khrushchev's mind. It was incredible to sit there and watch the lies coming out of his mouth."

Gromyko later argued that he had not lied. Two months later, he insisted that the weapons in Cuba were indeed defensive and that he had never said anything to Kennedy about nuclear missiles. In 1989, shortly before his death, he said, "Why didn't I mention it? Because President Kennedy—I do not know his concrete line of thought on this—did not ask about it. The words 'nuclear missiles' did not figure in the conversation. If he had asked me about it, I would have answered."

Gromyko recalled that in case Kennedy had asked about the missiles, he had been instructed to say that the Soviet Union was deploying a "small quantity of missiles of a defensive nature" in Cuba that would "never threaten anyone." If the President complained, he was to encourage quiet diplomacy.*

By Gromyko's much later account, he warned the President that the Soviet Union "will not remain a mere spectator" if a major war arose in connection with Cuba or anywhere else. He recalled that Kennedy replied that he had "no plans to attack Cuba" and said that he was "restraining those circles that support an invasion. . . . I am trying to prevent any actions that could lead to war."

Before Gromyko departed, Kennedy reminded him of what he had told Khrushchev in Vienna: the United States was a large country. So was the Soviet Union. History would judge their competition. Meanwhile, neither he nor the Chairman must "take actions leading to a confrontation of our two countries." Since his inauguration, he had tried to "adjust" American-Soviet relations. Laos had been "a success—so far," but not Germany or West Berlin. In light of Khrushchev's understanding of the United States, what had been happening in Cuba since July was "inexplicable."

Gromyko found the President "nervous, though he tried not to show it." When they parted at 7:18 P.M., the President said, "I hope you'll visit us here at the White House on several more occasions."

As soon as Gromyko left, Kennedy regretted his decision not to mention the missiles in Cuba. He may have been worried that, as after the Vienna summit, political foes might charge he had been too timid to confront his Soviet interlocutor.† Rusk and Thompson assured him that he had done the right thing.

---

*Although Gromyko did not say so, this would have given the Russians more time to rush the missiles to completion.

†Despite Kennedy's much-expressed indignation about leaks, in late October the President caused portions of his session with Gromyko to be leaked to the press. A State Department official allowed Max Frankel of the *New York Times* to take verbatim notes from the transcript to show "Gromyko's perfidy."

The President also had second thoughts about replying so favorably to the suggestion of a November summit with Khrushchev—especially if the Chairman planned to use it to brandish his missiles in Cuba and threaten the United States. Rusk said years later that the idea of the President and Khrushchev in the same room at the height of the Missile Crisis sent "chills up my spine." Thompson repaired Kennedy's mistake by telling Dobrynin that, under current conditions, a summit would not be "appropriate."

Robert Lovett found the President fuming that Gromyko had told him "more barefaced lies than I have ever heard in so short a time." Lovett recommended a blockade of Cuba, followed by gradual pressure against the Soviets, if necessary: "We would look ridiculous if we grabbed a sledgehammer to kill a fly. . . . We can always increase the tempo of combat, but it is very hard to reduce it once the battle is joined."

Walking in from the Rose Garden, Robert Kennedy asked pointed questions about a blockade, but Lovett felt that both brothers were by now almost agreed on "taking a relatively mild and not very bloodthirsty step first."

At a black-tie dinner on the seventh floor of the State Department, Gromyko raised a glass of California cabernet and said, "To the President." Rusk responded by toasting Khrushchev. By Khrushchev's later account, Gromyko reported to Moscow that the Secretary of State had been drinking heavily: "I never saw him in such a state. He was not himself."*

Ex Comm was meeting one floor below. A consensus was developing for a naval blockade and graduated response, which the group now referred to by the euphemism "quarantine," after Franklin Roosevelt's 1937 "quarantine-the-aggressor" speech. McNamara argued that, unlike an air strike, a quarantine would not foreclose other options. A straw vote found six members for an air strike, eleven for a quarantine.

At ten, the exhausted men left for the White House. Nine of the officials piled into Robert Kennedy's limousine to avoid attracting

*Khrushchev's memory is cast into doubt by the fact that in the same passage of his memoirs he also claimed that during this visit Rusk also told Gromyko about the U-2 pictures and said, "We know everything." It is possible that Gromyko portrayed Rusk as tipsy in order to feed the Chairman's conceits about the American lack of will. The Secretary of State used alcohol, but there is no evidence that any foreign diplomat ever saw him out of control.

attention with a fleet of cars. Sorensen felt as if a month had passed since the missiles were discovered.

In the upstairs Oval Room, under the President's questioning, the support for a quarantine seemed to unravel. Although he still had not determined his final course of action, Kennedy asked Sorensen for a television speech to be given on Monday night. If the missile secret reached the press, timing of the address could be moved up.

Friday morning, October 19. Before the President's departure on a campaign trip, Rusk, Bundy, and the Joint Chiefs told him that they now endorsed an air strike. Afterward Kennedy asked the Attorney General and Sorensen to pull Ex Comm together: "If you have any trouble, call me and I'll call off the trip and come back and talk to them." Sorensen found him impatient and "a bit disgusted" that people were still changing their minds—especially Bundy, with whom he usually worked so effortlessly.

Little Brother was watching. He later complained that first Bundy "was for a strike, then a blockade, then for doing nothing because it would upset the situation in Berlin, and then, finally, he led the group which was in favor of a strike—and a strike without prior notification, along the lines of Pearl Harbor." Sorensen recalled that "it was not one of Bundy's best weeks" and the President "didn't like it."

With his Irish demand for loyalty, Kennedy may have expected Bundy to realize that he was leaning heavily toward quarantine and help him get the Joint Chiefs on board. The President was carefully establishing a record of consultation with the Chiefs to clear himself of any future charges that he had failed to secure adequate military advice. Bundy almost surely felt his relationship with Kennedy was secure enough that at this moment he had not only the luxury but the duty to give him his best judgment.

Bundy reported to Ex Comm that morning that he had seen the President before departure. Speaking for himself, he now favored "decisive action with its advantages of surprise and confronting the world with a fait accompli." Sorensen said it was not fair to the President to reconsider a matter they had all decided on Thursday night. But Robert Kennedy insisted that the matter was so vital that people should still talk freely.

Repeating almost exactly his advice during the Berlin Crisis, Acheson declared that Khrushchev had presented the United States with a direct test of will: the sooner the showdown, the better. Taylor said it was "now or never for an air strike." If they were to attack on Sunday morning, the decision must be made at once. McNamara said that while he would order preparations, he did not favor a strike.

With a faint smile, the Attorney General said that he too had seen the President that morning. It would be very difficult for the President to order an air strike. For 175 years, the United States had not been the kind of country to wage sneak attack. Thousands of Cubans and Russians would be killed without warning. Better to act in a way that allowed the Soviets room to pull back from their "overextended position in Cuba."

Douglas Dillon recalled, "As he spoke, I felt that I was at a real turning point in history. . . . I knew then that we should not undertake a strike without warning. . . . With only one or two possible exceptions, all the members of the Ex Comm were convinced by Bob's argument." One need not question the Attorney General's eloquence to conclude that another reason his argument had such power was that few doubted whom he was speaking for.*

That evening, Bundy looked at new aerial pictures of Cuba. He was told that some of the MRBMs were apparently ready to fire. He called O'Donnell, who was staying with the President at the Sheraton-Blackstone in Chicago: the situation was "so hairy I think he'll want to come home."

News of trouble in Cuba was spreading. Salinger, who had not been told of the missiles, learned that Carleton Kent of the *Chicago Sun-Times* and the columnists Robert Allen and Paul Scott were about to report imminent American military action against Cuba. Kennedy asked him to tell Kent, "We are not planning to invade Cuba." He asked McNamara to talk to Allen and Scott. The Defense Secretary told his spokesman to deny a *Miami Herald* report of operational ground-to-ground missiles in Cuba.

Fortified by his first hot meal in days, sent over in a covered dish by a Washington hostess, Sorensen stayed up until three on Saturday morning to work on a draft of the President's television address after studying Woodrow Wilson's and Franklin Roosevelt's speeches asking Congress to declare the two World Wars.

*   *   *

*Dining once with other New Frontiersmen at Hickory Hill, where prayer before meals was obligatory, John Kenneth Galbraith marveled that "so many lifelong heretics should so suddenly become so devout from being in the house of the Attorney General of the United States who was also the brother of the President."

Saturday, October 20. In Moscow at the castellated Spiridonovka Palace, the Foreign Minister's official residence, Foy Kohler lunched with Frol Kozlov. The Ambassador had been told that despite his opposition to portions of Khrushchev's program at the Twenty-second Party Congress, Kozlov was still Khrushchev's most likely successor: he should try to get to know him.

Kozlov arrived late and was "very gross," recalled Kohler's political counselor, Richard Davies. "He sat with his elbows on the table, ate like a pig, and drank like a fish. He got thoroughly drunk—a nasty drunk. . . . Kozlov did not put himself out one whit. . . . Kohler made every effort to engage him in conversation. His replies were curt."

Kohler and Davies took Kozlov's boorishness as a deliberate "insult to the United States." Had they known about the missiles in Cuba, they might have wondered whether Kozlov now considered the Soviet Union to be so strong that he could openly indulge his instinctive hostility toward the Americans.

In Chicago, Salinger announced that the President was suffering from a cold and returning to Washington. At 1:35 P.M., Kennedy landed on the South Grounds by helicopter, staring silently out the window, chin in hand. He walked into the Oval Office, looked at Sorensen's draft of his television speech,* swam while talking to the Attorney General, and convened an NSC meeting at two-thirty in the upstairs Oval Room.

The CIA considered four MRBM sites to be operational: those missiles on launching pads could probably be fired within eight hours of a Soviet decision to attack. Two IRBM sites had been spotted: one of these might be operational within six weeks, the other in eight to ten. American spy planes had also found twenty-two Il-28 bombers (only one assembled), thirty-nine MiG-21 fighters (thirty-five uncrated), and twenty-four SAM sites.†

Robert Kennedy tried to give his brother the Ex Comm straw votes,

---

*Sorensen took notes: "The Soviets will probably be able to point to one or more U.S. statements in the past that our base structure, including missile bases, was clearly defensive in purpose. Don't see how to deal with this in the statement, but perhaps it could be stated that in the context of the then-publicly-known facts, these statements could not have had an ambiguous interpretation as to offensive-vs.-defensive distinctions."

†According to General Volkogonov in 1989, the Soviet Defense Ministry had planned a force of forty-two Il-28s, forty-two MiG-21s and twenty-four SAM batteries, as well as twelve missile-carrying PT-boats and cruise missile batteries.

but as when he met with the Joint Chiefs, the President had in mind the domestic political recriminations if his crisis management failed: "I don't want to see them. I may choose the wrong policy, and then the people who are right will have it in writing."

McCone warned that if the Kremlin learned that the United States had discovered the missiles, the Soviets might assume that America was about to go to war and order an immediate nuclear attack. Rusk, in his usual fashion, summarized the arguments for air strike and quarantine. He gave the President a handwritten endorsement of a quarantine, which Kennedy read and gave back.

McNamara argued that the Soviets would retaliate somewhere— probably in Berlin—whatever the United States did. They could not ignore thousands of Soviet deaths by air strike: "The U.S. could lose control of the situation, which could escalate to general war." Quarantine was the only military course compatible with America's leadership of the Free World. They would get the missiles out only if prepared to offer something in return: perhaps "the withdrawal of U.S. strategic missiles from Turkey and Italy, and possibly agreement to limit our use of Guantanamo to a specified, limited time."

Taylor warned that soon the missiles would be camouflaged and almost impossible to find. Gilpatric said, "Essentially, Mr. President, this is a choice between limited action and unlimited action, and most of us here think it's better to start with limited action."

The President said that before making his final decision, he wished to talk with specialists to make sure that a surgical air strike was absolutely impossible. Otherwise they could assume he would choose a quarantine. He predicted that the "domestic political heat" after his television speech would be "terrific."

He said he expected the Soviets to move on Berlin, but that would probably happen whatever he did. Perhaps this show of American strength would make the Soviet Union think twice before acting against Berlin. He said that "the worst course of all would be to do nothing." If the missiles were left in Cuba, both Khrushchev and Castro would seem able to do what they pleased in the world. With the Bay of Pigs prisoners still in Cuban jails, Castro could "shoot one hundred Americans a day with impunity."

Adlai Stevenson had flown down from New York. Last evening he had told a colleague that he would "insist for history we make one last day's effort to avoid a clash. . . . I'm fighting for getting ready . . . then split seconds to the UN and the OAS."

* * *

In 1960, Stevenson had been the most popular Democrat in the country. Now he served in a job he thought beneath him for a President he considered "cold and ruthless." He wrote one lady friend that he slept "with the help of God and Seconal." Three times he sent another lady friend a poem with the last line underscored: *"Humankind cannot bear very much reality."*

Kennedy knew that Stevenson was the only member of his government, with the possible exception of the Vice President, who had a serious independent political base. He knew that the old Illinois Governor, twice the Democratic nominee, was still more popular among many Democrats than he was. As long as Stevenson remained so, he would be able to exert liberal pressure on the President from within the government, especially on foreign policy. If he ever resigned in protest,* he could jeopardize Kennedy's support by the dominant wing of his own party.

At the same time as the President ostentatiously consulted his UN Ambassador, he worked to undermine him and coopt his national following. He hoped that by 1965, Stevenson's standing would be so diminished that without serious cost he could move him to the embassy in London, where his influence over a second Kennedy administration would be negligible.

Bundy years later remembered the President's relations with Stevenson as "a long and troubled story." The problems between the two men went back at least to Chicago in 1956, when Sorensen told Stevenson's staff that Kennedy would like to be Vice President. Stevenson said, "I like Jack Kennedy, admire him, but he's too young, his father, his religion." The nomination was thrown open. Nineteen fifty-six was the year that Robert Kennedy traveled with the Stevenson campaign and returned to tell his brother that Stevenson was "just not a man of action at all."

Kennedy's attitude was forever poisoned by 1960. In May, after winning the Oregon primary, he had arranged to call at the Governor's farm in Libertyville, Illinois. He had heard that Lyndon Johnson had invited Stevenson to "go out and corral some votes" against Kennedy, saying, "We'll teach that little prick a thing or two." Before going to Libertyville, he told his aide Hy Raskin, "I am going to find out if he is playing Johnson's game in trying to stop me. . . . If he wants to become Secretary of State, he'd better do something to earn it."

Kennedy told Stevenson that "Lyndon is a chronic liar. . . . He has been making all sorts of assurances to me for years and has lived up

---

*As he was contemplating doing against President Lyndon Johnson over Vietnam at the time of his death in 1965.

to none of them." The only way to treat the Texan was to beat him: "That fucking bastard can only understand power." Stevenson would not be moved.

Flying away from Chicago, Kennedy told Charles Bartlett, "Well, I learned one thing today and that is that Adlai Stevenson will never be my Secretary of State. I'm used to being turned down. I ask a hundred people a day if they will support me and about eighty-nine of them are still saying they are going to wait and see how this thing develops." Not Stevenson. "He said, 'Jack, I've decided I'm not coming out for you now. I'm going to hold back . . . because I can serve as a bridge between you and Lyndon Johnson.'"

Kennedy laughed bitterly. "I don't think Adlai realizes that Lyndon Johnson thinks that he's a fruit. . . . If he were a great diplomat, he would have come up with a better one than that."*

After the meeting, Stevenson called George Ball, his old Chicago law partner: "Kennedy behaved just like his old man. He said to me, 'Look, I have the votes for the nomination, and if you don't give me your support, I'll have to shit all over you.' . . . I should have told the son of a bitch off but, frankly, I was shocked and confused by that Irish gutter talk. That's pretty cheap stuff." Stevenson wrote Schlesinger that Kennedy was "*very* self-confident and assured and much tougher and bloodier than I remembered him in the past."

In July, nervous about draft-Stevenson demonstrations planned for the convention floor, Kennedy gave him another chance to join the bandwagon by delivering his nominating speech. Later, recounting Stevenson's reply that he was a "helpless pawn with all these forces," Kennedy was profane: "If he doesn't know how to do this, he's got no business being here."

On the weekend before the balloting, Joseph Kennedy clenched his fist and told a Stevenson aide, "Your man must be out of his mind," adding before he turned away, "You've got twenty-four hours." Robert Kennedy recalled that Stevenson "wasn't able to decide what he wanted. He wanted the nomination but he wasn't willing to fight for it. He wanted to keep his options open for Secretary."

---

*Kennedy was correct. Johnson would speak of "that fat ass Stevenson" as "the kind of man who squats when he pees," which suggested to Schlesinger that Johnson thought Stevenson a homosexual.

After the Libertyville meeting, Joseph Kennedy told Raskin, "I warned Jack it would be a waste of time because Stevenson was the kind of guy who normally would have volunteered his support as soon as it became apparent that Jack was the front-runner. Jack insisted on going all the way to Libertyville for nothing. All he got was some doubletalk. Fortunately we will win without him. I wouldn't trust him as Secretary of State anyway. He has too much trouble making up his mind."

Stevenson never understood how deeply he had alienated the Kennedys. He later said, "It never occurred to me I wouldn't become Secretary of State." The President-elect offered Justice, the London Embassy, or the UN, saying that he hoped "very much" that it would be the UN. Shocked, hurt, angry, Stevenson told his law partner Newton Minow, "I'm not going to take it. . . . I'm going to continue as we are—speeches, articles." Minow said, "Also you'll be on page forty-six in the *New York Times* with three lines of space."

George Ball recalled, "We sat up until 2 A.M. drinking brandy and talking about it. I told him he was temperamental and incapable of taking himself out of public life. . . . This was a new administration. . . . There was no telling what could turn out of it. I told him not to be an Agamemnon. . . . He always had an enormous capacity for dramatizing himself. . . . The thing that fascinated me about Adlai was that he accepted so easily the idea that he was a great historical figure moving back and forth on the scene. I think he always had Abraham Lincoln on his mind a good deal."

Stevenson told the President-elect in Georgetown that he could not accept the UN until he knew who would be Secretary of State. Kennedy said, "I'll be your boss. You can have a direct line to me." He took Stevenson out onto his front steps and announced his UN offer. The Governor said he wished to discuss how the job could be strengthened. Reporters asked, "Are we to understand you have not accepted it?" Stevenson said that his answer depended upon a further talk with the President-elect, "which I hope will be very soon."

"I hope it will be before the middle of next week," said Kennedy, who went back inside. Robert Kennedy recalled that his brother was "shocked" and "absolutely furious" that Stevenson publicized their bargaining, so furious that he "almost withdrew" the offer.

Unwilling to wind up on page 46 of the *Times,* the Governor used what few bargaining chips he possessed. Through several days of telephone talks with Kennedy and Rusk, he won the appearance but not the reality of a UN mission in New York that created foreign policy. As George Ball said, "History had passed him by."

In 1961, Kennedy spent no little amount of time keeping Stevenson happy. Were he not so concerned that the Governor might resign, he might have authorized military actions that might have made the Bay of Pigs less of a travesty.

By his second year in office, pressed by one crisis after another, more firmly established in the White House, Kennedy worried about Stevenson less and less. Although Rusk had backed Stevenson for

President in 1960, he now privately said that he would never confide his fallback position to the UN envoy: otherwise "he would reach that point in about the first five minutes of the negotiation."*

Harlan Cleveland, Assistant Secretary of State for UN affairs, noticed that "Kennedy was pragmatic, Stevenson more interested in long-range and the emotional side. Kennedy was not interested in long-range at all, he was interested in what to do next week."

Robert Kennedy said, "I don't like the word tough, but he was so untough. He didn't face reality in the world, in facing himself even. . . . Stevenson had a wonderful way of speaking, but he would get to the point and then move off it. . . . Stevenson would whine all the time. . . . Jack used to talk about him frequently—what a pain in the ass he was." The First Lady, who liked Stevenson and attended the theater with him in New York, conceded that "Jack can't bear being in the same room with him."

Kennedy encouraged her to pursue her friendship with the Governor. She painted a watercolor for his birthday and wrote him after a visit to the UN that "the whole atmosphere of that place is so charged with undercurrents and tension and excitement. . . . I was so lucky to have the chance to meet U Thant—and I loved him, but I'm not fickle." At a White House dinner, she confided in him about her marital relations in a manner that Stevenson found "most indiscreet."

Kennedy told a friend, "Look, Stevenson has had the two most shattering blows anyone could have had. He was twice defeated for President." George Ball recalled that once during troubles in the Congo, he called on Kennedy ("he was in the massage room at the White House, naked"), who asked him to call Stevenson in New York while he listened. Afterward he said, "Look, George, he lives in a microcosm that's totally different from the world of reality we live in here. Don't be as tough as you are with him."

At other times the President evinced the hostility of the younger man who knew he would never gain the approval of the older man he had dethroned. His treatment of Stevenson closely resembled the mix of thoughtfulness, wariness, and cruelty with which he treated Lyndon Johnson—and for most of the same reasons.

Kennedy told friends that despite Stevenson's great reputation as an intellectual, he read more books in a week than Stevenson did in a year. (This was probably true.) George Smathers thought that Ste-

---

*During Stevenson's tenure at the UN, Rusk heeded Stevenson's sensitivities by avoiding opportunities to speak in the General Assembly, as foreign ministers customarily do; he said that in light of his world stature Stevenson should be given a free hand in New York.

venson was "just not masculine enough for Jack Kennedy." The President asked Jacqueline why women liked Adlai so much and wondered aloud whether he was a "switcher": he had seen him in a Turkish bath in New York and doubted that he would be "much of a rival." He once told a reporter that he and Bobby had been having some fun "seeing how much old Adlai would stand for."

Oleg Cassini professed to remember an overcast Newport day when the President asked Stevenson to fly up by helicopter. Told of threatening skies, Kennedy said, by Cassini's account, "Good, he'll be airsick." When Stevenson arrived, "green at the gills," the President sat him on the deck of his boat in treacherous waters, where the Governor tried "unsuccessfully not to shiver in the wind and rain."

After Kennedy put him back onto the storm-tossed helicopter, Cassini said, "Mr. President, that is truly cruel and unusual punishment." By Cassini's account, Kennedy replied, "He could use it. It's good for his health."

From time to time Stevenson tried to increase his leverage in Washington, observing that a "wise politician" should never be far from a microphone. In December 1961, like a maiden prodding a suitor into marriage by waving a rival proposal, he told Kennedy that he was thinking of running for the Senate and wanted "a lot more autonomy and authority than in the past."

It did not work. "I don't understand that man and I never have understood him," the President told Kaysen afterward. "He's talking about being Senator from Illinois—well, if he wants to do that I wish him well. But I don't understand why he wants to be one among one hundred. . . . I know he's mad because I never offered him Secretary—but why didn't he ask me for it?" Kennedy refused Stevenson's request to issue a statement asking him to stay on at the UN.

The Governor never forgot that at the Inauguration he was the only Cabinet member to get no limousine, which he blamed on the "Irish Mafia" on Kennedy's staff. Of the President he carped, "That young man, he never says please, he never says thank you, he never asks for things, he demands them." The "avarice" of the Kennedys made him "sick." He was piqued when Peter Lawford announced that he was paying off Stevenson's campaign deficits.

For power he substituted the perquisites of power. Ball found him surrounding himself with "these rich females, this odd harem. . . . They gave him the best food in New York—he went to every first night in the theater. . . . He knew this was a very phony life, the UN, divorced from the reality of politics, living in the phony adulation of these women all the time. . . . They took care of him. . . . He talked about leaving the UN but he had no place to go."

Robert Kennedy recalled that his brother liked to "shock" Stevenson and "give him something he'd talk to his girls about." When Stevenson lectured the President at Hyannis Port about disarmament, he was horrified when Kennedy replied that disarmament was just "propaganda."

During these years Stevenson told one of his lady friends that he had trouble sleeping, "and I have the most terrible dreams when I do get to sleep"—nightmares about the world blowing up, "the death of mankind, the end of life on this planet."

Now in the Oval Room, Stevenson argued that the President's television speech on Cuba should include a proposal for negotiations with the Soviet Union: once the missiles were gone, the United States might be willing to discuss the "demilitarization" of Cuba, including both Soviet installations and the American base at Guantanamo. Perhaps they should consider withdrawing the Jupiters from Turkey and Italy.

McNamara had made a similar suggestion, but not as an offer before the escalation began. Sorensen said it was "not us but Russia that should be in the prisoner's dock." Dillon and McCone complained that starting with concessions would legitimize Khrushchev's action and give him an easy victory.

The President said that at this stage they could not consider giving up Guantanamo; that would suggest "that we had been frightened into abandoning our position." At an appropriate time, the United States would have to acknowledge its willingness to take strategic missiles out of Turkey and Italy, if the Russians raised the issue.

Stevenson did not give up: they should "offer to give up such bases in order to induce the Russians to remove the strategic missiles." Kennedy insisted that there would be "no bargains over our bases in Turkey and Italy."

On the Truman Balcony after the meeting, Robert complained to the President that Stevenson was "not strong enough or tough enough to be representing us at the UN at a time like this." They should "get someone else." The President replied that maybe Stevenson "went too far when he suggested giving up Guantanamo," but he had shown "plenty of strength and courage" to "risk being called an appeaser."

That evening Stevenson told O'Donnell, "I know that most of those fellows will probably consider me a coward for the rest of my life for what I said today, but perhaps we need a coward in the room when we are talking about nuclear war."

Bundy was informed that the *New York Times* had assembled a fairly accurate account of the crisis about to burst. Kennedy called James Reston: he was planning a speech on Monday. If the *Times* published, he "might well be confronted by a Moscow ultimatum" before he had a chance to speak. Reston worked to have the story quashed.

Before leaving Chicago, the President had called Jacqueline at Glen Ora and asked her to return with Caroline and John to the White House so that they could be together in case of sudden emergency. Swimming with Dave Powers on Saturday evening, he used the same words he had spoken while flying to London from the Vienna summit: "If we were only thinking of ourselves, it would be easy, but I keep thinking about the children whose lives would be wiped out."

Sunday morning, October 21. With the tang of autumn in the air, under a lowered sun, Washington had never looked more handsome. The President gave Ex Comm breakfast in the upstairs Oval Room. As McNamara recalled, Kennedy polled those present and found that the group was now in favor of an air strike, by nine to seven.

After Mass, the President returned to the room to question General Taylor and General Walter Sweeney, the tactical air chief who would command an air strike of Cuba, if ordered. The best they could offer was to destroy 90 percent of the known missiles. Since only about thirty of the forty-eight missiles presumed to be on Cuba had been found, an attack could thus leave as many as twenty-one untouched. McNamara and the two generals said that an initial attack would have to be followed by hundreds of sorties, leading almost inevitably to a full-scale invasion of Cuba.

Robert Kennedy arrived after a horseback ride at Hickory Hill, still wearing his riding clothes. He said they should start with a quarantine and thereafter "play for the breaks." McCone said that if it did not work, they must move on to air strike and invasion.

The President agreed. Rusk later said, "We did not *think* that Khrushchev would respond to the quarantine with a nuclear strike, but we couldn't *know* it." Even if he did not, the crisis could last for months. Robert Kennedy expected a "very, very difficult winter."

* * *

From the moment that the President was told of the missiles he had acted to ensure for himself and Ex Comm six days of quiet in which to scrutinize the problem from every angle. This may have been a legacy of what he had learned during the Berlin Crisis. Another President might have moved more hastily. The time that Kennedy bought for himself proved to be fortuitous: had he been compelled to make a decision within hours, he would probably have opted for an air strike.

Here the President also gained from his preference for secrecy and his superb sense of how to package foreign policy decisions for best advantage. From the start he knew that unless the missiles in Cuba and the American response were announced deftly, the world might be disgusted that the United States was risking nuclear war to remove missiles no more menacing than those along the Soviet border. Another President might not have taken such care to make sure that the missiles were not first revealed by the Russians, the *New York Times,* or CBS in a way that would undermine public support for his course of action.

Kennedy's six days of quiet deliberation were a gift that no American President in a similar quandary will probably ever enjoy again. Were the Missile Crisis to occur in the political and journalistic culture of three decades later, an American television network with access to a private satellite might well have discovered the missiles and announced them to the world only hours after the President had learned about them.

In the wake of the revelation, Allied leaders might have demanded that nothing be done, noting that the missiles were no greater danger than what Western Europe had endured for years. Republican campaigners would have demanded that the President fulfill his September warning by ordering an air strike and invasion. Others would question whether he had known about the missiles for weeks and been trying to conceal the embarrassing fact until after the November elections.

Amid such a noisy furor, it would have been much more difficult for Kennedy to hold public support for a moderate course of action. In the overheated domestic atmosphere, choosing anything less than air strike and invasion might have caused him to be denounced as an appeaser of Khrushchev.

On Sunday afternoon, the President called his NSC to the Oval Room. Rusk reported that State was drafting letters to forty-three heads of government, UN and OAS resolutions, a quarantine proclamation, and a list of precautions to be taken by American embassies around the world against riots and demonstrations. Admiral Anderson declared, "Mr. President, the Navy will not let you down."

After the Soviets detonated their first atomic bomb in 1949, American defense planners had begun drawing up plans for evacuation of the President and his highest officials. The Army Corps of Engineers built a huge secret underground shelter out of a mountain in the Virginia countryside called Mount Weather. If a nuclear attack seemed imminent, the President, other top leaders, and their families were supposed to rush there by helicopter.

Dean Rusk thought the plan "psychologically silly": after a nuclear exchange with the Soviet Union, "the first band of shivering survivors that could reach a President or a Secretary of State would hang him under the nearest tree." Nevertheless Kennedy was reminded to raise the matter with his wife.

Jacqueline Bouvier Kennedy's fastidious eye for art, furniture, and clothes, her indirect public manner, and her refusal to air political opinions all helped to obscure her influence on her husband's politics and his relations with other politicians. She said, "I think the best thing I could do was to be a distraction. Jack lived and breathed politics all day long. If he came home to more table thumping, how could he ever relax?"

When she asked him about Laos or another crisis dominating the headlines, he often told her, "Oh, gosh, kid, I've had that on me all day. Ask Bundy to let you see the cables." As she later recalled, she would read the cables until the flow of problems "depressed" her. After Kennedy received a notably imperious missive from de Gaulle, Bundy wrote her, "I am mindful of your warning not to fill your mind with official business, but on this one I have the President's very energetic approval for the notion that you will want to see it." She thanked him for letting her see his "treasure."

Arthur Schlesinger sent over a "glowing piece" from a London paper hailing the President as a new Henry V. She wrote back, "The Telegraph article is unbelievable! Couldn't you translate the Henry V part and send it to de Gaulle?"

Jacqueline's approach to life was less intellectual or moral than aesthetic. She saw international affairs (although not most of domestic politics) as a drama and her husband, in political terms, as a hero moving through a great historical pageant. She recalled growing up thinking that politics was "corny old men shouting on the Fourth of July" and that history was "something that bitter old men wrote."

Then she had realized that "for Jack, history was full of heroes"—the Knights of the Round Table, Melbourne, the protagonists of *Profiles in Courage.* In the spring of 1960, she had watched him read Mary Renault's *The King Must Die.*

The *Telegraph* piece was not the first time the parallel between her husband and Henry V had occurred to her. When the Grand Duchess of Luxembourg was scheduled to visit the White House, the First Lady asked Basil Rathbone to read the St. Crispin's Day speech from Shakespeare's play. The actor doubted that a speech about murdering kings was appropriate for a duchess.

She wrote Rathbone that *Henry V* was one of the President's favorites "for whatever lovely dreams of leading or being led on to victory lurk in his soul" and that the play "reminds me of him—though I don't think he knows that!" She insisted that "of all the speeches that make you care and want to make the extra effort—sacrifice, fight, or die—this is the one. The only person I would not wish you to say it in front of was Khrushchev, as we are not united in purpose*—but tiny Luxembourg. . . . We are all striving for the same brave things today."

On Friday evening, November 22, 1963, she asked the Attorney General, "What's the line between history and drama?"

The drama and high style later remembered of the Kennedy White House were Jacqueline's contribution. Before their marriage in 1953, when Kennedy gave a dinner party, a houseman would make do with a hot plate. For a period, the only liquor in his Georgetown house was Scotch, sent by Joseph Kennedy. A colleague recalled a Kennedy meal at which "we had chicken and we drank Scotch before, during, and after the dinner." One of the Congressman's aides noticed that he wore only four winter suits.

After Kennedy's election to the Senate in 1952, Joseph Kennedy urged his son to find a wife, worried that, like Stevenson, his son might become the victim of a whispering campaign that he was a homosexual. The elder Kennedy told his friend Dorothy Schiff, publisher of the *New York Post,* "We thought of Grace Kelly, but she was too Hollywood." He was delighted when his son shifted his courtship of Jacqueline Bouvier into high gear.

Her ability to invest her husband's career with romance was badly tested during their early marriage by his constant political travels and his uninterrupted pursuit of other women. But it survived. After the

---

*The First Lady was not immune to the Kennedy-Sorensen school of heroic rhetoric.

Los Angeles convention, she painted a portrait of him returning triumphantly in Napoleonic garb. That November, she marked her ballot only for her husband: "I didn't want to dilute it by voting for anyone else."

Entering the White House, she was appalled by the "Statler Hilton" decor of the Eisenhowers and "terrified" by the prospect of "all those eyes just staring," the aides who "hit the White House with their Dictaphones running." Ben Bradlee found her "nervous and distraught" when she heard he was keeping a diary. Staff members were told that "Mrs. Kennedy requests that you save all notes and memoranda you receive from her. . . . She will request these back for her files and her library at the end of the Administration."*

During the late 1950s, she had feared that she was a political liability to her husband and that everyone thought her a Newport snob who had bouffant hair and French clothes and hated politics: "Oh, Jack, I'm so sorry for you that I'm such a dud." He told her that he loved her as she was.

In the White House, probably no one was more surprised than he at her omnipresence on the covers of fan magazines, the larger crowds and cries of "Jackie!" when she appeared with him in public. She helped assuage her class-conscious husband's vague feeling of social and cultural inferiority; in November 1963, he encouraged her to show "those cheap Texas broads" what good taste was.

Noting his tendency to compartmentalize his relationships, Jacqueline later said, "Mine was the happiness compartment." He learned from her knowledge of drawing and French furniture; when she delved into eighteenth-century French history, he took the book from her and found out about Louis XIV's mistresses before she could.

The White House brought a regularity to their life together that had been absent during the years Kennedy spent campaigning for Presi-

---

*In 1965, when she read a draft of Arthur Schlesinger's *A Thousand Days,* she implored him to "take me out" of the book "wherever you can" and eliminate "things I think are too personal. *That* is the only thing that can remain private for JFK—With everyone writing books—there won't be one shred of his whole life that the whole world won't know about. But the world has no right to his private life with me—I shared all those rooms with him—not with the Book of the Month readers + I don't want them snooping through those rooms now—even the bathtub—with the children—Please take all those parts out."

When Schlesinger was publicly attacked for personal material that appeared in the book's prepublication serialization in *Life,* he replied, "This is exactly the kind of intimate detail which critics and readers would be delighted to read if I—or any other historian—came across it while writing about President Jackson or President Roosevelt."

dent. She arranged small dinners to divert him; sometimes she put on phonograph records such as Jimmy Dean's rendition of the ballad "PT-109," which she loved, or Lerner and Loewe's *Camelot,* after which there might be a moment of dancing. The President would vanish into his bedroom to work or make telephone calls, reappearing in time to bid their guests good night.

Still the marriage was subject to the tensions generated by a President unwilling to give up other women and a First Lady unwilling to perform domestic political errands. Lem Billings recalled Kennedy's exasperation about his wife's spending habits: "He just didn't like to spend money on little things. He was very much in the habit of spending a hell of a lot of money on his career. That was spent like there was no tomorrow. When he died, he had used up all his cash."

Mrs. Kennedy often departed alone for Glen Ora, New York, Hyannis Port, and Europe. When her husband persuaded her to make a Texas campaign trip in November 1963, it was to be the first time she had ventured west of Virginia since the Inauguration. During that same period, she had traveled abroad a number of times.*

Galbraith found that Jacqueline "had always a sharper view than her husband of the people around the Presidency, and while Kennedy leaned toward charity, she leaned to truth." Galbraith thought she "concerned herself excessively with dress and related artifacts of style," saying of General Lemnitzer, for instance, "We all thought well of him until he made the mistake of coming into the White House one Saturday morning in a sport jacket."†

In thanks for a volume of poetry, she wrote Roswell Gilpatric that a gift of such rare sensitivity could not have come from someone like "Antonio Celebrezze‡ or Dean Rusk."

The President's high opinion of men like Gilpatric, McNamara, Dillon, Bundy, Schlesinger, and Galbraith was bolstered by the fact

---

*In August 1962, when the Gallup poll asked Americans what they liked most and least about their First Lady, the most frequent comment on the latter list was "travels too much, away from family."

†One can imagine what she must have privately thought of the aesthetic presence on the New Frontier of Lyndon Johnson, whom Arthur Miller found at a White House dinner for André Malraux in May 1962 "wearing a ruffled blue shirt" and "almost demonstrably disdaining the occasion, standing with one knee raised and a shoe pressed against the immaculate wainscoting, studiously cleaning his fingernails with a file like an idler in front of a country store."

‡Anthony Celebrezze, former Mayor of Cleveland, succeeded Ribicoff in July 1962 as Secretary of Health, Education and Welfare.

that they met the First Lady's aesthetic standards. He was unaffected by her affection for Stevenson or her references to O'Donnell as "the wolfhound." He cautioned her to avoid saying even to him that she disliked some political figure because it would affect the way she acted toward the person.

Gilpatric recalled that "she was always asking me all kinds of questions about the Pentagon, about the flow of power. She had heard her husband mention all kinds of names of people at the Pentagon and she wanted to know what kind of power they had, whether they were motivated mostly by ambition or by their loyalty to the President. She was deeply concerned with how much they could be trusted. . . . She was very, very astute."

Jacqueline's knowledge of French, Spanish, and Italian, her sense of history and ease with foreign political figures (greater than her ease with their American counterparts), helped smooth the President's diplomacy. In private she was said to perform uncanny impersonations of dozens of world leaders she had met: Adenauer, the Shah, Queen Frederika of Greece, Sukarno, who during his Washington visit salaciously invited the First Lady to visit Indonesia without her husband.

She told the President that before they left the White House she hoped someone would ask her who was the greatest statesman she had ever met: "And it isn't going to be de Gaulle or Nehru or Macmillan or anyone. It's going to be Lleras Camargo of Colombia." This choice was in character: when the Kennedys went to Colombia in December 1961, President Alberto Lleras Camargo had proudly shown her through his presidential palace, a museum of Colombian history which inspired her in her restoration of the White House.

She enlisted Schlesinger and Goodwin to help save Abu Simbel and other Egyptian monuments threatened by the new Aswan Dam by securing funds from Congress and arranging a Tutankhamen show at the National Gallery. The mildly beneficial effect of the exercise on relations with Gamal Abdel Nasser did not enhance Kennedy's popularity among Jewish voters. Schlesinger wrote the First Lady that with the financial and technical problems solved, "this leaves the political problems with which the President will have to deal."

Jacqueline's political interests extended beyond Bogotá and the Nile. McNamara felt that Kennedy consulted her "on any number of issues—I don't mean in the sense of long, anguished discussions, but certainly she was informed of what was going on and expressed her views on almost everything." General Clifton said, "She wouldn't advise his staff, she would advise him. That's why nobody knew about it."

David Ormsby-Gore recalled that Jacqueline sent to the Library of Congress for books and articles on the background of political events, which she gave to the President—"her way of encouraging him to share his thoughts and troubles with her." Ormsby-Gore said that more than once he heard Jacqueline press the President to normalize relations with the Soviet Union.

While deliberating over the missiles in Cuba, he astonished her by calling her at midday and asking her to join him for a walk in the Rose Garden. "He was sharing with her the possible horror of what might happen," said Charles Spalding. "If it was earlier in their marriage, I don't think he would have called her then. But things were beginning to break up in his head."

Early in her husband's Presidency, she had arranged to see the White House bomb shelter, built during World War II four levels below the state floor. When the door was opened, a small army of Signal Corps men sprang to their feet. She glanced in and quickly left. "How amazing! I didn't expect to find so much humanity! I thought it would be a great big room that we could use as an indoor recreation room for the children. I even had plans for a basketball court in there."

Now the President asked his wife whether she wished to go to the government's great artificial cavern in the mountains. With her unerring sense of both history and drama, she told him that if nuclear war began she preferred to come over to the Oval Office and share whatever happened to him.

17

"The Moment We Hoped Would Never Come"

O N MONDAY, OCTOBER 22, HALE BOGGS, THE HOUSE DEMO-cratic Whip, was fishing in the Gulf of Mexico when a bottle was dropped by air into the water: "Call Operator 18, Washington. Urgent message from the President." The Air Force flew House Republican leader Charles Halleck from Indiana to Washington at almost the speed of sound. Other congressional leaders left the campaign trail boasting that the President needed their advice.

Dean Acheson flew to a SAC base north of London to brief David Bruce, who produced a bottle of Scotch from which they both drank. He left behind a CIA man to help Bruce show the U-2 pictures to Harold Macmillan. After peering at them, the Prime Minister said, "Now the Americans will realize what we here in England have lived through for this past many years." He could not know that was almost exactly what Khrushchev had said before sending his missiles to Cuba.

Flying on to Paris, Acheson slipped into the Élysée to brief Charles de Gaulle, who asked whether he had come to inform or consult. Acheson said, "We must be very clear about this. I have come to inform you of a decision which he has taken." The French President said he did not need to see the U-2 pictures: a "great nation" did not act if there were "any doubt about the evidence."

At Gettysburg, Eisenhower received a call from Kennedy, who told him of the speech planned for that evening. The General replied that without "all the background on file and communications and international conversation," he could not offer advice, but that whatever the government decided to do would have his support.

The President told him he hoped prominent Republicans would not make the crisis "a partisan thing." Eisenhower was "sure they wouldn't."

In Moscow, Colonel Oleg Penkovsky, who for eighteen months had been feeding thousands of pages of top-secret Soviet documents to British and American intelligence, was arrested. Richard Helms later said, "I remember very well that a meeting was scheduled with Penkovsky. We got no word and no word and no word. This really began to worry the hell out of me, and I went to McCone. . . . I burst through the door and said, 'It looks to me as though we've lost Penkovsky.' "

That the Russians should arrest the Western agent now, after months of surveillance, was no surprise. During the missile confrontation, the Kremlin could not afford to leave a traitor in a position from which he could do more damage to the Soviet cause. McCone considered the arrest strictly an operational intelligence matter and did not mention it to his colleagues on Ex Comm.

Had Penkovsky been arrested a year earlier, the United States might not have been able to establish so quickly that the U-2 pictures showed MRBMs and IRBMs. As Helms recalled, were it not for the information smuggled by Penkovsky to the West, "the President would have been up against a very tough decision because he didn't know if he could wait several days. Maybe they were in a firing position. How the hell is he going to know? Intelligence bought him the time he needed."*

---

*Raymond Garthoff, one of the CIA men who analyzed Penkovsky's take, wrote in 1987 that a CIA clandestine officer who managed the case told him in 1962 that, when Penkovsky was arrested, the agent sent the telephonic signal prearranged with his Western handlers to warn them against imminent Soviet attack: "Fortunately, his Western intelligence handlers, at the operational level, after weighing a dilemma of great responsibility, decided not to credit Penkovsky's signal and suppressed it. Not even the higher reaches of the CIA were informed of Penkovsky's provocative farewell." Garthoff wrote that he had not been able to confirm the report, but believed it to be true. Helms told the author in 1988 that he was more skeptical.

* * *

On Monday afternoon, tossing his coat over his shoulder, Robert Kennedy walked from Justice to the White House for a three o'clock NSC meeting. The previous week, he had been so preoccupied that when an aide brought in documents for signing, he had to remind the Attorney General that there was "a human being in the room." The aide said, "Something looks different here." Kennedy replied, "I'm older."

The President entered the Cabinet Room after a brief swim and luncheon with Jacqueline. He told his men that quarantine was going to be "a very tricky course, and we will never know whether this is the best course. . . . An air strike is tempting and I didn't give up on it until yesterday morning." As long as they could not be sure of annihilating all the missiles, a quarantine was "far less likely to provoke a nuclear response."

Placing missiles outside the Soviet Union was a "drastic change" in Soviet policy. If he did not act against them, the Russians might think he would not act elsewhere, especially in Berlin. "It would create grave problems in Latin America, where there would be a feeling that the balance of power in this hemisphere was shifting away from us, that the Russians could throw their weight around right on our own doorstep."

There was "a big difference" between the missiles in Cuba and those in Turkey and Italy: "Ours are an attempt to redress the balance of power in Europe. . . . But what is happening in Cuba is far different—a provocative change in the delicate status quo in this hemisphere. . . . The very secrecy of this operation, and attempts to guard that secrecy even by Khrushchev himself, poses an obvious danger to us that we can't ignore. . . . The next move is up to the Russians."

As Fidel Castro recalled, he was alarmed by the "movements in Washington, the convocation, the special meetings. . . . We understood by instinct, by smell, that something would happen."

That afternoon, preparing for the North American invasion that he believed to be imminent, he evidently mobilized 270,000 Cubans. His Army Chief of Staff, Sergio del Valle, estimated that they would suffer more than a hundred thousand casualties. But he insisted that the Cuban people were "ready to die defending the revolution." They were "utterly determined to fight to the last man."

* * *

At five-thirty, Kennedy opened his meeting with seventeen leaders of Congress, telling Everett Dirksen of Illinois, the chief Senate Republican, "Tonight you're going to get reelected." Dirksen knew that the President had been speaking for his opponent when called back to Washington: "That was a nice speech you gave for Sid Yates in Chicago. Too bad you caught that cold making it."

The merry atmosphere abruptly halted when Kennedy revealed the presence of missiles in Cuba. "Why, that's right next to my home state," cried George Smathers. "We never knew anything about it!"

Unlike his colleagues, Senator Richard Russell already knew about the missiles. Before going to Georgia, he had asked the White House for a briefing on Cuba. Bundy had warned the President that it would be "very bad for him to go home with an incomplete picture after he has asked for a briefing." The President had Lyndon Johnson confide the secret to his old friend during an automobile ride along the Potomac.

Now, as Kennedy described his quarantine plan, Russell scrawled, "Khrushchev believes what he says—we are afraid." When the President fell silent, Russell said he could not live with himself unless he spoke his mind. A quarantine was a "halfway measure. . . . If we let the Communists get away with it here, we'd be plagued by them for the rest of our lives." Why not "invade Cuba and remove the missiles physically, and at the same time remove Mr. Castro physically and set up a new and different government?"

Johnson evidently agreed but dared not speak out himself. Robert Kennedy noticed that as his brother defended the quarantine, the Vice President "was shaking his head, mad."

The President was astounded when Fulbright declared that a quarantine was the wrong decision, and that an invasion would be "less provocative and less inclined to precipitate a war with Russia."

Struggling to contain his anger, Kennedy looked at his abdomen and drummed the arm of his chair. He told Fulbright, "You're for an *invasion* of *Cuba,* Bill? You and Senator *Russell?* . . . Last Tuesday, I was for an air strike or an invasion myself, but after four more days of deliberations, we decided that was not the wisest first move. And you would too, if you had more time to think about it."

With the two Senate Democrats in open opposition, others complained that the quarantine was too slow and irrelevant to the scale of the danger. Some said they would back the President in public only because the hour was so dangerous. For several moments, everyone talked at once. Dirksen and Halleck told the President they would support him but, like de Gaulle, insisted that the record show they had been informed, not consulted.

Kennedy walked back to the family quarters with O'Donnell to dress for his speech. Mocking the leaders, he chirped, "Oh, sure, we support you, Mr. President. But . . . if it goes wrong, we'll knock your block off." Later he said, "The trouble is that when you get a group of Senators together, they are always dominated by the man who takes the boldest and strongest line. . . . After Russell spoke, no one wanted to take issue with him."

Dean Rusk lamented his failure to consult at least a few leaders earlier: "When you get the congressional leaders in there two or three hours before a major speech . . . which would precipitate a major crisis, about the only question for these Congressmen is 'Are you ready to support your country in a moment of crisis?'"

Most of the leaders did not fault Kennedy for his worry about leaks, but the bitter memory of being ignored during the first week of the Missile Crisis may have been one influence leading to the War Powers Act, enacted by Congress in 1973 in order to gain more authority over decision-making at times of foreign crisis.*

As the President donned a blue shirt for television, Sorensen noticed that he seemed more weary from his wrangling with the leaders than during the week of agonizing about Cuba. Kennedy said, "If they want this job, fuck 'em. They can have it. It's no great joy to me."

A message arrived from Harold Macmillan warning the President to prepare for Soviet retaliation against Berlin and the "weaker parts of the Free World defense system."

Rusk called Dobrynin to the State Department and gave him a copy of the President's speech. Uninformed by his own government about the missiles, the Ambassador said, "It is going to be terrible."† Rusk noticed that "Dobrynin seemed to age ten years while we were talking. It had a real physical impact on him, because he realized that this would be a major crisis. I didn't keep him too long, because I wanted him to get it on the wire back to Moscow."

---

*Gerald Ford, who was among the congressional leaders not consulted during the first week of the Missile Crisis, said in 1990, "Those of us who operated under the old rules think they were better than what we have to face today." As President, Ford thought the War Powers Act should be rescinded.

†At a January 1989 Moscow conference of American, Soviet, and Cuban officials and scholars on the Missile Crisis, Dobrynin noted that he had not been informed. Gromyko said, "What, Anatoly Fyodorovich, you mean that I did not tell you, the Ambassador, about the missiles in Cuba?"

Dobrynin: "No, you did not tell me."

Gromyko: "That means it must have been a very big secret!" [Laughter]

When Dobrynin emerged from the State Department, a reporter noted that he was "ashen-faced and visibly shaken." Asked if a crisis was about to explode, he replied, "What do you think?" He waved Rusk's manila envelope and slumped into his limousine.

In Moscow, Kohler received a cable from Rusk: "The following message from the President should be delivered to the Foreign Office for transmission to Khrushchev one hour before the delivery of the President's speech."

Drafted largely by Thompson, Kennedy's message did not open with the usual "Dear Mr. Chairman" but the discourteous "Sir." He had written that the one thing that had most concerned him was that Khrushchev's government would not understand American will: "I have not assumed that you or any other sane man would, in this nuclear age, deliberately plunge the world into war, which it is crystal clear no country could win and which could only result in catastrophic consequences to the whole world, including the aggressor."

Since Vienna, he had warned that the United States "could not tolerate any action on your part which in a major way disturbed the existing overall balance of power in the world." Now he was "determined" to remove the threat in Cuba: "At the same time, I wish to point out that the action we are taking is the minimum necessary. . . . I hope that your Government will refrain from any action which would widen or deepen this already grave crisis and that we can agree to resume the path of peaceful negotiation."

Soviet Foreign Ministry bureaucrats no longer slept through the day and worked through the night, as they once had done to keep in tune with Stalin. Long before dawn on Tuesday, by arrangement, Richard Davies brought the President's message for Khrushchev to the large double glass doors of the Foreign Ministry. Alarmed, a young Russian officer said, "This must be bad news you have for us." Davies said, "You'll have to decide for yourself."

At 6:55 P.M., Kennedy walked past Salinger and other aides, reporters, lights, cameras, and cables to his naval desk, covered with canvas and masking tape. Laced into his tight corset, he lowered himself mechanically onto two pillows, his back ramrod-straight. His face was thinner than usual, with dark rings about the eyes and deep creases in the forehead.

At seven, Evelyn Lincoln moved toward him with a hairbrush. As the television announcer began to speak, he waved her aside. Staring into the camera lens and then down at his script, the President began reading perhaps the most important address of the Cold War:

"Good evening, my fellow citizens. This Government, as promised, has maintained the closest surveillance of the Soviet military buildup on the island of Cuba. Within the past weeks, unmistakable evidence has established the fact that a series of offensive missile sites is now in preparation on that imprisoned island." Their purpose: a "nuclear strike capability against the Western Hemisphere."

The United States had found medium-range missiles "capable of striking Washington, D.C., the Panama Canal, Mexico City, or any other city in the southeastern United States, in Central America, or in the Caribbean area." Other uncompleted sites appeared to be designed to accommodate intermediate-range missiles capable of striking targets "as far north as Hudson Bay, Canada, and as far south as Lima, Peru."

This was "an explicit threat to the peace and security of all the Americas," defying tradition, the Rio Pact of 1947,* the September congressional resolution, the UN Charter, and his own public warnings of September 4 and 13.†

The buildup's size made it clear "that it has been planned for some months." Just last month, the Soviet government had said it had "no need" to locate its missiles outside the Soviet Union. "That statement was *false.*" On Thursday, Gromyko had "told me in my office that he was instructed to make it clear once again that Soviet assistance to Cuba—and I quote—'pursued solely the purpose of contributing to the defense capabilities of Cuba.' . . . That statement also was *false.*"‡

No nation could tolerate such "deliberate deception and offensive threats. . . . Nuclear weapons are so destructive and ballistic missiles are so swift that any substantially increased possibility of their use or any sudden change in their deployment may well be regarded as a definite threat to peace." For years, the United States and the Soviet

---

*The 1947 Inter-American Treaty of Reciprocal Assistance joined the United States with Latin American countries in common concern against aggression, including "an aggression which is not an armed attack."

†Including the references to tradition, the Rio Pact, and the UN Charter helped to divert public attention from the fact that the President had issued his first warning against offensive missiles in Cuba no earlier than September.

‡Sorensen had profited from reading Roosevelt's message to Congress asking for a war declaration after Pearl Harbor, in which the President said, "The distance of Hawaii from Japan makes it obvious that the attack was deliberately planned many days or even weeks ago. During the intervening time, the Japanese Government has deliberately sought to deceive the United States by false statements and expressions of hope for continued peace."

Union had never upset "the precarious status quo which insured that these weapons would not be used in the absence of some vital challenge." American missiles had never been sent to another nation "under a cloak of secrecy and deception."

But this "secret, swift, and extraordinary buildup," in an area "well known to have a special and historical relationship to the United States," this "sudden, clandestine decision to station strategic weapons for the first time outside of Soviet soil," was "a deliberately provocative and unjustified change in the status quo which cannot be accepted by this country, if our courage or our commitments are ever to be trusted again by either friend or foe." America's "unswerving objective" must be to prevent the missiles' use and to secure their elimination from the hemisphere.

Kennedy announced his *"initial"* course of action. (His official text italicized the word.) "To halt this offensive buildup, a strict quarantine on all offensive military equipment under shipment to Cuba is being initiated. All ships of any kind bound for Cuba from whatever nation or port will, if found to contain cargoes of offensive weapons, be turned back."*

There would be more "close surveillance" of Cuba. If the buildup continued, "I have directed the Armed Forces to prepare for any eventualities."† Any missile launched from Cuba against any nation in the hemisphere would bring "a full retaliatory response upon the Soviet Union." Guantanamo would be reinforced. The United States would ask for immediate meetings of the OAS and the UN.

"I call upon Chairman Khrushchev to halt and eliminate this clandestine, reckless, and provocative threat to world peace and to stable relations between our two nations. I call upon him further to abandon this course of world domination, and to join in an historic effort to end the perilous arms race and transform the history of man.‡

---

*A passage omitted in the final text from Sorensen's October 20 draft added, "Let me make it clear that this blockade will not only prevent completion of the current offensive buildup on Cuba. It will also require the Soviet Union to choose between fighting the American Navy in American waters, or abandoning its obligations to Mr. Castro."

†Douglas Dillon had tried and failed to insert a more blatant threat here: "Unless offensive military preparations are abandoned forthwith, military action to eliminate them will be required."

‡Sorensen's October 20 draft had Kennedy asking Khrushchev for a summit, ostensibly to discuss the missiles: "I am asking Soviet Chairman Khrushchev, who will shortly be coming to the United Nations meeting in New York, to meet with me at the earliest opportunity with respect to this provocative threat to world peace. . . . But we will not negotiate with a gun at our heads—a gun that imperils innocent Cubans as well as Americans. Our byword is: 'Negotiation yes, intimidation no.'"

"He has an opportunity now to move the world back from the abyss of destruction, by returning to his government's own words that it had no *need* to station missiles outside its own territory, and withdrawing these weapons from Cuba, by refraining from any action which will widen or deepen the present crisis, and then by participating in a search for peaceful and permanent solutions." The President warned against any "hostile move" where the United States was committed— especially against "the brave people of West Berlin."

Showing how long he expected the Missile Crisis to last, he warned that "many months of sacrifice and self-discipline lie ahead. . . . Our goal is not the victory of might, but the vindication of right. . . . God willing, that goal will be achieved.* Thank you, and good night."

At 7:17, the lights went dark. Kennedy said, "Well, that's it, unless the son of a bitch fouls it up."

Bundy recalled years later, "We sure didn't feel as good as that speech sounded." In retrospect, he wondered whether some of the President's language had not been overblown, pretentious, and excessively nerve-racking.†

The address was probably the most alarming ever delivered by an American President. Although it echoed Franklin Roosevelt's Pearl Harbor message in language and meter, Roosevelt's speech had been intended to calm the American people, Kennedy's to frighten them. Roosevelt's message was written to reassure Americans that the war would be won. Even without it, Pearl Harbor had already united the country behind the war effort. Kennedy knew that the missiles in Cuba were not open to such unambiguous interpretation as the attack on Hawaii.

Borrowing from the rhetorical tradition of his first State of the

---

Dillon had recommended an additional passage suggesting the President's personal disappointment with Khrushchev, along the lines of Khrushchev's statements against Eisenhower after the U-2 episode. Dillon advised, "No firm decision should be taken at this time that the President will see K at the UN if he comes. He might well wish to refuse to see him. My original thought for a meeting with K was *after* we had eliminated bases, which is quite different from talking *before* such action with missiles pointing down our throats."

*Sorensen's October 20 draft had flatly said here, "I tell you, therefore, that these missiles now in Cuba will someday go—and no others will take their place." The President may have felt it more prudent not to employ such an unambiguous statement that might later be used against him by domestic political opponents.

†Although Bundy also said that he knew of "no public document in the nuclear age that more faithfully reports a major course of action by a President, and the reasons for his choice."

Union message, Kennedy's address was designed to divert attention from his private belief that the missiles did not seriously increase the Soviet military danger and the fact that he had not warned Khrushchev against them until it was too late.* He knew that a less apocalyptic speech would not have been so successful in rallying Americans behind their President and lowering the "domestic political heat" he expected to feel after they learned that Keating had been right about missiles in Cuba after all.

In the "war room" of the Pentagon, eerie colored lights on the vast wall map glowed on, showing that theater commanders around the world were following Kennedy's order to throw all major U.S. commands on alert for the first time since the Korean War.

An official Cuban spokesman called the quarantine "not only an act of war but a provocation for tragic world events." Almost every major British newspaper wondered whether the President was overreacting: the British Isles had faced Soviet medium-range missiles for years. The pacifist British philosopher Bertrand Russell wired Kennedy, "Your action desperate . . . no conceivable justification." He wired Khrushchev, "Your continued forbearance is our only hope."†

Most Americans rallied around their President. In the *Atlanta Constitution,* Eugene Patterson wrote, "Now we are at a showdown that will test the nerve of America." *Time* predicted that Kennedy's "resolve" could prove "one of the decisive moments of the twentieth century."

Despite his private opposition to the quarantine, Richard Russell wrote a constituent that "all good Americans intend to support our Commander-in-Chief." The old diplomat Adolf Berle, who had stood with Franklin Roosevelt through the invasion of Poland and Pearl Harbor, wrote in his diary, "God help us all."

Barry Goldwater called Kennedy's action "welcome but belated." Hugh Scott complained that nothing the President had said would "remove five thousand Russians and a half-million tons of military

---

*In the speech, Kennedy mentioned his September warnings but placed greater emphasis on the violation of hemispheric security, the Rio pact, American traditions, the congressional resolution on Cuba, the UN Charter, and Khrushchev's and Gromyko's "deliberate deception" and use of a "cloak of secrecy." He noted that Americans had "become adjusted" to Soviet ICBMs and sea-launched missiles but that the missiles in Cuba added to the "already clear and present danger."

†Kennedy replied that Russell's attention "might well be directed to the burglar, rather than to those who caught the burglar."

supplies from Cuba."* The Republican chairman, William Miller, asked Americans to "pray" that Kennedy would not be governed by "the same timidity and indecision which doomed the Bay of Pigs." The Harvard *Crimson,* for which Kennedy had once written editorials, complained of his "frenzied rejection" of diplomacy.

Kenneth Keating declared that the President's speech had "taken Cuba out of politics." Richard Nixon saw his California campaign going up in smoke: "Now I knew how Stevenson must have felt when Suez and the Hungarian rebellion flared up in the last days before the election in 1956."

A Massachusetts schoolgirl wrote a friend, "Can you imagine not seeing another Christmas, Thanksgiving, Easter, birthday, dance, or even Halloween? . . . We're just too young to die."†

A Georgian wrote Kennedy, "Thank God you seem to be moving in the right direction at last. . . . What mystifies me is your apparent indignation that Khrushchev has lied to you. . . . Well, nobody else is surprised at him. . . . It must be a very bitter thought to you now to realize that if you had not sabotaged the Cuban invasion at the Bay of Pigs, this Cuban buildup would not have been possible. Well, maybe you will now learn and listen before it is forever too late."

In Madison Square Garden, eight thousand members of the Conservative Party booed the President and roared, "Fight! Fight! Fight!"

In Moscow, Khrushchev was surprised and angry. According to Mikoyan's son Sergo, the Chairman's first impulse was to order that the quarantine line be stormed and that work on the missile sites be sped up. The Deputy Premier cautioned him against precipitate action.

On Tuesday at 3:10 P.M. Moscow time, Kuznetsov summoned Kohler to the Foreign Ministry and gave him a letter from the Chairman to Kennedy. It lambasted the quarantine as a "serious threat to the peace" and a "gross violation" of the UN Charter, violating "freedom of navigation on the high seas." The "armaments now on Cuba, regardless of the classification to which they belong, are intended

---

*How might Scott have reacted had he known that over forty thousand Russians were in Cuba?

†Frazier Cheston, president of the National Association for Mental Health, advised American parents not to hide the crisis from their children: "It is possible for the adult to paint a picture of freedom and right versus slavery and wrong, and to point out that no effort is too great to protect the way of freedom."

exclusively for defensive purposes, to secure the Cuban Republic against attack by an aggressor." The President must "renounce" his actions.

Kuznetsov also gave Kohler a copy of an official Soviet statement to be broadcast by Radio Moscow at four. It told the Soviet people that Kennedy was placing Cuba "under naval blockade" and placing American forces in "combat readiness" but did not mention that these actions were in response to the installation of Soviet missiles in Cuba.

Khrushchev may have wished to conceal the fact of the missiles from the Soviet people in order to prevent them from being outraged in case they had to be removed. Silence about the missiles also helped Moscow to portray the President's actions as pure aggression.

Both Khrushchev's letter and this statement showed why in public and private he had been so careful to cast the buildup in Cuba as defensive. Contrary to later opinion that he had never prepared for the possibility that the President might discover and announce the missiles before he did, he had probably presumed that he could now argue that America was using brute force to strip "little Cuba" of the same kind of defense that the West had provided Turks and Italians: let the world declare Kennedy the transgressor and force him to abandon the blockade.

At times of Cold War crises like Suez, the U-2, and the Bay of Pigs, Khrushchev had indulged his penchant for fiery rhetoric only when there was little chance that it could inflame the situation to the point of nuclear war. The absence in both Soviet messages of provocative language and personal attacks on Kennedy (although the statement called the President's threat of retaliation for a nuclear attack "hypocrisy") showed the Chairman's effort to keep the atmosphere calm.

Both documents portrayed the President's actions primarily as a problem between the United States and Cuba. Perhaps the Russians felt that if they had to back down later, it would be far less embarrassing to do so under the fiction of resolving a conflict between the United States and a third country—not even a member of the Warsaw Pact—than to appear to be retreating from a naked confrontation between the superpowers.

The Soviet bloc announced a military alert, but this involved mainly mild and symbolic actions, such as cancellation of discharges and furloughs. Soviet forces were not redeployed or placed in high readiness. The State Department advised the White House that "the Soviet reaction thus far suggests a high degree of circumspection and implies that the Soviet Union may be carefully leaving the back door open for a retreat from the danger of general war over Cuba."

* * *

On Tuesday evening, Khrushchev made his first public appearance since the world had learned of the Missile Crisis. With Mikoyan, Kozlov, Brezhnev, and Romanian guests, he attended an American performance of *Boris Godunov,* starring Jerome Hines, at the Bolshoi Theater. (One wonders what went through the Chairman's mind when onstage a nobleman named Khrushchev was seized and beaten by peasants as anarchy spread through Russia.)

Had the Chairman wished to heat up the crisis, he would have boycotted an American performance. Not only did he attend but afterward he went backstage and raised a glass of champagne while Mikoyan toasted culture and American women.

That evening, Radio Moscow said that while the American blockade was "an act of piracy . . . an unheard-of violation of international law, the Soviet government could assure the United States "that not a single nuclear bomb will hit the United States unless aggression is committed." But work on the missile sites was still forging ahead. Soviet ships were still steaming toward Cuba.

On Tuesday morning in Washington, Kennedy woke up, relieved that the Soviets had not bombed the Jupiters in Turkey and Italy, sealed off the Dardanelles, or closed the Autobahn.

He had been deeply worried that Khrushchev would "close down Berlin." Etched in his mind was the knowledge that West Berliners were unlikely to survive a Soviet blockade longer than Cubans could survive the blockade imposed by the United States. Weeks later, Ben Bradlee found him haunted by the question of why Khrushchev did not blockade Berlin, as he had threatened at Vienna: the Chairman had "said it over and over and over again. And why didn't he do it?"

Bundy later felt that Kennedy and others "who feared reprisal in Berlin were taking too much counsel of our own long anxieties and too little note of demonstrated Soviet patience." Bundy believed that the Berlin crisis had been a showcase of "Khrushchev's unwillingness to risk open war."*

When the President met with Ex Comm, McCone warned that if the Russians threw a similar blockade around West Berlin, the West Ber-

---

*Along with other claims in his memoirs, Khrushchev said, "The Americans knew that if Russian blood were shed in Cuba, American blood would surely be shed in Germany." We cannot know whether this was armchair braggadocio or not.

liners were likely to cave in more quickly than the Cubans.* Yet Robert Kennedy noticed "a certain spirit of lightness . . . not gaiety, certainly, but a feeling of relaxation perhaps. We had taken the first step, it wasn't so bad, and we were still alive."

All agreed that if one of the U-2s now repeatedly photographing Cuba were downed, American bombers and fighters should destroy a SAM site, but only after the President's specific order. Kennedy asked McNamara to prepare for use of force against Cuba, if necessary: "I want to be able to feel that we will not have to waste any days having to get ready."

The President and Rusk had been worried that the OAS would not endorse the quarantine, which required a two-thirds vote. Without this sanction, the United States would have a harder time defending itself against Soviet charges of piracy. But at 4:45 P.M., all twenty members approved.

Ex Comm met at six o'clock. The President approved a reply to Khrushchev's letter, drafted by George Ball: "I hope that you will issue immediately the necessary instructions to your ships to observe the terms of the quarantine . . . which will go into effect at 1400 hours Greenwich time October 24." Bundy had scrawled in a final sentence—"We have no desire to seize a fire upon your march"—but struck it out.

The quarantine was to be composed of sixteen destroyers, three cruisers, an antisubmarine aircraft carrier, and six utility ships, with almost 150 others in reserve. Since for now petroleum, oil, and lubricants were not to be kept out of Cuba, all Soviet tankers would be let through.

Kennedy said that if a vessel refused to stop at the quarantine line, the Navy should try to avoid sinking the ship and killing Soviet troops:

---

*The CIA felt that even if the United States blockaded all shipments to Cuba except food or medicines, it was unlikely to topple Castro for many months: "There would be much confusion and disruption of life but . . . the regime would be likely to be able to prevent economic chaos and meet the basic needs of the population." As Castro's economy ground to a halt, the dictator could probably maintain control by increased resort to his Soviet-trained secret police and incitement of public rage against the North Americans. Anti-Castro revolutionaries inside Cuba were unlikely to move against him unless they saw evidence of an imminent American invasion.

Should Khrushchev blockade West Berlin, the CIA predicted that the sector would have enough food, fuel, medicines, and industrial material to survive and keep people employed for four to six months. The problem was psychological: "A total and uncontested blockade would cause the West Berliners to lose all hope in a matter of weeks." Even if the United States staged an airlift, as in 1948, "morale would deteriorate rapidly in the absence of a reasonable expectation that the U.S. would break the blockade."

fire at the rudder or propeller. McNamara noted that instead of board-ing the hostile vessel, the Navy could tow it to Jacksonville or Charleston.

The President was worried that they would "go through all of this effort and then find out there's baby food on it." He ordered the Navy to place highest priority on tracking the Soviet submarines sliding into the Caribbean and on the protection of American aircraft carriers and other vessels.

At 7:06 P.M., he nervously signed the formal instrument of quaran-tine. As popping flashbulbs cast ghostly shadows on the Oval Office walls, the President thrice had to ask what date it was. Reporters noticed that he was not dressed as fastidiously as usual. One side of his collar jutted over the lapel; the handkerchief in his breast pocket was not folded to keep the initials JFK from showing. Someone thought that for the first time in his life, Kennedy looked older than his age.

Usually the President signed a bill with numerous pens, which he handed out to the sponsors. This time he signed with one. He told his small audience, "We'll all be a lot wiser tomorrow."

Later he returned to his abiding anxiety: "The great danger and risk in all of this is a miscalculation, a mistake in judgment." He had lately read Barbara Tuchman's bestseller *The Guns of August,* about the faulty assumptions that had led to World War I. He was certain that neither the United States nor the Soviet Union wanted a showdown over Cuba but feared that misunderstanding and pride might force the two pow-ers into war.

At a Soviet Embassy reception that evening, a Soviet military at-taché loudly declared that Soviet captains heading for Cuba had been told to defy the American blockade: "If it is decreed that those men must die, then they will obey their orders and stay on course, or be sunk." This was said in the hearing of foreign guests, who could be relied upon to send it on to Western intelligence services.*

At 9:30 P.M., Robert Kennedy went to see Dobrynin in his third-floor apartment at the Soviet Embassy. As Dobrynin recalled, "Kennedy said that he came alone to share some thoughts with me, some concern about our relations in connection with . . . the Cuban crisis." The Attorney General mentioned the attaché's statement.

---

*The CIA reported the attaché's comment to the President the next morning. It also noted that the director of TASS, visiting Hiroshima, and a middle-ranking member of the Soviet UN delegation had made similar comments within Western earshot.

Dobrynin said, "He's the one who knows what the Navy is going to do, not I."

Robert reminded the Ambassador that in early September he had assured him that the Russians had no intention of placing offensive missiles in Cuba. Based on this and other similar assurances, the President had taken a "far less belligerent position" than people like Senator Keating and "assured the American people that there was nothing to be concerned about" in Cuba.

The President had thought he had built "a very helpful personal relationship with Mr. Khrushchev" with "mutual trust and confidence between them on which he could rely." By sneaking nuclear missiles into Cuba, the Soviet leaders had shown themselves to be "hypocritical, misleading, and false."

Dobrynin responded that Khrushchev had informed him there were no such missiles in Cuba. As far as he knew, there still were none. He asked why the President had not asked Gromyko about the missiles when they met last week: "He would have received a proper answer to the question." Kennedy replied by asking why Gromyko had not volunteered the information to the President. What orders had Soviet ships been given for the moment they encountered the quarantine line?

Dobrynin reported that Soviet captains "have an order to continue their course to Cuba." President Kennedy's action "contradicts international law." Soviet ships were "in international waters" and had "no reason to subordinate themselves to an arbitrary decision of the President of another country." Dobrynin felt that his response "made Kennedy a bit nervous."

The Attorney General said, "Our military vessels have an order of President Kennedy to intercept them." Dobrynin countered, "Ours have an order to continue on." Kennedy said, "I do not know how this will end."

Dobrynin cabled Moscow about the conversation. As he later recalled, "All my telegrams were coded. . . . From Western Union, a black man rode a bicycle, came to our embassy. We gave him the cables. And he, at such a speed—we tried to urge him on—rode back to Western Union, where the cable was sent to Moscow. . . . This was a nerve-racking experience. We sat there, wondering if he would be fast enough to deliver the important communication."

The Maharajah and Maharani of Jaipur, who had lavishly entertained Jacqueline Kennedy in India, had been scheduled to stay at the

White House and be feted at a private White House dinner dance on Tuesday night.

The President had no desire to look like Nero fiddling as Rome burned. Instead, the Jaipurs were installed in Blair House. The dance was changed to a small dinner to accommodate those overseas guests told of the cancellation too late to change their plans. The beautiful Maharani had just won a seat in the Indian Parliament on the Swatantra ("Goldwater") ticket. Kennedy teased her: "I hear you are the Barry Goldwater of India." He toasted her political debut and failed to persuade his old London friend J. J. "Jakie" Astor to respond.

After the meal, he sat with David Ormsby-Gore in the large center hall of the family quarters. Great-grandson of Lord Salisbury, Ormsby-Gore was a cousin of Kathleen Kennedy's husband, Lord Hartington. As a progressive Tory Member of Parliament and Minister of State for Foreign Affairs, he had concentrated on nuclear testing and disarmament.

After the 1960 election, the President-elect told him he must come to Washington as Ambassador. Flying from Key West to Washington the following March, he took the matter up with Macmillan. When the appointment was made, Ormsby-Gore wrote Kennedy, "I must let you know how privileged I feel to be accredited to the greatest country on earth at a period when it is under your exciting leadership." He was "convinced" that they could turn the tide of history "in our favour and that communism can be manoeuvred into a fatal decline."

Queen Elizabeth II knighted the new envoy before his departure. She wrote the President in the spring of 1962 that Ormsby-Gore was "highly thought of here": it was "excellent news that he and Cissie are making their mark in Washington."

The Ormsby-Gores were frequent Kennedy houseguests at Hyannis Port, Glen Ora, Newport, Palm Beach. The President said, "I trust David as I would my own Cabinet." He was amused when his British friend quoted Salisbury's observation that conducting foreign policy in a democracy was like playing bridge with "a number of people standing behind your chair advising you out loud which card you should play."

Sometimes the relationship was almost too close. In May 1962, Ormsby-Gore told the President that Macmillan was taking "an ostrich position" on the Congo and that the British negotiator, Lord Dundee, was "a fool." After a talk in July 1962, he promised Kennedy to "heed your parting advice about arguing our nuclear matters in terms of *our* interests, not yours."

When the Prime Minister indiscreetly sent congratulations to Edward Kennedy after his Senate primary victory in Massachusetts,

Ormsby-Gore wrote the President that Macmillan's "practically in-comprehensible message" was "wholly out of order." There would be "hell to pay if knowledge of its existence leaked out."

Despite his friendship with Kennedy, the Ambassador had wired Macmillan on Monday night that he could not believe that the missiles "so far landed" in Cuba posed "any significant military threat to the United States." Now he warned the President that many Englishmen were wondering whether the U-2 evidence that had started this crisis had been faked; couldn't the pictures be released? The Labour Party leader Hugh Gaitskell had even spoken of the "so-called missiles" in Cuba.

Salinger and David Bruce had made the same argument, but Ormsby-Gore's plea won the day: Kennedy sent for a file of U-2 pictures. As the other guests were served after-dinner drinks, he and his British friend combed through the prints for those that seemed most dramatic. He ordered their release the next day.

Robert Kennedy arrived, looking bleak and disheveled. He reported on his meeting with Dobrynin. Talking in machine-gun bursts, his eyes screwed tight, the President wondered aloud whether he should propose an immediate summit with Khrushchev. Then he reconsidered: as with Berlin, before any negotiation Khrushchev must be convinced of his determination to get the missiles out of Cuba. Before a summit took place—and it should—he wanted to have more cards to play.

Ormsby-Gore reminded him that the U.S. Navy had fixed the quarantine line at eight hundred miles: a Soviet ship would probably have to be intercepted just a few hours after the blockade began. Khrushchev had hard decisions to make. Every additional hour could make it easier for him to retreat gracefully. Why not draw the quarantine line closer to Cuba and give the Russians a little more time?

Kennedy called McNamara and ordered him, despite emotional Navy protests, to narrow the quarantine zone to a radius of five hundred miles from Cuba.

The President and Ex Comm were operating on the prudent assumption that there were nuclear warheads in Cuba, but American intelligence had found no conclusive evidence that the weapons had actually arrived.*

---

*McNamara observed in an October 22 background briefing of the press after Kennedy's speech, "Nuclear warheads are of such a size that it is extremely unlikely we would ever be able to observe them by the intelligence means open to us. I think

According to the Soviet general Dimitri Volkogonov, twenty warheads had indeed reached the island in late September or early October. Twenty more were aboard the *Poltava,* which had come to Cuba in mid-September, returned to Odessa, and was sailing again toward the island.*

Volkogonov recalled that the Soviets kept the twenty warheads "well away" from the MRBMs to reduce the danger that some madman could start a nuclear exchange. Had Khrushchev issued an order to prepare the missiles for war, it would have taken four hours to target them and fifteen minutes more for countdown.†

On Wednesday before dawn, Richard Davies took a list of quarantine rules to the Soviet Foreign Ministry. Stepping off the elevator onto a high floor, he saw a Russian wearing a gas mask rush by. He was certain that the scene had been staged for his benefit.

He told Soviet diplomats that if Americans were allowed to inspect ships in Leningrad, Odessa, or Vladivostok before their hatches were closed and they contained no contraband, they would be certified to pass through the American quarantine line. He later recalled, "This was high impertinence. Of course, they never let us into any of those places."

Still, the bureaucrats had clearly been ordered to do nothing that might in some small way escalate the crisis. Davies found that "in great contrast to the usual brusque and rude treatment," they were "gushingly polite," asking, "How are the children? . . . Are you happy in our country?"

Foy Kohler decided to keep his get-acquainted appointments with Soviet officials. To his surprise, no one canceled.

Soviet factories and farms held "spontaneous" demonstrations

---

it is almost inconceivable, however, that there would be missiles . . . without accompanying warheads."

The next day, the CIA told the President, "While we are unable to confirm the presence of nuclear warheads, photo coverage continues to reveal the construction at several sites of buildings which we suspect are for nuclear storage." October 24: "Nuclear storage sites apparently are being built on the basis of one site per missile regiment."

*American intelligence evidently had unverifiable information at the time that nuclear warheads had been loaded on the *Poltava* in Odessa and that, in the Atlantic, it made a rendezvous with three submarines from the Soviet Union's Northern Fleet.

†The missiles evidently had no permissive-action-link (PAL) device of the kind that the United States was introducing to prevent unauthorized arming of its nuclear warheads by anyone but the President. McNamara later recalled his worry that, during the crisis in Cuba, "some second lieutenant could start a nuclear war."

against the United States. In Moscow, a mob used pocket mirrors to divert the rays of the sun and blind workers inside the American Embassy. Shouting "Hands off Cuba!" the Russians threw rocks at the windows and dented Kohler's Cadillac. For safety, the Ambassador gathered American children at Spaso House.

Khrushchev wanted to send a new message to Kennedy. Had Thompson remained as Ambassador, he probably would have sent for him. Kohler he considered a bureaucrat who had contributed to the President's truculence over Berlin. Instead the Chairman tried his luck with another channel.

William Knox, president of the Westinghouse Electric International Company, was in Moscow to talk about patents. He had met Khrushchev in New York in 1960. On Wednesday, rising from lunch, he was told that the Chairman wished to see him within the hour. Arriving at the Kremlin, he noticed that Khrushchev was "very tired."

Khrushchev said that Monday had been a "very black day." Before the President's speech, Rusk and Gromyko had "practically agreed" on nuclear testing and Berlin negotiations. Despite his many difficulties with Eisenhower he believed, if the General were still in the White House, the Cuban problem would have been handled in a much more "mature" manner. He would hate to think that President Kennedy's handling of Cuba was connected with the congressional elections.

Repeating his private lament of 1960, the Chairman said that one reason negotiation with this President was so difficult was his youth: "How can I deal with a man who is younger than my son?" Kennedy had embarked on a "very, very dangerous" policy. He warned that if U.S. Navy ships stopped and searched an unarmed Soviet merchant vessel, Soviet submarines would sink them.

He offered his own definition of offensive and defensive weapons: "If I point a pistol at you like this in order to attack you, the pistol is an offensive weapon. But if I aim to keep you from shooting me, it is defensive, no?" The United States claimed that its Turkish bases were defensive, but what was the range of the missiles there?

For the first time to Western ears Khrushchev conceded that there were ground-to-ground missiles and nuclear warheads on Cuba.* The Cubans, he said, were "very volatile" people. The missiles would never be fired except on his order.

He told one of his favorite stories, about the man who fell on hard

---

*He probably said this to strengthen the Soviet position, not knowing that Kennedy was acting on the assumption that there were not only missiles but warheads.

times and had to live with a goat. He hated the smell but got used to it. Well, the Russians had been living with goats in Turkey, Greece, Italy, and other NATO countries. The Americans now had their goat in Cuba. "You are not happy about it . . . but you'll learn to live with it." He said he was anxious to see President Kennedy. At a summit, "without a circus atmosphere," they could resolve some of their problems.*

In a public reply to Bertrand Russell's telegram that same day, Khrushchev said that a summit might "remove the danger of unleashing a thermonuclear war. . . . When aggression is unleashed by the Americans, such a meeting will already become impossible and useless."

The Chairman probably made his summit offer in the hope that if Kennedy responded favorably, he might postpone plans for a quarantine and possible military action. Khrushchev could push the missiles toward readiness, send more warheads to Cuba, and meet the President with his negotiating leverage magnificently enhanced.

During the night, the *Poltava,* with its secret cache of twenty nuclear warheads, turned back before reaching the quarantine line. So did other Soviet ships whose hatches were wide enough to accommodate large missiles. Khrushchev almost certainly feared that the United States would intercept the vessels and examine and confiscate their precious cargo. But the *Yuri Gagarin* and the *Komiles* kept sailing toward Cuba, escorted by submarines.

On Wednesday morning, before the ten o'clock Ex Comm meeting in the Cabinet Room, the President told his brother, "It looks really mean, doesn't it?" McNamara told the group that the *Komiles* and the *Gagarin* were nearing the five-hundred-mile quarantine line. If they did not stop, the United States would have to intercept them or else declare that the quarantine was to be relaxed. Robert Kennedy wrote later, "This was the moment we had prepared for, which we hoped would never come."

McNamara reported that a Soviet submarine had moved between

---

*Khrushchev's advisers may have taken notice of Kennedy's comment at a February 1962 press conference that "if there was a major crisis which threatened to involve us all in a war, there might be a need for a summit." Khrushchev told Knox he was welcome to say whatever he wanted to the press, but Knox was close-mouthed. When he returned to New York on Thursday, Robert Komer of the NSC staff suggested that "in light [of the] possibility this guy has something, we should give him more attn. than routine CIA [debriefing]. Possible propaganda use." Knox was interviewed by State and the CIA, which sent the results to the President.

the two ships. The *Essex* had been ordered to signal it to surface and identify itself. If it refused, the *Essex* would force it to the surface with depth charges and small explosives. The Attorney General later wrote, "Was the world on the brink of a holocaust? Was it our error? A mistake? Was there something further that should have been done? Or not done?"

The President covered his mouth with one hand. The other he opened and closed into a fist. He and his brother stared at each other across the Cabinet table. Robert wrote, "It was almost as though no one else was there and he was no longer the President. . . . I thought of when he was ill and almost died, when he lost his child, when he learned that our oldest brother had been killed, of personal times of strain and hurt."

The President asked, "Isn't there some way we can avoid having our first exchange with a Russian submarine? Almost anything but that!"

"No, there's too much danger to our ships," McNamara replied. "Our commanders have been instructed to avoid hostilities if at all possible, but this is what we must be prepared for, and this is what we must expect."

"We must expect that they will close down Berlin," said Kennedy. "Make the final preparations for that." The Attorney General felt as if "we were on the edge of a precipice. . . . This time, the moment was now, not next week . . . not in eight hours 'so we can send another message to Khrushchev and perhaps he will finally understand.' . . . What could we say now—what could we do?"

At 10:25 A.M., McCone was handed a note. He said, "Mr. President, we have a preliminary report which seems to indicate that some of the Russian ships have stopped dead in the water." At 10:32, he said, "The report is accurate, Mr. President. Six ships previously on their way to Cuba at the edge of the quarantine have stopped or have turned back toward the Soviet Union."

Ex Comm learned that the twenty Russian ships nearest the barrier had stopped or turned back. The President ordered that "if the ships have orders to turn around, we want to give them every opportunity to do so. Get in direct touch with the *Essex* and tell them not to do anything but give the Russian vessels an opportunity to turn back. We must move quickly because the time is expiring."

Rusk nudged Bundy. With his pungent private rhetoric almost never used in public, he murmured, "We're eyeball to eyeball, and I think the other fellow just blinked."

This was soon the most famous utterance of the Missile Crisis, but Rusk was wrong. Khrushchev had decided not to test the quarantine with weapons-bearing ships. This assured that sensitive Soviet military technology would be kept out of American hands and gave the President time to consider his proposal for a summit.

Based on information we now have from Soviet sources, it meant that no more than forty-two of the eighty planned missiles and no more than twenty of the planned forty nuclear warheads made it to Cuba. Evidently none of the thirty-two intended IRBMs reached the island.

The Chairman's decision may have exacted a high domestic cost. The Soviets later found it so embarrassing that for years no Soviet commander conceded that the ships had ever turned around. Even in his memoirs, Khrushchev found the truth so painful to bear that he claimed his vessels had sailed "straight through."

Without the thirty-nine hours he was given before the quarantine began, Khrushchev might not have reversed himself. This demonstrated the President's wisdom in starting his response not with an irreversible air strike but with milder pressures that gave Khrushchev time to ponder his move.

At six o'clock that evening, Kennedy walked downstairs to the Situation Room in the West Wing basement. He was scheduled to speak to Harold Macmillan by telephone at seven.

That afternoon, Ormsby-Gore had told Bundy at the White House that "if there is not going to be a war," the Prime Minister wished to suggest a "Kennedy-Khrushchev summons" to a meeting on disarmament which, not inconveniently, would include Macmillan as a major player.* Before such a meeting, "there might have to be a standstill involving no import of arms and no blockade."

Having conveyed his leader's proposal, Ormsby-Gore disposed of it. He told Bundy that it was "not a good idea because the two sides are too far apart and because it leaves no room for the French." The President "should make it very plain to the PM that this is not an acceptable position and that the U.S. cannot stand down its blockade without progress toward the removal of the missiles."

---

*The Prime Minister may have been influenced by Labour leader Hugh Gaitskell's demand on Tuesday that Macmillan fly to Washington to discuss the blockade order with Kennedy. The shadow foreign minister, Harold Wilson, told a television audience the same day that the President should have taken the problem to the UN first.

During their conversation at seven, Macmillan asked Kennedy whether the turning back of the Soviet ships that morning meant that Khrushchev was now "frightened a bit."

The President said, "The ones that are turning back are the ones that we felt might have offensive military equipment on them, so they probably didn't want that equipment to fall into our hands." Other Soviet ships were now said to be approaching the quarantine line. "We ought to know in the next twelve hours whether they're going to submit or be searched."

Georgi Bolshakov had tried to deliver the message from Khrushchev and Mikoyan that the Soviet buildup on Cuba was purely defensive. By Robert Kennedy's own account, he refused to see him. After the President's Monday night speech, the Attorney General called Charles Bartlett: "Get ahold of Georgi and tell him how he betrayed us and how we're very disappointed."

Bartlett had never liked Bolshakov: "He was a pusillanimous little fellow, a comic, tough little guy, did a hundred and fifty push-ups . . . a primitive." But on Tuesday afternoon, he telephoned the Russian: "Georgi, the Attorney General is very disappointed in you." As Bartlett recalled, "Five minutes later, I got a call from Bobby, who'd obviously been tapping the lines and said, 'That wasn't very subtly done. I hope you can be a little more subtle.' "

On Wednesday, at Bolshakov's request, Bartlett lunched with the Russian, whom he found "puzzled and disturbed." Bolshakov pulled out his blue notebook and read him the notes of his meeting with Khrushchev and Mikoyan. He told Bartlett he "could not believe" that there were ground-to-ground missiles in Cuba. He warned that Soviet ships were "coming through" the blockade.

Coached by the Attorney General, Bartlett showed him two U-2 pictures of the MRBMs in Cuba. When Bolshakov tried to insist that they were merely SAMs, Bartlett asked him to inquire of his military attaché whether Russia had SAMs that were over fifty feet long. He told him that the plans to mount these missiles had to have been started in early summer. Bolshakov conceded that if things were as they appeared, he was in the position of having been deceived by his own government.*

---

*Documentation of Bolshakov's exposure to Robert Kennedy in October 1962 is, like that of all their meetings, sketchy. Sorensen's 1965 memoir *Kennedy* and Arthur Schlesinger's 1978 *Robert Kennedy and His Times* say that Bolshakov returned with a message from Khrushchev but not that he actually succeeded in delivering it to Robert. Other

Hours after his encounter with Bolshakov, Bartlett dined at the White House with the President and First Lady and a small group including the Robert Kennedys, the Radziwills, and Oleg Cassini. Bartlett proposed a celebration of the turning of the Russian ships that morning.

The President refused: "You don't want to celebrate in this game this early." Popping in and out during dinner, Bundy reported that the Soviet vessels were still staying away from the quarantine line. Kennedy said, "Well, we still have twenty chances out of a hundred to be at war with Russia."

At 10:50 P.M., after the guests had gone home, the President's telephone rang. He was read a new letter from Khrushchev:

> Imagine, Mr. President, that we had presented you with the conditions of ultimatum that you have presented us by your action. How would you have reacted to this? . . . Who asked you to do this? . . . You, Mr. President, are not declaring quarantines but advancing an ultimatum and threatening that unless we subordinate ourselves to your demands, you will use force.
>
> Consider what you are saying! . . . You are no longer appealing to reason, but wish to intimidate us. . . . And all this not only out of hatred for the Cuban people and their government, but also because of considerations having to do with the election campaign in the U.S.A. . . . The actions of the U.S.A. toward Cuba are outright banditry or, if you like, the folly of degenerate imperialism.
>
> Unfortunately such folly can bring grave suffering to peoples of all countries, not least the American people, since with the advent of modern types of armament, the U.S.A. has fully lost its invulnerability. . . . If someone had tried to dictate these kinds of conditions to you, you would have rejected it. And we also say—no. . . . We shall not be simply observers of the pirate-like actions of American ships on the high seas. We will be forced to take measures which we deem necessary and adequate to protect our rights.

---

sources improbably claim that Bolshakov gave the message to Kennedy but that it made the Attorney General so angry he refused to forward it to the Oval Office.

In a 1989 article in the Soviet journal *Novoye vremye,* Bolshakov claimed that he gave the message in person to Robert Kennedy on October 6, 1962: "As distinct from our past meetings, my host wore a dark formal suit, and his unruly shock of hair was neatly combed and parted. His face bore an impassive expression. . . . Robert was dry and formal. Everything was meant to impart an official character to our meeting." By Bolshakov's account, he lunched the next day with Charles Bartlett, who told him the President wanted Khrushchev's message "in detail in writing." This memory was certainly inaccurate: Bartlett did not learn of the missiles until October 22, along with the rest of the world.

Khrushchev may have intended this message to scare the President into accepting his demand for a summit; otherwise the Soviet Union would violate the quarantine, and who could know what might happen next?

The letter was the rudest any Soviet leader since Stalin had written to an American President, especially the suggestion that Kennedy had brought the world to the brink of war to improve the Democratic showing in the congressional elections. The challenge "Who asked you to do this?" implied that Kennedy was a timid youth forced to impose the quarantine by Cold Warriors in the State Department, Pentagon, and CIA, the Rockefellers, Morgans, and du Ponts.

The President called Bartlett at home. "You'll be interested to know I got a cable from our friend, and he said those ships are coming through. They are coming through tomorrow."

Kennedy wrote down the essentials of a reply to Khrushchev on a small White House pad. These were polished into a formal response with contributions from Sorensen, Bundy, Rusk, Ball, Gilpatric, and Thompson. It was taken to the Soviet Embassy at 1:45 A.M.

The President reminded Khrushchev that after receiving the "most explicit assurances from your government and its representatives, both publicly and privately," he had "learned beyond doubt what you have not denied—namely, that all these public assurances were false and that your military people had set out recently to establish a set of missile bases in Cuba." He hoped that the Chairman would repair the "deterioration in our relations."

On Wednesday afternoon, Stevenson had warned the President by telephone that the UN Secretary-General, U Thant, was going to propose a two-to-three-week suspension of both the quarantine and the arms shipments to Cuba.

Kennedy complained that this would compel the United States to lift the quarantine while the Soviet Union did no more than give its word that no more arms would be shipped to Cuba. Work on missiles already on the island would go on. Couldn't Thant wait until Thursday? Stevenson said, "He plans to do it tonight, and I believe we should answer it promptly."

On Wednesday evening, the Secretary-General made his proposal in identical letters to Kennedy and Khrushchev. George Ball asked Stevenson to deliver a letter from the President to Thant rejecting it.

Stevenson refused. He argued that Kennedy should at least be willing to discuss it.

Ball told him that he would have to ask the President to overrule him. When he called the White House family quarters at midnight, Kennedy had just received the shrill new message from Khrushchev.

Ball reminded him that within hours American and Russian ships could be firing at one another: perhaps Thant could be persuaded to intervene with the Russians "to hold their ships dead in the water until things could be better sorted out." This might give Khrushchev "a public excuse for doing what he might wish to do anyway." The President agreed that there was no harm in trying.

With this mandate, Ball called Stevenson and asked him to suggest the idea to Thant. At first the Governor demurred, unwilling to disturb Thant's sleep.* Under further pressure from Ball, he promised to try. At 12:20 A.M., he called Ball to say that Thant had agreed to issue such an appeal, but since communications at night were poor he would wait until morning.

Thursday, October 25. At the morning Ex Comm meeting, McCone reported that the previous day, in East Berlin, Gromyko had made the first public statement on Berlin by a high Soviet official since Monday: it "contained no hint of retaliatory measure against the Western position in Berlin."

The Soviets were still rushing work on the missiles. The CIA now considered two MRBM sites operational; three others would probably become operational today, a sixth by October 28. The agency suspected that three IRBM sites might become operational by December 1, two more by December 15. All twenty-four SAM sites were considered complete.

---

*This was not the first time that the Kennedys found Stevenson immobilized by his nineteenth-century manners. When Martin Luther King was jailed during the 1960 campaign, Stevenson had infuriated the brothers by refusing their request to call the civil rights leader's wife to express concern, saying that he and Mrs. King had "never been introduced."

Ball suggested years later that Stevenson's general relations with Thant were affected by his racial attitudes: "He thought he was a Burmese and could be as snobbish and race conscious as anybody. I remember that years ago, we'd walk across the [Chicago] Loop together, and some Negroes in an automobile would honk their horn at us, and Stevenson said, 'I don't think we ought to let those coons free.' It was a joke, but there was a lot of snobbism in him." As the Burmese broadcasting and information secretary, Thant had first met Stevenson in Burma just after the Governor's 1952 defeat. Thant found him "a very civilized and cultured gentleman with high ideals."

At 7:15 A.M., the tanker *Bucharest* had become the first Soviet ship to reach the quarantine line. Although tankers were excluded from the quarantine, some Ex Comm members had insisted that the vessel be stopped and boarded so that Khrushchev would "make no mistake of our will or intent."

The American destroyer *Gearing* challenged the tanker by flashing light. It replied, "My name is *Bucharest,* Soviet ship from the Black Sea, bound for Cuba." Unwilling to crowd Khrushchev, Kennedy let the *Bucharest* pass but ordered that it be trailed by American warships for later interception, if necessary.* He felt that eventually he would have to demonstrate American seriousness by stopping a Soviet ship. He ordered preparations to intercept an "appropriate" Soviet bloc vessel on Friday.

Rusk had arranged private briefings on Cuba for Congressmen and Senators around the country. Before the Ex Comm meeting was over, Salinger reported that Republican Congressman James Van Zandt, who was running for the Senate from Pennsylvania, had emerged from a New York briefing and chidingly told reporters that Kennedy had let the *Bucharest* pass through the quarantine.

The President had wanted to present the episode to the public in the best possible light. He cried, "What the hell is going *on* up there?" When Roger Hilsman called to explain, as Hilsman recalled, Kennedy gave him a "tongue-lashing that made the wires sizzle, and my morale, when I was finally permitted to hang up, was very low."

A few minutes later, Bundy called Hilsman. "I was in the room when the President was—er—talking to you, and I just wanted to say that it has happened to all of us."

At 1:15 P.M., Kennedy completed his negotiations with Stevenson about a reply to U Thant. Before dawn, he had sent Stevenson a copy of Khrushchev's new, threatening letter, in part to instill some respect in the UN envoy for the pressures under which he was laboring.

The final version of the President's message to the Secretary-General, issued at 2:19 P.M., said that while the solution to the Missile Crisis lay in removing offensive weapons from Cuba, Stevenson would be ready to discuss "preliminary talks to determine whether satisfactory arrangements can be assured." As Kennedy had expected,

---

*McCone later reported that, on hearing the *Bucharest* had been let through, Cubans had celebrated in Havana.

Khrushchev had approved Thant's Wednesday night proposal unconditionally.

At 2:26 P.M., Thant wrote Khrushchev to ask for Soviet assurances that ships sailing toward Cuba would keep away from the quarantine zone for a limited time in order to see whether discussions on a solution to the crisis could be started. In a message to Kennedy, he asked for a pledge that all American ships in the Caribbean would try to "avoid confrontation with Soviet ships in the next few days."

Stevenson went to the chamber of the Security Council. He did not know that for months the Soviet Ambassador, Valerian Zorin, had been suffering from mental deterioration. Arkady Shevchenko recalled that during private meetings, Zorin "would go silent and then look up at us in a daze, asking, 'What year is this?'"

Influenced perhaps by his illness, perhaps by faulty communication with the Foreign Ministry, Zorin had rejected Thant's standstill proposal at almost the same moment that Khrushchev was accepting it in Moscow. This afternoon, a full day after Khrushchev had told William Knox that there were ground-to-ground missiles and nuclear warheads in Cuba, Zorin continued to claim before the Security Council that there were no such missiles in Cuba and that the American U-2 evidence was "fake."

That morning the columnist William S. White had demanded Stevenson's resignation so that Kennedy could free himself from "unofficial experts who grandly ridiculed the fear of communism in Cuba." The *Chicago Tribune,* which had attacked Stevenson since his days in Springfield, inveighed against "wobblies" at the UN whose "built-in disposition" was to "have us surrender to the Soviet Union."

Delighted to show his mettle, especially after his struggles with Ex Comm on Saturday and Kennedy after midnight, Stevenson now seized the opportunity with both hands: "Do you, Ambassador Zorin, deny that the U.S.S.R. has placed and is placing medium- and intermediate-range missiles and sites in Cuba? . . . Don't wait for the translation! *Yes* or *no?*"

Zorin: "I am not in an American courtroom, sir, and I do not wish to answer a question put to me in the manner in which a prosecutor does—"

Stevenson: "You are in the courtroom of world opinion right now, and you can answer yes or no. You have denied that they exist, and I want to know whether I have understood you correctly."

Zorin: "Please continue your statement. . . . You will receive your answer in due course. Do not worry."

Stevenson: "I am prepared to wait for my answer until hell freezes over, if that's your decision. And I am also prepared to present the evidence in this room."*

The President watched the exchange on television: "I never knew Adlai had it in him. Too bad he didn't show a little more of this steam in the 1956 campaign." Illinois Republican friends who had always voted against Stevenson told him, "What a marvelous job you've done at the UN." His friend Jane Dick felt that he "seemed like a person who'd been purged of something. He was sitting on top of the world—to hell with it—he thought he had taken a long shot, and it had worked."

Before long Stevenson grimly realized that one of the moments for which future generations would remember him was his bellicose confrontation with a Soviet. He would have felt even more ambivalent about the exchange had he known that his victory had been scored against a sick man.

Sorensen said years later that while Kennedy thought Stevenson's performance "very good indeed," it made "no sense in logic. The one thing we were not prepared to do was wait till hell froze over. We wanted action from the Soviets fast."

The President wrote U Thant pledging to avoid a confrontation with Soviet ships during preliminary talks if the Russians should agree to keep away from the quarantine zone: This was "a matter of great urgency." Work on the missiles was continuing, and "certain Soviet ships are proceeding toward Cuba and the interception area."

During the three days after his television speech, Kennedy's crisis management had been almost flawless. To give the Chairman additional time he endured criticism by political opponents and the Joint Chiefs for reducing the quarantine zone. He had made every effort to avoid an inflammatory American-Soviet incident at sea.

Arriving late for a five o'clock Ex Comm meeting, he said that they must avoid a dangerous incident until after they had heard whether Khrushchev had accepted Thant's proposal to keep Soviet ships away from the quarantine line. Despite military opposition, Kennedy ordered that the *Bucharest* be allowed to sail on to Cuba: Khrushchev must not be pushed into "precipitous action. Give him time to con-

---

*Stevenson's deputy, Francis Plimpton, recalled that after the embarrassment of displaying doctored evidence during the Bay of Pigs (for which Kennedy privately called him "my official liar"), Stevenson was "reluctant" now to show the U-2 photographs of the missiles in Cuba: "It took a lot of persuading to get him to do it. He had to be convinced that it was OK."

sider. I don't want to put him in a corner from which he cannot escape."

The East German ship *Völker Freundschaft* [People's Friendship], with 1,500 passengers aboard, was nearing the quarantine line. Bundy advised the President that since its registry was not Soviet, stopping the vessel would not contradict his letter to Thant. McNamara warned that if they shot at or rammed the ship, injured passengers, and then found no missiles aboard, the world would wonder why "we allow Soviet ships through the quarantine but stop an East German ship." After an intense debate, Kennedy decided to let the vessel through.

Rusk reported that during the next two or three days, Thant would meet separately with Zorin and Stevenson "to arrive at a solution of the crisis or, if no solution is possible, to provide a basis for later action, having been unable to negotiate a settlement." These talks "must be limited to a very few days because the IRBM sites in Cuba are becoming operational, and the Il-28 bombers will soon be able to fly." Soon they must decide whether the Russians were "getting ready to talk" or "getting ready to attack us."

The President added jet and missile fuel to the contraband list. He approved planning for low-level evening spy flights, with pilots dropping flares on the IRBM sites. McNamara said the night flights would have a "psychological effect" and help to "convince the public that we are increasing the pressure on the Russians." The President ordered the Navy to follow the six Soviet submarines known to be near Cuba: they should be harassed and forced to surface in the presence of American warships.

Robert Kennedy reminded his colleagues that "fifteen ships have turned back, which is an impressive action taken by the Russians." The United States must "indicate clearly that we mean business, but we should avoid a direct confrontation now." Later they might decide "that it is better to avoid confronting the Russians by stopping one of their ships and to react by attacking the missiles already in Cuba."

The President warned, "We must act soon because work on the missile sites is still going on, and we must back up very soon the firmness we have displayed up to now. . . . Tomorrow we will know the Soviet response to U Thant's proposal." If Khrushchev refused it, the United States would have to ponder its "next major move." Bundy described what that next move would be: "Expand the blockade or remove the missiles by air attack."

CHAPTER

18

"I Don't See How We'll Have a Very Good War"

AT SEVEN O'CLOCK ON FRIDAY MORNING, OCTOBER 26, THE United States actively enforced its quarantine for the first time. The freighter *Marucla* was signaled by the American destroyer *Joseph P. Kennedy, Jr.*, on which Robert Kennedy had served in 1946.

Owned by Panamanians, registered in Lebanon, the *Marucla* was sailing under Soviet charter. A Navy boarding party studied its cargo manifest, looked into a hatch, satisfied itself that there was no contraband aboard, and allowed the ship to proceed. The President told Salinger, "The press will never believe we didn't stick the *Kennedy* in the way of the *Marucla* just to give the family publicity."

Down from New York to attend the ten o'clock Ex Comm meeting, Stevenson predicted that, in return for removing the missiles, the Russians would ask the United States to guarantee the territorial integrity of Cuba and dismantle the Jupiters in Turkey. McCone objected to Stevenson's comparison of the missiles in Turkey and Cuba:

those in Cuba were "pointed at our heart and put us under great handicap in continuing to carry out our commitments to the Free World."

Kennedy had concluded that quarantine alone would not work: the only way to get the missiles out would be "invading or trading." Mentioning a Brazilian proposal for a nuclear-free zone and territorial guarantee for all states in Latin America, he asked whether the United States "could commit ourselves not to invade Cuba."

McCone would not countenance the idea of "continued control of Cuba by Castro. Even if the Soviet missiles are removed, Castro, if he is left in control, will be in an excellent position to undertake the communization of Latin America."*

Someone renewed a proposal from the first week of the crisis: ask the Brazilian ambassador in Havana to advise Castro that he was being exploited by the Soviet Union and that any solution to the crisis would bring his regime's overthrow, if not his death. Hadn't the President said that only two things were not negotiable with Castro—military ties with Moscow and aggression against Latin America?

Kennedy doubted that the scheme would have any effect. With work being speeded up on the missile sites, he said he would give the New York talks forty-eight hours to succeed. If they failed, he would have to choose among three main alternatives.

The first was bargaining. Walt Rostow said, "The Soviets are evidently trying now to achieve a negotiation in which they either hold on to what they have in Cuba . . . (to be beefed up by future clandestine delivery of vital components, including nuclear warheads) or trade off what they have against some Western asset, notably Turkish and Italian missiles."

A second option: expand the quarantine to include petroleum, oil, and lubricants (POL). This would bring the Cuban economy "to a halt and radically limit military capabilities," reported the State Department. "The regime and the populace would be faced with the prospect of total economic collapse at the end of six months." This would "afford time for a face-saving resolution" and show that the United States would not bargain for the missiles' removal "against any Free World asset except the blockade itself."

Third, air strike. Kennedy was warned that such an attack "may force Khrushchev to react strongly and could result in some type of

---

*McCone's argument had its echo during the five months culminating in the Persian Gulf War of 1991, when advisers to President George Bush suggested expanding war aims beyond reversing the Iraqi seizure of Kuwait to using force to remove Saddam Hussein from power, thus preventing him from dominating the Middle East.

war." The Chairman "would not order launch of a missile from Cuba unless he is ready for war essentially on other grounds." More likely would be a "riposte in kind"—perhaps an attack on the Turkish missile base. But who could tell where the riposte would lead?

The previous day the Vice President had called the managing editor of the *Dallas Morning News,* Jack Krueger, and earned himself a political IOU by divulging what he had been hearing in the Cabinet Room: "It's fifty-fifty we hit Cuba, and if you get somebody up here and ready, I'll see to it he gets on the first press plane."

The Kennedy brothers would have been irate had they learned that at this moment of supreme danger the Vice President was leaking government secrets to improve his own sagging political position in Texas. Robert Kennedy was disparaging enough about Johnson's role in the crisis council: he later complained that Johnson "had the feeling that we were being too weak" but "never made clear what *he* would do."*

The President explained that Johnson was probably being influenced by militant congressional cronies. Laughing, the brothers considered asking others on Capitol Hill to telephone him and cavil that "the government is acting like a war party." Then they would see whether the Vice President changed his position.

* * *

*Even the number of Ex Comm meetings Johnson attended became a point of contention with Robert Kennedy. In October 1964, campaigning for a full term as President, Johnson told a Los Angeles audience, "I saw President Kennedy in the Cuban crisis in thirty-eight different meetings, and we got up to the last hours. Khrushchev had his missiles trained on this country that would completely wipe out San Francisco and Los Angeles. . . . I saw the generals with their stars come into the room and the admirals with their braid and the Secretary of State with all his diplomatic experience. I listened to every word. I never left home in the morning a single morning that I knew I would get back that night to see Lady Bird and those daughters."

Robert Kennedy ridiculed Johnson's boast during an oral history interview four months later: "He was never in on any of the real meetings. . . . He was there for the first meeting, I think. Then he went to Hawaii because they didn't want to . . . indicate that there was a crisis on hand. He wasn't there at all when the decisions were being made."

Kennedy maintained that Johnson had returned to the meetings no sooner than Saturday, October 27. In fact, the Vice President returned from his speaking tour on Saturday, October 20, and attended each of the 42 Ex Comm meetings held between the President's October 22 speech and the panel's disbandment on March 29, 1963, with the exception of five sessions in late December and early November.

Johnson complained in later years that "no man knew less about Congress than John Kennedy. . . . When he was young, he was always off to Boston or Florida for long weekends. . . . He was a Joe College man. He didn't have rapport with Congress. He didn't have affection for Congress. And Congress felt that he didn't know where the ball was."*

At Los Angeles in 1960, by Robert Kennedy's account, the new Democratic nominee for President allowed himself to be surprised, tricked, or blackmailed into accepting a running mate he did not want. According to Robert, his brother had intended to choose Senator Stuart Symington of Missouri.† But when Johnson snatched up his pro forma offer, Kennedy would not or could not summon the political courage to retrieve it.

That day he told his aide Hy Raskin, "Lyndon Johnson forced me to name him. You know we had never considered Lyndon, but . . . he and Sam Rayburn . . . reminded me that there would undoubtedly be a session of Congress between now and the election. If Lyndon was not the Vice Presidential candidate, there was a likelihood that some difficulties were in store for me. There was no time to try to figure it out or debate it. . . . Nixon will give us enough problems. There is no sense in inviting more from those Texas bastards."

The brothers promised each other never to reveal that Johnson had not been their first choice. In his father's style, Kennedy immediately focused on the virtues in Johnson's nomination. He reminded himself that it "wouldn't be worth being President" if Johnson stayed on as Majority Leader. Robert said that from the Senate Johnson would "screw" him "all the time." Flying back to Boston, Kennedy told newsmen, "Look what states I might be able to carry."

There is no record that he ever seriously conceded to Johnson or anyone else that he owed his Presidency to Johnson's presence on his

---

*This was in 1965, to the New Deal historian William Leuchtenburg. Johnson went on to complain that, on entering the White House, "all Kennedy had was leftover programs from Roosevelt, Truman, and Eisenhower" and that the President was "a little too conservative to serve my taste." No doubt Johnson said this to appeal to Leuchtenburg, but it certainly reflected his private impatience with Kennedy's caution about proposing domestic reform legislation that he feared would be defeated in Congress.

†Symington was so convinced he would be the candidate that he asked his friend Clayton Fritchey to draft an acceptance speech. Later Robert Kennedy told Charles Bartlett, "I hear your editor is mad because you thought that Stu Symington was going to be the nominee. . . . Well, you can tell him that I did too." He told the New Dealer James Rowe, "Don't you think this is a terrible mistake? Don't you think that Symington should be the candidate for the strength of the ticket?"

ticket: running with a non-Southerner, he would have been hard pressed to reclaim critical Southern states that had fallen to Eisenhower in 1952 and 1956.* As Bradlee noticed, "LBJ's simple presence seems to bug him. It's not very noble to watch, and yet there it is."

Johnson no doubt saw the Vice Presidency as a means of shedding his Southern label and gaining political obligations that would help him run for President in 1968. After the Bay of Pigs, when a dispirited Kennedy talked about retiring after one term, Lem Billings told him that Johnson's "every action" was based on a future campaign for the Presidency. Kennedy said that if Johnson were nominated, he would give him more support "than Eisenhower did to Nixon." Jacqueline reminded him that he had told her that Johnson's judgment was bad. He said that Johnson would be "better qualified four years from now than he is now."

At the time of the Inauguration, Johnson had given him a document ceding him unprecedented authority within the Executive Branch. The President managed to forget what he did with it. Johnson had asked Senate Democrats to allow him to keep presiding over their Democratic caucus. They turned him down. Kennedy felt that "the steam really went out of Lyndon when they wouldn't let him into that party caucus." The new Vice President made a habit of lolling about Evelyn Lincoln's desk, looking to see whether the President was in. Kennedy asked, "What is he doing in these offices?"

The President began their relationship with the ritual public announcement that Johnson would be the "most influential Vice President" in history. He sent advance texts of important speeches to Johnson and told Cabinet members, "Bring your problems to Lyndon or me." His effort to erode the Vice President's political standing had much to do with his failure to use Johnson's unexcelled skills to lobby Senators and Congressmen on behalf of Administration bills.†

Kennedy gave him charge of panels on space and equal opportunity, sent him on foreign trips, and listened to his (justified) complaints of bad treatment and ridicule by the White House staff, calling O'Donnell into the Oval Office to punish him in Johnson's presence as the designated whipping boy. Robert Kennedy insisted later that the President was displeased with Johnson's work on equal opportu-

---

*After the election, Nixon acidly wrote Henry Cabot Lodge that "as distinguished from the President-elect, I was always proud to appear with my running mate in every state in the nation."

†After the 1960 election Johnson had told a *New York Times* reporter that he expected to serve as Kennedy's domestic "troubleshooter" and felt certain that his knowledge of Congress could be "of considerable assistance in getting legislation passed."

nity and that he said, "That man can't run this committee. Can you think of anything more deplorable than him trying to run the United States?"

Even the Attorney General conceded that Johnson was "very loyal and never spoke against the President." Told of Johnson's letters to the octogenarian Senator from Arizona, prayerfully asking for "twenty more Carl Haydens," Kennedy said he received similar ones by the score, "but he only wants one of me." Johnson's circumspection stemmed from genuine allegiance as well as fear that if the President actively opposed him in 1968, he would have little chance for the Democratic nomination.

By 1962, Mrs. Lincoln noticed that Johnson's name "appeared less and less on the lists of those who were invited to crucial White House policy and planning meetings." When Kennedy said things like "We never got a thing done today—Lyndon never stopped talking," Johnson heard about it and told close friends, "President Kennedy has invited me to attend these NSC meetings on the condition that I do not express an opinion." During 1961, he spent a total of over ten hours of time in private with the President. By 1963, the figure declined to less than two.

Kennedy told Charles Bartlett, "When you get into an exciting one or when you get into a hot one, you just don't think to call people who haven't read the cables. . . . And Lyndon hasn't read the cables." By his second year in office, the President now viewed Johnson and Stevenson much less as Democratic mandarins to whom he still had to pay obeisance than as men who had stumbled politically and now depended on his goodwill.

He told Johnson's old right arm Bobby Baker (in Baker's recollection), "I know he's unhappy in the Vice Presidency. It's a horseshit job, the worst fucking job I can imagine. . . . I watch him in our Cabinet meetings . . . but he's so cautious that he won't say much or make major contributions. I *know* he's suppressing his instincts out of a sense of loyalty to me, but it would help if he'd speak up."

When Baker relayed the message, Johnson said, "If I speak one word of disagreement with the Cabinet and White House staff looking on, then they'll put it out . . . that I'm a damned traitor. . . . Oh, sure, Jack Kennedy's as thoughtful and considerate of me at those meetings as he can be, but I know his snot-nosed brother's after my ass, and all those high-falutin' Harvards, and if I give 'em enough rope they'll hang me with it." In later years Johnson said of his Vice Presidency, "I detested every minute of it."

* * *

For years he had been looking for ways to bring the *Dallas Morning News* into his camp. Its publisher, E. M. Dealey, who had insulted the President to his face as a man "riding Caroline's tricycle," distrusted Johnson as much as he reviled Kennedy.

Now Johnson told Jack Krueger by telephone to have one of his reporters "check in at the Washington Hotel, and don't call my office. Just be ready. He'll be told where to go from there." He warned, "Whoever you send, tell him he'd better not open his damn mouth about why he's sittin' here. . . . Not if he values his balls." Krueger sent a reporter named Hugh Aynesworth, who checked into the Washington and waited for his telephone to ring.*

John Scali, newly the diplomatic correspondent for ABC, was lunching at his State Department desk on Friday when Alexander Fomin, Counselor of the Soviet Embassy, called. "It's very important. Meet me at the Occidental in ten minutes."

Fomin was the Soviet official who had passed a message to the White House through Robert Estabrook of the *Washington Post* in March 1961. Bolshakov's usefulness as a channel to the Kennedys had been damaged when he was used to deceive them about the missiles. This created an opening for Fomin.

By Scali's count, he and Fomin had lunched seven times since their first meal at Duke Zeibert's restaurant in the fall of 1961. The Russian had told him he was new in Washington and wished to learn his way around. Scali found him "a quiet, reasonable, intelligent man who did not hesitate to depart when he felt it necessary from the standard Communist line." American intelligence told him that Fomin was a KGB colonel assigned to reorganize Soviet intelligence operations in the United States.

According to Fomin, he and Scali had lunched together on Monday, hours before the President's speech. Now at the Occidental restaurant, after a waiter took their order, Fomin said, "War seems about to break out. Something must be done to save the situation." Scali replied, "Well, you should have thought of that before you introduced the missiles into Cuba."

Fomin leaned across the table: "Perhaps a way can be found to solve this crisis. . . . What would you think of a proposition whereby we

---

*Johnson's favor evidently paid off. A *Morning News* editorial just after the Missile Crisis noted that the Vice President had been "one of the advocates of firmness in dealing with Castro and communism. . . . That he has worked unobtrusively but effectively toward that goal in the recent critical period is certain."

would promise to remove our missiles under United Nations supervision, where Mr. Khrushchev would promise never to introduce such offensive weapons into Cuba again? Would the President of the United States be willing to promise publicly not to invade Cuba?" If Stevenson suggested such a settlement at the UN, he said, Zorin would be interested.

Scali replied that he did not know whether Kennedy would make such a promise. Fomin said, "You find out immediately from your high-level State Department friends." Scali rushed back to the State Department, typed out a record of the conversation, and took it to Roger Hilsman.

Scali and the other Americans told of Fomin's approach presumed that it had been authorized by Khrushchev. In 1989, Fomin said he had acted on his own hook, although the conversation was reported to Dobrynin, who may have cabled it to Moscow. By then Fomin was ailing: time may have distorted his memory.

After Scali publicized his rendezvous with Fomin in *Family Weekly* in 1964, Charles Bartlett was told by his friend Alexander Zinchuk of the Soviet Embassy that Scali's story was "a phony" and that Fomin had been "acting on his own." As Bartlett recalled, "I think the implication was that Scali . . . might have been making more out of it than was there, that he was trying to get a little publicity."

Georgi Kornienko insisted in 1991 that Fomin was indeed free-lancing, that the KGB and others in the Washington embassy were working whatever American contacts they had to find a way out of the crisis.

In New York at almost the same hour, U Thant made virtually the same proposal to Stevenson that Fomin had made to Scali. Kennedy had no way of knowing whether the idea came from Khrushchev or was simply something the Secretary-General had dreamed up. Dean Rusk recalled that "the President never felt he had anything before him."

Several years later Thant revealed to the Secretary of State that the source of the proposal was a Soviet official. As Rusk recalled, "U Thant named the Russian. We knew he was a KGB man. . . . U Thant said Gromyko knew about it. That would have been very different, had we known that."*

If Kornienko's later argument was incorrect and the KGB was being used to submit identical secret proposals in New York and Washing-

---

*By Rusk's recollection, Dobrynin and Zorin had not been informed.

ton, Khrushchev was returning to his preferred method of defusing confrontation with the United States—sending a secret agent to make a suggestion for which the Chairman did not wish to take public responsibility.

In Moscow, Foy and Phyllis Kohler gave a luncheon at Spaso House for the novelist Irving Stone. Windows were shattered by rock-throwing Soviet students. "Usually they had concentrated on the Embassy proper," Kohler recalled. "It never happened again."

At 4:42 P.M., a breathless Soviet courier arrived at the Embassy with a long letter to Kennedy signed "N. Khrushchev" in violet ink. Richard Davies was astonished: the Embassy was usually asked to pick up such documents at the Foreign Ministry. The courier told him, "Please excuse the fact that there is no seal on this, but I came right from the Kremlin, and I was instructed to come right here and not to bother to go by the Ministry and have the seal put on it."

Looking at the letter, Davies saw other signs that the Chairman had been in a hurry: "It was all jumbled up. There were corrections made in violet ink in the same hand as that of the signature. . . . Words were crossed out, and other words written in." As with the Chairman's earlier letters, it was divided among several Embassy officers for speedy translation into English. Kohler cabled Washington that it might be a "breakthrough."

The President had been frustrated all week by the transmission delays from Moscow. The new letter did not arrive until six o'clock Washington time, eight hours after it had been given to Davies. Rusk summoned Ball, McNamara, Robert Kennedy, Bundy, Thompson, and others to his offices to read it with him as it rattled off the teletype:

> I would judge that apparently continuing to exchange opinions at such a distance, even in the form of secret letters, will hardly add anything to what each side has already said to the other. . . . I see, Mr. President, that you too are not devoid of a sense of anxiety for the fate of the world. . . .
>
> We must not succumb to intoxication and petty passions, regardless of whether elections are impending in this or that country*. . . . If

---

*Renewing his unsubtle accusation that Kennedy had devised his actions with one eye on the congressional elections suggested both the candor with which Khrushchev was

indeed war should break out, it would not be in our power to stop it. . . . I have participated in two wars and I know that war ends only when it has rolled through cities and villages, sowing death and destruction everywhere.

In the name of the Soviet Government and the Soviet people, I assure you that your conclusions regarding offensive weapons in Cuba are groundless. . . . You are a military man and, I hope, will understand me. Let us take, for example, a simple cannon. What sort of weapon is this—offensive or defensive? A cannon is a defensive weapon if it is set up to defend boundaries or a fortified area. But if one gathers artillery and adds to it the necessary number of troops, then the same cannons become offensive weapons, because they prepare the way for infantry to attack. The same happens with nuclear missiles. . . .

You are mistaken if you think that any of our weapons on Cuba are offensive. However, let us not quarrel now. It is apparent that I will not be able to convince you of this. But I say to you—you, Mr. President, are a military man and should understand—can one attack if one has on one's territory even an enormous quantity of missiles of various effective radiuses and various power, but using only these means. These missiles are a means of extermination and destruction. But one cannot attack with these missiles—even nuclear missiles of a power of a hundred megatons, because only people, troops, can attack. Without people, any weapons, however powerful, cannot be offensive.

Therefore, how can one give such a completely incorrect interpretation as you are now giving, to the effect that some sort of weapons on Cuba are offensive? All the weapons located there, and I assure you of this, have a defensive character, are on Cuba solely for the purpose of defense, and we have sent them to Cuba at the request of the Cuban government. You, however, say that these are offensive weapons.

Mr. President, do you really seriously think that Cuba can attack the United States, and that even we together with Cuba can attack you from Cuban territory? . . . Has something so new appeared in military strategy that one can think it is possible to attack this way? I say precisely, attack and not destroy, since barbarians—people who have lost their senses—destroy. . . .

You can regard us with distrust, but in any case you can be sanguine . . . that we are of sound mind and understand perfectly well that if we attack you, you will respond the same way. . . . My conversation with you in Vienna gives me the authority to talk this way. This shows that we are normal people, that we understand and evaluate the situation correctly. Therefore how can we permit the incorrect actions which you ascribe to us? Only lunatics or suicides, who themselves want to

---

speaking and the depth of his misunderstanding of the President's motives and his conviction that Kennedy was politically weak.

perish and to destroy the whole world before they die, could do this. We, however, want to live and do not at all want to destroy your country.

We want something quite different: to compete with your country on a peaceful basis. We quarrel with you, we have differences on ideological as well as economic questions that should be solved not by military means but by peaceful competition. . . .

You have now proclaimed piratical measures, employed in the Middle Ages, when ships moving in international waters were attacked. . . . Our vessels apparently will soon enter the zone your Navy is patrolling. I assure you that these vessels, now bound for Cuba, are carrying the most innocent, peaceful cargoes.

Do you really think that we occupy ourselves with nothing but the movement of so-called offensive weapons, atomic and hydrogen bombs? Although perhaps your military people imagine that these are some special sort of weapon, I assure you that they are merely the most ordinary, peaceful goods. Therefore, Mr. President, let us show good sense. I assure you that on those ships, which are bound for Cuba, there are no weapons at all. The weapons necessary for the defense of Cuba are already there. . . .

I don't know whether you can understand me and believe me. But I should like to have you believe in yourself and agree that one cannot give way to passions. It is necessary to control them. . . . Let us normalize relations. We have received an appeal from . . . U Thant. . . . His proposals amount to this: our side should not transport armaments of any kind to Cuba during a certain period while negotiations are taking place . . . and the other side should not take any sort of piratical actions against vessels sailing on the high seas. . . . This would be a way out of the situation that has been created, which would give people the possibility of breathing calmly.

You have asked . . . what provoked the delivery of weapons to Cuba. You raised this with our Foreign Minister. I will tell you frankly, Mr. President, what provoked it. We were very grieved by the fact—I spoke about it in Vienna—that a landing took place, that an attack on Cuba was committed, as a result of which many Cubans perished. You yourself told me then that this had been a mistake. I respected that explanation. You repeated it to me several times, pointing out that not everyone occupying a high position would acknowledge his mistakes as you had done.

I value such frankness. For my part, I told you that we too possess no less courage. We also acknowledged those mistakes which had been committed during the history of our state, and not only acknowledged, but sharply condemned them. If you are really concerned about the peace and welfare of your people—and this is your responsibility as President—then I, as the Chairman of the Council of Ministers, am concerned for my people. Moreover, the preservation of world peace should be our joint concern, since if, under contemporary conditions, war should break out, it would be a . . . worldwide, cruel and destructive war.

Why have we assisted Cuba with military and economic aid? . . . Our people once had a revolution, when Russia was still a backward country. We were attacked . . . by many countries. The U.S.A. participated in that adventure. . . . A whole book has been written about this by General Graves, who at that time commanded the U.S. Expeditionary Corps. Graves called it *The American Adventure in Siberia.* * We know how difficult it is to achieve a revolution and reconstruct a country on new foundations. We sincerely sympathize with Cuba and the Cuban people. . . .

You once said that the United States was not preparing an invasion. But you also declared that you sympathized with the Cuban counterrevolutionary emigrants, that you support them and would help them realize their plans against the present Cuban Government. It is also no secret to anyone that the threat of armed attack, aggression, has constantly hung and continues to hang over Cuba. It was only this that impelled us to respond to the Cuban Government's request to give it aid to strengthen its defensive capacity.

If the President and Government of the United States were to give assurances that the U.S.A. itself would not participate in an attack on Cuba and would restrain others from this kind of action, if you would recall your fleet, this would immediately change everything. I am not speaking for Fidel Castro. But I think that he and the Government of Cuba would probably declare demobilization and appeal to the people to get down to peaceful labor. . . .

Armaments bring only disasters. When one accumulates them, it damages the economy, and if one uses them, they destroy people on

---

*In *America's Siberian Adventure: 1918–1920* (New York: Jonathan Cape, 1931), Major General William Graves described his command of the limited expedition of American forces dispatched by Woodrow Wilson to Siberia in July 1918. Responding to requests by Britain, France, and Japan, the United States hoped to bolster any Russian government that would, unlike Lenin's, fight the Germans. In his book, Graves concluded that by sending the expedition, "the United States was a party to the efforts to overthrow the Soviets" and that "the various governments taking part in the intervention take very little pride in this venture. Who can blame them?"

This was hardly the first time Khrushchev had mentioned Graves's book to an American. He was always eager to show American visitors how the United States had wished to crush the Russian Revolution from its birth. During his Saturday afternoon meeting with Kennedy at Vienna, the Chairman noted that "the history of revolutions is very instructive. During the Russian Revolution, the revolutionaries were weak and a counter-revolution occurred. . . . Even the United States intervened." He went on to mention that he had "read a book by an American colonel entitled *U.S. Adventure in Siberia.* Notwithstanding all this, the revolution was victorious because the people were on its side."

both sides. . . . If people do not show wisdom, then in the final analysis, they will come to a conflict, like blind moles, and reciprocal extermination will begin.

Let us therefore show statesmanlike wisdom. I propose: we, for our part, will declare that our ships bound for Cuba will not carry any kind of armaments. You would declare that the United States will not invade Cuba with its forces and will not support any kind of forces that might intend to carry out an invasion of Cuba. Then the necessity for the presence of our military specialists in Cuba would disappear.

Mr. President, I appeal to you to weigh well what the aggressive, piratical actions, which you have declared the U.S.A. intends to carry out in international waters, would lead to. You yourself know that any sensible man simply cannot agree to this. . . . If you did this as the first step toward the uleashing of a war, well then, it is evident that nothing else is left to us but to accept your challenge.

If you have not lost your self-control and sensibly conceive what this might lead to, Mr. President, we and you ought not now to pull on the ends of the rope in which you have tied the knot of war, because the more the two of us pull, the tighter that knot will be tied. And a moment may come when that knot will be tied so tight that even he who tied it will not have the strength to untie it. . . . Let us not only relax the forces pulling on the ends of the rope. Let us take measures to untie the knot.

These, Mr. President, are my thoughts, which, if you should agree with them, could put an end to the tense situation which is disturbing all peoples. These thoughts are governed by a sincere desire to . . . remove the threat of war.

As the letter arrived in four parts, the diplomats read it with a microscope. Thompson suspected that the Chairman had sent it without clearance by the Presidium or Foreign Ministry. He knew that Khrushchev normally did not dictate such messages: he would speak in front of his colleagues and someone would write up his ideas.

Thompson thought that this letter had "all the earmarks of having been directly dictated by him—and probably under circumstances in which no one was able to change it or polish it or modify it. I think that he obviously was . . . under considerable strain."*

The essentials of the letter were promising but hardly acceptable to the United States. In exchange for the President's pledge not to invade Cuba and his relaxation of the blockade, Khrushchev was offering talks and a pledge not to bring in more weapons. Like earlier

---

*Three months later, Rusk privately told Senators, "We gather from what they have said to us since then that it was written and sent by him personally without general clearance topside in the Soviet Union."

offers, this would give the Russians time to rush the missiles to completion and, as Khrushchev knew, equip them with the warheads already in Cuba.

Rusk thought the letter showed the Chairman to be "disturbed" and "trying to find a way to get out" of his predicament. Ball agreed; it was "unquestionably a *cri de coeur* by Khrushchev." He could picture the "squat, morosely unhappy Chairman facing a blank wall and a doubtful future." He felt Khrushchev's "anguish in every paragraph."

Robert Kennedy agreed that the letter "had the beginnings perhaps of some accommodation." Dean Acheson found the text "confused and almost maudlin": Khrushchev must have been "either tight or scared." He thought his colleagues "too eager to liquidate this thing. So long as we had the thumbscrew on Khrushchev, we should have given it another turn every day."

Informed of Scali's talk with Fomin, Rusk took the newsman to the White House. Spotting Scali outside the Oval Office, Salinger thought he had sneaked in to try for an exclusive interview with the President. Rusk said, "It's okay, Pierre. I brought him here."

Kennedy wished to hear Scali's story from the horse's mouth and to allow him to tell Fomin that he had consulted the highest level of his government. He and Rusk operated under the very possibly false assumption that Fomin was acting as Khrushchev's agent, just as Bolshakov had done for seventeen months.

The President asked Scali to see the Counselor again "but don't use my name. That's against the rules. . . . Tell them you've gotten a favorable response from the highest authority in the government."

At 7:35 P.M., Scali met Fomin at the Sheraton Park Hotel. In his pocket was a handwritten note from Rusk: Scali should say that he had "reason to believe" the United States saw "real possibilities" in Fomin's offer but that time was "very urgent." When Scali conveyed this message over coffee, Fomin twice asked him for reassurance that it came from the highest American circles. Scali said, "If I lied about this at this critical moment . . . I would have to be the world's most irresponsible man."

Fomin said that since they were apparently agreed on UN inspection of Cuban bases, why not also ask the UN to inspect American bases in Florida and the Caribbean to ensure that American invasion forces were disbanded? Scali sharply replied that this was something new. Fomin shrugged; he was "just a small fry" and was only asking.

Scali said he was just a reporter but such a scheme would be politically difficult for the President, who was being pressured to invade Cuba immediately.

According to Scali, Fomin replied, "Very well. I will promise to pass this message on immediately to the highest Soviet leaders, and simultaneously to Mr. Zorin at the United Nations."

Khrushchev's letter demonstrated his awareness that Kennedy's blockade was working and could be tightened. To his amazement, the President had succeeded in gaining the support of the OAS, the UN, and most of the nations of the world.

He was unwilling to take the possibly nuclear risks that would grow out of a counterblockade of West Berlin. He knew that in the Caribbean, the United States enjoyed such conventional superiority that Soviet and Cuban forces could not hope to defy the invasion that would surely come.

Had Khrushchev's letter arrived punctually in Washington, Kennedy could have seized it as the basis for a settlement. Instead, the transmission delays meant that the President could not give him an answer on Friday night.

After reading the letter, Kennedy gave it to O'Donnell, who was "deeply moved" by it. Sorensen found the letter "long, meandering, full of polemics, but in essence appearing to contain the germ of a reasonable settlement."

That evening at ten, the President met with Ex Comm in the Cabinet Room. The ten days of pressures had depleted neither his sense of humor nor, evidently, his libido. Late in the second week of the crisis, he spotted one of the secretaries brought from the Commerce Department to cope with the increased White House workload and quietly told McNamara, "Get her name. We may avert nuclear war tonight."*

---

*Richard Goodwin had a similar experience during a March 1963 presidential visit to Costa Rica. In a hotel room on a high floor, Kennedy waved him over to the window and said, "Look down there, Dick . . . no, near those cars. Now that's one hell of a woman. . . . Why don't you . . ." As Goodwin recalled, the President's voice trailed off and he was not able to find out what Kennedy was about to ask him. Goodwin joked in his memoirs, "Perhaps he wanted some changes in the next day's speech."

Rusk and Thompson said that Khrushchev's letter was vague. It spoke of declarations by other people—the President would not invade, Castro would demobilize—but made no commitment for pulling out the missiles or for verification. Still, combined with Fomin's proposal, it could lead to an acceptable settlement. George Ball recalled that most of those in the room felt that Khrushchev's letter "seemed to be the break in the clouds we had been waiting for."

The President decided to treat the proposal suggested in the Chairman's letter and by Fomin as deserving a serious reply. Hilsman and his men were ordered to scrutinize it for hidden booby traps. After the meeting, Kennedy took Salinger into the Oval Office and said, "Do you think the people in that room realize that if we make a mistake there may be two hundred million dead?"

In Moscow on Friday night, Khrushchev proposed, "Why don't the members of the Presidium go to the theater tonight? Let's show both our own people and the entire world that, as far as we are concerned, the situation is still calm." The Chairman took Kozlov, Brezhnev, and other officials to a Cuban concert.

Like Khrushchev's well-publicized attendance at the Jerome Hines concert on Tuesday night, Gromyko felt such a gesture was "more reassuring than thousands of the most skillful lectures." Nor did it harm Soviet relations with Castro and his advisers, who were growing ever more nervous about an American-Soviet deal that would sell out their interests.

Saturday morning, October 27. Khrushchev sat in his Kremlin offices and listened as Malinovsky lectured in front of a map of the Soviet Union, using a pointer. He asked the Marshal and the other military advisers if they could assure him "that holding fast would not result in the death of five hundred million human beings."

As Khrushchev recalled, "They looked at me as though I was out of my mind or, what was worse, a traitor. The biggest tragedy, as they saw it, was not that our country might be devastated and everything lost, but that the Chinese or the Albanians would accuse us of appeasement or weakness." He wondered, "What good would it have done me in the last hour of my life to know that though our great nation and the United States were in complete ruin, the national honor of the Soviet Union was intact?".

Like Kennedy, he had been worried all week about the many hours each of his messages took to cross the Atlantic. Kharmalov, now the Soviet broadcasting chief, was called in to broadcast a new message to Kennedy over Radio Moscow. Melor Sturua of *Izvestia* was also summoned to pick up a copy. Peering through an open doorway at Khrushchev as he argued with his generals, Sturua noticed that the Chairman was "the most calm, the most rational man in the room."*

Khrushchev dictated his message, had it typed, corrected the draft, and had it retyped. Copies were sealed into envelopes and handed to Kharmalov and Sturua. As the *Izvestia* man recalled, his car was given a green light at every intersection from the Kremlin to his office on Pushkin Square. He wondered what was in the envelope. Did the Chairman's new message betoken "peace or war?"

On Saturday morning in Washington, Robert Kennedy entered the ten o'clock Ex Comm meeting with "considerable disquiet." He had just read a report from J. Edgar Hoover that Soviet diplomats in New York were thought to be preparing to destroy all their sensitive documents in anticipation of war.† The CIA reported that a Soviet tanker, the *Grozny,* had broken off from sister vessels to head toward the quarantine line.

As the Ex Comm meeting began (it was 5 P.M., Moscow time), Radio Moscow broadcast the new message from Khrushchev to Kennedy:

> You wish to ensure the security of your country, and this is under-standable. But Cuba too wants the same thing. . . . How are we, the Soviet Government, to assess your actions, which are expressed by the fact that you have surrounded the Soviet Union with military bases, surrounded our allies with military bases, placed military bases literally around our country, and stationed your missile armaments there? . . . Your missiles are stationed in Britain and in Italy and pointed at us. Your missiles are stationed in Turkey.

---

*Paul Ghali of the *Chicago Daily News* later reported on the basis of "diplomatic reports reaching Paris" that when Khrushchev raised the prospect of negotiation and with-drawal of the missiles, Malinovsky loudly complained that the Chairman was "upset-ting the whole Soviet military offensive structure" with a "stupid" and "senseless" move.

†Years later Dobrynin denied that official papers were burned but allowed that there were preparations for many contingencies. The Soviets in New York may have been trying to spook the Americans into thinking that they were nervelessly preparing for imminent war, like the gas-mask display for Richard Davies at the Foreign Ministry in Moscow.

You are worried by Cuba. You say that it worries you because it lies ninety miles by sea from the coast of the United States. But Turkey lies next to us. Our sentinels patrol back and forth and watch each other. Do you believe that you have the right to demand security for your country and the removal of such weapons that you call offensive, but do not accord the same right to us?

You have placed devastating missile weapons, which you call defensive, in Turkey, literally next to us. How then does recognition of our equal military capabilities square with such unequal relations between our two great states? . . .

It is good, Mr. President, that you have agreed to have our representatives meet and begin talks, apparently through the mediation of . . . Secretary-General U Thant. . . . I think that one could rapidly eliminate the conflict and normalize the situation. . . . This is why I make this proposal:

We are willing to remove from Cuba those weapons you regard as offensive. . . . Your representatives will make a declaration to the effect that the United States . . . considering the uneasiness and anxiety of the Soviet state, will remove its analogous weapons from Turkey. Let us reach agreement on the period of time you and I will need to bring this about. . . . Representatives of the UN Security Council could inspect on the spot the fulfillment of the pledges made. Of course, it is necessary that the Governments of Cuba and Turkey would allow these representatives to come to their countries. . . .

To give satisfaction and hope to the peoples of Cuba and Turkey and strengthen their confidence in their security, we will make a statement within the Security Council framework to the effect that the Soviet Government solemnly promises to respect the . . . sovereignty of Turkey, not to interfere in its internal affairs, not invade Turkey, not to make our territory available . . . for such an invasion, and that it would also restrain those who contemplate committing aggression against Turkey, either from Soviet territory or from the territory of Turkey's other neighboring states. The United States Government will make a similar statement . . . about Cuba.

It will declare that the United States will respect the inviolability of Cuba's borders and its sovereignty, will pledge not to interfere in its internal affairs, not to invade Cuba itself or make its territory available as a bridgehead for such an invasion, and will also restrain those who might contemplate committing aggression against Cuba, either from the territory of the United States or from the territory of Cuba's other neighboring states. Of course, for this we would have to agree with you on a certain time limit. Let us agree to some period of time, but without unnecessary delay—say, within two or three weeks, not longer than a month.

The weapons in Cuba, of which you speak and which disturb you, are in the hands of Soviet officers. Thus you can rule out any accidental use of them that would injure the United States. These weapons are stationed in Cuba at the request of the Cuban Government and are only for defensive purposes. Therefore if there is no invasion of Cuba, or attack on the Soviet Union or any of our allies, then, of course, these weapons are not and will not be a threat to anyone. For they are not for purposes of attack. . . .

The entire world is now apprehensive and expects reasonable actions from us. . . . Announcing our agreement would bring the greatest joy for all peoples. . . . It could serve as a good beginning and, especially, make it easier to agree on a nuclear test ban. . . . Our position and yours on this issue are very close together. All of this could possibly serve as a good impetus to search for mutually acceptable agreements on other controversial issues. . . . These are my proposals, Mr. President.

Why did Khrushchev up the ante overnight? His private Friday-evening letter had not mentioned Turkish missiles, only an American pledge not to invade Cuba.

Georgi Kornienko and other Soviets suggested in 1991 that on Friday night, the Chairman was convinced that a U.S. invasion of Cuba was imminent and that to achieve a quick settlement, he dropped his intention to demand removal of the Turkish missiles. They argued that by Saturday, surrounded by his generals, Khrushchev considered such an assault more remote and thus included the demand in his second letter.

On Saturday morning, a few minutes after ten, a report of Khrushchev's new message was handed to Kennedy, who read it aloud: "Premier Khrushchev told President Kennedy . . . he would withdraw offensive missiles from Cuba if the United States withdrew its rockets from Turkey."

Kennedy said, "That wasn't in the [Friday] letter we received, was it?"*

Bundy: "It's very odd, Mr. President. If he's changed his terms from a long letter to you and an urgent appeal from the Counselor [Fomin] only last night, set in a purely Cuban context, it seems to me . . . there's nothing wrong with our posture in sticking to that line. . . . I

---

*Once again, the President had switched on his secret tape recorder. This and other quotations from October 27 Ex Comm meetings that follow are taken verbatim from the transcript.

would answer back saying, 'I would prefer to deal with your . . . interesting proposals of last night.' " By "last night" Bundy meant Khrushchev's Friday letter.

Kennedy warned Ex Comm that the United States could be in "an unsupportable position" if it rejected Khrushchev's new demand to remove the Turkish missiles. He noted that last year they had "tried to get the missiles out of there because they're not militarily useful." To "any rational man," giving up the Turkish missiles would "look like a very fair trade." If the United States refused, "I think you're going to find it very difficult to explain why we are going to take hostile military action in Cuba. . . . I think we've got a very tough one here."

The President complained to Ex Comm that Khrushchev had issued the new demand "in a way that's caused maximum tension and embarrassment. It's not as if it was a private proposal, which would give us an opportunity to negotiate with the Turks. He's put it out in a way that the Turks are bound to say they don't agree to this."

McNamara: "How can we negotiate with somebody who changes his deal before we even get a chance to reply and announces publicly the deal before we receive it?"

Bundy said, "Let me suggest this scenario. . . . Privately we say to Khrushchev, 'Look, your public statement is a very dangerous one because it makes impossible immediate discussion of your private proposal and requires us to proceed urgently with the things that we have in mind.' " By this Bundy meant military action against Cuba.

He suggested sending Khrushchev a message, "by Fomin, for example, that last night's stuff [the Friday Khrushchev letter] was pretty good, *this* is *impossible* at this stage of the game, and that time is getting very short. . . . If they want to stop something further in Cuba, they have to do better than *this* public statement."

The President lobbied the men to accept the notion of bargaining over Turkey. The "best position now," he said, was to let Khrushchev know that the United States was "glad to discuss" Turkish missiles with him—"once we get a positive indication that they've ceased their work in Cuba."

Bundy warned that "if we sound as if we wanted to make this trade, to our NATO people and to all the people who are tied to us by alliance, we are in *real* trouble." World faith in the United States would suffer a "radical decline."

Kennedy: "Yes, but . . . if we reject it out of hand and then have to take military action against Cuba, then we also face a decline." He conceded that the allies would oppose a Turkey-for-Cuba trade: "They don't realize that in two or three days we may have a military strike which could bring perhaps the seizure of Berlin or a strike on Turkey.

"And then they'll say, 'By God, we should have taken it.' . . . What we're going to be faced with is: because we wouldn't take the missiles out of Turkey, then maybe we'll have to invade or make a massive strike on Cuba, which may lose *Berlin*. That's what concerns me." He concluded, "We're going to have to take our weapons out of Turkey."

Thompson opposed such an immediate trade: "The important thing for Khrushchev, it seems to me, is to be able to say, 'I saved Cuba, I stopped an invasion.' " As for "this Turkey thing," they could discuss it later.

Robert seconded Bundy's advice to respond to Khrushchev's Friday offer and brush aside the Saturday message. This was later made famous as the "Trollope ploy," after the ruse by which a maiden deliberately takes a suitor's remark to be a marriage proposal. The Attorney General advised his brother to just tell Khrushchev that he "made an offer, we accept the offer, and it's silly bringing up NATO at this time."*

The President doubted that it would work: "We can try this thing, but he's going to come back, I'm certain."

When the issue of Turkish missiles had earlier surfaced in Ex Comm, the President had insisted that there would be "no bargains over our bases in Turkey and Italy." During the first week of the crisis, some Ex Comm members had insisted that a basic principle of the nuclear age was that nuclear missiles should be installed openly and not in trouble spots like Berlin, Iran, Laos, or Cuba. Some worried that, as his price for dismantling the Cuban sites, Khrushchev would demand the sending of a UN team to "all the world's missile installations" and "major negotiations" on all foreign bases.

On Monday night after Kennedy's speech, reporters had asked McNamara on background why the Turkish missiles could not be traded for those in Cuba. Tortuously he replied, "There is no

---

*Especially during his 1968 presidential campaign, Robert took the credit for being the author of this idea. By then president of the World Bank, McNamara made a television commercial for the candidate praising his genius during the Missile Crisis in proposing that the President answer the earlier, more favorable letter. The gracious Bundy did not challenge their memories.

similarity between the provision of such weapons to nations under the threat of attack—and the clear threat of attack—and the stated threat of attack, on the other hand, versus the arming of Cuba, on the other, which obviously was not under the threat of nuclear attack or attack from this country."*

Rostow and William Tyler suggested to Rusk on Tuesday that the United States quietly persuade the Turks to phase out their IRBMs in favor of the submarine force already planned for the Eastern Mediterranean and agree with the Soviets not to station MRBMs in the Caribbean or Middle East. This would show Western European leaders that Washington was using the crisis not to abandon them but to pursue their long-term interests.

Walter Lippmann had drawn the Cuba-Turkey parallel in a Monday column: "If we use force to invade or blockade Cuba, we must be prepared for something around or in Turkey or some such place on the frontiers of the Soviet Union."

On Thursday he proposed a trade: "The only place that is truly comparable with Cuba is Turkey. That is the only place where there are strategic weapons right on the frontier of the Soviet Union. . . . The Soviet military base in Cuba is defenseless, and the base in Turkey is all but obsolete. The two bases could be dismantled without altering the world balance of power."

When Khrushchev's advisers read this column, they almost certainly suspected that it had been inspired by the White House. As Kennedy always complained, Khrushchev thought that Lippmann's columns spoke for the President. This was not illogical; when Lippmann saw the Chairman in April 1961, he had brought a private Berlin proposal that Khrushchev assumed to have come from Kennedy. The Russians may not have known that by May 1961, when Lippmann criticized the New Frontier as "the Eisenhower Administration thirty years younger," he had less access to the President than others like Reston maintained.

There is no evidence that Kennedy asked Lippmann to raise his trial balloon. It was a natural outgrowth of Lippmann's Monday column. It is doubtful that the President or his advisers would have undercut his Monday speech by suggesting a compromise even before the quarantine was announced.

---

* In 1989, McNamara conceded to Gromyko and other former Soviet officials in Moscow that he could understand how the Soviet Union "might well have interpreted" the Jupiters in Turkey "as showing signs of aggression." He noted that "there were actions by you which led us to feel the same way," such as the building of mammoth Soviet convention superiority in Europe.

Still, once Lippmann made his Thursday proposal, Kennedy may have thought it useful to call Khrushchev's attention to one route by which they could negotiate an end to the crisis. Had he wished to warn the Chairman away from such a route of bargaining, he could have easily asked Salinger to issue a statement to the effect that the United States could not accept the suggestions of a Turkey-for-Cuba trade that had appeared in public prints. Knowing Khrushchev might assume that Lippmann was proposing the trade on his behalf, the President let the column stand.

Now, after Saturday luncheon, the President scrawled notes for a new letter to Khrushchev and dictated them to Evelyn Lincoln. She felt that "by now the tension was unbearable."

A U-2, evidently on a routine air-sampling nuclear detection mission, strayed into Siberian air space over the Chukot Peninsula. Pursued by Soviet fighters, it returned safely to Alaska. The location of the incursion was enough to assure the Soviets that it was not a reconnaissance flight on the eve of an American surprise attack.

Khrushchev may have wondered whether this was a deliberate, provocative display of American superiority, like the one he had privately complained of to Kennedy just after the inauguration. It seems more likely that he quickly concluded that it had indeed been an accident. The episode may have made him more sensitive to the fact that the longer the Missile Crisis wore on, the greater was the danger of more accidents that could throw the two powers into military confrontation.

When the President was told of the accident, he noted that he had ordered such flights canceled. With a tense chuckle he said, "There is always some son of a bitch who doesn't get the word."*

At the afternoon Ex Comm meeting, the Joint Chiefs told Kennedy it was now time for a massive air strike and invasion of Cuba: the action should begin "no later than Monday morning, the 29th, unless there is irrefutable evidence in the meantime that offensive weapons are being dismantled and rendered inoperable."

This plea was interrupted by a bulletin: one of the U-2s photo-

---

*This was a Kennedy refrain. He said the same thing to his friend Bill Lawrence, for instance (using the term "bastard" instead of "son of a bitch") when he spotted the *New York Times* man wearing a Homburg rather than a top hat the night before the Inauguration.

graphing Cuba had been downed.* On Tuesday, Ex Comm had resolved that if a spy plane was fired upon over the island, the Tactical Air Command would retaliate by destroying a Soviet SAM site on Cuba. Such an attack could be launched within two hours of a presidential order.

Previously informed that all SAM sites in Cuba were under Soviet control, the President assumed that the U-2 downing was a deliberate Soviet action: "This is much of an escalation by them, isn't it?"

"Yes, exactly," said McNamara. He went on to say, "I think we can defer an air attack on Cuba until Wednesday or Thursday, but *only* if we continue our surveillance and . . . fire against anything that fires against the surveillance aircraft, and only if we maintain a blockade in this interim period."

Kennedy said, "We can't very well send a U-2 over there, can we, now? And have a guy killed again tomorrow?" General Taylor agreed: "We certainly shouldn't do it until we retaliate and say that if they fire again on one of our planes, then we'll come back with great force."

In fact, the U-2 downing had not been specifically ordered by Khrushchev or anyone in Moscow. Alexeyev recalled being told years later that on Saturday morning the Soviets on Cuba had discovered an American plane flying over the eastern part of the island.

According to Alexeyev, the Soviet command on Cuba had been given "no direct prohibition" against firing at American aircraft. Two Soviet deputy commanders had twenty minutes to decide whether or not to attack. After trying without success to reach their superior, they decided to fire at the plane on their own authority. An SA-2 was launched from a battery near the Cuban port of Banes, downing Anderson's plane on the first volley.†

---

*The dead pilot, Major Rudolph Anderson, had on Sunday, October 14, taken the U-2 pictures that alerted the United States to the missiles in Cuba.

†For almost three decades, the circumstances of who downed the U-2 were a mystery. Carlos Franqui, a Castro comrade who later left the country, claimed in 1981 that Castro went to the Soviet base at Pinar del Rio "with intent" to cause an incident that would show if "there was going to be a war or not." When a U-2 appeared on radar, he asked the Soviets how to shoot down an attacking plane. He pushed the vital button: "the plane came down amidst the consternation of the generals." This tale resembled George Washington chopping down the cherry tree in its tone and accuracy. Castro had actually remained in Havana throughout the crisis. In 1985, he said, "I did not have the honor of shooting down the spy plane."

The day after the downing, Castro wrote Khrushchev, "If we wanted to avoid the risk of a surprise attack, we had to order our artillerymen to open fire. The Soviet commanders can give you additional information on the airplane shot down."

Sergei Khrushchev recalled that when the Chairman was told of the U-2 downing, he was "very upset and considered it a big mistake on our part." Like the U-2 incursion over Chukot, it suggested that control of the crisis was being taken from his and Kennedy's hands. Sergei recalled his father's worry, "as a man who lived through two wars, and knowing what can happen in situations when troops are tense and located very close to one another," that "an unexpected decision, an unexpected shot . . . could lead to loss of control over events."*

Malinovsky immediately sent an angry reprimand to Soviet forces on Cuba: they had "hastily" shot down the plane while "an agreement for a peaceful way to deter an invasion of Cuba was already taking shape."

Cubans greeted news of the U-2 downing with wild celebration. Some in the Cuban leadership feared the incident would inflame the crisis. But as the Cuban official Jorge Risquet recalled, "We applauded the action. And we were very excited and our people were thrilled that such a thing had happened, because the people saw that they were not defenseless."

In the Cabinet Room late on Saturday afternoon, McNamara said he had reread Khrushchev's Friday letter: "My God! . . . I'd never base a transaction on *that contract*. . . . There's not a damned thing in it that's an offer.

"You read that message carefully. He didn't propose to take the missiles out. . . . It's twelve pages of—of fluff. . . . And *before* we got the damned thing read, the whole deal changed." By this he meant Khrushchev's Saturday message. "*Completely* changed. All of which leads me to conclude that the *probabilities* are that nothing's going to be signed quickly."

McCone: "I'd send him a threatening letter. I'd say, 'You've made public an offer [on Friday]. We'll accept that offer. But you shot down a plane today before we even had a chance to send you a letter, despite the fact that *you knew* that we were sending unarmed planes on a publicly announced surveillance. Now we're telling you, Mr. Khrushchev, this just one thing, that we're sending unarmed planes over Cuba. If one of them is shot at, we're going to take the [offensive] installations out, and you can expect it.'"

Lyndon Johnson asked for an explanation of why Khrushchev had

---

*Khrushchev had had a similar worry during the Friedrichstrasse tank confrontation in Berlin of October 1961.

increased his demands overnight. Thompson replied that the Chairman had either been overruled by colleagues or enchanted by public suggestions from Walter Lippmann and Bruno Kreisky, the Austrian Foreign Minister, that the crisis could be solved by a Cuba-for-Turkey trade.

Knowing his man, Thompson said, "Let's push harder. I think they'll change their minds when we take continued forceful action—stopping their ship or taking out a SAM site. That kills some Russians." He favored taking out a SAM base on Cuba without further warning "because I don't think giving an ultimatum is recommended."

Using a term later brought into common usage during his own long struggle in Vietnam, the Vice President said, "You warhawks ought to get together!"

Thompson declared, "We clearly have a choice here. . . . Either we go on the line that we've decided to attack Cuba . . . or we try to get Khrushchev back on the peaceful solution, in which case we shouldn't give any indication that we're going to accept this thing on Turkey. . . . It seems to me . . . they suddenly thought they could get up the price. They've upped the price, and they've upped the action.

"And I think that we have to bring them back by upping our action and by getting them back to this other thing without any mention of Turkey. . . . We ought to keep the heat on him and get him back on the line which he obviously was on the night before. That message was almost incoherent and showed that they were quite worried. And the Lippmann article and maybe the Kreisky speech has made them think they can get more."

As Bundy recalled, the President was now driven by hope raised by Khrushchev's Friday letter, anger at his hardening position, and worry that further incidents like the U-2 over Siberia and the Anderson downing might hurl the two powers into accidental collision, especially since the Joint Chiefs were increasing their demands for air strike and invasion.

Kennedy vetoed retaliation for the U-2 downing in Cuba. He told Thompson, "Well, I think . . . I'll just say [to Khrushchev], 'Of *course* we ought to try to go the first route which you suggest.' . . . But it seems to me we *ought* to have this discussion with NATO about these Turkish missiles."*

---

*By now State Department Intelligence had advised that if there were a Cuba-for-Turkey trade, Turkey, Iran, and other allies might see it as "a possible first move toward U.S. withdrawal from Europe . . . possibly an indication that the U.S. would not stand up to Soviet threats elsewhere, particularly in Berlin." Turkey would see the

He concluded, "We can't very well invade Cuba with all its toil, and long, as it's going to be, when we could have gotten them out by making a deal on the same missiles in Turkey. If that's part of the record, I don't see how we'll have a very good war."

Asked by Rusk to see Fomin, John Scali took the Russian to an empty ballroom at the Statler Hilton and demanded to know why Khrushchev had brought Turkish missiles into the bargaining. By Scali's account, the nervous Fomin said that perhaps the Chairman had been delayed in receiving his message from yesterday. Fomin reminded him that Lippmann had proposed a Cuba-for-Turkey trade.

Scali said, "I don't care . . . whether it was Walter Lippmann or Cleopatra. We are absolutely determined to get those missiles out of there. American invasion of Cuba is only hours away."*

For reasons of speed and to influence world opinion, Kennedy decided to publicize his next letter to Khrushchev. Late Saturday afternoon, he worked with Rusk, Ball, and Thompson on a draft. It complained that Khrushchev had brought European bases into the discussion while the bases in Cuba were being "feverishly" completed: "Time is running out, Mr. Chairman. . . . Work on these bases must be stopped at once and arrangements completed within a matter of days to dismantle them or I shall be obliged to undertake further steps to protect our security."

Robert Kennedy complained that this language was too negative. The President said, "If you disagree so violently, go and draft one yourself." The Attorney General took Sorensen into another room and brought back a new version.

After further revisions, Kennedy approved the final text.† It told

---

concession "as a move to bargain away installations of importance to the security of Turkey in order to achieve a greater measure of stability for the U.S. mainland." Soviet appeals to return to the era of Kamal Ataturk and resume friendly relations with Moscow "would fall upon more willing ears than in the past." The Turkish Foreign Minister had already declared in response to Khrushchev's public message today that abandonment of the bases in his country was "out of the question."

*Like the earlier Fomin-Scali conversations, this exchange has often been cited as a vital moment in the crisis. Noting the long transmission delays to Moscow, even through KGB channels, Georgi Kornienko argued in 1991 that Fomin's report of this talk could not have reached Khrushchev in time to influence his next move.

†The President had struck out a passage saying, "As I was preparing this letter, I learned of your public message attempting to connect NATO bases and Cuba. I must

Khrushchev that he had instructed his people in New York to talk with U Thant and the Soviets about "a permanent solution to the Cuban problem along the lines suggested in your letter of October 26th."

Under UN supervision, the Chairman would agree to dismantle and remove all weapons in Cuba "capable of offensive use" and keep them off the island. The President would respond by halting the quarantine and offering "assurances against an invasion of Cuba." He was "confident" that other nations in the hemisphere would do likewise.

Using the "Trollope ploy," the letter ignored Khrushchev's Saturday message, as Bundy had first suggested. It did not mention Turkish missiles. Kennedy did not want to put any concession on Turkey in writing. The furthest he was willing to go was to say that ending the crisis "would enable us to work toward a more general arrangement regarding 'other armaments,' as proposed in your second letter. . . . If . . . you are prepared to discuss a détente affecting NATO and the Warsaw Pact, we are quite prepared to consider with our allies any useful proposals."*

After the afternoon Ex Comm meeting, the Vice President had asked George Ball why the United States was not prepared to trade the Jupiters in Turkey for the missiles in Cuba. Ball replied that the previous week Ex Comm had concluded that such a deal "might be acceptable" if it would "save Berlin": NATO could defend Turkey instead "by assigning Polaris submarines to the area."

The President asked Thompson to deliver a copy of his letter and to explain it to Dobrynin. Thompson said, "No, you don't want me. You want a very personal message." That meant the Attorney General. As Jane Thompson recalled, her husband "tutored" Robert on "every comeback that Dobrynin could make."

Before his brother's departure, the President took him, Rusk, Bundy, McNamara, and Sorensen into the Oval Office. He told his brother, "Tell him if we don't get a reply by Monday, we'll start a military action against Cuba." In the presence of the four other trusted advisers, he asked him to give Dobrynin an additional oral message: the Turkish missiles must not be allowed to stand between war and peace.

---

tell you frankly that this is not a way to go forward with a settlement of the immediate crisis."

*This passage was as far as the President was willing to go in public to suggest that he was ready to meet the demand for removal of the Turkish missiles issued by Khrushchev's Saturday letter.

As Sorensen recalled, the President "recognized that for Chairman Khrushchev to withdraw the missiles from Cuba, it would be undoubtedly helpful to him if he could say at the same time to his colleagues in the Presidium, 'And we have been assured that the missiles will be coming out of Turkey.' "*

At 7:45 P.M., fifteen minutes before the President's letter was to be made public, Dobrynin arrived at the Justice Department. Robert Kennedy gave him a copy of the letter to Khrushchev and warned that if more American planes were downed over Cuba, the United States would retaliate. According to a memo he dictated soon thereafter, he told Dobrynin that "we had to have a commitment by at least tomorrow that those bases would be removed. This was not an ultimatum, I said, but just a statement of fact."†

By his own account, he told Dobrynin that once the Soviets agreed to dismantle the bases, "if Cuba and Castro ended their subversive activities in other Central and Latin American countries, we would agree to keep peace in the Caribbean and not permit an invasion from American soil."

Then he said that the President was willing to throw in the Turkish missiles:‡ "But it cannot be made part of a package and published. . . . Insofar as it involves a NATO decision, it must conform to standard procedures for NATO decision-making. Otherwise it would be very irregular for the President and he might be challenged for a decision taken by him alone."

By Kennedy's account, he told Dobrynin that "there could be no quid pro quo. . . . It was up to NATO to make the decision. I said it was completely impossible for NATO to take such a step under the

---

*In 1989, Sorensen offered a "confession": "I was the editor of Robert Kennedy's book [Thirteen Days]. It was, in fact, a diary of those thirteen days. And his diary was very explicit that this was part of the deal, but at the time it was still a secret even on the American side, except for the six of us who had been present at that meeting. So I took it upon myself to edit that out of his diaries."

†Long before the age of glasnost, in a book called President Kennedy's 1036 Days that was far more propaganda than history, Gromyko's son Anatoly claimed that the Attorney General added that "should war break out, millions of Americans would die." The United States was "trying to avoid this. . . . Any delay in finding ways out of the crisis was fraught with great danger." The younger Gromyko also wrote that Kennedy told Dobrynin that because of the U-2 downing, "the Pentagon was exerting strong pressure on his brother. . . . He did not exclude the possibility that the situation could get out of control and lead to irreparable consequences."

‡Recent Soviet accounts, including memoirs by Khrushchev not published until 1990, suggest that Kennedy also included the IRBMs in Italy.

present threatening position of the Soviet Union." But if four or five months elapsed, "I said I was sure that these matters could be resolved satisfactorily." He added that the understanding would be canceled at once if the Soviets tried to claim public credit for removing the Turkish missiles.

By Dobrynin's account, Kennedy also warned him that other Americans speaking with Soviets in Washington (presumably meaning Scali's talks with Fomin and perhaps Bartlett's with Zinchuk and Bolshakov) "do not reflect the views of the White House." Dobrynin should deal only with him.

According to Dobrynin, Kennedy's parting words were, "Time will not wait. We must not let it slip away." He said years later that the Attorney General "did not put forth any ultimatum. . . . But he persistently asked, it is true, to convey the President's request that if possible he wanted to receive an answer on Sunday."

The Ambassador wrote out a cable for Khrushchev and Gromyko. Presumably he worried that the Western Union man on the bicycle would not get the message to them in time.

When Robert stepped off the elevator on the second floor of the White House, his brother was dining with Dave Powers on broiled chicken. The President asked, "How did it go at the Embassy?" Robert reported that Dobrynin had preferred to meet at Justice. After listening to his account of their conversation, the President felt that the chance of settling the crisis by the end of the weekend was "a long shot at best."

When Ex Comm met at nine on Saturday evening, he approved the call-up of twenty-four air reserve squadrons: if American planes over Cuba were attacked on Sunday and the New York talks went nowhere, the United States should "take out" the SAM sites in Cuba. He noted that the *Grozny* was near the quarantine line. Stevenson should ask Thant to remind the Russians of their pledge to keep their ships out of Cuban waters during the UN talks.

Concealing his brother's Turkish missile concession, Robert said that the United States must not mention the subject of Turkey at a NATO meeting scheduled for Sunday: if the Soviets should "find, playing around and figuring on Turkey, we're willing to make some deal—if I were they, I'd push on that, and then I'd push on Italy, figuring that, well, if they're going to go on that, they can carry it one step further." If the United States was *"hard* on this thing," Moscow might solve the crisis "the way that they made the offer initially."

Deeply pessimistic, McNamara said, "I think . . . Bobby . . . we need to have two things ready—a government for Cuba, because we're going to need one . . . and secondly, plans for how to respond to the Soviet Union in Europe, because sure as hell they're going to do something there." Someone darkly joked, "Suppose we make Bobby mayor of Havana!"

They adjourned at almost midnight. The President arranged to review air-strike plans in the morning: "Now it can go either way." He and Powers went to the White House theater and watched one of his favorite actresses, Audrey Hepburn, in *Roman Holiday*.

Evidently only Rusk and the Kennedys knew that the President had taken one more secret precaution. After Robert departed to see Dobrynin, Kennedy and his Secretary of State had privately agreed that if Khrushchev did not accept the terms of the President's new letter by Monday, along with Robert's secret assurances about the Turkish missiles, U Thant should be quietly urged to propose a Turkey-for-Cuba trade. Kennedy would then publicly accept it.

Rusk called his friend Andrew Cordier, Dean of Columbia University's School of International Relations, who had served as a troubleshooter for Hammarskjöld. The President did not know him. Rusk dictated a statement to be issued by the Secretary-General and asked Cordier to give it to Thant "only after further signal from us."

Rusk said in 1987 that he felt Kennedy would have been ready to try the Cordier ploy on Monday "before we landed troops in Cuba, because landing those troops . . . would have been a major escalation from the Soviet point of view."

On Friday in Havana, Fidel Castro had warned Alexeyev that the United States was about to attack Cuba. By Alexeyev's account, the "fearful" Cuban leader asked to be taken into the Soviet Embassy bomb shelter.

With Alexeyev's help, Castro wrote a secret letter to Khrushchev predicting an American air strike or invasion within the next twenty-four to seventy-two hours. The morale of the Cuban people was "extremely high, and they will face the aggressor heroically." But should the United States succeed in occupying Cuba, the danger of allowing such aggression to go unchecked would be "devastating to humankind."

Castro implored Khrushchev to prevent the "imperialists" from gaining "the opportunity to launch the first attack in a nuclear war.

This would be "an act of self-defense" because there would be "no other solution, however harsh it might seem."

Alexeyev and Aragones years later defended Castro by saying that he was simply urging firmness against the United States. That was not Khrushchev's reading of the message; he assumed that Castro was urging him "to preempt the invasion and inflict a nuclear strike on the US."* For him, it was one more sign that control of the crisis was in danger of being snatched away from him and Kennedy.

By Saturday night, Khrushchev was more fearful than ever that the Pentagon would tighten what he considered to be its already strong grip on the President's decision-making. He had told Thompson in July of his suspicion that generals were in danger of seizing control of the United States government. He lived in a political culture where such things actually happened. When Dobrynin cabled Moscow of Robert Kennedy's comment that the Pentagon was pressuring his brother for an air strike, Khrushchev evidently read it to mean that the President was in danger of being overthrown.†

Alexeyev's telegram from Havana may have underscored the Chairman's fear of an immediate invasion in which many Soviets and Cubans would die. Castro's demand that the missiles be fired and the Anderson downing both sharpened Khrushchev's fear, like Kennedy's, that as the political and military atmosphere grew ever more frenzied, their two countries could be thrown into war by accident.

---

*The public revelation of Castro's demand displayed the political strains on Soviet historiography even four years after the start of *glasnost*. Between sessions of the American-Soviet-Cuban conference on the Missile Crisis in Moscow in January 1989, one participant told the *New York Times* that Castro had asked Khrushchev for a nuclear attack on the United States. The *Times* published the story. With President Mikhail Gorbachev about to leave for a difficult visit with Castro in Havana, the Soviet government may have considered it embarrassing to the Cuban leader if the story were left on the public record. Sergei Khrushchev was evidently prevailed upon to publicly deny the story, which he did.

The quotations from the Castro-Khrushchev correspondence in the preceding passage and in Chapter 19 come from a November 1990 *Le Monde* article by Jean-Edern Hallier, to whom Castro gave copies of his Missile Crisis correspondence with Khrushchev to defend himself against charges of having recklessly pushed the Chairman toward nuclear war.

†In his memoirs, Khrushchev said Dobrynin cabled that Robert Kennedy had wept and warned him, "If this situation continues much longer, the President is not sure that the military will not overthrow him and seize power. The American Army could get out of control." This recollection probably shows more about Khrushchev's own anxieties than about reality.

* * *

Sunday morning, October 28. Khrushchev awoke in his dacha outside Moscow. He drafted a response to Kennedy's Saturday night letter. A nervous messenger rushed it to Radio Moscow.

As Gromyko recalled, "Time was very dear to us at that moment. We had to take care not to allow delay to follow delay. . . . We had to strengthen the fundamental thing—to strengthen the situation for Cuba as an independent socialist state."

In Washington, Kennedy and his men awoke to a magnificent autumn morning. Walking into the White House, George Ball noted the South Grounds bathed in golden light and told McNamara, "It reminds me of the Georgia O'Keeffe painting that has a rose growing out of an ox skull."

A few minutes before nine, Washington time, Radio Moscow announced the broadcast of an important statement on the hour. Ignorant of the Cordier ploy, many members of Ex Comm supposed that if it was to be Khrushchev's rejection of Kennedy's Saturday night offer, the President would have to order an air strike on Cuba by Tuesday morning.*

At nine o'clock Washington time, an announcer for Radio Moscow began reading the new letter from Khrushchev to Kennedy, the tenth message between the two men since the Missile Crisis began:†

---

*Maxwell Taylor's personal assistant, William Smith, noted in 1989 that "every day that there was not U.S. military action was a day when those missiles became more ready to fire." He thought it would have been difficult for the President to long resist military pressures for an air strike.

McNamara insisted that he would have advised the President to postpone an air strike and invasion: "It would have been a bloody battle in which the Cuban and Soviet forces would have suffered a severe defeat with heavy casualties. I cannot believe there would not have been a Soviet military response." Raymond Garthoff has noted an estimate at the time that American casualties in a full-scale invasion of Cuba would be as high as twenty thousand.

McNamara felt that Kennedy "was intent on removing the missiles" but *without* running the huge risks that I think were associated with starting the military confrontation. And *nobody* knows where that would have ended. *Nobody.*" McNamara believed that the President would have tightened the quarantine to include petroleum and other Cuban necessities of life and/or resorted to the Cordier gambit: "Where that would have led had the missiles not been removed in a week, or two weeks, or a month, I'm not prepared to say." Sorensen agreed, while noting that Kennedy was "not a dictator," that there were "pressures on him from the military" and that "one man alone is not able to hold out against that rising tide indefinitely."

†Khrushchev was evidently so concerned about responding promptly to Kennedy's Saturday night letter (and presumably Robert Kennedy's request of Dobrynin for an

I have received your message of October 27. I express my satisfaction and thank you for the sense of proportion you have displayed and for recognition of the responsibility you now bear for the preservation of the peace of the world. I very well understand your anxiety and that of the American people about the fact that the weapons you describe as offensive are formidable weapons indeed. . . .

In order to eliminate as rapidly as possible the conflict which endangers the cause of peace . . . the Soviet Government, in addition to previously issued instructions to cease further work on weapons construction sites, has issued a new order to dismantle the weapons which you describe as offensive, and to crate and return them to the Soviet Union. . . .

"Dismantle . . . crate and return." Bundy was handed the first takes from Khrushchev's message while breakfasting in the White House Mess. Jubilant, he rushed out of the room and called the President. Thus the same man who had first alerted Kennedy to the Missile Crisis gave him what seemed to be the all-clear.

Bundy recalled, "It was a very beautiful morning, and it had suddenly become many times more beautiful. And I am sure the President felt the same way from the feeling between us as we talked about it. . . . We all felt that the world had changed for the better."

Khrushchev's words continued to blare out of speakers in American listening posts around the world:

Mr. President . . . I regard with respect and trust the statement you have made in your message . . . that there would be no attack or invasion against Cuba, not only by the United States but other countries of the Western Hemisphere. . . . Therefore the motives which induced us to give aid of this kind to Cuba have disappeared. . . .

We are prepared to reach an agreement to enable United Nations representatives to verify the dismantling of these weapons. Thus in view of the assurances you have given and our instructions for the dismantling, every condition has been met to eliminate the present conflict. . . .

Dean Rusk called the news to Robert Kennedy, who had taken his daughters to a horse show. Don Wilson, Acting USIA Director in Murrow's absence because of illness, recalled, "I felt like laughing or yelling or dancing." At the State Department, Harriman, Thompson, Edwin Martin, and William Tyler turned on Foy Kohler's old televi-

---

urgent reply) that once again he sent this reply by radio. Alexeyev wrote years later that broadcast of the message began even before the editing of its closing passages was completed.

sion set and watched the New York Giants play the Washington Redskins.

Khrushchev's message continued,

> I would like to say something about a détente between NATO and the Warsaw Pact countries, which you have mentioned. . . . Our people . . . have achieved tremendous successes since the October Revolution. . . . They want to . . . insure their further development on the road of peace and social progress. . . .
>
> We value peace perhaps even more than other peoples because we experienced the terrible war against Hitler. However our people will not flinch in the face of any ordeal. . . . Should the provocateurs unleash a war, they would not escape its grave consequences. But we are confident that reason will triumph, that war will not be unleashed, and that peace and security will be insured!

Bundy went to the family quarters and gave the full text to the President, who was leaving for ten o'clock Mass at St. Stephen's. Kennedy told Dave Powers, "I feel like a new man. Do you realize that we had an air strike all arranged for Tuesday? Thank God it's all over."

Dobrynin met Robert Kennedy at the Justice Department at eleven. Smiling, he said that everything was going to work out; Khrushchev wanted to send his "best wishes to the President."

When the President returned from Mass, he walked with springy step into the Cabinet Room. Sorensen thought he "looked ten feet tall." McNamara reported that the *Grozny* had stopped short of the line on Saturday night. Kennedy ordered the Navy to stop provocative operations by Cuban exiles that might reinflame the confrontation.

Rusk declared that all members of Ex Comm had helped to bring the "highly advantageous resolution" of the Missile Crisis. Bundy interrupted to say that everyone knew who were hawks and who were doves; today was the day of the doves.

The President warned them to be careful what they told the press: "Khrushchev has eaten enough crow. Let's not rub it in."* As for national euphoria, "that will wear off in about a week." After the

---

*In a background session, Rusk later told reporters, "When you're writing about this, don't make this appear to be a great capitulation on the part of the Russians. . . . We have no wish to make this situation more difficult than it already is by crowing. . . . It is not yet time to say this is over." Testifying to the difference between the journalism of 1962 and that of a later age, most of the reporters obeyed the request.

meeting, he remembered that Abraham Lincoln had been assassinated shortly after the greatest victory of his life. He told his brother, "This is the night I should go to the theater." Robert said, "If you go, I want to go with you."

The Attorney General's remark later entered the lore of the Missile Crisis as evidence of his fraternal loyalty. Actually, as he explained in a memo for his files, it referred to his disgust at the idea of Lyndon Johnson as President, having witnessed Johnson's "inability" to make "any contribution of any kind" during all the conversations.

After hearing of Khrushchev's message, the Vice President had invited Hugh Aynesworth of the *Dallas Morning News* to come to The Elms, the grand Washington home he had bought from the hostess Perle Mesta and equipped with Muzak, Texas paintings, and a swimming pool. Talking with Aynesworth as he and Lady Bird lounged in their bathrobes, Johnson gave his boss a grudging compliment: "He plays a damn good hand of poker. I'll say that for him."

In Havana, when Alexeyev heard about Khrushchev's message, he felt like "the most unhappy man on earth, as I imagined what Fidel's reaction to this would be." The Chairman had been so eager to resolve the crisis quickly that he did not take the time to first notify Castro, who evidently heard about the settlement on the radio.

Khrushchev wrote him, "We have just prepared our reply to the President's message. I am not going to reveal it to you, since you will hear about it on the radio. . . . At this stage of the crisis we would like to advise you not to let your feelings get the better of you." Castro must not down another U. S. plane: "The conflict is now coming to an end—with a favorable conclusion for you, since it will prohibit any invasion of Cuba. The mad militarists of the Pentagon clearly want to abort the agreement and drive you into actions that could be exploited against you. We urge you not to give them such an excuse."

Kicking the wall, shattering a mirror, Castro denounced the Chairman as a "son of a bitch . . . a bastard . . . an asshole," a leader with "no *cojones*" and later, a *"maricón"* [homosexual]. He refused Alexeyev's desperate telephone calls.

In Miami, Cuban exiles cried that they had been betrayed: Kennedy's no-invasion offer was "another Bay of Pigs for us. . . . We are just like the Hungarians now."

Soviet citizens were stunned by the broadcast of Khrushchev's message. All week the Soviet press, television, and radio had played down the gravity of the crisis. Now they learned that their leader was withdrawing missiles from Cuba that all week had been dismissed as an "American fabrication." And why had the Chairman allowed Kennedy to reject the demand to remove the Western missiles from Turkey?

Exhausted White House staff members gathered outside the Oval Office to watch the President board *Marine One* for the flight to Glen Ora, where he enjoyed a triumphant lunch with Jacqueline, the children, and Lem Billings. Afterward he returned to the White House and approved a response to Khrushchev drafted by Thompson and Ball, which was released to the press at 4:35 P.M.

In it, Kennedy wrote that he considered his weekend exchange of letters with the Chairman to be "firm undertakings" to "promptly be carried out. I hope that the necessary measures can at once be taken through the United Nations, as your message says, so the United States in turn can remove the quarantine."* Now they must turn to the problems of nuclear proliferation and the "great effort" for a test ban: "Perhaps now, as we step back from danger, we can together make real progress in this vital field."

Anxious that his fragile settlement not be criticized, the President asked McNamara and Gilpatric to bring the Joint Chiefs to the Cabinet Room. He told them, "I want to tell you how much I admire you and how much I benefited from your advice and your counsel and your behavior during this very, very difficult period."

Admiral Anderson cried, "We have been had!" The Air Force Chief of Staff, General Curtis LeMay, pounded the table: "It's the greatest defeat in our history, Mr. President. . . . *We should invade today!*" McNamara looked at Kennedy and noticed that "he was absolutely shocked. He was stuttering in reply."

The President told Schlesinger that during the final week of the congressional campaign, Republicans might "attack us on the ground that we had a chance to get rid of Castro and, instead of doing so, ended up by guaranteeing him against invasion. I am asking McNamara to give me the estimated casualties if we had attempted an

---

*Kennedy's earlier draft had been more specific: "I hope that the United Nations can immediately take the necessary steps to eliminate any need for surveillance on our part of Cuban territory. You have undertaken to remove what I have called offensive weapons from Cuba and I have assured you that no attack will be made on Cuba."

invasion. . . . The military are mad. They wanted to do this. It's lucky for us that we have McNamara over there."

Kennedy called the congressional leaders to the White House. Although he had cautioned others not to crow, he declared, "We've won a great victory. . . . We have resolved one of the great crises of mankind. . . . There will be another one—when and if the Chinese get the hydrogen bomb."

CHAPTER

19

"Now We Have Untied Our Hands"

On MONDAY, OCTOBER 29, DOBRYNIN BROUGHT ROBERT Kennedy a new private letter from Khrushchev to the President spelling out their secret agreement on Turkish missiles. Perhaps the Chairman was trying to defend himself against charges by his generals that he had been hornswoggled.*

By Dobrynin's account, Robert told him that it would be "very hard" for the United States to accept the letter, since withdrawal of the Turkish missiles had to be sanctioned by NATO. This would take time. He renewed his guarantee, on behalf of the President, that the missiles would be gone within four to five months.

The next day, Robert told Dobrynin that he and the President had

---

*Soviet radio that day called on the Kennedy administration to pay attention to "the people's wise demand" and "remove its rocket nuclear weapons from Turkey."

studied his letter overnight. There could be "no quid pro quo." In talking points for this conversation, he had written, "Take back your letter—Reconsider it & if you feel it is necessary to write letters then we will also write one which you cannot enjoy. Also if you should publish any document indicating a deal then it is off & also if done afterward will further affect the relationship."

He assured Dobrynin that the Turkish missiles would soon be gone but that it was "important not to publicize it" because he and the President would seem to be "purveying a falsehood to the American public." By Dobrynin's account, Khrushchev's message also raised the issue of Guantanamo, which Kennedy briskly dismissed.*

The Ambassador took back the letter, but Khrushchev's thirteenth-hour grab at a more favorable settlement had inflicted still another blow on trust between him and the Kennedys. When Dobrynin assured Robert that his government would not publish Khrushchev's secret Missile Crisis correspondence with the President, the Attorney General replied, "Speaking quite frankly, you also told me your government never intended to put missiles in Cuba."

The President's prohibition against public claims of victory over Khrushchev was based at least partly on his fear that, if provoked, the Chairman might reveal that it had not been such an American victory after all.

He remembered how in 1940 his own father and others had hurt Franklin Roosevelt by charging that FDR had made a "secret deal" with Churchill to bring the United States into Europe's war. As a Congressman, Kennedy himself had attacked Roosevelt's secret diplomacy at Yalta. Were Americans to discover that he had offered Khrushchev a secret concession to end the crisis, the President could have been badly damaged.

He knew that Khrushchev had much to gain from revelation of his secret concession. Not only would the Chairman seem more of a victor in the crisis, but were NATO to learn that the President had unilaterally pledged to scrap the Turkish missiles, it would have depreciated the value of other American commitments. It would have shown that in this confrontation, the Soviet Union was not the only superpower that had strong-armed a little ally for the sake of world peace.

---

*Walt Rostow warned Bundy on October 31 that the Russians were "re-raising" the issues of Turkey and Guantanamo "at levels short of formal diplomacy."

Thus Kennedy kept a sharp eye on reportage on the crisis. On the President's instructions, when Salinger was asked how many letters Kennedy had exchanged with Khrushchev during the thirteen days, the press secretary replied with a nonresponse: "Well, you are aware of the letters we have said anything about." Pressed further, he said, "I am going to stand on my answer."

The columnist Rowland Evans heard and wrote about Khrushchev's emotional Friday letter. The President ordered Salinger to officially deny that the letter had been "written by an agitated or an overwrought man." He was so furious about Evans's story that he did his own detective work to track down the leak. Told that Evans's source might have been a French diplomat with whom Evans had dined at Stewart Alsop's house, he ordered William Tyler to inform Ambassador Alphand of the President's view that "responsibility for the leak rests with a member of the French Embassy staff."

Alphand told Tyler that he had shown his copy of Khrushchev's letter to only one other person, his Counselor, Jean-Claude Winckler. The next day, Winckler confessed to Tyler that he had been the Frenchman at the Alsop dinner: he had mentioned a "peculiar" Khrushchev letter showing "great excitement and nervousness," but when Evans pressed for details he had "refused to discuss it."

Kennedy demanded that all outstanding copies of his correspondence with Khrushchev be retrieved. He told Ex Comm, which continued its meetings, "There's going to be press around all of you. They all want their own angles." The "only sources of information on the Cuban situation" should be Bundy and Sorensen: "We must make information available to the press in our own way, rather than have it leak out."

As with Vienna and his meetings with Gromyko, the President implemented this dictum in his own fashion. A few days later, he showed Walter Lippmann flattering excerpts from his crisis correspondence with Khrushchev. Just as he publicly took responsibility for the Bay of Pigs while privately blaming Eisenhower, the Joint Chiefs, and the CIA, Kennedy refrained from vulgar public gloating about the crisis while privately seeing to it that it was recognized as a triumph of his statesmanship.

When Bartlett asked him for a formal interview on the crisis, he refused: "After all, I would just be putting credit on myself. There's no point in sitting around patting myself on the back."

But presidential conversations on background with Bartlett, Lippmann, Sulzberger, and Bradlee and the usual skillful leaks by the White House staff ensured that Americans would know who had won the Missile Crisis. Discussing his confrontation with Khrushchev among intimate friends, the President modestly said, "I cut his balls off."*

The foreign editor of *Pravda,* Yuri Zhukov, rushed to Washington from Phillips Academy in Andover, Massachusetts, where he had been attending a Ford Foundation conference on American-Soviet relations. Known to be close to Khrushchev, Zhukov was primed to serve as his pathfinder before Soviet-American bargaining to tie up the loose ends of the agreement with Kennedy on Cuba.

He made appointments with Thompson, James Reston, and other Americans. Rusk told the President, "I guess Zhukov doesn't regard me as part of the ruling circle. He hasn't asked to see me." Over lunch, Salinger reminded Zhukov that high-ranking Russians had "deliberately lied" to Kennedy: if the Chairman's commitments on Cuba were not swiftly carried out, a renewed crisis was "inevitable."

Zhukov nodded: "If your President were to back down on his position, it would place Chairman Khrushchev in a most difficult position with Castro." What about a summit that would seal the agreements on Cuba and settle other problems? Salinger gave his "private" opinion that such a meeting would be "awkward" unless important results were assured. Zhukov assured him that Khrushchev would not soon reopen Berlin: "We do not want to solve this problem without your participation."

The Soviet Union had started dismantling the missile sites on Sunday, even before the President had replied to Khrushchev's public letter. Jackhammers were used to break up launching pads. Missiles were loaded onto ships bound for the Black and Baltic seas. When American spy planes flew over the ships sailing for the Soviet Union, Soviet crewmen waved cheerfully, pulling back tarpaulins to reveal the departing missiles.

Frustrated, Castro tried to thwart what was happening all around him. On Sunday, two hours after Khrushchev's letter was broadcast, he had thrown down his own demands: the United States must lift the military and economic blockade of Cuba, stop its subversive activities and violations of Cuban air space and territorial waters, and get out

---

*He even told Hugh Sidey that "the country rather enjoyed the Cuban quarantine. It was exciting, it was a diversion, there was the feeling we were doing something." He did hasten to add that "it might have been a different story if there had been thousands killed in a long battle."

of Guantanamo. He threatened to down American planes soaring across his island to photograph the Soviet retreat: "Whoever comes to inspect Cuba must come in battle array!"

U Thant flew to Havana. Wearing battle fatigues and a large pistol, Castro ranted at him for two hours against the United States. Thant pledged that if a UN team were allowed to inspect the Soviet offensive sites, Washington's no-invasion guarantee would go into effect. Castro denounced the proposal as "one more attempt to humiliate our country."

Havana street groups sang in Conga rhythm, "Nikita, Nikita / That which you give / Is not to be taken away!"

Castro declared, "Cuba does not want to be a pawn on the world's chessboard. . . . I cannot agree with Khrushchev promising Kennedy to pull out his rockets without the slightest regard to the indispensable approval of the Cuban government." Khrushchev's act was "immoral": "Friends simply just do not behave in this way!"

Khrushchev privately wrote Castro that he knew some Cubans "would have preferred that the missiles had not been withdrawn. . . . However as political figures and statesmen, we are the leaders of the masses and the masses do not know everything. . . . That is why we have to lead the way."

Without some kind of agreement with the United States, "a war would have surely ensued, causing millions of casualties, and the survivors would have blamed the leaders for failing to take the necessary steps to avoid it." The Chairman noted that Castro's cable of Saturday, October 27, had said "it was only a matter of time—twenty-four or seventy-two hours. Having received that alarming cable from you, knowing your courage, we gave your warning great credence. Didn't that constitute our consultation of you?"

Castro's cable had demanded that the Soviet Union be "the first to inflict a nuclear strike on the enemy's territory. You know very well where such an action would have led us. It would not have been a simple blow, but the beginning of a global thermonuclear war." Had the missiles been fired from Cuba, "the U.S. would have suffered enormous losses, but the Soviet Union and all the socialist bloc would have been greatly affected too. . . . The Cuban people would have heroically perished."

"If we do struggle against imperialism, it is . . . to lose the least in the struggle and regain the most afterwards in order to bring communism to triumphant heights. . . . The measures we have adopted have allowed us to reach the aim we sought when we decided to send you the missiles to Cuba. We have managed to obtain an agreement from the U. S. not to invade Cuba and not to allow its Latin American allies to do so. We have achieved all of that without a nuclear war."

Castro wrote Khrushchev, "We knew, without a doubt, that we would have been exterminated in case of a thermonuclear war. Still that did not lead us to ask you to remove the missiles. Nor did we ask you to give in. . . . Comrade Khrushchev, I did not suggest that the U. S. S. R. become the aggressor by striking first. . . . That would have been immoral and unworthy of me. I proposed that if the imperialists attacked Cuba and the Soviet military forces in Cuba assigned to defend us against foreign attack, we would retaliate and destroy them.

"Everyone has his own opinions. I believe that because of the Pentagon's dangerous character, it could have the motive and will to launch a preventive strike. . . . Comrade Khrushchev, I maintain my point of view. . . . I can only wish that I might be wrong and hope that you are doing the right thing. It is not just a few Cubans, as some might have told you, but many of them who in these moments are experiencing an indescribable amount of bitterness and sadness. There is already talk of a new invasion by the imperialists, proof that their promises are shortlived and unreliable."

Khrushchev felt deeply wounded by the rift with the protégé whom he considered "almost like a son." Almost tearfully he told a Cuban diplomat, "Because of Fidel I cannot sleep."

He knew that if Castro blocked the inspections of Cuba specified in his exchange of letters with Kennedy, the entire agreement might unravel: the United States could declare itself unbound by its no-invasion pledge. The Chairman was also concerned that Castro's loud complaints of betrayal would unsettle other Soviet clients and give ammunition to Khrushchev's own enemies in the Kremlin and Peking. He sent Mikoyan to Havana.

No Soviet leader was closer to Castro than Anastas Ivanovich Mikoyan, who in 1960 was the first high-ranking Russian to call on Castro. The normally impassive Armenian could not restrain his zeal for the young revolutionary. He once told Rusk, "You Americans must realize what Cuba means to us old Bolsheviks. We've been waiting all of our lives for a country to go Communist without the Red Army. It has happened in Cuba, and it makes us feel like boys again."

Born in 1895, Mikoyan had been a full member of the Presidium since 1935, far longer than Khrushchev or anyone else. It was said that if Russia returned to czarist rule, the new monarch would be heard to mutter, "Now, Anastas, what do I do?" Stalin called him "a genius in trade"; he was the man who brought Eskimo Pies to the Soviet Union. Khrushchev later recalled that during the Soviet crackdown in

Hungary, Mikoyan "threatened to do something to himself as a sign of protest."

He once told Mikoyan it was his bad luck to have been born one generation too late: otherwise he would have made a fortune. In 1957, the Armenian was the only member of Stalin's old circle to oppose the Anti-Party Group, a gamble for which Khrushchev was forever grateful.* Harriman was impressed by how frequently the Chairman referred to "Anastas and myself," almost suggesting that Mikoyan was part of a duumvirate.

On his way to Havana, Mikoyan stopped in New York to dine with Kuznetsov and Stevenson. He warned them that Castro might not accept ground inspections of Soviet military sites in Cuba. Arriving in the Cuban capital, he declared, "The Soviet people are with Cuba body and soul." During Mikoyan's second day of talks with Castro, his wife of forty years died in Moscow. So important was this mission that he did not return for her funeral.

Mikoyan found the Cuban leader morose and brittle. Castro told him it was not enough to apologize to him for Khrushchev's insolence; he must apologize to the Cuban people. When Mikoyan explained in a Cuban meeting hall, he was reputedly pelted with rotten fruit.†

American intelligence picked up signs that Castro might even try to expel the Russians from Cuba. The Secretary of State privately told Senators that if Soviet troops started shooting at Cubans, the United States would not accept "Hungarian-type action in this hemisphere" and "would have to do something immediately."

Rusk told Ex Comm that they did not have a "good contract with Khrushchev." An exchange of letters was not the same thing as a formal treaty: the United States must "get everything out of their language that we possibly can."

Kennedy told Sorensen that it would be "easy to get national support for getting the missiles out" but "much more difficult" to keep it for the final settlement. Robert Kennedy reminded his brother that

---

*Khrushchev did confide to the Yugoslav envoy in Moscow that Mikoyan had drafted his speech to the Central Committee during the Anti-Party Coup so that if the tide seemed to be going against Khrushchev, he could change it to suit the turn of events.
†Despite all this, Mikoyan and his son Sergo, who accompanied him on both the 1960 and 1962 trips, persisted in their enthusiasm for Castro. In a 1989 conversation with the author, Sergo Mikoyan, who emphatically criticized other shortcomings in Soviet foreign policy, refused to concede that Castro's thirty years in power had not been good for the island.

during the crisis, Stevenson had seemed "so upset, so disturbed." To negotiate against Zorin and Deputy Foreign Minister Kuznetsov at the UN, the President augmented Stevenson with the Republican John McCloy. To give Stevenson the bad news Kennedy sent Gilpatric and George Ball, who was not surprised that "Stevenson's nose was out of joint about it."*

In New York on Tuesday, October 30, Stevenson lunched with Kuznetsov, whom he had met in Moscow in 1958. The Russian buttered him up, saying that he had read all of Stevenson's books. In harmony with the message that Zhukov was spreading to all who would listen, he said he hoped not only to "wind up the Cuban affair" but also conduct a "general exploration of outstanding issues," including military bases around the world, and feel out the prospects for a Kennedy-Khrushchev summit.

This would have been in the Chairman's interest; he knew that Stevenson would be a more sympathetic negotiating partner than the hard young men of the New Frontier. The possibility of broader talks with Stevenson at the center was music to the Governor's ears. He quickly reported to Washington that Kuznetsov had been "extremely cordial" and was "very eager" to discuss the whole range of problems between their countries.

Kennedy was horrified not only by the idea of Stevenson renegotiating the American-Soviet relationship but by Kuznetsov's reference to military bases around the world, which almost certainly made him worry that the Soviets were once again going to try to establish a public link between the missiles in Cuba and Turkey.

Stevenson was ignorant of Robert Kennedy's secret assurances to Dobrynin. The President had no desire to give him information that he might one day use to vindicate his arguments within Ex Comm for a Turkey-for-Cuba trade: if Stevenson should ever be ridiculed for softness during the Missile Crisis, the temptation to hint that the President's ultimate deal with Khrushchev was exactly what he had originally proposed might be too great to resist. Kennedy cabled Stevenson to confine himself to winding down the Cuban crisis.

* * *

---

*The old Stevensonian Arthur Schlesinger recalled that in 1961, when McCloy and Arthur Dean went to the UN to work with Stevenson on nuclear testing and disarmament, the Governor had tried to ignore them: "They were up on the top story of the building, sore. Stevenson wouldn't even invite them to meetings. . . . I would take drafts up to them and get their stupid reactions. . . . McCloy and Dean had nothing of value to contribute and they took hours to do it."

Kuznetsov was worried about Castro's threat to attack American reconnaissance planes over Cuba. Knowing that a downing could reignite the crisis, he urged the Americans to limit themselves to the Cuban periphery. The President refused but took the precaution of approving the missions one by one.*

McCone warned Ex Comm that although the missiles in Cuba were leaving, "apparently everything else is being built up, including communication complexes and possibly even a submarine base." Assembly of Il-28 bombers was continuing.†

On Sunday, October 28, in the afterglow of Khrushchev's crowning letter, Kennedy had told Ex Comm not to "get hung up on the Il-28 bombers." But the Il-28s were capable of offensive use. He now asked Stevenson to tell Kuznetsov that the Il-28s should go. The Russian replied that this was a "new issue," not covered in the Kennedy-Khrushchev exchange of letters.

Thompson advised the President to give Khrushchev "something to show to his colleagues in the Kremlin." On Saturday evening, November 3, Robert Kennedy was sent to the Soviet Embassy.

Entertaining the Bolshoi Ballet, Dobrynin introduced the Attorney General to the beautiful prima ballerina, Maya Plisetskaya, who said, "You and I were born on the same day and same year"—November 20, 1925. Kennedy kissed her and promised to send her a present. In private, he told Dobrynin that if the Soviet Union started removing Il-28s and took them out within thirty days, "we would be prepared immediately to announce the removal of the quarantine."

The next day, over lunch at his country house in Stamford, Connecticut, McCloy told Kuznetsov, "You know what we want . . . namely, the elimination of Cuba as a Soviet military base in this hemisphere. . . . We think you should put heavy pressure on Castro to permit suitable inspection to take place."‡

---

*Ex Comm agreed that if a U-2 was attacked by a SAM site on Cuba, "we should probably assume that this is a deliberate Soviet decision." The United States would attack the SAM site by air strike, concurrent with a message from Kennedy to Khrushchev explaining "the vital necessity of continuing aerial surveillance." If a U-2 was downed, the United States would destroy the SAM site responsible, "communicate a second time with Moscow, and finally, in the absence of satisfactory assurances, eliminate the remainder of the SAM system" on Cuba.

†The CIA presumed that the Soviets had sent forty-two Il-28 bombers to Cuba, of which seven had been assembled. We now know that only twelve were actually delivered; three of these were earmarked for the Cuban Air Force and had yet to be uncrated.

‡Unaware of Kennedy's secret concession, McCloy also warned Kuznetsov not to bring the Turkish missiles into the negotiations: "It bears no relation to the Caribbean or the Western Hemisphere."

* * *

On Tuesday, November 6, Dobrynin gave Kennedy a letter from Khrushchev that rejected the President's Il-28 demand. Robert had what he later called "the most unpleasant conversation I have ever had with Dobrynin." Afterward he told his brother that perhaps he had seen the Ambassador too frequently: such familiarity made "statements by me at critical times less effective."

The President sent Stevenson and McCloy an angry cable that the Soviets seemed to be following their familiar course "in which bargains are fudged, secrecy prevents verification, agreements are reinterpreted, and by one means or another the Soviet government seeks to sustain and advance the very policy which it has apparently undertaken to give up."

Kennedy wrote Khrushchev that he was "surprised" at his charge that he was using the Il-28s to "complicate" the situation. His October 27 letter had referred to all weapons capable of offensive use. He had "no desire to cause you difficulties." But the Chairman must understand that the installation of missiles in Cuba had been a "deep and dangerous shock."

Not only did it "threaten the whole safety of this hemisphere, but it was, in a broader sense, a dangerous attempt to change the world-wide status quo. . . . Your Government repeatedly gave us assurances of what it was *not* doing . . . and they proved inaccurate."

Now it was "vital" to "reestablish some degree of confidence in communication between the two of us." The issue of verification in Cuba could "become very serious indeed." Kuznetsov and McCloy had "spoken as if this were entirely a problem for the Castro regime to settle." But this was an "explicit condition" of their exchange of letters. "The need for this verification is, I regret to say, convincingly demonstrated by what happened in Cuba in the months of September and October."

The President told Ex Comm that the situation was "capable of becoming dangerous very quickly." An earlier version of his letter had closed by threatening Khrushchev with "renewed action on our side."

That day Americans were voting in the midterm elections. Kennedy cast his ballot on Beacon Hill in Boston, flew by helicopter to Hyannis Port to see his father, and then returned to the White House, where he watched the returns with Jacqueline in the upstairs Oval Room.

The Gallup poll found that the Missile Crisis had improved the President's public approval rating from 66 to 74 percent. Harriman had complained in late October that the Republicans were already at work to "undermine" the President's acclaim. Congressman Thomas Curtis of Missouri charged that the crisis had been "contrived for election purposes." Barry Goldwater declared that the President's no-invasion pledge had "locked Castro and communism into Latin America and thrown away the key to their removal."

Kennedy did not resume campaigning. He knew the best way to help his party was to defend his management of the crisis. Cuban exiles were charging that the Soviets had not removed their nuclear missiles but had hidden them in Cuban caves. He asked Ex Comm to issue denials to "appropriate news editors.* The White House tried to keep the exiles from buying radio time.

After the President saw one exile unburdening himself on NBC's *Today* program, he gave an order that "within twenty-four hours our officials interrogate every Cuban refugee who was making statements about arms going to Cuba. The refugees are naturally trying to build up their story in an effort to get us to invade."

Kennedy knew that an unexpected visit from an FBI agent might not only yield information but instill a proper fear of the dangers of antagonizing the administration. The previous April, after steel magnates broke their pledge not to raise steel prices, as Robert Kennedy recalled, "I told the FBI to interview them all—march into their offices the next day." Some of the interviews took place at home, at night.†

The knock on the door chastened the steel men. One might imagine its impact on Cuban refugees of uncertain immigration status whose crime was indignation that the President might be consigning their country to Fidel Castro forever.

Kennedy told Ex Comm that he was not certain how much concern

---

*When the *Washington Evening Star* ran the caves allegation on its front page, Kennedy asked McCloy to speak with the *Star*'s editors to persuade them to "check such stories with the government before they print them."

†Robert Kennedy said later that the interviewing at night "was a decision the FBI made . . . nor did they discuss it with me, nor did I even know who they were interviewing." William Sullivan of the FBI agreed that "we were the ones who made the decision to interview at night, not Kennedy." Douglas Dillon recalled Robert's suspicions "that things like this might have been done on purpose by Edgar Hoover to embarrass him."

Even while Vice President, Lyndon Johnson used the same technique to throw his foes off balance. Two months after the President's steel showdown, when a Pecos, Texas, editor and the editor of *Farm and Ranch* were investigating his relations with the wheeler-dealer Billy Sol Estes, he asked Hoover, his old friend and Washington neighbor, to send agents to interview them. Hoover promised to "get started on it right away," but drew the line when Johnson asked him to do the same with a Florida Congressman who was calling for his impeachment.

he should show the public about Khrushchev's foot-dragging on the Il-28s. Four days before the election, when he informed the nation that the missiles were being removed, he did not mention the bombers. In case the Soviets refused to withdraw them, he did not want to risk the appearance that his efforts to close the crisis had ended in failure.

More Americans turned out on Election Day 1962 than for any off-year election in forty years. The Democrats gained four seats in the Senate and suffered a net loss of only two in the House, the best midterm showing of any party holding the White House since 1934. Political legend has had it that the Missile Crisis made the difference. After losing in California, Richard Nixon complained that "the Cuban thing" had kept him "from getting our message through."*

Actually, it is difficult to find a single race in which the crisis changed the outcome. Polls found that farm policy, civil rights, and other domestic issues had more impact than Cuba. The crisis doubtless gave a boost to many campaigners who were already in office. Congressman Curtis recalled that Cuba "gave all the incumbents running for reelection a great help: we were important."

Kennedy was delighted by the luster added to his political image by his party's defiance of electoral tradition but felt that on Capitol Hill he was "about in the position we were in the last two years." Looking forward to what he hoped would be a landslide reelection, he told friends, "Wait until 1964."

Alexander Zinchuk gave Charles Bartlett a new confidential message, which Bartlett reported to the President: "It would be a mistake to push Russia too hard now. . . . He feels their policy is to get the thing cleaned up as quickly as possible."† Khrushchev wrote the President four private letters refusing to withdraw the bombers before the quarantine was lifted.‡

---

*Nixon went on to perceptively speculate that Kennedy and Khrushchev might have made a secret "deal on NATO and the Warsaw Pact" to settle the crisis.

†Zinchuk's message must have come from an excellent source. As Bartlett reported the rest of the conversation to Kennedy, "The apparent justification . . . not the reason—for the sneak of the missiles into Cuba is to be the Turkish episode, which was done against their stern protests and maps were published in Turkey showing the targets in the SU. Khrushchev apparently was encouraged in acceding to the move by a desire to let you know how it felt to have those things moved in on you."

‡As of this writing, the contents of Kennedy's November 15 letter and Khrushchev's November 6, 12, 14, and 15 letters are still kept secret by the American and Soviet governments.

On Wednesday, November 14, Kennedy told Macmillan by telephone, "We might get the [Il-28] bombers out, but they want us to withdraw the quarantine and the overflights and have inspection of Florida as well as Cuba. . . . We might say the whole deal is off and withdraw our no-invasion pledge and harass them generally." The Prime Minister said, "You must not give in to him."

The Joint Chiefs advised Kennedy that if Khrushchev did not remove the Il-28s, the quarantine should be tightened to include petroleum, oil, and lubricants. If this failed, "we should be prepared to take them out by air attack."

In his concentration on the Il-28s, Kennedy had allowed himself to be distracted from two other elements of the Soviet offensive buildup. His November 7 letter had told Khrushchev that he attached the "greatest importance" to the Chairman's assurances to Kohler on October 16 that there would be no Soviet submarine base on Cuba, but he evidently did not pursue the matter further.

At the President's behest, McCloy complained to Kuznetsov about the Soviet regiments on the island, but Kennedy apparently contented himself with Soviet assurances that those military personnel associated with offensive systems on Cuba would be withdrawn.* His failure to clarify how many Soviets would be taken out of Cuba would come back to haunt him.

On Sunday, November 18, McCloy played Russian billiards and lunched with Kuznetsov at the Soviet retreat in Locust Valley, Long Island. Over coffee, McCloy told his host that removal of the Il-28s "cannot be indefinitely postponed."

He said that the President's offer to lift the quarantine had been "very difficult" for him to make since he had told the nation that he would not do so until UN observation of Cuba was assured: "We are neither trying to starve out the Cubans nor to be unresponsive to any constructive action taken by the Soviet Union."

McCloy gave him an ultimatum. Kennedy's next press conference would be on Tuesday at six o'clock: if the Soviets did not promise by then to withdraw the Il-28s, it would "put in question whether in fact we have an agreement with the Soviet Union" about Cuba. If the Il-28 problem was settled, the United States would "give our solemn decla-

---

*As Raymond Garthoff has noted, had Kennedy known that there were actually forty-two thousand, many of whom were not associated with the offensive weapons, he would have had to make a much larger issue about them. His September warning to Khrushchev had specifically included "any organized combat force in Cuba."

ration in the UN" not to invade Cuba and "use our good offices in connection with other Western Hemisphere countries to take the same position, assuming Cuba does not institute aggression against them."

Kuznetsov replied, "Please do not complicate the situation by insisting upon interminable inspection on the ground. It would be impossible to go all over Cuba turning over every stone, looking into every cave and bathroom to determine whether nuclear weapons still existed there."

McCloy said, "We are quite as anxious as the Soviet Union to wind up this transaction, for there are a number of things we ought to be discussing in order to keep this situation from arising again. Today it is Cuba and the combination of this bearded figure who is dictator of Cuba and certain miscalculation by the Soviet Union that almost brought us to war. Tomorrow it may be something else."

On Monday afternoon, November 19, Robert Kennedy informed Bolshakov that the United States had ceased low-level reconnaissance flights over Cuba, but that if the Il-28s did not go they would resume. And if Castro downed a U.S. plane, who could tell how the confrontation might escalate? He said he needed an answer before the President's press conference.

The Kennedys backed up their ultimatum with an even greater threat. That same day, the President sent a suggestion to NATO leaders that if the Il-28s were not promptly withdrawn, the United States might have to destroy them by air attack. This message was sent by means allowing it to be easily intercepted by the Soviet Union.

Another signal to Khrushchev and Castro may have been the destruction of a Cuban factory in mid-November by a Cuban exile sabotage team sent from the United States. The President had ordered covert action against Cuba canceled; a furious Robert Kennedy learned that nonetheless three commando teams had been sent. The factory explosion may have reminded the Soviets and Cubans that the Americans had the ability and intention to harass the Castro regime unless the Cuban problem was settled to its satisfaction.

In Havana, Castro had warned Mikoyan, "If you concede even a little to the Americans, they will immediately ask you for more and more, and they will not know when to stop. . . . To hell with the imperialists!" By Aragones's recollection, Mikoyan replied with a "long, confusing exposition on Soviet-Cuban friendship, on the overthrow of the czars and all kinds of things. . . . It was very confusing and surreal."

After days of bargaining, when Mikoyan asked Castro to break the deadlock with the United States by consenting to the removal of the Il-28s, the Cuban leader exploded. According to Aragones, he then leaned back, waved his hand, and cried, "Oh, to hell with the airplanes!"

Assuming that the three Il-28s destined for the Cuban Air Force had not yet been formally transferred, he knew it would be hard to keep the Russians from retrieving them. But he did have the power to veto on-site inspections of his island by outsiders, which he did.

On Tuesday, November 20, Dobrynin appeared at Justice: "I have a birthday present for you." This was a new letter from Khrushchev. In it, the Chairman complained that in their October correspondence, the President had not included "a single mention of bomber aircraft." Il-28s were obsolete and "cannot be classified as offensive types of weapons." But they would go within thirty days in exchange for the lifting of the quarantine.

Robert noted that Khrushchev's letter was "rather disorganized." Dobrynin told him that Khrushchev dictated such letters while walking around the room, never looking at the female stenographer.

The President concluded that Castro had given in because of the noisy, low-level U.S. spy flights over Cuba: he "could not permit us to indefinitely continue widespread flights over his island at two hundred feet every day, and yet he knew that if he shot down one of our planes, it would bring back a much more serious reprisal on him."

In the late afternoon, Bolshakov came to the Attorney General's office, where they had cocktails and watched the President's press conference on television. The President announced the removal of the Il-28s and the quarantine: "If we're successful in Cuba, we would be hopeful that some of the other areas of tension could be relaxed. . . . I think this is a very climactic period."

Bolshakov told Robert Kennedy that the President's statement had been "very good." Kennedy called Maya Plisetskaya in Boston and prodded his Russian friend to sing "Happy Birthday" to her.

The President immediately lifted the quarantine, terminated the SAC air alert, and ordered the release of all air reserves called up for the missile crisis. He cabled Macmillan, de Gaulle, and Adenauer, "It appears that at this second turning point in the Cuban crisis, Khrushchev has once again chosen the safer course."

* * *

The next day, Kennedy wrote the Chairman, "I have been glad to get your letter of November 20, which arrived in good time yesterday. As you will have seen, I was able to announce the lifting of our quarantine promptly at my press conference, on the basis of your welcome assurance that the Il-28 bombers will be removed within a month."

He regretted "that you have been unable to persuade Mr. Castro to accept a suitable form of inspection or verification in Cuba, and that in consequence we must continue to rely upon our own means of information. But as I said yesterday, there need be no fear of any invasion of Cuba while matters take their present favorable course."

Khrushchev could not have missed the meaning of the President's final seven words. Since Castro had refused the inspection of Cuba specified in their October exchange of letters, Kennedy had withheld a formal pledge not to invade Cuba. At his press conference, he had merely said, "For our part, if all offensive weapons are removed from Cuba and kept out of the hemisphere in the future, under adequate verification and safeguards, and if Cuba is not used for the export of aggressive Communist purposes, there will be peace in the Caribbean."

On Friday morning, November 23, the day after Thanksgiving, the President convened an Ex Comm meeting at Hyannis Port, including Rusk, McNamara, the Attorney General, Taylor, McCloy, Ball, Gilpatric, Sorensen, and Bundy. The Russians were pressing him for a formal document setting down the Kennedy-Khrushchev agreement on Cuba that could be registered with the UN.

Ex Comm produced a draft saying that as long as offensive weapons were gone from Cuba, the United States could "give assurances against invasion." Without the agreed-upon verification and other safeguards, such a promise would remain in force only if Cuba did not interfere with other means of gaining "satisfactory information"— namely, reconnaissance flights. The United States would continue to observe the Rio treaty and the UN Charter.

Kennedy instructed McCloy to tell Kuznetsov that since the Cubans had refused UN verification, this was "the most we can do." He did not want a "long and fruitless haggle" with the Russians over the document: "Some of these differences may wither away over time if things go well."

Aerial photography showed that within two weeks of Khrushchev's promise, the Il-28s were gone from Cuba. In New York, Kuznetsov pleaded with McCloy to delete the clause about gaining "satisfactory information," warning that it would inflame Castro. McCloy refused.

Through December, the Americans and Russians in New York and Kennedy and Khrushchev in their correspondence tried to agree on a joint declaration settling the Missile Crisis. They failed. The following month, Stevenson and Kuznetsov jointly asked U Thant to remove the matter from the Security Council agenda.

The President allowed his November 20 statement to stand as his final public word on the settlement. As Sorensen recalled, Kennedy "would have preferred a cleaner solution, but the way this worked out was really all right. We were able to continue our overflights, and Khrushchev got no no-invasion pledge."*

Khrushchev later claimed that his great missile gambit brought him what he wanted all along—an American promise not to invade Cuba. In the late 1960s, in his memoirs, he said that "for the first time in history," the "American imperialist beast was forced to swallow a hedgehog, quills and all. And that hedgehog is still in its stomach, undigested. . . . I'm proud of what we did."

This was an effort to put the best face on failure. The billion dollars earmarked for moving eighty MRBMs and IRBMs, related equipment and troops in and out of Cuba was a high price to pay for a flimsy no-invasion pledge that could be revoked at any time. With Castro's angry epithets ringing in their ears, potential Soviet clients no doubt reduced their expectation of how ardently Moscow might defend them against American threat.

The exercise did nothing to advance Khrushchev's ambition of improving the Soviet position in the nuclear balance of power. Much of the world took his haste to withdraw the missiles as hard evidence of Soviet nuclear weakness. As with the Berlin ultimata of 1958 and

---

*Although the Kennedy-Khrushchev agreement on Cuba was never formalized in a treaty, later Presidents and Soviet leaders treated it with almost the same reverence. In 1970, after the United States discovered construction of a Soviet submarine base in Cuba at Cienfuegos Bay, Richard Nixon's national security adviser, Henry Kissinger, examined the record of 1962 and told the President that the agreement was "never formally buttoned down."

Despite the ambiguity of the Kennedy-Khrushchev understanding about submarine bases, Kissinger proceeded as if submarines were as clearly prohibited from Cuba as long-range missiles or bombers. He told the Soviet chargé, Yuli Vorontsov, that the United States regarded the understanding as in effect. Happy to reaffirm the agreement for Castro, who was worried about a Nixon-inspired invasion, Vorontsov replied that the Soviets also saw it as "still in full force." TASS denied that the Soviet Union was building a submarine base in Cuba and confirmed its commitment to observe the 1962 understanding.

1961, he had challenged the United States and failed. The dismantled missiles and Il-28s sailing away from Cuba appeared to be the definitive rebuff to his claim in the Wars of Liberation speech that capitalism was in retreat.

Gromyko said in 1989 that "the world would have been better off" had Khrushchev not sent the missiles to Cuba. Georgi Arbatov of the U.S.A.-Canada Institute remembered the episode as a "humiliation": "The very fact that the missiles had to be withdrawn, and not on the most splendid terms, proves that it was a mistake."

Khrushchev had taken pains to build support among the Presidium for missiles in Cuba, but he found that while victory might have had a thousand fathers, defeat had only one. Many in Soviet politics came to see the gambit as an example of the "harebrained scheming" for which he was later thrown out of office.

The Chairman had once argued that a lean, powerful, minimum deterrent missile force that could destroy Western Europe and the American continent would be enough to restrain the West; Kennedy had acknowledged at Vienna that their two countries had nuclear parity.

For this approach the Missile Crisis* was the death knell. It suggested that Khrushchev's policy of nuclear blackmail was too dangerous. It gave his military opponents a second great victory, after that of July 1961, when the Chairman had to repeal his massive troop cut and increase defense spending in order to counter the Kennedy defense buildup and buy military support for his Berlin showdown.

In both the summer of 1961 and the fall of 1962, the Soviet military argued that if American nuclear strength had allowed Kennedy to thwart Khrushchev's assertions of Soviet power, the Soviet Union must now invest the resources to fully compete with the United States. At their Stamford luncheon, Kuznetsov notoriously warned McCloy, "You Americans will never be able to do this to us again."

Khrushchev was unwilling to allow the crisis to defeat his previous intention to resolve the most nagging problems of the Cold War. His brush with nuclear danger in the Missile Crisis increased his interest in a test ban and a period of Soviet-American détente.

More belligerent Soviet civil and military officials welcomed such a period of calm as a stopgap measure until that triumphant moment when the Soviet Union competed with the United States from a position of nuclear equality or, better yet, superiority.

---

*Or the "Caribbean crisis," as Russians have called it to this day, emphasizing not the Soviet offensive weapons but the American threat of aggression in the Caribbean.

*   *   *

During his lifetime, Kennedy virtually escaped criticism for the policies that moved Khrushchev to send missiles to Cuba and for the fact that he did not warn against the missiles until they were already reaching the island. No reporter ever questioned the President about either of these failures. Had Congress in 1963 investigated the origins of the crisis, as it had Pearl Harbor, Kennedy might have been badly embarrassed on the eve of his campaign for reelection.*

Most of the American press and public, relieved by the peaceful end to the crisis, were eager to accept the official version of events presented in Kennedy's October 22 speech—that Khrushchev had committed a "clandestine, reckless, and provocative" act in full knowledge that he was taking the world to the "abyss of destruction."

As with the Berlin Wall, the public's eagerness to believe in their President and the public relations talents of the Kennedy White House succeeded in diverting Americans at the time—and many historians later—from serious attention to his culpability in the Missile Crisis. Some later President, serving in an age of cynicism about the actions and motives of American leaders, would not have been so lucky.

With hindsight, it is more clear that had Kennedy not provoked Khrushchev by repeatedly heralding American nuclear superiority, indulging himself and his officials in talk that caused the Russians to fear an American first strike, and suggesting through Operation Mongoose and military preparations that the United States might invade the island in 1962, it is doubtful that Khrushchev would have felt compelled to take his giant risk on Cuba.

Had the President enough understanding of Soviet motives to issue the warning in March 1962 that he issued in September, Khrushchev would almost certainly have been deterred. The stakes would have been raised to a vital interest for which the United States had announced itself willing to go to nuclear war.

By the late 1970s, there was a substantial minority opinion that in the Missile Crisis the victor was not the American President. Senator Daniel Patrick Moynihan, who had served Kennedy as Assistant Secretary of Labor, complained in 1977 that by sending missiles to Cuba, Khrushchev should have expected "to have a lot of trouble with the

---

*As it did after the Bay of Pigs, the Kennedy administration headed off such hearings.

United States—and real trouble. All that happened was . . . 'OK, you can have your man down there permanently.' "

In 1982, the columnist George Will asked, "Why must Finland take care not to offend its Soviet neighbor, while Cuba exports subversion and expeditionary forces in this hemisphere and Africa? Because in 1962 the United States, which had might and right on its side, failed to achieve the only success worthy of the name—a severing of the Soviet military connection with Cuba."

Many critics have complained about what they consider to be the Kennedys' pledge not to invade Cuba. Close study of the settlement suggests that the President may have deliberately avoided such an unambiguous commitment. When an early draft of his October 27 letter to Khrushchev offered "binding assurances to respect the territorial integrity and political independence of Cuba," Kennedy struck this out and offered only "assurances against an invasion." The new language would not foreclose Mongoose-style attacks against the island.

He also watered down his no-invasion "assurances" by conditioning his October 27 offer on "effective United Nations arrangements." He may have anticipated that Castro would never accept on-site inspections. Even if Castro did, the ground teams could have gathered information that would be useful in American covert action against Cuba.

In his October 28 letter, Khrushchev tried to unilaterally improve the President's offer by referring to "your statement . . . that there would be no attack or invasion against Cuba." Kennedy caught the Chairman's trick. His reply to Khrushchev merely said that he would stand by what he had written on Saturday.

In his November 20 press conference statement, the President toughened his conditions: there would be "peace in the Caribbean" only if there were no more offensive weapons in Cuba, if there were "adequate verification and safeguards," *and* if there were "no export of revolution" from Cuba *and* if Cuba did not violate the Rio treaty and the UN Charter.*

These additional conditions, which were little noticed, had the effect of neutralizing Kennedy's no-invasion assurances. He knew that the UN Charter and the Rio Pact were so ambiguous that it would not be difficult, if necessary at some point, for the United States to declare

---

*An earlier draft added that the United States had "refrained from taking further military action against the Communist buildup in Cuba, but we are ready for whatever action might be required."

that Cuba had violated them and then invade.* And by late November, he knew that the chances of achieving the "adequate verification and safeguards" (defined with similar, probably intentional ambiguity) were almost zero.

One must therefore conclude that the President deliberately booby-trapped his no-invasion pledge in order not to rule out further American efforts to topple the Castro regime, including invasion. Here he employed his extraordinary powers of public presentation to distract the world from the fact that on this issue he had gotten the better of Khrushchev.

By November 1962, newly reeducated about the bloody cost of full-scale military force against Cuba, Kennedy was even less disposed to invade the island than before the Missile Crisis. But he was still unsettled by the idea of suffering the domestic and foreign political consequences of living with Castro until he left the White House in 1969. Especially if criticism of his settlement grew so brutal that it endangered his reelection, he probably wanted to be able to assure the American people that the agreement did not bind him to tolerate Castro forever.

In the wake of the Missile Crisis, Kennedy never spelled out in public the fact that Khrushchev had achieved no guarantee for Cuba against American invasion or attack. A major reason was no doubt the President's fear that if Khrushchev's retreat from Cuba looked too embarrassing, the Chairman might reveal Kennedy's secret deal on Turkey.

Nor did the President apparently gain any public Soviet pledge that Cuba would not be used to spread revolution throughout Latin America. He deleted from the draft of his October 27 letter to Khrushchev a demand for "binding assurances" from Cuba "that it would not seek, through military aggression or subversion, to interfere in the affairs of other American states." Robert Kennedy evidently made such a demand orally when he met with Dobrynin that Saturday evening.

No evidence now available suggests that Khrushchev met the de-

---

*Kennedy may have imposed the new conditions under pressure from the Joint Chiefs, who on November 16 recommended to the President that "any assurances to Castro be hedged by conditions protecting our obligations under the Rio Pact and linking the duration of the assurance to good behavior by Castro and the acceptance of air surveillance." A November 12 Ex Comm document noted that "if the Cubans started . . . to foment trouble in the hemisphere, it would be clear that the OAS under the Rio Treaty would have to take such action as might be necessary, up to and including invasion."

mand or that the President seriously raised the matter with the Russians again. At his November 20 press conference, he included Cuba's refraining from export of revolution among his conditions for peace.* Including this condition in what he intended as a definitive statement of the crisis settlement implied that Kennedy had done more than he really had to ensure that the Soviets would not use Cuba as a base from which to communize the hemisphere.

In the short run, this reinforced his efforts to ensure that Americans saw the Missile Crisis as a victory. Over the long run, it meant that each time something that could be taken as new evidence of revolutionary subversion of Latin America was revealed—arms caches, forged documents, sabotaged steel mills—the President would be forced to explain to an ever-more-angry domestic opposition why he did not intend to enforce the agreement with Khrushchev by invading Cuba.

Kennedy's successors paid the price for his effort to paper over the issue. In the 1970s and 1980s, when the Soviet Union used its Cuban base to nurture communism in Nicaragua, El Salvador, and other Latin countries, those Presidents had to deflect complaints from the American public that the Soviets had violated the Kennedy-Khrushchev agreement.

Later critics said that Kennedy should have threatened in November to tighten the quarantine or invade Cuba in order to win a settlement more favorable to the United States. In reply Bundy has sensibly noted that the President had imposed the quarantine simply to get offensive weapons out of Cuba: had he tried to barter it also for a Soviet pledge of good behavior in the Caribbean or removal of the entire Soviet military presence on Cuba, "we would have soon faced a rapid erosion of support at home and abroad."†

Thus Kennedy's management of the Missile Crisis achieved neither victory nor defeat. He simply accomplished his central purpose, the restoration of the status quo ante in Cuba, no more and no less. Khrushchev had pledged that the Soviet Union would not send offensive weapons to the island, but the importance of this pledge was soon diminished as the Russians improved their submarine strength in the

---

*On December 11, Rusk underscored the message by cabling McCloy to remind the Russians that "if Cuba undertook new acts of aggression, the U.S. and other American republics could not be expected to be bound by no-invasion assurances."

† Bundy, who on the eve of the crisis had defended the Il-28s in Cuba as acceptable, thought the President's November demand to remove the bombers "went right to the edge of what was prudent."

western Atlantic and Caribbean and installed in Cuba such potentially offensive weapons as the MiG-23 fighter-bomber, which could be quickly adapted to carry nuclear weapons.*

The chief effect of Kennedy's heavily qualified no-invasion assurance was not to bar Kennedy or his successors from invading Cuba but to compel that President to explain to world opinion why an invasion would not violate the Kennedy-Khrushchev understanding.

The victory Kennedy did score was with American opinion. In a drama far more compact and comprehensible to the general public than the abstractions of Berlin, he had seemed to throw down the gauntlet against Khrushchev and win. One American official called the Missile Crisis "the Gettysburg of the Cold War." Unaware of their President's responsibility for provoking the crisis, most Americans in 1962 saw it as a demonstration of firmness and mastery of Cold War statecraft that displaced previous anxieties that Kennedy had been too soft and inexperienced during the confrontations at the Bay of Pigs, Laos, Vienna, and Berlin.

Richard Rovere wrote in the *New Yorker* that Kennedy had achieved "perhaps the greatest personal diplomatic victory of any President in our history." *Newsweek* reported that Kennedy's behavior in the crisis "has given Americans a sense of deep confidence in the temper of their President and the team he had working with him." The hard-line columnist George Sokolsky said that Kennedy had "established that the 'soft' period in our history is over."

No longer was the President so rattled by the danger of being charged with appeasement. In December 1962, his poll ratings and congressional majority were little more favorable than those for the first twenty-one months of his Presidency. But in the wake of the near-unanimous acclamation, Kennedy felt far more politically self-confident to pursue the kind of Soviet détente that he might have preferred to have started in January 1961.

An improvement in relations would also reduce the danger that another confrontation like the Missile Crisis would spiral into nuclear war. Over dinner at the White House, the President reminded Ben Bradlee that one false step on Cuba could have wiped out "all of us at this table and our children."

* * *

*After the discovery of MiG-23 deliveries to Cuba in 1978 and 1982, the State Department ruled that as then configured they did not violate the Kennedy-Khrushchev agreement.

On December 1, the *Saturday Evening Post* published a Missile Crisis postmortem by Charles Bartlett and Stewart Alsop. What grabbed headlines was a blind comment by a "nonadmiring" official that at the decisive October 20 Ex Comm meeting, "Adlai wanted a Munich. He wanted to trade the Turkish, Italian, and British missile bases for the Cuban bases."*

The *New York Daily News* brayed, ADLAI ON SKIDS OVER PACIFIST STAND IN CUBA. Deeply hurt, Stevenson was convinced that Kennedy had inspired the article, perhaps to force his resignation. The President wrote him that he "did not discuss the Cuban crisis or any of the events surrounding it with *any* newspapermen."†

This was not true. While researching the article, Bartlett had mentioned Stevenson's apostasy to Kennedy over dinner. As Bartlett recalled, the President seemed "not too displeased that this had turned up," both to place Stevenson's suggestion on the historical record and because it had "rather shocked" him. Kennedy asked that a reference to Sorensen as an Ex Comm "dove" be deleted so that critics who knew he had been a postwar noncombatant would not leap on him. He asked no such favor for Stevenson.

The President knew that if a Turkey-for-Cuba trade was treated by the press as some kind of wild pacifist idea, the public might be less likely to suspect that this was exactly how he had secretly ended his confrontation with Khrushchev. Only in 1987, when Kennedy's willingness to consider an explicit Turkey-for-Cuba trade via Andrew Cordier finally became public, did Stevenson enjoy a measure of final vindication. Richard Harwood wrote in the *Washington Post,* "It now appears that Stevenson was not the only 'dove' at the White House during the crisis."

A week after the Alsop-Bartlett article appeared, Stevenson introduced Kennedy at a large Washington black-tie dinner. He looked and sounded drugged: "Ladies and gentlemen, / the auth-ore, / the pro-duc-ore, / the dye-rect-ore, / and the star / of Mr. Khrushchev's new play hit in Moscow, / 'A Funny Thing Happened to Me on the Way to Cuba,' / the President of the United States."

---

*Actually Stevenson had not mentioned Britain.

†Bartlett said that while researching the article, someone gave him a tip about Stevenson's performance. He confirmed it with members of Ex Comm: "Most of them did not like Adlai Stevenson and most of them were very happy to verify it." Robert Pierpoint of CBS reported that Bundy was the "nonadmiring" official: "It is well known in Washington that Bundy, a Republican, is not a friend of Stevenson's." Bundy denied it. George Ball thought it was Nitze. Others suspected Acheson. Ball was amazed that so many officials were leaking to Alsop and Bartlett after the President's order "that nobody was supposed to discuss this with anybody."

The audience roared. In keeping with his vow not to gloat in public about the Missile Crisis, Kennedy barely suppressed a smile. When he reached the lectern, he ignored his UN Ambassador. George Ball noticed that after the Alsop-Bartlett flap, Stevenson went "through the motions, making speeches, yet with a feeling in his heart that it didn't make any difference to the world if he fell over and had a heart attack."

During the second week of the crisis, the President had told Ormsby-Gore, "A world in which there are large quantities of nuclear weapons is an impossible world to handle. We really must try to get on with disarmament if we get through this crisis . . . because this is just too much."

The rendezvous with disaster also sharpened Khrushchev's interest in controlling nuclear weapons. After the acute phase of the crisis was over, Zhukov told Harriman that Cuba had shown that nuclear war was "unthinkable." They should "try to reach an agreement on nuclear testing." A test ban treaty would allow both sides to reduce defense spending and "concentrate on economic competition."

Harriman asked about China. Zhukov replied that there was not much time, but if Washington and Moscow achieved a test ban, "world opinion would force other nations, including China, to agree."

Rostow warned Bundy that having failed to redress the nuclear balance with missiles in Cuba, the Soviets would now try other means, such as nuclear weapons in space and a radically accelerated ICBM program. The United States should try to "maximize the influence in Moscow of those who may argue that the only realistic road to Russian security is by inspected arms control."

On October 30, Arthur Dean spoke to Kuznetsov in New York about a test ban treaty. In late November, when Mikoyan stopped in Washington, he told Kennedy that they "should proceed to a point-by-point negotiation of all outstanding questions." The Russians were waiting for "constructive proposals from the U.S." on Berlin. Bundy later told the President, "I suspect he may have to wait quite a while."

On Tuesday, December 11, Khrushchev wrote Kennedy a nine-page letter on Cuba and Berlin.* He promised to break the deadlock on a nuclear test ban.

---

*Still kept secret as of this writing.

* * *

After the Missile Crisis, Peking had denounced the Chairman for both "adventurism" and "capitulationism." Before the Supreme Soviet, Khrushchev retorted that the Chinese were more capitulationist than he: didn't they tolerate those "foul-smelling" colonial enclaves, Hong Kong and Macao, right on their doorstep?

Had the "loudmouths" been heeded, "we would have entered a new world war. . . . Our vast country could have withstood it, of course, but tens and tens of millions of people would have perished! And Cuba would have simply ceased to exist." For the first time, Americans had felt the "scorching breath of thermonuclear war on their own threshold.

"They began to realize that if a world war broke out, it would take place not somewhere across the ocean—in Europe or Asia—but everywhere, including the U.S.A., and would bring millions of Americans misery and death." The American elections had demonstrated this new humility. "The American people blackballed some of the more aggressive politicians, and first among them such a warmonger as Nixon."*

Reading the text, Kennedy called Arthur Schlesinger and read him two particularly well-drawn sentences,† saying, "Khrushchev certainly has some good writers." Schlesinger replied that they could do as well for him if only he would give two-hour speeches.

Responding to Khrushchev's latest letter, the President wrote, "We have come to the final stage of the Cuban affair between us, the settlement of which will have significance for our future relations and for our ability to overcome other difficulties. I wish to thank you for your expression of appreciation of the understanding and flexibility we have tried to display."

Referring to their "confidential channels," he wrote, "I have not concealed from you that it was a serious disappointment to me that dangerously misleading information should have come through these channels before the recent crisis." A Soviet diplomat had also used "a representative of a private television network as a channel to us.

---

*One Western intelligence report had it that thirty-five to forty high-ranking military officers who were members of the Supreme Soviet boycotted the session in protest of the Chairman's handling of the Missile Crisis.
†These were "At the climax of events around Cuba, there began to be a smell of burning in the air," and "Those militarists who boast that they have submarines with Polaris rockets on board, and other surprises, as they put it, against the Soviet Union, would do well to remember that we are not living in mud huts either." One of the speech writers was Fyodor Burlatsky.

This is always unwise in our country, where the members of the press often insist on printing at some later time what they may learn privately."*

Kennedy explained that "the competition for news in this country is fierce. A number of the competitors are not great admirers of my Administration, and perhaps an even larger number are not wholly friendly to yours. . . . It would be a great mistake to think that what appears in newspapers and magazines necessarily has anything to do with the policy and purpose of this government."

He looked forward to "your confidential letter and proposals on the test ban question, and I think there is every reason to keep working on this problem. I hope that in your message on this subject you will tell me what you think about the position of the people in Peking on this question."

On Wednesday, December 19, Khrushchev replied, "Now we have untied our hands to engage closely on other urgent international matters." The time had come to "put an end once and for all" to nuclear testing.

"Mr. President, you and your representatives point out that without at least a minimum number of on-site inspections, you will not manage to persuade the U.S. Senate to ratify an agreement. . . . Well, if this is the only difficulty . . . we are ready to meet you halfway."

He noted that Arthur Dean had told Kuznetsov that two to four annual on-site inspections on Soviet territory would be sufficient. To "overcome the deadlock," he offered "two to three inspections a year on the territory of each of the nuclear powers in the seismic areas where some suspicious earth tremors might occur."

Kennedy was exhilarated by Khrushchev's letter but puzzled by the reference to two to four inspections as being adequate. Dean denied having said so to Kuznetsov. White House staff members complained that Dean had a reputation for vagueness.†

Khrushchev may have confused the conversation with Jerome Wiesner's October suggestion to a Soviet scientist named Yevgeni

---

*This reference to John Scali may have been especially motivated by the leak to Scali, evidently by the Russians, of Khrushchev's November 20 letter to Kennedy. It suggested that the President wished his communications with Khrushchev through middlemen like Bolshakov to be classified into eternity. His worry that the Soviets would reveal his Turkish missile concession may have been newly aroused.

†Warren Heckrotte, one of the American test ban negotiators at Geneva, later said that he and most of his colleagues thought Kuznetsov's report to Khrushchev had been "a correct appraisal of what he thought he had been told."

Federov that one way to break the test ban deadlock would be for the Russians to offer three or four annual inspections: Kennedy might propose seven or eight, and they could split the difference.

The President wrote Khrushchev that on on-site inspections, "there appears to be some misunderstanding. . . . Ambassador Dean advises me that the only number which he mentioned in his discussions with Deputy Minister Kuznetsov was a number between eight and ten." This was a "considerable decrease," since the United States "had previously been insisting upon a number between twelve and twenty." He had hoped that the Soviet Union would "match" his concession.

Khrushchev was infuriated by Kennedy's rejection of his offer of a test ban treaty on what he thought to be roughly American terms. As Thompson said, the Chairman "probably thought it was deliberate."

Identified by the American press as having been used to deceive the President about the missiles in Cuba, Georgi Bolshakov was abruptly called back to Moscow. The Attorney General wanted to do something for him but did not want to be seen feting the Russian now publicly known to have been sent to trick his brother. He persuaded Bartlett to give Bolshakov a farewell luncheon at home.

Rising from the table, a Soviet diplomat gave a long speech brushing aside his country's lies about the missiles as a "misunderstanding." Driving Bolshakov away from the party, Robert asked him why he hadn't spoken up to support a citizen of the Soviet Union. Bolshakov said, *"He* doesn't know what *I* know."

He returned to Moscow as broadcasting chief of the Novosti Press Agency. The Attorney General sent him a handwritten note: "There is still peace even though you have been gone from the United States for more than two months. I would not have thought that possible. . . . I hope you are telling all your Communist friends what nice people we are over here—and that they believe you. . . .

"Give my best wishes to my friend Maya. Why don't you two jump into one of those brand new luxurious jet liners and fly over and see us. She could dance, I could sing, and you could make a speech. Best wishes from your friend, Bob."

The President closed the year by flying to Palm Beach. On Saturday, December 29, he and Jacqueline were driven in an open white car onto the Orange Bowl field in Miami, where forty thousand Americans and Cuban exiles welcomed the surviving veterans of the Bay of Pigs from Cuban jails.

When the rally was announced, Rusk and Bundy had opposed a presidential appearance. O'Donnell warned Kennedy, "It will look as though you're planning to back them in another invasion of Cuba." But the Attorney General said his brother's presence would help to soften his sense of guilt over the Bay of Pigs.

Even during the Missile Crisis, Robert had not forgotten the men. Preparing for a possible invasion of Cuba, he asked Brigade leaders whether they were ready to land in Havana, establish a new government, and release the 1,113 prisoners. In late November, he was told that if the men were not rescued soon, he would be "liberating corpses." Both Kennedys were grieved by the veterans' fate and knew that if they started dying in large numbers, it would renew calls for military action against Castro, tearing open the Cuban issue just after the delicate settlement had been reached with Khrushchev.

To fulfill Castro's demands, the Attorney General persuaded manufacturers to pledge $44 million in drugs, baby food, pharmaceuticals, and surgical, dental, and veterinary instruments.* The Department of Agriculture donated $9 million in powdered milk. Castro delayed the prisoners' release until the outstanding $2.9 million cash ransom from April was also paid. Robert turned to Cardinal Cushing, who quickly raised $1 million from "Latin American friends," to whom he promised repayment in three months. Lucius Clay helped to raise the remainder.

A list of cash contributors was never released. It was plausibly suggested that the Kennedy family may have donated some of the money. The President's 1960 campaign aide Hy Raskin understood that another "very substantial" sum came from "Jake the Barber" Factor, a wealthy California Democrat who had been imprisoned for a fraudulent stock deal. Factor's case for a presidential pardon had been argued by Governor Pat Brown before the Kennedy brothers, who had rejected it. Raskin recalled that Kennedy later changed his mind and granted the pardon.

By Christmas Eve, the last of the prisoners were airborne for Miami. The Attorney General said, "All right . . . what about Hoffa?"

At the Orange Bowl, Jacqueline told the men in Spanish that she hoped her son would grow up to be so brave. Cubans wept and shouted, "*Guerra! Guerra! Guerra!*" Pepe San Roman, the Brigade commander, gave the President the banner that had flown over the invasion site for three days: "We temporarily deposit it with you for your safekeeping."

---

*This was not all altruism. Windfall profits were promised by instant tax rulings allowing companies to take deductions at retail prices.

Unfurling the banner, Kennedy cried, "I can assure you that this flag will be returned to this brigade in a free Havana!"*

The text of the speech was given to Khrushchev. Deprived of a formal pledge not to invade Cuba, still burning over what he saw as the President's test ban double cross, straining to detect signs that Kennedy intended to exploit his advantage after the Missile Crisis, the Chairman may have wondered whether this challenge foretold some new effort to overthrow the Castro regime.

He wrote the President on New Year's Eve, "The year 1962 now passing into history witnessed events whose fatal development was possible to avert, thanks to the fact that both sides showed a sensible approach and reached a compromise."

In Washington, Dobrynin declared that chances for better relations with the United States were brighter than at any time since the long-ago springtime of 1960.

---

*After hearing about this challenge, Castro complained to a crowd that Kennedy had had too much to drink: "Never has a President so degraded the dignity of his position! This man acted like a vulgar pirate chief and freebooter to meet with these cowards and then say that their flag would return to a free Havana. . . . Kennedy the intriguer should stop dreaming. We *are* free, Mr. Kennedy!" In 1975, bitter members of the Brigade who felt betrayed by Kennedy and his successors demanded and obtained the flag's return from the John F. Kennedy Presidential Library.

CHAPTER

20

"The Peace Speech"

IN JANUARY 1963, IN THE CABINET ROOM, KENNEDY TOLD THE NSC OF his recent correspondence with Khrushchev about a nuclear test ban: a treaty affecting only the United States and Soviet Union would have "limited value," but "if it can help in keeping the Chinese Communists from getting a full nuclear capacity, then it is worth it."

The President was concerned about euphoric New Year's stories suggesting that the United States had stopped the advance of Soviet power in 1962. In a a background session, he told reporters that Khrushchev had been shown that in some areas America would do whatever was necessary: he might be more averse to future risky ventures like Cuba, but he had not abandoned his commitment to world communism.

While swimming with Dave Powers, Kennedy said, "Things are not as bad as they might be. . . . I only have to worry about Berlin, Cuba, Vietnam, Laos, and NATO." Arthur Schlesinger wrote Sorensen,

"We are for the moment between the acts, as far as the Cold War is concerned."

On Wednesday, January 9, Kennedy received a new letter from Khrushchev on nuclear testing. Despite the Chairman's anger about the confusion over verification, he agreed to relocate two of the ground stations in the Soviet Union if the Soviets could help decide where such installations would be located in the United States.

The CIA gave the President a message from a Soviet official that there was "simply no question" of improving Khrushchev's offer of two to four on-site inspections: since the Missile Crisis and the November elections, Kennedy enjoyed "great personal strength and prestige and hence can afford to circumvent Congress."

The President postponed a new series of underground tests in Nevada to allow American and Soviet test ban negotiators in New York to feel one another out. After the talks failed, he authorized the tests and privately resolved that six inspections would be "our rock-bottom number." He told Rusk and McNamara that a test ban wouldn't be worth the fight with Congress except for the chance to arrest the spread of nuclear weapons to other nations, especially China.

The chief American test ban negotiator, William Foster, told Kuznetsov in Geneva that if the Soviets accepted American ideas for inspection procedures, the United States could accept seven on-site inspections per year.

Foy Kohler complained by cable from Moscow that he was being kept in the dark about the test ban discussions: "I was considerably handicapped when I encountered Gromyko at an Indonesian reception last night." After consulting Kennedy, Rusk politely wired the Ambassador to butt out. When he saw Soviet officials, he should not bring up Cuba or Berlin, but was welcome to "express hope that current discussion on an atomic test ban will succeed."

Laconic and birdlike, Kohler moved about the Moscow Embassy with the gait of a cautious man. On weekends, a net was strung across the Spaso House ballroom, and he played badminton with his wife or members of his staff. When he left for Moscow, Rusk had reminded him that he would be "sitting on our Nuclear Target Number One." Kohler replied, "If I am, I only hope you don't miss."

Born in 1908, Kohler had joined the diplomatic service after graduation from Ohio State. He first served in Moscow in the late 1940s under Ambassador Walter Bedell Smith, Eisenhower's wartime chief of staff. Making use of Soviet eavesdropping on their telephones, Kohler would call his boss to say that a cable had come in asking him to see Molotov about such-and-such a matter. *"About what?"* asked the vinegary Ambassador. By the time Smith went to the Foreign Ministry, Molotov was fully prepared.

Kohler's wife, Phyllis, produced an English-language edition of the letters written by the Marquis de Custine about his Russian travels in 1839. The Soviets did not overlook her tacit suggestion that their government was just as despotic as that of Czar Nicholas I.

In 1952, Kohler's career was almost destroyed. Speeding home with his wife from a Washington dinner party at two in the morning, he lost control of his car and sheared off a telephone pole. Kohler was arrested for drunken driving. Police found classified documents in his possession that should not have been taken out of the State Department. Washington tabloids fanned the incident into a minor scandal.

Kohler had not spent years building alliances within the Foreign Service for nothing. Suspended for a month without pay, he was exiled to Ankara, where he helped to arrange the Voice of America's Russian-language service and eavesdropping stations along the Soviet border. In 1959, he was brought back to Washington as Assistant Secretary of State for Europe and the Soviet Union.

The Kohlers had first met John Kennedy in Athens in the late 1930s, when the son of the London Ambassador came through town and they were assigned to give him lunch and show him the local sights in an embassy car. After the 1960 election, Kohler assumed that he was too closely identified with Eisenhower to keep his job, but the President-elect thought it useful to keep a high official at State who had been deeply involved in Eisenhower's Berlin Crisis.

Kohler knew that in the Kennedys' struggle to bring the Foreign Service to heel, the President maintained civilized relations with the diplomats and let his brother lay down the law. Kohler met with Robert Kennedy alone only once, to discuss the government's secret plans for surveillance and, if possible, recruitment of Soviet officials in Washington. But as he recalled, during the Berlin Crisis, "Bobby would sit there across the table and look at me with those cold blue eyes as if to say, You son of a bitch, if you ever let my brother down, I'm going to knife you."

Like John Foster Dulles, Kohler believed that Khrushchev was more dangerous than Stalin; where Stalin had been a cynical, careful realist, Khrushchev was a Communist true believer and gambler. The Soviets were not happy that Kennedy had ignored their pleas to send them someone who had his ear: with Kohler in Moscow, was Dulles going to rule foreign policy from the grave?

The Senate confirmed his appointment after he answered questions about the old drunk-driving incident: "I don't make such mistakes a second time." Rusk told one diplomatic wife that he did not want a "cat session" but wanted to know whether Kohler had a drinking problem. When Kohler went to the Oval Office for a brief farewell talk before the President's noontime swim, Kennedy gave him no specific instructions and no private message for Khrushchev.

Kohler insisted on knowing what covert operations the CIA was running out of his Embassy: "It was standard for any self-respecting Ambassador." During a briefing at Langley, he learned that the United States had bugged the limousines of Khrushchev and other high Soviet officials. This exposed no vital secrets—the Soviets were too security-conscious—but did produce what Kohler considered "titillating stuff" on the personal relationships among those who ruled Russia.

Arriving in Moscow, the new Ambassador marveled that it was "an entirely different Soviet Union" from Stalin's day, with much more freedom of movement. He presumed that the Soviet servants in Spaso House were still working for the KGB. Sometimes he gave them copies of his invitation lists "so they wouldn't waste so goddamned much time finding out who the guests were."

In January 1963, the Soviets tried to recruit the sergeant who ran the U.S. Embassy's bachelor quarters. Four agents took him off to a militia station, where they accused him of sleeping with one of his Soviet maids and giving her forty rubles for an abortion. Following age-old custom, they showed him photographs of himself with the woman: since he had always been "proper" toward the Soviet Union, they were willing to forget the matter.

Kohler had the sergeant flown out of Moscow immediately. The President read his cables on the incident but was in no mood to sour the climate with the Soviets by making an issue of it. The episode remained unpublicized, one more of the many secrets jointly kept by the two governments.

In the wake of his Cuban failure, Khrushchev was fighting off a new challenge to his leadership by opponents in Moscow and Peking. In February, the Soviet government veered away from his policy of heading toward an open divorce from the Chinese, who were now asked for a conciliatory meeting "at any level and at any time."*

That month, the Soviets broke off their talks with the West on a test ban, the Chinese bête noire. The Soviet press increased its anti-American propaganda. Kohler cabled Rusk that there would be no progress on testing until the Soviet leadership "decides how to deal with the Chicoms and starts to do so."

Khrushchev's internal enemies had thrown a brake on his anti-Stalinist drive. Avant-garde music, art, and literature were denounced as a threat to Soviet national security. Out of his own philistinism and to buy support on more vital issues, Khrushchev had aligned himself with this new campaign. At a December closed-door meeting with four hundred writers and artists, he had castigated abstract painters (a "bunch of pederasts" who "wouldn't die for the Motherland") and quoted the Russian proverb that hunchbacks were straightened by the grave.

Leonid Ilyichev of the Central Committee stepped forward to denounce Yevtushenko's cry against anti-Semitism, "Babi Yar." When he insisted that there was no anti-Semitism in the Soviet Union, the artists and writers guffawed. Not to be outdone, Khrushchev declared, "Too many Jews in power always cause trouble. That is what happened in Hungary in 1956, and we had to go in and straighten out the mess."†

The Kremlin also turned its back on the Chairman's efforts to decentralize the economy, restrain the defense industry, and increase funding for agriculture. Key economic posts were assumed by men considered to be his foes. The French Kremlinologist Michel Tatu called it "Khrushchev's surrender."

In February, "campaigning" for reelection to the Supreme Soviet,

---

*The message went on to say that the Chinese must not "overestimate" their differences in the "struggle against imperialism." The "struggle for peace" and the "prevention of thermonuclear war," routinely included in such messages since 1960, were unmentioned. Bundy advised Kennedy that the message was "worth skimming through." On February 9, Khrushchev said, "We shall always be friends with the Chinese." This was roughly equivalent to his 1957 insistence under similar pressure that "we are all Stalinists."

†The CIA gave Bundy a report on the meeting, which Bundy found "fascinating." He asked Kennedy "whether we should find occasion to let the world know of Khrushchev's anti-Semitism." Richard Helms asked the President for permission to plant a magazine article "exposing Soviet religious persecution," including information on harassment of evangelical Christians and forcible removal of Jewish children to boarding schools: "In our negotiations with the writer and publisher, the right of final approval on content of the proposed article would be reserved for this Agency." Kennedy approved, deciding, as General Clifton told Helms, that "it wouldn't be too much of a needle to the Soviet Union."

the Chairman seemed at the end of his rope: "You know how old I am going to be soon.* Thank you for having gathered here to cheer me up." He warned that "enormous" sums would have to be spent on "military might." If defense were shortchanged for food and housing, Soviet voters should "condemn this as a crime."

Kohler cabled Washington that Khrushchev had seemed "listless and dispirited." He had denounced "the idea of making unrealizable promises," which the Ambassador considered "unconscious self-criticism."

The Gallup Poll found that Americans still considered Cuba and Castro to be the most important problem facing the country. Most Republicans disapproved of Kennedy's current handling of the matter. The Republican chairman in Houston, George Bush, demanded that Kennedy "muster the courage" to attack Cuba.

Senator Keating promised to "eat my hat" on the Capitol steps if the President could prove that all the offensive weapons were gone. Kennedy asked McCone for a "penetrating inspection which would probe the entire island." The CIA Director reminded him that it was impossible to "prove a negative."

When the inspection was done, McNamara gave a two-hour briefing on the results that was broadcast live by all three American television networks. Using pictures taken by U-2s and low-level Navy and Air Force planes, he declared that all the missiles and Il-28s were gone. Of Keating he said, "I don't own a hat and I hope he does, because he is going to have to eat it, based on the evidence that we presented today."

Dropping his claim about offensive weapons, Keating denounced the "sizable number of Soviet troops and military equipment" still on the island. Eisenhower wrote McCone that the Soviets were clearly "intent on making Cuba a much more formidable military power than any other Latin American nation." Goldwater demanded that the President "do anything that needs to be done to get rid of that cancer. If it means war, let it mean war."

Kennedy's advisers estimated that there had been twenty-two thousand Soviet military men, technicians, and other personnel in Cuba at the close of the Missile Crisis: if Khrushchev had kept his promise to withdraw those associated with the offensive weapons, seventeen thousand remained. (We now know that there were actually forty-two thousand Russians in Cuba at the end of the crisis and thus perhaps

---

*He would be sixty-nine in April.

as many as thirty-seven thousand in February 1963.)

In his November 6 letter to Khrushchev, the President had asked Khrushchev to withdraw the four reinforced Soviet regiments from Cuba. In his letter delivered November 20, the Chairman had promised to remove Soviet troops from Cuba in "due course." Kennedy did not press him about how many Soviets would remain on the island. As Bundy recalled, "We did not think some numbers of Soviet ground forces were a serious matter."

At a press conference on Thursday, February 7, the President was asked, "Are you just going to let them stay there?" He replied that the "kind of forces we are talking about" were not a "military threat" and noted that Khrushchev had promised to take them out in due time: "The time was not stated, and therefore we're trying to get a more satisfactory definition."

Over dinner with the Ben Bradlees, Kennedy said that seventeen thousand Soviet troops in Cuba was one thing viewed by itself, but something else again when one knew there were twenty-seven thousand American troops in Turkey, on the Soviet border. He warned the *Newsweek* man not to publish this information: "It isn't wise politically to understand Khrushchev's problems in quite this way."

Before another small dinner that month, the President complained to Bradlee, Theodore White, and Harry Labouisse, Ambassador to Greece, that he was "taking a beating" on the Soviet troops issue; soon Cuba would be like China in Truman's time. "Can you imagine the Russians backing up like this and not seeing it as a victory? We would never be allowed to back down like this. If we did, you can imagine what Congress and the press would say." Of the Republicans he carped, "Did you ever see such a rotten party?"

For reasons not apparent to the guests, the talk of Cuba moved Kennedy once again to talk about Turkey. Labouisse reminded him of a NATO Nike-Zeus program just begun on Crete: wait until the Russians described that as a new American missile base. Exasperated, Kennedy pulled out a card and scribbled a note. Bradlee told him that the working day was over; take it easy. The President replied, "If anything goes wrong, it's me they'll blame. . . . What the hell do we need those missiles for anyway?"

Kennedy's new interest in removing the Soviet troops from Cuba was rooted more in politics than national security. The CIA advised him that they might actually have the positive effect of restraining "Castro adventurism." Robert Kennedy privately said he would "rather have the Russians running the SAM sites than the Cubans running them."

The Attorney General and Rusk told Dobrynin that the American people were concerned that the Soviet forces on Cuba were being used to build an island "fortress" shielded by SAMs. On Monday, February 18, Dobrynin gave them Khrushchev's pledge to remove several thousand more troops within a month.

The President was able to announce by mid-March that four thousand more Russians had departed Cuba. Unless there was some great change in Soviet strategy, he told aides, the Cuban issue would be unimportant by 1964: not even the cleverest politician could easily revive an issue once the people had put it aside. As Bundy later recalled, "We did not think some numbers of Soviet ground forces were a serious matter."

But in April, Hanson Baldwin reported in the *New York Times* that "some intelligence experts" believed there to be as many as thirty to forty thousand Soviets still on the island. Baldwin's sources were probably officials disgruntled by the administration's effort to cool the issue.*

Furious, the President demanded to know who had talked to Baldwin. McCone's aide Walter Elder reported to Bundy that "no senior CIA officer has seen Baldwin socially for some time." (The relevant words in this sentence were probably "senior" and "socially.")

The day after Baldwin's story appeared, Richard Nixon told the American Society of Newspaper Editors, "We have goofed an invasion, paid tribute to Castro for the prisoners, then given the Soviets squatters' rights in our backyard. . . . We must no longer postpone making a command decision to do whatever is necessary to force the removal of the Soviet beachhead."

Richard Rovere wrote in the *New Yorker* that there was little doubt that "Cuba will be the principal issue in American politics between now and the next election."

Since March, Khrushchev had been staying in Pitsunda, where, as Michel Tatu observed, he "appeared more and more in disgrace." As during the Twenty-second Party Congress, his leading antagonist was evidently Frol Kozlov.

Born in 1908 to poor farmers, Kozlov liked to refer to himself as a "homeless waif." Trained as a metallurgical engineer, he had served as party leader of a steel plant and with the Central Committee in Moscow during the war. Kozlov concealed his ambition under a suave

---

*The Soviet evidence of many years later showed, of course, that these dissenters were correct.

Leningrad manner. A British diplomat observed, "He is probably the only citizen in the entire Soviet Union who wears a button-down shirt." Once a Malenkhov protégé, he was one of the few high Soviet officials to come to Khrushchev's aid in 1957.

The Chairman made him a Deputy Premier, along with Mikoyan, after which he served as a secretary of the Central Committee. He told Harriman in 1959 that Kozlov was his most likely successor: "Despite his white hair, which ladies love, Kozlov is young, a hopeless Communist. When we pass on, we will rest easily because we know Kozlov will carry on Lenin's work . . . I recommend him. He is modest and not such a brute as we."

Thompson cabled home that if Kozlov ever took power, he was not likely to keep it: Khrushchev had probably chosen him "as a front man while the power struggle would be decided behind the scenes."

Despite the Chairman's near-endorsement, Kozlov had carved out a position to Khrushchev's right. By April 1963, his platform of neo-Stalinism, increased military spending, conciliation with Peking whatever the cost to American relations, and reversal of Khrushchev's "one-man rule" was coming into vogue.

On Wednesday, April 3, in Washington, Dobrynin reflected his country's new hard line when he handed Robert Kennedy a scathing indictment of American foreign policy. Kennedy read it and said it was "so insulting and rude" that he would not give it to the President; if Dobrynin wanted to "deliver that kind of message," he should "go to the State Department and not talk to me again." Dobrynin thrust out the paper and said, "Take it!"

Kennedy refused. Dobrynin took his advice and went to the State Department. Their angry encounter may have occasioned the moment when, as Jacqueline recalled, the Attorney General telephoned the Kremlin late at night "in a rage about something." He was apparently trying to reach Bolshakov and received no answer.

Never again did the President's brother assume the role of chief intermediary with the Soviet Union. He recalled, "That really was the end of our relationship." Increasingly engaged by the gathering storm over civil rights, he continued to advise the President on Soviet affairs but for the most part gave up his Soviet portfolio.

That same week Khrushchev sent the President his first private letter in three months. In it, he discussed the Soviet troops on Cuba and complained about the American position on on-site inspections.

A week later, the President sent a three-page reply.* He told Bohlen, who was briefly back from Paris, "I don't see any reason for me ever to see Khrushchev again. There is nothing to be gained from it. But I am glad I saw him once. It was valuable in terms of the effect on me."

In Moscow in early April, eight full members of the Presidium appeared together in Moscow without Khrushchev, ostensibly to greet visiting French Communists. Not since Stalin's death had so many high officials gathered in public in the Chairman's absence. It has been speculated that Kozlov used the occasion to convene the Presidium meeting for a move against Khrushchev.

On Wednesday, April 10, *Pravda* announced that the Central Committee would meet in May to examine "current ideological tasks." Kozlov was said to have ordered this meeting in the Chairman's absence, upending Khrushchev's plans. There were rumors that at the May session Khrushchev would be forced to resign.

Within twenty-four hours of *Pravda*'s announcement, Kozlov suffered a near-fatal seizure. Some called it a heart attack, some a stroke. Whatever kind of seizure it was, it was so severe that Kozlov was removed from Soviet politics forever. Twenty-one months later, he died.†

---

*Both letters are still withheld from public view by the American and Soviet governments as of this writing.

†Had Kozlov not been stricken at this exact moment, Khrushchev might possibly have been ousted so that Kozlov could lead the Soviet Union into a neo-Stalinist age in which he could court the Chinese and renew the old American confrontation. From the closed Soviet society of 1963 we have no concrete evidence of foul play. Kozlov had indeed suffered previous coronaries, the worst in April 1961. One Moscow rumor had it that on the evening of April 10, Khrushchev and Kozlov had a violent telephone argument that brought on Kozlov's seizure.

The Soviet leader with the most to gain from Kozlov's removal, of course, was Khrushchev. The Chairman was hardly reluctant to use homocide for political advantage. In the 1930s and 1940s, he had been knee-deep in mass murder in the Ukraine and Poland. As he once told Llewellyn Thompson, he and his colleagues may have caused Stalin to die of his stroke by refusing him proper medical help. Later that year, Khrushchev was only too delighted to have the secret police chief Lavrenti Beria murdered. In 1956, he did not flinch from the slaughter of thirty thousand Hungarians.

Leonid Brezhnev had almost as much to gain. (During this period, he may have been conspiring against Khrushchev's life. See Chapter 24.) Kozlov's incapacitation allowed him to take Kozlov's job as general supervisor of the Party apparatus, while remaining Soviet President. Many presumed that he was now in line to be Khrushchev's successor, despite the reassignment of Kozlov's jobs to both Brezhnev and Nikolai Podgorny.

* * *

Once Kozlov was gone from the Soviet political scene, Soviet policy toward the United States showed immediate signs of softening. *Pravda* reprinted a *Washington Post* article hailing President Kennedy's "sincere efforts" for peace. *Kommunist* published a "long-lost" Lenin document sanctioning the occasional need to make concessions to the "bourgeois powers" for the sake of Soviet economic development.

On Friday, April 12, less than two days after Kozlov's incapacitation, Khrushchev received the *Saturday Review* editor and old champion of détente, Norman Cousins, at Pitsunda. Before Cousins's departure, Kennedy had told him that Khrushchev no doubt sincerely believed "that the United States reneged on its offer of three inspections. But he's wrong."

Perhaps Cousins could convince the Chairman that it was an honest misunderstanding: "I genuinely want a test ban treaty." Rusk added that the United States could not reduce its demand for eight inspections.* Perhaps American and Soviet negotiators could resolve everything else and then let Khrushchev meet with the President to work out this final issue.

When Cousins and his two daughters arrived at Khrushchev's estate, the Chairman was standing in the driveway, wearing a large gray fedora and a green-and-tan tweed cape. As the girls swam in the indoor-outdoor pool, he and Cousins sat on the adjoining glass-enclosed terrace. Cousins did not know about the drama between Khrushchev and Kozlov but noticed that, unlike December, when he had called on the Chairman in Moscow, Khrushchev seemed "weighted down, even withdrawn," and "under considerable pressure."

Leaning forward, the Chairman said, "If the United States really wanted a treaty, it could have had one. . . . We wanted a treaty and the United States said we couldn't get one without inspections. So we agreed, only to have you change your position."

Cousins reported the President's position. Khrushchev said, "A misunderstanding?" He cited Wiesner's assurance "that the United States was ready to proceed on the basis of a few annual inspections. Ambassador Dean told Khrushchev the same thing." After Cuba,

---

Khrushchev was not about to let one man again hoist himself into the position of chief heir and putative challenger. Western intelligence could not conclude for certain whether Brezhnev or Podgorny now ranked higher in the hierarchy of power.

*This was at a time Kennedy had privately told his Secretary of State that six inspections would be his "rock-bottom" position.

there had been a "real chance" for both countries to advance the peace. He had thought they were close to agreement on nuclear testing. He had persuaded the Council of Ministers to offer two to three inspections. Kennedy had made him look "foolish."

Cousins said, "The President would like to hold the question of inspections for last, and then you and he would work out this problem together."

Khrushchev shook his head: "For various reasons I cannot go to Washington,* and I would assume that the President right now has good reasons for not coming to Moscow. . . . If you go from three to eight, we can go from three to zero." His scientists and generals were pressing for a green light for a new series of nuclear tests. "I think I might decide to give it to them."

Cousins said, "Your final response is that you are probably going to resume atomic tests. . . . This destroys any possibility that other nations can be persuaded not to test. . . . Last summer, President Kennedy was informed by a Soviet representative that missile bases were not being installed in Cuba. Perhaps it will be said that this was a misunderstanding. . . . Perhaps one misunderstanding can cancel out another."

Khrushchev said, "You want me to accept President Kennedy's good faith? All right, I accept President Kennedy's good faith. . . . You want me to set all misunderstandings aside and make a fresh start? All right, I agree to make a fresh start. . . . And we will give you something you don't really need. We will give you inspections inside our country to convince you we aren't really cheating. We make our offer, you accept it, and there's no more nuclear testing. Finished. If the President really wants a treaty, here it is."

Cousins said, "The President has come down a great deal from the original twenty-two inspections, but he knows of no way he can come all the way down to three. The Senate would never accept it."

Khrushchev pulled a watch out of his breast pocket and toyed with it. "I cannot and will not go back to the Council of Ministers and ask them to change our position to accommodate the United States again. Why am I always the one who must understand the difficulties of the other fellow? Maybe it's time for the other fellow to understand *my* position."

* * *

---

*After his close call, he may have been afraid to leave the Soviet Union at this moment. The Anti-Party Coup had taken place while he was out of the country.

On Monday, April 22, Cousins went to the Oval Office. Kennedy asked him whether Khrushchev's "place on the Black Sea" was "as nice as they say." When the editor described their badminton game, the President said, "Sounds as though he's in good condition." Cousins related the internal pressures on Khrushchev to take a hard line on nuclear testing.

Kennedy replied that the CIA was telling him the same thing. "One of the ironic things about this entire situation is that Mr. Khrushchev and I occupy approximately the same political positions inside our governments. He would like to prevent a nuclear war but is under severe pressure from his hard-line crowd. . . . I've got similar problems. . . . The hard-liners in the Soviet Union and the United States feed on one another, each using the actions of the other to justify his own position."

The President understood Khrushchev's difficulties but could not "cut down" the number of inspections: "As it is, we'd have a real battle on our hands to get a treaty through the Senate, even if the Russians agreed to everything we asked."

In September, when the two sides had seemed deadlocked on nuclear testing, Bundy had written Kennedy, "I do think it is getting to be time to consider a top-level and politically savvy visitor to Moscow, and my own candidate would be Harriman."

Now the suggestion was revived. In late April, Harriman went to see Khrushchev as the President's emissary. For the seventy-one-year-old man, it was the triumph of his efforts to work his way back into the center of American-Soviet affairs.*

Born in 1891, he was the son of Edward H. Harriman, the Union Pacific railroad baron who amassed a fortune of more than $70 million. After Groton and Yale, the young man had combined casual investment banking with serious polo playing. In 1924, when the newborn Soviet Union was seeking foreign capital, he secured a manganese concession; when it flagged, he renegotiated the franchise with Leon Trotsky.

Harriman's liberal older sister, Mary, and Governor Al Smith

---

*That same month, the last Jupiter missile left Turkey. NATO had formally decided in January 1963 to remove the IRBMs from both Turkey and Italy, to be replaced by ten Polaris submarines. McNamara recalled years later that at the end of the Missile Crisis, "right away I went back to the Pentagon and ordered them withdrawn, cut up and photographed so that I could personally see that those missiles had been destroyed."

helped to bring him into the Democratic Party. In 1940, he went to Washington as a dollar-a-year man to help improve American rail capacity in preparation for war. He persuaded Harry Hopkins to let him carry his bag on his famous visit to Churchill in January 1941. Franklin Roosevelt appointed him "expediter" of aid to Great Britain.

That August, Harriman and Churchill's supply minister, Lord Beaverbrook, went to see Stalin about aid to the Soviet Union. The dictator accused them of wishing to see Hitler destroy the Soviet regime, then struck the best deal he could. A grinning Litvinov said, "Now we shall win the war!" In the tradition of Rooseveltian statecraft, Harriman bypassed the U.S. Ambassador in Moscow, Laurence Steinhardt, and commiserated with Stalin about the poor quality of both of their countries' envoys.

In 1943, Harriman took over the embassy in Moscow. With immense distaste, his aide George Kennan brought him morning cables at Spaso House, where Harriman worked in his dark bedchamber, wearing a silk dressing gown and red Morocco slippers. No longer in such desperate need of Western help, the Russians were already growing more bellicose. In March 1945 at Warm Springs, Roosevelt banged his fist on his wheelchair: "Averell is right. We can't do business with Stalin."

Under Truman, Harriman was Ambassador to London, Secretary of Commerce, and a White House foreign policy aide. In 1954, he overcame his wooden oratory and near-indifference to state issues to be elected Governor of New York. With Truman's support, he ran vainly for the 1956 Democratic nomination. Defeated for reelection by Nelson Rockefeller, he planned a regenerative trip to the Soviet Union.

He asked Llewellyn Thompson by letter to tell the Russians "that I would like to come to the Soviet Union if I can have a talk with Khrushchev."* In June 1959, Harriman arrived in Moscow, ostensibly as a commissioned writer for *Life.* As he did with other American leaders who resisted Cold War dogma, Khrushchev granted him a well-publicized audience that would strengthen him politically. That September, he gave Harriman an additional boost by allowing him to host his famous New York encounter with the American ruling class.

---

*Thompson replied he had recently seen Mikoyan, who was "very drunk" and said that, while he had disliked Harriman, he had liked his daughter, Kathy. During a wartime discussion of some Lend-Lease request, Mikoyan had been "annoyed" by Harriman's insistence on being told what the Russians planned to do with the aid. Mikoyan had said that Kathy, on the other hand, "was the only woman he had ever known who could drink like a man and not show any effects of it."

Harriman's support for Kennedy in 1960 was in no way sentimental. He had first met the young man in 1945 at the UN conference in San Francisco. With characteristic foresight, he invited him up for a drink. But his attitude toward the candidate was tinctured by his old antipathy toward Joseph Kennedy and the son's failure to oppose Joseph McCarthy.

Worried about a Catholic nominee, Harriman wrote Galbraith, "There won't be the same vindictive talk as in '28, but what will happen when they get in that booth and commune with their faith (or prejudices)?" When he learned of Kennedy's success in the West Virginia primary, he told his wife, Marie, "It's just shocking. . . . They have just used their money to buy their way. They simply bought the election."

Like other frugal, rich men in politics, Harriman wanted to be wanted for himself, not his money. But in early October, the Kennedys used a middleman to suggest that they expected thirty-five thousand dollars for the fall campaign. To avoid jeopardizing his chances to return to government, he ponied up.

After the election, he wrote Kennedy, "Yours was a great victory, even though it was a bit close in some states. . . . I glad that New York gave you a good solid majority of over 400,000 (not quite the 500,000 that I had been predicting)." He kept the President-elect well abreast of his November meetings with well-placed Russians and the messages from Khrushchev.

But Kennedy saw Harriman mainly as a rich, stubborn, slightly deaf old man, a failed politician and, perhaps, too soft on the Russians. When James MacGregor Burns in 1959 imagined who might get key diplomatic jobs in a Kennedy government, Sorensen advised him that Harriman's inclusion in the list was "farfetched." Robert Kennedy asked Harriman's friends Galbraith and Schlesinger, "Are you sure that giving Averell a job wouldn't be just an act of sentiment?"*

The most the new President would offer was an ill-defined job as "roving ambassador." Harriman told a friend in April 1961, "I am not yet in the inner circle of this administration. . . . I started as a private with Roosevelt and worked to the top. That is what I intend to do again."†

---

*A pre-Inaugural note from Robert Kennedy testified to Harriman's distance from the center of the new government: "My home number is now EL 6-6174. I hope you will have a chance to call me and come out for a meal. Many thanks for all your kindnesses to me over this past year."

†He indiscreetly went on to say that Kennedy had erred in appointing Bundy; as a Republican he simply would not feel free enough to criticize Eisenhower's errors. He

To almost everyone's surprise, he turned out to be right. Impressed by his successes on Laos, Kennedy promoted him in November 1961 to Assistant Secretary of State for the Far East. Harriman said, "Damn, I was hoping it was Europe." That month, when Khrushchev congratulated him on his seventieth birthday, Harriman replied that if the Chairman would agree with the Americans on Laos, this would "release me to work on other situations." In 1962, he wrote Beaverbrook, "I seem to be thriving on what little work I am doing."

He channeled his restlessness into sporadic attacks on the permanent bureaucracy and demands for "young blood," which further endeared him to the Kennedy brothers. In April 1963, he became Under Secretary for Political Affairs, the number-three officer in the State Department. After being sworn, he said privately, "This place is dead, dead, dead. What I want to do is to give it a little of the crusading spirit of those earlier times."

Jacqueline Kennedy wrote Marie Harriman, "Isn't it marvelous about Averell—everybody is so happy. Now that he has had more government jobs than anyone else since John Quincy Adams, don't you think we should hang his picture in the Green Room?"

Despite this comeback, the Kennedys had seemed to keep Harriman at arm's length from his first love. The President consulted him on Khrushchev and Soviet affairs before Vienna largely because his sister Eunice twisted his arm. During the Berlin Crisis, Harriman's arguments for diplomacy before tanks were sent down the Autobahn were ignored. His views were not asked during the Missile Crisis; he had been forced to call Schlesinger in hopes of getting advice to Kennedy.*

Overimpressed by quickness, the President may have mistaken Harriman's bad hearing and sluggish speech for dimwittedness, which he may have deemed fine for negotiation but not for policy-making. Before October 1962, he may have been chary to be seen soliciting advice from someone known to be close to the Russians.

But after earning his spurs in the Missile Crisis, Kennedy could afford to use Harriman on the Soviet Union. He knew that Kohler had no particular commitment to improved relations and that Khrushchev did not especially like him. Just as Roosevelt had used special envoys

---

said that the President had also erred by expressing doubt as to whether the American system or communism would triumph in the end: this might seem reasonable at home but had "unfortunate echoes" abroad.

*The advice was that Khrushchev was not behaving like someone who wanted war: "If we do nothing but get tougher and tougher, we will force them into countermeasures. We must give Khrushchev an out."

to circumvent Joseph Kennedy in London, the President sent Harriman to Moscow. He wrote Khrushchev, "You and your colleagues have known him well and I put great hope in the results of his discussions with you."

Through the early spring, Kennedy and Khrushchev had complained to each other through Dobrynin and the State Department about Laos. The Soviet Ambassador noted that in defiance of the Geneva agreement, American troops and planes were still operating in Laos, along with "adherents of Chiang Kai-shek."

The President had replied that the North Vietnamese were defying the pact by sending "large numbers" of troops into Laos, from which to interfere in the "internal affairs" of South Vietnam. He said that all American military personnel, except for a handful of diplomatic attachés, had been withdrawn by the agreed-upon deadline of October 1962.*

Khrushchev now told Harriman that the deterioration in Laos was unpleasant for the Soviets, who had a "very limited" ability to influence the situation. Harriman reminded him that the United States had twisted General Phoumi's arm to accept the 1962 agreement. Khrushchev replied, "In Russia, the expression is that one twists something else." Laughing, Harriman conceded that if Washington had "followed the Russian method, Phoumi would have agreed sooner."

Harriman told Khrushchev that nothing would please Kennedy more than to relax tensions everywhere: "The President looks upon Laos as a symbol. . . . If we can't cooperate in that case, how could we hope to cooperate in other fields?" He said that the United States had "definite information" that the Viet Minh were operating in Laos.

The Chairman asked, "Are you a religious man?" Harriman replied that his grandfather was a minister. Khrushchev said, "Will you swear on a Bible that the Viet Minh are there?" Harriman agreed: "Would Mr. Gromyko be willing to swear on a Bible that the Chiang Kai-shek forces are there?"

Khrushchev reminded him that Gromyko was a nonbeliever: per-

---

*The only American planes in Laos, he said, were there in response to Souvanna Phouma's "request for air supply," carrying "food, clothing, medicines, and other necessities" to people who, through Pathet Lao "intransigence and harassment," could not otherwise obtain them. As for the alleged supporters of Chiang Kai-shek, these were "small, independent bands of former Chinese Nationalist regulars who wander back and forth in the remote areas of the Burmese-Thai-Lao borders and who are engaged in various types of trade."

haps he could instead use a copy of *Das Kapital* or "swear by the beard of Karl Marx": "Let's each bet a million dollars on whether or not the Viet Minh are there. You have many millions and would not mind losing one."

Harriman said that he would be willing to give a million dollars to get the Viet Minh out of Laos. He reminded Khrushchev that when he was Ambassador to Moscow, he had seen Stalin in this same office to talk about the Poles. Stalin had cried, "The Poles! The Poles! Can't you think of anything to talk about except the Poles? They have made trouble all through history and they always will." He said that he suspected the Chairman felt the same way about the Laotians.

Khrushchev responded by raising the subject of Germany. Harriman said, "Germany? Can't you think of anything else to talk about? The President is concerned about Cuba." Khrushchev ridiculed Kennedy's worry about troops in Cuba and rattled off a list of countries where the United States kept forces. For the millionth time, he warned that if the West tried to cross the GDR after a peace treaty, the rockets would fly and the tanks would burn.

By Harriman's account, he laughed, saying, "I know you're too sensible a man to want to have war." The Chairman replied, "You're right."

Harriman went on, "We want to advance our mutual good, but Cuba is a case in point. There are many foolish voices in the United States calling for rash action. The President needs help in keeping those sentiments under control. We would appreciate anything you could do to help him . . . if you can do it without hurting your own national interests. You should know that the President has been quite willing to help you personally, provided it does not hurt our national interests." He said that he had a "very serious suggestion to make."

Khrushchev slapped the table. "Out with it!"

"Come to an agreement on the test ban. This would enable you to devote much more of your resources to civilian production." Harriman said that Berlin should be "put on ice": "Why don't the Soviets want to get on with important things, such as a test ban?"

The Chairman said that he and his comrades regarded Harriman with highest esteem. "We would like to return our relations to the state they were in during the period when you served here. . . . So I will propose a deal with you." Why not combine a test ban with a German settlement? Harriman replied that the United States could not buy a "pig in a poke" but was "always ready to talk about both the test ban and about the German settlement."

Smiling, Khrushchev told Harriman he was an "old diplomat" who knew "how to talk without saying anything."

* * *

In early May, Georgi Bolshakov wrote Robert Kennedy that wherever he spoke, "everybody is anxious to get an answer to only one question: can we live in peace with you? And everyone I've met gives only one answer: we not only can, but must. . . . Now, as before, I am with Novosti Press Agency and I am taking care of the 'New Frontiers' in television. My friends jokingly call me 'Telstar.' Anastasia . . . thanks you both for the gift.*

"Greetings and best wishes to you from Maya [Plisetskaya]. We share your desire to have a get-together. . . . We hope to have a chance to see each other, to chat, to sing together, and let those who can, dance.† Our greetings to Ethel and to your large family. We were glad to learn that your family is due to increase around June, so we'll be delighted to send to you one more *Matrushka* for the new arrival."

Bolshakov added a jarring note: "Rest assured, Robert, we are doing our best to secure peace. Speaking quite frankly, certain hopes were set on your brother, but now these hopes are diminishing."

Since the previous autumn, Alpha 66, Commandos L-66, and other free-lance radical exile groups had conducted hit-and-run strikes against Cuban installations. Operating from Florida and the Bahamas, they also fired torpedoes against Cuban and Soviet ships. The Soviet government complained in late March that U.S. "encouragement of such actions" violated the settlement of the missile crisis.

Rusk told Kennedy that the raids "may complicate our relations with the U.S.S.R. without net advantage to us": "Better if they are going to be done that we do it." The President authorized a statement that the United States would "take every step necessary" to stop raids from its territory. Exiles were detained and speedboats impounded. Nelson Rockefeller told the press he hoped Kennedy had not made his decision to "appease the Soviets," but "what other reason" could there be?

The NSC's new Standing Group on Cuba, successor to Ex Comm, considered what Bundy called the "gradual development of some form of accommodation with Castro." In April, the Cuban leader

---

*Launched in July 1962, the thirty-five-pound American Telstar communications satellite had transmitted the first live television broadcast between North America and Europe. The Kennedys had sent Mrs. Bolshakov a pair of shoes.
†This a reference to Robert's comment in November to the Bolshoi dancers that he could not do the two-step.

announced that "U.S. limitations on exile raids" were "a proper step toward accommodation."

Castro was still unhappy with the Russians. After Khrushchev learned that he had gone so far as to schedule a meeting with Chinese officials, he invited Castro to the Soviet Union and gave him one of the warmest welcomes ever granted a foreign leader. During his forty-day visit, Castro inspected the Northern Fleet and Soviet missile bases, reviewed the May Day parade from the Lenin Tomb, and spent dozens of hours with Khrushchev at the Kremlin and Pitsunda. In Kiev, he was provided with a voluptuous blonde who caught his eye.

Defending his settlement of the Missile Crisis, the Chairman noted that Stalin would never have taken such a risk as sending missiles to defend the island. According to Khrushchev, he did not tell Castro about Kennedy's secret Turkish missile concession because the President had "asked me to keep it secret." He increased Cuban sugar subsidies and promised to forget about the old-line Cuban Communists who had given Castro so much trouble. By the end of his trip, Castro openly praised the Russians for risking "a severe war in defense of our little country. . . . *That* is communism!"

In April, the CIA predicted to Kennedy that the Soviet Union would "maintain some sort of a military presence" on Cuba as a "tripwire deterrent against a U.S. invasion" and turn their attention to the subversion of Latin America: "There is a good chance that Castro's position in Cuba a year from now will be stronger than it presently is and that in Latin America the Communists will have recovered some of the ground lost in the Missile Crisis."

The President knew that Castroite revolutions throughout the hemisphere could not only endanger Western security but cause him grave political problems when he ran for reelection—especially because he had inspired the false impression in November that his Cuban settlement included a ban against Cuban subversion of Latin America.

During a November Ex Comm meeting, Kennedy had asked for a long-range plan to "keep pressure on Castro and to bolster other regimes in the Caribbean." He knew that new American covert action against Castro would force him to worry about his internal stability and relax his hemispheric ambitions.

Bundy warned that "useful organized sabotage is still very hard to get." Nevertheless Robert Kennedy told the Standing Group in May that the United States "must do something against Castro, even though we do not believe our actions would bring him down." The following month, the President approved a new CIA program to sabotage Cuban power stations, petroleum refineries, storage facilities, factories, railroads, and highways.

Kennedy and Macmillan were worried that time was running out if they were to achieve a test ban treaty that might keep nuclear weapons out of the hands of China and other countries. They sent Khrushchev a joint letter saying that the difference between his proposal of three inspections and theirs of seven "should not be impossible to resolve." On the automatic seismic stations, their differences appeared "fairly narrow."

The President and the Prime Minister were prepared to send "very senior representatives who would be empowered to speak for us and talk in Moscow directly with you." They hoped to bring the matter "close enough to a final decision so that it might then be proper to think in terms of a meeting of the three of us at which a definite agreement on a test ban could be made final."

On Wednesday, May 8, Khrushchev wrote Kennedy that he had learned the President's test-ban proposals by heart "just as we used to learn 'Pater Noster.' " He had already once agreed to two or three inspections in order to help him with his Senate. For this all he had gotten was Western haggling over numbers and conditions.

Was the President just going through the motions for domestic political reasons? If there was no real hope for an agreement, the Soviet Union would have no choice but to strengthen its security. Nevertheless, the Soviet Union was willing "to receive your highly placed representatives."

The harshness of Khrushchev's response grew partly from his genuine exasperation and partly from his own domestic anxieties. He felt that Kennedy had already bamboozled him once over a test ban. In the wake of his recent political scare with Kozlov, he was hardly going to go on the written record with language that would allow the President to make him look "foolish" before his colleagues again.

In Washington, Dobrynin privately suggested that the Chairman was willing to be more flexible. He told Wiesner that there had been too much public discussion about numbers: five or six inspections "might have been acceptable, had things gone differently." He told Chester Bowles that if they could not agree on a test ban now, "it would be tragic and the rift would last for many years": perhaps they could agree on a "lump sum" of inspections—"say, twenty-five or twenty-seven over a period of five years."

* * *

Kennedy and Macmillan proposed to Khrushchev that their special envoys arrive in late June or early July. The Chairman agreed but was impatient and worried that his diplomatic bureaucracy might sabotage the bargaining. He would have preferred a summit with the President. He was willing to take Rusk.

In February, Alexander Fomin had renewed his connection with John Scali and suggested that Rusk visit the Kremlin.* Gromyko reminded Kohler that he had traveled to the White House three times, but the Secretary of State had never been to Moscow. In mid-May, Khrushchev himself raised the suggestion in a letter to Kennedy.

The President did not want to undercut his test ban negotiator or involve his Secretary of State in bargaining that might fail. He replied that Rusk was "prepared to come at any time in July or August that is convenient to you."

After seeing Khrushchev in April, Norman Cousins had urged Kennedy to make some kind of dramatic peace offer to the Soviets. In early May, Sorensen asked him for ideas for a June commencement speech the President was scheduled to deliver at American University in Washington.

Kennedy had decided that the time had come for a major address on peace. Coming just before the bargaining in Moscow, it would show the Russians his sincerity and prepare Congress and the American people to support the test ban treaty that emerged. He would emphasize the peaceful and positive in the American-Soviet relationship, unleavened by threat, boast, or lecture.

Bundy asked the White House staff to send their best thoughts to Sorensen and say nothing to anyone else. They did not solicit official suggestions from other departments. Sorensen drew on contributions from Cousins, Bundy, Thompson, Kaysen, Bowles, Schlesinger, and others, language deleted from the Inaugural Address and Kennedy's 1961 UN speech as well as that drafted for the ill-fated 1962 television exchange with Khrushchev.

As Sorensen worked on the text, the President flew westward. On Wednesday, June 5, he stopped in El Paso, where he met at the Cortez Hotel with the new Governor of Texas, John Connally, and the Vice

---

*Fomin was clearly well informed on high-level Soviet thinking. He complained that the Kennedy administration had "double-crossed" Moscow by reneging on its promise to accept two or three inspections.

President. O'Donnell later recalled the stop with "no pleasure."

Kennedy said, "Well, Lyndon, do you think we're *ever* going to have that fund-raising affair in Texas?" Connally said, "Fine, Mr. President, let's start planning your trip."

Kennedy flew on to Honolulu, where he addressed the U.S. Conference of Mayors about civil rights and approved a draft of what he had now taken to calling "the Peace Speech." A copy was transmitted to the White House, where Carl Kaysen was told to clear it with Rusk, McNamara, and Taylor. Not by accident, it was too late for their bureaucracies to dilute the rhetoric.

While the President was in Hawaii, Khrushchev sent him and Macmillan an irascible letter designed probably to soften them up before the test ban negotiations. He questioned their sincerity and complained once more about inspections: success would depend on what their envoys brought in their baggage to Moscow.

On Sunday night, June 9, the President flew eastward, scrawling last-minute changes into his text. By telephone, Kaysen suggested minor revisions to respond to Khrushchev's latest letter. Arriving at Andrews on Monday at 8:51 A.M., Kennedy was rushed to the White House, where he changed his shirt, and then to American University. Tired reporters on *Air Force One* and the Washington diplomatic corps had been told that this address would be "of major importance."

The President began by saying that world peace was "a topic on which ignorance too often abounds. . . . What kind of a peace do I mean and what kind of a peace do we seek? Not a Pax Americana enforced on the world by American weapons of war. Not the peace of the grave or the security of the slave.

"I am talking about genuine peace—the kind of peace that makes life on earth worth living, the kind that enables men and nations to grow and to hope and to build a better life for their children. . . . Not merely peace in our time, but peace for all time."

He spoke of peace "because of the new face of war." Total war made no sense in an age when great powers had "relatively invulnerable nuclear forces," when one nuclear weapon had "almost ten times the explosive force delivered by all of the Allied air forces in the Second World War," when deadly nuclear poisons could be carried "to the far corners of the globe and to generations yet unborn."

Some counseled delay until the Soviets became more enlightened:

"I hope they do. I believe we can help them do it." But assuming that peace was impossible was "a dangerous, defeatist belief. It leads to the conclusion that war is inevitable—that mankind is *doomed,* that we are gripped by forces we cannot control. . . . Our problems are manmade. Therefore, they can be solved by man.* And man can be as big as he wants. . . . Man's reason and spirit have often solved the seemingly unsolvable—and we believe they can do it again."

Therefore, "let us reexamine our attitude toward the Soviet Union. . . . As Americans, we find communism profoundly repugnant. . . . But we can still hail the Russian people for their many achievements—in science and space, in economic and industrial growth, in culture and acts of courage."

Both the American and Soviet peoples abhorred war: "Almost unique among the major world powers, we have never been at war with each other." No nation had ever suffered more than the Soviet Union during the war. At least twenty million had died. A third of its territory "was turned into a wasteland, a loss equivalent to the devastation of this country east of Chicago." Their most basic link was "that we all inhabit this small planet. We all breathe the same air. We all cherish our children's future. And we are all mortal.

"Let us reexamine our attitude toward the Cold War." The one place where "a fresh start is badly needed" was a test ban treaty, allowing the nuclear powers to deal with "one of the greatest hazards which man faces in 1963, the further spread of nuclear arms. It would increase our security. It would decrease the prospects of war."

Near the end of the speech, Kennedy announced that the United States would not test in the atmosphere "so long as other states do not do so." Khrushchev, Macmillan, and he had agreed on high-level test ban discussions in Moscow: "Our hopes must be tempered with the caution of history, but with our hopes go the hopes of all mankind."

This lyrical address was easily the best speech of Kennedy's life. Read three decades later, the words do not exert the power they did at the time. The reason for that power was their startling dissonance with the shrill alarums of the President's first two years in office. The speech was light-years from Kennedy's Salt Lake City jeremiad of the 1960 campaign and his muscle-flexing Inaugural Address.

---

*This sentence was fortunately changed from the earlier draft: "Therefore, they are man-sized."

No Cold War President, save Eisenhower after Stalin's death,* had so publicly endorsed the need to find a way out of the conflict. Even during the détente of 1959–1960, with no need to worry about reelection, Eisenhower had been too timid about raising public expectations to educate Americans about why better Soviet relations were in their interest.

Later historians have cited the American University speech as evidence that Kennedy's turbulent experience managing Soviet relations, especially through the Missile Crisis, had brought some kind of epiphany, showing the error of his ways, allowing his idealism to prevail at last over caution and political calculation.

Certainly Berlin and Cuba had shown him the dangers of eternal Cold War, but there was not a sentence in this speech with which he would have privately disagreed in 1960. The change was not in Kennedy but in what he perceived to be his political environment.

In 1960, he had had to win an election at a time of high tension with Moscow. During his first two years, he had felt compelled to demonstrate to the American people, Allied leaders, and Khrushchev that he was capable of tough leadership of the Free World. By 1963, most Americans felt he had proved his mettle by facing down the Russians over Cuba. Now he could advocate better relations without fear of being branded a "weak sister."

The American University speech, though deeply felt, was as much the product of political calculation as any address Kennedy ever gave. It was designed to build public support for the test ban treaty he hoped to achieve, to mollify Khrushchev after the misunderstanding over inspections, and overcome any Soviet skepticism that he was willing to jeopardize his domestic position in order to push a controversial agreement through the Senate.

The speech may also have been intended to offer the Chairman a shining inducement for an American-Soviet entente. In early June, Chinese officials were about to descend on Moscow in hopes of resolving their Soviet quarrel at the expense of the United States.

* * *

---

*In an April 1953 address to the American Society of Newspaper Editors, Eisenhower described the price of an eternal arms race: "Every gun that is fired, every warship launched, every rocket fired signifies . . . a theft from those who hunger and are not fed, those who are cold and not clothed. . . . This is not a way of life at all. . . . Under the cloud of threatening war, it is humanity hanging from a cross of iron." These words were also a perfect distillation of Khrushchev's private feelings on the subject.

The following week, the President's speech brought 896 letters to the White House: only 25 were hostile. During the same seven days, 28,232 people wrote Kennedy about a bill on the cost of freight. He told aides, "That is why I tell people in Congress that they're crazy if they take their mail seriously."

When the Voice of America broadcast the speech to the Soviet people in Russian, the Soviet government jammed only one paragraph, which mentioned "baseless" Soviet claims about American purposes. Kennedy's text appeared in the Soviet press. Citizens tore out copies and carried them in wallets and purses.

When the British Labour leader Harold Wilson called on Khrushchev, he found the Chairman deeply impressed that the President had been willing to say such things in public. Khrushchev later said that it was "the best speech by any President since Roosevelt."*

Robert Kennedy read intelligence reports saying that the speech had changed Khrushchev's opinion of American aims. The new British Ambassador in Moscow, Humphrey Trevelyan, felt that "for the first time" Soviet leaders now felt that Kennedy "was someone who was genuinely working for a détente and with whom they could do business."

The President's first choice to be his Moscow test ban negotiator had been McCloy. The Chase Manhattan Bank chief had acquitted himself well in the New York talks after the Missile Crisis, Khrushchev liked him, and, best of all, he was an eminent Republican. But McCloy declined, pleading the call of business for oil clients.

With great ambivalence, Rusk nominated Harriman. He was worried about Harriman's aversion to the bureaucracy and his sentimental attachment to the Soviet Union. Kennedy felt this was exactly the right set of messages to send to Khrushchev. The day after Rusk made his suggestion, George Ball, perhaps acting on the Secretary's behalf, told the White House that Harriman might not be such a good idea after all. Resorting to one more Trollope ploy, Kennedy ignored the second message from State and told Rusk that he accepted his suggestion.

Dutifully Rusk cabled Kohler, "We now propose to send Harri-

*Valentin Falin recalled that Soviet officials in Moscow assumed that the speech would cause the President "enormous troubles in his own country" because it was "totally out of tune with the views of very powerful circles who were seeking a U.S.-Soviet confrontation."

man." He cabled Bohlen that the President had chosen Harriman "because of his tested diplomatic skill and his ability to get past technical obstacles to agreement." A Soviet diplomat in Washington told an American, "As soon as I heard that Harriman was going, I knew you were serious."

On Thursday, June 20, the United States and the Soviet Union signed an agreement in Geneva establishing a "hot line" for messages between their two heads of government. Washington had proposed such a channel since early 1961 without success.

Only after the near-fatal hours of delay during the Missile Crisis, when the Kennedy-Khrushchev exchanges depended on Radio Moscow and the Western Union man on the bicycle, did the Russians listen to reason. Kennedy said, "We can't go through this kind of thing again."

The two leaders approved a wire-telegraph-teleprinter circuit leading through London, Copenhagen, Stockholm, and Helsinki. Messages would be sent in code during crises when every second would count. When the new hot line was tested, technicians in Moscow were baffled by the first message sent from Washington: "The quick brown fox jumps over the lazy dog."

The seventeen years of disarmament negotiations had been so barren that the hot line accord was only the second major agreement to emerge from the talks.* Kennedy promised to "bend every effort to go on from this first step." Two evenings later, he boarded *Air Force One* for his first trip to Europe since Vienna.

---

*The first was a 1959 ban on nuclear explosions in Antarctica, which was ratified in 1961.

CHAPTER

21

The Spirit of Moscow

KENNEDY'S EUROPEAN TRIP WAS INTENDED TO IMPROVE HIS standing among the Allies and hence his freedom of action on the world stage. A left-wing French newspaper called it "Kennedy's seduction voyage."

The President knew that the one leader in Western Europe least open to seduction was Charles de Gaulle. It did not go unnoticed that his schedule did not include a visit to Paris. De Gaulle was as unhappy about a détente with Khrushchev as about American pressure to sign a test ban treaty that would force him to give up his dream of a mighty French nuclear arsenal, enshrining his country as a major world power.

Bohlen had quietly told the French Foreign Minister, Maurice Couve de Murville, that Kennedy wanted de Gaulle to pay a return visit to Washington sometime in 1963: if France would join "any test ban agreement which might be reached," forswearing its own nuclear program, the President "would be prepared to discuss what the U.S. might do to help in those circumstances."

To show his lack of interest, de Gaulle replied that a trip in 1963 would not be very convenient: that fall he must entertain the Grand Duchess of Luxembourg and visit the Shah of Iran. Instead, he would be pleased to call on Kennedy around Easter 1964—but not in Washington, where the visit would be too highly publicized. Bohlen cabled Washington that de Gaulle was stalling in order to ensure "some concrete beginning at least of his nuclear force."

During the overnight air journey from Washington to Bonn, the President recalled driving through Germany in 1939 with his friend Byron White, now one of his appointees on the Supreme Court. Young Nazis with armbands had thrown bricks at their car with its English license plates. He remembered the hate in their faces.

In a welcoming address at the Bonn airport, Adenauer wasted no time in reminding his visitor that at American University "you said, Mr. President, that the United States would make no deal with the Soviet Union at the expense of other nations."

In Cologne, Frankfurt, and other cities, hundreds of thousands of West Germans shouted "Ken-ne-dy! Ken-ne-dy!" William Tyler of State felt that the President's popularity "went far beyond anything that could be accounted for by any act. . . . Something about him . . . just seemed to echo in the hearts and voices of all the people when they greeted him."

Kennedy told the Chancellor, "Don't tell me these families just happened to have American flags in their homes." Riding into Wiesbaden, with its large American population, he passed a sign saying, "Ask Not What You Can Do for Your Ford Dealer, Ask What Your Ford Dealer Can Do for You."

At the General von Steuben Hotel, he met with Kohler, who had flown in with his wife from Moscow to obtain "fresh views and instructions from the 'big boss,'" as he wrote a friend. He reported that Khrushchev seemed ready for a test ban: he needed something to justify his split with the Chinese and his efforts for peaceful coexistence.

As they departed, Phyllis Kohler turned around and saw the President standing on a balcony, "waving and smiling and looking like a Greek god." Disapproving of what she had heard of his private life, she silently mused about how in politics image did not always conform to reality.

*   *   *

Kennedy arrived in West Berlin on Wednesday, June 26, in time for the fifteenth anniversary of the Berlin Airlift. Lucius Clay had been worried that a trip to Berlin might endanger the President's life. When he found that Kennedy was unfazed by his warning, he said, "You haven't had any reception yet. You just wait until you get to Berlin. You're going to see something you've never really seen before."

Shortly after noon, the President mounted a flag-draped platform on the steps of the City Hall, where in August 1961 crowds had cried out against their "betrayal" by the West.

Today a million roaring West Berliners jammed the plaza. Standing among the "enormous, swelling, heaving, delirious multitude that was capable of almost anything," William Manchester noted that Kennedy looked "handsome, virile, and—yes—Aryan." Trained by hard experience to distrust such mass emotion, Adenauer asked Rusk, "Does this mean Germany can one day have another Hitler?"

Back in Washington, Robert Kennedy had urged his brother to say something to the West Berliners in German. Flying in on *Air Force One*, the President had asked O'Donnell, "What was the proud boast of the Romans? . . . Send Bundy up here. He'll know how to translate it into German." Bundy later recalled that his boss "had no feeling for any foreign language. So there we were on the goddamn airplane coming down on Berlin while he repeated the phrase over and over again . . . and it worked. God, how it worked!"

As the crowds shrieked, Kennedy spoke in rhythmic, precisely delineated phrases that turned his words into a kind of angry poetry:

> Two thousand years ago,
> two thousand years ago,
> the proudest boast was
> *"Civis Romanus sum."*
> Today,
> in the world of freedom,
> the proudest boast is
> *"Ich / bin / ein / Berliner!"**

Theatrically he swept his hand across his abdomen, snatched up his pages of text, and turned his profile to the crowd.

Hearing this boast in German from the leader on whom their city

---

*In his Boston accent, this came out, "Ish/been/ine/Bee-leen-ah!"

depended for its life, the West Berliners let out almost an animal howl.* Gerhard Wessel, Adenauer's military intelligence chief, said years later, "Never underestimate the psychological influence of this one sentence. . . . With the Germans, it was the decisive sentence that changed the feeling, made them feel that Kennedy was a great President and a friend of the Germans."

Kennedy was moved and disconcerted by the emotion. Toying with his tie and lower lapel, he took the edge off what he had said by evoking laughter: "I appreciate my interpreter translating my German!"

He had always resolved to avoid the crowd-baiting demagoguery of his political Boston grandfathers, but not today. His juices were flowing from the most responsive audience of his life, his admiration for the West Berliners' bravery, his eagerness to reassure them that he would not sell them down the river to Khrushchev as part of a détente.

He may have been affected by whatever sense of guilt he felt about his complicity in the Berlin Wall, which he had seen for the first time that morning. Just as when he had remorsefully greeted the Bay of Pigs prisoners at the Orange Bowl, he allowed the emotions of this day to carry him beyond what he had wanted to say:

> There are many people
> in the world
> who really don't understand,
> or say they don't,
> what is the great issue
> between the Free World
> and the Communist world.
> *Let them come to* BERLIN!
>
> There are some who say
> that communism
> is the wave of the future.
> *Let them come to* BERLIN! . . .
>
> And there are even a few
> who say
> that it's true

---

*With some chagrin Bundy later realized that Kennedy should have said *"Ich bin Berliner"* because this was more grammatical—" and also because *'ein Berliner'* colloquially can mean a doughnut. Fortunately the crowd in Berlin was untroubled by my mistake; no one in the square confused JFK with a doughnut."

that communism is an evil *system,*
but it permits us to make economic progress.
Lass' sie nach Berlin kommen.
Let THEM *come to Berlin!*

For the first time in his life, the President publicly denounced the Berlin Wall:

Freedom has many difficulties,
and democracy is not perfect.
But we have never had to put a *wall* up
to keep our people in,
to prevent them from leaving us!

He went on, "It is, as your Mayor has said"—even in this agitated mood, Kennedy was cautious enough to put his words in Willy Brandt's mouth—"an offense not only against history but an offense against humanity, separating families, dividing husbands and wives and brothers and sisters, and dividing a people who wish to be joined together." With the exception of three tiny references later in his tour, each less than a sentence, the President never publicly mentioned the Berlin Wall again.

The speech has been best remembered for the line *"Ich bin ein Berliner."* Three decades later, after the end of the Cold War and reunification of Germany, the peroration of Kennedy's address has far greater impact:

So let me ask you
as I close
to lift your eyes beyond the dangers of today
to the hopes of tomorrow,
beyond the freedom merely of this city of Berlin,
or your country of Germany
to the advance of freedom everywhere,
beyond the Wall
to the day of peace with justice. . . .

Then we can look forward
to that day
when this city will be joined as one—
and this country and this great continent of Europe—
in a peaceful and hopeful globe.

When that day finally comes—
as it will—
the people of West Berlin
can take sober satisfaction in the fact
that they were in the front lines.

Had Khrushchev taken Kennedy's city hall oration as literally as Kennedy had his Wars of Liberation address in 1961, the good done by the American University speech might have been eroded. Luckily the Chairman took the longer view and wrote it off as Cold War rabble-rousing, a rhetorical form with which he had had no small acquaintance.*

American diplomats in Europe were told to explain to their host governments that the President had not quite meant to say that the West could not work with the Communists. To counteract the impassioned words at the city hall, Bundy inserted some conciliatory language into the next speech of Kennedy's tour.

When the President left the divided country, he was so cheered by the four-day adulation that he told a German crowd he would leave an envelope for his successor, saying, "To be opened at a time of some discouragement." In it would be a note: GO TO GERMANY. He added, "I may open that envelope myself some day." After the plane was airborne, he told Sorensen, "We'll never have another day like this one as long as we live."

Bundy had given his boss a West German poll: "You beat de Gaulle in a close election in Germany—but his popularity was then and yours is now."

From Berlin, the President flew to Ireland. Bundy had felt that the stop would unnecessarily prolong the trip. O'Donnell told Kennedy that he scarcely needed more Irish-American votes: "People will just say it's a pleasure trip." But his boss replied, "I am the President of the United States—not you."

Arriving in Dublin, Kennedy announced that he would support the

---

*In a speech two weeks later Khrushchev said, "If one reads what he said in West Germany, and especially in West Berlin, and compares this with the speech at the American University, one would think that the speeches were made by two different Presidents." Kennedy was "competing with the President of France in courting the old West German widow. Both try to win her heart, which has already grown cold and which often prompts its possessor to utterly unconstructive thoughts. And if this widow is courted the way these two wooers woo her . . . the widow can become conceited and think that the solution of world problems really depends on her."

1968 candidate for President of the United States who would appoint him ambassador to Ireland. He met cousins in Dunganstown, sang "Danny Boy" with balladeers at Bunratty Castle, and quoted Joyce before the Irish parliament, the first time the blasphemer had been mentioned in that chamber, except during debates on censorship.

Flying on to England, the President went to the great house Chatsworth and knelt at his sister Kathleen's grave before taking a helicopter to Macmillan's country house, Birch Grove, in Sussex, where they were to discuss test ban strategy.

Depressed more than usual, the Prime Minister was reeling from a sex-and-security scandal. His Defense Minister, John Profumo, had that month admitted that he had shared the chorine Christine Keeler with a Soviet military attaché, Captain Yevgeny Ivanov, and then lied about it.* David Bruce had cabled Washington that most British voters thought Macmillan should leave office: "Conservatives are now beginning actively to consider when and by whom Macmillan should be replaced."

Kennedy's special relationship with the Prime Minister had its limits. Disturbed by the possibility of sharing Macmillan's bad publicity, especially while he was building support for better relations with Moscow, he had pondered canceling the visit.† Instead, his staff had informed the British he regretfully could not stay longer than twenty-four hours (this after four days spent touring Ireland!) and to ask for a change of venue from London to Sussex, where the meeting would attract less attention.‡

Macmillan wrote in his diary of his irritation by stories "that the President has 'snubbed me' ": the truth would one day out if and when Kennedy revealed his "self-invitation" to Birch Grove.

The day before he left for Europe, Kennedy complained, "I don't know why we didn't get wind of this Profumo thing ages ago. After

---

*In 1989, Ivanov said, "When I read that I'd tried to get Keeler to ask Profumo about rockets, I had to laugh. It would have been moronic to even think about it." He attributed the scandal to "some sort of group" that was "interested in Profumo's downfall. What group, I don't know. He had enemies and they needed material to compromise him." He claimed to know that Khrushchev "didn't spend one second on the whole thing."

†The *Washington News,* for instance, demanded that the President cancel his visit because it would lend "prestige and support for the foundering government of Prime Minister Macmillan. . . . We can think of no better time for an American President to stay as far as possible from England."

‡From Birch Grove, the President called O'Donnell and Powers in Brighton, where they were planning a party with reporters and the *Air Force One* crew: "Thanks for leaving me stranded. I suppose you've been cooking up this little party for a week or more. Who's there? What's going on? I suppose you've got a big drink in your hand."

all, we give our military secrets to Britain and we have to check the
character of its high officers. . . . But then, the CIA never does tell me
anything."

Bruce sent him an "eyes only" message in Bonn: "current gossip"
about the Profumo affair, and "many other people totally un-
connected with it, is of a variety and virulence almost inconceivable. . . . Thus far, no American government official has, to my knowledge, been involved . . . nor have I reason to believe any will become
so, unless by innuendo."

Last on the schedule was two days in Italy, where Kennedy met the
newly elected Pope Paul VI, President Antonio Segni, Prime Minister
Giovanni Leone, and other Italian leaders. Kennedy had asked Rusk
to arrange a night for him in a relaxing, beautiful spot somewhere in
Italy. The Secretary of State secured the Rockefeller Foundation's
magnificent villa on Lake Como. Years later he recalled that when the
President arrived, he dismissed the servants and security men: "It was
strongly suspected that Kennedy had not spent the night alone."

On Monday, July 1, while the President was on Lake Como, his
Attorney General saw James Horan and Dom Frasca of the *New York
Journal American.* They had published a front-page story that one of the
"biggest names in American politics" had been involved with a New
York woman named Suzy Chang, who had been associated with Christine Keeler and her friend Mandy Rice-Davies during a Manhattan
visit in 1962.

Robert Kennedy asked who the high official was. The newsmen
said, "The President." They played back a tape of their telephone
interview with one of Miss Chang's acquaintances. Robert asked
whether the story was corroborated by another source. They answered affirmatively but refused to reveal it. Courtney Evans of the
FBI, whom Robert had asked to monitor the meeting, recorded that
it "ended most coolly" amid "almost an air of hostility between the
Attorney General and the reporters."

The next day Robert asked J. Edgar Hoover if the Bureau could find
out exactly what Keeler and Rice-Davies had been doing in New York.
There turned out to be no convincing evidence that Chang, Keeler,
or Rice-Davies were among the women said to sometimes drift into
the President's Carlyle penthouse. Nonetheless the Attorney General
would not have been overanxious to fear that the Profumo-Keeler
furor would make the sexual entanglements of national leaders fair
game for the press.

The British scandal had shown that if a public figure was involved in a liaison that could damage him if revealed, he might be vulnerable to blackmail. Reporters might now assert that it was in the public interest to reveal what they knew of the private affairs of those leaders most responsible for the security of the West. For the Attorney General, this was not an enchanting prospect. In July 1963, the President was himself in danger of suffering his own sex-and-security scandal.

A comprehensive history of John Kennedy's sexual behavior is far outside the scope of this volume, but what we know of the President's relationships with women raises an important question about his leadership and diplomacy.

Kennedy knew that sexual compromise and blackmail was one of the oldest instruments of espionage. In the America of the early 1960s, if the President was shown to have slept with a woman not his wife, his political career would have been gravely damaged. If that woman was shown to be connected in some important way with a Soviet bloc government, he would have almost surely been thrown out of office.

Every one of his major foreign policy decisions would be called into question: had the Soviets blackmailed the President to pull punches toward the Soviet Union or its allies out of fear of exposure? Other American leaders would be investigated for signs of similar compromise in a red scare that would dwarf the McCarthy period.

Whether the President wished to sleep with women not his wife does not concern the historian of his diplomacy. What is of importance is that from all the evidence we have, Kennedy made no systematic effort to ensure, by security investigation or otherwise, that all of the women with whom he was involved lacked the motive or the ability to use evidence of their relationship to blackmail him on behalf of a hostile government or organization.

Herve Alphand, the French Ambassador in Washington, wrote in his diary that the President's "desires are difficult to satisfy without raising fears of scandal and its use by his political enemies. This might happen one day, because he does not take sufficient precautions in this Puritan country."

If Sam Giancana ever threatened, for instance, to publicize evidence of Kennedy's relationship with Judith Campbell, the President could have been faced with a choice between giving in to whatever demands Giancana made or allowing himself to be driven out of office. What President could survive the revelation that he had knowingly slept with the mistress of a Mafia chief?*

We know that during the 1950s and early 1960s, there was a serious effort by Soviet bloc intelligence to sexually compromise Western officials who exerted major influence on their countries' policy toward the Soviet Union. In 1958, for example, the French Ambassador in Paris, Maurice Dejean, known to be close to de Gaulle, was enticed into an affair with a KGB swallow, then beaten up by a thug posing as her husband.

According to a defector, the Soviet secret police had been told that "Nikita Sergeyevich himself" wanted Dejean caught. The Ambassador was inevitably called on by a Soviet official, who assured him that while it "took a lot of doing," the thug would "keep quiet in the interest of Soviet-French relations."

Since Dejean was considered to have a promising future in French politics, the Soviets evidently did not try to push him into a major act of disloyalty while in Moscow. Presumably they felt that he would be more useful once he was back in Paris and more able to further the old Soviet goal of dislodging France from the Western orbit.†

The Secret Service lacked the resources or the mandate to investigate the background of each woman who arrived in the presidential bedroom.‡ The Service had to take the same approach to the matter as Dean Rusk, who said years later that he was Kennedy's Secretary of State, "not his chaperone."

The President was hardly unaware that the Soviets used sex for

---

*From the available information, Kennedy did not know of Campbell's relationship with Giancana at the time they met but continued the affair after he found out, perhaps as a method to keep in touch with the Mob boss, possibly out of worry that if he broke it off too hastily, she would be more likely to lash out against him.

†Richard Davies of the American Embassy recalled the Llewellyn Thompsons as "envious" of the fact that Soviet painters, writers, and composers barred from their embassy were officially encouraged to frequent the Dejeans' salon. After the French learned from a Soviet defector in 1963 that the Ambassador had been compromised, de Gaulle ordered an investigation. Dejean was recalled from Moscow and interrogated. He was later said to have been brought to the Élysée Palace, where the President looked down his nose and dismissed him with a single sentence: *"Eh bien, Dejean, on couche!"* ("So, Dejean, one enjoys the women!")

During the same period, the KGB evidently made an effort to bring the Canadian Ambassador to Moscow, John Watkins, a secret homosexual, into camp. And according to a Czech defector, a KGB seductress was photographed in the early 1960s in bed with a Conservative member of the British Parliament. When the Tory refused to work for the Soviets, the pictures were published in a leaflet and sent to the London press. He was defeated for reelection.

‡One agent is said to have said that the Service's worst fear was that the Soviets would "plant a broad" on the President.

blackmail. When Thompson once explained to him how unmarried young Marines guarded the Moscow Embassy, he found Kennedy "very upset" by the possibility of compromise by the Soviets: "Jesus, Tommy! You mean to tell me that they're in there and they have no women for one solid year? My God, what do they do about women?"*

Once before, a romance had threatened Kennedy's career. It was in early 1942, as a Naval Intelligence officer, that he was involved with Inga Arvad Fejos, a married woman and reputed recent mistress of Axel Wenner-gren, a Swede blacklisted by the State Department for his close association with Hermann Göring and other Nazi leaders. She was photographed at the 1936 Olympics sitting with Hitler, who found her "the perfect example of Nordic beauty."

She was a tall, blond former Miss Denmark who declaimed against the "damned dirty Jews" and was, by specific order of Franklin Roosevelt's Attorney General, under FBI surveillance as a possible Nazi spy. This resulted in such entries in her Bureau file as the following: "On February 6, 1942, she visited Kennedy in Charleston, South Carolina, the two spending three nights together in the same hotel room and engaging in sexual relations on numerous occasions."

Testimony to Kennedy's political cynicism at the time was his willingness to be involved with a woman who was hardly critical about Hitler† and whose movements and connections he knew to have inspired official concern that she was working against the United States. That winter he wrote her, "I've returned from an interesting trip, about which I won't bore you with the details, as if you are a spy I shouldn't tell you and if your [sic] not you won't be interested. But I missed you."‡

In March 1942, Kennedy wrote Lem Billings that Arvad was "head-

---

*Kennedy's worry proved to be farsighted three decades later when Marine guards at the Embassy were accused of having traded sex for secrets.
†Of an interview with Hitler, she wrote that he was "exceedingly human, very kind, very charming. . . . He is not evil as he is depicted by the enemies of Germany. He is without a doubt an idealist; he believes that he is doing the right thing for Germany and his interests do not go any further."
‡Another letter Kennedy wrote her from Charleston, South Carolina, sounded as if it had been written by Kennedy's father: "Don't you people in Washington have anything to talk about except a fan dancer and a movie actor being paid $1200 a year? With everything in the world going down the drain and . . . especially all that dough being spent, they just boil and stew over a stinking little bit of New Dealism of which there have been other and better examples for the last ten years. I think that everything up there has gotten too complex for the average Congressman. . . . The only thing that continually measures up to expectations is you."

ing for Reno. It would be certainly ironical if I should get married while you were visiting Germany." That summer: "As you probably have not heard—Inga-Binga got married—and not to me—She evidently wanted to leave Washington and get to N.Y. so she married someone she had known for years but whom she didn't love. I think it would have been much smarter for her to take the train. . . . Anyway she's fine—and that leaves the situation rather blank."

The affair almost caused Kennedy to be cashiered from the Navy. It was later said that to disrupt the relationship, which had the potential to harm not only Kennedy's future but that of his older brother and father, Joseph Kennedy used his influence with the Roosevelt administration to have him transferred to a PT-boat in the Pacific. Privately the President recalled, "They shagged my ass out of town to break us up." J. Edgar Hoover came to regret his role in the episode, telling an aide that if Kennedy had not commanded the PT-109, he would never have become President.*

Perhaps the knowledge that he had cheated fate by winning the Presidency in spite of the Arvad files reinforced Kennedy's sense that his private behavior was unlikely to cause him public embarrassment. His lawyers, his father, and his brother Robert evidently used financial payoffs, legal action, and other kinds of threats to silence women who had been involved with Kennedy and, for breach of promise or other reasons, threatened to go public.

Kennedy knew the rules of the game in that era compelled opposing candidates and the mainstream press not to use sordid information learned about a leader's private life unless it was judged to affect his public performance. During the 1952 Senate campaign against Henry Cabot Lodge, when someone unearthed a picture of Kennedy and a naked woman on a beach, he said, "Don't worry. Cabot will never use it." He was right, but the naked woman was neither a Soviet bloc agent nor a Mafia moll.

Although he was fascinated by what he learned about the love lives of Castro, Goulart, and other leaders, the President felt that the private behavior of a chief of government should be beyond the vulgar curiosity of the public. Over a private dinner at the White House, when someone once brought up the subject of Lenin's mistresses, he received a stony stare from the head of the table.

---

*Charles Colson of the Nixon White House recalled in 1975 that the FBI furnished him information on the Kennedy-Arvad affair in 1971 or 1972, presumably for use against the Democrats.

For Kennedy, a security check performed on every woman he saw before he saw her might have removed some of the appeal of the tryst. Like his father, he enjoyed defying the rules and getting away with it. It is hard to imagine Truman or Eisenhower forming a gambling pool with close friends, as this President is said to have done, to be claimed by "the first man to have sex with someone other than his spouse inside the Lincoln Bedroom."

Kennedy considered his public performance and his private behavior to be two areas of his life that had no serious connection. He conducted the former with a consistent sense of responsibility, the latter with the fatalism that Billings noted, living "for the moment, treating each day as if it were his last, demanding of life constant intensity, adventure, and pleasure." Of his relations with women, the President is said to have told an intimate, "They can't touch me while I'm alive. And after I'm dead, who cares?"

During the 1950s, his father and his lawyers might have been relied upon to constrain forces that wished to do him ill. But once he moved into the White House, the stakes were no longer one Senator's career but the entire world. By pursuing women whose full backgrounds he evidently could not know, Kennedy caused his Presidency to be a potential hostage to any resourceful group in American society that might have wished to bring him down—the Teamsters, the Mafia, the Radical Right—and every hostile intelligence service in the world.

Ellen Fimmel Rometsch was the twenty-seven-year-old wife of a West German airman attached to the West German military mission in Washington. Born in Kleinitz, East Germany, she was a member of two Communist Party organizations before fleeing to the West in 1953 at the age of seventeen. Her parents and other relatives stayed behind.

In April 1961, she and her second husband, Sergeant Rolf Rometsch, arrived in Washington. "We were so hard up that Ellen did some work on the side as a model," he later said. "I had no idea of irregular conduct." Working at all hours of the day and night, she told friends that she was a model.

Clad in a skin-tight costume with black fishnet stockings, she started working as a hostess at the Quorum Club, the private suite in the Carroll Arms Hotel across from the Senate office buildings frequented by members of Congress, their staff, and lobbyists. The club's proprietor was Bobby Baker of Alabama, the onetime protégé of Lyndon Johnson, fixer and secretary of the Senate known as "the hundred-and-first Senator."

Later Rometsch attended the notorious parties held at Baker's Southwest Washington town house. Rometsch's quickly expanding acquaintanceship on Capitol Hill and Embassy Row and in the Executive Branch evidently included at least one member of the Soviet Embassy and, according to the FBI, the President.

Her loud name-dropping and conspicuous spending were what attracted the FBI's attention. Informed of the Bureau's investigation in late July or early August 1963, Robert Kennedy demanded her immediate expulsion from the country. With less than a week's notice, Rometsch and her husband were rushed to West Germany by one of Robert's aides. "My chief at the Embassy told me I had to go back to Germany because of my wife's behavior," Rolf said later. "I was told it was because of security reasons."

Here the matter might have rested but for the gathering Senate probe into Baker's kickbacks, favors, and women that later sent the Alabaman to prison. On October 26, 1963, the *Des Moines Register* reported Rometsch's expulsion and said she had been "associating with congressional leaders and some prominent New Frontiersmen" and that she was angry that her "important friends" had not prevented her departure. Republican Senator John J. Williams of Delaware demanded an inquiry.

Robert Kennedy asked his trusted friend LaVern Duffy, an investigator who had worked closely with him, Salinger, and O'Donnell on the Labor Rackets Committee, to fly immediately to West Germany, calm the woman down, and keep her quiet. By the time reporters were swarming around her family house in Linderhausen, a guard was there to wave them off with a shotgun. Perhaps tipped off by Washington and uneager to antagonize the Americans, the Bonn government issued a statement that Rometsch had had no East German contacts: "The whole thing seems harmless."

The Attorney General asked J. Edgar Hoover to help persuade the Senate leaders, Dirksen and Mansfield, to avert a Senate investigation that, he warned, would taint Republicans as well as Democrats. Sticking in the knife, Hoover replied that Robert already had "a complete memorandum upon this matter," which he should read to Mansfield and Dirksen himself. Kennedy was reduced to making his request again. The Director acceded.

As a result of Hoover's meeting with the two Senators at Mansfield's home, Rometsch's relationship with the President remained a national secret. FBI agents stormed the office of a congressional photographer, confiscating prints and negatives of the German woman. The President and his brother acquired one more unwanted debt to Hoover.

The following week, the President passed out some disinformation to Ben Bradlee. He told the *Newsweek* man that he intended to see Hoover regularly, as Franklin Roosevelt had done, "with rumors flying, and every indication of a dirty campaign coming up." He shook his head: "Boy, the dirt he has on those Senators. You wouldn't believe it."

He described a picture of Ellen Rometsch that, he said, the Director had brought to a recent lunch, showing her to be "a really beautiful woman." Hoover had told him, he said, that she now wanted to return to the United States to marry a Senate investigator: the Senate aide "was getting for free what Elly was charging others a couple of hundred dollars a night." As for Baker, Kennedy had told Bradlee the previous month that he was "primarily a rogue, not a crook. He was always telling me he knew where he could get me the cutest girls, but he never did."

In a 1965 oral history interview, Robert Kennedy put his own slant on what little was publicly known about the Rometsch episode: "I spoke to the President about it—and it didn't involve anybody at the White House—but I thought that it would just destroy the confidence that the people in the United States had in their government and really make us a laughingstock around the world. I suggested that maybe Hoover should meet with Mike Mansfield and Dirksen and explain what was in the files. . . . Some of the girls just obviously told lies about it. . . . But we had it under control."

Had the Attorney General and Hoover failed to get the Rometsch matter "under control," were the President forced to resign in 1963 or 1964 in a sex-and-security scandal, the politics of the United States could have been poisoned for a generation. The American Right and others might have explained Kennedy's failure to exploit the American nuclear advantage at the Bay of Pigs, in Laos and Berlin, and during the Missile Crisis as the result of the President's compromise by Soviet bloc intelligence.

In a climate in which every American decision of the Cold War would be scrutinized for signs that American officials were secretly laboring under the thumb of the Russians, what American leader would have had the courage to bring similar suspicion on himself by pressing ahead for better relations with the Soviet Union?

* * *

On Tuesday, July 2, 1963, at an East Berlin sports arena, Nikita Khrushchev praised the "sober appraisal" of the world in Kennedy's American University speech. Before thousands of cheering Communists, he said that the Soviet Union was ready to agree on a limited test ban, covering the atmosphere, outer space, and under water. Combined with the "simultaneous signing of a nonaggression pact" between East and West, such a treaty would create a "fresh international climate."

The Chairman dropped his earlier demand for an unpoliced moratorium on underground testing but withdrew his offer of on-site inspections: the Soviet Union would never "open its doors to NATO spies." He later said that the Soviet Union would no more allow inspectors to travel about than Orientals would allow other men into their harems.

Kennedy heard about Khrushchev's speech while flying from Naples to Andrews. Thompson advised that by withdrawing his offer of on-site inspections, the Chairman had probably "yielded to military pressure."

Carl Kaysen wrote Willy Brandt from Washington that while Khrushchev had proposed only a limited test ban, it "could go a long way toward helping to close the door to further diffusion of nuclear weapons." Perhaps the Russians were "feeling the same concern" as the United States about China: "The President is sure that it would be unwise for us to ignore the opportunity that this signal might present."

On the fourth of July, Mikoyan attended the Independence Day reception at Spaso House. He told Kohler, "We are for ending the Cold War." The next day, when Chinese officials arrived in the Soviet capital for their much-ballyhooed talks, Khrushchev insulted them by flying from East Berlin to Kiev without stopping in Moscow.

At his river dacha in Kiev, with crops being harvested in the distance, the Chairman told Paul-Henri Spaak, the NATO Secretary-General, that there would be no war, probably none for generations, but it was up to the West whether or not the Soviet Union adopted a hard or soft policy.

Turning to Berlin, he told the Chekhov story of the peasant arrested for stealing bolts from the railroad track for fishing lines. He told the judge that an accident was impossible: villagers had been stealing them for years. Khrushchev told his visitor that he would keep taking bolts from Berlin, but never too many at a time. Spaak warned him not to link the issue to a test ban: "You will lose all in an impasse if you adopt this."

Harold Macmillan wrote Kennedy that if the Chairman "really drops the offer of inspection," they should seek the "very big prize" of a limited ban: "Then we may be able to approach much more effectively the problems that we have with France, Germany, etc., and Khrushchev also may be able to do something with China."

Drafting negotiating instructions for Harriman, the President considered how the negotiations might be shaped to keep China from going nuclear.* He had warned André Malraux, the French Culture Minister, in January that a nuclear China would be a "great menace in the future to humanity, the Free World, and freedom on earth" and was ready to sacrifice hundreds of millions of its own people for its "aggressive and militant policies." Kennedy had told aides that he was even willing to accept some Soviet cheating as long as a comprehensive test ban denied China the Bomb.

By 1963, Peking required no further Soviet help to join the nuclear club. A comprehensive test ban might deny China the excuse that its nuclear testing was merely in emulation of the Soviets and Americans. It might embolden Khrushchev to impose new political and economic sanctions, but in recent years these had failed to dampen Chinese radicalism.

There were top-secret proposals in the State Department to ask the Soviets to remove their nuclear umbrella from China in exchange for "a secret undertaking not to support Chiang's efforts to return to the mainland" or abandonment of the American commitment to German reunification. Thompson told the President that the Soviets might warn those Chinese leaders eager for nuclear weapons, "Don't do this, or else," leaving open the possibility of a preemptive strike against Chinese nuclear installations.

One of Harriman's briefing papers proposed "radical steps in coop-

---

*Preparing for Vienna two years earlier, Kennedy's advisers had proposed suggesting to Khrushchev an American-Soviet condominium for a "stable, viable world order," including restraint of China's radical aggressiveness. But in 1961, the Chairman had not yet decided to jeopardize his alliance with Peking.

eration with the U.S.S.R.," such as "Soviet or possibly joint U.S.-U.S.S.R. use of military force" against China. One proposal was to order Soviet and American bombers to drop explosives on the Chinese nuclear facility at Lop Nor. Only one would detonate: no one would ever know which. Another idea was to use Nationalist Chinese agents to sabotage the installation in a fashion that appeared to be an industrial accident.

Walt Rostow wrote the President, "We have both a national interest and a duty to history in conducting the Harriman probe." Thompson advised that it was almost impossible to prod Khrushchev into any serious discussion of China, but Kennedy asked Harriman to go as far as he could to explore some kind of understanding on the problem. Harriman told him that to succeed he would need something to sweeten the pot: one "obvious possibility" was the Multilateral Force (MLF).

In 1962, the Kennedy government had promoted this plan for a nuclear arsenal under joint European-American control in order to alleviate doubts by Western European leaders, especially de Gaulle, that the United States would risk nuclear war for them. The impetus for MLF faded as France pulled away from the Western military alliance. And after the Missile Crisis, few wondered whether Kennedy would risk nuclear confrontation with the Soviet Union.* When Bundy observed that MLF had "had it," the President replied, "Where have *you* been?"

Kennedy now told Harriman that he should use MLF as a bargaining chip with Khrushchev if it could purchase an understanding on China. Other advisers felt that the President was willing to trade MLF for a comprehensive test ban with an acceptable quota of inspections. Kennedy told Harriman that with the success of his trip to West Germany he now had some "cash in the bank there" and would "draw on it if you think I should."†

Macmillan was pressing for an American-Soviet-British summit to be convened at the time a test ban was signed. With elections ahead and the Profumo scandal still unfolding, his party was in need of a shot in the arm. The Prime Minister wished to restore the tradition

---

*The European allies might have wondered about his commitment to NATO had they known about his secret deal to give up the Turkish missiles.

†Harriman had earlier told Schlesinger he was certain the Soviet Union would not agree to an acceptable inspections quota unless he had "some goodies in my luggage." Unaware of the secret Missile Crisis settlement, he said he regretted that the United States had "unilaterally" pulled the Jupiters out of Turkey: he wished he could trade them now.

of British participation in East-West summits, broken at Camp David and Vienna, and to end his career by basking in the acclaim for the test ban for which he had fought so long.

Kennedy told Harriman that if a summit would clinch Khrushchev's approval of a treaty, he was willing to have a summit. But he thought that the French and West Germans would be provoked by the presence of the dovish Macmillan, and that the size of such a meeting would make it too formal.

The President felt that any summit should be choreographed for the purpose of gaining congressional and public support in the United States for the finished treaty. He remembered how Wilson in 1919 had met in triumph with the leaders of Europe and then returned home to have the Senate thwart his dream of American membership in a vibrant League of Nations.

On Monday, July 15, Harriman's five-man delegation and a British team led by Macmillan's Minister for Science, Lord Hailsham, arrived in Moscow.* Harriman told reporters that if Khrushchev was as interested in a test ban as Kennedy and Macmillan, "we ought to be out of here in two weeks." Gromyko led the Soviet delegation, which Harriman and Hailsham considered a good omen.

The Chairman greeted the negotiators at the Kremlin: "Why don't we have a test ban? Why don't we sign it now and let the experts work out the details?" Harriman pushed forward a blank pad: "Here, Mr. Khrushchev, you sign first and I'll sign underneath."

He gave Khrushchev a letter from Kennedy. Commending Harriman, the President wrote that he still hoped to achieve a comprehensive test ban and regretted their disagreements about inspections: "I can only repeat again that there simply is not any interest in using such inspections for espionage of any sort, but I know from your recent statements that you have not accepted this explanation."

Nevertheless the Chairman told Harriman that he had no further interest in inspections: "The trouble with you is that you want to spy. . . . You're trying to tell me that if there's a piece of cheese in the room . . . the mouse won't go and take the cheese."

---

*Macmillan had initially wanted Ormsby-Gore to head his delegation but decided that the leader should be someone of Cabinet rank who was not so close to Kennedy. Harriman privately thought Hailsham too much a product of the British amateur tradition, ill-prepared and consumed with desire to get a treaty at almost any cost. In return, Hailsham thought Harriman "a man very much after his best, tired and becoming a little deaf."

He produced a draft of a limited test ban that would take effect upon signature by the Soviets, Americans, British, and French. Harriman and Hailsham naturally insisted on the deletion of France, while conceding that France's later adherence to the treaty would be "very important." Harriman took the opportunity to mention the danger from China. Khrushchev replied that Peking would not have nuclear weapons "for years" and that their arsenal could not remotely compete with those of the United States and the Soviet Union.

He also presented the draft of a nonaggression pact. The Russians had for years tried to interest the Americans in such a treaty.* Harriman declared that such an accord would require extensive consultation with America's Western allies that might delay a test ban for a long time. He did not see how the United States could accept it unless aggression was defined to include interference with access to West Berlin.

Khrushchev charged that Bonn was preventing Kennedy from accepting a nonaggression pact: "You conquered the Germans and now you are afraid of them."

Kennedy kept tight strings on Harriman and his colleagues. He had told Harriman that he did not want daily summaries of the test ban talks but a blow-by-blow description of every meeting "so we can appraise it ourselves." To prevent leaks, he established a secret channel, code-named BAN: outside the West Wing, Harriman's cables were shared only with Rusk, McNamara, McCone, Thompson, and William Foster of the Arms Control and Disarmament Agency.

After reading Harriman's report of his meeting with Khrushchev, the President cabled back, "You are right to keep French out of initial treaty, though I continue to be prepared to work on French if Soviets will work on Chinese." He was still "convinced that Chinese problem is more serious than Khrushchev suggests."

In a private meeting, Harriman should remind the Chairman "that relatively small forces in hands of people like Chicoms" could be very dangerous to us all. "You should try to elicit Khrushchev's view of means of limiting or preventing Chinese nuclear development and his willingness to take Soviet action or to accept U.S. action aimed in this direction."

---

*Before Harriman's departure from Washington, Alexander Zinchuk of the Soviet Embassy had told an American official that a nonaggression pact was needed to reassure those concerned that a limited test ban would not include a moratorium on underground testing.

* * *

Walking into Spiridonovka Palace for the first day of formal talks, Harriman told his colleagues that the first time he had been in that building was in 1943, for an American-Soviet conference on a postwar United Nations.

When the sessions began, he demanded improvement of foggy language that seemed to prevent use of nuclear weapons even in self-defense. An Anglo-American draft would allow peaceful nuclear explosions in the prohibited environments if all signatories agreed. Gromyko complained that this would reduce the treaty's appeal to other potential signatories.

Another Anglo-American clause allowed a signatory to withdraw from the treaty if some other country set off a nuclear explosion that it considered a danger to its security. Gromyko complained that this clause would raise doubts about the seriousness of the signatories. What was more, the Soviet Union claimed as its inherent right the abrogation of any treaty that violated its national interest.

Harriman knew that without a withdrawal clause, the Senate might refuse to ratify the treaty out of fear that it would allow China to move ahead of Moscow and Washington in nuclear development. The talk grew so heated that at one point he picked up his papers and threatened to leave. Finally, the Westerners traded the peaceful explosions clause in exchange for a weasel-worded provision for withdrawal.

Gromyko made such a fierce demand for a nonaggression pact that Harriman wondered whether the Russians would walk out of the talks. He promised Gromyko to send the President a sympathetic report on the Soviet position. In Washington, Thompson thought that had gone "a little bit beyond" Harriman's instructions and was "an unnecessary concession." But it worked.

The final obstacle: how could nations not formally recognized by others, such as East Germany and China, sign the treaty without being recognized? Hailsham complained to Macmillan by cable that Harriman's rigidity on this issue was in danger of scuttling the talks.

At Thursday noon, July 25, Ormsby-Gore arrived at the White House to argue against Harriman's position. The Americans had just called from Moscow to say that a solution had been found: each nation would sign the treaty in association with only those nations it approved of. Kennedy was on the telephone with Macmillan. Grinning, he told the Prime Minister, "Don't worry. David is right here. It's been worked out and I've told them to go ahead."

Macmillan was jubilant. As he wrote in his diary, he had "prayed hard for this, night after night." He rushed out of the room to tell his wife the joyful news, after which he burst into tears. He cabled the President, "I found myself unable to express my real feelings on the telephone tonight. . . . I do understand the high degree of courage and faith which you have shown."

That evening, Harriman, Hailsham, and Gromyko initialed the most important arms-control accord since the start of the Cold War. Harriman looked at Hailsham's ornate initial and said, "Did you see his 'H?' It was very beautiful!"

During the talks, at a reception for the Hungarian Prime Minister, Janos Kadar, Khrushchev had told Harriman he was glad to see "the imperialist." The American replied, "When you came to my house in New York, you called me a capitalist. Is this a promotion or a demotion?"

Khrushchev said, "A promotion. . . . An imperialist is a capitalist who interferes in other countries—for example, as you are in South Vietnam." He went on to ask, "Why don't we have a nonaggression pact?" Harriman had a "better idea": swap commanders. The new NATO commander, General Lemnitzer, could go to Warsaw and Marshal Andrei Grechko to Paris. The Chairman called Grechko over: "I understand you are going to Paris." When the Marshal shook his head, Khrushchev said, "No, let's have a nonaggression pact."

Harriman reminded him that an Amateur Athletic Union team from the United States was competing against a Soviet team in Lenin Stadium. The Chairman said he had never been to a track meet. He turned up at the stadium with Kadar, Brezhnev, and their wives. Harriman and the Kohlers joined them in the official box. As American and Soviet runners strode the field, arm in arm, Harriman and Khrushchev rose to accept a vast ovation. Harriman saw tears in the Chairman's eyes.

After the treaty was initialed, Harriman went to the Kremlin. Reaching up with both arms, Khrushchev gave his tall friend a bear hug and cried, *"Maladyets!"** As arranged with Kennedy, Harriman raised the subject of China.† He said that the President felt "great concern over Chinese development of nuclear weapons" and tried to explore Khrushchev's knowledge and attitude about Peking's nuclear program. Khrushchev was monosyllabic.

---

*"Good work!" or "Well done!"
†When Harriman had stopped in London to see Macmillan, the Prime Minister took him aside and agreed that the China issue was "so sensitive" that Harriman should raise it alone with the Chairman, without Hailsham present.

Harriman persisted. "Suppose we can get France to sign the treaty? Can you deliver China?" The Chairman said, "That is your problem." Harriman tried again: "Suppose their rockets are targeted against you." Again Khrushchev was silent. Harriman did not raise the possibility of an American-Soviet attack on Chinese nuclear sites.*

Brightening, the Chairman took his visitor across the Kremlin courtyard, shaking hands and pinching a girl on the cheek. Introducing "Gospodin Garriman," he shouted, "We've just signed the Test Ban Treaty! I'm going to take him to dinner. Do you think he deserves it?" The slaves of communism cheered.†

During dinner, Harriman mentioned that Robert Kennedy would "very much like to visit the U.S.S.R."; perhaps the Chairman could invite him. Khrushchev replied that if he did so he would be expelled from the Party, given some of the Attorney General's anti-Soviet speeches.

Later he wrote the President, "Mr. Harriman showed himself worthy of the recommendation that you gave him in your letter. Furthermore we never doubted this." Ormsby-Gore reported to Kennedy that Macmillan was in "a state of euphoria." Arthur Schlesinger wrote Harriman, "I am damn glad that you are in the government!" The editors of the *Bulletin of the Atomic Scientists* moved the hands of their Doomsday Clock back to twelve minutes before midnight.

When the impending treaty was announced, the Chinese delegates sent to Moscow to discuss their differences with the Russians had stalked home and excoriated the test ban as a device to perpetuate the Soviet-American monopoly on power. The Sino-Soviet divorce came into full public view.

Harriman had cabled Washington, "It is becoming crystal clear that the Soviets have as their objective . . . an attempt to isolate the Chicoms." He felt that by including many other countries, "particularly the underdeveloped," in the treaty, Khrushchev felt he could pressure Peking to stop its nuclear program.

---

*A State Department official recorded in October 1964 that "a search of our records of the Test Ban Treaty negotiations in Moscow fails to reveal any Harriman proposal for a joint U.S.-U.S.S.R. effort to slow down Red China's nuclear weapons development."

†Harriman later recorded that the "manner in which he takes advantage of any opportunity to talk to the people" was "typical of Khrushchev." He remembered how when Stalin left the Kremlin to go to his dacha, "he traveled at high speed. . . . Traffic at intersections was held up as he sped through, behind bulletproof glass, with the blinds of his car windows drawn."

This was why the Chairman placed "maximum importance" on getting France to sign. That summer he joked, "De Gaulle has said that he wanted his own nuclear umbrella, but to construct a nuclear umbrella is not such a simple thing. One may end up both without one's pants *and* without the umbrella!"

Kennedy had earlier written de Gaulle that a test ban treaty was important as a means to limit the dangerous increase in the number of nuclear powers: "I must say frankly, they occupy me considerably." He tried to entice the Frenchman by offering him the technical information that he would have otherwise acquired through atmospheric testing. Under the terms of the Atomic Energy Act, he declared France a nuclear power, making it eligible for nuclear assistance without new legislation.

After the treaty was initialed, the President beseeched de Gaulle by letter not to "make an early final decision": "We have always hoped to have the participation of France in banning tests. . . . All that I am urging now is that it would be to our common advantage for our three Governments to explore these questions."

In Paris, the French President declared that as long as Russia and America retained their capacity to destroy the world, France would not be diverted "from equipping herself with the same sources of strength."* Several days later he added that he was not impressed by the adhesion of dozens of Third World nations: "It is rather like asking people to promise not to swim the Channel." He rejected the President's offer of nuclear cooperation as a violation of French sovereignty.†

Kennedy was disappointed and angry. He knew that a boycott by the French and Chinese meant that the treaty would probably fail as a means of stopping the spread of nuclear weapons. With more emotion than foresight, he carped that "Charles de Gaulle will be remembered for one thing only—his refusal to take that treaty."

*　*　*

---

*David Klein of the NSC reported, "Curiously enough, he chose *not* to denounce the test ban agreement but merely to minimize it. . . . This probably reflects an awareness on his part that even in France there is popular support for the Moscow action."

†Ormsby-Gore cabled Macmillan, "The President has just heard that the French Ambassador in Moscow was advising de Gaulle to try to do a deal with the Soviet Union to obtain nuclear information in order to rid himself of his hateful Atlantic links." This referred to Maurice Dejean, whose ridiculous suggestion possibly reflected the strength of his compromise by Soviet intelligence, of which Western authorities were still unaware.

Tuesday, January 30, 1962: Khrushchev's son-in-law, Alexei Adzhubei, and his wife Rada arrive at the White House for luncheon with Kennedy. Years later, after the Missile Crisis, Fidel Castro said it was this meeting "that started everything."

Left: Secretary of Defense Robert McNamara, whose public statements during the spring of 1962 evidently encouraged the Soviets to suspect that the United States might be planning a preemptive nuclear attack against the Soviet Union.

Below: In April 1962, Fidel Castro (*second from right*) at a Havana rally. At this moment he was privately warning Khrushchev and the Soviets that the United States was about to invade Cuba. Fourth from right is Major Rolando Cubela, known to the CIA as AM/LASH, who in 1963 agreed to murder Castro on the Agency's behalf.

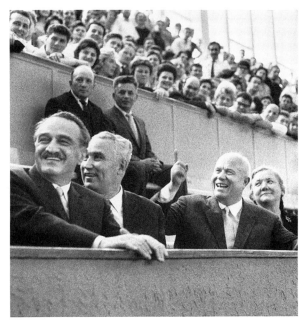

Above: In the Kremlin, Khrushchev and his advisers. Determined to thwart a U.S. invasion of Cuba and to bolster the world's perception of Soviet nuclear might, he decides in April 1962 to slip MRBMs and IRBMs onto the island.

Right: His spirits boosted by the knowledge that he has found a way out of his political predicament, Khrushchev attends a Benny Goodman concert, Moscow, May 1962, along with Mikoyan, Kozlov, and Nina Petrovna.

Opposite, upper left: CIA Director John McCone, who in August 1962 privately demanded that Kennedy investigate the possibility that Soviet strategic missiles might be going into Cuba.

Opposite, upper right: McGeorge Bundy, Kennedy's national security adviser, who gave him the news over breakfast on Tuesday, October 16, 1962.

Opposite lower: Kennedy reveals the Soviet gamble to the world—and his response, Monday, October 22, 1962.

Right: The Soviet Embassy, Washington, Tuesday evening, October 23, as Robert Kennedy meets secretly upstairs with Ambassador Anatoly Dobrynin.

Bottom: In Moscow that same evening, an obviously troubled Khrushchev tries to convey calm by attending an American performance of *Boris Godunov*, along with (*far left*) Brezhnev, three Romanian officials, and Mikoyan.

November 1962: The missiles sail from Cuba.

Mikoyan arrives in Havana to mollify the irate Castro. He is followed by aides, including his son Sergo (*top of ramp*).

December 1962 (*above*): On NBC's *Today* program, an upset Adlai Stevenson defends himself against anonymous Kennedy administration charges that he "wanted a Munich." *Below:* At the Orange Bowl, a thousand Bay of Pigs prisoners ransomed from Castro present Kennedy with their Brigade flag. He promises to return it in a "free Havana." (Thirteen years later, Brigade veterans took it back.)

Above: In January 1963, Khrushchev arrives in East Berlin to bless the Wall and signal that he does not intend to reopen the Berlin Crisis. Third from right is East German party leader Walter Ulbricht. *Left:* To stop provocations that might reinflame the Missile Crisis, U.S. agents arrest exile commandos operating against Cuba, March 1963.

Kennedy in West Berlin, June 1963. The President rides through crowds with Mayor Willy Brandt and Konrad Adenauer, views the Wall for the first time, and assures a vast throng that when Germany is reunited, "the people of West Berlin can take sober satisfaction in the fact that they were in the front lines."

July 1963: During test ban bargaining in Moscow, Khrushchev attends a track meet with Averell Harriman and U.S. Ambassador Foy Kohler. Brezhnev is at left.

In August at the Kremlin, before the treaty signing, Khrushchev, Gromyko, and Dobrynin (*seated fourth from left*) receive a U.S. delegation including Senators Leverett Saltonstall and J. William Fulbright, Kohler, and Dean Rusk.

Visiting Khrushchev's estate at Pitsunda on the Black Sea, Rusk strolls with his host and tests the water in the Chairman's beloved indoor-outdoor pool.

Above: In September 1963, the President is startled by the public support for the Limited Test Ban in Salt Lake City, where he had given perhaps his most anticommunist speech of the 1960 campaign.

Right: U.S. Ambassador Henry Cabot Lodge calls on South Vietnamese President Ngo Dinh Diem in Saigon while encouraging the coup that leads to Diem's murder.

The President speaks outdoors at Fort Worth, Friday morning, November 22, 1963.

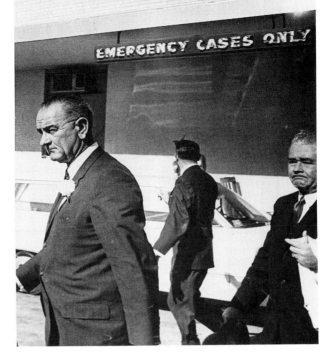

Right: Lyndon Johnson, now President, leaves Parkland Memorial Hospital, Dallas, wondering whether a conspiracy is underway to kill all high-ranking leaders of the U.S. government.

Below: Robert and Jacqueline Kennedy at Andrews Air Force Base that evening.

Above: After taking a special overnight train from Kiev, Khrushchev signs the memorial book for Kennedy at Spaso House, Saturday, November 23, 1963. Gromyko and Kohler are behind him.

Right: Worried that the Soviet Union might be blamed for the assassination, Mikoyan passes the late President's coffin and eternal flame at Arlington National Cemetery, Monday, November 25, 1963.

Above: Ten days after Kennedy's murder, still looking stunned, Khrushchev walks through a snowy forest outside Moscow with the Finnish President, Urho Kekkonen.

Below: In April 1964, Leonid Brezhnev fetes Khrushchev on his seventieth birthday while secretly plotting to overthrow and perhaps even kill him.

Nevertheless on Friday evening, July 26, the President spoke on television from the Oval Office "in a spirit of hope": the worlds of communism and free choice had been caught for eighteen years in a "vicious circle of conflicting ideology and interest. . . . Yesterday a shaft of light cut into the darkness."

The Limited Test Ban was the product of "patience and vigilance. We have made clear, most recently in Berlin and Cuba, our deep resolve to protect our security and our freedom against any form of aggression. . . . This treaty is not the millennium. . . . But it is an important first step, a step towards peace, a step towards reason, a step away from war. . . ."

If it proved to "symbolize the end of one era and the beginning of another," both sides could "gain confidence and experience in peaceful collaboration." Less than an hour's nuclear exchange "could wipe out more than three hundred million Americans, Europeans, and Russians, as well as untold numbers elsewhere." As Khrushchev had warned the Chinese, "the survivors would envy the dead."

The treaty would reduce radioactive fallout and retard "the spread of nuclear weapons to nations not now possessing them. . . . I ask you to stop and think for a moment what it would mean to have nuclear weapons . . . in the hands of countries . . . stable and unstable, responsible and irresponsible, scattered throughout the world."

While danger remained "in Cuba, in Southeast Asia, in Berlin," for the first time in years "the path to peace may be open. No one can be certain what the future will bring. . . . But history and our own conscience will judge us harsher if we do not now make every effort to test our hopes by action."

Without revealing its provenance, Kennedy quoted the same Chinese proverb he had quoted to Khrushchev at Vienna: "A journey of a thousand miles must begin with a single step. My fellow Americans, let us take that first step."

The President flew to Hyannis Port, where Harriman arrived on Sunday with a great jar of caviar from Khrushchev: "But I'm not sure you like caviar very much." Recalling his difficulty in extracting thirty-five thousand dollars from the multimillionaire in 1960, Kennedy replied, "We're going to take it whether we like it or not."

The President sent a copy of the treaty to Harry Truman in Independence, Missouri. With his tape recorder running, he called his predecessor and said, "Well, I think Averell Harriman did a good job." Truman replied, "I'm writing you a personal, confidential letter about certain paragraphs in it. . . . But I'm in complete agreement with what—what it provides. . . . My goodness life, maybe we can save a total war with it."*

Kennedy was more anxious about Eisenhower. When the Moscow negotiations were almost finished, he had sent Rusk and McCone up to Gettysburg. Eisenhower told them, "The big stumbling block to the treaty will be China and France." Rusk predicted that the Soviets might impose sanctions against Peking. McCone said that "China's possession of the Bomb" was still "several years off."

The General was not sold on the treaty. More conservative than during his Presidency, he was also influenced by his friend Lewis Strauss, an old warrior against a test ban who had preceded McCone as Chairman of his Atomic Energy Commission.† He told Rusk and McCone, "Five years ago, we were fully confident of our own superiority in nuclear science." But now the Soviets might be ahead in antimissile development: "An agreement would favor them."

He did not like the President's compromise on the withdrawal clause: "We might not be able to disclose the intelligence sources that tell us the Russians have been cheating."

Rusk assured him that "there is no direct relationship between this treaty and other issues such as Cuba, Laos, and Vietnam." The Limited Test Ban was "not an indication that we are ready to accept the status quo." The United States would "continue to push in these unrelated areas."

Kennedy abandoned the idea of signing the treaty at a Moscow summit with Khrushchev. He did not want to have to fight off Macmillan, whose presence might encourage the Chairman to pressure him for further concessions. He did not like the imagery of going to Khrushchev's lair to sign a document that his domestic foes would portray as a gift to the Russians.

Instead he decided to implicate key Senators—the more conservative, the better—by sending them to Moscow in a delegation headed

---

*Not by accident did Kennedy mention Harriman, to whom Truman was still close. The former President sent him three minor quibbles with treaty language. The President replied, "You have flagged three of the difficult and sensitive parts of the treaty, and I want you to know that if you ever want the assignment of keeping an eye on Averell Harriman, we will be delighted to have your help."

†Strauss had written him in March, "I should remind you that the Russians proposed three on-site inspections during your Administration (in 1960) and the proposal was treated by us as totally inadequate. . . . We may be on the point of stopping our development of small, clean weapons again while the Russians continue to impose on our good faith."

by Rusk. Republicans were resistant. Everett Dirksen and Bourke Hickenlooper refused to make the trip. George Aiken of Vermont recalled that Mansfield twisted his arm: "Mike started out by saying 'Don't say no, don't say no.'... Although I would have given anything not to have gone, I agreed." He was joined by Leverett Saltonstall of Massachusetts.

The Democrats were represented by Senators Fulbright, John Sparkman of Alabama, and John Pastore of Rhode Island. Rusk had advised the President that "rather than fool around and sort of reach out into left field for somebody like Keating ... we go with these three Democrats and two Republicans. And then if the Republicans appear ... to be niggardly about this, I think they'll be the ones to suffer."

Kennedy was worried that Stevenson's presence might incite the American Right. As Sorensen recalled, "Adlai wanted to go. He deserved to go. But Kennedy was alarmed about Woodrow Wilson and the Senate." Stevenson reminded the President that with his 1956 test ban proposal, he had "started this whole thing."* Khrushchev made it easier by insisting that U Thant attend the signing. Kennedy called Rusk: "If U Thant goes, then Adlai can go. ... It ought to be sold on that basis."

In Moscow on Monday morning, August 5, Rusk called on Gromyko at the Foreign Ministry. Showing that his office windows faced westward, Gromyko told Rusk that he often looked out and wondered what was "really happening" in the West.

When the Americans went to the Kremlin, Khrushchev told Rusk that the Limited Test Ban was merely a first step. They must now face the problem of Germany. Rusk politely said that Germany was "fundamental" and that Americans understood why the Soviet Union was so concerned.

The Chairman chided him for referring to some countries as "the East" instead of "socialist." Rusk noted that some Americans regarded the Kennedy administration as socialist. Khrushchev asked, "What kind of a man would say a thing like that?"

Fulbright recalled the Chairman's tea with the Foreign Relations Committee four years before: if the American South could get along with the "damned Yankees," the United States and the Soviet Union could get along.

---

*Recalling the "abusive attacks" Stevenson had endured in 1956, John Steinbeck wrote him that he had suffered from "the dangers of getting seven years ahead of history."

Khrushchev needled Stevenson about his harassment of Zorin in the Security Council during the Missile Crisis: "What's happened to you, Stevenson, since you started working for the United States government? We don't like to be interrogated like a prisoner in the dock." Wounded, Stevenson later lamented that the Chairman no longer thought him "objective."

After a gala luncheon, brandy, and speeches, a Soviet orchestra played Gershwin's "Love Walked In" as the beaming Khrushchev led Thant and the Americans, British, and Russians into a white marble Kremlin hall, gleaming under television lights. Rusk, Gromyko, and the Earl of Home signed the treaty. As they clinked glasses of champagne, Russians cried out, "Peace and friendship!" Glenn Seaborg wrote in his diary, "A glorious day!"

During dinner, Khrushchev recalled the failed "Spirit of Geneva" and the failed "Spirit of Camp David." Now he said, "Let's create a new Spirit—of Moscow!"

At Spiridonovka Palace, Rusk fulfilled Harriman's pledge by discussing a nonaggression pact with Gromyko. Khrushchev had earlier assured him that such an agreement was like mineral water, refreshing and invigorating: no one would win, no one would lose. Rusk had told him it was more like the Kellogg-Briand Pact of 1928, which had aspired to outlaw war but had left Americans in "considerable frustration."

He told Gromyko that the United States hoped to reduce its military budget, but this would depend on other East-West agreements. Washington was ready to discuss how to prevent new tensions over Germany, including new arrangements for access to West Berlin. His talks with Dobrynin had succeeded only in "boring each other."

Perhaps he and Gromyko could take a "fresh look" at the problem during the UN General Assembly session in the fall: "We don't believe this matter is urgent or critical unless one chooses to make it so. . . . We readily concede that the Soviet Union is a great power, but so are we."

Rusk, Dobrynin, Gromyko, Foy and Phyllis Kohler, and Llewellyn and Jane Thompson flew to Gagra and motored to Pitsunda. Neither American Ambassador had ever been honored with an invitation to Khrushchev's Black Sea estate. Gromyko laughingly warned Rusk not to swim toward Turkey. The Secretary of State may have wondered whether Gromyko was making an oblique, taunting reference to Kennedy's Turkish missile concession.

When they arrived, the Chairman showed off his indoor-outdoor pool, pressing a button to open the glass wall: "We close it in the winter. . . . You get the illusion of the sea." At the mandatory huge lunch, Phyllis Kohler was placed at the Chairman's right. Khrushchev murmured to Jane Thompson, "These stupid protocol men! This is not the seating I asked for."

The Chairman could not resist challenging his guest of honor to badminton, which they played on the large Oriental rug, the French doors opened to the breeze. After losing by four to one, Rusk later said, "Khrushchev is pretty good with a racket. Basketball is my game, and we didn't play that."

The two men strolled off into the woods and stopped under a tree. Khrushchev told him, "I've never understood why you Americans are so stubborn about Berlin. De Gaulle doesn't want a war over Berlin and Macmillan certainly doesn't. Why is it only the Americans?" Rusk thought to himself, *What do I tell the son of a bitch?* He improvised: "Mr. Khrushchev, you've just got to assume the Americans are goddamn fools."

After the Americans departed, Khrushchev learned of the death of the Kennedys' prematurely born second son, Patrick. He called Rusk in Moscow and asked him to convey his sympathies.

Kennedy sometimes derided large families, saying that state nurseries would do the job better. As Jacqueline recalled in her notes, "He never wanted them all crowded together like Bobby and Ethel—so small children in the middle were miserable and their parents harassed—But he always wanted a baby coming along when its predecessor was coming up—That is why he was so glad when he learned I was having Patrick."

For the President, the baby's death cast a shadow across the success of the Limited Test Ban. Macmillan wrote him by hand, "The burdens of public affairs are more or less tolerable, because they are, in a sense, impersonal. But private grief is poignant and cruel."

With the approaching test ban fight in the Senate, Kennedy had little time to linger on his private grief. He feared that the coalition of Southern Democrats and Republicans that was blocking his civil rights bill would deny him the needed two-thirds vote for his test ban treaty. Already Senators were charging that Harriman had made a "secret deal with Khrushchev" to win an agreement.

McNamara privately told the Joint Chiefs, "If you insist in opposing this treaty, well and good, but I am not going to let anyone oppose it out of emotion or ignorance." During a fortnight of meetings he resolved their anxieties about Soviet cheating and promised to improve detection methods, prepare for atmospheric tests on short notice if the treaty were abrogated, and continue underground testing. General LeMay was persuaded that the treaty would help to divide the Chinese and Russians.

The President was told that congressional mail was running fifteen to one against the treaty.* His aides were astonished when he told them that, if necessary, he would "gladly" forfeit his reelection for the sake of the treaty. In early August, he said he could name fifteen Senators who would probably oppose anything with his name attached, "and not all of them are Republicans." If the vote were held that day, he thought the treaty would be defeated.

Before the Senate Foreign Relations Committee, McNamara made a conservative argument for the treaty, warning that if testing continued in all environments, the United States would probably lose its technical lead. Kennedy told Senators that the nation did not need a hundred-megaton bomb, that neither side needed further tests to develop an antimissile missile, and that no amount of Soviet underground testing or undetected cheating could reverse the American lead.

The President was furious to hear that McCone was sending CIA nuclear specialists to persuade Senators that the Soviets had cheated during the testing moratorium. His relations with McCone had plummeted since the Missile Crisis. Robert Kennedy complained that when the Cuban issue was reinflamed in February, McCone had hurt the President by reminding Senators that he had not been the one to underestimate the possibility of missiles in Cuba in the summer of 1962.†

---

*Scanning a report on White House mail, the President observed, "The category that leads the list again this week is requests to the Kennedy family for money. . . . I also see that we have received more letters on the White House animal pets than on the financial crisis of the United Nations. Nuclear testing is far down the list, but most of the people who write . . . are against the ban." (As reported by the *New York Times*, Khrushchev's gift dog Pushinka and Caroline's terrier Charley were the new parents of a litter of puppies. Many Americans had written to the President offering to adopt them.)

†Richard Helms recalled, "It was ironic, as far as I was concerned, to hear that the President's intelligence chief, the one guy who for whatever reason was right—that this should have soured his relationship with the President."

The Attorney General suspected that with an election year looming, McCone might now be a Trojan horse, "playing with the Republicans." Bundy told a CIA man, "I'm so tired of listening to John McCone say he was right I never want to hear it again."

Spearhead of the opposition to what it called "the Treaty of Moscow" was the deeply anticommunist physicist Edward Teller, father of the hydrogen bomb. In confidential testimony, he insisted that the United States must continue its secret high-altitude testing if it hoped to develop a means of destroying Soviet missiles in flight; the Russians had performed antimissile tests during their 1962 series.* A later witness warned that this could place the United States "at the mercy of the dictators who already control a third of the world."

Others demanded that reservations be attached to the treaty. Arthur Dean warned against such renegotiation with Moscow and the more than a hundred nations expected to sign, perhaps "throwing away any possibility of further negotiations with the Soviet Union." Hickenlooper demanded to see Khrushchev's private correspondence with Kennedy.

Rusk volunteered to show the letters to Senate leaders. Smathers warned colleagues that if they became public, Khrushchev might say, "The hell with you, Mr. Kennedy, I am never going to write a letter to you again."

Richard Russell opposed the treaty on grounds that it lacked safeguards against cheating: "Those Russians . . . have never yet carried out any agreement they've made." Bundy later thought that had the President been willing to ask Lyndon Johnson to work on Russell, the Georgian might have changed his mind. But as with Stevenson, by 1963 Kennedy was less willing than ever to give his Vice President a chance to renew his political influence.

Foreign Relations recommended the Limited Test Ban Treaty to the Senate with only one dissenting vote, cast by Democrat Russell Long of Louisiana. Barry Goldwater demanded that ratification be contingent on withdrawal of all Soviet forces from Cuba. He claimed that not "ten men in America" knew the full truth about Cuba, the test

---

*Fulbright warned the President by telephone that "Teller made some impression on some of the members. . . . He is such an actor. I mean, he's John L. Lewis and Billy Sunday all wrapped up in one." Kennedy replied, "Well, there's no . . . doubt that any man with complete conviction, particularly who's an expert, is bound to shake anybody who's got an open mind."

ban treaty, or other commitments made to governments "dedicated to our destruction."

Kennedy replied at a press conference: "There are no commitments, and I think that Senator Goldwater is at least one of the ten men in America who would know that is not true." Asked if he cared to comment further, the President had 1964 in mind: "No, not yet, not yet."

As the treaty went to the Senate floor, Kennedy was still worried about Eisenhower's ability to sink it. The President had one particular source of leverage. Soon after the Inauguration, his Justice Department had interviewed Bernard Goldfine, the Boston textile manufacturer whose favors to Eisenhower's chief of staff, Sherman Adams, had forced Adams to resign.

Suffering from arteriosclerosis, Goldfine now claimed that his gifts to Adams had included not only lodging and the famous vicuña coat and rugs but more than $150,000, slipped to Adams over five years. The accusations seemed to be corroborated by a series of cashier's checks that Adams had given his Washington landlady.

Robert Kennedy's lieutenants worried that Goldfine's flagging memory and crying jags, evidently induced by his illness, might impede his credibility on the witness stand. Aides to Mortimer Caplin, Director of the Internal Revenue Service, felt that the paper trail demonstrated Adams's guilt. They strongly recommended prosecution.

The Attorney General could not have been displeased by the prospect of using Adams to tarnish the record of Eisenhower, who so disapproved of his brother and who still commanded such influence on public opinion. In February 1961, he wrote in his notes that he was "not optimistic" about winning the case but thought "there is probably a fifty-fifty chance."

He gave the case to William Hundley, conveniently an Eisenhower holdover at Justice. Adams admitted receiving money from unremembered donors, but not from Goldfine. Citing Goldfine's weakness as a witness, the gaps in the evidence, and the possibility that people might claim that they had given Adams money out of disinterested patriotism, the Attorney General's subordinates recommended against prosecution. Internal Revenue officials wondered whether the case was quashed for political reasons.

The President later told Joseph Alsop that he sent the evidence against Adams to Eisenhower at Gettysburg. No doubt Kennedy believed that if Adams were not prosecuted, Eisenhower might feel grateful. According to Alsop, the General sent word back that he hoped Adams would be spared further humiliation. Robert Kennedy later insisted that this was not the reason he ultimately decided against prosecution. Nevertheless the President was evidently content to let Eisenhower think so.

Bobby Baker claimed in 1978 that when Eisenhower learned of the evidence against Adams, he instructed Everett Dirksen to ask Kennedy, "as a personal favor to me," to kill the case: "He'll have a blank check in my bank if he will grant me this favor." According to Baker, the President agreed: when his brother balked, he said, "If you can't comply with my request, then your resignation will be accepted."

A cryptic exchange of letters between Eisenhower and Dirksen in 1962 suggests that Baker's story may be accurate. In a January 10 letter to the General, Dirksen wrote that Eisenhower's old congressional liaison Bryce Harlow "spoke to me about one of your former staff members—I am sure you will recall it—and I discussed it with the President on Monday morning at breakfast. I believe everything is in proper order." Eisenhower replied, "I am particularly indebted to you for following through the matter mentioned in your second paragraph."

Dirksen wrote him the next month that "the matter which you asked Bryce to talk to me about quite a while back about an individual has been gotten back on track." Eisenhower thanked him "for your effort on behalf of an individual for whom we both have a high regard. I cannot tell you how delighted I am that, finally, he seems assured that the matter is indeed on the track."

Late in the test ban struggle, Dirksen was still publicly undecided. Frederick Dutton of State felt that the Republican leader had "backed and filled" to prevent the treaty from becoming a "clear-cut accomplishment of the Administration useful in '64." Smathers recalled that Kennedy thought of Dirksen as "a fellow who could go either way at most any time." The President laughed about having heard Dirksen give the best speech ever made for the Marshall Plan while in the House and the best speech against it while in the Senate.

By Baker's account, Kennedy called Dirksen to the White House to ask for support on the test ban treaty: "Ike said I had coin in his bank and you say I have coin in yours. . . . I want you to reverse yourself and come out for the treaty. I also want Ike's public endorsement of the treaty before the Senate votes. We'll call it square on that other matter." According to Baker, Dirksen replied, "Mr. President, you're a hell of a horse trader. But I'll honor my commitment, and I'm sure that General Eisenhower will."

Dirksen endorsed the treaty, reminding other Republicans that their 1960 platform had called for a test ban. By his own account, he told the President, "My mind is made up. I shall support the treaty, and I expect some castigation for my vote." Kennedy replied, "Everett, have you read *The Man and the Myth?* . . . You do not know what castigation is."*

Despite his earlier coolness, Eisenhower also backed the treaty, adding that he presumed it would not prevent the use of nuclear weapons in the event of war.† He may or may not have pulled his punches in exchange for the President's decision to spare Adams, but on November 23, 1963, he privately complained to Lyndon Johnson about the "tactics" employed by Kennedy's Justice Department and IRS.

The Limited Test Ban passed the Senate on Tuesday, September 24. Eleven Democrats were opposed—all Southerners, except for the maverick conservative Frank Lausche of Ohio. Eight Republicans were opposed—all Westerners, except for Margaret Chase Smith of Maine. Sorensen felt that "no other accomplishment in the White House ever gave Kennedy greater satisfaction."

The President departed that day for a western "conservation" tour in preparation for 1964. He would need new sources of support to make up for the southern states he expected to fall away as a result of his support for civil rights. In 1960, the only western states he had carried were Nevada, New Mexico, and Hawaii.

Starting in Duluth, Bismarck, Cheyenne, and Laramie, Kennedy spoke on conservation and did not say a word about the Limited Test Ban. Presidential aides feared that if he mentioned the treaty, he might be booed. But when he spoke in Billings, Montana, he could not help but praise Mansfield for his help in passing a treaty that was a first step toward "a more secure world." The audience cheered.

Kennedy told another Montana audience that while the competition with communism would dominate the rest of their lives, the United States should compete not in nuclear violence but to show the world which society was "happier."

---

*J.F.K.: The Man and the Myth was a hostile biography of the President by Victor Lasky that made national bestseller lists. In his history of the treaty, Glenn Seaborg concluded that the test ban would not have been defeated had Dirksen maintained his opposition but that the margin of victory would have been "certainly affected."
†He did not publicly mention his concerns about the withdrawal clause or about the fact that it might allow the Soviets to leap ahead of the West in antimissile weapons.

On Thursday, September 26, he went to the Mormon Tabernacle in Salt Lake City. This was where, exactly three years before, the Democratic nominee had strained to affirm his anticommunism, branding Khrushchev the "dictator" of the "enemy" Communist system, "implacable, insatiable, unceasing" in its drive for world domination.

Now he said that "the Communist offensive, which claimed to be riding the tide of historic inevitability, has been thwarted and turned back in recent months." The Limited Test Ban was "important as a first step, perhaps to be disappointed, perhaps to be ultimately set back. But at least in 1963, the United States committed itself, and the Senate of the United States, by an overwhelming vote, to one chance to end the radiation and the possibilities of burning."

The day before he had flown over the Little Big Horn, "where General Custer was slain, a massacre which has lived in history, four hundred or five hundred men. We are talking about *three hundred million* men and women in twenty-four hours. I think it is wise to take a first step to lessen the possibility of that happening." The crowd gave him a standing ovation.

Reporters told Salinger that Kennedy seemed to have found a powerful new issue for 1964. "Yes, you're right," he replied. "We've found that peace is an issue." After his return to Washington, the President told Ormsby-Gore over dinner that he was determined to maintain the momentum of the test ban treaty and that he hoped to visit the Soviet Union at the first suitable moment.

The Limited Test Ban never fulfilled Kennedy's and Khrushchev's hopes. The treaty reduced the amount of strontium 90 in the atmosphere, but its failure to stop all forms of nuclear testing kept it from throwing a serious damper on the nuclear arms race.

Had the President been willing to seize Khrushchev's offer of two to three on-site inspections in December 1962, he might have had a chance to close a comprehensive test ban. But that month he was still enmeshed in the unresolved issues of the Missile Crisis. Had he sprung such a surprise on the American people so soon after the shock of Cuba, his critics might well have killed it by charging that the test ban was part of some secret concession to Khrushchev in return for withdrawing the missiles.

By the time Kennedy might have been ready to fight for a comprehensive treaty in the spring of 1963, Soviet hard-liners had pushed the Chairman to withdraw his proposal for on-site inspections and retreat to a limited test ban. In May 1960, the world was robbed of the chance for a comprehensive ban by the U-2 affair and the collapse of the Paris summit. Three years later, the stars once again fell out of alignment. The nuclear arms race roared on.*

William Attwood was a former *Look* editor who had served for two years as Kennedy's Ambassador to Guinea and was now an American delegate to the UN. On Monday, September 23, he stood in the corner at a New York cocktail party given by an ABC correspondent named Lisa Howard.

The Cuban Ambassador to the UN, Carlos Lechuga, told Attwood that Castro had hoped to establish some sort of contact with Kennedy in 1961, but the Bay of Pigs had ended any chance of that. He complained about the continuing exile raids against Cuba but said that Castro had liked the tone of Kennedy's American University speech. Perhaps Attwood could make a quiet visit to Havana.

The encounter was not accidental. Lisa Howard had told Attwood that after interviewing Castro in April she was convinced he wished to restore communications with the United States. She offered to hold a party at which he could speak informally with Lechuga.

Before Attwood agreed, he wrote a memo asking for permission to make "a discreet inquiry into the possibility of neutralizing Cuba on our terms." There was reason to believe that Castro was unhappy with the Russians and suffering from the American trade embargo. If the approach proved successful, it could "remove the Cuban issue from the 1964 campaign. He showed his memo to Stevenson, who said, "Unfortunately the CIA is still in charge of Cuba." Stevenson mentioned the initiative to Kennedy and reported to Attwood that the President had not objected.

Attwood saw Robert Kennedy the day after his rendezvous with Lechuga. Robert told Attwood that a Havana visit would be too risky. It was bound to leak. If it failed, the Republicans would call it "appeasement" and demand a congressional investigation. But the general idea was worth pursuing. He told Attwood to stay in touch with Bundy and his staff man on Cuban affairs, Gordon Chase.

The Attorney General consulted his brother, who declared himself willing to normalize relations if Castro ended the Soviet bloc military

---

*In the 1980s, horrified at the escalation of the nuclear arms race, Macmillan scored Kennedy for his failure to risk a fight for a comprehensive test ban: "I mean weakened by constantly having all those girls, every day. . . . He was weak in pressing the Russians for seven inspections instead of three. If we could have had that, it would have eventually led to no testing in the air at all."

presence on his island, broke ties with the Cuban Communists, and stopped the subversion of Latin America.*

The CIA forged ahead with the sabotage program approved by the President in June to foster "a spirit of resistance and disaffection which could lead to significant defections and other by-products of unrest."†

As Robert Kennedy recalled, "There were ten or twenty thousand tons of sugar cane that was being burned every week through internal uprisings." Bundy gave the President "the after-action report on the Sawmill sabotage enterprise. . . . A quick first glance suggests that it is a businesslike report of adventure which you would find interesting."

The NSC's Standing Group on Cuba had asked the CIA in the spring of 1963 to assess the effects of Castro's possible death. The Agency replied that "his brother Raul or some other figure in the regime would, with Soviet backing and help, take over." If Castro were by chance assassinated, "the U.S. would be widely charged with complicity."

The CIA resumed its plotting against the Cuban leader. In January 1963, Desmond FitzGerald, who had replaced William Harvey as manager of covert action against Cuba, suggested that a tiny explosive be installed in a rare seashell to be left in a place where Castro might skin-dive and pick it up. This proved to be beyond the Agency's technical capability.

At the beginning of September, a CIA man in São Paulo, Brazil, met with a well-placed Cuban official named Rolando Cubela. Codenamed AM/LASH, Cubela was a doctor and onetime student guerrilla leader who had murdered Batista's military intelligence chief in 1956 and seized the Presidential Palace in advance of Castro's arrival. Cubela said that he resented the Soviet presence in Cuba and that Castro had

---

*During his visit with Khrushchev in August, Rusk had once again asked him to reduce the Soviet presence on Cuba.

†George Denney of State proposed that some Central American leader "be induced to assume a David role in which he employs ridicule and invective to make of Castro an enraged and impotent Goliath, thereby substantially reducing Castro's prestige and conspiratorial effectiveness throughout Latin America." Radio Havana's broadcasts of Castro's speeches could be interrupted by "someone with a quick and acid wit" to taunt the Cuban leader by "mimicking his voice" or saying, "Fidel, you are lying! . . . Come on, Fidel, shave. . . . Fidel, you butcher! . . . You're lying again, you ape." Denney felt that such "affronts to Castro's personal vanity might make him wilder and more open to terror than existing economic and political pressures."

betrayed the revolution: he was ready to attempt an "inside job."

Soon after the meeting, Castro went to a Brazilian Embassy reception in Havana and warned that if American leaders tried to do away with the leaders of Cuba, "we are prepared to fight them and answer in kind. United States leaders should think if they are aiding terrorist plans to eliminate Cuban leaders, they themselves will not be safe." Nervous CIA men wondered whether Castro had chosen the Brazilian Embassy to make his threat in order to signal his knowledge of the São Paulo meeting.

Gordon Chase of the NSC gave Bundy a copy of a press account of Castro's Embassy appearance, writing that a friend had speculated "that Castro may have had a few too many to drink at the cocktail party."

CHAPTER

22

Fragile Opportunities

B Y OCTOBER, KENNEDY WAS STARTING TO PLAN HIS 1964 CAM-
paign. As his brother recalled, the President was worried that
he had not gotten himself across "as a person with much compassion"
and that the American people "didn't feel personally involved with
him."*

That autumn, Kennedy's popularity had dropped to its lowest point
ever—59 percent, compared to the post–Bay of Pigs high of 82.

*In 1959, James MacGregor Burns had observed that Kennedy was not the kind of
man at whose funeral strangers would cry. In August 1963, William F. Buckley, Jr.,
complained in the *National Review* about the "slickness" of Kennedy's performance:
"He is surrounded by vain sycophants who seek to transmute his dismaying record
into one great, endless, triumphal parade." This was "politically reassuring, but only
for so long as the people continue in their drugged state. How would they respond
to a totally different figure?"

Gallup suggested that a major reason was the President's June civil rights bill and related measures: by 46 to 12 percent, Americans thought that he was "pushing integration too fast."

Kennedy had originally expected his 1964 opponent to be Nelson Rockefeller, which disturbed him because he believed that the New York Governor would have beaten him in 1960. Theodore White told him that Rockefeller "likes you." The President replied, "I like him too, but he'll get to hate me. It's inevitable." Then Rockefeller's candidacy was harmed by his remarriage to a divorcée who had given up her children.

Now Kennedy was anxious about the new Governor of Michigan, George Romney. The silver-haired former American Motors chief and devout Mormon had met a payroll and looked, far more than Kennedy, like a President. Kennedy told his Navy friend Paul Fay, "You have to be suspicious of somebody as good as Romney. . . . Imagine someone we know going off for twenty-four or forty-eight hours to fast and meditate, awaiting a message from the Lord whether to run or not to run."

The President was hoping for Goldwater: "Give me good old Barry. I'd never have to leave this Oval Office." As Robert Kennedy recalled, "We had worked with Goldwater and we just knew he was not a very smart man and he's just going to destroy himself." He recalled his brother's concern "that he would destroy himself too early and not get the nomination."

Kennedy asked his aides to avoid mentioning Romney but use every chance to cite Goldwater as of White House stature. With "Mr. Conservative" as his opponent, he expected to win a historic landslide and a congressional majority that would enable him to do the many things he had postponed during his first term. At the top of the list was expanding the improvement in Soviet relations begun with the Limited Test Ban.

In the summer of 1963, Rusk had reminded him of their understanding that for financial reasons he would serve only one term at State: if the President wanted "a fresh start in my job in preparation for the forthcoming election," he would be glad to quit. Kennedy said, "Don't raise that question again with me. I like your guts. And there are too few people around here that have got any guts."*

---

*Unwilling to make Rusk an instant lame duck by divulging their one-term understanding, the President was content to give Schlesinger and other critics of the Secre-

Cruising off Hyannis, he mused about replacing Rusk during the second term with McNamara: "But then if I don't have McNamara at Defense to control the generals, I won't have a foreign policy." Harriman felt he deserved consideration on the strength of his test ban success. Told that Bundy might get the job, one official at State said he wished Bundy and his staff would move "over to this building, just to get them off the phone."

Robert Kennedy told Justice Douglas of his interest in State. As Douglas recalled, he raised the matter with the President, who "indicated a great interest." The President knew that appointing his brother to State might help Robert to win the 1968 Democratic presidential nomination. He told Bradlee in early 1963 that his brother might run someday, "but certainly not in 1968." At the moment he was about to pass into history, he did not wish to be mired in renewed charges that the Kennedys were trying to lock up the White House.

But by fall he was asking Charles Bartlett, "Who do you think it'll be in '68—Bobby?" Bartlett found him "apprehensive" about the prospect. "Jack talked about how '68 was going to be a contest between Bobby and Lyndon Johnson, and I don't think he took cordially to it at all." Charles Spalding recalled the President's feeling that his brother "was overly ambitious" and that "Bobby was hard-nosing it."

After the Missile Crisis, Kennedy had once spoken with his friend Philip Graham, publisher of the *Washington Post,* about getting the 1968 nomination for McNamara. Graham wrote him that the Secretary of Defense "might (just might) be ready to be a Tribune of the People in six (or sixteen) years."

To almost anyone else in public life, McNamara would have seemed a bizarre choice. He was a Republican with no electoral experience, abrasive, and intolerant. What the President saw was his competence, incorruptibility, and freedom from political cant. McNamara may have seemed a natural response to Kennedy's growing conviction, as he had said at Yale, that the problems of the 1960s were more administrative than ideological.

McNamara may have also seemed a solution to his Bobby-in-1968 problem. When Kennedy had resigned his Senate seat to become President, he had arranged for one of his Harvard roommates, Benjamin Smith, to hold the seat until Edward was old enough to run for it. He may have expected McNamara to hold the Oval Office for Robert, perhaps even naming the President's brother as Vice President and, by tacit agreement, renouncing reelection.

---

tary of State the impression that he was going to take their advice and fire Rusk after the election.

In a 1965 oral history interview, Robert said that the Missile Crisis had shown his brother "what can happen to a country and how much depends on a particular individual. . . . And we thought that McNamara was that individual."

To a Democrat like O'Donnell, the notion was heresy. He doubted that when the time came, the President would ever have thrown in his hand with a Republican political neophyte. He felt that by the fall of 1963, the President was "on to" what O'Donnell considered to be the gaps in McNamara's political judgment.

In the fall of 1963, the drought-plagued Soviet harvest fell catastrophically short, even by the usual standard, of feeding the Soviet people. Khrushchev devised a crash program to produce one hundred million tons of chemical fertilizer per year by 1970. He told the Presidium that in the meantime there were two solutions: starve the people, as Stalin and Molotov had, or purchase grain from the West.

Secretary of Agriculture Orville Freeman told a September Cabinet meeting that the Russians were interested in buying American grain. Sorensen recalled this as the only time "when a subject spontaneously raised at a Cabinet meeting produced a valuable discussion."

Bundy reported to Kennedy that selling sixty-five million bushels of wheat to the Russians would not make a dent in the American surplus. It would produce jobs, improve the U.S. balance of payments, and reduce federal storage costs. Other Western nations had sold wheat and flour to the Soviet bloc for years.

Hubert Humphrey knew that a wheat sale would help Minnesota farmers. He and Freeman, the former Governor of Minnesota, agreed it was "acceptable to sell the Soviets anything they can't shoot back at you." O'Donnell and O'Brien argued that a wheat sale would be "politically disastrous" in 1964, hurting the President with German-Americans, Polish-Americans, and Irish Catholics. Usually O'Donnell kept Lyndon Johnson away from the Oval Office, but knowing that the Vice President would oppose the sale, he prompted Kennedy to ask for his advice.

Johnson refused to state an opinion. He knew that such remarks often found their way into the newspapers as examples of disloyalty that could undermine his place on the 1964 ticket. He told the President, "Kenny and I will talk it over later, and he'll let you know how I feel about it." Later he told O'Donnell, "Selling this wheat to Russia would be the worst political mistake he ever made."

Freeman found Kennedy "very nervous" about the wheat sale. During the Berlin Crisis, Congress had passed an amendment barring sales of subsidized commodities to unfriendly nations. Robert Kennedy advised his brother to ignore it as a nonbinding declaration of interest, but the President did not wish to appear as if he were cutting corners to help the Russians.

He cut a deal with Mansfield and Humphrey: to buy the acquiescence of Congress, the strongly anti-Communist maritime workers, and other unions, any grain shipped to Russia must travel on American ships. In early October, Thompson saw Dobrynin, who agreed. Kennedy was amazed; American shipping rates were among the world's highest. Gallup found that by 60 to 31 percent, Americans approved of "our selling surplus wheat to Russia."

Then the agreement almost collapsed. As Freeman recalled, the Russians realized that with the cost of American freight tacked on, the wheat was "damned expensive." Kennedy and Sorensen joked that probably some Soviet political commissar had authorized the use of U.S. vessels before a commercial commissar explained how costly it would be.

Finally the Soviets were persuaded to take hard durum wheat, of which there was a large American supply and hence a large government subsidy. This reduced the price. "Once the first sale had been made, it went on from there," said Freeman. "But politics almost jammed it up."

On Wednesday, October 2, at the Soviet Mission in New York, Rusk told Gromyko that Berlin was still their number-one point of confrontation: "Certainly no question about that." Nevertheless the last two years had removed the "fever of the situation." East Germany was no longer "bleeding" emigrants. West German trade with the East was now "something like five billion dollars a year." Hadn't Mr. Khrushchev said that trade meant peace?

Gromyko complained once more of Bonn's obstruction of a German peace treaty. Rusk replied once more that the U.S. government was "no monkey on a stick, manipulated by West Germany"; while a peace treaty was "important," there seemed no solution now. Better to let their relations develop and let time heal the problem, especially now that Adenauer was stepping down as Chancellor.* They must "avoid a crisis from which neither side would benefit."

* * *

---

*In favor of his Finance Minister, Ludwig Erhard.

For most of 1963, Berlin had been quiet. In the wake of the Missile Crisis, Khrushchev did not wish to test Kennedy's will.* In January 1963, he reminded an East German Party Congress that with Soviet help they had built the wall allowing them to control their borders and resist those who would weaken the GDR.

By the fall, Khrushchev could not easily ignore the Berlin issue. Domestic critics already angry about the Limited Test Ban and wheat sale would argue that he was abandoning Soviet demands in order to curry favor with the West. In October, the Soviets resumed petty harassment of American soldiers on the city's access routes. Guards stopped two American troop convoys on the Autobahn.

Usually they counted the soldiers and waved them on. This time, the troops were ordered to disembark and line up for head counts. When their commanders refused, an eastbound convoy was detained for fifteen hours, a westbound convoy for fifty-two. A Soviet jet also buzzed an American reconnaissance plane.

On Thursday, October 10, Gromyko went to the White House for his first visit with Kennedy since the start of the Missile Crisis. He found the President "smiling and as usual in a good mood."

They spoke of how to expand the progress of the Limited Test Ban: new safeguards against surprise attack and accidental nuclear war, prohibition of underground nuclear testing and bombs in space, a U.S.-Soviet moon project. Gromyko asked for increased trade, a German peace treaty, and a nonaggression pact.

Kennedy revealed that while American soldiers were to get a salary increase, he intended to "flatten" his next defense budget, "unless, of course, some crisis should develop." Perhaps the Soviets could also put a lid on military spending. He assured Gromyko that the number of American troops in Europe would shrink in 1964. Perhaps the Russians could reciprocate. A formal agreement "would raise difficulties in view of the difficult inspection problem."

Gromyko praised the American University speech. The President said that he and Khrushchev must "do everything possible to prevent us from colliding." It was "helpful" that Soviet troops were leaving Cuba, but the problem remained. More incidents on the access routes

---

*The President had refused the counsel of advisers such as Robert Komer of the NSC, who wrote Bundy at the end of October 1962, "We may have a first-class chance of getting some kind of a viable standstill arrangement on Berlin. Now would be the time to beat up Adenauer . . . and offer the Soviets a deal."

to Berlin should be avoided as an "unnecessary nuisance and irritation."

That evening, at a Soviet Embassy dinner, Rusk proposed mutual destruction of all American B-47 and Soviet Badger bombers. This would be easy to verify and a move toward nonproliferation: "If these aircraft should become obsolete in five years . . . why couldn't we destroy them in three years? That would give us some disarmament and would also be beneficial in other respects." One supersonic bomber equaled the cost of "maintaining a whole university in an underdeveloped country. . . . It would be nonsense to give such bombers to the less developed countries."

Gromyko replied that they should work on rockets as well. Rusk agreed; the United States was "prepared to discuss the question of nuclear delivery vehicles across the board." But "we must start somewhere and move ahead." After B-47s and Badgers, he and Gromyko might find other classes of weapons that would "lend themselves to a similar approach."

When Gromyko issued his standard complaint about American bases, Rusk recommended that he ask Malinovsky how many bases the United States had abandoned since 1948. Gromyko would be amazed. If the job proved too big for the Soviet Defense Ministry, he would give him the figures himself.

Gromyko raised the old Soviet suggestion of nuclear-free zones around the world. Rusk said the United States would not object, as long as the idea won the consent of those countries involved. In Latin America, for example, Cuba would be the main problem. In Africa, the stickler would be Egypt.

As for the Middle East, Rusk went on to suggest that "perhaps something could be worked out" to deal with Israel. Was this a quiet invitation, like Harriman's on China in July, for the Soviet Union to join the United States to keep the Israelis out of the nuclear club?

Israel had begun building a nuclear reactor in the Negev desert in the late 1950s. Prime Minister Ben-Gurion claimed that the Dimona plant was a "textile factory," but said, "It is not impossible for scientists in Israel to do for their own people what Einstein, Oppenheimer, and Teller—all three Jews—have done for the United States."

Kennedy's private attitude toward the Jewish state had always resembled the suspiciousness of Stevenson far more than the enthusiasm of Humphrey. He admired Stevenson in 1956 for resisting large Boston Jewish contributors who asked him to endorse the attack on

Suez. In 1960, he asked Theodore White, "Teddy, tell me why the Jews in Israel are so different from the Jews in this country. They are so tough."*

In 1961 and 1962, the President quietly attempted to defuse the Middle East powder keg with a plan to allow free Palestinian emigration to Israel and the Arab countries. He deployed his aide Myer Feldman, who was Jewish, and others to win Israeli acceptance, but failed.† Kennedy had little to gain by turning the screws on Jerusalem before 1964—especially since, as he told Bradlee, the "only people" who really gave during political campaigns now were Jews. Like so much else, he may have been deferring serious pressure on Israel until after his reelection.

What could not wait was keeping Israel from gaining the Bomb. In 1962, Jerusalem declared that there were no nuclear weapons in the Middle East and that Israel would never be the first to introduce them. This denial did not foreclose the manufacture of devices that would require minutes of work before they became nuclear bombs.

At Kennedy's behest, Feldman negotiated a secret pact with the Israelis for regular American inspection visits to the Dimona reactor in exchange for Hawk antiaircraft missiles, long sought by Ben-Gurion. The administration defended the missile transfer, the first serious American military aid to Israel, as a response to the Soviet SAMs given to Egypt.

In March 1963, Bundy gave the President a CIA report on "what we know at this moment on nuclear capabilities in the UAR [Egypt] and Israel. It is clearly not enough and we are pushing ahead on arranging for another inspection of the Israeli activities." By October, Kennedy was irritated with the Israelis for failing to live up to their half of the secret bargain: Americans were not gaining sufficient access to their nuclear installations.‡

---

*White, who was Jewish, felt "disappointed" by Kennedy's suggestion that "Jews in this country aren't tough." A black eavesdropper would not have been delighted to hear what Kennedy said next. White's notes: "He says there [are] all these brilliant N[egro] leaders, really brilliant. . . . In no other people is the gap between the [leaders] and the led so [great]." Kennedy was not immune to ethnic stereotype. In 1959, after NBC's *Meet the Press* tackled the subject of whether a Catholic could be elected President, he angrily telephoned the program's Jewish moderator, Lawrence Spivak, and outraged him by asking, "How would *you* like it if someone did a program on 'Are Jews Honest?' "

†In a 1964 oral history interview, with his usual presumption that he was the arbiter of good Americanism, Robert Kennedy said of Feldman, "His major interest was Israel rather than the United States."

‡Gromyko claimed years later that the President told him there were "two groups of the American population which are not always pleased when relations between our two

Bundy later said, "My recollection is that close concern with this issue ended with the death of Kennedy." Had the President lived, his second term might have seen a serious effort to deprive Israel of the Bomb.

At Pitsunda in August, Khrushchev had told Rusk, "If you want to, go ahead and fight in the jungles of Vietnam. The French fought there for seven years and still had to quit in the end. Perhaps the Americans will be able to stick it out for a little longer, but eventually they will have to quit too."

Kennedy was swiftly resolving the ambiguities in his policy toward Vietnam. In January 1962, he had asked the NSC to reread Khrushchev's Wars of Liberation speech: "We are embarked on a major effort here, and it is not going to be an easy one." He worried about what would happen in Vietnam "when the Chinese get missiles and bombs and nuclear weapons." The NSC responded with paramilitary plans including the famous "strategic hamlets," the fortification of a thousand villages against Viet Cong guerrillas by barbed wire and ramparts.

Rusk privately told senators in March 1962 that despite Soviet "protestations that they would like to get that situation settled down, agents and cadres and personnel and very limited amounts of supplies continue to go into South Vietnam." It was "just possible that Moscow is losing its influence, its ability to influence that situation."

In an April letter, Galbraith implored the President to consider that the Soviets might not be "particularly desirous" of causing trouble in Southeast Asia; he should "impress upon all concerned the importance of keeping American forces out of actual combat commitment." Queasier than ever about joining an Asian land war on the side of a regime that he considered unloved by its own people, Kennedy told Harriman that month that they must "seize upon any favorable moment to reduce our involvement," although that moment "might yet be some time away."

---

countries are eased." One was "ideological," the other "of a particular nationality who think that, always and under all circumstances, the Kremlin will support the Arabs and be an enemy of Israel. This group has effective means for making improvement between our countries very difficult." Gromyko presumed that Kennedy "meant the Jewish lobby." His account does not quite ring true: American supporters of Israel were more inclined to link détente with harm to the Jewish state in the 1970s than the early 1960s. Nevertheless, in the fall of 1963, Kennedy and Rusk were indeed casting about for some kind of cooperation with the Russians to keep Israel from going nuclear.

President Ngo Dinh Diem had refused to sign the July Geneva agreement on Laos, complaining that it coddled the Viet Cong and would lead to Vietnam's neutralization. Kennedy turned him around with a private assurance that Laos "will not be used for military or subversive interference in the affairs of other countries."

Khrushchev proved unwilling or unable to restrain Hanoi. Only one third of the nine thousand North Vietnamese advisers and combat troops in Laos were withdrawn. Several hundred per month slipped into South Vietnam. Harriman complained that the Geneva agreement had been broken "before the ink was dry."

After the Missile Crisis, Walt Rostow urged Bundy to consider using the strengthened American position "to induce or force the Soviet Union to honor its pledge given at Geneva that infiltration into South Vietnam via Laos would end after the Laos settlement."

By January 1963, a CIA estimate called the war "a slowly escalating stalemate." When the Army Chief of Staff, General Earle Wheeler, returned from an eight-day tour of South Vietnam, he told Kennedy that political restrictions on attacks against Communist sanctuaries in Laos and Cambodia were making "victory more remote." He and the CIA proposed "a coordinated program of sabotage, destruction, propaganda, and subversive missions against North Vietnam."

Bundy advised the President that the program would "encounter all the difficulties of an operation in a denied area, but there is agreement that it is worth trying." The Joint Chiefs that spring ordered "nonattributable" hit-and-run operations against the North. Conducted by the South Vietnamese, the attacks were supported by American "matériel, training, and advisory assistance."

As Rusk recalled, the failure of the Laos accord and Khrushchev's inability to restrain the North Vietnamese were "a bitter disappointment" to Kennedy. Both President and Secretary viewed the failure as a demonstration of Communist unwillingness to honor international agreements. In June 1963, just before Kennedy left for Europe, Rusk and McNamara proposed a sequence of covert and overt pressures that would lead to "the initiation of military action against North Vietnam."

The President approved the program's first stages. To control the approaches to Thailand and mountain trails into South Vietnam, U.S. advisers would encourage right-wing and neutralist military action against the Pathet Lao, aided by American air strikes and Special Forces units on the ground. The American Embassy in Vientiane was told that the purpose was to show the Pathet Lao that they "may no longer instigate such actions with impunity."

* * *

President Diem was fast losing the support of the South Vietnamese people. A mandarin Catholic, born in 1901, Diem had once studied for the priesthood. During World War II, he had resigned from the cabinet of the Vietnamese Emperor, Bao Dai, whom he considered "an instrument in the hands of French authorities." After the French defeat at Dien Bien Phu in 1954, Diem ran for chief of state of South Vietnam. Backed by the United States, he won a gratifying 98.2 percent of the vote.

A growing number of generals and citizens objected to what they thought to be Diem's dabbling in military matters, his authoritarian rule, cronyism, and nepotism. They hated his peremptory younger brother and principal adviser, Ngo Dinh Nhu, and Nhu's wife, an elegant tigress who demanded the substitution of Catholic stricture for traditional Buddhist laws on marriage, sex, and divorce.

Three days after Kennedy's election in 1960, a group of colonels staged an unsuccessful coup. George Carver of the CIA believed they "wanted to preempt any risk that a new Catholic American President might throw the full weight of American support" behind Diem.

In May 1963, thousands of Vietnamese gathered to celebrate Buddha's birth and protest a ban by the Diem government against the display of religious flags. As government forces broke up the crowd, seven or more Buddhists were killed. In mid-June, a Buddhist monk sat in a Saigon intersection and set himself aflame. Madame Nhu denounced the Buddhist leaders as "Communist dupes" and dismissed the suicide as a "barbecue."

Rusk worried about the perception of "a large Buddhist majority tyrannized by the Catholic minority." As a Catholic, Kennedy was not insensitive to the domestic political problem of seeming to support such persecution. In July, on his return from Europe, he asked aides, "How could this have happened? Who are these people? Why didn't we know about them before?"*

With his usual reflex of self-protection by appointment of blue-chip Republicans, Kennedy accepted the long-standing offer of his old

---

*One cannot help but note this additional instance of Kennedy's tendency to divert blame for disagreeable developments by complaining about faulty intelligence. With the Berlin Wall, the missiles in Cuba, and the Buddhist persecutions, he made a large point of complaining that he had not been sufficiently warned. As with the Wall and the missiles, he had actually been given more than enough information to know that Diem had been provoking the Buddhist majority to an extent that would undermine his regime.

Massachusetts foe Henry Cabot Lodge to serve as Ambassador to Saigon. Knowing his low private opinion of Lodge's political talents, O'Donnell, O'Brien, and Powers were shocked. He defended his choice by telling them that the idea of mixing Lodge up in such a hopeless mess as Vietnam was "irresistible."

Ngo Dinh Nhu warned South Vietnamese generals in August that the Limited Test Ban might foretell wholesale American "appeasement" of communism and that Saigon must be ready to stand alone. Diem declared martial law. Nhu's shock troops raided pagodas in five cities and arrested 1,400 Buddhist monks and nuns.

Harriman concluded that the United States could no longer support the Diem-Nhu government. On Saturday, August 24, he and Roger Hilsman, now Assistant Secretary of State for the Far East, drafted a cable to be signed by George Ball authorizing Lodge in Saigon to set the wheels in motion for a coup.

The message informed the new envoy that the "U.S. government cannot tolerate a situation in which power lies in Nhu's hands." If Diem refused to remove him and redress the Buddhist problem, "we must face the possibility that Diem himself cannot be preserved." Lodge was asked to carry this message to "key military leaders" and also to "make detailed plans as to how we might bring about Diem's replacement should this become necessary."

Harriman and Hilsman wanted to send the message immediately to prevent Nhu from strengthening his position. Rusk, McNamara, McCone, and Bundy were all out of town. When Michael Forrestal of the NSC staff read the cable by telephone to the President at Hyannis Port, Kennedy asked, "Can't we wait until Monday, when everybody is back?" Forrestal told him that Harriman and Hilsman wanted to "get this thing out right away."

Ball called Hyannis Port. The President was concerned that he might not like the leader who succeeded Diem: but "if Rusk and Gilpatric agree, George, then go ahead." Gilpatric recalled that while he was "somewhat unhappy" about the cable, he thought it a decision for State, not Defense. Rusk later said that if Ball, Harriman, and Kennedy were willing to send it, "I wasn't going to raise any questions." The message went to Saigon on Saturday night.

On Monday morning at the White House, Kennedy was astonished when McNamara, McCone, and Taylor all loudly objected to the sending of the cable. Taylor charged that an "anti-Diem group centered in State" had exploited the absence of principal officials to send out a message that would otherwise have never been approved. They did not recommend that the President embarrass himself by revoking the cable. Forrestal offered to resign and take the blame. Kennedy snapped, "You're not worth firing."

Harriman's involvement in the President's embarrassment sapped the goodwill he had accumulated with Kennedy by his Limited Test Ban success. Robert Kennedy noted that after what he called "that famous weekend," Harriman seemed to age ten years.

The Voice of America on Monday broadcast a statement, cleared by State, that the U.S. government might "sharply reduce its aid to Vietnam" unless Diem dismissed those responsible for the pagoda raids. Lodge fired off an angry cable to Washington that the broadcast had just destroyed the chance of "achieving surprise" with a generals' coup.

At a Wednesday NSC meeting, the State Department argued that the United States "must decide now to go through to a successful overthrow." Just retired from Saigon, Ambassador Frederick Nolting warned that if Diem and Nhu were jettisoned, the world would conclude that Washington had reneged on its commitments. Perhaps still smarting from the knowledge that he had blown his hard-won position with the President, Harriman excoriated Nolting's record and political judgment.

Kennedy later told Charles Bartlett, "My God, my government's coming apart!" Robert Kennedy recalled that week as "the only time, really, in three years that the government was broken in two in a disturbing way." He later said, "Diem was corrupt and a bad leader . . . but we inherited him." He thought it bad policy to "replace somebody we don't like with somebody we do because it would just make every other country nervous as can be that we were running coups in and out."

General Taylor had sent a cable to Saigon saying that "authorities are now having second thoughts" about Diem. This infuriated the President, who did not wish to appear as if he was waffling. Lodge replied, "We are launched on a course from which there is no respectable turning back: the overthrow of the Diem government. . . . There is no possibility, in my view, that the war can be won under a Diem administration." He urged an "all-out effort to get the generals to move promptly."

Kennedy cabled Lodge, "I know that failure is more destructive than an appearance of indecision. . . . When we go, we must go to win, but it will be better to change our minds than fail." He authorized Lodge to approach the coup leaders. On Saturday, August 31, General Paul Harkins, commander of the U.S. military advisers in South Vietnam, told the conspiring generals that the U.S. government would back a move against Diem. But they were mistrustful of where Washington really stood and nervous about the continuing strength of Diem loyalists. They told him that the idea was dead.

At an NSC meeting, Lyndon Johnson spoke up. During his 1961 trip to the region, he had lauded Diem as the "Winston Churchill of Southeast Asia." Now he exhorted the President to "stop playing cops and robbers," talk "straight" with Diem, and "go about winning the war."

Those in the room who opposed Diem knew that since the Missile Crisis the Vice President's meager influence on foreign policy had been evaporating. Some suspected that he might even be dismissed from the Kennedy ticket in 1964, in which case his views on Vietnam would be meaningless.

In September, the Buddhist protesters in South Vietnam were joined by students, many of them children of the urban elite on whom Diem should have been able to rely for support. Robert Kennedy interrogated McNamara and other advisers about whether the war could be won with Diem and Nhu. Forrestal suspected that the President had "stoked up" the Attorney General to "ask those unpleasant questions" on his behalf.

On Tuesday, September 10, after a thirty-six-hour visit to South Vietnam, Major General Victor Krulak reported to the President that Diem's political problems were "not great." His traveling partner, Joseph Mendenhall of State, foresaw "a large-scale movement to the Viet Cong" if at least Nhu did not go. Kennedy asked, "Did you two gentlemen visit the same country?"

Lodge cabled a recommendation for selective cuts in U.S. economic aid that would encourage the generals to act against Diem.* The President was worried that such cuts might antagonize Diem and Nhu into making some kind of quick peace with Hanoi. Since no coup seemed imminent, he opted instead for a set of gradually escalating

---

*He also suggested that Vietnam be taken up with Khrushchev, should the Chairman attend the fall UN General Assembly session. Harriman replied that there was "no current indication" that Khrushchev was coming to New York: "I doubt, in any event, that Khrushchev would be willing, given the present state of Soviet problems with the Chicoms, to discuss with a U.S. representative the Vietnam problem in realistic terms."

pressures that would force Diem to fire his brother and reform his government.

In late September, McNamara and Taylor led a ten-day mission to South Vietnam. The Secretary of Defense warned Diem of the "disturbing probability" that the war effort would be damaged by his government's "political deficiencies." Diem blamed the "vicious" American press: actually, he had been "too kind to the Buddhists." The student demonstrators were "immature, untrained, and irresponsible." He told McNamara that he was "preparing a dossier" on the Americans plotting against him.

On Wednesday, October 2, McNamara and Taylor reported to the President that the "great progress" in the military effort could be endangered by "further repressive actions by Diem and Nhu." They recommended new cuts in economic aid. The U.S. government should remain "cryptic." As the U.S. cutbacks became known, various elements of South Vietnamese society could draw their own conclusions. McNamara predicted that this would "push us toward a reconciliation with Diem or toward a coup to overthrow Diem."

Glad to be offered a Vietnam policy that most of his high officials could accept, Kennedy told the NSC that they must "all sign on" to the plan with "good heart."

In Saigon three days later, one of the anti-Diem conspirators, Major General Duong Van "Big" Minh, met with Lucein Conein of the CIA. He wanted assurance that the United States would not obstruct a coup "in the very near future."

Informed of the meeting, Washington cabled Lodge that while it did not "wish to stimulate a coup," it would not "thwart a change" or deny a new regime assistance "if it appeared capable of increasing the effectiveness of the military effort, ensuring popular support to win the war, and improving working relations with the U.S."

David Smith, chief of the CIA station in Saigon, informed McCone that one of General Minh's three contingency plans involved the assassination of Nhu and the youngest Dinh brother, Ngo Dinh Can. McCone replied that the United States "certainly cannot be in the position of stimulating, approving, or supporting assassination." Still, it was "in no way responsible for stopping every threat of which we might receive even partial knowledge."

Meeting privately with the President and Attorney General, McCone spoke in standard circumlocutory terms about Minh's plan. He told Kennedy that there was no serious alternative to Diem: "If I was manager of a baseball team and I had one pitcher, I'd keep him in the box whether he was a good pitcher or not." Assuming that Kennedy agreed with him, McCone cabled his Saigon station to tell the generals that the United States would not even discuss assassination.*

On Tuesday, October 29, Lodge cabled that a coup attempt was "imminent." The President advised that he should discourage the group unless there was "substantial possibility of quick success": "A miscalculation could result in jeopardizing the U.S. position in Southeast Asia."

Lodge replied, "Do not think we have the power to delay or discourage a coup. . . . These men are obviously prepared to risk their lives and they want nothing for themselves."

Bundy cabled back, "We do not accept as a basis for U.S. policy that we have no power to delay or discourage a coup." He instructed Lodge to reject appeals for American intervention, mediate an indecisive struggle, and offer asylum to the plotters if their attempt failed. "But once a coup under responsible leadership has begun, and within these restrictions, it should succeed."

On Friday, November 1, Lodge went to the Presidential Palace. Diem rhapsodized about the success of the war and then said, "I know there is going to be a coup, but I don't know who is going to do it." Lodge did not reply. Before he left, Diem told him, "Please tell President Kennedy that I am a good and frank ally and that I would rather be frank and settle questions now than talk about them after we have lost everything."

While Lodge was speaking with Diem, Conein brought a pistol, hand grenades, a radio, and a bag containing the South Vietnamese equivalent of $42,000 to the headquarters of the Saigon Joint General Staff. General Minh told Conein, "In case we fail, you're going with us."

The coup leaders captured the airport, radio station, and Defense Ministry. Diem called Lodge: "Some units have made a rebellion and I want to know what is the attitude of the U.S." Lodge replied that it was early morning in Washington: "The U.S. government cannot possibly have a view." He said, "If I can do anything for your physical safety, please call me."

---

*American acquiescence in the plot was never conditioned on sparing the lives of Diem and his brothers: this would have compromised Washington's effort to plausibly deny involvement in the coup.

Rebel troops captured the Presidential Palace the next day. Diem and Nhu had fled. After failing to win asylum from the Nationalist Chinese, they surrendered. The coup leaders asked Conein for a plane to fly the brothers nonstop to a distant point from which they could not try to launch a countercoup. They were told that, in the absence of preparations that would have implicated the U.S. in the coup, such a flight could not be arranged for twenty-four hours.

Diem and Nhu were hustled from a Catholic church into an armored personnel carrier. As the vehicle paused before a railroad crossing, the brothers were shot and repeatedly stabbed to death.

In the Situation Room, Kennedy was monitoring the coup when told of the murders. He rushed out of the room. Forrestal felt that the assassination "shook him personally" and "bothered him as a moral and religious matter. It shook his confidence, I think, in the kind of advice he was getting about South Vietnam."*

That fall, the President was afflicted anew by the issue of Soviet troops in Cuba. In October, Joseph Alsop reported that Khrushchev had assured Harriman in Moscow that all Soviet troops would eventually leave Cuba, adding that they disliked the steamy climate. The State Department replied that it knew of no Soviet promise that any troops would be withdrawn from Cuba beyond "a substantial number."

At an October 31 news conference, Kennedy said only that "the numbers have steadily been reduced." After a luncheon with Ohio editors a week later, he was reported as saying that he "expects nearly all of them to be out by the end of the year." Gordon Chase warned Bundy that such "overly optimistic expressions" might come back to "haunt" the President.†

---

*Eisenhower wrote Nixon, "I rather suspect the Diem affair will be shrouded in mystery for a long time to come. No matter how much the Administration may have differed with him, I cannot believe any American would have approved the cold-blooded killing of a man who had, after all, shown great courage when he undertook the task some years ago of defeating communism's attempts to take over the country."

Galbraith wrote Harriman, "The South Vietnam coup is another feather in your cap. Do get me a list of all of the people who told us there was no alternative to Diem." (The cautious Harriman told his secretary, "File and don't answer.")

†As with Kennedy's intentional public fuzziness about whether or not the Soviets had pledged not to use Cuba as a base for subversion of Latin America, his effort to suggest that Khrushchev had agreed to pull Soviet ground forces out of Cuba came back to haunt at least one later President. In August 1979, the Chairman of the Senate Foreign Relations Committee, Frank Church, Democrat of Idaho, disclosed discovery of a Soviet combat brigade on Cuba and asked President Jimmy Carter to insist on its

The Special Group had approved twenty new covert operations against Cuba for the remainder of 1963. In late October, Desmond FitzGerald met with AM/LASH. To satisfy Cubela's insistence on a meeting with Robert Kennedy, FitzGerald identified himself as a "personal representative" of the Attorney General. He said that a coup against the Cuban leader would have the full backing of the United States government.

That month, Hurricane Flora had swept across eastern Cuba. The storm killed a thousand Cubans and ravaged the region responsible for half of Cuban sugar and nearly all the island's coffee. Castro charged on television that the CIA was "stepping up its activities against Cuba in the wake of the devastation." Citing instances of infiltration, sabotage, and murder, he said, "This was the kind of aid the United States sent to Cuba after the hurricane."

Jean Daniel, editor of the French socialist *L'Observateur,* was scheduled to interview Castro. At William Attwood's request, Ben Bradlee arranged for Daniel to go to the Oval Office before he went to Havana.

On Thursday, October 24, Kennedy told him he had approved of Castro's demands for justice while fighting in the Sierra Maestra. But he was President of the United States, "not a sociologist." Castro had allowed himself to become a Soviet agent. "I know that through his fault—either his 'will to independence,' his madness, or communism—the world was on the verge of nuclear war in October 1962."

Daniel asked him what the United States expected to gain from its economic blockade of Cuba. The President said, "Are you suggesting that the political effectiveness of the blockade is uncertain? You will see when you go to Cuba whether it is or not." Continuation of the

---

"immediate withdrawal." As a junior Senator in 1962, at the behest of the Kennedy administration, Church had publicly denied Kenneth Keating's charges about missiles in Cuba. Facing a difficult reelection in 1980 (he ultimately lost), Church did not wish to be caught on the wrong side of the Cuban issue for the second time.

The Soviet brigade was probably a descendant of one of the four Soviet combat teams sent to Cuba in 1962. Still Soviet Ambassador, Anatoly Dobrynin told Secretary of State Cyrus Vance that it was not Moscow's problem if American intelligence was so incompetent that it had not spotted the troops for seventeen years. The State Department declared that ground forces did not "figure" in the American-Soviet understandings on Cuba of 1962 and 1970. Under heavy Carter administration pressure, the Soviets would pledge only to make no change in the troops' status. Souring congressional and public attitudes toward the Soviet Union, the flap delayed consideration of Carter's SALT II treaty until chances for Senate ratification were killed by the Soviet invasion of Afghanistan four months later, leading to the harsh Cold War climate of the early Reagan years.

blockade would depend on whether Castro kept up his efforts to subvert Latin America.

A week later, Attwood told Bundy that Castro's doctor and aide-de-camp, Major Rene Vallejo, had called Lisa Howard to say that Castro wanted an American official to fly from Key West to a "secret airport" near Havana.

After consulting the President, Bundy told Attwood that Kennedy wanted to "know more about what is on Castro's mind before committing ourselves to further talks on Cuba." On Monday, November 18, Attwood reached Vallejo, who told him that Castro would instruct Lechuga to discuss an agenda with him.

In Miami that same day, the President spoke to the Inter-American Press Association. Sorensen knew that the audience was "a very tough anti-Castro group." Kennedy had asked him for a speech that would open a door to the Cuban leader. He told the journalists that all that kept Cuba apart from the United States was that it was being exploited "by external powers to subvert the other American republics. . . . As long as this is true, nothing is possible. Without it, everything is possible."

Bundy told Attwood by telephone that once Attwood and Lechuga had drawn up an agenda for his visit to Havana, the President would instruct him on what to say to Castro. But first Kennedy had to visit Texas.

In early November, the Soviets resumed their harassment of ground and air traffic to Berlin. Rusk called Kohler, who was on a golfing trip in England: "You'd better get the hell back to Moscow." The Russians let an Anglo-American convoy down the Autobahn only after forty-one hours of detention.

On Thursday, November 7, at the Kremlin celebration of the forty-sixth anniversary of the Bolshevik Revolution, Khrushchev warned, "If the Americans attack Cuba, we shall attack America's allies who are even closer to the Soviet Union." He accused Western diplomats of "rejoicing that we are arguing with the Chinese" and warned the Soviet Union had greater disputes with the West: "The Chinese and we have the same future."

Foy Kohler could not believe that the euphoria over the Limited Test Ban had been only three months before. He suspected that the Berlin harassments and Khrushchev's rhetoric might be the Chairman's effort to mollify generals and other leaders apprehensive about the American détente. He asked Khrushchev, "Where is the Spirit of

Moscow? . . . I haven't heard any toasts *I* could drink to."

Looking startled, Khrushchev asked him to offer a toast. Kohler replied that it was the Chairman's party, not his. Khrushchev declared, "The Ambassador refuses to make a toast. The Spirit of Moscow is the spirit of peace with all countries who want to live with us. I drink a toast to the Spirit of Moscow. Peace for all the world!"

That afternoon, the Chairman told American businessmen visiting under the aegis of *Time* that Western intransigence was the reason for the incident in Germany: "We decided . . . to put our armored cars across the Autobahn to test your nerves and see if you would start shooting or not. And we were glad you didn't."

Chauncey Cook, president of General Foods, asked about East Germans killed while trying to cross the Berlin Wall. Khrushchev shot back, "If you start throwing hedgehogs under me, I shall throw a couple of porcupines under you. . . . In your country, children are killed in a church for the sole reason . . . that they are black instead of white."

Khrushchev complained of the slow pace of Soviet-American trade: "Businessmen go wherever they can make a profit. Well, here you can, if you want to. Perhaps someone has played a bad joke on you and told you that if you don't trade with us, we'll cease to exist. . . . We never had a war with you. Sure, there was a little trouble after our revolution, when you poked your nose into our country. But we gave you a kick in a certain place and that was the end of that!"

The Americans did not know that, at that moment, a Yale political science professor named Frederick Barghoorn was in Lubianka Prison, where he had been locked up with a copy of Dreiser's *An American Tragedy*.

On Halloween night, Barghoorn had met Kohler's deputy Walter Stoessel for drinks and was returned to the Metropole Hotel by a U.S. Embassy driver. As he walked in, a young Russian thrust a roll of old newspapers into his hands. KGB agents handcuffed him and took him away. On Tuesday, November 12, the Soviets announced that he had been "arrested as a spy."

Barghoorn had served in the Moscow Embassy with Kohler in the 1950s. A well-known Soviet expert and frequent traveler to Moscow, he had taken a Yale Russian seminar to the Soviet Union in March, reporting to Kohler on Khrushchev's "renewed campaign to bring the more independent intellectuals to heel."

Kohler cabled Rusk that Barghoorn's arrest was probably in "retaliation" for the FBI's arrest in New York two days earlier of Igor Ivanov, a Soviet undercover agent. He presumed that the Russians wanted "trading material." Years later he speculated that KGB files on Barghoorn "had not been kept up. They had had a lot on him when he was there working in the Embassy and they hadn't realized how important he'd become in the field of Soviet scholarship."

Furious about the arrest, Kennedy asked Bundy to make sure that Barghoorn was actually innocent of espionage. Richard Helms reported back that the professor had "no ties to the CIA or Army."

Kohler had earlier been asked to identify a Soviet group whose American visas could be canceled if there should be another Autobahn incident. Bundy cabled him that the President "authorizes you in your discretion" to do so now "if you consider it likely to help in showing clearly our judgment that it is wholly inappropriate to retaliate for real spies against bona fide scholars."

Kohler warned that Barghoorn had "obviously had numerous contacts with Soviet citizens" and that the "Soviets no doubt feel they can work up a case of 'espionage' which will appear plausible, at least to the Soviet audience."

He saw Zorin and Smirnovsky to express Kennedy's "grave concern" about Barghoorn's "unwarranted arrest" and complained that the Embassy had not been notified for twelve days. He cabled Washington that "Zorin, despite his past role as Soviet 'hatchet man,' was embarrassed and . . . seemed to me to lack the usual conviction." Smirnovsky was "clearly uncomfortable and appeared downcast throughout the session."

On Thursday morning, November 14, at the last press conference of his life, Kennedy twice declared that Barghoorn was "*not* on an intelligence mission of any kind": especially after the Autobahn incident, the atmosphere with Moscow had been been "badly damaged."

Kohler cabled Washington that his "initial reaction" had been to boycott a ceremony planned the next day to celebrate the thirtieth anniversary of Soviet-American diplomatic relations: "However, the meeting will of course include many well-intentioned Soviet citizens with whom we will wish to maintain future contacts, since we must continue to operate in this society." He sent one mid-level officer.

At Saturday noon, Gromyko called in Kohler and said that Khrushchev had "personally" decided to expel Barghoorn from the Soviet Union in response to Kennedy's "deep concern," expressed at his news conference. The Soviets now had the "expectation" that Ivanov would also be released. If the U.S. government should try to "publicly justify" Barghoorn's conduct and thus cast doubt on his arrest, the Soviet Union would publish the results of its "investigation." Barghoorn was released the next day.

The Soviet defector Yuri Nosenko later told American authorities that General Oleg Gribanov of the KGB had asked him to locate a potential American hostage who could be traded for Ivanov. He had suggested Barghoorn: the professor had served in the State Department and accepted grants from American foundations that could be portrayed as having intelligence connections. Gribanov had beamed: "It's clear. He's a spy."

With Khrushchev away from Moscow, the KGB chief, Vladimir Semichastny, had called Brezhnev, who approved the plan. Brezhnev may not have comprehended how the arrest would poison American relations. Even if he did, he and his collaborators were unlikely to be troubled by the prospect of undermining Khrushchev's détente.

By Nosenko's recollection, the Chairman was "stunned" to hear of Kennedy's personal indignation about Barghoorn: he asked what idiot had authorized this mad venture. Semichastny pointed to Brezhnev, who, by Nosenko's account, said, "Oh, no! They didn't tell me he was a friend of Kennedy's. I did not approve such a thing."

After Barghoorn's release, Walter Stoessel cabled Bundy, "I would think it prudent . . . if at all possible, to confine our public comment to a brief statement that we welcome the action of the Soviet government in removing a major irritant in U.S.-Soviet relations. . . . I would hope, in any case, we could refrain from any 'chest-beating' or intimation that the Soviets had knuckled under." The President asked Thompson to quietly inform Dobrynin that he appreciated Khrushchev's personal intervention in the case.

On Thursday, November 21, Thompson reported back that Dobrynin had "said he would transmit the message, but made no comment other than to express surprise at the amount of the reaction here. I indicated to him that we had taken some action to try to keep this from getting out of hand but did say that this affair had been far from helpful in our relations." This message was transmitted to the President in Texas.

Kennedy and Khrushchev had not directly corresponded since early October. On Thursday, October 10, after the Chairman signed the Limited Test Ban treaty at the Kremlin, Zorin had handed Kohler a letter from Khrushchev to the President suggesting that they seek solutions to other "ripe" issues such as Berlin, nuclear proliferation, bombs in orbit, and the fear of surprise attack.

Ten days later, the State Department sent Bundy a draft reply saying, "I am convinced then that the possibilities for an improvement in the international situation are real. . . . These opportunities, however, are still fragile ones, and we must be constantly on guard to move forward, lest our hopes of progress be jeopardized." After the President read the draft, Bundy scrawled, "Approved. Let's get it out."

Later, Bundy was informed that "due to clerical misunderstanding in the State Department," the President's reply to Khrushchev was never sent. Had Kennedy learned of the error, the air of the Oval Office would have rocked with epithets about bureaucratic incompetence. But the President never found out, because Bundy was not told that the letter had gone unsent until December 1963.

Waiting in Moscow for Kennedy's reply, Khrushchev might have wondered why Kennedy had not responded to his cordial letter about new opportunities for peace. As the weeks passed in silence, his dark imagination may have begun to take over: was the President about to turn his back on their emerging détente? The proud, vulnerable, ever-anxious Chairman refused to be the first to break the silence. This was how the private correspondence between Kennedy and Khrushchev died.

CHAPTER

23

"Now Peace Is Up to You"

ALL AUTUMN IT HAD BEEN COLD AND RAINY IN WASHINGTON. AS Robert Kennedy recalled, by mid-November 1963, his brother was feeling "rather gloomy." One reason for the President's melancholy may have been that the bloom seemed to be fading from the rose of rapprochement with the Soviet Union.

Another source of gloom was Vietnam. As Kennedy had feared, the coup in Saigon was producing more turmoil. Soon he would have to decide how far the United States would go to defend South Vietnam. Still another source was the prospect of running for reelection against the John Birch Society and millions of others who were seething over civil rights and the Soviet détente.

Nowhere was the hatred more intense than in Texas, where the President was to make a "nonpolitical" tour. Whatever its billing, the trip's main purpose was to raise campaign money and resolve a bitter feud between the state's two senior Democrats, the conservative Governor John Connally and the liberal Senator Ralph Yarborough. Kennedy feared that the feud between the two men might harm his chances to win the state in 1964.

From Dallas, the President was to fly to a Democratic fund-raising dinner in Austin, where he would be introduced by his Vice President. Defensive about the second largest city in his home state, Johnson remembered that Stevenson had been spat upon during an October visit. He told aides that he intended to open his speech with a joke: "Mr. President, thank God you made it out of Dallas alive!"

Kennedy spent the last weekend of his life at Palm Beach with his Harvard friend Torbert Macdonald, with whom he had dined at the Carlyle on the eve of the Missile Crisis. Macdonald recalled, "It was like being back in 1939, when there was nothing of moment on anybody's mind."

Bundy sent the President weekend reading: "A paper showing the German military mind at work. . . . Zbigniew Brzezinski meets the press, and I think you may find it more interesting in that it shows a somewhat more balanced view than some other remarks of his. . . . George Ball's views on the handling of less developed countries. . . . A good summary of the situation in Yemen. . . . The joys of public celebration in Indonesia."

On Saturday morning, Kennedy and Macdonald flew to Cape Canaveral and joined Lyndon Johnson to watch a Polaris missile firing. Returned to Palm Beach the next day, the President bet his chum that the Chicago Bears would defeat the Green Bay Packers and collected his money after they watched the victory on television. That evening, they screened the new film of Henry Fielding's bawdy classic *Tom Jones.*

Before Kennedy's Florida trip, the FBI and Secret Service had received information that anti-Castro exiles might erupt in violence against him. During the Canaveral visit, the President had ordered a Secret Service agent to "keep those Ivy League charlatans off the back of the car." This was the same occasion on which he overruled the agents and told his Vice President to "get in my plane," laughingly asking, "Don't you fellows want McCormack as President?"

On Monday, Kennedy returned to Washington on *Air Force One.* His back hurt. Lying on his stateroom bed, he summoned George Smathers from the front of the plane: "God, I wish you could think of some way of getting me out of going to Texas. . . . Look how screwed up it's going to be. You've got Lyndon, who is insisting that Jackie ride with him. You've got Ralph Yarborough, who hates Lyndon, and

Johnson doesn't want Yarborough with him. Connally is the Governor.

"They're all prima donnas of the biggest order, and they're all insisting that they ride either with me or with Jackie. The law says the Vice President can't ride with the President. I've got to start off my speech by saying what a fine guy Johnson is, then what a fine guy Connally is, and then Yarborough, and they all don't like each other. I just wish to hell I didn't have to go. Can't you think of some emergency we could have?"

Smathers reminded him how the Vice President was looking forward to entertaining the President and First Lady at the LBJ Ranch at the end of the trip: "Even if you declared war, Johnson would never forgive you if you didn't go."

He recalled going with Kennedy to the ranch after the 1960 election. Johnson had roused Kennedy before dawn, after which he gave him a high-powered rifle and took him off in his white Cadillac. When a deer sauntered by, Johnson cried out, "Shoot! Shoot!" Kennedy used his rifle and rushed back to the car, trying to put the "defenseless beautiful deer" out of his mind. He later carped to Smathers, "That will never be a sport until they give the deer a gun."*

On Tuesday, November 19, Bundy dropped by the Oval Office before flying with McNamara to Honolulu for a meeting on Vietnam. John, Jr., gave Bundy a mock serving of what he called his "cherry vanilla pie." Bundy pronounced it "delicious" and said farewell to his boss.

That afternoon, Richard Helms and a CIA Latin America expert named Hershel Peake called on Robert Kennedy. As Helms recalled, "We had been for a long time looking for hard evidence that the Cubans were exporting revolution to Latin America."

Now his men had discovered a three-ton Cuban arms cache left by terrorists on a Venezuelan beach, as well as blueprints for a coup against President Romulo Betancourt, whom Castro reviled as a "bourgeois liberal." Starting with the strangulation of Caracas auto traffic, the plan was to seize control of Venezuela by halting the national elections scheduled for the first of December. So far, no American officials knew about the new evidence except for the CIA.

---

*After the Inauguration, Johnson had presented him with the deer's mounted head and insisted that it go on the Oval Office wall. In a gesture that was a more gallant concession than the Vice President ever knew, Kennedy installed the trophy in a nearby room.

Helms knew that in response to the evidence Kennedy "wasn't going to invade Cuba, for goddamn sure." He presumed that any efforts the President was making for an accommodation with Castro were at best "a feint": "Like most two-track policies, try everything." He was certain that the administration's "real energy" on Cuba was going into covert action.

Helms had brought Peake to provide technical details that would help him to make "an undeniable case." He told the Attorney General, "You told me that the reason the President wasn't pressing Castro any more aggressively was the lack of hard evidence. Well, here it is." Helms produced one of the rifles from the arms cache. As he later recalled, Robert "didn't fight me about it." Instead he called the President and said, "I'm going to send these guys over."

The two CIA men went to the West Wing and waited in the Cabinet Room, leaving on the long table the briefcase containing what Helms recalled as "this vicious-looking weapon." At 6:15 P.M., they handed Kennedy the rifle. As the President scrutinized it, Helms showed him how its Cuban coat-of-arms had been sanded off.

At his press conference exactly one year ago tomorrow, Kennedy had settled the Missile Crisis by pledging peace in the Caribbean "if all offensive weapons systems are removed from Cuba" and "if Cuba is not used for the export of aggressive Communist purposes." When they learned of this evidence showing that Cuba was being used to export communism, would his Republican critics demand that he disturb the peace in the Caribbean?

They were likely to press for fresh belligerent action against Cuba, perhaps renewal of the naval blockade, which would further sour the new relationship with Moscow. Kennedy knew that if he did nothing, word of the evidence from Venezuela would almost certainly be leaked to the press. With the election year one month away, his critics would demand to know why he was allowing Khrushchev to welsh on his promises without penalty.

The President was not about to discuss such political matters with the chief of covert operations. He let Helms see nothing but delight that the CIA had found evidence of Castro's malign intentions for Latin America. He reminded Helms that he was leaving soon for Texas: "Great work. Be sure to have complete information for me when I get back from my trip. I think maybe we've got him now."

* * *

On Wednesday, November 20, visiting his old political base in Kiev, Khrushchev received the Danish Foreign Minister, Per Haekkerup, who gave him a teak and black leather rocking chair and said he hoped that the Chairman would rock in the "same rhythm" as President Kennedy.

Khrushchev laughed; rocking in the same rhythm was "important." Turning solemn, he warned that the West had underestimated the seriousness of the Autobahn incidents in early November: the Soviet position on Berlin was "very firm."

That morning in the Oval Office, Kennedy greeted three high school students from West Berlin. Dillon called him to warn that the Soviet wheat deal was stirring up hornets on Capitol Hill. A letter arrived from Professor Barghoorn: "I am personally convinced that it was only because of your vigorous action that I was released."

Sorensen brought in two copies of the speech the President would give at the Trade Mart in Dallas. With his sense of drama that rivaled his wife's, he liked the idea of being Daniel in the lion's den. Donning reading glasses, Kennedy sat in his rocking chair and read Sorensen's text, which criticized voices "wholly unsuited to the sixties" which assumed "that vituperation is as good as victory and peace is a sign of weakness."

He called in Michael Forrestal: "I want you to organize an in-depth study of every possible option we've got in Vietnam, including how to get out of there. We have to review this whole thing from the bottom to the top."

That evening, he and Jacqueline held their annual reception for the Supreme Court and other members of the judiciary. Since the death of their infant son, she had eschewed Washington, planning to re-emerge at a state dinner for the new West German Chancellor, Ludwig Erhard, on Monday night, November 25. But after a telephone call from her husband, she hastened back by chopper from Wexford, their new country place near Middleburg, to help him greet the seven hundred guests.

After performing as host, the President went to his office to look at cable traffic and then took the elevator to the family quarters. The Attorney General stopped by, just back from New York, where he had attended the premiere of the film *It's a Mad, Mad, Mad, Mad World.* Later that evening at Hickory Hill, he and dozens of friends would celebrate his thirty-eighth birthday.

The President told him that the political fights would make the Texas trip "more interesting." But as Robert recalled, he complained of "how irritated he was with Lyndon Johnson, who wouldn't help at all in trying to iron out any of the problems in Texas, and that he was an S.O.B."

Another reason for Kennedy's anger was his suspicion that Johnson was promoting himself for 1968 at his expense. The President had hoped that, as in 1960, Johnson would bring him the votes of Southerners who found Kennedy too liberal. Instead, the Vice President was speaking out for civil rights more than he ever had as a Senator from Texas.

Kennedy privately spoke of replacing Johnson with another Southerner, perhaps Governor Terry Sanford of North Carolina. While he might never have followed through on this threat, he knew that if Johnson felt he was in trouble, he might be more inclined to toe the President's line in the months to come.*

That evening Kennedy reminded George Ball by telephone that Henry Cabot Lodge was flying back from Saigon to discuss the future course of American involvement in Vietnam. "I'll be back from Texas Sunday. Come out to Camp David. Cabot Lodge will be there and we can go over these things."

At Thursday noon, November 21, the President and First Lady flew to Texas. Sitting in his compact airborne office, Kennedy riffled through briefing books on the Erhard visit. He told O'Donnell and Powers, "You two guys aren't running out on me and leaving me stranded with poor Jackie at Lyndon's ranch. If I've got to hang around there all day Saturday, wearing one of those big cowboy hats, you've got to be there too."

At the Rice Hotel in Houston, the President confronted his Vice President about his hostility to Yarborough and his failure to help resolve the Connally feud. As usual, Johnson controlled himself in Kennedy's presence but, as someone noticed, he "left that suite like a pistol." Jacqueline asked, "What was that all about? He seemed mad." The President said, "That's just Lyndon. He's in trouble." He later told her that Johnson was "incapable of telling the truth."†

---

*As Robert Kennedy recalled, "They took a poll down in Texas, and Lyndon Johnson lost a great deal of his popularity . . . in the South and was a burden rather than a help." John Connally years later recalled that Johnson was "very concerned" that the Attorney General would persuade his brother to dump him from the ticket: the Vice President implored him to make sure that Texas was "in line" for 1964.

†Of this meeting, Arthur Schlesinger later wrote in his notes, "Johnson's st[oc]k was never lower—and he knew it."

That evening, Schlesinger viewed *From Russia with Love* in the White House theater. Sorensen predicted that the President would enjoy it. He did not know that Kennedy had already seen the film in October with Ben Bradlee, who had noted that he "seemed to enjoy the cool and the sex and the brutality."

On Friday morning, November 22, Kennedy walked out of the Hotel Texas in Fort Worth to address a rally across the street. In 1960, he had pledged a United States that was not first *if* but "first period." Now he spoke in the cadences he expected to use in 1964. His administration had built "a defense system second to none." The United States was "stronger than it has ever been in its history."

Sounding like Khrushchev, he boasted about space and economics: "In December—next month—the United States will fire the largest booster in the history of the world, putting us ahead of the Soviet Union in that area for the first time in our history. . . . In 1962 and the first six months of 1963, the economy of the United States grew not only faster than nearly every Western country—which had not been true in the fifties—but also grew faster than the Soviet Union itself."

At a Chamber of Commerce breakfast, he reminded his audience that the Pentagon was using planes and helicopters built in Fort Worth: "So wherever the confrontation may occur—and in the last three years it has occurred on at least three occasions: in Laos, Berlin, and Cuba; and it will again—wherever it occurs, the products . . . and the men of Fort Worth provide us with a sense of security. . . .

"I am confident, as I look to the future, that our chances for security, our chances for peace, are better than they have been in the past. And the reason is because we are stronger. And with that strength is a determination to not only maintain the peace, but also the vital interests of the United States. To that great cause, Texas and the United States are committed. Thank you."

He returned to his hotel suite and read a full-page advertisement in the *Dallas Morning News:* WELCOME MR. KENNEDY TO DALLAS. It asked why he had allowed "thousands of Cubans" to be jailed and wheat sold to those who were killing Americans in Vietnam: "Why have you scrapped the Monroe Doctrine in favor of the Spirit of Moscow? . . . Mr. Kennedy, we DEMAND answers to these questions and we want them now."

Jacqueline felt sick. Her husband shook his head: "We're heading into nut country today." Pacing the room, he said, "You know, last night would have been a hell of a night to assassinate a President. . . . There was the rain and the night, and we were all getting jostled. Suppose a man had a pistol in a briefcase."

She thought the fantasy an expression of her husband's "Walter Mitty streak," his way of shaking off the ad. She recalled that everywhere she had ever traveled with him, he had been bathed in affection. She could not even imagine someone throwing a tomato at him.

During the flight to Dallas, Kennedy asked O'Donnell, "What kind of journalism do you call the *Dallas Morning News*? You know who's responsible for that ad? Dealey. Remember him? After that exhibition he put on in the White House, I did a little checking on him. He runs around calling himself a war correspondent, and everybody in Dallas believes him."

In the President's morning *Intelligence Checklist* were situation estimates on Saigon, Cyprus, and Korea, reports on Vietnam casualties and on Khrushchev's warning in Kiev that the Soviet position on Berlin was "very firm." To buoy the President's spirits in this month of troubles, one of the CIA analysts had included the bullfighter's verse that the President had recited at State on October 16, 1962, just after he was told about the missiles in Cuba:

> *Bullfight critics ranked in rows*
> *Crowd the enormous Plaza full;*
> *But only one is there who knows,*
> *And he's the man who fights the bull.*

Dean Rusk, five Cabinet colleagues, and Salinger were flying from Honolulu to Tokyo, where they were to arrange a presidential trip to Japan for early 1964. Bundy and McNamara were at the Pentagon working on the 1965 military budget for presentation to the President at Hyannis Port on the day after Thanksgiving.

Robert Kennedy had driven home for luncheon after a meeting about his war against organized crime. At State, George Ball was discussing the Soviet wheat deal by telephone with a Treasury official. At the Metropolitan Club, Llewellyn Thompson was lunching with Dean Acheson. In Moscow, Foy and Phyllis Kohler were dining at Spaso House.

At CIA headquarters in Langley, Richard Helms was sitting down to luncheon with John McCone. All morning, they had answered questions from watchdog members of the President's intelligence oversight board. Now the grilling was over and they could unwind.

The two men and several colleagues took their meal in a small room next to the Director's office that McCone called the "French Room," perhaps in honor of a friendly intelligence service. Furnished with a round table, television, and easy chairs, the chamber was one of a maze of holding rooms designed by Allen Dulles so that visitors who did not wish to encounter one another did not risk doing so.

A door flew open. McCone's aide Walter Elder cried out, *"President Kennedy has been shot!"*

Someone turned on a television set. McCone cried, "My Lord! I must get over and see Bob." Despite their quarrels over Cuba and the test ban, he remembered how Robert and Ethel had looked after him upon the death of his first wife. He convened the CIA's emergency Watch Committee and ordered himself driven to Hickory Hill.

Helms recalled, "We all went to battle stations over the possibility that this might be a plot—and who was pulling the strings. We were very busy sending messages all over the world to pick up anything that might indicate that a conspiracy had been formed to kill the President of the United States—and then what was to come next."

CIA men were staggered to learn that they could not locate Nikita Khrushchev. They agonized over every imaginable conspiracy. Could there be a plot, perhaps by the Chinese, to murder the leaders of both superpowers? Was the Soviet leader staying away from Moscow in anticipation of an American nuclear strike in revenge for a Soviet plot against the President?

"We were very high in tension about any indicators which would support such a theme," recalled Helms. "So if Khrushchev was missing from Moscow, we were worried about it."

At Parkland Memorial Hospital in Dallas, Secret Service agents sequestered Lyndon Johnson as doctors labored over the dying President. "In that little clinic where they hid me, I was scared," Johnson recalled. "They were telling me that it could be a massive plot to kill the whole structure of government."

When McCone walked into Robert Kennedy's upstairs library at Hickory Hill, the Attorney General was anchoring his tie with a PT-109 tie clip, preparing to rush to Andrews and an Air Force plane for Dallas. Then the White House telephone rang. Robert said, "He had the most wonderful life." Later: "God, it's so awful. Everything was really beginning to run so well."

His principal mission since John Kennedy's first Senate campaign had been the advancement of his brother's career. Now the assignment had instantly shifted to his brother's legacy. Even as he reeled from the Dallas news, he had the presence of mind to call Bundy and ask whether the personal letters and papers of a President who died in office belonged to his relatives.

Bundy obtained an affirmative opinion from the State Department and ordered that the combinations on the safes containing John Kennedy's private files be changed immediately.

In Dallas, the new President was sped through red lights to the Dallas airport, Love Field. In the Secret Service's haste to get Johnson out of Dallas, he was separated from General Clifton and the "bagman" carrying the satchel with coded instructions for nuclear attack.

If the Soviet Union now sent missiles and bombers across the DEW Line, it would have taken the two men at least thirty minutes to reach the President. An officer at the White House switchboard in Dallas informed the Pentagon that McNamara and the Joint Chiefs "are now the President."

Over the Pacific, Rusk announced Kennedy's death over the sound system of the Cabinet plane: "May God help our country." As others sobbed, he ordered the jet to turn around and fly to Washington. Sealed in a tube thirty-five thousand feet high while his country was in trauma, he had never felt so helpless. He wondered aloud "who has his finger on the nuclear button." The consensus aboard the plane was that the assassination was "the opening shot of a plot."

At the Pentagon, General Taylor agonized over the fact that Johnson knew so little about what was in the satchel. On becoming Vice President, he had inexplicably refused to be briefed on its contents.* If an emergency was imminent, the U.S. nuclear arsenal would have had to be put on hold while the new President was led through the documents for the first time.

Llewellyn Thompson first dismissed the news from Dallas as a bad joke. Then he left Acheson to brood over Johnson's sparse knowledge of foreign affairs and the Soviet Union. He recalled how the dead President had "drained me dry of all I knew. And on the rare occasions when there was a difference of opinion between us, he was right and I was wrong." That evening he told Jane, "It was too good to be true."

In Paris, Chip Bohlen felt "as though the future had retreated to the present:" "There was an unknown quality about Kennedy, despite

---

*Under Eisenhower, Richard Nixon was fully briefed.

all his realism, that gave you infinite hope that somehow or other he was going to change the course of history."

As *Air Force One* flew to Washington bearing the thirty-fifth and thirty-sixth Presidents, the skies of the southeastern United States were scanned for "unidentified, unfriendly" aircraft. Johnson was appalled to be reminded that six Cabinet members were over the Pacific. A member of the press pool, Charles Roberts of *Newsweek,* wondered, *Will the Russians do anything while we're in the air during this two-hour flight?*

Before midnight in Moscow, Andrei Gromyko was given a TASS report on Dallas. He instantly thought of his final conversation with Kennedy just the previous month. He called Kohler at Spaso House, where a night duty officer had "bowled over" the Ambassador and his wife by bringing the news to their bedroom. Gromyko told him that his government would express condolences "at the highest level."

In Washington, the Secret Service urgently asked the State Department if it had a file on one Lee Harvey Oswald, an ex-Marine who had defected to the Soviet Union, married a Russian, and returned to the United States in 1962. George Ball ordered up the large dossier. U. Alexis Johnson approved an investigation "to see if our handling of the case had been OK."

They wondered whether the assassination had been ordered by the Kremlin. Thompson told them Communists did not work this way: the Russians might kill defectors but not chiefs of state. They would never set a precedent that might be awkward for them. Harriman agreed. Alex Johnson observed that Americans might react to Oswald's professed Marxism by undoing all of Kennedy's careful work for détente.

On the Cabinet plane, Rusk read teletype copy on Oswald's ties to the Soviet Union: "If this is true, it is going to have repercussions around the world for years to come."

In Paris, AM/LASH had been meeting with a CIA case officer, who had just given him a ballpoint pen containing a poison needle destined for Castro. Cubela thought the pen fit for an amateur. He told the CIA man that he was more interested in rifles with telescopic sights and explosives from which Castro could be killed from a distance. After the thunderbolt from Dallas, the two men adjourned.*

---

*Years later Bundy, who insisted that Kennedy never authorized the CIA to kill Castro, said, "We thought . . . that the CIA at least after the Bay of Pigs was a disciplined part

* * *

At the Pentagon, Robert Kennedy told Ed Guthman, "People just don't realize how conservative Lyndon really is. There are going to be a lot of changes." He and Taylor and McNamara took a helicopter to Andrews.

Landing in the dark at about five-thirty, Robert saw a crowd of newsmen and Washington officials gathering there to welcome his brother home. He wished to avoid the crowd but also to be at Jacqueline's side as soon as possible. He found a deserted Air Force truck, jumped over the tailgate, and sat there among pieces of military equipment.

Suddenly he remembered the last time he had been at this spot—at Saturday noon, October 20, 1962, when Jack had returned with his "cold" from Chicago. It struck him that then he had been standing on the airstrip, waiting for his brother; now he was crouching in the back of a truck.

At the White House, before a wall-sized screen in the Situation Room, gimlet-eyed staff members were mesmerized by a network broadcast of videotaped highlights of the Kennedy Presidency. The slender young man on the screen was shouting to a million shrieking Germans, *"Ich bin ein Berliner!"*

Aboard *Air Force One,* O'Donnell seized another Kennedy man by the arm and pointed at the broad shoulderblades of Lyndon Johnson: "He's got what he wants now. But we take it back in '68."

The new President was met at Andrews by Bundy, Ball, and McNamara, with whom he boarded an Army helicopter, saying, "It was an awful thing. . . . Horrible. . . . That little woman was brave. . . . Who would have thought this could happen? . . . You fellows know I never aspired to this. . . . Kennedy could do things I know I couldn't."

In his congressional manner he asked, "Any important matters pending?" There were none. McNamara described the Pentagon's worldwide alert; if the assassination proved to be the prelude to an enemy attack, the United States would be ready with an overwhelming counterstrike.

After landing on the South Grounds, Bundy walked with Johnson

---

of the Executive." He blamed the Cubela incident on "outrageous insubordination. . . . It was loose management, the worst single result of an administrative untidiness that in some other contexts was enormously constructive."

toward the West Wing: "There are two things I am assuming, Mr. President. One is that everything in locked files before two P.M. today belongs to the President's family, and the other is that Mrs. Kennedy will handle the funeral arrangements." Johnson replied, "That's correct."

The sirens of Washington wailed through the night. Dillon had trouble sleeping. Bundy could not put out of his head the German word *Unsinn*—absurdity. Later he wrote in his journal that the "real sadness" was "not at predictable moments—but whenever one got hit at some unguarded opening by a fresh thought of loss and change. I remember such starts in passing the Rose Garden, in coming to the elevator to the second floor, in admiring the new red rug in his office which he never got to see."

At the White House, Schlesinger encountered Adlai Stevenson, who had flown down from New York. In 1952, the Harvard historian had written speeches for the Democratic nominee. Tonight he noticed that Stevenson's "glee at Kennedy's murder could not be suppressed. There was a smile on his face. It was a half smile. I was just sick at heart that night. I loved Stevenson, but I never felt the same way about him after that."

In West Berlin, people carried blazing torches through dark streets. The city hall square was renamed John F. Kennedy Platz. In Paris, Charles de Gaulle said, "I am stunned. They are crying all over France. It is as though he were a Frenchman, a member of their own family." Retired from office, Harold Macmillan remembered the "splendid, young, gay figure" in June stepping from the helicopter in Sussex.

Kennedy's enemies were not silent. Peking schoolchildren applauded when told of the assassination.* A Chinese editorial cartoon showed the President lying on his face, his necktie stamped with dollar signs: KENNEDY BITING THE DUST. Madame Nhu declared, "The chickens have come home to roost" and wrote to Jacqueline Kennedy, "Extreme graciousness with communism does not protect from its tortuous blows."

Called in Kiev by Gromyko, Khrushchev burst into tears. He was further staggered to learn that the President had been killed in the

---

*As they did in more than one school in Dallas.

presence of his wife and that she had been "sullied" by her husband's blood.

Adzhubei recalled the day as a "personal tragedy" for Khrushchev: "He didn't know the history of America, of course, because he was not very well educated, but he knew that in the U.S. when it happened, it wasn't for the first time. It was a shock."

The Chairman realized that his absence from Moscow would fuel American suspicions. At a time of such uncertainty, he should not remain away from his capital. In light of his current problems with China, his conspiratorial bent may have led him to wonder whether Kennedy's murder was part of a plot against both leaders working for a Soviet-American détente. He boarded a special all-night train back to Moscow.

Shocked by news of Oswald's Soviet connections, Soviet officials feared that the Soviet Union was about to be blamed for the assassination. The Russians knew Lyndon Johnson as an emotional Texan and more thoroughgoing Cold Warrior than Kennedy; might the new President retaliate in some way?

Soviet troops around the world were placed in readiness. Soviet intelligence agents were sent out to question anyone who might have known Oswald in the Soviet Union. The Foreign Ministry was told to be "vigilantly circumspect" and "report anything, no matter how small." During Johnson's first hours in office, the Soviet government evidently received a private assurance from the new President that there would be no reprisals.

From the moment of Kennedy's death, the Soviet press exerted itself to prove that the assassination had been inspired not by Communists but the American Right. Not only would this divert suspicions from Moscow, but if the American people blamed ultraconservatives for their President's murder, it would undermine the Right's ability to jeopardize American-Soviet relations.

TASS reported, "From the moment of Kennedy's arrival in Dallas, small groups of ultra-right-wing elements had demonstrated in different sections of the city under Confederate flags and slogans hostile to Kennedy. . . . In the speech President Kennedy was scheduled to deliver at luncheon, the text of which was found in his pocket, he denounced his ultraconservative opponents."

Izvestia: "All the circumstances of President Kennedy's tragic death give grounds for believing that the assassination was conceived and executed by ultra-right-wing fascist and racist circles . . . displeased by any step aimed at relaxing international tension and improving Soviet-American relations."

Pravda ran a large front-page photograph of the late President. As if the Berlin and Cuba confrontations had never happened, *Pravda* noted "Kennedy's steps toward cleansing the international situation" and how they had "met with sharp attacks from American 'madmen.'" Soviet radio played Slavic funeral dirges. Soviet television aired film of the Inaugural Address and the American University address.

On Moscow streets, Soviet citizens praised Kennedy for the Limited Test Ban and the wheat sale. An elderly woman said, "He was so young! Those wretches! In his own country! Wasn't he protected?" Another Muscovite: "Here was a man who tried to do good and they would not let him live."

Fidel Castro had been lunching with Jean Daniel at Varadero when told that the President was wounded. He said that if Kennedy could be saved, he was "already reelected." Major Vallejo tuned in a Miami radio station and translated the English words: "Wounded in the head . . . pursuit of the assassin. . . . President Kennedy is dead." Castro rose: "Everything is going to change. . . . At least Kennedy was an enemy to whom we had become accustomed."

After twenty minutes, he said, "They will have to find the assassin quickly, but very quickly. Otherwise you watch and see—I know them—they will try to put the blame on us for this thing." Driving away, he and Daniel heard on the car radio that the suspected assassin was married to a Russian. Castro said, "There, didn't I tell you? It'll be my turn next."

The radio announced that the suspect was a Castro admirer and member of the Fair Play for Cuba Committee. Castro said, "If they had proof, they would have said he was an agent, an accomplice, a hired killer. In saying simply that he is an admirer, this is just to try and make an association in people's minds between the name of Castro and the emotion awakened by the assassination."

Castro canceled his engagements. Like the Russians, he worried that the United States might now use the excuse of Oswald's admiration for him as a pretext—in his case, for the air strike and invasion so long sought by the CIA and the Pentagon.

He went on television to insist that he was not behind the assassination: despite Kennedy's "hostile policies toward us," the news of his death was "grave and bad." The information about Oswald was "a Machiavellian plan against Cuba. Oswald never had contacts with us. . . . But in the dispatches he's always presented as a pro-Castro Communist. This is all part of a defamatory campaign against the U.S.S.R. and Cuba. . . . What is behind this assassination no one knows."

* * *

On Saturday morning, November 23, Kohler convened his staff to reminisce about the late President. The Foreign Ministry called to say that Khrushchev was coming to Spaso House. Shortly after noon, the red-eyed Chairman started up the stairs, followed by Gromyko and Smirnovsky. Even the stone-faced Foreign Minister had tears in his eyes.

Kohler took Khrushchev by the arm to a small table bearing a condolence book and a black-draped photograph of the late President inscribed to Kohler. A Marine stood at attention beside the table. The Chairman and Kohler did not say a word. The only sound in the room was the whirring of newsreel cameras. The Chairman put on his gold-rimmed spectacles and bent over to sign the book. Still silent, he posed for pictures with the Ambassador and their aides.

Then Kohler took his guest into a parlor with fireplace called the Fawn Room. As he recalled, "Khrushchev did all of the talking." The Chairman took pains to demonstrate that the Soviet Union had nothing to do with Kennedy's death. He told Kohler that his government had always deplored assassinations. The Mensheviks and Black Hunters had been the assassins in Russia—not the Bolsheviks. The Bolsheviks, he said, had not favored political murder.

After he briefly reminisced about Kennedy at Vienna, Khrushchev and his entourage returned to their black limousines. Later that day, the Chairman wrote Lyndon Johnson that the "villainous assassination" was a "heavy blow." Gromyko wrote Rusk that the "best monument to the deceased" would be to continue their efforts to ease world tension begun with the Limited Test Ban that Kennedy had "evaluated highly."

Bundles of letters from Soviet citizens delivered to the U.S. Embassy broke through the arid language of diplomacy. One Comrade Babitchev wrote Johnson, "I am sure that you will continue the course of the late Mr. Kennedy who was so dear to all of us. His great deeds will live forever! . . . Death to the villainous butchers!!"

A Kharkov student wrote, "Let the American people be merciless and severe in the punishment of the assassins, who wish to sabotage the cause of peace between our people." Tatyana and Yevgenya Shcherbakov of Bryansk wrote, "Let the thought that the grief is shared by one hundred million Russian women help Mrs. Kennedy to survive her grief."

Vladimir Abrosichkin of Moscow sent Kohler a poem about the "villainous act of the mad reactionaries":

> He was endeavoring to meet us.
> He was searching a way to secure peace.
> The darkness of death has stopped his marching.
>
> The lowered flags are silent.
> The President's throne has been rocking.
> A flock of black crows whirls over Washington.
>
> Terror and blackmail are in the order of things in that country,
> Where money is law, power, and force.
> Shame, America! You keep silent while they kill your sons.

A Muscovite named Lazarev sent more verse:

> Chairman Khrushchev stood silent for minutes. . . .
> He stood for us, the Russians.
> The eagle's pinions have wilted.
> Damn the assassin, who took away his life!
> All people's friend is lost.
> The star's light has faded.
> We see him off on his last journey.
> Americans! Do find another one to substitute for him,
> And let it be a new Lincoln.

On Sunday afternoon, November 24, Lyndon Johnson kept the dead President's appointment with Lodge and told him that he was not willing to "lose Vietnam": "Tell those generals in Saigon that Lyndon Johnson intends to stand by our word."

When Lee Harvey Oswald was shot to death, Thompson considered it a diplomatic catastrophe— "just as the funeral was about to restore our foreign image." *Pravda* asked, "Who led Ruby to the jail that was so carefully guarded? . . . There can only be one answer: It was done by the same people who prepared and committed the infamous assassination of the President, the same 'ultras' who are now trying to put the blame . . . on American Communists and . . . the Fair Play for Cuba Committee."

When Kennedy's British friend Henry Brandon, of the *Sunday Times*, went to the Soviet Union a month later, he was startled to find the mourning was "almost more intense in Moscow than in Washington." Time and time again he was asked, "Do you think Johnson organized the assassination?"

Khrushchev had first thought of sending Gromyko to Kennedy's funeral but concluded that sending Mikoyan would make a stronger statement. On Monday, before the Washington ceremonies, Dillon was "scared to death that Mikoyan might be shot at."

At Rusk's request, Thompson insisted to the Soviet Embassy that Mikoyan had excellent reasons not to walk in the funeral parade: age, his recovery from surgery, and hepatitis. But the Armenian insisted on walking with de Gaulle* and other world leaders behind the coffin. In Moscow, a tearful Nina Khrushchev led members of the Soviet-American Friendship Society to Spaso House, where they signed the funeral book.

The President was buried at Arlington National Cemetery, on the slope below the Custis-Lee Mansion. Charles Bartlett had told the Secretary of Defense about the spring day in 1963 when he and Kennedy had looked through the Smithsonian's air and space exhibits and then driven over to Arlington.

Shown through the old edifice at the top of the hill, the President had said, "Wouldn't this be a fine place to have the White House? . . . I could stay here forever." With tears in his eyes, McNamara said that the gravesite would be "almost a shrine."

Robert Kennedy consoled Jacqueline by noting that "if Jack had been shot after the Bay of Pigs, he would have looked like the worst President." After the burial, she stood in a White House receiving line. When the Duke of Edinburgh arrived, she reminded Angier Biddle Duke that while flying to London after Vienna, he had told her that the wife of a chief of state did not curtsy to royalty. Now, looking "like a dim, lost leaf," she said, "Angie, I'm no longer the wife of a chief of state."

Watching Mikoyan moving up the line, the widow noticed that he was trembling all over, looking "terrified." By her later account, she told the Soviet official, "Please tell Mr. Chairman President that I

---

*Arriving in Washington, de Gaulle said, "The people of France insisted that I come." Later, when Lyndon Johnson asked him to proceed with the American visit in the spring of 1964 that de Gaulle had reluctantly promised Kennedy, the Frenchman infuriated Johnson by insisting that his attendance at Kennedy's funeral had liquidated his promise.

know he and my husband worked together for a peaceful world, and now he and you must carry on my husband's work." Rusk's memory of what the widow said was more terse: "My husband's dead. Now peace is up to you."

Mikoyan blinked and covered his face with both hands. For the rest of his visit, he could not stop himself from repeating the widow's appeal.

Lyndon Johnson asked Sorensen what he thought of the possibility of foreign involvement in the assassination. He showed him an FBI report, which Sorensen pronounced "meaningless." The new President knew that if Kennedy had been murdered by another government, it could, as Rusk had feared, distort American foreign policy for years. Gallup found that many Americans thought that the Soviet Union, Cuba, or "the Communists" were involved.

George Kennan wrote Kohler that the key question was "not whether Oswald was the assassin, about which there seems not much room for doubt, but the curious background of his own murder. I am not by nature a suspicious person, but . . . I fairly bristle with doubts, and I think it terribly important, not least from the standpoint of our international relations, that the background of this affair be exhaustively examined and brought to light."

Richard Helms found Lyndon Johnson distracted well into 1964 by his worry that Kennedy had been assassinated by conspiracy. As Helms recalled, the Agency was "very helpful to Johnson on this" and met the new President's request for an independent CIA study. Motion pictures of the Dallas motorcade and autopsy photographs were sent over to the Agency.

A week after Dallas, Johnson persuaded Chief Justice Earl Warren to chair a blue-ribbon panel to investigate the crime. If the rumors were not halted and "the public became aroused against Castro and Khrushchev, there might be war."

When the Warren Commission concluded in September 1964 that no foreign government was involved, the Soviet weekly *Za Rubezhom* published a summary of the report, along with quotations from Western papers doubting that Oswald acted alone. Soviets suspected that the President had been murdered by the CIA, which could not forgive him for the Bay of Pigs and the Soviet détente; the Mafia, which hoped to recover lost Cuban properties; or Johnson himself, who they presumed could not have come to power any other way.

* * *

In the spring of 1967, the first stories were published suggesting that Castro had caused Kennedy's murder in retaliation for CIA murder plots against him. Johnson asked the FBI to investigate and called in Helms, by then CIA Director. He was shocked to be informed, as he later said, "that we were running a damn Murder, Incorporated, in the Caribbean."

More than three years in the White House, reelected by a landslide, Johnson still suffered from comparison with the leader who was now so flawless in public memory. He seemed to have an almost psychological compulsion to believe that Kennedy had brought his tragic fate upon himself. He privately insisted that "Kennedy was trying to get Castro, but Castro got him first."

As early as December 1963, Johnson had told Helms that the assassination had been divine retribution for the murder of President Diem. He said the same to Salinger, who related to Robert Kennedy that Johnson had told him that someone he knew while growing up had run into a tree and struck his head, which made him cross-eyed: that was God's retribution for people who were bad. You had to be careful of cross-eyed people because God put his mark on them.*

When Rolando Cubela's rendezvous with the CIA was revealed during investigations by the Senate Intelligence Committee in 1975, some wondered whether AM/LASH was a Cuban double agent who had told Castro of American plotting against him and inspired a fatal counterplot. By then Cubela had been arrested by Cuban counterintelligence and imprisoned. Were he a double agent, he would have been unlikely to be sentenced, as Cubela was, to death.†

Interviewed in Havana by the House Assassinations Committee in 1978, Castro said, "Who here could have planned something so delicate as the death of the United States President? That would have been insanity." He noted that murdering Kennedy brought to office a man who would have been expected to be tougher toward Cuba.

Castro argued that he did not intend his Brazilian Embassy warning in September 1963 about American conspiracies against him to be taken as a physical threat. The military power of the United States to retaliate against Cuba for an attempt against its President's life was so great that such an action would be "suicidal."

Beyond Lee Oswald's peculiar brand of Marxism, his two years in the Soviet Union (and rumored connections to Soviet intelligence that

---

*This may have referred to the fact that the late President's left eye was off center.
†The sentence was commuted to thirty years by Castro's personal intervention.

were unproven aside from his marriage to a Russian woman said to be the niece of a secret police officer), and a possible visit to the Cuban and Soviet embassies in Mexico City in September 1963, there is little evidence that the Russians had anything to do with the Kennedy assassination.

One might imagine a scenario under which some rogue element of Soviet intelligence or Soviet leaders might have had something to gain from Kennedy's death. Enemies of Khrushchev's détente might have presumed that Johnson would be a more doctrinaire Cold Warrior. Enemies of Khrushchev might have reasoned that a Kennedy assassination would rob the Chairman of the argument that he should be kept in power because of his indispensable personal relationship with the American President.

We know that in the early 1960s, Soviet intelligence agents and higher officials such as Brezhnev did not flinch from contemplating what they referred to as "wet operations" against political figures in the Soviet bloc, the Third World, and the West. But even these Russians would probably have been reluctant to assassinate a President of the United States and thereby risk an American retaliatory attack.

In January 1964, the CIA received a coded message from a KGB officer in Geneva. Member of a Soviet disarmament delegation, Yuri Nosenko was a defector-in-place from whom the Agency hoped to gain many years of information on Soviet intelligence. Now he told Langley that his superiors had ordered him home within five days. Anxious that his treason had been discovered, he persuaded them to bring him to the United States.

Of the assassination Nosenko told his CIA handlers, "I can unhesitatingly sign off to the fact that the Soviet Union cannot be tied into this in any way." He said that as a counterintelligence officer against the Americans and British, he had supervised Oswald's case when the twenty-year-old American came to Moscow in 1959: the Soviet government had known nothing about him until he was already in the country.

By Nosenko's account, the KGB did not know that Oswald had been a Marine on the Japanese base from which U-2 planes flew into the Soviet Union and would not have cared anyway. Oswald had been found "mentally unstable" and not very intelligent. Nosenko said that when Oswald tried to kill himself rather than accept Moscow's demand that he leave the country, Soviet intelligence had "washed its hands" of him.

Nosenko's story strained credulity. It was difficult to imagine that the Russians would have been so indifferent to a man who was only the third American Marine to defect to Moscow and who knew at least a few details about the spy planes that for three years had defied the Russians' desperate efforts to down them.

The Agency did not know whether to take Nosenko's tale as evidence of Soviet innocence in the assassination or of Moscow's desire to clear its name, which suggested that perhaps it indeed had something to hide. Nosenko's performance under interrogation was not encouraging. He failed lie detector tests and proved ignorant of facts about the American presence in Moscow that an official of his professed background would have been expected to know.

The CIA counterintelligence chief, James Angleton, suspected that the Russians had planted Nosenko not only to allay suspicion about its complicity in Dallas but to divert attention from Soviet agents within American intelligence. For four years, the Russian was locked into a sealed vault, denied reading material, human company, toothbrushes, and toothpaste, and subjected to hostile interrogation in an effort to break him down.

The effort failed. Helms said, "I don't think there has ever been anything more frustrating in my life." Nosenko was freed and given a new home and American citizenship. The CIA remained divided about whether he was a legitimate defector or not.*

In the fall of 1963, mobsters like the Louisiana and Texas chieftain Carlos Marcello, Santos Trafficante, Sam Giancana, and their associate James Hoffa were irate with the Kennedy brothers for prosecuting them more vigorously than ever before. When Hoffa heard the news from Dallas, he said, "Bobby Kennedy is just another lawyer now."

They were also disgusted by the President's understanding with Khrushchev after the Missile Crisis, which suggested that Castro might remain permanently in power, denying the Mafia franchises in Cuba that had been said to yield more than a billion dollars a year

---

*The most extended published exposition of the theory that Oswald murdered the President on Moscow's behalf was a 1977 volume subtly entitled *Khrushchev Killed Kennedy* by a British solicitor named Michael Eddowes, who claimed also to have refused a recruitment attempt in London by Yevgeny Ivanov, the Soviet agent involved with Christine Keeler and John Profumo.

Eddowes postulated that the real Oswald never returned from the Soviet Union and was replaced instead by a Soviet lookalike who assassinated Kennedy on Khrushchev's orders. In the early 1980s he persuaded the Texas courts to open Oswald's grave and find out who was really buried there. The answer turned out to be Oswald.

before 1959. Both Oswald and Jack Ruby had close connections to organized crime figures that were not apparent to the public in the immediate aftermath of the assassination.

During the spring and summer of 1963, Oswald stayed in New Orleans with his Uncle Charles "Dutz" Murret, who had long served as his surrogate father.* Murret was a New Orleans bookmaker and associate of local mobsters named Sam Saia and Nofio Pecora, both known for their closeness to Carlos Marcello. In August 1963, Oswald was arrested after a street quarrel over his championship of the Fair Play for Cuba Committee and was evidently bailed out by one of Pecora's associates.

As an adolescent on the West Side of Chicago, Ruby ran errands for Al Capone and later worked for Paul Dorfman of the local Scrap Iron and Junk Handlers Union, whom Robert Kennedy later described in *The Enemy Within* as "a major operator in the Chicago underworld." A staff member of the Senate's Kefauver Committee, which examined organized crime in 1950, found that Ruby was "a syndicate lieutenant who had been sent to Dallas to serve as a liaison for Chicago mobsters."

During the months before the assassination, Ruby was evidently in touch with Robert "Barney" Baker, described by Robert Kennedy as Hoffa's "ambassador of violence," another Hoffa lieutenant named Murray "Dusty" Miller, and the same Nofio Pecora who was affiliated with Carlos Marcello and Oswald's uncle. In the early 1970s, John Roselli, the West Coast partner of Sam Giancana and Santos Trafficante who was involved in the CIA's plots against Castro, told reporters that Ruby was "one of our boys," designated to keep Oswald from giving information to federal investigators that might implicate the Mob.

In 1959, Ruby had gone to Cuba one or more times to see Lewis McWillie, manager of the Tropicana nightclub, owned by a Trafficante associate, and perhaps to see Trafficante himself in a jail outside Havana.† Ruby was evidently also involved in Mafia gunrunning—first to Castro, with the aim of keeping the Mob on his good side, then to anti-Castro guerrillas after the Cuban leader evicted organized crime from Havana.

After the assassination, the CIA hastened to cover its own tracks. If even routine Agency monitoring of Oswald during his defection and return from the Soviet Union were fully revealed, it might have

---

*Oswald's actual father died before his birth.
† The Tropicana was where the young Senators John Kennedy and George Smathers had one year earlier met the singer Denise Darcel.

excited a nation raw with grief to suspect that Oswald had been hired by the CIA to murder a President who in 1963 was thwarting what were popularly thought to be the Agency's cherished aims of removing Castro and keeping the Cold War at full throttle.

If the American people had learned in the last weeks of 1963 that the CIA had cooperated with the Mafia in an effort to assassinate Castro and that the scheme might have culminated in the death of the President, there would have been serious demands, as Kennedy had threatened after the Bay of Pigs, to shatter the Agency into a thousand pieces and scatter it to the winds.

By withholding this information from the Warren Commission, the CIA bought time in the hope that it could be kept from the public forever. This was not to be: the murder attempts against Castro were unveiled by the mid-1970s. In the same way that the Kremlin brought suspicion on itself by its elaborate efforts to deny involvement in the Kennedy assassination, CIA critics wondered whether the Agency had covered up its links to the Mafia and anti-Castro exiles because it had something more sinister to hide.

We will probably never know beyond the shadow of a doubt who caused John Kennedy to be murdered and why. So much conflicting and unverifiable information and disinformation has been generated by so many intelligence services and other groups for a thousand different reasons that, three decades later, it is almost impossible to imagine an explanation of the crime grounded on a single coherent body of evidence that will silence all but extreme skeptics.

Fascinated by political courage and by men dying young, acquainted more than most of his predecessors with the darker side of American politics and foreign policy, Kennedy knew that he was subjecting himself to physical danger by unleashing a vast effort to topple Fidel Castro and then restraining it, by electrifying Americans against the Soviet Union and then relaxing tensions—and, perhaps, by flirting with organized crime figures who wanted Cuban concessions back and then allowing his Attorney General to prosecute them more vigorously than ever before.

What is consistent with virtually every major serious explanation of who killed the President is that he was murdered, to one degree or another, as a result of his public policies. Kennedy never gave up his awareness of how intention could be sabotaged by accident and miscalculation. Contrary to most American leaders, he was always more willing to incur physical than political risks. Characteristically it was about his physical survival, not his political survival, that he said in the fall of 1963, "Whoever wants to get me will get me."

Told about the suspected assassin, Jacqueline Kennedy lamented that her husband's death had been robbed of meaning: "He didn't even have the satisfaction of dying for civil rights. It had to be some silly little Communist." But if martyrdom is defined as dying in the pursuit of public purpose, then John Kennedy's murder was martyrdom enough.

During her final fortnight in the White House, as Lyndon Johnson went to work in the West Wing, Mrs. Kennedy scrawled a letter to the leader of the Soviet Union. The letter was written on White House stationery in her stylish, looping hand that looked more like printing than script.

It closed the cycle of private correspondence between the two most powerful men in the world, begun with the surprise letter from Pitsunda in September 1961 that Georgi Bolshakov had concealed in a newspaper and delivered to the Carlyle. When the widow finished writing, she attached a note saying, "Important/Mrs Lincoln/This is my letter to Khrushchev to be delivered to him by Ambassador Thompson"*:

Dear Mr. Chairman President

I would like to thank you for sending Mr. Mikoyan as your representative to my husband's funeral. He looked so upset when he came through the line, and I was very moved. I tried to give him a message for you that day—but as it was such a terrible day for me, I do not know if my words came out as I meant them to.

So now, in one of the last nights I will spend in the White House, in one of the last letters I will write on this paper at the White House, I would like to write you my message. I send it only because I know how much my husband cared about peace, and how the relation between you and him was central to his care in his mind.

He used to quote your words in some of his speeches—"In the next war the survivors will envy the dead." You and he were adversaries, but you were allied in a determination that the world should not be blown up. You respected each other and could deal with each other. I know that President Johnson will make every effort to establish the same relationship with you.

The danger which troubled my husband was that war might be started not so much by the big men as by the little ones. While big men

---

*In fact, the letter was delivered through normal channels.

know the needs for self-control and restraint—little men are sometimes moved by fear and pride. If only in the future the big men can continue to make the little ones sit down and talk, before they start to fight—I know that President Johnson will continue the policy in which my husband so deeply believed—a policy of control and restraint—and he will need your help.

I send this letter because I know so deeply of the importance of the relationship which existed between you and my husband, and also because of your kindness, and that of Mrs. Khrushcheva in Vienna. I read that she had tears in her eyes when she left the American Embassy in Moscow, after signing the book of mourning. Please thank her for that.

Sincerely,

Jacqueline Kennedy

Epilogue

The Culmination

AFTER THE KENNEDY FUNERAL, LYNDON JOHNSON GAVE MIKOYAN only thirty-five seconds in the State Department receiving line, one of the new President's shortest encounters. Soviet diplomats worried that Johnson might be demonstrating American indignation about Lee Harvey Oswald's Soviet history.

They were relieved the next day when Johnson saw the Deputy Premier in the Oval Office. He promised to live by whatever pledges the late President had made to Khrushchev on Cuba. He wished to continue their private correspondence. He gave Mikoyan a letter reminding the Chairman that he had "kept in close touch" with the improvement in American-Soviet relations and was "in full accord with the policies of President Kennedy."

Nevertheless Khrushchev remained "worried" about Kennedy's murder and "how events would develop." He thought Johnson "reactionary" and "inflexible." As his son Sergei recalled, "We didn't

believe Johnson, didn't trust him." The Chairman's advisers reminded him of Johnson's intimacy with Texas oil and gas interests,
which they considered to be anti-Soviet, perhaps a party to the assassination. They warned that Johnson "smells oily."

On the morning after New Year's 1964, Dobrynin gave Rusk the
first major letter for the new President from Khrushchev. The long,
rambling screed was a condescending lesson in history and geopoli-
tics evidently intended to educate a foreign policy novice from Texas.
Denouncing "colonializers" and "imperialism" as the causes of
war, it insisted that Taiwan was an "inalienable part" of People's
China and that all "war bases" on foreign lands should be "liquidated." The Italian Fascists had christened the Mediterranean *"mare
nostrum"* to pose as the heirs of the ancient Romans. So much blood
had been spilled in nineteenth-century Paraguay that its population
was "still smaller than before this war." All territorial disputes should
be settled "exclusively by peaceful means."
Reading the letter at the LBJ Ranch, the disappointed Johnson
thought it "designed for propaganda purposes rather than serious
diplomacy."* He replied by urging that in settling territorial disputes
they consider not only established borders but such internationally
recognized features as the demilitarized zones in Korea and Vietnam
and the access routes to Berlin. Use of force should be considered to
include "aggression, subversion, or clandestine supply of arms."
McNamara suggested reduction of U.S. production of fissionable
materials for nuclear weapons to demonstrate his peaceful intentions
to Khrushchev. In his first State of the Union message, Johnson announced a 25 percent cutback in enriched uranium production. He
told the Russians in February that he would make a further cutback
and urged them to do the same. He negotiated with Khrushchev by
letter and through Dobrynin and Kohler.
When the talks were stalled in mid-April, he informed the Chairman
that he would announce his new reduction three days hence at a New
York press luncheon. As he was about to speak, he was handed a

---

*Harlan Cleveland wrote Rusk that as usual Khrushchev "has to tramp through all
those familiar themes before getting to what he has to say—just as Beethoven, in
opening the fourth movement of his Ninth Symphony, reiterates all the themes from
the first three movements before stating the theme of the fourth." In the Missile Crisis,
"the President received a couple of letters from Khrushchev that were full of nonsense. . . . But those letters contained individual paragraphs, here and there, which
we picked up and built on to bring about the great nuclear deconfrontation. Have we
lost our touch?"

message from Khrushchev allowing him to announce that the Soviet Union would stop construction of two new plutonium reactors and "substantially reduce" enriched uranium production.

Dobrynin suggested that a Johnson-Khrushchev summit "could be useful for both countries." The new President replied that a summit would raise "unrealistic expectations." There were "distinct disadvantages to my leaving the country during my first year in office." With no Vice President to share the "burdens of leadership," he was trying to persuade Congress to pass Kennedy's tax cut, civil rights, and other legislation. He told friends, "Khrushchev didn't think I was going to be a sap."

Soon after Johnson's return from Dallas, McCone had quietly shown him evidence of the Cuban arms cache and Venezuelan coup plans that Helms had shown the late President three days before his murder. Johnson warned Mikoyan during their meeting that Castro's campaign to subvert Latin America was straining American-Soviet relations. Mikoyan's black eyes flashed: Cuba had no desire to subvert anyone! How could a tiny nation bother anyone, let alone a great power?

The United States gave the evidence from the Venezuelan beach to President Betancourt, who at the end of November demanded a partial air and naval blockade of Cuba to prevent the export of weapons. Nervous after the Kennedy assassination that the warlike Johnson would use any pretext to invade, Castro charged the CIA with "faking" the evidence as part of a "plot" against him. He warned Venezuela and other "lackey" nations that if they tried to invade his island, "they would not last twenty-four hours."

Speaking before the Central Committee, Khrushchev agreed that the evidence had been "invented": "I want to tell you frankly, gentleman aggressors: do not play with fire! You must realize that if tension is fanned and a threat against Cuba is created, it cannot but affect the entire international situation."

Had Kennedy lived, the Venezuelan evidence might have forced him to choose between suffering election-year charges of appeasement or taking action against Cuba that could reignite the Missile Crisis. Helms believed that had Kennedy not been killed, the pro-Castro revolutionaries would have proceeded with their plot against Betancourt. If it had succeeded, Kennedy would have been under ferocious pressure to act boldly and stop the overthrow of other Latin American governments.

Johnson did not wish to start his Presidency and run for election by renewing the crisis over Cuba. He knew that Americans, still numb and mourning, were not likely to be responsive to Republican slurs against the sainted President's policies. Thus he contented himself with lobbying OAS members to condemn Castro's efforts against Venezuela with a threat to use "armed force."

The new President read a memo from William Attwood on his efforts to see Castro, but Johnson was not interested in a Cuban rapprochement. He told Attwood merely that he had read his account "with interest." Later Attwood heard from Gordon Chase that there was "no desire among the Johnson people to do anything about Cuba in an election year."

Helms found that Johnson lacked Kennedy's emotional commitment to covert action against Castro. The new President ordered the CIA to halt the sabotage program. As Helms recalled, "He saw little point in pressing Cuba." Helms found Johnson more absorbed in "Vietnam, whether or not the Kennedy assassination was a conspiracy, civil rights, and the 1964 election. Maybe he saw Cuba as an obsession of Robert Kennedy's."

Desmond FitzGerald told his agents in 1964 that "if Jack Kennedy had lived, I can assure you we would have gotten rid of Castro by last Christmas."

Returning from a Saigon trip in March, McNamara recommended new assistance to South Vietnam. He told the President that since Diem's murder, the situation had "unquestionably been growing worse." Roughly 40 percent of the countryside was under Viet Cong "control or predominant influence."* The political fate of General Nguyen Khanh, who had overthrown the military junta, was "uncertain."

Johnson approved a document pronouncing Vietnam a "test case" of American capacity to cope with the wars of national liberation proclaimed by Khrushchev. Worried that the Republicans might use the Vietnam issue against him, he authorized his aides to draft a bipartisan congressional resolution allowing him to run the war as he saw fit and to remove the issue from the fall campaign.

On Sunday, August 2, in the Gulf of Tonkin, the U.S. destroyer *Maddox* zigzagged along the bays and islands on the North Vietnamese coastline. Loaded with eavesdropping devices, the ship gathered information on Soviet-built SAMs and radar stations. The *Mad-*

---

*The Americans also found that the Diem regime had falsified information on the progress of the war effort to make it seem more hopeful than it actually was.

dox was also in contact with South Vietnamese commandos who had raided nearby islands two nights before. It sailed outside the three-mile territorial limit established by the French colonials but inside the twelve-mile limit set by China and other Communist nations.

Three North Vietnamese boats fired torpedoes at the ship. *Maddox* gunners and jets from the nearby *Ticonderoga* fired back, crippling two of the vessels and sinking the third.

President Johnson rejected further reprisals. Using the hot line to Moscow for the first time, he cabled Khrushchev that he did not wish to widen the conflict but hoped that North Vietnam would not attack other American vessels in international waters.

The *Maddox* and another destroyer, the *C. Turner Joy,* were ordered to sail eight miles off the North Vietnamese coast, four miles off the offshore islands. The commandos from the South resumed their operations. On Sunday evening, intercepted radio messages gave the *Maddox* commander, Captain John Herrick, the "impression" that Communist patrol boats were about to attack. With air support from the *Ticonderoga,* the *Maddox* and *Turner Joy* began firing.

Maddox officers reported twenty-two enemy torpedoes, none of which scored a hit, and two or three enemy vessels sunk. But when the firing stopped, Herrick warned his superiors that the "entire action leaves many doubts"; no sailor on either destroyer had seen or heard enemy gunfire. An "overeager" young sonar operator who had counted torpedoes may have been misled by "freak weather effects."

Nevertheless the President ordered bombing of North Vietnam for the first time and unveiled the document now christened the Gulf of Tonkin resolution. Language was broadened to authorize Johnson to "take all necessary measures" to protect American forces and "prevent further aggression." The Senate passed it with only two dissenters.

Eager to preserve the American détente, Khrushchev evidently privately urged Hanoi to stop trying to "liberate" the South. He responded to pleas for new military help by advising negotiation.

Kennedy had told Mansfield, O'Donnell, Bartlett, and others that he planned to withdraw American forces from Vietnam after he was reelected and the political risks diminished. But as January 1965 came about, Kennedy might have worried that cries of "Who Lost Vietnam?" would undermine his other ambitions with the Soviet Union, the second-term domestic program he had so long postponed, and his ability to name his successor in 1968.

Rusk, McNamara, Bundy, and the other advisers who guided Lyndon Johnson into major involvement in Vietnam might have done the same with the President who four years earlier had brought them to power.* Rusk noted years later that had Kennedy "decided in 1963 on a 1965 withdrawal, he would have left Americans in a combat zone for political purposes, and no President can do that."

Dictating his memoirs in the late 1960s, Khrushchev noted that Johnson "got sucked in up to his neck in the Vietnam War, but that was his personal stupidity. Perhaps Kennedy would have been equally stupid. I'm not in a position to judge that now." In 1966, the Soviet government declared that America suffered a "strange and persistent delusion" if it thought that relations with the Soviet Union could be improved despite the war in Vietnam.

In April 1964, when Khrushchev turned seventy, President Leonid Brezhnev led a large official group to the Chairman's residence in Moscow. Wiping away a tear, he kissed the guest of honor and read out a proclamation: "We wish you at least as many more years and hope that you will live them as brilliantly and fruitfully as you have those already passed." *Pravda* devoted seven of its eight pages to Khrushchev's birthday.

By now, the Chairman was thinking about retirement: "We're old-sters. We've done our bit. It's time to yield the road to others." Sergei Khrushchev noticed that his father's strength was waning: "His eyes ached from the endless reading, and more and more frequently he asked one of his assistants, or one of his children, to read to him aloud."

Khrushchev's colleagues were growing ever more indignant about the Chairman's personality cult and the Chinese quarrel, his agricul-tural failures, and his military meddling and arbitrary decision-mak-ing. With Kennedy gone, Khrushchev could no longer cite his per-sonal relationship with the President as evidence of his indispensability. They wondered whether Johnson's accession would doom the American détente the Chairman had so touted, but which had so far brought the Soviet Union so relatively little.

In July, Khrushchev sent Adzhubei to West Germany, where he met with Ludwig Erhard and Willy Brandt to pave the way for an official visit by the Chairman. Having shown the East Germans eighteen months before that he was unwilling to initiate another Berlin crisis,

---

*The scholar Eliot Cohen makes the argument that their common experience of the Missile Crisis led these men to propose a similar calibrated, gradual application of force to North Vietnam. Cohen does not go so far as to say so, but one suspects that, presented in these terms, the first major bombing plans for Vietnam in 1965 might thus have struck Kennedy, had he lived, as eminently rational.

Khrushchev now had high hopes for rapprochement and lucrative trade with Bonn. Moscow rivals were shocked by what they suspected to be his impending sellout of the GDR and the use of his widely disliked son-in-law for secret diplomacy.*

Rumors were spread that in Bonn, when Adzhubei was privately asked how better relations would affect the Berlin Wall, he had replied that when Khrushchev came and saw what good guys the West Germans were, the Wall would disappear without a trace. Told of the rumors, the Chairman asked Adzhubei to "write an explanation for the Presidium."

Two months after Adzhubei's Bonn visit, a West German technician, Horst Schwirkmann, came to Moscow to check the FRG Embassy for eavesdropping devices. When he found them, he sent a high-voltage jolt through the lines, which gave KGB listeners a painful shock. The secret police saw their opportunity to sabotage Khrushchev's rapprochement with West Germany. While touring the Zagorsk Monastery, Schwirkmann was shot in the buttocks with nitrogen mustard gas that could have killed him.

The outraged West Germans announced that Khrushchev could not visit Bonn until the case was satisfactorily resolved. The Soviet apology in October was unusually specific: "Those who indulge in such actions are trying to undermine the good relations between our two countries." But it was issued too late. By then, Khrushchev had been ousted by men who had other ideas about relations with West Germany.

John Kennedy's near-canonization and Barry Goldwater's nomination prevented the campaign of 1964 from becoming the rancorous struggle over foreign policy that the late President had feared. Contrasting himself with Goldwater and his "Why Not Victory?" platform, Lyndon Johnson campaigned as a centrist.

The President asked Khrushchev through Norman Cousins to "keep out of the election": he wished to defeat Goldwater soundly and must not appear to be the Kremlin's candidate. During a Moscow visit, David Rockefeller of the Chase Manhattan Bank told the Chairman of Johnson's hope that they could establish "relations of the sort

---

*Not long afterward Gromyko told a visitor, "Why was Khrushchev overthrown? Because he sent Adzhubei to Bonn, of course." This comment reflected Gromyko's tunnel vision more than reality, but the Adzhubei mission no doubt contributed to Khrushchev's downfall.

which you had with President Kennedy," which were "very useful in times of conflict."

Khrushchev felt that Johnson had "turned out to be a clever man." He was relieved that the President had not reversed Kennedy's policies, even under pressure from Goldwater. He presumed that once the Texan was elected by a landslide, he and Johnson could resume and augment the détente begun with Kennedy.

The Chairman did not know that his closest colleagues had been plotting against him for months. According to the KGB chief Vladimir Semichastny, Brezhnev asked him in June 1964 whether Khrushchev could be poisoned or his plane sabotaged when he returned from a visit to Nasser in Cairo.

By Semichastny's account, he replied that he was "not a murderer." Not only were the Chairman's crewmen devoted to him but Gromyko and others would be aboard the plane. There was further talk of stopping Khrushchev's train and arresting him on his way back from a Swedish visit in July.*

That same month Khrushchev asked Brezhnev to resign the Presidency in favor of Mikoyan in order to "concentrate" on his Central Committee duties. Brezhnev may have taken this as Khrushchev's signal that he would not be the Chairman's successor.†

Brezhnev may have felt even more unsettled by Khrushchev's call for a November Central Committee meeting. A Western reporter was told that the meeting would see "many changes at the top. Almost all the leaders except Khrushchev will be affected." Sergei Khrushchev recalled that his father was planning to add younger men to the Presidium "who would one day take over." These included Adzhubei, Kharmalov, and Yuri Andropov, who had served as Ambassador to Budapest during the Hungarian revolution.

In September, Sergei was called by a security agent named Vasily Galyukov: "I've found out that there is a plot against Nikita Sergeyevich! I wanted to tell him about it in person. . . . I can't go to

---

*The historian William Taubman correctly suggests that this charge should be treated with some caution: by the time Semichastny made it in 1989, there was considerable political gain to be had from criticizing the by-then-despised Brezhnev.

†Brezhnev may have heard that Khrushchev complained to his son and others that Brezhnev lacked the strength of character to succeed him. Khrushchev recalled that, in the prewar Ukraine, Brezhnev had been nicknamed "the Ballerina": "Anyone who wants to can turn him around."

Semichastny. He's actively involved in the plot himself, along with Shelepin, Podgorny, and others.''

Sergei picked up Galyukov at a Moscow street corner. At dusk, walking through a glade outside the city, Galyukov told him of "innuendos, hints, tête-à-têtes" and repeated references to "November." Sergei hoped that "this bad dream would pass, that everything would be cleared up and life would roll along again as before." Yet he knew that "things would never be the same again."

The Chairman did not normally discuss high politics with his son. When Sergei criticized Lysenko's approach to genetics, the father said, "Don't stick your nose into what isn't your business." As Sergei recalled, "Not only would I have to violate this taboo, I was intending to accuse his closest associates and comrades-in-arms of conspiracy."

On Sunday, September 27, after breakfast at the dacha, he strolled with his father through a meadow: "You know, an unusual thing happened. . . . Maybe it's nonsense, but I don't have the right to keep it to myself." After hearing the story, Khrushchev told his son that he had been right to tell him, but he could not believe that Brezhnev, Podgorny, and others could unite against him: "They're completely different people."

The next evening, the Chairman told him that he had shared the tale with Podgorny, who had laughingly said, "How can you think such a thing, Nikita Sergeyevich?" Sergei was mortified. His father asked him, as a precaution, to bring Galyukov to see Mikoyan, who would "take care of everything." Mikoyan duly interviewed the security agent and assured Khrushchev that there was nothing to worry about.

Sergei concluded that his father "did not want to believe that such a turn of events was possible. After all, the people accused had been his friends for decades! If he couldn't trust them, whom could he trust? What's more, my seventy-year-old father was tired, tired beyond measure, both morally and physically. He had neither the strength nor the desire to fight for power."

On Monday evening, October 12, as the sun sank into the Black Sea, Khrushchev was strolling along his beach with Mikoyan when called back for an urgent telephone call from Mikhail Suslov of the Presidium. Into the receiver he barked, "I'm on vacation. What could be so urgent? . . . What do you mean, you all 'got together'? We'll be discussing agricultural questions at the November plenum. There'll be plenty of time to talk about everything!"

Suslov persisted. Khrushchev agreed to fly the next day to Moscow.

Resuming their stroll, he told Mikoyan, "You know, Anastas, they haven't got any urgent agricultural problems. I think that call is connected with what Sergei was telling us." He told his ancient comrade that if it turned out to be like 1957, he would not put up a fight.

Nina Petrovna was relaxing at a Czechoslovak spa with Viktoria Brezhnev. It was later said that Brezhnev had arranged the vacation to deprive Khrushchev of advice from his perceptive wife.

When Khrushchev and Mikoyan landed in Moscow, they were met only by Semichastny, who said, "They've all gathered at the Kremlin. They're waiting for you." At the old fortress, Khrushchev was indicted for rashness, egotism, nepotism, confusion, "harebrained scheming," and mismanagement of farming and industry. He had been undignified in public and had damaged relations with China.

Mikoyan courageously proposed that Khrushchev keep one of his posts. Someone said, "You'd better keep your mouth shut or we'll take care of you too." Mikoyan replied, "We're not carving up a pie here. We're deciding the fate . . . of a great country. Khrushchev's work is the party's political capital. Kindly do not threaten me."

According to one account, Khrushchev said, "I ask you to forgive me if I ever offended anyone. . . . I can't remember all the charges, nor will I try to answer them. I'll just say one thing: my main failing . . . is being too good, too trusting, and perhaps also that I myself didn't notice my own failings. But you, all of you present here, didn't tell me openly and honestly about my shortcomings."

He defended his settlement of the Caribbean crisis: "You accuse me of pulling out our missiles. What do you mean, that we should have started a world war over them? How can you accuse me of undertaking some sort of Cuban adventure when we made all decisions relating to Cuba together?

"Or take the erection of the Berlin Wall. Back then, you all approved the decision, and now you're blaming me. For what, for goodness' sake? . . . Anyone can talk. But to decide what to do concretely— none of you could suggest anything then, and you can't even now." Relations with China were "quite complex, and they'll get even more sticky. You're going to come up against great difficulties and complexities in four or five years."

He said this would be his last political speech—"my swan song, so to speak." When he asked to make one request of the November Central Committee plenum, Brezhnev interrupted: "There will be no request!"

Khrushchev evidently broke down and cried. Then he composed himself. "Obviously it will now be as you wish. What I can say—I got what I deserved. I'm ready for anything. . . . We face a lot of problems, and at my age, it isn't easy to cope with them all. We've got to promote younger people. Some people today lack courage and integrity. . . . But that's not the issue now. Someday, history will tell the whole, profound truth about what is happening today."

That evening he told Mikoyan, "Could anyone have dreamed of telling Stalin that he didn't suit us anymore and suggesting that he retire? Not even a wet spot would have remained where we had been standing. Now everything's different. . . . That's my contribution."

On Wednesday morning, Khrushchev faced the Presidium for the last time. He was stripped of his Party and government posts, which went to Brezhnev and Kosygin. As Adzhubei recalled, Khrushchev sat slumped in a chair, "hanging his head, not raising his eyes, seeming very small, as if the force had suddenly gone out of his strong body."

Before noon, he returned home, saying, "That's it. I'm retired." He handed his briefcase to Sergei and never opened it again.* The spurned leader and his son walked in silence, followed by Yelena Khrushchev's dog Arbat. Sergei recalled that previously Arbat had not shown much interest in his father, but from this day forward the dog never left his side.

That evening, Mikoyan came to assure Khrushchev that he would have a pension, a dacha, and a city house for life: he had suggested his hiring as a consultant, but that was rejected. Khrushchev thanked him: "It's good to know you have a friend at your side."

The Armenian seized his old partner and kissed him on both cheeks. Then Khrushchev watched him walk quickly to the garden gate. He never saw Mikoyan again.

On Thursday, Lyndon Johnson was riding through noisy campaign crowds in Brooklyn. With complex irony, he had come to aid Robert Kennedy's campaign for the New York Senate seat held by Kenneth Keating. Over the President's limousine radio came a TASS report that Khrushchev had abruptly "resigned" for "reasons of health."†

On Friday, the Chinese detonated their first nuclear weapon. Unlike

---

*After his father's death, Sergei found in it a memo on McNamara's counterforce doctrine.

†Charles Bartlett called his friend Alexander Zinchuk of the Soviet Embassy. "You can't let us have an election in peace. Two years ago you messed things up in Cuba, and now we're trying to decide who's going to be President, and you've thrown Khrushchev out." Zinchuk noted that Khrushchev's ouster had deflected attention from the arrest of Johnson's close aide Walter Jenkins on a morals charge: "When Jenkins got into trouble, we realized that President Johnson was in trouble. So we decided to help. And when a Russian decides to help, no sacrifice is too great!"

his predecessor, Johnson remained calm. From a CIA briefing, he knew that the Chinese would have to travel a long and expensive road before they developed accurate ICBMs; some future President would have to deal with that problem.

A fortnight later, Johnson kept his office by the greatest majority in a contested Presidential election. No longer so beholden to his predecessor's legacy, he now confronted two Soviet leaders who would not allow their predecessor's name to be publicly spoken or published. The years of Kennedy and Khrushchev were over.

Twenty-five years to the week after Johnson's election, the Berlin Wall collapsed. The close of the Cold War epoch allows us to see more clearly than ever the chief importance of the Kennedy-Khrushchev period.

These were the years in which humankind came closer than any other time to nuclear incineration, and in which the United States and the Soviet Union began the greatest arms race in human history. Both leaders ended their two nuclear crises without war and took steps to control nuclear weapons, but these achievements are not mitigated by the darker side of their legacy.

More than perhaps any other man who might have dominated the Soviet government during the decade after Stalin's death, Khrushchev was committed to improving the lot of the Soviet consumer by holding down military spending. The problem was that, in contrast to the late 1980s, no Soviet leader of that era could have renounced Soviet imperial ambitions in favor of stengthening the domestic economy and kept power. Nor was Khrushchev willing to relinquish the dream of world communism.

Thus he had to resort to a combination of public lies about Soviet military predominance and to nuclear blackmail. This strategy was not so dangerous when waged against Eisenhower. The old General's profound understanding of the actual correlation of forces enabled him to operate in private from a presumption of American preponderance. His domestic prestige allowed him to refrain in public from shattering Khrushchev's assertions about Soviet strength, to keep down American defense spending, and to respond to such challenges as Khrushchev's Berlin ultimatum with poise.

Khrushchev did not comprehend how dangerous his strategy had become once Kennedy had entered the White House. Practiced against a President who lacked Eisenhower's consistency, his determination to avoid alarming the American people about Soviet behavior, his understanding of the arms race and his domestic political strength, it meant years of almost unrelenting crisis.

Throughout those years, Kennedy showed a fine sensitivity to the dangers of misperception and accident and a talent for intense crisis management. He pushed for a test ban more persistently than almost anyone else who might have been President.

But throughout his term, Kennedy rarely showed the magnanimity that should have been expected of a superior power. Instead he aroused the Western world to an hour of imminent danger that did not exist, provoked the adversary by exposing Soviet nuclear weakness to the world, and unwittingly caused the Soviets to fear that he was on the verge of exploiting American nuclear strength to settle the Cold War on American terms, perhaps even in a preemptive strike.

One effect of this was Khrushchev's dangerous efforts to assert what power he did have in Berlin and Cuba. The more lasting effect was the Kremlin's decision, hardened between the summer of 1961 and the end of 1962, to damn the Soviet consumer and make the mighty reach for nuclear parity or superiority. Had Khrushchev or a successor been encouraged to pursue the previous policy of minimum deterrence, the arms race of the next two decades could have been avoided.

We cannot know for certain whether continued nuclear imbalance between the two powers would have brought more dangerous episodes like Berlin and Cuba, or whether a more leisurely arms race would have retarded the collapse of communism and the end of the Cold War. More conclusive answers to these questions must await the day when historians from all countries gain unfettered access to archives for the period in the Soviet Union and the West.

We do know that by 1970 the Soviet Union could claim rough nuclear equality with the United States. Khrushchev had predicted that by that year the Soviet economy would be the strongest on earth and that by 1980 Soviet sports and national defense would be conducted by spontaneous initiative of the masses. Instead, 1980 found the Soviet economy mired in a terminal stagnation that led to the rise of Mikhail Gorbachev.

Berlin never again became a flashpoint between East and West. By 1971, Soviet strategic power was so great that the Kremlin no longer needed to exploit the vulnerable Western position in the city to force the West to move on other Cold War issues. Under the stimulus of Chancellor Willy Brandt's *Ostpolitik*, the four occupying powers signed an agreement declaring "the frontiers of all states in Europe inviolable," in exchange for a Soviet guarantee not to interfere with Western access rights to Berlin.

Fidel Castro claimed credit for the rise of Soviet strategic power in the late 1960s, boasting that were it not for Khrushchev's humiliation over Cuba, the Russians would never have made the effort to catch up. Brezhnev was displeased by Castro's economic mismanagement and his support of what he considered to be hapless, unpredictable guerrillas in Venezuela, Colombia, and Guatemala.

But in 1968, Castro was one of the few Communist leaders willing to back the Soviet invasion of Prague. By the mid-1970s, he was siphoning roughly one half of all Soviet economic and military assistance to the Third World. Extending his revolutionary ambitions to Africa, Castro sent Cuban combat forces to Angola and Ethiopia. In the early 1980s he became a political and military godfather to the Nicaraguan Sandinistas and the guerrillas of El Salvador.

Kennedy's death did not halt American assassination attempts against the Cuban leader; these evidently ended only in 1965. A decade later, Henry Kissinger's State Department contacted Cuban diplomats about relaxing tensions, an effort renewed by the Jimmy Carter administration until Castro in 1980 expressed his feelings toward the United States by sending it tens of thousands of Cuban criminals and mental patients in the notorious Mariel boat lift. The Ronald Reagan administration revived Castro's anxieties about a new American invasion by threatening to go "to the source" of Central American upheaval.*

Dictating his memoirs after the invasion of Prague, Khrushchev had called Brezhnev's decision "a mistake" but insisted that "time will heal the wounds. . . . The Czech people, in the end, will fall into step with the people of the other socialist countries, and especially with the Soviet people. . . . Our goals are the same—to be side by side in the fight for socialism and communism. I think all will turn out well in the end."

Khrushchev failed as a prophet. Two decades later, when Mikhail Gorbachev made it clear that he would no longer use Soviet tanks and lavish economic aid to prop up puppet governments unsupported by their people, Eastern Europe threw off the shackles of communism and East Germany rejoined the West. In Havana, Fidel Castro gasconaded against Gorbachev's heresies and agonized over how to preserve his regime in an age in which Moscow no longer had the enthusiasm or the ability to sign his large annual check.

In the Soviet Union after 1964, like the beautiful Lara in *Doctor Zhivago*, Nikita Khrushchev was as "forgotten as a nameless number on a list that afterward got mislaid." As Sergei recalled, "The new

---

*The Cuban official Jorge Risquet argued in 1991 that "at a certain point, the U.S. did not have the forces to wage two wars simultaneously. . . . Therefore we have always been grateful for the Vietnamese people, who for many years kept away the danger of a war in our area."

regime didn't publicly analyze or criticize the decade just past, or even my father's indisputable errors. He simply vanished—along with all his victories and defeats, all his virtues and shortcomings, all the love of his friends and the hatred of his enemies."

At the beginning of 1965, Brezhnev and Kosygin took away the old man's houses and banished him and Nina Petrovna to a green log cottage near an apple orchard outside Moscow, a world away from the estate in Pitsunda and the indoor-outdoor pool. Deeply dispirited, he told his family, "I've got to learn how to kill time."

Wrapping himself in a green-and-beige cloak given him by a French textile magnate during his 1960 visit to de Gaulle, he would pick up brushwood and start a bonfire that reminded him of his youth herding sheep and horses in Kalinovka. With Arbat at his side, he stared at the fire for hours and told his son and daughters about his hungry childhood and the nightingales and warm summer nights of the Ukraine.

When Brezhnev heard that he was dictating his memoirs, Khrushchev was called in to the Central Committee. He told them, "You can take everything away from me. My pension, my dacha, my apartment. . . . So what! I can still make a living. I'll go to work as a metalworker—I still remember how it's done. If that doesn't work out, I'll take my knapsack and go begging. People will give me what I need. . . . But no one would give you a crust of bread. You'd starve!"

The first volume was published in the West in 1970 as *Khrushchev Remembers.* Called in once again by the Central Committee, he roared, "It's been six years since I was in office, six years since you blamed me for everything. You said that once you were rid of Khrushchev everything would go smoothly. . . . Our agriculture is foundering. . . . The stores are empty. . . . We bought grain from America in 1963 as an exception, but now it's become the rule. Shame on you!"

On the quarrel with China: "Six years have passed, and relations have only worsened. Now everyone can see the causes are deeper. . . . It will take new people both here and in China who are able to look at the problem in a new way and throw off old encrusted views."

Asked to sign a carefully worded statement that he had "never passed on memoirs" to the West, he refused, then reconsidered: "I've done what you asked. I signed. Now I want to go home. My chest hurts." After returning home, he sat down at the edge of the woods and suffered a heart attack. The following spring, he complained, "No one needs me anymore. I'm just wandering around aimlessly. I could go hang myself and no one would even notice."

In September 1971, Khrushchev died. Sergei wondered whether any high Soviet official would come to call; most of them had at least professed to be close to his family. "Unfortunately a certain degree of culture and intellect is required to understand this," he wrote. "Not one of them called." Among the blizzard of messages from Soviets and Westerners were letters from Llewellyn Thompson and Jacqueline Kennedy Onassis.

Three years later, a second volume of Khrushchev's memoirs was published. It included a tribute to the man who in Khrushchev's memory was no longer the militant Kennedy of early 1961 but the President who conceded at Vienna that American and Soviet power were equal and who collaborated with him to avoid war in Berlin and Cuba and usher in the détente of 1963. Sergei recalled that his father "trusted Kennedy and felt human sympathy toward him, and such likes and dislikes played a big part in Father's life."

In the memoirs, Khrushchev conceded that their backgrounds were "poles apart": "I was a miner, a metal-fitter, who by the will of the Party and the people rose to be the Prime Minister of my country. Kennedy was a millionaire and the son of a millionaire. He pursued the goal of strengthening capitalism, while I sought to destroy capitalism and create a new social system, based on the teachings of Marx and Engels."

Still, in the Caribbean crisis, the two leaders had found "common ground and a common language." Kennedy "knew that war brings impoverishment to a country and a disaster to a people, and that a war with the Soviet Union wouldn't be a stroll in the woods. . . . He showed great flexibility and together we avoided disaster."

In September 1959, during their first encounter, Khrushchev had predicted to Kennedy and other Senators that their grandchildren would live under communism. He would have been staggered to learn that his grandchildren would live in a Soviet Union that was lurching, however ambivalently, toward freedom. When Mikhail Gorbachev resolved to improve the Soviet living standard, people remembered where they had heard this before. Many began referring to the Khrushchev decade as "our first *perestroika.*"

Alexei Adzhubei had been out of public life for years. Returning to Moscow in the late 1960s, Jane Thompson saw him "struggling to get this huge sack of potatoes into the back of a little car." She did not greet him: "It would have embarrassed the bejeezus out of him. Later we heard that he was sent out to Alma-Ata or Mongolia to run a paper. Then we heard he'd come back."*

---

*Actually Adzhubei was asked to leave Moscow for a job in the Soviet Far East. He threatened to write an official complaint to U Thant at the UN. Surprisingly this worked. Sergei Khrushchev later suggested that the authorities also talked to Adzhubei "about some other matters," implying that Adzhubei may have agreed to distance himself from his father.

Liberated by *glasnost,* Adzhubei told a reporter in the late 1980s, "The Khrushchev period was the first act in a great drama—the drama of a society recovering its vision. I'm reminded of one of those Greek tragedies in which the first words shatter the audience. The first words in our drama were spoken by Khrushchev. The culmination is taking place now."

Sergei Khrushchev agreed: "Freedom and *glasnost* are far ahead of those days, but that's where it all started." He wrote Gorbachev, "Your style of work, your quick reactions, your urge to see life with your own eyes and to become personally involved and make decisions independently, all remind me a great deal of my father. . . . Khrushchev is a part of our history and, in my opinion, far from the worst part."

Asked if his father should be reburied in the Kremlin Wall, the son laughed; buried near him in Moscow were artists, poets, writers, and soldiers alongside whom Khrushchev had fought: "I think it's better if he stays where he is. He's in very good company."

Jacqueline Kennedy Onassis flew to Moscow in 1976 for the first time, making the trip she would almost certainly have made with her husband, had he lived. A New York book editor working on a volume called *In the Russian Style,* she lunched at Spaso House and viewed a Kremlin exhibition of Russian costume from the eighteenth and nineteenth centuries, the period limned by Lesley Blanch in *The Sabres of Paradise,* which she had recommended to Khrushchev in Vienna.

In February 1989, Sergei Khrushchev arrived in the United States for the first time since accompanying his father on the long-ago American tour. Stopping at Harvard, he lectured one evening in halting English at the Kennedy School of Government. Hecklers took out shoes and banged them on tables.

With his father's aplomb, Khrushchev did not skip a beat: "Thank God that the only questions that divide us are which shoes, left or right?" The room resounded. He went on: "One should not just criticize a person. One should also study history and understand its origins in order not to encounter it again. . . . We have come to understand how poorly we know one another. The results of this misunderstanding have led to many missteps, even at the highest level."

Of that history he said, "For you in the West, it's interesting information about the guy who lives next door. For us, it's our future, which has always flowed out of our past."

ACKNOWLEDGMENTS

As I have suggested in the preface, I am first of all grateful to the hundreds of scholars who have scrutinized the issues, events, and personalities treated in this volume. I am only sorry that there are not enough pages to list in the Selected Bibliography every title that has influenced me since I began reading and thinking about John Kennedy, Nikita Khrushchev, and American-Soviet relations as a schoolboy in Illinois.

I have many others to thank. Stephen Ambrose, James Blight, James MacGregor Burns, Mary Graham, and Strobe Talbott provided critical readings of the manuscript. Priscilla Johnson McMillan, who knew and has written about both Kennedy and Khrushchev, provided the author with lodging and counsel during long periods of research in Cambridge and Boston. Sister Cynthia Binder and Maryam Mashayekhi helped to gather research materials in Washington.

American, Soviet, British, German, and French alumni of the

Kennedy-Khrushchev years, as listed in the General Sources, agreed to be interviewed and, in some cases, provided access to private papers and diaries. I wish to pay tribute to those Americans, Soviets, and Cubans who participated in the Hawk's Cay, Cambridge, Moscow and Antigua conferences on the Missile Crisis, an invaluable source that might otherwise have been lost to history. Zvi Dor-Ner and Adrianna Bosch of WGBH-TV, Boston, kindly provided me with raw transcripts of the interviews conducted with Americans and Soviets for *War and Peace in the Nuclear Age.* Vladislav Zubok, James Blight, Benina Berger-Gould, and Peter Collier were good enough to share additional materials mentioned in the Notes.

For a decade of research help, I thank John Wickman, Martin Teasley, David Haight, and their colleagues at the Eisenhower Library; William Johnson, Barbara Anderson, Suzanne Forbes, Henry Gwiazda, Ronald Whealan, Michael Desmond, Alan Goodrich, and the staff at the Kennedy Library; as well as those men and women at the other archives listed in the General Sources.

Everyone at HarperCollins has helped to make publication of this book a pleasure. My publisher and friend Edward Burlingame was intensely involved with the volume at every stage, operating as he always does in the most distinguished tradition of American book publishing. He was abetted by Christa Weil and Kathy Banks of Edward Burlingame Books, as well as William Shinker, Buz Wyeth, Joseph Montebello, Karen Mender, Steven Sorrentino, Sheryl Fuchs, and their HarperCollins colleagues.

Research for this book was fascinating because by the late 1980s, virtually every week saw the opening of new American and Soviet sources that changed what we knew about Kennedy, Khrushchev, and their era. The appearance of important new sources continued during this book's production process, requiring the author to lard materials into the volume as late as the page-proof stage. Bill Luckey, C. Linda Dingler, Kim Lewis, Dot Gannon, and others in the HarperCollins production department responded to this challenge with high effectiveness and grace, and they deserve my gratitude. I also thank Janet Baker, who copy-edited the book; and Vincent Virga, who edited the photograph section.

During the six years of composition, my literary agent Timothy Seldes has always been a wise and faithful counselor. I am grateful to Afsaneh Mashayekhi for her consistent support, and to her and many other friends and family for putting up with the author's long absorption in the years of Kennedy and Khrushchev.

GENERAL SOURCES

Selected Bibliography

The following list includes published works cited in the Notes. For reasons of space, it does not cover the full range of secondary sources that have influenced the author's thinking on the issues and events treated in this volume.

Abel, Elie. *The Missile Crisis.* Philadelphia: Lippincott, 1966.

Adams, Sherman. *Firsthand Report.* New York: Harper, 1961.

Adenauer, Konrad. *Erinnerungen: 1959–1963.* Stuttgart: Deutsche Verlags-Anstalt, 1968.

Adler, Richard. *"You Gotta Have Heart."* New York: Donald I. Fine, 1990.

Adomeit, Hannes. *Soviet Risk-Taking and Crisis Behavior.* London: Allen & Unwin, 1982.

Allison, Graham T., *Essence of Decision: Explaining the Cuban Missile Crisis.* Boston: Little, Brown, 1971.

Alsop, Stewart. *The Center: People and Power in Political Washington.* New York: Harper, 1968.

Ambrose, Stephen E. *Eisenhower: The President.* New York: Simon and Schuster, 1984.

———. *Nixon: The Education of a Politician, 1913–1962.* New York: Simon and Schuster, 1987.

———. *Nixon: The Triumph of a Politician, 1962–1972.* New York: Simon and Schuster, 1989.

———. *Rise to Globalism.* New York: Penguin, 1988.

———, with Richard H. Immerman. *Ike's Spies: Eisenhower and the Espionage Establishment.* New York: Doubleday, 1981.

Andrew, Christopher M., and Oleg Gordievsky. *KGB: The Inside Story.* New York: HarperCollins, 1990.

Attwood, William. *The Twilight Struggle: Tales of the Cold War.* Harper, 1987.

Baker, Bobby, with Larry L. King. *Wheeling and Dealing: Confessions of a Capitol Hill Operator.* New York: Norton, 1978.

Baker, Leonard. *The Johnson Eclipse: A President's Vice Presidency.* New York: Macmillan, 1966.

Ball, Desmond. *Politics and Force Levels: The Strategic Missile Program of the Kennedy Administration.* Berkeley: University of California, 1981.

Ball, George W. *The Past Has Another Pattern.* New York: Norton, 1982.

Barnet, Richard. *The Alliance: America, Europe, Japan.* New York: Simon and Schuster, 1983.

———. *The Giants: Russia and America.* New York: Simon and Schuster, 1977.

Barron, John. *KGB: The Secret Work of Soviet Secret Agents.* London: Corgi reprint, 1975.

Berg, Raisa. *Acquired Traits.* New York: Penguin reprint, 1990.

Bergquist, Laura, and Stanley Tretick. *A Very Special President.* New York: McGraw-Hill, 1965.

Berle, Beatrice, and Travis Beal Jacobs, eds. *Navigating the Rapids: 1918–1971: From the Papers of Adolf A. Berle.* New York: Harcourt, 1973.

Beschloss, Michael R. *Kennedy and Roosevelt: The Uneasy Alliance.* New York: Norton, 1980.

———. *Mayday: Eisenhower, Khrushchev and the U-2 Affair.* New York: Harper, 1986.

———, and Thomas E. Cronin. *Essays in Honor of James MacGregor Burns.* Englewood Cliffs, N.J.: Prentice-Hall, 1988.

Bishop, Jim. *A Bishop's Confession.* Boston: Little, Brown, 1981.

———. *The Day Kennedy Was Shot.* New York: Random House, 1968.

Blair, Clay, Jr., and Joan Blair. *The Search for JFK.* New York: Putnam, 1976.

Blakey, Robert, and Richard Billings. *The Plot to Kill the President.* New York: Times Books, 1981.

Blechman, Barry, and Stephen Kaplan. *Force Without War.* Washington, D.C.: Brookings, 1978.

Blight, James G., and David A. Welch. *On the Brink: Americans and Soviets Reexamine the Missile Crisis.* New York: Farrar, Straus, 1989.

Bohlen, Charles E. *Witness to History, 1929–1969.* New York: Norton, 1973.

Bourne, Peter G. *Fidel: A Biography of Fidel Castro.* New York: Dodd, Mead, 1986.

Bowles, Chester. *Promises to Keep: My Years in Public Life, 1941–1969.* New York: Harper, 1971.

Bradlee, Benjamin C. *Conversations with Kennedy.* New York: Norton, 1975.

Branch, Taylor. *Parting the Waters: America in the King Years, 1954–63.* New York: Simon and Schuster, 1988.

Brandon, Henry. *Special Relationships.* New York: Atheneum, 1988.

Brandt, Willy. *Begegnungen und Einsichten.* Hamburg: Hoffmann & Campe Verlag, 1976.

Brodie, Fawn. *Richard Nixon: The Shaping of his Character.* New York: Norton, 1981.

Brook-Shepherd, Gordon. *The Storm Birds: Soviet Postwar Defectors.* New York: Weidenfeld, 1989.

Brown, Thomas. *JFK: History of an Image.* Bloomington, Ind.: Indiana University, 1988.

Brune, Lester H. *The Missile Crisis of October 1962: A Review of Issues and References.* Claremont, Calif.: Regina, 1985.

Bundy, McGeorge. *Danger and Survival: Choices About the Bomb in the First Fifty Years.* New York: Random House, 1988.

Burner, David, and Thomas West. *The Torch Is Passed: The Kennedy Brothers and American Liberalism.* New York: Atheneum, 1984.

Burns, James MacGregor. *Edward Kennedy and the Camelot Legacy.* New York: Norton, 1976.

———. *John Kennedy: A Political Profile.* New York: Harcourt, 1959.

Burrows, William E. *Deep Black: Space Espionage and National Security.* New York: Random House, 1986.

Carbonell, Nestor T. *And the Russians Stayed: The Sovietization of Cuba.* New York: William Morrow, 1989.

Cassini, Oleg. *In My Own Fashion.* New York: Simon and Schuster, 1987.

Cate, Curtis. *The Ides of August: The Berlin Wall Crisis, 1961.* New York: M. Evans, 1978.

Catudal, Honoré Marc. *Kennedy and the Berlin Wall Crisis.* Berlin: Verlag, 1980.

Chang, Gordon H. *Friends and Enemies: The United States, China and the Soviet Union, 1948–1972.* Stanford: Stanford University, 1990.

Chayes, Abram. *The Cuban Missile Crisis.* New York: Oxford, 1964.

Cline, Ray S. *The CIA Under Reagan, Bush & Casey.* Washington, D.C.: Acropolis, 1981.

Clubb, Oliver. *China & Russia: The "Great Game".* New York: Columbia, 1971.

Cohen, Stephen F. *Sovieticus: American Perceptions and Soviet Realities.* New York: Norton, 1985.

Cohen, Warren I. *Dean Rusk.* Totowa, N.J.: Cooper Square, 1989.

Colby, William. *Lost Victory.* Chicago: Contemporary, 1989.

Collier, Peter, and David Horowitz. *The Fords: An American Epic.* London: Collins, 1988.

———. *The Kennedys: An American Drama.* New York: Summit, 1984.

Corson, William R., and Robert T. Crowley. *The New KGB: Engine of Soviet Power.* New York: Morrow, 1985.

Cousins, Norman. *The Improbable Triumvirate: John F. Kennedy, Pope John, Nikita Khrushchev.* New York: Norton, 1972.

Crankshaw, Edward. *Khrushchev: A Career.* New York: Viking, 1966.

Davis, John H. *The Kennedys: Dynasty and Disaster.* New York: McGraw-Hill reprint, 1984.

———. *Mafia Kingfish: Carlos Marcello and the Assassination of John F. Kennedy.* New York: McGraw-Hill, 1989.

Deakin, James. *Straight Stuff: The Reporters, the White House and the Truth.* New York: William Morrow, 1984.

De Gaulle, Charles. *Memoirs: Renewal, 1958–1962.* London: Weidenfeld and Nicholson, 1971. Translated by Terence Kilmartin.

Demaris, Ovid. *The Director: An Oral Biography of J. Edgar Hoover.* New York: Harper's Magazine, 1975.

Destler, I.M. *Presidents, Bureaucrats and Foreign Policy.* Princeton: Princeton University, 1974.

———, Leslie H. Gelb and Anthony Lake. *Our Own Worst Enemy: The Unmaking of American Foreign Policy.* New York: Simon and Schuster, 1984. Hereafter cited as Destler.

Detzer, David. *The Brink: Cuban Missile Crisis, 1962.* New York: Crowell, 1979.

Dinerstein, Herbert S. *The Making of a Missile Crisis.* Baltimore: Johns Hopkins, 1976.

Divine, Robert A. *Blowing on the Wind: The Nuclear Test Ban Debate, 1954–1960.* New York: Oxford, 1978.

———. *Foreign Policy and U.S. Presidential Elections: 1952–1960.* New York: New Viewpoints, 1974.

Donmen, Arthur J. *Conflict in Laos: The Politics of Neutralization*. New York: Praeger, 1964.

Donovan, Hedley. *Roosevelt to Reagan: A Reporter's Encounter with Nine Presidents*. New York: Harper, 1985.

Donovan, James B. *Challenges: Reflections of a Lawyer-at-Large*. New York: Atheneum, 1967.

Douglas, William O. *The Court Years*. New York: Random House, 1980.

Eddowes, Michael. *Khrushchev Killed Kennedy*. Privately published, 1975.

————. *The Oswald File*. New York: Clarkson N. Potter, 1977.

Eisenhower, Dwight D. *The White House Years: Waging Peace, 1956–1961*. New York: Doubleday, 1965.

Enthoven, Alain, and Wayne Smith. *How Much is Enough?* New York: Harper, 1971.

Epernay, Mark (John Kenneth Galbraith). *The McLandress Dimension*. Boston: Houghton Mifflin, 1963.

Epstein, Edward Jay. *Legend: The Secret World of Lee Harvey Oswald*. New York: McGraw-Hill, 1978.

Exner, Judith. *My Story*. New York: Grove, 1977.

Faber, Harold, ed. *The Kennedy Years*. New York: Viking, 1964.

Fay, Paul B., Jr. *The Pleasure of His Company*. New York: Harper, 1966.

Ferrell, Robert H., ed. *Off the Record: The Private Papers of Harry S. Truman*. New York: Harper, 1980.

Finder, Joseph. *Red Carpet*. New York: Holt, 1983.

Firestone, Bernard J. *The Quest for Nuclear Stability: John F. Kennedy and the Soviet Union*. Westport, Conn.: Greenwood, 1982.

Fisher, Eddie. *Eddie: My Life, My Loves*. New York: Harper, 1981

FitzSimons, Louise. *The Kennedy Doctrine*. New York: Random House, 1972.

Foreign Relations of the United States: 1950. Washington, D.C.: U.S. Government Printing Office, 1975.

Fox, Stephen. *Blood and Power: Organized Crime in Twentieth-Century America*. New York: Morrow, 1989.

Frankland, Mark. *Khrushchev*. London: Harmondsworth, Penguin, 1966.

Franqui, Carlos. *Family Portrait with Fidel*. New York: Vintage reprint, 1984. Translated by Alfred MacAdam.

Fulbright, J. William, with Seth P. Tillman. *The Price of Empire*. New York: Pantheon, 1989.

Gaddis, John Lewis. *The Long Peace: Inquiries into the History of the Cold War*. New York: Oxford, 1987.

————. *Russia, the Soviet Union, and the United States*. New York: Oxford, 1978.

————. *Strategies of Containment: A Critical Appraisal of Postwar American Security Policy*. New York: Oxford, 1982.

Galbraith, John Kenneth. *Ambassador's Journal*. Boston: Houghton Mifflin, 1969.

————. *A Life in Our Times*. Boston: Houghton Mifflin, 1981.

Gallagher, Mary Barelli. *My Life with Jacqueline Kennedy*. New York: McKay, 1969.

Gallup, George H., ed. *The Gallup Poll: Public Opinion, 1935–1971*. New York: Random House, 1972. Hereafter cited as *Gallup*.

Garthoff, Raymond. *Detente and Confrontation: American-Soviet Relations from Nixon to Reagan*. Washington, D.C.: Brookings, 1985.

————. *Intelligence Assessment and Policymaking: A Decision Point in the Kennedy Administration.* Washington, D.C.: Brookings, 1984.

————. *Reflections on the Cuban Missile Crisis.* Washington, D.C.: Brookings, 1987. Hereafter cited as Garthoff.

————. *Reflections on the Cuban Missile Crisis* (second edition). Washington, D.C.: Brookings, 1989. Hereafter cited as Garthoff (1989).

Gehlen, Reinhard. *The Service: The Memoirs of General Reinhard Gehlen.* New York: Popular Library, 1972.

Gelb, Norman. *The Berlin Wall: Kennedy, Khrushchev and a Showdown in the Heart of Europe.* New York: Times Books, 1986.

George, Alexander L., and Richard Smoke. *Deterrence in American Foreign Policy.* New York: Columbia, 1974.

Geyer, Georgie Anne. *Guerrilla Prince: The Untold Story of Fidel Castro.* Boston: Little, Brown, 1991.

Giancana, Antoinette, and Thomas C. Renner. *Mafia Princess.* New York: Avon reprint, 1984.

Goldman, Marshall I. *Gorbachev's Challenge: Economic Reform in the Age of High Technology.* New York: Norton, 1987.

Goldwater, Barry M. *With No Apologies.* New York: William Morrow, 1979.

————, with Jack Casserly. *Goldwater.* New York: Doubleday, 1988.

Goodwin, Doris Kearns. *The Fitzgeralds and the Kennedys.* New York: Simon and Schuster, 1987.

Goodwin, Richard N. *Remembering America: A Voice from the Sixties.* Boston: Little, Brown, 1988.

Graves, Robert. *Oxford Addresses on Poetry.* London: Cassell, 1962.

Griffith, William E. *Albania and the Sino-Soviet Rift.* Cambridge, Mass.: MIT, 1963.

————. *The Sino-Soviet Rift.* Cambridge: MIT, 1964.

Gromyko, Anatoly. *1036 dnei prezidenta Kennedi [The 1036 Days of President Kennedy].* Moscow: Politizdat, 1971.

————. *Vneshnaya politika SShA: uroki i deistvitel'nost', 60-70-e gody [U.S.A. Foreign Policy: Lessons and Reality, the 1960s and 1970s].* Moscow: Mezdunarodnaya Otnosheniya, 1978.

Gromyko, Anatoly, and Andrei Kokoshin. *Bratya Kennedi [The Kennedy Brothers].* Moscow: Mysl, 1985.

Gromyko, Andrei. *Memoirs.* New York: Doubleday, 1989. Translated by Harold Shukman.

Grossman, Michael Baruch, and Martha Joynt Kumar. *Portraying the President: The White House and the News Media.* Baltimore: Johns Hopkins, 1981.

Gunther, John. *Inside Europe.* 1937.

————. *Procession.* New York: Harper, 1965.

Guthman, Edwin O. *We Band of Brothers.* New York: Harper, 1971.

————, and Jeffrey Shulman. *Robert Kennedy: In His Own Words: The Unpublished Recollections of the Kennedy Years.* New York: Bantam, 1988.

Halberstam, David. *The Best and the Brightest.* New York: Random House, 1963.

————. *The Powers That Be.* New York: Knopf, 1979.

Haldeman, H.R., with Joseph DiMona. *The Ends of Power.* New York: Times Books, 1978.

Hammer, Armand, with Neil Lyndon. *Hammer.* New York: Putnam, 1987.

Hammer, Ellen J. *A Death in November: America in Vietnam, 1963.* New York: Dutton, 1987.

Hammer, Manfried, et al. *Das Mauerbuch.* Berlin: Oberbaum, 1984.

Hearst, William Randolph, Jr., Frank Conniff and Bob Considine. *Ask Me Anything: Our Adventures with Khrushchev.* New York: McGraw Hill, 1960.

Herken, Gregg. *Counsels of War.* New York: Knopf, 1985.

Heymann, C. David. *A Woman Named Jackie.* New York: Lyle Stuart, 1989.

Higgins, Trumbull. *The Perfect Failure: Kennedy, Eisenhower and the CIA at the Bay of Pigs.* New York: Norton, 1987.

Hilsman, Roger. *To Move a Nation: The Politics of Foreign Policy in the Administration of John F. Kennedy.* New York: Doubleday, 1967.

Hirsch, Richard, and John Trento. *The National Aeronautics and Space Administration.* New York: Praeger, 1973.

Hofmann, Gunter. *Willy Brandt: Porträt eines Aufklärers aus Deutschland.* Hamburg: Rowohlt, 1988.

Höhne, Heinz, and Hermann Zolling. *The General Was a Spy.* New York: Coward, McCann and Geoghegan, 1972.

Holloway, David. *The Soviet Union and the Arms Race.* New Haven: Yale, 1983.

Horelick, Arnold L., and Myron Rush. *Strategic Power and Soviet Foreign Policy.* Chicago: University of Chicago, 1966.

Horne, Alistair. *Macmillan: 1957–1986.* London: Macmillan, 1989.

Hurt, Henry. *Reasonable Doubt.* New York: Holt, 1985.

Hyland, William and Richard Shryock. *The Fall of Khrushchev.* New York: Funk & Wagnalls, 1968.

Isaacson, Walter and Evan Thomas. *The Wise Men: Six Friends and the World They Made.* New York: Simon and Schuster, 1986.

Jahn, Hans Edgar. *An Adenauers Seite.* Munich: Langen Müller, 1987.

Jaipur, Maharani of. *A Princess Remembers.* Delhi: Tarang reprint, 1984.

Johnson, Haynes. *The Bay of Pigs.* New York: Norton, 1984.

———, and Bernard M. Gwertzman. *Fulbright: The Dissenter.* New York: Doubleday, 1968.

Johnson, Lyndon B. *The Vantage Point: Perspectives on the Presidency, 1963–1969.* New York: Holt, 1971.

Johnson, Priscilla. *Khrushchev and the Arts: The Politics of Soviet Culture: 1962–1964.* Boston: MIT, 1965.

Kalb, Madeleine G. *The Congo Cables: The Cold War in Africa.* New York: Macmillan, 1982.

Kaplan, Fred. *The Wizards of Armageddon.* New York: Simon and Schuster, 1983.

Karnow, Stanley. *Vietnam: A History.* New York: Penguin reprint, 1984.

Kearns, Doris. *Lyndon Johnson and the American Dream.* New York: Harper, 1976.

Kelley, Kitty. *Jackie Oh!* New York: Ballantine reprint, 1978.

———. *His Way: The Unauthorized Biography of Frank Sinatra.* New York: Bantam reprint, 1987.

Kennan, George F. *Memoirs: 1950–1963.* Boston: Little, Brown, 1972.

Kennedy, Edward M., ed., *The Fruitful Bough.* Privately published, 1965.

Kennedy, John F. *Profiles in Courage.* Harper, 1964.

———. *The Strategy of Peace.* New York: Harper, 1960.

———. *Why England Slept.* New York: Wilfred Funk, 1940.

Kennedy, Robert F. *The Enemy Within.* New York: Harper, 1960.

———. *Thirteen Days: A Memoir of the Cuban Missile Crisis.* New York: Norton, 1969. Hereafter cited as RFK13.

Kennedy, Rose Fitzgerald. *Times to Remember.* New York: Doubleday, 1974.

Kern, Montague. *The Kennedy Crises: The Press, the Presidency and Foreign Policy.* Chapel Hill: University of North Carolina, 1983.

Khrushchev, Nikita S., *Khrushchev Remembers.* Boston: Little, Brown, 1970. Translated and edited by Strobe Talbott. Hereafter cited as NSK1.

———. *Khrushchev Remembers: The Glasnost Tapes.* Boston: Little, Brown, 1990. Translated and edited by Jerrold L. Schechter with Vyacheslav V. Luchkov. Hereafter cited as NSK3.

———. *Khrushchev Remembers: The Last Testament.* Boston: Little, Brown, 1974. Translated and edited by Strobe Talbott. Hereafter cited as NSK2.

Khrushchev, Sergei N., *Khrushchev on Khrushchev: An Inside Account of the Man and His Era.* Boston: Little, Brown, 1990. Edited and translated by William Taubman. Hereafter cited as SNK.

King, Larry, with Peter Occhiogrosso. *Tell It to the King.* New York: Jove reprint, 1989.

Kissinger, Henry A. *White House Years.* Boston: Little, Brown, 1979.

Kistiakowsky, George B. *A Scientist at the White House.* Cambridge: Harvard, 1976.

Klurfeld, Herman. *Winchell: His Life and Times.* New York: Praeger, 1976.

Knightley, Phillip, and Caroline Kennedy. *An Affair of State: The Profumo Case and the Framing of Stephen Ward.* New York: Atheneum, 1987.

Koch, Thilo. *Tagebuch aus Washington.* Frankfurt: Fischer Bücherei, 1965.

Koerfer, Daniel. *Kampf ums Kanzleramt; Erhard und Adenauer.* Stuttgart: Deutsche Verlags-Anstalt, 1987.

Kohler, Foy D. *Understanding the Russians.* New York: Harper, 1970.

Kokoshin, Andrei, and Sergei Rogov. *Serye kardinaly belogo doma* [*Gray Cardinals of the White House*]. Moscow: Novosti, 1986.

Kraft, Joseph. *Profiles in Power: A Washington Insight.* New York: New American Library, 1966.

Kroll, Hans. *Lebenserinnerungen eines Botschafters.* Cologne: Kiepenheuer und Witsch, 1967.

Kutler, Stanley I. *The Wars of Watergate.* New York: Knopf, 1990.

Lacey, Robert. *Ford: The Men and the Machine.* Boston: Little, Brown, 1986.

LaFeaber, Walter. *America, Russia and the Cold War, 1945–1975.* New York: John Wiley, 1976.

Laqueur, Walter. *A World of Secrets: The Uses and Limits of Intelligence.* New York: Basic, 1985.

Lash, Joseph P. *A World of Love: Eleanor Roosevelt and Her Friends, 1943–1962.* New York: Doubleday, 1984.

Lasky, Victor. *It Didn't Start with Watergate.* New York: Dial, 1977.

———. *J.F.K.: The Man and the Myth.* New York: Macmillan, 1963.

Lawrence, Bill. *Six Presidents, Too Many Wars.* New York: Saturday Review, 1972.

Lebow, Richard Ned. *Between Peace and War: The Nature of International Crisis.* Baltimore: Johns Hopkins, 1981.

Legvold, Robert. *Gorbachev's Foreign Policy: How Should the U.S. Respond?* New York: Foreign Policy Association, 1988.

Leonhard, Wolfgang. *Child of the Revolution.* Chicago, Regnery, 1958.

——. *The Kremlin Since Stalin.* New York: Praeger, 1962.

Lewis, John Wilson, and Xue Litai. *China Builds the Bomb.* Stanford: Stanford University, 1988.

Lieberson, Goddard, and Joan Meyers, eds. *John Fitzgerald Kennedy: . . . As We Remember Him.* New York: Atheneum, 1965.

Lincoln, Evelyn. *Kennedy and Johnson.* New York: Holt, 1968.

——. *My Twelve Years with John F. Kennedy.* New York: McKay, 1965.

Linden, Carl A. *Khrushchev and the Soviet Leadership, 1957–1964.* Baltimore: Johns Hopkins, 1966.

Lippmann, Walter. *Conversations with Walter Lippmann.* Boston: Atlantic Monthly, 1965.

Logsdon, John M. *The Decision to Go to the Moon: Project Apollo and the National Interest.* Cambridge: MIT, 1970.

Lowell, Robert. *For the Union Dead.* New York: Farrar, Straus, 1964.

Lukas, J. Anthony. *Nightmare: The Underside of the Nixon Years.* New York: Viking, 1976.

MacDuffie, Marshall, *The Red Carpet.* New York: Norton, 1955.

MacMahon, Edward B., and Leonard Curry. *Medical Coverups in the White House.* Washington, D.C.: Farragut, 1987.

Macmillan, Harold. *At the End of the Day.* New York: Harper, 1973.

——. *Pointing the Way: 1959–1961.* New York: Harper, 1972.

——. *Riding the Storm: 1956–1959.* New York: Harper, 1971.

MacNeil, Robert. *The Right Place at the Right Time.* Boston: Little, Brown, 1982.

Mahoney, Richard D. *JFK: Ordeal in Africa.* New York: Oxford, 1983.

Manchester, William. *The Death of a President: November 20–25, 1963.* New York: Harper, 1967.

——. *One Brief Shining Moment: Remembering Kennedy.* Boston: Little, Brown, 1983.

——. *Portrait of a President: John F. Kennedy in Profile.* Boston: Little, Brown, 1962.

Marchetti, Victor, and John Marks. *The CIA and the Cult of Intelligence.* New York: Dell reprint, 1975.

Martin, David C. *Wilderness of Mirrors.* Harper, 1980.

Martin, John Bartlow. *Adlai Stevenson and the World.* New York: Doubleday, 1977.

——. *It Seems Like Only Yesterday.* New York: Morrow, 1986.

Martin, Lawrence. *The Presidents and the Prime Ministers: Washington and Ottawa Face to Face.* New York: Doubleday, 1982.

Martin, Ralph. *A Hero for Our Time: An Intimate Story of the Kennedy Years.* New York: Macmillan, 1983.

Mazo, Earl. *Richard Nixon.* New York: Harper, 1959.

McCauley, Martin, ed. *Khrushchev and Khrushchevism.* London: Macmillan, 1987.

McDougall, Walter A. *. . . the Heavens and the Earth: A Political History of the Space Age.* New York: Basic, 1985.

McGehee, Ralph W. *Deadly Deceits: My 25 Years in the CIA.* New York: Sheridan Square, 1983.

MccGwire, Michael. *Military Objectives in Soviet Foreign Policy.* Washington, D.C.: Brookings, 1987.

McLellan, David S., and David C. Acheson, eds. *Among Friends: Personal Letters of Dean Acheson.* New York: Dodd, Mead, 1980.

McMillan, Priscilla Johnson. *Marina and Lee.* New York: Harper, 1978.

McNamara, Robert S. *Blundering into Disaster.* New York: Pantheon, 1986.

McNeil, Neil. *Dirksen: Portrait of a Public Man.* Cleveland: World, 1970.

McSherry, James E. *Kennedy and Khrushchev in Retrospect.* Palo Alto: Open-Door Press, 1971.

Medved, Michael. *The Shadow Presidents: The Secret History of the Chief Executives and Their Top Aides.* New York: Times Books, 1979.

Medvedev, Roy. *All Stalin's Men.* New York: Anchor/Doubleday, 1984. Translated by Harold Shukman.

———. *Khrushchev.* New York: Doubleday, 1983. Translated by Brian Pearce.

Micunovic, Veljko, *Moscow Diary.* New York: Doubleday, 1980. Translated by David Floyd.

Miller, Arthur. *Timebends: A Life.* New York: Grove, 1987.

Miller, Merle. *Lyndon: An Oral Biography.* New York: Putnam, 1980.

Miroff, Bruce. *Pragmatic Illusions: The Presidential Politics of John F. Kennedy.* New York: McKay, 1976.

Moldea, Dan E. *The Hoffa Wars: Teamsters, Rebels, Politicians and the Mob.* New York: Paddington, 1978.

Moran, Lord. *Winston Churchill: The Struggle for Survival, 1940–1965.* London: Constable, 1966.

Morley, Morris H. *Imperial State and Revolution: The United States and Cuba, 1952–1986.* London: Cambridge, 1987.

Morris, Charles R. *Iron Destinies, Lost Opportunities: The Arms Race Between the U.S.A. and the U.S.S.R., 1945–1987.* New York: Harper, 1988.

Mosley, Leonard. *Dulles: A Biography of Eleanor, Allen and John Foster Dulles and Their Family Network.* New York: Dial, 1978.

Navasky, Victor S. *Kennedy Justice.* New York: Atheneum, 1971.

Neustadt, Richard E. *Presidential Power: The Politics of Leadership.* New York: Wiley, 1960.

Neustadt, Richard E., and Ernest R. May. *Thinking in Time: The Uses of History for Decision Makers.* New York: The Free Press, 1986.

Newhouse, John. *War and Peace in the Nuclear Age.* New York: Knopf, 1989.

Nitze, Paul H. *From Hiroshima to Glasnost.* New York: Grove, 1989.

Nixon, Richard. *RN: The Memoirs of Richard Nixon.* New York: Grosset & Dunlap, 1978.

———. *Six Crises.* New York: Doubleday, 1962.

Novosti. *Nikita Khrushchev: Life and Destiny.* Moscow: Novosti, 1989.

Nye, Joseph S., Jr. *Bound to Lead: The Changing Nature of American Power.* New York: Basic, 1990.

Oberg, James E. *Red Star in Orbit.* New York: Random House, 1981.

———. *Uncovering Soviet Disasters: Exploring the Limits of Glasnost.* New York: Random House, 1988.

O'Donnell, Kenneth P. and David F. Powers with Joe McCarthy. *"Johnny, We Hardly Knew Ye": Memories of John Fitzgerald Kennedy.* Boston: Little, Brown, 1972. Hereafter cited as Odon.

Opotowsky, Stan. *The Kennedy Government.* New York: Dutton, 1961.

Pachter, Henry M. *Collision Course: The Cuban Missile Crisis and Coexistence.* New York: Praeger, 1963.

Paper, Lewis J. *The Promise and the Performance: The Leadership of John F. Kennedy.* New York: Crown, 1975.

Parmet, Herbert S. *Jack: The Struggles of John F. Kennedy.* New York: Dial, 1980.

————. *JFK: The Presidency of John F. Kennedy.* New York: Dial, 1983.

Paterson, Thomas G., ed. *Kennedy's Quest for Victory.* New York: Oxford, 1989.

Pearson, John. *The Life of Ian Fleming.* London: Pan reprint, 1966.

Penkovsky, Oleg. *The Penkovsky Papers.* New York: Ballantine reprint, 1982.

Petschull, Jürgen. *Die Mauer.* Munich: Stern 1981.

Phillips, David Atlee. *The Night Watch.* New York: Ballantine reprint, 1977.

Pierpoint, Robert. *At the White House: Assignment to Six Presidents.* New York: Putnam, 1981.

Pistrak, Lazar, *Khrushchev's Rise to Power.* New York: Praeger, 1961.

Plimpton, George, and Jean Stein. *American Journey: The Times of Robert Kennedy.* New York: Harcourt, 1970.

Powers, Richard Gid. *Secrecy and Power: The Life of J. Edgar Hoover.* New York: Free Press, 1987.

Powers, Thomas. *The Man Who Kept the Secrets: Richard Helms & the CIA.* New York: Knopf, 1979.

Prados, John. *The Soviet Estimate: U.S. Intelligence Analysis and Russian Military Strength.* New York: Dial, 1982.

Prittie, Terrence. *Willy Brandt.* New York: Schocken, 1974.

Public Papers of the Presidents of the United States: Dwight D. Eisenhower, 1953–1961. U.S. Government Printing Office, 1954–1961. Hereafter cited as DDEPP.

Public Papers of the Presidents of the United States: John F. Kennedy, 1961–1963. U.S. Government Printing Office, 1962–1964. Hereafter cited as JFKPP.

Quirk, John Patrick. *The Central Intelligence Agency.* Guilford, Conn.: Foreign Intelligence Press, 1986.

Rabinowitch, Alexander. *Revolution and Politics in Russia.* Bloomington, Ind.: Indiana University, 1972.

Ranelagh, John. *The Agency: The Rise and Decline of the CIA.* New York: Simon and Schuster, 1986.

Report to the President by the Commission on CIA Activities within the United States, Nelson A. Rockefeller, Chairman. Washington, D.C.: U.S. Government Printing Office, 1975.

Reston, James, Jr. *The Lone Star: The Life of John Connally.* New York: Harper, 1989.

Roberts, Chalmers M. *First Rough Draft.* New York: Praeger, 1973.

Rositzke, Harry. *The CIA's Secret Operations.* New York: Reader's Digest, 1977.

————. *The KGB: The Eyes of Russia.* London: Sidgwick & Jackson reprint, 1983.

Rostow, W.W. *The Diffusion of Power.* New York: Macmillan, 1972.

————. *Open Skies.* Austin: University of Texas, 1982.

Rovere, Richard. *Final Reports.* New York: Doubleday, 1984.

Rowan, Carl. *Breaking Barriers.* Boston: Little, Brown, 1991.

Rusk, Dean, with Richard Rusk. *As I Saw It.* New York: Norton, 1990.

Rust, William J. *Kennedy in Vietnam.* New York: Scribners, 1985.

Sakharov, Andrei. *Memoirs.* New York: Knopf, 1990. Translated by Richard Lourie.

Salinger, Pierre. *With Kennedy*. New York: Doubleday, 1966. Hereafter cited as Sal.

Salisbury, Harrison. *A Journey for Our Times*. New York: Harper, 1983.

———. *Without Fear Or Favor: The New York Times and Its Times*. New York: Times Books, 1980.

Saunders, Frank, with James Southwood. *Torn Lace Curtain*. New York: Holt, 1982.

Scheim, David E. *Contract on America: The Mafia Murder of President John F. Kennedy*. New York: Shapolsky, 1988.

Schick, Jack M. *The Berlin Crisis, 1958–1962*. Philadelphia: University of Pennsylvania, 1971.

Schlesinger, Arthur M., Jr. *The Cycles of American History*. Boston: Houghton Mifflin, 1986.

———. *Kennedy or Nixon: Does It Make Any Difference?* New York: Macmillan, 1960.

———. *Robert Kennedy and His Times*. Boston: Houghton Mifflin, 1978. Hereafter cited as AMSRK.

———. *A Thousand Days: John F. Kennedy in the White House*. Boston: Houghton Mifflin, 1965. Hereafter cited as AMSTD.

Schmidt, Helmut. *Menschen und Mächte*. Berlin: Siedler Verlag, 1987.

Schoenbaum, Thomas J. *Waging Peace and War: Dean Rusk in the Truman, Kennedy and Johnson Years*. New York: Simon and Schuster, 1988.

Schorr, Daniel. *Clearing the Air*. Boston: Houghton Mifflin, 1977.

Seaborg, Glenn T. *Kennedy, Khrushchev and the Test Ban*. Berkeley: University of California, 1981.

———. *Stemming the Tide: Arms Control in the Johnson Years*. Lexington, Mass.: Lexington, 1987.

Searls, Hank. *The Lost Prince: Young Joe, the Forgotten Kennedy*. Cleveland: World, 1969.

Sejna, Jan. *We Will Bury You*. London: Sidgwick & Jackson, 1982.

Shell, Kurt L. *Bedrohung und Bewährung: Führung und Bewölkerung in der Berlin Krise*. Cologne: Westdeutscher Verlag, 1965.

Shevchenko, Arkady N. *Breaking with Moscow*. New York: Knopf, 1985.

Shulman, Marshall. *Beyond the Cold War*. New Haven: Yale, 1966.

———. *Stalin's Foreign Policy Reappraised*. Cambridge: Harvard, 1963.

Sick, Gary. *All Fall Down: America's Tragic Encounter with Iran*. New York: Random House, 1985.

Sidey, Hugh. *John F. Kennedy, President*. New York: Atheneum, 1963.

———. *John F. Kennedy, President* (second edition). New York: Atheneum, 1964. Hereafter cited as Sidey (1964).

Simmonds, George W., ed. *Soviet Leaders*. New York: Crowell, 1967.

Slater, Ellis D. *The Ike I Knew*. Privately published, 1980.

Slusser, Robert M. *The Berlin Crisis of 1961*. Baltimore: Johns Hopkins, 1973.

Smith, Jean Edward. *The Defense of Berlin*. Baltimore: Johns Hopkins, 1963.

Smith, Joseph Burkholder. *Portrait of a Cold Warrior*. New York: Putnam, 1976.

Smith, Wayne. *The Closest of Enemies*. New York: Norton, 1987.

Spector, Leonard C. *Nuclear Proliferation Today*. New York: Vintage reprint, 1984.

Sorensen, Theodore C. *Kennedy*. New York: Harper, 1965. Hereafter cited as Sor.

Steel, Ronald. *Walter Lippmann and the American Century*. Boston: Atlantic Little, Brown, 1980.

Stein, Jean, and George Plimpton. *American Journey: The Times of Robert Kennedy.* New York: Harcourt, 1970.

Stoughton, Cecil, and Chester V. Clifton. *The Memories: JFK, 1961–1963.* New York: Norton, 1973.

Strauss, Franz-Josef. *Die Erinnerungen.* Berlin: Siedler, 1989.

Stromseth, Jane E. *The Origins of Flexible Response.* New York: St. Martin's, 1988.

Stützle, Walther. *Kennedy und Adenauer in der Berlin-Krise, 1961–1962.* Bonn: Verlag Neue Gesellschaft, 1973.

Sullivan, William, with Bill Brown. *The Bureau: My Thirty Years in Hoover's FBI.* New York: Pinnacle reprint, 1979.

Sulzberger, C.L. *The Last of the Giants.* New York: Macmillan, 1970.

Summers, Anthony. *Conspiracy.* New York: Paragon reprint, 1989.

———. *Goddess: The Secret Lives of Marilyn Monroe.* New York: Onyx reprint, 1986.

———, with Stephen Dorril. *Honeytrap: The Secret Worlds of Stephen Ward.* London: Weidenfeld, 1987.

Szulc, Tad. *Fidel: A Critical Portrait.* New York: Morrow, 1986.

Talbott, Strobe. *The Master of the Game: Paul Nitze and the Nuclear Peace.* New York: Knopf, 1988.

Tatu, Michel. *Power in the Kremlin.* New York: Viking, 1969. Translated by Helen Katel.

Taubman, William. *Stalin's American Policy.* New York: Norton, 1982.

Taylor, Maxwell. *Swords and Plowshares.* New York: Norton, 1972.

Terrill, Ross. *Mao: A Biography.* New York: Harper, 1980.

Theoharis, Athan G., and John Stuart Cox. *The Boss: J. Edgar Hoover and the Great American Inquisition.* Philadelphia: Temple, 1988.

Thomas, Hugh. *Cuba: The Pursuit of Freedom.* New York: Harper, 1971.

Thomas, Liselotte, et. al. *Walter Ulbricht.* Berlin: Staatsverlag der Deutschen Demokratischen Republik, 1968.

Thompson, Kenneth W., ed. *The Kennedy Presidency: Seventeen Intimate Perspectives of John F. Kennedy.* Lanham, Md.: University Press of America, 1985.

Travell, Janet. *Office Hours: Day and Night.* Cleveland: World, 1968.

Trewhitt, Henry L. *McNamara.* New York: Harper, 1971.

Turner, Stansfield. *Secrecy and Democracy.* Boston: Houghton Mifflin, 1985.

Ulam, Adam. *Expansion and Coexistence: Soviet Foreign Policy, 1971-73.* New York: Praeger, 1974

———. *The Rivals: America and Russia Since World War II.* New York: Viking, 1971.

U.S. Arms Control and Disarmament Agency. *Documents on Disarmament, 1961.* Washington, D.C.: U.S. Government Printing Office, 1962.

U.S. Congress. *Memorial Addresses and Tributes in Eulogy of John Fitzgerald Kennedy.* Washington, D.C.: U.S. Government Printing Office, 1964.

U.S. House of Representatives. *Investigation of the Assassination of President John F. Kennedy.* Washington, D.C.: U.S. Government Printing Office, 1979. Hereafter cited as *Assassination Report.*

U.S. Senate. *Executive Sessions of the Senate Foreign Relations Committee (Historical Series): 1961–1963.* Washington, D.C.: U.S. Government Printing Office, 1984–1986. Hereafter cited as DFR by year.

———. *Joint Appearances of Senator John F. Kennedy and Vice President Richard M.*

Nixon: Presidential Campaign of 1960. Washington, D.C.: U.S. Government Printing Office, 1961.

———. *The Speeches of Senator John F. Kennedy: Presidential Campaign of 1960.* Washington, D.C.: U.S. Government Printing Office, 1961. Hereafter cited as PCS.

———. *The Speeches of Vice President Richard M. Nixon: Presidential Campaign of 1960.* Washington, D.C.: U.S. Government Printing Office, 1961.

U.S. Senate, Select Committee on Intelligence Activities. *Interim Report: Alleged Assassination Plots Involving Foreign Leaders.* Washington, D.C.: U.S. Government Printing Office, 1975. Hereafter cited as *Assassination Plots.*

Vidal, Gore, and Robert J. Stanton. *Views from a Window: Conversations with Gore Vidal.* Secaucus, N.J.: Lyle Stuart, 1980.

Von Hoffmann, Nicholas. *Citizen Cohn.* New York: Doubleday, 1988.

Walton, Richard J. *Cold War and Counterrevolution: The Foreign Policy of John F. Kennedy.* New York: Penguin reprint, 1972.

Watt, D.C. *Survey of International Affairs, 1961.* London: Oxford, 1965.

Weinberg, Steve. *Hammer: The Untold Story.* Boston: Little, Brown, 1989.

Weintal, Edward, and Charles Bartlett. *Facing the Brink: An Intimate Study of Crisis Diplomacy.* New York: Scribner, 1967.

Weissman, Steve, and Herbert Krosney. *The Islamic Bomb.* New York: Times Books, 1981.

West, J.B., with Mary Lynn Kotz. *Upstairs at the White House.* New York: Warner reprint, 1974.

White, Theodore H. *In Search of History.* New York: Harper, 1978.

———. *The Making of the President: 1960.* New York: Atheneum, 1961.

———. *The Making of the President: 1964.* New York: Atheneum, 1965.

Wills, Garry. *The Kennedy Imprisonment: A Meditation on Power.* Boston: Little, Brown, 1982.

Wise, David. *The Politics of Lying: Government Deception, Secrecy and Power.* New York: Random House, 1973.

Wise, David, and Thomas B. Ross. *The Invisible Government: The CIA and U.S. Intelligence.* New York: Vintage reprint, 1974.

Wofford, Harris. *Of Kennedys and Kings: Making Sense of the Sixties.* New York: Farrar, Straus, 1980.

Wright, Lawrence. *In the New World: Growing Up with America, 1960–1984.* New York: Knopf, 1987.

Wyden, Peter S. *Bay of Pigs: The Untold Story.* New York: Simon and Schuster, 1979.

———. *Wall: The Inside Story of Divided Berlin.* New York: Simon and Schuster, 1989.

Zolling, Hermann, and Uwe Bahnsen. *Kalter Winter im August.* Oldenburg: Gerhard Stalling, 1967.

Manuscript Collections

Joseph and Stewart Alsop Papers, Library of Congress, courtesy of Joseph Alsop.

Lord Beaverbrook Papers, House of Lords Record Office, London.

Adolf A. Berle Diary, Franklin D. Roosevelt Library.

Charles Bohlen Papers, Library of Congress.

Chester Bowles Papers, Yale University Library.

John Mason Brown Papers, Harvard University.

James MacGregor Burns Papers, private possession, Williamstown, Mass., courtesy of James MacGregor Burns.

Homer Capehart Papers, Indiana State Library, Indianapolis, Ind.

Everett Dirksen Papers, Dirksen Congressional Leadership Research Center, Pekin, Ill.

John Foster Dulles Papers, Dwight D. Eisenhower Library and Princeton University.

Dwight D. Eisenhower Papers, Dwight D. Eisenhower Library.

Federal Bureau of Investigation Files, Washington, D.C.

Foreign Office Archives, Public Record Office, Kew Gardens, Surrey, U.K.

J. William Fulbright Papers, University of Arkansas.

John Kenneth Galbraith Papers, John F. Kennedy Library.

W. Averell Harriman Papers, Library of Congress, courtesy of Pamela Harriman and Clark Clifford.

Christian Herter Papers, Dwight D. Eisenhower Library and Harvard University.

Bourke B. Hickenlooper Papers, Herbert C. Hoover Library.

Roger Hilsman Papers, John F. Kennedy Library.

Lyndon B. Johnson Papers, Lyndon B. Johnson Library.

John F. Kennedy Papers, John F. Kennedy Library.

Robert F. Kennedy Oral History Collection, John F. Kennedy Library.

Robert F. Kennedy Papers, John F. Kennedy Library.

Foy D. Kohler Diary and Papers, University of Toledo and private possession, Tequesta, Florida, courtesy of Foy D. Kohler.

Arthur Krock Papers, Princeton University.

Walter Lippmann Papers, Yale University.

Henry R. Luce Papers, Library of Congress and private possession, New York, courtesy of Henry Luce III.

John Bartlow Martin Papers, Princeton University.

John J. McCloy Papers, Amherst College.

Wayne Morse Papers, University of Oregon, Eugene.

Richard Nixon Papers, National Archives, Alexandria, Va.

Richard Nixon Papers, National Archives, Laguna Niguel, Calif.

Lauris Norstad Papers, Dwight D. Eisenhower Library.

Drew Pearson Papers, Lyndon B. Johnson Library.

Dean Rusk Collection, University of Georgia, Athens.

Richard Russell Papers, University of Georgia, Athens.

Pierre Salinger Papers, John F. Kennedy Library.

Arthur M. Schlesinger, Jr., Papers, John F. Kennedy Library.

George Smathers Papers, University of Florida, Gainesville.

Howard Snyder Diary, Dwight D. Eisenhower Library

Theodore C. Sorensen Papers, John F. Kennedy Library.

Adlai E. Stevenson Papers, Princeton University.

Llewellyn E. Thompson Papers, family possession, Washington, D.C., courtesy of Jane Thompson.

Harry S. Truman Papers, Harry S. Truman Library, Independence, Mo.
Time Archives, Time & Life Building, New York, courtesy of Henry Luce III.

Records of Conferences

Proceedings of the Hawk's Cay Conference on the Cuban Missile Crisis, David A. Welch, ed. Marathon, Florida, March 5–8, 1987, sponsored by the Carnegie Corporation, the Alfred P. Sloan Foundation and the Center for Science and International Affairs, Harvard University. Participating former American officials included George Ball, McGeorge Bundy, Abram Chayes, Douglas Dillon, Raymond Garthoff, Robert McNamara, Arthur Schlesinger, Jr., Theodore Sorensen and Maxwell Taylor. Hereafter cited as HCCT.

Proceedings of the Cambridge Conference on the Cuban Missile Crisis, David A. Welch, ed. Cambridge, Mass., October 11–12, 1987, sponsored by the Ford Foundation and the Center for Science and International Affairs. Soviet participants were Fyodor Burlatsky, Sergo Mikoyan and Georgi Shakhnazarov. Former American officials present included McGeorge Bundy, Raymond Garthoff, Robert McNamara and Theodore Sorensen. Hereafter cited as CCT.

Proceedings of the Moscow Conference on the Cuban Missile Crisis, Bruce J. Allyn, James G. Blight and David A. Welch, eds. Moscow, January 27–28, 1989, sponsored by the Institute for the Study of the U.S.A. and Canada, the Carnegie Corporation and the Center for Science and International Affairs. Among former and current Soviet officials present were Alexander Alexeyev, Georgi Arbatov, Georgi Bolshakov, Fyodor Burlatsky, Anatoly Dobrynin, Valentin Falin, Alexander Fomin, Andrei Gromyko, Sergei Khrushchev, Sergo Mikoyan and Georgi Shakhnazarov. Participating former American officials included Robert McNamara, McGeorge Bundy, Theodore Sorensen and Pierre Salinger. Among Cuban participants were Emilio Aragones, Jorge Risquet and Sergio del Valle. Hereafter cited as MCT.

Proceedings of the Antigua Conference on the Cuban Missile Crisis, James G. Blight and David Lewis, eds. Antigua, January 3-7, 1991, sponsored by the Center for Foreign Policy Development, Brown University. This was comprised of Americans and Soviets who had attended the earlier conferences, as well as a Cuban delegation including General Fabian Escalante. Hereafter cited as ACT.

Author's Interviews

This list includes formal interviews conducted by the author as well as conversations that enhanced his understanding of the issues treated in this volume:

Robert Amory, Jr., William Attwood, Charles Bartlett, Richard Bissell, Dino Brugioni, McGeorge Bundy, James MacGregor Burns, Clark Clifford, Ray S. Cline, Thomas Corcoran, Ernest Cuneo, Richard Davies, François de Laboulaye, Sir Philip de Zulueta, Douglas Dillon, Robert Donovan, John Eisenhower, Milton Eisenhower, Gerald Ford, Clayton Fritchey, J. William Fulbright, Andrew Goodpaster, Edwin Guthman, Karl Harr, Richard Helms, Frederick Holborn, Frank Holeman, Lawrence Houston, Philip Kaiser, Sergei Khrushchev, James Killian, Robert King, Boris Klosson, Foy Kohler, Clare Boothe Luce, Henry Luce III, Arthur Lundahl, Carl Marcy, Priscilla Johnson McMillan, Robert McNamara,

Cord Meyer, Sergo Mikoyan, Newton Minow, Luvie Pearson, Claiborne Pell, Robert Pierpoint, Hy Raskin, Henry Raymont, Sergei Rogov, Walt Rostow, Franklin Roosevelt, Jr., Dean Rusk, Roald Sagdeev, Oleg Sakhalov, Ray Scherer, Dorothy Schiff, Herbert Scoville, Earl E.T. Smith, Lawrence Spivak, Mary Ann Stoessel, Melor Sturua, Jane Thompson, Vladimir Toumanoff, Robert Tucker, Sander Vanocur, Frank Waldrop, Gerhard Wessel.

Oral Histories and Interviews by Others

This category includes oral histories conducted for the Columbia University Oral History Project and the John F. Kennedy Library. It also includes records of interviews conducted by WGBH-TV, Boston, for the PBS series "War and Peace in the Nuclear Age," kindly provided to the author, and by John Bartlow Martin for *Adlai Stevenson and the World,* located in the Martin Papers at Princeton. These are all cited in the (Chapter) Notes.

NOTES

Additional abbreviations used in Notes:

conv	Conversation with the author
CR	*Congressional Record*
DDEL	Dwight D. Eisenhower Library
FBI	Federal Bureau of Investigation Files
FO	British Foreign Office Archives
int	Interview by the author
int JBM	Interview by John Bartlow Martin
int WGBH	Interview by WGBH-TV
Izv	*Izvestia*
JFKL	John F. Kennedy Library
L	*Life* Magazine
memcon	Memorandum of conversation
NW	*Newsweek* Magazine
NYHT	*New York Herald Tribune*
NYKr	*The New Yorker*
NYT	*New York Times*
oh	Oral history, John F. Kennedy Library
oh COHP	Oral history, Columbia Oral History Project
PA	"The President's Appointments," 1961–1963. John F. Kennedy Library
Prav	*Pravda*
SEP	*Saturday Evening Post*
SR	*Saturday Review*
tel note	Record of telephone call
T	*Time* Magazine
USN	*U.S. News & World Report*
WP	*Washington Post*
WS	*Washington Star*

1. Almost Midnight

JFK awakens: *Pittsburgh Press* 10/15/62, PA 10/14/62. Unless otherwise noted, the chief reference for the timing and location of JFK's appointments and movements throughout this book is PA. Niagara-Buffalo scenes: *Buffalo Evening News*, NYT 10/15/62, FBI memo, 10/11/62. "Sudden shift": *New York Mirror* 10/15/62. Stevenson's trip to New York: *Newsday*, NYT 10/15/62, Bartlow Martin *Stevenson* 719–20. Carlyle suite is described in Sidey oh, Gallagher 185, Ralph Martin 402. Automat scene: Lundahl int, Lundahl oh, Brugioni int. Bissell int, *Life* 11/2/62, *Look* 12/18/62, Burrows 122, David Martin 142–3. Kremlinologists on NSK and missile placement: Thompson oh, Bundy int, Davies int. General sources on 10/16/62: Abel 43–54, 99–116. *The President's Intelligence Checklist:* Wise and Ross 238–9, SEP 7/27/63, RFK oh. "The Saudis, fed": *The President's Intelligence Checklist* 10/15/62, JFKL.

JFK hears about Goulart: Bradlee 151. "Talks like when drunk": Bundy-JFK 9/15/61, JFKL. Ben Bella arrival: NYT 10/16/62, WS 10/16/62, *New York World Telegram* 10/16/62. Missile discovery, call to Bundy and Bundy reaction: Bundy-JFK 3/4/63, JFKL, Cline int, Bundy int, Lundahl int, Lundahl oh, *Look* 12/18/62, SEP 12/8/62, Cline 219–21, Bundy 684–5, Ralph Martin 459. Bundy notifies JFK and JFK reaction: Bundy int, Transcript of Martin Agronsky interview with Bundy, 1964, Schlesinger Papers, AMSTD draft, Richard Neustadt and Graham Allison, "Afterword" in RFK13 122, Bundy 414, RFK13 1, Abel 44. AMSTD draft is cited instead of AMSTD in cases in which the draft offers a slightly fuller treatment of the event or issue described. Helms sees RFK and Helms on Kennedys and Mongoose: Helms int. Special Group (Augmented) 10/16/62 meeting and Mongoose: CIA memcon 10/4/62, JFKL, Helms int, Prados *Presidents' Secret Wars* 213, *Assassination Plots*, 147. See Notes for Chapters 6 and 14.

JFK reluctance to approve invasion: McNamara int, MCT. "The top priority": *Assassination Plots* 144, Thomas Powers 138. On CIA collaboration with Mafia, see Notes for Chapter 6. RFK views U-2 pictures: Helms int, Bundy int, AMSRK 506–7. JFK request of Sorensen and result: Sorensen oh. On failure to warn Soviets, see Notes for Chapter 15. JFK appearance on 10/16/62 morning and aides' reactions: Odon 310–11, Sal 249–50, Sidey (1964) 271–2, Parmet *JFK* 284–5. On JFK taping system, see Bouck oh and Notes for Chapter 13. 10/16/62 morning meeting: Transcript and tape recording in JFKL. Also see Notes for Chapter 16. Kohler visit with NSK: Kohler int, Kohler-Rusk 10/16/62, Kohler Diary 10/16/62, JFKL, NYT 10/27/62, Davies int. NSK vacation and vacation routine: SNK 27–8, 79–80, 199, Sergei Khrushchev int.

NSK and *War and Peace:* Harriman-NSK memcon 6/23/59, JFKL and DDEL, Frank Roberts in McCauley 222. Throughout the Notes, memcons are cited by date of meeting. JFK at State: Abel, 53–4. Bullfighter's verse: NW 11/12/62, RFK oh, Graves 4. Bohlen dinner: Bohlen notes, Bohlen oh, Susan Mary Alsop-Jacqueline Kennedy, 9/19/62, JFKL, Bohlen 489–90, Ralph Martin 458–9, Alsop conv. Berlin on "presentiment": Sulzberger 922. Spalding, Manchester, Rostow on JFK: Spalding oh, Manchester *Portrait* 236, Rostow oh. Joseph Kennedy's pessimism: Beschloss *Kennedy and Roosevelt* 65, 160–1, 184–6, 190–1, 204, 167–9. JFK to Smathers on best way to die: Smathers int. JFK watches jet and pantomimes death: Manchester *Death* 121, Ralph Martin 545, Kearns Goodwin 743–6. JFK said similar things to Priscilla Johnson McMillan, Ted Reardon, LeMoyne Billings and Charles Spalding. See also Chapter 23. "He just figured": Kearns Goodwin 743–6.

"Notoriously poor," "whoever wants" and "Get in my plane": W.C. Sullivan-D.J. Brennan 12/1/63, FBI. JFK to Vidal on Wallace book: Vidal 273. "The best job" and "You never know": RFK oh, Bartlett int. JFK anger at Kohler report: RFK13 5–6. "How an immoral gangster" and "It had all been lies": RFK oh. Eisenhower on Cold War: DDEPP 12/8/53. This and all succeeding references to the *Public Papers* series and similar anthologies are cited by date instead of page. JFK reading of *Fail Safe:* Sulzberger 935. NSK remembers JFK's 1959 lateness: See Notes for Chapter 8.

2. *"He's Younger Than My Own Son"*

JFK arrival in Washington: Holborn int, WP 9/17/59, WS 9/17/59. *Caroline:* Sor 100, Lincoln *My Twelve Years* 125–5. JFK driving: Lincoln *My Twelve Years* 31–2, Sor 25. O'Leary: Gallagher 17, Bradlee 43. JFK attitude toward seeing NSK: Holborn int. Gallup Poll: T 9/28/59. JFK envy of Humphrey audience with NSK: Holborn int. Humphrey article: L 1/12/59. Menshikov's efforts to reach JFK, JFK arrival in office and walk to Capitol: Holborn int. DiSalle meeting: *Cleveland Plain Dealer* 9/17/59, Sor 131, Holborn int. JFK tardiness noted by NSK: See Notes for Chapter 8. NSK meeting with Senators: JFK undated notes in JFKL, Gwirtzman oh, Marcy, Fulbright ints, *Boston Globe, Christian Science Monitor*, NYT 9/17/59. NSK meeting with JFK: Odon 294, NSK2 488, Holborn int. NSK "impressed": NSK1 458. "Dear Jack": Fulbright to JFK, September 1959, quoted in Johnson and Gwirtzman 165.

JFK Columbus report on meeting: *Cincinnati Enquirer* 9/17/59. "I don't believe it": PCS, New Castle, Pa., 10/15/60. JFK early international education: Parmet *Jack* 38–83, Burns *Kennedy* 29–48, Blairs 56–114. Joe, Jr., Soviet trip: Searls 77–78. "Joe seems": AMSRK 19–20. Rose Kennedy trip: Rose Kennedy 206–10. Gunther quote: Gunther *Inside Europe* 511. "Finished Gunther": AMSTD 82. JFK Russian history course: Report card in JFKL. JFK to Billings is in letter 5/3/39. Photocopies of the JFK-Billings letters and other Billings material cited in this book were kindly shared with the author by Peter Collier. NSK and subway: Crankshaw 84–95. "Met a girl": JFK-Billings 5/28/39. "Crude, backward": Burns *Kennedy* 38. JFK on *Blind Date:* Parmet *Jack* 99–100. JFK visits Bohlen: Bohlen oh, Bohlen notes in Bohlen Papers, Bohlen 476. "Had a great": JFK-Billings 7/17/39.

"It seems": JFK-Billings 2/12/42. JFK on UN is in *New York Journal-American* 4/30/45. JFK on FDR and Poland: Lasky *JFK* 99–100. JFK on "sick Roosevelt": CR 2/21/49. JFK visit with Eisenhower: JFK-Krock, undated, 1951, Krock Papers. JFK on Algeria and Poland: Burns *Kennedy* 199, Parmet *Jack* 401–8, copies of speeches in JFKL, JFK and Democratic debate: AMSTD 298–301, AMSRK 417–9. "The barbarian": Parmet *Jack* 318–9. JFK to Kennan: 2/13/58, JFKL, and Kennan 267–8fn. "New shortcut": CR 8/14/58. Burns conversation: 7/17/59 transcript in Burns Papers and Sorensen Papers. On the 1960 campaign and international relations generally, see Divine 183–287. Thaw after Camp David: Beschloss *Mayday* 7–8, 216–242. Rochester speech: copy in JFKL, 10/1/59. *Washington Star* quote: WS 10/4/59. "Clumsy attempt": NYT 5/18/60. "Living through": Sor 149.

JFK St. Helens episode: *Oregonian* 5/17/60–5/25/60, telephone interviews with the high school principal, Len Monroe, and Wallace Thompson, who asked the question. Hugh Scott demand and JFK defense: CR 5/23/60. "When one apologizes": T.A. Hawkins-JFK 5/29/60, JFKL. "Saying or implying": Thomas Lee-JFK 5/18/60, JFKL. "YOU'RE UNFIT": Edward Stettedahl-JFK 5/24/60, JFKL. LBJ on apology: Lasky *JFK* 357, Sor 149. Kendall memo, May 1960: U-2 file, DDEL. Nixon on JFK comments: Beschloss *Mayday* 319. "New cold air": T 6/13/60. Jackson on "tough line": Divine *Presidential Elections* 211. Second thoughts: *Gallup* May-June 1960. JFK twelve-point speech: CR 6/14/60. East-West climate in summer 1960: Beschloss *Mayday* 305–41. A NYT survey (9/26/60) showed that NSK's trip to New York helped to make foreign policy the leading concern of US voters.

Nixon on JFK and NSK: U.S. Senate *Speeches of Nixon* 194–5. Nixon boasts of experience: Brodie 421. Nixon on Eisenhower attitude toward him: Transcript of an Alsop interview with Nixon, undated, 1958, Alsop Papers. Critics on PT-109: Burns *Edward Kennedy* 312. JFK on Foreign Relations: Marcy int. Schlesinger on experience: Schlesinger *Kennedy or Nixon* 32, NYT 8/25/88. JFK defense: f.e., PCS, 9/29/60, Syracuse, N.Y. "Put us on the defensive": Beschloss *Mayday* 319. Rostow warning: Rostow oh. Nixon to Rogers: 11/4/60, Nixon Papers. Kennedy at Mormon Tabernacle: PSC 9/23/60. Galbraith to Harris: 9/27/60, Galbraith Papers. Jacqueline on JFK experience is in an undated note to Schlesinger, Schlesinger Papers. Schlesinger on subject: AMSTD 424. Stevenson to JFK on experience: undated, Stevenson Papers. Bowles to JFK: 10/17/60, JFKL. US preponderance: Nye 69–112. "Like sausages": Prados *Soviet Estimate* 77.

Nixon, Eisenhower and missile gap: Alsop interview with Nixon, undated, 1958. Alsop Papers, Bissell int, Goodpaster int, Beschloss *Mayday* 153–4, 237, Ambrose, *Eisenhower* 561–3, 487. Wiesner "astounded": Herken 133. Eisenhower and Dulles briefing: Dulles-Eisenhower 8/3/60, DDEL. JFK and SAC briefing: Wheeler, Sorensen, McCone ohs, Sor 610–3. JFK on missile gap: *Wilson Quarterly,* Winter 1980. JFK on overreliance on nuclear: PCS, Portland, 9/7/60. JFK on Soviet growth: Detroit, 9/5/60, and Greenville, 9/17/60, PCS. Actual position of American and Soviet economies: Nye 5–13, 69–130. Dulles on caution: Thomas Powers 201. Nixon suspicion of Dulles: Kissinger 11. JFK on prestige: Detroit, 10/26/60, and Queens, 10/27/60. Gallup Poll: *Gallup* 11/30/60. "I ask you": PCS, York, Pa., 9/16/60. JFK, Cuba and 1960 campaign: Smathers int, *Diplomatic History,* Winter 1984, Divine *Presidential Elections* 242–86, Goodwin 124–6.

Goodwin on Cuba and "How would we": Goodwin 75, AMSTD 224. Eisenhower anger at Allen: Howard Snyder Diary 10/26/60, DDEL. Drafting of statement on Cuba and text: Goodwin 125, NYT 10/21/60. Nixon reaction and call to Seaton: Goodpaster int, Nixon *Six Crises* 353–4. Nixon on Dulles briefing: Nixon *Six Crises* 354. Bundy to JFK: 3/14/62, JFKL. White House on JFK "not told": 3/20/62 statement, JFKL. JFK request, Dulles statement, McCone call: Robert Donovan tel note, Nixon tel note, 3/20/62 statement, DDEL. Goodpaster on Dulles briefing: Goodpaster int. Goodwin 1981 quote is in Parmet *JFK* 48. Goodwin 1988 quote is in Goodwin 172–4. "Put into a corner": Goodpaster int. Nixon in fourth debate: NYT 10/22/60. JFK on not favoring intervention and "major blunder": NYT 10/22/60–10/23/60. Stevenson on JFK mistake: Stevenson-Barbara Ward 10/28/60, Stevenson Papers.

Stevenson to JFK on Berlin: 8/17/60, Stevenson Papers. "Can you possibly": PCS, Wilmington, Del., 10/16/60. JFK on Quemoy and Matsu: statement issued in Georgia, PCS 10/10/60. Republicans on comments and JFK drops issue: NYT 10/13/60–10/17/60. JFK and Nixon on NSK in debates: U.S. Senate *Joint Appearances* 9/26/60 and 10/7/60. "The American people have": Frankland 159. "The battle between": NSK2 489. "Political advertising is": Prav 2/28/63. NSK assurances about Eisenhower and embarrassment: Beschloss *Mayday* 216–7, 238–42. NSK on Stevenson: NSK2 488. NSK-Stevenson 1958 meeting: Robert Tucker notes 8/5/58, Stevenson Papers. Tucker conv. Bulganin public letter and aftermath: Divine *Blowing* 100, Divine *Presidential Elections* 139, 157–9, Ambrose *Eisenhower* 349–50, Eisenhower-Bulganin 10/21/56, DDEL.

Menshikov-Stevenson meeting and its origins: Stevenson 1/16/60 memo, Stevenson Papers, Tucker conv, Bartlow Martin *Stevenson* 471–5. Mikoyan to Eisenhower on NSK 1956 "vote": Memcon 1/17/59, DDEL. NSK to colleagues on 1960 candidates: Shevchenko 108–9, NSK2 488–9, Harriman 12/14/60 memcon on meeting with Menshikov. *Izvestia* on JFK: Izv 7/15/60. Other Soviet journalistic comments: *Reporter* 12/8/60. Washington establishment on JFK as playboy: Burns conv. Reston question: Rostow oh. "You all went": Crankshaw 3. On NSK background, see Notes for Chapter 7. "He's younger than my own son" and similar comments were made by NSK on many occasions from 1960 through 1962. See, for example, William Knox account of NSK conversation in *New York Times Magazine* 11/18/62 and Walter Lippmann account in USN 5/1/61. KGB profiles: Corson and Crowley 271.

"Mr. Nixon has dressed": Prav 8/31/60 and Sal 221. "Roosevelt!": Beschloss *Mayday* 340. Lodge to NSK: Lodge-Christian Herter 2/9/60 in DDEL, NSK2 489–90, Nixon tel note 2/27/60, Nixon Papers. I have taken the liberty of inserting articles in cables cited throughout this book, except in cases in which meaning might be altered. Thompson to Nixon: 8/13/60, Nixon Papers. On Harriman's background, see Notes for Chapter 20. Harriman October message: Isaacson and Thomas 603. NSK keeps fliers to elect JFK: Sal 230, Shevchenko 109, NSK1 458, NSK2 490–1. Spaso House luncheon, Thompson-JFK history, NSK to Thompson before election: Jane Thompson, Klosson ints, Thompson oh. Eisenhower years as Dark Age: Kennan oh, Bohlen notes, Jane Thompson int, Kennan 178–87, Bohlen 441–3. Hyannis Port luncheon and NSK telegram: Bohlen notes, copy of telegram in JFKL, Sor 211–2, 231, Bradlee 32–4, 227, Odon 225–6, Bohlen 474.

3. *"Our Clue to the Soviet Union"*

Bohlen-JFK relationship in 1960: Holborn int, Bohlen oh. For Bohlen's background and personality, principal sources are Bohlen, Bohlen oh, Isaacson and Thomas, Brandon 79–80. "Ugly record": Mosley 311. Senate fight: Isaacson and Thomas 566–70. "It would build him": Tel note, Dulles Papers, DDEL. Bohlen's removal from Moscow: Bohlen-Thompson 1/11/57, Thompson-Bohlen 1/17/57, Bohlen-Dulles 1/25/57, Bohlen-Thompson 1/28/57, Bohlen Papers, Jane Thompson int. "At this great distance": quoted in Kennan-Bohlen 7/23/73, Bohlen Papers. Bohlen drafting of JFK reply and consultation with Eisenhower: Bohlen 474, Sor 231, tel note in Herter Papers 11/10/60, DDEL. Text of reply is in JFKL and NYT 11/11/60. Menshikov sessions: Douglas oh, Bowles oh,

Bohlen 475–6. Menshikov reporting and NSK recognition of distortions are in Shevchenko 196–7, Beschloss *Mayday* 203–4, memcon of Lodge meeting with Eisenhower 9/25/59, DDEL. *"Nash Durak":* NW 12/25/61.

Kuznetsov on NSK "education": Lodge memcon 9/19/59, DDEL. Menshikov-Stevenson contacts: Stevenson memcon of Menshikov meeting 11/16/60, Stevenson Papers, Stevenson-JFK 11/22/60, JFKL. On Korneichuk background, see Pistrak 177–9. Korneichuk-Harriman contacts and Harriman report: Harriman-JFK, 11/12/60 and 11/15/60, JFKL and Harriman Papers. Menshikov-Harriman contacts: Harriman memcons 11/21/60 and 12/14/60, JFKL and Harriman Papers. Rostow-Wiesner Moscow meetings: Rostow memo 11/27/60–12/7/60, JFKL, Rostow oh, AMSTD 301–4. RFK-Menshikov luncheon: RFK-Rusk 12/18/60, RFK Papers. Menshikov-Salisbury contacts: Salisbury memo 12/15/60, JFKL. Principal sources for impending Sino-Soviet split are CIA memo 4/1/61, JFKL, Gaddis *America* 223–4, Gaddis *Strategies* 194–5, Ulam *Expansion* 623–5, Ulam *Rivals* 286–308. NSK to Adenauer: quoted in H. Carleton Greene-Ralph Murray 2/13/59, FO. "If the imperialists": NSK2 255.

"Only when the Americans": Andrei Gromyko 251–2. NSK on Mao: SR 9/7/74. Sino-Soviet tensions in 1959–1960: Terrill 281–2, Clubb 435–7, Hyland and Shryock 4–17, Tatu 101–6, Linden 101–4, Ulam *Expansion* 634–5. 81-party meeting: 4/1/61 CIA memo, NYT 12/2/60 and 2/12/61. "Blame when things": Penkovsky 264. NSK 1960 domestic problems: Beschloss *Mayday* 323–5, Tatu 114–22, Linden 105–6, Ulam *Rivals* 305–13, Ulam *Expansion* 634–40. Thompson-Herter 1/29/60 on Sino-Soviet friction is in DDEL, as are Thompson-Herter 10/14/60 and 11/28/60. The 99-page CIA memo is that of 4/1/61 cited above. "Whole way of doing business": Thompson-Rusk 2/2/61, JFKL. NSK curiosity about JFK: Shevchenko 110, NSK2 492. JFK at Palm Beach during interregnum: Lincoln *My Twelve Years* 199–200, Odon, 229. JFK sees Hammer: Weinberg 140, Hammer 312–4. JFK has Bruce see Menshikov: Kennan oh. Soviet views of JFK cabinet are in Anatoly Gromyko 104–10.

NSK on Dillon is in NSK2 378. "The most dangerous": Mosley 6. On NSK general view of how US appointments are made, see Frankland 160. NSK at New Year's 1961 reception: Prav 1/2/61, NYT 1/2/61, Jane Thompson int. Kennan-JFK meeting: Kennan oh. Drafting of JFK inaugural address: Sor 240–3, Lincoln *My Twelve Years* 216–20. JFK-Stevenson conversation: Bartlow Martin *Stevenson* 571–2. JFK on minimum wage: Nixon *Memoirs* 235. Text of inaugural speech: JFKPP 1/20/61. Radio Moscow: NYT 1/21/61. Goldwater on speech: Jack Bell oh. Menshikov reaction: Sidey 40. Soviet telegram to JFK is in JFKL. NSK call to Thompson: Jane Thompson, Klosson ints. NSK-Thompson 1/21/61 meeting is documented below. Thompson background and personality and relations with NSK: Thompson oh, Jane Thompson, Klosson, Davies, Rusk, Toumanoff, Kohler, Bundy ints, McMillan conv, NYHT 2/26/58, *New York Times Magazine* 3/11/62, L 8/10/62.

Bohlen on NSK: Bohlen to the Norwegian Ambassador in Moscow, Eric Braadland, 7/30/58 and 7/31/59, Bohlen Papers. NSK to Harriman: Harriman memcon 6/23/59, JFKL. Thompson to NSK on Bohlen's comment: Thompson memo 9/29/59, DDEL. "Most striking thing": Thompson-Bohlen, 1957, Thompson Papers. "I have built up": Thompson to DFR 2/13/61. Canadian envoy on NSK and Thompson: Micunovic 412. Jane Thompson and Khrushchevs: Jane Thompson int. "As I was taking": Thompson-Herter, 11/13/59, DDEL. Dacha trip: Jane Thompson, Klosson ints, *Look* 8/14/62, SNK 72–4. NSK after U-2 downing: NYT 5/10/60, Salisbury 489–90. NSK-Thompson September exchange: Thompson-Herter 9/8/60 and 9/9/60, DDEL, NYT 9/9/60. NSK-Thompson 1/21/61 meeting: Thompson-Rusk 1/21/61 and 1/24/61, JFKL. JFK on first morning in White House: AMSTD draft. Truman on JFK: NYT 7/3/60.

"A certain wariness": Bundy int. Rusk-Thompson: 1/23/61, JFKL. Bartlett-Kennedy dinner: Bartlett int, Bartlett oh, Rostow *Diffusion* 170. "Everyone had told him": Bergquist 11. Soviets run inaugural text: Allen Dulles-Goodpaster 1/23/61 JFKL. Jamming reduced: NW 2/6/61. RB-47 release: Thompson-Rusk 1/24/61, Rostow oh, T 2/3/61, NYT 1/26/61, Wise 324–6, Sal 138–1, Sidey 51–7, Lincoln *My Twelve Years* 233–6, JFKPP 1/25/61. KGB man on concessions: Estabrook memo 3/20/61, JFKL, cited below. Concealed American incursion: Rusk-Thompson 2/2/61, JFKL. JFK efforts to improve American-Soviet climate: AMSTD 304. Requests to remove anti-Soviet language and reaction: Sylvester oh, NYT 1/28/61, 1/31/61, 4/14/61, Trewhitt 89–90, 164–5. Eisenhower "exercised": Howard Snyder Diary 5/27/59, DDEL. Lifting of crabmeat ban: Rusk-JFK 2/26/61, JFKL, Hammer 314–27, Weinberg 142–5, NYT 3/10/61.

On Edwin Walker, see NYT 9/30/62, *Overseas Weekly* 4/16/61, Trewhitt 90–2, McMillan 259–300. Eisenhower on NSK 1/6/61 speech: Goodpaster int, NYT 1/19/61. JFK reaction to speech: SEP 3/31/62, RFK oh, McNamara int. Thompson on speech: Thompon on speech: Thompson-Herter 1/19/61, DDEL and JFKL. Arthur Schlesinger, Jr., has written that JFK responded to NSK's 1/6/61 speech "by devoting his inaugural address a fortnight later almost exclusively to foreign affairs." (AMSRK 421–4, also in testimony to the Senate Foreign Relations Committee, 5/10/72) In fact, what Schlesinger calls JFK's "inaugural rodomontade" cannot be blamed on Khrushchev's speech because the latter was not released to the West until 1/18/61 (NYT 1/19/61), by which time the inaugural address had been almost completely written. "You've got to understand it": Ralph Martin 351.

4. Novosibirsk

State of the Union scene: NYT 1/30/61 and 1/31/61, Sidey 5–9. Writing of speech and text: Sor 292, NYT 1/30/61, JFKPP 1/30/61. Text of NSC-68 is in *Foreign Relations of the United States: 1950*, vol. 1, 22–44. On provenance of "hour of maximum danger," see Herken 49–50, Kaplan 144–73. Eisenhower's 1961 State of the Union: DDEPP, 1/12/61. JFK January 1961 foreign policy review: Helms, Bundy, Rusk, McNamara ints. Thompson displayed his advanced knowledge of the Sino-Soviet split on such occasions as his secret testimony before the Foreign Relations Committee: DFR, 2/13/61. On JFK inclination to crisis, see Miroff 12–13. JFK at Los Angeles: NYT 7/15/60. JFK and McCarthy: Burns *Kennedy* 131–55, Parmet *Jack* 288–325. Soviet unhappiness with State of the Union: NYT 2/11/61, Prav 2/5/61, Izv 2/10/61. U.S. Minuteman launching and Soviet reaction: Herken 153, MccGwire 51, 483.

Report on Jupiters to Turkey and Ryzhov reaction: Rabinowitch 286. McNamara background session: Jack Raymond memo 2/6/61, Krock Papers, McNamara int WGBH, McNamara int, Charles Murphy-Lauris Norstad 2/11/61,

Norstad Papers, Trewhitt 20–1. "Terrible mistake": McNamara int. WGBH. JFK reaction: Taylor 205, JFKPP 2/8/61, McNamara int, McNamara int. WGBH. Origin of Defense Intelligence Agency: Trewhitt 85. "No, not really": Lodge-Herter 2/9/60, DDEL. "Both to get your advice": Rusk-Thompson, 1/25/61, JFKL. Bohlen's and Thompson's reappointments had been reported in NYT 1/8/61. Thompson arrival in Washington: T 2/10/61, DFR 2/13/61, Jane Thompson int. "It's wonderful": Jane Thompson int. Thompson tutorial for JFK: Thompson-Rusk 2/2/61. JFKL. Eisenhower machinery on Soviet relations: Goodpaster int, Solarium exercise file in DDEL, Kennan 181–2.

JFK February meetings on Soviet relations: 2/11/61 memcon, JFKL, Rusk, Bundy ints, Kennan, Bohlen, Thompson ohs, JFKL, NYT 2/10/61, 2/12/61, 2/19/61, Thompson-DFR 2/13/61, Weintal and Bartlett 13, AMSTD 303–6, Sor 510, 541–2, Cohen 135–6. "All Senators": Bundy int. "A good deal": Bohlen-Thompson 3/10/61, Bohlen and Thompson Papers. Bohlen on JFK and Soviet relations: Bohlen notes and oh. Rusk on JFK eagerness for summit: Rusk int. On Rusk background and personality, see Rusk, Schoenbaum, Cohen, Halberstam *Best* 307–29. "I am more comfortable": *New York Times Magazine* 3/18/62. "I don't think": USN 9/11/61. Rusk on word "feel": Halberstam *Best* 312. Rusk to Bohlen is 6/27/73, Bohlen Papers. Rusk and Marshall: Rusk 130–5, Halberstam *Best* 320–1. "Act the position": RFK oh. Rusk on leaks and "There are some things": Rusk int and Schoenbaum 280.

McNamara obtains JFK promise on appointments: McNamara int, RFK oh. Bowles on Rusk insecurity: Bowles oh. "The land didn't": Halberstam *Best* 313. Rusk misapprehension about veterinarian: AMSTD 432. "G-A-L": Halberstam *Best* 314. Rusk and Lee: Rusk 55, Schoenbaum 34. "I feel deeply": Schoenbaum 94. Rusk on Truman and Hiroshima: Rusk 122. Rusk opposition to Kennan: Schoenbaum 137–8. Acheson on "Purple Heart": Halberstam *Best* 324. Rusk irritation with White House aides: Rusk-John Foster Dulles 5/6/53, DDEL. "Half the men": Adolf Berle Diary 7/6/60, FDRL. Stevenson intention to appoint Fulbright: Sulzberger 683. "He likes to call" and Acheson-JFK meeting: Acheson oh. Lovett and meeting with JFK, see Bowles oh, Lovett oh, Halberstam *Best* 4–10, Isaacson and Thomas 592–7. "Henry Stimson was one": Odon 235. Rusk to JFK: 11/22/60, JFKL.

Rusk memo on conversation with Hammarskjöld: 11/30/60, JFKL. Rusk summoned to see JFK, preparation and meeting: Bowles, Lovett ohs, Bowles 299–302, Rusk int. "That was never a problem": Rusk int. JFK and RFK differ on Fulbright: RFK oh, Bartlett oh, Bowles oh. FBI eavesdropping on Fulbright call: S. B. Donahue-A.H. Belmont 9/23/60, FBI. JFK consideration of Bruce and decision to appoint Rusk: RFK 2/9/61 memo, quoted in AMSRK 222–3, and RFK oh. JFK calls Rusk, Rusk reaction and second meeting: Rusk int. "The best man": T 12/26/60. "I must make the appointments": Galbraith *Ambassador's Journal* 6. Rusk's article, "The President," was in *Foreign Affairs*, April 1960. "Soft sentimentalism": JFK *Strategy* 7. "Kennedy had the impression": Rusk int. Thompson insistence on JFK seeing NSK: Thompson oh, Jane Thompson int. "I believe that Soviet policy": Thompson-Rusk 1/28/61, JFKL. "Really felt he had": Bohlen oh. "I think we'll go": Sidey 164.

"I have to show him": Odon 286. "Am interested in harmonious": undated notes in JFKL. Bundy on "opening ploy": Bundy int. JFK first letter to NSK,

2/22/61, is in JFKL. NSK and marshals speeches and Slusser opinion on Presidium meeting: Rabinowitch 281–92. Soviet demarche to Adenauer: Rusk-JFK 2/17/61 and Soviet memo attached, JFKL. On the Congo problem in early 1961, see Kalb 3–239, Mahoney 3–88, Clare Timberlake and G. Mennen Williams to DFR 2/6/61. "They say that in the Congo": NYT 11/8/60. "I find it difficult": JFKPP 2/15/61. JFK instructions to Thompson on Congo: Memo of talking points, undated, February 1961, JFKL. Thompson-NSK meeting at Novosibirsk: Jane Thompson, Klosson ints, Thompson-Rusk 3/10/61, Bohlen-Thompson 3/10/51, NW 3/20/61, NYT 3/4/61, 3/8/61, 3/7/61, 3/10/61, Sidey 163–4.

Some of the contents were revealed by the CBS Bonn correspondent Daniel Schorr, which horrified Thompson (Rusk-Thompson 3/17/61 and Thompson-Rusk 3/18/61, Schorr conv). NSK at Academy City: Roald Sagdeev conv, Berg 335–6. Estabrook was close enough to Schlesinger for instance, to sponsor him for membership in the Metropolitan Club. (Estabrook-Harriman 4/19/61, Harriman Papers) Fomin background: Andrew and Gordievsky 473. His name appears on a list of NSK traveling party in DDEL. Bartlett, Brandon and Russians: Bartlett int, Brandon conv. Hoover warning about "compromised" journalist: Lewis Strauss Diary 3/16/62, Hoover Library. Estabrook-Fomin conversation: Estabrook memo 3/20/61, JFKL. On JFK and test ban through 1960, see AMSTD 452–3, Sor 617, Seaborg 3–25, Sorensen oh. "Jack was not passionate": Ralph Martin 504.

JFK in campaign on test ban: PCS, Milwaukee and Madison, Wisc., 10/23/60. On JFK and test ban, early 1961: Seaborg 30–53, AMSTD 453. "If we could gain" and "serious effort": Seaborg 3/21/61 talks: Seaborg *Kennedy* 54–5, Sor 617, AMSTD 453–4. Gromyko-JFK 3/27/61 meeting: Bowles-Thompson 3/27/61, JFKL, NYT 3/19/61 and 3/22/61, Sidey 82–3. On Laos problem in early 1961, see Bohlen oh, Rostow oh, Winthrop Brown to DFR 2/2/61, Rusk to DFR 4/11/61, Bowles to DFR 5/17/61, LBJ to DFR 5/25/61, Donmen 94–183, Parmet *JFK* 131–42, AMSTD 320–42, Hilsman 105–31. "Disunity and the failure": 2/11/61 memcon, JFKL. JFK movement of Marines: Donmen 189–91. JFK and guerrilla war: Sidey 74 and JFKPP 3/24/61. JFK threat and Gromyko approach to Stevenson: JFKPP 3/23/61 and Bartlow Martin *Stevenson* 613–5. NSK in late March 1961: Thompson-Rusk 3/20/61, Tatu 124–40, Linden 105–16. NSK and intelligence: Corson and Crowley 271, SNK in MCT.

Bissell 3/29/61 report: Wyden *Bay* 139–40 and Maxwell Taylor, "Taylor Committee Report and Memorandum for Record of Paramilitary Study Group Meetings," 5/17/61–6/18/61. Hereafter cited as Taylor Report. Stalking of Castro: Thomas Powers 154.

5. *"I'm Not Going to Risk an American Hungary"*

Discussion of Cuba during February meetings and Bohlen views: 2/11/61 memcon, JFKL, Kennan oh, Bohlen notes, Bohlen 477–8. On history of Cuba and its relations with the U.S., see Hugh Thomas 1–1180. On Castro background, see Szulc, Bourne, Geyer. Castro on maturing in a "pseudo-republic": Szulc 96–99. Castro accusing father and "hatred" of society people: Szulc 114, 123. Castro's court defense is reconstructed in Szulc 294–8. CIA support of Castro movement and "I have sworn": Szulc 427–9, 51. British report from Havana: A.S. Fordham-

Lloyd 7/4/58, FO. Gardner message to Nixon: 12/5/58, Nixon Papers. Nixon's possible Havana career: Mazo 35. Rebozo and Nixon: Lukas 362–3. Nixon-Gardner appointment: 12/5/58, Nixon Papers. Eisenhower on Pawley: Eisenhower-Taylor 6/26/61, DDEL. CIA and Indonesia: Ambrose *Ike's Spies* 249–51. Pawley Havana mission: 10/3/60 Nixon staff note, Nixon Papers, Higgins 40–1.

"The Revolution begins" and "If the Americans don't": Szulc 459, 482–3. "The wishes of the President's doctor": D.F. Muirhead-Henry Hankey 4/9/59, FO. Trujillo's treatment of Batista: Dalton Murray-Hankey 8/26/59, FO. Herter on Castro: Memcon of Eisenhower meeting 4/18/59, DDEL. "I couldn't get anywhere": Bundy int. Castro history with communism: Szulc 50–1, 141–2, 148–50, 162, 172–3, 181–99, 444–5, 453–5. Soviet-Cuban history: ACT, Hugh Thomas 731, 793, 967, 1265–6. Alexeyev background and role in Cuba: Alexeyev int WGBH, Alexeyev in MCT, Alexeyev in *Ekho Planety* (Moscow), November 1988, Alexeyev interview in *Argumenty i fakty* (Moscow), 3/11/89–3/17/89, Szulc 507–8, 510–11, 522, Barron 23, 202, Andrew and Gordievsky 467–8. Eisenhower to Cabinet on Soviets and Cuba: Memcon 6/7/59, DDEL. "This meant death" and "When I handed": Alexeyev int WGBH. Castro on embargo: Sulzberger 518. Eisenhower on blockade: Krock memcon of Eisenhower meeting 7/7/60, Krock Papers.

Thompson on Soviets and "this Cuban thing": Thompson-Herter, 1960, DDEL. NSK on Monroe Doctrine and comments by aides, Guevara, Eisenhower: NYT 7/10/60, Szulc 518–9. JFK relationship with Smathers: Smathers int, Raskin int, Spivak conv. *Nation* 12/7/64, T 5/4/62, Kelley *Jackie* 137. July 1956 yacht trip and Pearson on "estrangement": Smathers int, Kelley *Jackie* 135–6, Pearson in WP 12/23/66. JFK and Smathers in Havana: Smathers int, Earl Smith conv, *Times* (Havana) 12/23/57, 12/25/57. Mrs. Lansky on Kennedy and Havana women: Transcript of "60 Minutes," CBS-TV, 6/25/89. "Kennedy wasn't a great casino man" and "I don't think I ever heard": Smathers int. JFK on "bloody and repressive" dictatorship: PCS, Cincinnati, 10/6/60. Richard Helms presumes that JFK and Smathers would have been routinely surveilled. (Helms int) Castro on "rich illiterate": Ralph Martin 323.

JFK questions Bergquist: Bergquist 20–1. JFK seeks advice from Smith and Smathers: Smathers int, Earl Smith conv, Holborn int. Betty Spalding on Florence Smith: Blairs 319. "Nightclub-style evening": Clayton Fritchey conv. Smith appointment to Switzerland: NYT 2/7/61, 2/23/61, USN 3/6/61. Bohlen on JFK reaction to Swiss refusal to accept Smith: Bohlen oh, Bohlen notes. Smathers on lobbying JFK on Cuba: Smathers int, Smathers oh. JFK on Castro and Bolivar: JFK *Strategy* 132–3. "I don't know why": Ralph Martin 509–10. "There are two people": Goodwin 172. JFK at Cincinnati: PCS 10/6/60. Rusk on JFK antagonism for Castro: Rusk int. Nixon to Hall on badgering Eisenhower: 10/5/60 memo, Nixon Papers. "Are they falling": Wyden *Bay* 29. January 1960 planning against Castro regime: Wyden *Bay* 19–27, Ambrose *Eisenhower* 555–7, Eisenhower memcon 1/25/60, DDEL.

"A Program of Covert Action": 3/16/60, DDEL. Nixon suspicion about Cuba invasion delay and of CIA "liberals"; Thomas Powers 201, Kissinger 11, Kutler 201. JFK November 1960 briefings by Dulles and Bissell: NYT 11/19/60, Amory int, Amory oh, Bissell int, Thomas Powers 113, AMSTD 231–2, Sor 291–2. Assessments of JFK used by CIA: Corson and Crowley 30–2. On JFK-Arvad affair, see Notes for Chapter 21. Joseph Kennedy-Hoover relationship is documented in Joseph Kennedy FBI Files, FBI. Nixon on Eisenhower and JFK blame for Cuba: Nixon-Pawley 5/8/63, Nixon Papers. JFK announcement of Hoover and Dulles reinstatement: Bradlee 33–4. Dulles on Cuba and "Sino-Soviet bloc": Dulles to DFR 1/1/61. Eisenhower to JFK on Cuba, 1/19/61: Clark Clifford notes 1/24/61, JFKL, Clifford conv. 1/28/61 NSC meeting: Memcon and General David Gray, "Summary of White House Meetings," 5/9/61, JFKL.

Evolution of invasion plan: Wyden *Bay* 86–92, Higgins 61–94. Bundy to JFK on Defense and CIA attitude toward invasion: 2/8/61, JFKL. Bundy to JFK on moving Bissell to State: 2/25/61, JFKL. JFK worry that Cuba would be another Hungary: Goodwin 174. On JFK worry about Cuba-Berlin connection, see Notes for Chapter 6. JFK request for quieter landing: 2/9/61 memcon, JFKL. JFK worry about "spectacular" plan and CIA response: Wyden *Bay* 499–101, National Security Action Memorandum #31, JFKL, AMSTD 240–3. Bundy to JFK on "remarkable job": 3/15/61, JFKL. Failure to realize that "melt into the mountains" option was gone: Wyden *Bay* 102–3, AMSTD 243. Fulbright memo to JFK: Marcy int, Fulbright-JFK 3/29/61, JFKL, Fulbright 164–5. JFK in Palm Beach: NYT 4/2/61, 4/3/61, PA. Schlesinger journal entry is in AMSTD 249.

Bundy on JFK "really wanted to do this" and "There are candidates": Bundy int. Joseph Kennedy 1961 political views: Waldrop, Corcoran ints, Manchester *Portrait* 185. Bundy rolling eyes: Bundy int. Joseph Kennedy influence on RFK appointment: Smathers int, Clifford conv. 4/4/61 meeting: NYT 4/5/61, Rusk int, Wyden *Bay* 146–52, Higgins 110–13, Taylor Report. On leaks about Cuba invasion, see *Journalism Quarterly*, vol. 63, 1986, "The Bay of Pigs and the *New York Times.*" Harrison-Schlesinger talk: Harrison conv, Harrison oh, Schlesinger-JFK 4/6/61, JFKL. *New York Times* leak and JFK reaction: NYT 4/7/61, Catledge 259–62, Salinger 146. Daniel on Dryfoos action: NYT 6/2/66. NSK skepticism about Cuba invasion reports: Corson and Crowley 271. "The Cuban coast": NSK1 492. NSK on "aggressive American monopolists": NYT 1/3/61.

Scant mention of Cuba in Thompson talks: Thompson-Rusk 1/21/61, 3/10/61, JFKL. Schlesinger-Kornienko talk: AMSTD 262–4 and Schlesinger-JFK 4/12/61, noted in AMSTD draft. Vladislav Zubok of the U.S.A.-Canada Institute, Moscow, has also kindly shared material from his interviews with Kornienko. JFK on NSK reading of Lippmann: Lisagor oh. NSK restores postponed Lippmann visit: Steel 526. NSK and Pitsunda estate: *Atlantic*, September 1963, Cousins 83–5, SNK 124–42, T 8/16/63. "It's coming from your ally": NSK-Eric Johnston memcon 10/6/58, DDEL. Lippmann-NSK interview: notes in Lippmann Papers, NW 4/24/62, Steel 526–8, Text in USN 5/1/61 and WP 4/17/61–4/19/61. NSK political exploitation of space: McDougall 231–99, NSK2 53–7, Oberg *Red Star* 28–30. Soviet space misfire during NSK 1960 UN visit: Oberg *Uncovering* 151, 163, 303 and McDougall 242–4. Bondarenko accident: Oberg *Uncovering* 159–62. Gagarin flight: NYT 4/13/61–4/15/61, Prav 4/13/61–4/15/61, Oberg *Uncovering* 161–2, McDougall 244–9, Oberg *Red Star* 50–98.

NSK on meaning of Gagarin success: Thompson-Rusk 4/13/61, JFKL, McDougall 248–9. JFK statement on Gagarin: 4/12/61, JFKL. JFK on dictatorship's "advantages": JFKPP 4/12/61. "This is the end" and "frustration, shame": "Man into Space," NBC-TV, 4/12/61, T 4/21/61. "Russian housing is lousy": Bergquist 12. Sorensen notes JFK irritation: Wyden *Bay* 165. "I know everybody is grabbing": Wyden *Bay* 165. "Under no circumstances": Goodwin 174. Telegram from Marine colonel and JFK approval of Saturday airstrikes: Taylor Report, Wyden *Bay* 168–70, Higgins 126–30. Saturday airstrikes, exile landing in Miami and Castro government reaction: NYT 4/16/61, AMSTD 270–1. Stevenson defense of cover story and discovery of lie: Charles Yost int JBM, Bartlow Martin *Stevenson* 627–8, Wofford 348–50, Higgins 130–1. "I've got to resign": Jane Dick into JBM. Stevenson criticism of JFK "boy commandos" and "Cuban absurdity": Bartlow Martin *Stevenson* 634, Stevenson-Agnes Meyer 5/14/61, Stevenson Papers.

Stevenson cable to Rusk: 4/16/61, JFKL. "He did *not* fuss": Bundy int JBM. Glen Ora: Bartlett oh, Bartlett int, NW 12/19/60, Billings oh. Billings oh refers in this case to the transcript of an interview with LeMoyne Billings, kindly shared with the author by Peter Collier. Rusk-JFK Sunday telephone conversation: AMSTD draft, Schlesinger 12/31/64 interview of Bundy and Jacqueline Kennedy interview, V, 4, both noted in AMSTD draft, Higgins 132, Bundy in NYT 6/12/85. Bundy-Bissell-Cabell-Rusk talks: Cabell-Taylor 5/9/61, JFKL, Higgins 133–4, Wyden *Bay* 199–200. JFK reproaches himself: Billings Diary 4/29/61. JFK later told Schlesinger that he felt that cancelling the second airstrike was an error but not a decisive one. (Schlesinger journal 5/23/61, noted in AMSTD draft). Cabell Monday morning appeals: AMSTD 273–4, Higgins 135, Wyden *Bay* 205–6. Start of the invasion: Higgins 138–43, Wyden *Bay* 206–35. NSK hears of invasion: Radio Moscow 4/17/61, Sergei Khrushchev conv, ACT, NSK1 492.

6. "A Big Kick"

Castro's 4/16/61 speech: NYT 4/17/61. NSK on Castro calling his movement "socialist": NSK1 492. *Pravda* on Dulles movements: Prav 4/18/61. *Izvestia* quotation: Izv 4/17/61. Eden quotation: Eden-Lord Beaverbrook 4/20/61, Beaverbrook Papers. JFK calls RFK: RFK oh, RFK 6/1/61 memo, RFK Papers, AMSRK 444. "Rather be called an aggressor": RFK 6/1/61 memo, RFK Papers. RFK-Guthman exchange: Guthman 110–4. Thompson's departure: Jane Thompson int. Insult to Freers: Memo attached to copy of Freers-Rusk 4/18/61 cable in JFKL, also NYT 4/19/61. Moscow demonstration: Prav 4/19/61, NYT 4/18/61, Klosson int. Other demonstrations: NW 5/1/61, L 4/28/61. 4/18/61 Congressional breakfast: Memcon in JFKL, NW 5/1/61. JFK to exile leaders on Cuba and Berlin was in December 1962: Carbonell 190. "I think you will find": Bundy-JFK 4/18/61, JFKL.

JFK-Reston conversation: Schlesinger journal 4/18/61, noted in AMSTD draft. I have restored the President's actual language, which Schlesinger softened in the published version of *A Thousand Days.* American officials react to NSK message: AMSTD 276–7. JFK response to NSK: 4/18/61, JFKL. Tuesday night meeting in Cabinet Room: Rostow oh, RFK oh, Sor 307, Sidey 131–4, Collier and Horowitz *Kennedys* 271, Wyden *Bay* 269–72, Higgins 467–8. Wednesday morning events: RFK 6/1/61 memo, RFK Papers, Taylor Report, Higgins 148–9, Wyden *Bay* 272–88. JFK and First Lady in bedroom: Jacqueline Kennedy interview, V, 7. cited in AMSTD draft. Rose Kennedy on call to her husband: Rose Kennedy Diary 4/19/61, quoted in Rose Kennedy 400. Robert Kennedy on need to act and Rostow reply: Rostow oh, Rostow *Diffusion* 210–1. Mao on West as "paper tiger" appears in the CIA 4/1/61 memo on the Sino-Soviet split, as does NSK's reaction.

RFK-JFK: 4/19/61 draft, RFK Papers. Jacqueline on "very boring" gift: Billings oh. "Everybody really seemed to fall apart": RFK memo 6/1/61, RFK Papers. Bowles on consensus and Wednesday evening meeting: Bowles oh, Bowles 329–30, RFK 6/1/61 memo, RFK oh. For Sorensen's background, see *Reporter* 2/13/64, Sor 16–7, Medved 260–83. Burns's conclusion: Burns *Kennedy* 281. "The impression should never be given" and "the basis for our judgment": Sorensen-Burns 10/17/59 and 10/27/59, Sorensen Papers. Burns reply, 11/1/59, is in Sorensen Papers. Effect of book on Burns-JFK relations: Burns conv and Burns oh. On the entire episode, see Beschloss in Beschloss and Cronin 66–74. "I felt I could have had," "The only human being who mattered," "His work of art": Medved 260–2. "A Kennedy speech has to have class": Bartlow Martin *It Seems* 195. "I do not want current": Sorensen oh COHP.

Parmet's verdict on *Profiles* authorship: Parmet *Jack* 320–3. JFK on Sorensen's increasing resemblance: Manchester *Portrait* 115–6. Neustadt on JFK and Sorensen: Notes of Schlesinger interview with Neustadt, 9/15/64, Schlesinger Papers. JFK on RFK 1959 attitude toward Sorensen: Raskin int. "To prove ourselves": Medved 261. JFK-Sorensen Wednesday night meeting and afterward: Sidey 138, AMSTD 287. Bohlen on JFK "looking forward": Bohlen oh and notes. JFK-Sorensen walk: Sor 308. JFK speech to the editors is in JFKPP, 4/20/61. The final exclamation point is in the original. Cuban exile reaction: NYT 4/21/61. Menshikov's cancellation: Bartlow Martin *Stevenson* 632. RFK on speech: RFK 6/1/61 memo, RFK Papers. Goodwin criticism of speech and JFK reply: Goodwin 180–1. Goldwater on "apprehension and shame": NYT 4/21/61, 4/23/61. Norstad on worst defeat since 1812: Sulzberger 743.

Thompson on JFK speech: Thompson-Rusk 4/21/61, JFKL. Yevtushenko poem: Prav 10/14/62. JFK press conference comments on Bay of Pigs and Vanocur question: JFKPP 4/21/61 and Vanocur int. "Allen and Dick didn't just *brief* us": SEP 6/24/61. Donovan on "preposterous praises": Hedley Donovan 77–8. "My God, the bunch": Jacqueline Kennedy interview, V, 4–5, noted in AMSTD draft. JFK on Allen Dulles assurance: Jack Bell oh. JFK attributes same quote to Joint Chiefs: Arthur Krock memcon on meeting with JFK 5/5/61, Krock Papers. "I'll bet Dean Rusk": Weintal and Bartlett 149. "We can't win them all": AMSTD draft, based on Schlesinger journal 4/21/61. I have again restored the President's actual language, softened in the published *A Thousand Days*. NSK Saturday message to JFK: Freers-Rusk 4/22/61, JFKL. "He's got this very good habit": Bundy int. State announcement on "extended debate": NYT 4/29/61.

"How could I have been so stupid?": Sor 309. "It was Eisenhower's plan": Wofford 355. JFK on "albatross": Bergquist 11. Bundy on JFK effort to make invasion plan work: Bundy oh COHP. Schlesinger on "intoxication": AMSTD 206. "You always assume": Schlesinger journal 4/21/61, noted in AMSTD draft. For documentation of Adenauer visit, see Notes for Chapter 11. "He would have thought more about the Russian aspect": Bundy int. RFK opinion that JFK "never would have tried this operation": RFK memo 6/1/61, RFK Papers. Dulles comments in his notes, Dulles Papers, Princeton University, are quoted in Lucien Vandenbroucke, "The 'Confessions' of Allen Dulles," *Diplomatic History*, Fall 1984. I have not applied for permission to examine the Allen Dulles Papers because of the extraordinary demands imposed by their proprietors for influence on the content of books in which quotations from them will appear.

Bissell on dropping five times the tonnage of bombs: Interview in WS 7/20/65. Bissell and Castro assassination: Bissell int, Thomas Powers 146–9, 153–4, Wyden *Bay* 23–5, 40–1, 109–110. JFK conversation with Fleming: Pearson 382–4, Brandon conv. CIA effort to dust Castro's shoes with depilatory: *Assassination Plots* 72–3. J.C. King memo on "thorough consideration": *Assassination Plots* 92. Bissell request of Dr. Gottlieb: Thomas Powers 146. Edwards-Maheu September 1960 meeting: *Assassination Plots* 74, Joseph Smith 240. For documentation on Trafficante and Ruby, see Notes for Chapter 23. Maheu-Giancana October 1960 meeting: Thomas Powers 147–9. Bissell on "ultimate cover": Wyden *Bay* 41. In the Nixon Papers appears an announcement of "Maheu & King Associates, Inc., Consultants in Management, Government and Public Relations," with offices in Washington, Beverly Hills and San Francisco. King was also friendly with Nixon's Cuban-American friend Bebe Rebozo. (King-Nixon, 12/4/52, Nixon Papers)

King-Nixon relationship and Nixon on King as "alter ego": King-Nixon tel note 10/29/54, Nixon Papers, *St. Louis Post-Dispatch* 9/19/54. Nixon told reporters that King was "an expert on domestic and international communism" and that his internal security work had given him "a keen insight into the immense danger and possibility of subversion in the United States." The Vice President's appointment of a liquor executive caused him to receive many protest letters from temperance advocates, which are also in the Nixon Papers. King later said that when Nixon hired him, he told him that one of his main duties was to "protect" him so that he had time to read and think: "He needed protection and I, as the only male member of his immediate staff in those days, was the chief buffer." (NYT 9/7/73) Similarly in my King int.

King accompanied Nixon to Vienna, where they met with exile victims of the foiled Hungarian revolution. In June 1959, he accompanied Nixon and his wife Pat to the Soviet Embassy in Washington to meet the visiting Deputy Premier Frol Kozlov. Afterward King wrote the Vice President to thank him for the "considerable thrill": "I used to be so absorbed in my Russian pursuits of old that I would dream of being in Moscow, and so you can see that the Embassy provided a special meaning." (King-Nixon, 7/5/59, Nixon Papers) This was three months before King's partner Maheu met with Sam Giancana about killing Castro.

Pawley call to Rose Mary Woods and Nixon reply: Woods-Nixon note 1/4/60, Nixon Papers. Nixon-Pawley lunch and letter to Pawley: Nixon-Pawley 1/12/60, Nixon Papers. Nixon-King 1/12/60 meeting: 1/12/60 note, Nixon Papers. Nixon and Mahev: King int. Pawley to Nixon, 7/18/60, is in Nixon Papers. Nixon's interest as President in obtaining the CIA file on Cuba: John Ehrlichman notes, 9/18/71, published in Appendix 3 of U.S. House Judiciary Committee, *Statement of Information*, May–June 1974, AMSRK 486–8. In the ultimately decisive tape of his 6/23/72 Oval Office conversations, Nixon asked his aide H.R. Haldeman to tell the CIA that since an investigation of the Watergate break-in might reopen the "whole Bay of Pigs thing," the FBI should be put off the trail for the good of the country. (Tape in Nixon Papers, Alexandria, Va.) Nixon's interest in O'Brien's relationship with Hughes: Lukas 173–81, Ambrose *Nixon: Education* 421–3, Kutler 202–5, Haldeman 109, 133–5, 144–7, 159–60.

Nixon's first serious public criticism of JFK was in a Chicago speech of 5/5/61 (NYT 5/6/61 and *Chicago Tribune* 5/6/61). He had waited until late spring in order to give the new President a decent interval of national unity (Nixon-William

Rogers 4/29/61, Nixon Papers) CIA-Mafia plotting against Castro, March–April 1961: Wyden *Bay* 38–45, 109–110. Rusk, McNamara, Bundy, Sorensen insistence on ignorance of a CIA plot: Rusk int, *Assassination Plots* 120, 157–159. JFK to Szulc on assassination: *Assassination Plots* 138–9, and Szulc in *Esquire,* February 1974. JFK to Goodwin on assassination: WP 7/21/75. JFK to Martin on "skirtchaser" rumors: Bartlow Martin *It Seems* 211. "You're all looking to tag me": Bradlee 49. Ford on CIA secret report ruining Presidential reputations: Schorr 143–4. "A lot of people probably lied": Helms int. Bissell "pure personal opinion": Davis *Kennedys* 543–50. McNamara on CIA as "highly disciplined": *Assassination Plots* 158.

"There are two things you have": Thomas Powers letter in *Times Literary Supplement* 4/21–27/89. Helms said the same thing to the current author. (Helms int) JFK to Smathers on assassination: Smathers oh, Smathers int. Thomas Powers on CIA officials walking "a fine line": Thomas Powers in *Times Literary Supplement* 4/21/89. Hoover to RFK on Edwards-Maheu relationship and planning against Castro: Davis *Kennedys* 385–6, AMSRK 493–4. No record of JFK-RFK investigation of "dirty business" and "contacts": Helms int. RFK on crime as "number one concern": Davis *Kennedys* 367. "I'd like to be remembered": Opotowsky 74–5. RFK target list: Blakey and Billings 169. Marcello deportation: Davis *Mafia Kingfish* 90–3. "Here I am, helping the government": Samuel Giancana file, FBI, Fox 341. Critics argument about JFK-Giancana alliance: Fox 333–5. Trafficante-Marcello rumored contribution to Nixon: Moldea 198. Hunter to Nixon, 12/13/59, on Hoffa meeting: quoted in Drew Pearson, WP 2/5/61.

Pearson on Teamster help in Ohio and Hunter-Hoffa 12/8/60: WP 1/4/61. Eisenhower on Sinatra in Kennedy activities: Slater 240. Justice report on "show girls" in JFK suite: Kelley *His Way* 293. Joseph Kennedy's presence at Cal-Neva Lodge is attested to by Hy Raskin: Raskin int and unpublished manuscript. Visits by gangsters are noted in Kelley *His Way* 304. Giancana post-election boast: Exner 194. JFK-Campbell relationship: Exner 49–252. White House telephone logs: *Assassination Plots* 194. Smathers on Campbell being taken into private quarters and JFK-Thompson talks about her and other women: Smathers int, Raskin int. In her memoir, Exner refers to a "railroad lobbyist": Exner 129–31. Joseph Kennedy's rumored crime associations: Blakey and Billings 274–98. Winchell on "top New Dealer's mistress": Klurfeld 95 and Klurfeld conversation with Ernest Cuneo, reported to the author by Mr. Cuneo.

Campbell's claim of secret meetings and sealed envelopes and explanation of why she did not say so earlier: *People* 2/29/88 and *Donahue,* Los Angeles, transcript #030188, February 1988. Roselli egging on Giancana: Fox 338–9. Giancana on knowing "all" about Kennedys: Giancana file, FBI. Sorensen on official log as "far from complete": Sorensen int JBM. JFK throws *Time* into fireplace: Collier and Horowitz *Kennedys* 271. RFK on being "through a lot of things together": RFK oh. "He felt very strongly": RFK 6/1/61 memo, AMSRK 446. JFK to Clifford on "second Bay of Pigs": Clifford oh, Clifford conv. *Christian Science Monitor* 7/24/75. Press on digging out of rubble: for example, NYT 4/30/61. JFK on giving job to LBJ: Billings Diary 5/7/61. JFK on "tragic administration": Billings Diary 4/29/61. On JFK and Billings: Michaelis 127–89, Collier and Horowitz *Kennedys* 62–7, 79–80, 90–2.

Billings on why never married: Billings oh. JFK on "especially sickening letter":

JFK-Billings 5/3/39. Billings on late April luncheon: Billings Diary 4/29/61. "It was the only thing on his mind": Ralph Martin 336. JFK on keeping Dulles in office: AMSTD 290. "Dulles is a man": Sidey 146–7. JFK and Eisenhower at Camp David: Eisenhower interview by Malcolm Moos, 11/8/66, DDEL, Eisenhower memo 4/22/61, DDEL, NYT 4/23/61. JFK "unimpressed" by Eisenhower: Billings Diary 4/29/61. JFK-Goldwater meeting: Goldwater *Goldwater* 136–8. JFK-Nixon meeting: Nixon in *Readers Digest,* November 1964, Nixon *Memoirs* 232–6, NYT 4/21/61. Bundy to JFK on "heaviest Republican pressure": 2/19/63, JFKL. "That's what's really important": Sor 294. RFK refuses CIA: RFK oh, Sidey 149. Brandon encounters Bundy: Brandon oh. Bundy resignation letter to JFK: undated, JFKL, Kissinger to Bundy: 5/5/61, JFKL.

Bundy move to West Wing basement: Bundy int, Destler, 186–7, Sidey 151. JFK establishes Taylor board: JFK-Taylor 4/22/61, JFKL, and Taylor Report. Bowles and NSC meeting: Bowles oh, Bowles 330–2, Goodwin 186–8. Rusk worry about missiles in Cuba: Rusk to DFR, 5/3/61. Further post–Bay of Pigs deliberations: AMSRK 446–9, 458–60, Higgins 151–171. Taylor Report conclusion: Taylor Report and Taylor-JFK 6/13/61, JFKL. RFK on Cuban matter sliding: RFK 6/1/61 memo, RFK Papers. Doolittle Report conclusion appears in U.S. Senate *Final Report of the Senate Select Committee on Intelligence* 52–3. Arnold Smith on NSK after Bay of Pigs: 4/26/61, Bohlen papers. NSK and Soviet shortcomings: See, for example, Tatu 127–40. Shevchenko on effect of Bay of Pigs in Moscow: Shevchenko 109–10. Soviet attitudes toward JFK after Bay of Pigs: Klosson int, Kohler int, RFK oh, Chayes oh, AMSTD draft, Shevchenko 110, 117, Corson and Crowley 271, Ulam *Expansion* 653, Andrew and Gordievsky 468–9. Van Fleet affair: NYT 11/1/61, 11/2/61.

NSK "impression that Kennedy was indecisive": Shevchenko 110. Eastern European to Bowles: Bowles oh. NSK says father not a rich man: quoted in Ulam *Expansion* 650. JFK to Adenauer on summit: 5/16/61, JFKL. Bohlen on summit as "dead": Bohlen notes. For documentation of Bolshakov gambit, see Notes for Chapter 7.

7. The Secret Agent

Bolshakov's first meeting with RFK and generally: RFK oh, Holeman int, Guthman int, Bartlett int, Bolshakov in *Novoye vremya* (Moscow) 1/27/89, NW 12/24/62, Salinger in *Macleans* 11/28/83, AMSRK 499–501, Bradlee 194, Guthman 119, Symington 144, Salinger 184, 187. Vladislav Zubok has kindly shared material from his interview with Adzhubei. "I'd like to meet", "I'm the only person" and "Georgi was being tailed": Holeman int. "An important agent": *Macleans* 11/28/83. Holeman in 1952 motorcade: Nixon-John Madigan 11/13/56, Nixon Papers. Holeman persuades Press Club to admit Soviets: Holeman int. Gvozdev query about Lebanon and reply: Holeman int. "I keep telling them": Rose Mary Woods-Nixon, after Holeman conversation, 12/18/58, Nixon Papers. "Frank Holeman, Boy Spy": Woods-Frank Holeman tel note 1/8/59, Nixon Papers. "The Russians feel war is close": William G. Key-Nixon 7/17/58 (copies sent to Allen Dulles, John Foster Dulles, J. Edgar Hoover, 7/18/58), Nixon Papers.

"Don't worry about Berlin": Woods-Nixon 12/18/58, Nixon Papers, and Holeman int. NSK "very interested" and "would bid very high": Woods-Nixon 12/

18/58 and Woods note 1/8/59, Nixon Papers. Nixon probable consultation of Eisenhower and Foster Dulles: Goodpaster int and Holeman int. Gvozdev's life after leaving Washington: Holeman int and Barron 508. Holeman encountered Gvozdev in the Soviet Union while accompanying Nixon on his 1959 visit. (Holeman int) JFK-Adenauer on "faced with the problem": 5/16/61, JFKL. Bohlen on summit conditions, JFK instruction to RFK on "leaning" toward summit and Bolshakov reply: Bohlen notes, RFK oh. "They didn't want to go": RFK oh. "Bobby was my client": Holeman int. "My guy wants to see": Guthman 119 and Guthman int. "My interest was in making sure": Holeman int. Bolshakov Washington acquaintanceship: NW 12/24/62.

"I unfortunately": RFK oh. Thompson on "error of judgment," JFK reaction to this advice, Rusk and Bundy attitudes toward and knowledge of channel: Thompson oh, Jane Thompson int, Rusk int, Bundy int. Symington on "insinuating jocularity" and "dangerous game": Symington 145. JFK appeared before photographers with Soviet delegations including Bolshakov, for instance, on 6/26/61 and 11/25/61. See documentation in Notes for Chapters 10 and 13. FBI surveillance while Bolshakov dined at Holeman home: Holeman int. "I don't think Bobby thought": Bartlett int. NSK on Gromyko dropping trousers was said during Harold Macmillan's 1959 Soviet trip: Macmillan *Riding* 589–635. Molotov to Vienna and NSK worry about Molotov loyalists: Medvedev *All Stalin's Men* 106–7. Sergei Khrushchev believes that his father removed Molotov from Ulan Bator because the Mongolians disliked having an envoy in whom NSK obviously had so little confidence. (Sergei Khrushchev conv)

Shelepin criticism of NSK foreign policy: Simmonds 92. "Each crisis that I've faced so far": Sidey (1964) 141. "Keep pushing us all over": quoted in Lasky *JFK* 569, based on Lasky conv with Nixon. "Getting involved in a fight": Odon 286. "The worse I do" and "If I had gone": AMSTD 292, based on Schlesinger journal 5/3/61 and 5/7/61, as noted in AMSTD draft. "I would assume you would share": JFK-Adenauer, 5/16/61, JFKL. Johnson fear about summit: Merle Miller 287. "Soviet rulers usually pay": Bohlen notes. "Recent events make a meeting": Thompson-Rusk 5/4/61 and 5/6/61, JFKL. JFK relief about Shepard success: Sidey 157–8. "Wasn't too happy to note": Billings Diary 5/7/61. "It will fall into our laps": AMSTD 334. Brown request for airstrikes: Brown-Rusk 4/26/61, JFKL. Joint Chiefs plans for move against North: Parmet *JFK* 148. "Afford to make another mistake": Billings Diary 5/7/61.

"The life of a single farm boy": Salisbury *Without Fear* 292. "The head of the Army said": RFK memo 6/1/61, RFK Papers. "If the Marines aren't willing": Rostow oh and RFK oh. "The Communists could send five men": RFK memo 6/1/61, RFK Papers. JFK refuses troops to Laos and "We would be into Laos": Odon 267–9, Schlesinger journal 5/7/61, noted in AMSTD draft, RFK 6/1/61 memo, RFK Papers. Geneva talks and JFK to Harriman: AMSTD 337, AMSRK 702–3. Johnson "very depressed": Johnson-DFR 5/25/61. RFK consults Bolshakov and worry about "tunnel": RFK oh, RFK 6/1/61 memo, RFK Papers. NSK at Tbilisi: Lucius Battle-Bundy 5/25/61 and NYT 5/13/61. Vanocur scoop on summit: Vanocur int, Sidey 159–62. JFK-Menshikov 5/16/61 meeting: 5/16/61 memcon, JFKL. Bohlen-Rusk conversation: Bohlen-Bundy 5/16/61, JFKL. On JFK-Diefenbaker relations: RFK oh, Lawrence Martin 180–90.

Memo embarrassment and "I didn't think": Lawrence Martin 191, Bradlee 67,

181–5. Tree-planting ceremony and JFK injury: Sidey 165–6 and Lieberson 132, the latter of which includes photographs of JFK wincing in pain. JFK condition: Lincoln *My Twelve Years* 260–1 and Odon 288. Announcement of summit: TASS statement of 5/19/61 and NYT 5/20/61. Fulbright on "nervousness": DFR 5/20/61. Jacksonville and Carson City citizen reactions: USN 6/5/61. "Mr. Khrushchev may not see": NYkr 6/3/61. Biddle cable: Biddle-Rusk 5/31/61, JFKL. *Newsweek* report and Gore and Hickenlooper on summit: NW 5/29/61. Ball and Goldberg on summit: Sulzberger 755–6 and Ralph Martin 350. Mansfield to JFK on summit, 5/26/61, is in JFKL. Reston column (NYT 4/30/61) was reprinted in *Pravda* 5/5/61. JFK in mid-May 1961: Sidey (1964) 160–1.

JFK decision to make second State of the Union: Sorensen oh, Sidey 123, 172. JFK speech text is in JFKPP 5/25/61. Sorensen on likelihood of Rockefeller in 1964: Sorensen oh. Advice to JFK to distance himself from Project Mercury: McDougall 309–10. "Is there any place we can catch them?": Sidey 122. "In the eyes of the world": Hirsch and Trento 108. JFK consideration of moon program: Sor 523–6, McDougall 317–22, Sidey 113–23. Eisenhower resistance of moon race: Ambrose *Eisenhower* 640–1. "Almost hysterical": Eisenhower draft letter 6/22/61, DDEL. Eisenhower to Borman: 6/18/65, DDEL. Prescott Bush on inflation: NYT 5/26/61. Joseph Kennedy on unbalanced budget: Corcoran int. JFK reads briefing materials: Rostow *Diffusion* 224, Sidey 166–70. "Here are the beginnings": Bundy-JFK 5/26/61, JFKL. State Department on NSK at Vienna: State Department, "Scope Paper," 5/23/61, JFKL.

CIA profiles: Office of Current Intelligence, "Khrushchev: A Personality Sketch" and "Khrushchev: The Man and His Outlook," 9/11/59 and 5/25/61, DDEL and JFKL. 1960 CIA assessment of NSK personality and quotation from Wedge letter: Bryant Wedge in *Transaction* October 1968. Transcripts of other American conversations with NSK are in DDEL and JFKL. "You are like a nightingale": NSK-Reuther memcon 10/30/59, DDEL and JFKL. "The way Soviet leaders": Stevenson-JFK 5/25/61, JFKL, and Bartlow Martin *Stevenson* 638–41. Bohlen to JFK on NSK: Bohlen notes and Sulzberger 758. Lippmann to JFK on NSK: Lippmann oh, Bundy-JFK 5/29/61, JFKL, and Steel 532. NSK background and personality: NSK1, NSK2, NSK3, Pistrak, Crankshaw, Medvedev and SNK, as well as biographical material in DDEL and JFKL. "A working man's Cambridge": Prav 12/13/62. McDuffie on 1946 NSK meeting: McDuffie 199–200.

Secret Speech text: NSK1 559–618. "We are all Stalinists": Leonhard 232. "You are afraid to face" and "The fool didn't": Micunovic 270–1. "The post of Prime Minister": NSK-Hubert Humphrey memcon 12/3/58, JFKL. American-Soviet differences on priority business at summit: Thompson-Rusk 5/24/61, 5/30/61, JFKL. On the Berlin problem 1945–1960, see Schick 3–133, Slusser in Blechman and Kaplan 303–408. "We don't even have to fire them": NSK-Humphrey memcon 12/3/58, JFKL. Dulles and Mikoyan on East German government: Memcon 1/17/59, DDEL. NSK to Humphrey on German reunification: NSK-Humphrey memcon 12/3/58, JFKL. Stevenson on Germany never reunified: Newton Minow conv, Minow int JBM. Eisenhower on West Germany as "magnet": Eisenhower-Bernard Law Montgonery 7/14/53, DDEL. West Germany achieves sovereignty: Ambrose *Eisenhower* 216–7.

"We knew that officially they would not": Sergo Mikoyan at Harvard University, 2/13/89–2/15/89. I am indebted to Benina Berger-Gould and Priscilla Johnson

McMillan for sharing with me their notes and records of these sessions. NSK fear of nuclear FRG and Rapacki Plan: Ulam *Expansion* 610–3, Ulam *Rivals* 288–94. Eisenhower on NSK "manufactured crisis": Eisenhower 336fn. On Eisenhower-NSK Camp David sessions, see Beschloss *Mayday* 187–215. Eisenhower concessions on Berlin and Germany are noted in AMSTD 348. NSK advisors advise softpedal Berlin: Gelb 70. NSK to Kroll: NYT 1/2/61. JFK views on Berlin before 1961: JFK *Strategy* 96–8, 212–4, AMSTD 346–7, CR 6/14/60. JFK request of NSK for time to prepare Berlin position: Sor 542. JFK omission of Berlin in State of Union and explanation: JFKPP 1/30/61, 2/1/61.

Thompson on NSK would "almost certainly proceed": Thompson-Rusk 2/4/61, JFKL. JFK instruction to Thompson on Berlin: Martin Hillenbrand-Thompson 2/20/61, JFKL. JFK-Adenauer communiqués: JFKPP 4/13/61 and statements in JFKL. "Surprised at the unanimity": Thompson-Rusk 3/10/61, JFKL. "All my diplomatic colleagues": Thompson-Rusk 3/16/61, JFKL. Lippmann-NSK on Berlin: Lippmann 51–2, Steel 526–8, WP 4/17/61–4/19/61. "If I go to a cathedral": Sulzberger 572. On NSK eagerness to show toughness with President, see Beschloss *Mayday* 215–20, 239, 257, 300–1, 304–7. Acheson April Berlin advice: Acheson-JFK 4/3/61, Bundy-JFK 4/4/61, AMSTD 346, Isaacson and Thomas 609–11. Schlesinger objected to Acheson's presentation in a memo to JFK, (4/6/61, JFKL) "All discussion on Berlin": *Der Tagesspiegel* 3/9/61. Lightner on hard line: Lightner-Rusk 5/25/61, JFKL. Thompson May Berlin advice: Thompson-Rusk 5/30/61, JFKL.

"At one extreme are" and "There is a chance": Bundy-JFK 5/29/61, JFKL. RFK to Bolshakov on Berlin commitment: RFK oh. JFK at Hyannis: Sidey (1964) 144. Joseph Kennedy before JFK arrival: Saunders 38 and Edward Kennedy 264. JFK decides on gift for NSK and asks father for money: Billings oh and Edward Kennedy 264. Boston Armory dinner is described by Richard Rovere in NYkr 6/17/61 and Rovere 158–60. Speech text is in JFKPP 5/29/61. JFK on Samuel Adams in campaign: 9/16/60, Pikesville, Md., PCS. NSK departure for Vienna: U.S. Embassy Prague cable to U.S. State Department 5/31/61, JFKL, NYT 5/29/61. 6/1/61, 6/2/61 and Medvedev 179–80. NSK and Thompson at ice show: Thompson-Rusk 5/24/61 and 5/30/61, JFKL, NYT 5/25/61. JFK meeting with Ben Gurion and departure: NYT 5/28/61, Lincoln *My Twelve Years* 262, Sidey 173–4. JFK to Salinger on deprecating chances for success: Sal 169, 175–7. RFK on being "reasonably hopeful" about Vienna: RFK oh.

8. *"Not as a Cripple"*

JFK arrival at Orly: NYT 6/1/61, NW 6/12/61, Sidey 175–6. Rose Kennedy on arrival: Rose Kennedy 492. Billings on JFK sensitivity about family on trips: Billings oh. Motorcade into Paris and arrival: Lincoln *My Twelve Years* 262–3, Odon 288, Sidey 177–8. JFK interest in and study of de Gaulle: AMSTD draft, AMSTD 103, Sor 560–1. "Even when there is": Wahl-Bundy, undated, May 1961, JFKL. "Somewhat fumbling": de Gaulle 254. De-Gaulle-JFK conversations: memcon of JFK meeting with Congressional leaders 6/6/61, JFKL. Bohlen oh, Bohlen notes, Bohlen 479–80, de Gaulle 254–9, AMSTD 349–58, Sor 559–62, Sulzberger 759–62, Odon 290–1. De Gaulle to Eisenhower on Berlin, 1960: Herter-Dillon

5/16/60, JFKL, and Couve de Murville oh. Luncheon: AMSTD 350–1 and AMSTD draft, based on Jacqueline Kennedy interview, V, 46–7, Schlesinger Papers.

"The more you become": de Gaulle 256. Trujillo murder and reaction in Paris: Rusk to DFR 12/20/61, Bowles oh, NYT 6/1/61, Sal 172–3, Sidey 187–8. "Influence which stretches": NW 6/12/61. Versailles dinner: NYT 6/1/61, L 6/9/61, Odon 289, Kelley *Jackie* 170, AMSTD 354–5. "You've studied": Bohlen oh, Bohlen notes. "I have more confidence": Manchester *Shining* 186. JFK on Friday night: NYT 6/2/61, Harriman-JFK, "Current Status of Cease-fire Issue," undated, Harriman Papers, Halberstam *Best* 74–5. JFK Paris departure and flight to Vienna: Abram Chayes oh, Kohler int, Jane Thompson int, Sorensen oh, NYkr 6/17/61, Sidey 192. JFK refusal to go to Europe as cripple was voiced to General Chester Clifton: Stoughton and Clifton 7. JFK on Roosevelt and Kuriles was spoken at Salem, Mass.: CR 2/21/49. Radford-Snyder conversation: Radford told this story to Arthur Krock, who recorded it in a memo, 2/9/72, Krock Papers. India Edwards on JFK illness and Sorensen reply: NYT 7/5/60.

Break-ins at doctors' offices: Parmet *JFK* 121. Casey investigation of JFK health and Moley on "palpable mental lapses": Raymond Moley-Nixon 12/14/60, Nixon Papers. Lord Moran and Churchill: See Moran. JFK's Addison's disease and its concealment: MacMahon and Curry 122–36, Blairs 561–79, Parmet *Jack* 190–2, 308–9, Kearns Goodwin 734–5. JFK managers and Travell on JFK health: Parmet *JFK* 18–20. JFK's back problem: Kearns Goodwin 646–7, 700–1, 735, 774–6. Blairs 24. JFK to Billings on back: Billings oh. "Born with an unstable back": Blairs 24. Jacqueline Kennedy on procaine treatments: AMSTD draft, based on Jacqueline Kennedy interview, I, 11–3, Schlesinger Papers. JFK resort to bathtub: Odon 288. Travell in Paris: Travell 398–99. Burkley's distress: Burkley oh, Parmet 121–2.

Max Jacobson and relationship with JFK: NYT 12/4/72–12/6/72, 12/8/72, 12/10/72, 12/12/72, 1/16/73, 2/24/73, 2/25/73, 4/19/73, 6/24/73, 10/29/73, 3/24/74, 4/26/75, 6/25/75, 5/30/79, Fisher 81–4, 97–8, 102, 236–7, 261–6, 282–3, 313–4, Heymann 296–319. On Jacobson and JFK, the Heymann account is the most thorough available, based on what Heymann describes as a "lengthy unpublished memoir," other Jacobson records and interviews with Jacobson's son Thomas, wife Ruth and friend Ken McKnight, as well as Jacobson patients including Charles Spalding and Truman Capote. Like such subjects as the Kennedys and the Mafia and JFK and Judith Campbell, the details of the JFK-Jacobson relationship are extremely difficult to confirm with the same assurance as more orthodox diplomatic history. One must also remember that the Jacobson family has as large an interest in rehabilitating the reputation of the late doctor as the Kennedy family does in distancing the President from him. Thus I have treated this material cautiously.

"Acute amphetamine poisoning": NYT 12/4/72. Deletion from autopsy report and RFK possible involvement: Dr. John K. Lattimer in *Resident and Staff Physician*. May 1972, and Davis *Mafia Kingfish* 291–4. Spalding concern about JFK exhaustion in 1960: Heymann 297–8. "Dr. Jacobson's here": Saunders 206. "I said that if I ever heard": NYT 12/4/72. Jacobson and JFK in 1963: NYT 12/4/72. Manchester on Novocaine injection: Manchester *Shining* 167. Jacobson's presence in Paris and Vienna: Heymann 302–6, citing Jacobson unpublished manuscript.

"The last thing": Heymann 311. "I don't care if it's": Heymann 313. JFK aversion to "leading strings": AMSTD 123. NSK Vienna arrival: NYT 6/3/61, Sidey 191. CIA interest in Molotov: Flora Lewis in NYT 11/18/86, the likelihood of which is suggested for the current author by Richard Helms. (Helms int)

"A militaristic exercise": NYT 6/3/61. JFK Vienna arrival: NYT 6/4/61, Lincoln *My Twelve Years* 268–9, Sidey 191–2. CIA involvement in foreign welcomes: Helms int. Billings on arrival: Billings oh. American residence scene: Jane Thompson int, Sidey 192. "Khrushchev is supposedly": Heymann 305. JFK meets NSK: NYT 6/4/61, NW 6/12/61, Odon 292–4, Lincoln *My Twelve Years* 268–9, Sidey 192–3, conv with David Wise, then of the *New York Herald Tribune*, who was present. "After all the studying": Odon 293. Holeman-Gvozdev rendezvous: Holeman int. 1955 CIA briefings of Eisenhower: Goodpaster int, Goodpaster memo 6/28/55, DDEL. "He must have thought": Odon 293. JFK and NSK on Thompson: NW 6/12/61.

As noted in the text, the principal source for my account of what Kennedy and Khrushchev said to each other at Vienna is the official American memoranda of conversations. They include separate memcons for 6/3/61 (12:45 P.M., luncheon, 3 P.M.) and 6/4/61 (10:15 A.M., luncheon, 3:15 P.M.) They were released to the author, with some excisions, by the Archivist of the United States in response to "your appeal of the decision of the Director of the John F. Kennedy Library to continue the national security classification" of the records. (Deputy Archivist Claudine Weiher letter to the author, 9/5/90) I must note the abuse of the classification process that caused these transcripts to be withheld for twenty-nine years. The content of the Kennedy-Khrushchev talks is scarcely unknown to the Soviet government. In 1965, Schlesinger and Sorensen published highly revealing accounts of the Vienna summit based on their access to official records. Official records of the 1960 Eisenhower talks with Khrushchev have been publicly available since 1982.

My account of the talks is enhanced by "Talking Points Reviewing Conversations between President Kennedy and Chairman Khrushchev," June 3–4, 1961, undated (declassified December 1989) and the memcon of JFK's 6/6/61 meeting with Congressional leaders, JFKL. I have also drawn on my interviews with Rusk, Bundy and Kohler, who were present during portions of the talks, and the accounts in AMSTD 358–74, Sor 543–51, Bohlen 480–2, Odon 294–7, Sal 177–82, Kohler 330, Rusk to DFR 6/16/61, Bradlee 124–6 and Sidey 159–67. I have additionally used Soviet sources on the summit, including Andrei Gromyko 136–7, 175, NSK1 458, NSK2 492–509, SNK 50–1, Adzhubei int WGBH, Falin int WGBH, Burlatsky int WGBH, Shevchenko 110–1, Sergei Khrushchev conv. Saturday JFK-NSK luncheon: 6/3/61 luncheon memcon, JFKL, Sal 178, NSK1 458, NSK2 491, AMSTD 361–2, Sor 544–5.

NSK more temperate with Eisenhower during walk in the woods: Adams 454–55. NSK and JFK stroll in garden: 6/3/61 luncheon and 3 P.M. memcons, JFKL, Odon 296. Summit talks and Iran: Sick 8–9, *Dallas Morning News* 6/6/61. NSK happiness over JFK comment on America-Soviet power in balance: SNK 106. JFK to Eisenhower: Eisenhower memcon 4/22/61. Joint Chiefs anger: Herken 157. Brandon on JFK after first day: Brandon 169, Brandon conv. "Is it always like this?": Thompson oh. "May I be permitted": Heymann 305. JFK returns to quarters: Lincoln *My Twelve Years* 268–75. "You seemed pretty calm": Odon

295-6. "He really believes it": Thompson-Rusk 2/2/61, JFKL. "I think his problem": Bartlett int. Press briefing on first day: NYT 6/4/61, NYkr 6/17/61, Sal 179-80. Randolph Churchill boredom and departure: NYT 6/4/61, NYkr 6/17/61, Russell Baker in NYT 12/9/87.

Jacqueline and Nina Petrovna on Saturday: NYT 6/2/61, 6/4/61, NYkr 6/17/61, Philip Geyelin conv. "The American princess" and "I'd like to shake": NYT 6/4/61. NSK on Jacqueline and Rose Kennedy: NSK2 498-9. Rose Kennedy on Nina Petrovna: Rose Kennedy 404-5 and Ralph Martin 482. De Gaulle and Jacqueline on Nina Petrovna: Sulzberger 914-16. Nine Petrovna personality and background: Salisbury *Journey* 485-90, Kohler int, Jane Thompson int. Jacqueline on Adzhubei: Sulzberger 914-6. Presence of Eunice: Billings oh. Travell in journal: Travell 401. "Quick with her tongue": NSK2 499. Jacqueline's conversation with NSK: AMSTD draft, based on Jacqueline Kennedy interview, V, 33-4, AMSTD 366-7. Bohlen's view of JFK on first day: Bohlen 482-3, Bohlen oh, Bohlen notes. Thompson's view: Thompson oh, Jane Thompson int.

Kohler's view: Kohler int. JFK resolved that NSK would "understand": RFK oh. "You aren't going to make a Communist": Rusk int. JFK at Mass and NSK lays wreath: NW 6/12/61, Odon 297. "Rusk, you make" and Rusk fear: Schoenbaum 335, Rusk 220. "I greet you on a small piece": NYT 6/5/61.

9. *"He Just Beat Hell Out of Me"*

Bolshakov to RFK in May: RFK oh. On Open Skies, see Rostow *Open Skies.* "I can't leave here without giving": Odon 297. "No, we're *not* going": Sidey 200. Mrs. Kennedy and Mrs. Khrushchev luncheon: NYT 6/5/61. Nina Petrovna on Jacqueline: *McCalls,* July 1963, and Jane Thompson int. JFK presents gift to NSK: Billings oh. NSK gifts are noted in draft JFK-NSK 6/10/61 thank you note, unsent, JFKL. De Gaulle's recommendation on what JFK should tell NSK on Berlin: Odon 288-92. NSK on JFK at end of Sunday afternoon session: NSK2 500-1. "In diplomacy, you almost never use": Rusk int. Soviet *aide-mémoire* on Berlin is in JFKL. JFK worry about "Spirit of Vienna": Kern 65. Bohlen briefing and Kennedy asks Salinger to publicize "somber" mood: Lisagor oh and Sal 182.

Reston-JFK interview: NYT 6/5/61, Sal 182, Halberstam *Best* 75-7, Odon 298. "It was like riding": Heymann 306. Jacqueline and letter to de Gaulle: Heymann 306. JFK on NSK aboard plane: Geyelin conv. JFK to O'Donnell on Berlin: Odon 292, 299-300. JFK London arrival: NYT 6/5/61, Lisagor oh, Macmillan *Pointing* 355-6. "Laid great hopes" and "met a man": Macmillan *Pointing* 385, 400. "The driver escorted me through": Heymann 306-7. Macmillan-JFK talks: 6/5/61 memcon and Bundy-Rusk, 6/5/61, JFKL. "Let's not have a meeting": Macmillan interview with Schlesinger, 5/20/64, notes in Schlesinger Papers. JFK-Macmillan early relationship: de Zulueta int. Brandon oh, Macmillan *Pointing* 306-7, Horne 281-97. Bruce on Macmillan: Bruce-Rusk 12/13/61, JFKL. "I value our friendship": Macmillan-JFK 5/25/61, JFKL.

"Half his time thinking": Alistair Horne in *National Review* 1/30/87. "You know how it is when you meet": Macmillan interview with Schlesinger, 5/20/64, notes in Schlesinger Papers. Macmillan on JFK account of NSK meeting: Macmillan *Pointing* 357. NSK at Indonesian reception: NYT 6/7/61, T 6/16/61, UPI dispatch 6/6/61. NSK comparison of JFK and Eisenhower: NSK1 458, NSK2 497-8.

"Too intelligent and too weak": Burlatsky int WGBH and in CCT. NSK astonishment at JFK undercutting arguments and worry about "very small majority": letter to Nehru, quoted in Macmillan *Pointing* 398–9. "More the look of an advisor": Burlatsky at Harvard, 9/27/88. "This guy was here": Burlatsky int WGBH. Sergei Khrushchev on NSK opinion of JFK: SNK 50–1, Sergei Khrushchev at Harvard, 2/13/89–2/15/89, Sergei Khrushchev conv. Sergei Khrushchev on "flight to Mars": SNK 51.

Kornienko on NSK and 1959 report on JFK: Schlesinger journal, 8/23/62, noted in AMSTD draft. JFK at Radziwill christening party: William Douglas-Home oh, NYT 6/6/61, NYkr 6/17/61, Evangeline Bruce conv, Alsop conv, Collier and Horowitz *Kennedys* 278, Kern 64. JFK autographs picture: Lincoln *My Twelve Years* 270–6. "Met Queen Mary and was at tea": JFK-Billings, August 1938. Palace use of Radziwill titles: Sulzberger 1011, Kelley *Jackie* 189. Jacqueline inquiry and Duke reply: Manchester *Death* 611. Jacqueline trip to Greece: L 6/16/61, NYT 6/7/61, Ralph Martin 355. JFK-Sidey interview on plane: Sidey oh, Sidey 203–5. JFK scribbles Lincoln quotation: Lincoln *My Twelve Years* 274. "Well, I want you to know that I've now got": Bartlett int. Bundy to Sorensen on Vienna speech: 6/5/61, JFKL. JFK meeting with Congressional leaders: Memcon 6/6/61, JFKL, Kern 64–5.

Scene of JFK Vienna speech: NYT 6/7/61, NW 6/19/61. Text is JFKPP 6/6/61. *New York Times* headline: NYT 6/7/61. Padong seizure, JFK reaction and Rusk comment: USN 6/19/61, Rusk to DFR 6/16/61. Thompson on NSK and Laos: Parmet *JFK* 139–41. "We both look at the same set of facts": Thompson-Rusk 2/1/61–2/2/61, JFKL. JFK instruction to Harriman: Isaacson and Thomas 616. JFK later mused with Ormsby-Gore on NSK feeling that JFK had acted belligerently. (AMSTD draft) JFK's three requests of Congress to increase defense are in JFKPP, 1/30/61, 3/28/61 and 5/25/61. NSK on "feeling sorry for Kennedy": NSK2 499. Bolshakov on NSK changing mind before Vienna: RFK oh. For documentation of NSK plans on testing, see Notes for Chapter 12. Billings on JFK after Vienna: Billings oh. Harriman and William O. Douglas used similar language to describe JFK's reaction. (Seaborg 67 and Douglas oh)

RFK on JFK after Vienna: RFK oh. "Like dealing with Dad": Collier and Horowitz *Kennedys* 277–8. Bradlee on JFK after Vienna and hears JFK read from transcript: Bradlee 125. Excerpts appear in press: for instance, L 6/16/61. "While JFK was giving us his lecture": McLellan 209–10. Mansfield on NSK attitude toward JFK: Mansfield oh. "Khrushchev scared the poor little fellow": Ralph Martin 352. Johnson dropped to knees: Kern 263. "What was I supposed to do": David Powers oh COHP. Bolshakov to Holeman on Vienna: Holeman int. JFK at Palm Beach after Vienna: Sidey oh, L 6/16/61, NYT 6/11/61, Sidey 205–7. Salinger announcement of JFK malady: NYT 6/9/61, 6/13/61. "As de Gaulle says": Odon 298. Rusk on keeping NSK ultimatum secret: NYT 6/12/61. *Pravda* publication of *aide-mémoire:* Prav 6/10/61. JFK return to Washington: NYT 6/13/61, T 6/23/61, Sidey 209, RFK oh.

JFK on what went wrong: Ormsby-Gore interview with Schlesinger, 3/5/65, noted in AMSTD draft. "The first effort by Khrushchev": RFK oh. "We may drift to disaster": Macmillan *Pointing* 389. JFK inquiry about available supplies: Lemnitzer-JFK 6/14/61, JFKL.

10. The Ticking Clock

NSK 6/21/61 speech: Prav 6/22/61, NYT 6/22/61, USN 7/3/61, T 6/30/61. "The hands of the clock": NSK2 503. NSK on 6/24/61 and 6/25/61: Prav 6/25/61 and 6/26/61, Izv 6/25/61, Radio Moscow 6/25/61, Slusser 19. NSK-JFK on Strelka is 6/15/61, JFKL. "How did this dog": Schlesinger interview with Jacqueline Kennedy, V, 33–4, noted in AMSTD draft. Strelka's arrival is also noted in Traphes Bryant oh, NYT 6/21/61 and Odon 300–1. NSK enjoyed placing emblem: Adzhubei int WGBH. "Strelka and Belka, not Rover": PCS, Portland, Ore., 9/7/60. JFK-NSK thank you note is 6/21/61, JFKL. American-Soviet television debate and Soviets visit with Salinger: Sal 180–7. JFK meeting with Soviet delegation: WP 6/28/61, Sal 187–8, Sidey 213–5. Mansfield on Berlin: Mansfield oh, NYT 6/15/61, USN 7/10/61, T 6/23/61, NW 6/26/61. JFK on Mansfield statement: JFKPP 6/28/61.

Drummond on JFK statement: quoted in Nixon *Six Crises* 336fn. JFK as "the tiger": Sidey 218fn. Adenauer wish for Eisenhower and Dulles: RFK oh, Acheson oh. Among sources on Adenauer's background and character are Gunther *Procession* 453–6, Brandt 48–61, Jahn, Koerfer 181–368. Adenauer attitude toward 1960 Presidential campaign: William Tyler oh, Jahn 393–8, Stützle 21–2, 37–43, Strauss 355–6, Koerfer 529–31, Prittie 283–4. JFK in *Foreign Affairs:* October 1957, "A Democrat Looks at Foreign Policy." Adenauer fear of Stevenson at State: Schlesinger int JBM. JFK thinks Adenauer almost openly pro-Nixon: Sor 541. Adenauer closeness to Nixon: Nixon-Adenauer, 9/19/60, Nixon Papers, NYT 11/10/60. Adenauer's diffidence about reunification: 3/16/60 memcon of Adenauer-Herter talk at Herter's home, DDEL.

JFK-Adenauer April 1961 meetings and their background: Jahn 401–4, Stützle 89–90, Koerfer 533, USN 4/24/61. Kissinger-JFK is 4/6/61, JFKL. JFK on Adenauer: AMSTD draft, based on Jacqueline Kennedy interview, V, 43–4, VI, 1–4, Sor 559. "Repetitious assurances": Sor 559. Adenauer on JFK: Barnet 223, Koerfer 532, Prittie 283–4. Wessel on Bay of Pigs and Vienna: Wessel int. 6/29/61 NSC meeting: memcon, JFKL, Acheson oh, Catudal 143–7, Sor 583–9, AMSTD 381–3. Acheson previous attitude toward JFK: Isaacson and Thomas 590–1. Acheson refusal of NATO and "DA is buoyed": Acheson oh, Isaacson and Thomas 609. Acheson on "gifted amateur" and JFK response: Acheson oh. "Three essentials": Catudal 145, Zolling 78, Brandt 21. Von Eckhardt mission is noted in Harriman-Archibald Cox 7/28/60 in Harriman Papers. JFK to Polish-American Congress: PCS, Chicago, 10/1/60.

"This is almost an invitation": Wyden *Wall* 72fn. RFK on wish not to "be on the other side": AMSRK 509. *Newsweek* article and JFK response: NW 7/3/61 and 7/10/61, NYT 7/1/61, NYHT 7/6/61. NSK on "reports" of mobilization: NYT 6/30/61. NSK to Roberts: Roberts account in McCauley 222, WP 7/12/61, NYT 7/14/61, SEP 10/21/61. David Klein supposition: Kern 80–1. NSK at Independence Day reception: Klosson int, Jane Thompson int, Sherry Thompson conv, NYT 7/5/61. NSK on scrapping force reduction: Prav 7/10/61, USN 7/24/61. "Should we break them off": JFK-Bundy 7/10/61. JFK with officials at Hyannis Port: NYT 7/9/61, T 7/14/61, AMSTD 388–9, Catudal 160–3. McCloy to Eisenhower on "another session with the Russians": 7/7/61, McCloy Papers. 7/13/61 meetings: 7/13/61 memcon, JFKL, Bohlen oh, McNamara int. AMSTD 389–90.

Kennedy officials on torpor: Chayes oh, JFK in JFKPP 12/17/62. Actual story on reply to aide-mémoire: Bundy-JFK 7/21/61, JFKL, and Martin Hillenbrand in Catudal 153–4. "Shorter, simpler version": Sor 587. "And I was goddamned": Kohler int. The reply was sent on 7/17/61: NYT 7/18/61, text in JFKL. "I am shocked that it could be": JFK-Bundy 7/10/61, JFKL. "All had to be done or redone": RFK oh. Galbraith on "fully automated foreign policy": Epernay 57–74. "Really objects to my being President": Berle 750. "They're not queer": Robert Monagan oh. Galbraith on State Department: Galbraith-JFK 8/15/61, JFKL. "Damn it, Bundy and I": AMSTD draft. Bundy activities: Bundy int, Cohen 100, Destler 184–94. Acheson on resigning if Bundy at NSC: Isaacson and Thomas 598. JFK-Bundy relationship: Bundy int, Bundy in *Foreign Affairs*, April 1964, Bundy in *Massachusetts Historical Society*, vol. 90, 1978, Rusk int, Lisagor oh, Halberstam *Best* 43–7, 59–63, Bundy letter to author 1/1/90.

"McBundy": Lincoln *My Twelve Years* 239. "I hope he leaves a few": SEP 3/10/62. "You can't beat brains": Bradlee 134 and NW 3/4/63. Bundy notes to JFK: Bundy-JFK 54/63, 8/21/63, 12/23/61, JFKL. "I think the White House should gang up": Bundy-JFK 10/28/63, JFKL. "A semi-comedy of low-level": Bundy-JFK 9/17/62, JFKL. Bundy to JFK on reregistering as Democrat: Bundy conv and address at Women's National Democratic Club, 1990. Bundy poem to JFK: Bundy-JFK, undated, JFKL, Bundy int, WP 1/25/74. The horse show took place on 5/19/62. JFK Madison Square Garden party: Adler 222–7. Bundy background: Bundy int, NW 3/4/63, T 11/15/63, SEP 3/10/62, *New York Times Magazine* 12/2/62, Hilsman 44–6, Halberstam *Best* 40–63. "The worst-conducted campaign": NW 3/4/63. "Wars are full of glory" and "Why did we all so much": Bundy-John Mason Brown 10/6/43, 1/2/49, Brown Papers. "Far from compelling": Galbraith *A Life* 363. "I go to Temple Israel": Bundy-Brown 10/7/52, Brown Papers.

Cutler offer of job: Bundy int. "Felt no great love": Bundy-Bohlen 11/18/73, Bohlen Papers. Bundy persuades JFK to appoint Kirk: Bundy int. Bundy on attending school with JFK, advising on run for Senate and exchange on Furcolo: Bundy int. Bundy aid to JFK campaign and Shriver meeting: Bundy int. JFK interest in Bundy for State: NW 3/4/63, Odon 235, 243. Bundy appointment as security adviser: Bundy int. "The President called it a pig pen": Bundy-O'Donnell 1/5/62, JFKL. "I am not an Ian Fleming fan": NW 3/4/63. "He was having one of his pretty girls" and "It wasn't that he was ungenerous": Ralph Martin 300–1. Menshikov on Americans "won't fight": NYT 7/16/61 and 7/21/61, NYHT 7/16/61, USN 7/31/61, NYkr 8/5/61. "Maybe we were wrong": Burlatsky at Harvard, 9/27/88.

Bolshakov on Menshikov to NSK: RFK oh. Americans see Menshikov: USN 8/7/61, 7/15/61 Nitze memcon, noted in AMSTD draft. Rowen-Kaysen exercise: Sorensen oh, Sorensen int WGBH, Carl Kaysen int WGBH, Herken 159–60, Kaplan 299–301. 7/19/61 meetings: 7/19/61 memcon, Bundy-JFK 7/19/61, Sorensen-JFK 7/19/61, JFKL, Sorensen oh, McNamara int, Sorensen int JBM, RFK int JBM, Sor 590–1. Eisenhower on "right and ready": DDEPP 3/11/59. "I think the evidence is clear": Eisenhower-McCloy 6/22/61, DDEL. "If Mr. Khrushchev believes": Sor 588. McNamara and flexible response: Trewhitt 25, 80, 103. Kissinger on emergency declaration: Kissinger-Bundy 7/14/61, JFKL. "An alarm bell": Sorensen oh. Tax increase suggestion: Walter Heller-Sorensen 7/18/61, JFKL, T 8/4/61, RFK oh, Odon 278–9.

JFK interest in shelters: Bundy int, JFK-Bundy 7/5/61, 7/7/61, RFK oh, Sorensen oh, Bundy in Thompson 206–9, AMSRK 428, Sor 613, Kaplan 307–14, Catudal 171–2. "Gentlemen, you might": Catudal 182fn. "If I were you": Bundy 375. Acheson's SEP article was 3/7/59. It was unearthed and described by Marquis Childs. (WP 7/28/61) "There was absolutely no thought": McNamara int WGBH. McNamara assertion that JFK agreed to no first use: Bundy 376, McNamara int. "Nobody ever knew": Bundy 378. Writing of JFK 7/25/61 address and scene of delivery: T 8/4/61, NW 8/7/61, NYT 7/26/61, 7/27/61, Sor 591–2, Sidey 229–32, Lincoln *My Twelve Years* 278–9, Manchester *Portrait* 26–7. "A little shooting pain": AMSTD draft, based on Jacqueline Kennedy interview, VI, 3. JFK speech is in JFKPP 7/25/61. "That boy is cool": Leonard Baker 101.

Nixon on speech: *Dallas Morning News* 7/29/61. Letters and telegrams to White House: NYT 8/5/61. Hartmann on JFK: *Los Angeles Times* 7/28/61. *Indianapolis News* comment: 7/28/61. TASS claim: NYT 7/27/61. *Times* headline is *The Times* (London), 7/26/61. David Bruce on Berlin: Bruce-Rusk 7/17/61, JFKL. Reston on negotiable issues: NYT 7/26/61, 7/29/61. Higgins on JFK thoughts: NYHT 7/27/61. McCloy visit to Soviet Union and NSK: McCloy notes in McCloy Papers, Prav 7/27/61, NYT 7/28/61, 8/1/61, *Manchester Guardian* 8/23/61, AMSTD 392, Isaacson and Thomas 613–4. "Really mad on Thursday": McCloy-JFK 7/29/61, JFKL. "Believe you should report": Rusk-McCloy 7/29/61, JFKL. "We were not in control": Burlatsky at Harvard, 9/27/88. "A record number of refugees": Macmillan *Pointing* 392. Alphand complaint: Bundy-Battle 7/13/61, JFKL.

Fulbright on Berlin: NYT 8/3/61, Marcy int. *Der Tagesspiegel* on Acheson and Korea is 8/2/61. "Realistic" formula: *Neues Deutschland* (East Berlin), 8/2/61. "A variety of comment": Bundy-JFK 8/4/61, JFKL. Bundy explanation of remark: Bundy int, Bundy 682. Wonder about Fulbright suggestion: Koch 60, Catudal 200–3. JFK sees McCloy: NYT 8/1/61. "If we expect the Soviets": Thompson-Rusk 3/16/61, JFKL. "Khrushchev is losing East Germany": variations of this comment appear in Rostow oh, Rostow *Diffusion* 231, AMSTD 394.

11. "A Wall Is a Hell of a Lot Better Than a War"

Early August Moscow meetings: Prav 8/6/61, NYT 8/6/61, NYHT 8/4/61, Griffith 83–4. NSK-Ulbricht exchanges on border closing: Jan Sejna in *Der Spiegel* 8/16/76, Sejna 112–5 and Wyden *Wall* 85–90, drawing on an interview with Sejna. Sejna was deputy defense minister and Warsaw Pact liaison officer for Czechoslovakia. As Catudal notes, his recollections must be regarded with some caution. (Catudal 50fn) Other sources include Sergo Mikoyan and Sergei Khrushchev at Harvard, 2/13/89–2/15/89, Burlatsky at Harvard, 9/27/88, Zolling and Bahnsen 102–4, Liselotte Thomas 211. NSK August speeches, response and Penkovsky: Thomas Hughes memo 8/7/61, JFKL, Prav 8/8/61, Izv 8/9/61, NYT 8/8/61–8/10/61, Wyden *Wall* 116–21, Garthoff 40–1, David Martin 111–7. Fanfani-NSK meeting: Salinger-JFK 8/8/61, JFKL, NYT 8/3/61, 8/5/61, 8/28/61, Watt 243. JFK on possible border closing: JFKPP 8/10/61.

Rusk meeting with Adenauer: Memcon 8/10/61, JFKL. NSK 8/11/61 and 8/12/61 appearances: Prav 8/12/61, 8/15/61, NYT 8/12/61. "A check list of the actions": Bundy-JFK 8/4/61, JFKL. Presidential fallout shelter: NYT 4/4/75. Soviet trawlers: D.J. Brennan-William C. Sullivan 9/3/63, FBI Files. JFK 8/12/61

activities: 8/12/61 PA, NYT 8/13/61. Border closing scene: *Der Tagesspiegel* 8/15/
61, Wyden *Wall* 150–2, Catudal 257–61. Washington response: Rusk int, Kohler
int, Kohler oh, Ausland in *Foreign Service Journal,* July 1971, Kohler 333, Gelb
167–81, Wyden *Wall* 170–6, 213, Catudal 22–35, Cate 304–7. JFK notified and
response: Rusk int, Kohler int, 8/13/61 PA, "Statement concerning travel restrictions in Berlin," 8/13/61, JFKL, Wyden *Wall* 26–9, 176–7, Catudal 35–8, Weintal
and Bartlett 211. "We kidded among ourselves": NSK2 506.

Brandt notified and response: Brandt 13, 18, Wyden *Wall* 152, 162–3. Zolling
and Bahnsen 16–18. On Brandt, background and relations with Adenauer, see
Brandt, Prittie, Hofmann. Brandt on JFK: Brandt 70–1. Brandt first White House
meeting: Rusk-JFK 3/10/61, JFKL, Brandt 80–1. "*Kennedy* is making mincemeat":
Wyden *Wall* 164. "On August thirteenth" and "The curtain went up": Wyden
Wall 164. "The Soviet Union had defied": Brandt 25. JFK 8/14/61 meeting:
Slusser 149. Bundy-Amory meeting: Amory int, Amory oh, Wyden *Wall* 217–8.
Bundy on "clear initiative": AMSTD 398. "More and more pressure": JFK-
McNamara 8/14/61, JFKL. "What steps will we take": JFK-Rusk 8/14/61, JFKL.
JFK-Kennan meeting: Kennan oh, 8/15/61 PA, Isaacson and Thomas 614.
Brandt at *Rathaus:* Petschull 155–7, Zolling and Bahnsen 144–5, Wyden *Wall*
225–6.

Brandt-JFK letter and JFK reaction: *Frankfurter Allgemeine Zeitung* 8/19/61, NYT
8/20/61. *Vierteljahrschefte für Zeitgeschichte,* vol. 33, 1985. Brandt 31, Wyden *Wall*
224. Adenauer notified about closing, response and slur against Brandt: NYT
8/17/61, Zolling and Bahnsen 11–2, 141 Stützle 133–40, Koerfer 544–5, Prittie
286. Smirnov to Adenauer: Watt 250. Reports on flagging morale in West Berlin:
Wyden *Wall* 226. "Remember that what is at stake": Rostow-Bundy 8/16/61,
JFKL. JFK calls LBJ: NYT 8/18/61, Leonard Baker 69–70, Odon 303, Lincoln
Kennedy and Johnson 174–5. "The President sent me a message": Macmillan *Pointing* 393. JFK silence: JFKPP 8/13/61–8/20/61. Reports of JFK shock, "Actually
he saw" and "Why would he put up": Odon 303.

Fifteen years "to get out of their jail": NYT 9/6/61. This was in a James Reston
column written after a conversation with JFK. JFK pique at failure to warn of Wall:
Allen Dulles and Robert Amory, quoted in Catudal 242. The FRG intelligence
chief Reinhard Gehlen also insisted that previous warning would have been
almost impossible. (Wessel int, Gehlen 239, Höhne and Zolling 221–2) Wessel,
as Gehlen's successor, cooperated with Höhne and Zolling in their research.
(Wessel int) "Today, the endangered frontier": JFKPP 7/25/61. "May have given
advance encouragement": Bundy 367–70. Paques and Whalen: Rusk int, Barron
31, Marchetti and Marks 214–5, Gelb 142fn. "After they put the Wall up because
I was disgusted": RFK oh. Eisenhower revulsion: Eisenhower interview with
Moos 11/8/66, DDEL.

"If we had acted vigorously": Acheson oh. "We might have been able to have
stopped": Clay oh. Couve de Murville on "immediate reaction": Couve de Murville oh. Leonhard on probable East Berlin reaction: Leonhard *Kremlin*. JFK
mentioned his Potsdam meeting with Eisenhower to Brandt: Brandt 73. A photograph exists of the occasion and is reprinted in Lieberson 46. "Had we torn it
down": Sorensen oh. "Until the other side is just too tired": Burlatsky at Harvard,
9/27/88. Strauss on risking World War III: Quoted in Bundy 367. "As you know,
Eastern Berlin": JFKPP 10/11/61. Brief JFK references to Wall: JFKPP 12/17/61,

3/10/62, 5/18/63. "It would also have been better": Bundy 370. "I want to see at first hand": NYT 8/19/61. Johnson delegation to FRG and West Berlin: Jack Bell oh, Clay oh, Bohlen oh, RFK oh, L 8/25/61, NW 11/20/89, T 8/25/61, Bohlen notes, Bohlen 483–5, Jahn 425–6, Brandt 31–4, Cate 404–36, Wyden *Wall* 227–34, Merle Miller 286–90, Roberts 229. Leonard Baker 71–7, Jahn 425–6, Isaacson and Thomas 615.

JFK awaits word from Berlin: RFK oh, Sidey 199–200, Wyden *Wall* 229–30, AMSTD 396–7. JFK learns news: PA 8/20/61, Sor 594, Wyden *Wall* 233. American troops arrive in Berlin: Petschull 173–6, Wyden *Wall* 232–4. JFK on Sunday and refuses LBJ visit: PA 8/20/61 and NYT 8/21/61. "We are going to pass through": JFKPP 8/21/61. "Has tasted blood": Roberts 229. Commander deference to Soviet request: Schick xv. Eisenhower-Dulles meeting: Dulles-JFK 8/20/61, JFKL. JFK asks Rusk to suggest means for negotiation: 8/3/61 memcon, Rusk-JFK 8/2/61, Bundy-JFK 8/3/61, JFKL. "Felt that a turning point": Sor 594. "I want to take a stronger": JFK-Rusk 8/21/61, JFKL. JFK preparation to bargain: AMSTD 398–40. "His own immediate concern" Bundy-JFK 8/21/61, JFKL. Soviet statement on "extremists": NYT 8/25/61. Statement possibly issued in NSK absence: Slusser 143–9, 169. NSK to Fanfani on negotiation: NYT 8/28/61. Pearson visit with NSK and origins: Luvie Pearson conv, SEP 4/7/62, NYT 8/28/61, WP 8/28/61, Prav 8/25/61 and 8/29/61, Izv 8/25/61.

12. "I Want to Get Off"

JFK learns of Soviet tests: Bundy int, Bundy in *Foreign Affairs*, April 1964, Bundy-Salinger 9/5/61, JFKL, Sor 619, AMSTD 459, AMSTD draft. I have restored the President's original language, softened by Schlesinger. July Gallup Poll: *Gallup* 7/12/61. "Assuming as I did then": Eisenhower-Herter 6/16/61, Herter Papers. Joint Chiefs pressure: Sor 618. George Ball had recommended deferring "any announcement of test resumption until at least of the year." (Ball-JFK, 8/4/61, JFKL) "We simply cannot be sure" and JFK consideration of limited ban: JFK-Macmillan 8/3/61, JFKL, AMSTD 458–9. JFK authorizes resumption preparations and offers new concession: Seaborg 71–8. JFK to Pearson and Pearson to NSK: Pearson-NSK 9/1/61, 9/5/61, JFKL. JFK statement on Soviet resumption, 8/30/61, is in JFKL. "Must have thought there was something sinister" and JFK comments on resumption: RFK oh and RFK 9/1/61 memo, quoted in AMSRK 429.

NSK and Sakharov on 7/10/61: Sakharov 215–7. NSK Cherkasky story is in "Khrushchev: A Personality Sketch," cited in Notes for Chapter 7. Burlatsky on NSK demanding much: Burlatsky int WGBH and in CCT. Sergei Khrushchev on Soviet military leaders: Sergei Khrushchev at Harvard, 2/13/89–2/15/89. 8/31/61 NSC meeting: RFK oh, RFK 9/1/61 memo in AMSRK 429–30, AMSTD 448–9, Seaborg 82–4. "I should have had him involved" and "But now he realized": Collier and Horowitz *Kennedys* 271–2, LBJ on RFK: Wofford 418. Generally on RFK and background, see AMSRK. Jacqueline on "immigrant side": Collier and Horowitz 264. "In many ways, Jack still felt": Collier and Horowitz *Kennedys* 254. "I like Luce": AMSTD 63. FDR and stamp collection: Beschloss *Kennedy and Roosevelt* 106.

"My, he's unassimilated": Collier and Horowitz 218. "He really doesn't": This comment was made about Smathers (Bartlett oh). RFK as "sissy": Rose Kennedy in "The Journey of Robert F. Kennedy," ABC-TV, 1969. Joseph Kennedy and Washington dowager: Thomas Corcoran int. "It won't go over with the WASPs": Bradlee 67–8. "Lives the life we'd all": Exner 112. RFK and Guevara: AMSRK 801–2. RFK and counterinsurgency: AMSRK 46–7. Joseph Kennedy on leaving Korea and Berlin: AMSRK 84–5. "Everybody in Embassy": RFK-Paul Murphy, undated, July 1948, quoted in AMSRK 79–80. "We can look back": *Boston Advertiser* 1/16/49. "President Roosevelt felt": "A Critical Analysis of the Conference at Yalta," RFK Papers. "Something to die for": RFK-Joseph Kennedy, undated, October 1961, quoted in AMSRK 91–2. "I felt at the time": Stein and Plimpton 50.

RFK analyzing statistics: Bartlett int. "Really very cross": AMSRK 109. RFK-Douglas trip: Douglas oh, Douglas 306–7. "Qualifies as colonialism": NYT 1/2/56 and AMSRK 128. "All I ask is that before": 10/10/55 Georgetown University text in RFK Papers. Wofford on RFK 1957: Wofford 32–3. RFK and 1956 campaign: AMSRK 133–6. RFK-Giancana exchange: Fox 338–9. Documentation of JFK-RFK interest in National Crime Commission and Hoover annoyance is in 1959–1960 JFK FBI Files, FBI. RFK to Nixon: 7/25/59, Nixon Papers. "When you get to the White House": quoted by John P. Roche in *National Review* 7/22/ 88. Ehrlichman infiltration of Rockefeller party is traced in June 1960 Ehrlichman notes in Nixon Papers. Joseph Kennedy's prediction of JFK and RFK futures: SEP 9/7/57. Joseph Kennedy-Hoover relations and memory of Murphy-Jackson involvement in diplomacy: Joseph Kennedy FBI Files and Beschloss *Kennedy and Roosevelt* 200, 213–4, 231, 253.

Rayburn to JFK: 12/15/60, JFKL. Mail to Democratic National Committee: T 1/13/61. "Bobby did not want": Demaris 180–3. RFK early 1961 limited exposure to Soviet affairs: Kohler int, Guthman int, Helms int. "Third toughest job": Caplin conv. "By far the smartest": Vincent Dooley oral history in Russell Papers. Eisenhower brothers: Milton Eisenhower int. "The Second Most Important": Collier and Horowitz *Kennedys* 289. "There's only one way": Stein and Plimpton 127. "Wasn't too happy": Billings oh. RFK in 1960 campaign: AMSRK 192–221. RFK to Harriman: Collier and Horowitz 288–91. "McClellan didn't press!": AMSRK 150–1. Rusk on never being pushed into swimming pool: Rusk int. 1962 Gallup Poll: *Gallup* 8/19/62. Robinson to Eisenhower: 6/23/61, DDEL. RFK prosecution of Cassini and Landis: Navasky 378–91, AMSRK 387–91. RFK ferocity about Castro: Helms int.

"You see, I was nothing": RFK oh. Soviet resumption and JFK response: T 9/22/61, Smathers int, AMSTD 459–60, Seaborg 85–6. JFK meets aides in bedroom: AMSTD draft, briefer version in AMSTD 459–60. "I understand full well": Gavin-Rusk 9/2/61, JFKL. JFK call to Rusk and note: AMSTD 460, Sor 620. JFK learns of second Soviet test and response to neutralist resolution: Sidey 203, Parmet *JFK* 201, AMSTD 520. "I had no choice": Sidey 245. "It isn't time yet": AMSTD 398. "What choice did we have?": Bartlow Martin *Stevenson* 661. "A time of sustained and draining": Bundy 363, 681. "Fall 1961": Lowell 11–2. Reston on JFK frustration: NYT 9/6/61. Sulzberger-NSK interview: NYT 9/8/61, 9/11/ 61, 9/13/61, 6/26/70, Sulzberger 786–806, Marina Sulzberger 246–7. Private note was sent through the Paris Embassy. (Cecil Lyon-Sorensen 9/10/61, JFKL)

Sulzberger sees JFK: Sulzberger 809. Lemnitzer 9/13/61 briefing: SIOP-62 briefing 9/13/61 memcon, JFKL, Scott Sagan in *International Security,* Summer 1987, Prados *Soviet Estimate* 116–9. "Khrushchev certainly drew": Bartlow Martin *Stevenson* 661. JFK to Stevenson on UN to West Berlin: Bartlow Martin *Stevenson* 660, Schlesinger int JBM. Rostow on "Nkrumah's plans": Rostow-JFK, September 1961, JFKL. JFK on "two possibilities about Berlin": Schlesinger journal 9/5/61, quoted in AMSRK 431. JFK to Wechsler is in *New York Post* 9/21/61–9/22/61. Wechsler-JFK relationship was described to the author by Joseph Rauh. (Rauh conv) JFK learns of Hammarskjöld death; Sidey 248–50. Gromyko-Rusk September 1961 talks: Rusk-JFK 9/20/61, Bundy-Tazewell Shepard 9/23/61, JFKL, NYT, 9/22/61, 9/24/61, 9/28/61, 9/29/61, 10/1/61, 10/6/61, T 9/29/61, NW 10/2/61, 10/9/61, Watt 266.

Sinatra at Hyannis Port: Kelley *His Way* 318–9, Saunders 82–5. JFK writing of UN speech and flight to New York: Sor 521. Bolshakov call to Salinger: Sal 191. On Salinger background and personality: Lisagor oh, Pierpoint conv, Sal, Deakin 162–91, Bartlow Martin *It Seems* 176. White on Salinger: White (1961) 51. Pierpoint on Salinger: Pierpoint 129. Pierpoint conv. "He looks more": Sal 50. JFK on Salinger life: Cassini 324. Lisagor on Salinger: Lisagor oh. "More than a little surprised": Sal 18–9. "No one who followed": White (1961) 52. JFK-Salinger effort for government censorship: Sal 154–60, Krock 375, Deakin 177–9. Soviets see Salinger and Salinger sees JFK: Sal 191–4. Jacobson treatment of JFK before speech: NYT 12/4/72, Heymann 308–9. First page of JFK 9/25/61 reading copy is reproduced in NW 10/9/61. Text: JFKPP 9/25/61. RFK on "Meet the Press": 9/24/61 "Meet the Press" transcript, Library of Congress.

Soviets see Salinger again: Sal 193–66. Bundy sends "intelligence material": Bundy-JFK 9/27/61, JFKL, Helms int. Salinger sees Bolshakov: Sal 197–9.

13. "Dear Mr. President" and "Dear Mr. Chairman"

Salinger takes letter to Newport: Sal 198–200. Contents of 9/29/61 NSK-JFK letter: Sor 515, 552, 599, *Macleans* 11/28/83, Sal 198–200. In this and other cases noted in the text and below, the exact contents of some JFK-NSK letters remain unreleased after three decades. Khrushchev-Eisenhower correspondence: Kohler-Calhoun 3/22/60, DDEL, Kohler int, Goodpaster int, Eisenhower-NSK 3/19/60, list of Eisenhower-Bulganin letters, DDEL. "You and I must recognize": Eisenhower-NSK 3/12/60, 4/1/60, DDEL. JFK reaction to NSK letter: Bundy int, Rusk int, Kohler int, Sal 199–200, Sor 553, Ralph Martin 503. "Have Bundy and Sorensen": JFK memo 10/3/61, JFKL. JFK-Sulzberger meeting: Sulzberger 808–813. "Really the first time": Odon 304. JFK on Gromyko 1945: Sulzberger 811.

On Gromyko background and personality: Rusk, Klosson, Davies, Kohler, Jane Thompson ints, Andrei Gromyko, Simmonds 164–70, Shevchenko 143–62, 167–71, 196–208, *New York Times Magazine* 5/24/59, Medvedev *Stalin's Men* 82–112. Gromyko comparison with Talleyrand: for example, Shevchenko 153. Gromyko on personality: Shevchenko 146. Harriman estimate: NYT 7/4/89. "Impatience, coldness": K.B.A. Scott minute 3/5/59, FO. Daughter on Gromyko: Shevchenko 155. Gromyko on father: Shevchenko 146. Molotov on "Litvinov liberalism": Shevchenko 147. Paulina Molotova exile and return: Medvedev *Stalin's Men* 96–103. Stalin's aides joke about Gromyko fate: Shevchenko 146. Vishinsky charge and punishment: Shevchenko 148. Molotov firing and Shepilov appointment: Medvedev *Stalin's Men* 105–6.

NSK on Gromyko: Shevchenko 104, 146. Description of Gromyko at UN is based on this author's viewing of news film of the event in National Archives, Washington, D.C. Leisure activities: Shevchenko 149, 156–7. "Profit is the pitiless filter": Andrei Gromyko 75. "Leave the Secretary": Weintal and Bartlett 159. JFK-Gromyko meeting: NYT 10/4/61, 10/7/61, 10/8/61, T 10/13/61, SR 1/9/71, Sor 599, Sidey 261–2, Odon 304–6. JFK to Lippmann on meeting: Lippmann oh. Content of meeting leaked: Salisbury *Without Fear* 285. "I think the Russians": Macmillan *Pointing* 403.

JFK reply to NSK 9/29/61 letter (official text still unreleased) and NSK-JFK correspondence generally: Bundy int, Rusk int, Kohler int, *Macleans* 11/28/83, Sor 552–5, 599, Sal 197–200. Bundy on Smirnovsky: Bundy-JFK 10/20/61. NSK opens Twenty-second Party Congress: Prav 10/18/61, NYT 10/18/61, McSweeney-Rusk 10/19/61, JFKL. White House reply: NYT 10/18/61. JFK-Dealey encounter: Manchester *Death* 48–9, 85. American sources for early 1961 estimate of Soviet missiles: Prados *Soviet Estimate* 192–26. CIA 9/6/61 assessment: CIA, "Current Status of Soviet and Satellite Military Forces and Indications of Military Intentions," 9/6/61, JFKL, Prados *Soviet Estimate* 117–8. Hilsman on Soviet ICBM system obsolescence: Hilsman 164. JFK thinking on revealing Soviet inferiority: Hilsman 162–5. "When I get up": Sidey 282. Gilpatric background: T 7/6/62, Trewhitt 11.

Gilpatric speech and origins: Rusk int, McNamara int, Bundy int, Hilsman oh COHP, Gilpatric int WGBH, Hilsman 162–5. Alsop on "human lubricant": Alsop-JFK, undated, JFKL. JFK on "second most attractive man": Bradlee 230. "I think it's that father image": Kelley *Jackie* 204. "To convince the Soviet Union": Gilpatric int WGBH. "Were allowed to continue": Hilsman 163, Hilsman oh COHP. "John Kennedy isn't": Wyden *Wall* 258. Gilpatric speech text: *Documents on Disarmament* 542–50, Defense Department press release, 10/21/61, JFKL. "Mr. Khrushchev must know": *Department of State Bulletin* 1961. "Not trade places": JFKPP 11/8/61. Herter to Eisenhower, 10/31/61, and Eisenhower reply, 11/4/61, are in Eisenhower and Herter Papers. Chou En-lai behavior at and departure from Party Congress: NYT 10/20/61, Prav 10/24/61, Linden 133fn, Griffith 94.

"Bolt from blue": Herken 88–101. Thirty-megaton Soviet blast: NYT 10/24/61. Malinovsky to Party Congress: Prav 10/25/61, NYT 10/24/61. Checkpoint Charlie confrontation: Clay-Dowling 10/31/61, Norstad Papers, Clay oh, Falin int WGBH, NYT 10/26/61, 10/28/61, Jean Edward Smith 319–21, Gelb 250–60, Wyden *Wall* 260–7. Clay appointment: Clay oh, NYT 8/31/61. "I'm a President's man": Wyden *Wall* 214. RFK-Bolshakov talks on confrontation: RFK oh. Falin on American suggestion: Falin int WGBH. Adzhubei on NSK calmness: Adzhubei int WGBH. "Can't turn their backs": NSK2 506–7. Falin on orders to destroy Wall: Falin int WGBH. NSK said so too. (NSK2 506–7) Clay did order Army engineers in West Berlin to build a wall in the forest and practice knocking it down. (Catudal 133) "Closer to the third world war": Falin int WGBH.

NSK hopes for Party Congress: Ulam *Expansion* 656–62, Tatu 141–5. Stalin removal from Lenin tomb and other de-Stalinization orders: NYT 11/12/61, NW 11/13/61. Troika dropped and Thant election: Watt 294. Rusk on Thant: Rusk to DFR 9/20/61. NSK on 11/7/61: NYT 11/8/61. NSK to Kroll: Kroll 527. Bolshakov to RFK on Party Congress and JFK comment: RFK notes 11/7/61, quoted in AMSRK 499. "Raising of the price": Bundy-JFK 12/12/61, JFKL. "I am conscious": JFK-NSK 11/16/61, JFKL. Vietnam conflict, 1961: Rust 21-73, Karnow 247-54, Halberstam *Best* 64-151. RFK advised that Vietnam better place to fight: Rust 34. "Join with you in an intensified": JFK-Diem 5/8/61, JFKL. "Now we have a problem": Halberstam *Best* 76. Rostow on NSK strategy: Rostow-JFK 6/26/61, JFKL. Taylor-Rostow recommendation: Taylor-JFK 11/1/61, JFKL. McNamara-Joint Chiefs reaction: McNamara-JFK 11/8/61, JFKL.

"It will be just like Berlin": Schlesinger journal 11/13/61, quoted in AMSRK 705. Rusk-McNamara to JFK, 11/11/61, is in JFKL. Lemnitzer on "planned phase": Rust 63. JFK-Krock luncheon, 10/11/61, is in Krock memo, Krock papers. "A determined attempt": JFK-NSK 11/16/61, JFKL. JFK to Diem on "Our indignation" is 12/15/61, JFKL. "We must work with certain countries": JFKPP 11/16/61. JFK-Adenauer November 1961 talks: NYT 11/23/61, T 12/1/61, Jahn 433-4, Strauss 357-67, Koerfer 613. Briefing of Adenauer: Amory oh, Gaddis *Strategies* 207, Enthoven and Smith 132-42. Lemnitzer complaint about briefing: Lemnitzer-Norstad 11/25/61, Norstad Papers. NSK in November 1961: Slusser 459-65. Salinger to Kharmalov on Soviet interview of JFK: Sal 192-3, 200. NSK instructions to Adzhubei: Adzhubei int WGBH. Adzhubei dinner with Salinger: Sal 200-2.

CIA on Adzhubei: Office of Current Intelligence, Adzhubei profile, 6/8/61, Helms-Hugh Cumming, 7/26/60, JFKL. "Khrushchev hesitates to grant": Thompson-Rusk 7/28/61, JFKL. Other sources on Adzhubei background: Adzhubei, "Retracing an Anniversary from Contemporary History," *Ogonyok* (Moscow) October 1989, Adzhubei int WGBH, CIA profile 1/30/62, JFKL, Jane Thompson int, Kohler int, *Reporter* 8/4/60, Beschloss *Mayday* 52-3, 201, 218. NSK on Stalin's wife: NSK1 44. "Exuberant people": 6/8/61 CIA profile, JFKL. "It may have shocked": Prav and Izv 10/28/61. Crankshaw on Adzhubei: Crankshaw 260-1. Adzhubeis' Paris trip: 1/30/62 CIA profile, JFKL. 11/24/61 JFK meeting with aides: Kaysen-JFK 11/22/61, 12/9/61, Kaysen-Bundy 11/13/61, McNamara int, Kaysen int WGBH, Harold Brown int WGBH, Sorensen int WGBH, McNamara int WGBH, Kaplan 257, Herken 151-5. Enthoven on "rubble": quoted in Herken 154. Eisenhower on going "completely crazy": Kistiakowsky 293.

"To be honest with you": Bundy notes, January 1962, JFKL. Adzhubei-JFK encounter: Adzhubei int WGBH, NYT 11/26/61, T 12/1/61, Sal 203-4. Text is from NYT 11/29/61. "It was very cold": Adzhubei int WGBH. JFK taping system: Bouck oh, Powers oh COHP, inventory of tapes in JFKL, WP 2/5/82. Eisenhower taping system: T 11/5/79. Taps on Amory, Baldwin, Norman telephones: Amory conv, Lasky *Watergate* 72-4. Bradlee writes that after the President found that Norman had divulged a new development in military technology in *Newsweek*, the reporter was "investigated from hell to breakfast." (Bradlee 155-6) "My God, they wiretapped": Lasky *Watergate* 71. Kennedy alumni find "inconceivable": Hedley Donovan 84. RFK use of tapes for *Thirteen Days:* WP 2/5/82. Report of RFK request for press eavesdropping: Lasky *Watergate* 75-84. Walters on JFK eavesdropping on wife and brother: Stephen Ambrose notes after a November

1990 conversation with Walters, kindly shared with the author by Professor Ambrose.

"Your arrogant Russian friend": Sal 204–5. RFK on Adzhubei: RFK oh. "Subscribe": NW 12/4/61. *Izvestia* runs interview: Izv 11/28/61, L 12/8/61, NW 12/11/61, NYT 12/7/61. Salinger on alteration: Sal 206. "As you know, I had an interview": JFK-NSK draft of letter sent 12/2/61. NSK 12/9/61 speech: Prav 12/10/61. Thompson to NSK about Christmas: Jane Thompson int. Request thwarted: NYT 12/16/61. Joseph Kennedy illness: NYT 12/20/61, RFK oh. RFK-JFK speak of 1961 and Russians: RFK oh. "Who would want to read": Abel oh. Bundy on no "nuclear pushiness": Bundy 366–85. "Great crises make great men": JFK *Profiles* 49. JFK on Liddell Hart credo: AMSTD 110. Bundy on NSK rigidity: Bundy 384–5. Sergei Khrushchev on Berlin Crisis: CCT, Sergei Khrushchev at Harvard, 2/13/89–2/15/89. "It is my earnest hope" and "At the Vienna meeting": JFK-NSK 12/29/61 and NSK-JFK 12/29/61.

14. *"Your President Has Made A Very Bad Mistake"*

"The main achievement" and NSK unusual mood: NYT 1/2/62. Rumors about NSK and other evidence of NSK internal difficulties, early 1962, and Soviet official response: George Ball-Thompson 1/26/62, JFKL, Myron Rush in *Current History,* October 1962, NYT 2/6/62, 2/9/62, USN 1/15/62, 1/29/62, NW 2/19/62. NSK at Minsk: Prav 1/13/62. *L'Unità* story: *L'Unità* 2/5/62, McMillan 477. Bohlen on NSK not in serious trouble: Bohlen notes, Bohlen Papers. McCone on NSK status: McCone-JFK, "Appraisal of Soviet Intentions," 1/5/62, JFKL. Thompson on Sino-Soviet quarrel: Thompson-Rusk 2/18/62, JFKL. Bolshakov to Bradlee: Bradlee-RFK 1/10/62, RFK Papers. NSK frustrated Party Congress hopes and other problems, early 1962: Frankland 190–1, USN 5/14/62, Tatu 176–225, Linden 118–40, USN 5/14/62, NW 6/11/62. "Our Nikita Sergeyevich": Izv 6/11/61. "Sure Success for Novel": NYT 1/28/62.

"Geared to whether Khrushchev": Thompson to DFR 4/3/62. Rusk-Kennedy and State-White House relationship: Bohlen oh, Jack Bell oh, Dutton oh, USN 7/31/61, *Commonweal* 3/29/63, *Harper's* November 1961, NR 7/24/61, Halberstam *Best,* 35–7, 344–6, Weintal and Bartlett 149–66, Galbraith *A Life* 402–6, Trewhitt 253–4, Hilsman 34–5, 59–60, Bohlen 474–6, Cohen 213–6. JFK to aides on *Life* profile (6/8/62) and to White on Rusk: White notes in Schlesinger Papers, JFKL. "How do you fire": Hilsman oh, COHP. "He always gives me": Cassini 327. JFK to Hilsman on "no Dean Acheson": Hilsman oh, COHP, and Hilsman 53. JFK-Rusk relationship as of early 1962: Schoenbaum 263–89, Rusk 292–5. "Would never follow anything up": RFK oh. JFK calls Rusk "Dean": tel note 7/30/63, JFKL. "You know, it is very significant": Rusk-Bohlen 6/27/73.

"My relationship with President Kennedy": Rusk int. Rusk effort to rehabilitate Davies: Schoenbaum 200–1. "Robert Kennedy wanted people": Rusk int. Rusk complaint about RFK demand and JFK response: Rusk int, RFK oh. Schlesinger notes on Rusk: Schlesinger notes in Schlesinger Papers. JFK to O'Donnell on replacing Rusk: Odon 281–2. "A tremendous operations man" and "A good errand boy": Hilsman oh, COHP, Douglas oh, and White notes in Schlesinger Papers. Rusk worry about casual note-taking: Rusk int. "Scaring the hell out of the desk officer": Schoenbaum 274. "Pretty rough": Schlesinger, Sr., notes on

AMSTD draft. Rusk on Schlesinger: Schoenbaum 286–7, Rusk int. Reston on records "poorly kept": Sal 208 and NYT 12/29/62. "It isn't worth being Secretary": Halberstam *Best* 63. "For God's sake, try to get": Destler 184.

Bolshakov-Smirnovsky dinner with Bradlee-Weintal: Bradlee-RFK 1/10/62, RFK Papers. Bolshakov also told Bartlett, Lippmann and Bradlee that JFK should send an envoy to Moscow to whom he was personally close: Bartlett-JFK, undated, 1962, and Bartlett int. Bolshakov to Salinger on television exchanges and RFK visit: NYT 3/1/62, Sal 207–210. RFK letter to NSK and reply are noted in JFKL inventory of JFK-NSK letters. Adzhubeis visit to Washington: Adzhubei int WGBH, Thomas Mann-Rusk 1/26/62, JFKL, JFKPP 1/31/62, NYT 1/25/62, MW 2/5/62 and 2/12/62, USN 2/12/62. *Good Housekeeping*, July 1962, Roberts 205–7. Castro on seeing copy of Adzhubei report of JFK talk: Jean Daniel in *New Republic* 12/14/63 and NYT 12/12/62. Salinger and Harriman conferred on how to react to this public report: Salinger-Harriman tel note, 12/11/63, Harriman Papers.

Castro to Szulc on JFK-Adzhubei talk: Szulc 578–9. Bundy contemporaneous recollection: Roberts 206–7. JFK and Macmillan at Bermuda: David Bruce-Rusk 12/13/61, JFKL, Schlesinger interview with Macmillan 5/20/64, notes in Schlesinger Papers, AMSTD 489–51, Seaborg *Kennedy* 125–31, Horne 321–4. Sorensen recalled (int JBM) that Macmillan was "always writing letters to Kennedy" and suggested that "it got to be a nuisance." Bundy warned JFK on 10/27/61 (memo, JFKL) that Macmillan was "trying to get you hooked to an agreement not to test without his consent," which Bundy thought "dirty pool." JFK wish not to use Nevada test site: Seaborg *Kennedy* 136–7. Macmillan to JFK on "dictators, reactionaries": Macmillan *At the End* 156. "Why are we taking so much trouble": AMSTD draft, Kohler int. JFK and Macmillan to NSK on "common measure" is 2/6/62, JFKL.

NSK-JFK February–March exchanges: NSK-JFK 2/10/62, 2/21/62, 3/3/62, 3/10/62, 3/20/62, JFK-NSK 2/6/62, 2/13/62, 2/15/62, 2/21/62, 2/24/62, 3/5/62, 3/7/62, JFKL. JFK private views on testing: NSC memcom 2/27/62, JFKL. JFK on resumption: JFKPP 3/2/62, Bradlee 61–3. JFK preparation for television exchange: Sor 557–8, 730. Bolshakov to Salinger on exchange cancellation and JFK reaction: Sal 214–7. Bolshakov to Sorensen on Soviet response to resumption: Sor 558. Thompson-Gromyko Berlin meetings and Soviet harassment: JFK-Norstad 2/26/62, Norstad Papers, Hillenbrand oh, Kohler int, McNamara int, NYT 1/3/62, 1/29/62, NW 1/15/62, NW 2/5/62, T 1/26/62, Ulam *Expansion* 661–3.

Thompson on Berlin: Thompson to DFR 4/3/62. Possibilities of space cooperation: JFK-NSK 2/21/62 and 3/7/62, NSK-JFK 2/21/62 and 3/20/62, JFKL, JFKPP 2/21/62, NYT 2/22/62 and 3/18/62, *Business Week* 3/24/62. NSK-JFK messages were so frequent during this period that General Clifton wrote Bundy of "rumblings among my press contemporaries" that "the President himself is not personally considering the messages that go from here to there because the U.S. replies are being returned so rapidly. . . . Because the President is young . . . he is very vulnerable to the unwarranted accusation that he shoots from the hip" (Clifton-Bundy, March 1962). "DAVE, KENNY, TED": JFK note on Bundy-JFK 3/23/62, JFKL. Jacqueline in Mountbatten apartment: Galbraith *A Life* 411.

Hoover 3/22/62 lunch with JFK and finds Campbell relationship over: *Assassination Plots* 126–31, AMSRK 494–5. JFK and McNamara in Berkeley and at Vandenberg: PA 3/23/62, McNamara int. JFK in Santa Monica: Raskin int and Raskin unpublished ms. JFK in Palm Springs: JFK-Eisenhower 3/8/62, DDEL, Pierpoint conv, Raskin int, Summers *Goddess* 294–6. Dobrynin arrival and background: NYT 3/31/62 and 4/24/62, NW 5/7/62, USN 2/26/62 and 3/26/62, T 3/23/62, *New York Times Magazine* 7/29/62. Menshikov recall and demotion: Kohler int, Davies int, Thompson on Dobrynin: Thompson to DFR 4/3/62. "Suddenly all the diplomats": *New York Times Magazine* 7/29/62,. Thompson on Dobrynin: Thompson to DFR 4/3/62. "The best ambassador": NW 12/24/62. "Hated Bolshakov's guts": Holeman int. Menshikov to Stevenson: December 1961, Stevenson Papers. "All that will stop": Sal 220–1.

Rusk-Dobrynin Berlin talks: Hillenbrand oh, Kohler int, Rusk int, NYT 4/13/62, 4/17/62, 4/21/62, NW 3/23/62, USN 4/30/62. Clay return: Clay oh, NW 4/23/62. Clay wrote Eisenhower (2/28/62, DDEL), "When I reach the President, I get support. Short of the President, it is a different story. I am afraid delegation of authority is a thing of the past." Rusk on "no room for maneuver": Seaborg *Kennedy* 146. American resumption is described in NW 4/23/62 and *Life,* quoted in Wright 35. Sakharov on Soviet intelligence effort to probe tests: Sakharov 225. Anti-missile tests: Rusk int, Seaborg *Kennedy* 152, 271–3, Rusk 602. McNamara briefing: McNamara to DFR 2/8/62, McNamara int, McNamara int WGBH. JFK-Alsop interview: SEP 3/31/62, McNamara int, Roberts 202–3. *Pravda* "astonished": Prav 3/31/62.

Effect on NSK of Alsop interview: Tatu 218–9. Salinger-NSK visit: Sal 222–37, Schlesinger-Salinger 5/8/62, Salinger Papers, NYT 5/13/62, *Look* 8/14/62. Arbatov on "phony missile launch sites": MCT and Stephen Ambrose notes of meeting with Arbatov, Moscow, November 1990. Nightly cable to Adenauer: Sal 233. Castro on "Marxist-Leninist program": Szulc 568–9. Eisenhower on "definite opportunity": Eisenhower-Charles Percy 11/23/62, DDEL. Bundy on "latest estimate": Bundy-JFK 3/31/62, CIA, "The Situation and Prospects in Cuba," 3/21/62, JFKL. Castro and Bay of Pigs anniversary: NW 3/19/62, 3/26/62, 4/30/62. Castro spring 1962 problems: Szulc 569–6, Bourne, 232–7. Bundy wrote JFK (6/2/62, JFKL) of the "growing tension between the 'new' and the 'old' Communists" in Cuba. Cuban intelligence on "all means possible": *New Republic* 12/14/63.

Dulles to Senators: Dulles to DFR 5/2/61. "This man with ice water": Rusk int. McNamara on "hysterical": *Assassination Report* 157–8, Parmet *JFK* 217. "Terrors of the earth," OAS expulsion, economic blockade: Davis *Kennedys* 394. Szulc 571–5. "My idea is to stir": RFK 11/7/61 memo, RFK Papers. Operation Mongoose, general: Bissell int, Amory int, Amory oh, McNamara int, Helms int, Bissell int, Prados *Secret Wars* 210–3, *Assassination Plots* 139–45, *Miami Herald* 11/21/62, CIA 11/28/61 estimate, JFKL, Taylor Branch and George Crile III in *Harper's,* August 1975, Thomas Powers 132–8, Davis *Kennedys* 393–9, 428–9, 433–4, 835–9, AMSRK 477–80, Szulc 562–76, Garthoff 5, 17–8, 78–9, 90, David Martin 126–44. "Bobby was his brother's": Helms int. RFK and Matahambre mines: Thomas powers 138–41. "Nutty schemes": Helms int. March 1962 estimate: CIA 3/21/62 estimate, JFKL.

Poison pills to Roselli and Puerto Rico training: Thomas Powers 148–9. JFK initiation of most covert activities: Quirk 197. Diplomat on Castro as "romantic": A.S. Fordham-Lloyd report 7/14/59, FO. Castro son's Moscow visit: NYT 11/12/

61. Soviet-Cuban relations, spring 1962: Hugh Thomas 1377–84, Hyland and Shryock 28–31. Castro and NSK alarm each other about invasion: *New Republic* 12/14/63, Szulc 578–80, Igor Statsenko, "On Some Military-Political Aspects of the Caribbean Crisis," *Latinskaya Amerika* (Moscow) November-December 1973. JFK disinclination to invade, Soviet-Cuban perception and Gromyko reply: McNamara and Gromyko in MCT. Thompson on Soviets and Cuba: Thompson to DFR, 4/3/62. "Public balancing act": Bundy-JFK 9/17/62, JFKL. JFK on "outside Communist penetration": JFKPP 4/20/61. Reston on "limit" to JFK promise: NYT 4/20/61.

JFK on Castro threat to Guantanamo: JFKPP 3/21/62. "Let the U.S. make a move": USN 9/17/62. Harris to JFK on public opinion: Harris-JFK 10/4/62, JFKL. *Chronicle* poll: Kern 101. NSK belief in military-political power brought by numbers of nuclear weapons and delivery systems: Bundy int, Bundy 419–20, MccGwire 22–5. JFK on Vietnam after 1964: Odon 16–7, 413–4, AMSRK 708–23, George Ball 366–7. NSK knew that most of Party Congress opposed de-Stalinization: Burlatsky int WGBH and Burlatsky at Harvard, 9/27/88. NSK-Mikoyan relations and discussion of missile gambit: Sergo Mikoyan in CCT, MCT, at Harvard 2/13/89–2/15/89, Mikoyan conv, Sergei Khrushchev conv, Sergo Mikoyan in *Latinskaya Amerika,* January 1988. Lebow on expense of missile gambit: *Political Science Quarterly,* Fall 1983. JFK at news conference on missile firing from close range or five thousand miles: JFKPP 3/7/62.

Secrecy as Soviet norm: Burlatsky int WGBH, Shakhnazarov in MCT. American concession that NSK stealth and dishonesty helped American case: RFK oh, Bundy in CCT, Sorensen in MCT. JFK to Bundy 10/16/62 news: Bundy int. Malinovsky on Turkish bases: Burlatsky in CCT. NSK to Stevenson on Turkish bases: Tucker notes 8/5/58, Stevenson Papers. NSK to Harriman and Pearson on bases: NSK-Harriman memcon 6/23/59, JFKL, SEP 4/27/62, WP 8/28/61, Luvie Pearson conv. Mikoyan attitude to NSK misile gambit: Sergo Mikoyan in CCT, MCT, at Harvard 2/13/89–2/15/89 and Sergo Mikoyan conv. "Naturally tormented our leadership": Sergei Khrushchev in MCT. "Only two thoughts": Sergo Mikoyan in CCT. Mikoyan love of Castro: Sergo Mikoyan conv. "All these thoughts kept churning": NSK1 493–5. NSK at Varna 5/16/62 and Sofia 5/19/62: Prav 5/17/62 and 5/20/62.

NSK reveals missile gambit to Gromyko: Gromyko in MCT and Gromyko in Izv 4/15/89, "On Glasnost Now and Secrecy Then," *Observer* (London) 4/2/89, Alexeyev in *Argumenty i fakty* 3/11/89–3/17/89. NSK on talkative Presidium: Burlatsky in CCT. NSK reveals scheme to only five: Sergo Mikoyan in CCT and MCT, also NSK1 498–9. NSK on secret meeting after Bulgaria visit: NSK1 494–5. NSK and Malinovsky on how long Soviet invasion of nearby island would take: Sergo Mikoyan in CCT. CIA estimate of $1 billion for missile gambit: CIA, "The Crisis: USSR/Cuba," 10/25/62, JFKL. Soviets had never moved nuclear missiles beyond borders: Thompson oh, Bundy int. Gromyko felt Malinovsky supported scheme: Gromyko in MCT and in Izv 4/15/89. Sergei on "usual way to check himself": Sergei Khrushchev in MCT. "It wasn't until after two or three": NSK1 499.

Gromyko relieved by NSK insistence: Gromyko in MCT and in Izv 4/15/89. "Let's send Marshal Biryuzov": Sergo Mikoyan in MCT. Volkogonov on order to

Malinovsky: MCT. Alexeyev on appointment and told of missile gambit: Alexeyev int WGBH, MCT, Mikoyan in CCT, Alexeyev in *Argumenty i fakty,* 3/11/89–3/17/89, *Ekho Planety,* November 1988. Rashidov mission and aftermath: Szulc 576–7, Alexeyev int, Alexeyev, Risquet, Mikoyan, Volkogonov and Aragones in MCT, Castro in *Le Monde* 3/22/63. Castro on NSK proposal: Szulc 576–81, *New Republic* 12/14/63. "Once more, I have raised": Szulc 576. "He did not necessarily think through": Burlatsky in CCT, Burlatsky int WGBH, MCT. Gromyko-Dulles exchange: Gromyko in Izv 4/15/89. Arbatov on "closed coterie": MCT. Gromyko on necessity for secrecy: MCT.

Fulbright on missiles in Cuba: CR 6/29/61. No formal warning before May 1962: Bureau of Intelligence and Research memo, October 1962, JFKL. NSK on "threat": NSK-JFK 4/22/61, JFKL. "Very emotional man": Burlatsky int WGBH and in CCT. "It was high time": NSK1 494, also Volkogonov and Sergei Khrushchev in MCT.

15. *"No One Will Be Able Even to Run"*

Benny Goodman in the Soviet Union and NSK on jazz: Adzhubei int WGBH, Jane Thompson int, NYT 5/31/62, 6/2/62, 7/5/62, 7/9/62, NW 6/11/62, SNK 206. JFK to NSK on Goodman and Salinger: JFK-NSK 6/5/62, JFKL. Laos, spring 1962: RFK oh, Laos 1962 file in Harriman Papers, Rusk and Chayes to DFR 7/13/62, *Diplomatic History,* Spring 1979, Hilsman 136–55, Donmen 200–80. "I fear there is little": Rusk to DFR 3/29/62. JFK to Adzhubei on Southeast Asia: Sal 213–4. JFK to NSC on Laos: 1/18/62 memcon. JFK February press conference: JFKPP 2/21/62. "Combined bluff with real determination": Sor 645–8, Sor oh. JFK on Laos to Alsop: SEP 3/31/62. Thompson says "highly significant": Thompson-Rusk 5/14/62, also Thompson-Rusk 5/15/62, Harriman Papers. NSK on "reckless game": NW 6/11/62. Rusk draft of JFK-NSK letter: 5/11/62, Harriman Papers. RFK-Bolshakov exchanges on Laos: RFK oh.

"Good news has come": NSK-JFK 6/12/62, JFKL. Fate of Laos settlement: Hilsman 151–5, Donmen 281–303, Rust 76–7. Raul-Aragones Moscow mission: Mikoyan in CCT, Aragones and Risquet in MCT. Risquet on Cuban suggestion and Aragones on NSK reaction: MCT. NSK on 7/4/62: Jane Thompson int, NYT 7/5/62. NSK to JFK on Berlin: NSK-JFK 7/5/62, JFKL. Bolshakov on Berlin: RFK oh and Bolshakov memo 6/18/62, RFK Papers. Bundy on "buzzing incident": Bundy-JFK 7/17/62, JFKL. JFK-Dobrynin 7/17/62 meeting: memcon, JFKL. Dean comment in Geneva and Rusk-JFK reaction: Seaborg 162–3, Adrian Fisher oh. McNamara background and personality: McNamara int, McNamara int WGBH, Kohler int, Henry Trewhitt conv, Hilsman oh, Sylvester oh, Lovett oh, Dutton oh, T 2/11/91, SEP 8/5/61, L 3/30/62, *Reporter* 1/18/62, *Harper's* August 1961, NW 12/26/60, 5/12/62, Trewhitt, Burner and West 105–6, Halberstam *Best* 214–47, 258–9, Alsop 127–9.

"Who are smarter than I am": Trewhitt 29. "He really runs": Burner and West 103. "Bob suffers fools badly": Trewhitt 96. "I have never taken actions": Trewhitt 106–7. "I tried to persuade Dean": Kohler int. JFK admiration of McNamara: RFK oh. "Men can't understand": Bradlee 230–1. "Why is it they all": Halberstam *Best* 220–4. On "Hickory Hill seminars," see Schlesinger Papers. "The Kennedys—I like": Halberstam *Best* 220–4. "He'll come in": Cassini 327.

JFK on administrative solutions: JFKPP 6/11/62. O'Donnell warning: Vanocur int. "Everyone ought to run": Bradlee 162. Alsop on McNamara's "complicated business": Kern 120. "Bob is your great discovery": Joseph Alsop-JFK, undated, JFKL. "Somewhat crowded, rigidly": Trewhitt 27. "I agree that I don't": Collier and Horowitz *Fords* 248–9. Kennedy failure to exploit McNamara 1960 vote: McNamara int.

"Liberal outlook": Odon 237. "More money than I'm ever going" and "How many other": Trewhitt 7 and Collier and Horowitz *Kennedys* 254. JFK-McNamara Georgetown meeting and appointment: McNamara int, David Bell oh, Odon 236–8, Lincoln *My Twelve* 211–3, Sidey 14, Trewhitt 7–10, Halberstam *Best* 220–4. "Impressed with the fact": RFK oh. "You can never substitute emotion": Trewhitt 119. "I've got to think precisely": Trewhitt 296. "The most dangerous man": Trewhitt 83. "The other guy hasn't a chance": Trewhitt 250. Reston on McNamara: quoted in Hilsman 43–4. Worry about McNamara taking life and "another Forrestal": Trewhitt conv, Trewhitt 271. McNamara demand on Vietnam: McNamara int. McNamara and counterforce and Chicago speech: McNamara int WGBH, Trewhitt 122–5. "He was listening to his Whiz Kids": Trewhitt 115. NSK on counterforce: Prav 7/11/62, NYT 7/12/62.

"I don't know anybody who thinks": McNamara int WGBH, McNamara int, McNamara in HCCT. "We launched our missiles": Rusk int WGBH, Rusk int. NSK on anti-missile missile and Pentagon response: Prav 7/18/62, 7/19/62, NYT 7/17/62. RFK Moscow possibility: RFK oh and Thompson oh. Jacqueline on Glenn: Sulzberger 915. Galbraith trial balloons and JFK reaction: Bradlee 114. RFK on Kohler: RFK oh. Kohler background: Kohler int, NYT 6/29/62, NYT 10/21/64, Wise 100. Kohler on JFK: Kohler int. "If you send people": Bartlett int. Bolshakov-Holeman July luncheon: Holeman int and Holeman memo 7/11/62, JFKL. NSK to Nixon on Captive Nations: Nixon *Memoirs* 207–8. Mrs. Khrushchev–Jane Thompson exchange: Jane Thompson int. Khrushchev-Thompson farewell dinner: Jane Thompson int, NYT 7/25/62, Thompson-NSK 10/8/62, Thompson Papers.

"Seldom has there been such a lack": NW 7/9/62. NSK internal problems, summer 1962: Tatu 229–60. "Khrushchev at Bay": Rostow *Diffusion* 251–2, Rostow oh, T 8/25/87. Cline reaction and Rostow unconcern on Cuba: Prados *Soviet Estimate* 134 and Sulzberger 918. "No one will be able even to run": Acheson to Truman 5/3/62, Truman Papers. JFK on space: JFKPP 8/22/62 and 9/12/62. Estimates of MRBM and IRBM range: *Aviation Week* 11/12/62, Garthoff 20n. Count of Soviet personnel, Il-28s, anti-aircraft sites, MRBMs, IRBMs for Cuba: Castro in *New Republic* 12/14/63, AMSRK 504. Soviet troops kept in secrecy: CCT, MCT. Possibility of NSK fall trip and possible content of bargaining: Hilsman-Rusk 9/20/62, JFKL. Dobrynin to Rusk: Bundy-JFK 8/31/62, JFKL, Rusk to DFR 9/5/62. Chinese on Rusk proposal: Griffith *Sino* 351, Ulam *Expansion* 664–6. Mongoose activity: Davis *Kennedys* 397–9, Thomas Powers 129–30, AMSRK 477–80, Prados *Secret Wars* 194–207.

Discussion of Castro "liquidation": *Harpers* July 1975, Goodwin 189, Thomas Powers 129–30, *Assassination Plots* 105, 161, AMSRK 497–8. 8/30/62 U-2 incident and NSK response: NYT 9/5/62, Prav 9/6/62, *Business Week* 9/8/62, NW 9/17/62, Rusk to DFR 9/5/62. CIA surveillance of Soviet ships: Prados *Soviet Estimate*, Laqueur 159–60, Burrows 116–23. Schlesinger on support of uprising: Schlesinger-JFK 9/5/62, and JFK-Schlesinger 9/5/62, JFKL. Missile force size: Garthoff (1989) 18–20, ACT. Alexeyev on Biryuzov's belief: MCT. Sergo Mikoyan on "absolutely Russian": CCT. Castro on disguise as agricultural products: Mikoyan in CCT. Agent and refugee reports: 10/18/62 William K. Harvey summary of agent reports since July 1962, JFKL, also Frank Sievarts official history, "The Cuban Crisis, 1962," written for State Department internal use on the basis of official sources, 1963, JFKL. Hereafter cited as Sievarts history.

"Clearly something new": CIA, Office of Current Intelligence, Current Intelligence Memorandum 8/22/62, JFKL, McCone suspicions of nuclear missiles in Cuba: Bundy int, Helms int, Rusk int, SEP 7/27/63. McCone alert of JFK and JFK response: Laqueur 165–9, Prados *Soviet Estimate* 127–50. U-2 8/29/62 flight: Hilsman memo 2/5/63, Hilsman Papers. Carter on "crash program": Carter to DFR, 9/5/62. Rusk on Soviet buildup: Rusk to DFR, 9/5/62. Marine rehearsal and Castro interpretation: Arbesu and Risquet in MCT, Garthoff 36. Keating and other charges on coverup: Keating in *Look* 11/3/64. Keating suspicion of bugging: Lasky *Watergate* 81–2. Helms on Keating charges: Helms int. JFK on "fifty thousand-odd Cuban refugees": JFK to Theodore White 2/13/63, in White notes, Schlesinger Papers. Republican demands for blockade: *National Review* 9/25/62, 10/23/62, Garthoff 16.

Nixon on "clear and present danger": NYHT 11/4/62. Rebozo sends article: Rebozo-Nixon 9/10/62, Nixon Papers. Houston security incident: SAC Houston-J. Edgar Hoover 9/17/62, FBI. Congressional authority for reservists callup: NYT 9/22/62. Cuban banners in Houston: J. Edgar Hoover-Chief, Secret Service 9/14/62, FBI. JFK defers action through first two years and plans for 1962 election: Odon 307. *New Republic* on JFK and *The King and I:* 10/1/62. McCone background and personality: Amory int, Hilsman oh, Amory oh, R.O. L'Allier-W.C. Sullivan 9/28/61, FBI, SEP 7/27/63, NYT 9/27/61, T 10/6/61, L 10/6/61, Cline 215–9, Thomas Powers 159–67, Halberstam *Best* 152–5, Phillips 151–2, Laqueur 79–81, Alsop 232–3, 244–5, Hilsman 46–7, Wise and Ross 193–9. "He liked Ethel": RFK oh. "Snob and a puritan": David Martin 186. JFK on money and religion: AMSTD 72. McCone and Cal Tech professors on test ban: Wise and Ross 192–4, Halberstam *Best* 152–5.

"An operator, not a policy-maker": Divine *Blowing* 256–8. McCone denounces test ban: McCone-Krock 2/23/61, Krock Papers. Kistiakowsky on McCone and public opinion: Kistiakowsky 197–203, 261–2, 281–5, 372–3. "Let's look forward" and "Phi Beta Kappas": McCone-Nixon 11/10/60, Nixon Papers, and McCone-Krock 2/23/61, Krock Papers. Charge of war profiteering and McCone response: Halberstam *Best* 152–5. JFK thinks of RFK for CIA and decides on McCone: RFK oh, Sor 630–1. O'Donnell indignation about appointments: Vanocur int. "McCone is an alley fighter": Hilsman oh, Hilsman 46–7. Eisenhower to McCone on appointment: 9/27/61, DDEL. McCone arrival at CIA: David Martin 118. McCone and Kirkpatrick report: Ranelagh 380–1, Wise and Ross 192–3. Cline on McCone and assassination: Cline 215–9, 224. McCone belief in importance of nuclear balance: Bundy int, Bundy 419–20. McCone sees Gilpatric and questions Cuba buildup: Detzer 63–4, Abel 16–8. McCone worry about excommunication: *Assassination Plots* 105.

RFK on McCone's prescience before Missile Crisis: RFK oh. RFK on missiles as "major political problem": RFK memo 9/11/62, RFK Papers. RFK-Dobrynin

9/4/62 meeting: RFK oh, RFK13 2–4. "We did it because of the requirements": Bundy int and Bundy in Thompson 210. Sorensen on JFK drawing line: HCCT. O'Donnell chiding of RFK on *Thirteen Days:* This exchange, circulated among Kennedy aides and Cabinet members, was told to the author by a fellow scholar. Dobrynin-Sorensen 9/6/62 meeting and Sorensen report to JFK: Sor 667–9. Udall sees NSK: NYT 10/1/62, NW 10/29/62, *Atlantic,* September 1963. Frost sees NSK: NYT 9/9/62, *Atlantic,* September 1963. "How like you": Frost-JFK 7/24/62, JFKL. Secret Service analysis of wine: R.H. Jevons-Mr. Conrad 9/21/62, FBI. One of the Republicans who adopted Frost's crack was Nixon: *Reader's Digest,* November 1964.

JFK on Frost comment: Sulzberger 929. TASS 9/11/62 statement: Kohler-William Tyler 6/11/63 and Kennan-Rusk 9/13/62, JFKL. JFK response: JFKPP 9/13/62. NSK to Austrian: Tatu 240–1, Garthoff 12–3. "More rude noises": Kaysen-JFK 9/21/62, JFKL. Bundy on need for "fairly tough talk": Bundy-JFK 9/15/62, JFKL. *Omsk* arrival and unloading: Detzer 69, Garthoff 19. 9/5/62 U-2 flight: Hilsman 2/5/63 memo, Hilsman Papers. 9/9/62 U-2 incident in China: Prav 9/10/62. *Poltava* arrival, 9/15/62: Garthoff 19. 9/17/62 U-2 flight: Hilsman memo 2/5/63, Hilsman Papers. Reports to JM/WAVE: Harvey memo 10/18/62, JFKL, Rusk int, Sievarts history, RFK13 6–7, 9/19/62 CIA estimate and McCone reaction: 9/19/62 Special National Intelligence Estimate, JFKL, Sievarts history, Prados *Soviet Estimate* 127–39, Wise and Ross 292. McCone letter to Nixon: McCone-Nixon 9/29/62, Nixon Papers.

Castro port announcement: NYT 9/25/62. CIA postmortem on agent reports and Rusk comment: Rusk int, Hilsman 2/5/63 memo, JFKL, Wise and Ross 292–4. JFK comparison to Pearl Harbor: RFK oh. Geneva progress: Seaborg *Kennedy* 167–71. NSK to JFK on limited ban: NSK-JFK 9/4/62, JFKL. JFK on "serious effort": JFK-NSK 9/15/62, JFKL. NSK agrees to target date: NSK-JFK 9/28/62, JFKL. Bolshakov sees NSK and Mikoyan: RFK oh, Bartlett int, Bartlett oh, Bartlett-RFK 10/26/62, RFK Papers, SEP 12/8/63, Sor 668, AMSRK 502, Garthoff 27, 27n, 28n. Bartlett-Zinchuk luncheon: Bartlett int. Thank-you note and Bundy comment: 10/10/62 draft, JFKL. "I am glad that we can continue": JFK-NSK 10/8/62, JFKL. Bay of Pigs prisoners plight and Donovan October 1962 mission: James Donovan 84–109. JFK on freeing prisoners: Odon 275–7. "Millions for defense": Safire-Nixon, 1961, Nixon Papers. See also *Dallas Morning News* 10/12/62.

Goodwin-Goulart mission: Haynes Johnson 273–5. RFK on sending equipment to Cuba: 9/11/62 memo, RFK Papers, AMSRK 470–1. "Before Donovan signs on" and "I got the message": Helms int and J. Swift-Bromley Smith 10/9/62, JFKL. Rusk on "umbrella" and 10/10/62 comment: Roberts 203, NYT 10/11/62. JFK asks for Berlin plans and expects crisis: Hilsman-Rusk 9/20/62, Kaysen-Lincoln 9/29/62, Kaysen-JFK 9/29/62, Rusk to DFR 9/5/62, Rusk int, Sorensen oh, USN 9/3/62, Sor 668–89. CIA on Il-28s and Hughes-Bowles-Dobrynin talks: Thomas Hughes conv, Bowles oh, Garthoff in HCCT, Bowles 418, Roberts 210. Work sped up in Cuba: Bundy 405. Gromyko-Dorticos meeting: Gromyko and Mikoyan in MCT. Bundy on "Issues": 10/14/62 transcript, ABC-TV. NSK at Chinese dinner: NYT 10/15/62, Hyland and Shryock 53–4. Elder to McCone: David Martin 142–3.

16. "He's the One Playing God"

10/16/62 Cabinet Room scene: RFK oh, Lundahl int, Lundahl oh, Sidey (1964) 272–3, Burrows 124–5, *Look* 12/18/62. Gilpatric on JFK at meeting: Parmet *JFK* 284–5. JFK-Bohlen talk: Bohlen notes, Bohlen 488–9. 10/16/62 morning meeting dialogue: Transcript and tape, 10/16/62, JFKL. Draft to "Mr. F.C." and attached note: undated, Sorensen Papers. Bundy on NSK being "much too sensible": Bundy 419. Bundy on JFK 1962 belief that U.S. on defensive: Bundy 418–9. Kohler's cables and JFK reaction: Kohler-Rusk 10/16/62, JFKL, Kohler Diary 10/16/62, and RFK oh. History of IRBMs in Europe: Sievarts history, William Bundy memo on Jupiters and overseas bases 10/20/62, JFKL, Garthoff 43n, Ambrose *Eisenhower* 447, 495, 553. Eisenhower-McElroy exchange: 6/5/59 memcon, DDEL.

Harr on "public relations": Harr conv, Harr-Eisenhower 10/14/59, DDEL. Rusk on missiles obsolescence: Rusk int, NYT 8/7/87. JFK request for review of missiles in Turkey and result: Rusk-DFR 1/11/63, Garthoff 43n. Rostow on failure of diplomacy to extract missiles: Rostow oh. NSK fear of nuclear weapons in FRG: See, for instance, Ulam *Expansion* 610–1, 663–4. 10/16/62 evening meeting dialogue: Transcript and tape, 10/16/62, JFKL. Formosa Straits crisis of 1958 and JFK view: JFK *Strategy* 102–4, staff memo to JFK on Formosa-Cuba parallel 9/7/62, JFKL. McNamara on NSK view of Soviet Union as "numerically behind": MCT. JFK private view of Monroe Doctrine: Norbert Schlei oh, AMSRK 505. JFK publicly on Doctrine: JFKPP 8/29/62. JFK angry at secrecy and deception: RFK oh, RFK13 5–6. Krock on JFK and Monroe Doctrine: NYT 9/14/62, 9/18/62.

Bundy on feeling of being "deliberately deceived" and Sorensen on difficulty had Soviets announced missiles: MCT, Bundy int. "I would have been impeached": RFK13 45. "Have you forgotten": Odon 316. JFK-Stevenson 10/16/62 meeting: L 12/14/62, Abel 49, Bartlow Martin *Stevenson* 720. Stevenson 10/17/62 note and JFK reaction: copy in JFKL and Sorensen int JBM. Bohlen refusal of JFK plea to stay and RFK reaction: Bohlen oh, Bohlen notes, RFK oh, Bohlen 489–93.

"The campaign is over": Sidey (1964) 278. JFK at Waterbury: JFKPP 10/17/62. Blight and Welch on two schools: Blight and Welch 7–8, 200–21. Volkogonov on 1962 Soviet nuclear strength: MCT. Rusk on his Ex Comm function and RFK reaction: Rusk int, RFK oh, RFK alleges Rusk breakdown and Rusk response: RFK oh, Rusk int. RFK as de facto leader: Abel 57–8, George Ball 290. "We all knew Little Brother": Abel 58.

On handling missiles like U-2 episode: 10/17/62 memcon, JFKL, Sievarts history. Sorensen ulcers: NYHT 10/3/62. Sorensen record of options: Sorensen notes, 10/17/62, JFKL. Sorensen and RFK meet JFK at National Airport: Sorensen oh. 10/18/62 morning Ex Comm meeting: Sorensen notes and memcon, JFKL, Sievarts history, *President's Intelligence Checklist* 10/18/62, JFKL. JFK on where would be "if Khrushchev knocks off Berlin": Weintal and Bartlett 65–9. Sorensen draft of television address and "airtight letter": 10/18/62 draft and "Synopsis of President's Speech," undated, Sorensen Papers. Stevenson on *"talking* with K": 10/17/62 note, JFKL. Sorensen relinquishes idea of letter to NSK: Sor 685–6. Thompson on probability of Soviet ships deferring to blockade: Thompson oh, Jane Thompson int, Sievarts history. Rusk on going "down with a bang": Sievarts history. Acheson-JFK talk: Acheson oh, Acheson in *Esquire*, February 1969.

Rusk, Thompson, Bundy advise JFK before Gromyko talk: David Klein-Bundy 10/17/62, Bundy-JFK 10/18/62, Rusk-JFK 10/18/62, Roberts 211. JFK-Gromyko 10/18/62 talk: memcon 10/18/62, JFKL, Sievarts history, Gromyko in Prav 1/23/63, Gromyko in Izv 4/15/89, Gromyko in MCT, Burlatsky in CCT, Andrei Gromyko 175–9, RFK oh, RFK 13 17–20, Abel 75–7, Sor 689–91, NW 10/29/62, NYT 10/19/62, 10/20/62, 10/27/62. JFK regrets silence about missiles and Rusk, Thompson response: Cohen 154. JFK second thoughts about summit: Garthoff 28. Rusk on "chills up my spine": Rusk int. "More barefaced lies" and RFK questions: Lovett oh. Gromyko toast: Sievarts history, NSK3 174–5. Frankel notes on Gromyko-JFK meeting: Salisbury *Without Fear* 285. Rusk use of alcohol: Galbraith *A Life* 402–3, Alsop 186. 10/18/62 evening Ex Comm meeting: Sievarts history, RFK13 21–2.

JFK sees aides, 10/19/62 morning: RFK 10/31/62 memo, RFK Papers. Odon 321. RFK and Sorensen on Bundy oscillations: RFK oh, Sorensen int JBM. 10/19/62 morning Ex Comm meeting: memcon, JFKL, "Steps which would make air strike more acceptable to blockade group," 10/19/62, CIA memo 10/19/62, Sievarts history, RFK 10/31/62 memo, RFK Papers, RFK13 22–3, Abel 83–90. Dillon on RFK arguments: Abel 81, Stein and Plimpton 136–7. Galbraith on "heretics" at Hickory Hill: Galbraith *A Life* 496. Bundy calls O'Donnell in Chicago: *Look* 12/18/62. JFK and McNamara plug leaks: Sylvester oh, Sievarts history, Abel 83–4, Bundy 402–3. Sorensen work on draft of television speech: 10/20/62 draft, Sorensen Papers, Sor 691–3. 10/20/62 luncheon with Kozlov: Kohler int, Davies int, Kohler Diary 10/20/62.

JFK 10/20/62 return and afternoon NSC meeting: 10/20/62 memcon, JFKL, Sorensen 10/20/62 notes, Sorensen Papers, Sievarts history, Sorensen int JBM, George Ball 295–6, Sor 695–6, Odon 321–6, Abel 91–9, RFK13 25–8, NYT 10/21/62, RFK interview with Schlesinger 4/6/64, Schlesinger Papers, Bartlow Martin *Stevenson* 723–4, Stevenson-Schlesinger, January 1963, undated, JFKL. Stevenson on "effort to avoid a clash": Phillip Klutznick int JBM. Stevenson on JFK as "cold and ruthless" and generally: Adlai Stevenson III int JBM, Minow int JBM, Minow conv, Ball int JBM, Sulzberger 923–4, Bartlett int, Bartlett oh, Bartlow Martin *Stevenson* 530. Stevenson suffering and *"Humankind cannot bear"*: Marietta Tree int JBM, Bartlow Martin *Stevenson* 592. "A long and troubled story": Bundy int. "I like Jack Kennedy": Minow int JBM. "Just not a man of action": AMSRK 136. "We'll teach that little prick" and "I am going to find out": Raskin int and unpublished ms.

"Lyndon is a chronic liar": AMSTD draft. "That fucking bastard": Adlai Stevenson 111 int JBM. "Well, I learned one thing": Bartlett int and in Thompson 10–2. LBJ on "fat ass" Stevenson: Schlesinger int JBM. Joseph Kennedy to Raskin: Raskin int and unpublished ms. JFK and Stevenson at Libertyville: Minow int JBM, Minow conv, Ball int JBM, Odon 178, Raskin ms. *"Very* self-confident": Bartlow Martin *Stevenson* 508. JFK on Stevenson as "helpless pawn": Sorensen int JBM. Joseph Kennedy gives "twenty-four hours": Bartlow Martin *Stevenson* 522. "Wasn't able to decide": RFK oh. "It never occurred to me": Schlesinger oh COHP, Schlesinger int JBM. JFK offers three jobs: Bartlow Martin *Stevenson* 557–65. "I'm not going to take it": Minow int JBM. "We sat up until 2 A.M.": Ball int JBM. "I'll be your boss" and JFK-Stevenson to press: Bartlow Martin *Stevenson* 261–5. RFK on JFK reaction: RFK oh, RFK int JBM, Sorensen int JBM.

"History had passed him by": Ball int JBM. "Kennedy was pragmatic": Cleveland int JBM. "I don't like the word tough": RFK int JBM. "Jack can't bear": Lash 541. "The whole atmosphere": Jacqueline Kennedy-Stevenson 2/9/63, Stevenson Papers. Jacqueline on marital relations: Tree int JBM. "Look, Stevenson has had": Ball int JBM, Schlesinger int JBM. Ball on JFK talk in massage room: Ball int JBM. "Just not masculine enough": Smathers int. JFK on Stevenson as "switcher" and in Turkish bath: Collier and Horowitz *Kennedys* 233, William Douglas-Home oh. "Seeing how much old Adlai": Hedley Donovan 76. Rusk avoids General Assembly: Rusk int JBM.

Stevenson at Newport anecdote: Cassini 325–6. Stevenson on "wise politician": Bowles oh. Stevenson-JFK talk on Senate run: Bartlow Martin *Stevenson* 676–8. "I don't understand that man": Kaysen int JBM. Stevenson deprived of limousine: Bartlow Martin *Stevenson* 575. "That young man": Halberstam *Best* 27. Stevenson on "avarice" and Lawford announcement: Bartlow Martin *Stevenson* 812, 575. Ball on "rich females": Ball int JBM. RFK on JFK liking to "shock" Stevenson: RFK int JBM. Stevenson on nightmares: Bartlow Martin *Stevenson* 594, 807. RFK-JFK after meeting: RFK oh, Odon 322–3. Stevenson to O'Donnell: Odon 326. *New York Times* leak quashed: Sievarts history, Schlesinger-Reston memcon 12/24/64, Schlesinger Papers, Ball in HCCT. JFK calls Jacqueline and swims with Powers: Odon 325.

10/21/62 morning meetings: memcon, JFKL, McNamara notes 10/21/62, CIA Current Intelligence Memo 10/21/62, Sievarts history, Taylor in HCCT, Taylor in WP 10/5/82, Rusk int. 10/21/62 afternoon meeting: Bundy, "Tentative Agenda," 10/21/62, NSC Action Memorandum 10/21/62, Sievarts history, JFKL. Presidential evacuation plans and shelter: Goodpaster int, Rusk int, USN 10/7/89. Jacqueline on being "distraction": *Good Housekeeping* September 1962. "Oh gosh, kid" and reading cables: AMSTD draft, Bundy-Jacqueline Kennedy 10/30/62, JFKL. "I am mindful of your warning" and Jacqueline response: Bundy-Jacqueline Kennedy and Jacqueline Kennedy-Bundy, both undated, JFKL. *Telegraph* article: Schlesinger-Jacqueline Kennedy, undated, and Jacqueline Kennedy-Schlesinger 1/18/63, Schlesinger Papers. Jacqueline's aesthetic approach: Galbraith *A Life* 411–2.

Jacqueline on "corny old men," heroes in history, *The King Must Die:* White *Search* 518–24, Manchester *Death* 623. Jacqueline Kennedy-Rathbone: Heymann 377–8. "What's the line": White *Search* 524. JFK bachelor life: *Good Housekeeping* September 1962. Joseph Kennedy worry about whispering campaign and veto of Grace Kelly: Priscilla McMillan conv, Dorothy Schiff int. Napoleonic portrait: Faber 112–3. "I didn't want to dilute": AMSTD 118. Jacqueline unhappiness about being First Lady: Franklin Roosevelt, Jr., int, Heymann 247–337, Bradlee 152–3, Saunders 68, West 291–4, Kelley *Jackie* 95–159. Request to return memos: Letitia Baldrige to staff 5/29/63, JFKL. "Take me out": Jacqueline Kennedy-Schlesinger note, undated, 1965, Schlesinger Papers. Schlesinger defense of *A Thousand Days:* Schlesinger-Bohlen, 1965, Schlesinger Papers.

"Oh, Jack, I'm so sorry": AMSTD draft. JFK surprise at her popularity and "cheap Texas broads": based on unpublished draft of Manchester *Death*, noted in Pearson Papers, 1967. "Happiness compartment": AMSTD draft. Billings on

Jacqueline's spending: Billings oh. Jacqueline travel during Presidency: Ralph Martin 474–5, Bishop *Day Kennedy* 23. Galbraith on "sharper view" and Lemnitzer: Galbraith *A Life* 411. Jacqueline on poetry: Halberstam *Best* 36. Gallup on Jacqueline: *Gallup* 9/23/62. Miller on LBJ at White House: Arthur Miller 508. Jacqueline on "wolfhound": Ralph Martin 318. JFK caution not to say she disliked: Manchester *Death* 82. Jacqueline political influence: Ralph Martin 320, Heymann 347–9.

Jacqueline impersonations of leaders: Heymann 340. "And it isn't going to be de Gaulle": Manchester *Death* 610. "This leaves the political problem": Schlesinger-Jacqueline on Abu Simbel: 1963, Schlesinger Papers. Jacqueline-JFK relationship as Missile Crisis grows and her desire to remain with him: AMSTD draft, Ralph Martin 465, Odon 324–5, Parmet *JFK* 277–98.

17. "The Moment We Hoped Would Never Come"

Boggs, Halleck, other leaders notified: Sievarts history, Mansfield oh, Halleck oh, Boggs oh, Hickenlooper oh in Hickenlooper Papers, *Look* 12/18/62, L 11/2/62. Acheson sees Bruce and Macmillan briefing: Acheson in *Esquire* February 1969, T 11/2/62, Sievarts history, Chester Cooper oh, Acheson oh, Horne 364–5. Acheson briefs de Gaulle: T 11/2/62, Acheson oh. JFK-Eisenhower call: Eisenhower interview with Moos 11/8/66, Eisenhower 10/22 memcon, DDEL. Penkovsky arrest and contribution: Helms int, Garthoff in HCCT, Garthoff 39–41, Roberts 211, Blight and Welch 208. Bundy told the current author of his conviction that Penkovsky's importance had been exaggerated in the literature on the period, and noted that in the text of his history of nuclear weapons *Danger and Survival* he had managed to avoid even a single reference to the spy. (Bundy int)

RFK before 10/22/62 NSC meeting: Guthman 122–3, Guthman int. 10/22/62 NSC meeting: memcon, JFKL, and NSC "Record of Actions" 10/22/62, Sievarts history. Castro alarmed by Washington movements and mobilizes: Detzer 184 and del Valle in MCT. JFK meeting with Congressional leaders: Smathers int, Russell oh and notes in Russell Papers, RFK oh, Fulbright oh, Marcy int, Hickenlooper oh, Hickenlooper Papers, Lundahl oh, George Darden oh in Russell Papers, MacNeil 205–7, RFK13 31–3, Odon 327–8, Sidey (1964) 283. JFK mocks leaders: Odon 328. "When you get the Congressional leaders": Rusk int. "Those of us who operated": Gerald Ford int. Dobrynin-Gromyko exchange: MCT, also Shaknazarov in CCT, based on talk with Dobrynin, Harriman oh COHP.

"If they want this job": Sorensen draft of *Kennedy* in Sorensen Papers. I have restored JFK's original language. Macmillan message: Macmillan-JFK 10/22/62, JFKL, Sievarts history. Rusk-Dobrynin meeting: Rusk int, NYT 10/23/62, Sievarts history, Harriman oh COHP, Shaknazarov in CCT, Garthoff 15. Rusk cable delivery: Rusk-Kohler 10/22/62, Kohler int, Davies int, Davies oh COHP, Davies memo on October 22–8, 1962, undated, kindly provided by Davies to the author. JFK Oval Office scene: L 11/2/62, Sidey oh. JFK speech is in JFKPP 10/22/62. Sorensen and Dillon language appears in drafts for 10/22/62 speech, JFKL. "Well, that's it": Ralph Martin 467. "We didn't feel as good": Bundy int and Bundy in HCCT. Bundy criticism of speech: Bundy in CCT, Bundy 457–8.

Pentagon war room scene and activity: *Foreign Service Journal* July 1971, L

11/30/62, Garthoff 37–8. Cuban statement: *New Orleans Times-Picayune* 10/23/62. The only British newspaper that did not suggest a Presidential overreaction was Lord Beaverbrook's *Daily Express.* (10/24/62) Lord Russell to JFK and JFK reply: T 11/2/62, Detzer 203–4. "Now we are at a showdown": *Atlanta Consitution* 10/23/62. *Time* on JFK resolve: T 11/2/62. Russell on "all good Americans": Russell-Arthur Burdett 10/24/62, Russell Papers. Berle comment: Adolf Berle Diary, 10/22/62, Berle Papers. Goldwater on JFK action: NYT 10/23/62. Hugh Scott and William Miller comments: *New Orleans Times-Picayune* 10/23/62. *Crimson* complaint: Detzer 191. Keating reaction: NYT 10/23/62, 10/24/62. Nixon on campaign damage: Nixon *Memoirs* 244.

"Can you imagine": *Boston Herald* 10/26/62. Frazier Cheston to parents: *Boston Herald* 10/25/62. Georgian to Kennedy: Richard Edmonds-JFK 10/24/62, JFKL. Conservative Party rally: Detzer 187. NSK and Mikoyan reaction to JFK speech: Mikoyan in MCT, Garthoff 33–4. Kuznetsov summons and NSK letter: NSK-JFK 10/23/62 and attachments, JFKL. Soviet alert and NSK at Bolshoi and State Department reading: Garthoff 41–2, Hilsman-Rusk 10/24/62, T 11/2/62, NSK1 497. Radio Moscow announcement: 10/23/62 text in JFKL. For other world reaction, see CIA memo 10/23/62, JFKL. JFK relief on 10/23/62 morning: RFK13 35. JFK mystification about failure to blockade Berlin: Bradlee 124–5, Sulzberger 926–7. Bundy on JFK fear of Berlin reprisal: Bundy 421–2 and Odon 318–9, 329–31. NSK on Russian and American bloodshed: NSK1 500.

10/23/62 morning Ex Comm meeting: Bundy memcon, JFKL, Hilsman-Rusk 10/23/62, Hilsman Papers. JFK-NSK 10/23/62 and drafts are in JFKL. CIA estimates on blockades of Cuba and West Berlin: CIA, "The Possible Role of a Progressive Economic Blockade Against Cuba," 10/25/62, "Survivability of West Berlin," 10/23/62, "Effect on Cuba of a Blockade Covering All Goods Except Food and Medicines, 10/23/62, JFKL. 10/23/62 evening Ex Comm meeting: Bundy memcon, JFKL. JFK signs quarantine: NYT 10/24/62, Sievarts history, Abel 135–6, L 11/2/62. JFK on risk of miscalculation and *The Guns of August:* RFK13 40. Soviet military attaché comment and CIA report to JFK: Abel 134. RFK-Dobrynin 10/23/62 evening meeting: RFK13 41–4, Dobrynin in MCT. "All my telegrams were coded": Dobrynin in MCT. Jaipurs dinner: Jaipur 284–5, AMSTD draft.

JFK–Ormsby-Gore relationship: de Zulueta int, David Bruce oh, AMSTD 423–4, NYT 10/18/61, Macmillan *Pointing* 338–9, Sor 559, Odon 94, 266–7. "I must let you know how privileged": Ormsby-Gore–JFK 5/18/61, JFKL. Elizabeth II on envoy: Elizabeth II–JFK 5/14/62, JFKL. "I trust David": Barnet *Alliance* 211. "A number of people": Ormsby-Gore-JFK 5/18/61, JFKL. Ormsby-Gore on "ostrich position": Ormsby-Gore–JFK 5/26/62, JFKL. "Heed your parting advice" and "practically incomprehensible message": Ormsby-Gore-JFK 7/13/62, 9/19/62, JFKL. Ormsby-Gore wires Macmillan, Gaitskell suspicion and Ormsby-Gore–JFK 10/23/62 evening talk: AMSTD draft, AMSTD 815–8, RFK13 44–5, Abel 138–40, 148. McNamara 10/22/62 background briefing: transcript, JFKL. CIA to JFK on storage sites: estimates, 10/23/62, 10/24/62, in JFKL.

No conclusive evidence of warhead arrival: Rusk int, Sievarts history, Garthoff in HCCT, 10/25 afternoon meeting memcon, JFKL. Volkogonov on twenty warheads: MCT. U.S. information on warheads on *Poltava:* Garthoff 21–2. Davies delivers quarantine list: Davies int. Soviet demonstrations: Davies int, Kohler int,

Kohler Diary 10/24/62, NYT 10/25/62. NSK-Knox talk: *New York Times Magazine* 11/18/62, Associated Press London dispatch 10/25/62, T 11/23/62, Prav 10/25/62, Kohler-Rusk 10/25/62, Rusk-Kohler 10/27/62, Hilsman-Rusk 10/26/62, JFKL. Komer on Knox: Komer-Bundy 10/25/62, also Klein-Bundy 10/30/62, JFKL. NSK reply to Russell: NSK-Russell 10/24/62, *Foreign Broadcast Information Service*.

10/24/62 morning Ex Comm meeting: CIA, "The Crisis: USSR/Cuba," 10/24/62, Ex Comm Record of Action 10/24/62, JFKL, RFK13 45–52. JFK on "major crisis" and "need for a summit": JFKPP 2/14/62. "We're eyeball to eyeball": SEP 12/18/62. NSK on ships sailing "straight through": NSK1 496. Ormsby-Gore to Bundy, 10/24/62: Bundy-JFK 10/24/62. Macmillan-JFK talk, 10/24/62: Macmillan *At End* 196–203. Gaitskell and Wilson comments: CIA, "The Crisis," 10/24/62. RFK on Bolshakov effort to deliver NSK message: RFK oh. Bartlett meeting with Bolshakov and RFK reaction: Bartlett int, RFK oh, Bartlett-RFK 10/26/62, RFK Papers, Garthoff 27, Sor 668, AMSRK 502, Bolshakov in *Novoye vremye*, nos. 4–6, 1989, NW 12/24/62, *Look* 12/18/62.

As suggested in the text, exactly what NSK and Mikoyan said, exactly what was reported, by whom and to whom has been obscured by the fog of history. Sorensen writes that NSK and Mikoyan gave Bolshakov the message, but not that RFK delivered it. *Newsweek* reported that shortly before JFK's 10/22/62 speech, Bolshakov brought a false message to RFK, who refused to send it to the White House. *Look* reported that Bolshakov sought out RFK and said that NSK wanted JFK to know that no weapon capable of hitting U.S. soil will be placed in Cuba. Zinchuk is not mentioned in these accounts.

JFK 10/24/62 dinner and JFK call to Bartlett: Bartlett int, Cassini 323, Abel 214. NSK-JFK 10/24/62 letter is in JFKL. JFK reply: JFK notes, 10/24/62, and JFK-NSK 10/25/62, JFKL. Stevenson-JFK 10/24/62 call and Stevenson refusal and acceptance of Ball request: Ball int JBM, George Ball 301–2, Abel 157–8. Stevenson refusal to call Mrs. King: Branch 360. "He thought he was a Burmese": Ball int JBM. "A very civilized": Thant int JBM. 10/25/62 morning Ex Comm meeting: Sievarts history, 10/25/62 memcon, JFKL, Bundy, Ex Comm Record of Action 10/23/62, CIA, "The Crisis," 10/25/62, Hilsman-Rusk 10/25/62, JFKL. Van Zandt indiscretion and JFK reaction: Hilsman 45, 213, Abel 161–2. JFK-Stevenson, 10/25/62, on reply to Thant: Sievarts history. JFK-Thant 10/25/62 is in JFKL.

Thant-NSK, 10/25/62, and Thant-JFK are in JFKL. Zorin's infirmity: Shevchenko 114. Zorin claim that missile evidence is "fake": Sievarts history. White demand for Stevenson resignation: *Rochester Democrat-Chronicle* 10/25/62. *Chicago Tribune* on "wobblies," 10/25/62. Stevenson-Zorin exchange: NYT 10/26/62, Sievarts history. "I never knew Adlai had it in him": Odon 334. Republican friends approve: Jane Dick int JBM. Sorensen on Stevenson performance: Sorensen int JBM. JFK on "urgency": JFK-Thant 10/25/62, JFKL. Plimpton on Stevenson reluctance to show U-2 pictures: Jane Dick int JBM. 10/25/62 Ex Comm meeting, 5 P.M.: memcon, JFKL, Bundy, Ex Comm Record of Action 10/25/62, JFKL.

18. *"I Don't See How We'll Have a Very Good War"*

Quarantine enforced, 10/26/62: Sievarts history, Abel 173–4, RFK13 59–61. "The press will never believe": Sal 271. 10/26/62 morning Ex Comm Meeting:

10/26/62 memcon, JFKL, CIA, "The Crisis," 10/26/62, Record of Action 10/26/62, JFKL, Sievarts history, Abel 175–6, RFK13 63–4. Rostow on Soviet effort for negotiation, State on POL blockade, warning about NSK reaction to air strike: Rostow-Ex Comm 10/26/62, Hilsman-Rusk 10/26/62. LBJ talk with Krueger: Hugh Aynesworth in *Washington Times* 10/26/87. RFK and JFK on LBJ in Ex Comm: RFK oh. LBJ and Missile Crisis in 1964 campaign: RFK oh, White (1965). LBJ Ex Comm attendance: Rostow-LBJ 10/5/68, LBJ Daily Diary 10/24/62–10/30/62, Lyndon B. Johnson Library. "No man knew less": William Leuchtenburg in *American Heritage,* May-June 1990. JFK intention to choose Symington: RFK oh, Clayton Fritchey conv, Bartlett int, Bartlett oh.

"Lyndon Johnson forced me": Raskin int and unpublished ms. JFK focuses on LBJ virtues: RFK oh and Roberts. "LBJ's simple presence": Bradlee 194–5. JFK, Billings, Jacqueline on LBJ for President: Billings Diary, April-May 1961. "The steam really went out": Bradlee 226. "What is he doing in these offices?": Lincoln *Kennedy and Johnson* 149–50. "Most influential Vice President" and domestic "troubleshooter": NYT 11/10/60. O'Donnell as whipping boy: Odon 7–9. "That man can't run" and "very loyal": RFK oh. JFK on "twenty more Carl Haydens": Bradlee 217. LBJ less exposure to JFK and "We never got a thing": Lincoln *Kennedy and Johnson* 161, 182. "President Kennedy invited me": Thompson 101.

"When you get into an exciting one": Bartlett oh. "I know he's unhappy" and "If I speak one word": Bobby Baker 115–7. "I detested every minute": Kearns 164. Dealey distrust of Johnson and Krueger dispatch of Aynesworth: *Washington Times* 10/26/87. *Dallas Morning News* on LBJ "firmness": 10/30/62. Scali-Fomin history and in Missile Crisis: Fomin and Scali in MCT, ACT, Sievarts history, NW 8/17/64, *Family Weekly* 10/25/64, Abel 177–80, Hilsman 217–9, 222–3, Odon 334–6, Sal 271, 274–80, Scali, Salinger and Hilsman in "ABC News Reports," 8/13/64, transcript. James Blight kindly shared material on Kornienko's views. Fomin 1989 version: MCT, ABC-TV "World News Tonight," 1/29/89, Garthoff (1989) 80–1n. The Turkey-Cuba parallel was also suggested to the West by Soviet Ambassadors Nikita Ryzhov in Turkey and Nikolai Mikhailov in Indonesia. (Garthoff 50–1) Zinchuk on Scali story and Bartlett comment: Bartlett oh and Bartlett int.

Thant-Stevenson proposal and Rusk view: Rusk int JBM, Thant int JBM, Garthoff 51–2, Komer-Bundy 10/26/62, Sievarts history. Kohler luncheon for Stone: Kohler Diary 10/26/62 and Kohler int. NSK letter delivered: Davies int, Davies oh, Kohler-Rusk 10/26/62, NSK-JFK 10/26/62, JFKL. State Department group reads NSK letter: Thompson oh, RFK13 64–9, George Ball 303–5, Acheson in *Esquire,* February 1969, Abel 179–85, Sievarts history. NSK on *America's Siberian Adventure* at Vienna: 6/3/61 afternoon memcon, JFKL. Rusk to Senators on NSK letter: Rusk to DFR 1/13/63. O'Donnell and Sorensen reaction to NSK 10/26/62 letter: Odon 335–6, Sor 712–3. JFK to McNamara on secretary: King 88. 10/26/62 evening Ex Comm meeting: 10/26/62 memcon, JFKL, Sievarts history, RFK13 68–9, Abel 185–6, Bundy in HCCT.

Goodwin on JFK in Costa Rica: Goodwin 221. JFK and Ex Comm members on open installation of missiles and NSK possible demand for foreign bases negotiations: Sievarts history. McNamara to press on Turkey-Cuba trade: Background briefing transcript, 10/22/62, JFKL. Rostow and Tyler to Rusk on Turkish aspect: Rostow-Tyler to Rusk 10/23/62, JFKL. Lippmann on Cuba-Turkey parallel and trade: WP 10/22/62 and 10/25/62, Kern 129–30. Lippmann access to JFK reduced in 1961: Steel 531–2. McNamara on Jupiters in 1989: MCT. NSK party to theater, 10/26/62: Gromyko in Izv 4/15/89, NSK1 497. NSK sees military advisers and issues message, 10/27/62: NSK1 498–9, Sturua in MCT, Sturua conv, NSK to Cousins (SR 10/15/77), Sturua in Izv 2/6/89.

Soviet internal debate: Garthoff 46–8, Tatu 229–97, Hyland and Shryock 45–65, Linden 146–73. RFK 10–27–62 morning "disquiet": RFK13 71–2. NSK-JFK 10/27/62 message is in JFKL. Delivery: Davies-Kohler 8/22/67, kindly provided to the author by Davies. Paul Ghali report on Malinovsky reaction to negotiation: *New Orleans Times-Picayune* 11/2/62. Dobrynin denial that papers were burned: MCT. Burning report: RFK13 71, Garthoff in HCCT. Dobrynin on "whether it was in connection with my cable": MCT. Kornienko information was related by Kornienko to Vladislav Zubok and provided to this author. JFK failure to reveal RFK concession to Ex Comm: Transcript of tape of 10/27 Ex Comm meetings, JFKL. See also Blight, Welch and Bruce J. Allyn in *International Security,* Winter 1989–1990. 10/27/62 Ex Comm meetings: Memcons and transcripts in JFKL, Bundy and Sorensen in HCCT, Clifton-JFK on military readiness, 10/27/62, CIA, "The Crisis," 10/27/62, Ex Comm Record of Action, 10/27/62, Rostow-Ex Comm 10/27/62, Hilsman-Rusk 10/27/62, Abel 187–202, RFK13 73–4.

Excerpt from McNamara commercial is in "The Journey of Robert F. Kennedy," ABC-TV, 1969. Lincoln on "unbearable" tension: Lincoln *My Twelve Years* 327–9. 10/27/62 U-2 incidents: Hilsman-Jacqueline Kennedy 3/6/64, Hilsman Papers, Sievarts history, RFK 75–7, Hilsman 220–3, Abel 189–90, 195–6, Garthoff 52–3, 56–7, Mikoyan and Burlatsky in CCT, Igor Statsenko in *Kommunist vooruzhennykh sil* (Moscow), October 1987. JFK to Lawrence before Inauguration: Lawrence 256. U-2 downing not specifically ordered: Alexeyev in MCT. Franqui 1981 claim: T 3/16/81. Castro in 1985 on plane downing: Szulc 583–5. Sergei Khrushchev on NSK "very upset": MCT. Malinovsky reprimand to Soviet forces on Cuba: MCT. Cuban celebration of downing: Risquet in MCT. Castro-Khrushchev letter, 10/28/62, was published in *Le Monde* 11/24/90. State on Cuba-Turkey trade: Hilsman-Rusk 10/27/62, Hilsman Papers. JFK-NSK 10/27/62 draft: draft in McCloy Papers. RFK and Sorensen rewrite: RFK-Sorensen drafts, JFKL, RFK13 79–82, Abel 189–90.

JFK-NSK 10/27/62 is in JFKL. LBJ and Ball on why U.S. could not trade Jupiters: 10/27/62 memcon, JFKL. JFK asks Thompson to see Dobrynin and Thompson reply: Jane Thompson int. "Tell him if we don't get a reply": *International Security,* Winter 1989–1990. Sorensen on JFK recognition of helpfulness of assurance on Turkey: MCT, *International Security,* Winter 1989–1990. Sorensen 1989 "confession": MCT. Possible specific inclusion of Italy Jupiters: NSK3 179. RFK-Dobrynin 10/27/62 meeting: Dobrynin in MCT, RFK13 83–7, AMSRK 521–2, Garthoff (1989) 88n. RFK sees JFK and Powers, 10/27/62 evening: Odon 339–41. JFK and Powers see *Roman Holiday:* Odon 341. JFK agrees to Cordier gambit: Rusk int, Bundy int, Rusk to James Blight 2/25/87, read aloud by Bundy in HCCT, NYT 8/28/87, Blight and Welch 173–4, Garthoff 59–60.

Castro-Alexeyev 10/26/62 meeting, message to NSK and NSK interpretation: Alexeyev int WGBH, Alexeyev in MCT, NSK3 177, *Le Monde* 11/24/90, Alexeyev in *Ekho planety,* November 1988. *Times* story and Sergei Khrushchev denial: NYT 1/29/89, 1/30/89, Garthoff (1989) 92n. NSK to Thompson on danger of American generals: Jane Thompson int. NSK on RFK-Dobrynin meeting: NSK1 497–8. NSK issues message, 10/28/62: Gromyko in MCT. "It reminds me": Ball in HCCT. Ex Comm supposition of possible air strike and Smith, McNamara, Sorensen views of JFK next step: HCCT, CCT, MCT, Sievarts history, Abel 194–5. Broadcast of NSK-JFK 10/28/62 message: NYT 10/29/62, Alexeyev in MCT, Burlatsky, Mikoyan in CCT. Bundy on news of NSK 10/28/62 message: Martin Agronsky interview for NBC-TV, "NBC White Paper," 1964, Schlesinger Papers. RFK and others notified: RFK13 87–8, Abel 204–7. Diplomats watch Giants-Redskins game: Tyler-Kohler 10/31/62, Kohler Papers.

"I feel like a new man": Odon 341. RFK-Dobrynin 10/28/62 meeting: Dobrynin in MCT, RFK13 88. 10/28/62 morning Ex Comm meeting: 10/28/62 memcon, CIA, "The Crisis," 10/28/62, Sievarts history, Hilsman-Rusk 10/28/62, JDKL, Ralph Martin 471. JFK on NSK eating "crow" and going to theater: Ralph Martin 471, RFK13 88, Abel 210. Rusk advice to reporters: Abel oh, Meg Greenfield in NW 10/18/62, Abel 207. RFK on LBJ "inability": RFK 11/15/62 memo, RFK Papers. LBJ to Aynesworth: *Washington Times* 10/26/87. Alexeyev on NSK message: MCT, Alexeyev int WGBH. Khrushchev-Castro, 10/28/62, is in *Le Monde* 11/24/90. Castro anger at NSK message: Risquet in MCT, Alexeyev int WGBH, Castro in *Le Monde* 3/22/63, Castro to George McGovern in NYT 8/15/75, Detzer 260, Bourne 239–41, Szulc 585–7. Cuban exiles upset: NYT 10/29/62, *Miami Herald* 10/29/62, 10/30/62. Soviet press on "American fabrication" and citizens stunned by NSK message: NYT 10/29/62, NW 11/12/62.

JFK departure and return: PA 10/28/62. JFK-NSK 10/28/62 and earlier draft is in JFKL. JFK-Joint Chiefs meeting: McNamara int, Garthoff 58–9. JFK to Schlesinger: Schlesinger journal 10/29/62, noted in AMSRK 524–5, also Schlesinger in HCCT. "We've won a great victory": There are several versions of this comment, including those in Boggs oh and Roberts 217.

19. *"Now We Have Untied Our Hands"*

RFK-Dobrynin 10/29/62 and 10/30/62 meetings: Dobrynin in MCT, AMSRK 523 and RFK notes 10/30/62, RFK Papers. Soviet radio, 10/29/62, on "wise demand": Radio Moscow, 10/29/62, text in JFKL. Rostow warning on Soviets "reraising" Turkey and Guantanamo issues: Rostow-Bundy 10/31/62, JFKL. Joseph Kennedy charge of Roosevelt "secret deal": Beschloss *Kennedy and Roosevelt* 14–6, 213–5. Salinger response on number of NSK-JFK letters: Salinger briefing transcript, 10/29/62, JFKL. Evans on NSK 10/26/62 letter, JFK effort to find leak: Tyler oh, JFK at Ex Comm memcon 11/2/62, Tyler memos 11/2/62, 11/6/62, JFKL. JFK to Ex Comm on dealing with press: Sorensen int JBM. JFK shows NSK correspondence to Lippmann: Lippmann oh. "I would just be putting credit": Bartlett oh and Bartlett int.

JFK background conversations with Bartlett, Sulzberger, Bradlee: Bartlett int, Sulzberger 926–9, Bradlee 122–6. "I cut his balls off": Manchester *Shining* 215. "The country rather enjoyed": Sidey 381. On Zhukov at Andover conference, I have benefited from an unpublished piece kindly provided by my old history teacher Harrison Royce of Phillips Academy. NSK-Zhukov ties: Zhukov memcon

9/15/59, DDEL, Slusser 190–1, Sulzberger 801–5. Zhukov Washington appointments and Rusk comment: Harriman-Reston memcon 10/30/62, Harriman Papers, Sal 280–2. Missile sites dismantled and Soviet crews cooperate: Sievarts history, Ex Comm memcon 11/3/62, Defense Department memo 2/12/63, JFKL. Castro 10/28/62 demands: NYT 10/29/62. "Whoever comes to inspect Cuba": Abel 212. Thant mission to Cuba: Mikoyan in CCT, Thant int JBM, NW 11/12/62, Abel 212–3. "Nikita, Nikita": Abel 213, *Reporter* 12/6/62.

NSK on Castro as "son" and "cannot sleep": Bourne 243. Khrushchev-Castro, 10/30/62, and Castro-Khrushchev, 10/31/62, are in *Le Monde* 11/24/90. Mikoyan to Rusk on Castro: Rusk int. Mikoyan background: Sergo Mikoyan conv, Medveyev *Stalin's Men* 28–60, Bureau of Intelligence and Research profile in Sorensen Papers, Sulzberger 622, 557, Micunovic 265–79, NYT 10/16/64, Eisenhower Diary 1/12/59, Eisenhower memcon 3/26/59, Lodge-NSK memcon 9/18/59, DDEL, Stevenson-Mikoyan memcon 7/31/58, Stevenson Papers. "Anastas and myself": Harriman-NSK 6/23/59 memcon, JFKL. Khrushchev on Mikoyan and Hungary: NSK3 123. Mikoyan to Kuznetsov and Stevenson on Castro opposition to inspections: Rusk to DFR 1/11/63, McCloy notes 10/29/62, McCloy Papers, Garthoff 63–5. Mikoyan mission to Cuba: Mikoyan in CCT, Sergo Mikoyan conv, Rusk to DFR 1/11/63, NW 11/12/62, 11/26/62, T 11/29/62, Sergo Mikoyan in *Latinskaya Amerika*, January 1988, NSK1 500, 504, Garthoff 64–5. Report on Mikoyan pelted with fruit: Sejna 54.

NSK on Mikoyan during Anti-Party Coup: Micunovic 278–9. Sergo Mikoyan enthusiasm for Castro: Sergo Mikoyan conv. Rusk on "Hungarian-type action": Rusk to DFR 1/11/63. Rusk to Ex Comm on no "good contract": 11/6/62 Ex Comm memcon, JFKL. JFK to Sorensen on "easy to get national support": Sorensen into JBM. RFK to JFK on Stevenson: RFK oh, RFK int JBM. Ball on Stevenson attitude to McCloy appointment: Ball int JBM, also Charles Yost int JBM. Schlesinger on McCloy and Dean, 1961: Schlesinger int JBM. Stevenson-Kuznetsov 10/30/62 luncheon and JFK reaction: Stevenson-Rusk 10/30/62, JFKL, Sorensen int JBM, NW 11/12/62, Kuznetsov-Stevenson memcon 10/30/62, Schlesinger-JFK 10/30/62, RFK int JBM, McCloy-Rusk tel note 10/29/62. Kuznetsov urging of U.S. to stay on Cuban periphery and JFK response: WP 10/9/87, Garthoff 62.

McCone on buildup, Thompson on offer to Soviets and JFK on situation: Ex Comm memcons 11/1/62–11/18/62, JFKL. JFK on I1–28 bombers: Ex Comm memcon 10/28/62, JFKL, Garthoff 65–8. Ex Comm on U-2 attack by SAMs on Cuba: Memo for Ex Comm, "Revised course of action in the contingency that a surveillance plane is shot at or destroyed," 11/8/62, JFKL, *Political Science Quarterly,* Fall 1980. JFK instruction that Il-28s should go and Kuznetsov response: Ex Comm memcon 11/2/62, JFKL, McCloy-Kuznetsov 11/5/62, McCloy Papers, Garthoff 68–9. RFK-Dobrynin 11/3/62 meeting: Bromley Smith note, JFKL. McCloy-Kuznetsov 11/4/62 luncheon: memcon, McCloy Papers. RFK-Dobrynin 11/6/62 meeting: AMSRK 526, RFK oh. JFK on "bargains are fudged": JFK-Stevenson and McCloy, 11/3/62, JFKL.

JFK "surprised" at NSK charge: JFK-NSK 11/6/62 and draft, JFKL, Garthoff 69. JFK Boston trip and watches returns: NYT 11/7/62. Gallup on JFK approval: *Gallup* 8/19/62, 12/5/62. Harriman on acclaim being undermined: Harriman-RFK, undated, Harriman Papers. Curtis and Goldwater on crisis and settlement:

NYT 11/6/62, *Journal of American History,* vol. 73, 1986, T.J. Paterson and W.G. Brophy, "October Missiles and November Elections." Cuban exile charges, JFK asks for denials, White House tries to impede purchase of radio time, JFK interrogation order: Ex Comm memcon 11/12/62, JFKL. JFK to McCloy on *Washington Star* allegation: Ex Comm memcon 11/6/62, JFKL. RFK on FBI interviews of steel men: RFK oh. Sullivan and Dillon on FBI interviews: AMSRK 402–7.

LBJ request for Hoover help and Hoover response: C.D. DeLoach-Mr. Mohr 6/28/62, J. Edgar Hoover-Al Rosen 7/3/62, FBI. JFK unsure about public attitude on Il-28s: Ex Comm memcon 11/3/62, JFKL. Silence on bombers: JFKPP 11/2/62. 1962 election results: *Journal of American History,* vol. 73, 1986, NYT 11/8/62. Nixon on "Cuban thing" and JFK "deal": *Los Angeles Times* 11/8/62. Limited importance of Cuban issue in election results and Curtis on issue: *Journal of American History,* vol. 73, 1986. JFK on results and "Wait until 1964": Bartlett int and Harris-JFK 11/19/62, JFKL. Zinchuk message: Bartlett-JFK 11/6/62, JFKL, Bartlett int. JFK-Macmillan 11/14/62 telephone talk: Macmillan *At the End* 215.

Joint Chiefs demand POL and air attack: Maxwell Taylor talking paper 11/16/62, JFKL, Garthoff 71–2. JFK-NSK on submarine base, 11/7/62, is in JFKL. See also 11/5/62, 11/6/62 Ex Comm memcons and Garthoff 75–6. McCloy to Kuznetsov on four regiments and Soviet assurances: Stevenson-Rusk 11/18/62 and Garthoff 77. McCloy-Kuznetsov 11/18/62 luncheon: memcon, JFKL and McCloy Papers, Stevenson-Rusk 11/19/62, Garthoff 72–3. RFK-Bolshakov 11/19/62 meeting: AMSRK 526. JFK suggestion to NATO leaders: Garthoff 73. Exile destruction of Cuban factory: Garthoff 79. Castro warning to Mikoyan and Mikoyan reply: Mikoyan in CCT, Risquet and Aragones in MCT. Castro final decision on planes: Aragones in MCT. RFK-Dobrynin 11/20/62 meeting: Abel 211–2.

NSK-JFK 11/20/62 letter: Ex Comm 11/20/62 memcon, WP 10/9/87. JFK on why Castro gave in: JFKPP 12/17/62. RFK, Bolshakov and JFK press conference: AMSRK 526–7 and JFKPP 11/20/62. Earlier drafts of JFK statement are in Sorensen Papers. JFK ends quarantine and alert: Defense Department memo on Missile Crisis operations 2/12/63, JFKL, Garthoff 73–4. JFK to Macmillan, de Gaulle, Adenauer, 11/20/62, is in JFKL. See also Garthoff 73. JFK-NSK, 11/21/62, is in JFKL. 11/23/62 Ex Comm meeting: memcon, Bundy-JFK 11/22/62, 11/23/62, 11/24/62, JFKL, Sorensen int JBM, 11/23/62 instructions to McCloy, McCloy Papers. Il-28s gone from Cuba: Sievarts history. Kuznetsov plea to delete clause and McCloy response: Stevenson-Rusk 11/25/62, McCloy Papers. December negotiations and conclusion: McCloy-Bundy 11/22/62, Rusk-Stevenson 12/11/62, McCloy-Kuznetsov 12/20/62, McCloy Papers, Stevenson and Kuznetsov to Thant 1/7/63, JFKL, Garthoff 81–3.

Sorensen on JFK attitude to crisis solution: Sorensen oh. Cienfuegos episode: Garthoff 97–106, Kissinger 632–5. NSK on U.S. swallowing "hedgehog": NSK2 512. Gromyko on world "better off" and Arbatov on "humiliation": MCT. "You Americans": Bohlen 495–6. Moynihan on Missile Crisis "defeat": *Playboy,* March 1977. Will on JFK failure: NW 10/11/82, also in WP 9/3/87. JFK dilutes assurances: JFK-NSK 10/27/62 and 11/20/62 drafts, JFKL. Joint Chiefs on hedging assurances and invasion possibility: Joint Chiefs-JFK 11/16/62, and Ex Comm memcon, JFKL. Bundy defense of JFK failure to broaden quarantine: Bundy 408. Rusk-McCloy, 12/11/62, is in JFKL.

State Department acceptance of MiG-23s in Cuba: Garthoff 103–4. On "Gettysburg": Sor 724. Rovere on "personal diplomatic victory": quoted in *New Republic* 12/1/62. *Newsweek* on JFK in crisis: NW 11/12/62. Sokolsky on end of " 'soft' period": *Miami Herald* 11/1/62. JFK poll ratings, December 1962: *Gallup* 12/5/62. "All of us at this table": Bradlee 119–78. Bartlett-Alsop article: SEP 12/8/62. On the entire flap, see Bartlow Martin *Stevenson* 741–8, Stevenson-Schlesinger memo, January 1963, undated, JFKL, Acheson int JBM, RFK int JBM, Schlesinger int JBM, Bundy int JBM, Roberts 207–9. "Did not discuss the Cuban crisis": JFK-Stevenson 12/5/62, JFKL. JFK to Bartlett on Stevenson suggestion and request to help Sorensen: Bartlett oh and Bartlett int, Stewart Alsop-Schlesinger 8/25/65, Schlesinger Papers.

Harwood in *Washington Post:* WP 8/29/87. Bartlett on research for article: Bartlett oh, Bartlett int, Bartlett int JBM. Pierpoint, Ball speculations: Pierpoint conv, Ball int JBM, NYT 12/12/62. Stevenson at Joseph P. Kennedy, Jr., Foundation dinner: JFKPP 12/6/62, and author's viewing of film of event in National Archives. "Through the motions, making speeches": Ball int JBM. JFK to Ormsby-Gore on new need for disarmament: AMSRK 530. Zhukov-Harriman conversation: 10/31/62 memcon, Harriman Papers. Rostow to Bundy on Soviet future plans: Bundy-JFK 11/17/62, JFKL. Dean-Kuznetsov 10/30/62 meeting: Seaborg *Kennedy* 179–80. Mikoyan-JFK meeting and Bundy comment: Bundy-JFK 12/7/62, Rusk-JFK 11/29/62, JFKL, Sievarts history, NYT 11/30/62, Garthoff 81, Rostow oh. Chinese on "adventurism": Abel 213, Linden 155.

NSK retort: Prav 12/13/62, Burlatsky int WGBH. Hilsman-Ball analysis 12/13/62 is in Hilsman Papers. Possible military boycott: Garthoff (1989) 48. JFK admires text: AMSTD draft, citing Schlesinger journal 12/25/62. "We have come to the final stage": JFK-NSK 12/14/62, JFKL. NSK-JFK, 12/19/62, and JFK reaction: letter in JFKL, Bromley Smith-Bundy 12/20/62, JFKL, Seaborg *Kennedy* 178–82. Dean denial and reputation: Seaborg *Kennedy* 175–81. JFK at Orange Bowl: JFKPP 12/29/62, *Miami Herald* 12/30/62, Collier and Horowitz *Kennedys* 300–1, Odon 276–7. "Never has a President": NW 1/14/63. Brigade demands flag return: NYT 3/12/75. RFK efforts to free prisoners: Clay oh, RFK oh, USN 1/7/63, NW 4/30/62, 1/14/63, AMSRK 468–9, Carbonell 184–91, Navasky 327–46, Thompson 57–8.

"Very substantial sum" from Factor: Raskin int and unpublished ms. "What about Hoffa?": AMSRK 537. NSK to JFK, 12/31/62, is in JFKL. Dobrynin on chances for better relations: Cousins 68–73.

20. *"The Peace Speech"*

JFK to NSC: Hilsman notes, 1/22/63, Hilsman Papers. JFK in background session: USN 1/14/63, 1/21/63. "Things are not as bad": Odon 350–1. "We are for the moment": Schlesinger-Sorensen 1/2/63, Schlesinger Papers. NSK-JFK, 1/9/63, is in JFKL. CIA on Soviet official's message: CIA memos, 1/16/63 and 1/31/63, JFKL. JFK decisions on testing and on six inspections as "rock-bottom": AMSTD 181, 895–7, Seaborg *Kennedy* 185–92. JFK to Rusk and McNamara on testing: 2/8/63 memcon, JFKL. Foster to Kuznetsov on seven inspections: Seaborg *Kennedy* 189. "I was considerably handicapped" and Rusk reply: Kohler-Rusk 1/22/63 and Rusk-Kohler 1/23/63. Kohler background and personality: Kohler int, Kohler, NYT 10/21/64, Koh oh, Davies int, Jane Thompson int. "Sitting on our Nuclear Target" and Kohler-Bedell Smith exchange: Kohler int.

Kohlers first meet JFK and Kohler reappointment by JFK: Kohler int. "Bobby would sit there": Kohler int. Kohler on NSK and Stalin: Kohler int and Kohler 128–31. "I don't make such mistakes": NYT 10/21/64. Kohler farewell talk with JFK: Kohler int. "It was standard" and CIA briefing: Kohler int. "Entirely different Soviet Union" and Soviet servants: Kohler int. Foiled Soviet recruitment effort: U.S. Army Moscow-State 1/19/62, JFKL, Kohler int. Request of Chinese for conciliatory meeting: Prav 2/14/62, 3/14/63, Tatu 319–24.

February Soviet coolness and Kohler on no testing progress: Kohler-Rusk 1/27/63, 3/13/63, 3/16/63, JFKL, Tatu 310–9. "We shall always be friends": NYT 2/10/62, Tatu 319–24. Campaign against Soviet artists: Priscilla Johnson 101–339. December NSK meeting with artists: Prav 12/22/62, Davies-Rusk 1/1/63, JFKL, Linden 159–61. CIA report on meeting and Bundy reaction: Bundy-JFK, January 1963, JFKL. Helms request for planted article and JFK approval: Helms-Chester Clifton 1/4/63, Clifton memo 1/17/63, Helms int. Process of "Khrushchev's surrender": Tatu 298–314. Kohler on NSK "listless" speech: Kohler-Rusk 2/27/63, 2/28/63, JFKL. Gallup on Cuba: *Gallup* 3/22/63. Bush on JFK and Cuba: *Boston Globe* 6/12/88. Cuban troop issue reemerges: Bundy in *Massachusetts Historical Society,* vol. 90, 1978, NYkr 3/2/63, 5/4/63, USN 2/18/63. JFK asks McCone for inspection and reply: McCone-Hilsman tel note 2/4/63, Hilsman Papers, JFK memo 2/4/63, JFKL.

Eisenhower on Soviet "intent on making Cuba": Eisenhower-McCone, November 1962, DDEL. Forty-two thousand Soviets actually on Cuba and Bundy view: MCT and NYT 10/23/79. "Are you just": JFKPP 2/7/63. JFK to Bradlee and White on Soviets on Cuba: Bradlee 131–3, White notes, 2/13/63, Schlesinger Papers. Bundy on Soviet forces in Cuba: NYT 10/23/79. CIA on "Castro adventurism": CIA 4/22/63 estimate, JFKL. RFK on Russians running SAM sites: RFK oh. Concern expressed to Dobrynin and Dobrynin reply: NYT 2/11/63, RFK oh. JFK March announcement on Soviet departure: JFKPP 3/21/63. Baldwin in *Times,* JFK reaction and Elder report: NYT 4/20/63, Elder-Bundy, April 1963, JFKL. Nixon to editors and Rovere on Cuba: NYkr 5/4/63. NSK further internal problems: T 5/3/63, USN 4/1/63 and 5/6/63, Hyland and Shryock 67–97, Tatu 298–351, Linden 146–59.

Kozlov background and personality: K.B.A. Scott minute 3/5/59, FO, Livingston Merchant-Kozlov memcon 7/3/59, Eisenhower-Kozlov memcon 7/1/59, 1959 CIA profile, DDEL, Hyland and Shryock 70–3. "Homeless waif" and "Despite his white hair": Harriman-NSK memcon 6/23/59, JFKL. Kozlov was present during this meeting. Thompson on Kozlov as "front man": Thompson-Herter 7/17/59, DDEL. RFK-Dobrynin 4/3/63 meeting: RFK oh, AMSRK 597–8. RFK calls Kremlin in "rage": Jacqueline Kennedy, quoted in Bradlee 193–4. "This really was the end": RFK oh. NSK-JFK and JFK-NSK April letters are dated 4/3/63, 4/11/63, JFKL. "I don't see any reason": Sulzberger 978. April Soviet political events and Kozlov seizure: Prav 4/10/63, Tatu 341–9. Moscow rumor of NSK-Kozlov violent argument: Tatu 341, Hyland and Shryock 80. NSK and genocide in Ukraine and Poland: Crankshaw 96–147. NSK on possibly causing Stalin's death: Jane Thompson int.

NSK and Beria murder, Hungary: Medvedev *Khrushchev* 62–8, Crankshaw 186–90, 241–3, NSK1 334–41. Brezhnev 1963 promotion and Western uncertainty about Brezhnev and Podgorny status: Tatu 349–51. "Oh, he's a very sick man!": Tatu 348. NSK-Cousins 4/12/63 meeting: Cousins 95–110. JFK-Cousins 4/22/63 meeting: Cousins 111–20. "I do think it is getting": Bundy-JFK September 1962, JFKL. McNamara on Jupiters removal: CCT. Harriman background and JFK-Harriman history: Isaacson and Thomas 40–6, 601–9, 616–9, Halberstam *Best* 191–9, NSK2 350–2, Philip Kaiser conv, Dorothy Schiff int. "Now we shall win the war!": Isaacson and Thomas 213. "Averell is right": Isaacson and Thomas 249. Harriman-Thompson on 1959 Soviet trip, 12/1/58, and Thompson reply, 12/16/58, are in Thompson Papers.

"There won't be the same vindictive": Harriman-Galbraith 1/25/60, Harriman Papers. "It's just shocking": Salisbury *Journey* 243. "Yours was a great victory": Harriman-JFK 11/12/60, JFKL. JFK 1960 attitude to Harriman: RFK oh, Isaacson and Thomas 603–4, Halberstam 73–5. Sorensen to Burns on Harriman appointment, is in Burns file, Sorensen Papers. "Are you sure that giving Averell": AMSTD 149. RFK to Harriman on home number, 1/10/61, is in Harriman Papers. "I am not yet in the inner circle": Sulzberger 753. "Damn, I was hoping": Isaacson and Thomas 619. "Release me to work": Harriman-NSK 11/14/61, Harriman Papers. "I seem to be thriving": Harriman-Beaverbrook 11/21/62, Beaverbrook Papers. Jacqueline Kennedy letter: 3/15/63, Harriman Papers. Harriman on State as "dead, dead, dead": Schlesinger journal 4/14/63, cited in AMSTD draft. Eunice intervention before Vienna: Halberstam *Best* 75. Harriman during Berlin and Missile crises: AMSTD 383, Sor 589, Isaacson and Thomas 627–9.

JFK-NSK on Harriman, 4/23/63, is in JFKL. Dobrynin on U.S. and Chiang forces in Laos and JFK reply: 1/4/63 Dobrynin memcon, 1/23/63 draft reply, 1/10/63, Dobrynin-Kuznetsov-Harriman memcon, Harriman Papers. NSK-Harriman 4/26/63 meeting: memcon, Harriman Papers. Bolshakov-RFK, 5/10/63, is in RFK Papers. Winter and spring 1963 attacks against Cuba: Summers *Conspiracy* 325, 424–5, AMSRK 539–45, NYT 4/21/63, Garthoff 90–3. Soviet complaint: Soviet Foreign Ministry to U.S. Embassy Moscow, 3/27/63, 3/29/63, JFKL. Rusk on raids and Soviet relations: Rusk-JFK 3/28/63, JFKL. U.S. statement: AMSRK 540, *Assassination Report*, vol. V, 11–3. Rockefeller reaction: NYkr 5/4/63. Standing Group and "accommodation": AMSRK 538, *Assassination Plots* 173. Castro on "U.S. limitations on exile raids": AMSRK 542.

Castro visit to Soviet Union: NSK1 504–5, NSK2 511, NSK3 181–3, Szulc 589–91, USN 5/13/63. Castro provided with blonde and not told of Turkey concession: Geyer 294, NSK3 182. CIA April prediction on Soviets in Cuba: 4/22/63 estimate, JFKL. JFK on keeping "pressure on Castro": Ex Comm memcon 11/29/62, JFKL. Sabotage, early 1963: Prados *Secret Wars* 215–7, *Assassination Plots* 172. JFK approves new sabotage program, June 1963: AMSRK 543, *Assassination Plots* 172–3, 337. JFK-Macmillan to NSK on testing, 4/15/63, is in JFKL. NSK-JFK, 5/8/63, is in JFKL. Dobrynin to Wiesner and Bowles on NSK flexibility: Thompson oh, Bowles oh, Wiesner-Dobrynin 5/16/63 memcon, JFKL, Cohen 162. NSK and special envoys and Rusk: JFK-NSK 5/13/63, NSK-JFK 5/15/63,

JFKL. Fomin-Scali February 1963 talk: Scali-Robert Manning tel note 2/19/63, JFKL.

NSK-JFK, 4/29/63 and 5/8/63, and JFK reply, 5/13/63, are in JFKL. Cousins urges peace offer and Sorensen asks for ideas: Cousins 122–4, Sor 730, AMSTD 900. JFK decides on major peace address: Bundy in *Massachusetts Historical Society,* vol. 90, 1978, NYkr 6/22/63, AMSTD 900. Bundy and Sorensen prepare speech: Sorensen oh COHP, Sor 730–1, Kaysen interview with Schlesinger 8/6/64, Schlesinger Papers. JFK-LBJ-Connally 6/5/63 meeting, El Paso: Reston 237–41, Odon 356. JFK on "the Peace Speech": Odon 357. Clearance process: Thompson oh, Salinger (Honolulu)-Kaysen (White House) with JFK text for Kaysen clearance, 1:55 A.M., E.S.T., 6/9/63, AMSTD 900, Sor 731. NSK to JFK and Macmillan, 6/8/63, is in JFKL. JFK return to Washington and address "of major importance": Sor 731. American University address: JFKPP 6/10/63 and drafts in JFKL.

Eisenhower on arms race: DDEPP 4/16/53. Chinese mission to Moscow: George Denney-Rusk 7/25/63, Gordon Chang in *Journal of American History,* "JFK, China and the Bomb," March 1988. White House mail on speech and JFK reaction: AMSTD 910. Soviet public learns of and reacts to speech: Kohler-Rusk 6/11/63, Sor 733, Seaborg *Kennedy* 218, Barnet *Giants* 24–5. NSK to Wilson and "best speech by any President": NYT 6/11/63, Sor 733. RFK reads intelligence reports: RFK oh. Falin on speech: Falin int WGBH. Trevelyan on speech: Trevelyan oh. McCloy refuses appointment for testing negotiations: Isaacson and Thomas 630. Rusk nominates Harriman, Ball criticizes and JFK overrules: Kaysen-Schlesinger interview in Schlesinger Papers, AMSTD 902–3, AMSTD draft. "We now propose" and "because of his tested": Rusk-Kohler 6/8/63 and Rusk-Bohlen 6/14/63, JFKL.

"As soon as I heard": AMSTD 903. "Hot line" achieved and background: Davies oh, Davies int, *Business Week* 4/13/63, 6/29/63, *Defense Nationale* (Paris) July–December 1983, "Le Teletype Rouge," NW 12/24/62, NYT 6/21/63, USN 7/1/63, Sor 724–6, Sulzberger 980, Salisbury *Without Fear* 54. "Bend every effort": JFKPP 6/20/63.

21. The Spirit of Moscow

Origins and announcement of JFK European trip: USN 6/10/63, Seaborg *Kennedy* 224, Odon 338, AMSTD 881–4, 887, Rovere 160–2. Negotiations on de Gaulle U.S. trip: JFK-Bohlen 6/14/63, Bundy-Tyler 6/14/63, Bohlen-Rusk 6/15/63, 6/19/63, JFK-Bohlen 7/10/63, 11/4/63, JFKL. JFK reminiscence during flight to Bonn: Michaelis 155–6, Ralph Martin 488, Cologne reception: NYT 6/24/63, Tyler oh. "Don't tell me these families": Tyler oh. Ford advertisement in Wiesbaden: NYkr 7/13/63. "Fresh views and instructions": Kohler-Truman Landon 5/4/63, Kohler Papers. Kohler sees JFK and Phyllis Kohler reaction: Kohler int, NW 7/15/63, NYT 6/21/63. Clay on JFK Berlin visit: Clay oh.

JFK at City Hall: JFKPP 6/26/63, NYT 6/27/63, Manchester *Shining* 207–8, The current author has also viewed film of the speech in National Archives. Adenauer to Rusk on "another Hitler": Gelb 226. Genesis of *"Ich bin"*: Bundy int. NYkr 7/13/63, Odon 361, Bradlee 95–6, Bundy 390, 683, Ralph Martin 489, Wyden *Wall* 282–3. "Never underestimate the psychological": Wessel int. JFK next speech was at Free University of Berlin: JFK 6/23/63, Kraft 167. JFK on envelope and to Sorensen: JFKPP 6/23/63, Sor 601. Bundy to JFK on poll, 6/19/63, is in JFKL. Bundy and O'Donnell on Ireland trip and JFK reply: Odon 358–9. JFK in Ireland: Odon 361–71. JFK trip to Chatsworth and Birch Grove: Odon 361, 371, Horne 512–8. Profumo-Keeler scandal: "BOWTIE" files, FBI, Knightley and Kennedy, Summers and Dorril.

Ivanov on scandal, 1989: WP 5/19/89. Bruce on Macmillan possible replacement: Bruce-Rusk 6/19/63, JFKL. Cancellation demanded and JFK staff reduces visibility of visit: Knightley and Kennedy 196–207. Macmillan on JFK "snub": Horne 512. JFK on "Profumo thing": Heckscher oh, and Charles Heckscher memo, 6/19/63, Schlesinger Papers. Bruce on "current gossip": Bruce-JFK 6/21/63, JFKL. JFK to O'Donnell and Powers in Brighton: Odon 372. JFK in Italy, request of Rusk and Rusk recollection: Odon 372–4, AMSTD 887–8, Schoenbaum 282. RFK sees Horan and Frasca: C.A. Evans-J. Edgar Hoover 7/3/63, FBI. RFK request of Hoover on Keeler and Rice-Davies and response: C.W. Gates-J. Edgar Hoover 6/29/63, W. Branigan-W.C. Sullivan 7/23/63, Evans-Belmont 7/24/63, FBI, Knightley and Kennedy 202–7.

Alphand on JFK "desires": Ralph Martin 342. Campbell-Giancana-JFK triangle: Exner 63–299, Exner in *People* 2/29/88, Kelley *His Way* 293–4. Dejean episode: Davies int, Kohler int, de Laboulaye conv, Barron 170–92. Watkins and Tory politician episodes: Barron 243–4, David Martin 166–7, Ladislav Bittmann in Oversight Subcommittee of House Intelligence Committee hearings, 2/19/80. Secret Service agent on "broad": Lasky *Watergate* 17. "Not his chaperone": Rusk int. Thompson to JFK on Marines and "Jesus, Tommy!": Jane Thompson int. Arvad episode: Waldrop int, Inga Arvad Fejos file, FBI, Blairs 129–52, Kearns Goodwin 630–5, Parmet *Jack* 88–94, Theoharis and Cox 334–5. "Damned dirty Jews": 6/24/42 summary, Arvad file, FBI. FBI on 2/6/42 JFK-Arvad encounter, Arvad on Hitler, "I've returned," "Don't you people": 6/24/42 summary and Arvad file, FBI. "Heading for Reno": JFK to Billings: 3/11/42, July 1942. Hoover to aide on PT-109 and keeps JFK file: Wofford 215n. Charles Colson on FBI and JFK-Arvad affair: NBC-TV, "Today," 2/7/75, noted in 2/14/75 FBI memo, FBI.

"You can't fire Hoover": This was said to Timothy Seldes, then of Doubleday, who was working on publication of Truman's memoirs. Kennedy handling of possible embarrassment by women: JFK FBI file, FBI, NYT 12/17/77, Ralph Martin 163. JFK notes on *Caroline:* WP 5/29/87. "The first man to have sex": Prospectus for "The Politicians, the Gangsters and the Stars" by Patricia Lawford and Ted Schwarz. "They can't touch me": Ralph Martin 312. "We were so hard up": *London Daily Mirror* 10/25/63. Rometsch episode: RFK oh, Rometsch file, FBI, Evans-Belmont 10/21/63, 10/25/63, 10/28/63, J. Edgar Hoover-Clyde Tolson 10/28/63, 11/7/63, FBI, NYT 10/29/63, 12/1/64, 12/9/64, WS 10/28/63, 10/29/63, 12/1/64, 12/4/64, 12/5/64, 12/9/64, WP 12/3/64, 12/10/64, *New York Post* 10/29/63, *Des Moines Register* 10/30/63, 10/31/63, Bradlee 227–9, Branch 911–4, Bobby Baker 77–80. Rometsch expulsion reported: Clark Mollenhoff in *Des Moines Register* 10/26/63. JFK to Bradlee on Rometsch and Baker: Bradlee 231–5. "I spoke to the President": RFK oh.

NSK in East Berlin: Prav 7/3/63, NYT 7/3/63. Thompson's advice on speech: Thompson oh, Jane Thompson int. Kaysen to Brandt, 7/5/63, is in Harriman Papers. Mikoyan at Spaso House, 7/4/63: NW 7/15/63, NYT 7/5/63. NSK insults Chinese: Chang in *Journal of American History*, March 1988, NYT 7/4/63,

USN 7/22/63. NSK-Spaak meeting: Harriman-Embassy Brussels 7/13/63, Harriman Papers, Seaborg *Kennedy* 230. Macmillan to JFK, 7/4/63, is in JFKL. On Limited Test Ban generally, see videotape of Kennedy Library conference on the subject, 1988. JFK instructions to Harriman: Thompson oh, Kaysen-Harriman 7/5/63, Harriman Papers, 7/18/63 JFK memcon, JFKL. Advisers to JFK before Vienna: State to JFK 5/25/61–5/26/61, JFKL. JFK to Malraux and aides on nuclear China: Tyler oh. Test ban chances of stopping nuclear China: Chang 237–8, 243.

"Secret undertaking," Thompson suggestion: JFK-Harriman 7/15/63, Harriman Papers, Chang 242–5, Chang in *Journal of American History,* March 1988. Proposals for "radical steps," explosives on Lop Nor, industrial sabotage: Chang in *Journal of American History,* March 1988. "We have both a national interest": Rostow-JFK 7/8/63, JFKL, also Rusk memo 7/5/63, Rusk-Harriman 7/2/63, Harriman Papers. Thompson on NSK discussion of China: Thompson oh. JFK instruction to Harriman and reply: Chiang in *Journal of American History,* March 1988, AMSTD draft. History of MLF: Bundy int, Seaborg *Stemming* 83–94, Herken 174–5, Bundy 503–4. Harriman on "goodies in my luggage": AMSTD 903, AMSTD draft. Macmillan presses for summit: Seaborg *Kennedy* 258. Harriman on "two weeks": Seaborg *Kennedy* 251. Gromyko heads Soviet delegation and NSK-Harriman 7/15/63 meeting: Seaborg *Kennedy* 238. JFK-NSK, 7/15/63, is in Harriman Papers. Macmillan original desire for Ormsby-Gore, Harriman and Hailsham on each other: AMSTD draft, AMSTD 905.

Zinchuk on nonaggression pact: Bartlett int. JFK tight strings on Harriman delegation: Benjamin Read oh, Sorensen int JBM, Schlesinger interview with Adrian Fisher 4/2/65, Schlesinger Papers. "You are right to keep French": JFK-Harriman 7/15/63, Harriman Papers. Harriman on 1943 talks: NW 7/29/63. Debate on nuclear weapons in self-defense, withdrawal clause, nonaggression pact, unrecognized signatories: AMSTD 906–7, John McNaughton contingency paper 7/20/63, Harriman Papers, JFK memcon 7/18/63, 7/23/63, JFKL, Thompson oh, Seaborg *Kennedy* 249–50. Moscow-London-Washington 7/25/63 exchanges on treaty conclusion: Harriman, "Personal notes on meeting with Gromyko," 7/25/63, Harriman Papers. "Prayed hard for this" and "I found myself unable": 7/27/63 cable and Diary in Horne 522. "Did you see his 'H?' ": Seaborg *Kennedy* 256.

NSK-Harriman at Kadar reception: Harriman memcon 7/20/63, Harriman Papers. NSK and Harriman at track meet: Harriman-DFR 7/29/63. NSK-Harriman meeting after treaty initialling: 7/26/63 memcon, Harriman papers, Roberts 218–9. State official on Harriman China proposal: John de Martino-Benjamin Read 10/2/64, Harriman Papers. NSK-Harriman at dinner: 7/26/63 memcon, Harriman Papers. "Mr. Harriman showed himself": NSK-JFK 7/26/63, JFKL. "A state of euphoria": Ormsby-Gore–JFK 8/2/63, JFKL. "I am damn glad": Schlesinger-Harriman 7/28/63, Harriman Papers. *Bulletin of the Atomic Scientists* moves hands: Seaborg *Kennedy* 285–6. Chinese stalk home from Moscow: Thomas Hughes-Ball 8/21/63, JFKL. "It is becoming crystal": Harriman-Rusk 7/23/63, Harriman Papers. "De Gaulle has said that he wanted his own": Seaborg *Kennedy* 999.

"I must say frankly" and JFK efforts to entice de Gaulle: JFK memcon 7/22/63, 7/23/63, JFK-de Gaulle draft 7/3/63, JFK-de Gaulle 7/24/63, Bohlen-Bundy

8/6/63, JFKL. "We have always hoped to have": JFK-de Gaulle 7/24/63, JFKL. Report on de Gaulle performance: David Klein-Bundy 7/30/63, JFKL. Ormsby-Gore to Macmillan on Dejean: Bundy-JFK, July 1963, JFKL. "It is rather like people": AMSTD 914. JFK reaction and on de Gaulle refusal: JFK-Macmillan, undated, and AMSTD 914. JFK television speech on test ban: JFKPP 7/26/63 and NYT 7/27/63. JFK sees Harriman at Hyannis Port: AMSTD draft, tape of Bundy-JFK telephone call 7/25/63, JFKL. JFK-Truman conversation: tape, 7/24/63, 7/26/63, JFKL.

Truman sends quibbles and JFK reply: JFK-Truman 7/26/63, 7/30/63, Truman-JFK 8/16/63, JFKL. Rusk-McCone-Eisenhower meeting: 7/24/63 memcon, DDEL. Strauss to Eisenhower on test ban, 2/21/63, is in DDEL. Eisenhower reply is 3/16/63, DDEL. JFK abandons Moscow signing: Seaborg *Kennedy* 258. JFK recruits senators for Moscow signing: Aiken oh, JFK-Dutton tape 7/30/63, JFK-Rusk tape 7/30/63, JFKL. "Adlai wanted to go" and Stevenson reminds: Sorensen int JBM. "If U Thant goes, then Adlai can go": Tape, 7/30/63, JFKL. Steinbeck to Stevenson: Bartlow Martin *Stevenson* 770. Rusk-Gromyko 8/5/63 meeting: Rusk-Ball 8/5/63, JFKL, Seaborg *Kennedy* 260–1. NSK and American delegation 8/5/63 meeting: Rusk-Ball 8/6/63, 8/7/63, JFKL. NSK-Stevenson exchange: Bartlow Martin *Stevenson* 769.

Treaty signing ceremony and Seaborg diary entry: NYT 8/6/63, Seaborg *Kennedy* 260–1. NSK on "Spirit of Moscow": Kohler int. NSK and Rusk on nonaggression pact: AMSTD 917–8. Rusk-Gromyko exchange: Rusk-Ball 8/6/63, 8/7/63, JFKL. American delegation to Pitsunda: Jane Thompson int, Kohler int, Davies int, Rusk int, Rusk-Ball 8/9/63, JFKL. NSK to Rusk on Patrick Kennedy: NYT 8/12/63. "He never wanted them all": Jacqueline Kennedy-Schlesinger, undated, Schlesinger Papers. "The burdens of public affairs": Macmillan-JFK, 8/14/63, JFKL. McNamara persuades Joint Chiefs: JFK memcon 7/18/63, JFKL, Chang in *Journal of American History,* March 1988, USN 8/5/63, Trewhitt 252–3. JFK on Senate obstruction, Congress mail and forfeiting reelection: Sorensen oh, Cousins 128–35, Sor 737–40, Seaborg *Kennedy* 263–5.

"The category that leads the list again this week": Cousins 129. McNamara to Foreign Relations: Seaborg *Kennedy* 266 and Chang in *Journal of American History,* March 1988. JFK arguments to Senate: JFK-Mansfield 8/12/63 tape, JFKL. JFK fury about McCone lobbying: Halberstam *Best* 153–4, Herken 182. RFK on McCone reminders and as Trojan Horse: RFK oh, Hilsman oh, SEP 7/27/63. "I'm so tired": Thomas Powers 162. "It was ironic": Helms int. Teller and later testimony: NYT 8/21/63, Seaborg *Kennedy* 271–5. Fulbright-JFK on Teller: 8/23/63 tape, JFKL. Dean on renegotiation: Seaborg *Kennedy* 274–5. Hickenlooper demand and Rusk, Smathers responses: DFR 8/28/63. Russell on treaty: Earl Leonard oh in Russell Papers. Bundy on failure to use LBJ: Bundy in *Massachusetts Historical Society,* vol. 90, 1978. Foreign Relations approves and Goldwater opposition: Seaborg *Kennedy* 281, NYT 9/25/63, 9/28/63. "There are no commitments": JFKPP 9/12/63.

Goldfine case pursued and dropped: Caplin conv, William Hundley oh, AMSRK 385–6. Caplin aides recommendation: Caplin conv. Eisenhower-Dirksen exchanges: Eisenhower-Dirksen 1/16/62, 2/5/62, 2/21/62, 5/11/62, Dirksen-Eisenhower 1/10/62, 2/16/62, DDEL. Dutton on Dirksen "backed and filled": Dutton-Rusk 9/7/63, JFKL. Smathers recalls JFK on Dirksen: Smathers oh. Baker account of JFK-Dirksen talk: Bobby Baker 97–9. "My mind is made up": U.S. Congress *Memorial Addresses* 7. Seaborg on Dirksen influence: Seaborg *Kennedy* 279–80. Eisenhower support for treaty: NYT 8/27/63. Eisenhower complaint about JFK Justice and IRS: Eisenhower-LBJ memcon 11/23/63, DDEL. Senate test ban passage and Sorensen on JFK reaction: NYT 9/25/63, Sor 740. JFK motive for Western tour: Edward Cliff oh, Douglas oh, Odon 379, Bradlee 212–4. JFK in Montana and at Salt Lake City: JFKPP 9/25/63–9/26/63.

Salinger on "peace issue": Halberstam *Best* 295–7. JFK on Soviet trip: Brandon 200. Limited effect of test ban: Bundy 460–1, Seaborg *Kennedy* 285–301. Macmillan on JFK "weakness": Horne 525. Attwood effort for Cuba rapprochement: Attwood oh, Attwood conv, RFK oh, Helms int, Attwood in *Virginia Quarterly Review,* Autumn 1983, Attwood 257–60, Szulc 588–9, Bundy in *Massachusetts Historical Society,* vol. 90, 1978. Rusk to NSK on Soviet presence in Cuba: Rusk int. "A spirit of resistance": *Assassination Plots* 177–82, 337. Denney proposal: Denney-Crimmins 7/25/63, JFKL. "There were ten or twenty thousand": RFK oh. Bundy on "after-action report": Bundy-JFK 10/11/63, JFKL. CIA on Castro death: *Assassination Plots* 172. FitzGerald on seashell explosive: AMSRK 485, *Assassination Plots* 85–6. Cubela background and contact of CIA: AMSRK 546–7, Summers *Conspiracy* 321–4. Castro at Brazilian Embassy and CIA reaction: *Baltimore Sun* 9/9/63. Chase on Castro at Brazilian Embassy: Chase-Bundy 9/10/63, JFKL.

22. Fragile Opportunities

JFK worry about not getting himself across: RFK oh. Burns on JFK in 1959: Burns conv, Burns oh. Buckley on JFK "slickness": *National Review* 8/13/63. JFK poll ratings drop: Louis Harris–JFK 9/3/63, JFKL, *Gallup* 3/27/63, 5/19/63, 7/7/63, 8/25/63, 9/20/63, 11/10/63, USN 7/8/63, "Is Kennedy in Political Trouble at Home?" JFK expectation of Rockefeller in 1964: Sor 184, 614, Bradlee 121. JFK to White on Rockefeller: White notes 2/13/63, Schlesinger Papers. JFK on Romney: Harris-JFK 11/19/62, JFKL, Bartlett int, Bartlett oh, RFK oh, Bradlee 195, Fay 259. JFK on Goldwater: Bartlett int, RFK oh, Odon 13, Fay 259. JFK expectations for second term: RFK oh, Rostow oh, AMSTD 921–2. Rusk-JFK on 1963 possible resignation: Rusk int.

"But then if I don't have McNamara": Galbraith *A Life* 406. Harriman, Bundy prospects for State: RFK oh, T 3/15/63. RFK prospect for State and Presidency: Bartlett int, Bartlett oh, Billings oh, Douglas 308, Bradlee 146, Ralph Martin 565. Graham to JFK on McNamara, undated, 1962, is in JFKL. JFK arranges Benjamin Smith appointment: Burns conv, Odon 243–4. RFK on McNamara in 1968: RFK oh. O'Donnell on McNamara: Vanocur int. Failed Soviet harvest and wheat deal: RFK oh, Thompson oh, Freeman in Thompson 169–71, Odon 381–2, Sor 741–3, 753, AMSTD 920, 1018, Linden 187–91. Gallup on wheat sale: *Gallup* 10/25/63. Rusk-Gromyko 10/2/63 meeting: memcon, JFKL, USN 10/7/63.

NSK in East Berlin, January 1963: NYT 1/17/63, Slusser 469. Komer on Berlin deal: 10/29/62 memo, JFKL. Berlin problem resumes, fall 1963: McCloy memo on FRG trip, October 1963, McCloy Papers, T 10/18/63, Bundy-JFK 11/9/63. Gromyko-JFK 10/10/63 meeting: 10/10/63 memcon, JFKL, Andrei Gromyko 181–2, NYT 8/27/63. Ben-Gurion on Dimona: Weissman and Krosney 111. JFK and Israel: Bundy int, Bundy-JFK 8/16/63, 9/26/63, AMSTD 566–7, Sor 558, Bundy 509–10, Parmet *JFK* 225–35. JFK to White on Jews and Negroes: White notes 6/27/60, Schlesinger Papers. JFK to Spivak: Spivak conv. JFK on Jewish contributors: Bradlee 200. Jerusalem on nuclear weapons, 1962: Spector 122. Feldman negotiates pact and Washington on Hawk transfer: Bundy int, Bundy 510–1, *Journal of American History*, vol. 73, 1986. "What we know at this moment": Bundy-JFK 3/23/63, JFKL. JFK irritation, October 1963: Bundy int. "My recollection": Bundy 510. Gromyko on JFK on American Jews: Andrei Gromyko 181–2.

JFK and Vietnam, general 1962–1963: Rust 60–182, Colby 82–171, Karnow 247–348, Hammer 103–320. "We are embarked": 1/18/62 NSC memcon, JFKL. Rusk on Vietnam: Rusk to DFR, 3/9/62. Galbraith on Southeast Asia: Galbraith-JFK 4/4/62, Harriman Papers. JFK on seizing "favorable moment": Rust 73. Diem refusal to sign and turnaround: Rust 75–6. "Before the ink was dry": Rust 77. "A slowly escalating stalemate": CIA Current Intelligence Memorandum 1/11/63, JFKL. Wheeler report and CIA proposal: Rust 85–6. "Encounter all the difficulties": Bundy-JFK 1/12/63, JFKL. Rusk on JFK and Laos accord failure: Rust 88. Rusk-McNamara June proposal and JFK response: Rusk-JFK 6/17/63, JFKL, Rust 89–90.

Diem background: Rust 3–7. Carver on 1960 coup: Rust xvii, 1, 8–20. Rusk and JFK worry about Buddhists and Catholics: Rust 94–107. JFK to aides on Lodge: Odon 16. Nhu on test ban: Rust 106. Failed August 1963 coup attempt: Hilsman 482–98, Hammer 166–98, Rust 108–30, Colby 128–58. 8/28/63 NSC meeting: memcon, JFKL. "My God, my government's": Bartlett oh, Bartlett int. RFK on JFK policy toward Diem: RFK oh. Taylor cable and JFK, Lodge response: Taylor-Harkins 8/28/63, JFKL, Rust 123–4. "I know that failure": JFK-Lodge 8/29/63, JFKL. LBJ at NSC meeting: Rust 129.

Forrestal on RFK, September 1963: Rust 132. Krulak, Mendenhall reports and JFK response: Rust 134–9. McNamara-Diem September 1963 meeting: 9/29/63 memcon, JFKL. McNamara-Taylor 10/2/63 report to JFK and JFK response: McNamara-Taylor 10/2/63, JFKL, Rust 143–4. October 1963 movement toward coup: Rust 144–57, Hammer 207–79, Colby 148–54. Lodge-Diem 11/1/63 meeting: Rust 157–63. Diem coup: Rust 163–78, Hammer 280–311, Colby 152–8. Forrestal on JFK reaction: Rust 175. Eisenhower to Nixon on Diem affair, 11/11/63, is in DDEL. Galbraith-Harriman on coup: 11/4/63, Harriman Papers.

Alsop report on Soviets in Cuba and State reply: Izv 11/13/63, 11/17/63, NYT 10/20/63, 11/13/63. JFK on "reduced" numbers: JFKPP 10/31/63. JFK at editors luncheon and Chase warning: Chase-Bundy 11/13/63, JFKL. The 1979 Cuban brigade affair: Garthoff *Detente* 828–48. Special Group approval of new operations and Fitzgerald-AM/LASH meeting: AMSRK 547–8. Hurricane Flora and Castro reaction: USN 11/4/63, NW 11/4/63, NYT 10/29/63, 11/1/63. Daniel-JFK 10/24/63 meeting: *New Republic* 12/14/63. Attwood prepares for Havana visit: RFK oh, Sorensen oh, Attwood oh. JFK Miami speech: JFKPP 11/18/63, Sorensen oh COHP, Sor 723. "You'd better get the hell": Kohler int. NSK-Kohler on 11/7/63: NYT 10/24/63, 11/8/63, Prav 11/8/63, 11/13/63, USN 11/18/63, Kohler Diary 11/7/63, Kohler int. *Time* 11/7/63 visit with NSK: NYT 11/7/63, 11/8/63, Sidey og, Kohler-Rusk 11/8/63, JFKL.

Barghoorn arrest, general: Kohler int, Davies int, Mary Ann Stoessel conv,

NYT 11/17/63, Bohlen-Thompson 3/10/61 (on Barghoorn Moscow visit), Bohlen Papers, Kohler-Barghoorn 5/17/62, Barghoorn-Kohler 4/20/63, Kohler Papers, Kohler Diary 10/31/63–11/21/63, Rusk-Kohler 11/12/63, Bundy-Kohler 11/12/63, Denney-Rusk 11/12/63 ("Soviet motives in Barghoorn case obscure"), Bromley Smith-Bundy 11/12/63 ("Helms says Barghoorn has no ties to CIA or Army"), Kohler-Bundy 11/13/63, Kohler-Rusk 11/13/63, Rusk-Kohler 11/13/63, Kohler-Rusk 11/14/63, Bruce-Bundy 11/16/63, Stoessel-Bundy 11/16/63, Kohler-Rusk 11/18/63, JFKL. Kohler on KGB files: Kohler int. JFK on Barghoorn: JFKPP 11/14/63. Gromyko-Kohler 11/16/63 meeting: Kohler-Rusk 11/16/63, JFKL. Nosenko on Barghoorn affair: *Listener* 5/22/75, Barron 85–7. Thompson 11/21/63 report on Dobrynin talk: Thompson-Dobrynin memcon 11/21/63, JFKL.

Zorin delivers NSK-JFK 10/10/63 letter: Kohler-Rusk 10/10/63, JFKL. JFK-NSK draft by State and Bundy inscription, 10/20/63, is in JFKL. "Clerical misunderstanding": Note to Bundy 12/9/63, JFKL.

23. *"Now Peace Is Up to You"*

Cold and rain in Washington: Martin *It Seems* 242. RFK on JFK gloom: RFK oh, Manchester *Death* 11. Vietnam, November 1963: Rust 175–82, Hammer 312–20. Genesis of Texas trip and JFK worry about feud: RFK oh, Odon 3–22, Reston 240–64. Johnson on Austin speech: Wright 47, Raymont conv. Macdonald on last weekend: Lieberson 217. Weekend reading: Bundy-JFK 11/16/63, JFKL. JFK to Canaveral and watches football and *Tom Jones:* Smathers int, NYT 11/17/63, Manchester *Shining* 263–8. Warnings about Florida trip and JFK orders to Secret Service: FBI 11/18/63 and 11/19/63 memos, W.C. Sullivan-D.J. Brennan 12/1/63, FBI, Bishop *Day Kennedy* 27, Manchester *Death* 37. JFK to Smathers, 11/18/63: Smathers int. Smathers on 1960 LBJ Ranch visit: Smathers int.

LBJ brings mounted head: Manchester *Death* 118–9. Bundy sees JFK, 11/19/63: Manchester *Death* 12. Helms-Peake 11/19/63 visit to RFK and JFK: Helms int and PA 11/19/63. Discovery of Venezuela arms cache: Helms int. See additional documentation in Notes for Epilogue. "Great work": Helms int and Joseph Smith 7–8. NSK-Haekkerup talk: NYT 11/21/63, 11/23/63. JFK Oval Office activities, 11/20/63: PA 11/20/63, Manchester *Shining* 268–9, Manchester *Death* 10–15. Judiciary reception and Jacqueline return: Manchester *Death* 15–29, Ralph Martin 547–8. RFK sees "Mad, Mad World" and visit with JFK: FBI memos 11/4/63, 11/5/63, W.V. Cleveland-C. Evans 11/17/63, FBI. JFK irritation with LBJ on civil rights: RFK oh. JFK thoughts of Sanford: Lincoln *Kennedy and Johnson* 199–207.

RFK on Texas poll and Connally on LBJ as "very concerned": RFK oh, Connally at LBJ Library symposium, March 1990, aired on C-SPAN, 9/4/90. "I'll be back from Texas Sunday": Manchester *Death* 29. JFK on plane to Texas and to O'Donnell, Powers: Manchester *Death* 65–70. JFK-LBJ Rice Hotel confrontation: Schlesinger-Manchester memcons 11/20/64, 1/6/65, 3/25/65, Manchester *Death* 82. Schlesinger sees *From Russia with Love* and JFK reaction to film: Manchester *Death* 89–90, Bradlee 221. JFK in Fort Worth: JFKPP 11/22/63. JFK sees *Morning News* and "hell of a night": Manchester *Death* 121–2, Odon 23–6. 11/22/63 *Intelligence Checklist:* RFK oh. Rusk, Salinger, Bundy, McNamara, RFK, Ball, Thompson, Acheson, Kohler whereabouts at noon 11/22/63: Rusk int, Bundy int, Jane Thompson int, Kohler int, Manchester *Death* 139, 140–1, 192, George Ball 310–5.

Helms-McCone 11/22/63 luncheon: Helms int. McCone reaction to assassination and "We all went to battle stations": Helms int. CIA loses location of NSK: Corson and Crowley 32–5. "We were very high in tension": Helms int. "In that little clinic": Bishop *Bishop's Confession* 418–9. McCone at Hickory Hill and "most wonderful life": Manchester *Death* 256–7. RFK asks Bundy about papers, Bundy orders locks changed: Manchester 257–8, 403. LBJ to Love Field, "Are now the President," Taylor seething: Bishop *Day Kennedy* 271, Manchester *Death* 261–4. Rusk on Pacific plane: Rusk int, Freeman in Thompson 163–6, Manchester *Death* 356–7. Thompson reaction to assassination: Thompson oh, Jane Thompson int, Manchester *Death* 261. Bohlen reaction: Bohlen oh, Bohlen notes. Flight to Washington: Manchester *Death* 339–52. Roberts worry about Russians: Charles Roberts oh.

Gromyko learns news and calls Kohler: Kohler int, Andrei Gromyko 182. Oswald dossier ordered and Thompson reaction: Manchester *Death* 364–5. "If this is true": Rusk int, Manchester *Death* 356–7. AM/LASH meeting in Paris: *Assassination Plots* 88–9, AMSRK 547–8. "We thought . . . that the CIA": Bundy in *Massachusetts Historical Society*, vol. 90, 1978. RFK at Andrews: Manchester *Death* 377–9. "He's got what he wants: Bishop *Day Kennedy* 617. "It was an awful thing": Bishop *Day Kennedy* 415. McNamara to LBJ on Pentagon alert: Manchester *Death* 345–6, 402–3. Bundy to LBJ on South Grounds: Manchester *Death* 403. Dillon sleeping trouble and Bundy in journal: Manchester *Death* 416, 424, 445. Schlesinger on Stevenson: Schlesinger int JBM.

De Gaulle and Macmillan on assassination: Rusk int, Horne 574–6, Macmillan *At End* 471–5. Chinese and Madame Nhu reaction: NYT 11/25/63. NSK reaction to assassination: Adzhubei int WGBH, SNK 50–4. NSK wonder about conspiracy and return to Moscow: Adzhubei int WGBH, NYT 11/23/63. Soviet effort to learn more about Oswald: Shevchenko 123–4. LBJ assurance on no reprisals: Shevchenko 123. Soviet press on assassination and citizens reaction: Tass 11/23/63, Izv 11/23/63, Prav 11/23/63, NYT 11/23/63, 11/24/63, 11/25/63. Castro learns of assassination: *New Republic* 12/21/63. Castro television speech: NYT 11/24/63. Kohler staff meeting and NSK-Kohler talk: Kohler int, Kohler Diary 11/23/63, NSK2 514, NYT 11/24/63. NSK-LBJ and Gromyko-Rusk, 11/23/63, are in LBJ Library and Kohler Papers. Soviet citizen letters are in Kohler Papers. LBJ-Lodge 11/24/63 meeting: Manchester *Death* 543, Halberstam 298–9.

Thompson on Oswald death: Manchester *Death* 527. *Pravda* on Ruby: Prav 11/27/63. Brandon on Soviet mourning and conspiracy questions: Brandon oh, Brandon 198–203, Brandon conv. NSK sends Mikoyan and Dillon fear of incident: NYT 11/24/63, 11/5/63, George Ball 314. Thompson on Mikoyan not walking: Jane Thompson int, Manchester *Death* 574. Nina Khrushchev signs book: Manchester *Death* 598, 654. De Gaulle visits Washington and refuses to return: Rusk int, Bohlen notes, Manchester *Death* 611–4. Bartlett to McNamara on JFK visit to Arlington: Bartlett oh, Bartlett int, Manchester 491–5. "If Jack had been shot": Brandon 201–2. "Angie, I'm no longer": Manchester *Death* 610–1. Jacqueline to Mikoyan: Manchester *Death* 609–10, Rusk int.

LBJ worry about conspiracy: Manchester *Death* 481, Rowan 232–3, NYT 4/26/75. Gallup on suspicions of conspiracy: *Gallup* 12/6/63. Kennan on Oswald:

Kennan-Kohler 11/26/63, Kohler Papers. Helms on LBJ distraction and CIA study: Helms int. LBJ persuades Warren: Manchester *Death* 630. Soviet reaction to Warren Commission findings: *Za Rubezhom* (Moscow) 10/14/64. LBJ asks investigation of 1967 stories: Thomas Powers 156–7. "A damn Murder, Incorporated": *Atlantic*, July 1973. "Kennedy was trying to get Castro": NYT 6/25/76. LBJ to Helms and Salinger on divine retribution: RFK oh, Halberstam 292. Revelation of Cubela plotting and Cubela fate: Summers *Conspiracy* 321–4, 400–2, 411. "Who here could have planned": *Assassination Report*, vol. 3, 216, 220. Oswald wife and KGB and Oswald Mexico City visits: Summers *Conspiracy* 160–1. Soviet "wet operations" of early 1960s: Andrew and Gordievsky 464–5, Barron 413–47.

Nosenko: Helms int, Epstein 3–50, 257–74, Barron 85–7, 452, David Martin 111–4, 200–8. For Eddowes theory, see Eddowes. Oswald exhumation: NYT 10/5/81. "Bobby Kennedy is just another lawyer": Fox 181. Mafia disgust with Missile Crisis settlement: Scheim 193–5. Oswald and Murret and Pecora: McMillan 161–2, 309–14, Summers 449–51. Ruby and Capone, Dorfman, "Barney" Baker, Miller, Pecora, Roselli: Davis *Kennedys* 559–62, Summers 246, 432–51. Oswald New Orleans mailing address and seen with anti-Castroites: Summers 290–8. RFK to Goodwin on organized crime and assassination: Goodwin 465, Bobby Baker 393.

Ruby visits to Cuba and gunrunning: Davis *Kennedys* 552–3, 559–61, Summers 440–5, Scheim 104–6. Rusk in retirement was indignant about Allen Dulles's failure to reveal the CIA's anti-Castro plotting to the Warren Commission. (Rusk int) "He didn't even have the satisfaction": Manchester *Death* 407. Jacqueline Kennedy-NSK, 12/1/63, is in JFKL and Manchester *Death* 653–4.

Epilogue: The Culmination

LBJ-Mikoyan 11/26/63 meeting: Mikoyan in MCT, Prav 11/27/63, NYT 12/4/63, NSK1 505, Weintal and Bartlett 116. LBJ-NSK, 11/25/63, is in Johnson Library. NSK "worried" and receives reports on LBJ: Sergei Khrushchev conv, Sergei Khrushchev at Harvard, 2/13/89–2/15/89, Shevchenko 123–4, NSK3 181, Crankshaw 285–6. NSK New Year's letter, delivery and LBJ reaction: NSK-LBJ 12/31/63, Johnson Library, LBJ *Vantage Point* 464–5, Robert McCloskey briefing 1/3/64, Johnson Library. Cleveland on letter: Cleveland-Rusk 1/4/64, Harriman Papers. LBJ reply: LBJ-NSK 1/18/64, Johnson Library, LBJ *Vantage Point* 465–6. U.S. enriched uranium cutback and Soviet response: Seaborg *Stemming* 21–3, 35–50, LBJ *Vantage Point* 465–7. Dobrynin and LBJ on summit: NYT 4/18/64, LBJ *Vantage Point* 468.

"Khrushchev didn't think": Bishop *Bishop's Confession* 417–9, also LBJ-Turner Catledge memcon 12/15/64, Krock Papers. McCone sees LBJ on arms cache, evidence to Betancourt, LBJ reaction: Helms int, T 7/3/64, USN 12/23/63, 2/10/64, 3/9/64, NYT 11/30/63, 12/4/63, 12/7/63, 12/10/63, *Department of State Bulletin* 12/9/63, 12/16/63, 8/10/64, Joseph Smith 374–78. Castro and NSK reactions: NYT 12/7/63, 12/8/63, 1/18/64, Prav 12/13/63. LBJ stops Attwood gambit: Attwood oh. "He saw little point in pressing Cuba": Helms int. "If Jack Kennedy had lived": Joseph Smith 377. LBJ and Vietnam, spring 1964, and Gulf of Tonkin incident: Karnow 319–86, LBJ *Vantage Point* 112–9. NSK to Hanoi on negotiation: Karnow 328. "Got sucked in up to his neck": NSK3 181. JFK on withdrawing from Vietnam: Odon 16–7, AMSRK 708–23, George Ball 366–7. Rusk on 1965 withdrawal possibility: Rusk 441.

Missile Crisis impact on Vietnam decision-making: Eliot Cohen in *The National Interest,* Winter 1986. NSK 70th birthday celebration: SNK 52–6, 337–8, NYT 4/18/64. "We're oldsters": SNK 28. Discontent with NSK in Moscow: Tatu 364–98. Adzhubei mission and Schwirkmann incident: *L'Humanite* 11/9/64, *Le Monde* 1/7/65, SNK 132–3, Tatu 388–91, Linden 201, Hyland and Shryock 161, Barron 10–11, 120, Crankshaw 285–6. Gromyko on Adzhubei mission's impact on NSK ouster: Tatu 389. Rockefeller-NSK meeting: Finder 182–9. NSK on LBJ as President: NSK3 181. Plotting against NSK: SNK 45–155. Brezhnev as "the Ballerina": SNK 32.

NSK ouster: SNK 145–62, 223, Medvedev *Khrushchev* 235–45, Adzhubei in WP 10/15/89, Sergei Khrushchev in NYT 10/23/88, Tatu 394–423, Linden 202–30. Report of Brezhnev role in Nina Khrushchev's absence: Sejna 92–3. LBJ learns of NSK ouster and Chinese nuclear test: NYT 10/19/64, 10/28/64, LBJ *Vantage Point* 468–70. Zinchuk to Bartlett: Bartlett int. Stagnation of 1980 Soviet economy: Goldman 1–41. Mikhail Gorbachev's aide Georgi Shakhnazarov said that the price of parity was "the stagnation of our economy. We paid a high price for parity." (CCT) 1971 Berlin agreement: Bundy 385–8. Castro and Soviets after 1963: Szulc 595–683, Hugh Thomas 91–106, Wayne Smith 84–257. End of plotting against Castro: Szulc 600. Reagan government threats against "the source": Risquet in MCT, Garthoff 106, USN 3/8/62, NYT 9/15/83. Risquet on Vietnam: ACT. NSK on Prague invasion: NSK3 139–41.

NSK in retirement: SNK 163–331, Medvedev *Khrushchev* 250–5. "You can take everything": SNK 247. "It's been six years": SNK 303–4. "Unfortunately a certain degree": SNK 340. Letters from Jane Thompson and Jacqueline Onassis: Jane Thompson int, SNK 341. NSK on JFK in memoirs: NSK2 513–4. NSK to senators on grandchildren living under communism: NYT 9/17/59 and JFK notes, 9/16/59, JFKL. "Our first *perestroika*": *Financial Times* 4/29/88. "Struggling to get this huge": Jane Thompson int. Adzhubei's fate after 1964: Adzhubei int WGBH, NYT 11/14/64. "The Khrushchev period was the first act": WP 10/15/89. "Freedom and *glasnost* are far ahead": *Boston Globe* 2/18/89.

Sergei Khrushchev to Gorbachev, 1986, is in SNK 315–6. "I think it's better if he stays": NYT 10/23/88. Jacqueline Onassis 1976 Soviet visit: Mary Ann Stoessel conv, NYT 7/20/76, 11/2/76, 4/5/77. Sergei Khrushchev at Harvard and on future: *Harvard Crimson* 2/16/89, *Boston Globe* 2/18/89, Sergei Khrushchev conv, NYT 10/13/88.

INDEX